Lecture Notes in Computer Science 720

Edited by G. Goos and J. Hartmanis

Vladimír Mařík Jiří Lažanský
Roland R. Wagner (Eds.)

Database and Expert Systems Applications

4th International Conference, DEXA '93
Prague, Czech Republic, September 6-8, 1993
Proceedings

DEXA 93

Springer-Verlag
Berlin Heidelberg New York
London Paris Tokyo
Hong Kong Barcelona
Budapest

Series Editors

Gerhard Goos
Universität Karlsruhe
Postfach 69 80
Vincenz-Priessnitz-Straße 1
D-76131 Karlsruhe, Germany

Juris Hartmanis
Cornell University
Department of Computer Science
4130 Upson Hall
Ithaca, NY 14853, USA

Volume Editors

Vladimír Mařík
Jiří Lažanský
Faculty of Electrical Engineering, Czech Technical University
Technicka 2, 16 627 Prague, Czech Republic

Roland R. Wagner
Inst. for Informatics & Research Inst. for Applied Knowledge Processing (FAW)
J. Kepler University Linz
Altenbergerstraße 69, A-4040 Linz, Austria

CR Subject Classification (1991): H.2, H.4, H.5.2, I.2.1, I.2.4-5

ISBN 3-540-57234-1 Springer-Verlag Berlin Heidelberg New York
ISBN 0-387-57234-1 Springer-Verlag New York Berlin Heidelberg

Printed in Germany

Typesetting: Camera-ready by author
Printing and binding: Druckhaus Beltz, Hemsbach/Bergstr.
45/3140-543210 - Printed on acid-free paper

Foreword

The Database and Expert Systems Applications (DEXA) Conferences are traditionally thought as a wide platform for the exchange of ideas, experience and opinions among theoreticians and practitioners active in the areas of database and artificial intelligence technologies and coming from all over the world.

Despite the applications aspect occurring in the name of the conference, the Program Committee arranged – as it has become tradition – the necessary balance between theoretical and practical points of view.

This volume contains the best 78 contributed papers which have been carefully selected during a tight reviewing process involving comments of many international experts by the Program Committee from a total of 269 submissions. The scope of the papers in this proceedings covers the real hot topics in both the areas of database and AI systems. The database sessions are primarily devoted to *object-oriented data modeling*, *distributed databases*, *active database aspects*, *database optimization*, and *performance evaluation*; among the specialized systems *spatial* and *geographic databases* have been stressed. Artificial Intelligence is represented in particular by papers on *expert systems applications*, *knowledge engineering* and *distributed AI systems*. While some of the topics, as for example *hypertext/hypermedia* and *user interfaces*, are important for both database and AI systems, some fields, in particular *software engineering* and *legal systems*, are even aimed at integrating the results achieved in both fields.

DEXA'93 is the 4th conference in the line and has some new features. After Vienna (1990), Berlin (1991), and Valencia (1992), this conference takes place in the capital of an East-European country, thus providing an ideal forum for the advancement of the East-West scientific cooperation.

This conference is the first organized in cooperation with the IEEE Computer Society; this is an important feature confirming that the DEXA Conferences have gained a certain recognition among many international database and AI events. All the individuals involved in the preparation of this conference consider this fact as a great honour.

We would like to express our thanks to all institutions actively supporting this event, namely to

Research Institute for Applied Knowledge Processing (FAW), Linz
Czech Technical University, Prague
IEEE Computer Society
Allen-Bradley, A Rockwell Int. Comp., Milwaukee, WI.
Austrian Computer Society (ÖCG)
Gesellschaft für Informatik (GI)

Our thanks are also due to all individuals who took an active part in the dissemination of information and in the encouragement of many potential contributors. In this respect, the activities of the following people are highly appreciated: P. Dražan (The Netherlands), A. Hameurlain (France), F. Golshani

(U.S.A.), T. W. Ling (Singapore), J. Debenham (Australia), F. Galindo (Spain), D. Karagiannis (Germany), B. Pernici (Italy), E. Lum (Hong Kong), and J. Wand (Canada).

We also would express our thanks to all members of the Program Committee and the Organizing Committee as well as to all referees supporting the selection of the contributions with valuable evaluations often given on short notice.

Vienna, Prague, Linz
June 1993

A Min Tjoa
V. Mařík
J. Lažanský
R. R. Wagner

General Chair

A Min Tjoa	University of Vienna, Austria

Program Committee Chair

Vladimír Mařík	Czech Technical University, Czech Republic

Organizing Committee Chair

Roland R. Wagner	J. Kepler University, Austria

Program Committee

Afsarmanesh H.	University of Amsterdam, The Netherlands
Appelrath H. J.	University of Oldenburg, Germany
Bauknecht K.	University of Zürich, Switzerland
Bench-Capon T.	University of Liverpool, United Kingdom
Bing J.	NRCCL Oslo, Norway
Bratko I.	University of Ljubljana, Slovenia
Croft B.	University of Massachusetts, USA
Cellary, W. S.	Technical University of Poznan, Poland
Debenham J.	University of Technology, Sydney, Australia
Dražan P.	RIKS Maastricht, The Netherlands
Eder J.	University of Klagenfurt, Austria
Furtado A. L.	University of Rio de Janeiro, Brazil
Galindo F.	University of Zaragoza, Spain
Gardarin G.	INRIA, France
Golshani F.	Arizona State University, USA
Gottlob G.	Technical University of Vienna, Austria

Hajičová E.	Charles University, Czech Republic
Hawryszkiewycz I.	University of Technology, Sydney, Australia
Henderson P.	University of Southampton, United Kingdom
Hirota K.	Hosei University, Japan
Hong J.-K.	IBM Tokyo, Japan
Hsiao D.	Naval Postgraduate School, USA
Jarke M.	University of Aachen, Germany
Kamel M.	Naval Postgraduate School, USA
Kambayashi Y.	IMEEI, Japan
Kappel G.	University of Vienna, Austria
Karagiannis D.	University of Vienna, Austria
Kroha P.	University of Dortmund, Germany
Lažanský J.	Czech Technical University, Czech Republic
Lochovsky F.	HKUST, Hong Kong
Lum V.	Chinese University of Hong Kong, Hong Kong
Müller G.	University of Freiburg, Germany
Motiwalla J.	University of Singapore, Singapore
Neimat M.-A.	HP Laboratories, USA
Neuhold E.	GMD-IPSI, Germany
Olive A.	Universitat Politecnica de Catalunya, Spain
Ozsoyoglu G.	University Case Western Research, USA
Papazoglou M.	National University, Australia
Quirchmayr G.	J. Kepler University, Linz, Austria
Ramos I.	Technical University of Valencia, Spain
Rolland C.	University Paris I, France
Rollinger C.-R.	University of Osnabrück, Germany
Roussopoulos N.	University of Maryland, USA
Saltor F.	Facultat d'Informatica, Spain
Sernandas A.	University of Lisbon, Portugal
Smith J. C.	University of British Columbia, Canada
Specht D.	Produktionstechnisches Zentrum Berlin, Germany
Štěpánková O.	Czech Technical University, Czech Republic
Tanaka K.	Kobe University, Japan
Thanos C.	IEI-CNR, Italy
Thoma C. H.	Ciba-Geigy, Switzerland
Van Dorsser C.	ORIGIN, The Netherlands
Vidyasankar K.	Memorial University of Newfoundland, Canada
Wagner R. R.	J. Kepler University, Linz, Austria

Organizing Committee:

Wagner G.	J. Kepler University, Linz, Austria
Kouba Z.	Czech Technical University, Prague, Czech Republic
Lhotská L.	Czech Technical University, Prague, Czech Republic
Přeučil L.	Czech Technical University, Prague, Czech Republic
Vlček T.	Czech Technical University, Prague, Czech Republic

List of Referees

Each paper was carefully reviewed by three referees. Most of this work was done by the Program Committee. However, invaluable help was provided by other referees listed below:

Aberer K.	Jirků P.	Polák J.
Adelsberger H.	Junkermann G.	Popper M.
Amano H.	Kanet J.	Price B.
Arikawa M.	Klas W.	Pröll B.
Bayle A.	Klir G.	Psutka J.
Berka P.	Kobe U.	Přeučil L.
Bradbury W.	Kotek Z.	Qianshan H.
Brayshaw M.	Kouba Z.	Retschitzegger W.
Brázdil P.	Král J.	Rausch-Schott S.
Búcha J.	Kramosil I.	Rodriguez H.
Castellanos M.	Kraus K.	Röhner F.
Cortes-Rello E.	Kroha P.	Roos N.
Csonto J.	Kunishima T.	Schutzelaars A.
Demlová M.	Kusaku K.	Starzacher P.
Dorffner G.	Kwak S.	Stumptner P.
Drobnič M.	Lee J.	Šonka M.
Emmerich W.	Leung K.S.	Štěpánek P.
Falby J.	Lhotská L.	Takahashi J.
Findler N.	Löhr N.	Takeda K.
Fischer G.	Macháček M.	Traunmüller R.
Friedrich G.	Maruyama H.	Ulje I.
Garcia-Solaco M.	Matoušek V.	Urbančič T.
Grobelnik M.	Mayorga I.	Ushakov I.
Hájek P.	Mladenič D.	Van d. Baaren J.
Halaška I.	Motta E.	Vlček T.
Hameurlain A.	Mozetic I.	Watt S.
Harmanec D.	Muth P.	Winkelhofer A.
Hlaváč V.	Nakamura Y.	Wolfmayr K.
Horáček P.	Pastor J.A.	Wu X.
Hori M.	Pizzarello A.	Yoshida N.
Hořejš J.	Plášil F.	Zdráhal Z.
Hudec B.	Pokorný J.	Zheng Y.

Table of Contents

Invited Talk

Topic 1: Data Models

Topic 2: Distributed Databases

Topic 3: Advanced Database Aspects

Topic 4: Database Optimization and Performance Evaluation

Topic 5: Spatial and Geographical Databases

Topic 6: Expert Systems and Knowledge Engineering

Topic 7: Legal Systems

Topic 8: Other Database and AI Applications

Topic 9: Software Engineering

Topic 10: Hypertext/Hypermedia and User Interfaces

Information Handling – A Challenge for Databases and Expert Systems

Ralph Busse, Adrian Müller, Erich J. Neuhold

GMD–IPSI
Dolivostr. 15, D–64293 Darmstadt, FRG
e–mail: {busse,amueller,neuhold}@darmstadt.gmd.de

Abstract The increasing availability of a broad range of information types like textual documents, audio and video data, and hyper-linked information structures imply a need to reformulate the task of information handling systems. An integrated heterogeneous information pool of interlinked multimedia data forms the center of such a system. In order to create and utilize this pool components involving many interoperating humans and also active (intelligent) system support are needed. In this paper we focus on the acquisition, offer, and retrieval of information performed around this pool of multimedia data. We discuss requirements, approaches and (partial) solutions in areas like storage, information modelling, semi-automatic acquisition, retrieval and visualization of multimedia data, and sketch implemented systems that integrate some of these aspects. The discussions will identify needs and show techniques to embed expert system functionality into each single step of the process of information handling. An integrated prototype, which is currently under development at GMD-IPSI, will be outlined at the end of this paper.

1 Introduction

In former times, the materialization of verbal knowledge in books, and then the creation of public libraries, started new eras in information handling and in interhuman communication. Nowadays, knowledge is more and more stored in electronic libraries and made available through information servers in networks. The necessity of being 'up to date' and the immense growth of electronic information require on-line access to the data. Furthermore, the central storage of information and its replicability create new means of information delivery. Broadcasting through a network is the fastest way to provide many people with actual information. This requires adequate representation of all potential information. Not only size and structure of the data items increase. New media like video or audio, for example, provide a new quality of stored data, because they add temporal aspects to all tasks that are performed around a database.

Taking all these demands into account, the challenges to database development can be sketched as:

- appropriate modelling of multimedia data
- effective storage and retrieval of mass data
- synchronization and real-time assertions for temporal data
- automatic acquisition of external data

- unified modelling layer for a simple access to all kinds of data
- integration of network services into information management systems

All these new requirements go beyond the capabilities of traditional database management systems. Most of the tasks are already solved, as long as they are viewed separately. E.g., CAD/CAM applications and desktop publishing programs are publicly available. But the integration of all these requirements into a new database concept remains to be done. The object-oriented paradigm of database design seems to be a good basis for this integration. Thus, the major goal of database development can be summarized as:

Databases must efficiently store all kinds of data and provide integrated and unified manipulation methods.

Traditional retrieval systems are designed for effectiveness in searching and finding single records or simple sets of data in large but poorly structured databases. This becomes obvious if one takes a closer look at the quality measures that have been formulated several decades ago and are still in use. *Recall* (the ratio of relevant documents retrieved) and *precision* (the degree of 'noise' in the result set) are purely quantitative rules of success.

The new and promising results in information acquisition and storage imply a need to develop new paradigms for the design and construction of intelligent multimedia information systems. New challenges for information handling systems – to provide access to complex information structures and to support users in preparation of large and rich structured data – have to be adopted in two domains. On the one hand there is a need to build new kinds of general purpose retrieval tools. On the other hand existing applications have to incorporate novel information structures without loosing their acquainted usage. These future systems have to address more qualitative goals like:

- mediation of dependencies of information, not leaving users alone in 'hyperspace',
- visualization of complex information structures and
- integration of several types of media within one unique metaphor of man-machine interaction.

New theories and technologies that have been developed in the area of information retrieval to reach these design goals should be transferred to existing applications in the domain of databases and information systems (e.g. business and engineering systems, bulletin boards, library systems, or electronic newspapers). These systems should be endowed with components capable to handle new electronic media like video, audio, interactive maps and pictures to overcome the existing paradigm of pure information managing. This integration leads to promising approaches like

- presenting data as instantiations of concepts and ideas, i.e., cooperation of users and machines via active media and
- intensifying the productivity of the human mind (by abstracting from physical or spatial aspects of information storage and retrieval and offering cognitive models of the underlying information sources)

The formulation of clear and procedural design guidelines for information handling systems and the development of active multimedia systems in the way sketched here is a long-range goal. Research at GMD–IPSI and other locations has started to tackle certain aspects. The overall goal is the development of fully functional prototypes which can mutually be combined to integrate the benefits of distinct research areas.

The big amount of automatic processing and the high degree of user interaction reveal a big need of integrating techniques from the area of knowledge processing to allow information handling systems to take decisions and to guide the user in his or her tasks. Instead of providing stand-alone expert systems, active system support is achieved by embedding knowledge based assistance components into the system.

In the following we will take a look at different aspects of information handling. Section 2 presents an overview of the whole 'process of information handling'. The single steps in the information flow from information sources to terminal applications are depicted and related to each other. Section 3 sheds some light on information acquisition and storage mechanisms appearing in that environment. Structural enrichment, schema integration and concepts for modelling videos are the selected topics. New developments in retrieval techniques are presented in section 4. Multimodal dialogues and interface mechanisms to heterogeneous databases lead up to virtual-reality visualizations of complex data. The last section of this paper will then be used to present the MultiMedia Forum, an integrated information system prototype under development at GMD–IPSI.

2 The Process of Information Handling

The main functionality of an information handling system is the acquisition and maintenance of data together with a support of appropriate retrieval mechanisms. This overall scope can be divided into two general parts, that can be roughly entitled as *import* (*acquisition* and *creation*) and *export* (*offer* and *retrieval*). The import part is responsible for populating the information base. It acquires data from many different sources and has to prepare it for appropriate usage. The second part is concerned with all aspects of retrieval of this data and the presentation of the results to the user. In addition to query mechanisms and visualization techniques, it may provide sophisticated user guidance to assist the user in his or her search for the desired information. Both tasks have to be based on a common metaphor for the handled data. An appropriate modelling is necessary to connect these two parts through the shared information base.

Figure 1 shows further refinements of this whole process of information handling. The graphic mirrors the information flow from the information sources to the terminal application programs and the user. Interconnections between the different actions, like cooperating editors and cycles (e.g. storage of retrieved or edited data) are not taken into account. In the following, we will take a look at the different parts of the information processing task.

2.1 Information Acquisition

Information Import. When an information system has to be built up, it has to be filled with data. The information to be gathered in this state of information handling is of diverse nature and comes in many different structures from many different sources. In addition to existing internal and external databases with more or less structured data, information can reside in simple text files, in expert systems, or in on-line databases

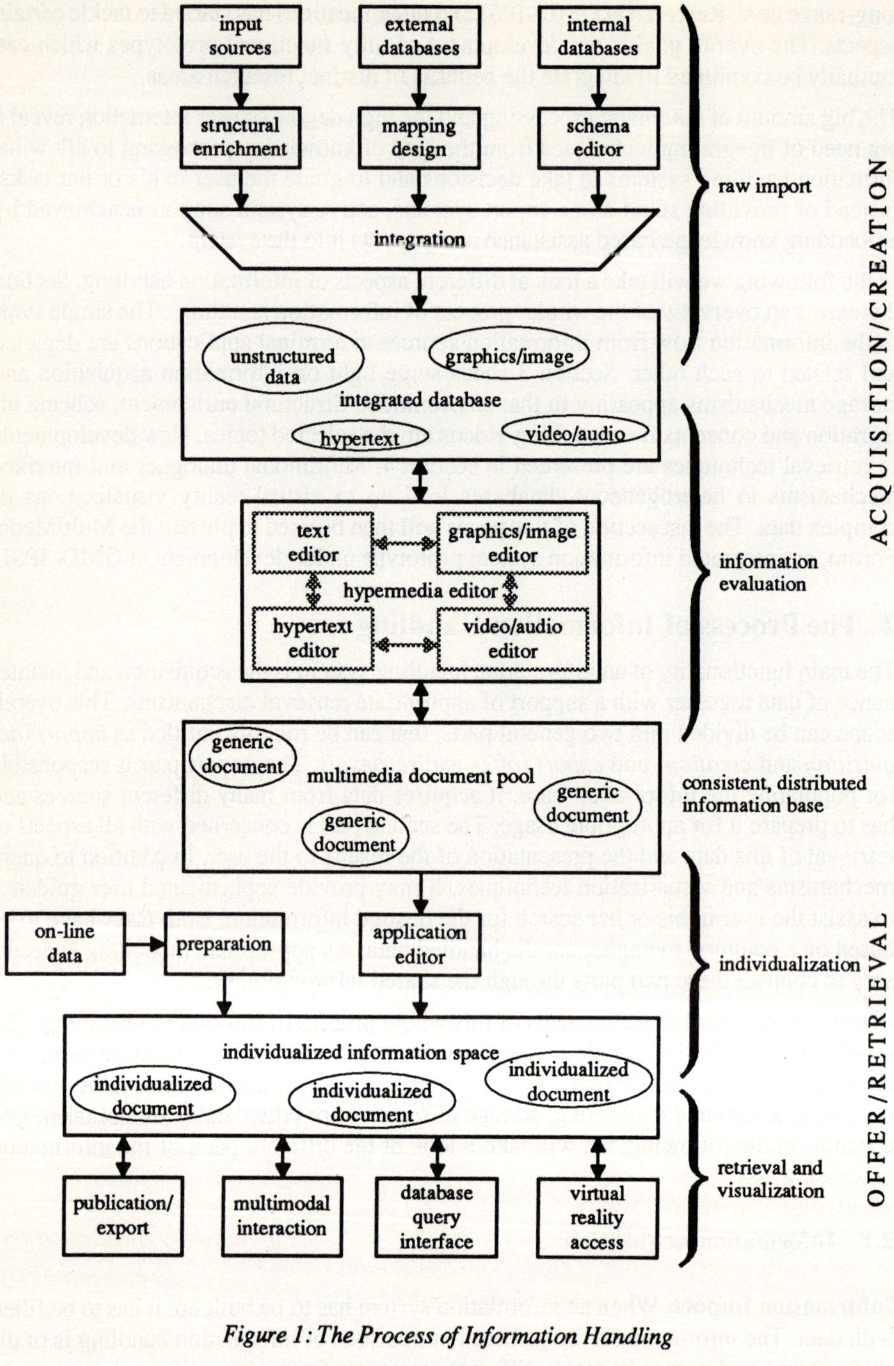

Figure 1: The Process of Information Handling

with special retrieval interfaces. Moreover, there could even be the need to integrate non-electronic data like printings or pictures into the information pool, by converting it to an electronic representation [39], or at least by handling references to it.

In contrast to specialized databases that normally handle only one type of data, the database that will be used as a repository for an information system has to cope with many different types of data at the same time:

- numerical data (measurements, tables, statistics, stock market information)
- textual data (reports, excerpts, articles, books)
- 'hypertext' (text chunks that are connected through links, e.g. lexica)
- graphics (charts, blueprints, technical figures)
- images (digitized photos and paintings, bitmaps, phototypesetting layouts)
- audio (speeches, music, sounds)
- animation (animated charts, 3D presentation)
- video (movies, documentations, sport takes, commercials)

⇒ 'hypermedia document' = A network of all these data types.

It is necessary to provide appropriate storing mechanisms for all of these manifestations. Images and videos are very space consuming, audio and video data need time information and synchronization capabilities. Hypertext has to be broken up into storable data items without losing the connecting links [41]. Furthermore, even data of the same kind can be structured in many different fashions and has to be adapted to the internal structure of the information base when it shall be used in the information management system. Data representations found in internal or external databases have to be integrated into one logical database using integration editors that are based on semantic knowledge [20]. Flat data like ASCII files need structural enrichment to be accessible at a finer granularity [13][14][15]. Accesses to on-line databases and expert systems through an information network have to be supported by some procedural capabilities of the system. A good basis for all of these tasks is given with the *object-oriented* paradigm. The AMOS project, for example, uses the object-oriented database system VODAK [27] for modelling analogue and digital videos [37]. The 'Structured Document Base' SDB exploits the object-orientation of C++ to provide an SGML specific interface to a relational database [21].

The inflationary growths of the available information and the immense sizes of the new data types give more and more a substantial need for (at least partially) automated information acquisition and enrichment. To achieve this, the techniques of artificial intelligence and cognitive sciences must be exploited.

Information Evaluation. The simple import of existing data is by far not sufficient to form an integrated information base. The data has to be viewed and checked and made consistent[1] with the previous content of the database. This task of *value adding* encompasses conversion of this information, selection of relevant parts, deletion of others, and addition of further knowledge. Besides obeying consistency, the data should be as little redundant as possible. The separate information has to be classified and must be interrelated with other information in the database by establishing links. All those tasks need sophisticated assistance tools that guide the reviewer and support decisions. Furthermore, each type of data will need its own editing tool. Text editors and graphics tools are well known. Video and audio editors are more and more available and have to be integrated into the database environment [38][47]. Hypertext editors have to be augmented to hypermedia editors and will be used to interconnect all the different parts of the information. SEPIA, a cooperative editing tool, and TEDI, a terminology editor, are examples for such editors [35][46]. The evolution of existing schemas and the derivation of new schemas from old ones need to be supported, as well.

Although parts of this evaluation may be automated [22], most of the work will be up to human reviewers. Due to the size of this project and to different experiences there will be several reviewers working on the same data. It will be necessary to define specifications and to support cooperative work, task flow management and versioning for an effective way of working the information up [23][46].

2.2 Multimedia Document Pool

When the information is imported and revised it will result in a set of information 'chunks' containing the different kinds of data, a set of links modelling the relationships between them, and a set of constraints that guarantee consistency. This result will be called a *raw document* because it can be seen as a hypermedia document without any layout information. These documents should be independent of a special format and a concrete medium to allow maximal reuse. The 'neutral' database where these documents are stored is called the *multimedia document pool*. Physically, it will be stored in the same database as the imported data, but it provides a different view on this data. While the structure of the imported data is mainly determined by its sources, the structure of the documents provides a more logical access to the information. Simple navigations along semantic links and sophisticated retrieval mechanisms on this information network provide access to all data that has been stored in the database. In our institute we use the object-oriented database system VODAK and the hypermedia server *HyperBase* [41] in parallel. The integration of these systems is part of the development of an integrated information system prototype as described in section 5.

To achieve maximal benefits of the expensive gathering of data, this pool should be accessible via electronic networks by providing interfaces to X.400 electronic mail, ISDN network bridges or others [22]. Special requirements for a multimedia archive are currently being investigated in the GAMMA project [49].

---

1. This notion of *consistency* differs from database consistency: Two different values for one attribute would be a *conflict* in a database, but may represent the *consistent* information 'There are conflicting values for that item' in an information base.

2.3 Information Retrieval

Individualization. Once this generic information pool has been created, it can serve as a basis for different information system tasks. A *distribution system* can offer this information in the form of an electronic newspaper [23] or deliver it on CD-ROM to some customers [22]. *Retrieval tools* can be invoked by users that need specific information on some topic [48][51]. In a *publication environment*, the information will be further edited and provided with a final layout before it is sent to press [22].

In all these processes *individualization* plays an important role, because it tailors the subsequent retrieval process. It restricts the content of the multimedia document pool to an individualized scope and supports some pre-formatting of the data structures to allow easier access [22]. Information offering systems (like the *Multimedia Forum* discussed in the last section of this paper) need to be adapted to the individual information structure, which results from the individualization step, and therefore knowledge about the needs and wishes of the users (modelling of user requirements, adapting machine learning techniques to information retrieval) has to be considered. Using expert systems techniques helps to produce the right kind of information space on the right media and at an acceptable cost for various individuals and groups.

Retrieval Concepts. The availability of new information sources like the individualized multimedia document pool stresses the need to relieve users from the burden of acquiring database-specific knowledge as well as from general retrieval expertise. One way in this direction is to interweave different retrieval paradigms (e.g. relational databases as opposed to full-text retrieval systems, browsing of hyper-linked information items contrasting interactive 3D-visualizations of information spaces) into new and integrated forms of the retrieval process. This should be accompanied by the theory-based development of methods and tools for intelligent user support, which should consider the well-known domain structure of the current information space.

Clarifying the user's informational needs is a complex task which should take into account several topics, which have been (partly) treated independently in the past:

- provide unique access to heterogeneous data sources (OODBM, RDBM, full-text retrieval, on-line systems, plain text) and data types (multimedia data, hyper-linked and unstructured information, video, audio etc.)
- provide terminological support by combining the benefits of controlled vocabularies with adaptive semantic or statistic networks of terms
- adjust relevance measurement dynamically due to the current retrieval situation

These points show the significance of new theories for information retrieval in complex information systems since it is impossible to improve the mere technical process of data searching without considering the user's state of mind, as it might be reflected in his/her actions on the system's interface. The goal here is to be able to offer the user as easily as possible at each point of time the 'needed' (in terms of size and contents) kind of information

Interface Design. Users need cooperative support in performing complex information handling tasks. This requires an interpretation of the user's actions in a larger context as e.g. his or her last query issued. The user interface should possess knowledge about the underlying information structure and the current state of interest the user is in. This is why one line of research at GMD-IPSI concentrates on the development of on-line support in query formulation whereas another research goal is the development of an integrated concept and document representation framework. At each point of time the user should be able to formulate (based on his/her knowledge) an information request that results in the proper presentation of precisely the information he/she requested. This may be in the form of retrieval results [48][51] but also in the form of an information offer [23].

The prototypes developed so far combine several research disciplines with human computer interaction in the context of information systems. Linguistic research and speech act theory is the basis for modelling and structuring multimodal dialogues (enabling the system to guide the user but react flexible in case he/she disagrees). Case-based reasoning and task-parsing modules augment information systems with intelligent user guidance (e.g., comparing the user's actions with expert strategies and offering the user to complete a task automatically, if desired). The combination of natural language generation techniques with active help systems (e.g., providing dynamically created text to comment on current (critical) situations [10]) helps to avoid confusing users by either lengthy dialogues or potentially misunderstandable graphical feedback.

Certainly, the best cooperative support is not worth mentioning it if it is not embedded in a convenient user interface. The design should be consistent with the underlying data (e.g., generating the interface out of database structure and contents) and it should allow direct and interactive manipulation of the data representation (like presenting countries as interactive maps). But whereas the term 'user interface' in the context of retrieval systems is typically associated with traditional graphical interfaces (window systems, QBE tables etc.), an appropriate treatment of complex information structures should consider new dimensions of interfaces e.g. 3D-visualization or even virtual reality scenes that can be manipulated by the new hardware gadgets that currently appear.

2.4 Integrating new Technologies

The development of new hardware, software and communication technologies together with falling prices and increasing availability of these products open the door for new dimensions of data storage and human-computer interaction. That means, research in the domain of information systems has to address an increasing group of naive users as well as the fact that the shift from prototypes to widely used applications becomes faster and faster.

Since it is hard to foresee the inventions of the next years, it is difficult to formulate requirements for today's research. Here is a summary of current activities at GMD-IPSI which tries to integrate new technologies in existing information handling systems:

- Optical and semantic structure recognition: Automated insertion of textual data into databases without losing structural information.
- Multimedia database system: Integration of analogue and digital video and audio data into the object-oriented database system VODAK.
- Multimedia archives in public networks: Development of representation and distribution strategies to access multimedia data through a telecooperation network.

- Cooperative authoring systems: Synchronous and asynchronous work of several authors on the same publication, represented in four *versioned activity spaces* and emphasizing *group awareness*.
- Virtual reality: 3D-visualization of complex information structures (i.e., data combined with its dependencies and access methods) and new techniques of interaction in 3D-space (like gesture recognition).
- Large displays: Using Liveboards for computer assisted (tele-)classrooms or (tele-)meeting rooms with interactive manipulation of multimedia information.
- Visual Query Languages: Extending the query language of an object-oriented DBMS with visual query patterns, thus enabling graphical and exact querying in a new metaphor of man-machine interface.
- Dictionary of Art: Development of a complete publication system that covers both information acquisition and individualized retrieval of an encyclopedia of art.

3 Integrating Heterogeneous Information into a Database

When a database is to be used in an information management system, it has to provide a combination of capabilities that goes beyond the functionality of simple databases of today. In this section we investigate three selected topics that are related with the acquisition and storage of information. Section 3.1 describes a tool for structuring flat texts, thus making them manageable for databases. Section 3.2 is concerned with the general notion of *schema integration*, i.e. the provision of a unified view on existing external databases. The last part of this section sketches a further challenging topic, the representation of video and audio in a database.

3.1 Structural Enrichment of Flat Information

When text shall be stored in a database, two aspects should be considered: *granularity* and *standardization*. Simple storage of a text as a whole does not make much sense, because it impedes both subsequent processing and access to the information inside of that text. Single information items like authors, creation date, section headings, or figure titles, should be accessible in a query without reading the whole document. This refinement of granularity can be achieved by adding structural information to the text. This structural information, however, should follow standardized rules, so that retrieval on all stored texts can be done with the same type of query.

One such structuring standard is SGML (Standard Generalized Markup Language)[25]. The main idea is to add *tags* to the text that identify the different structural components independent of font and layout information. For example, a tag for a headline could be <level one headline> instead of (16pt Roman, centered). This system-independent separation of the logical structure from the physical appearance improves the reusability of documents and provides good means for storing them in databases [21].

Unfortunately, many texts that shall be used in an information system come as plain ASCII files and have to be tagged first. The DREAM-parser (Document structure REcognition And Markup [14]) that has been developed at IPSI, uses implicit structural information of a given text to convert it automatically to a tagged SGML document. The basis of such a conversion are prefixes and key-words (e.g. 'Date:','From:'), embedded font change information, indentations and empty lines. The expected structure of a given document is described in a declarative *document structure definition (DSD)*. This is a set of rules describing the structural composition of single components together with recognition information. When the current part of the document matches the recognition patterns of a currently active rule, the formatting commands inside of that rule will be executed and the tagged portion of the text will be copied to the output.

Example:

An entry of an (imaginary) bibliographic database like

```
AN  12345
TI  PASCAL, User Manual and Report
AU  Kathleen Jensen
    Wirth, Niklaus
SO  SPRINGER Verlag New York Heidelberg Berlin, Jahr: 1978
PX  ISBN: 3–387–90144–2
TX  Description of the PASCAL standard.
YR  19870711
```

uses line prefixes to distinguish the meaning of the different items. The DSD of such a bibliographic item could, besides others, contain the following two rules:

```
<!ELEMENT bibitem    – – (docnr, title, authors, source, isbn?, abstract?, date)>
<!ELEMENT docnr      – – cut(^"AN" " "+), copy([0–9]+), cut($)>
```

The first rule specifies, that the structural entity 'bibitem' is made up of a sequence of seven substructures. The question marks declare isbn and abstract as optional. The second rule defines the recognition pattern of the document number, the first part of our bibitem. When the current input line matches the "AN" at the beginning of the line, followed by a sequence of digits after at least one space, then only the number will be copied to the output, tagged as <docnr>. A set of twelve of such rules suffices to convert the bibliographic item to the following SGML document:

```
<bibdoc><bibitem>
  <docnr>12345</docnr>
  <title>PASCAL, User Manual and Report</title>
  <authors>
    <author>
      <name><fname>Kathleen</fname><lname>Jensen</lname></name>
    </author><coauthor>
      <name><lname>Wirth</lname><fname>Niklaus</fname></name>
    </coauthor>
  </authors>
  <source>SPRINGER Verlag New York Heidelberg Berlin, Jahr: 1978</source>
  <isbn>ISBN: 3–387–90144–2</isbn>
  <abstract>Description of the PASCAL standard.</abstract>
  <date> <year>1987</year> <month>07</month> <day>11</day> </date>
</bibitem></bibdoc>
```

While tagging can now be done automatically, the definition of the different DSDs remains a manual task. Current work investigates the benefits of using 'learning by example' for this task [34]. Instead of defining the DSD directly, the reviewer tags some example documents at his wishes. A learning system generalizes these markups to a DSD and tags some more documents. Interactive corrections by the reviewer will then step by step refine the definition to a DSD that accepts all necessary documents [13].

Furthermore, this structural enrichment can be used to assist the process of scanning printed documents. The additional layout information that has been detected by a scanning tool [39], e.g. fonts or two-dimensional placement, can be fed into the enrichment component to achieve maximum benefit of the available structural knowledge [12].

3.2 Integration of External Databases

For a reasonable supply of information it is necessary to access external databases. This external data has to be represented in a way that fits locally stored information to allow common manipulation. This mapping of external formats to a unified view is known as *schema integration*. The main problem of this task is the *design autonomy* of the external databases. They use different data models (*heterogeneity*), model different aspects of the real world (*perspective*), and even the same situation may be represented in many different ways (*semantic relativism*) [3][43].

The problem of heterogeneity can be solved by mapping the exported schema of each external database onto a *local schema*, i.e. a representation of its structure in terms of the local data model [28]. Therefore, the local data model must provide means for an adequate modelling of the export schemas (*semantic model*) and for the specification of the procedural parts of this mapping. Both demands can be captured by an *object-oriented database* like VODAK [27]. *Objects* with *properties* and *methods* are the basis for storing the external information. A well-defined interface for their manipulation prevents abuse of the properties and hides the external accesses (*transparency*). Complicated actions on an external database can thus look like simple property accesses. Aggregation of objects into *classes* and *inheritance mechanisms* allow to define *relationships* between these objects and certify the semantic power of the object-oriented model.

After this mapping, each export schema is accessible as a disjoint local schema. Although this allows a unified access, overlapping information of the different sites introduces high redundancy and conflicts. Furthermore, the different schemas are not connected and related information has to be collected explicitly during retrievals. Therefore, the goal of schema integration is to create one (partial) overall schema that combines all needed information from all databases with as little redundancy as possible. In a *preintegration phase*, the assertions and constraints of the different local schemas are collected. Then the schemas are being *compared*, and correspondences between the different entities, mapping instructions and additional constraints are defined. Finally, the single schemas have to be *transformed* to conform to the global view, before they will be *merged* into the large schema. While complete integration is neither realistic nor required, a methodology is still necessary to dynamically integrate those portions of external databases, which are needed to create a sufficient view for the application domains.

Example:

In this example we assume a situation where two sources of personal data shall be integrated into one class. The first one could be an on-line server containing information on all employees, the second one a local relational database on members of a special working group. Figure 2 shows the local schemas that represent the external databases and a possible mapping to one integrated class.

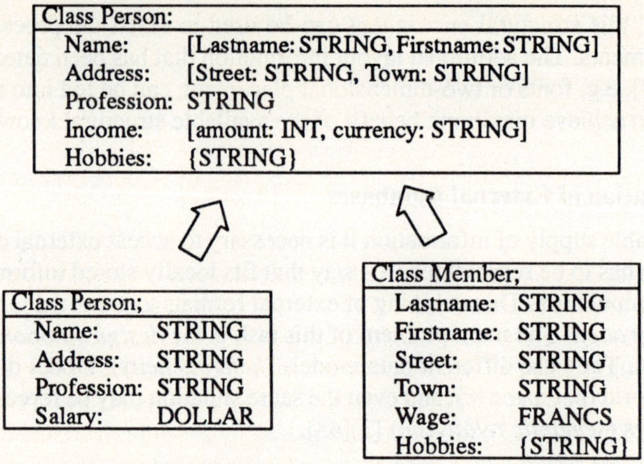

Figure 2: Simple Integration of two Similar Classes

The first problem to be solved in this integration step is the detection of corresponding items and their respective semantics. While the name information can be expected to be a key for the person, the addresses stored in both sources may differ (e.g. company address versus home address). 'Salary' and 'Wage' have to be compared and then combined, e.g. by selecting one or summing up both. All these mappings, not forgetting the separation of first name and last name in the left local schema, must be expressible in the system.

Schema integration methodologies that have been developed until now can be divided into two major categories. Methods using upward inheritance or correspondence assertions and integration rules [3][43] can be categorized as *strict integration.* They are sound, but at the same time intolerant and restrictive. *Heuristic techniques* like best paths, spanning trees and structural similarity [17][30][33] allow a more practicable handling of the problems but lack in soundness. The declarative integration methodology developed at our institute [40] extends strict unification techniques in such a way, that even structural heterogeneity can be treated to a large degree. In addition, we use background knowledge in the form of a fuzzy terminological network to make more real world semantics about local schemas explicit. The overall paradigm of our methodology is the undiscriminated assistance of top down as well as bottom up semantic integration. The result of an interactive integration procedure assisted by this methodology is a partially integrated schema together with mappings for transforming requests to the external databases [11].

3.3 Storing Videos and Audios in Databases

The simplest approach for adding multimedia information like video or audio to a database is to store only references to the external sources and to add some descriptive data like size or contents [36]. Together with some predefined functions for presentation, an integrated access to this data is given. However, there are almost no manipulation capabilities and neither persistency nor locking mechanism are available, because the sources reside outside of the database.

While this solution remains the only possible way for integrating analogue data, digitized videos and sound samples can be directly stored in the database by the use of long fields or better by object-oriented modelling [26][38]. The advantage of storing the data in the database itself is the applicability of database features like *data independence*, *persistency*, and *recovery* to this data. However, when a database stores these multimedia types, it must be able to cope with the following three qualities: *data volume*, *time dependency*, and *interaction* [37].

Data Volume. Videos and audios need immense storage and bandwidth capacities. 90 minutes of a standard video format take 41 gigabytes of memory and need a transmission rate of 60 million bits per second! In spite of growing capacities, compression algorithms are a basic need for effective work with this data. When lossless compression algorithms are not powerful enough, loss of information is accepted to gain higher reduction ratios (e.g. JPEG). Normally, this loss is invisible, because high resolution images contain a lot of noise, but repeated compressing and decompressing during an editing session accumulates the deviations to an unacceptable degree and gives need for special editing mechanisms [37]. In addition to single frame compression, videos can be further reduced by exploiting common contents of consecutive frames (e.g. MPEG). Referencing techniques instead of copying, partial access and continuous loading in the background are further items that have to be observed in an implementation.

Time Dependency. Videos and audios have to be presented as a predefined sequence of presentation states with determined durations. First of all, the system must provide means for the definition of temporal information and its synchronization. To avoid unnecessary dependencies between different media, timing should not be based on one selected information stream. All temporal data should be related to one abstract time scale as a global reference. To be able to satisfy these timing requirements, the database must provide some real-time assertions. Synchronicity measurements like *speed ratio* or *jitter* can be used to detect the current presentation quality and to change some parameters, if necessary [2]. When, for example, the transmission speed is too small, some frames of the currently displayed video may be dropped to achieve the original presentation speed. The third important point of time-dependent, and thus time-consuming media, is the need for parallel tasks. Otherwise, the presentation of a video would block the whole database for the duration of the presentation.

User Interaction. As opposed to simple data, it is not desirable that the result of a query, which may be a video, can only be presented as a whole. The user must be able to pause the presentation, to wind or rewind, to continue, or to abort the presentation (*movie actions*). He or she must be able to change window sizes, volume and brightness (*scaling actions*), and to follow links in the presentation of hypermedia documents (*decision actions*). The functionality of a VCR constitutes a good basis for a user interface. It can be extended with direct positioning capabilities and editing functions.

Object-oriented databases provide good means for modelling the content and behaviour of multimedia information and for implementing the functionality of presentation devices. However, the need for special buffering mechanisms and the assertion of real-time aspects go beyond the usual capabilities of such object-oriented models. Therefore, it will normally be necessary to add new predefined datatypes to the database system, which implement at least the basic features. The higher level objects can then be constructed from these basic items. Furthermore, the representations should be modelled as implementation independent as possible. Inheritance mechanisms can then be used to integrate new standards without changing existing applications. These investigations constitute the work of the AMOS project in our institute. Media and device information are being implemented on top of (and inside of) VODAK, and synchronization features are taken from 'Imestre' [47].

4 Retrieval and Visualization

To releave users from the burden of acquiring database-specific knowledge (as suggested in the first section of this paper) domain-knowledge has to be embedded in the retrieval systems which access an individualized information pool. A typical example of mixing structured and unstructured information is academic information about research projects, topics, companies and people. The systems discussed in the following sections use the CORDIS (Community Research and Development Information Service) data, which provide information about European Community research programs, funded projects, contact persons etc.. The originally unstructured data has been converted to relational and hyper-linked information spaces [15] and it has been enriched with multimedia information (pictures, maps, videos), whereby the original information (records and text documents) is still accessible. Terminological knowledge for the area of computer science is accessible through a module called *Knowledge Explorer* [29], which has conceptual knowledge of (parts of) the database domain and provides content-based reformulation suggestions.

Users typically do not search for independent information items but for relevant information objects, e.g., research programs and projects, which fulfill certain conditions (topic, duration, nationality of partners etc.). An appropriate information handling system must possess the capability to store, control and retrieve unstructured, structured and multimedia information. Furthermore, it should mediate between different national languages and different domain-specific terminologies. And, as we already mentioned in previous sections of this paper, it should give intelligent support to (novice) users, who are unfamiliar with the domain and/or the retrieval system.

In the following sections, we discuss three systems developed at GMD-IPSI, which are designed to integrate at least some of the outlined divergent tasks. Section 4.1 describes MERIT, which provides a so-called multimodal dialogue retrieval interface (using the CORDIS database as an example). In section 4.2 we introduce TORI (and its enhanced version HYDRA), which combines different retrieval paradigms. The last approach discussed in section 4.3 outlines an intuitive 3D-visualization tool for complex information structures in the CORDIS domain.

4.1 Multimodal Dialogues

Multimedia information pools require various means of accessing and interfacing information. As the information structure becomes complex, most interfaces allow users to investigate the information items directly. This interface design reduces the distance between the user's intentions and the objects taking part in his/her actions to a minimum [24]. But this exploratory approach to information retrieval has to face problems of disorientation (which are also well-known in hypertext applications) arising from browsing in unknown information spaces. One way to overcome the deficiencies is to combine the direct manipulation of objects with cooperative system responses.

The design of MERIT (Multimedia Extensions to Retrieval Interaction Tools) is built around such a kind of hybrid interaction style, integrating graphical and natural language components in a multimedia environment. Since man-machine interactions regarding cooperation as a dialogue between two partners are often referred to as the conversation metaphor this approach is called *multimodal conversation* or *multimodal dialogues* [44].

The main difference between direct manipulative interface systems and the conversational approach of MERIT is that user inputs (mouse clicks, menu selections, help-calls) are interpreted as dialogue acts, i.e., they do not rise function calls etc. directly but are treated as dialogue statements. An underlying conversational roles network *COR* ([44], details of the formalism can be found in [42]) defines the generic dialogue acts available (e.g. requesting or offering information, answering, evaluating). It can be regarded as a recursive state-transition network, where transitions are instances of dialogue acts connecting follow-up dialogue states. An attempt to combine this speech act oriented dialogue model with Rhetorical Structure Theory [31] was made by [32]. Mai-

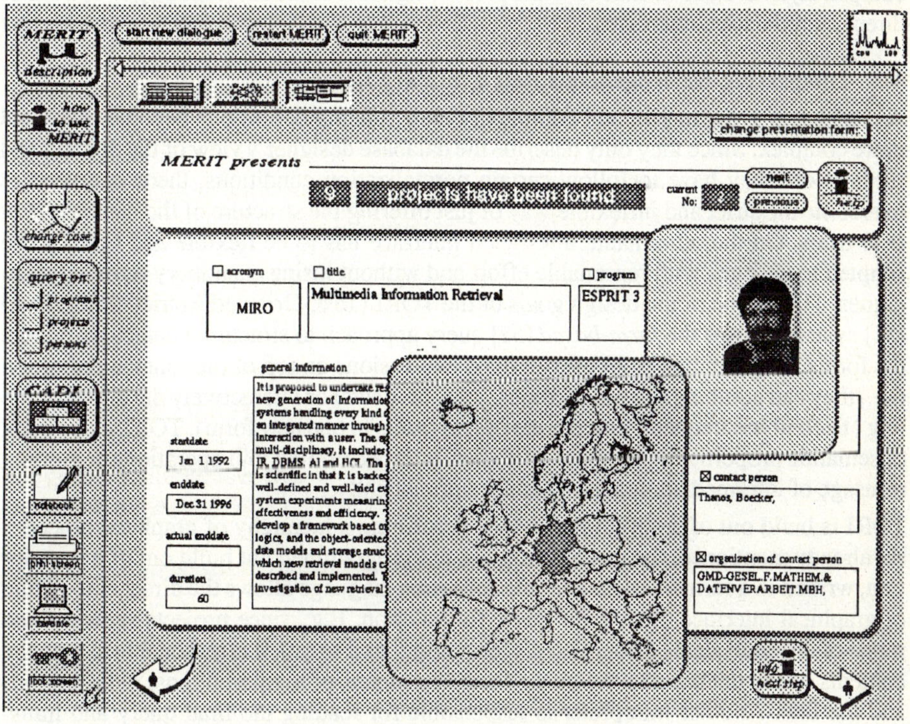

Figure 3: Sample Screen of MERIT

er & Sitter describe a framework for integrating a natural language generation component into the dialogue manager of MERIT.

The COR network describes the illocutionary level of dialogues but does not supply means for a specification on the thematic or topical level. Since we argued for cooperative support with respect to information-seeking strategies, we have to supply prescriptive additions to the dialogue model. Based on the classification of dialogues in information systems [5], Belkin, Cool, Stein and Thiel [4] developed a set of typical dialogue plans or scripts. On the implementation level in MERIT, dialogues are presented as a sequence of dialogue steps as described in the COR network. The selection of a certain dialogue plan based on past experience (in previous dialogues) is pursued in the area of case-based reasoning. These ideas have been adopted to the requirements of a user-guidance component [50][45].

Another knowledge-based component of MERIT supports flexible control of visual dialogues. At any time during a guided interaction the user must have the opportunity to withdraw a step, reject a system's offer, start a sub-dialogue etc. The MERIT *Presentation Manager* automatically maps information structures and dialogue act types to graphical presentations, e.g., mapping relational information spaces to ring presentations or visualizing iconic dialogue control objects. This mapping is guided by specialized knowledge bases to find the most appropriate representation with respect to human cognitive and perceptual capabilities (e.g. using spatial grouping of objects and different colouring to indicate the degree of similarity [45]). This leads to a reduction of the complexity of the user interface while preserving most of the useful dialogue options of direct manipulative interfaces.

4.2 Integrating Heterogeneous Retrieval Paradigms

As databases grow in size and complexity their schema definitions become more and more complex. Since they only describe the database designer's view of the domain and furthermore they have to follow certain normalization conditions, there is a need to overcome the strict and inflexible way of just offering the structure of the database *as it is* to users. On the other hand, a retrieval interface has to be flexible and needs to be adapted to changes with reasonable effort and without losing customary retrieval techniques. This is one of the design goals of the TORI (Task-Oriented Retrieval Interface) [51] system. It uses the *form-based* [52] query approach to structured databases, where the forms are generated from user-defined expressions on top of the schema definition (i.e., they can combine several relations, joins or views) or interactively during run-time (e.g., to combine frequently used parts of two forms in one new form). TORI keeps track of semantic properties of database attributes, thus performing join operations or guiding re-usage of intermediate retrieval results automatically.

TORI is build out of several interpreters, describing a hierarchy of graphical objects[2]. As already mentioned, the query-forms are not programmed but build out of a description, written in a formal language. This definition language allows the direct embedding of graphical interface objects for query formulation. E.g., since projects show a fixed range of different status ('completed', 'executing' and so on), it is reasonable to map the contents of the database to the query-forms by means of toggle-buttons, radio-buttons and the like. Another interpreter is responsible for reading the final query and transforming it to the underlying DBMS. The complete interface of TORI is based on collections of graphical objects, which are also accessible to these interpreters. This allows a unique integration of graphical means to express Boolean conditions between different forms[3] with objects representing limited ranges of database contents and general means like text input fields or sliders for numerical values. Furthermore, TORI also uses graphical objects to display multimedia information (video, pictures), so that there is one unique layout design of query- and result-forms, even for multimedia data.

While relational databases are appropriate for large amounts of structured data, traditional full-text information retrieval systems cope with unstructured data (e.g. bibliographic records, long textual documents). The flexibility of the design of TORI enabled us to integrate two retrieval paradigms into one system. We used the RDBMS Sybase to store the relational structured part of the CORDIS domain, offering complex boolean queries and conditions on strongly typed attribute fields. INQUERY, an experimental IR system using Bayesian inference nets [8], allows sophisticated queries for unstructured data like "find projects *related* to the *area* of database research" and returns belief values for retrieved documents, thus enabling a ranking of result items. The HYDRA approach [16] uses an *embedded full integration* approach, where the two retrieval systems process mutually independent, but share an integration phase for the retrieval results. HYDRA, which in fact is realized through several add-ons to the kernels of INQUERY and SYBASE, could be build on top of TORI with just a few refinements of the TORI interpreters. As a consequence, the user interface changed only slightly (only two additional graphical objects in the appropriate query-forms), hiding the underlying mechanisms from the user but allowing queries like "find 'ESPRIT 3' projects *related* to the *area* of database research, *starting* 1993, and *sort* the results by *relevance*".

The direct-manipulative interface of TORI is essential for the dynamic and flexible style of building the system but again raises the problems of disorientation, which have been addressed in MERIT with the dialogue-oriented interaction techniques. In contrast to this approach, TORI employs task-models to capture the user's behaviour [19]. Single information seeking activities are seen as embedded sub-tasks in a higher-level task context where information is assembled to solve a given problem. TORI monitors those intermediate steps and tries to interpret them as goal-driven behaviour. This happens in an external module (the *task-parser*) which can suggest follow-up steps to reach a recognized plan (which may not be obvious to find for the user inside the TORI system).

4.3 Content-based Visualization of Complex Information Structures

Interface design has seen two dimensions of complexity. Starting from one-dimensional ASCII terminals the next paradigm has been the two-dimensional desktop metaphor, resembling piles of documents, folders and so on. Current hard- and software develop-

2. TORI objects are mapped to OSF/Motif objects and widgets, thus enabling dynamic re-configuring of windows if appropriate. One non-standard resource of TORI objects is the interaction language. The entire system can be switched to another interaction language with one call to the object interpreter, including natural language special character support.
3. This is necessary to overcome most of the restrictions, which are inherent to form-based interfaces, e.g., difficulties to specify nested queries.

ments open the door for the three-dimensional representation of information spaces, using human capabilities of spatial perception. Based on the content-based interface design proposed in [1], Hemmje [18] developed an 3D interface to INQUERYs representation of dependent information. This approach tries to overcome the deficiencies of INQUERY (a retrieval system with a command-line based interface) and the HYDRA approach (combining search techniques for relational and unstructured data but requiring the users to formulate his/her information need in terms of an unknown information spacc) by visualizing the data itself.

Vector-based query techniques are widely distributed in information retrieval [1]. The process of retrieval typically is based on a cycle of query-formulation and result-evaluation, which adjusts the query vector to the assumed information need of the user. This new vector has to be mapped to the underlying data structure (the index from terms to documents) and the process iterates.

The central idea of visualizating information spaces is to omit the intermediate process of mapping from terms to documents (and vice versa) and to visualize the index structure itself. Hemmje [18] introduces the concept of *content-based search paths* which can be adjusted interactively. The immediate responses of the systems allows a direct browsing of the term-document structure and thus frees the users from the need to find the correct terms. Zooming techniques and the representation of the index structure as cone-tress [9] facilitate an overview of potentially large information spaces. New kinds of input devices like data-gloves and space-balls are currently integrated to provide adequate control facilities [6].

5 Conclusions

Instead of summarizing the different topics discussed in the previous sections we would like to sketch the ongoing development at GMD-IPSI of an integrated prototype, which in fact summarizes several aspects and systems described here. The concept of an integrated prototype is twofold: on the one hand, it should integrate existing tools and applications to demonstrate their usability and on the other hand, it should address new domains of information handling to challenge the development of new concepts.

The *Multimedia Forum* [37], an SGML-based information service, is such an integrated prototype. It is a kind of 'multimedia-review' of current events, interviews, publications and films and offers a hyper-linked information pool to its readers. The Multimedia Forum uses several tools described in this paper (e.g., the DREAM parser to enrich plain text with structural information, the SDB database layer [21] for storage and retrieval of hyper-linked information etc.).

The information pool can be read from several users and it is maintained from a newly developed editor's workbench, which provides means to access and import all kind of data, synchronous displaying of video/audio information [47], hyper-link editing and retrieval. The Multimedia Forum is already in use and provides a current survey of research activities, social events, news and so on.

Future work at GMD-IPSI will be integrated into the Multimedia Forum in order to test mutual combinations of up to now isolated solutions. Next steps will be to integrate document recognition techniques, to design multimedia document management tools, and to add editor support to handle documents with time-dependent information (e.g. video editing). Since the information pool of the Multimedia Forum itself is an individualized information space, newly developed techniques for information handling systems – acquisition, storage, distribution, retrieval and visualization – will be incorporated into the system in the future.

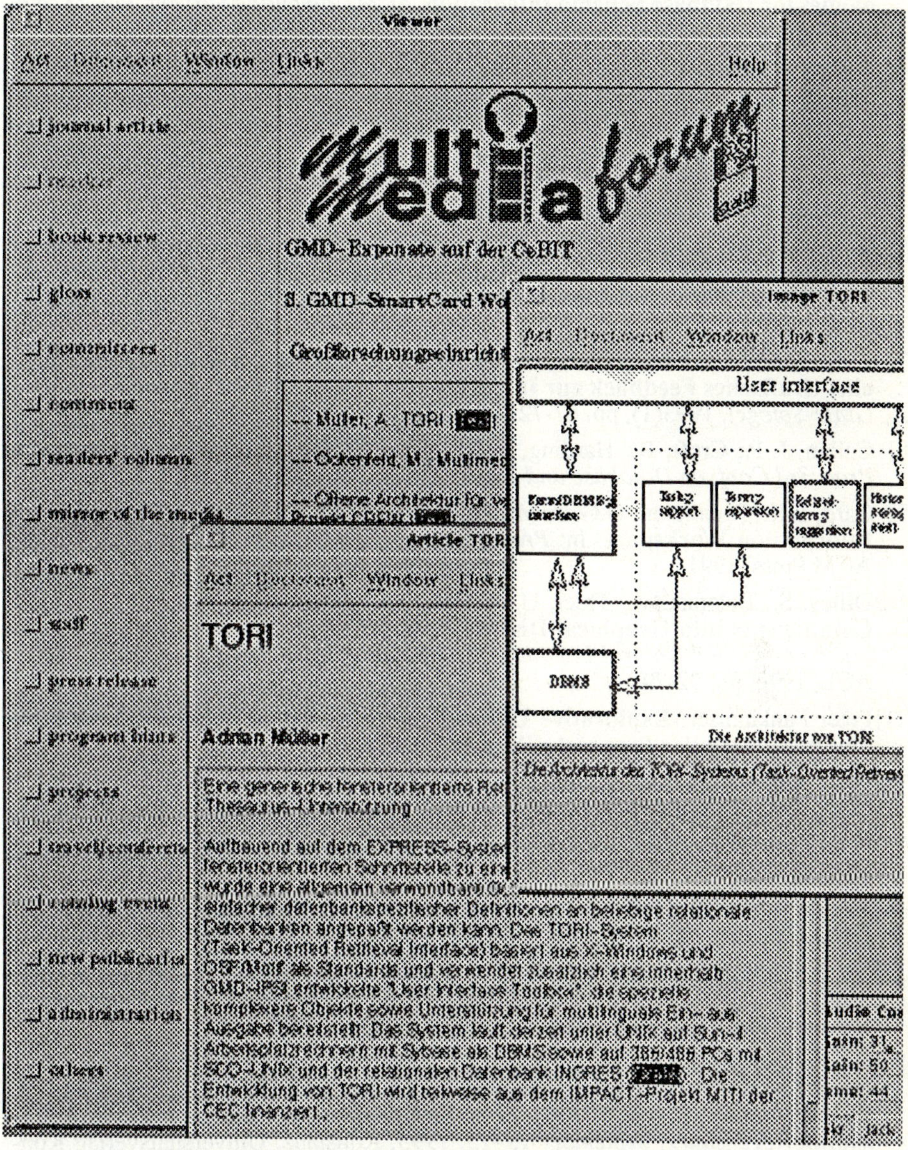

Figure 4: Multimedia Forum, Displaying an Article on TORI

References

[1] Agosti, M., Gradenigo, G. & Marchetti, P.G.: **Architecture and Functions for a Conceptual Interface to very large Online Bibliographic Collections.** In: *Intelligent Text and Image Handling*, RIAO 91, Barcelona, Spain, April 1991

[2] D. P. Anderson, G. Homsy: **A Continuous Media I/O Server and Its Synchronization Mechanism.** *Computer, Vol. 24, No. 10, October 1991;* pp. 51–57

[3] C. Batini, M. Lenzerini, and S. V. Navathe: **A Comparative Analysis of Methodologies for Database Schema Integration.** *ACM Computing Surveys, Vol. 18; No. 4, 1986;* pp. 323–364

[4] Belkin, N.J., Cool, C., Stein, A. & Thiel, U.: **Scripts for Information Seeking Dialogues.** Paper presented at: *AAAI Spring Symposium on Case-Based Reasoning and Information Retrieval, Stanford, California, March 23-25, 1993.*

[5] Belkin, N.J., Marchetti, P.G. & Cool, C.: **BRAQUE: Design of an Interface to Support User Interaction in Information Retrieval.** In: *Information Processing & Management. Special Issue on Hypertext* 29(4).

[6] Bordegoni, M. & Hemmje, M.: **A Dymamic Gesture Language and Graphical Feedback for Interaction in a 3D User Interface.** To appear in: *Proc. of the Eurographics '93, Barcelona, Spain, Sept. 6-10, 1993.* Oxford, Great Britain: Blackwell, 1993.

[7] Bordegoni, M., Hemmje, M. & Effenberger, D.: **Eine dynamische Gestensprache. Grafisches Feedback zur Interaktion in einem 3D-User Interface.** In: *Der GMD-Spiegel*, 1993(1), pp. 67-72.

[8] Callan, J. P.; Croft, B.; Harding, S. M.: **The INQUERY Retrieval System.** In: *Proc. 3rd Conf. on Database and Expert Systems Applications*, Sept. 1992.

[9] Card, S.K., Robertson, G.G. & Mackinlay, J.D.: **The Information Visualizer, an Information Workspace.** In: *Proceedings of CHI'91*, New Orleans, April 1991, ACM Press, 1991

[10] Dilley, S., Bateman, J., Thiel, U. & Tißen, A.: **Integrating Natural Language Components into Graphical Discourse.** In: *ANLP '92, Proc. of the 3rd Conference on Applied Natural Language Processing, Trento, Italy, March/April 1992.* ACL, 1992, pp. 72-79.

[11] Peter Fankhauser: **Explorative Unification for Semantic Database Interoperability.** *Dissertation Proposal, GMD–IPSI, May 1993*

[12] Peter Fankhauser, Jörg Schmidt, Xu Yi: **STREAM Research and Development Plan.** *GMD-IPSI internal draft, 1992*

[13] Peter Fankhauser, Xu Yi: **MarkItUp! – An Incremental Approach to Document Structure Recognition.** *Internal Draft.*

[14] Tilman Göttke, Peter Fankhauser: **DREAM2.0 User Manual.** *Arbeitspapiere der GMD 660, July 1992*

[15] Gu, J. & Thiel, U.: **Automatically Converting Linear Text to Hypertext. A Case Study.** In: Frei, H.P. & Schäuble, P. (eds.): *Proc. of Hypermedia '93, Zürich, Switzerland, March 2-3, 1993.* Berlin: Springer, 1993, pp. 220-231.

[16] Gu, J., Thiel, U. & Zhao, J.: **Efficient Retrieval of Complex Objects: Query Processing in a Hybrid DB and IR System.** To appear in: Knorz, G., Krause, J. & Womser-Hacker, C. (eds.): *IR'93. Proc. 1st German Natl. Conf. on Information Retrieval, Regensburg, September 13–15, 1993*, Konstanz: Universitätsverlag Konstanz, 1993.

[17] S. Hayne, Sudha Ram: **Multi–User View Integration System (MUVIS): An Expert System for View Integration.** *Proceedings of the 6th International Conference on Data Engineering*; Feb. 1990

[18] Hemmje, M.: **Eine inhaltsorientierte, intuitive 3D Benutzerschnittstelle für Information Retrieval Systeme.** In: *Proceedings of GI–IR Tagung*, Regensburg, Sept. 1993 (forthcoming).

[19] Hoppe, H.U. & Schiele, F.: **Towards Task Models for Embedded Information Retrieval.** In: *Proceedings of CHI '92, May 3-7, 1992, Monterey, CA.*

[20] Gerald Huck: **SED – A Graphical Schema Editor for VML.** *Diploma Thesis at TH Darmstadt, 1992*

[21] Christoph Hüser: **Report on a Prototypical Interface for Structured Documents and its Application to the IEN Scenario.** *Technical Report 75/GMD/IPS/DS/L/047/b0, TELEPUBLISHING Project, RACE-Programme, August 1991.*

[22] Christoph Hüser, Thomas Kamps, Wiebke Möhr, G. Quirchmayr, R. Bilboul, M. Doubleday, R. Woodham, R. Minio, Anne Ankrah, J. Wheeler: **AP1: Requirements, Publishing Process and Environment.** *Technical Report R2042/GMD/IPS/DS/R/008/b1, EUROPUBLISHING Project, RACE–Programme, March 1993*

[23] Christoph Hüser, Anja Weber: **The Individualized Electronic Newspaper: An Application Challenging Hypertext Technology.** *In: Ralf Cordes, Norbert Streitz (ed.): Hypertext und Hypermedien 1992: Konzepte und Anwendungen auf dem Weg in die Praxis; GI–Fachtagung München. Springer Verlag, Heidelberg 1992.*

[24] Hutchins, E.L., Hollan, J.D., & Norman, D.: **Direct Manipulation Interfaces.** In: Norman, D.A. & Draper, S.A. (eds.): *User Centered System Design: New Perspectives on Human Computer Interaction*, 87–124. Hillsdale, NJ: Erlbaum, 1986.

[25] ISO–IS8879: **Information Processing – Text and Office Systems – Standardized Generalized Markup Language (SGML).** *Ref. No. ISO 8879–1986(E); International Organization of Standardization, 1986.*

[26] Wolfgang Klas: **Tailoring an Object-Oriented Database System to Integrate External Multimedia Devices.** *Proceedings of 1992 Workshop on Heterogeneous Databases and Semantic Interoperability, February 1992, Boulder, Colorado*

[27] Wolfgang Klas et al.: **VODAK Design Specification Document.** *GMD–IPSI internal draft, November 1992*

[28] Wolfgang Klas, Gisela Fischer, Karl Aberer: **Integrating a Relational Database System into VODAK using its Metaclass Concept.** *Arbeitspapiere der GMD No. 738, Sankt Augustin, March 1993*

[29] Kracker, M.: **A Fuzzy Concept Network Model and its Applications.** In: *Proc. of the FUZZ-IEEE '92, San Diego, March 1992*, pp. 760-768.

[30] D. Lin, D. McGregor: **A Distributed Approximation Algorithm for the Steiner Problem in Graphs and its Application in Natural Language Understanding.** *Proceedings of the 13th Conference on Graphtheoretic Concepts in Computer Science (WG87), 1987*

[31] Mann, W.C. & Thompson, S.A.: **Rhetorical Structure Theory: Description and Construction of Text Structures.** In: Kempen, G. (ed.): *Natural Language Generation.* Dordrecht/Netherlands: Martinus Nijhoff Publishers, 1987, pp. 85–96

[32] Maier, E. & Sitter, S.: **An Extension of Rhetorical Structure Theory for the Treatment of Retrieval Dialogues.** In: *CogSci '92, Proc. of the 14th Annual Conference of the Cognitive Science Society, Bloomington, Indiana, July 1992.* Hillsdale, NJ: Erlbaum, 1992, pp. 968-973.

[33] Ashish Mehta, James Geller, Yehoshua Perl, Peter Fankhauser: **Algorithms for Access Relevance to Support Path–Method Generation in OODBs.** *RIDE–IMS, Vienna, April 93.*

[34] D. H. Mo, I. H. Witten: **Learning Text Editing Tasks from Examples: a Procedural Approach.** *Behavior & Information Technology, Vol. 11 (1), 1992*, pp. 32–45

[35] Wiebke Möhr; Lothar Rostek: **TEDI: An Object-Oriented Terminology Editor.** *In: Terminology and Knowledge Engineering. Proceedings of the TKE' 93, Cologne, August 1993; INDEKS–Verlag (to appear)*

[36] Thomas C. Rakow: **Der V² Video-Server – Analoges Video mit Datenbankmanagementsystemen.** *GMD-Spiegel 3/4 92, Sankt Augustin, Nov. 1992*, S. 67–69

[37] Thomas C. Rakow, Michael Löhr, Frank Moser, Erich J. Neuhold, Klaus Süllow: **Einsatz von objektorientierten Datenbanksystemen für Multimedia–Anwendungen.** To be published in: *it + ti – Informationstechnik und Technische Informatik, Themenheft „Multimedia", Oldenbourg Verlag, München, Juni 1993.*

[38] Thomas C. Rakow, Peter Muth: **The V³ Video server – Managing Analog and Digital Video Clips.** *Demonstration description at SIGMOD '93, Washington DC, May 1993.*

[39] Jörg Schmidt, Wolfgang Putz: **Knowledge Acquisition and Representation for Document Structure Recognition: the CAROL Project.** *Proceedings of the Ninth IEEE Conference on Artificial Intelligence in Applications, Orlando/Florida March 1–5, 1993, IEEE Computer Society Press 1993*

[40] Michael Schrefl, Erich J. Neuhold: **Object Class Definition by Generalization using Upward Inheritance.** *Proceedings of the 4th International Conference on Data Engineering, IEEE, 1988*; pp. 4–13

[41] Helge Schütt, Norbert Streitz: **HyperBase: A Hypermedia Engine Based on a Relational Database Management System.** *In: A. Rizk, N. Streitz, J. André (eds): Hypertext: Concepts, Systems, and Applications (ECHT' 90), Cambridge University Press, Cambridge, 1990.* pp. 95–108

[42] Sitter, S. & Stein, A.: **Modeling the Illocutionary Aspects of Information-Seeking Dialogues.** *Information Processing & Management, Vol. 28 (2)*, 1992, pp. 165-180.

[43] Stefano Spaccapietra, Christine Parent, Y. Dupont: **View integration: a step forward in solving structural conflicts.** *LBD, DI, EPF Lausanne 90, to appear in IEEE Transactions on Knowledge and Data Engineering, October 1992*

[44] Stein, A. & Thiel, U.: **A Conversational Model of Multimodal Interaction.** Paper presented at: *HCIC '93, Human Computer Interaction Consortium 1993 Winter Workshop, Atlanta, GA, Jan. 23-26, 1993.*

[45] Stein, A., Thiel, U. & Tißen, A.: **Knowledge-Based Control of Visual Dialogues in Information Systems.** In: Catarci, T., Costabile, M.F. & Levialdi, S. (eds.): *AVI '92, Proc. of the 1st International Workshop on Advanced Visual Interfaces, Rome, Italy, Mai 27-29, 1992.* World Scientific Series in Computer Science, Vol. 38, Singapur et al.: World Scientific Press, 1992, pp. 138-155.

[46] Norbert Streitz, Jörg Haake, Jörg Hannemann, Andreas Lemke, Wolfgang Schuler, Helge Schütt, Manfred Thüring: **SEPIA: A Cooperative Hypermedia Authoring Environment.** *Proceedings of the ACM Conference on Hypertext (ECHT' 92), Milano, Italy, 1992*, pp.11–22

[47] Süllow, K.L: **Technologien zur spontanen Nutzung von digitalen Videos**, In: *Der GMD-Spiegel*, 1993(2), (forthcoming)

[48] Thiel, U., Hemmje, M., Kerner, A., Kracker, M., Sitter, S., Stein, A. & Tißen, A.: **Towards a User-Centered Interface for Information Retrieval: The MERIT System.** In: *Arbeitspapiere der GMD No 699*, Sankt Augustin: GMD, Nov. 1992.

[49]Heiko Thimm, Thomas C. Rakow: **Accessing Multimedia Archives in a Public Mail Network: Specification of the User's Perspective for the Applications Information Archive and Work Flow Mangement.** *Working Paper, GMD-IPSI, Feb. 1993*

[50]Tißen, A.: **Knowledge Bases for User Guidance in Information Seeking Dialogues.** In: Wayne, D. G., et al. (eds.): *IWIUI '93, Proc. of the 1993 International Workshop on Intelligent User Interfaces, Orlando, FL, January 4-7, 1993.* New York: ACM Press, 1993, pp. 149-156.

[51]Zhao, J., Kostka, B. & Müller, A.: **An Integrated Approach to Task-Oriented Database Retrieval Interfaces.** In: Richard Cooper (ed.). *Interfaces to Databases 1992, Proc. of the First International Workshop on Interfaces to Database Systems. Glasgow, July 1-3, 1992.* Berlin et al.: Springer, 1992. pp 51-68.

[52]Zloof MM. **The Query-by-Example Concept for User-Oriented Business Systems.** In: Sime ME, Coombs MJ (ed). *Designing for Human-Computer Communication.* London et al.: Academic Press, 1983, pp. 285-309.

Context Versions in an Object-Oriented Model

Lina Al-Jadir, Gilles Falquet, Michel Léonard [1]

Université de Genève
Centre Universitaire d'Informatique
24, rue Général-Dufour, 1211 Genève 4, Switzerland
tél.: +41 22 705.77.70, fax: +41 22 320.29.27
(aljadir | falquet | leonard)@cui.unige.ch

Abstract. The concept of context in an object-oriented database model is first presented in this paper. A context is an associative abstraction of the schema which consists of a structure, rules and methods. A connection function is used to compute objects associations according to the context structure and rules. Then the concept of dynamic context is introduced. A dynamic context is composed of context versions and allows to model objects life-cycles. A Petri Net describes conditions under which objects may go from one context version to another.

Keywords: object-oriented model, context, evolution, context version, life-cycle, dynamic context.

1 Introduction

Database applications are becoming larger and more complex. Domain modelling often gives complicated schemas which are difficult to understand globally. Furthermore, cycles in schemas introduce semantic ambiguity. As a consequence, the database programmer or end-user is not always able to fully and correctly understand and exploit the stored data. This led to the definition of views and contexts. The context concept was introduced in [6] to ease database querying. In this paper, we extend it by adding to its definition rules and methods.

Structural and dynamic aspects are often separated in DBMS. The form and the behaviour of objects change over time. Objects have a different structure and respond to different rules and methods at different periods of their life-cycle. By introducing context versions, we will be able to follow the evolution of objects in their context.

The paper is organized as follows. In section 2, we mention related approaches. In section 3, we present the Farandole 2 object-oriented data model. In section 4, we develop the notion of context: we present its structure, rules, connection functions and methods. In section 5, we present dynamic contexts with context versions.

---

1. This research was supported by the Swiss National Funds for the Scientific Research (FNRS) under grant no. 20-34056.92.

2 Principal Approaches

Views, which are well known in the relational model as a tool to simplify data access, are still not well defined in the object-oriented model. Several proposals have been given in different papers [16, 8, 11, 1]. Roles in [13, 14] have been defined to express the different behaviours of an object during its life-cycle.

Shilling and Sweeney's Views. In [16], the notion of view is introduced in an object-oriented model. A view is defined on a class. It gives:

- Multiple interfaces: a class may have a different set of methods in two different views. Furthermore, the same method may have a different implementation in two different views.
- Visibility of instance variables: a view allows to show or hide instance variables of a class. It allows also to specify if an instance variable is modifiable or read-only.
- Copies of instance variable sets: a view allows to have multiple activations for the same interface, which means multiple copies of instance variables to occur within an object instance.

An object instance is member of a view instance if it has been created in the view instance or if it has joined the view instance explicitly by an operation. An object instance may participate in many view instances but it has the same object identifier. To access an object, we have to give the object identifier and the view instance identifier.

Heiler and Zdonik's Views. In [8], the view notion is introduced in the functional model FUGUE. The concepts of this model are: objects, functions and types. Functions, when applied to objects, access their attributes, perform operations on objects, or test constraints on them. A function has a signature (types of its input and output arguments) and an implementation. Types specify the functions that can be applied to objects.

A view makes visible certain information from the base, possibly transformed, and hides information which is not specifically included in the view. A view is defined as a set of types and a set of objects, V = [T: {types}, O: {objects}]. A type in a view is a derived type, i.e. it is defined in terms of data abstractions over some base type in the schema, or a new type. The functions of a derived type use functions of the base type.

The set of objects in a view is computed by a query over the database. The query language contains predicate-based selection functions, collection manipulation functions (union, intersection, difference, flatten) and join function which produces a set of tuples. Updates to objects in a view can be implemented in terms of updates to objects of the database.

Two properties are defined: type-closure of a view and value-closure of a view. Type-closure means that for any type t defined in a view V, the definition of V is not missing any types that are needed by functions(t). Value-closure means that it's not possible to cause an object to disappear in the view V by updating its attributes in the view. However, it's possible to cause an object to disappear from a view by updating it in the database. A program always executes in a single view so an object is not visible in two views simultaneously.

Morsi, Navathe and Kim's Views. In [11], a view is defined in an object-oriented model to show certain classes and properties (instance variables and methods) in the same class hierarchy. A view has to be consistent with the underlying database schema. Two invariants have to be verified. The first requires that the set of properties of a class in a view is a subset of its underlying properties. The second requires that the objects of a class in a view is a subset of its underlying objects.

Operations on views are the following:

- class: add, hide, modify (name), categorize (i.e. include all leaf classes which have a common superclass into a single class category).
- property: add, hide, modify (name, class domain, class origin).
- ISA relationship: add, hide.

Pernici's Roles. In the ORM model [13, 14], a class is defined as follows: class = (cn, $\{R_0 = \langle rn_0, P_0, S_0, M_0, Ru_0 \rangle, R_1 = \langle rn_1, P_1, S_1, M_1, Ru_1 \rangle, ..., R_v = \langle rn_v, P_v, S_v, M_v, Ru_v \rangle\}$), where cn is the class name and R_i's are roles that describe different behaviours of an object of the class cn at different stages of its life-cycle. Each role R_i named rn_i, consists of a set of properties P_i, a set of states S_i, a set of messages M_i and a set of rules Ru_i. A property is an instance variable of the class. In a given role, an object is in one of the states S_i. A message can be received or sent by an object. Only the messages that modify the state of an object are considered. A rule indicates which messages can be sent or received for each state and which are the allowed state transitions. Two categories of rules exist: state transition (dynamic) and integrity rule (static).

Each class has a base role R_0 which describes the initial characteristics of an object upon its creation and global properties concerning its evolution. Properties in R_0 are relevant to different roles. Messages in R_0 allow to add, delete, suspend and resume a role instance. States in R_0 are active and suspended. An object becomes active when it is created. A suspended object can neither send, nor receive a message. Rules in R_0 specify transitions between roles and global constraints for a class. Upon the creation of an object in a class, role R_0 is instantiated. Other roles must be explicitly instantiated for an object. They may be instantiated many times for each object of a class.

3 The F2 Model

The Farandole 2 (F2) model is an object-oriented model based on the following concepts: object, class, attribute, generalization/specialization and key [2, 5].

A *class* assembles objects of the same nature. Two types of classes exist: *atomic* classes and *tuple* classes. Integer, real, string, boolean, etc... are examples of atomic classes. These classes have an inferior and a superior bound that delimit the set of their objects. Student, room, course, etc... are examples of tuple classes.

An *attribute* corresponds to a function defined between an *origin* class and a *domain* class, it links objects of these classes. The origin of an attribute must be a tuple class, while the domain of an attribute may be a tuple class or an atomic class. An attribute can be mono- or multi-valued depending on its *maximal cardinality*. It's possible to specify the minimal number of values that an object takes on an attribute by giving its *minimal cardinality*. The minimal cardinality of an attribute, when it is superior to zero, expresses a referential integrity rule.

The objects of a class have an object identifier *oid* and a *value*. Atomic objects are self-identifying, i.e. their oid is equal to their value. The value of an object o in a tuple class C is a tuple formed by the oids of objects linked to o through the attributes of C.

The *generalization/specialization* mechanism allows to specialize a class in subclasses. We call *superclass* of a class C the class from which C has been directly derived. We call *subclass* of a class C the classes directly derived from C. A subclass has a unique superclass (which forbids multiple inheritance in F2). A subclass inherits all the attributes of its superclass and recursively all those of its ancestors. It can have its own additional attributes.

A *key* of a tuple class C is a minimal subset of attributes of C (locally defined or inherited) so that if two objects of C have the same values on these attributes, they are identical (i.e. they have the same oid and consequently the same values on all attributes). A class can have several keys or none. A subclass inherits the keys of its superclass and can have its own additional keys.

Example 3.1: We take the example of a fictive university database and give some class definitions in the F2 data definition language. The class CourseHours is an integer atomic class.

class CourseHours: intType (8..21);

The class Department is a tuple class with three attributes. The attribute in_faculty has minimal cardinality 1 et maximal cardinality 1. Its minimal cardinality means that if a faculty is deleted, all its departments are also deleted. The other attributes have by default minimal cardinality 0 and maximal cardinality 1. The class Department has a key on the attributes dept_acronym and in_faculty.

```
class Department (dept_acronym: SmallText
                  in_faculty: Faculty * 1..1
                  dept_name: LongText)
    key (dept_acronym, in_faculty);
```

The class BigDepartment is a subclass of the class Department.

```
subclass BigDepartment of Department
         (budget: Real);
```

4 Four Steps to Contexts

In the F2 model we introduced the context concept. A context, named cn, is a structure S which is subject to a set of rules R and to which a set of methods M is attached: context = <cn, S, R, M>. A connection function, applied on a context, is used to compute objects associations according to the context structure and rules.

4.1 Step 1: Context Structure

A *context* is an abstraction of the schema constituted by nodes and arcs where:

- a *node* is a pair (N_i: C_i) where N_i is the name of the node and C_i the name of the class on which the node is defined. (The name of the class alone is not sufficient because we can define several nodes on the same class, especially in the case of cyclic schemas cf. §4.3).
- an *arc* is a triple (N_i, A_{ij}, N_j) where N_i and N_j are the names of the nodes that the arc links, and A_{ij} is the name of the attribute on which the arc is defined. The origin class of A_{ij} is the class of N_i and the domain class of A_{ij} is the class of N_j.

A context is represented by a directed connected graph (nodes of atomic classes are not shown to avoid overloading of the graph).

Example 4.1: We build the context "courses planning" (fig. 1). A room *ro* is in a building *bld* described by an acronym, a name, and an address. The room *ro* is identified by a number and contains a number of places. It is reserved for a course *co* at a day of the week between two hours. A course *co* is identified by a number and has a name. It is given in the department *d* of the faculty *f* and is taken by a number of students. Other classes and attributes of the schema are not relevant to this context.

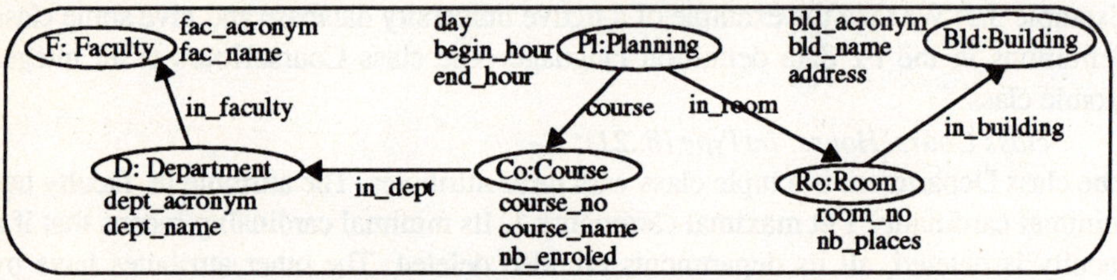

Fig. 1. Context "courses planning"

4.2 Step 2: Context Rules

Objects in a node are objects of the corresponding class which satisfy the rules of the context. There are two types of rules:

- *<path operator value>*: *path* is a list [N_1 A_1 N_2 A_2... N_s A_s N_{s+1}] such that all the nodes N_i ($1 \leq i \leq s+1$) are distinct, and arc A_i ($1 \leq i \leq s$) goes from N_i to N_{i+1} or from N_{i+1} to N_i (a path is non-directed and it is denoted by $N_1.A_1.A_2 \ldots .A_s$); *operator* belongs to the set of operators OPER = {'=', '≠', '<', '≤', '>', '≥', '∈', '∉', '⊆', '¬⊆', '⊇', '¬⊇'}; *value* is an atomic value or a set of atomic values.

- *<path1 operator path2>*: *path1* and *path2* are two paths starting from the same node; *operator* belongs to OPER.

Example 4.2: In the context "courses planning", we add on the node Co:Course the rule: Co.in_dept.in_faculty.fac_acronym = "E", to show only courses of the Economics faculty. This mechanism avoids to overload the schema by adding new subclasses (EconomicsFaculty and OtherFaculty) and provides genericity. In fact, by modifying this rule we can use the same context for courses planning of other faculties. We add another rule on the node Pl:Planning : Pl.course.nb_enroled ≤ Pl.in_room.nb_places.

On the one hand, it is easier to extract rules by examining a context than the whole schema. On the other hand, encapsulating a rule at the level of the schema is rigid. The solution we suggest is more flexible because it allows us to use the same schema with different rules in different contexts. This point is interesting for the evolution of the behaviour of the domain.

Example 4.3: Suppose that we are in housing shortage period and there is a lack of university buildings. We create a context identical to the context "courses planning" but without the last rule so that the number of students in a course can be bigger than the number of places of the room where the course is given. This allows us to treat exceptional cases.

4.3 Step 3: Connection Function

To each subset of tuple nodes (i.e. defined on tuple classes) in a context is associated a unique non-ambiguous semantics. It is given by the *connection function*. Let St be a state of the database and N a subset of tuple nodes in the context K, N = {N_1: C_1, N_2: C_2, ..., N_p: C_p}. The connection function *connect* applied on the context K, on the set N, on the database state St produces a set of tuples [N_1: o_1, N_2: o_2, ..., N_p: o_p] where o_i is the identifier of an object of the class of N_i. The tuple [N_1: o_1, N_2: o_2, ..., N_p: o_p] belongs to connect(K, N, St) if:

- the objects are linked through *all* the paths of the context located between the nodes of N, and
- the objects verify the rules on the paths of the context located between the nodes of N.

Example 4.4: We take the context "courses planning" with the two rules seen in §4.2. Suppose that the database is in the state given by figure 2. The results of the connection

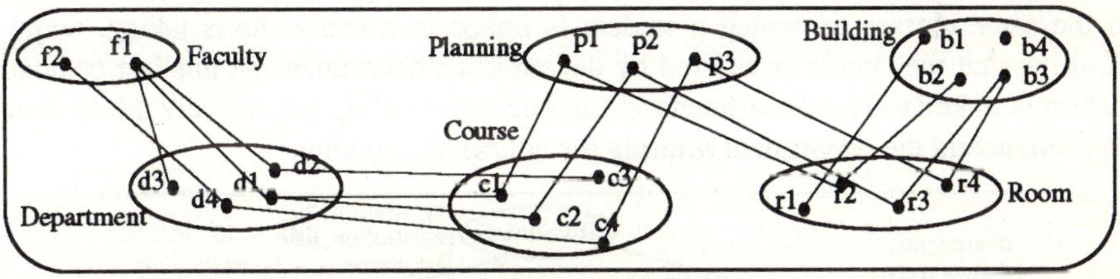

Fig. 2. Database state St

function on different sets of nodes in this context are given in figure 3.

The tuples of a context are not stored, they are computed by the connection function from the objects of the database. An object can appear in nodes of several contexts; it is always identified by the same oid.

When the graph of a context is cyclic, i.e. two nodes are linked by more than one path, each path expresses a semantics. The semantics given by the context is the conjunction

Connect ("courses planning", {Bld}, St):

Bld
b1
b2
b3
b4

Connect ("courses planning", {Ro, Bld}, St):

Ro	Bld
r1	b1
r2	b2
r3	b3
r4	b3

Connect ("courses planning", {Co, Pl, Ro, Bld}, St):

Co	Pl	Ro	Bld
c1	p1	r2	b2
c2	p2	r3	b3
c4	p3	r4	b3

Connect ("courses planning", {F, D, Co, Pl, Ro, Bld}, St): (Economics faculty has oid f1)

F	D	Co	Pl	Ro	Bld
f1	d1	c1	p1	r2	b2
f1	d1	c2	p2	r3	b3

Fig. 3. Connection function on context "courses planning"

of the semantics of all paths that link the two nodes.

Example 4.5: Suppose we take the context given in figure 4. The nodes Stu:Student and

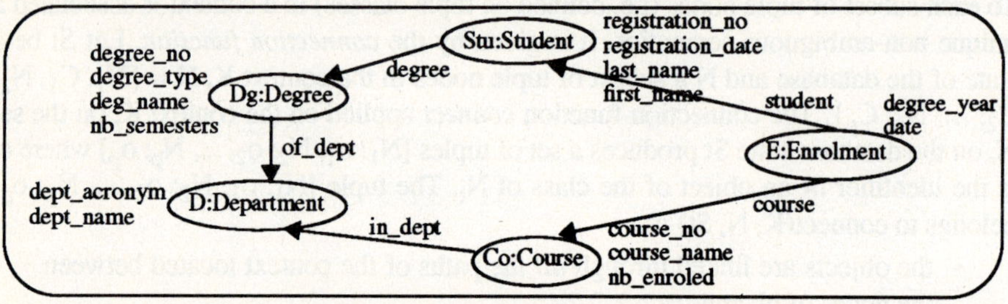

Fig. 4. Context "enrolment in courses in his department"

Co:Course are linked by two separated paths. On the one side, a student *stu* has enroled in a course *co*. On the other side, a student *stu* takes a degree *dg* of a department *d* that offers a set of courses *co*. The semantics of the context (with all its tuple nodes) is: a student *stu* takes a course *co* given in his department *d*. Figure 5 shows another context, on the same classes, in which a student is linked to a course he is taking, without requiring that the course be offered by the student's department. In this last context a student is linked to two departments *d1* and *d2* representing respectively the student's department and the department offering the course he is taking.

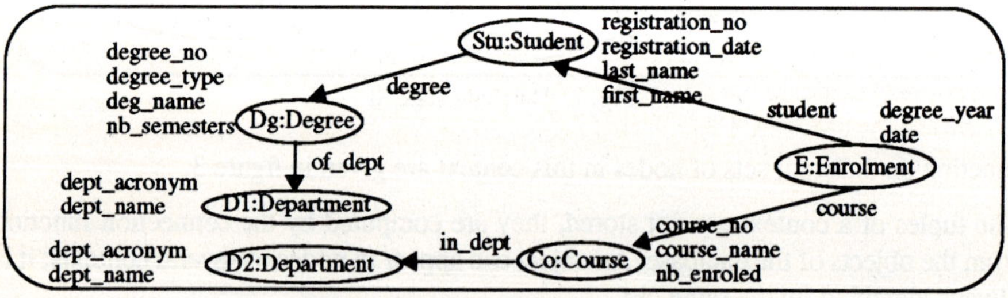

Fig. 5. Context "enrolment in courses"

Let $\mathcal{N}$ be the set of all the tuple nodes of a context K. The *total connection function* on context K *total_connect* is defined as the union of all the connections on K on the powerset of $\mathcal{N}$: total_connect (K, St) := $\bigcup_{X \in 2^{\mathcal{N}}}$ connect(K, X, St)

4.4 Step 4: Context Methods

Computed attributes are managed by context *methods*. Methods are attached to contexts instead of classes. The advantages are that a method may access data in several classes and not only one, and the same attribute may be computed according to different methods in different contexts.

Example 4.6: A student succeeds the first year if he satisfies the conditions of his educational program. The conditions are not the same for all the faculties. The attribute succeed_1st_year of node Stu:Student is computed by a method, according to the conditions of the student's faculty and the student's marks (fig. 9).

```
method Stu.succeed_1st_year in context  "1st year student of Economics
Faculty" is
begin
        theResults := select R from [Stu R] where Stu = self
        -- get the results of this student (self) from the connection on
        -- [Stu:Student R:Results] in this context
        if average(mark(theResults)) ≥ 4.0 and min(mark(theResults)) > 2.0
        then return true else return false
end;
```

5 Context Versions

We introduce now the notion of *context version* to express the dynamics of objects in a context. We take as an example the context "StuMgmt" (student management). While a student is in the university, he goes through several stages: registration, years of study, leave. A stage requires information that is not useful for another stage and it is governed by rules and methods that are not available to another stage.

Example 5.1: Information about high-school diploma is required at the registration of a student but it is not useful later. So, we will make it visible in the registration stage and hide it in the others. The method wich computes the attribute succeed_1st_year (cf. §4.4) will be visible only in the first year stage.

We will implement each stage that we want to keep by a context version. We will now consider a context, as defined in the previous sections, as a version of a dynamic context. A *dynamic context* is defined as follows:

dynamic context = (cn, {V_0 = <vn_0, S_0, R_0, M_0>, V_1 = <vn_1, S_1, R_1, M_1>, ...,
V_s = <vn_s, S_s, R_s, M_s>}, PN)

where cn is the dynamic context name, V_0 is the generic version, each V_i ($1 \le i \le s$) is a context version described by its name vn_i, its structure S_i, its rules R_i and its methods M_i and finally PN is the Petri Net associated with the dynamic context. The generic version assembles nodes, arcs, rules and methods that are common to all the versions of a dynamic context. The Petri Net describes the life-cycle of the dynamic context's objects and gives the allowed transitions between context versions. A place in the Petri

Net corresponds to a context version and a transition corresponds to an event.

Example 5.2: Figure 6 shows the Petri Net associated with the dynamic context

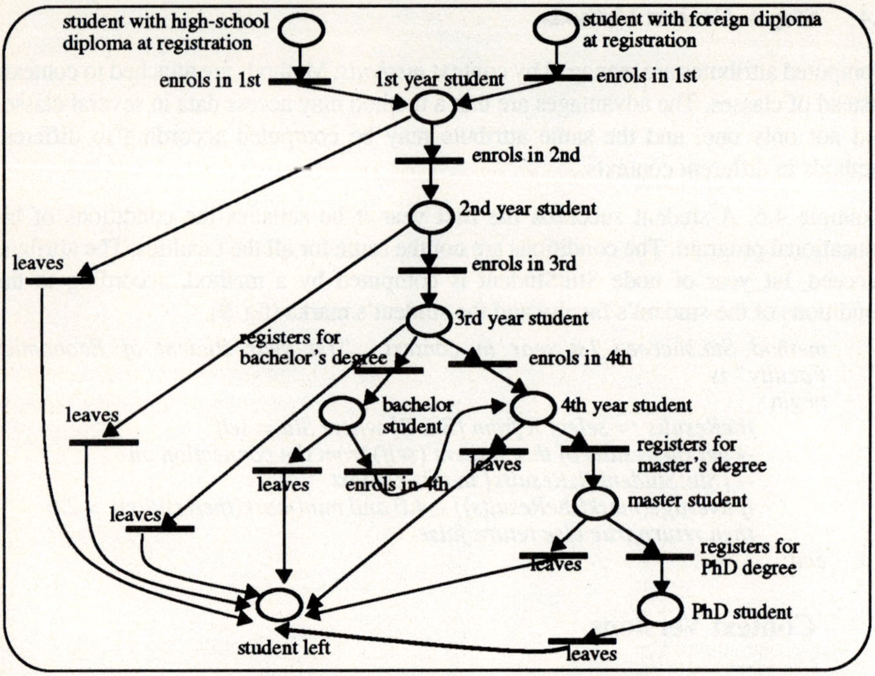

Fig. 6. Petri Net of dynamic context "StuMgmt"

"StuMgmt". It describes a student's stages in the university. Its generic version contains the node Stu:Student. At the student's registration, we keep different pieces of information about him such as his file number, last name, first name, etc. A student who has high-school diploma is accepted without conditions. A student who has a foreign

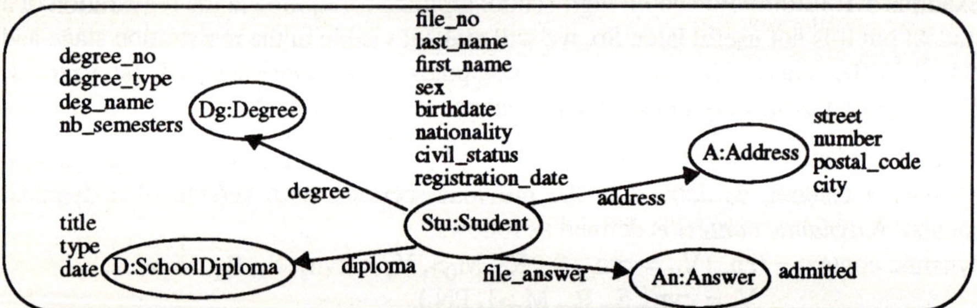

Fig. 7. Version "student with high-school diploma at registration" of context "StuMgmt"

school diploma may be admitted if he has a good average mark or honors, or he may pass admission exams. In these cases, we have to store his average mark, honors and admission exams marks. We described the same stage (registration) in two different situations. Two parallel versions allow us to store different data on which a different registration procedure is applied (fig. 7, 8). The result of this procedure is kept in the

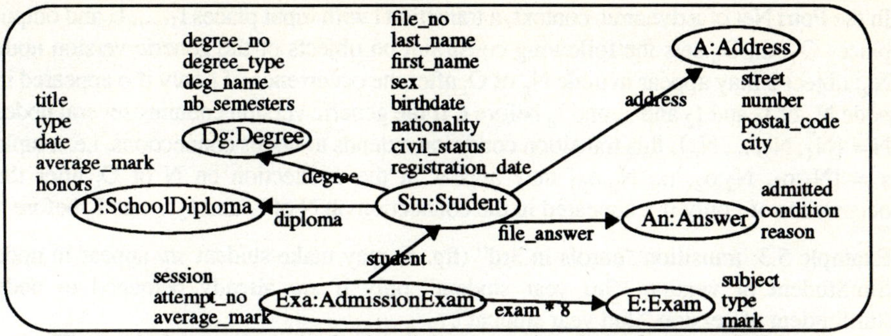

Fig. 8. Version "student with foreign diploma at registration" of context "StuMgmt"

file_answer attribute which is computed by a method of the context version.
If a student fullfils the admission conditions, he is enroled in first year. In the version "1st year student", we store new information: his registration number, status, current semester, first-year courses enroled in, and marks (fig. 9). Versions "2nd year student",

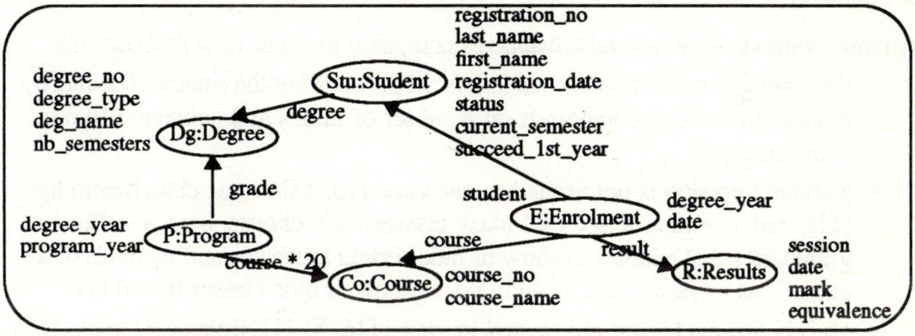

Fig. 9. Version "1st year student" of context "StuMgmt"

"3rd year student" and "4th year student" are similar to that one.
In the version "bachelor student", we store the title of the thesis, the advisor professor, the date and the mark the student gets (fig. 10). Versions "master student" and "PhD

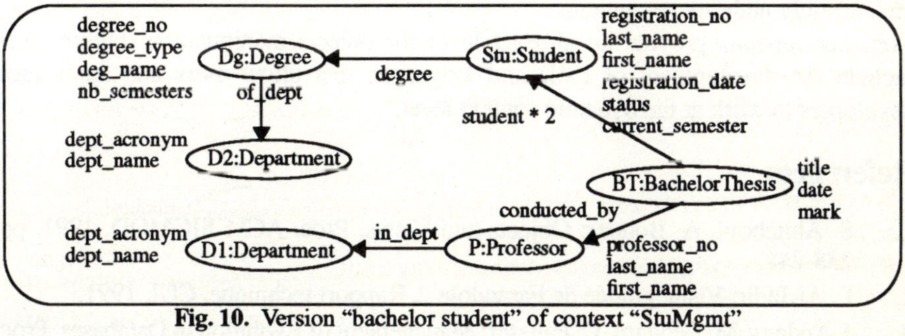

Fig. 10. Version "bachelor student" of context "StuMgmt"

student" are similar to that one. In the version "student left", we store leave date and leave reason (graduated, didn't pay fees, asked to leave, etc...).
This example is a simplification of the domain where more complicated cases occur.

In the Petri Net of a dynamic context, a transition t with input places $I_1, ..., I_n$ and output places $O_1, ..., O_n$ sets the following constraint on objects of the generic version node N_g: object o may appear in node N_g of O_i after the occurrence of t only if o appeared in node N_g of I_1 and I_2 and ... and I_n before t. If the generic version contains several nodes $N = \{N_1, N_2, ..., N_p\}$, this transition condition extends to nodes connections, i.e. a tuple $x = [N_1{:}o_1, N_2{:}o_2, ..., N_p{:}o_p]$ may appear in the connection on N of O_i after the occurrence of t only if x appeared in the connection on N of I_1 and I_2 ... and I_n before t.

Example 5.3: transition "enrols in 3rd" (fig. 6) may make student *stu* appear in node Stu:Student of version "3rd year student" only if *stu* already belonged to node Stu:Student of version "2nd year student".

6 Conclusion

We first introduced contexts as a structure, rules and methods and then added dynamic contexts with contexts versions that allow to consider the dynamic aspect of objects in the database.

Dynamic contexts have several advantages compared to usual view mechanisms:

- the connection function is not a join of all the nodes of the context. It is more flexible as we can compute it on a subset of nodes and achieve different connections.
- a context version is not limited to one class [16, 13] or one class hierarchy [11], but contains a set of linked classes. We choose here a different granularity that enables to show or hide certain attributes and methods of a class C, as in views, and, in addition, to show or hide classes linked to C.
- objects life-cycles are not treated in views [16, 8, 11]. Roles [13] allow to model objects life-cycles in only one class. Context versions are less restrictive, as we can have several nodes in a generic version and follow the evolution of their interconnected objects through different versions.

Static contexts have been implemented in the Farandole 2 DBMS. Dynamic contexts are currently under development.
Contexts versions provide an abstract level for objects manipulation. Future work include the development of tools and languages that allow users and application developers to work at the dynamic context level.

References

1. S. Abiteboul, A. Bonner: Objects and Views, Proc. ACM SIGMOD, 1991, pp. 238-247.
2. L. Al-Jadir: Visite guidée de Farandole 2, Rapport technique, CUI, 1991.
3. J. Andany, M. Léonard, C. Palisser: Management of Evolution in Databases, Proc. 17th VLDB Conference, 1991, pp. 161-170.
4. R. Bursens, J. Guyot: Temps + Dynamique + Référentiel = Histoire, Proc. Journées Bases de Données Avançées, INRIA, Port-Camargue, 1987, pp. 187-203.

5. T. Estier, G. Falquet: Le petit Manuel de Farandole 2, Rapport technique, Cahiers du CUI, no 54, 1992.
6. G. Falquet: Interrogation de bases de données à l'aide d'un modèle sémantique, Thèse de doctorat, Université de Genève, 1989.
7. G. Falquet: F2: an Object-Oriented Database Model with Semantic Contexts, Rapport technique, Cahiers du CUI, no 52, 1990.
8. S. Heiler, S. Zdonik: Object Views: Extending the Vision, Proc. Data Engineering Conf., 1990, pp. 86-93.
9. W. Kim, H.T. Chou: Versions of Schema for Object-Oriented Databases, Proc. 14th VLDB Conference, 1988, pp. 148-159.
10. T. Libourel: Introduction de relations pour exprimer l'évolutivité dans un système d'objets, Thèse de doctorat, Université de Montpellier II, 1992.
11. M.M.A. Morsi, S.B. Navathe, H. Kim: A Schema Management and Prototyping Interface for an Object-Oriented Database Environment, In: F. Van Assche, B. Moulin, C. Rolland (eds.): Object Oriented Approach in I.S., IFIP, North-Holland, 1991, pp. 157-180.
12. C. Palisser: Le Modèle de Versions du Système CHARLY, Proc. 6èmes Journées Bases de Données Avancées, INRIA, 1990.
13. B. Pernici: Requirements specifications for object-oriented systems, In: A. Flory, C. Rolland (eds.): Nouvelles perspectives des systèmes d'information, INFORSID, Eyrolles, 1990, pp. 41-63.
14. B. Pernici: Objects with Roles, IEEE Conf. on Office Information Systems, 1990, pp. 205-215.
15. E. Sciore: Using Annotations to Support Multiple Kinds of Versioning in an Object-Oriented Database System, ACM Transactions on Database Systems, vol. 16, no. 3, september 1991, pp. 417-438.
16. J.J. Shilling, P.F. Sweeney: Three Steps to Views: Extending the Object-Oriented Paradigm, Proc. OOPSLA, 1989, pp. 353-361.
17. A.H. Skarra, S.B. Zdonik: Type Evolution in an Object-Oriented Database, In: B. Shriver, P. Wegner (eds.): Research Directions in OO Programming, MIT Press, 1987, pp. 393-415.

Towards Class-less Object Models for Engineering Design Applications

Margret Groß-Hardt* Gottfried Vossen †
University of Giessen University of Muenster

Abstract

Engineering design applications have specific requirements to database support not yet completely met by existing systems. We argue that one reason is the inability of current object models to capture the needs of design applications appropriately. We show how to combine concepts from prototype programming languages with a versioning mechanism for objects into a new model which does without the notion of a class. The idea is that objects can freely exist in a database, have multiple versions, and can share structure and behavior with others. In addition, working with design objects is done both associatively (via user-defined identifiers) and declaratively (via collections as a query tool).

1 Introduction

Recently, it has been argued [17, 19, 21] that traditional models for object-oriented databases (OODBs) are not adequate for some of those applications which originally triggered the development of this database technology. Indeed, in order for a data model to be useful in engineering design applications, it must reflect and support the specific database requirements of these domains. In this paper, a dedicated object model is outlined, which combines recently proposed concepts from prototype-based programming languages with versioning. The model does not know classes, but objects, which may associatively be named by a user, can freely exist in a database; in addition, they can reference each other, reuse structure and/or behavior of other objects, and may exist in multiple versions.

Traditional models for OODBs [6] center around the notion of a class. Thus, they resemble the common approach of defining a schema first and then introducing *instances*. This receives justification by the fact that a large database is commonly *designed* before it is *used*. However, engineering applications can hardly be well-supported following this approach. Indeed, a designer in a CAD

---

*AG Informatik, University of Giessen, Arndtstraße 2, D-35392 Giessen, Germany

†Institut für Wirtschaftsinformatik, University of Muenster, Grevenerstr. 91, D-48159 Muenster Germany

environment thinks in terms of concrete design objects he or she is working on, and not about the structure or behavior of a class of which these objects may be instances in the first place. It therefore makes sense to adopt concepts and techniques from prototype-based programming languages [7] to this context.

Prototype languages like SELF [20] or Garnet [13] allow objects to share structure and behavior not via membership in the same class, but via reference to the same prototype. For creating similar objects, prototypes may be cloned, without the need to care for corresponding format descriptions and appropriate initialization. In addition, objects which are unique w.r.t. structure and/or behavior need not be put into a class, but can exist independently.

It has also been long recognized that design applications need versioning, since the objects under design typically exist in many versions while being constructed. In response to this, various systems like Orion [10] and Ode [1] already include a versioning mechanism, but there is no true incorporation of that mechanism into the underlying object model. The work described in this paper is an attempt to combine the two: *class-less object modelling and built-in versioning.* We do not claim that our model can serve as a replacement for other OO models; however, we will indicate that it is better suited for design applications than "general-purpose" models.

The basic idea underlying the model is to have objects freely exist in a database. Objects still have a structure and a behavior, but can additionally be versioned. Thus, each object in our model has an identifier, an associated set of versions, and a set of messages it understands. Versions in turn have a number and a value, where values are elements of domains that are described by types. As will be seen, objects can be composed of other objects, and can interact. Finally, objects can inherit structure and or behavior from other objects. Clearly, a declarative way of querying and updating a database is still desirable. To this end, we introduce the notion of a *collection*, which generally is an arbitrary set of objects or versions; however, it seems useful to identify a number of collections which have specific properties. For example, *configurations* are consistent sets of versions, or *constellations* are collections containing an object together with all its subobjects. Thus, a database in our model can be grouped into a variety of application-dependent collections, which can then be subject to user operations.

In Section 2, we describe the basic ingredients of our model; in particular, we define objects, versions, values, types, and domains. In Section 3, we present a graphical tool, *object trees*, for describing composition relationships between objects or versions; these trees are useful for introducing collections with specific properties. In Section 4 we discuss related work, and in Section 5 we present some conclusions as well as questions deserving further study.

2 Basic Concepts

We assume the reader to be familiar with the basic principles of object-orientation [3]. They imply that data models for OODBs should center around the notion of a class, which is a container for objects, and encapsulates structure and behavior. We want to do without classes and therefore advocate the view that objects

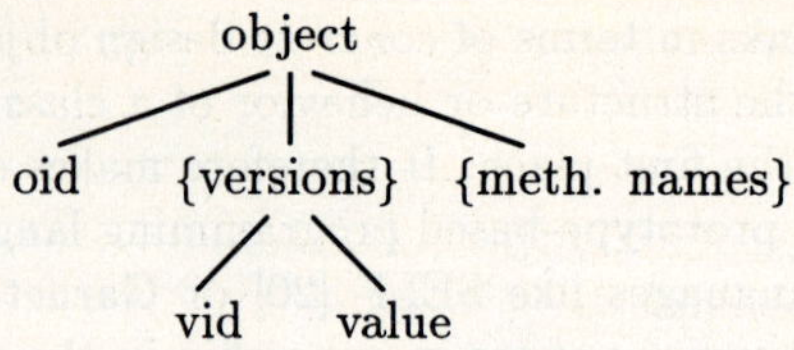

Figure 1: Objects in CLOOD.

have an existence of their own, have a value, and understand methods. Since the object model we introduce in this section is targeted especially at design application, we additionally want them to have versions.

The basic ingredients of CLOOD (Class-Less Object-Oriented Data model), the model we introduce in this paper, are objects, which have an identifier, versions, and behavior. Versions are numbered and have values, while behavior is represented through message names (cf. Figure 1).

We define the various components formally in the remainder of this section. To this end, we assume that the following finite and pairwise disjoint sets are given: A union $\mathbf{D}$ of distinct sets of atomic values, like integers, strings, etc., a set $\mathbf{A}$ of attribute names, a set $\mathbf{O}$ of object identifiers (oid's), a set $\mathbf{V}$ of version numbers, and a set $\mathbf{M}$ of message names. For an arbitrary subset $O \subseteq \mathbf{O}$, which might represent a current database state, we define a set $\mathrm{Val}(O)$ of *values* over O as follows:

(i) $\mathbf{D} \subseteq \mathrm{Val}(O)$, (ii) $O \subseteq \mathrm{Val}(O)$, (iii) $\mathtt{nil} \in \mathrm{Val}(O)$,

(iv) if $v_1, \ldots, v_n \in \mathrm{Val}(O)$, $A_1, \ldots, A_n \in \mathbf{A}$ s.t. $A_i \neq A_j$ for $i \neq j$, $n \geq 1$, then $[A_1 : v_1, \ldots, A_n : v_n] \in \mathrm{Val}(O)$,

(v) if $v_1, \ldots, v_n \in \mathrm{Val}(O)$, then $\{v_1, \ldots, v_n\} \in \mathrm{Val}(O)$.

Notice that values may contain oid's at any level of nesting, so that complex aggregations can be constructed. In what follows, the universe of all values will be denoted $\mathbf{Val} := \bigcup_{O \subseteq \mathbf{O}} \mathrm{Val}(O)$.

We do not associate values with objects directly, as in [6], but we associate them with object versions: Versions are pairs consisting of a version identifier (vid) and a value. The versions of a particular object are formally given through a mapping $\mathrm{vers} : \mathbf{O} \rightarrow 2^{\mathbf{V} \times \mathbf{Val}}$ which assigns a set of versions to an object $o \in O, O \subseteq \mathbf{O}$. Hence, for each such o, $\mathrm{vers}(o) = \{(v_0, val_0), \ldots, (v_n, val_n)\}, n \geq 0$ (each object is assumed to have at least one version, the *default version*; clearly, if all objects currently in the database have one version only, the database is in fact unversioned). We require that version numbers associated with one object are distinct and that version values are indeed "valid", i.e., $val_i \in \mathrm{Val}(O)$ for $0 \leq i \leq n$.

For a given oid and some version number, it is often useful to talk about the value associated with them. To this end, function value : $\mathbf{O} \times \mathbf{V} \rightarrow \mathbf{Val}$

determines the value of an object version, such that the following holds:
$(\forall\, O \subseteq \mathbf{O})(\forall\, o \in O)(\forall\, v \in \mathbf{V})(\forall\, val \in \mathrm{Val}(O))$

$$\mathrm{value}(o, v) = val \iff (v, val) \in \mathrm{vers}(o)$$

In what follows, we will frequently refer to the following running example: Consider a microprocessor μP, which consists of an execution unit, a control unit and several registers. The execution unit currently exists in two versions which vary in their *a*rithmetic–*l*ogical–*u*nit–component (one version refers to bit–slice–alu *alu49*, the other to *alu38*). In total, there are three alu–objects. The control unit *cu* and the registers *r*0 to *r*7 are not specified further. At the level of values, we thus have the following sample set of objects:

value(μP, 0) = [execUnit : *exec51*, controlUnit: *cu*, registers : *datareg*]
value(*exec51*, 0) = [alu : *alu49*, accu : *accuReg*]
value(*exec51*, 1) = [alu : *alu38*, accu : *accuReg*]
value(*datareg, 0*) = {*r*0, *r*1, ..., *r*7}
value(*alu49*, 0) = [slices : {*alu52*}, #slices : 4]
value(*alu38*, 0) = [oplength : 32, addertype: 'von-Neumann']
value(*alu52*, 0) = [oplength : 8, addertype: 'parallel']

Notice that except the execution unit, all objects are unversioned (only their default version currently exists).

Our exposition so far allows values to be non-sensical. For example, we could have included value(*rom99*, 0) = [name : 35, age : 111] above. To avoid such situations, we introduce a type concept next, define the type of an object and then require that the version values of one object stem from a single domain.

A set $T(\mathbf{A})$ of *types* over a given set $\mathbf{A}$ of attributes is defined as follows:

(i) $B \subseteq T$, where B is a finite set of base types;

(ii) `oid` $\in T$; none $\in T$;

(iii) if A_i are distinct attributes from $\mathbf{A}$ and $t_i \in T$, $1 \leq i \leq n$, then $[A_1 : t_1,\ \ldots,\ A_n : t_n] \in T$;

(iv) if $t \in T$, then $\{t\} \in T$.

We also write T instead of $T(\mathbf{A})$ if $\mathbf{A}$ is immaterial. As usual, we want to use types as descriptions of domains; to this end, we introduce the following. For $O \subseteq \mathbf{O}$, a mapping dom : $T(\mathbf{A}) \to 2^{\mathrm{Val}(O)}$ is recursively defined as follows:

(i) $(\forall\, b \in B)\ (\exists!\ d \subseteq \mathbf{D})\ \mathrm{dom}(b) = d$;

(ii) dom(`oid`) = O; dom(none) = `nil`;

(iii) $\mathrm{dom}([A_1 : t_1,\ \ldots,\ A_n : t_n])$
$:= \{[A_1 : v_1, \ldots, A_n : v_n] \mid (\forall\, i, 1 \leq i \leq n)\ v_i \in \mathrm{dom}(t_i)\}$;

(iv) $\mathrm{dom}(\{t\}) := \{\{v_1,\ \ldots,\ v_n\} \mid (\forall\, i, 1 \leq i \leq n)\ v_i \in \mathrm{dom}(t)\}$.

We now require that each value in some object version must be from the domain of a type, and additionally all versions of the same object have the same type, i.e., $(\forall\ o \in O)(\exists!\ t \in T)(\forall\ (v, val) \in \text{vers}(o))\ val \in \text{dom}(t))$.
Notice that this is not a restriction in our model, since the `nil` value is available for objects, and empty set and empty tuple can be used as values. It follows from the above requirement that we disallow heterogeneous sets in our model; in other words, Val(O) can actually be written as $\text{Val}(O) := \bigcup_{t \in T} \text{dom}(T)$. For all values $val \in$ **Val**, we can now speak about their type; let $\text{type}(val) := t$ if $val \in \text{dom}(t)$. In addition, it will be safe to speak about the type of an object o, denoted type(o), since all versions of o have the same type. Some types in our running example are

type(μP) = [execUnit : `oid`, controlUnit : `oid`, registers : `oid`],
type($alu38$) = [oplength : `int`, addertype : `string`].

As seen, objects may be specializations of other objects. Since the objects we consider are uniquely typed, this amounts to a subtyping relationship (with `none` as smallest type), and also gives rise to inheritance (*is-a* relationships) at the level of structure; details can be found in [21]. We mention that the behavioral aspect of our model vastly follows that of class-based models [6], with the difference that behavior is directly attached to objects, not to classes.

3 Object Trees. Collections

So far our model allows the creation of versioned objects, which may be aggregated from other objects. Clearly, a mechanism is needed which helps to keep track of the various versions of an object, the objects they are comprised of, the versions of these subobjects, and so on. In this section, we will introduce such a mechanism, which is called *object trees.*

Basically, an object tree abstracts from a given object and its versions in that it restricts the attention to composition (i.e., aggregation links between objects), and ignores atomic values at all levels (thus, object trees will not be isomorphic images of given objects, but only exhibit part of the information contained therein) and — for the time being — also inheritance. Since associated with a given oid are versions, which again comprise objects and their versions, it seems appropriate to employ *and/or graphs*, a well-known data structure for describing, for example, decomposable production systems in artificial intelligence [15], in that respect. Informally, and/or graphs are directed, bipartite graphs consisting of *and nodes* as well as *or nodes* s.t. edges exist only between these two sets of nodes; direct successors of an or node represent alternatives, while direct successors of an and node represent mandatory components of this node.

We will here use and/or trees (not general and/or graphs) in the following way: or nodes will be used to represent objects, whose direct successors are the currently available versions; and nodes, on the other hand, represent versions whose direct successors represent subobjects that are referred to by this version. As will be seen, object trees are useful tools for defining various specific collections over databases in our model. We mention that the use of and/or graphs in this context has originally been suggested in [12] and later again in [8], where this type of graph has been exploited for data management in a CAD and in a CASE context, resp. It should also be mentioned that we restrict the attention here to trees instead of more general graphs for reasons of simplicity; however, there is no conceptual reason for this restriction.

Object trees can be thought of as a unit of allocation to designers within a specific application. That is, if a designer wants to work on some object, a long-time check-out for this object and its components has to be made. However, a designer will typically not be interested in all existing versions of an object in question; instead, he will primarily look at configurations, which select a particular version for each object appearing in a large composition. Eventually, he will alternatively be looking just at the composition structure of some (large) object under design, which will be captured by constellations. As will be shown, object trees ease the construction of configurations and constellations.

Before we define object trees formally, we introduce a straightforward way of labeling aggregation links. To this end, let attr(v) denote the attribute names at the top-most level of a tuple value v. For example, attr(value(μP, 0)) = {execUnit, controlUnit, registers}. An aggregation link of the form $v \rightarrow v'$ exists between two non-atomic values v and v' with *link label ll* as follows:

(i) $ll = \emptyset$, if v is the object identifier v'.

(ii) $ll = *$ if v is a set-value and v' is contained in v,
e.g., value(*datareg, 0*) $\stackrel{*}{\rightarrow}$ *r0*.

(iii) $ll = A$ if v is a tuple-value, $A \in$ attr(v) and v' is the value of A,
e.g.,value(μP, 0) $\stackrel{\text{controlUnit}}{\longrightarrow}$ *cu*.

(iv) $ll = l1.l2$, if $l1$, $l2$ are link labels s.t. $v \stackrel{l1}{\rightarrow} v'$ and $v' \stackrel{l2}{\rightarrow} v''$, and $v' \notin O$,
e.g., value(*alu49, 0*) $\stackrel{\text{slices}}{\longrightarrow}$ {*alu52*} and {*alu52*} $\stackrel{*}{\longrightarrow}$ *alu52*,
so value(*alu49, 0*) $\stackrel{\text{slices.*}}{\longrightarrow}$ *alu52*.

Notice that aggregation links are defined between non-atomic values. The associated label describes the nesting structure between them without "going through" an object. Transitivity as defined in (iv) always has intermediate values which are not objects; for example, value(μP, 0) $\stackrel{l1}{\rightarrow}$ *exec51* $\stackrel{l2}{\rightarrow}$ *alu49* is impossible since *exec51* $\stackrel{l2}{\rightarrow}$ *alu49* is not defined.

Our next goal is to introduce object trees. As was mentioned above, object trees represent information about the composition of objects with respect to their different versions. Hence they will have two types of nodes, labeled with object identifiers or version identifiers, resp. Edges always connect different types of nodes, and edge labels either carry the version number of the (version) node the edge is directed to, or a link label representing the nesting structure between adjacent nodes. More precisely, we have:

An *object tree* is a directed, labeled tree $T = (N_T, E_T, \text{nlabel}_T, \text{elabel}_T)$, where

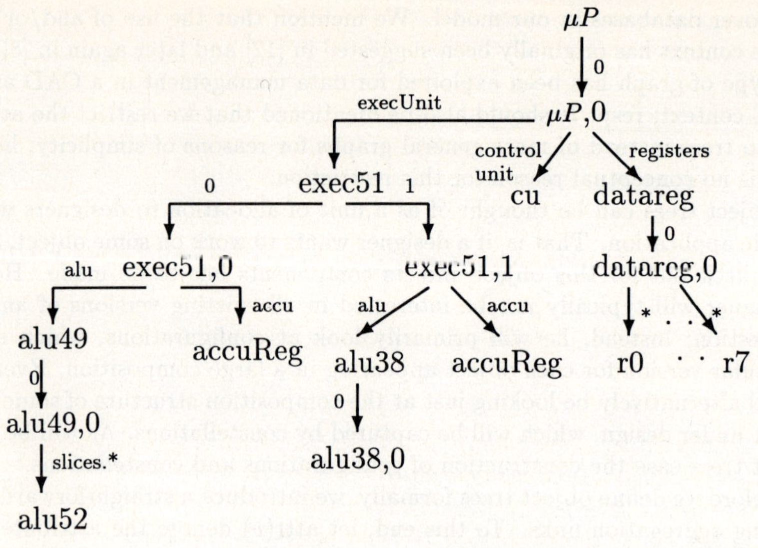

Figure 2: Object tree for object μP.

- the node set N_T is a subset of $O \cup (O \times \mathbf{V})$,
- the edge set E_T is a subset of $(O \times (O \times \mathbf{V})) \cup ((O \times \mathbf{V}) \times O)$ s.t. for all nodes $o \in O$ and $(o', v) \in (O \times V)$ the following holds

  (i) $\forall\, (o, (o', v)) \in E_T : o = o'$

  (ii) $\forall\, ((o', v), o) \in E_T : \text{value}(o', v) \xrightarrow{ll} o$, for a valid link label *ll*.

- nlabel is a function assigning each node representing some $o \in O$ the label 'o', and each node representing $(o, v) \in (O \times \mathbf{V})$ the label 'o, v',
- elabel assigns each edge $(o, (o', v)) \in E_T$ the version number v, and each edge $((o, v), o') \in E_T$ a link label *ll* s.t. $\text{value}(o, v) \xrightarrow{ll} o'$.

It follows that in the traditional terminology of and/or graphs, nodes representing objects are the or nodes, while those representing versions are the and nodes.

As an example, Figure 2 shows the object tree for the microprocessor object from our running example. The outgoing edges from the (only) microprocessor version points towards object nodes *exec51*, *cu* and *datareg*. The edge towards *alu52* must be labeled 'slices.*'. Notice control unit and register versions have been omitted from this figure to improve its readability.

If an object node has only one outgoing edge, this is always directed towards its default version and hence labeled zero. The leaves of an object tree are always versions. All objects comprising the "root object" are explicitly represented in the tree. Hence, up to atomic values the representation of an object as object

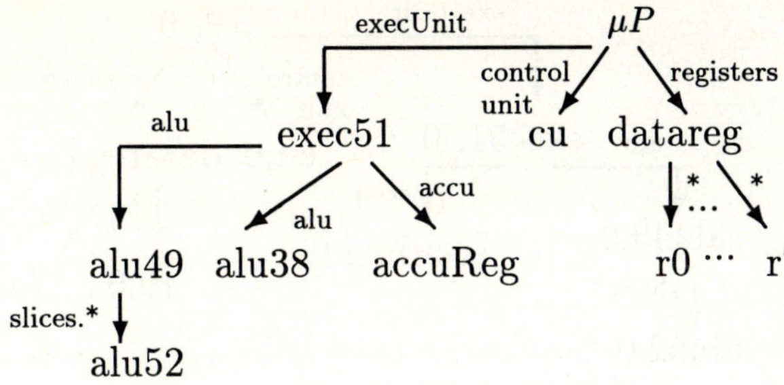

Figure 3: A constellation tree.

tree is "composition equivalent" to the notation which was introduced in Section 2; however, some form of normalization of the latter is needed for this to hold, which in essence gets rid of unnecessary tuple or set brackets; we assume that object descriptions have been normalized in this way before an object tree is constructed.

Given an object tree, it is easy to derive two other types of trees from it, one containing purely composition information (which will be referred to as constellation), the other capturing the intuitive notion of a configuration. Such derivations can straightforwardly be done using the specific properties of and/or graphs.

The first type of derived tree, called *constellation tree*, is modeled after the notion of constellation from [5]; it is intended to describe object composition without any references to existing or used versions. So, given an object tree T, a constellation tree CS_T is derived from T as follows:

- Starting from the root r of T, consider all paths of length 2 (i.e., ignoring or nodes) starting at r and introduce an edge in CS_T for each such path;
- repeat the above for each node newly added to CS_T;
- stop if no further such path exists.

For example, Figure 3 shows a constellation tree constructed from the root of the object tree which was shown in Figure 2. Notice that a constellation tree contains only oid's as node labels. Clearly, constellation trees can also be derived from a given object tree T for any root of a subtree of T.

Our second type of derived tree, called *configuration tree*, is modeled after the common notion of configuration, i.e., a set of versions, one for each object in question (which together represent a preliminary or final version of the entire artifact under design). Thus, a configuration tree will be a tree whose nodes represent versions; given an object tree T, a configuration tree CF_T is derived from T as follows: Starting from the root of T, move downwards through the alternating or/and layers of T, and do the following at each layer:

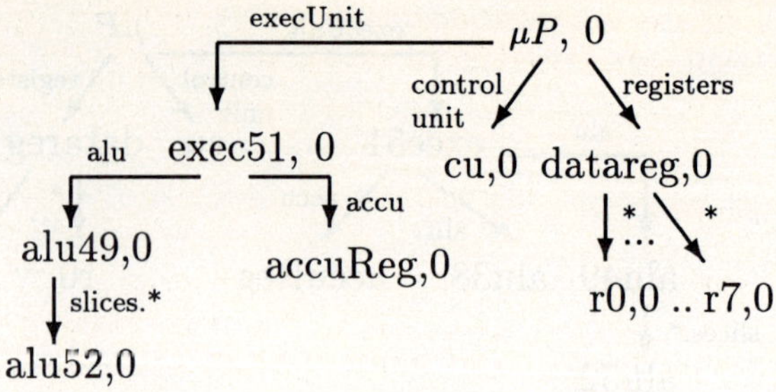

Figure 4: A configuration tree.

- For each or node reached, include exactly one successor in CF_T (and the connecting edge);
- for each and node reached, include all successors in CF_T (and the connecting edges);
- finally, shortcut the resulting tree as follows: condense each edge of the form $(o, (o, v))$ into the node labeled (o, v).

For example, Figure 4 shows a configuration tree derived from the object tree shown in Figure 2.

We finally mention that the derived trees introduced above can alternatively be defined in purely graph-theoretic terms; details are omitted.

Clearly, in a database context it is desirable to query declaratively, i.e., to specify which conditions a result should satisfy without saying how to construct it. To this end, it is reasonable to have sets of object(–version)s available against which queries can be directed. We introduce *collections* for that purpose, where collections are arbitrary sets of objects or versions with generally distinct types.

In general, an *object collection* is an arbitrary subset of O, while a *version collection* is an arbitrary subset of $O \times \mathbf{V}$, where $O \subseteq \mathbf{O}$, for example, collections are: $K_1 = \{\mu P, \textit{exec51}, \textit{cu}, \textit{alu38}, \textit{alu49}\}$, $K_2 = \{(\textit{alu38}, 0), (\textit{datareg}, 0)\}$, $K_3 = \{(\textit{alu38}, 0), (\textit{datareg}, 0), \textit{exec51}\}$. Thus, collections can intersect, be nested into each other, or be disjoint. In particular, individual objects or versions can be members of several collections simultaneously.

While collections in the most general sense may be such that there is no link relationship between their objects or versions, specific collections can be formed for which this is the case. To this end, let an object tree T and a constellation tree CS_T derived from T be given. Then a *constellation* is simply the set of objects represented by the nodes of CS_T; hence, a constellation can be considered a specific object collection.

An example of a constellation is the set of all objects from the microprocessor example. Another constellation is $\{\textit{datareg}, r0, \ldots, r7\}$, but $\{\textit{exec51}, \textit{accuReg}, \textit{alu38}\}$ is not a constellation, since e. g. *alu49* is missing.

Next, given an object tree T and a configuration tree CF_T derived from T, a *configuration* is the set of versions represented by the nodes of CF_T. Hence, a configuration can be considered a specific version collection.

4 Related Work

Work that is related to ours basically falls into three categories: (1) object models which allow for some liberal form of typing; in particular, objects are allowed to change their type during their lifetime; (2) proposals suggesting to incorporate ideas from prototype languages into OODBs; (3) proposals regarding object models suited for engineering design. We consider each category in turn.

The data model of *Melampus* [4] provides a mechanism named *aspects* [16] to allow objects to change their type and to model objects that have many types. In brief, an aspect extends an existing object with additional state and behavior while maintaining its identity; an object may enjoy many aspects simultaneously, and these can vary over time. By having many aspects, an object is an instance of many types, instead of being an instance of a unique class defined via multiple inheritance. Object references are to particular aspects, and behavior depends on the aspects referenced. Aspects cannot be simulated in our model, since it requires versions of an object to share the same behavior; corresponding extensions appear reasonable. In the data model of Iris [22], objects are also allowed to acquire or lose types dynamically; this can be simulated in the language we are designing for our model. A different proposal to capture the issue of evolution was made in [9], where the concept of *or-objects* is introduced. These are intended to model incomplete specifications, in which choices to be made during a design process are not fixed from the beginning. Or-objects are instances of *or-types*, which encapsulate different design alternatives, and thus allow storing incomplete information. It is again easily verified that or-objects can be simulated using versions; in addition, our model comprises adequate mechanisms to manage such versions, which are missing in the work of [9].

The proposal described in [17] is among the first to go in the direction of class-less models and uses concepts from prototype languages [11, 20]. *Object hierarchies* are models for real-world entities; each object in a hierarchy represents some information about an entity. An object may have some state and some behavior, and additionally inherits behavior from its parent. When a message is sent to an object, it either responds directly, or *delegates* the message to its parent, so that inheritance is determined on a per-object basis. An existing hierarchy can be *cloned*, and an object can be extended with the behavior of another object. *Template hierarchies* provide *prototypes* from which instances may be cloned. While this approach concurs with ours in the avoidance of classes, it seems that our model is easier to use, since we do not need an entire hierarchy for a single object; in addition, there are no versions in the proposal of [17].

Work on dedicated object models for engineering applications goes back to [2]; more recent proposals are [14] and [18]. The SHOOD model of [14] is a concrete proposal for a specialized object model. Here the rationale is to design a library of meta-classes, from which dedicated classes for design objects can be instantiated. The authors emphasize the view that classes need to be available in the first place before objects can be created; this has been questioned in our paper. The model underlying PLAYOUT [18] follows the same philosophy: Database support for design environments needs a dedicated class library. Notice that our approach does not exclude the possibility of creating specific collections which resemble the role of classes; however, we do not wish a designer to bother about class definitions before the actual objects exist. As was mentioned earlier, the use of and/or graphs was also explored in [12]. There, these graphs were used as the central tool of data modeling (in the context of a semantic model implemented atop a relational database) and of configuration management. Our approach differs from this in that we use and/or graphs only as a supporting aid for collection definition (and management).

5 Conclusions and Future Work

In this paper we have described the basics of an object model which combines concepts from prototype languages with a versioning mechanism needed in engineering applications; there are no classes in this model, and versioning is directly built-in. As such, the CLOOD model seems more appropriate for design applications than class-based models, or models without built-in versions. On the other hand, we do not claim that CLOOD will have major applications outside design domains. Indeed, the general philosophy behind our approach is that future data models will have to be tailored towards specific application areas; in order to be well-suited for technical and other non-standard applications, domain-specific models will be needed which clearly depart from the "general purposeness" of traditional data models.

Clearly, the mechanisms we have developed in this paper with respect to object modeling cannot be used in a database environment without appropriate means for declarative querying and updating. To this end, a future goal of our work is the design and implementation of a language based on collections. In addition, a variety of other issues deserve further study; for example, we do not yet make a distinction between versions and *variants*, which is common in design environments. Two versions of a given object can be considered variants of each other if they differ by value only, but not by composition. Also, configurations are commonly considered as units of consistency in a design database; to this end, integrity constraints are needed which do not yet appear in our model. It might also be desirable to easily keep track of the derivation history of a version; mechanisms for this need to take the interaction between versioning and inheritance into account. Finally, we plan to incorporate the model into a real-world design environment to obtain a feasibility evaluation.

References

[1] R. Agrawal et al.: Object Versioning in Ode; Proc. 7th ICDE 1991, 446–455

[2] D.S. Batory, W. Kim: Modeling Concepts for VLSI CAD Objects; ACM TODS 10, 1985, 322–346

[3] E. Bertino, L. Martino: Object-oriented Database Management Systems: Concepts and Issues; IEEE Computer 24 (4) 1991, 33–47

[4] F. Cabrera et al.: The Melampus Project: Toward an Omniscient Computing System; IBM Research Report RJ7515, San Jose 1990

[5] W. Cellary, G. Vossen, G. Jomier: Multiversion Object Constellations for CAD Databases; Techn. Report 9105, AG Informatik, Univ. Giessen, 11/91

[6] O. Deux et al.: The Story of O_2; IEEE TKDE 2, 1990, 91–108

[7] C. Dony, J. Malenfant, P. Cointe: Prototype-Based Languages: From a New Taxonomy to Constructive Proposals and their Validation; Proc. OOPSLA '92, 201–217

[8] J. Ebert, G. Vossen: Object Constellations and Configurations in CASE Applications; Technical Report, University of Giessen, in preparation

[9] T. Imielinski et al.: Incomplete Objects — A Data Model for Design and Planning Applications; Proc. ACM SIGMOD 1991, 288–297

[10] W. Kim et al.: Features of the ORION Object-Oriented Database System; in: W. Kim, F.H. Lochovsky (eds.): *Object-Oriented Concepts, Databases, and Applications*, Addison-Wesley 1989, 251–282

[11] H. Liebermann: Using Prototypical Objects to Implement Shared Behavior in Object Oriented Systems; Proc. OOPSLA '86, 214–223

[12] D. McLeod, K. Narayanaswamy, K.V. Bapa Rao: An Approach to Information Management for CAD/VLSI Applications; Proc. ACM SIGMOD Database Week "Engineering Design Applications" 1983, 39–50

[13] B.A. Myers, D.A. Guise, B. Vander Zanden: Declarative Programming in a Prototype-Instance System: Object-Oriented Programming without Writing Methods; Proc. OOPSLA '92, 184–200

[14] G.T. Nguyen, D. Rieu, J. Escamilla: An Object Model for Engineering Design; Proc. ECOOP 1992, Springer LNCS 615, 233–251

[15] N.J. Nilsson: *Principles of Artificial Intelligence*; Springer-Verlag 1980

[16] J. Richardson, P. Schwarz: Aspects: Extending Objects to Support Multiple, Independent Roles; Proc. ACM SIGMOD 1991, 298–307

[17] E. Sciore: Object Specialization; ACM TOIS 7, 1989, 103–122

[18] E. Siepmann, G. Zimmermann: An Object-Oriented Datamodel for the VLSI Design System PLAYOUT; Proc. 26th ACM/IEEE Design Automation Conference 1989, 814–817

[19] J.D. Ullman: A Comparison of Deductive and Object-Oriented Database Systems; Proc. 2nd DOOD Conference, Springer LNCS 566, 1991, 263–277

[20] D. Ungar, R. Smith: Self: The Power of Simplicity; Proc. OOPSLA '87, 214–242

[21] G. Vossen: On Formal Models for Object-Oriented Databases; EMISA Forum 2/1992, 22–40

[22] K. Wilkinson et al.: The Iris Architecture and Implementation; IEEE TKDE 2, 1990, 63–75

Semantic Relativism in Conceptual Modeling

Jaroslav Pokorný

Department of Software Engineering, Charles University, Prague
Malostranské nám. 25, 118 00 Praha 1, Czech Republic

Abstract. A functional approach to conceptual modeling integrating recent semantic database models is presented. The notion of attribute (MAT78], [DKMS86], [ZLA85], [POK89]), [POK90]) as a basic modeling construct is used. The presented results show how to deal exactly with so called semantic relativism, i.e how to express that two different semantic database models have the same expressive power. We show that it is easy to reach the property for many of well-known semantic database models.

1 Introduction

Until now a part of theoretical research on database management systems has focussed on so called semantic (conceptual, entity-oriented, or object-oriented) database models. The strength of semantic database models is that are conceptually oriented. The intuitive nature of the notion "conceptually" has led to their wide use in modeling of the object system, but rather in the business sphere, where it is not so important what is exactly meant by this notion. On the other hand, new technologies (KMBSs CAD/CAM, office automation, etc.) need express a broader range of knowledge and more complex structures of objects.

One of research branches in this area integrates the structural features of the prominent semantic database models into a formal, coherent framework [HUL87], [POK89]. A second fundamental theme arising in semantic database models focuses on the development of formal methods for comparing of the information capabilities of conceptual schemes expressed in these models [HUL87], [HY84], [DMS88], [DM90], [POK89], [HEU90].

With connection to the comparing of semantic data models an interesting observation may be gained. The expressive power of a given semantic database model depends on a few number of basic constructs only. Most of interesting "semantic" constructs in semantic database models are redundant, i.e they don't increase the expressive power of these models.

The possibility of various ways of modeling the same object system is called a *semantic relativism.* The existence if this phenomenon was observed (only as a hypothesis) by Klein and Hirschheim who note in [KH87] that the possibilities of all E-R approaches are approximately the same. Saltor in [SAL87] relates the problem to derivability of external schemas and studies the semantic relativism using an extended E-R-A metamodel.

Another authors give a similar (but imprecise) opinion [BRO84], [HK87]: the semantic database models distinguish each other in that, how many integrity constraints (ICs) they absorb into basic constructs and how many of them must be formulated explicitly. Many people mean that with powerful tools of the second type the semantic models offer practically the same chances for the conceptual modeling. Unfortunately, the fact is not true. As we shall see, explicit IC only "filter" information coming into a database. The expressiveness of a database model is given by its basic modeling constructs.

In general, our approach is based on the notion of function. This notion covers naturally all structures allowed in the recent database models. As manipulating tool for functions we have a typed lambda calculus at disposal. Moreover, the approach is inspired by transparent intensional logic (TIL) [TIC82], [MP81].

The structure of the paper is as follows. In Sect. 2, we provide basic notions concerning a type system classifying functions. In this section we also introduce a version of typed lambda-calculus. In Sect. 3, we review the possible worlds philosophy and specify some important notions used in the conceptual modeling. The notions of definability and informational equivalence are introduced in Sect. 4. In Sect. 5 we formalize a notion of database model dominance and expressive power of semantic database models. We show how selected database models can be proved to be the "same" (in the sense of their expressive power). They make to possible to construct conceptual schemas that are equivalent even in a heterogeneous user environment.

2 Types and a Lambda Calculus - Basic Definitions

In order to integrate modeling constructs of different semantic database models, it is first necessary to introduce concept of a type system.

The existence of some *(elementary) types* $S_1, ..., S_k$ ($k \geq 1$) is assumed. They constitute a *base* B. More complex types are obtained in the following way.

If $S, R_1, ..., R_n$ ($n \geq 1$) are types, then

(i) $(S : R_1, ..., R_n)$ is a (functional) type

(ii) $(R_1, ..., R_n)$ is a (tuple) type.

The set of *types* $\mathcal{T}$ over B is the least set containing types from B and those given by (i)-(ii).

When S_i in B are interpreted as non-empty sets, then $(S : R_1, ..., R_n)$ denotes the set of all (total or partial) functions from $R_1 \times ... \times R_n$ into S, $(R_1, ..., R_n)$ denotes the Cartesian product $R_1 \times ... \times R_n$.

An important elementary type is $BOOL$ defined as the set {TRUE,FALSE}. The type $BOOL$ allows to type such objects as sets and relations. Sets and relations are modelled as unary and n-ary characteristic functions, respectively.

The fact that X is an object of type $R \in \mathcal{T}$ will be written alternatively X/R or "X is the R-object".

For example, mathematical functions may be easily typed. Arithmetic operations +, -, *, / are examples of $(REAL : REAL, REAL)$-objects. Logical connectives, quantifiers and predicates are also typed functions: (e.g., and/$(BOOL : BOOL, BOOL)$, R-identity $=_R$ is $(BOOL : R, R)$-object, universal R-quantifier Π_R and existential R-quantifier Σ_R are $(BOOL : (BOOL : R))$-objects). R-singularizer $I_R/(R : (BOOL : R))$ denotes the function whose value is the only member of a R- singleton and in all other cases the application of I_R is undefined.

We can observe that functional and relational objects can be homogeneously viewed both in a functional manner.

A version of the typed lambda calculus with tuple types directly supports manipulating of objects typed by $\mathcal{T}$. Starting with a collection $\mathcal{FUNC}$ of constants, each having a fixed type, and denumerable many variables of each type, the *language of (lambda) terms* $\mathcal{LT}$ is defined as follows: Let types R, S, $R_1, ..., R_n$ ($n \geq 1$) are elements of $\mathcal{T}$.

(1) Every variable of type R is a term of type R.

(2) Every constant (a member of $\mathcal{FUNC}$) of type R is a term of type R.

(3) If M is a term of type $(S : R_1, \ldots, R_n)$, and $N_1, \ldots, N_n$ are terms of types $R_1, \ldots, R_n$, respectively, then $M(N_1, \ldots, N_n)$ is a term of type S.

(4) If $x_1, \ldots, x_n$ are different variables of the respective types $R_1, \ldots, R_n$ and M is a term of type S, then *lambda* $x_1 \ldots x_n(M)$ is a term of type $(S : R_1, \ldots, R_n)$

(5) If $N_1, \ldots, N_n$ are terms of types $R_1, \ldots, R_n$, respectively, then $(N_1, \ldots, N_n)$ is a term of type $(R_1, \ldots, R_n)$.

(6) If M is a term of type $(R_1, \ldots, R_n)$, then $M[1], \ldots, M[n]$ are terms of respective types $R_1, \ldots, R_n$.

Terms can be interpreted in a standard manner by means of an *interpretation* assigning to each function symbol from $\mathcal{FUNC}$ an object of the same type, and by a *semantic mapping* [ ] from $\mathcal{LT}$ into all functions given by the type system $\mathcal{T}$.

According to semantics of the quantifiers and the singularizer, we can write simply **foreach** $x(M)$ instead of $\Pi(lambda\ x(M))$. Similarly, **forsome** $x(M)$ replaces $\Sigma(lambda\ x(M))$. Finally, we write $I(lambda\ x(M))$ shortly as **onlyone** $x(M)$ and read "the only x such as M". (Naturally, $M/BOOL$.)

For the purposes of formal defining of basic database notions, we won't require an arbitrary language $\mathcal{LT}$. We call a language $\mathcal{LT}$ *database-applicable* iff it has the following properties: $BOOL$ and $REAL$ are among the types of B, there is a distinguished binary predicate $=_R$ for any type R among constants of $\mathcal{FUNC}$, there are logical connectives, R-quantifiers and R- singularizer (for any R) among constants of $\mathcal{FUNC}$.

All another $\mathcal{LT}$s may be considered as an extension of a given database-applicable language $\mathcal{LT}$. We will assume a fixed interpretation assigning to symbols of $\mathcal{FUNC}$ in $\mathcal{LT}$ their intended interpretation. In the remainder of the paper, we consider database-applicable languages $\mathcal{LT}$ only.

3 Conceptualization of the Object System

In this section we briefly review possible world semantics used in the natural language analysis based on intensional logic [TIC82],[MP81].

Recall that the intuitive idea behind the possible worlds model is that, besides the true state-of-affairs, there are a number of other thinkable (logically consistent) possible states-of-affairs (relative to the given natural language $\mathcal{L}$) which constitute the logical space of $\mathcal{L}$ - possible worlds.

For example "actor" does not denote a set of objects but rather the property of being an actor. The actual class of actors is dependent on the actual state-of-affairs (actors exist in a world with theaters) and, possibly, on time (new actors are coming, etc.). On the other hand, the expression "integers" clearly denotes the set of integers (in the usual sense).

Similarly, there is a difference e.g. between expressions "a film which they are showing at a given theater" and "the count". The former denotes a function which can be applied to theaters and gives a film (or nothing). We emphasize that this function can not be computed from the definition of participating notions in the language expression; its value is dependent on a given possible world and a time moment. On the other hand, the application of the function count to a (finite) set of objects returns always the cardinality of the set (independent on possible worlds and time).

Thus, we can distinguish between two categories of functions: *empirical* and *analytical*. A function the domain of which is the logical space (elementary type W) is called *intension*. Range of these functions are again functions defined (possibly) on time moments. Functions which are not intensions are *extensions*.

Using the type system $\mathcal{T}$ introduced in Sect. 2, we will consider some base B (*epistemic base*) containing elementary types $BOOL$, W (possible worlds), T (time moments), IND (individuals). Then intensions are objects of type $((R : T) : W)$ for any type R of $\mathcal{T}$. (We abbreviate the fact as R_{TW}.) For example, *individual concepts* are IND_{TW}-objects, *properties of R-objects* are $(BOOL : R)_{TW}$-objects, *propositions* are $BOOL_{TW}$-objects.

Thus, "the cast for Hamlet" denotes an individual concept, 'actor' denotes a property of individuals, 'the cast for Hamlet is Olivier' denotes a proposition. The proposition is defined in a world with theaters and is, e.g., false in the time when Olivier is dead.

The associated value of an intension applied to a given world (and, usually, a given time moment) gives, usually, an extension. Then, e.g., the extension of an individual concept is an *individual*, the extension of a property of R-objects is a *class of R-objects*, the extension of a proposition is its truth value. (Thus, classes are aggregates defined by properties of objects.)

The last but not least example of a conceptual object is an *attribute*, in general, an $(S : R_1, \ldots, R_n)_{TW}$ - object (for any types S, R_i). It is appropriate to type a universum in the base. This process is called a *sortalization*. As usually, we shall distinguish entity and descriptive sorts. For example, "film which they are showing at a given theater at a given date" is a $(FILM : THEATER, DATE)_{TW}$-object, i.e. an attribute, the type of which is defined over the base $B' = \{BOOL, W, T, FILM, THEATER, DATE\}$.

At the conceptual level, a *database concept* is defined as a tuple of attributes [ZLA85]. A description of these attributes is called a *conceptual schema*.

According to our formal tools, both last objects can be viewed as terms of an appropriate language $\mathcal{LT}$; names of attributes can be conceived as typed variables of $\mathcal{LT}$ with the only interpretation - the related attributes.

On the database level only extensions of attributes are kept. However, when we want to distinguish between meaningful and meaningless databases described by a conceptual schema, some (explicit) ICs are needed. Given the attribute set $\{A_1/R_1, \ldots, A_k/R_k\}$, an IC is given by an appropriate lambda term *lambda* $c(M)$, where $c/(R_1, \ldots, R_k)$ and $M/BOOL$. ICs approximate values of attributes in the actual world.

The notion of attribute seems to be the fundamental in conceptual modeling:

(i) The structure of attribute conceived as a complex object covers all known similar notions known from the semantic database models [POK89].

(ii) Given the extension of an attribute it is possible to generate the set of *basic propositions*. For the above attribute they are denoted by sentences such as "They are showing the film 'Amadeus' at the Metro on March 8th".

The set of basic propositions and their logical consequences creates an *information base* (it is called the *information capability* of an attribute in [DMS88]). Clearly, a part of information capability of a set of attributes can be gained by an appropriate language $\mathcal{LT}$ used as a query language or view definition tool.

Example 1: Let the following schema be a fraction of a "culture" information system in a city.
Entity sorts: $THEATER, FILM, ACTOR$
Descriptive sorts: $BOOL, DATE, ADDRESS, PRICE$
Attributes:

$A_1/((BOOL : THEATER, DATE) : FILM)$
$A_2/((BOOL : ACTOR) : FILM)$
$A_3/(ADDRESS : THEATER)$
$A_4/((BOOL : PRICE) : FILM, THEATER, DATE)$

Notice that attributes are denoted by symbols here. Their semantics (hidden in names of attributes) are the following: A_1: theaters with dates where they are showing a given film, A_2: actors which are starring in a given film, A_3: address of a given theater, A_4: seat prices for a given film in a given theater on a given date.

IC C_1: They are not showing the same film in two different theaters on the same day. C_1 can be formalized by the following term:
lambda A_1

foreach $t_1, t_2, f_1, f_2, d(A_1(f_1)(t_1, d)$ **and** $A_1(f_2)(t_2, d)$ **implies** $f_1 = f_2) \diamond$

4 Definability and Informational Equivalence of Attributes

The schema in Example 1 may be hardly considered as conceptual. For example, entity sorts in the schema are not equipped by appropriate identifying attributes. Furthermore, the attribute A_1 is redundant. Indeed, A_1 is definable over A_4 by the following term (we will omit the dependence on possible worlds and obvious types of variables):

$$\textit{lambda } f \textit{ lambda } th\ d(\textbf{forsome } p(A_4(f, th, d)(p)))$$

In general, the notion of *definability* of attribute over a set of attributes is conceived with respect to the set $\mathcal{FUNC}$ of analytical functions given by the choice of the language $\mathcal{LT}$ (see [DKMS86]). (In the case of A_1 $\mathcal{FUNC}$ contains the existential quantifier only.) We say that an attribute A is definable over attributes $A_1, \ldots, A_m$, $(m \geq 1)$ w.r.t. a language $\mathcal{LT}$, iff there is a term U such that

(i) variables A_i $(1 \leq i \leq m)$ are the only free variables in U,
(ii) no subterm of U is logically true or logically false,
(iii) for each $w \in W$ and $t \in T$ $A_{tw} = U_{tw}$,
(in other words, $A = U$ in all database states).

A trivial example of definability is obtainable by construction of the so called *rotation* of an attribute. For example, $A_{11}/(THEATER : FILM, DATE)$ defined as

$$\textit{lambda } f\ d \textit{ lambda } th(A_1(f)(th, d))$$

is a rotation of A_1. Moreover, with respect to C_1, this rotation is *singular*, i.e. it is specified by a term

$$\textit{lambda } f\ d \textbf{ onlyone } th(A_1(f)(th, d)$$

The so called *reversed attribute* A' is another rotation of a given attribute A. The reversed attribute A'_1 is specified by

$$\textit{lambda } th\ d \textit{ lambda } f(A_1(f)(th, d))$$

The sets A, B of attributes are said to be *informationally equivalent* [DMS88] iff each attribute in A is definable over B and vice versa. (Thus, e.g. all rotations of a given attribute are informationally equivalent.) In [DKMS86] it is proved that given two informationally equivalent sets of attributes the associated information capabilities of these attribute sets are the same. Thus, attributes are "information containers" and all definable attributes yield derived information (propositions) only.

In consequence, inversed attributes in SDM, "inversed" roles in the Binary model with roles, etc., have not any positive influence on the expressive power of these database models. Explicitly defined ICs also do not extend the information capability of attributes. They give only "filter" non-admissible data coming into a database.

5 Expressive Power of Object-oriented Database Models

We extend the notion of informationally equivalent attribute sets to schemes. Schemes $S_i = (B_i, P_i, I_i)(i = 1, 2)$ are said to be *informationally equivalent* iff P_1 and P_2 are informationally equivalent and I_1 may be converted into I_2 by appropriate substitutions of attributes and vice versa. The substitutions are made in accordance with mutual definability of the respective attribute sets.

This is correct, if one assumes certain "compatibility" of types in B_1 and B_2. The types in B_1 that are not in B_2 must be expressible by means of substitution as types of B_2 and vice versa.

A *substitution*, θ_{ij}, is a finite mapping from B_i to $\mathcal{T}_j$ $(i \neq j)$. $B_i\theta_{ij}$ stands for the result of applying θ_{ij} to B_i. Thus, we can assign a new base of elementary types, B_i', to B_i. A substitution can be written as a set of bindings enclosed in curly braces.

Example 2: Let $B_1 = \{BOOL, S_1, S_2, S_3\}$ and $B_2 = \{BOOL, R_1, R_2\}$ and $\theta_{12} = \{S_3 \leftarrow (BOOL : (BOOL : R_1))\}$ and $\theta_{21} = \{R_1 \leftarrow (S_1, S_2)\}$. After applying the substitution we obtain bases B_1' and B_2'. It is easy to verify that $B_1' = B_2'$. ◇

If for substitutions θ_{12} and θ_{21} we have $B_1' = B_2'$, then B_1 and B_2 are said to be *unifiable*. In practice, we specify a substitution by a system of bindings. For example, bases specified in the example 2 are unifiable. It implies, that a notion denoting an object of type R_2 is expressible by a couple of notions of type (S_1, S_2).

The substitution θ_{ij} is not only a formal construction as should be to seem from the above construction. Let us to consider, for a moment, the base $B_3 = \{BOOL, S_1, S_2, S_3, R_1, R_2\}$, i.e. $B_3 = B_1 \cup B_2$. Then, e.g., S_3 given by the binding

$$S_3 \leftarrow (BOOL : (BOOL : R_1))$$

has one possible interpretation expressing an association (a bijection) of objects o/S_3 to objects $o'/BOOL : (BOOL : R_1)$. On an intuitive level, the base B_3 makes an integration environment for "miniworlds" given by bases B_1, B_2. In other words, there is a so called integration attribute *Is-explained-as* of type $((BOOL : (BOOL : R_1)) : S_3)$. The reversed attribute to it can be called *Is-covered-by*/ $(S_3 : (BOOL : (BOOL : R_1)))$. Notice that *Is-explained-as* and *Is-covered-by* are rather generic names for expressing these semantic connections. Thus, a unification of bases is designer-oriented (empirical) process.

The above integration attributes are in a good accordance with our intuition. They express a deepness of our notions used in modeling of the object system.

Example 3: Assume that the object system is defined over the base

$B_1 = \{THEATER, BOOL, ACTOR, STREET, HOUSE\#\}$.

Another possibility how to model the same starts with basic sorts given by the base

$B_2 = \{BOOL, ACTOR, ADDRESS\}$.

In the case, theaters are modelled, e.g., as classes of actor groups which are playing in particular plays. So, we can specify these facts by the attribute *is-explained-as*$_{THEATER}$ of type $((BOOL : (BOOL : ACTOR)) : THEATER)$, i.e. to each theater a class of actor groups is assigned. Similarly, the sort *ADDRESS* can be conceived as the couple $(HOUSE\#, STREET)$, the attribute *is-explained-as*$_{ADDRESS}$ of type $((HOUSE\#, STREET) : ADDRESS)$ describes this fact. ◇

To formalize the idea of "the same expressiveness" of two models, the following definition were proposed in [POK89].

Definition: Let Γ_1 and Γ_2 be two semantic database models and $\mathcal{LT}_1$ and $\mathcal{LT}_2$ be the respective database - applicable languages of terms which differ mutually in B_1 and B_2 only. Let B_1 and B_2 be unifiable. Then Γ_2 *dominates* Γ_1 if for each conceptual schema S_1 in Γ_1 there is a conceptual schema S_2 in Γ_2 such as S_1 and S_2 are informationally equivalent. We say that Γ_1 and Γ_2 have the *same expressive power* if each of them dominates the other.

In [POK89] the equivalence of a functional version of the Binary model to E-R model was briefly proved. Also a statistical classification was proved to be redundant as a modeling construct added to a semantic model.

We now give a proof of the first (slightly modified) statement in detail.

Statement 1: Assume that the E-R model uses basic constructs of respective (generic) types $(BOOL : E_1, \ldots, E_n)$, i.e. *relationships*, where $n \geq 2$, $(D : E_1, \ldots, E_n)$, i.e. *monovalued attributes*, and $((BOOL : D) : E_1, \ldots, E_n)$, i.e. *multivalued attributes*, where $n \geq 1$, and the Binary E-R model using basic constructs of respective (generic) types $(BOOL : O_1, O_2)$, (O_1, O_2), where at least one O_i is E. Then both models have the same expressive power.

Proof: First we provide a base unification. We will suppose that

$B_1 = \{E_1, E_2, \ldots\}$, $B_2 = \{E_1, E_2, \ldots, R, \ldots\}$

and $R \leftarrow (E_1, \ldots, E_n)$. It is sufficient to prove that the Binary model dominates the E-R model. We give a transformation for n-ary relationship only. Let S_1 be a conceptual schema containing object $RS/(BOOL : E_1, \ldots, E_n)$. We define $A_i/(E_i : R)$, $1 \leq i \leq n$, in S_2 as

$$A_i = \textit{lambda } r \textbf{ onlyone } e_i(RS(r) \textbf{ and } r[i] = e_i)$$

Now we provide a variable substitution $r \leftarrow (s_1, \ldots, s_n)$. Then RS is given by term

$\textit{lambda } s_1 \ldots s_n \bigwedge_{i=1}^{m}(A_i(r) = s_i) =$
$\textit{lambda } s_1 \ldots s_n \bigwedge_{i=1}^{m}(\textbf{onlyone } e_i(RS(s_1, \ldots, s_n) \textbf{ and } s_i = e_i) = s_i) =$
$\textit{lambda } s_1 \ldots s_n \bigwedge_{i=1}^{m}(RS(s_1, \ldots, s_n) \textbf{ and } s_i = s_i)$
$\textit{lambda } s_1 \ldots s_n \bigwedge_{i=1}^{m} RS(s_1, \ldots, s_n) = RS.$

Monovalued and multivalued attributes are expressed in the similar way. ◇

Remark: We shall call the E-R model described in the Statement 1 as a *standard E-R model.*

The following statement characterizes a power of the class construct. We prove that semantic models (particularly the standard E-R model) with the class construct are not more general than the the original model.

Statement 2: Let Γ be the E-R model model as in the Statement 1. The Γ and Γ augmented by the class construct (of type $(BOOL : E)$) have the same expressive power.

Proof: We begin with a base unification. We suppose that

$B_1 = \{E_1, E_2, \ldots, S_T, \ldots\}$, $B_2 = \{E_1, E_2, \ldots, T, \ldots\}$

and the unification is given by the substitution $S_T \leftarrow (BOOL : T)$. If $\Gamma_1 = \Gamma \cup \{$ class construct$\}$, then we must prove that Γ dominates Γ_1. Let S_2 be a conceptual schema containing objects $CL_i/(BOOL : T)$ where $1 \leq i \leq s$. We define $R_T/(BOOL : T, S_T)$ such that

$$R_T(t, g) = TRUE \text{ if and only if } t \in g.$$

a) $CL_i = \textit{lambda } r$ (**forsome** $d(R(r, d)$ and $d = g_i)) =$
lambda $r(R(r, g_i)$, where g_i/ST.

b) $\textit{lambda } rd(\bigvee_{i=1}^{s}(d' = CL_i \textbf{ and } CL_i(r))) =$
$\textit{lambda } rd(\bigvee_{i=1}^{s}(d' = \textit{lambda } r'(R(r', g_i)) \textbf{ and } R(r, g_i)))$
After a variable substitution $d' \leftarrow d$, where $d'/(BOOL : T)$ we obtain
$\textit{lambda } rd(\textbf{forsome } (d = \textit{lambda } r'(R(r', g_i)) \textbf{ and } R(r, g_i))) =$
$\textit{lambda } rd(R(r, d) = R$ ◇

We can conclude, that the Binary model appears to be sufficient enough for a conceptual modeling. On the other hand, many natural n-ary relationships must be decomposed into binary ones. Experiences with the conceptual model HIT [DKMS86] show that attributes of so called simple types (like attributes in example 1) cover naturally most of situations in a conceptual modelling. The future is in the functional data model.

6 Conclusion

In this paper, we have shown that a theoretical framework based on the lambda calculus and the intensional logic can be adapted to deal with important features of semantic database models. We have also proposed a possibility how to compare two semantic database models. The expressive power of models depends on basic objects given in the conceptual realm (a certain "similarity" of sorts) and on basic constructs allowing to construct conceptual bridges between notions in different conceptual schemes.

The results have a positive influence on an integration process of heterogeneous databases, a specification of external views in different variants of a semantic model etc.

Future research in the area should focus on the following problems: a construction of natural query languages based on the above ideas; finding a kernel of a conceptual schema (i.e. informationally equivalent non-redundant set of attributes).

References

[BRO84] Brodie,M.L.: On the development of Data Models. In: On conceptual modeling, Brodie,M.L., Mylopoulos,J., and Schmidt,J.W. /eds./, Springer Verlag,New York,1984

[DKMS86] Duží,M., Krejčí,F., Materna,P. ,Staníček,Z.: HIT Method of Data Base Design (a Functional Approach to Information Representation). RR., Techn. Univ. Brno, 1986

[DMS88] Duží,M., Materna,P., Staníček,Z.: Information Capability of a Database Schema. Kybernetika, 24, 3, 216-226, (1988)

[DM90] Duží, M., Materna, P.: Attributes: Distinguishing capability versus infromational capability. Comp. and AI, 9, 2, 169-185 (1990)

[HEU90] Heuer, A.: Equivalent schemes in semantic, nested relational, and relational database models. MS, TU Clausthal, West Germany

[HK87] Hull,R.,King,R.: Semantic Database modeling: Survey, applications, and research issues. ACM Comp. Surv., 13, 201-260 (1987)

[HUL87] Hull R.: A survey of theoretical research on typed complex database objects. Chap.5 in: Databases (J. Paredaens, ed.), Academic Press, London, 1987, pp. 193-256.

[HY84] Hull,R.,Yap,C.K.: The format model:a theory of database organization. JACM, 31, 3, 518-537 (1984)

[KH87] Klein,H.K., Hirschheim,K.A.: A Comparative Framework of Data modeling Paradigms and Approaches. The Comp.Journ., 30,1,(1987)

[MP81] Materna,P.,Pokorný,J.: Applying Simple Theory of Types to Databases. Information Systems,6,4, 283-300 (1981)

[POK89] Pokorný, J.: A function: unifying mechanism for entity-oriented database models. Entity-Relationship Approach, C.Batini (Ed.), Elsevier Science Publishers B.V. (North-Holland) 1989, pp. 165-181

[POK90] Pokorný, J.: Integration of relational, functional and logical databases. Invited paper on Int. Conf. on Engineering Information in Data Bases TEXNODATA '90, Berlin, 1990

[SAL87] Saltor,F.: Semantic relativism in databases. RR 18/87, Dep. de Lieng. i Sist. Inf., Universitat Politecnica de Catalunya, Barecelona, 1987

[TIC82] Tichý, P.: Foundation of Partial Type Theory. Reports on Math.Logic,14, 55-72 (1982)

[ZLA85] Zlatuška,J.: HIT Data Model. Database from the Functional Point of View. VLDB'85, Stockholm, 1985

Animation Support for a Conceptual Modelling Language *

Thorsten Hartmann, Ralf Jungclaus, Gunter Saake

Abt. Datenbanken, Techn. Universität Braunschweig
POBox 3329, D–38023 Braunschweig

E-mail {hartmann|jungclau|saake}@idb.cs.tu-bs.de

Abstract

The first phase in developing information systems is often called conceptual modelling phase. The model constructed is the first formal document describing the desired system. The conceptual model must deal with structural *and* behavioural aspects of the world. The complexity of such a model often prevents a detailed understanding by the later users. One way to estimate if (s)he really gets what (s)he wants are prototype systems constructed by conventional programming. We propose a way to construct prototypes from formal specifications by means of transformation into a kernel language that can be executed in a suitable distributed runtime environment. We introduce the modelling language, the basic execution mechanism, and the basic architecture of the runtime system.

1 Introduction

A large number of software systems can be characterized as information systems. The purpose of an information system is to represent parts of the world usually called Universe of Discourse (UoD) through a computer system. An information system is *embedded* in the real world and therefore the first steps in designing such systems is the integrated modelling of the parts of the UoD that are to be computerized later and the environment using this system. Following [7] the relevant aspects of the UoD are static and dynamic. Usually this phase of system design is called *conceptual modelling*.

On the one hand the conceptual model must be depicted in a formal way since it will be used by system developers as the *basis for following implementation steps*. Thus the derivation of knowledge for the design process must be possible. On the other hand it serves as the contract between system developers and

*This work was partially supported by the CEC under ESPRIT-2 BRA WG 3023 IS-CORE (Information Systems – COrrectness and REusability). The research work of Ralf Jungclaus and Thorsten Hartmann is supported by Deutsche Forschungsgemeinschaft under Sa 465/1-3.

users and must therefore be *readable by domain specialists.* These requirements contradict each other.

In general it seems not to be possible to have a declarative, formal specification of a conceptual model developed by a computer scientist that is also easily understandable by users. A way out of this dilemma can be given by *early prototyping* or *animation* of the model, providing help to understand the specification by way of *testing* prototypes generated from the specification.

The formalisms usually adopted for conceptual modelling like the ER-model and its extensions [2, 5], semantic data models [21] as well as informal approaches like data flow diagramms or JSD [11] are not sufficient for a detailed modelling of real world aspects. Either they only provide means to model the structural components of a UoD or they do not integrate the structural and behavioural aspects. Only very few modelling resp. knowledge representation approaches address the problem explicitly, among them TAXIS [20], RML [6], Object/Behaviour Diagramms [14], and CMSL [26].

One way to overcome the problem of integrating the structural and behavioural part of a system description is an *object-oriented viewpoint.* Regarding a system as communicating objects seems to be a natural way to represent the relevant aspects of the real world [3]. Objects, encapsulating an internal state and providing an external operation interface may be used to describe the system as a whole when they are connected via communication links.

In our approach the specification of a UoD can be depicted as a system of interacting components. The characteristics of this approach can be summarized as follows: All system components have a *local state.* Thus, state information is localized in the components. The components evolve during time, i.e. their state changes over time. Autonomous components do not influence each other. All components of a system may themselves be structured and composed of smaller subparts.

The approach to conceptual modelling of dynamic information systems described here integrates formalisms known from semantic data models, object oriented methods and formal approaches to software specification. The goal is to define a declarative formalism for system specification using results from algebraic specification of abstract data types [27], algebraic specification of processes [10, 19] and logical modelling of reactive systems [17].

The language TROLL [13] developed on the basis of [25] will only be sketched here. Key concepts can also be found in [12, 8].

2 Animation vs. Implementation

Following the specification of the desired information system, the next step is known as *design phase.* In the design phase, a declarative specification is transformed into an operational description that can then be implemented on a computer system. The design process can and should be guided by information derived from the conceptual model specification. The derived knowledge can also be used to automatically construct parts of the design. We therefore distinguish between two orthogonal directions: *Animation*: automatic construction of executable specifications from conceptual model specifications on the same level of abstraction. *Implementation*: realisation of abstract concepts with concrete ones using services provided by the underlying sub-systems like database systems, operating systems and communication software.

On each level in the stepwise design process an animation must be possible. That is, starting with the conceptual model which contains mainly declarative components and can therefore only be executed to some extent, we reach more and more operational specifications during the design/implementation process.

During the conceptual modelling phase the animation is used to *validate* a conceptual model developed so far. This means, that the users, together with the specifier, can test the specification with respect to the desired functionality. In the successive design steps the animation can serve as a test of the functionality of the more concrete system specification.

This does not mean however that animation is a way to *verify* parts of the design. We think, that the main function of animation is a *verification against informal requirements* as described in some kind of requirements analysis *before* any formal conceptual model is constructed. In contrast to design steps formulated in a formal language that can be formally checked against the previous, more abstract level, the original conceptual model can only be *tested* against the requirements of the user *by means of experiment.*

For animation we transform constructs from the conceptual model specification into equivalent executable constructs where this is possible. One may say that this approach is near to an automatic implementation constructed from the conceptual model. But this is not quite right. For animation purposes it is irrelevant to ask for efficiency, ergonomic user interfaces, security etc. The main task of the animation is to show the functionality of the UoD model.

Design and implementation on the other hand serves the purpose to construct an efficient, ergonomic and secure system. The abstractly described data and communication structure of the conceptual model is refined into concrete data structures and communication between the computational processes described on a lower level of abstraction. During design and implementation the transition from a *problem oriented* descripton to a *solution oriented* description is taken. Nevertheless, some techniques used for the automatic translation of abstract specifications into executable ones may be adopted for the design and implementation.

3 TROLL Concepts and Language Features

3.1 Basic Concepts

Nowadays, the object oriented paradigm is not only used in the realm of programming languages but also for the design of software, databases and information systems [15, 3]. We can identify the following basic ideas adopted from the areas programming languages and databases [1].

Objects are entities encapsulating an internal state and providing an external interface. In databases we can find a varying degree ranging from fully encapsulating the internal structure to a completely visible state in form of attributes. Objects are uniquely identifiable, i.e. we may distinguish between objects that are in the same state and between different states of an object. Objects can communicate with each other by sending messages. These messages are sometimes answered by the receiver. An object locally determines how to react on the receipt of a message. Objects can be classified due to similar structure and observable behaviour. In programming languages classes are usually described as the *type* of objects whereas in databases classes serve as templates for instances as well as containers for instances of the class [1]. Classes are embedded in an inheritance hierarchy. In programming languages this feature is used to describe code reuse. More generally we can also look at the *concrete properties* of an instance that can be inherited by subinstances.

For the conceptional modelling approach adopted for the language TROLL, we have to abstract from the operational point of view of programming languages respectively the access oriented view of databases and introduce declarative constructs to describe the possible *evolution* of objects and thereby the evolution of the system as a whole. The concepts of TROLL can be characterized as follows:

- Objects are the basic building blocks to describe a system of interacting components.
- The internal state of an object can only be changed by means of *events.*
- Objects may be persistent.
- The evolution of an object is described by the possible sequences of event occurrences and communication with other objects.
- The internal state of an object is encapsulated. Parts of this state however can be observed by means of *attributes.*

Additionally to these concepts TROLL introduces various abstractions that help to structure specifications:

- Objects are classified in *classes* with a unique name space.
- Objects may be *aggregated* to *composite objects* [8].
- Object may be connected via *relationships* [12].

For the specification of objects in TROLL we use a variety of formalism that are integrated into the object oriented framework. For the description of various properties we use a sorted first order logic. The behaviour in terms of possible event sequences and possible attribute evolutions is described with a linear first order temporal logic dialect [22] respectively a CSP [10] based language.

3.2 Basic Language Features

The specification of object systems in TROLL [13] starts with the specification of *templates* which together with a suitable identification mechanism are used to describe object classes. We do not only describe the static aspects of objects but also their *behaviour*.

As a starting point we will specify an object class account. The description of a class containing accounts starts with an identification mechanism introducing *external* names for account objects (here natural numbers) and continues with the specification of a suitable template:

```
object class Account
  identification No:nat;
  template
    attributes
      constant Holder:|BankCustomer|;
      Balance:money; CreditLimit:money;
    events
      birth open; death close;
      new_credit_limit(Amount:money);
      withdraw(Amount:money); deposit(Amount:money);
    constraints
      initially CreditLimit = 0 and Balance = 0;
      (Balance < 0) ==> sometimef(Balance >= 0);
    valuation   variables m:money;
      { m > CreditLimit } ==> [new_credit_limit(m)]CreditLimit = m;
      [withdrawal(m)]Balance = Balance - m;
      [deposit(m)]Balance = Balance + m; ...
  behavior
      permissions   variables m,m1:money;
        { Balance = 0 } close;
        { m <= (Balance+CreditLimit) } withdraw(m);
        { (sometime(after(deposit(m1)))) and
          (m1 > CreditLimit) and (m <= m1) } new_credit_limit(m);
end object class Account;
```

The declaration of attributes and events defines the *signature* of the object instances of class Account. Attributes are strongly typed. Data types itself are not specified together with the specification of an object society but are assumed to be predefined using a suitable formalism for specification of abstract data types. A special data type is |BankCustomer| which denotes *internal* identifiers of objects.

In the event section the state changing operations on objects are declared. We distinguish between *birth*, *death*, and *update* events that create, destroy or update objects respectively. Optional event parameters are used to define more specific state changes as well as data interchange between objects during communication.

In the constraint section we introduce constraints on attribute evolutions. In this example, we specify that the initial value of the attributes CreditLimit and Balance, i.e. the value after the birth event occured, must be zero.

The valuation section describes effects that events have on attribute values. The rules in this section are formulae in a restricted positional logic [4]. These formulae have a rather operational meaning: *after* the occurrence of an event for example withdraw instantiated with the value m the attribute Balance has the value Balance-m. The rules may be applicable in only certain object states which is described with a first order condition.

In the behaviour section we describe the allowed event sequences on the object state *over time*. In this example we only introduce *permissions*, i.e. *preconditions* on event occurrences. These preconditions are formulated as first order conditions on object states or temporal logic rules referencing the past evolution of the object at hand. The second rule states that a requested update operation is only allowed to occur after the preceding request is followed by an update_failed, withdraw, or deposit event.

For a more detailed specification of behaviour it is also possible to specify events and event combination that must be part of a life cycle: *obligations* or *liveness properties* and events that occur by the initiative of the object itself: *commitments*.

3.3 Structuring Object Societies

Objects and object classes can be in various relation to each other. They can be structured in *composite objects*, they can be embedded in a class hierarchy (*specialization*) and they may be connected with *relationships*. Since the specialization hierarchy and relationships are not needed for the description of animation and the execution model in the rest of the paper, we will only introduce composite objects and communication relationships inside composite objects.

A composite object in TROLL can be defined using *component constructors* in the components section of a template description. Let us suppose a fragment of a specification of a bank object that is constructed from a manager object taken from class Person (not further specified here), a set of Account objects, and a list of Person objects:

```
object Bank
  template
    components
      Manager:Person; Accounts:SET(Account); ServQueue:LIST(()Person);
      ...
    events
      birth establish; death close_down;
      open_account(No:nat); close_account(No:nat);
      ...
    behavior
      permissions   variables n:nat;
        { not Accounts.IN(Account(n)) } open_account(n);
        { sometime after(open_account(n)) } close_account(n);
        ...
    interaction   variables n:nat;
      open_account(n) >> Accounts(Account(n)).open;
      open_account(n) >> Accounts.INSERT(Account(n));
      ...
  end object Bank;
```

With the specification of *components* special events and attributes to alter and observe the structure of the composite object are introduced. The composition is *event driven*, i.e. special events are used to introduce and delete component objects to/from the composition. The components may be *single valued*, *set valued*, or *list valued* (see example).

Important in this discussion is the *interaction* section. In the interaction part we define the communication relationships inside the composition. Events occurring in the composite object force other events to occur. E.g. the event `open_account` *calls* for the events `Accounts.INSERT` and `open`. The calling relationship denotes *synchronous*, *directed* communication between objects.

4 Towards Animation of Conceptual Models

On the one hand a modelling language like TROLL should be sufficiently powerful to represent the relevant details of a given UoD. It should be declarative, that is, it must show *what* the user wants to have and not *how* it can be realized. It has been argued that such modelling or specification language need not (necessarily) be executable [9]. Here we want to stress that some kind of execution capability is necessary to *validate* the constructed model of the real world in terms of what the user intended to have. The problem is merely to *identify* parts of the model that *cannot* be executed (in finite time) and warn the user of an animation system if he tries to execute these constructs.

The declarative language constructs in TROLL are mainly the conditions for allowed object evolution in terms of event sequences and attribute evolution sequences (temporal constraints) formulated using temporal logic.

In particular temporal logic preconditions for events may involve checking the history back to the birth event. Since this approach is not practical (not even for prototyping), we tried to find a reduced set of information about the history that is sufficient to evaluate these conditions [24]. Some of the techniques applied there may also be used to check the conditions on the future attribute evolution. Techniques as for example *integrity preserving transactions* have been worked out in [16].

If the conditions used in the specification are of an appropriate form or if the user is warned of conditions that may not be handled this way the problem of animating a model can be tackled. We adopt the well known idea of a *kernel language* over which the higher level language constructs are defined. Thus the problem of executing the language TROLL reduces to executing the kernel constructs and warn the user if such a transformation cannot be given. The kernel language contains only restricted first order formulae, no inheritance, only simple forms of complex objects etc.

Also the kernel language contains declarative features, for example the behavioural component dealing with communication of objects. Event calling can be regarded as (synchronous) message passing. The model applied is more powerful than one could see in the first examples. See for example a decimal counter object [23]. In this object the digits of a decimal counter are represented as attributes. Upon counting the digits are incremented starting with the leftmost digit Digit(1) and successively higher digits if necessary:

```
object Counter
  template
    attributes Digit(nat):nat;
    events birth CreateCounter; Count; IncDigit(nat);
    constraints variables n:nat; Digit(n) <= 9;
    valuation variables n:nat;
      [ CreateCounter ] Digit(n) = 0;
      { Digit(n) < 9 } ==> [ IncDigit(n) ] Digit(n) = Digit(n) + 1;
      { Digit(n) = 9 } ==> [ IncDigit(n) ] Digit(n) = 0;
    interaction variables n:nat;
      Count >> IncDigit(1);
      { Digit(n) = 9 } ==> IncDigit(n) >> IncDigit(n+1);
end object Counter
```

This object specification contains some language features not introduced up to now. In the attributes section we introduce an infinite set of attributes, one for each natural number or equivalently an *infinite array.* These attributes are set to zero with the first valuation rule. This is an example of a non executable construct. The only way to execute this construct is to delay the execution to the first *read* on this attribute (some kind of *lazy execution*). This can be done by transforming the attributes into objects with initialization upon first read.

More problematic in the sense of execution are the conditions posed on the valuation and calling rules. The conditions for the calling rules say that the rules are only evaluated if their conditions hold in the current state. The event to increment single decimal places IncDigit calls (recursively) for an arbitrary number of other IncDigit events depending on the current state of the object. In this case it can be derived easily (at least for a human being) that all IncDigit-instantiations are different, the argument strictly increases. This may not always be the case. Consider e.g. the same event being called *twice.* Conceptually, calling is synchronous, even more, all events in such an event chain occur in parallel, they transform one object state into the next state. Does such an event occur *twice*? Another questions concerns valuation rules. Some events in such an event chain defined by calling may change the value of *the same* attribute. What is the new attribute value in the next state? Clearly we need some form of an *execution model* for event occurrences and calling relationships.

If we want to execute a specification, we must *analyze* such calling rules. Since the problem in general is undecidable due to first order conditions for calling and valuation rules this can only be done at execution time, i.e. we detect conflicts and possibly also infinite calling chains. We will now introduce an informal execution algorithm that can be implemented using traditional programming language technology. The general problem is to execute an event e in an object o. *Conceptually* the following algorithm defines the execution model:

1. Collect the set E of events called by e. This may involve other (part-)objects of o and transitive calling of events. This step is problematic since it may

not terminate. Introducing a set E insures the absence of duplicates of events, i.e. events do not occur *twice* in a calling chain.

2. Check conflicts in terms of valuation rules. For every x∈E the set of affected attributes A_x is determined. These sets must be *pairwise* disjoint. If conflicts are encountered: **abort**.
3. Check if all preconditions for events in E hold. If not: **abort**.
4. Evaluate all valuation rules and determine the next (temporary) object state in terms of new attribute bindings.
5. Check integrity rules for all rules containing attributes affected in 2. If at least one rule is violated: restore the old state and exit.

The execution of a calling chain must therefore be encapsulated as an *ACID* transaction. For an implementation of this execution model we do not want to be restricted to a single workstation architecture. So the objects involved in communication may be distributed over a network.

5 Animation Support

The operational properties of TROLL partly coincide with the capabilities of object-oriented programming languages and databases. We therefore translate the TROLL-kernel language to *Sather*, a language developed at ICSI (Berkeley) that is based on *Eiffel* [18]. Additionally we build a runtime system dealing with communication in a network of workstations. The runtime package handles the distributed management of state information on different database systems, the automatic routing of event callings, and the necessary transaction protocol.

The structure of the system is depicted in Figure 1. Each node in the system

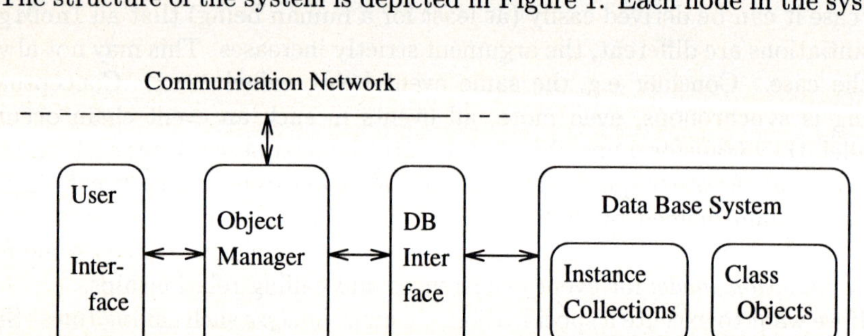

Figure 1: Architecture of Runtime/Animation System

contains an object manager that provides protocols for object communication and access. As long as we have no mechanism for object migration, the class objects on each node manage the actual existing class population. For migration of instances some further concepts like e.g. duplication of class objects are needed. For each node there exists a database component with a simple interface to the runtime system. This interface provides protocols for object read/write and transaction management. It allows an easy integration of different database systems.

The user interface can use the protocol of the object manager to *access* objects via their external names handled in the class objects, *trigger* events, or observe attributes. Currently a simple graphical interface is under development showing existing classes (on a node), lists of their instances, mouse driven selection of instances, event triggers, and observing actions.

The implementation of event calling chains can be sketched in the following way. Event calls are routed via the object managers in the network (algorithm step 1) the set of events is constructed iteratively. Information about the instances and their location can be found in the object manager class-location tables and in the class objects.

The event calling is described as a tree. The runtime conflict detection, the detection of violated preconditions, computation of new attribute values, and checking of constraints is done in the objects itself that have an executable form (compiled Sather objects). Therefore the set of events constructed so far as well as the set of affected attributes must be contained in the communication of the different object managers. This method is not always efficient but sufficient for *prototyping*.

The transactional behaviour of the algorithm is realised with the transaction protocol provided by the database interface. The transaction runs with a *two phase commit protocol*. The object managers use an asynchronous communication protocol to really achieve a parallel execution of events.

6 Conclusion and Future Work

Prototyping or animation eases the *validation* of a conceptual model under construction. It must be performed together with the user. The quality of the conceptual model is increased and possible flaws are found early during the modeling and/or design process. The animation is not restricted to the modeling phase but can be applied in any stage during the design of the software or information system. Animation however, means not *verification* of design. It is only meant to support the understanding between domain specialists (users) and modelling specialists (computer scientists).

After having defined the executable language kernel and implementing the first animation prototype, we will formalise the transformation TROLL to TROLL-kernel. In fact the kernel was developed with respect to the needed functionality of the full language and ideas for the transformation.

We are aware of the restrictions of our simple execution model. Up to now we may execute simple event calling chains. For latter stages in the design process we have to *refine* or *implement* events on the conceptual level with *event sequences* on a more detailed level. These event sequences must be executed as (sub)transactions in their own right. Therefore we will have to integrate a nested transaction facility into the execution model.

Acknowledgements

We are grateful to Cristina Sernadas who developed the basic features of TROLL with us. For many fruitful discussions on the language we are grateful to all other members of IS-CORE, especially to Hans-Dieter Ehrich, Amílcar Sernadas, José Fiadeiro. For implementation work we thank our students Jan Kusch and Urs Thürmann.

References

[1] M. Atkinson, F. Bancilhon, D. DeWitt, K. R. Dittrich, D. Maier, and S. B. Zdonik. The O-O Database System Manifesto. In W. Kim, J.-M. Nicolas, and S. Nishio, editors, *DOOD*, North-Holland, 1990, pages 40–57.

[2] P. P. Chen. The Entity-Relationship Model – Toward a Unified View of Data. *ACM TODS*, 1(1):9–36, 1976.

[3] D. de Champeaux and P. Faure. A Comparative Study of Object-Oriented Analysis Methods. *JOOP*, 3(2):21–33, 1992.

[4] J. Fiadeiro, C. Sernadas, T. Maibaum, and G. Saake. Proof-Theoretic Semantics of Object-Oriented Specification Constructs. In R. Meersman, W. Kent, and S. Khosla, editors, *Object-Oriented Databases: Analysis, Design and Construction (4th IFIP WG 2.6 Working Conference DS-4)*, pages 243–284, Amsterdam, 1991. North-Holland.

[5] M. Gogolla and U. Hohenstein. Towards a Semantic View of an Extended Entity-Relationship Model. *ACM TODS*, 16:369–416, 1991.

[6] S. Greenspan, A. T. Borgida, and J. Mylopoulos. A Requirements Modelling Language and its Logic. In M. L. Brodie and J. Mylopoulos, editors, *On Knowledge Base Management Systems*, pages 471–502. Springer, 1986.

[7] J. J. van Griethuysen. Concepts and Terminology for the Conceptual Schema and the Information Base. Report N695, ISO/TC97/SC5, 1982.

[8] T. Hartmann, R. Jungclaus, and G. Saake. Aggregation in a Behavior Oriented Object Model. In O. Lehrmann Madsen, editor, *Proc. ECOOP'92*, pages 57–77. Springer, LNCS 615, Berlin, 1992.

[9] I.J. Hayes and C.B. Jones. Specifications are not (necessarily) executable. Technical Report UMCS-89-12-1, Univ. of Manchester, 1989.

[10] C.A.R. Hoare. *Communicating Sequential Processes.* Prentice-Hall, 1985.

[11] M. A. Jackson. *System Development.* Prentice-Hall, New Jersey, 1983.

[12] R. Jungclaus, T. Hartmann, and G. Saake. Relationships between Dynamic Objects. In H. Kangassalo, H. Jaakkola, K. Hori, T. Kitahashi, editor,

Seminar on Information Modelling and Knowledge Bases. IOS Press, Amsterdam, 1993, pages 425–438.

[13] R. Jungclaus, G. Saake, T. Hartmann, and C. Sernadas. Object-Oriented Specification of Information Systems: The TROLL Language. Technical Report 91-04, TU Braunschweig, 1991.

[14] G. Kappel and M. Schrefl. Object/Behavior Diagrams. In *Proc. Data Engineering*, pages 530–539, IEEE Computer Society Press, 1991.

[15] W. Kim and F. H. Lochovsky, editors. *Object-Oriented Concepts, Databases, and Applications.* ACM Press/Addison-Wesley, New York, 1989.

[16] U. W. Lipeck. Transformation of Dynamic Integrity Constraints into Transaction Specifications. *TCS*, 76:115–142, 1990.

[17] Z. Manna and A. Pnueli. *The Temporal Logic of Reactive and Concurrent Systems. Vol. 1: Specification.* Springer-Verlag, New York, 1992.

[18] B. Meyer. *Object-Oriented Software Construction.* Prentice-Hall, Englewood Cliffs, NJ, 1988.

[19] R. Milner. Operational and Algebraic Semantics of Concurrent Processes. In J. van Leeuwen, editor, *Formal Models and Semantics*, pages 1201–1242. Elsevier, 1990.

[20] J. Mylopoulos, P. A. Bernstein, and H. K. T. Wong. A Language Facility for Designing Interactive Database-Intensive Applications. *ACM TODS*, 5(2):185–207, 1980.

[21] J. Peckham and F. Maryanski. Semantic Data Models. *ACM Computing Surveys*, 20(3):153–189, 1988.

[22] G. Saake. Descriptive Specification of Database Object Behaviour. *DKE*, 6(1):47–74, 1991. North-Holland.

[23] G. Saake. Objektorientierte Spezifikation von Informationssystemen: Konzepte und Sprachvorschläge. Habilitationsschrift, TU Braunschweig, 1992

[24] S. Schwiderski and G. Saake. Monitoring Temporal Permissions using Partially Evaluated Transition Graphs. In U. Lipeck and B. Thalheim, editors, *Proc. Modelling Database Dynamics, Volkse 92*, pages 196–217. Workshops in Computing, Springer, Berlin, 1993.

[25] A. Sernadas, C. Sernadas, and H.-D. Ehrich. Object-Oriented Specification of Databases: An Algebraic Approach. In P.M. Stocker and W. Kent, editors, *Proc. 13th VLDB'87*, pages 107–116. VLDB Endowment Press, Saratoga (CA), 1987.

[26] R. J. Wieringa. A Conceptual Model Specification Language (CMSL Version 2). Technical Report IR–248, Vrije Universiteit, Amsterdam, 1991.

[27] M. Wirsing. Algebraic Specification. In J. Van Leeuwen, editor, *Handbook of Theoretical Computer Science, Vol. B: Formal Models and Semantics*, pages 675–788. Elsevier, Amsterdam, 1990.

A Unifying Model of Data, Metadata and Context

Toncan Duong, John Hiller, Uma Srinivasan
School of Computer Science & Engineering, University of New South Wales, Kensington, Australia

Abstract. In this paper, we define *Context* as a data structure that gives the meaning and the environmental information of the detail data, and discuss two of its main features—*nested structure* and *role dynamism*. Then we propose a Context Model that unifies detail, meta and contextual data. We also discuss a Context-oriented query mechanism and illustrate the model by query examples.

1. Introduction

Context has been used loosely in Information Systems to denote the usage, the environment, the hidden meaning of a term but it has not been defined rigorously. In this paper, we will adapt the definition used in the Webster New Collegiate Dictionary (G. & C. Merriam Co. 1977) and define it to the degree that we see suitable for the multidatabase application.

According to the dictionary, *Context* has two meanings: *i)- As the parts of a discourse that surround a word or passage and can throw light on its meaning, ii)- As the interrelated conditions in which something exists or occurs: ENVIRONMENT.*

The definition of *Context* refers to assumed knowledge which is not explicitly represented. In a single environment, users and applications understand the meaning, assumption and rules of the data. However, when more than one information system needs to be accessed by the same application, or where the data from different systems needs to be integrated to provide a composite view, the limits in representation can become evident [SG89,YJ91, SM91b, KE91].

Generally, there are two approaches to resolve semantic heterogeneity. The *Mapping* approach uses a functional language like IPL [KE91] directly links one concept to another. The *Conceptual* approach employs a common conceptual structure where each concept may refer to, the structure imparts more meaning to the original concept and helps to resolve the differences [SM91a, SM91b, CH91].

In this paper, We argue that the *Conceptual* approach is more flexible and natural. In particular, Context is seen as a structure that stores the meaning, the usage, the environment, and the rules that relate to particular data.

Three basic issues of *context modelling* will be discussed, namely (i) What is *Context?*, (ii) Is it possible to *distinguish* contextual and detail data?, (iii) How does context get *represented?*,

We propose a unifying model that treats detail and contextual data similarly. This model supports four types of abstractions for its data organization (subsumption, aggregation, association and membership), and has a flexible data structure that can represent different forms including rules and constraints. A context oriented query mechanism will be discussed, and this will be followed by examples which illustrate the importance of context in information retrieval and data conflict resolution.

The remainder of this paper is organized as follows. Section 2 discusses the main features of context modelling including a definition of context, the cognitive consideration, and a suitable data structure. Section 3 discusses a flexible representation of context. In section 4 we provide query examples. In section 5 we summarize and compare our work with other approaches. Finally, section 6 concludes the proposal and expands issues that need further research and development.

2. Characteristics of Context

In this section, we will define the term Context as it is used in this paper, and discuss how to model it in a multidatabase environment. We propose a nested data structure that can support various levels of abstraction and different forms of data, including rules and constraints. As we do not distinguish between detail and contextual data, the contextual data can be represented by the same structures (set, list, tuples,...) as used in the representation of detail data. Further, the same language can be used to retrieve and manipulate both.

2.1. Context = Metadata

A traditional view of metadata refers to the schema of an information system like the relational data dictionary and directory [CO90, DK87]. We adopt an extended view and classify the data as detail or metadata depending on its role.

When an instance of data needs other data to clarify its meaning, to define its structure, to describe its usage, or to specify its environment, the latter data acts as a descriptor and has the role of the *metadata* whereas the data that is being described is called the *detail data*. It should be noted that we use the term 'data' to refer to an abstract representation which can be a simple integer like 1,2,3... or a complex document like an encyclopaedia.

This extended view of metadata is *equivalent* to context as described in the introduction and includes the schematic description as used in the traditional view. In the following, we will give a precise definition and then use the terms context and metadata interchangeably.

Definition: Context is defined as a data structure that gives the meaning and the environmental information of the detail data. The environment here means the scope of the data, the constraints and rules that the data need to follow.

Some of the metadata relate to the schematic constructs of a particular data model such as relation, attribute, tuple. In this paper, the discussion will be limited to only the non-schematic metadata in a multidatabase environment, the schematic counterpart will be treated separately.

2.2. Issues in context modelling

We classify data as detail or contextual according to its role as being described or describing another piece of data. Usually the amount of detail data is larger than the one of metadata, nevertheless, they can be modelled similarly. Here we will discuss the three major issues: cognitive considerations, the uniform treatment of detail and metadata, and the structure of contexts.

2.2.1. Cognitive considerations

To use a piece of data effectively, we need to provide a description that is adequate for the purpose and omit all else. Recall that to have an optimum *cognitive load*, users need to handle only the important data and not the baggage. For example, "exchange_rate=70.6", will be understood to most people in Australia to refer to "the official exchange rate of Australian to US dollars", the contextual data like "$A ->$US" is implied for this group of users. Similarly, the statement "exchange_rate = 70.2" will be sufficient for most people in Papua New Guinea. However, when these two systems need to interchange data, the context becomes important and each exchange_rate needs to be described by either "$A ->$US" or "Kina ->$US".

Part of contextual data often can be used in multiple contexts, for example, "money in $A" is contextual data for various contexts that is related to a variety of money such as salary, traffic_fine, local_subscription. The connections between a context and its detail data can be modelled in various ways such as domain approach [HI88], metadata rules [SM91], linguistic matching [DH92a]. It is beyond the scope of this paper to study the connection issue and we will not discuss it further.

To keep the cognitive load manageable, contextual data needs to be organized into a logical structure that allows the user to nominate a suitable abstraction level for a particular task. Our model supports four types of organization, namely subsumption, partition, connection and grouping. These four types correspond to the abstractions of specialization, aggregation, association and membership.

Subsumption

Contextual data may be grouped into levels in which each outer level includes the inner levels, this allows a user to choose a particular level that contains just enough contextual data for the application. Subsumption corresponds to the Specialization abstraction denoted by $\subset$, such as "microEconomy $\subset$ economy".

Aggregation

Contextual data may also be partitioned into modules so that the user needs to handle only one module at a time. It should be noted that we use the term 'partition' loosely and allow overlapping for the common contextual data. The partition organization corresponds to the Aggregation abstraction in the sense that the modules of contextual data that describe common detail data are aggregated into groups. For example, the contextual data for the sport car MX5 may be partitioned into two modules, design and manufacturing, these two modules are related by aggregation and form a new aggregate context of Design & Manufacturing.

Association

Context_i is connected to context_j ($\text{context}_i \mapsto \text{context}_j$) when context_i describes part of the contextual data of context_j (this contextual data becomes the detail data of Context_i). This corresponds to the association abstraction in which one concept may lead to another concept. For example, the context Einstein refers to the context Relativity as one of his proposed theories.

Membership

A Membership relationship relates an individual contextual data value to the group (context) it belongs to. Context can be nested in that contexts themselves can be the contextual data of another context. It should be noted that membership is subtly different from aggregation; the former focuses on the relationship between a group and its element, whereas the latter focuses on the relationship between elements that form the group.

2.2.2. Role identification

Smith and Smith have noted the variety of logical representations and stated "Relationship, Entity, Component, Category, Attribute, and Instance are just different interpretations of the same Abstract Objects" [SM78]. According to the definition (§2.1), detail data is data that is described by another data, but the detail data of one application can be the contextual data in another. For example, "future stock" is detail data in the context of a "trading floor" in the "New York stock market", but the same "future stock" may also be the context for the "trade price" detail of "999".

So, the label of a piece of data as contextual or detail, may change according to the application. Our approach does not distinguish specific data as contextual or detail and use a flexible representation that can support both (§ 3).

2.2.3. The organization of contexts.

Contexts can be nested and the discussion on the logical structure (§2.2.1) applies also to the organization of contexts. We model contexts by a network of directed lattice, in which the arrow points from a describing context to the context being described (fig.1).

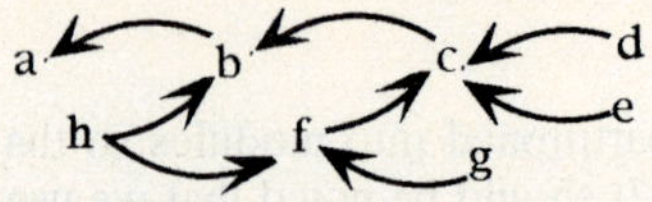

Fig.1 - Context is a lattice of information that describes a particular term

There are four types of arcs corresponding to the four types of abstraction. In the following, we will use annotated arrows to represent these arcs.

a) Subsumption:

$$(c1 \xrightarrow{s} c2 \xrightarrow{s} c3) \rightarrow (c1 \xrightarrow{s} c3)$$

- c1, c2, c3 are the contexts related by subsumption; the dark arrow denotes a logical deduction.

b) Aggregation:

$$(\{c1,c2\} \xrightarrow{a} c3) \leftrightarrow (\{c2,c1\} \xrightarrow{a} c3)$$

- For clarity reason, we only discuss a simple kind of aggregation (not ordered).

•• The symbol $\leftrightarrow$ denotes the equivalence between the two different forms.

c) Association:

There may be different routes connecting any two contexts, the choice of a particular route may depend on the amount of contextual information required. For example, figure 2 depicts a fictitious accident 'Chenoble', in which there are two possible routes for the context population. If the application requires maximum coverage, then route 2 is used and gives <Chenoble is an accident at Rusena which has 200,000 people>, otherwise, route 1 is used and gives only <Chenoble affects 200,000 people>.

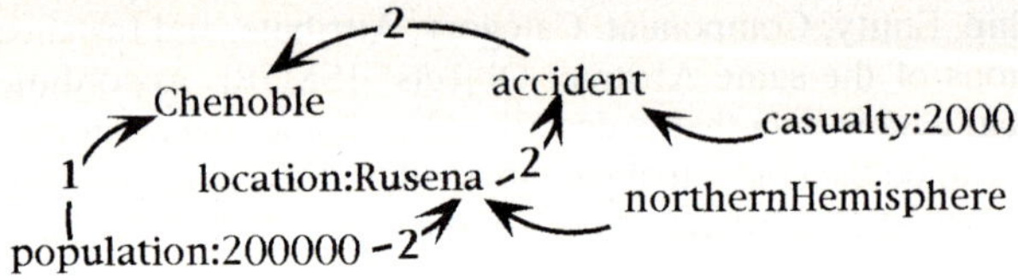

Fig.2 - Different routes connecting a context to the term it describes.

c) Membership:

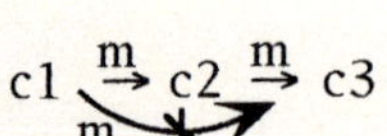

- Context 1 is a member of context 2 and context 2 is a member of context3, then context 1 cannot be a member of the context 3.

3. Context representation

To effectively model a context, the representation is required to support different forms of data including rules and constraints. The role of particular data can be either detail or contextual, and both roles need to be supported fully. The representation should also support a nested structure and the four types of abstraction as discussed in §2.2.1 and §2.2.3.

Most of the current data models distinguish metadata and detail data. Also the query language in these systems usually limits to the retrieval of the detail data from a specification of the metadata, the reverse and the associated query are poorly supported [CH89]. An example is the SQL query, "retrieve currency from stock where exchange=NY". The reverse query like "What is the contextual information of NY used in the stock exchange?" cannot be answered easily by these systems. Also, the constraints and rules in these systems are normally hidden from the users, the questions like "What are the constraints related to the data of currency?" or "Are any rules set for the currency used in the NewYork stock exchange?", are normally difficult to get executed.

Also, the conventional data model emphasizes the extension of data, actually it is considered as a faux pas to have an empty attribute. However, the intension of the data is as important as the extension in context modelling. Consider the five attributes in the description "Chenoble was an accident at location Rusena which has a population 200000 and is located at the northern hemisphere, had 2000 casualties" (fig.2). Only three attributes have value (location:Rusena, casualty:2000, and population:200000). The remaining two attributes, accident and northernHemisphere, do not have any value.

§2.2.1 and §2.2.3 have discussed the four abstractions and their use in context modelling. Our representation projects these four dimensions to give a linear representation which is written such that the left hand side is either a subsuming context, or an aggregate context, or an associated context of the right hand side.

4. Context application in Multidatabase environment

In this section we will illustrate the use of context to integrate data for a multidatabase environment. The example makes use of the variety in brand names for a drug type, the terms used are fictitious and do not correspond to what are being used in reality, for example, pamol is merely an imaginary drug name produced by the fictitious Pam Pharmaceutical.

Example: There are two independent databases, Pam belongs to the Pam Pharmaceutical and GP belongs to a medical centre called GP. The Pam database contains a set of information about the drug that it manufactures or distributes, and the GP database contains a set of relevant information about its patient. The details of their data are as follows:

<u>Pam pharmacy</u>

Objects,
{d1,d2,d3,...}

Data,
drugName: { panadol, tylenol, ampicillin, penicillin, septran, glucose, valium,... }
drugCode: { 1234P, 2345C,... }
manufacturer: { glaxo, biotech,... }
drugCategory: { scheduled, otc,... }
drugType: { paracetamol, antibiotics, intravenous,... }
drugForm: { tablet, capsule,... }
packaging: { <units:200, form:tablet>.carton, <units:50, form:capsule>.box,... }
symptom: { fever, headache }
impactTime: { oneHour, twoHour,... }

<u>GP medical centre</u>

Objects,
{p1,p2,p3,...}

Data,
patientName: { joe, jack, jill, henry,... }
drugName: { panadol, benadril, moxacin,... }
dosage: { onceDaily, twiceDaily,... }
symptom: { fever, headache, bodyAche, cold... }
diagnosis: { chestInfection, tonsilitis, cold,... }

Figure 3 has the patient p1 in the GP database. This patient has the name joe and is diagnosed as suffering cold based on his symptom of headache. A drug called pamol has been prescribed for his treatment. Though it is known that the drug has a symptom published by its manufacturer, GP has no such detail in hand. Also, the database has a rule to classify different brand names to their drug type. In the diagram, each arrow starts from the describing data to the described data and is annotated by a character such as a, as, s to denote the abstraction as aggregation, association or subsumption.

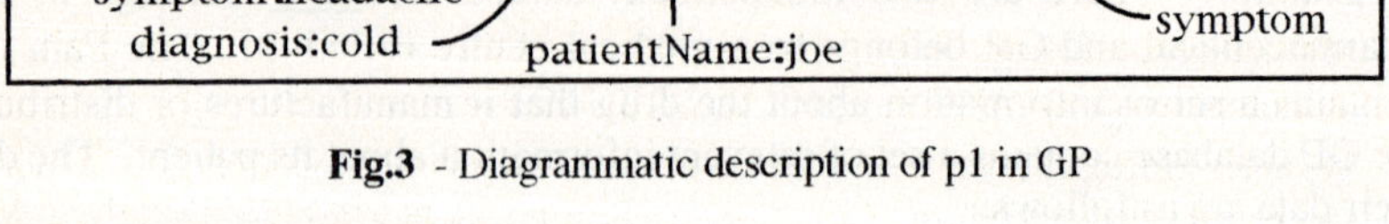

Fig.3 - Diagrammatic description of p1 in GP

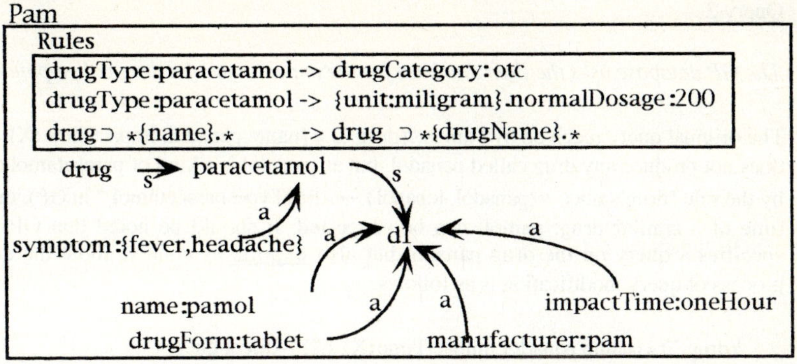

Fig.4 - Diagrammatic description of d1 in Pam

Figure 4 is a diagrammatic description of the drug d1 in the Pam database, d1 has a name pamol and is manufactured in tablet form, it is useful to the symptoms of fever or headache and has an impact time of one hour. Also, d1 belongs to a drug type called paracetamol, and there are two rules in relate to its usage: 1) all paracetamol can be sold over the counter (otc), 2) the normal dosage is 200 milligram. There is another rule in the database that specifies the equivalence of name and drugName in the context of drug ($*$ is a wild-character denoting one or more occurrence of context, and it can be ø).

Query 1

The GP database asks the Pam database for the symptoms of drug pamol.

The query can be expressed as ?(drug ⊃ $_*${name:pamol, symptom:X}.d1). "⊃" denotes the subsumption abstraction, "{...}" denotes the aggregation abstraction, and "*" is a wild-character for one or more occurence of any context. As GP contains only the intension of symptom, "drug ⊃*{symptom}.d1", its extension needs to be retrieved from Pam, ,

It should be noted that the symptom of a drug, "drug ⊃*{symptom}.*", is different from the symptom of a patient, "patient ⊃*{symptom}.*", they are distinguished by their respective contexts .

When the query gets executed at Pam, because the context pamol does not contain any data about its symptoms, the query is modified and directed to the generalized context, paracetamol.

?(drug ⊃*{name:pamol, symptom:X}.d1) is expanded to include a generalized context Y, and becomes ?(drug ⊃ Y ⊃{name:pamol, symptom:X}.d1). Y is related to d1 by subsumption, (Y ⊃{A}.X→ {A}.Y ⊃{A}.X). Y is matched to paracetamol, and the query becomes ?(drug ⊃{symptom:X}.paracetamol ⊃{name:pamol}.d1). This modified query can be executed and returns *(X ={fever, headache}, Context= paracetamol–generalized*).

Query 2

The GP database asks the Pam database for the impact time of a drug called panadol.

The original query received by Pam is ?(drug ⊃ ∗{name:panadol, impactTime:X}.d2). Pam does not produce any drug called panadol, but as panadol is a kind of paracetamol (deduced by the rule "drugName: v{panadol, tenanol} → drugType: paracetamol " in GP), the impact time of a similar drug, pamol, can be suggested. It should be noted that GP not only specifies a query on the drug panadol but also exports its context about the drug. The process of query modification is as follows:

?(drug ⊃ ∗{name:panadol, impactTime:X}.d2) – direct query
?(drug ⊃ {impactTime: X}.paracetamol ⊃ {name:panadol}.d2) – generic query
?(drug ⊃ paracetamol ⊃ {impactTime: X, name:Z}.d3) – similar query

?(drug ⊃ paracetamol ⊃ {impactTime: X, name:pamol}.d3)
(X= oneHour, Context = pamol.–similar)

5. Discussion and Comparison with Other Approaches.

Most of the current proposals address the issue of context as a solution to an existing problem such as user aids [MO86], system maintenance [DK87, HB91], and data conflict [SM91a]. Consequently, they are designed to work well in a particular domain of application but insufficient to provide a general framework that includes considerations of the user's cognitive load, navigation, and retrieval. Also, it is essential that context can support multiple viewpoints, and dynamism in the sense that a context may get defined depending on the other contexts. We argue that our approach is a step in the right direction and the following contains a comparison with some current models.

[SM91b] discussed the importance of context matching in a source-receiver model, and proposed a rule-based representation for metadata. Attributes are divided into primitive and semantically definable, the primitive attributes are self-understood whereas the semantically definable attributes need other attributes to provide the meaning. One particular feature of that proposal is to allow the semantics of an attribute dynamically determined by the value of some other attributes, and rules are used to express such relationship.

The proposed model includes this rule-based approach, a context rule such as, $(metadata^1:value^1 \rightarrow metadata^2:value^2)$.detail assigns $(metadata^2:value^2)$ as the semantics to the detail based on the value of $metadata^1$. Moreover, as the model has a flexible representation, other forms such as $(metadata^1 \rightarrow metadata^2)$.detail or $(metadata^1:value^1 \rightarrow metadata^2)$.detail can be expressed.

[MC82] criticized the lacking of support to metadata management at current data models and has addressed some general issues like its access and manipulation. Though the author argued for the advantages of using the same DBMS tools for both detail and metadata, the two concepts were actually treated separately. The integration of data and metadata was at the tool level whereas our approach distinguishes the two only by the role that the data currently plays. The result is a more direct representation that supports multiple levels of abstraction and the user can select a suitable level for a particular application.

Association is an important abstraction in context modelling, this has not been supported in most current proposals. For example, the context of "Australian-Economy" may associate to the context of "The current President of USA", it then also associates with the generalized context of "The Presidents of USA". However, it will not associate with the "Musical Endowment" which is a more specialized context of "The current President of USA". Provided $C^1 \supset C^2$, then $C^2.x \rightarrow C^1.x$, because C^1 contains every contextual data of C^2 including the one used for association. The reverse is not always true.

Carnot system being developed at MCC is an ambitious project that aims to integrate separately developed information systems by providing a common semantic communication layer [CH91]. The approach uses an existing global *ontology*, the Cyc knowledge base, for relating concepts expressed in the individual system, it emphasizes a global consistency in which there is one unique context for each concept. On the contrary, we argue for a different paradigm in which there may be many ontologies [DH92b], and emphasize the pragmatism of data. For example, the decision of uranium mining has been a heated argument between the Conservationist and the Materialist; each has its own context. Our approach is to support multiple viewpoints and makes use of the contract/negotiation mechanism to achieve an agreement for a particular purpose [DH92a]. This corresponds to an aggregation of two incompatible contexts (partitions) and the choice of a particular context may depend on the selection rule.

The statements of "Conservationist ⊃ uraniumMining.decision:against" and "Materialist ⊃ uraniumMining.decision:for" are the respective positions of the Conservationist and Materialist. These two contexts may be aggregated to form a new context, Machiavellianism, that has a selection rule based on the economy indicator.

∧(economy:bad,
  {Conservationist ⊃ uraniumMining.decision:against,
   Materialist ⊃uraniumMining.decision:for})
→ materialist ⊃ uraniumMining.decision:for

6. Summary

The proposed model distinguishes from previous approaches in the way that it unifies the detail data, metadata and contextual data, and we believe that the following goals have been achieved:

1. The model is natural as it does not distinguish the type of data as being detail, meta or contextual. Only the role of the data in a particular application being used by the user, is important. Also it supports all four major abstractions, subsumption, aggregation, association and membership by the same generic representation.
2. The same query feature is available to a user for both the detail and contextual data, including those peripheral information that may relate to the subject. The user may specify a certain context for his/her query and only the specified contextual data are returned.
3. It supports loosely specified query and provides a flexible query strategy that makes use of the subsumption relationship. When the query needs to change to a similar query, the user is prompted for the actual context being used.
4. The model can handle multiple viewpoints in the sense that incompatible contexts can be aggregated to form a composite context, a selection rule is used to dynamically determine which particular context should be used based on the current value of the control data when the rule is invoked.

This paper has discussed an effective and natural framework that can support equally the detail and contextual data needed by a user or a system to perform a task. We envisage its major application in multidatabase environment which require the context as well as the detail data for the cooperation between databases. Some further works in this area are:

- Incorporate Negotiation Mechanism into the Context Model, this is essential for an intelligent cooperated system of autonomous databases.
- Model the merging of different contexts, in particular, when there are conflicts in rules, domains and constraints. This involves various issues such as maintenance, authorization, and versioning.
- Model the integration between a database context (public) and the private context used by a particular user. This provides information customization in that the same set of data gets used in different ways depending on the individual's context..

Acknowledgements

The authors would like to thank YK Chan, Werasak Kurutach, Anne H.H. Ngu for their useful discussion and insightful comments.

7. References

[CH91] Christine Collet, M. Huhns, & W.Shen, *Resource Integration Using a Large Knowledge Base in Carnot,* (IEEE COMPUTER, Dec-91, p.55-62)

[CH89] Y.K.Chan & J.Hiller, *A domain based browsing system*, (The Australian Database Conference, Aug 1989)

[CO90] E.Codd, *The Relational Model for Database Management, Version 2,* (Addison-Wesley, 1990)

[DH92a] T.Duong, J.Hiller, & A.Ngu, *A Framework of Flexible and Dynamic Integration for Multidatabases,* (Proceedings of The International Conference on Intelligent & Cooperative Information Systems, May '93, p.43-54).

[DH92b] T.Duong, J.Hiller, *Modelling the Real World by Multi-World Data Model,* (Proceedings of The International Conference on Intelligent & Cooperative Information Systems, May '93, p.279-290).

[DK87] D.Dolk & R.Kirsch II, *A Relational Information Resource Dictionary System,* (Communications of the ACM, Vol 30, No.1, Jan-87, p.48-61)

[HB91] C.Hsu, M.Bouziane, & L.Rattner, *Information Resources Management in Heterogeneous, Dostributed Environments: A Metadatabase Approach,* (IEEE Transactions on Software Engineering, Vol. 17, No.6, Jun-91, p.604-625)

[HI88] J.Hiller, *Domains and Mappings in Relational Data Bases*, (ASWEC 88, Canberra, May 1988)

[KE91] W.Kent, *Solving Domain Mismatch and Schema Mismatch problems with an Object-Oriented Database Programming Language*, (Proc. of the 17th Intl Conf on Very Large Data Bases, Sep-91, p.147-160).

[MC82] J.McCarthy, *Metadata Management for Large Statistical Databases,* (Proc. of the 8th Intl Conf on Very Large Database Systems, 1982, p.470-479)

[MO86] A.Mottro, *Baroque : a browser for Relational Databases*, (ACM Trans on Office Information Systems, Vol. 4, Apr-86, p.164-181.

[SG89] A. Sheth & S. Gala, *Attribute relationships : an impediment in automating schema integration* ,(NSF Heterogeneous Workshop, Eds. C. Yu & P. Scheuermann, Evanston, Illinois, Dec -89, p.1-7).

[SM78] J.Smith & D.Smith, *Principles of Database Conceptual Design*, (Proc. of the NYU Symposium on Database design, 1978, p.35-49)

[SM91a] M. Siegel & S. Madnick, *Context Interchange: Sharing the Meaning of Data* (SIGMOD RECORD Vol.20, No.4, Dec-91, p.77-78).

[SM91b] M. Siegel & S. Madnick, *A Metadata Approach to Resolving Semantic Conflicts*, (Proc. of the 17th Intl Conf on Very Large Data Bases, Sep-91, p.133-144).

[WM90] Y.Richard Wang, & S.E.Madnick, *A Polygen Model for Heterogeneous Database Systems: The Source Tagging Perspective*, (Proc. of the 16th Intl Conf on Very Large Data Bases, Oct-90, p.519-538).

[YJ91] Clement Yu, Biao Jia, Wei Sun, & Son Dao, Determining Relationships among Names in Heterogeneous Databases, (SIGMOD RECORD Vol.20, No.4, Dec-91, p.79-80).

Information Brokers: Sharing Knowledge in a Heterogeneous Distributed System

Daniel Barbará[1] and Chris Clifton[2]

[1] Matsushita Information Technology Laboratory
2 Research Way
Princeton, N.J. 08540. USA
[2] Northwestern University
Department of EECS
2145 Sheridan Road
IL 60208-3118. USA

Abstract. A large percentage of valuable electronic information is not stored in conventional database systems. Very often, applications have to deal with heterogeneous services such as electronic libraries, airline reservation systems or weather information services. Many times, finding these services and information can be an overwhelming task. In this paper, we describe a tool to facilitate the finding of such information. The cornerstone of the service is the idea of a broker. A broker indexes services and objects by their describing properties. A query to a broker returns enough information to contact the service and get the object or information needed. The type and amount of information indexed by the broker depends on the information that is known and available about the service or object. We present a simple but powerful design for the broker that is flexible enough to accommodate a wide variety of information providers. We also present a complete architecture for our distributed information system.

1 Introduction

There has been a growing interest in recent years in developing techniques to provide interoperability for data stored in conventional database management systems. (For a good survey, see [7].) However, in practice a large percentage of valuable information is not stored in such systems, but as a wide variety of unstructured and semi-structured data such as electronic mail, documents, files and spreadsheets. In addition, applications must deal with heterogeneous *services* such as an electronic library, an airline reservation system or a weather information service. Many times, finding these services can be itself an overwhelming task.

Consider for example an application for organizing a convention. This application might involve finding out possible locations (hotels, convention halls), setting up arrangements with airline companies, catering services and so on. A first step could involve finding out information sources that contain addresses for the possible service providers. A source containing information about hotels, for instance may be managed by a relational database system. Then the application will issue an SQL query to retrieve the data. In other cases, this information can be found by some special server that understands a fixed set of commands.

It is clear that in this environment interoperation will surely involve human intervention. However, the system can provide a set of tools for interoperation including tools for resource discovery, data translation, activity management and automated processing. At the Matsushita Information Technology Laboratory (MITL) we are developing some of this interoperation tools. These tools operate in an environment with *objects* and *services*. Objects and services can be located anywhere on the network. The internals of an object or service can be arbitrary; however, objects and services have one or more *properties* that describe their contents and functionality. For instance an hotel information service may be described by keywords (hotel, accommodations), the type of interface required to access it (SQL), and its location (host and port). This paper focuses in describing one of such tools: the resource and information discovery system.

In the recent past, various research efforts (e.g. [11, 6]) have aimed to address the problem of distributing and retrieving information electronically. However, the common denominator in their work is the belief that every provider of information will abide by their protocols and architecture, thereby enforcing a standard in information sharing. We believe that it is very unlikely that this standardization will become a reality. There is simply too great a diversity of autonomous organizations involved in providing information to hope for any kind of universal agreement. Heterogeneity in accessing methods and architectures is a fact of life which any useful system will have to deal with.

In our mind, an architecture that addresses the problem of global, autonomous, shared information exchange, must follow three principles:

- No explicit cooperation from information providers is assumed. The system can adapt to a spectrum of conditions from no cooperation at all to a very tight coupling with information providers. In other words, we should be able to support information providers *without change*.
- The system must be scalable; i.e. the addition of a new information provider or a new user should not affect other components of the system or require major modifications of the software.
- It is better to accept incomplete or partial results in the information search than to require all of the information system components to maintain a perfect, consistent view.

In this paper we briefly describe such an architecture (currently under development at MITL, in the context of the Gold project) and we focus in one of its components: the information broker. A broker is an agent that takes queries from users and returns information provider locations.

The authors of [13] have correctly identified the problem of finding information in a global Internet as an important challenge for the database community. Since the standard services for locating resources (such as the X.500 directory standard [10]) are hierarchical, and hierarchical searches are quite cumbersome and inefficient, the need exists for non-procedural languages, such as relational languages to enter the picture by accessing the information directly. The key for efficient query processing in this vast environment is to cache data at various levels of the system. Brokers can be seen as a tool to cache metadata indices to the information. We identify a simple but powerful data model that proves to support a wide variety of models of information providers.

This paper is organized as follows. Section 2 reviews related work. Section 3 contains a brief description of the architecture. Section 4 describes the brokers and shows how the model used for them can support a variety of information providers. Section 5 offers conclusions and defines avenues for future research.

2 Related Work

Considerable work has been done in the area of heterogeneous databases ([12, 16]). Much of this work tries to create a single *multidatabase* out of a heterogeneous collection of databases. The problem with these methods is that considerable work must be done up-front to build a global schema, ([4, 17, 5]), and this global schema must be updated every time a new information provider (database) is added. This does not scale well to the number and diversity of information providers we envision.

Profile [14] is an attribute-based naming service for large networks. It allows users to retrieve information about resources associated with the attributes. A name server keeps links to a collections of resources administered by a user or an organization. Name servers are viewed as forming a loosely coupled federation. In this sense, the architecture of Profile resembles our own architecture. However, there are two main differences. First, all involved servers follow the same set of protocols. Second, attributes are of the form *tag* = *value* (for instance, *name* = *Peter*). As we describe later, brokers provide a more flexible definition for attributes.

The systems that come the closest to our goals are WAIS [11] and Distributed Indexing [6]. WAIS is also designed as a global-scale service. A directory of databases is used to find the appropriate database, this is similar to our broker. WAIS, however, relies on a fixed protocol (based on ANSI Z39.50) to connect servers and consumers. This has many disadvantages, not the least of which is that "The success of this system lies in a "critical mass" of users and servers. This protocol, then, could be used on any electronic network from digital networks to phone lines." ([11]). Distributed Indexing talks less about the database/application interface, however the index brokers are much more closely tied to the databases (and are not allowed to be out of date.) This approach violates our goal of supporting existing servers without change. The information providers are assumed to run a *site broker* responsible for remembering the queries that the brokers used to build their indexes. When an update occurs, the site broker applies the stored queries against the updates and forwards the appropriate changes to the index brokers. This schema obviously does not scale well.

R. Golding in [9] describes an architecture to provide good scalability and availability of an information service. The paper emphasizes the issue of how to maintain information servers implemented by distributed databases using weak-consistency protocols. It briefly addresses the issue of discovering information in the Internet, by suggesting that a database location server can be built using their protocols. Again, this solution requires collaboration among the sites that support this database location server. Although this solution can be easily weaved into our own architecture, we do not require this to be the case.

Finally, the architecture described in [15] is the closest to our own. Our brokers corresponds to the agents in that architecture. That paper, however, focuses more in the problem of how to disseminate information in the system. Our paper, in contrast, focuses on the support that the brokers have to give and the ways they can be used to obtain information.

3 Architecture

The Gold distributed information system consists of four types of processes: information providers, information users, information brokers, and translators. Providers and users are the core of the system, brokers and translators are the glue that ties the (autonomous, heterogeneous) users and providers. However, we wish to place as few a-priori constraints on providers and users as possible, so as not to limit the capability of future providers and users that may wish to join the system. As a result information brokers act as a "lowest common denominator" that can communicate with all users and providers. Brokers act as an *index* that allows users to specify simple queries and responds with the provider (and often the specific object on that provider) that contains the requested information. The user then goes directly to the provider (possibly using the services of a translator) to obtain the information. A sample network is shown in Figure 1.

This paper describes the model that brokers support and its usage. We also describe the minimum requirements of users and providers; although this is a small part of this paper.

3.1 Information Providers

Information providers are a widely varied set of databases. (Note that database is used in a loose sense; we expect providers to be based on DBMS's, file systems, on-line information systems, and perhaps platforms of which we have not yet conceived.)

The level of indexing support needed by the provider varies with the provider type. A DBMS may provide an address, interface (such as SQL), and schema synopsis. The user then issues a query to the DBMS to get the specific information desired. A file system accessed via FTP (File Transfer Protocol), on the other hand, may wish to index each file individually so that the broker provides

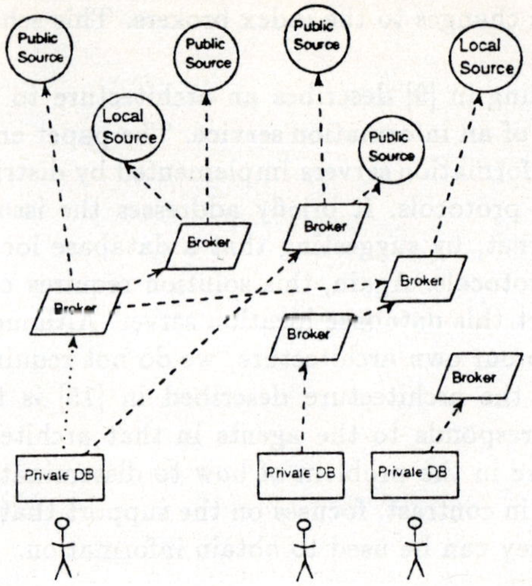

Fig. 1. The Gold environment.

the complete path name (as the provider has no efficient mechanism to allow the user to determine which file contains the desired information.)

Providers may support a variety of interfaces. For example, a relational database may support a variety of query languages. In addition, certain "canned queries" may be made available through the broker, for users who do not understand the query language. These might return a complete table rather than just the tuples desired, but at least the user is able to access the information.

We will give examples of a few types information providers when we discuss brokers and indexing.

3.2 Users

When we refer to information users, we are bundling the applications program (for example, a workstation-based multimedia interface) along with the end user of the information. We assume that users are running applications which generate broker queries. An example of such applications is the Gold software which includes a mailer that allows the user to store and retrieve messages in a private database (see [2]) The software indexes every message by its contents and provides a simple query language to look for stored messages. The same index will be used to keep information about brokers, translators and information providers. The same query language will be used to pose queries to all brokers in the information exchange network. (The details of the query language are beyond the scope of this paper.)

3.3 Translators

Translators are simply services that help users and providers of information to communicate. Since we do not impose constraints on the interfaces used by providers and users, we expect incompatibilities. Translator services can allow incompatible users and providers to communicate without requiring changes to the user or provider interfaces.

In the next section, we describe the issues involved in the design of the brokers.

4 Brokers

An information broker exists to connect users and providers of information. The broker is in essence an index that takes queries from users and returns provider locations. Brokers specialize in certain types of information. Users can index a broker (its address) in their personal databases according to the topics that the broker offers. The broker makes no guarantees about the information provider. It simply tries to be as up-to-date as possible in the contents and location of the provider. The amount and quality of the information kept by the broker depends on the degree of collaboration that the provider is willing to offer. At the lowest end, the broker is responsible for updating its own information. We make no assumptions about the degree of collaboration obtained from information providers.

Brokers are, in principle, autonomous entities. They might belong to a user, an organization, or form part of a service that spans several organizations in the Internet. In that sense, two brokers that specialize in the same topics but belong to two different organizations can be totally independent of each other. They might not follow any kind of consistency protocol (not even eventual consistency); the responsibility of keeping them consistent falling to two independent entities. On the other hand, these two brokers might be part of a service that spans several organizations and implements some consistency protocol (For instance, the weak-consistency protocols presented in [9])

Each information broker consists of two parts: An index engine, and an update handler. These run as separate processes. We will start by discussing the query and indexing protocol, which are handled by the index engine. We will then discuss registering information providers and maintaining the index, tasks that are performed by the update handler.

The information broker provides two things to the user process: A provider address, and an object describing the information. By convention this object consists of two parts: An interface, and interface-specific information to point to the registered information. For example, a file system on machine "Hamaguri" might register this paper as follows:

Keywords: Distributed Information Finding
Address: Hamaguri
Interface: NFS (Network File System)
File Name: /pub/goldpaper

Note that the broker only needs to understand the address (for reasons described later) and the keywords used to index this object. It is up to the user process to understand the rest of the object (and to decide if it can access this file using NFS, or if it must search for a translator.)

We have tried to make the broker extremely simple. One reason for this is efficiency: We want brokers to easily handle requests from many users. A more important reason is that a simple broker is easier to interact with. This results from our goal of supporting as wide a variety of users and providers as possible, while requiring a minimum of changes to the users and providers.

The index engine stores information about objects and services as a collection of words that describe their properties. One can think about the data stored in the index engine as a relation with the following schema:

property	distance	identifier	tag

It is worth pointing out that the applications dealing with the engine do not use the names of the attributes mentioned above. They are presented here just to clarify the explanation. Although we use SQL in what follows to explain the concepts, the engine "understands" a simpler language that does not require the attribute names. Also, it is important to notice that these attributes do not have to be atomic. The index engine supports a nested relation, i.e., each of the attributes above can indeed be viewed as a relation. For instance, the identifier could be a relation with attributes Address, Interface, Port and an ID that serves as the identifier for the information provider. (In [18] the authors prove that nested relations can be very efficient in supporting storage and retrieval of complex objects such as documents.) As we will show in the examples of the next subsection, this gives considerable power to the engine, allowing it to represent a wide spectrum of providers.

4.1 Examples

A relational database A very different example of information we would like to index is a relational table. The following is the relation EMPLOYEE that we use for this discussion.

Ename	Extension	Salary	Department
Chris	120	42K	EECS
Daniel	106	57K	MITL
Chuck	111	70K	MITL

We must first note that there are two approaches we can take: Placing a description of the table in the index, or placing the data (or excerpts of the data) into the index. As an example of the former method, we might index EMPLOYEE as one set (distance 0) of boolean keys, and "Attribute Ename Extension Salary Department" as another set. Note that we could instead specify that the attributes were close to each other (distance greater than 0) rather than distance 0, however this would make little sense as there is no concept of order of the attributes in a relation - the distance between all attributes is the same. We could also attach a textual description of the relation, indexed with relative keys in the same way as the body of an email message.

The second alternative, indexing the data, is a simple extension to the above. We could, for example, decide to index the table on all **Enames** and **Department** We simply add (boolean) keys "Chris EECS," "MITL Daniel," and "Chuck MITL," to the index (with distance 0 between keys from the same tuple.) We use boolean keys because it makes no sense to give a relative distance between tuples, as tuple order is not important to a relation. It is worth noting that this method does not allow us to specifically request a table containing someone named **Chris** in department **EECS**; if a different table contained someone named **EECS** in department **Chris** it would be returned as well. Extending the broker to handle every case such as this results in a broker that is a superset of all the information providers. This violates our goal of providing a simple information finding mechanism that can support a variety of information providers, including those that we have not yet conceived of. We do not see this as significant; the job of the information broker is simply to find a reasonable set of possible providers of the desired information. Complex queries should be posed to the provider of the information.

The result of a request to the broker

find [Chris, EECS](0)

would be

Address:	DBServer
Interface:	SQL
Relation Name:	Employee
Relation Schema:	Ename: Char(20), Extension: Integer, Salary: Integer, Department: Char(4)

Some users may not know the SQL interface, to provide information from the SQL database to these users we can use the information broker to fake a simpler interface. For example, if we assume that the SQL interface responds to SQL queries received on port 1524, we can simulate an Email Server interface as follows:

Address:	DBServer
Interface:	Email Server
Port:	1524
Message_ID:	Select * From Employee

A user (or application) which understands the Email Server interface would simply request Message_ID "Select * From Employee" from the "Email Server" at address DBServer port 1524. The DBMS would see an SQL query, and return the appropriate table. This method requires no changes to either the DBMS or application: We are saving the information on how to access the DBMS (not just where it is) in the information broker. The provider could simply index both the SQL and Email interface descriptions (using the same keys); the user would receive both in response to the query, and could decide which interface (SQL or Email Server) it preferred.

A restaurant information provider The following example shows how the server information can be further categorized using the "tag" attribute. Assume a server that has information about restaurants. The broker that knows about this server has the information stored in the following way:

property	distance	identifier	tag
chinese	a	id1	Chicago
chinese	b	id2	New_York
thai	b	id3	New_York

The identifier id1 would be:

Address: Restaurant_Server
Interface: Email Server
Port: 1535
Message_ID: Select * From Chicago_Restaurants where type = "chinese"

similarly, id2 would be:

Address: Restaurant_Server
Interface: Email Server
Port: 1535
Message_ID: Select * From New_York_Restaurants where type = "chinese"

and id3:

Address: Restaurant_Server
Interface: Email Server
Port: 1535
Message_ID: Select * From New_York_Restaurants where type = "thai"

A query regarding chinese and thai restaurants in New York would be:
find (New_York : chinese) or (New_York : thai) [3]

Finding code via FTP Another example would be indexing program source code available via FTP. Here distance could be very useful, for example to find a program containing a routine multiply that operates on a matrix multiplicand. We could specify that we want programs where multiplicand and matrix are close, as well as multiply and multiplicand. This would find the desired program in cases where multiplicand was a local variable (and thus matrix and multiply were close) as well as those where multiplicand is a global (and thus close to both its definition and the routine that uses it, even though the definition and routine are not close.)

The "index card" returned for a program would be simple:

Address: progserv.COM
Interface: ftp
Port: 21
Path: /pub/programs/MatrixMultiply.c

[3] The syntax (x:y) means tuples with tag x and property y

Probabilistic searches In [3], a data model that includes probabilities associated with the values of relational attributes is described, along with the set of relational operators for the model. In it, each attribute A (with the exception of the key), is a probabilistic function that assigns a value in the interval $[0, 1]$ to elements of the domain of A. Implementing this probabilistic model requires the support for nested relations, since each attribute can be best viewed as a relation with attributes that include probabilities and descriptions. Thus, the index engine can support this model, while benefiting from its richness. The following is an example.

property	distance	identifier	tag
science_fiction	-	0.6 [DB1] 0.25 [DB2] 0.15 [DB3]	Bob
law	-	0.9 [DB1] 0.1 [DB4]	Jane

In the previous example, the broker is pointing to three different providers that contain information about "science_fiction": DB1, DB2 and DB3 (this in turn are records that indicate address, access method and so on), while to find information about "law," the user must access either DB1 or DB4. The broker has probabilities associated with each provider. This distribution has some semantics associated with it: in the example it indicates, the preference that "Bob" gives to each of these providers when looking for information about "science_fiction" (Notice that another entry for the property "science_fiction" can exist, being tagged by a name other than "Bob"; this entry would indicate preferences by other user.) By using this construction, the broker can implement the notion of *collaborative filtering*, i.e., people helping one another in filtering information by means of annotating their reactions to the sources they have used. (The idea of collaborative filtering has been implemented by other means in Xerox's Tapestry [8], a repository of documents.)

Different semantics are possible for this probability functions. For instance, the probabilities may express the "expertise" of the provider about the topic and they might be inferred from data given by the providers themselves. The probabilistic model enriches the usage of the broker even further, by allowing a variety of semantics to be associated with the index information.

4.2 Distance Attribute

For each pair of properties a and b associated with a provider there can be three types of relationships between them. Namely, the distance between a and b can be positive, zero or undefined. Using this distances, a set of properties K can be organized in many ways, grouping the properties in classes that reflect the relationship among the properties included in each class.

4.3 Finding Brokers

Because brokers specialize in certain types of information, the user must first find the right broker to find the desired information providers. This is easily handled: Brokers simply register themselves with other brokers as providers of their specialty.

This does not solve the problem of finding an initial broker. This is similar to the problem of finding a name server in a network. Although we could "hard code" a broker location into user processes (or ask the human end user), we plan to use a local-area broadcast when no broker is known. Local area nets that do not contain an information broker can contain a stub broker that will respond to this message with the location of a remote broker.

4.4 Updating Information

Owing to the wide variety of information providers, we support a variety of techniques for keeping information in a broker up to date. These methods do not guarantee that the broker reflects the current state of the information provider. Delays in notifying the broker of the deletion of an indexed object result in some inefficiency as users request unavailable items. This inefficiency can be traded off with the expense of keeping the broker updated. More serious is the problem of not finding information of interest; the tradeoff here is between the expense of updating the broker and the cost of not finding information.

5 Conclusions

In this paper we have presented an architecture for distributing and finding information in a distributed heterogeneous system. We believe that our approach has the merits of accommodating a vast variety of information providers without asking them to abide to any specific protocols. We can take advantage of any degree of collaboration that these sources can offer, but we are also able to function without requesting any extra work from the providers.

We have shown that our design of the brokers allows us to accommodate a wide spectrum of information sources, while keeping the model simple enough for the user.

Work is already proceeding on various parts of this project. A prototype index engine has been completed and will be used as the basis for the information brokers. We will add to the Gold Mailer interface the functions required to handle distributed information finding. We have started designing a broker update process to interface with the index engine for automatic update support.

We plan to implement the capabilities of *continuous queries* as described in [1] to monitor for sources of information. (A continuous query acts as if it were executed in a system at every instant of time). Using continuous queries, we will be able to let the user formulate queries such as: "find information sources that contain topics covered by DB1," where DB1 is a provider known to the user.

Another idea is to do mining of information in the metadata supported by the brokers. We plan to come up with techniques that will identify interesting patterns of information and thus help the user to be aware of potential sources of interest.

References

1. D. Barbará and R. Alonso. Answering Continuous Queries in General Environments. Technical report, MITL, January 1993.
2. D. Barbará, C. Clifton, F. Douglis, H. Garcia-Molina, S. Johnson, B. Kao, S. Mehrotra, J. Tellefsen, and R. Walsh. The Gold Mailer. In *Proceedings of the Ninth International Conference on Data Engineering, Vienna, Austria*, April 1993.
3. D. Barbará, H. Garcia-Molina, and D. Porter. The Management of Probabilistic Data. *IEEE Transactions on Knowledge and Data Engineering*, 4(5):487–502, October 1992.
4. C. Batini, M. Lenzerini, and S.B. Navathe. A Comparative Analysis of Methodologies for Database Schema Integration. *ACM Computing Surveys*, 18(4):323–364, December 1986.
5. B. Czejdo, M. Rusinkiewicz, and D. Embley. An Approach to Schema Integration and Query Formulation in Federated Database Systems. In *Proceedings of the Third International Conference on Data Engineering, Los Angeles*, February 1987.
6. P.B. Danzig, J. Ahn, , and K. Obraczka. Distributed indexing: A scalable mechanism for distributed information retrieval. In *Proceedings of the Fourteenth Annual International ACM/SIGIR Conference on Research and Development in Information Retrieval, Chicago, Illinois*, October 1991.
7. A. Elmagarmid and C. Pu. Special issue on heterogeneous databases. *ACM Computing Surveys*, 22(3), September 1990.
8. D. Goldberg, D. Nichols, B.M. Oki, and D. Terry. Using the Collaborative Filtering to Weave an Information Tapestry. *Communications of the ACM*, 35(12):61–70, December 1992.
9. R.A. Golding. A weak-consistency architecture for distributed information services. Technical Report UCSC-CRL-92-31, University of California, Santa Cruz, June 1992.
10. International Telegraph and Telephone Consultative Committee (CCITT). *The Directory*, 1988. Recommendations X.500, X.501, X.509, X.511, X.518-X.521.
11. B. Kahle. Wide area information server concepts. Technical Report Anonymous FTP from think.com:/public/wais/wais-8-aXX.tar.Z, 1989.
12. W. Litwin, L. Mark, and N. Roussopoulos. Interoperability of Multiple Autonomous Databases. *ACM Computing Surveys*, 22(3):267–293, September 1990.
13. J. J. Ordille and B.P. Miller. Database Challenges in Global Information Systems. In *Proceedings of ACM-SIGMOD 1993 International Conference on Management of Data, Washington, D.C.*, June 1993.
14. L.J. Peterson. The Profile Naming Service. *ACM Transactions on Computer Systems*, 6(4):341–364, November 1988.
15. M. F. Schwartz. The Networked Resource Discovery Project. In *Proceedings of the IFIP XI World Congress, San Francisco*, pages 827–832, August 1989.
16. A. P. Sheth and J.A. Larson. Federated Database Systems for Managing Distributed Heterogeneous and Autonomous Databases. *ACM Computing Surveys*, 22(3):183,236, 1990.
17. S.P. Sheth, J.A. Larson, A. Cornelio, and S.B. Navathe. A Tool for Integrating Conceptual Schemas and User Views. In *Proceedings of the Fourth International Conference on Data Engineering, Los Angeles, California*, February 1988.
18. J. Zobel, J.A. Thom, and R. Sacks-Davis. Efficiency of Nested Relational Document Database Systems. In *Proceedings of the Seventeenth International Conference on Very Large Databases, Barcelona*, September 1991.

A Customized Multidatabase Transaction Management Strategy

Jiansan Chen, Omran A. Bukhres, and Jamshid Sharif-Askary

[1] Department of Computer Sciences, Purdue University, West Lafayette, IN 47907, USA, {jchen, bukhres}@cs.purdue.edu

[2] Harris Corporation, P.O. Box 430, Melbourne, FL 32902, USA

Abstract. Many algorithms have been proposed for multidatabase transaction management. However, very few provide mechanisms for multidatabase administrators and application programmers to customize their own transaction management strategies to suit the conditions found in different application environments. This paper describes a customized multidatabase transaction management strategy implemented in the InterBase System [8]. The strategy is based on a fully decentralized multidatabase architecture. It consists of a semantic-based commit method and a customized concurrency control algorithm that allow multidatabase administrators to change global concurrency control approaches and application programmers to individually customize their commit decisions, as guided by the semantics of global transactions and the transaction management strategies of underlying systems.

1 Introduction

A multidatabase system (MDBS) is a federation of pre-existing, autonomous, and usually heterogeneous database systems (called local database systems, or LDBSs) supporting global applications (or transactions) accessing data at more than one LDBS. Such a federation should allow pre-existing applications on individual LDBSs to be executed without modification. This federation is thus significantly different from traditional homogeneous distributed systems. An MDBS therefore supports the following two types of transaction:

- **Global transactions**: transactions under the control of the MDBS, which may access more than one LDBS (or site); and
- **Local transactions**: transactions under the control of individual LDBSs, which access only a single site. These are either generated by a single site or subtransactions of global transactions. The MDBS is only aware of those local transactions that arise from global subtransactions.

A global transaction manager (GTM) enables an MDBS to coordinate the execution of global transactions. Ideally, the GTM should enforce the ACID (Atomicity, Consistency, Isolation, and Duration) properties on global transactions. This objective has been the subject of extensive investigation in the years following the initial representation of the requirements of MDBS transaction management problem in [14]. Examples of proposed algorithms growing out of these research efforts include [1, 6, 24, 19, 7, 11, 13, 22]. However, all algorithms developed to date arise from specific application environments. For example, the compensation approach proposed in [19] is valid only when all global transactions are compensatable and local transactions have no influence on global subtransactions. This is because the operations of an MDBS are constrained by its component pre-existing LDBSs, and the ACIDity of global transactions is thus hampered by the *autonomy* of the LDBSs [2]. While LDBSs incorporate their own concurrency controllers to ensure that local transactions are run in a serializable fashion, improper synchronization may arise at the global level, as illustrated in [12]. An LDBS may also unilaterally commit or abort a global subtransaction executed as a local transaction without consulting the GTM, making the possibility of leaving a global transaction in an unacceptable state. This may occur because each LDBS in an MDBS sees itself as isolated, unaware of the existence of other LDBSs and the MDBS. It has been shown that the atomicity of global transactions is incompatible with the full retention of the autonomy of LDBSs [23]. The enforcement of the ACIDity of global transactions may be further complicated by the incorporation into an MDBS of information systems such as CAD and CAM databases that may not support ACID transactions.

The standardization of MDBS transaction management is so far proven to be beyond reach. Given the variability of application environments, it may instead be the advantages to selectively utilize the semantics of global transactions and transaction management strategies of the LDBSs themselves. Such an approach has the potential to reduce the complexity and improve the performance of global transaction management, while still supporting the correct synchronization and commitment of global transactions in their corresponding application environments. For example, the best global transaction management strategy in a situation where all global transactions are retrieve-only is to *do nothing*. On the other hand, if strict two-phase locking is employed as the local concurrency control strategy by a group of LDBSs, global serializability can be maintained by executing global transactions on the corresponding LDBSs in the same relative execution order. In an application in which all global transactions are reversible in any circumstance, compensation can be used as the global com mit strategy. We therefore see that the application environments in which an MDBS operates may impose very different requirements on transaction management strategies. These requirements may range from very loose control, where no correctness criterion must be maintained, to a very tight enforcement of the ACIDity of global transactions. It is neither possible nor necessary to require that the ACIDity of global transactions be uniformly enforced in all circumstances. Transaction management approaches must be tailored to their application environments, exploiting the transaction management strategies of the underlying systems and the semantics of global transactions to reduce the complexity and improve performance of MDBS transaction mangement. MDBS administrators and application programmers should have at their disposal flexible transaction management strategies for customized control of the synchronization and commitment of global subtransactions. This approach should optimally be based on a decentralized MDBS architecture rather than on the less reliable centralized one. Unfortunately, little work has been done on this issue.

This paper presents such a customized transaction management strategy, as implemented in the InterBase System at Purdue University. Section 2 discusses the decentralized MDBS architecture used as the basis for this strategy. A customized distributed concurrency control algorithm is presented in Section 3, while the semantic-based commit method is set forth in Section 4. A conclusion and directions for future research appear in Section 5.

2 The Decentralized MDBS Architecture

Many proposed MDBS transaction management strategies are based on centralized MDBS architectures [24, 7, 11, 22]. While such an architecture is easy to design and implement, it is vulnerable to the failure of the central node, which could incapacitate the entire system. A distributed system such as the MDBS architecture used in this paper, shown in Figure 1, is not vulnerable to such failures. The MDBS consists of a Global Transaction Manager (GTM) and a set of interfaces. The GTM is responsible for controlling the execution of all MDBS transactions. For each MDBS transaction T_i, a GTM process GTM_i, which is responsible for the consistent and reliable execution of T_i, is invoked from the machine where T_i is issued. GTM_i is therefore coincident with the life cycle of T_i.

Each MDBS transaction consists of a set of subtransactions, each of which consists of operations on or a service request to an LDBS. The scheduling order[3] of these subtransactions within the MDBS transaction is determined before the execution of the transactions. Before a transaction is executed, it requests all corresponding MDBS interfaces to arrange the scheduling order of its subtransactions on the corresponding LDBSs so as to prevent any MDBS inconsistencies its execution may cause. When executing a global transaction, a GTM process only interact with relevant MDBS interfaces, without the need to communicate with other GTM processes. Each GTM process can thus run independently and the GTM is made a distributed entity.

An MDBS interface I_j is superimposed on an LDBS L_j, which is integrated into the MDBS. This interface receives execution requests for subtransactions of MDBS transactions to be executed at L_j, determines their scheduling order, creates *MDBS interface processes* to execute them in the pre-determined scheduling order, and recovers them from errors. MDBS interfaces must be in continuous

[3] The scheduling order of subtransactions at a site determines the order of these subtransactions scheduled for execution.

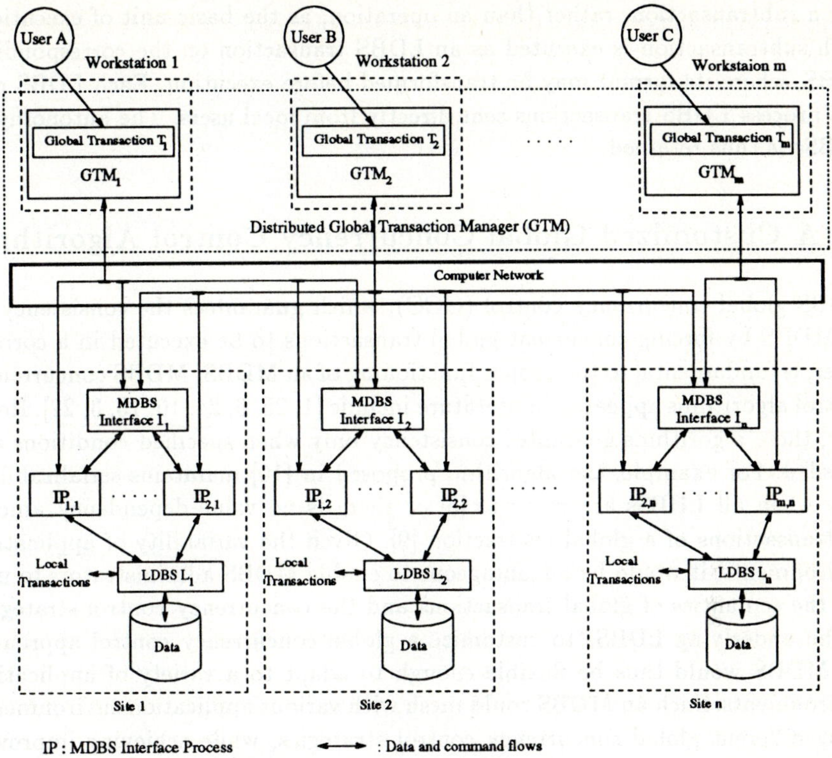

Fig. 1. The MDBS architecture

operation. Since an MDBS interface interacts only with those global transactions that have a subtransaction at its associated site, it can run independently from other MDBS interfaces. That is, all MDBS interfaces and GTM processes are independent MDBS components, a fully distributed MDBS system is therefore established.

Let us envision an example how a global transaction is executed. Global transaction T_1, executed by the GTM process GTM_1, communicates with MDBS interfaces I_1 and I_2 and MDBS interface processes $IP_{1,1}$, and $IP_{1,2}$. Interfaces I_1 and I_2 determine the scheduling order of and schedule the execution of T_1 on Sites 1 and 2. $IP_{1,1}$ and $IP_{1,2}$ are created by I_1 and I_2 to execute T_1 on Sites 1 and 2, respectively, and communicate directly with T_1 for their execution. The execution of T_1 therefore depends upon the coordination of GTM_1, I_1, I_2, $IP_{1,1}$, $IP_{1,2}$, as well as LDBSs L_1 and L_2; this coordination is performed via computer network.

Unlike many other systems [24, 7, 13, 22, 3], the approach proposed here makes no assumption regarding LDBSs. The interfaces provided by LDBSs may be services, query languages, or transaction languages. The MDBS thus schedules a subtransaction, rather than an operation, as the basic unit of execution. Each subtransaction is executed as an LDBS transaction on the corresponding LDBS, where its format may be transformed before execution. Each LDBS can also process LDBS transactions sent directly from local users. The autonomy of LDBSs is thus retained.

3 A Customized Global Concurrency Control Algorithm

MDBS global concurrency control (GCC), which guarantees the consistency of an MDBS by forcing concurrent global transactions to be executed in a correct order, is fundamental to the proper functioning of an MDBS. MDBS concurrency control algorithms appeared in literature include [1, 25, 6, 24, 10, 13, 3, 22]. However, these algorithms guarantee consistency only when specified conditions are satisfied. For example, the algorithm proposed in [10] maintains serializability only when all LDBSs are *rigorous* [5] or there is no value dependency among subtransactions of a global transaction [9]. Given the variability of application environments, it would be advantageous to enable MDBS administrators to utilize the semantics of global transactions and the concurrency control strategies of the underlying LDBSs to customize a global concurrency control approach. An MDBS would thus be flexible enough to adapt to a variety of application environments. Such an MDBS could mesh with various application environments using different global concurrency control strategies, while achieving improved performance.

The customized concurrency control algorithm presented here is a variation of that presented in [8]. It requires that all MDBS interfaces be numbered from I_1 to I_n in some specified order. When a global transaction T_i interacts with the relevant MDBS interfaces to determine the scheduling order of its subtransactions, it must *lock* the MDBS interfaces in an ascending order corresponding to their numbers. This approach is thus similar to the linear ordering of resources locks. After T_i *unlocks* a relevant MDBS interface, it cannot *lock* any further MDBS interfaces. T_i must *unlock* all relevant MDBS interfaces after the scheduling order of its subtransactions is determined. On the other hand, an MDBS interface can determine the scheduling order of a corresponding subtransaction of T_i only when T_i *locks* the MDBS interface. In this way, this algorithm is similar to two-phase locking. If an optimistic concurrency control algorithm is used, a NOLOCK message is returned by the corresponding MDBS interface as the reply for the first *lock* call. Upon receiving such a message, T_i stops the locking process and executes its subtransactions immediately.

By combining *two-phase locking* [15] and the *linear ordering of resources locks* [17], this algorithm permits deadlock-free, totally distributed, and correct synchronization of concurrent scheduling order requests from global transactions. The execution of a global transaction is thus performed in at least two separate phases. In the first phase, the relative scheduling order of a global transaction with respect to other global transactions at each participating site is determined. In the second phase, the global transaction is executed in the relative scheduling order determined in the first phase.

The relative serialization order (RSO) of a global transaction on different LDBSs can be customized according to the semantics of global transactions and the particular transaction management strategies used by the underlying LDBSs. For example:

1. if global transactions are all read-only applications or MDBS consistency is not required, the RSO can be interpreted as *No Order*;
2. if the underlying LDBS supports two-phase commitment, the RSO can be determined by the order of the prepare-to-commit states of subtransactions on the LDBS;
3. if *local conflicts* can be forced on the underlying LDBS [13], the RSO coincides with the order of obtaining the *ticket* [13] at the LDBS; the ticket method introduces a data item called *ticket* at a local site and requires each global subtransaction to access the ticket at the local site; direct conflicts are thus created among all global subtransactions executed at the same site;
4. if there is no value dependency among subtransactions of a global transaction, the RSO can be determined by the commit order of subtransactions on the corresponding LDBSs;
5. if the underlying LDBS is rigorous, the RSO can be determined by the commit order of subtransactions on the LDBS; and
6. if the underlying LDBS supports both two-phase locking and two-phase commit, and Timestamp or Commit Order is used as the GCC strategy, the RSO can be determined by the prepare-to-commit order.

Therefore, this algorithm guarantees that the RSO of global transactions on different sites is consistent with their pre-determined relative scheduling order, ensuring that global transactions have the same RSO at all sites. The semantics of the RSO on MDBS interfaces can be changed dynamically by MDBS administrators through a well defined RPC primitive gcc. As demonstrated in [6], when global transactions have the same RSO at all sites, global serializability is preserved in the presence of local transactions. This algorithm therefore guarantees MDBS consistency if a uniformed RSO can be determined on all LDBSs.

Let us envision an MDBS consisting of three LDBSs L_1, L_2, and L_3. Assume that L_1 supports two-phase commitment, L_2 is rigorous, and L_3 is a relational database that allows users to create relations and access data. To maintain global serializability, MDBS interface I_1 associated with L_1 uses the order of prepare-to-commit states of subtransactions on L_1 as the RSO of the subtransactions, MDBS interface I_2 associated with L_2 uses the commit order of subtransactions on L_2 as the RSO of the subtransactions, while MDBS interface I_3 associated with L_3 creates a relation with some data item as the ticket and uses the order of update operations on the ticket as the RSO of the subtransactions. Moreover, if all global transactions on this MDBS are read only, the MDBS administrator can change the GCC strategy to NOORDER. All three MDBS interfaces will then change their GCC strategies accordingly, allowing all subtransactions on LDBSs associated with these MDBS interfaces to be executed in any order and thus improving performance. The customization of the GCC strategy of an MDBS is thus determined by both the semantics of global transactions and the transaction management algorithms used by the LDBSs.

The advantages of this algorithm is that concurrency control decisions concerning a global transaction T_i is made independently either within GTM_i that executes T_i or within individual MDBS interfaces that execute subtransactions of T_i, based on locally available or customized information. This algorithm is therefore fully decentralized, the GTM can then be distributed among machines where global transactions are issued. This approach is therefore both flexible and reliable, in contrast to algorithms proposed in [1, 25, 6, 10, 22],

4 The Semantic-based Commit Method

The control of atomicity in MDBSs is of critical importance to the preservation of transaction atomicity and MDBS consistency in presence of global transaction aborts and failures. Since the recovery procedures of each LDBS ensure the atomicity and durability of local transactions and global subtransactions, MDBS commitment needs only be concerned with ensuring that each global transaction either commits or aborts at all sites. This task, however, has proved to be extremely difficult, because each LDBS can unilaterally commit/abort a global subtransaction, making the possibility of leaving a global transaction in neither a commit nor an abort situation. The obstacle can be alleviated by redoing or retrying [4, 18] unilaterally aborted subtransactions or by semantically undoing (compensating) unilaterally committed subtransactions. It is also possible to utilize the semantics of global subtransactions to user-customize the commitment of global transactions and improve their performance. Consider a global transaction consisting of two subtransactions, one retrieve-only and the other involving some updating in an environment in which all LDBSs support two-phase commitment. If we ignore the semantics of the global transactions, two-phase commitment will be applied to both subtransactions. Although this approach guarantees correct execution, its performance is not optimal, because other local transactions or global subtransactions may be blocked by the data read by the retrieve-only subtransaction before the global transaction is committed. Incorporating the semantics of the individual global transactions yields enhanced performance. In this case, *do nothing* and two-phase commitment act as the commit protocols for the retrieve-only and updating subtransactions, respectively. This ensures other local transactions or global subtransactions will not be blocked by the data read by the retrieve-only subtransaction before the global transaction is committed.

To support user-customized commitment and to facilitate the incorporation of different commit protocols within an MDBS transaction, this method requires a subtransaction to be decomposed into an *execution step*, an optional *confirm step*, and an optional *undo step*. These steps are determined from the semantics, rather than from the syntax, of a subtransaction. It is therefore the application programmer's responsibility to define the execution step, confirm step, and undo step for a subtransaction. The following provides guidelines for the definition of these steps in different instances.

For a *compensatable* subtransaction S_i [15], the execution step includes all the operations of S_i, and the undo step contains the compensating operations for S_i. No confirm step needs to be defined for S_i.

For a read-only subtransaction (S_i), or if the data modified by S_i need not be consistent, or if the consistency of the MDBS can be maintained by the semantics of the global transactions, then only the execution step for S_i must be defined. Clearly, in this case, the execution step includes all the operations of S_i.

The situation is more complex for a noncompensatable subtransaction S_j of a global transaction T_i. Depending upon the nature of S_j, two options are available, generating different versions of the execution, confirm, and undo steps:

- If S_j must be run independently from T_i, i.e., S_j is beyond the control of T_i, the execution step includes all the operations of S_j from the beginning to the prepare-to-commit state of S_j, the confirm step those from that state to the commitment of S_j, and the undo step those from that state to the abortion of S_j. The execution step completes first. During the commitment of T_i, if S_j must be committed, the confirm step is issued to bring S_j to completion; otherwise, the undo step is issued to undo the execution of S_j. In this way, S_j is executed as two separate local transactions. One typical application of this commit method can be found in airline ticket reservation systems, where users can reserve a ticket and then purchase or cancel the reservation.
- If T_i and S_j are capable of intercommunication, allowing T_i to control the execution of S_j, then the execution step is defined as S_j itself. At the prepare-to-commit state of S_j, after making a report to T_i regarding its success, S_j awaits a signal from T_i. Again, during the commitment of T_i, if S_j must be committed, the confirm step is issued to trigger S_j to commit; otherwise, the undo step is issued to trigger S_j to abort. In this way, S_j is executed as a single local transaction. This sequence is very similar to the *two-phase commit protocol*.

A graphical illustration of this commit method is given in Figure 2. The critical state encompasses a variety of situations, including the final state of compensatable subtransactions or read-only subtransactions and the prepare-to-commit state of two-phase commit subtransactions.

One of the advantages of this commit method is that its semantic structure

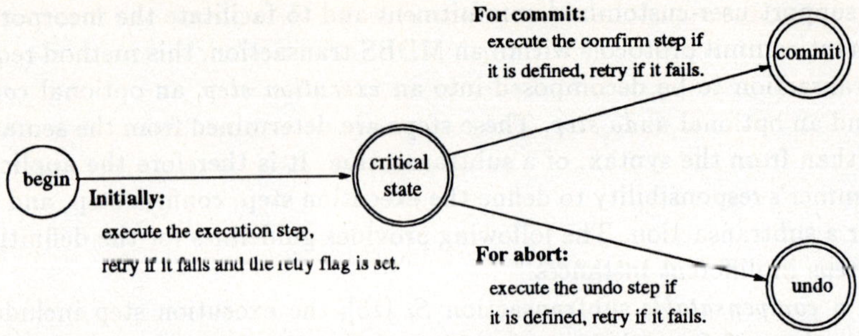

Fig. 2. The state machine of the semantic-based commit method for a subtransaction

allows application programmers to customize their own necessary commit decisions, as guided by the semantics of the global subtransactions and commit protocols of the underlying systems, using a uniform syntax for different commit protocols. This method is capable of determining from the definition of a subtransaction what kind of commit protocol should be used. The semantics-based commit method is therefore both flexible and simple and can be used in a variety of application environments.

As an example, let us consider a global transaction T_i which transfers money from Bank 1 to Bank 2. Assume that the LDBSs associated with the both banks support two-phase commitment. T_i can be decomposed into two subtransactions $T_{i,1}$ and $T_{i,2}$, where $T_{i,1}$ withdraws money from Bank 1 and $T_{i,2}$ deposits money into Bank 2. Regardless of the semantics of T_i, both $T_{i,1}$ and $T_{i,2}$ can use two-phase commitment as their commit protocol, an approach which guarantees the correctness of T_i but is inefficient. A better execution protocol for T_i would execute $T_{i,1}$ to its prepare-to-commit state, from which T_i would be aborted or $T_{i,2}$ executed; if $T_{i,2}$ is committed, $T_{i,1}$ and T_i would be committed; otherwise, $T_{i,1}$ and T_i would be aborted. This execution protocol eliminates an unnecessary costly exchanges of remote information required in a uniformly two-phase commit scenario. If Bank 2 is geographically well remoted from the originating machine of T_i, this savings could be significant. To implement this protocol, $T_{i,1}$ should consist of an execution step of withdrawal from Bank 1, a confirm step that triggers $T_{i,1}$ to commit, and an undo step that triggers $T_{i,1}$ to abort, while $T_{i,2}$ should consist only of an execution step of depositing money into Bank 2. A second advantage of this execution protocol is that the LDBS that executes $T_{i,2}$ does not need to support two-phase commitment and still guarantees the correct execution of T_i.

As a more complicated example, let us postulate that an airline ticket-purchasing global transaction T as follows:

1. obtain information from a customer;
2. make alternative possible reservation for the customer with different airlines;

3. allow the customer to select a preferred reservation;
4. purchase the reserved ticket selected by the customer, if payment can be made with the credit card provided by the customer;
5. cancel the reservations not purchased by the customer; and
6. generate a report.

Clearly, the first step of T can be defined as a read-only subtransaction; a ticket reservation, purchasing, and cancellation actions can be seen as the execution, confirm, and undo steps of a corresponding subtransaction; and the subtransactions involving credit-card payment and generating report require only an execution step.

This semantic-based commit method offers a practical solution, and details of its implementation are provided. A uniform syntax is used to specify subtransactions which would be applicable to both nested and multi-level transaction environments [16]. This method is therefore more flexible than those proposed in [19, 20, 21, 26], which are designed for multi-level transaction environments only[4].

5 Conclusion and Future Work

This paper presents a decentralized and customized solution to the problem of MDBS transaction management, as implemented in the InterBase System at Purdue University. The approach presented here is based on a fully decentralized multidatabase architecture. It includes a semantic-based commit method to allow users to customize their control of the correct update of global transactions. MDBS consistency is guaranteed by a customized global concurrency control algorithm which takes into consideration the semantics of global transactions, the variability of application environments, and the requirements imposed by MDBS administrators.

The solution presented here offers the flexibility of utilizing a variety of transaction management approaches in different application environments, taking advantage of the inherent features of the transaction management strategies used by underlying systems and the semantics of global transactions. The complexity of MDBS transaction mangement is thus reduced; and the performance is simultaneously improved.

There are many issues to be considered in the implementation of such a customized solution. These include the execution protocol for this approach and Remote Procedure Calls supporting this approach. These also include recovering MDBS from a component crash, reactivating a crashed component, efficient handling of requests from several global transactions at an MDBS interface simultaneously, and the creation of network connections among system components.

[4] The commit/abort status of a subtransaction in a nested transaction must comply with its governing transaction, while a subtransaction in a multi-level transaction has no such restriction.

For the sake of simplicity, these issues have not been addressed here. They must, however, be always kept in mind in developing an MDBS system and will be dicussed in upcoming articles.

Although the customized approach presented here is far from being perfected, it has the potential to offer an innovative and effective solution to the problems of MDBS transaction management. Its benefits have been demonstrated through a trial implementation of the InterBase System at Bell Northern Research Inc. A performance evaluation of this strategy is being investigated, and detailed performance results will be reported at a later time. Future research will further illustrate the benefits inherent in this customized MDBS transaction management strategy.

References

1. R. Alonso, H. Garcia-Molina, and K. Salem. Concurrency control and recovery for global procedures in federated database systems. In *IEEE Data Engineering Bulletin*, pages 5–11, September 1987.
2. N. S. Barghourti and G. E. Kaiser. Concurrency Control in Advanced Database Applications. *ACM Computing Surveys*, 1991.
3. R.K. Batra, M. Rusinkiewicz, and D. Georgakopoulos. A decentralized deadlock-free concurrency control method for multidatabase transactions. In *Proceedings of International Conference on Distributed Computing Systems*, June 1992.
4. Y. Breitbart, H. Garcia-Molina, and A. Silberschatz. Overview of multidatabase transaction management. *The VLDB Journal*, 1(2):181–239, October 1992.
5. Y. Breitbart, D. Georgakopolous, M. Rusinkiewicz, and A. Silberschatz. On Rigorous Transaction Scheduling. *IEEE Transactions on Software Engineering*, 17(9):954–960, 1991.
6. Y. Breitbart and A. Silberschatz. Multidatabase update issues. In *Proceedings of the ACM SIGMOD Conference on Management of Data*, pages 135–142, June 1988.
7. Y. Breitbart, A. Silberschatz, and G. Thompson. Reliable transaction management in a multidatabase system. In *Proceedings of the ACM SIGMOD Conference on Management of Data*, pages 215–224, May 1990.
8. O. A. Bukhres, J. Chen, W. Du, A. K. Elmagarmid, and R. Pezzoli. InterBase : An Execution Environment for Global Applications over Distributed, Heterogeneous, and Autonomous Software Systems. *IEEE Computer*, August 1993. (to appear).
9. W. Du and A. Elmagarmid. Quasi Serializability: a Correctness Criterion for Global Concurrency Control in InterBase. In *Proceedings of the 15th International Conference on Very Large Data Bases*, pages 347–355, Amsterdam, The Netherlands, August 1989.
10. W. Du, A. Elmagarmid, and W. Kim. Maintaining Quasi Serializability in Multidatabase Systems. In *Proceedings of the 7th Intl. Conf. on Data Engineering*, pages 360–367, Kobe, Japan, April 1991.
11. W. Du, A. Elmagarmid, and W. Kim. Maintaining transaction consistency in multidatabases using quasi serializable executions. In *Proceedings of COMPCON SPRING'91*, pages 152–155, San Francisco, California, 1991.

12. W. Du, A. Elmagarmid, Y. Leu, and S. Ostermann. Effects of autonomy on maintaining global serializability in heterogeneous distributed database systems. Technical Report CSD-TR-835, Department of Computer Science, Purdue University, December 1988.
13. D. Georgakopoulos, M. Rusinkiewicz, and A. Sheth. On serializability of multidatabase transactions through forced local conflicts. In *Proceedings of the 7th Intl. Conf. on Data Engineering*, pages 314–323, Kobe, Japan, April 1991.
14. V. Gligor and R. Popescu-Zeletin. Transaction management in distributed heterogeneous database management systems. *Information Systems*, 11(4):287–297, 1986.
15. J. N. Gray. Notes on Database Operating Systems. In *Operating Systems: An Advanced Course, Lecture Notes in Computer Science*, pages 624–633. Springer-Verlag, Berlin, 1978.
16. Jim Gray and Andreas Reuter. *Transaction Processing: Concepts and Techniques.* Morgan Kaufmann Publishers, Inc., 1992.
17. J.W. Havender. Avoiding Deadlock in Multitasking Systems. *IBM Systems Journal*, 7(2):74–84, 1968.
18. M. Hsu and A. Silberschatz. Unilateral commit: A new paradigm for reliable distributed transaction processing. In *Proceedings of the 7th Internatonal Conference on Data Engineering*, pages 296–304, Kobe, Japan, April 1991.
19. H. Korth, E. Levy, and A. Silberschatz. A Formal Approach to Recovery by Compensating Transactions. In *Proceedings of the 16th International Conference on Very Large Data Bases*, Brisbane, Australia, August 1990.
20. E. Levy, H. Korth, and A. Silberschatz. An optimistic commit protocol for distributed transaction management. In *Proceedings of the ACM SIGMOD International Conference on Management of Data*, Denver, Colorado, May 1991.
21. E. Levy, H. Korth, and A. Silberschatz. A theory of relaxed atomicity. In *Proceedings of the ACM SIGACT-SIGOPS Symposium on Principles of Distributed Computing*, August 1991.
22. S. Mehrotra, R. Rastogi, Y. Breitbart, H. F. Korth, and A. Silberschatz. The concurrency control problem in multidatabases: Characteristics and solutions. In *Proceedings of the ACM SIGMOD Conference on Management of Data*, pages 288–297, 1992.
23. James G. Mullen, Ahmed K. Elmagarmid, Won Kim, and Jamshid Sharif-Askary. On thc impossibility of atomic commitment in multidatabase systems. In *Proceedings of the International Conference on Systems Integration*, pages 625–634, Morristown, New Jersey, June 1992.
24. C. Pu. Superdatabases for composition of heterogeneous databases. In *Proceedings of the International Conference on Data Engineering*, pages 548–555, February 1988.
25. K. Vidyasankar. Non-two phase locking protocols for global concurrency control in distributed heterogeneous database systems. In *CIPS Edmonton*, 1987.
26. H. Wächter and A. Reuter. The ConTract Model. In Ahmed K. Elmagarmid, editor, *Database Transaction Models for Advanced Applications.* Morgan Kaufmann, 1992.

Interoperability between a Distributed System and a Database System

Adriana Danes, François Exertier, Samer Haj Houssain

Unité Mixte Bull–IMAG
2, rue Vignates
38610 Gières – FRANCE

Abstract. An approach to provide interoperability between an object–oriented distributed system (Guide) and an object–oriented database system (O2) is presented. Our major goal is to enrich Guide with database functionalities, like efficient and secure processing of high amount of data. Our approach is based on an export/import mechanism that allows a Guide application to ask for remote processing of data stored in the O2 system. A client–server architecture has been implemented for the interconnection and a first prototype allows to validate our approach and to make some performance evaluation.

1 Introduction

Interoperability is one of the key issues in information technology today. It is a technique for controlling, exchanging or sharing information between two or more systems. Some goals of the interoperability are:

- to provide access to information that is stored within different systems,
- to facilitate cooperation between programs that create or manipulate information (i.e. invoke each other to retrieve data or perform services).

Interoperability has been particulary studied in the area of database systems. Federated database systems [1, 2] and multidatabases [3] are examples of interoperability. Interoperability between object–oriented systems is addressed by the OMG (Object Management Group) work. The OMG has defined an architecture allowing several heterogeneous object–oriented systems to cooperate. This architecture is currently becoming an industrial standard, called CORBA for Common Object Request Broker Architecture [8]. It provides interoperability between applications on different machines by interconnecting multiple object systems through a remote object invocation mechanism.

The work presented in this paper concerns interoperability between Guide [5], an object–oriented distributed system, and O_2 [6] an object–oriented database system. The main goal of Guide – O_2 interoperability is to provide Guide users with database services in order to build new applications that use both distribution and database services. This interoperability saves us the work of integrating database functionalities within the Guide system. Moreover, interoperability has been achieved with as few modifications as possible to the Guide system and language.

The paper is organized as follows. Section 2 contains a brief description of the two systems and motivations for making them interoperate. In Section 3 the Guide_O2 object concept is introduced: it is the cornerstone of our interoperability paradigm and defines the way the two systems interoperate. Section 4 describes how the support for interoperability has been implemented and how it works. The final two sections present some experimental results and conclusions on the accomplished work, as well as possible future work.

2 General Description

2.1 Objectives

The Guide system provides an environment for the development of distributed applications on a local network [5]. Data handled by Guide applications are persistent and governed by an object–oriented model. Although Guide provides persistence, it is not a database system. For instance, it doesn't provide support for efficient manipulation of high amounts of data or transaction management.

Our aim is to make possible that Guide applications access and update large amount of persistent, reliable, secure and shared data via the interoperability with the O_2 system. Guide is thus enriched with database functionalities like collection manipulation and associative access facilities, without modification of Guide's model or system.

To satisfy this goal, an one–way interoperability from Guide to O_2 is sufficient. This means that the Guide system is able to access and manipulate data managed by the O_2 system, but the contrary is not possible.

2.2 The Guide System and Language

One important feature of the Guide project is a strong integration between the Guide language and the Guide system, through an object paradigm [4]. The idea is to embody the main abstractions provided by the system in language constructs: so, the language supports directly the object model on which the system is built. The main features of the language are separate definition of types and classes, strong typing, support for complex persistent objects, and location transparency.

Types and classes. A type is an interface description that specifies the behavior of all objects of a given type through operations (method signatures) that can be applied to these objects and their visible state variables (attributes). A class specifies a particular implementation of a type. It includes a description of the internal state of the object (the instance variables) and the code of the methods.

Subtyping, subclassing and inheritance. A subtyping relationship defines a hierarchy between types. This hierarchy is simple, i.e. a type has only one supertype. The subtyping hierarchy is paralleled by a subclassing hierarchy, which allows sharing implementations between objects that already share a common behavior.

Object storage. It is organised as a two–level storage. The Storage System is the lower level in charge of the long term storage of persistent objects. Upon this, the Virtual Object Memory (VOM) supports the execution of applications. Both storage levels are distributed. When a method is called on an object, this object is loaded in the VOM of the current node. If the object was already loaded in the VOM of a distant node, the application diffuses on that node.

2.3 The O2 System

O_2 is an object–oriented database management system with a complete development environment and a set of user interface tools [6]. The core of the system is O_2ENGINE – an object database engine. O_2ENGINE stores structured and multimedia objects, provides disk management, transaction management, concurrency, recovery, security and data administration. Two kinds of interface are supported by O_2ENGINE, a language interface (C and C++) and the O_2 environment which includes a query language (O_2Query), an object language (O_2C), a user interface generator, a graphic programming environment, and an interface (O_2API) allowing direct access to the O_2ENGINE primitives.

O_2 handles values and objects. Values are typed while objects belong to classes. A type defines a data structure and a class is defined by a type and its methods. Types are constructed recursively from atomic types and type constructors (*tuple*, *list* and [*unique*] *set*). Values cannot be shared but objects can.

Attributes and methods are private by default. They may be accessible outside the class if they are declared public, read or write.

O_2 provides particularly efficient collection manipulation facilities: sets' union, intersection or difference; filters and iterations on collections; set or list comparison, etc..

Values and objects are persistent only if they are attached to a persistent root (reachability model). This can be done explicitly by naming or implicitly through composition links.

2.4 Remarks on Similarities and Differences

Both systems are based on object–oriented models. Some of the differences between the two models are:

- The type and class concepts are different from Guide to O_2. An O_2 type defines a data structure while a Guide type defines an object interface. An O_2 class is comparable to a Guide type and a Guide class is a particular implementation of a Guide type.
- O_2 provides the set and list constructors at programming language level. Collection manipulation is efficiently implemented. To enhance associative access performance, the definition of indexes on collections is possible. In Guide, the definition of collections is entirely left to the user's charge.
- O_2 supports multiple inheritance while Guide does not.

Although Guide provides data persistency, it does not support transactions.

3 Principles and Design Choices

This section describes the principles of the Guide – O_2 interoperability. It presents issues and solutions for the design of Guide applications manipulating data stored and managed by the O_2 system.

The aim of the Guide – O_2 interoperability is to make possible that Guide applications create, access and invoke methods (operations) on some objects stored in the O_2 system. We call them *Guide_O_2* objects. These objects have the following characteristics:

- they are implemented in the O_2 system, so they are stored in the O_2 storage and their operations execution take place in the O_2 system,
- operations applied to Guide_O_2 objects are invoked from Guide applications.

In this way, Guide_O_2 objects may benefit from the database functionalities implemented in O_2, as well as from the security and reliability properties offered to data stored in O_2.

Guide applications which use Guide_O_2 objects are called *Guide_O_2 applications*. These applications are composed of:

- Guide objects, stored in Guide,
- Guide_O_2 objects, stored in O2 and accessible from Guide,
- O_2 objects which cannot be accessed directly from Guide but may be accessed through the Guide_O_2 objects.

The design of Guide_O_2 applications needs the definition of objects stored in both systems. Considering the Guide_O_2 objects, in addition to their O_2 definition (structure and behavior description), an interface must be provided on the Guide side.

We consider as very important the following constraints: Guide_O_2 objects manipulation (creation or method invocation) should be expressed at the language level in the same manner as any Guide object manipulation, and no extension to the Guide language should be necessary to write Guide_O_2 applications. It is necessary to have Guide types and classes, that we call *Guide_O_2 types* and *Guide_O_2 classes*, which provide the interface to create and invoke operations on Guide_O_2 objects.

3.1 Guide_O2 Objects Definition

This section examines two possible ways of defining Guide_O_2 objects: using the O_2 programming interface, or using the Guide language. The choice of the Guide language seems better because it is used to develop the main part of the application which is stored and executed in the Guide system. However, using the O_2 programming interface presents some advantages:

- Describing the structure and behavior of Guide_O_2 objects in Guide should imply their translation in O_2C. Conversely, O_2 specification of the Guide_O_2 objects, implies the translation in Guide of only the type specifications necessary to use Guide_O_2 objects within a Guide application. Method code is not translated in Guide because method execution takes place in the O_2 system.
- The structure description of the Guide_O_2 objects can benefit of the O_2 constructors. Their behavior description may directly use database functionalities like filters and iterations on collections. The expression of these functionalities is actually not possible in the Guide language, so using directly the O_2 programming interface avoids us to extend the Guide language.
- The fact that Guide_O_2 objects are specified in O_2 makes possible the use of already existing O_2 classes.

All these considerations lead us to choose the first option, at least for the prototyping phase, despite the inconvenient of using two languages.

So, Guide_O_2 objects will be defined through O_2 class definitions and O_2 method body definitions. Once defined, they are made visible from the Guide side: we say that O_2 *export* these classes to the Guide world and that Guide *import* them. The result of importing an O_2 class in Guide is a new Guide type specification, which is called a *Guide_O_2 type*.

Such a type contains a method signature for each method of the corresponding O_2 class. Guide_O_2 type method signatures are obtained by translating the O_2 method signature in Guide language. Type specification translation from O_2 to Guide obey to correspondence conventions not detailed here. Guide_O_2 types do not contain state variables (attributes) because data carried by Guide_O2 objects is stored in the O_2 system, not in Guide. Still, a Guide_O2 application must be able to access and modify attributes (if it is allowed by the access rights). So, for each public attribute, two methods appear in the Guide_O_2 type: one to access, the second to modify the attribute value. If the access right is restricted, read or write, only one method will appear in the Guide_O_2 type (figure 1).

3.2 Guide_O2 Application Design

Three phases can be distinguished in the design of a Guide_O_2 application:

1. The user has to decide which objects are to be managed by Guide and which by O_2. Generally Guide_O_2 objects are those who need database manipulations, security and recovery mechanisms.

2. The definition of the Guide_O_2 objects is made writing O_2 class and method definitions. These classes, and if necessary other existing O_2 classes, are imported into Guide. The Guide_O_2 types are obtained.
3. Finally, Guide objects are defined. Guide type and class definitions may use the obtained Guide_O_2 types: they may contain composition links towards Guide_O_2 types (see figure 1), but they may not be defined as subtypes of Guide_O_2 types. This rule derives from the main principle of the Guide – O_2 interoperability: objects that need database manipulations are stored in the O_2 system (there is no migration of objects between O_2 and Guide), so it makes no sense for a Guide object to inherit a property which is defined and executed in the O2 system (in our conception, operations on Guide objects are defined and executed exclusively in the Guide system).

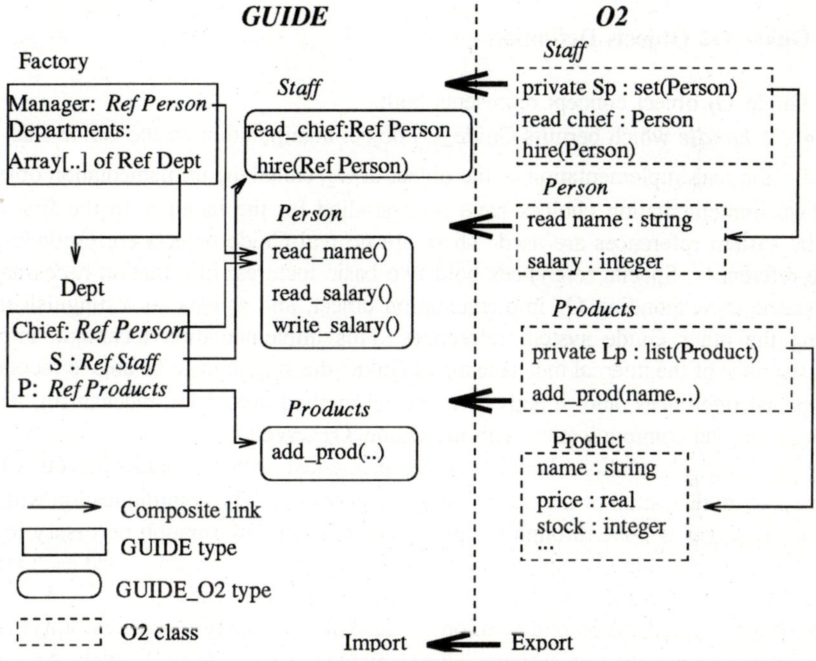

Fig. 1. Specification of a Guide_O_2 application.

An important feature of a Guide_O_2 application is that its O_2 part must be completely defined in O_2: accordingly to our unidirectional interoperability, Guide types may not be used in the definition of O_2 classes, and so, O_2 objects may not contain references to Guide objects.

An O_2 class may have one or more superclasses. When importing such a class in Guide, the Guide_O2 type will contain method signatures for all the public properties, including all the inherited ones.

Figure 1 gives an example of Guide_O_2 application. The O_2 classes Staff, Person and Products are imported into Guide. The Guide classes Factory and Department use the resulting Guide_O_2 types. Note that when importing an O_2 classe in which a method parameter or a method result is an object (see Staff definition), the class of this object (Person) must also be imported.

4 Implementation Aspects and Architecture

The Guide – O_2 interconnexion is based on a client–server architecture. A client is any Guide application which invokes a Guide_O2 object. A server, built upon the O2API interface, receives the requests which are implemented as remote procedure calls. Requested operations are executed in the O_2 system and the results are returned to the client. The Guide_O_2 server is in fact an O_2 client (the O_2 system is also designed with a client–server architecture).

4.1 Guide_O2 Objects Definition

The Guide_O_2 object concept represents both:

- a *handle* which permits Guide_O_2 object manipulation on the Guide side,
- the real implementation of the object in O_2, called the implementation object.

Two implementation choices have been studied for the handles. In the first one, special system references are used. There are no real Guide objects corresponding to these references. Special references hold two basic features: information necessary to access the corresponding O_2 implementation object, and a mark to distinguish them among the other Guide system references. This implementation technique implies modifications of the internal mechanisms of Guide: the system must be able to recognize the special references, and to activate a special method invocation mechanism, which implements the communication with the Guide_O2 server.

In the second solution, handles are implemented as real Guide objects called *proxys*. No modification of the Guide system is necessary. The communication with the Guide_O_2 server is done through the proxy object itself: information necessary to access the corresponding O_2 implementation object is stored in the proxy, and each proxy method contains the implementation of the Guide_O_2 server calls.

We have adopted the second solution because of its generality and flexibility: communication between the two systems is implemented as a Guide application. As a consequence, Guide interoperability with another object–oriented database system could be easily developed on the basis of the same mechanism; moreover, interconnections with different object–oriented databases could coexist. Finally, this solution satisfies the constraint to make as few modifications as possible to the Guide system.

Proxies are instances of Guide_O_2 classes which implement the imported types (the Guide_O_2 types). The generation of these classes is part of the import mechanism. The body of each method of a Guide_O_2 class contains a call to the Guide_O_2 server through a RPC mechanism.

4.2 Guide_O2 Object Management

This section presents the management of the correspondence between proxy objects and their implementation in O_2. Then, Guide_O_2 object creation and invocation mechanisms are presented in more details.

"Proxy to implementation object" correspondence is implicit: the proxy object holds the information needed to find the O_2 object. This information is a logical identifier managed by the Guide_O_2 server. Logical identifiers are necessary because O_2 clients cannot directly access persistent object identifiers: only run time handles on objects are available to O_2 users when accessing an O_2 object. Our solution consists in keeping a persistent list in O_2 for each exported O_2 class. Such a list, called Correspondence List (CL), contains all the objects of the class having a proxy in Guide. The logical identifier holds to the position in the list where the implementation object is inserted. In fact, such a list is a persistent root which allows to retrieve an implementation object using its logical identifier.

These lists are also used to manage the inverse correspondence. An element of a list stores, in addition to the implementation object, the Guide reference of the proxy object (unlike O_2 ones, Guide references can be accessed by the users). This correspondence is necessary for methods returning a Guide_O_2 object.

Guide_O2 Object Creation. The creation of a Guide_O_2 object, on request of a Guide_O_2 application, consists of the following operations: creation of a proxy object in Guide, creation of an implementation object in O_2, and assignment of a logical identifier to the new object (this identifier is stored in the proxy and the corresponding CL entry is filled with the new O_2 object and the reference of its proxy).

Method Invocation on a Guide_O2 Object. Method invocation on a proxy induces the execution in O_2 of the corresponding method on the implementation object. This object is accessed using the logical identifier stored in the proxy. If the result of the execution is an O_2 object whose class has been exported, the reference of the corresponding proxy has to be returned. But, there are situations where a resulting O_2 object has no proxy in Guide, for instance if it was created as a side effect of a method execution. In this case the caller is notified to create the proxy, and a second call is necessary to send the new proxy reference to the Guide_O_2 server to update the corresponding CL. So, a Guide_O_2 object may be created in two different ways: either explicitly, when a Guide application invokes the New method on a Guide_O_2 class, or implicitly, after a method execution on a Guide_O_2 object returning an O_2 object (instance of an exported class) which has not yet a proxy in Guide.

Guide_O2 Objects Consistency. Any implementation object is persistent, since inserted in a persistent list. But, if its proxy in Guide is not attached to a persistence root, it will be destroyed by the garbage collector. So the proxy's reference stored in the CL becomes invalid. The adopted solution is based on the exception mechanism provided by Guide.

When an invalid reference use is attempted, a system exception is raised. The associated treatment creates a new proxy object and updates the corresponding CL.

Conversely, under normal operation, the logical identifier stored in a proxy is always valid because of the persistence of the CL lists. But, if the O_2 system fails after a Guide_O_2 object creation, the update of the CL is lost and the logical identifier becomes invalid. The proposed solution is to trigger a *validate* operation in O_2 after any Guide_O_2 object creation.

A complete solution to the consistency problems, which takes into consideration failures on both Guide and O_2 sides, could be proposed only by implementing a distributed transaction mechanism. This is not yet possible because of the lack of transactional mechanisms in the Guide system.

4.3 The Guide_O2 Server

This server accesses directly O_2ENGINE, the kernel of the O_2 system, through the O_2API interface. O_2API [7] is organized as a library of C functions which may be called from C or C++ programs.

For each exported O_2 class, a set of procedures is generated and included in the Guide_O_2 server: one for the creation of a Guide_O_2 object on user request, one for each public method of the Guide_O2 class, and a procedure to update the CL of the class, when a Guide_O_2 object is created as a side effect of a method execution.

The server also provides some general interest procedures for the O_2 session initialization, and for validating or aborting the modifications performed since the beginning of the session or since the last validation point.

4.4 Export/Import Mechanisms

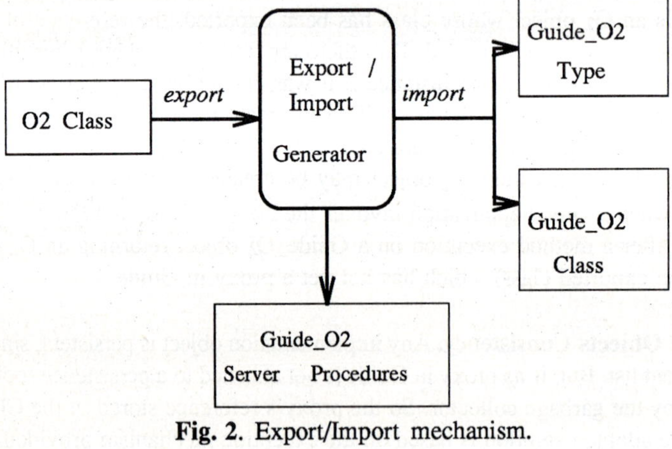

Fig. 2. Export/Import mechanism.

The export/import mechanism is represented in figure 2. For each imported class, a Guide_O_2 type and a Guide_O_2 class are generated. The Guide_O_2 methods contain the implementation of the communication with the Guide_O_2 server.

The server is obtained by linking together the server procedures generated for the exported classes, the general interest procedures, and the server skeleton. The SUN *rpcgen* compiler is used to generate the client stubs (linked to the Guide system) and the server skeleton (linked to the server).

5 Experiments and Measurement Results

We have implemented a first prototype to validate our interoperability model and to make some performance evaluation measurements. The export/import generator was not implemented in this prototype, so the server procedures and the Guide_O_2 types and classes have been written by hand.

Some application examples have been developed on this prototype. They allowed us to test Guide_O_2 object manipulations: object creation and method invocation. Performance evaluations were done using an application that implements research operations on collections of different sizes. This application has been implemented in two ways. In the first case, the collections are implemented in Guide ; the research is implemented as a scan. The second implementation uses interoperability, so collections are implemented as Guide_O_2 objects, research operations are invoked from the Guide side and performed in O_2. Time measurements include in this case the communication overhead(1). Two cases were considered for the collections implemented in O_2: with and without an index defined on the research path.

Time (seconds)		1rst collect	2nd collect	3th collect	4th collect	5th collect
Collection size		500	1000	5000	10000	20000
Guide	cold	1,399	2,485	20,187	58,685	163,089
	warm	0,152	0,468	1,567	3,503	152,421
O_2 (no index)	cold	0,461	0.848	3,658	5,777	12,156
	warm	0,460	0,649	2,812	5,596	11,884
O_2 (index)	cold	0,139	0,142	0,143	0,149	0,164
	warm	0,106	0,115	0,123	0,128	0,125

The results show that most of the time, it is more interesting to implement collections manipulated by a Guide_O_2 application in O_2. This is especially true for big collections,

(1) In the considered configuration Guide and O_2 systems are running on the same station.

but if the O_2 indexing facility is used, the programmer can also take benefits from implementing small collections in O_2.

6 Conclusions

Related Work. There are some similarities between the proposed architecture and the federated database architecture proposed by Heimbinger and McLeod in [1]. This architecture provides mechanisms for interconnecting database systems into a loosely coupled federation in order to share and exchange information.

Guide is not a database system but provides a persistent object repository. The Guide – O_2 interconnection can be considered as a federation because Guide applications may access data stored in the O_2 system via the export/import mechanism, comparable to the export/import schema mechanism of the federated database approach.

There are however many differences. First, the Guide – O_2 federation is more tightly coupled. There is no negotiation between O_2 and Guide concerning the exported/imported classes. Instead, Guide users can ask for new O_2 classes to be written and added to an O_2 schema, in order to import them.

Lessons and Open Issues. Implementing Guide – O_2 interoperability mechanisms at application level allowed us to quickly develop a first prototype and to make some experiments. Moreover the main interest of implementing interoperability as an application is generality. If another object–oriented database system is to be used, the export/import generator would have to generate the same kind of proxies but different server procedures.

The implemented mechanisms provide Guide users with efficient and safe manipulation of large collections of data in the O_2 system. Experiments proved that it is more efficient to use the O_2 system as a repository for collections with more than 5000 elements.

However, there are two aspects of our prototype who need more study. First, the problem of consistency between objects stored in O_2 and their proxies (see 4.2), should be solved through the implementation of persistent and distributed transaction management mechanisms; the proposed ad hoc solution is incomplete and expensive. Secondly there are some difficulties in designing Guide_O_2 applications: it seems necessary to provide a set of simple and clear strategy rules to facilitate designers' work and to ensure efficiency. If the use of efficient database functionalities improves performance, communication overhead and uncontrolled proxy proliferation lead to efficiency decrease.

Future work. Implementation of the export/import generator should be the first step. Then a detailed study of the global consistency problems is necessary to identify mechanisms to be implemented for consistent distributed processing support.

In a more general perspective, the use of an Object Request Broker like those proposed by the OMG in the CORBA architecture [8] could save the work of translating object invocations into RPC calls. The fact that the CORBA architecture deals with object identification could also avoid us to handle our own global object identifier (for Guide–O_2 objects).

Finally, the experiment presented in this article might be the first step towards a distributed database environment. Distributed database applications could be developed using Guide as a platform for distribution, to which different object–oriented database systems are connected.

References

1. D. Heimbigner and D. McLeod: A Federated Architecture for Information Management. ACM Transactions on Office Information Systems, Vol. 3 , No. 3, pp. 253–278, July 1985.

2. A. Seth and J. Larson: Federated Database Systems for Managing Distributed, Heterogeneous, and Autonomous Databases. ACM Computing Surveys, Vol.22 (No.3) , pp. 183–235, September 1990.

3. W. Litwin, L.Mark and N. Roussopoulos: Interoperability of Multiple Autonomus Databases. ACM Computing Surveys, Vol.22 , No. 3, pp. 267–293, September 1990.

4. S. Krakowiak, M. Meysembourg, et Al: Design and Implementation of an Object–Oriented Strongly Typed Language for Distributed Applications. Journal of Object–Oriented Programming, Vol. 3 , No. 3, pp. 11–22, Sept./Oct. 1990.

5. R. Balter, J.Bernadat, D. Decouchant, et Al: Architecture and Implementation of Guide, an Object–Oriented Distributed System. Computing Systems (Usenix), Vol. 4, No 1, pp. 31–67, 1991.

6. O. Deux et Al.. The O2 system. Communications of ACM, Vol. 34, No. 10, pp. 34–48, October 1991.

7. The O2 Application Designer's, The O2 Programmer's Manual, The O2API Programmer's Manual, V 4.0, O2 Technology, 7 rue du Parc de Clagny 78035 Versailles cedex– France , June 1992.

8. OMG: The Common Object Request Broker : Architecture and Specification, No 91.12.1, OMG, Boston, December 1991.

Reservation Commitment and Its Use in Multidatabase Systems

James G. Mullen, Jin Jing, and Jamshid Sharif-Askary

[1] Dept. of Computer Sciences, Purdue University, West Lafayette, IN 47907, USA
[2] Intergraph Corporation, Huntsville, AL 35894, USA
[3] Harris Corporation, P.O. Box 430, Melbourne, FL 32902, USA

Abstract. This paper discusses a new atomic commitment protocol, called *reservation commitment*, and its implementation in multidatabase systems. The implementation discussed does not require component systems to provide a visible prepare-to-commit state (as does two phase commitment) and does not require component system modification. The reservation commitment protocol will work for cases not handled by the compensation approach and can be used to increase the number of cases where compensation will work. Finally, The reservation commitment protocol avoids the blocking of local read-only transaction that occurs in two phase commitment, and can take advantage of data and transaction semantics to decrease the level of blocking of local update transactions.

1 Introduction

Multidatabase systems combine autonomous and heterogeneous component (or local) database systems into a unified global database system. Transactions represent logical units of work in database systems, and in multidatabase systems there are two types of transactions: global transactions and local transaction. Global transactions are submitted to the multidatabase system and are divided into subtransactions, with one subtransaction per local (or component) system that the global transaction accesses. Local transactions execute at a single local database system and are submitted directly to the local system.

One of the most difficult problems with implementing reliable transaction management in multidatabase systems is the problem of atomic commitment of global transactions, i.e. ensuring that if any of the subtransactions of a global transaction are committed, then all of the subtransactions will be committed. (see, for example, [4]). In this paper, we present the reservation commitment approach and discuss its use in multidatabase systems. We compare the reservation commitment approach to two phase commitment and compensation.

2 Reservation Commitment

Reservation commitment is an atomic commitment protocol that uses a reservation phase which attempts to ensure that the global transaction can execute successfully (without actually executing it). Unfortunately, because of failures, it is impossible for the reservation phase to guarantee that the *first* attempt to execute the global transaction will succeed, so the goal of the reservation phase becomes that of guaranteeing that each subtransaction of the global transaction can *eventually* be executed successfully. That is, each of the subtransactions is guaranteed to eventually commit if it is re-executed when it aborts.

An important (and in our opinion reasonable) assumption made is that integrity constraint transaction failures (transaction failures caused by the state of the database) are the only phenomenon that can cause a transaction that is repeatedly submitted to abort *indefinitely* (this assumption is also made, in effect, in [3] and [5]). For example, consider the case of a transaction that is trying to withdraw $100 from an account with under $100. This transaction could fail indefinitely, if no other transaction deposited more money into the account. Therefore, the goal of reservation becomes that of ensuring that integrity constraint transaction failures cannot occur. If the other kinds of failures (such as media, system, and communication failures) could exist indefinitely, any transaction management approach would seem to have difficulties.

Figure 1 provides a pictorial representation of the reservation commitment protocol. When a transaction is initiated by a user, the reservation phase is started. If all necessary reservations succeed, then the execution phase begins, otherwise, an unreservation phase begins where all successful reservation are undone. In the execution phase, the subtransactions are executed (and reservations are undone) as many times as is necessary until all of them successfully commit.

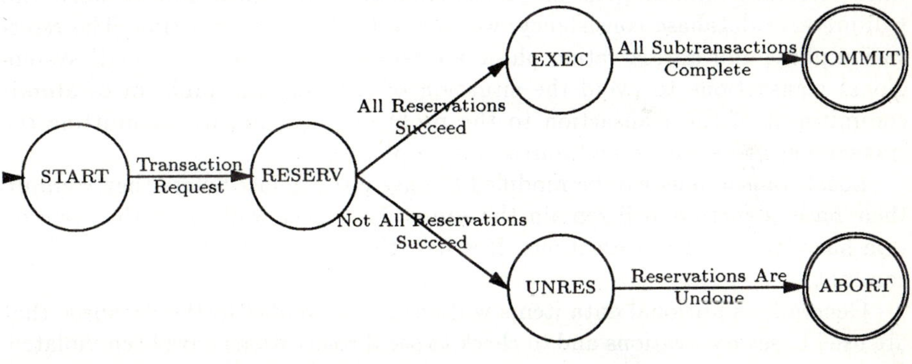

Fig. 1. Reservation Commitment Protocol.

3 Reservable Transactions

In this section, we discuss a multidatabase implementation of reservation commitment which we call *reservable transactions*. In our approach, we construct global transactions in a certain way, modify local transaction programs that access globally accessible data, and create additional data items that are used to manage the reservation process. However, our implementation scheme does not require component database system programs to be modified, which is often an extremely difficult, if not practically impossible, task.

Only global transactions need to use an atomic commitment protocol, so global transactions will use reservation commitment, and local transactions will simply make sure that they do not violate reservations.

Global transactions will be modified in the following way:

- For each subtransaction, a reservation transaction will be created that reserves the subtransaction (if necessary), and an unreservation transaction will be added that undoes the effects of the reservation (if necessary).
- Integrity constraint checks from the subtransactions can be removed (since it will be reserved), and commands to undo the subtransaction's reservation should be added.

We will call this enhanced global transaction a reservable transaction, and it will have the following structure:

1. n single system reservation transactions.
2. 1 "execution (phase)" transaction with n subtransactions. Each subtransaction will have a "standard" part (that does the work of the subtransaction), and an "unreservation" part.
3. n single system unreservation subtransactions.

So, reservable transactions are actually a set of global transactions. However, since reservable transactions are considered to be a logical unit of work and will preserve database consistency, we choose the name transaction. The reservation phase and unreservation phase are represented by a set of single system global transactions to avoid the situation of reducing the problem of atomic commitment of the transaction to the problem of atomically committing the transaction's reservation and unreservation phases.

Local transactions will be modified to have a check just before they commit; their basic structure will remain the same. The check will see if the transaction has violated any reservations. If it has, then it will abort, otherwise it can commit.

Generally, additional data items will need to be added to the database that are used to set reservations and to check to see if reservations have been violated. Examples of such data items are given in the following section. A formal model and proofs of the correctness of reservable transactions, as well as a transaction management approach and a discussion of related work, are presented in [2].

4 Example Reservable Transactions

4.1 Generic Reservable Transaction Example.

A generic method for implementing reservable transactions is to completely lock the data from updates in the reservation stage. For any data item(s), one data item that will function as the lock needs to be added. The lock will have two possible values: "locked" and "unlocked". Non-read-only local transactions and reservation transactions abort if the lock is set. Reservation transactions set the lock if it is not already set, and the data value(s) in the database will not cause their corresponding execution subtransaction to abort. The unreservation transaction releases the lock. In general, this method should work regardless of the semantics of the data item(s) involved, however, local update transactions will be blocked. Read-only local transactions will be free to execute, since the reservation does not actually perform the effects of the (reservable) transaction, there is no danger of the local transactions reading a value that was written by a transaction that will later be aborted. By using the semantics of the transactions and data involved, one can reduce the blocking of local update transaction also, as the following example will illustrate.

4.2 Bank Account Example.

Suppose that there are bank accounts stored in a database that have the following transactions defined for them:

- Local Transactions: Deposit, Withdraw, Interest Payment
- Global Transactions: Deposit, Withdraw

Suppose also that accounts cannot have a negative amount, and that similarly there is a maximum limit (say $100,000) on accounts (possibly for insurance purposes).

To implement reservation, two data items, *lower_limit* and *upper_limit*, could be added. All transactions would need to preserve the following property:

$$minimum \leq lower\_limit \leq amount \leq upper\_limit \leq maximum$$

Local transactions and execution subtransactions would simply modify *amount* as usual (but abort if the above property was violated). Withdraw reservations would increase *lower_limit* by the amount of the withdrawal. Deposit reservations would decrease *upper_limit* by the amount of the deposit. This example uses data and transaction semantics to reduce local update transaction blocking, because only local update transactions that would violate the above property would be blocked.

5 Transaction Method Comparison

The compensation approach does not block local transactions, but it will not work for certain cases where reservation commitment will work. Compensation fails for the bank account example because the operations are not commutative. That is, if local interest payments are allowed (in effect multiplication), they will not commute with deposits and withdrawals (additions and subtractions). For example, suppose that the account initially has $100, and then a withdraw transaction that withdraws \$100 is executed that will later be compensated. Then suppose a local transaction makes an interest payment of 1% before the compensation is performed (i.e. when the account has \$0). After the compensation is performed the account will have \$100 when it should have \$101, and therefore database consistency will not be preserved.

Even if local interest payments are eliminated (we will refer to this as Example 4.2′), compensation will still not work due to the minimum and maximum value restriction on the account. Suppose that there is \$0 in account A and that a transfer transaction deposits \$100 in A. The compensation of this transaction would be to withdraw \$100 from A. However, suppose another transaction withdraws this money before the compensation can be performed. The result would be that the compensation could fail indefinitely. If, however, reservation was used to ensure the account would not go below \$100, then the compensation could succeed. So, in this example, compensation alone will not be successful, but it's use in conjunction with reservation will be successful.

If local interest payments, and the minimum and maximum are removed (we will refer to this as Example 4.2″), then compensation will work and will not block. However, if this is the case, then reservation will not block either. Since there are no limits, there will be no possible integrity constraint violations, and therefore the execution phase of reservable transactions will be implicitly reserved (i.e. the reservation phase could be eliminated).

In general, reservation commitment avoids the blocking of read-only local transactions that occurs between the first phase and second phase when using two phase commitment (e.g. example 4.1) and can use data and transaction semantics to reduce the blocking of local update transaction that are also blocked when using two phase commitment (e.g. examples 4.2, 4.2′, and 4.2″). In addition, reservation does not require all component systems to provide a visible prepare-to-commit state as does 2PC.

Table 1 summarizes our comparison.

	COMMITMENT METHOD		
EXAMPLE	2PC	Reservation	Compensation
4.1 Generic Case	Blocks All Local Transactions	Blocks Local Update Transactions	Does Not Work
4.2 Bank Account local transactions: withdraw, depost, interest minimum and maximum limit	Blocks All Local Transactions	Blocks Some Local Update Transactions	Does Not Work
4.2′ Bank Account local transactions: withdraw, deposit minimum and maximum limit	Blocks All Local Transactions	Blocks Some Local Update Transactions	Works if Reservation Used
4.2″ Bank Account local transactions: withdraw, deposit NO minimum and maximum limit	Blocks All Local Transactions	No Blocking	No Blocking

Table 1. Transaction Example Comparison of Commitment Methods.

6 Conclusions

In this paper we have presented the reservation commitment protocol and a multidatabase implementation of this protocol called reservable transactions. In summary, we see the disadvantages of our approach as follows:

- Local transactions that modify globally accessible data must be modified.
- New data items must be created.
- Constructing global applications becomes more complex.

The advantages of our approach are that it:

- Avoids component system modification.
- Handles cases not covered by compensation.
- Does not block read-only local transactions and can use data and transaction semantics to reduce the blocking of local update transactions.
- Can be used to increase the applicability of compensation.

We feel that the reservation approach presented here is particularly appropriate for multidatabase environments built from off-the-shelf (but non-preexisting) software components. In such environments, local system autonomy is clearly a consideration, however, there are no pre-existing applications that need to be modified; all applications can be designed with reservation in mind from the beginning. Such environments occur frequently in the development of customized information system at companies such as the Harris Corporation.

We are currently implementing support for reservation commitment in the InterBase-Star multidatabase prototype system (based on the InterBase system [1]) at Purdue University.

References

1. O. A. Bukhres, J. Chen, W. Du, A. K. Elmagarmid, and R. Pezzoli. InterBase : An Execution Environment for Global Applications over Distributed, Heterogeneous, and Autonomous Software Systems. *IEEE Computer*, Aug. 1993. (to appear).
2. A. K. Elmagarmid, J. Jing, J. G. Mullen, and J. Sharif-Askary. Reservable transactions: An approach for reliable multidatabase transaction management. Technical Report SERC-TR-114-P, Department of Computer Science, Purdue University, April 1992.
3. M. Hsu and A. Silberschatz. Unilateral commit: A new paradigm for reliable distributed transaction processing. In *Proceedings of the 7th Internatonal Conference on Data Engineering*, pages 296–304, Kobe, Japan, Apr. 1991.
4. J. G. Mullen, A. K. Elmagarmid, W. Kim, and J. Sharif-Askary. On the impossibility of atomic commitment in multidatabase systems. In *Proceedings of the International Conference on Systems Integration*, pages 625–634, Morristown, New Jersey, June 1992.
5. P. Muth and T. Rakow. Atomic commitment for integrated database systems. In *Proceedings of the 7th Intl. Conf. on Data Engineering*, pages 296–304, Kobe, Japan, Apr. 1991.

Predict Query Processing Cost in a Distributed Database System*

Weiyi Meng[1], Chengwen Liu[2], Wei Sun[3] and Clement Yu[4]

[1] State University of New York, Binghamton, NY 13902-6000
[2] DePaul University, Chicago, IL 60601-2302
[3] Florida International University, Miami, FL 33199
[4] University of Illinois at Chicago, Chicago, IL 60680

Abstract. The configuration of a distributed database system consists of a network and a number of local configurations. A local configuration (LC) consists of a CPU, some I/O devices and a local DBMS, etc. at its site. To improve the performance of the distributed database system, one way is to change one or more LCs. If, at each site, the old LC may be replaced by one of several possible new LCs, then a large number of different new configurations may be formed, each will have different performance. The objective is to find a new configuration satisfying a certain performance goal at the minimum additional cost. It may not be practical to enumerate all possible configurations and conduct an experiment for each configuration to find the performance since the number of different configurations can be prohibitively large. In this paper, we propose a methodology that predicts the performance of all different configurations based on experiments on a very limited number of configurations. Our experimental results indicate that the proposed methodology fairly accurately predicts the performances of new configurations.

1 Introduction

A distributed database system (DDBS) consists of many LCs connected by a communication network, where a LC consists of various hardware and software components at a site, such as local database management system (DBMS), CPU and I/O devices, etc. Given all LCs and the network, a *system configuration* (or simply a *configuration*) is formed. Clearly, the performance of a DDBS depends on the underlying LCs and the network.

Consider the following scenario: an existing DDBS can no longer satisfy the new performance requirement and, as a result, one or more LCs of the distributed system need to be upgraded. Suppose that each LC may be replaced by one of several new LCs and an administration has to decide on a specific configuration, within a given budget, to satisfy certain performance requirements, say the response time of the entire system to a typical query must not exceed a pre-set value. From these choices of LCs, many different configurations can be

* Research supported in part by NSF (IRI-9111988) and AirForce (AFOSR 93-1-0059).

formed. To find the configuration with the desired property, one way is to carry out a performance evaluation for each possible configuration and compare the results. However, the number of all possible configurations may be so large that one simply can not afford to do all the experiments. Also, actually changing LCs to test the performance of the system can be very disruptive to the normal operation. Another possible way is to use an analytical model [14, 8, 13, 15, 21] to do performance analysis. However, analytical models usually involve substantial statistical assumptions on job arrival rate and service rate, which may not be true in practice. In this paper, we propose to carry out the experiments for a small number of configurations only and then predict the results for other configurations based on these experimental results. This method has a good potential of predicting result well, since the performance evaluation is based on actual experimental results and the special characteristics of query processing is captured into the modeling process.

In this paper, we assume that a configuration is upgraded by changing one or more LCs while preserving the network. The differences between old LCs and new LCs are restricted to CPU's and I/O devices in this study, though this may be relaxed (see Section 6). The response time to a single typical query will be used as the performance measurement in our discussion. Each configuration of an N-site system can be represented by a vector of N components $(lc_1, lc_2, \ldots, lc_N)$, where lc_k represents the LC at site k, k=1,...,N.

The rest of this paper is organized as follows. In Section 2, we briefly describe query processing in a DDBS. The basic methodology for predicting the result of a configuration from the result of another configuration is proposed in Section 3. In Section 4, the basic methodology is further generalized by removing certain assumptions adopted in Section 3. Experimental results for the proposed methodology are provided in Section 5. Section 6 concludes the paper.

2 Distributed Query Processing

In a distributed relational database system, data is stored at different sites connected through a network. Each site is managed by a local DBMS. Relations may be fragmented [3, 20, 16, 4] or not fragmented [7, 9]. When a query is received by the system at a site, called *query site*, the query optimizer parses the query and determines a strategy to process it. The strategy usually consists of decomposing the query into several subqueries and assigning them to the local DBMSs at different sites. Processing of these subqueries can take place in parallel at different sites. The partial results from the processing sites are then combined to produce the final result.

When the relations are fragmented, the *fragment and replicate* strategy [5, 18] is normally used to process distributed queries. For example, this strategy is used in *distributed Ingres* [17]. For a given query, the system first decides a set of processing sites at which subqueries are actually processed and then decides which relation should remain fragmented and which relations should be replicated at the processing sites. If all the referenced relations are not fragmented, the strategy of single site processing [7, 9] or the *partition and replicate* strategy [19] can be used to determine an execution plan. No matter which strategy is used, substantial data transfer may be required to replicate relations before a subquery can be processed at a site. In order to reduce communication cost, some of the relations/fragments may be locally reduced (by projection and selection) before being sent to other sites. By observing the query processing strategies used by existing systems (e.g., distributed INGRES and R^*) and other proposed strategies [19], we find that the actions of each processing site can be partitioned into three phases, *planning phase, data preparation phase* and *subquery processing phase.* In the planning phase, user queries are decomposed into subqueries according to some optimization criteria. In the data preparation phase, data needed to process the subqueries are transferred to their respective sites. In the subquery processing phase, subqueries are processed locally in parallel and partial results produced by subqueries are sent to the *assembling site* to form the answer. In this paper, we concentrate on the data preparation phase and the subquery processing phase only since the time for planning is usually small in comparison to the time used by other phases [1, 11].

Without loss of generality, we use the fragment and replicate to present our methodology for performance prediction in this paper. With minor modification, the methodology should also be applicable when a different algorithm is chosen.

Based on the fragment and replicate algorithm, the actions in the data preparation phase are: (1) perform local reduction (selection/projection), if any; and then (2) send/receive data to/from other site(s) through the network; and (3) union the fragments of the same relation into a relation. During the reduction, actions of CPU and I/O interleave and overlap. Idle time may occur before and/or during the union. This is because for the union to start, at least two fragments of the same relation must be available at a site. Otherwise, the site has to wait until the fragments arrive. Changing the CPU or I/O device at one site may affect the idle time at another site. If at a site reductions need to be performed on more than one relation, then the reductions are performed in a given order. When all reductions on all relations at a site are completed, the obtained data of each relation is packaged and sent to other sites in the same order in which reductions are performed.

After the data preparation phase, one fragment of the fragmented relation and all other involved whole relations are present at each processing site. The subquery processing phase can now start. For a processing but non-assembling site, the actions in this phase are: (1) process the subquery and then (2) send the locally obtained result to the assembling site. It is assumed that all local operations are performed before any processed data is sent to the assembling site, i.e., no pipelining actions take place. If the assembling site is also a processing site, then the actions in this phase are: (1) process the subquery; (2) receive data from other sites; and (3) perform the assembling. Idle time can occur since only after the partial results from at least two subqueries are present in this site, can assembling be started. If the assembling site is not a processing site, then the actions in this phase are: (1) receive data from other sites and (2) perform the assembling. Since an assembling and non-processing site can be regarded as an assembling and processing site needing zero processing time, we may assume the assembling site is also a processing site. It is possible for the first phase at one site to overlap the second phase of another site. In general, the assembling site may or may not be the same as the query site. Without loss of generality, we may assume they are the same since otherwise we can simply add to the response time the time needed to transfer the result from the assembling site to the query site.

Example 1. Suppose the query $Q = \sigma_p(R_1) \bowtie R_2$ *is submitted, where* R_1 *and* R_2 *are two relations,* σ_p *is the selection operator with predicate* p *and* $\bowtie$ *is the natural join. Assume both* R_1 *and* R_2 *have three disjoint fragments, i.e.,* $R_i = \bigcup_{j=1}^{j=3} F_{ij}$ *and* $F_{ij} \cap F_{ik} = \phi$ *for* $j \neq k$*, where* F_{ij} *is the fragment of* R_i *at site* j*.*

Suppose the optimizer has chosen Site 1, Site 2 and Site 3 to be the processing sites, and has decided to fragment R_2 *and replicate* R_1*. Then, by our assumption, the selection on every fragment of* R_1 *will be done first. Thus, it suffices to replicate the result of* $\sigma_p(R_1)$ *at each processing site. The reduced fragment* $\sigma_p(F_{11})$ *of* R_1 *at site 1 should be sent to site 2 and site 3, the reduced fragment* $\sigma_p(F_{12})$ *should be sent to site 1 and site 3, and the reduced fragment* $\sigma_p(F_{13})$ *should be sent to site 1 and site 2. The three reduced fragments are then unioned together to produce* R_1^p*, the result of* $\sigma_p(R_1)$*, at sites 1, 2 and 3, respectively. Subsequently, the original query* Q *has been decomposed into the following three subqueries:* $Q_i = R_1^p \bowtie F_{2i}$*, for* $i = 1, 2$ *and* 3*.*

The three subqueries will be processed in parallel at the respective sites (Q_i *at site* i*). Then the results obtained at each site are sent to an (assembling) site where they are unioned to produce the answer.* ■

Knowing the time needed for each phase at the query site and the planning time, the total time spent at the query site, which is the response time of the system to the query, can be easily computed.

3 Basic Methodology

Our methodology consists of two steps: in the first step, we carry out one experiment for the existing configuration (i.e., run the typical query in the existing system) and save the needed information for the second step; in the second step, we use the saved information in the first step to predict the response time of the typical query under other configurations.

In this section, we assume that the criteria used by the query optimizer to decompose the submitted query and to decide the data transfer across the sites for the query are independent of the system configuration. *This assumption will be removed later.* Under this assumption, for a given query, the optimizer will always choose the same relation to remain fragmented regardless of the underlying configuration. This assumption also implies that for a given query and a given site the amount of data processed at this site as well as the amount of data which needs to be sent/received by this site will not change even if the configuration changes. Because of the implication, we call this assumption the *data invariant assumption.*

3.1 Experiment on the Existing Configuration

Let α denote the existing configuration. Let $F_{1i}, \ldots, F_{x_i i}$ be the fragments on which reductions are to be performed in the given order at site i. Let ds_{ki} be the size of F^r_{ki} which is F_{ki} after reduction. Let T_{ki}, T^{cpu}_{ki} and T^{io}_{ki} be the total time, the CPU time and the I/O time needed to pack F^r_{ki} into packages and put these packages into network, respectively, k=1,...,x_i. Let arr$_{wji}$ be the time when F^r_{wj} arrives at site i from site j. If F^r_{wj} is too big to be held in one package, then arr$_{wji}$ is the time when the last package of F^r_{wj} arrives at site i.

By carrying out the experiment for the existing configuration, we can determine and save the information for each processing site i as indicated in Table 1. We will discuss in the next subsection how these information can be used to predict the performance of other configurations.

(1) CPU time, I/O time and the total time needed for local reduction
(2) CPU time, I/O time and the total time needed for subquery processing
(3) Size of each reduced fragment ds_{ki}, k=1,...,x_i
(4) Total, CPU and I/O times for packaging each reduced fragment
    T_{ki}, T^{cpu}_{ki}, T^{io}_{ki}, k=1,...,x_i
(5) arr$_{wji}$, where site j is a processing site and w=1,...,x_j
(6) (if site i is not the assembling site) the size of the data needs to be sent to the assembling site in the subquery processing phase; (if site i is the assembling site) the arrival times of data from other processing sites in the subquery processing phase

Table 1. Saved information for each site under configuration α.

3.2 Performance Prediction for Other Configurations

Two configurations differ by one LC at site i if they have different LCs at site i but they have the same LC at each site j, $j \neq i$. Let β be a configuration that differs from α by n LCs at sites $s_1, \ldots, s_n$, $1 \leq n \leq N$ (N is the number of sites in the network). Let $C_\beta = \{\gamma_1, \ldots, \gamma_n\}$ be a set of n configurations such that the LC of γ_i at site s_i is the same as that of β at site s_i and γ_i differs from α by exactly the LC at s_i, i=1,...,n.

For example, if $\alpha = < lc^*_1, lc^*_2, lc^*_3, \ldots, lc^*_N >$ and $\beta = < lc^\#_1, lc^\#_2, lc^*_3, \ldots, lc^*_N >$, then $C_\beta = \{\gamma_1, \gamma_2\}$ with $\gamma_1 = < lc^\#_1, lc^*_2, lc^*_3, \ldots, lc^*_N >$ and $\gamma_2 = < lc^*_1, lc^\#_2, lc^*_3, \ldots, lc^*_N >$ because β differs from α by only two LCs $lc^\#_1$ and $lc^\#_2$.

Now we consider how to predict the response time of the typical query under configuration β from the information saved when the typical query is run under configuration α. The prediction of the performance of β is done in two steps. In the first step, we predict the impact on a given site s_i when the LC of site s_j is changed. That is, for each γ_j in C_β, we predict the impact on a given site s_i when the configuration of α is replaced by γ_j. It is possible that j = i. When s_j varies among different sites, all individual impacts on site s_i can be obtained. In the second step, we use the individual impacts on site s_i obtained in the first step, to predict the total time needed by site s_i.

Impact of One Site on Another Site. Recall that $\gamma_j \in C_\beta$ is a configuration that differs from α by exactly the LC at site s_j. Now we discuss the impact on the arrival times arr_{wji}, w=1,...,x_j, of data from site s_j to site s_i when the local configuration of α at site s_j is replaced by that of γ_j at site s_j. Without loss of generality, we assume both the CPU and I/O device at site s_j are different for configuration α and configuration γ_j.
Data preparation phase: We now predict the arrival time arr_{wji} of F^r_{wj} from site j to site i when the configuration α is changed to γ_j. Let cpu^τ, io^τ and tot^τ be the CPU time, I/O time and the total time for site s_j to complete its local reduction under configuration τ, respectively. When the experiment for configuration α is done, cpu^α, io^α, tot^α, ds^α_{wj}, $\mathrm{arr}^\alpha_{wji}$, etc. are recorded. In addition to the recorded information, we also know the manufacturer-provided information: r^α_{cpu} — the processing rate of the CPU at site s_j under configuration α and r^α_{io} — the accessing rate of the I/O device (the number of I/Os per second) at site s_j under α. Similarly, we know $r^{\gamma_j}_{cpu}$ and $r^{\gamma_j}_{io}$. Thus, cpu^{γ_j} and io^{γ_j} can be computed:

$$cpu^{\gamma_j} = \frac{r^\alpha_{cpu}}{r^{\gamma_j}_{cpu}} * cpu^\alpha, \qquad io^{\gamma_j} = \frac{r^\alpha_{io}}{r^{\gamma_j}_{io}} * io^\alpha \tag{1}$$

Let olp^τ be the overlap time between CPU and I/O device for the local reduction at site s_j under configuration τ. Then

$$tot^\tau = cpu^\tau + io^\tau - olp^\tau \tag{2}$$

Thus, predicting tot^{γ_j} is equivalent to predicting olp^{γ_j}.

Since olp^τ is defined to be the overlap time between CPU and I/O devices at site s_j, it can be considered a function of cpu^τ and io^τ. The following properties of an overlap function with two arguments, say z=f(x,y), can be observed: (1) if x=0 and/or y=0, then z=0, (2) z is an non-decreasing function of x and y, and (3) $z \leq \min\{x, y\}$.

It is easy to see that the function f(x,y)=$a * \min\{x, y\}$, where $0 \leq a \leq 1$ is independent of CPU and I/O devices, satisfies all the three properties. Thus,

$$olp^\tau = a * \min\{cpu^\tau, io^\tau\}, \quad 0 \leq a \leq 1 \tag{3}$$

could be a reasonable formula to estimate olp^τ.

By using cpu^α, io^α, tot^α and formula (2), olp^α can be computed. By using olp^α, io^α, cpu^α and formula (3), a value of a can be computed. By using this value of a and io^{γ_j}, cpu^{γ_j} and formula (3), olp^{γ_j} can be estimated. Finally, by using olp^{γ_j}, io^{γ_j}, cpu^{γ_j} and formula (2), tot^{γ_j} can be predicted. Our experimental results [12] indicate that accurate total time estimation can be obtained by using this method.

Similarly, $T^{\gamma_j}_{wj}$ can be predicted, w=1,...,x_j.

Knowing tot$^{\gamma_j}$, $T^{\gamma_j}_{wj}$ and the time when the data preparation phase starts, T_0, the arrival time of F^r_{wj} from site s_j to site s_i can be estimated by

$$arr^{\gamma_j}_{wji} = T_0 + tot^{\gamma_j} + \sum_{y=1}^{w} T^{\gamma_j}_{yj} + c * ds_{wj} + d_{wj} \tag{4}$$

where c is the transmission rate, ds_{wj} is the size of F^r_{wj} and d_{wj} is the network contention delay. However, since ds_{wj} is a constant for given j and w due to the data invariant assumption (i.e., $\mathrm{ds}^{\gamma_j}_{wj} = \mathrm{ds}^{\alpha}_{wj}$), $c * ds_{wj} + d_{wj}$ in formula (4) can be combined into one constant b_{wj}. Thus, the estimation formula becomes

$$arr^{\gamma_j}_{wji} = T_0 + tot^{\gamma_j} + \sum_{y=1}^{w} T^{\gamma_j}_{yj} + b_{wj} \tag{5}$$

By using tot$^{\alpha}$, arr$^{\alpha}_{wji}$, T$^{\alpha}_{yj}$ and formula (5), a value of b_{wj} in formula (5) can be computed. By using this value of b_{wj} and tot$^{\gamma_j}$ and $T^{\gamma_j}_{yj}$, y=1,...,w, the value of arr$^{\gamma_j}_{wji}$ can be computed from formula (5).

If site s_j and site s_i are the same, then no data transfer is needed. Thus, there is no need to estimate the arrival time in this case.

Subquery processing phase: In this phase, only the assembling site may receive data from other sites. Therefore, site s_i is regarded as the assembling site while site s_j remains to be a typical processing but non-assembling site. Without loss of generality, assume the local processing at site s_j yields data of non-zero size. Site s_j can influence the assembling site by sending the data to the assembling site earlier or later. Therefore, we need to predict the arrival time of the data from site s_j to the assembling site under configuration γ_j as we have done in the data preparation phase. Clearly, the same prediction method as used in the data preparation phase can be used here.

Impact of Multiple Sites on One Site. We now predict the total time needed by the data preparation phase and the subquery processing phase at site s_i under configuration β.

Data preparation phase: From the previous discussion, we know that for any processing site s_i, the following information is either recorded or estimated: the time when the local reduction is completed, the times when data from other sites arrive at site s_i and the corresponding data sizes. Note that the unioning of two fragments of the same relation is done by appending one fragment to another. Thus, the time needed for the union is proportional to the size of the appending fragment and has nothing to do with where the appending fragment is from. Therefore, if ds is the size of an appending fragment, then the time needed to union this fragment and the current fragment at site s_i can be computed by $h{*}ds$, where h is a factor depending on the current combination of CPU and I/O device at site s_i. The value of h can be determined by using the same technique as that for predicting the total time of local reduction for a site under configuration γ_j. We assume fragments from remote sites are always the appending fragments. Let $F_1, \ldots, F_W$ be all the reduced fragments to be sent to site s_i from other sites. F_k has size ds_k, k=1,...,W. Without loss of generality, let arr_k be the arrival time of F_k, k=1,...,W, such that $arr_1 \leq arr_2 \leq \cdots \leq arr_W$.

The following algorithm can be used to compute the total time needed by the data preparation phase at site s_i:

```
INPUT:    arr_1,...,arr_W, ds_1,...,ds_W, h
          t  — local reduction time at site s_i
          T_0 — the starting time of data preparation phase
OUTPUT:   T_d — the total time for the data preparation phase at site s_i
BEGIN
   X = T_0 + t; /* X traces the time when data preparation phase ends */
   FOR k = 1 to W, STEP 1
   {
      If arr_k ≤ X, then X = X + h*ds_k    /* no idle time */
      Else X = arr_k + h*ds_k; /* X + idle_time + h*ds_k, where idle_time=arr_k − X */
   }
   T_d = X − T_0; print(T_d);
END.
```

Subquery processing phase: Since assembling is basically fragment-unioning and we know the starting time of the subquery processing phase at each site (X in the above algorithm), it is easy to see that the total time needed by the subquery processing phase at the assembling site can be predicted in the same way as we did for the data preparation phase.

4 Elimination of Data Invariant Assumption

Without the data invariant assumption, different relations may be chosen to remain fragmented by the query optimizer for different configurations. Let D_τ be the chosen decomposition when τ is the configuration. Clearly, $D_{\tau_1} = D_{\tau_2}$ implies that when the system configuration is changed from τ_1 to τ_2 (or vice versa) the data invariant assumption is true. Thus, if we know the experiment result for (τ_1, D_{τ_1}), then the performance of (τ_2, D_{τ_2}) can be predicted if $D_{\tau_1} = D_{\tau_2}$ by using the method developed in Section 3.

For a query involving m relations, there are m possible decompositions each corresponds to a different choice of the relation that remains fragmented. Usually, m$\leq$4. Let D_i be the decomposition when relation R_i remains fragmented, i=1,...m. Despite the large number of different configurations, $D_1, \ldots, D_m$ are all the possible decompositions. Thus, if we can carry out an experiment for each decomposition in advance and save the necessary information, then a prediction bed can be built such that when we need to predict the performance for a configuration β, we can first determine D_β, suppose $D_\beta = D_k$, $1 \leq k \leq m$, and then we can use the saved information of the experiment for D_k to do the prediction.

Now we discuss how to carry out an experiment for each decomposition. The fragment and replicate algorithm tends to fragment the relation with the largest size so that the job load of each processing site is more balanced. Thus, to carry out the experiment for a given D_i, we only need to make the size of relation R_i large enough. Note that we do not need to physically increase the number of tuples in relation R_i. We only need to change the statistical entry for the size of R_i in the data dictionary. In this way, each D_i, i=1,...,m, can be generated for the same configuration α. Since the size of R_i is not physically changed, the experiment carried out for D_i under α uses real relation size.

5 Experimental Results

Experiments were carried out to investigate the validity of our methodology. Our experimental environment consists of 5 dedicated workstations connected by an Ethernet local area network. Each workstation, which serves as a LC, has its own disk drive and its own local DBMS as shown in Table 2. It is a small heterogeneous environment. The Sun-3/50 workstations are running Sun UNIX 4.2 release 3.4 and the Sparc station is running Sun UNIX 4.2 release 4.0.

Workstation	Workstation Type	CPU	Disk Drive	DBMS
WS_1	Sun 3/50	68020	Micropolis 1355	SunIngres 3.0
WS_2	Sun 3/50	68020	Micropolis 1325	SunIngres 3.0
WS_3	Sun 3/50	68020	Micropolis 1325	SunIngres 3.0
WS_4	Sun Sparc 1+	SPARC	Quantum ProDrive 105S	SunIngres 6.3
WS_5	Sun 3/50	68020	Micropolis 1558	SunIngres 3.0

Table 2. Local Configurations of Workstations.

The database used for our testing consists of a set of relations which are fragmented and distributed among three sites [1, 22] . All relations have the same set of attributes satisfying the Wisconsin benchmark requirement [2]. The size of each relation ranges from 0.3 megabyte to 4.2 megabytes. A primary index and a secondary index are built on two of the attributes such that various queries with or without index for join can be designed. Some attributes are used as selection attributes giving various selectivities.

On top of the local DBMSs, is a special version of our experimental distributed query processing system [11, 22], which collects detailed information of communications and usages of local resources.

Assume that the existing configuration $\alpha = \{WS_1, WS_2, WS_3\}$. Then for configuration $\beta = \{WS_1, WS_4, WS_5\}$, the set of configurations, each differs from α by exactly one LC, is $C_\beta = \{\gamma_2, \gamma_3\}$, where $\gamma_2 = \{WS_1, WS_4, WS_3\}$ and $\gamma_3 = \{WS_1, WS_2, WS_5\}$.

The information as listed in Table 1 is collected and saved for configuration α. To predict the response time for β, we first estimate the impact on each site when configuration α is changed to configurations γ_2 and γ_3 by using the information collected for configuration α and formulas (1) to (3). The response time for β is the sum of the query planning time, the total time of the data preparation phase, and the total time of the subquery processing phase. Query planning time is estimated by applying the information collected under α to formulas (1) to (3). The total times for the data preparation phase and the subquery processing phase are obtained by the algorithm given in section 3 and the information obtained for α, γ_2 and γ_3 in the first step.

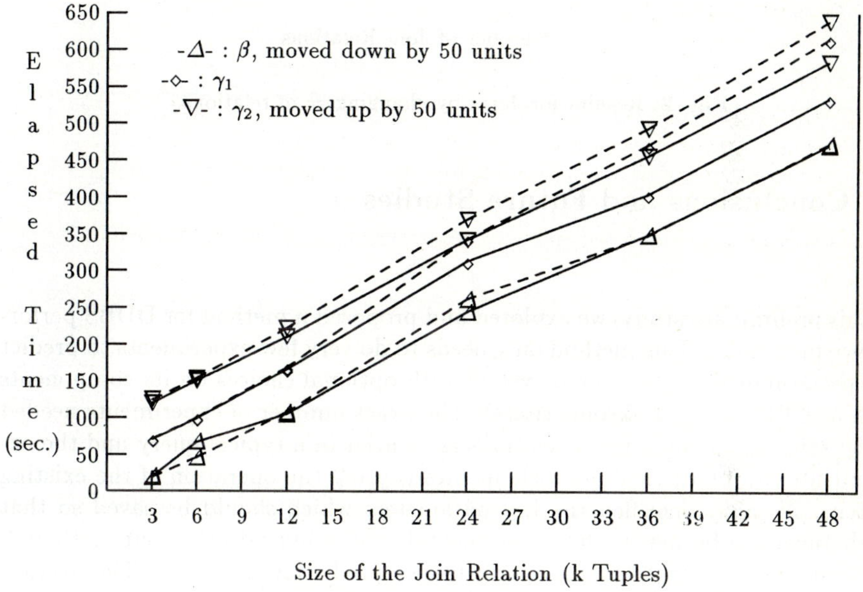

Fig. 1. Results for 2-way Join by changing relation sizes.

Experiments were performed with various queries by changing the sizes of the relations, the number of relations for join, existence of selection clauses and indices for join or selection. Because of space limitation, we can not present all the results here. As a result, in Figures 1 and 2, we only present the results for a subset of the queries we tested. The solid lines represent the actual response times and the dashed lines represent the estimation results. Note that the lines for configuration β are moved down by 50 units and those for γ_2 are moved up by 50 units in order to avoid overlaps with the lines of γ_1. Our experimental results indicate that our methodology can predict response time of a query rather accurately without actually performing the experiment for a given configuration.

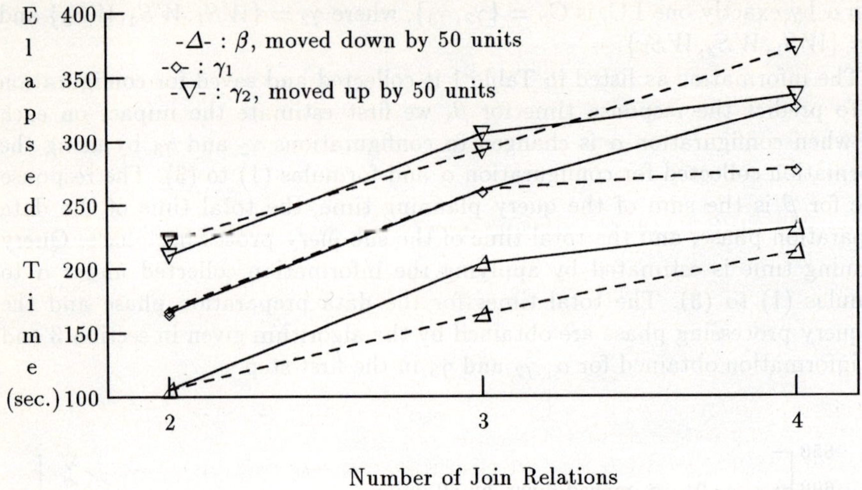

Fig. 2. Results for Joins by changing # of relations.

6 Conclusions and Future Studies

In this preliminary study, we explored and proposed a method for DDBS performance prediction. This method only needs to do very few experiments to predict the performance of distributed system with optional choices on its components such as CPU and I/O of some site(s). The exact number of experiments needed is the same as the number of relations referenced in a typical query and the experiments can be carried out without interrupting the operation of the existing system. We also identified the key parameters which should be saved so that predictions can be made. Our experimental results indicate that our methodology can provide fairly accurate performance prediction of DDBS. The average error is about 8%.

Although we presented our methodology based on the fragment and replicate algorithm, we believe that the methodology can be applied to other distributed query processing algorithms, for example [19, 10], with minor changes since performing local reduction, transmitting data across different sites and executing subqueries are common in distributed query processing algorithms.

It is very interesting to extend the proposed methodology such that the changes to LC are not restricted to only CPU and I/O devices. For example, changes may include the main memory size [6], local DBMS and operating system. In this case, the methodology is still applicable with minor modifications. For example, benchmark experiments may be needed to obtain estimates of the amount of overlap between CPU and I/O operations. We will carry out experiments to verify the extended methodology.

References

1. Agrawal, P., D. Bitton, K. Guh, C. Liu and C. Yu, *A Case Study for Distributed Query Processing* , Int'l Symposium on Databases in Parallel and Distributed Systems, Austin, Dec. 1988, pp. 124-130.
2. Dina Bitton, David J. DeWitt and Carolyn Turbyfill, *Benchmarking Database Systems: A Systematic Approach.* Proc. of VLDB, 1983, pp8-19.
3. Ceri, S., Negri, M. and Pelagatti, G., *Horizontal Partitioning in Database Design,* ACM SIGMOD, 1982.
4. Chen, J.S.J. and Li, Victor, *Optimizing Joins in Fragmented Database Systems on a Broadcast Local Network.* IEEE TSE, Vol.15, No.1, Jan. 1989, pp. 26-38.
5. Epstein, R., Stonebraker, M. and Wong, E., *Distributed Query Processing in Relational Database Systems.* ACM SIGMOD 1978.
6. Garcia-Molina, H., *Performance Through Memory.* Proc. of the ACM SIGMETRICS Conf., 1987, pp. 155-162.
7. Haas, L.M., Selinger, P.G., and Bertino, E., *R*: A Research Project on Distributed Relational DBMS,* Database Engineering, Vol. 5, No. 4, Dec. 1982, pp. 66-75.
8. Jenq, B-C., Kohler, W., and Towsley, D., *A Queueing Network Model for a Distributed Database Testbed System.* IEEE TSE, Vol.14, No.7, July 1988.
9. Mackert, L. and Lohman, G., *R* Optimizer Validation and Performance Evaluation for Distributed Queries,* Proc. of VLDB, Aug. 1986, pp. 149-159.
10. Liu, C. and Yu, C., *Validation and Performance Evaluation of the Partition and Replicate Algorithm,* Proc. of Int'l Conf. on Distr. Compu. Sys., 1992, pp. 400-407.
11. Liu, C. and Yu, C., *Performance Issues in Distributed Query Processing.*IEEE Trans. on Parallel and Distributed Systems, 1993 (to appear).
12. Meng, W., Liu, C., Sun, W., and Yu, C., *Distributed Database System Performance Prediction.* CS-TR-92-18, Dept. of CS, State Univ. of NY at Binghamton, 1992.
13. Mikkilineni, K.P. and Su, S.Y.W., *Evaluation of Relational Join Algorithms in a Pipelined Query Processing Environment.* IEEE TSE, Vol.14, No.6, 1988.
14. Pramanik, Sakti, *Performance Analysis of a Database Filter Search Hardware,* IEEE Trans. on Computer, Vol.35, No.12, Dec. 1986, pp. 1077-1082.
15. Pu, C. and J. M. Wha, *Performance Evaluation of Global Reading of Entire Databases* , Int'l Symposium on Databases in Parallel and Distributed Systems, Austin, Dec. 1988, pp. 167-176.
16. Segev, A., *Optimizing 2-way Joins in Horizontally Partitioned Database Systems.* Computer Journal, Vol.30, No.5, Oct. 1987, pp. 458-468.
17. Stonebraker, M. and Neuhold, E., *A Distributed Data Base Version of INGRES,* Second Berkeley Workshop on Distributed Data Management and Computer Networks, Berkeley, CA, 1977, pp. 19-36.
18. Yu, C.T., et al., *Query Processing in a Fragmented Relational Distributed System: Mermaid.* IEEE TSE, Aug. 1985, pp. 795-810.
19. Yu, C.T., Guh, K. C., Brill, D., Chen., A.L.P., *Partition Strategy for Distributed Query Processing in Fast Local Networks,*IEEE TSE, June, 1989, pp. 780-793.
20. Yu, C.T., and Chang, C.C., *Distributed Query Processing.* ACM Computing Surveys, Vol.16, No.4, December 1984, pp. 399-433.
21. Yu, P.S. and Dias, D.M., *Performance Analysis of Optimistic Concurrency Control Schemes for Systems with Large Memory,* Proc. of SIGMETRICS, 1989, pp. 238.
22. Yu, C. and Liu, C., *Experiences with Distributed Query Processing* , Proc. IEEE Data Engineering, Feb. 1990, pp. 192-199.

CoBase: A COOPERATIVE QUERY ANSWERING FACILITY FOR DATABASE SYSTEMS*

Wesley W. Chu
Department of Computer Science, University of California
Los Angeles, CA 90024

Abstract. A new generation of database that integrates knowledge base technology with database systems is presented for providing cooperative (approximate and conceptual) query answering. Based on the database schema and application characteristics, data are organized into type abstraction hierarchies. The higher levels of the hierarchy provide a more abstract data representation than the lower levels. Generalization (moving up in the hierarchy), specialization (moving down in the hierarchy) and association (moving between hierarchies) are the three key operations in deriving cooperative query answers. A relaxation manager is included to provide control for query relaxations. An Explanation System is also included to describe the relaxation process and provide the nearness of the approximate answer. We have demonstrated the feasibility and functionality of CoBase on top of a transportation relational database. The CoBase methodology has also been adopted in the knowledge based multimedia medical distributed database project [5] at UCLA.

1 Introduction

Consider asking a query of a human expert. If the query you pose has no answer, or the complete data for an answer is not available, you do not simply get a null response. The human expert attempts to understand the gist of your query, suggesting or answering related questions, inferring an answer from data that is accessible, giving an approximate answer. The goal of cooperative database research is to create computer databases with these characteristics [8]. The key is the integration into the database system of a knowledge base which can represent the data semantics.

In conventional database, if required data is missing, if an exact answer is unavailable, or if a query is not well-formed with respect to the schema, the database just returns a null answer or an error. An intelligent system would be much more resourceful and cooperative, permitting conceptual level queries (containing concepts that may not be expressed in the database schema) when the user does not know the precise schema, providing approximate answers when some data is missing, or even volunteering associative (relevant) information to the query answer. Cuppens and Demolombe [6] provide cooperative answers by rewriting the query to add variables to the query vector, which carry relevant information to the user. The rewrite is not a generalization of the query,

*This research is supported by DARPA contract N00174-91-C-0107.

rather, it extends the query to provide more information. Motro [15] proposes allowing the user to select the direction of relaxation and thus to indicate which relaxed answers may be of interest. Hemerly, et.al [10] uses a predefined user model and maintains a log of previous interactions to avoid misconstruals when providing additional information. All the above approaches are rule-based and difficult to scale up. To remedy such shortcomings, we are developing a knowledge-based facility for providing a structured approach to cooperative query answering in database (CoBase). Gaasterland [9] uses a similar approach for query relaxation, but presented in terms of logic programming. They also propose several relaxation control strategies.

In this paper we shall first present the concept of type abstraction hierarchy [2] to provide a structured approach to query modification and explicit cooperative operators for query relaxation. Next, we present the cooperative SQL primitives and selected examples. Then, we discuss relaxation control for providing efficient query processing and filtering out unsuitable answers for the user. We then present the pattern-based approach for providing association information to query answers. Finally, we discuss the technology transfer of CoBase to transportation and medical database applications.

2 Structured Approach to Cooperative Query Answering

Cooperative query answering relaxes a query scope to enlarge the search range, or relaxes an answer scope to include additional information. Enlarging and shrinking a query scope can be accomplished by viewing the queried objects at different conceptual levels, since an object representation has wider coverage at a higher level, and, inversely, narrower coverage at a lower level. Although linking different level object representations can be made in terms of explicit rules [6], such linking lacks a systematic organization to guide the query transformation process. To remedy this problem, we propose the notion of a *type abstraction hierarchy* (TAH) [2,4] for providing an efficient and organized framework for cooperative query processing. TAH emphasizes the abstract representation of object instances (Fig. 1). For example, "runway_length_range" in the domain of *range* (e.g. 4,000 to 8,000 ft.) is a more abstract representation than "runway length" in the domain of *length* (e.g. 6,000 ft). Abstraction of atomic values can be *combined* to form abstraction of complex values. For example,

Airport(location, runway length, runway width, parking space)

can have a more abstract representation

Airport(location area, runway length range, runway width range, parking area)

Since a higher-level and more abstract object representation corresponds to multiple lower-level and more specialized object representations, querying an abstractly represented object is equivalent to querying multiple specialized objects. In general, such an abstraction can enlarge the scope of a concept and relate neighborhood or associative concepts through high-level object representations or the rules referencing these representations.

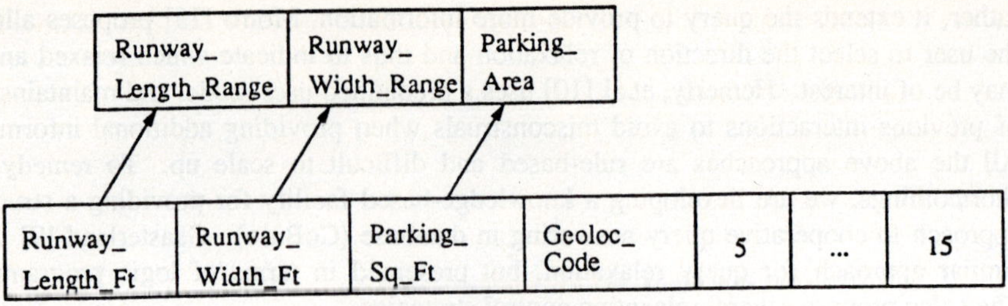

1a. Tuple Abstraction Hierarchy

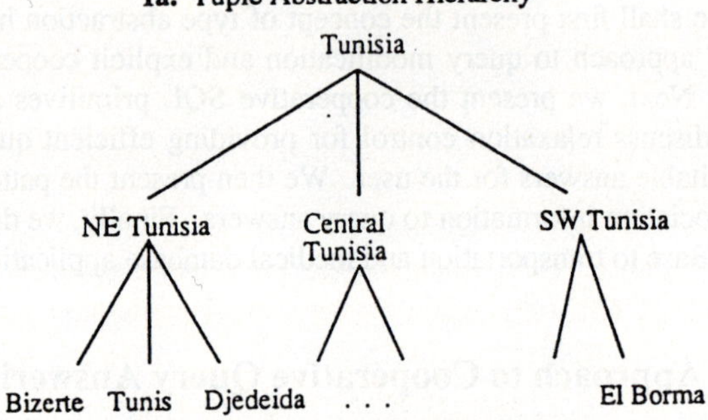

1b. Attribute Value Abstraction Hierarchy

Figure 1. Type Abstraction Hierarchies

The notion of multi-level object representation is not captured by the conventional semantic network and object-oriented database approaches for the following reasons: Grouping objects into a class and grouping several classes into a super-class only provide a common "title" (type) for the involved objects without concern for the object instance values and without introducing abstract object representations. Grouping several objects together and identifying their aggregation as a single (complex) object does not provide abstract instance representations for its component objects. Therefore, an object-oriented database deals with information only at two general layers: the meta-layer and the instance layer. Since forming an object-oriented type hierarchy does not introduce new instance values, it is impossible to introduce an additional instance layer. In the proposed type abstraction hierarchy, instances of a super-type and a sub-type may have different representations and can be viewed at different instance layers. Such multiple layer knowledge representation is essential for cooperative query answering.

Transferring a query between different abstraction levels is achieved by *query abstraction* and *query refinement*. Such a process consists of converting object types, attribute names, and domain values between different knowledge levels. A *query refinement process* converts a query Q to more specific query representations according to the type abstraction hierarchy.

The query modification, either upward or downward, is invoked recursively depending on the requirement and knowledge availability. Since TAH depends on query and application contexts, they are localized and will be small in size. Further, TAH provides a structured way for query modification which is different from the rule-based approach [6]. Thus, using our proposed structured approach to derive cooperative query answering is scalable to problems with large knowledge and data bases. We have developed techniques to generate TAH automatically from databases when given an application context and a set of queries [13].

Query modification may also be specified explicitly by the user through a set of cooperative operations with a pre-specified relaxation range and specification. Therefore, we have extended SQL to CSQL to include these cooperative operations as well as the relaxation control operations, which will be discussed in the next section.

3 Cooperative SQL (CSQL)

3.1 CSQL Cooperative Operators

The cooperative operations consist of the following four types: context free, context sensitive, control, and interactive operations.

Context free operations. *Approximate* operator, ^, relaxes the specified values within the approximate range that is predefined by the user. For example, ^9am will be changed to the interval (8am, 10am).

Between specifies the interval for an attribute. For example, time *between* (7am, 9am) transforms into (7am, 10am). The transformed interval is prespecified either by the user or the system.

Within specifies a set membership for an attribute value. For example, airport *within* {'LAX','BURBANK'}

Context sensitive. *Near-to* is used for specification of geographical nearness. For example, *near-to* 'Bizerte' requests the list of cities located within a certain Euclidean distance (depending on the context) from the city 'Bizerte'.

Similar-to is used to specify a set of objects semantically similar to the given object. It is a multiple attribute operator with a weight assigned to each of the attributes. The attributes may be also be expressed in non-numerical values for specifying the similarity abstractions. The similarity set is derived from the pre-specified nearness ranking formula. The size of this set is bound by a pre-specified nearness threshold.

Control Operators. *Relaxation-order* specifies the order of the relaxation. For example, *relaxation-order (runway_length runway_width)* indicates that if no exact answer is found, then *runway_length* should be relaxed first. If still no answer is found, then relax the runway width.

Not-relaxable specifies the attributes that should not be relaxed. For example, *not-relaxable (location_name)* indicates that condition clause containing *location_name* must not be relaxed.

User/System interaction operators. *Nearer, Further* provide the user with ability to control the relaxation scope of *near-to* interactively. *Nearer* reduces the distance by a pre-specified percentage, while *further* increases the distance by a pre-specified percentage.

3.2 Examples

In this section we present a few selected examples that illustrate the capabilities of the cooperative operators. The corresponding TAHs used for query modification are shown in Fig. 1 and the relaxable ranges are shown in Table 1.

Approximate operator relaxation range:

Relation Name	Attribute Name	∧ Range
aports	runway_length_ft	500
aports	runway_width_ft	10
aports	parking_sq_ft	100000
geoloc	latitude	0.001
geoloc	longitude	0.001

Near-to operator relaxation range:

Relation Name	Attribute Name	Near-To Range	Near/Further
aports	aport_name	100 miles	50%
geoloc	location_name	200 miles	50%

Table 1. Relaxation Range for the Approximate and Near-to Operators

Query 1. List all the airports with the runway length greater than 7500 feet and runway width greater than 100 feet. If there is no answer, relax the runway length condition first. The following is the corresponding CSQL query:

select aport_name, runway_length_ft, runway_width_ft
from _aports
where runway_length_ft > 7500
and runway_width_ft > 100
relaxation-order runway_length_ft, runway_width_ft

Based on the TAH on runway length and also the relaxation order, we relaxed the query to:

select aport_name, runway_length_ft, runway_width_ft
from _aports
where runway_length_ft ≥ 7000
and runway_width_ft > 100

If this query yielded no answer, then we proceed to relax the range *runway width*.

Query 2. Find all the cities with their geographical coordinates near the city Bizerte in the country Tunisia. If there is no answer, the restriction on the country should not be relaxed. The near-to range in this case is pre-specified at 100 miles. The corresponding CSQL query is as follows:

select location_name, latitude, longitude
from geoloc
where location_name near-to 'Bizerte'
and country_state_name = 'Tunisia'
not-relaxable country_state_name

Based on the TAH on location Tunisia, the relaxed version of the query:

select location_name, latitude, longitude

from geoloc
where location_name *in* {'Bizerte', 'Djedeida',
'Gafsa,'Gabes', 'Sfax', 'Sousse', 'Tabarqa','Tunis'}
and country_state_name_= 'Tunisia'

Query 3. Find all the airports in Tunisia *similar to* the Bizerte airport. Use the attributes *runway_length_ft, runway_width_ft* as criteria for similarity. Place more similarity emphasis on runway length than runway width; their corresponding weight assignments are 2.0 and 1.0, respectively. The following is the *CSQL* version of the query:

select aport_name
from _aports, geoloc
where aport_name *similar-to* 'Bizerte'
based-on ((runway_length_ft 2.0) (runway_width_ft 1.0))
and country_state_name_ = 'TUNISIA'
and geoloc.geo_code = _aports.geo_code

To select the set of the names of the airports that have the runway length and runway width similar to the ones for the airport in Bizerte. We shall first find all the airports in Tunisia, and therefore transform the query to:

select aport_name
from _aports, geoloc
where country_state_name_ = 'TUNISIA'
and geoloc.geo_code = _aports.geo_code

After retrieving all the airports in Tunisia, based on the runway length and runway width and their corresponding weights, the similarity of these airports to "Bizerte" can be computed by the pre-specified nearness formula (e.g. weighted mean squared error) [14]. The order in the similarity set is ranked according to the nearness measure, and the size of the similarity set is determined by the pre-specified nearness threshold.

4 Relaxation Control

When a query is not answerable, some of its attribute values can be relaxed to provide a wider search scope. As a result, approximate answers are derived. However, without control over relaxation, we may generate more approximations than the user can handle. For example, if we are looking for an airport with a 7000 ft. runway in Bizerte, and assuming that there is no airport in Bizerte which meets the specifications, there are many ways to relax the query in terms of location and runway length. The generalization/specialization operations effectively broaden the search scope of the original query. If, in addition, we know that the user is interested only in the airports in NE and SW Tunisia, and does not wish to shorten the required runway length, the system can eliminate the search in the Central Tunisia, and also avoid airports with short runways, as shown in Fig. 2. As a result, we can limit the query relaxation to a narrower scope by trimming the type abstraction hierarchies. Thus, the system's performance and the relevance of the answer is improved.

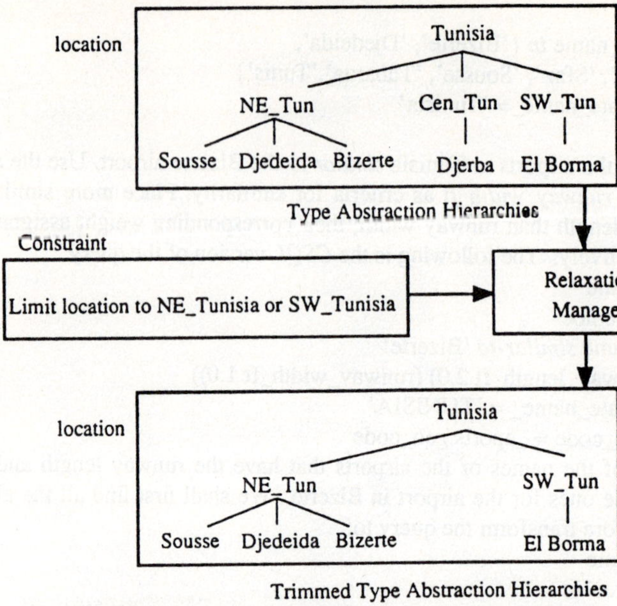

Figure 2. Relaxation Manager using the trimmed TAH

The policy for relaxation control depends on many factors, including user profile, query context, attribute relaxation order (e.g. relax location first, then runway length), relaxation level, and the number of answers as well as rules to combine these factors over multiple attributes. The *Relaxation Manager* combines these rules via certain policies (minimizing search time or nearness, for example) to restrict the search for approximate answers.

Figure 3 shows an overview of the CoBase architecture. CoBase stores the Type Abstraction Hierarchy and relaxation ranges for the explicit cooperators in a LOOM [11] knowledge base. LOOM is a knowledge representation system developed at USC/ISI. When CoBase asks queries, it can either use the Paramax Loom Interface Module (LIM), or directly query the underlying relational database (eg. Oracle and SyBase).

CoBase's control mechanisms include a graphical user interface and an Explanation System. The relaxation manager controls the search for approximate answers by directing the individual relaxation modules. Each module is a separate relaxation operator. The architecture is highly modular allowing easy expansion and modification to the system.

Figure 4 depicts the data flow of the CoBase System. When a query is presented to CoBase, the system first relaxes any explicit cooperative operators in the query. The modified query is then presented to the underlying database system for execution. If no answers are returned, then the cooperative query system, under the direction of the Relaxation Manager, relaxes the queries by query modification using the trimmed type abstraction hierarchies. The relaxed query is executed, and, if there is no answer due to overtrimmed TAHs, the relaxation manager will deactivate certain relaxation rules, restoring part of a trimmed TAH to broaden the search scope until an answer is found.

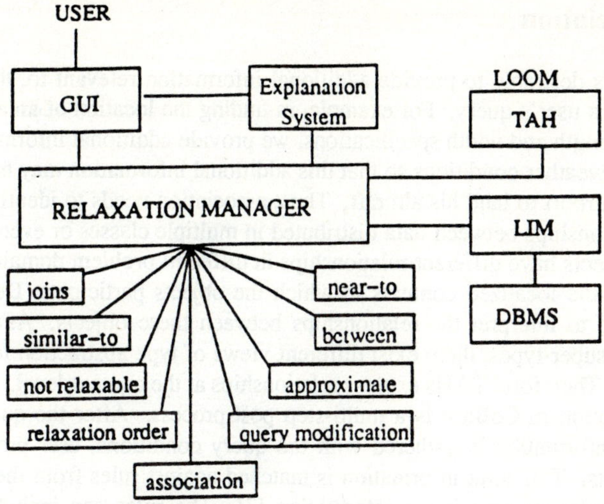

Figure 3. CoBase Architecture

When an approximate answer is returned, the user may wish for an explanation of how the answer was derived, or to be presented with an annotated relaxation path. A context-based semantic nearness will be provided, allowing the system to rank the approximate answers (in order of nearness) against the specified query. A graphical user interface displays the query, query results, TAHs and explanations of the relaxation processes. A user is able to construct his own TAH of an attribute, tuples or types, and is also able to modify the existing TAH in the KB. There is a directory/dictionary of KB that specifies all the available TAH's in the system.

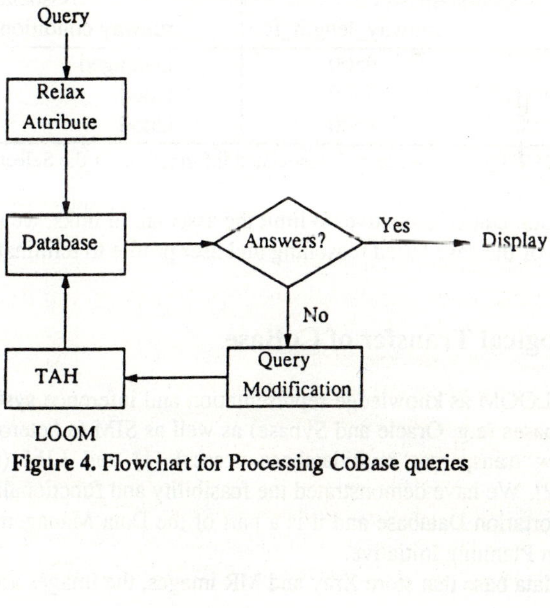

Figure 4. Flowchart for Processing CoBase queries

5 Association

Often it is desirable to provide additional information relevant to, though not explicitly stated in, a user's query. For example, in finding the location of an airport satisfying the runway length and width specifications, we provide additional information about the runway and weather conditions so that this additional information may help the pilot select a suitable airport to land his aircraft. Thus, association needs to identify the dependencies and relationships between data distributed in multiple classes or even multiple databases. Since objects have different relationships in different problem domains, it is necessary to focus on the localized contexts in which the objects participate. Domain knowledge is then used to interpret the relationships between these objects. As an object can have multiple super-types, there exist different views of type abstraction for different problem contexts. Therefore, TAHs express relationships at the context level.

Association in CoBase is a multi-step post-process. After the query is executed, the answer information is gathered with the query conditions, user profile and application constraints. This joint information is matched against rules from the knowledge base to identify relevant associative information [3]. The rules can include any CoBase construct, such as conceptual conditions (e.g. runway_length_ft = *short*) or explicitly cooperative operations (city *near-to* 'Bizerte'). For example, consider the query

select name, runway_length_ft
from airports
where runway_length_ft > 6000

Based on the joint information, associated information on runway conditions and weather for the corresponding airports is retrieved from the knowledge base. The associated information is appended to the query answer, as shown in Table 2.

Query Answer		Associated Info	
name	runway_length_ft	runway condition	weather
Jerba	9500	Damaged	Sunny
Monastir	6500	Good	Foggy
Tunis	8500	Good	Good

Table 2. Query Answer and Associated Information for the Selected Airports.

Since association can be transitive, to limit the association links, we are currently investigating the use of the case based reasoning and user profile to terminate the association.

6 Technological Transfer of CoBase

CoBase uses LOOM as knowledge representation and inference system and supports relational data bases (e.g. Oracle and Sybase) as well as SIM (a heterogeneous distribution layer to allow transparent multidatabase access) [1] and LIM (the Loom Interface Module) [7,12]. We have demonstrated the feasibility and functionality of CoBase on top of the Transportation Database and it is a part of the Data Management provision of the Transportation Planning Initiative.

In medical data base that store Xray and MR images, the images are evolution and temporal based. Further, these images need to be retrieved by object feature or contents rather than patient ID. The queries asked are often conceptual and not precisely defined. We need to use knowledge about the application (e.g. age class, ethnic class, disease class, bone age etc.), user profile and query context to derive such queries [5]. Further, to match the feature exactly is very difficult if not impossible. For example, if the query "Find the treatment methods used for tumors on 12-year-old Korean males," can not be answered, based on the TAH shown in Fig. 5, we can relax "tumors " to "tumor class X", and "12-year-old Korean male" to "pre-teen Asian," which results in the following relaxed query: "Find the treatment methods used for the tumor class X on pre-teen Asians." Further, we can obtain such relevant information as the *success rate, side effects,* and *cost of the treatment* from the association operations. As a result, query relaxation and modification are essential to process these queries. We have applied the CoBase technology to the medical imaging data base. The TAH can be constructed based on the available application domain and medical knowledge available in the textbooks and/or literatures. Once the TAH's for the medical domain and application have been constructed, query relaxation and modification can then be carried out in the same manner as in the transportation domain.

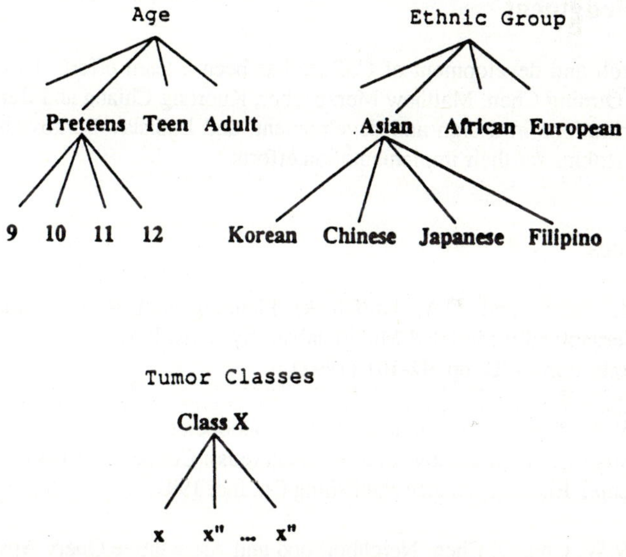

Figure 5. Type Abstraction Hierarchies for the Medical Query Example

We are currently working on the explanation system to provide effective summary of the relaxation process and the estimation of nearness measure. The explanation is particularly useful when the relaxation involves in multi-variables.

7 Conclusions

We have presented a structured approach that uses *type abstraction hierarchy* for providing query modification. Such an approach provides multi-level knowledge representation, and is also scalable to large systems. We have also extended the SQL and LIM to CSQL and CLIM. These extended languages consist of cooperative operators that allow the user to explicitly specify relaxation ranges and relaxation control. Based on user profile and application contexts, the relaxation manager limits the search scope and also filters out the unsuitable answers. To provide relevant information to the query answers, a *pattern-based* framework is used for deriving associative (relevant) information. An explanation facility is included which summarizes the query modifications and relaxation process, and also provides the nearness of the approximate answer to the exact answer. CoBase stemmed from the Transportation Planning application, which requires querying a large number of databases with different schemas. It has also been implemented on a knowledge-based medical imaging database, which provides approximate answers to medical queries.

Acknowledgment

The research and development of CoBase has been a team effort. I would like to acknowledge Qiming Chen, Matthew Merzbacher, Kuorong Chiang and Berthier Ribeiro for their contributions in design and development, and Ladislav Berkovich, Gladys Chow, and Jason Robins for their implementation efforts.

References

1. Y. Arens and C.A. Knoblock: Planning and Reformulating Queries for Semantically-Modeled Multidatabase Systems. ISMM International Conference: Baltimore, MD, pp. 92-101 (1992)

2. W.W. Chu, Q. Chen and R. Lee: Cooperative Query Answering via Type Abstraction Hierarchy. In S.M. Deen (eds): Cooperating Knowledge Based Systems. Elsevier Science Publishing Co. Inc, 1991.

3. W.W. Chu, Q. Chen: Neighborhood and Associative Query Answering. Journal of Intelligent Information Systems, Vol. 1, No.3/4, 355-382 (1992)

4. W.W. Chu, Q. Chen: A Structured Approach for Cooperative Query Answering. To appear in the IEEE Transactions on Knowledge and Data Engineering (1994)

5. W.W. Chu, A.F. Cardenas, and R. Taira: A Knowledge-based Multimedia Medical Distributed Database System - KMeD. Technical Report 93-005. UCLA Computer Science Department (1993)

6. F. Cuppens, R. Demolombe: Cooperative Answering: A Methodology to Provide Intelligent Access to Databases. Proc. of the 2nd international conference on expert database systems, pp 333-353 (1989)

7. T.W. Finin, D.P. McKay and A. O'Hare: The Intelligent Database Interface. Proceedings of the 7th National Conference on Artificial Intelligence (AAAI), Artificial Intelligence (1990)

8. T. Gaasterland, P. Godfrey and J. Minker: An Overview of Cooperative Answering. Journal of Intelligent Information Systems. Vol 1. 123-157 (1992)

9. T. Gaasterland, P. Godfrey and J. Minker: Relaxation as a Platform for Cooperative Answering. Journal of Intelligent Information Systems. Vol 1. 293-321 (1992)

10. A. Hemerly, M. Casanova and A. Furtado: Exploiting User Models to Avoid Misconstruals. Proc. of the Workshop on Non-Standard Queries and Answers: Vol. 2, Tolouse, France (1991)

11. R. MacGregor: The Evolving Technology of Classification Based Knowledge Representation Systems. Workshop on Formal Aspects of Semantic Networks (1989)

12. D.P. McKay, J. Pastor and T.W. Finin: View-Concepts: Knowledge-Based Access to Databases. ISMM International Conference, pp. 84-91 (1992)

13. M. Merzbacher, W.W. Chu: Pattern-Based Clustering for Database Attribute Values. AAAI Workshop on Knowledge Discovery (1993)

14. A. Motro: VAGUE: A User Interface to Relational Databases that Permits Vague Queries. ACM Transactions on Office Information Systems. 187-214 (1987)

15. A. Motro: FLEX: A Tolerant and Cooperative User Interface to Databases. IEEE Transactions on Knowledge and Data Engineering. 231-245 (1990)

"Duplicate Deletion in a Ring Connected, Shared-Nothing, Parallel Database System"

Abdelguerfi M., Grant K[1]., Murphy E., Patterson W.[1]
Computer Science
University of New Orleans
New Orleans, LA 70148

Stelly J.
Mathematics
University of New Orleans
New Orleans, LA 70148

Abstract. The problem of detecting and removing duplicates tuples within a parallel database is one which has far reaching implications. An efficient solution for these problems would have a positive impact in many areas of Computer Science. We have compared the performance of three algorithms for duplicate detection and removal in a ring-connected, shared-nothing, parallel database system. Each algorithm uses a different pre-processing method to reduce the size of the data set which must be processed. It is shown that in a parallel environment (as described above) pre-processing of the database (in the algorithms we've tested) achieves too little reduction in run-time to offset the added cost of its execution.

1 Introduction

Detecting and removing duplicates [1,2] appears in a number of applications such as relational and object oriented databases, protocol verification and image processing. For example, in relational databases, primitive operations such as projection, set union, aggregate functions, etc.., generally require the detection and removal of duplicates.

Duplicate detection and removal is a computationally intensive task. In the past, several specialized architectures were proposed to improve the performance of this operation. In [3], a bus connected cellular array of specialized processing elements is used to detect and filter out duplicates. ICL's Content Addressable File Store (CAFS) is a specialized add-on hardware accelerator that uses a bit-array filtering technique to perform duplicate detection and removal [4].

Recent trends in database technology suggest that the efficient handling of very large databases can be best undertaken by shared-nothing [5] parallel database systems [6]. Unlike conventional mainframes, the above parallel systems can usually be scaled up to meet future performance needs of conventional database software.

In this paper, three parallel algorithms for the duplicate detection and removal operation on a unidirectional, ring-connected, message-passing, parallel database system are analyzed and compared. The effect on parallel algorithms of the number of processors, the size of the horizontal fragments, tuple size, and the duplication factor is investigated. It is shown that in a parallel environment (as described above) pre-processing of the database (in the algorithms we've tested) achieves too little reduction in run-time to offset the added cost of its execution. The experimental vehicle is a unidirectionally ring-connected array of general purpose T800 NMOS

[1]The work of Dr. Wayne Patterson and Kevin Grant was funded in part by The Louisiana Consortium for Computing Science and Engineering (LCCSE).

transputers (see Figure 1). The ring topology is attractive for parallel processing because of its simplicity and ease of scale.

2 Description of Programs

Each of the three programs used in this research contains at least one phase during which local duplicate removal is performed. When this is done, it occurs in parallel in each node of the ring simultaneously. Teuhola and Wegner's local duplicate removal algorithm (known as "DDT") was used for this purpose because of its minimal space requirement and average linear time complexity [7,8].

The global duplicate detection scheme used in one of our three programs uses hash based bit-array. Specifically, this technique involves the construction of a bit-array in each node by applying a hashing function (the same function is used by all nodes) to each tuple stored within that node. Each application of the hashing function to a tuple yields an index into the bit-array. The indexed bit is then set. Bit-arrays are passed around the ring and processed at each node until each bit-array has been processed for every tuple at every node except for the one at which it finally arrives (which is also its node of origin). This node may use this completely processed bit-array to determine which of its locally stored tuples may or may not be duplicates of other tuples stored at other nodes around the ring. It does this by applying the hashing function to all of the tuples stored locally and checking the bit of the bit-array at the site indicated by the hashing function. A value of "0" in this location indicates that there is no duplicate tuple to be found at any other node (note that this does not rule out the possibility of a duplicate tuple residing at the same node). If such a duplicate tuple had existed the bit being examined would have been set when the bit-array was processed at the node in which the duplicate existed. A "1" in this location indicates that the tuple may or may not have a duplicate elsewhere around the ring. This is so because it is possible for two different tuples to hash to the same location in the bit-array.

Either of the two preprocessing techniques discussed above has the same effect upon the duplicate deletion program. Specifically, each technique partitions the set of tuples stored locally into two groups. The first group does not need to be hashed around the ring. In the algorithm in which the local duplicate removal preprocessing technique is used (DHD) this is because the first group of tuples are those tuples which have been determined to be duplicates of other tuples stored at the same site. These tuples can be deleted immediately. In the algorithm in which the global duplicate removal preprocessing technique is used (Bit-Array) the first group contains those tuples such that we already know that there is no duplicate of any of those tuples anywhere else within the ring. These tuples can be stored locally as being unique provided that before doing so the algorithm checks for the presence of duplicates within this group.

2.1 The First Algorithm — Hash-DDT (HD)

Our first algorithm does not contain a preprocessing step. It is included to enable us to determine the degree of advantage or disadvantage in using any preprocessing step at all. The algorithm performs as follows:

> We assume as our initial state that all of the tuples upon which the algorithm is to work are distributed evenly around the ring in a random fashion.

Each tuple is then hashed on those attributes within itself whose duplicates we wish to remove from around the ring. The hashed tuple is then passed around the ring to that node which is the result of the hashing function.

At this point, it must be the case that for any tuple in the database for which duplicates exist, the tuple and all of its duplicates are all contained within the same node. We then perform a phase of local duplicate removal.

As all duplicates have now been removed from the database we pass all of the remaining tuples around the ring to the front end for presentation to the user.

This is equivalent to allowing the user of a database distributed in this fashion to do a projection on the set of tuples and then have all duplicates removed from the set of tuples created by this operation.

2.2 The Second Algorithm - DDT-Hash-DDT (DHD)

The second algorithm is identical to the first except that before the tuples are hashed around the ring they are preprocessed by being passed through the local duplicate removal algorithm. This was done to avoid wasting run-time by passing around the ring tuples whose status as duplicates can be determined locally.

2.3 The Third Algorithm - Bit-Array (BA)

The third algorithm is identical to the first in all ways save that before the tuples are hashed around the ring we construct and pass around the ring a bit-array to which information about the tuples contained therein is added at each node. Upon its return to its node of origin the bit-array contains information about the tuples present in every node around the ring except for those at its point of origin. Each tuple is then compared against the bit-array as a result of which many of those tuples which do not have duplicates residing elsewhere around the ring are identified immediately and stored locally as being unique without having to be hashed around the ring and processed at another site.

3 Comparison of Performance

3.1 The Global Approach

A "global approach" to duplicate detection and removal is any approach in which, for a given node, information is gathered from all other nodes and used to determine the uniqueness of tuples stored at that node. The Bit-Array algorithm is an example of this. The information gathered by a node allows it to pre-determine the uniqueness of many, but not necessarily all, of the unique items stored locally.

Our work suggests that the processing time used by techniques of this nature will tend to suffer due to a hidden feature of this approach. In order to be accomplished by all of the nodes in a network, each node must gather information about the tuples stored at all other nodes. The information gathered by any node will be different from the information gathered by any other node, as the information a node uses to judge the uniqueness of its own tuples must not contain information about the presence of its own tuples in the network (otherwise all of the tuples in every node would show up as duplicates all of the time). Thus, a network of N nodes must produce N different collections (in our case, bit-arrays) of such information, each of which must contain information about the tuples stored at the other N-1 nodes. The complexity of this operation is thus: $N \times (N-1) \times (|R|/N)$ where $|R|$ is the size of the set of all tuples distributed around the ring and optimal parallelism is assumed. This simplifies to $|R| \times (N-1)$. From this it can be seen that the run-time of algorithms using this approach will suffer not only as the number of tuples contained within the network increases, but also as the number of nodes of which the network is constructed increases. This happens because with each increase in the number of nodes in the network, each bit-array must include information about more and more tuples (all tuples except the shrinking few stored within the node for which the information is being gathered). The overhead time needed to transmit the bit-arrays from node to node will also increase as the number of nodes increases.

The important question is whether or not the decrease in run-time gained by the use of such a pre-processing strategy will more than offset the extra time used in executing it. With regards to the Bit-Array algorithm, our results demonstrate that this is not the case.

3.2 The Local Approach

A "local approach" to duplicate detection and removal is any approach in which, for a given node, information already stored locally is used to determine the uniqueness of tuples stored at that node. The DHD algorithm is an example of this. As implemented in this algorithm, the information already stored within a node allows it to pre-determine the "duplicate-ness" of many, but not necessarily all, of the duplicate tuples stored locally. In most of the cases that we studied the percentage of the sets of duplicates that will be contained within the same node after a random distribution of tuples is such a small percentage of the total that an insufficient number of duplicate tuples are pre-processed out of consideration to offset the extra run-time taken up by the pre-processing algorithm. It must be noted, however, that comparisons between the DHD algorithm and the HD algorithm (which is identical to DHD except that it contains no pre-processing step) indicate that in most cases the extra work saved by this pre-processing strategy *almost* completely offsets the extra run-time necessary to execute it.

Number of Tuples vs. Time. The distance between the run-times of the Bit-Array and DHD algorithms holds almost constant over the entire range of data taken. While not easily seen in the graph, the run-time of the algorithm HD drops away from both of them to the extent of about a third of a second. With both pre-processing techniques, the amount of time saved by the pre-processing step fails to compensate for the amount of work that must be done to execute it. The more tuples that the pre-processing routine must process the more that this disadvantage adds up. This suggests that there would be no point further along in the graph (at points with higher values for the "number of tuples parameter") at which any of these lines will cross over each other. Thus the HD algorithm consistently shows the best performance.

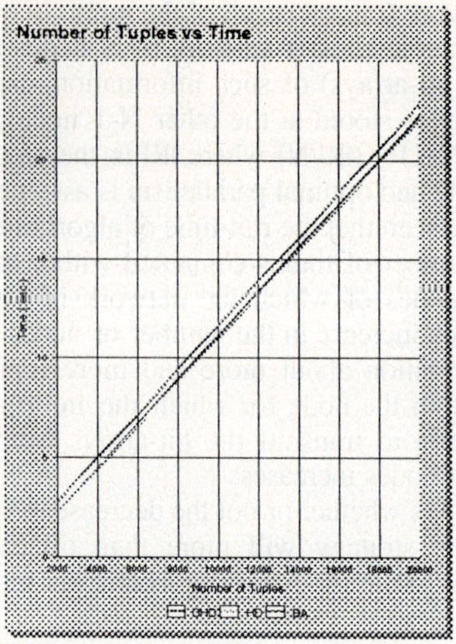

Fig. 1 Tuple size = 295 INT16's (590 bytes). Ring Size = 10 nodes.
Percentage Duplication » 27%

Tuple Size vs. Time. The difference between the run-times for the HD and Bit-Array algorithms is almost constant over the range of this graph. DHD's run-time, however, drops away from both HD and Bit-Array's run-times to the extent of about four tenths of a second over the range covered by this graph. While DHD starts out using more run-time than HD, the run-times for the two algorithms converge at a tuple size of about 295 INT16's or 590 bytes. From these trends, we can conclude that the DHD algorithm will perform better for all tuple sizes beyond 590 bytes and that the Bit Array algorithm will never outperform either of the others.

Fig. 2 Number of Tuples = 20,000. Ring Size = 10 nodes.
Percentage Duplication ≈ 27%

Ring Size vs. Time. There are two primary influences on the nature of the graph of ring size vs. time. First, the time that it takes to hash all of the randomly distributed tuples into their destination nodes increases linearly with an increase in the number of nodes in the ring (remember that the number of tuples in the system is held constant). Second, the run-time of the local duplicate removal subroutine used by all three of these algorithms decreases linearly (on the average) with decreases in the number of tuples that must be processed (with each increase in the size of the ring, the number of tuples that must be processed by each node decreases). The rise in the run-time of the algorithms in this graph is the result of both of these effects acting on each of these three algorithms simultaneously (the fact that the graphs of the run-times are curved, rather than linear, as the above would suggest, is because we are graphing time against the number of nodes in the ring, not the number of tuples being processed by each node) . In no case does the time gained by the greater parallelization of the local duplicate removal step offset the greater amount of hashing that must be done to execute it. The Bit-Array algorithm suffers more than the others here because of the extra hashing that it must do (when hashing the bit-arrays around the ring during the pre-processing step).

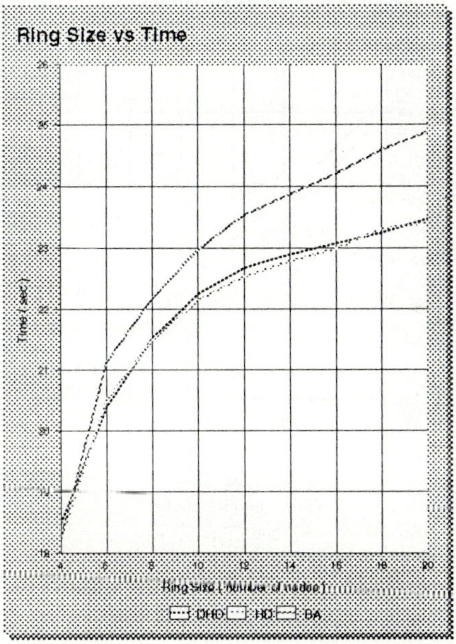

Fig. 3 Tuple size = 295 INT16's (590 bytes). Number of Tuples = 20,000.
Percentage Duplication ≈ 27%

Percent Duplication vs. Time. There are only two major components to the HD algorithm. First, all tuples are hashed around the ring into their perspective nodes. Second, the local duplicate removal subroutine is run at each node. The percentage of duplication of tuples can have little effect on the total time spent hashing tuples around the ring, as long as after all of the hashing is done the tuples are still more or less evenly distributed. This is true of the data sets used at all points on the graph except where there is 100 percent duplication (where all tuples are duplicates of each other). Hence we conclude that the primary cause for the behavior of the HD algorithm in this graph is the way in which the run-time of the local duplicate removal subroutine is affected by the percentage of duplication within its data set. This accords with the conclusions of the Teuhola and Wegner regarding their DDT algorithm. They state that the higher the percentage of duplication within the data set, the faster the DDT algorithm will run (when the size of the data set is held constant). As usual, the behavior of the other two algorithms is almost identical to that of HD (except that Bit-Array takes slightly longer to run in each case) leading us to believe that the effect of the percentage of duplication within its data set on the local duplicate removal subroutine is the primary determinant of the behavior of these two algorithms as well. The Bit-Array algorithm continues to take more time than the other two here because of the extra time spent processing the bit-array. We note that as the percentage of duplication increases, the number of tuples that the Bit-Array algorithm can pre-process out of consideration as being unique will decrease, leading to a slightly worsening run-time for the Bit-Array algorithm (relative to the other two). Close examination of the graph will reveal that this is, in fact, the case.

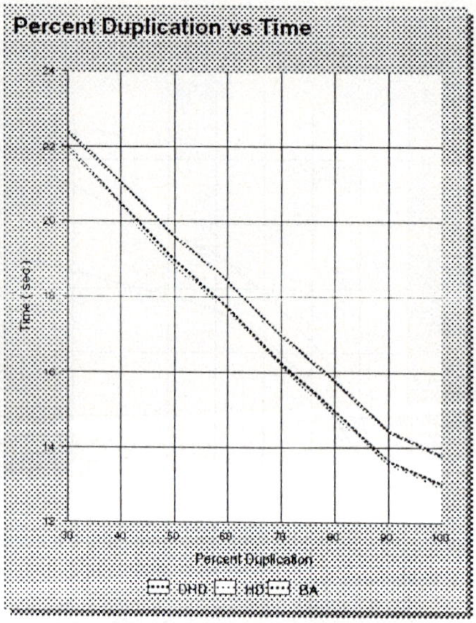

Fig. 4 Tuple size = 295 INT16's (590 bytes). Number of Tuples = 20,000.
Ring Size = 10 nodes

4 Conclusion

Our work leads us to believe that any "global approach" to the problem of pre-processing in a duplicate detection and removal algorithm on a unidirectional ring should be avoided. The primary reason for this is that algorithms of this type are prone to worsening performance as ring size is increased. Close examination of the problem suggests that this behavior would be exhibited on other network configurations as well. Our global approach program (Bit-Array) demonstrates this, and further indicates that there may be problems in finding global approach algorithms such that the run-time benefits gained from their use offset the run-time lost by their execution. The "local approach" to this problem suffers from the fact that that the chances of sets of duplicate tuples residing in the same node after a random distribution are so small, that the number of tuples thus found and removed is insufficient to offset the time used in executing this algorithm. It should be noted that some of the problems mentioned above are algorithm dependant, and it that may be possible to find more efficient local or global pre-processing algorithms who's run-time benefits do offset their deficits.

In almost all cases the algorithm HD outperformed the other two, although the run-time differences between HD and DHD were always minimal. Much of the data taken (particularly that appearing in the graph "percent duplication vs. time") suggests that the performance of all of these algorithms is largely determined by the behavior of the local duplicate removal algorithm used by each. The algorithm we selected performs better as the percentage of duplication is increased. This suggests that the performance of such a duplicate detection and removal algorithm may be optimized for the database in which it is being used via the selection of a local duplicate removal whose performance is optimal for the percentage of duplication most often encountered. It may also be possible to construct an adaptive algorithm that keeps statistics on the amount of duplication previously present and selects the best local duplicate removal algorithm based on its own estimation of present needs. Future work will include more testing of the algorithms with much larger data sets to determine how these algorithms will function in very large databases and an investigation into the effects (if any) that different amounts of data skewing (among the processors) will have on run-time.

References

1. Abdelguerfi, M., Sood, A.K., "Computational Complexity of Sorting and Joining Relations with Duplicates," *IEEE Transactions on Knowledge and Data Engineering*, in print, to appear December 1991.

2. Frieder, V. A. Topkar, R.K. Karne, and A. K. Sood, "Experimentation with Hypercube Database Engines", *IEEE Micro,* February 1992, pp.42-56.

3. Abdelguerfi, M., Sood, A.K., ""A Bus Connected Cellular Array Unit for Relational Database Machines, in Database Machines and Knowledge Base Machines, edited by M. Kitsuregawa, and H. Tanaka, 1988, Kluwer Academic Publishers, pp. 243-256

4. Maller, V.A., "Information Retrieval Using the Content Addressable File Store, *Proceedings of the IFIP-80 Congress,* North Holland, 1980, pp.187-190.

5. Stonebroker, M., "The Case for Shared-Nothing," *Database Engineering*, Vol. 9, No.1, 1986, pp.

6. Abdelguerfi, M., Lavington, S., "Parallel database and Knowledge-Base Systems," in: Emerging Trends in Database and Knowledge-Base Machines: the application of parallel architectures to smart information systems, (editors: M. Abdelguerfi and Simon Lavington), IEEE Computer Science Press, Advances Series, (to appear: September 1993).

7. Teuhola, J., Wegner, L., "Minimal Space Average Linear Time Duplication Deletion", *Communications of the ACM*, Vol. 34, No. 3, 1991, pp. 62-73

8. Teuhola, J., Wegner, L., "Technical Correspondence: Duplication Deletion Revisited", *Communications of the ACM*, Vol. 35, No. 7, 1992, pp. 99-107.

On Temporal-fuzziness in Temporal Fuzzy Databases

Werasak Kurutach
School of Computer Science and Engineering

James Franklin
School of Mathematics
The University of New South Wales, Australia

Abstract. We propose a framework for a database model unifying both imprecision and time aspects of data. Particularly, we emphasize that the fuzzy meanings of linguistic data can change with time; we call this property *temporal-fuzziness*. The major problems arising from the lack of the ability to handle this property have been studied, i.e. users and databases misinterpret the meaning of data. Thus, it is essential to treat temporal-fuzziness within an appropriate framework like ours. In our work, we employ concepts based on fuzzy set theory - possibility theory and linguistic variables - for modeling and evaluating uncertain/imprecise data from three domain types, i.e. quantitative, qualitative, and multivalued logic data domains. To model past data, the tuple time stamping method and the discrete time conceptual model are utilized. We introduce three kinds of measures for each domain type to evaluate data. They can provide upper bounded, lower bounded, and approximate answers to queries. Then, the Temporal Fuzzy Data Model and a metadatabase are proposed. The concept of metadatabase allows the time-variant property of fuzzy meanings to be modeled. Since based on the relational model, our model has a uniform and simple structure.

Key Words: fuzzy data, temporal data, time, temporal-fuzziness, measures, subjectivity, objectivity, qualitative data, quantitative data

1 Introduction

Imprecision and time are two important aspects of data and information used by human beings in various disciplines. Any data processing system supporting such activities needs to be able to handle them effectively. During the last decade, database models incorporating those two aspects of data have received extensive attention. Recently, temporal database researchers have taken into consideration the appearance of uncertainty and fuzziness in stamping time and time-varying data [5, 6, 8]. In the AI community, there are however several discussions on the connections among time, uncertainty, and fuzziness, which are inherent features of human knowledge [4, 13]. From another perspective, a major problem in handling both temporal and fuzzy data is the treatment of the meaning of fuzzy data represented as linguistic values. The meaning of a linguistic value can be defined as a fuzzy subset of a universe of discourse and characterized by a compatibility function, $c : U \rightarrow [0, 1]$. By the nature of the real world, the meaning of a fuzzy term can change with the context and the context is variable with time. Consequently, the meaning of a fuzzy term is time-variant, and we call this property *temporal-fuzziness*. For example, at two points in time, a fuzzy term *high salary* may have two different meanings in terms of dollars. Generally, fuzziness of data is measurable in either objective or subjective terms. For example, *Youth* is measurable in objective terms via *Age* while *Attractiveness* is purely subjective in nature. More precisely, the meaning of a fuzzy term of the former type (called *an objectively-based type*) can be expressed as a fuzzy subset of the objectively measurable values. This is not the case for the latter type (called *a subjectively-based type*).

In the literature on temporal and fuzzy databases, no researcher has considered the temporal-fuzziness property of fuzzy data. It has been implicitly assumed that the meaning of a fuzzy term stored in a database does not change. Since the primary aims of temporal fuzzy databases are to model more realistic and natural data, and to make information systems more intelligent, the assumption is a major obstacle. This work develops a framework for a database model which represents not only crisp/fuzzy data and their time aspect but also the meanings of fuzzy terms at various times. This contribution provides a further step in achieving those initial purposes. Now two major problems arising from the lack of an appropriate treatment of the temporal-fuzziness property shall be pointed out. The first problem is the misinterpretation of data which is represented in fuzzy terms, e.g. the meaning of the term *high* for the attribute SALARY in the database state at time t1 can be different from the meaning for the state at time t2. The other is the misinterpretation of query specifications which may be the expressions of linguistic values, so that the answer is not what the user expects, e.g. in the query "Give the names of employees who earned a high salary in 1985", it may not be clear whether the user aims at the meaning of *high salary* as of 1985 or as of the time the query is asked.

The paper is organized as follows. Section 2 presents an example and discusses the problems in queries. Section 3 reviews the primary concepts which are used as tools in our work. In section 4, we discuss the main types of domains which most databases concern, and propose the notions of their measures. Then, based on these, the model to handle temporal fuzzy data is proposed. A metadatabase to represent temporal-fuzziness of such data is described. Finally, section 5 concludes our work and discusses some possible extensions.

2 Example

This section determines problems in querying a simple temporal fuzzy database which has no support for the temporal-fuzziness property. To make it simple to discuss our main point, we will be concerned with *precise valid time* only. Valid time is the time when the event takes place in the real world [11].

We suppose a temporal fuzzy database comprising a relation whose schema is *Employee(Name, Age, Salary, Motivation)*. The following two snapshots of

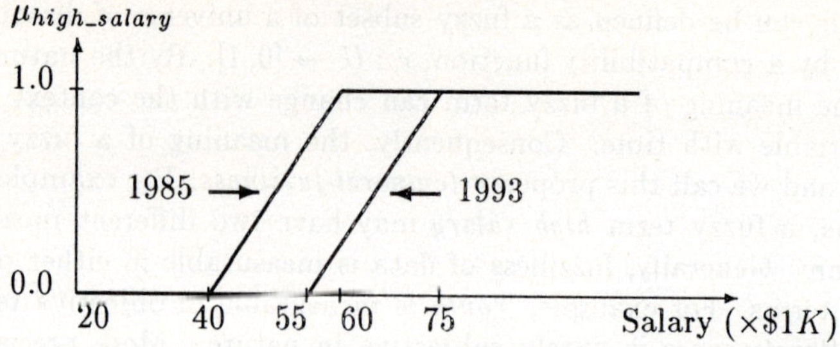

Figure 1: The meanings of *high salary* in 1985 and 1993

the database will be considered.

In *January 1985*, the state of the database is

Name	Age	Salary	Motivation
T. Jones	mid-age	$60K	high
J. Neil	young	$35K	low
N. Brooks	45	high	middle

In *January 1993*, the state of the database is

Name	Age	Salary	Motivation
T. Jones	mid-age	$77K	low
J. Neil	around-31	$60K	high
N. Brooks	53	$65K	middle

Age and *Salary* may have crisp or objectively-based fuzzy values. Let consider only *Salary* here and assume that the salaries of the employees are in the range $10K-$70K in 1985 and $20K-$90K in 1993. Such change may affect the interpretation of fuzzy data of *Salary*, i.e. the same fuzzy data at both times may have different meanings. The meaning of a fuzzy data value of *Salary* can be interpreted by defining a function to evaluate the grade of membership (the compatibility) for each value drawn from its corresponding domain. For example, the function defining the *high salary* in 1985 and 1993 might be expressed by Eqs. 1 and 2, respectively (see Figure 1). This is the temporal-fuzziness which arises in objective fuzzy values.

$$T(x;40K,60K) = \begin{cases} 0 & \text{if } x < 40K, \\ (x-40)/(60-40) & \text{if } 40K \le x \le 60K, \\ 1 & \text{if } x > 60K. \end{cases} \tag{1}$$

$$T(x;55K,75K) = \begin{cases} 0 & \text{if } x < 55K, \\ (x-55)/(75-55) & \text{if } 55K \le x \le 75K, \\ 1 & \text{if } x > 75K. \end{cases} \tag{2}$$

In contrast, the ***motivation*** attribute has subjectively-based fuzzy values. The motivation of an employee is not objectively measurable, but comes from the subjective opinion of an observer. Hence the meanings of its values cannot be expressed in the same manner as the fuzzy values of *age* and *salary*. In fuzzy databases, the fuzziness of values of this kind is treated by the similarity relation of the values. Normally a similarity relation is defined for the values in the same domain at a specific time. This similarity relation possibly changes from time to time (maybe due to the change of the observer or a change in the criteria used by the observer). Consequently, this may require a similarity measurement of the values across time. For example, it may be desirable to measure the compatibility of the value *highly motivated* in 1985 and in 1993. The temporal-fuzziness of subjectively-based fuzzy values must be dealt with in such a case.

All fuzzy database researchers proposed their models concentrating on snapshot databases only, and none has clearly classified the concepts of the two fuzzy data types as we described above [1, 10, 9]. Therefore, the scope of their models has been restricted.

In the temporal database area, most of the work [3, 7, 12] are concerned with crisp data which have no problems caused by temporal-fuzziness. Here, we will discuss queries of fuzzy data in the time dimension and illustrate some of the problems that can arise:

Q1: When did T. Jones earn a high salary?
The problem for this query is what the reference time point of the *high salary* the user intends to refer to. If it is the present time (when the query is issued), the currently valid function will be used for interpreting the fuzzy term. For example, if the reference time is 1993, Eq. 2 must be used to evaluate T. Jones' salary in each year. As a result, a part of the answer will be 1985 and 1993 with the compatibility values 0.33 and 1.0 respectively. But if the reference time is the time of earning, the equation valid at each particular earning time will be used. For example, T. Jones earned high salary in 1985 and 1993 with the compatibility value 1.0 (by Eq. 1) and 1.0 (by Eq. 2), respectively.

Q2: Whose salary in 1993 is much higher than in 1985?
This query uses a fuzzy comparator (*much higher than*) which complicates the evaluation. It will be more complex if the two operands are fuzzy terms. However, the interpretation of a fuzzy term is not a problem since the compatibility function which is valid at the time the value is held will be used.

Q3: Whose motivation in 1985 is higher than in 1993?
The *motivation* data are subjective in nature, and the motivation of a group of persons can be relatively measured at the same time. The query asks for the comparison of motivation data measured at different times. The problem is whether *high motivation* in 1985 is really higher than *nearly high motivation* in 1993.

Q4: Was N. Brooks' salary high throughout the period 1985-1993?
This query has the same problems as Q1 and perhaps Q3. Moreover, the answer of this kind of query is not necessarily *yes* or *no*. It may be a value of multivalued logic, i.e. it is true to some degree.

3 Background Concepts

In this section we shall provide some basic concepts which are used in the fuzzy database literature and also present the notation used in the paper. More detailed discussions can be found in [14] and [15].

Definition 3.1 *Let U be a set of objects, called the universe of discourse. An element of U is denoted by u. A fuzzy subset F of U is characterized by a membership or compatibility function $\mu_F : U \rightarrow [0,1]$. μ_F is called the grade of membership or compatibility value of u in F. F is denoted by $\{ \mu_F(u_i)/u_i \}$, where $u_i \in U$.*

For the sake of computational efficiency and ease of use, we will use trapezoidal functions which are sufficient in practice in defining grades of membership. A trapezoidal membership function can be defined as follow:

$$T(x;a,b,c,d) = \begin{cases} 0 & \text{if } x < a \text{ or } x > d, \\ (x-a)/(b-a) & \text{if } a \leq x < b, \\ 1 & \text{if } b \leq x \leq c, \\ (d-x)/(d-c) & \text{if } c < x \leq d, \end{cases} \quad (3)$$

The parameters a, b, c, d are adjustable to reflect the meanings of the designated fuzzy terms. In general, trapezoidal functions are defined on the continuous domain $\Re$, but we apply them to discrete domains in the concept of relational databases. We regard our discrete domains as subsets of $\Re$, and we are interested in only those values in the subsets. To make a trapezoidal function applicable for this work, the following constraint must be enforced: $lo \leq x, a, b, c, d \leq up$, where lo and up are the lower and the upper bounds of the universe of discourse, respectively. The constraint is valid and consistent with the concept of domains in the relational database model. That is, a domain is conceptually a set of all possible values allowed for its corresponding attribute, and hence shall have the lower and upper boundary values. From this perspective, the domain of an attribute is a universe of discourse.

Based on the concept of fuzzy sets, the theory of possibility has been proposed to clarify the role of the notion of a fuzzy restriction in information processing [15]. Zadeh used this as a basis to develop a meaning representation language called PRUF [16]. We adopt this approach by employing a possibility distribution to represent the meaning of a fuzzy term stated in a proposition. A fuzzy proposition can induce a possibility distribution as formally defined below.

Definition 3.2 *If F is a fuzzy subset of U characterized by its membership function $\mu_F : U \rightarrow [0,1]$, then the proposition "$Y$ is F" induces a possibility distribution Π_Y on U that is equal to F. This signifies that the proposition "Y is F" has the effect of constraining the values that may be assumed by Y, with the possibility distribution Π_Y identified with F.*

Definition 3.3 *A linguistic variable is characterized by a quintuple* $(X, T(X), U, G, M)$ *in which* X *is the name of the variable;* $T(X)$ *(or simply* T*) denotes the set of names of linguistic values of* X*, with each value being a fuzzy variable denoted generically by* X *and ranging over a universe of discourse* U *which is associated with the base variable* x*;* G *is a syntactic rule for generating the names in* T*; and* M *is a semantic rule for associating with each* t *in* T *its meaning, which is a fuzzy subset of* U.

4 Modeling Temporal-Fuzzy Data

The discussion here is divided into three parts. Firstly, the primitive data domains and their basic measures are defined. Secondly, a temporal fuzzy database model is proposed. Lastly, we present a metadatabase which collects the meanings of the fuzzy terms at various times.

4.1 Definitions of The Fuzzy Data Domains

Basically, there are three primitive types of data to be represented in a database model - quantitative data (e.g. age), qualitative data (e.g. color), and multivalued logic data in the unit interval [0,1] (e.g. degrees of attraction). In the relational database model, each element of a domain is of the same structure. This results in the homogeneity of the represented data. To extend the representational power, we may need to sacrifice this homogeneous property [2]. In the following, we will determine quantitative and qualitative data domains. Multivalued logic data can be treated as a special case of quantitative data.

Domain of quantitative data

Data representation and interpretation. A quantitative data domain is an extension of a numerical data domain to allow the representation of fuzzy data. A numerical data domain is called *the basic domain* of its corresponding quantitative data domain. Quantitative data to be representable are numerical values (e.g. 30), (objectively-based) linguistic values (e.g. *young*) and interval values (e.g. [young, rather old]). However, noncontiguous intervals, e.g. *John's age is in either [20,23] or [25,27]*, are not supported due to their little need in practice and computation inefficiency. Based on the linguistic variable concept (from Definition 3.3), a semantic rule M can assign the meanings to those representable values in a quantitative data domain. Such meanings can be characterized by trapezoidal functions defined on the corresponding basic domain. For example, a numerical value 30 is characterized by $T(x; 30, 30, 30, 30)$. In the case of an interval value, the convex hull of two trapezoidal functions (for two ending values of the interval) has to be calculated to obtain a new trapezoidal function which characterizes the meaning of the interval value.

Even though there is a nonhomogeneity in the representation level, the meaning level is homogenous, i.e. it is in the form of fuzzy subsets, defined by trapezoidal functions, of the basic domain. Thus, any operation to manipulate data needs to be processed at the meaning level, that is, the level of functions.

Measures for data evaluation. Three measures are examined to allow a user to enquire three kinds of information when uncertain/imprecise data are concerned - the upper bounded information using the possibility measure, the lower bounded information using the necessity measure and the approximate information using the proximity measure. These measures can be defined as follows.

Definition 4.1 *(Possibility and Necessity Measures) Let F be a fuzzy subset of U characterized by the membership function μ_F, Π_X be a possibility distribution of a variable X which takes values in U, and π_X be the possibility distribution function of X. The possibility measure, the possibility that the value of X belongs to F, and the necessity measure, the necessity that the value of X belongs to F, are respectively defined by*

$$P(F \mid \Pi_X) = \sup_{u \in U} \min(\pi_X(u), \mu_F(u)) \tag{4}$$

$$N(F \mid \Pi_X) = \inf_{u \in U} \max(1 - \pi_X(u), \mu_F(u)) \tag{5}$$

Definition 4.2 *(Proximity measure) Let D be a quantitative domain and $u, u' \in D$. The meanings $M(u)$ and $M(u')$, as defined in Definition 3.3, are characterized by $T(x; a, b, c, d)$ and $T(x; a', b', c', d')$ respectively. The proximity of u and u' is determined by the proximity index*

$$P_x(u, u') = \frac{\nabla A}{\Delta A + \nabla A} \tag{6}$$

where $\Delta A = \int_{\min(a,a')}^{\max(d,d')} |T(x; a', b', c', d') - T(x; a, b, c, d)| dx$

$\nabla A = \int_a^d T(x; a, b, c, d) dx + \int_{a'}^{d'} T(x; a', b', c', d') dx - \Delta A$

Equation 6 is depicted in Figure 2. A proximity measure can be viewed as a fuzzy relation between two data values with the reflexivity and symmetry properties. It allows users to enquire about what is being stored in the database (not possible or necessary information), and may be used to reduce redundancy of information, e.g. redundant tuples resulting from the projection operation.

Domain of qualitative data

Data representation and interpretation. A qualitative data domain is an extension of its *basic domain* which is a pool of non-numerical values called *atomic qualitative values.* For example, a basic domain of hair colour may be a set { red, blonde, ...}. Qualitative data to be representable are an atomic qualitative value (e.g. blonde) and a possibility distribution on a basic domain (e.g. {1.0/red, 0.8/pink}). The latter is introduced to represent imprecise/uncertain information. Subjectively-based fuzzy terms such as *Motivation* are generally represented as qualitative data.

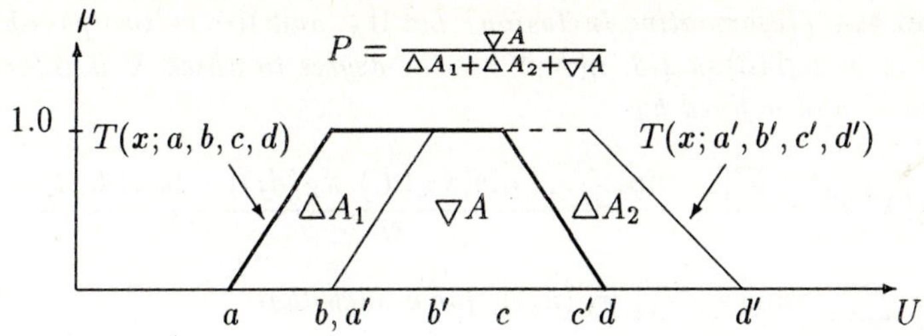

Figure 2: The depiction of the proximity measure definition

To obtain a homogeneously semantic framework, we propose that a qualitative value of type 1 be translated into type 2, i.e., into the form of possibility distribution on itself. For example, the value *red* is interpreted as $\{1.0/red\}$. In addition, since sometimes the atomic values of a basic domain have inherently imprecise meanings, the degree of similarity between the values is required for measuring their nearness. Therefore, a relation called a similarity relation has to be maintained in the metadatabase for a basic domain.

Measures for data evaluation. Like quantitative data domains, three measures, possibility, necessity and proximity measures, are proposed. However, the measures here must take into consideration the similarity relations of the elements that may exist in some basic qualitative data domains. We also assume that the semantics of qualitative data of an object's attributes are normalized. The measures are defined as follows.

Definition 4.3 *(Possibility and Necessity Measures) Let $D = \{d_1, d_2, \ldots, d_n\}$ be the basic domain of a qualitative data domain, and let S_{im} denote a similarity relation on D, $S_{im} : D \times D \longrightarrow [0,1]$. Also, let Π_X and Π_Y be respectively possibility distributions of variables X and Y which take values in the qualitative data domain based on D, and π_X and π_Y be the possibility distribution functions of X and Y respectively. The possibility measure, the possibility that the information of X is described by Y, and the necessity measure, the necessity that the information of X is described by Y, are respectively defined by*

$$P(\Pi_Y \mid \Pi_X) = \sup_{1 \leq i,j \leq n} (\min(\pi_X(d_i), \pi_Y(d_j)) \times S_{im}(d_i, d_j)) \quad (7)$$

$$N(\Pi_Y \mid \Pi_X) = 1 - \sup_{1 \leq i,j \leq n} (\min(\pi_X(d_i), 1 - \pi_Y(d_j)) \times S_{im}(d_i, d_j)) \quad (8)$$

Before defining the proximity measure, we need to define the notion of *informative inclusion.* Informally, it is characterized as the degree to which information described by a possibility distribution is mostly included or closest to the one expressed by another distribution. This concept of informative inclusion is primarily the effect of the similarity relation between the elements of the universe of discourse.

Definition 4.4 *(Informative Inclusion) Let* Π_X *and* Π_Y *be two possibility distributions as in definition 4.3.* $\eta(X,Y)$ *is the degree to which* X *is informatively included in* Y *and defined by*

$$\eta(X,Y) = \frac{\sum_{i=1}^{n} \sup_{1\le j\le n}[\min(\pi_X(d_i), \pi_Y(d_j)) \times S_{im}(d_i,d_j)]}{N} \tag{9}$$

where $N = \sum_{i=1}^{n} \min(\pi_X(d_i), \pi_Y(d_k))$*, for* k *such that*

$$\min(\pi_X(d_i), \pi_Y(d_k)) = \frac{\sup_{1\le j\le n}[\min(\pi_X(d_i),\pi_Y(d_j))\times S_{im}(d_i,d_j)]}{S_{im}(d_i,d_k)}$$

The proximity measure of two possibility distributions is then defined by analogy with the concept of the traditional equivalence relation, where two set X and Y are equivalent if and only if $X \subseteq Y$ and $Y \subseteq X$.

Definition 4.5 *(Proximity measure) Let* Π_X *and* Π_Y *be respectively possibility distributions of variables* X *and* Y *which take values from a qualitative data domain. The proximity relation of* X *and* Y *is characterized by the proximity index*

$$P_x(X,Y) = min(\eta(X,Y), \eta(Y,X)) \tag{10}$$

4.2 A Temporal Fuzzy Data Model

This subsection determines the *Temporal Fuzzy Database Model* which is able to represent both imprecise and temporal data. A fuzzy database consists of a set of *fuzzy relations* which can store both precise and imprecise data.

Definition 4.6 *Let* $R = \{A_1, A_2, \ldots, A_n\}$ *be a relation scheme, where each* $A_i, 1 \le i \le n$*, is called an attribute. For each attribute* $A_i, 1 \le i \le n$*, there is the corresponding nonempty and finite set* D_i *called a domain. A domain can be either a quantitative data domain, a qualitative data domain or a unit interval domain. A fuzzy relation* r *over the relation scheme* R *is a subset of the Cartesian product* $D_1 \times D_2 \times \ldots \times D_n$*.*

A temporal fuzzy relation is a fuzzy relation expanded into the (valid) time dimension to retain the history of data. We choose the discrete time model in which time is viewed as being isomorphic to the integers. Each integer corresponds to the location of an indecomposable unit of time (called *a chronon*) in the time line. A variable *now* is used to denote the present time.

Definition 4.7 *Let* $R = \{A_1, A_2, \ldots, A_n\}$ *be a relation scheme of a fuzzy relation* r*, and* A_{T_b} *and* A_{T_e} *be interpreted time attributes. For both* A_{T_b} *and* A_{T_e}*, there is the corresponding domain* D_T *which is a set of chronons, denoted by integers, and a variable now.* R_T *is said to be a relation scheme of a temporal fuzzy relation if* $R_T = R \cup \{A_{T_b}, A_{T_e}\}$*, and a temporal fuzzy relation is defined as* $r_T \subset D_1 \times D_2 \times \ldots \times D_n \times D_T \times D_T$*, where* D_i *is the corresponding domain of* $A_i, 1 \le i \le n$*.*

Primarily, *a time-independent key* (K_{TI}) is defined as a set of attributes that satisfies the two time-independent properties - uniqueness and minimality. In our temporal fuzzy database model, a K_{TI} has to have a precise value, and, for any time instant t, there are no two tuples s_1 and s_2 such that $s_1[K_{TI}] = s_2[K_{TI}]$ and time intervals in both tuples contain t. Another important issue is removal of identical tuples in a relation. Since our model allows us to have fuzzy data, the concept of proximity relations that are described in the previous subsection is to be employed for defining the duplication of tuples.

Definition 4.8 *Let r_T be a temporal fuzzy relation over a scheme $R_T = \{A_1, A_2, \ldots, A_n, A_{T_b}, A_{T_e}\}$, and s_i and s_j be a pair of tuples in r_T. s_i and s_j are said to be* α-duplicated) *if and only if* $\inf_{1 \leq k \leq n} P_x(s_i[A_k], s_j[A_k]) > \alpha$

If two tuples are α-duplicated, they need to be combined using the union operation and/or the convex hull operation.

4.3 Structure of the MetaDatabase

This subsection determines the construction of a metadatabase for handling the *temporal-fuzziness* property. A primary purpose of metadata is to provide the ability to recognise the intentions of users and to prevent users from misinterpreting the answers to queries. The methods in this subsection are used for modeling two main kinds of metadata - the definitions of the meanings of linguistic values and the similarity relations of fuzzy qualitative data. The metadatabase contains metadata at the same level as the system catalog, and users should be allowed to access this data (with some restriction) to discover the meanings of fuzzy terms in various contexts.

Recall that the meanings of linguistic values are defined by parameter-based functions which are trapezoidal functions in our case. The meaning of a linguistic value is generally dependent on the contexts *where* and *when* it is used. The relationship among the contexts, fuzzy terms and their definitions is modeled in a relation called *a meta-relation.* A specific format of relation scheme is employed to define the structure of a meta-relation, i.e.

$$\text{MetaRel (Rel\_Name, Att\_Name, Fuzzy\_Term, Definition, } T_b, T_e)$$

Rel_Name takes its value from the set of relation names and *Att_Name* from the set of attribute names. The domain of *Fuzzy_Term* will be the set of linguistic values from the quantitative data domains used in the database. A value of *Definition* is taken from a set of trapezoidal functions defined on the basic quantitative data domain. T_b and T_e are defined in the same manner as A_{T_b}, A_{T_e} mentioned in definition 4.7.

The next type of metadata is the similarity relations of basic qualitative data domains. We assume that a basic qualitative data domain has only one similarity relation in any context, except time, e.g. the similarity relation of a domain *color* can be applied to the colors of both cars and hair. There are two main kinds of similarity relations in the context of time - one for values used in the same period and the other for values used in different periods. Firstly, the representation of the similarity relation of a basic qualitative domain whose elements are used in the same period of time will be determined. The schema of the relation is defined by

$$\text{Sim\_Name}(\text{Ele\#1}, \text{Ele\#2}, \text{Degree}, T_b, T_e)$$

where *Sim_Name* is any relation name corresponding to the basic domain, *Ele#1* and *Ele#2* are attributes taking values from the basic domain, *Degree* has a value in the unit interval [0,1] representing the degree of similarity, and T_b and T_e are defined as previously. Any two tuples whose non-time components are *identical* and time intervals are consecutive are required to be coalesced. This is enforced as an integrity constraint.

Lastly, we will describe the representation of the similarity relation of a basic qualitative domain whose elements are used in different periods of time. In this case, the schema of the relation is defined by

$$\text{Sim\_Name}(\text{Ele\#1}, T_{s_1}, T_{e_1}, \text{Ele\#2}, T_{b_2}, T_{e_2}, \text{Degree})$$

where *Sim_Name*, *Ele#1*, *Ele#2* and *Degree* are defined as the former case, T_{b_1} and T_{e_1} represent as time interval on *Ele#1*, and T_{b_2} and T_{e_2} represent as time interval on *Ele#2*. When this kind of meta-relation is not defined, then by default the values from a basic domain which are used at different times are *uncomparable*. That is, there is no association among them.

5 Discussion and Conclusion

In the literature, researchers introduced uncertainties and/or fuzziness into time data. Some are in the database area [5, 6, 8], while others are in the AI domain [4, 13]. Our work is orthogonal to theirs. We introduce uncertainties and fuzziness into non-time data in temporal databases and show how to handle the changeable meaning of those data in the time dimension. This is the first work to do so. From a fuzzy database perspective, we have examined a new concept of measures in the domain of qualitative data which model subjectively-based fuzzy terms. Moreover, we have proposed the notion of proximity measures for fuzzy data that can provide the approximate answer to a query, in addition to the upper bounded and lower bounded answers. We also examined structures of a metadatabase to handle time-varying meanings of fuzzy data. All structures are based on the relational model. Therefore, they are quite simple, and the relational algebra can be directly applied. Our work can be extended in many possible directions. First, transaction time (see [11]) can be introduced to keep track of the evolution of the database itself. Second, valid time can be expanded to be imprecise. Third, the individual view of each user on the meanings of fuzzy data may be incorporated. Currently, we are developing a query language capable of supporting the temporal-fuzziness property.

In conclusion, we contended that both time and imprecision aspects of data are important. We also emphasized that when both features are concerned, a property of fuzzy data called *temporal-fuzziness* will arise. A major problem caused by this property is the misinterpretation of fuzzy data by both users and

DBMSs, and this is a major obstacle to an intelligent system. Our proposed framework is developed for a treatment of temporal-fuzziness property and is a further contribution to intelligent system development.

Acknowledgments: The authors are grateful to Prof. John Hiller for helpful suggestions on the initially proposed ideas.

References

[1] Buckles B. P. and Petry F. E., A Fuzzy Representation of Data For Relational Databases, Fuzzy Sets and Syst. 7, 1982, 213-226

[2] Buckles B. P. and Petry F. E., Uncertainty models in information and database systems, J. Inform. Sci. 11, 1985, 213-226

[3] Clifford J. and Croker A., The Historical Relational Data Model (HRDM) and Algebra Based on Life Spans, Proc. 3rd Int. Conf. Data Engineering, Feb. 1987, 528-537

[4] Dubois D. and Prade H., Processing Fuzzy Temporal Knowledge, IEEE Trans. Systems, Man, and Cybernetics, Vol. 19, No. 4, July/August 1989, 729-744

[5] Dutta S., Generalized Events in Temporal Databases, Proc. 5th Int. Conf. on Data Engineering, Los Angeles, CA, Feb 1989, 118-126

[6] Dyreson C. E. and Snodgrass R. T., Historical Indeterminacy, Technical Report TR-91-30a, Dep. of Computer Science, Univ. of Arizona, April 1992

[7] Gadia S. K. and Yeung C-S, A Generalized Model for A Relational Temporal Database, Proc. ACM SIGMOD Int. Conf. Management of Data, June 1988, 251-259

[8] Kouramajian V. and Elmasri R., A Generalized Temporal Model, Technical Report, Univ. of Texas at Arlington, 1992

[9] Prade H. and Testemale C., Generalizing Database Relational Algebra for the Treatment of Incomplete or Uncertain Information and Vague Queries, Inform. Sci. 34, 1984, 115-143

[10] Shenoi S. and Melton A., An Extended Version of the Fuzzy Relational Database Model, Inform. Sci. 52, 1990, 35-52

[11] Snodgrass R. and Ahn I., A taxonomy of time in databases, SIGMOD Record 14, 1985, 236-246

[12] Snodgrass R., The Temporal Query Language TQuel, ACM Trans. on Database Systems, Vol. 12, No. 2, June 1987, 247-298

[13] Vitek M., Fuzzy information and fuzzy time, Proc. IFAC Symp. Fuzzy Information, Knowledge Representation and Decision Analysis, Marseille, France, 1983, 159-162

[14] Zadeh L. A., The Concept of a Linguistic Variable and its Application to Approximate Reasoning, Infor. Sci. 8, 1975, 199-248 (I) and 301-357 (II)

[15] Zadeh L. A., Fuzzy sets as a basis for a theory of possibility, Fuzzy Sets and Syst., Vol. 1, No.1, 3-28

[16] Zadeh L. A., PRUF-a meaning representation language for natural language, Int. J. Man-Machine Studies 10, 1978, 395-460

Object-based Schema Integration for Heterogeneous Databases: *A Logical Approach*

Frederick N. Springsteel
Computer Science Department, Missouri University,
Columbia, MO USA [1]

ABSTRACT. *Given the large number of conceptual schema design tools and methodologies in use today, conversion efforts need strategies by which any source schemas can be easily integrated in heterogeneous database systems. We discuss the design and analysis of strategies for multiple schema/view integration with an extensible redesign system that is object-based, as defined herein. Our focus is on well-defined, clearly identifiable objects; E-R schemas describable in linear form, or in graphical (E-R Diagram) form with annotations. E-R schemas are a composite class of basic objects: E-sets (of entities) and R-sets (of relationships), each of which is extended. E-sets are described by structured sets of keys, lists of attributes (with domains), indexes, and textual constraints. R-sets are structured lists of E-set names with a description of their participation in the R-set ["one" or "many"], and textual constraints, e.g. foreign keys. We propose a design for the missing step: a Graphic Schema Algebra to merge various conceptual schemas, to provide a leverage point for interoperation.*

1 Introduction to Object-based Integration

Lately, the goal of "interoperability" has almost replaced actual integration efforts. We interpret this term to imply the empowerment of the DBA to operate in any one (or more) of a diverse federation of databases, from one meta-system, thereby simulating the original goal of merged schemas and migrated data.

Our goal is to produce higher-level schemas and action mappings which effectively combine different source schemas, that may have originated in very different data models with distinct DBMSs. All essential parts of this "meta-model schema" will be provided visually, via semantic/graphic metadata. However, to ensure true interoperability as we define it also requires solutions to the problems of (a) mapping user requirements to the metamodel, for design of new applications; (b) inversely, mapping from many existing DBMS applications to a representative conceptual schema in the metamodel; (c) for operation purposes, to have a common physical design tool for the translation of metamodel schemas into any appropriate DBMS, and a recursion-enabled query language for information retrieval; and (d) an extended ability to declare new complex objects via Abstract Data Types (ADTs) at the meta-modelling level.

We first contend that "problems" (a) - (d) have actually been solved, at least in principle. We then propose the missing last step: (e) a Graphic Schema Algebra to merge the various conceptual schemas from (a) and (b), without which there is no leverage point even for [weak] interoperation. We suggest an intuitive, visual, generic meta-model interface, and a rule-driven knowledge-based integration mechanism.

1.1. The need for meta-model integration of objects in schemas

In this context the problem of view/schema integration can be seen as the need to incorporate multiple user groups' views, or any multiple data schemas, into one global schema. The multiple schemas may even be from different data models for a heterogeneous DBMS such as MULTIBASE [Lan]. For simplification, we shall assume the given inputs are a pair of schemas. Then the integration of N schemas may be done in pairs, applied to all the intermediate resulting schemas, via repeated uses of our approach in a two-way merge-tree of depth O(log N). Using a merge of pairs the user can follow the process at all times and help decide the appropriate resolution of conflicts [BATI86].

The main problem for our generic strategy is to decide whether or not two given objects are truly "integrable", in a sense to be defined by the rules, and if so then to produce their integrated form. This paper will examine this problem for meta-objects, i.e. schemas, as a general problem which, when specialized to certain scenarios, represent a range of specific combinatorial problems, some of which have tractable solutions (in polynomial-time) and others of which do not.

A truly model-independent integration tool that will be useful for both schemas and transactions will have to capture the semantics of complex objects, including operations on them. The clear implication for strategic approaches is that the generic metamodel must be extensible: it must allow new data models and new operations.

1.2. The state of integration research

In the current research state of the art, the needs of schema/view/object integration are not being fully met in the following areas: Generality, Extensibility, and Evaluability.

Generality issues: Interoperable systems generally need to capture different types of information, using possibly different data models, at the various levels of: External, Conceptual/Logical and Physical Design; and to be able to handle meta-data information like textual annotations and logic-based constraint rules. Current methods of (homogeneous) view/schema integration, tied as they are to one fixed data model, are inflexible and cannot fulfill all demands made on them by the most general integration efforts.

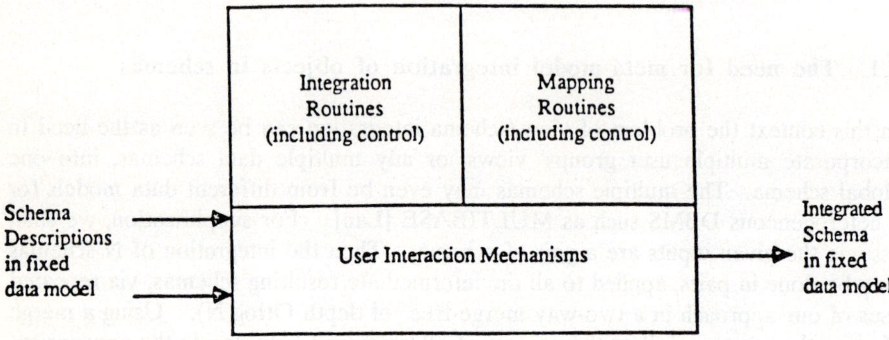

FIGURE 1. Architecture of current integration efforts

Extensibility issues: Existing DB design and integration tools do not separate the integration tools from the control mechanism used and, thus, are difficult to extend. An integrator architecture that clearly distinguishes integration rules from control functions is needed, such that new functionality will be added by changes of the rule set rather than the control program. This allows logical independence from the special viewpoint of one data model. Figure 1 shows the schematic architecture of current tools with control built into the integration routines. Figure 2 gives a strategic design for our extensible, rule-based integrator.

Evaluability: Basically *there is no comprehensive theory of objects,* nor even an attempt to base schema integration rules on a sound theoretic foundation. As a result it is difficult currently to determine the correctness of existing object integration strategies.

In section Two we outline our principles and approach to the above problems, with an emphasis on algorithms in section Three. We also discuss notions that need to be clarified to help establish a secure natural theory of integration: ***consistency,*** *e.g. of naming conventions;* ***equivalence of objects,*** *in this case E-R Schemas; and important relationships between objects in distinct schemas, i.e.* ***interschema connections.*** Section Three summarizes results and prospects.

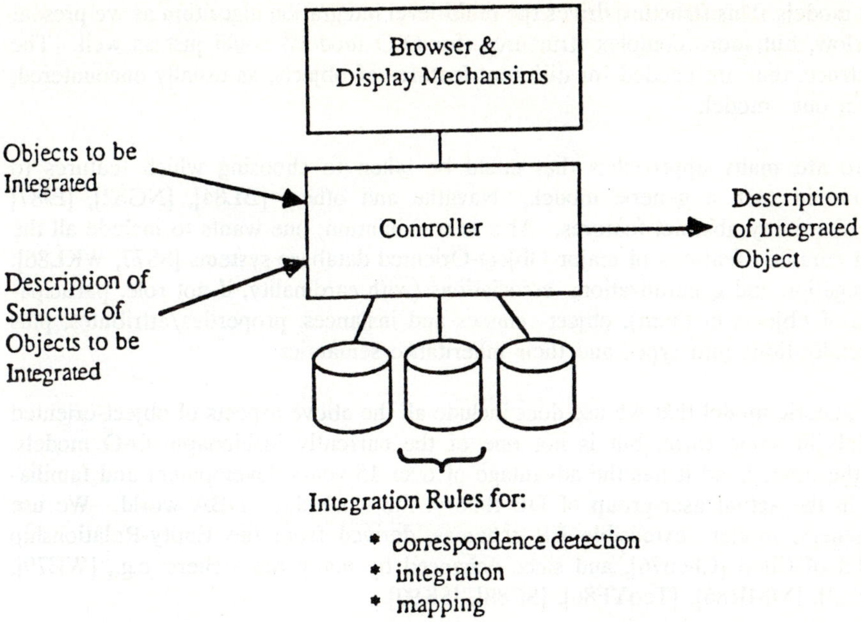

FIGURE 2. Architecture of an extensible integrator

1.3. Mappings for both data and operations

Integration efforts could benefit from a rule-based approach in the mappings area both by saving labor and by avoiding needless obsolesence. We suggest that objects be represented in meta-model schemas, by interactive conversion of the input schemas [NG82], to allow mappings that exploit new information gathered during the process, such as metadata and units. Because our meta-model schemas are visual, being based on E-R schemas, it should be more natural and intuitive for the humans monitoring the process.

When mapping data and operations, the integrity constraints must be mapped in a consistent manner, to be able to integrate correctly. Existing tools usually can handle simple (e.g. key) constraints and often append unstructured lists of constraints without analyzing them. There are many opinions on how best to attack the mapping problems in any integration process [BATI86].

2 The Generic Model: a meta-database approach

The main goal of this introduction of a generic-object model (for databases) is to represent the main given schemas that need to be integrated, and to do so in an abstract, hierarchial structure: the ER schema, which is neutral between the standard data models. This structure drives the multi-level integration algorithm as we present it below, but more complex structures (for O-O models) could just as well. The constructs that are needed for different features of objects, as usually encountered, are in our model.

There are many approaches that could be taken to choosing which features to include in such a generic model. Navathe and others [BL84], [NG82], [El87] describe many abstract features. At a very minimum, one wants to include all the most common features of major Object-Oriented database systems [SS77, WKL86]: aggregation and generalization, associations (with cardinality, if not role, participations of objects in them), object classes and instances, properties/attributes, plus specializations into types and their inheritance semantics.

The generic model that we use does include all the above aspects of object-oriented models in some form, but is not one of the currently fashionable O-O models. On the other hand it has the advantage of over 15 years development and familiarity in the actual user-group of DB theory: the workaday DBA world. We use as generic model extensible ER schemas, derived from the Entity-Relationship model of Chen [Chen76], and since enhanced by many researchers; e.g., [WE79], [JNS83], [MMR86], [TeoYF86], [SC88], [SK90].

Because integration of large databases involves a HUGE number of decisions, the only manageable structure for doing so is a visual, multi-level hierarchy. Our meta-model (extended E-R) schemas are viewed as "information-organizing" hierarchies. The process of intergation can then be conducted in a top-down, depth-first, recusrsive descent manner, as is most natural on hierarchies. Because KB invocations mark the decision points, coinciding with subroutine (stacking) calls, difficult decisions can be delayed until later in the session.

Specifically, and in outline form, we identify the following E-R features as approximate semantic counterparts to Object-Oriented terminology:

E-R FEATURES	**OBJECT-ORIENTED TERMS**
entity (set)	**object (class)**
entity (instance)	**object (instance)**
attribute [value]	**property [value]**
relationships:	**associations:**
many-related	**N-marked**
one-related	**1-marked**
subset/sub-entity	**subclass/subobject**
superset	**aggregation/superclass**
ISA-relationship	**IS-A assocaiation**
multiple subset-of	**multiple inheritance**
dependent entities	**generalized objects**
ID-relationship	**IS-TYPE-OF association**

Composite entity	**Compound objects**
required subset	HAS-A-associated object

As far as we can see, there is no major schema feature of O-O models, represented in diagrams by circles and arrows, that cannot be represented by the boxes (entities), diamonds (relationships) and ovals (attributes) of the extended E-R model's graphs. We note that all the associations we have seen are between exactly two objects - classes and/or instances. So, O-O acts like a (generalized) Binary Data Model, whereas the most common E-R model [Ull88] allows K-ary relationships, K > 2. On the other hand, complex objects, where several objects are PART_OF related to one (e.g., an automobile) are non-trivial in any model.

2.1 Structure of the Generic Model

Henceforth we shall work with examples, [E-R] schemas that can all be realized within the following structures, with [options]:

schema	=	**Sname (E-set; R-set),** where the basic forms are
E-set	=	(Ent [, Ent]*) /* one or more entities */
R-set	=	(Rel*) /* any number of relationships */
Ent	=	Ename (Key(s); **Att(s)**; Index(es); "Text")
Rel	=	Rname (**E-seq**; [Att(s)]; "Text"), where
E-seq	=	{Ent_1, $card_1$; ... ; Ent_k, $card_k$}, for k > 1, and
Att	=	Aname:data_type [definer, domain, units]
Index	=	Aname:index_type, and **card** is "1" or "m".

Other component structures may be added as extensions to our system, freely, as long as they are precisely definable as above. However, many commonly used features are definable as sub-cases of the above structures, e.g. a subset entity of the Chen model [Chen76] is any SubEnt related by a special "ISA" relationship:
ISA ({SubEnt, m; Ent, 1}, - , [Text]).

The above structures will be encoded into the rules input to the Controller Algorithm; in the next section we show a version of it that results from using the above schema's structure rules, but we only mean the algorithm seen here as a prototypical "case" of the generic algorithm. Because schema structures are adaptable, i.e. modifiable to particular modeling tasks, we so achieve a separation of the used model's details from the more general integration strategy. This is a main step towards our model-independent goal, more so than prior integration strategies [Bati86]. This is prompted by our strong belief that control mechanisms can and should be as general as possible; our structure-driven approach allows that, in a rule-based environment.

Representation of schemas as schema-trees: Each schema in the above form can be considered a linear expression of its sub-schema hierarchy, or tree. We get a tree because each Rel has as sub-node a copy of each Ent_i in its E-sequence, with the associated $card_i$ as edge label. Thus a schema corresponds to a (unique) schema-tree, as its preorder traversal; cf. Figures 3, 4, and 5, below. A similar "hierarchialization" occurs with any structured model.

2.2 Integration Process Control: the generic algorithm

The control process, labeled "Controller" in Figure 2, reads two specific input schemas, in some known structure as above, e.g. the schema-tree's preorder traversal, .nd generates calls to the Integration Rules. may require querying the user.) The basic control strategy is to attempt semantic matching within syntactic categories, moving down the levels of the hierarchy given by the used model's structure by recursive descent. In a more general strategy than shown here, the major control logic would be: "find corresponden-ces in categories of the meta-model, resolve non-matches among objects, and recurse down the hierarchial (meta-shema) tree".

If two compared objects, and their substructures, are found to correspond, then the nature of the correspondences and the integrated result are next determined, when necessary by referral to the user. The process is invoked recursively to ensure that substructures can be integrated, and that they are integrated, before completion of the process that called them: the integration of the compared structures. Naturally, various safeguards and subtleties are to be observed to prevent infinite recursion and unbounded stacking.

A "model-ruleless" integration process would not have even the benefits of current fixed-model strategies. Thus, we assume that our integrator's rule-base contains: the used model's structure, detailed integration rules, and the general business rules of the enterprise neccessary to make the kinds of decisions seen below. In traces below, Domains and Units are implicitly used to help make decisions, but are omitted. Data_types are implicit below also. Before outlining the generic integration control algorithm, we give an example of its application to three Views of an enterprise's conceptual database, which employ life-like attributes. The following schemas, given also as schema-trees, can almost be integrated without reference to a user's special knowledge.

View1: Payroll (E1, E2; R1)

E1 = EMPL (SSN, Atts, Name:hash, "employees"), where
Atts = {SSN, Name, Dept, JobCode, Rate, Hours, NumDeps},

E2 = PLAN (Code, {Code, Level, PlanName}, PlanName:inv, "med")

R1 = EMPLAN ({E1, m; E2, 1}, --, "SSN is PK, Code is FK")

View1: **Payroll (E1, E2; R1)**

E1 = EMPL (SSN, Atts, Ruleset1)   where

Atts = {SSN, Name, Dept, JobCode, Rate, Hours, NumDeps},

E2 = PLAN (Code, {Code, PlanName, Level}, Ruleset2)

R1 = EMPLAN ({E1, m; E2, 1}, --, PK(SSN) & FK(Code))

Schema-tree:

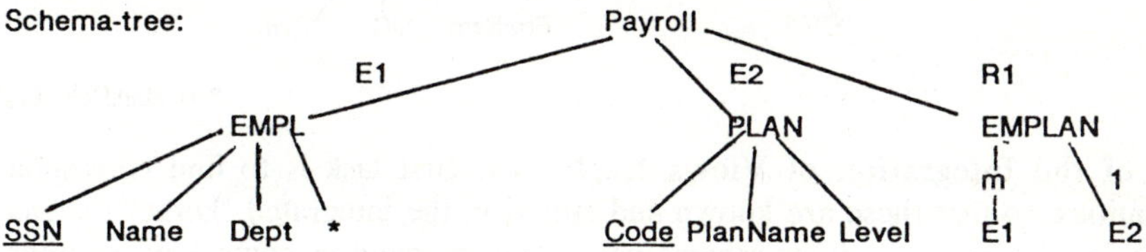

* = JobCode/Rate/Hours/NumDeps

View2: **Personnel (E1, E2; R1)**

E1 = EMPLYE (ID#, Atts, RuleSet1'),   where

Atts = {ID#, Name, Addr, Skills, HourRate, HireDate},

E2 = DEPT (Dnum, {Dnum, Dname}, RuleSet2')

R1 = WORKS_IN ({E1, m; E2, 1}, JC, PK(ID#) & FK(Dnum))

Schema-tree:

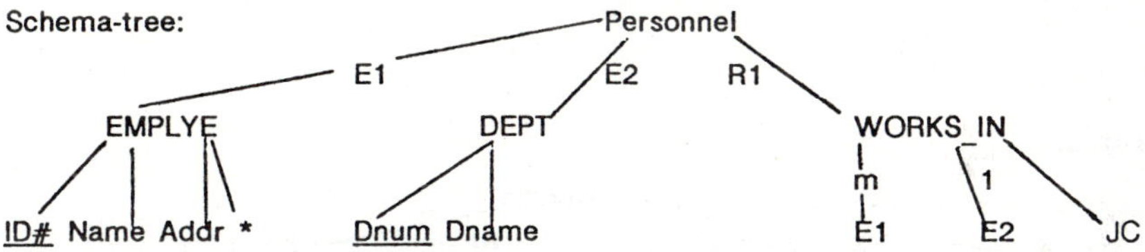

where   * = Skills, HourRate, HireDate

View3: **Managers (E1, E2, E3; R1, R2)**

E1 = EMPLOYEE (ID#, Atts, RuleSet1") where

Atts = {ID#, Names, Skill},

E2 = DEPTS (Dept#, {Dept#, Name}, RuleSet2")

E3 = PROJECTS (Proj#, {Proj#, ProjNam, Duration}, --)

R1 = PAID_BY ({E1, m; E2, 1}, {JC, Title}, PK(ID#) & FK(Dept#))

R2 = PART_OF ({E1, m; E3, n}, {Start, Role, End}, PK({ID#,Proj#}) & FK(ID#) & FK(Proj#))

Schema-tree:

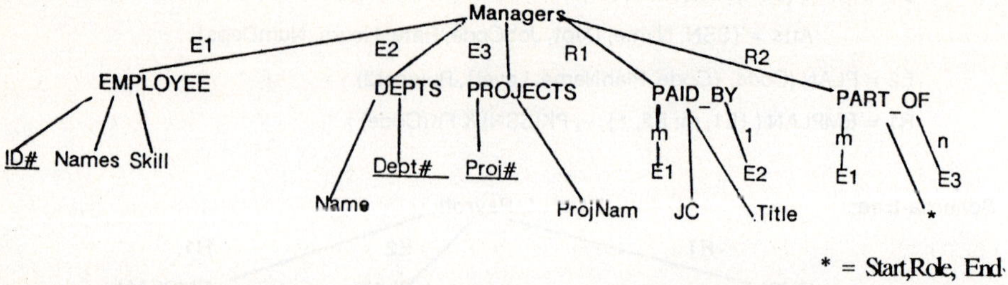

Trace of the Integration of Views 1,2,3: The first task is to find corresponding Entities, so that these are known and stored in the integrated "kernel" schema built up by the process. [Our schema-pairs strategy requires some kind of intermediate schema, so we shall make use of it.] To reduce confusion, we shall treat the second input schema as the curent result, into which the first schema is being integrated, although both may be "source" schemas. First we integrate View_1 into View_2. Due to their name similarity and/or to their like-domain keys, the E1s of both views are integrated under the user-favored name of EMPLYE, with Key ID#, and common attributes Name and (Hour)Rate. The attribute Dept is (domain-/unit) equivalenced to Dnum, and so is not in the new E1, whose other attributes are the union of the old E1s'. The two other Ents have no commonality, so are not integratable, but are unioned into the kernel schema **(View_2')**. The two input Rels are between different objects, and so become R1 and R2 in View_2', whose "upper conceptual" schema-tree is:

Schema-tree:

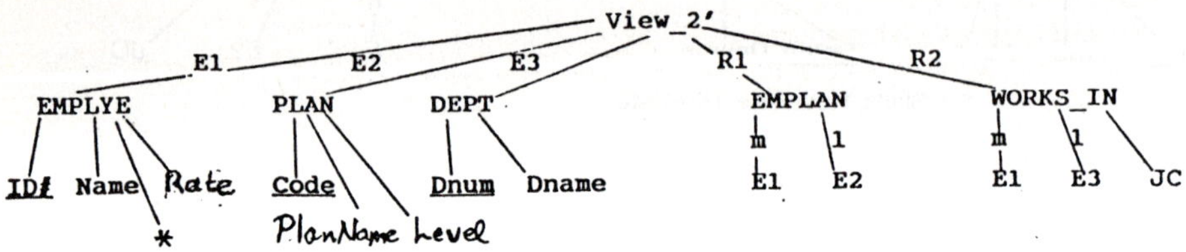

where * = Skills/Hiredate/Hours/NumDeps

Integration of View_3 into View_2': By conflict rules, naming conventions of the Manager's view (View_3) prevail in the result below. Thus, the Ents are named EMPLOYEE, DEPTS, PROJECTS, and the (previous) PLAN; the Department entities are identical here, up to names, by domains and keys. Thus, the same-cardinality Rels, PAID_BY and WORKS_IN, can then be integrated as relating the same objects in the same way, despite the attribute Title of the former, which is unioned to the common JC. Thus we obtain:

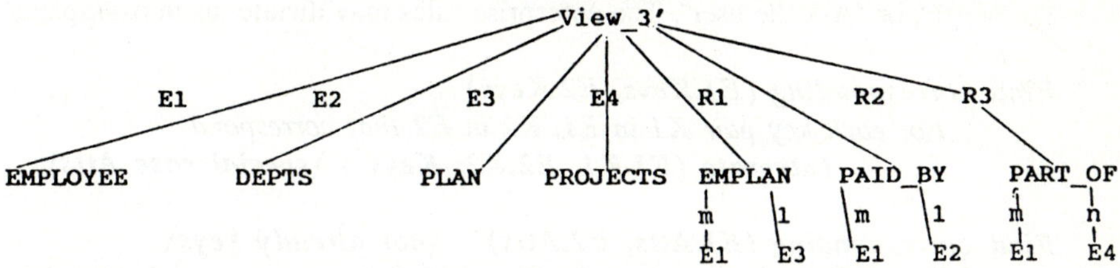

THE SCHEMA INTEGRATION CONTROL ALGORITHM:

We now exemplify our strategy of a generic control algorithm, assuming the reader's understanding of the above example. Many details are omitted.

Integrate (S1, S2: schemas): \Given the "schema" structure rules\

begin \find corresponding Ents before looking at Rels [El87] \

Find_corresponding (S1.E-set, S2.E-set) \search entity pairs

Correspondence may be detected by matching names or by looking inside the entities to detect matching keys. The generic algorithm controls the search among likely entity pairs, while particular integration rules may look inside Atts, or interact with the user.

For each Ent pair E1 in S1, E2 in S2 found to correspond
Integrate (E1,E2: Ents) \mappings are generated here

For each non-corresponding Ent in S1 or S2
Union (Ent, IS.E-set) ***\IS is the Integrated_Schema***

For each Rel pair R1 in S1, R2 in S2 found to correspond
Integrate (R1,R2: Rels) \mappings are generated here

For each non-corresponding Rel in S1 or S2
Union (Rel, IS.R-set)

end

The calls to integrate entity (or relationship) pairs are handled by the same sturcture-driven strategy. For example, to complete Integrate(E1,E2: Ents) the substructure calls are:

begin

Integrate (E1.Ename, E2.Ename)

/Integration of atomic objects, like names, needs to be handled by a given integration rule; possible ones include "Use name from scheme 1", or "Ask the user". The enterprise rules may dictate, as in examples./

Find_corresponding (E1.Keys, E2.Keys)

For each key pair K1 in E1, K2 in E2 that correspond

Integrate (E1.K1, E2.K2: Keys) \special case Atts

Find_corresponding (E1.Atts, E2.Atts) \not already keys

For each attribute pair A in E1, A' in E2 that correspond

Integrate (E1.A, E2.A': Atts)

For each non-corresponding Att in S1 or S2

Union (Att, IS.E-set)

Integrate (E1.Indexes , E2. Indexes) \using the rule base

Integrate (E1.Texts, E2.Texts) \using the rule base

end

2.3 Special Integration Problems: some complexity issues

While our algorithm lacks a physical realization at present, it appears capable of utilizing the best features of any proven scheme integrator, by imitating its behavior in the rule-set. In this section we try to anticipate some potential problems that might limit the usefulness of model-independent integration.

While the preceding generic algorithm can indeed guide a model-independent scheme integrator, there are special problems that could arise in using it. Depending on the user-given set of integration rules, a generic strategy may be slower (or faster) than a hardcoded single-model integrator, it would seem. Concerns of this nature need quantified measures to test them.

We focus here on the structural component-matching strategy that drives our algorithm. Other issues about decisions seem equally important: (i) context, (ii) commitment level in the hierarchy, (iii) timing, and (iv) user-dependence versus rule-dependence, for decisions. We have preliminary ideas about the former two areas and general ideas about the latter two, so we leave them to sequel work. On the nature of the structural conditions, however, one can make observable predictions based on scientific knowledge of tree pattern-matching versus graph isomorphism.

A Tractable Scenario: Suppose that the integration rules make almost all correspondence decisions on the basis of naming conventions. If a commitment is made to integrate "no matter how compatible" (or incompatible) two schemas are, then any two scheme-trees can be integrated. However, suppose that we are integrating views in a connected database, that we seek to deal with pairs that overlap, and that a further criterion is set that at least X% of both schemas should be very compatible, say isomorphic.[1] One can then reach decisions about whether X% of Scheme A and of Scheme B each have isomorphic sub-schemas, using well-known position-tree matching and standard node-numbering tree isomorphism algorithms. Metrics of "compatibility" are needed before one can make stronger statements than this, but most theorists would agree that this scenario suggests at least polynomial-time complexity, i.e. tractability.

An Intractable Scenario: Suppose we did not use tree-like hierarchies to structure our schemas, but employed standard E-R diagrams. Obviously they are not trees but complicated networks of many possible cycles. Holding constant the criterion of X% compatibility, but now of graphs, one can easily run afoul of the Subgraph Isomorphism Problem and its well-known NP-complete complexity. This could happen because X% of Scheme A may be 100% of Scheme B! No algorithm is known for deciding whether one graph is isomorphic to a subgraph of another, which runs in less than exponential time.

We take these two (simplistic) scenarios as additional, accruing evidence that a hierarchial structure is preferable over a general graphical structure. Furthermore, obvious network navigation problems would destroy the simplicity of our recursive descent algorithm, beyond recognizable utility. For this reason, even for source schemas from the object-oriented model with its very rich connections, a simple translation to neutral-model schemas seems worthwhile and at least deserving of further study.

The scenarios above are idealistic in their concept of isomorphism; the structure of connections is syntactic. Truly systematic information equivalence of schemas must also consider semantic information, such as constraints, keys, and domains. The author described "data-dependency equivalence" for E-R diagrams as name-compatibility plus FD-equivalence of their relational scheme forms [JNS83]. The application of that work here leads to the following rather more semantic description of scheme "isomorphism":

Two (ER) schemas, S1 and S2, are *(semantically)* <u>*equivalent*</u> if their total structures are conformable in these senses:

1. All S1 names are compatible with all S2 names, under the rules of naming standards;
2. S1 and S2 are data-dependency equivalent [JNS83];

---

[1] The value of X is debatable; it may depend on the rigor and philosophy of the rule-set.

3. The domains in S1 and S2 are compatible;
4. Textual constraints are compatible or resolvable.

This definition leaves a few questions to be resolved by local rules of integration, because we believe there is no such thing as "universal isomorphism" of informational structures. However, the science of the organization of information should nonetheless keep trying to reach agreement on certain required criteria, by which to know when two forms are non-superficially the same.

4. SUMMARY AND FUTURE PROJECTED RESEARCH

Because we have aimed to demonstrate the feasibility of a model- independent approach to schema integration, rather than to produce hasty tools, it would be appropriate here to summarize by comparing other approaches to ours. This task is facilitated by the comprehensive survey paper [Bati86] of Batini, et alia, which describes twelve previous approaches from various viewpoints, such as these aspects of the surveyed integrators:

(i) Schemas input method: Of the six approaches that are explicit about it, four use binary arity of input schemas ([Bati86], [CaVi83], [TeoYF86], [WE79]); the other two use N-ary inputs. On the choice of a "ladder" versus "balanced tree" organization of the N schemas to be integrated by the pairing methods, there is no consensus; the four above split evenly. We feel that this should be a non-issue, because either choice leads to O(N) integrations. However, we prefer the structure of the balanced binary tree; they are only O(log N) deep. The main advantage is that the user/integrator combine each given pair of the original schemas first into |_N/2_| schemas, each roughly twice the size of the smaller of the pair, and then proceed with half as many remaining schemas, at each depth of the merge tree.

(ii) Activity flow: Most of the previous approaches focus on three successive activities: Comparing, Conforming, and Merging (C,C,M). These take place between the constructs in the respective schemas with restart from either of the latter, from Conforming in [BL84] AND [El87], or from Merging in [ME84], [NG82], [WE79]. A few of the approaches mention the Pre-integration activity of getting all the inputs in the same model ([El87], [ME84], [NG82]). The automated flow of activities from Preintegration to the cycle C -> C -> M, and back to the first C, takes some of the burden off of the users, to free them for appropriate human activities: making the finer semantic distinctions, and the positive or negative correspondence decisions. Thus, we prefer this cycle.

(iii) Integration order of constructs in the model: From the seven approaches, of those mentioned above, which divide the process into two stages for constructs, fully five handle entities/objects first and then a different construct, either relationships ([BL84], [El87]) or connections/functions for the objects strategies ([El87],

[NG82], [Yao]). We follow their consensus for treating entities first, via correspondence and integration rules, so that the knowable identifications in the E-sets can be used to help integrate the higher-level R-sets.

FUTURE RESEARCH NEEDS: Specific areas needing the most attention:

Description-driven integration: Designers need to integrate schemas in different data models, so an integrator tied to a fixed model is inadequate. A hard-coded integrator also misses a main chance to be an aid in other stages of the process. It is some-times necessary to integrate metadata that belongs to no data model, such as physical design choices or requirements-tracing information. In future object-oriented systems, it will be necessary to integrate more general object definitions, e.g. Abstract Data Types, that combine data and operations. We have recognized this model-independent need, and intend to address it.

Automated generation of mappings for both data and operations: Any general integrator should generate mappings between the original schemas and the output schemas. In addition, when databases are interoperably integrated, queries and updates against the resulting schemas must be mapped to the original schemas. When views are integrated, old transactions against the individual views may need to be replaced by transactions against the global schema. Difficult problems arise in the areas of query optimization (using unions and outer-joins) and in update mapping, a form of the View Update Problem.

Integrity constraints: Because existing DBMSs have been notoriously poor in expressing them, these constraints are often implicitly buried in the physical implementation structure. During the integration process, especially of heterogeneous data-bases, it is essential to extract this information, make it explicit, and map it to the constructs of the target model. Which constructs should be provided in the integrator, to capture semantic constraints, is a matter of research.

Another interesting problem connected with this area is to deal with the inheritance of constraints defined on complex objects. How to express the inheritance semantics and to embed them into the appropriate mapping rules is a non-trivial problem! In summary of much of our aim, however, the use of semantic data in support of integration of database schema and transactions is crucial to improve the quality of integration. Many specifics are as yet weakly defined, and their elucidation will require deeper research. However, we consider an extensible integrator as the clearly superior environment to incorporate new semantic rules incrementally.

****

REFERENCES

[BL84] Batini,C. and Lenzerini,M. 1984 A methodology for data schema integration into the entity-relationship model. *IEEE Trans. Software Engr.*, SE-10,6 (Nov) 628-644.

[Bati86] Batini,C., Lenzerini,M. & Navathe,S. **A comparative analysis of methodologies for database schema integration**, *ACM Computing Surveys*, v.15, no.4, Dec. 1986, 323-364.

[CaTuL90] Casanova,M., Tucherman,L. & Laender,A. Algorithms for designing and maintaining optimized relational repre-sentations of ER schemas, *Proc. 9th Intl. Conf. ER Approach*, Lausanne, 1990, 361-374.

[CaVid83] Casanova,M. & Vidal,V. Towards a sound view integration methodology, *Proc. 2nd ACM SIGMOD-SIGACT Symp. on Prin. DB Systems*, Atlanta, March 1983, 36-47.

[Chen76] Chen,P. The Entity-Relationship Model: Toward a Unified View of Data, *ACM Trans. Database Systems*, Vol.1(1), March 1976, 9-36.

[El87] ElMasri,R., Larson,J. & Navathe,S. Integrated algo-rithms for federated databases and logical database design. *Tech. Report, Honeywell Corp. Research Center*, 1987.

[ElWie79] Elmasri,R. & Wiederhold, G., Data model inte-gration using the structural model, *Proc. ACM SIGMOD Intl. Conf. Mgt. of Data*, Boston, June 1979, 191-202.

[JNS83] Jajodia,S., Ng,P. & Springsteel,F., The problem of equivalence for Entity-relationship Diagrams, IEEE Trans. on Software Engr., SE-9, 5, (Sept. 1983), 617-630.

[Lan] Landers,T. & Rosenberg,R. An overview of MULTIBASE, in: Distributed Databases, H.J. Schneider, ed., North-Holland.

[ME84] Mannino,M. & Effelsberg,W., 1984. A methodology for global schema design. Tech. report No. TR-84-1, Univ. Florida Comp. & Info. Sci. Dept., Sept. 1984.

[MMR86] Makowsky,J., Markowitz,V. & Rotics,N., Entity-Relationship Consistency for Relational Schemas, ***Proc. 1st Intl. Conf. Database Theory***, Rome, Sept. 1986, 18pp. *(pre-print)*

[NG82] Navathe,S. & Gadgil,S. 1982. A methodology for view integration in logical database design, *Proc. 8th Intl Conf. on VLDB*, Saratoga, CA.

[ParSp90] Parent,C.& Spaccapietra,S., View Integration: A step forward in soving structural conflicts, research report, LBD, Dept. Inform., EPFL, Lausanne-Ecublens, Suisse, 1990.

[SC88] Springsteel,F. & Chuang,P. ERDDS: the intelligent E-R-based Database Design System, *Proc. 7th Intl. Conf. on E-R Approach*, 1988, Rome, Italy, 211-230.

[SK90] Springsteel,F. & Kou,C. Reverse Data Engineering of E-R-Designed Relational Schemas, *PARBASE-90: Two-track Conf. on Databases, Parallel Architectures, and their Applications*, Miami Beach, Florida, March 1990, 438-440.

[SS77] Smith,J. & Smith,D. 1977. Databse abstraction: aggregation and generaliztion, *ACM Trans. Database Sys.* 2,2 (June 1977), 105-133.

[TeoYF86] Teorey,T., Yang,D. & Fry,J. A logical design methodology for relational databases using the extended entity-relationship model, ACM Computing Surveys, 18,2, (June 1986), 197-222.

[Ull88] Ullman, J.D., Principles of Database and Knowledge-Base Systems, Vol.1, Computer Science Press, 1988.

[WE79] Elmasri, R. & Wiederhold, G., Data model integration using the structural model, *Proc. ACM SIGMOD Intl. Conf. Mgt. of Data*, Boston, June 1979, 191-202.

[WKL86] Woelk,D., Kim,W. & Luther,W. 1986. AN object-oriented approach to the multimedia databases, *Proc. ACM SIGMOD Intl. Conf. Mgt. of Data*, Washington.

[Yao] Yao,B., Waddle,Y. & Housel,B. View modeling and integration using the functional data model, IEEE Trans. on Software Engr., SE-8, 6, 544-553.

Heterogeneous Multilevel Transaction Management with Multiple Subtransactions

Jari Veijalainen

Technical Research Centre of Finland (VTT)
Laboratory for Information Processing
Lehtisaarentie 2A, SF-00340 Helsinki, Finland
(veijalainen@tik.vtt.fi)

Abstract. Heterogeneous transaction management has been an active research field for a few years. Based on the degree of local transaction autonomy we distinguish between update autonomous, semi-autonomous, and non-autonomous multidatabase systems. In the semi-autonomous environments one problem is the inter-site correctness problem, i.e. that a mix of pre-existing local and global transactions might not enforce any unique global consistency or might violate local consistency. Independently of this, it is not possible to dynamically detect exactly those global subtransactions that have local RW conflicts, without considerably restricting at least some aspect of local autonomy. No optimal global syntactical conflict detection mechanism is practical and even a syntactically correct mechanism is difficult to achieve, without restricting autonomy. Semantically oriented multilevel transaction management scheme with multiple subtransactions per site is therefore favourable. The binary valued concept of consistency should also be replaced. Locally serializable schedules (LSR) seems to contain all reasonable RW schedules in the environment.

1 Introduction

A conventional distributed or centralized database management system should guarantee *atomicity* [3] for the execution of the DML command sequence belonging to a transaction. Only consistency preservation of the application programs, called here transaction *correctness assumption* (TCA), is assumed as an "axiom" when constructing them. Heterogeneous transaction management addresses the problems of using pre-existing database systems as building blocks of a distributed heterogeneous database system [6]. The overall architecture is similar to that of a distributed database system, i.e. the global transactions fulfil TCA and access the global system through a well-defined global database interface (GI) offered by the global data manager GDM [6]. *Local transactions*, submitted through a local database interface (LDBI), are typical of the heterogeneous transaction management, especially in *semi-autonomous environments* [14], where local data can be updated both globally and locally.

An often adopted approach in heterogeneous environments, called here *single subtransaction at site* (SSS), means that there is at most one subtransaction at a site for each global transaction. The necessity to allow more than one subtransaction for recovery purposes is widely recognized in autonomous environments (see e.g. [4,7,8,12,13,18]). We call this principle *multiple subtransactions at site* (MSS).

2 Autonomy and the intersite correctness problem

Autonomy is widely recognized as an important issue in distributed system design [11]. We assume here that the reader is familiar with the basic ideas and definitions presented e.g. in [13, 14]. We just shortly discuss the relevant aspects of *site* autonomy in the setting of Fig. 1.

Organizational autonomy (O-autonomy) is the most fundamental type of autonomy. It means that the organization is not controlled by other organizations, as concerns how it organizes its data processing. An organization is *D-autonomous* (design autonomous) with respect to a computer system (or a part of it) if it has full organizational self-determination towards the system in a design phase. Further, a (part of a) computer system is D-autonomous with respect to an organization if the organization is *not* D-autonomous with respect to the system.

For the global transaction management it is crucial, to which extent *local database management system* (LDBMS), *local application system* (LAS), local conceptual schema (Local Sch in Fig. 1), or Export schema (Export Sch) are D-autonomous towards foreign organizations or global database administrator (GDBA). A D-autonomous LDBMS cannot be expected to be changed in any way when the global transaction mechanism is set up[1], and thus global subtransactions cannot be distinguished from the local transactions by it. Impossibility to modify local applications (LA) in LAS, add new ones or remove old ones, might make it impossible to reach all globally consistent states (completeness) or guarantee that only globally consistent states are reachable (soundness) [13]. Impossibility to change local schema to support global level logs (cf.[1,6,7,12,16]) makes it difficult a reasonable implementation of the transaction management components at site (see Fig. 1). Finally, some global database applications might be impossible to program if the necessary local data are not accessible, because the export schema does not contain the necessary metadata.

A local organization is *local transaction autonomous* (LT-autonomous) if it is able to modify existing local updating applications in LAS, implement new ones, and start these as local transactions through Local Application Interface (LAI). It is *effectively* LT-autonomous if it does this irrespective of the global considerations. The major concern resulting from the preservation of LT autonomy is: does the set of the existing global and local transactions preserve both the global and local consistency in any *serial* execution, i.e. is TCA valid during the existence of the system? Who says what "consistent" means, i.e. is there a GDBA?

Assume that the local consistency constraints enforced by local transactions La and Lb are $0 < v(a) < 10$ and $0 < v(b) < 10$ at sites a and b, respectively. Let $v(a) < v(b)$ be a global constraint. Then a global retrieval transaction G perceives an inconsistent value constellation in a serial schedule

(1) $W_{La}(a,6)\ C_{La}\ W_{Lb}(b,3)\ C_{Lb}\ R_G(a)\ R_G(b)\ C_{Ga}\ C_{Gb}$, whereas in

(2) $W_{La}(a,3)\ C_{La}\ W_{Lb}(b,6)\ C_{Lb}\ R_G(a)\ R_G(b)\ C_{Ga}\ C_{Gb}$

the values retrieved are globally consistent. All values are still locally consistent.

The pro–blem cannot be solved even if there was a global transaction which always enforces the global constraint, as there is no guarantee that the local transactions L_a and L_b do not necessarily enforce it under LT-autonomy. Consequently, no global TCA-based transaction mechanism can guarantee global consistency, if local transactions violate it. Neither can such a mechanism guarantee local consistency if global transactions do not obey it. *Serializable garbage is as useful as serial garbage.*

---

[1] This aspect alone is often defined as D-autonomy of a LDBS [8] or even autonomy.

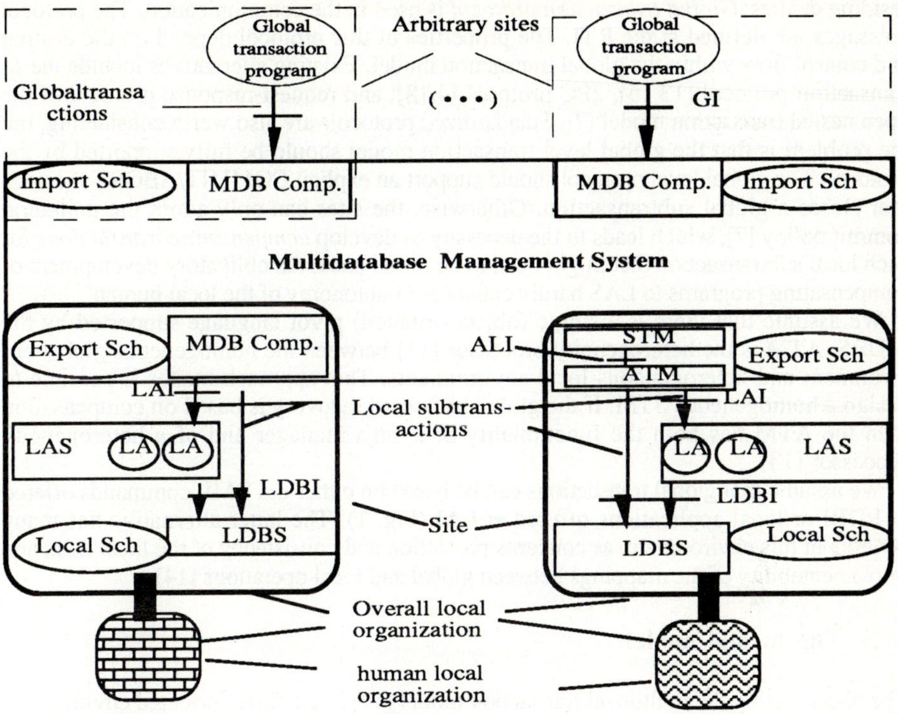

Legend:

Local Database Management System:	LDB(M)S	Abstract Local Interface:	ALI
Local Dabase Interface :	LDBI	Site Transaction Manager:	STM
Local Application (System):	LA(S)	Abstract Local Transaction Manager:	ATM
Local Application Interface:	LAI	Remote Transaction Interface:	RTI
		Global Transaction Manager:	GTM

Fig. 1. The model of the environment of concern.

The intersite correctness problem is not trivial because of site autonomy. It can only be solved by semantical analysis of the data and transactions– and the possible changes in LAS. It must be solved, otherwise there is no much sense in setting up TCA-based global transaction management mechanisms. One direction is to develop new correctness concepts, which are based on probability or fuzziness (see [13]). The transaction model should also support (application) semantics. Therefore, we discuss below the *heterogeneous multilevel transaction model* giving also further arguments for this approach.

3 A heterogeneous multilevel transaction model

3.1 The underlying transaction management architecture

Globally, we assume that there is a GTM (see Fig. 1) which can be distributed and/or replicated. A GTM takes care of handling the global transactions, together with the STMs residing at sites. *Global transaction protocol* is used in the communication. The protocol messages are defined at the RTI. The properties of this protocol depend on the nesting and control flow within the global transaction model. Existing alternatives include the S-transaction protocol [13,15], 2PC protocol [4,18], and request-response protocol of the open nested transaction model [7]. Standardized protocols are also worth considering, but the problem is that the global level transaction model should be fully supported by the protocol. The global level protocol should support an explicit COMMIT/ABORT message that closes a global subtransaction. Otherwise, the sites can only adopt the unilateral commit policy [7], which leads to the necessity to develop *compensating transactions* for each local subtransaction that might need to be rolled back. An obligatory development of compensating programs to LAS hardly enhances D-autonomy of the local human

We assume that there is a single (object-oriented) pivot language supported by the MDBS. ATM is the heterogeneity processor [11] between the homogeneous global environment and heterogeneous local environments. This approach makes it possible to design a homogeneous STM. If the global backward recovery is based on compensation then the ATM has both the functionality of a saga manager and of a heterogeneity processor [13].

We assume that global transactions can be based on either the DML commands offered at LDBI or local applications offered at LAI (Fig. 1). The latter alternative has many benefits in this environment, as concerns protection and consistency of the local data, and implementability of the mappings between global and local operations [14].

3.2 The formal model

The idea of using the multilevel transaction model [17] in an object-oriented environment has been followed by GMD-IPSI [7]. The model below is a slightly modified version of [MVN93].

We distinguish between the *transaction* and *conflict definitions* and *executions* (*instances*)., respectively. The transaction definitions are set up in the database design phase and materialized as local transaction programs in LA, and method specifications offered at RTI and GI. The conflict definitions *CONi* are also set up in the design phase based on the semantical analysis (cf. the intersite correctness problem). They are materialized to CON_i during the execution of transactions by the STMs, ATMs, and LTMs (in [17], the conflict definitions between operations remain implicit, and the conflict relations observed are always particular instances, pertaining to particular schedule).

Trees model executions. Global transactions are trees with a root T_k at level 3 (corresponding to GI) and one or several *global subtransactions* $T^i{}_{kj}$ (corresponding to ith RTI) and possibly one (abort A_{kj} and) commit operation C_{kj} at level 2. There might be more than one global subtransaction at the same site (MSS). Each global subtransaction $T^i{}_{kj}$ has one or several *local subtransactions* $T^i{}_{kjs}$ at level 1 (corresponding to LAI) and possibly one (abort $A^i{}_{kjs}$ and) commit operation $C^i{}_{kjs}$, which closes the global subtransaction. Local subtransactions and *local transactions* $T^i{}_{ltu}$ are trees with a single root at level 1 and leaves $R_{kjst}[X^i]$, $W_{kjst}[X^i]$, and possibly $C^i{}_{kjst}$ or $A^i{}_{kjst}$ at level 0. The latter actions model local commit and abort.

Heterogeneous Multilevel Schedule S =(T, G, GS, LS, RW, $<_0$), where T is a set of global and local transactions, is the following system:

L_0 schedule over T, RW, consists of the set of level 0 operations and a total (temporal) order $<_0$ among them.

At L_0 the conflict specification CON_0 is the usual one, i.e. two actions conflict if at least one of them is W and they access the same data item X^i. The conflict relation $CON_0(RW)$ contains exactly the conflicting pairs in RW, in the order in which they appear in RW. W-Actions are not considered conflicting if they are locally aborted. A locally aborted R-action might be considered conflicting if it belongs to a resubmitted local subtransaction (cf. [16]).

L_1 schedule over T, LS, consists of local transactions, local subtransactions, and A and C actions. Order $<_1$ is deduced from the L_0 order site-wise: $a^i_{kjs} <_1 a^i_{rth}$ iff for each of their child actions a^i_{kjsw} and a^i_{rthv} it holds $a^i_{kjsw} <_0 a^i_{rthv}$. Conflict specification CON_1 contains those L_1 operation pairs which do not always commute. Commuting is defined (site-wise) among all local transaction and subtransaction operations for a particular environment. Conflict relation $CON_1(LS)$ contains those actions that are in conflict in LS. Axiom 1 must be valid, i.e. $(a^i_{krt},a^i_{ijs}) \notin CON_1(LS)$ if they do not have conflicting L_0 actions in $CON_0(RW)$. Especially locally aborted *regular* local subtransactions and local transactions do not appear in $CON_1(LS)$. CON_1 is thus context-dependent, because CON_0 is.

L_2 schedule over T, GS, consists of level 2 actions, i.e. global subtransactions and A and C actions. Order $<_2$ is deduced from the order $<_1$ site-wise: $a^i_{kj} <_2 a^i_{rt}$ iff for each of their child actions a^i_{kjs} and a^i_{rth} it holds $a^i_{kjs} <_1 a^i_{rth}$ and for each local transaction a^i_{lou} it holds $a^i_{kjs} <_1 a^i_{lou} <_1 a^i_{rth}$ or $a^i_{lou} <_1 a^i_{kjs}$ or $a^i_{rth} <_1 a^i_{lou}$.

Conflict specification CON_2 contains those global subtransaction operation pairs (GS^i_k,GS^i_s) which do not always commute with each other at level 2. If (LS^i_{kg},LT^i_j), and (LT^i_j,LS^i_{uh}), appear in CON_1 for some local operation LT^i_j then (GS^i_k,LT^i_j) and (LT^i_j,GS^i_u) appear in CON_2., provided LT^i_j does not commute with one of the global subtransactions. Also all conflicting local transaction pairs (LT^i_j,LT^i_r),.. (LT^i_r,LS^i_{uh}) which connect global subtransactions, belong to CON_2. The instance $CON_2(GS)$ then contains the directly or indirectly conflicting global subtransaction pairs (a^i_{kt},a^i_{sy}) in GS and pairs (LT^i_j,LT^i_r) and (a^i_{kt},LT^i_j) which are in LS.

L_3 schedule over T, G, consists of global roots. Order $<_3$ is deduced from the order $<_2$ by combining: $T_k <_3 T_r$ iff for each of their child actions a^i_{kj} and a^i_{rt} at the same site it holds $a^i_{kj} <_2 a^i_{rt}$ and otherwise for all L_0 level child actions $a^s_{kw} <_0 a^t_{rw}$ holds.

Schedule S is *serial* if no L_0 action is both preceded and followed in $<_0$ by two different L_0 actions belonging to another transaction.

The *serialization orders* $\leq_i$ are defined in the following way:

(i) $\leq_0 = CON_0(RW)$

(ii) $\leq_1$: $a^i_{stw} \leq_1 a^i_{tuk}$ iff $\exists$ a^i_{stwy} and a^i_{tukv} in CON_0.

(iii) $\leq_2$: $a^i_{st} \leq_2 a^i_{tu}$ iff $\exists$ a^i_{stw} and a^i_{tuk} in $(CON_1 \cap \leq_1)^*$,

(iv) $\leq_3$: $T_s \leq_3 T_t$ iff $\exists$ (a^i_{st},a^i_{tu}) in $(CON_2^* \cap \leq_2)$,

* above denotes that the relation has been enhanced with global (local) subtransaction pairs $(a^i_{st(w)},a^i_{tu(k)})$ that are in an indirect conflict through local transactions.

3.3 The serializability

If the local schedulers allow cycles among incomplete transactions then one cannot prove $\leq_1$ acyclic for all schedules. We distinguish between *complete* and *incomplete* transactions [3,16]. The complete local transactions are closed with local commit or abort action, otherwise they are incomplete. A global transaction is complete if all its R and W operations are locally committed or aborted, and a commit action occurs at each level above. Furthermore, if some subtransactions have been compensated then each necessary compensating action is complete. *Committed projection* of S, C(S), only contains complete transactions of S.

Following [17] we define: schedule S is *heterogeneous 3-level serializable* iff $\leq_i$ of C(S) is acyclic for each i = 0,1,2,3 (see [10] for further details). S is locally *serializable* (LSR) if $\leq_1$ of C(S) is acyclic.

If no locally aborted R or W actions occur in $\leq_0$ (cf. above), then all actions in $\leq_0$ also occur in some local committed projection $C^i(RW)$. Consequently $\leq_1$ of C(S) is a subset of the union of local serializability relations $SG(C^i(RW))$. Because LTM guarantees acyclicity for the corresponding $SG(C^i(RW))$, $\leq_1$ is acyclic as part of it; S is in LSR. It is evident that quasi-serializable (QSR) [5] and two-level serializable (2LSR) schedules [9] are proper subsets of LSR under the above assumption concerning $\leq_0$.

4 Global schedulers

4.1 Basic problems

In order to guarantee heterogeneous 3-level serializability, global and local schedulers should keep $\leq_i$ acyclic for C(S). For $\leq_0$ and $\leq_1$ this is guaranteed by the LTMs, for $\leq_2$ and $\leq_3$ by the global level schedulers residing at GTM and STMs. *Syntactic* schedulers inherit all conflicts from $\leq_0$ up to $\leq_3$, *semantic* ones use CON_1 and CON_2 to reduce them. To keep the relations acyclic, a scheduler either a) tries to ascertain that two subtransactions do not have conflicting L_0 actions; or b) it tries to find out in which order the local subtransactions are in $\leq_1$; or c) it tries to enforce a certain order for the local subtransactions in $\leq_1$ by regulating their *submission* order (or the order of local commit actions); or d) it aborts local and global subtransactions to keep $\leq_2$ and $\leq_3$ acyclic.

When is $\leq_2$ acyclic? At least if SSS holds for C(S) then there cannot be cycles in it [18]. Still different global subtransactions at different sites might be serialized in $\leq_2$ so that $\leq_3$ becomes cyclic [6]. Under MSS and and LT-autonomy, even $\leq_2$ might be cyclic, because conflicting local transactions can interleave between two directly non-conflicting local subtransactions (under presumed commit policy [7]). This makes the usage of syntactic schedulers uninteresting under the conditions stated.

Option c) above is often offered as a solution to keep $\leq_3$ acyclic. Under LT-autonomy local transactions can be interleaved with two local subtransactions and reverse $\leq_1$ against the submission order, unless the local scheduler is rigorous [2]. We call this L1–*ordering problem*. It is relevant even under SSS, because it affects acyclicity of $\leq_3$. The problem must be solved, whether or not semantical information is used (as long as CON_2 is non-empty), as the examples show. Semantical schedulers are more viable, because by using the information in CON_1 it is possible to forget indirect conflicts. A special case is that CON_1 and CON_2 do not contain local operations at all. In that case acyclicity of $\leq_2$ is easier to achieve [10]. For syntactical schedulers it is enough to assume that local schedulers are rigorous. Another solution is to enforce additional conflicts to keep the desired order [2], but this restricts D-autonomy of the local schemas (cf. above).

4.2 Optimality, Correctness, and Axiom 1 Coherence of schedulers

The main difficulty of a global scheduler under LT-autonomy is that has *no or not enough information* of the local transactions during run-time, assuming LTMs are D-autonomous (option b) above being unrealistic). The lack of exact information means that it cannot exactly form CON_1 or CON_2 and $\leq_2$, but it must *approximate* them. Let $\leq_{s2}$ here denote the view of the global scheduler on $\leq_2$, and so on. Now one can postulate criteria for a global scheduler:

Optimality: if (a^i_{rt}, a^i_{su}) occur in $\leq_{s2}$ then (a^i_{rtec}, a^i_{suwb}) occur in $\leq_0$ of C(S)
Correctness: If (a^i_{rtec}, a^i_{suwb}) occur in $\leq_0$ of C(S) then (a^i_{rt}, a^i_{su}) occur in $\leq_{s2}$.
Axiom 1 Coherence: if (a^i_{rt}, a^i_{su}) is in CON_{s2} then (a^i_{rtec}, a^i_{suwb}) is in $\leq_0$ of C(S).

Optimality, as defined above is extremely difficult to achieve under D-and LT-autonomy, because the global scheduler should have complete information of $\leq_0$ or at least of the decompositions of the global subtransactions into elementary R and W actions. Correctness is also difficult to achieve, if LDBS applies e.g. triggers which are not known to the global (syntactical) scheduler (see [14]).

Semantical global schedulers need neither be correct nor optimal in the above sense. Still, Axiom 1 should be valid, i.e. the last property should hold. Because CON_{s2} is instantiated based on the same (incomplete) information as $\leq_{s2}$, this is difficult to achieve. Further research is needed to understand better these problems.

5 Conclusions

We have handled above transaction management issues in a heterogeneous, semi-autonomous environment. The main result is that there is no much sense in trying to develop TCA-based management mechanisms without semantical analysis of the operations and data. Inter-site correctness problem, i.e. the question of the correctness of the overall transaction mix consisting of local and global transactions, is here central. The very concept of consistency should also be developed further, based perhaps on probability theory of fuzziness. Architecturally, we suggest a multilevel transaction approach, where local applications can be used as part of the global transactions and where semantics heterogeneity are explicitly addressed. A new class of schedules, locally serializable schedules (LSR) is recognized in this framework. It seems to contain all interesting schedules in this environment. Optimality, correctness and Axiom 1 coherence characterize diverse global schedulers.

Acknowledgements. The work presented in this paper was mainly performed while the author was visiting GMD-IPSI in Darmstadt, Germany. Special thanks go to Prof. Dr. Erich J. Neuhold for the invitation. I also thank him and Peter Muth for the discussions concering the contents of this paper.

6 References

1. R. Alonso, H. Garcia-Molina, K. Salem: Concurrency Control and Recovery for Global Procedures in Federated Database Systems. In: W. Kim et al. (eds.): Database Engineering 6, IEEE CS Press, USA 1987. pp. 129 - 135.
2. Y. Breitbart, D. Georgakopoulos, M. Rusinkiewicz, A. Silberschatz: On Rigorous Transaction Scheduling. IEEE Trans. on SE 17, 954 - 960 (1991).
3. P.A. Bernstein, V. Hadzilacos, N. Goodman: Concurrency control and recovery in database systems. Addison-Wesley Publ. Comp., USA 1987.
4. Y. Breitbart, A. Silberschatz, G.R. Thompson: Reliable Transaction Management in a Multidatabase System. Proc. ACM SIGMOD'90 pp. 215 - 224.
5. W. Du, A.K. Elmagarmid: Quasi Serializability: a Correctness Criterion for Global Concurrency Control in InterBase: Proc. VLDB'89, pp. 347 - 355.
6. V. Gligor, R. Popescu-Zeletin: Transaction Management in Distributed Heterogeneous Database Management Systems. Inform. Syst. 11, 287 - 297 (1986).
7 P. Muth, T. Rakow: Atomic Commitment for Integrated Database Systems. Proc. IEEE Data Engineering'91, pp. 296-304.
8. S. Mehrotra, R. Rastogi, A. Silberschatz, H.F. Korth: A Transaction Model for Multidatabase Systems". Proc. ACM PODC'92.
9. S. Mehrotra, R. Rastogi, H.F. Korth, A. Silberschatz: Non-Serializable Executions in Heterogeneous Distributed Database Systems. Proc. PDIS'91, IEEE CS Press, pp. 245-252.
10. P. Muth, J. Veijalainen, E. Neuhold: Extending Multi-Level Transactions for Heterogeneous and Autonomous Database Systems. Arbeitspapiere der GMD(IPSI) Nr. 739. Germany, March 1993.
11. A.P. Sheth, J.A. Larson: Federated Database Systems for Managing Distributed, Heterogeneous, and Autonomous Databases. ACM Comp. Surveys 22, 183-236 (1990).
12. H.-J. Schek, G. Weikum, W. Schaad: A Multi-Level Transaction Approach to Federated DBMS Transaction Management.Proc. IMS'91, IEEE CS Press, pp. 280-287.
13. J. Veijalainen: Transaction Concepts in Autonomous Database Environments. ISBN 3-486-21596-5, R. Oldenbourg Verlag, Munich, Germany 1990.
14. J. Veijalainen, P. Muth: Transaction Management issues in Multidatabase Environments. Arbeitspapiere der GMD(IPSI), Nr. 691, Darmstadt, Germany, Oct. 1992.
15. J. Veijalainen, F.Eliassen, B.Holtkamp: The S-transaction Model. Ch 12 in: A. Elmagarmid (ed). Transaction Management for Advanced Database Applications. Morgan Kaufmann Publishers, Inc. USA, 1992, pp. 467-513.
16. J. Veijalainen, A. Wolski: Prepare and Commit Certification for Decentralized Transaction Management in Rigorous Heterogeneous Multidatabases. Proc. IEEE Data Engineering'92 IEEE CS Press, pp. 470-479.
17. G. Weikum: Principles and Realization Strategies of Multi-Level Transaction Management. ACM TODS 16, 132-180 (1991).
18. A. Wolski, J. Veijalainen: 2PC Agent Method: Achieving Serializability in Presence of Failures in a Heterogeneous Multidatabase.Proc. IEEE PARBASE-90. pp. 321 - 330.

Inheritance Conflicts in Object-Oriented Systems

Tok Wang LING and Pit Koon TEO

Department of Information Systems and Computer Science
National University of Singapore

Abstract. Inheritance conflicts in class hierarchies are avoidable through design that considers application semantics. An algorithm, in the form of IF-THEN statements, is presented that resolves any name conflicts in class hierarchies. Several examples are given which show that conflicts arise because of poor design. These conflicts can be resolved by redesigning the schema, renaming properties, redefining (or overriding) an overloaded property, factoring attributes to a more general class, removing redundant ISA relationships and/or explicitly selecting an inheritance path.

1 Introduction

In the object-oriented (OO) paradigm, classes related through the ISA relationship are organised into a class hierarchy. The class hierarchy provides an inheritance mechanism which allows a class to inherit properties (attributes/methods) from its superclasses, if any. In a single inheritance situation, a class A has only one direct superclass B. If both A and B define a property p, then A has a conflict situation which is resolved by adopting a precedence rule that chooses A's property. This is the generally accepted way of handling single inheritance situations. In a multiple inheritance situation, a class A has two or more direct superclasses B1, B2, .., Bn (n>1). Consider the case in which each Bi (1≤i≤n) has commonly named properties p1,..,pk (k≥1). Many OO database systems (OODBMSs) treat this as a conflict situation and provide several techniques to resolve it, e.g. choosing the first in a list of superclasses[6], using type information[5], explicitly choosing the required property to inherit[4] etc.

In this paper, we show that these techniques are not satisfactory because they do not examine the reasons why conflicts arise. We propose that these conflicts are avoidable if application semantics are considered during the schema design stage. An algorithm, in the form of IF-THEN statements, is presented that resolves any name conflicts in class hierarchies. The approaches we adopt include redesigning the schema, renaming properties, redefining an overloaded property, factoring attributes to a more general class, removing redundant ISA relationships and explicitly selecting the desired property.

Section 2 provides some background information while Section 3 provides a motivating example. In Section 4, a model of inheritance is proposed. A design algorithm is given in Section 5 which resolves conflicts in ISA hierarchies. Examples are given in Section 5 to substantiate our approach. Section 6 concludes. Many of the examples are illustrated using Entity Relationship diagrams[3].

2 Background

Several interpretations of the ISA relationship exist[2]. One such interpretation imbues the class hierarchy with a set inclusion semantics: Given classes A, and B, A ISA B implies that an instance of A is also an instance of B. This interpretation is adopted in situations where the class hierarchy is used to organise and classify concepts. Such a class hierarchy has been called a classification hierarchy[9]. Classification hierarchies are typically used to model ISA relationships in database schema design. When the class hierarchy is used as a model of concept classification, the order of superclasses is insignificant in a multiple inheritance situation. For example, consider the classic University database schema in which a TEACHING_ASSISTANT class is a subclass of both EMPLOYEE and STUDENT classes. The order of STUDENT and EMPLOYEE does not, and should not affect the semantics of the subclass TEACHING_ASSISTANT.

Another interpretation treats each subclass of a class hierarchy as a specialisation of its superclass(es). Therefore, given classes A and B, A ISA B implies that A inherits all properties of B (possibly redefined). Further, A can specify some extra properties beyond what B possesses. This interpretation is typically adopted in situations where a superclass shares code with its subclass(es). Such a hierarchy has been called a specialisation hierarchy[9]. Code sharing via the ISA hierarchy is predominantly used in OO programming languages. In some of these languages, e.g. Flavors, to handle code sharing in multiple inheritance situations, an ordering is imposed on the superclasses so that a class that inherits from superclasses A and B is different from a class that inherits from B and A. Intuitively, this is a straightforward way of handling multiple inheritance in a programming language, and it has been adopted in some OODBMSs, e.g. ORION[6], to handle conflicts in class hierarchies. This approach is, however, inadequate, as will be discussed in the next section.

An important property of the ISA relationship is that it is transitive, i.e. given classes A, B and C such that A ISA B and B ISA C, we can infer that A ISA C, i.e. an instance of A is also an instance of C.

3 Motivating Example

Several resolution techniques have been proposed for OODBMSs to handle conflicts in multiple inheritance situations[4,5,6,7]. An example of such a situation is given in Figure 1, which is adapted from [6]. The class SUBMARINE needs to determine which 'SIZE' attribute to inherit from its two direct superclasses. The method used in ORION[6] is to choose the first in the list of superclasses. An order is, therefore, imposed on the superclasses of SUBMARINE so that 'SIZE' is taken from, say, WATER_VEHICLE if it is the first in the list. This approach is somewhat arbitrary and may not yield the required semantics. For instance, given that superclasses A and B of a class C have commonly named attributes p and q, then no ordering of A and B will allow C to inherit A's p and B's q. POSTGRES [7] does not allow the creation of a subclass that inherits conflicting attributes (e.g. SUBMARINE). This approach is not flexible when compared to that in O2, which allows the explicit selection of the properties to inherit. O2 emphasises the path along which the property is to be inherited from. We feel, however, that the path is not important compared to the identity of the source class which defines (or redefines) the property and from which the property is inherited. For example, if 'SIZE' is defined in VEHICLE, but not in MOTORISED_VEHICLE and WATER_VEHICLE, then SUBMARINE inherits 'SIZE' from VEHICLE directly. There are two paths to VEHICLE from SUBMARINE, but either path will lead to the same result. IRIS[5] uses type information to resolve conflicts, e.g. by choosing a more specific type to inherit. It is not clear how type specificity is determined in IRIS.

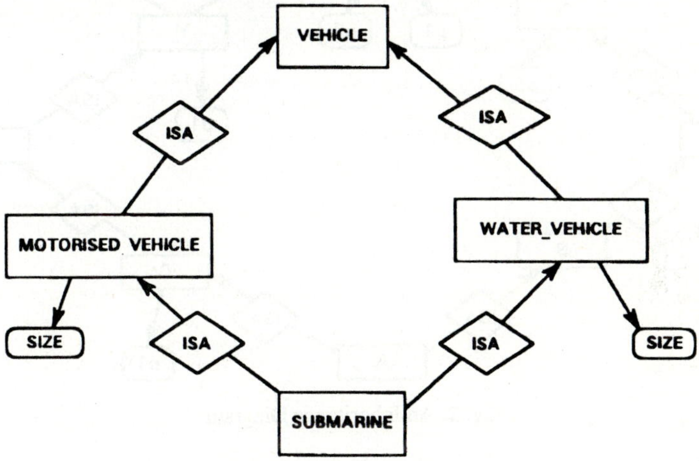

Fig. 1. Motivating Example

Many of these techniques do not examine the semantics of the properties involved in a conflict situation. The reasons why conflicts occur are not examined. Further, these techniques resolve conflicts only after the schema has been completed and implemented. In Section 5, a design methodology is proposed which resolves conflicts at the design stage. Our approach is thus proactive, as opposed to the reactive approach used in most OODBMSs. Although we recommend identifying and resolving inheritance conflicts during the design stage, there may be valid reasons for implementing a schema without removing all conflicts (e.g. user requirements). The reactive techniques of [4,5,6,7] can then be used to resolve such conflicts.

4 A Model of Inheritance

A property is *specified* in a class if it is either defined or redefined for the class. A *redefined* property overloads a similarly named property in some superclass(es) of the class. A class can inherit properties from its superclasses, if any. An inherited property is *well-defined* if it is specified in one and only one superclass, possibly indirect. A *conflict situation* exists when an inherited property is not well-defined, i.e. two or more superclasses specify the same property.

We will use ER diagrams to illustrate our notion of inheritance conflicts. Classical ER diagrams are structural and do not have the notion of methods. However, for ease of explanation, methods are depicted in our ER diagram in a similar manner as attributes. Only properties specified in an entity (class) are represented in ER diagrams.

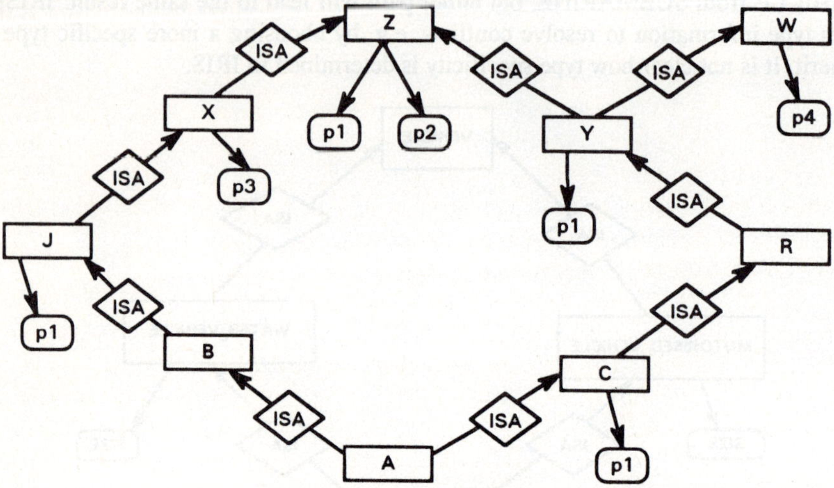

Fig. 2. An Inheritance Diagram

In Figure 2, p1 and p2 are defined in class Z, and p3 and p4 are defined in classes X and W respectively. Property p1 is redefined in classes Y, J and C and hence are explicitly represented as properties of these classes in the ER diagram. Class B inherits p1 from class J and p2 and p3 from classes Z and X respectively, while class C inherits p2 and p4 from classes Z and W respectively. Since these properties are inherited rather than specified in the classes, they are not explicitly shown on the ER diagram. Note that classes B and C have commonly named properties p1 and p2, but only p1 contributes to a conflict situation in class A. Property p1 is not well defined in A (there are two classes J and C (at least) which specify p1), but p2 is well defined (only class Z defines p2). In most OODBMSs, class A would be treated as having two conflict situations, one involving p1 and the other involving p2. Furthermore, in resolving the inheritance of p2 in class A, most systems would ask for the path of inheritance, either from B or from C. In our approach, p2 is specified in class Z and therefore the path of inheritance for this case is immaterial; either way through B or C will still converge to class Z.

In our model, properties with distinct names have different semantics. We refer to this as the *unique name assumption*. If properties with distinct names have the same semantics, we rename these properties to ensure that properties with the same semantics have the same name. However, properties with the same name need not necessarily have the same semantics. For example, in Figure 2, property p1 in class

C has a different semantics from p1 in class Y. Whenever a property p is renamed to p', it is important to rename all properties with the same semantics as p to p' in order to ensure the same consistency of meaning. This observation is important because renaming is one way to resolve conflicts in inheritance hierarchy, as we will see in the next section.

5 Avoidance of Conflicts

In this section, we introduce a design methodology which resolves conflicts in ISA hierarchies at the design stage. Our design methodology is guided by a set of IF-THEN statements, covering both single inheritance (SI) and multiple inheritance (MI) situations. Briefly, conflicts in SI situations are resolved by choosing the properties of a subclass over similarly named properties in its direct superclass. Conflicts in MI situations arise because of the following reasons. First, there may be redundant ISA relationships. By removing redundant ISA relationships, conflicts are resolved. Second, the design may be poor or erroneous. For instance, for a given subclass, the intersection of its superclasses may be empty, which suggests an erroneous design. A schema redesign will resolve the conflict. Third, given a subclass, some properties of its superclasses may have the same name and semantics. To resolve such a conflict, we either explicitly choose a superclass to inherit the property from or use a process called factoring (see Section 5.4) which moves a conflicting property to a more general class in order to resolve the conflict. Fourth, given a subclass, some properties of its superclasses may have the same name but different semantics. Renaming is recommended to resolve the conflict. The detailed algorithm is given below. Examples are given in subsequent subsections to describe the situations covered by the algorithm.

```
Given an OO schema design with ISA hierarchies,
FOR each conflict situation in the hierarchy DO
 IF it is a single-inheritance situation THEN        /* Case I : SI (Section 5.1) */
    adopt precedence rule that prefers subclass properties; ensure semantics is understood
 IF it is a multiple-inheritance situation THEN
    /* Check for ISA redundancy arising from ISA transitivity property */
   IF conflict arises because of ISA redundancy THEN
      /* Case II : MI with ISA Redundancy (Section 5.2) */
      resolve conflict by removing ISA redundancy
   ELSE
     BEGIN
        Let the MI conflict situation be represented by classes A, B1,..,Bn (n>1)
        where B1,..,Bn are the nearest superclasses of A that specify a property p.
        /* Note that a superclass of some Bi may itself specify a property p. */
        /* Check the semantics of p in B1,..,Bn */
        IF semantics of p is the same in B1,..,Bn THEN
        BEGIN  /* Check if the intersection of B1,..,Bn is empty */
           IF intersection of B1,..,Bn is empty THEN
           /* Case III: MI - same semantics (Empty Subclass) (Section 5.3) */
              Design Error, since class A (which is the intersection of B1,..,Bn) is empty
```

```
ELSE    /* Case IV: MI - same semantics (Factoring)  (Section 5.4) */
   IF there exists a more general class K which is UNION of B1,B2,..,Bn THEN
        factor  p to class K    /* for factoring see Section 5.4 */
   ELSE
       Resolve the conflict by either:
       (a) creating a general class K that is the UNION of B1,B2,..,Bn and
           factoring p to K. Add new ISA relationships Bi ISA K for i=1,..,n.
           For each maximal superclass Ci of Bi such that K is a superset of
           Ci, add the ISA relationship Ci ISA K and remove the redundant
           ISA relationship Bi ISA K.
           IF there exists a class Y such that Y is a minimal superset of K THEN
                       insert new ISA relationship K ISA Y.
           /* Option (a) removes data redundancy but may create some ISA
                redundancies which will be removed by applying Case II      */
       OR
       (b) Explicitly choosing one superclass to inherit the property.
             /* data redundancy exists which must be managed.  */
END
ELSE
  BEGIN    /* Case V: MI - properties with different semantics  (Section 5.5)*/
    Let G1,G2,..,Gm be sets of mutually exclusive classes from B1,..,Bn such that
    classes in a group share the same semantics for p. The groups G1,G2,..,Gm
    have pairwise different semantics for p. Resolve the conflict in A by:
    (a) redefining p in class A, /* not a good solution; see Section 5.5  */  or
    (b) Renaming p in Gj to, say, p_Gj for j=1,..,m to reflect their different
        semantics. To conform to the unique name assumption, each p in the
        schema that has the same semantics as p_Gj must be renamed to p_Gj.
      FOR each group Gj (j=1,..,m) with 2 or more classes having property p_Gj DO
          /* An MI situation exists between class A and  classes in Gj;  */
          /* p_Gj has the same semantics in the classes of Gj            */
          Resolve the conflict in class A using the method described in cases III & IV
      ENDFOR
   END
 END
ENDFOR
```

5.1 Case I : Single Inheritance Situation

Conflict situations in single inheritance systems are relatively easy to overcome, since we can adopt the rule that the properties in a subclass take precedence over similarly named properties in its direct superclass. However, it is important to ensure that application *semantics* are well understood. Consider the ER diagram in Figure 3. From a conventional database design viewpoint, Figure 3 is erroneous because, given that MANAGER ISA EMPLOYEE, it is strictly not correct to have 'PHONE#' as a single valued attribute in EMPLOYEE and as a multivalued attribute in MANAGER. The correct semantics, from this perspective, is that the attribute 'PHONE#' in EMPLOYEE should also be multivalued. This multivalued attribute is then inherited directly by MANAGER, without any redefinition. In this case, the majority of employees will have only one telephone number as the value of the multivalued attribute 'PHONE#'. However, this semantics cannot express the fact that only a manager can have multiple 'PHONE#'. The OO approach allows us to express this fact by making use of the ability of a subclass to redefine an inherited attribute. In Figure 3, for instance, MANAGER can override the single-valued attribute 'PHONE#' from EMPLOYEE and redefine it as a multivalued attribute 'PHONE#'. This interpretation retains the semantics of the application more closely than defining 'PHONE#' as multivalued in EMPLOYEE.

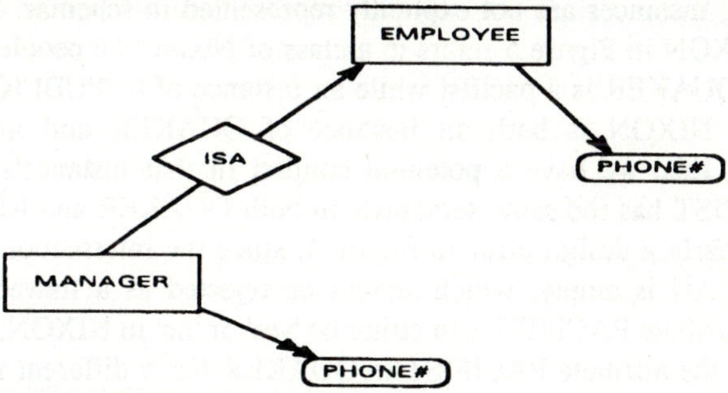

Fig. 3. 'PHONE#' is overridden in MANAGER and treated as multi-valued

5.2 Case II : Multiple Inheritance with ISA Redundancy

Redundant ISA relationships arise because of the transitive property of ISA, i.e. given A ISA B, B ISA C and A ISA C, A ISA C is redundant since it can be deduced from the other two ISA relationships. Many multiple inheritance situations can be reduced to a straightforward single inheritance situations by removing redundant ISA relationships, as illustrated in Figure 4. Figure 4 is adapted from [8] and shows an example in which the value of the color attribute for CIRCUS_ELEPHANT is supposedly ambiguous. However, note that the ISA link between ELEPHANT and CIRCUS_ELEPHANT is redundant and can be removed.

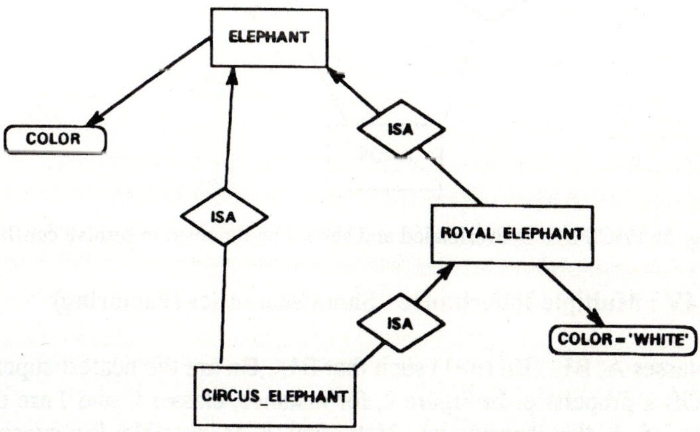

Fig. 4. Removing Redundant ISA Relationship

5.3 Case III : Multiple Inheritance - Same Semantics (Empty Subclass)

Consider classes A, B1,B2,..,Bn such that B1,B2,..,Bn are the nearest superclasses of A that specify a property p. If the semantics of p is the same in B1,B2,..,Bn and the intersection of B1,B2,..,Bn is empty, then there is a design error. This is because class A (the intersection of B1,B2,..,Bn) is empty. Figure 5 illustrates this situation.

The example schema shown in Figure 5 is adapted from [8]. In conventional database design, instances are not explicitly represented in schemas. Therefore, we assume that NIXON in Figure 5 refers to a class of Nixon-like people. In Figure 5, an instance of QUAKER is a pacifist while an instance of REPUBLICAN is not. If an instance of NIXON is both an instance of QUAKER and an instance of REPUBLICAN, then we have a potential conflict in that instance's belief. If the property PACIFIST has the same semantics in both QUAKER and REPUBLICAN, then there is clearly a design error in Figure 5, since the intersection of QUAKER and REPUBLICAN is empty, which should be rejected as a flawed design. The single-valued attribute PACIFIST can either be 'yes' or 'no' in NIXON, but not both.

Note that if the attribute PACIFIST in QUAKER has a different meaning from the attribute PACIFIST in REPUBLICAN (i.e. their semantics is different), then either choosing a specific property to inherit or changing the attribute name in either one or both superclasses will resolve the conflict. (See Section 5.5). For example, the PACIFIST attribute in REPUBLICAN can be renamed as PARTY-PACIFIST. Then an instance of NIXON will inherit two distinct attributes, viz. PACIFIST and PARTY-PACIFIST, thus removing any potential conflict.

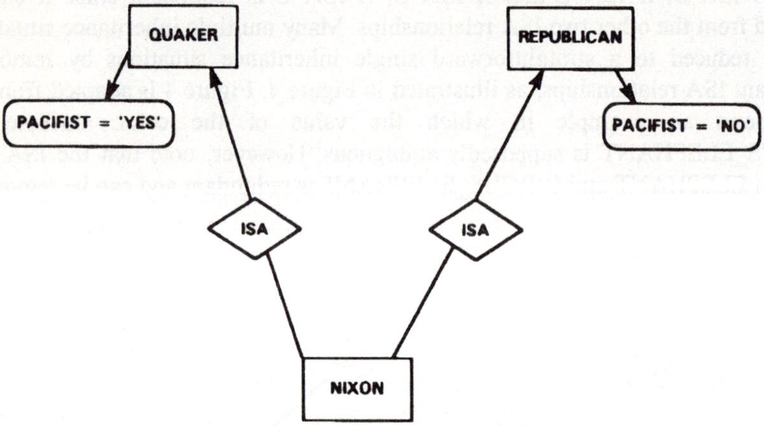

Fig. 5. 'PACIFIST' is overloaded and should be renamed to resolve conflict

5.4 Case IV : Multiple Inheritance - Same Semantics (Factoring)

Consider classes A, B1,..,Bn (n>1) such that B1,..,Bn are the nearest superclasses of A that specify a property p. In Figure 2, for instance, classes C and J are the nearest superclasses of A that specify p1. Note that it is possible for superclasses of B1,B2,..,Bn to specify a property p. For example, in Figure 2, p1 is also specified in class Z which is a superclass of C and J, and in class Y, which is a superclass of J. If p has the same semantics in B1,.., Bn, and the intersection of B1,..,Bn is not empty, the conflict in class A can be resolved by one of the following two possible cases:

(Case A) If the search for a class K in the hierarchy such that K is the union of B1,..,Bn succeeds, then perform the following steps:

(i) If K has a property p, rename the p in K to p'. Note that p' has a different semantics from the p in B1,..,Bn. For each p in the schema that has the same semantics as p', rename p to p'. This conforms to the unique name assumption (see Section 4). Then specify p in K with the same semantics as p in B1,..,Bn.

(ii) If a superclass of Bi (i=1,..,n), say Bi', lying between Bi and K, specifies a property p, then redefine the property p in Bi to explicitly inherit p from K. This prevents Bi from inheriting the property p of Bi' (whose semantics is different from p of Bi). If no superclass of Bi (i=1,..,n), lying between Bi and K specifies a property p, then remove p's definition from Bi. This ensures that Bi inherits p from K.

(iii) explicitly state that class A inherits p from K. This prevents A from inheriting p from any superclass of A lying between A and K that specifies a property p.

The execution of steps (i), (ii) and (iii) is called *factoring* p to K. Note that there can be multiple paths from A to K, but it is only important to note that A's p is taken from K.

(Case B) If no class K can be found such that K=UNION(B1,..,Bn), then consider creating a class K such that K=UNION(B1,..,Bn) and inserting K into the class hierarchy together with ISA relationships Bi ISA K, for i=1,..,n. Then factor p to K. For each *maximal* superclass Ci of Bi such that K is a superset of Ci, (i.e. there does not exist a superclass Ci' of Bi such that K is a superset of Ci' and Ci' is a superclass of Ci), we add the ISA relationship Ci ISA K and remove the redundant ISA relationship Bi ISA K. For any class Y such that Y is a *minimal* superset of K(=UNION(B1,..,Bn)), i.e. there does not exist a superset Y' of K such that Y' is a proper subset of Y, then insert the ISA relationship K ISA Y. Note that redundant ISA relationships may be created. However, these redundancies will be removed by using the method in Section 5.2.

In Figure 2, for instance, let the semantics of p1 in classes C and J be the same. Then class A has a conflict situation which can be resolved as follows:

(Case A) If Z=UNION(C,J), we (i) rename p1 in Z to p1', rename each p1 in the schema with the same semantics as p1' to p1', and specify p1 in Z with the same semantics as that in C and J, (ii) remove p1 from J and redefine p1 in class C so that p1 is explicitly inherited from Z; this prevents class C from inheriting p1 from Y, (iii) state in class A that p1 is explicitly inherited from Z; this prevents class A from inheriting p1 from class C. Note that there are two paths from A to Z, but either path will yield the same result.

(Case B) If Z is a superset of UNION(C, J), consider creating a class K such that K=UNION(C,J) and inserting it into Figure 2, together with the ISA relationships J ISA K, C ISA K and K ISA Z. Then factor p to K. For each maximal superclass S of C such that K is a superset of S, insert S ISA K and remove the redundant relationship C ISA K. For instance, assuming that K is a superset of R, Y and W

(the superclasses of C) respectively, then S = W (i.e. W is maximal) and therefore we add W ISA K and remove C ISA K. Similarly, if X is a maximal superclass of J such that K is a superset of X, we insert X ISA K and remove J ISA K.

As another example, assume in Figure 1 that 'SIZE' has the same semantics in both MOTORISED_VEHICLE and WATER_VEHICLE. It is better to factor 'SIZE' to a more general class, say VEHICLE, provided all vehicles have 'SIZE' as an attribute, i.e. VEHICLE is a union of MOTORISED_VEHICLE and WATER_VEHICLE. If VEHICLE is not a union of MOTORISED_VEHICLE and WATER_VEHICLE, then create a class K which is a union of these two classes, and K ISA VEHICLE. Three ISA relationships need to be created, viz. MOTORISED_VEHICLE ISA K, WATER_VEHICLE ISA K and K ISA VEHICLE. Then 'SIZE' can be factored to K. Moreover, the two redundant ISA relationships MOTORISED_VEHICLE ISA VEHICLE and WATER_VEHICLE ISA VEHICLE will be removed by our algorithm, as described in Case II (Section 5.2).

Sometimes, it may not be agreeable to create additional classes in order to resolve conflicts. In this case, the user may explicitly choose to inherit from one of B1,..,Bn. However, this option means that for each instance of A, the property p is redundantly stored in each of B1,..,Bn. For example, in Figure 1, the user may choose to select the 'SIZE' attribute from, say, WATER_VEHICLE. Then, for each instance of SUBMARINE, the 'SIZE' attribute is redundantly represented in MOTORISED_VEHICLE and WATER_VEHICLE. This redundancy is clearly not desirable.

5.5 Case V : Multiple Inheritance (Properties with Different Semantics)

Consider classes A, B1,B2,..,Bn such that B1,B2,..,Bn are the nearest superclasses of A that specify a property p. Let G1,G2,..,Gm be mutually exclusive groups formed from B1,B2,..,Bn such that each class in a group shares the same semantics for p. The semantics of property p is different across the groups G1,..,Gm. To resolve the conflict in class A, we propose that one of the following two options be adopted:

(Option A) the user can redefine or overload the property p in class A. Note that in some systems, e.g. O2, the user can also explicitly select a particular p to inherit from one of G1,..,Gm. We do not advocate either redefinition or explicit selection of p, because it precludes A from inheriting p with different semantics from G1,..,Gm.

(Option B) the property p can be renamed in each group Gj (for j=1,..,m) to p_Gj, since they have different semantics. Each p in the schema that has the same semantics as p_Gj must also be renamed to p_Gj. This is to conform to the unique name assumption (Section 4). For each group Gj (j=1,..,m) with two or more classes having property p_Gj, a multiple inheritance situation exists between A and the classes in Gj. Since the semantics of p_Gj is the same for the classes in Gj, the techniques in Sections 5.3 and 5.4 can be used to resolve the conflict in class A.

As an example, consider Figure 1 again. If the interpretation of 'SIZE' in MOTORISED_VEHICLE and WATER_VEHICLE is 'engine size' and 'capacity' respectively, then the semantics of 'SIZE' in these two classes is clearly different.

The two approaches described above can be used to resolve this conflict: First, the user can redefine the 'SIZE' attribute to have its own semantics in SUBMARINE. It is also possible for the user to explicitly select a required interpretation of 'SIZE' for SUBMARINE, i.e. choose the superclass required. Either way, it is not possible to access both the 'engine-size' and 'capacity' of an instance of SUBMARINE. Second, the user can rename the 'SIZE' attribute in either one or both superclasses, and inherit the renamed attribute(s). This conforms to the unique attribute name assumption and allows an instance of SUBMARINE to have both interpretations of 'SIZE'.

5.6 Conflicts in Specialisation Hierarchies

It is possible to define two classes A and B such that A inherits B's code without necessarily implying that each of A's instance is also an instance of B, i.e. there is no set inclusion semantics. Consider the following two class definitions from [1] (using a C++ like notation):

```
class supplier {    Name nm;
                    Addr addr;
          public :  supplier(Name xname, Addr xaddr); /* constructor */
                    Name name();
                    Addr address(); }
class item {        Name nm;
          public :  item (Name xname); /* constructor */
                    Name name(); }
```

In [1], a class stockitem is subsequently defined as a derived class of both supplier and item.

```
class stockitem: public item, public supplier {
                    int consumption;
          public :  int qty;
                    stockitem(Name iname, int xqty, int xconsumption,
                              Name sname, addr saddr);
                    int reorder_qty();
                    Name suppliername();
                    Name itemname();
                    Name name(); }
```

The class stockitem is specified to share code/properties with supplier and item. A conflict then arises because the method name() defined in both supplier and item has the same name. The method used in [1] is to use explicit qualification to resolve this conflict. Therefore, if it is required that the name() function of stockitem yields the supplier's name, then name is redefined as:

```
Name stockitem::name()
{ return supplier::name() ; }
```

Similar changes to the above code are required if item name is required. This example illustrates that an attempt to share in object-oriented languages may produce a conflict situation which typically is resolved using some language feature (e.g. explicit qualification as the example shows).

6 Conclusion

In this paper, we showed through several examples the reasons why conflicts can arise in multiple inheritance systems. We also discussed the conflict resolution techniques adopted by several object-oriented database systems, e.g. ORION, O2 and POSTGRES. The main fault with these techniques is that they operate at a syntactic, rather than a semantic, level.

We propose that conflicts can be avoided if more thought is given to application semantics during the design stage. Conflicts are removed by redesigning the schema, by renaming the properties in order to satisfy the unique attribute name assumption, by removing redundant ISA relationships, by factoring properties to a more general class, by overriding (or re-implementing) an overloaded property and by explicitly choosing an inheritance path in order to preserve the advantage of name overloading. An algorithm, in the form of IF-THEN statements, is given to resolve conflicts in ISA hierarchy in a systematic manner.

References

1. R. Agrawal, N. H. Gehani: ODE (Object database and environment): The language and the data model. Proc. ACM-SIGMOD Intl. Conf. on Management of Data. 1989, pp. 36-45.
2. R.J. Brachman: What IS-A is and isn't. Computer. Vol 16 No 10, Oct 1983, pp. 30-36.
3. P.P. Chen: The entity-relationship model: toward a unified view of data. ACM Transactions on Database Systems. Vol 1 No 1, 1976.
4. O. Deux et al: The story of O2. IEEE Transactions on Knowledge and Data Engineering. Vol 2 No 1, Mar 1990, pp. 91-108.
5. D. Fishman et al: IRIS: An object oriented database management system. ACM Transactions on Office Information Systems. Vol 5 No 1, Jan 87, pp. 48-69.
6. W. Kim: An introduction to object-oriented databases. MIT Press, Cambridge, Mass., 1990.
7. L. Rowe, M. Stonebraker: The Postgres data model. The Postgres Papers, Memo No. UCB/ERL M86/85. University of California, Berkeley, Jun 1987 (Revised).
8. D. Touretzky: Implicit Ordering of Defaults in Inheritance Systems. Proc. AAAI-84, Austin, Texas, 1984, pp. 322-325.
9. S. Zdonik D.Maier: Fundamentals of object-oriented database systems. Readings in Object-Oriented Database Systems. Morgan Kaufman, San Mateo, Ca., 1990, pp. 1-32.

Managing Derived Data in Intelligent Database Systems: An Implementation Study

J. Leon Zhao

Graduate School of Business Administration
The College of William and Mary, Williamsburg, Virginia 23187, USA

Abstract: Knowledge-directed inference in intelligent database systems derives large amounts of data that require new functionalities not available in conventional database management systems. This paper presents a front-end implementation of the *selective materialization paradigm* proposed in a previous study for efficient management of derived data. Empirical results obtained in this study demonstrate that selective materialization can be very cost effective compared to current approaches in other research prototypes. In addition, this paper introduces several concepts and algorithms key to the implementation, such as the minimal derivation graph, the rule transformation algorithm, and physical rule/data graphs.

1. Introduction

Intelligent database systems (IDSs) are being developed to produce information from the data contained in large shared databases, using knowledge-directed inference [Brod88, Ston89, Kers90, Ston92]. Efficient management of derived data is a major issue in IDSs due to two factors: the large volume of these data and the chaining effect in the inference process [SeZh91]. Managing derived data is different from managing base data. While changes to base data are usually done directly by users, changes to derived data must be done automatically by the database management system. Consequently, techniques and algorithms for maintaining derived data must be developed and implemented in IDSs.

There are a number of research systems that integrate rule systems into a DBMS, for example, Postgres [StRH90], Starburst [Haas90], Iris [WiLH90], LDL [Chim90], RDL1 [KiMS89], DIPS [SeLR90], and Ariel [Hans89]. Currently, rule systems in these prototypes focus on supporting database services such as triggers, integrity constraints, data security, and relational views. With regard to managing derived data, these research prototypes materialize either all data objects, such as DIPS [SeLR90], or none of the data objects, such as LDL [Chim90].

Most previous research on data materialization in relational DBMSs ([BlLT86], [Hans87], [SePa89], [SeFa91], [Rous91]) has been limited to when and how to materialize results of a relational query in a centralized or a distributed DBMS. These studies have established that to improve processing efficiency or to meet requirements on response time, derived data may be maintained on secondary storage rather than recomputed when they are needed. However, the issue of selecting the point of materialization in a large inference network (or graph) was not addressed in those studies.

In an earlier paper [SeZh91], the authors proposed a selective materialization paradigm and analyzed the chaining effect when selecting derived relation for materialization in an inference network. Maintaining a derived relation in this case has two potential benefits. First, queries to the derived data will be answered more quickly, thus realizing better performance, and, second, subsequent rules on the chain will be processed more efficiently as well. In [SeZh91], the authors also developed a decomposition-based optimization algorithm to identify points in the rule/data graph, where local decisions are optimal; the result is a set of derived relations whose materialization decisions have been made and a set of optimization problems corresponding to subgraphs of the original graph.

This paper presents a front-end implementation of the selective materialization paradigm, referred to as the *Materialization Assisted Rule System (MARS)*. Experimental results presented in this paper demonstrate that the selective materialization paradigm is more cost effective than either the approaches of "materialize all" or "materialize none" currently utilized in other systems.

The following section delineates the prototyping environment of MARS and some basic concepts, including a brief introduction to Postgres, the rule language, and the concept of rule transformation. Section 3 describes the system architecture of the MARS prototype and its components, the algorithms of rule transformation and data propagation. Section 4 presents two experiments that demonstrate the cost-saving potential of the selective materialization paradigm. Finally, section 5 discusses the merits and limitations of the MARS prototype system and suggests future research directions.

2. The MARS Prototyping Environment

The MARS prototype is implemented in the front-end of the Postgres DBMS as illustrated in figure 1. As the first step of prototyping efforts, the front-end implementation serves as a testbed to provide further evidence on the importance of the selective materialization paradigm in addition to the results of theoretical computation in [SeZh91].

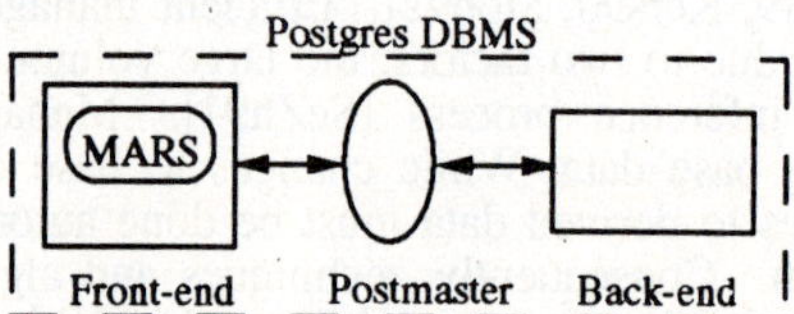

Figure 1. The front-end implementation of MARS

2.1. Postgres as the Prototyping Platform

Postgres is an extensible relationally-based DBMS designed to deal with many advanced database issues such as complex data types, user-defined procedures, triggers, and rules [Ston91]. It is composed of three main components: the front-end, the postmaster, and the back-end. Postgres provides a front-end library that enables applications to send a query command to the back-end, name a buffer space, direct query results to the named buffer, and extract data elements from the buffer.

Although Postgres rule system consists of two rule managers, a relational-level rule manager and a tuple-level rule manager, it does not make use of the selective materialization paradigm. Consequently, the rule managers are not used in the implementation of the MARS prototype.

2.2. Rule Definition

An inference rule is defined with a command that has the syntax of

define_rule id head content

For example, rule r1 is given by

define_rule r1 perform (company.name, company.ltype, byear = 5, solvent = "no")
where company.cftd > 0.13 and company.tdta > 0.70

A syntactical analysis of rule r1 gives

id = "r1"
head = "perform"
content = "(company.name, company.ltype, byear = 5, solvent = "no")
where company.cftd > 0.13 and company.tdta > 0.70"

Notice that the content of rule r1 is based on PostQuel (the Postgres data language) [StRH90].

2.3. Rule Storage Format

In this prototype, information about rules and their interrelationships is stored in three relations: the rule_body relation, the rule_text, and the rule_status relation. The status is 1 if the relation is materialized (or a base relation) and 0 otherwise. The schemas of the rule definition relations are

rule_body[body,id]   rule_text[id,head,content]   rule_status[predicate,status]

Now, considering that the relation associated with the "perform" predicate of rule r1 in the previous subsection is not materialized and "company" is a base relation, the rule definition relations will contain the following when r1 is defined.

rule_body["company","r1"]
rule_text["r1","perform", "(company.name, company.ltype, byear = 5, solvent = "no")
where company.cftd > 0.13 and company.tdta > 0.70"]
rule_status["company",1]
rule_status["perform",0]

2.4. Minimal Derivation Graph

The data propagation algorithm requires the concept of *Minimal Derivation Graph* (MDG). The inter-relationships among a group of rules may be represented with a rule/data graph as shown in figure 2(a), where a black dot is a base object, a shaded dot indicates a materialized object, and a white dot represents a non-materialized object. The arrows denote rules that interconnect the objects.

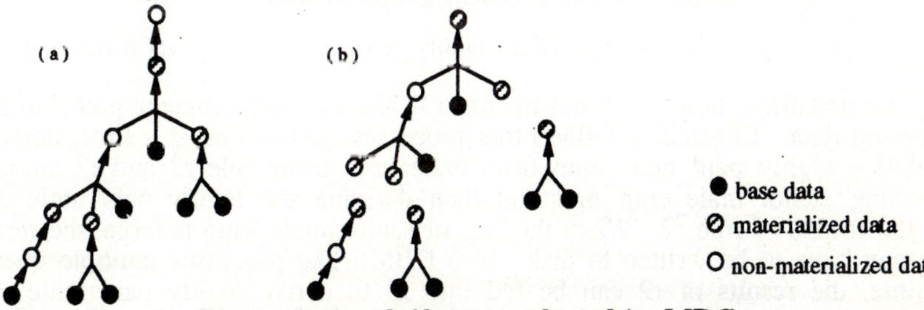

Figure 2. A rule/data graph and its MDGs

An MDG is a subgraph that consists of a minimal set of interrelated rules and data objects where every chain of data flow starts with a materialized or base data and ends with a materialized data. The boundary data nodes of an MDG are either source nodes or destination nodes. Using this concept, the rule/data graph in figure 2(a) may be partitioned into four subgraphs in the form of MDGs, as shown in figure 2(b).

2.5. Rule Transformation and Physical Graphs

First, we define the concepts of *logical graph* and *physical graph.* A logical graph is defined by users based solely on logical sequence of data derivation. A physical graph is the result of rearranging the interconnections among rules based on the logical graph and materialization decisions.

Rule transformation is the process of converting a logical rule/data graph into a physical graph, given the materialization decisions on the derived objects in the graph. *Rule transformation* is similar to query rewrite in conventional DBMSs [Ston92], both involving conversion of logic expressions.

Rule transformation enables users to concentrate on the logical correctness of the rules and leave the physical implementation to the system. The system optimizes the materialization decisions and transforms the logical rules into physical ones without users' intervention.

To illustrate the concept, consider a relation emp(id,sex,age,salary) and rules r1, r2, and r3. Assume that attributes are unique.

r1: IF emp(sex="male") THEN male_emp(id,age,salary).
r2: IF male_emp(age>50) THEN senior_male_emp(id,age,salary).
r3: IF senior_male_emp(salary>50k) THEN highly_paid_senior_male_emp(id,age,salary).

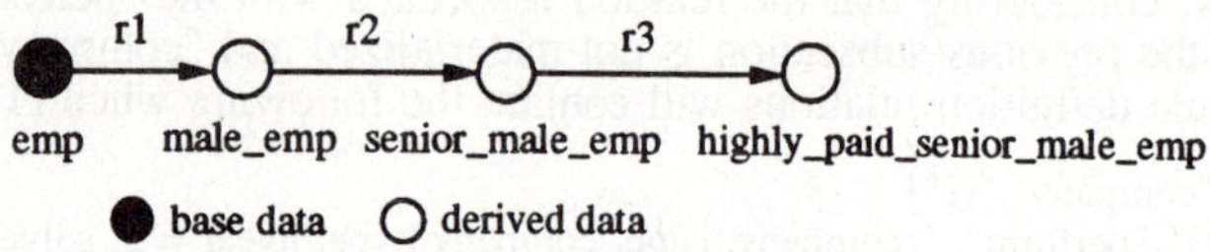

Figure 3. A simple logical graph

The logical rule/data graph of this example is given in figure 3. Supposing that the optimal materialization decision is to materialize the results of rule r2, i.e., male_emp, then the physical rule/data graph will be as in figure 4, where r3' is the result of combining rules r2 and r3.

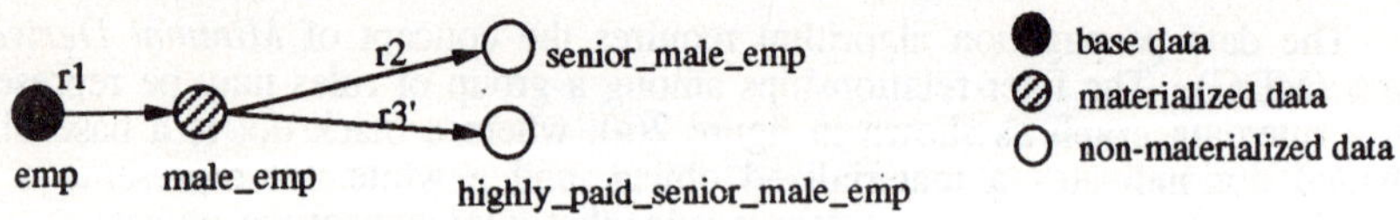

Figure 4. The physical graph of figure 3

r3': IF male_emp(age>50,salary>50k) THEN highly_paid_senior_male_emp(id,age,salary).

The transformation of r2 and r3 into r3' allows more efficient processing of the derived data. Consider a DBMS that processes queries one at a time, deriving the relation highly_paid_male_emp from male_emp using rule r2 and r3 amounts to deriving senior_male_emp first and then deriving the highly_paid_male_emp using the results of rule r2. When the size of senior_male_emp is large, the results of r2 may have to be written to disk. In a DBMS that processes multiple queries at a time, the results of r2 can be fed into r3 to derive highly_paid_male_emp without writing intermediate results to disk, thus reducing processing time. By transforming r2 and r3 into r3', highly_paid_male_emp will be derived directly, thereby avoiding the derivation of intermediate results. This example illustrates the basic idea of rule transformation that applies to more complex situations with any number of rules.

3. The MARS System and Algorithms

MARS is composed of three basic components: a rule transformer, a retrieval manager, and an update manager. The system architecture is illustrated in figure 5.

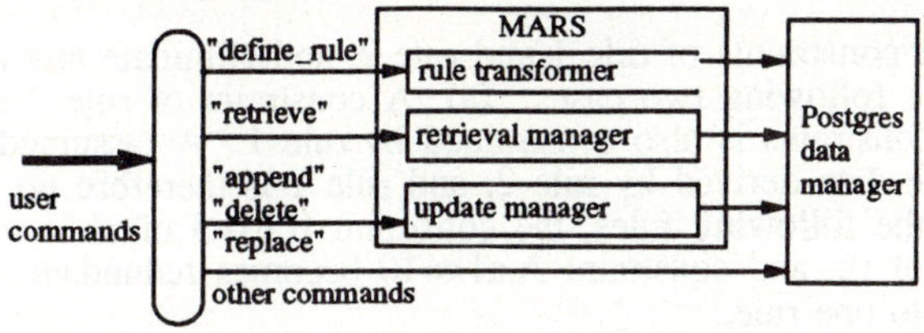

Figure 5. System architecture of the MARS prototype

When a rule is defined, the rule transformer combines it with the rules existing in the system. The retrieval manager is called upon when a retrieval query requests non-materialized data objects, and the update manager deals with commands that append to, delete from, or modify a base data object.

3.1. The Rule Transformation Algorithm

With the algorithm, each rule is transformed by combining it with all rules that derive its antecedent data. To simplify the prototype programming, it is assumed that the order of defining rules of a rule/data graph is such that rules closer to the base data are defined first. To introduce the algorithm below, two generic rules, rule 1 and rule 2, are denoted. Let rule 1 be defined on the data derived by rule 2, i.e., the direction of data flow is [rule 2] --> [rule 1]. The basic procedure of transforming rule 1 and rule 2 into a new rule is given below.

(0) Stop the transformation if the head predicate of rule 2 is materialized.

(1) Determine the feasibility of transformation. Stop the transformation if not transformable. The transformability of rules is limited by the first-order logic on which the PostQuel language is based. Rule 1 and rule 2 cannot be combined if rule 1 constrains an attribute that is computed in rule 2. For instance, the following rules r1 and r2 cannot be combined, where the rules are defined using an English-like syntax.

r1: IF B(b1>10) THEN C(c1=B.b1)
r2: IF A(a1>5) THEN B(b1=A.a1*A.a2)

Suppose r1 and r2 are combined into r1', then we have

r1': IF A(a1>5,a1*a2>10) THEN C(c1=A.a1*A.a2)

Unfortunately, the clause a1*a2>10 in r1' is not a first-order logic clause and is therefore invalid in PostQuel or any other first-order language.

(2) Determine the satisfiability between rules 1 and 2. Stop the transformation if rule 1 is not satisfiable. The results of rule 2 does not satisfy rule 1 in the following two cases. (a) An attribute assigned with a constant in rule 2 is constrained in rule 1, but the assigned constant does not satisfy rule 1. For instance, such is true for the following rules r1 and r2 because B.b1 is assigned a value of 30 in r2, while r1 asserts a condition of B.b1<10.

r1: IF B(b1<10) THEN C(c1=B.b2)
r2: IF A(a1>5) THEN B(b1=30,b2=A.a3)

(b) An attribute selected in rule 2 never satisfies a constraint clause of rule 1. For instance, in the following rules r1 and r2, attribute B.b1 is selected in r2 from A.a1. Since r2 ensures that the value of B.b1 is larger than 10, the data values of the attribute B.b1 will never satisfy r1.

r1: IF B(b1<5) THEN C(c1="x")
r2: IF A(a1>10) THEN B(b1=A.a1,b2=A.a3)

(3) Combine the constraints of rule 1 and rule 2, and eliminate any redundant constraints as in the following two cases. (a) A constraint of rule 2 is redundant if the attribute it constrains is also constrained by rule 1. As assumed above, rule 1 is defined on the data derived by rule 2, and rule 1 is therefore no less restrictive than rule 2. In the following rules, the constraint B.b1<5 of r1 is more restrictive than A.a1<=10 of r2, and constraint A.a1<=10 becomes redundant after r1 and r2 are combined into one rule.

r1: IF B(b1<5) THEN C(c1="x")
r2: IF A(a1<=10) THEN B(b1=A.a1,b2=A.a3)

(b) A constraint of rule 1 is redundant if it constrains an attribute assigned with a constant in rule 2 because that assignment clause will disappear after transformation. For example, the combination of the following two rules, r1 and r2, gives r1', and the constraint B.b2=10 needs to be eliminated since it is redundant.

r1: IF B(b2=10) THEN C(c1="x")
r2: IF A(a1<5) THEN B(b1=A.a1,b2=10)
r1': IF A(a1<5) THEN C(c1="x")

Notice that rule r1' does not retain all the information contained in rules r1 and r2. This is not a problem since rule r1 still exists. The transformation r1' is merely to enable the derivation of predicate C from A without going through predicate B.

(4) Substitute the predicate and attribute variables of rule 1 with appropriate ones of rule 2. This step can be explained through the following two rules.

r1: IF B(b2>10) THEN C(c1="x")
r2: IF A(a1<5) THEN B(b1=A.a1,b2=A.a2)

Assuming that predicate B is not materialized and that rules r1 and r2 are transformable and satisfiable, the constraints of r1 and r2 can be combined in Step (3), resulting in

r1': IF A(a1<5) AND B(b2>10) THEN C(c1="x").

Since predicate B will disappear and B.b2 is equivalent to A.a2, the substitution of predicate and attribute gives

r1': IF A(a1<5) AND A(a2>10) THEN C(c1="x"),

which is essentially

r1': IF A(a1<5,a2>10) THEN C(c1="x").

Although the procedure of substituting predicates and attributes is more complex when joins are involved, the principle of substitution remains the same.

3.2. Data Propagation and Rule Chaining

There are four Postgres commands for data manipulation, "retrieve", "append", "delete", and "replace". The "append," "delete", and "replace" commands are called collectively as updates, while "retrieve" commands are termed queries.

3.2.1. The Query Propagation Algorithm

When MARS receives a retrieval command, it propagates the query process:

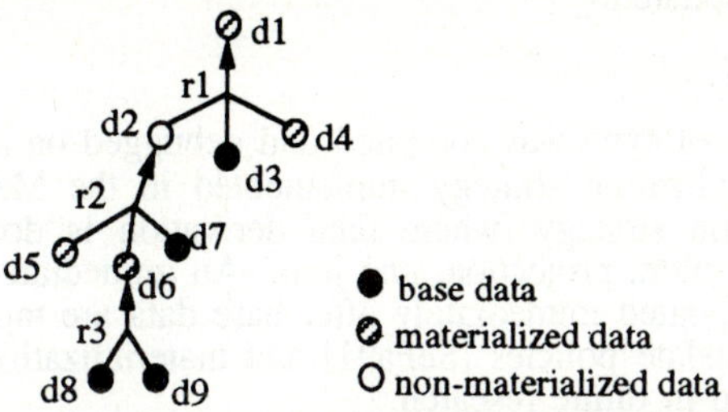

Figure 6. Data propagation through an MDG

- If the retrieval accesses a non-materialized data object, all rules that are needed to recompute the data object will be activated. For example, if the data object d2 of figure 6 is requested by a retrieval query, rule r2 will be activated.
- If an activated rule accesses a non-materialized data object, all other rules deriving the non-materialized data object will also be activated. This is the case for r2 since it accesses d6 which is not materialized. As a result, rule r3 is also activated.
- This recursion will continue until all newly activated rules do not access non-materialized data objects. The process of searching rules that are needed to derive a given data object is commonly referred to as *backward chaining*.
- Once the backward chaining is done, non-materialized data objects will be derived in the reversed order that the rules are activated until the data objects accessed by the retrieval command are derived. Using the example in figure 6, d6 is derived first and then d2. This process of deriving non-materialized data objects from materialized or base data is usually called *forward chaining*.

3.2.2. The Update Propagation Algorithm

Considering the MARS receives an append command to a base data object (the procedures for deletion and replacement are similar), an update propagation proceeds as follows:

- MARS searches for materialized objects along the chain of rules by traversing the physical rule/data graph from the body predicate affected to its head predicate. Given that base data d8 in figure 6 is accessed with an append query, the first materialized data along the chain of rules starting with d8 is d1.
- If a materialized data is reached through the traversal, MARS creates a differential file containing the base data appended.
- A backward chaining starts with the materialized data, e.g., d1 in the example. This process creates the minimal derivation graph (MDG) that includes the materialized data object as a destination node and the base data object as a source node.
- When the backward chaining is complete, a differential file corresponding to each destination node of the MDG will be created by a forward chaining using the differential file corresponding to the base data object updated by the append command. For the example, this amounts to generating a differential file for the destination node d1 given the activated rules, r1, r2, and r3 and the differential file for the source node d8.
- The destination differential file is then used to append the destination object, d1 in the example.

- This update propagation continues to the subsequent MDG in the same rule/data graph until all materialized data objects, reachable by the append command, are updated.

4. Experiments

The MARS prototype was compiled and debugged on a Sun Sparc II workstation. The materialization strategy implemented in the MARS prototype is the direct materialization strategy, where data derivation is done through relational operations, i.e., selection, projection, and join. An immediate update policy, where materialization is updated immediately after base data are modified, is used in this prototype. Other update policies [SeFa91] and materialization strategies [SeZh93] will be implemented in future research.

4.1. Experimental Procedure

The experimental procedure that is used to obtain empirical results is introduced below. Example 1 is described with the logical and physical rule/data graphs in figures 7 and 8 respectively. The relational schemas of the data objects and logical rule definitions for example 1 are given below.

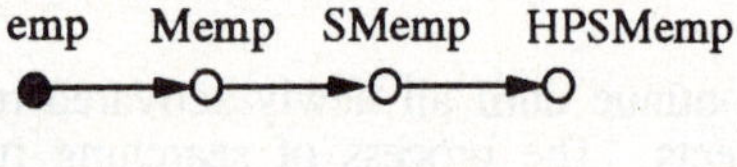

Figure 7. The logical rule/data graph of example 1

Example 1:

schemas

emp(eid, ename, sex, age, salary) Memp(eid, sex, age, salary)
SMemp(eid, sex, age, salary) HPSMemp(eid, sex, age, salary)

rule definitions

define_rule r1 Memp (eid=emp.eid,age=emp.age,salary=emp.salary) where emp.sex="m"
define_rule r2 SMemp (eid=Memp.eid,age=Memp.age,salary=Memp.salary)
 where Memp.age>50
define_rule r3 HPSMemp (eid=SMemp.eid,age=SMemp.age,salary=SMemp.salary)
 where SMemp.salary>50k

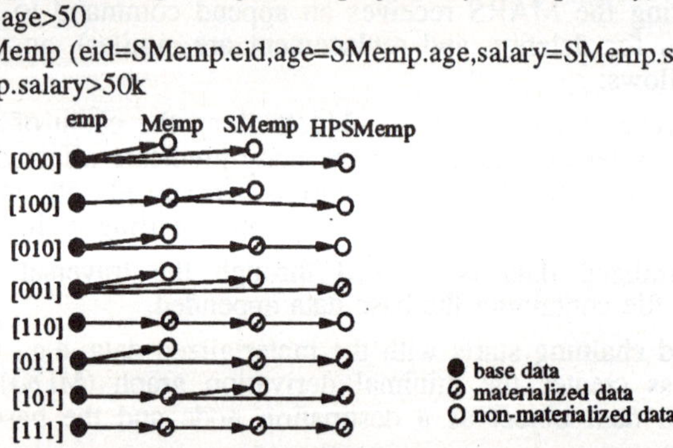

Figure 8. The physical rule/data graphs of example 1

Given a logical rule/data graph and a set of materialization decisions about the derived objects, the sequence of actions in each test are as follows.

(1) Create the relations in the Postgres database for the given rule/data graph. In the example, the following command creates the emp relation.

create emp(name=char16,eid=int2,sex=char,age=int,salary=int2)

(2) Append the rule status relation with tuples that represent the materialization decisions; where 1 denotes materialization and 0 means no materialization. The table below illustrates the content of the rule_status relation when the physical graph with a materialization decision of [010] is used (see figure 8).

rbody	mstatus
emp	1
Memp	0
SMemp	1
HPSMemp	0

(3) Transform the logical rules. Rule transformation is performed automatically as the rules are defined. The physical rules resulting from the transformation are appended to the rule_text relation. At the same time, the unique rule bodies are extracted automatically from the rule definition and appended to the rule_body relation. Given the rule_status table above, the rule definitions in example 1 would be transformed into the ones shown in the following table, where the rule with the id "r2r1" is the result of combining rules r1 and r2.

id	head	content
r1	Memp	(eid=emp.eid,age=emp.age,salary=emp.salary) where emp.sex="m"
r2r1	SMemp	(eid=emp.eid,age=emp.age,salary=emp.salary) where emp.age>50 and emp.sex="m"
r3	HPSMemp	(eid=SMemp.eid,age=SMemp.age,salary=SMemp.salary) where SMemp.salary>50k

body	id
emp	r1
emp	r2r1
SMemp	r3

(4) Effectuate the physical rules by issuing the command "set_rule". The three rule definition relations, namely, rule_status, rule_text, and rule_body, are buffered to expedite the rule chaining processes.

(5) Initialize the base relations with tuples. For each tuple appended into a base relation, the relevant rules are activated to update the materialized relations. This update propagation initiates the rule-derived relations that are specified to be materialized in the rule_status relation.

(6) Activate the timer by the command "start_test".

(7) Run the test in a batch mode. Each test consists of a combination of update and retrieval commands.

(8) Record the time consumed by the test using the command "end_test".

(9) Diseffectuate the rules by "unset_rule".

4.2. Experimental Results

This section reports the results of two experiments, each of which consists of a series of tests that are characterized in two dimensions: query composition and rule materialization decision. A query composition is given by specifying the type and frequency of query commands in a test. To simplify the experiment, the types of query commands are limited to "retrieve" and "append". A rule materialization decision specifies the materialization status of the relations.

It should be noted that the experiments are not random. Since materialization decisions are heavily dependent on the parameter values, such as selectivity and query-to-update ratios, there would be cases where the best decision is either "materialize all" or "materialize none". The objective of the experiments is to substantiate the fact that there are realistic cases where selective materialization outperforms both "materialize all" and "materialize none" approaches.

4.2.1. Experiment I

A test in experiment I is composed of 100 append queries to relation emp, 5 retrieval queries to relation Memp, 1 retrieval query to relation SMemp, and 1 retrieval query to relation HPSMemp. Each test takes one of the eight materialization combinations shown in figure 8. Before each test, the emp relation is initialized with 900 tuples that are generated randomly. When all derived relations are materialized, relations Memp, SMemp, and HPSMemp are initialized with 445, 167, and 56 tuples respectively. The results of experiment I are shown in figure 9 where the horizontal axis specifies the rule materialization decisions and the vertical axis gives the total response time for all queries and updates of each test.

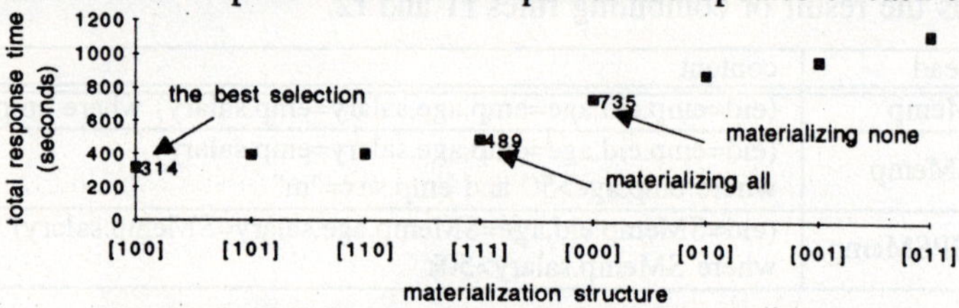

Figure 9. Total response times of experiment I

The results depicted in figure 9 show that the selective materialization resulting in the lowest computing cost for the experimental condition is [100], i.e., only the derived relation Memp should be materialized. This selective materialization strategy saves about 60% relative to the "materialize all" strategy and about 140% relative to the "materialize none" strategy. Figure 9 indicates that materializing relations SMemp and HPSMemp increases the overall computing cost under the given conditions.

4.2.2. Experiment II

In this experiment, a join rule is added to example 1, resulting in example 2 and the logical graph in figure 10. The added rule and data objects of example 2 are shown below. Some physical graphs of example 2 are given in figure 11.

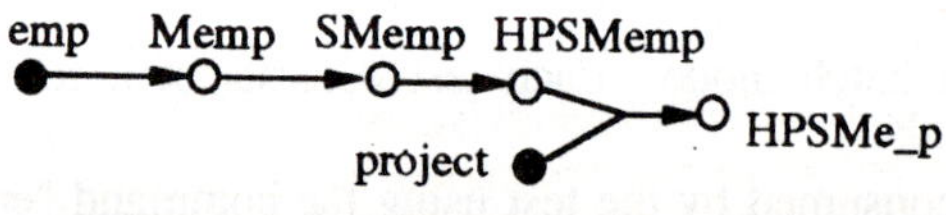

Figure 10. The logical graph of example 2

project(pname, memo, eid)
HPSMe_p(eid, pname, memo)
define_rule r4 HPSMe_p (eid = HPSMemp.eid, pname = project.pname,
memo = project.memo) where HPSMemp.eid = project.eid

In this experiment, the initial sizes of emp, Memp, SMemp, and HPSMemp are 250, 121, 31, and 13 respectively. The project relation is initialized with 1000 tuples and the initial size of HPSMe_p is 107. The queries in the test include 75 appends to emp, 1 retrieval to Memp, 1 retrieval to SMemp, 1 retrieval to

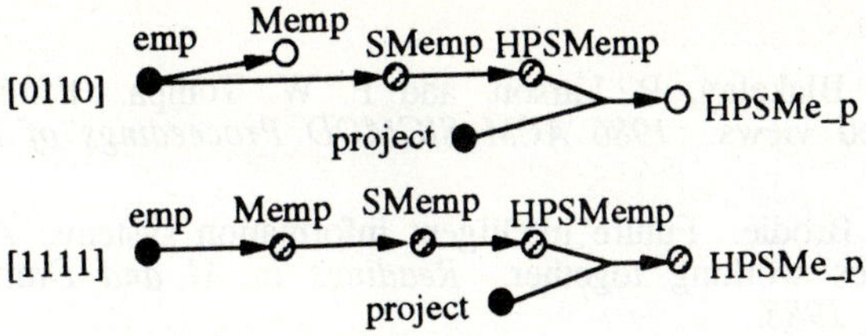

Figure 11. Some physical graphs of example 2

HPSMmep, and 20 retrievals to HPSMe_p.

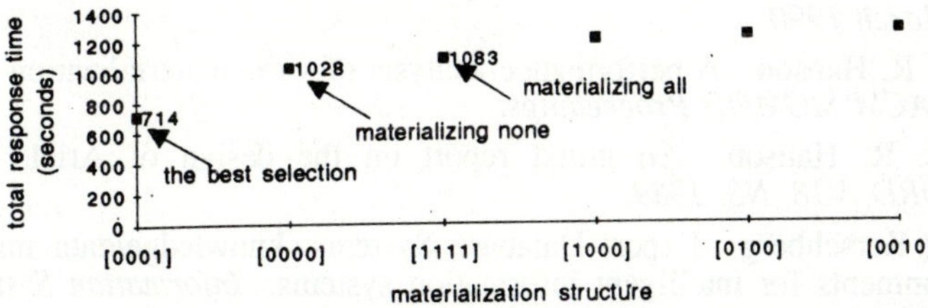

Figure 12. Total response times of experiment II

As shown in figure 12, the best materialization decision is [0001], i.e., only the derived relation HPSMe_p is materialized. The cost savings of the selective materialization strategy is about 40% relative to the two special strategies that materialize either all or none of the derived relations. Notice that results are presented only for some of the tests that include the best and worst cases.

5. Conclusion

A prototype rule system termed *Materialization Assisted Rule System* (MARS) was implemented in the front-end of the Postgres DBMS to demonstrate the practicality and the benefits of the selective materialization paradigm proposed in a previous study [SeZh91]. Concepts and algorithms were developed as the implementation requires, which include the minimal derivation graph, the logical and physical rule/data graphs, and the algorithms of rule transformation, query propagation, and update propagation. The concept and algorithm of rule transformation is an important contribution of this study. As explained previously, rule transformation enables the independence of rule definition and rule implementation. With the system taking charge of materialization decisions and rule transformation, users can focus on the logic correctness of rules without worrying about the efficiency issues of implementing them.

As illustrated by the experimental results, the selective materialization paradigm is very beneficial and the cost savings is as much as 140%. Considering that the MARS prototype is a front-end implementation, these results are significant. MARS favors non-materialization to materialization since the recomputation of non-materialized data is a more standard operation of Postgres.

A back-end implementation of the concepts and algorithms developed in this paper is under investigation to make the selective materialization more efficient. In addition, the rule materialization framework developed in [SeZh93] for individual rules will be implemented as well. The back-end implementation will result in new relational operators such as one that can inform the materialization status of a derived relation to the data manager.

References

[BlLT86] J. A. Blakeley, P. Larson, and F. W. Tompa. Efficiently updating materialized views. *1986 ACM SIGMOD Proceedings of Management of Data.*

[Brod88] M. L. Brodie. Future intelligent information systems: AI and database technologies working together. *Readings in AI and Databases, Morgan Kaufmann, 1988.*

[Chim90] D. Chimenti et al. The LDL system prototype. *IEEE Trans. on Knowledge and Data Engineering (TKDE), V2, N1, March 1990.*

[Haas90] L. Haas et al. Starburst mid-flight: as the dust clears. *IEEE TKDE, V2, N1, March 1990.*

[Hans87] E. R. Hanson. A performance analysis of view materialization strategies. *1987 ACM SIGMOD Proceedings.*

[Hans89] E. R. Hanson. An initial report on the design of Ariel. *SIGMOD RECORD, V18, N3, 1989.*

[Kers90] L. Kerschberg. Expert Database Systems: knowledge/data management environments for intelligent information systems. *Information Systems, V15, N1, 1990.*

[KiMS89] J. Kiernan, C. de Maindreville, and E. Simon. The design and implementation of an extendible deductive database system. *SIGMOD RECORD, V18, N3,. 1989.*

[Rous91] N. Roussopoulos. An incremental access method for viewcache: concept, algorithms, and cost analysis. *ACM TODS, V16, N3, 1991.*

[SeFa91] A. Segev and W. Fang. Currency-Based Updates to Distributed Materialized Views. *Management Science, July 1991.*

[SeLR90] T. Sellis, C.-C. Lin, and L. Raschid. Coupling Production Systems and Database Systems: A Homogeneous Approach. *Univ. of Maryland, UMIACS-TR-87-68.1, 1990.*

[SePa89] A. Segev and J. Park. Updating Distributed Materialized Views. *IEEE TKDE, V1, N2, June 1989.*

[SeZh91] A. Segev and J. L. Zhao. Data Management for Large Rule Systems. *VLDB Conference, 1991.*

[SeZh93] A. Segev and J. L. Zhao. Rule Management in Expert Database Systems. *Management Science (forthcoming).*

[Ston89] M. Stonebraker. Future Trends in Database Systems. *IEEE TKDE, V1, N1, 1989.*

[Ston91] M. Stonebraker, et al. Postgres Reference Manual V3.1. *Comp. Sci., UC Berkeley, CA 94720, USA.*

[Ston92] M. Stonebraker. The Integration of Rule Systems and Database Systems. *IEEE TKDE, V4, N5, 1992.*

[StRH90] M. Stonebraker, L. A. Rowe, and M. Hirohama. The Implementation of POSTGRES. *IEEE TKDE, V2, N1, 1990.*

[WiLH90] K. Wilkinson, P. Lyngbek, and W. Hasan. The Iris architecture and implementation. *IEEE TKDE, V2, N1, 1990.*

An Integrated Calculation Model for Discovering Functional Relations from Databases

Ning Zhong Setsuo Ohsuga
Research Center for Advanced Science and Technology
The University of Tokyo
4-6-1 Komaba, Meguro-ku, Tokyo 153, Japan

Abstract. This paper presents an integrated calculation model for discovering automatically the functional relations from databases. This calculation model is a fundamental one for developing KOSI which is one of sub-systems of the GLS discovery system implemented by us. In this model, the process of discovering the functional relations from databases is a process based on incipient hypothesis generation and evaluation, and AI techniques and statistical methods are cooperatively used in multiple learning phases for performing multi-aspect intelligent data analysis and learning.

1 Introduction

Knowledge discovery in databases is becoming an important topic in AI and is attracting the attention of leading researchers in databases[5]. The functional relations are a kind of important regularity hidden in databases [6, 7]. There are two basic methods for discovering the functional relations from data: (1) traditional statistical methods such as regression analysis [4]; (2) machine learning methods such as data-driven discovery [3].

There are two main advantages of traditional statistical methods. First, the uncertainty and incompleteness of sample data can be fairly processed; Second, the discovered functional relations can be used for prediction and inference. For example, regression analysis can be used for finding a structural relation (i.e., a kind of functional relation) hidden in the data. The discovered structural relation (e.g., it is represented by the regression model) can be used for inferring, predicting and supporting human decision making. However, traditional statistical methods have also their limits. Main limits among these ones are (1) the algorithm of traditional statistical methods is too inflexible and ignores the domain knowledge; (2) the statistical models elicited from sample data cannot be easily managed/refined; (3) the sample data used in statistical methods, sometimes, cannot be directly collected (e.g., the collected sample data cannot be directly used in regression analysis, until they are preprocessed by human being into a suitable form). On the other hand, Langley et al. developed a system called BACON using a machine learning method for discovering scientific (numeric) laws from scientific (numeric) data in the domains of physics and chemistry [3]. The main advantage of the BACON system is that data-driven heuristics can be used for discovering a wider class of numeric laws. However, the object of BACON is only scientific (numeric) data in the domains of physics and chemistry; its capability for processing the uncertainty and incompleteness of data is weaker, and it has not integrated with knowledge-driven methods.

Our purpose is to discover the functional relations from databases. That is, our learning/discovering object is databases. Therefore, the features of databases (e.g., databases are not always complete but contain uncertain and incomplete data, databases are generally very large and complex and so on), which are different from other learning/discovering objects, are considered in developing our method [6]. Thus, our purpose is more general than BACON's one in the following three aspects:

- Not only process scientific data from physical and chemical experiment but also from other fields in which may contain more uncertainty and incompleteness.
- Not only discover scientific laws but also more general functional relations.
- Not only discover exact functional relations but also approximate functional relations.

To achieve our purpose, we introduce an integrated calculation model for discovering automatically the functional relations from databases. In this model, the discovery process is the one based on incipient hypothesis generation, evaluation and refinement as shown in Figure 1. In this process, AI techniques and statistical methods are cooperatively used in multiple learning phases for performing multi-aspect intelligent data analysis and learning. First, a new attribute is generated as a function of existing attributes (i.e., a hypothetical functional relation). This is called *attribute calculation.* This includes generating new attributes by cooperative use of model-driven/data-driven heuristics and qualitative/quantitative calculation. Second, new generated attributes are added to the original database, and then they are evaluated by statistic inference such as regression analysis. This includes selecting the statistical strategies and methods that should be used, as well as controlling the statistical process using conceptual knowledge. Moreover, the discovered functional relation is represented as a production rule and a set of data for showing its error, so that it can be easily used, managed and refined.

In the following sections, we describe how to generate new functional relations by attribute calculation; how to evaluate the generated functional relations by statistical methods; and finally we give concluding remarks, as well as our related researches and some further research subjects.

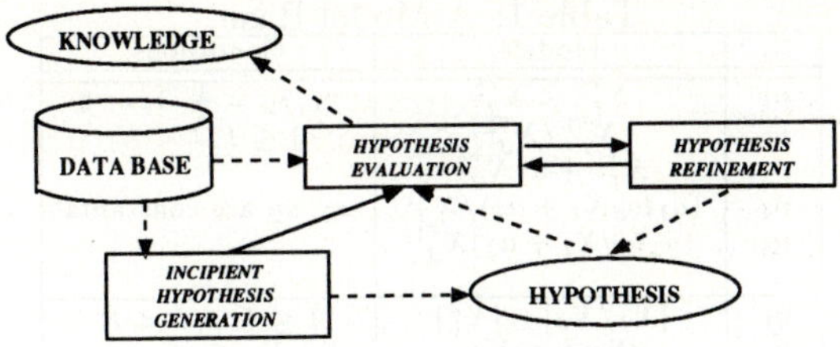

Figure 1: The process of knowledge discovery from databases

original attributes							new created attributes			
x_1	...	x_I	...	x_J	...	x_N	x_{N+1}	x_{N+2}	...	x_K
x_{11} x_{12} ⋮ x_{1m}	...	x_{I1} x_{I2} ⋮ x_{Im}	...	x_{J1} x_{J2} ⋮ x_{Jm}	...	⋮	⋮	⋮	...	⋮

Figure 2: The original attributes and new created attributes in a database

2 Attribute Calculation

As stated in Section 1, *attribute calculation* is a method of generating a new attribute as a function of the given set of attributes. The primitive way of generating functions is the exhaustive method. As shown in Figure 2, let $A = \{X_1, X_2, \ldots X_N\}$ be a initial set of attributes, and S be a set of mathematical operations including the four fundamental operations of arithmetic, log and so on (i.e., $S = \{+, -, \times, \div, log, \ldots\}$). Let X_K ($K > N$) be a new attribute generated by the mathematical operations among any attributes of $X_1 \sim X_{K-1}$ (i.e., $X_K = f(X_I, X_J)$, $1 \leq I, J < K$). First, a sequence composed of some elements of $A \cup S$ is generated. Then, check the sequence. If the sequence is syntactically illegal, it is put away and another sequence is generated. If it is a legal mathematical expression, this one is a hypothetical functional relation and it is statistically evaluated. This method, however, is very inefficient. In order to improve its efficiency, a method of controlling the creation by cooperative use of a model base and data-driven heuristics is introduced [7].

2.1 A Model Base

The different models of functions that are considered to appear very often are given as a model base as shown in Table 1. Only these types of functions that exist in this model base are found/created. Thus, the extent and the content of

Table 1: A Model Base

No	Models	Conditions
p_1	$X_I^{r_1} \times X_J^{r_2}$	$r_1, r_2 = \frac{1}{2}$, 1, or 2
p_2	$X_I^{r_1} / X_J^{r_2}$	$1 \leq I, J < K$
p_3	$X_I^{r_1} + a_1 X_J^{r_2}$	
p_4	$(a_1 log X_I + a_2)/X_J^{r_1}$	a_1, a_2 are constants
p_5	$(a_1 log X_I + a_2) X_J^{r_1}$	
...	...	...
q_1	$[X_I/X_J] \otimes [X_L^2]$	$1 \leq I, J, L < K$
q_2	$X_I \propto_Q X_J$	$X_I, X_J \in$ *cluster-1*
...	...	...

search are confirmed by the content of the model base. In Table 1, *Conditions* are used for representing the condition of which a model should satisfy. The notation $[x]$ represents the qualitative value of quantity x, and the notation $\otimes$ represents one of the four fundamental operations of arithmetic. Thus, $X_I \otimes X_J$ means $X_{I_i} \otimes X_{J_i}$, $i = 1 \sim m$.

In current system, only linear function and quadratic function are considered (i.e., $r_1, r_2 = \frac{1}{2}$, 1, or 2 as shown in Table 1). Moreover, q_1, q_2 in Table 1 can be used for incremental discovery. Sometimes, the quantitative functions cannot be discovered from current databases, but the qualitative functions (e.g., $[X_I/X_J] \otimes [X_L^2]$ shown in Table 1) can be created. In this case, the qualitative functions are first created and stored in a model base, and then when the data in a database is added, these qualitative functions are used for controlling further search, or it is used in the evaluation by a statistical method.

2.2 Heuristics

Two kinds of heuristics, Heuristics-Type-1 and Heuristics-Type-2, are used in our approach for processing data with more uncertainty and incompleteness, and extending the capability of knowledge discovery.

2.2.1 Heuristics-Type-1

Heuristics-Type-1 is based on heuristics used in BACON. Three basic heuristics are as follows:

- If $X_I \propto_{Q+} X_J$, then define the ratio X_I/X_J and examine its values.
- If $X_I \propto_{Q-} X_J$, then define the product $X_I X_J$ and examine its values.
- If the results calculated by using above heuristics are nearly constant, then the result of the calculation is that a function is created.

Where, $X_I \propto_{Q+} X_J$ (or $X_I \propto_{Q-} X_J$) means that X_I increases (or decreases) as X_J increases ($I \neq J$), and the "near constant" is evaluated by a method called *dynamic adjustment of error* [7].

Above three basic heuristics can be extended for controlling the discovery of more complex functions. For example,

- If $(X_{I_{i+1}} - X_{I_i}) \propto_{Q+} (X_{J_{i+1}} - X_{J_i})$,
  then calculate $(X_{I_{i+1}} - X_{I_i})/(X_{J_{i+1}} - X_{J_i})$.
- If $\log X_I \propto_{Q+} \log X_J$, then calculate $\log X_I / \log X_J$.
- If $(X_I/X_J)^2 \propto_{Q+} X_I/X_J$ and $(X_I/X_J)^2$ increases faster,
  then calculate $(X_I/X_J)^{1/2}$.

The goal of these heuristics and calculations, however, is to find "constants" (or near constants) as far as possible. The prerequisite used above heuristics is that attributes X_I and X_J have to be monotonic increasing/decreasing. Therefore, if only use these heuristics for discovering the functional relations from real databases, then their usefulness is quite limited. On the other hand, the ability of discovery using these heuristics is also limited. For example, it is difficult to discover the approximate quadratic function such as $Y = a_0 + a_1X^1 + a_2X^2 + \varepsilon$ from a database.

2.2.2 Heuristics-Type-2

In order to resolve issues of Heuristics-Type-1, Heuristics-Type-2 is used. It is based on the process of *generation & evaluation* shown in Figure 1. The scope of calculation for generating new attribute X_K is limited by a model base shown in Section 2.1, and the following heuristics are used in the process of *generation*:

- If $X_I \overset{not}{\propto_Q} X_J$, but $X_I \dot{\propto}_Q X_J$ (or $[X_I] \dot{\propto}_Q \{X_J\}_I$, then hypothesize that there is an approximate functional relation between X_I and X_J.

- If there is not monotonicity among X_I, X_J, X_L $(1 \leq I, J, L < K)$, but $f(X_I, X_J) \dot{\propto}_Q X_L$, then hypothesize that there is a functional relation among X_I, X_J, X_L, and $X_K = g(f(X_I, X_J), X_L) = g(X_I, X_J, X_L)$.

- If $X_I \overset{not}{\propto_Q} X_J$, but just exist one and only one point x_0 $(x_0 \in X_J)$ makes the first-order derivative of the hypothetical $X_I = f(X_J)$, $X'_I = f'(x_0) = 0$, and the sign of the value $f'(X_J)$ is changed when the value of X_J passes x_0, then hypothesize that there is an approximate quadratic functional relation between X_I and X_J.

- If the calculations are also fail when using above heuristics (including Heuristics-Type-1), but new generated attributes are more than two ones, then evaluate whether an approximate functional relation among them exists or not by using statistical methods which will be stated in Section 3.

Where, $\propto_Q$ (or $\dot{\propto}_Q$) denotes (approximate) monotonic increasing/decreasing, $[X_I]$ denotes the qualitative value of attribute X_I defined by *landmark* [2], and

$\{X_J\}_I$ denotes the clusters of attribute X_J which correspond with the defined qualitative value $[X_I]$. Thus, $X_I \dot{\propto}_Q X_J$ (or $[X_I] \dot{\propto}_Q \{X_J\}_I$) means that X_I (or $[X_I]$) increases/decreases approximately as X_J (or $\{X_J\}_I$) increases approximately. The "approximation" can be defined by the following method:

> Evaluate the uncertainty of contradictory values, which destroy the monotonicity between attributes if they exist, by calculating their probability. If their probability is larger than the *threshold value*, then define the qualitative values of attribute X_I, and form the clusters of attribute X_J. Then evaluate the uncertainty of contradictory values, which destroy the monotonicity between qualitative values $[X_I]$ and clusters $\{X_J\}_I$.

Thus, if we use a material database shown in Table 2 as an example [1], then we can find an approximate functional relation between attributes ZrO_2 and TiO_2 by using the following steps:

*step*1 : If the calculations are fail using Heuristics-Type-1, then evaluate the uncertainty of contradictory values by calculating their probability. Because their probability is larger, define the qualitative values of attribute ZrO_2 by using background knowledge and/or meta knowledge about the method called *the division of ranges* [7] as follows:

$$[ZrO_2]_1 = [100 \sim 95],\ [ZrO_2]_2 = (95 \sim 85],$$
$$[ZrO_2]_3 = (85 \sim 75],\ [ZrO_2]_4 = (75 \sim 65].$$

*step*2 : Form the clusters by using qualitative values $[ZrO_2]$ defined in *step1*. That is, the following clusters can be formed for attribute TiO_2:

$$\{TiO_2\}_1 = \{0.1, 0.2, 0.3, 1.0, 2.0\},\ \{TiO_2\}_2 = \{0.0, 5.5, 8.3, 10.5\},$$
$$\{TiO_2\}_3 = \{18.3\},\quad \{TiO_2\}_4 = \{30.0\}.$$

*step*3 : Check if the contradictory values exist between $[ZrO_2]$ and $\{TiO_2\}$. Here, value 0.0 in $\{TiO_2\}_2$ is a contradictory value because it destroys the monotonicity between $[ZrO_2]$ and $\{TiO_2\}$.

*step*4 : If there are contradictory values, then evaluate the uncertainty of contradictory values. That is, calculate their probability. For example, the probability of value 0.0 in $\{TiO_2\}_2$ is $\frac{1}{13}$ for the sample material database shown in Table 2.

*step*5 : If the probability of contradictory values is smaller than the *threshold value*, then hypothesize that there is an approximate functional relation between attributes ZrO_2 and TiO_2.

These hypothetical functional relations are first stored in a model base using qualitative equations (e.g., $X_I \dot{\propto}_Q X_J$ shown in Table 1). Then they are evaluated by the statistical methods as stated in Section 3.

Table 2: A sample material database

No	Y_2O_3	TiO_2	ZrO_2	...
1-1	2.5	1.0	96.5	...
.	2.0	2.0	96.0	...
.	1.7	18.3	80.0	...
.	.	30.0	70.0	...
.	.	1.0	97.0	...
.	.	5.5	92.0	...
.	.	1.0	96.0	...
.	.	10.5	88.0	...
.	.	8.3	90.0	...
.	.	0.1	95.4	...
.	.	0.2	99.8	...
.	.	0.0	94.0	...
.	.	0.3	98.2	...
...	...	...	...	...

3 Evaluation by Regression Analysis

In general, regression analysis is a statistical method for finding a structural relation (i.e., a kind of functional relation represented by regression model) among variables (attributes) from sample data, with which the value of the objective variable can be predicted/inferred by the values of descriptive variables. In our application, the goal of evaluating the hypothetical functional relations by regression analysis is to find the optimal regression model (i.e., the best structural relation) among variables of which there is a hypothetical linear (or quadratic) functional relation stored in a model base.

If it is hypothesized that there is a linear (or quadratic) functional relation between X_I and X_J by the heuristics as stated in Section 2.2, then let $Y = X_I$ be an objective variable, X_J be a descriptive variable, and ε be the residual variance with normal distribution of average 0 and dispersion σ^2. The number of descriptive variables can be more than one. In order to evaluate the hypothetical functional relations, several methods of regression analyses such as multiple regression, polynomial regression etc. are prepared at the moment. These regression models are obtained by the Least Square Method based on H transformation and a criterion called AIC [8, 4], and are used as the prototypes for further constituting the production rules in a knowledge-base [8].

There are two main different points between our method and traditional statistical ones. One of these is that the objective variable and the descriptive variables used in regression analyses may be new attributes automatically generated by attribute calculation stated in Section 2. Another different point is that the control knowledge is used for selecting automatically the method of regression analysis that should be used. Let this kind of control knowledge be called meta-level knowledge (meta control in short), because it is mainly used for controlling and deciding how to use object-level knowledge [6, 7, 8].

The functional relation that has been evaluated by statistical methods is represented as a production rule and a set of data for showing its error [7]. This production rule is added into a knowledge-base and can be immediately used in inference integratedly with the domain knowledge. For example, it is used for supporting human decision making. Or it is refined/managed [8].

4 Concluding Remarks

We briefly presented an integrated calculation model for discovering automatically the functional relations from databases. In this model, the process of discovering the functional relations from databases is a process based on incipient hypothesis generation and evaluation. The most important feature of our approach is cooperative use of AI techniques and statistical methods.

This calculation model is a fundamental one for developing KOSI (Knowledge Oriented Statistic Inference) which is one of sub-systems of the GLS discovery system developed by us [6, 7, 8]. We are also developing another sub-system called IIBR (Inheritance Inference Based Refinement) for managing and refining the knowledge discovered by KOSI [6]. Thus, KOSI and IIBR can perform multi-aspect intelligent data analysis and learning by using multiple learning phases such as attribute calculation, statistic inference, management and refinement, in which multiple kinds of learning/discovery methods are used integratedly. KOSI and IIBR constitute a promising framework for discovering the functional relations from databases.

We have tested or are testing several databases in fields such as economics, zoology, material science and so on. These tests show the usefulness of our approach. Future work involves to use cooperatively the discovered functional relations with analogy reasoning, to develop a general user interface, and to apply our approach to more real problems and application fields.

References

[1] Y.W. Lu et al. (eds.). *User Manual of Advanced Material Data System.* Institute of Material Science, TsingHua University, (1990).

[2] K.D. Forbus. Qualitative Process Theory. *Artificial Intelligence*, Vol.24, (1984) 95-168.

[3] P. Langley and J.M. Zytkow. Data-Driven Approaches to Empirical Discovery. *Artificial Intelligence*, Vol.40(No.1-3), (1989) 283-312.

[4] Y. Sakamoto, M. Ishiguro, and G. Kitagawa. *Information Statistics.* Kuritsu Publish Ltd. Japan, (1983). (in Japanese).

[5] G.P. Shapiro and W.J. Frawley (eds.). *Knowledge Discovery in Databases.* AAAI Press and The MIT Press, (1991).

[6] N. Zhong and S. Ohsuga. GLS - A Methodology for Discovering Knowledge from Databases. *Proc. the 13th International CODATA Conference entitled "New Data Challenges in Our Information Age"*, (1992).

[7] N. Zhong and S. Ohsuga. Attribute Calculation in Knowledge Discovery in Databases. *(to appear in) Journal of Japanese Society for Artificial Intelligence*, Vol.9 No.1, (1994).

[8] N. Zhong and S. Ohsuga. Knowledge Discovery and Management in Integrated Use of KB and DB. *Ohsuga et al. (eds.) Information Modelling and Knowledge Bases: Foundations, Theory and Application*, (IOS Press, Amsterdam, 1992) 480-495.

On the Maintenance of Implication Integrity Constraints*

Naci S. İshakbeyoğlu** and Z. Meral Özsoyoğlu

Computer Engineering and Science Department
Case Western Reserve University
Cleveland, Ohio 44106

Abstract. Semantic integrity constraints are utilized for enforcing the integrity of the database as well as for improving the efficiency of the database utilization, as in semantic query optimization. In this paper we address the problems related with maintaining a sound and nonredundant set of constraints satisfied by the database in the case of updates to the constraint base. We consider implication constraints as semantic integrity constraints. The constraints are represented as conjunctions of inequalities. We present a methodology to determine whether a constraint is redundant or contradictory with respect to a set of constraints. It is based on the partitioning of the constraint base which, we show, improves the efficiency of the algorithms that check whether a constraint is redundant or contradictory with respect to a constraint base.

1 Introduction

Constraints are assertions on permissible or consistent database states. They specify certain properties of data to be satisfied by valid instances of the database. In general, constraints can be classified [26] as i) structural constraints, and ii) semantic integrity constraints. Structural constraints (also called dependency constraints) concern only equalities among values in the database and are utilized in database design and normalization. Functional dependencies are example to such constraints. Semantic integrity constraints depend on the semantics of domain elements, and/or concern the actual values stored in the database. They are clauses of inequality predicates containing comparison operators $<, \leq, =, \neq, >$, and $\geq$. For example, in an Employee-Manager-Department database, a semantic integrity constraint may be as follows: *only managers make more than 80K* (employee.Sal > 80K → employee.Job = 'Manager'). Such a constraint is also called an implication constraint.

There are two main problems regarding the maintenance of integrity constraints. One is called the integrity enforcement, i.e., the problem of checking whether updates to database such as inserting/deleting tuples invalidates the constraints or not. This problem is discussed in [19, 2, 11, 5, 12, 18]. In this paper, we address the second

* This research is supported by the National Science Foundation under grant IRI-9008632, and FAW Award IRI-9024152. Part of the research has been carried out while the authors were at Dept. of Computer Engineering and Information Sciences, Bilkent University, Ankara, Türkiye.

** The research of this author is partially supported by the Scientific and Technical Research Council of Türkiye.

problem of maintaining semantic integrity constraints. That is, given a set of constraints (constraint-base) and a database, the problem is how to maintain a sound and nonredundant set of constraints satisfied by the database in the case of updates (i.e. constraint insertion and deletion) to the constraint base. It is necessary to keep a consistent set of constraints. Maintaining a nonredundant set is useful because both the maintenance algorithms discussed here and the methods in the integrity enforcement get more costly – exponentially in the former case – when the size of the constraint set gets bigger. The constraints are clauses of inequality predicates containing comparison operators $<, \leq, =, \neq, >$, and $\geq$. One first needs algorithms to check whether a constraint to be inserted is redundant or contradictory to a set of constraints. A given constraint is said to be redundant with respect to a set of constraints if all the database instances satisfying the constraint set also satisfy the given constraint. A constraint is said to be contradictory to a (satisfiable) set of constraints if it makes the constraint set unsatisfiable when inserted into the set. Checking whether a constraint is redundant or contradictory with respect to a set of constraints is in general exponential with the number of constraints in the constraint-base. We propose algorithms that are based on partitioning of the constraint set according to the domains of the attributes, by utilizing the fact that values belonging to different domains cannot be compared with each other. That is, in order to check whether a given constraint is implied by a set of constraints, it is sufficient to consider only those partitions with constraints having attributes with common domains as the given constraint. Moreover, if there are two such partitions for example, to check the redundancy of a constraint with respect to the constraints set, we in fact need to check the redundancy of this constraint with respect to these two partitions separately, which is more beneficial than checking the redundancy of the constraint with respect to the unpartitioned constraint base. A similar argument also applies to checking for contradiction.

For showing that a constraint is implied by a constraint set, we need an inference mechanism. In [13] we propose a sound and complete refutation procedure, called System R, for this purpose. The procedure is based on a resolution rule for inequalities which is more general than the resolution rule for propositional calculus.

Checking the redundancy/contradiction of a constraint with respect to a constraint base does not solve the maintenance problem completely. A nonredundant/noncontradictory constraint that is also satisfied by the database may cause some other constraints to be redundant when inserted into the constraint base. Such constraints are removed so that the resulting constraint base is free from redundancy and contradiction.

The rest of the paper is organized as follows. The implication constraints and the related background including System R are given in section 2. Also some of the previous work is listed. In section 3, the difficulty of the maintenance of a constraint base is shown, as well as some assumptions made for simplicity in the previous section are explained. Section 4 formally describes how a constraint set is partitioned. In sections 5 and 6, algorithms and their costs are given for checking the redundancy and the contradiction of a constraint with respect to constraint set, respectively. Section 7 presents the concluding remarks. Due to space limitations, we omitted the proofs of lemmas and theorems in the paper, which can be found in [14].

2 Basic Concepts and Previous Work

2.1 Implication Constraints

Let $R = R_1, R_2, ..., R_n$ be a schema for relations and $r_1, r_2, ..., r_n$ be the respective instances of the relations. We refer to an attribute X of R_i as $R_i.X$. For simplicity, we do not prefix the attribute names with their relation names by assuming that all attribute names in the database schema are unique (this can be achieved by renaming the attribute names). The *database instance* r is the relational algebra expression $r_1 \times ... \times r_n$ for database R.

We will utilize the fact that the attributes belong to different domains. Let DOM_1, $DOM_2, \cdots, DOM_{nd}$ be the domains that attributes in R belong to. A predicate $X\theta Y$ is meaningful only if both X and Y belong to the same domain. Thus, we associate each predicate P in the constraint set to a domain, named DOM_P, which is the domain of the variables in predicate P.

We have two major assumptions. The first is the nonempty relation instances. Each relation instance r_i is nonempty, and so is r. The other is that the domains of all the attributes are fully ordered dense domains like rational numbers, or unordered domains like character strings. The reasons for these assumptions will be apparent later.

We use P_i to denote a predicate of the form $X\theta Y$ where X is an attribute, θ is a comparison operator from $\{\geq, >, \neq, =, <, \leq\}$, and Y is either an attribute (other than X) or a constant. The negation of a predicate P_i is denoted as $\neg P_i$ (or $\bar{P}_i$) which is obtained by replacing $X\theta Y$ with $X\theta' Y$ where θ' is the inverse of θ, e.g., $<$ and $\geq$. An implication constraint is denoted as a clause $P_1 \vee ... \vee P_k$ where P_i's are predicates. We assume no duplicate predicates in a constraint.

Example 1. Consider an Employee-Department database. Then a constraint "All managers earn more than 80K" is the clause

(emp.Job≠"Manager") ∨ (emp.Salary>80K).

To be more intuitive, we can also represent it in various forms such as

(emp.Job="Manager") → (emp.Salary>80K) or

(emp.Job="Manager") ∧ (emp.Salary≤80K) →

where "→" denotes the logical implication.

We have selected a simple, yet meaningful class of constraints which makes the maintenance problem plausible. Similar constraints are utilized in some semantic query optimization systems [24, 25, 29].

A constraint $P_1 \vee ... \vee P_k$ is said to be satisfied by the database instance r iff there is some tuple in r that makes at least one predicate P_i true when the constraint is instantiated with the tuples. Constraints should not be *unsatisfiable* or *tautology*. For $P_1 \vee ... \vee P_k$ to be unsatisfiable, each P_i must be unsatisfiable in the form of $X > X$, $X < X$ or $X \neq X$. For the constraint to be tautology, $(P_1 \wedge ... \wedge P_k)$ must be unsatisfiable. These two conditions can be checked efficiently by using a graph representation for the conjunction [13]. Constraints should not contain *redundant* predicates either. Consider a constraint $(X \leq 3) \vee (Y \geq 3) \vee (X \leq Y)$. Here $X \leq Y$ is redundant. It is easier to see this in the conjunctive representation of the constraint, i.e., $(X > 3) \wedge (Y < 3) \wedge (X > Y) \rightarrow$. In the conjunction $(X > 3) \wedge (Y < 3) \wedge (X > Y)$, predicate $X > Y$ is implied by the other two, thus it is redundant. Using the transitive reduction of a directed graph [1], a nonredundant subset of a conjunction of inequalities can be found in polynomial time [28]. In this paper, without loss of generality we assume that constraints are not unsatisfiable or tautologies, and also do not contain redundant predicates.

2.2 A Deduction System for Constraints

It is indispensable to keep a consistent set of constraints. For efficiency, it is also desirable to keep a nonredundant set. Thus, when a new constraint C is to be inserted into the existing constraint-base $S = \{C_1, C_2, ..., C_n\}$, we need to check if S implies C and if S implies $\neg C$ for redundancy and contradiction checking respectively. In this section we briefly describe a resolution based deduction system (System R) for this purpose, which is sound and complete[3] as shown in [13].

System R: The refutation procedure is actually a more general form of the resolution for propositional calculus [10, 7] with the following inference rule:

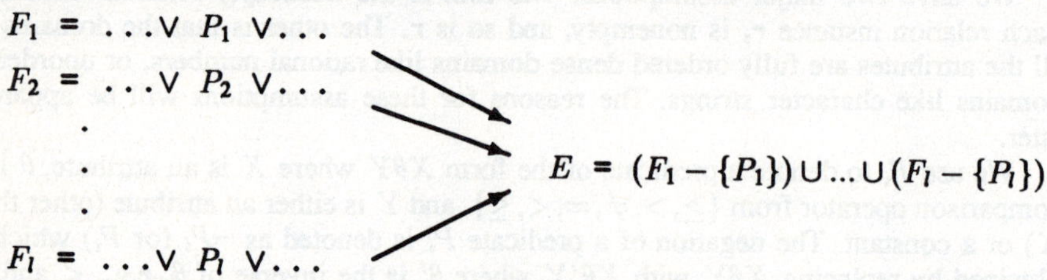

where $F_1, ..., F_l$ be distinct constraints containing predicates $P_1, ..., P_l$ respectively such that all these predicates belong to the same domain and the conjunction $(P_1 \wedge ... \wedge P_l)$ is *minimally* unsatisfiable, i.e., all of its proper subsets are satisfiable. Each $(F_i - \{P_i\})$ is F_i with predicate P_i removed. $F_1, ..., F_l$ are called the *premises*, and E is the *resolvent*. Whenever the empty clause □ is derived, then the input set of constraints is found to be unsatisfiable. To check the redundancy (contradiction) of a constraint C with respect to a constraint set S, □ must be derived from set $S \cup \{\neg C\}$ $(S \cup \{C\})$.

Example 2. Let S contain $C_1{=}(X > 5) \vee (W \leq 8)$, $C_2{=}(W > 12)$, $C_3{=}(Y < 5)$, and $C_4{=}(X \leq Y)$. Suppose W belongs to DOM_1 and X and Y belong to DOM_2. Then the derivation of □ can be represented by the following figure:

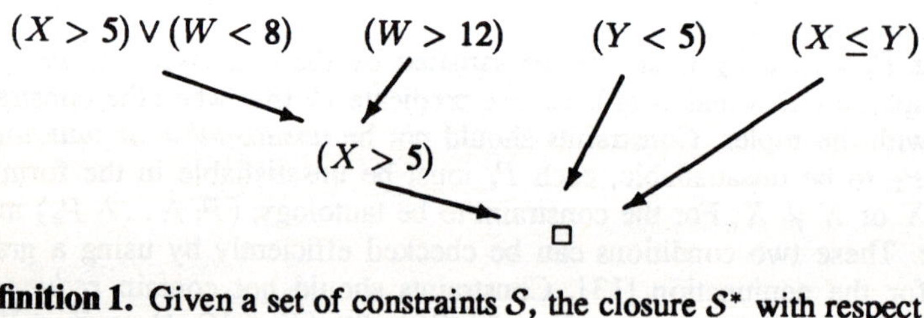

Definition 1. Given a set of constraints S, the closure S^* with respect to S is defined recursively as follows:

[3] That is, all the derived constraints from a constraint set S are those that are implied by S, and all the constraints that are implied by S are derivable from S and tautology constraints, by using System R. Note that, each constraint in S is satisfiable and is not a tautology.

$\mathcal{S}^0 = \mathcal{S}$
$\mathcal{S}^i = \mathcal{S}^{i-1} \cup \{E \mid E$ is a resolvent of constraints $F_1 \cdots F_l$ in $\mathcal{S}^{i-1}$ and E is not in $\mathcal{S}^{i-1}\}$.

Whenever $\mathcal{S}^n$=$\mathcal{S}^{n+1}$, $\mathcal{S}^*$ is found to be $\mathcal{S}^n$. The condition "E is not in $\mathcal{S}^{i-1}$" guarantees that a constraint is derived only once. The procedure terminates either as soon as □ is derived (in this case $\mathcal{S}^*$ contains □), or a saturated set $\mathcal{S}^*$ is obtained that contains all the derivable constraints from $\mathcal{S}$ but □. Since there are a finite number of predicates, say N, in $\mathcal{S}$, the size of $\mathcal{S}^*$ is bounded by 2^N where the largest constraint contains all N predicates, and all others are its subsets. Note that $\mathcal{S}$ here may denote the set S of constraints of the constraint base and a given constraint C, i.e., $S \cup \{C\}$, or S and the negation of the given constraint, i.e., $S \cup \{\neg C\}$.

2.3 Previous Work

There have been extensive research regarding the maintenance of integrity constraints. In the literature, the term maintenance refers to two different problems in general. One is the problem of keeping a consistent set of constraints when new facts or tuples are inserted (or deleted from) into a (relational) database [19, 18, 12]. The other, the one we discuss here, is concerned with the redundancy and contradiction of a constraint set when new constraints are inserted into (or deleted from) the constraint base [5, 17, 3, 4, 16]. Another related problem is the containment and disjointness of the conjunctive queries [27, 15, 8]. [9] describes a logic for reasoning about probabilities.

There are differences between the above work and ours. In [4], the class of constraints are first-order formulas without inequalities. In this paper, the constraints are only clauses of inequality predicates where the variables are attribute variables. (Note that there is no relational predicates in the constraints). First order logic is undecidable, whereas for the class of constraints we consider, there are decidable proof procedures, i.e. the procedure always terminates [13]. Since the deduction system for clauses of inequalities described in this paper is decidable, satisfiability refers to finite satisfiability in our case. Instead of working on the efficiency of the theorem prover itself as in [17], we try to partition the constraint set and then check the unsatisfiability of each partition by a proof procedure, e.g., in [13]. The class of constraints we consider here or its special cases have also been utilized in semantic query optimization [24, 29]. The constraints in [3] contain inequalities as well as universal and existential quantifiers. In this paper, there are no quantified variables, but the variables in the constraints are universally quantified implicitly. We give redundancy/contradiction checking algorithms that are based on partitioning of the constraint set. The work in [27, 15, 8] is concerned with two conjunctions. In our case, we consider a conjunction (or in clausal form) and a *set* of constraints. The work in [6] is related to ours as it concerns the consistency of a rule-base, differs in that their formulas are active rules that derive new database facts, whereas we consider a passive constraint base that do not insert any tuples to the database.

3 Maintenance Problem and Unsatisfiability

There are two different levels of *unsatisfiability* mentioned in this paper. The first is the unsatisfiability of a conjunction of (inequality) predicates. This can be tested in polynomial time under the assumption that the size of the domain of attributes is greater than the number of attributes in the conjunction. (Without this assumption, checking the unsatisfiability of a conjunction of predicates with inequalities is NP-Complete [22].) A polynomial time algorithm can be given [28, 13] by using a graph representation for conjunctions.

As discussed in section 2, we do not allow the ordered discrete domains such as natural numbers[4]. The reason is that in such domains we need to take into consideration the consecutiveness of the elements of those domains. When checking the unsatisfiability of a conjunction of predicates, this brings extra burden. Consider, for instance, the conjunction $(X > 5) \wedge (X \neq 6) \wedge (X < 7)$. Suppose X's domain is natural numbers. This conjunction is then unsatisfiable. But, to check the unsatisfiability of the conjunction, one needs the information that 5, 6 and 7 are consecutive and there are no other natural numbers between them. For the simplicity of the unsatisfiability checking algorithm, we do not consider such cases (see also [3]).

The second kind of unsatisfiability concerns a set of constraints $S \cup \{C\}$ or $S \cup \{\neg C\}$ denoted by S. Each constraint consists of inequality predicates as defined above. We assumed that each relation instance is non-empty at any time so that the database instance "r" is non-empty. The reason is that without this assumption there may not be any contradiction in the constraint-base. Consider the two constraints $r.X > 5$ and $r.X < 5$. These two constraints are satisfied at the same time only if r is empty. But in most cases, r is not empty and thus we should not allow such contradictions in the constraint-base.

Deciding whether a set S of constraints is satisfiable or not is also an NP-complete problem as it is a general case of the SAT problem for propositional calculus, which is NP-complete [14].

Thus, for a given set of constraints S and a constraint C, there is no known polynomial algorithm to determine if S implies C (or $\neg C$). In the rest of the paper, we discuss methods for solving this problem by utilizing the fact that the attribute variables belong to different domains. Accordingly, S is disjointly partitioned into its subsets and instead of considering the set of all constraints, only the constraints in relevant partitions are used to check whether they imply C or $\neg C$. Although this does not change the complexity in asymptotic sense, it is expected to result in significant improvement in practice since size of a partition in general is much smaller than the size of the constraint base.

4 Partitioning the Constraint Set S

In this section, we define how S is partitioned into its disjoint partitions with respect to the domains of (attribute) variables.

Let $DOM_1, \cdots, DOM_{nd}$ be the domains of all attributes in the database schema. Every predicate $X\theta Y$ in S is also associated to one domain; it is the domain of variable X. If Y is also a variable, its domain is the same as the domain of X since the comparison can be between two values belonging to the same domain. Given a set Z of constraints, the domain set with respect to Z, DS_Z, is the set of domains that the predicates in Z belong to.

Example 3. For the set of constraints S in Example 2 the domain set is $DS_S=\{DOM_1, DOM_2\}$, where $DS_{\{C_3,C_4\}}=\{DOM_2\}$, and $DS_{C_2}=\{DOM_1\}$.

[4] Note that ordered dense domains such as rational numbers are allowed.

Union operation. Let S_1 and S_2 be any sets of constraints. They are merged into one set S_3 only if $DS_{S_1} \cap DS_{S_2} \neq \emptyset$. DS_{S_3} becomes $DS_{S_1} \cup DS_{S_2}$.

Then the constraint set S is partitioned as follows: start with $C_1, \cdots, C_n$ of S, having domain sets $DS_{C_1}, \cdots, DS_{C_n}$ respectively. Apply the union operation as long as no application is possible. The resulting sets $S_1, S_2, \cdots, S_d$ are the disjoint partitions of S such that $DS_{S_1}, \cdots, DS_{S_d}$ are all pairwise disjoint.

Example 4. Consider a constraint base S={C_1, C_2, C_3, C_4} where C_1=($U \neq$ "a") $\vee$ ($X > Y$),C_2=($Z \leq 10$),C_3=(U = "a"), and C_4=($W > V$) $\vee$ ($V < 8$). Suppose U belongs to DOM_1, X,Y,Z to DOM_2, and W and V to DOM_3. Then the domain sets are DS_{C_1}={DOM_1,DOM_2}, DS_{C_2}={DOM_2}, DS_{C_3}={DOM_1}, and DS_{C_4}={DOM_3}. It can be seen that C_1, C_2, and C_3 are merged into one set S_1 by the union operation. The partitions of S are then S_1={C_1, C_2, C_3}, and S_2={C_4} with domain sets DS_{S_1}={DOM_1,DOM_2} and DS_{S_2}={DOM_3}. Note that $DS_{S_1} \cap DS_{S_2} = \emptyset$.

It can be observed that, in order to apply the resolution rule of System R, the premises must contain predicates belonging to the same domain.

Lemma 2. *Let $F_1, \cdots, F_l$ be the premises of a resolution step with the minimal unsatisfiable conjunction ($P_1 \wedge \cdots \wedge P_l$) where $P_1 \in F_1$, ..., $P_l \in F_l$. Then, predicates $P_1, \cdots, P_l$ belong to the same domain.*

In the following sections, we give methods for checking redundancy and contradiction of a constraint C with respect to a constraint set S based on the partitioning defined above.

5 Checking for Redundancy

In this section, we give an algorithm that checks whether a constraint C is redundant with respect to a constraint set S by using the partitions of S. Since it is an exponential task to check the unsatisfiability of $S \cup \{\neg C\}$, it will be shown that it is more efficient to use the partitions of S instead of S itself. We assume that S={$C_1, \cdots, C_n$} is currently partitioned into $S_1, \cdots, S_d$ with corresponding domain sets $DS_{S_1}, \cdots, DS_{S_d}$. We use *constraints* and *clauses* interchangeably.

To see that S implies C, we need to check if $\Box$ is derivable from $S \cup \{\neg C\}$ in System R. Let C be $P_1 \vee P_2 \vee \cdots \vee P_k$. Then $\neg C$ is k different singleton clauses (each containing exactly one predicate) $\bar{P}_1, \cdots, \bar{P}_k$, where $\bar{P}_i$ is P_i's negation. $S \cup \{\neg C\}$ contains $n+k$ clauses. Since each of these k clauses are singletons, in the new partitioning of $S \cup \{\neg C\}$, no partitions of S will be merged. Rather, each $\bar{P}_j$ is to be inserted into S_i if $DOM_{P_j} \in DS_{S_i}$. The following is the formal definition of the partitions of $S \cup \{\neg C\}$.

Definition 3. Partitions of $S \cup \{\neg C\}$. We define

$$S'_i = S_i \cup \{\bar{P}_j \mid DOM_{P_j} \in DS_{S_i}\}, \quad 1 \leq i \leq d, \quad 1 \leq j \leq k,$$

S_{rest} = the set of predicates $\bar{P}_j$ not inserted into any partition above.

Then $S \cup \{\neg C\} = S'_1 \cup \cdots \cup S'_d \cup S_{rest}$.

Example 5. Consider S={C_1, C_2, C_3, C_4} in Example 4 where C_1=($U \neq$ "a")$\vee$($X > Y$), C_2=($Z \leq 10$), C_3=(U = "a"), C_4=($W > V$) $\vee$ ($V < 8$),

DS_{C_1}={DOM_1, DOM_2}, DS_{C_2}={DOM_2}, DS_{C_3}={DOM_1}, DS_{C_4}={DOM_3}.

Suppose the given constraint C is $(X \geq Z) \vee (Y \leq 10) \vee (W \neq 6) \vee (T > 8)$ and the domains of the predicates are DOM_2,DOM_2, DOM_3,DOM_4 respectively. $\neg C$ is the set of four clauses $(X < Z)$, $(Y > 10)$, $(W = 6)$, and $(T \leq 8)$. Then, the new partitioning is as follows:
S'_1={C_1, C_2, C_3,$(X < Z)$,$(Y > 10)$}, S'_2={C_4,$(W = 6)$}, S_{rest}={$(T \leq 8)$},
$DS_{S_1}=DS_{S'_1}$={DOM_1,DOM_2}, $DS_{S_2}=DS_{S'_2}$={DOM_3}.

Our purpose in the partitioning is to show that if $S\cup\{\neg C\}$ is unsatisfiable, then it is necessary and sufficient that some partition S'_i is unsatisfiable. It is shown [14] that if a constraint is implied by a set of constraints, then one of the partitions alone implies this constraint. In other words, several partitions do not come together to imply a constraint.

Now we give the main result achieved by partitioning S. The algorithm that checks the redundancy of a constraint with respect to a set of constraints is based on the following lemma.

Lemma 4. *Let S be a satisfiable set of constraints partitioned into $S_1, \cdots, S_d$ according to the domains that variables in S belong to. Let C be a given constraint. $S \cup \{\neg C\}$ is partitioned into $S'_1, \cdots, S'_d, S_{rest}$ as defined above. Then, $S \cup \{\neg C\}$ is unsatisfiable (or equivalently □ is derivable in System R) if and only if there exists an i $(1 \leq i \leq d)$ such that $S'_i \neq S_i$ and S'_i is unsatisfiable.*

The following algorithm checks if a constraint is redundant with respect to a set of constraints S. The correctness of the algorithm follows from Lemma 4.

Algorithm **Redundancy.**
Input. A set of constraints S partitioned into $S_1, \cdots, S_d$.
A constraint $C = P_1 \vee \cdots \vee P_k$, which is not a tautology or unsatisfiable.
Output. "Yes" if C is redundant, "No" otherwise.
Begin /* $\neg C$ is the set of clauses $P_1, \cdots, P_k$. */
for i=1 to d
  $S'_i = S_i \cup \{P_j \mid DOM_{P_j} \in DS_{S_i}\}$.
  if $S'_i \neq S_i$ then
    if S'_i is unsatisfiable by using System R, then return "Yes"
end;
return "No"
End.

Example 6. Consider the previous example. S'_1 was found to be {C_1,C_2,C_3,$(X < Z)$, $(Y > 10)$}. Since S'_1 is unsatisfiable, the algorithm returns "Yes". If S'_1 were not unsatisfiable, then the algorithm would continue calculating S'_2. □ can be derived from S'_1 in two resolution steps. First, $(X > Y)$ is derived from C_1 and C_3. Then, □ is derived from clauses $(X > Y)$, $(Z \leq 10)$, $(X < Z)$, and $(Y > 10)$.

The Cost of the Algorithm : We need to compare the cost of checking the unsatisfiability of $S \cup \{\neg C\}$ without partitioning with the cost of the algorithm Redundancy. Given any set S, checking its unsatisfiability in System R is not a deterministic process. □ can be derived in more than one ways since at a time there are usually more than one constraints to be derived. For the comparison, we use a deterministic algorithm corresponding to the nondeterministic algorithm of System R.

The time required by the algorithm Redundancy to check whether a given constraint C is redundant w.r.t. a set S of constraints is [14] $d * K^{(n/d)} * O(\frac{n+k}{d})$, where d is the number of partitions, k is the number of predicates in C, n is the number of constraints in S, and K is the number of predicates in each constraint of S. worst case, all S_i's are augmented to become S_i''s. Assume Without the partitioning, the cost [14] is $Cost(S \cup \{\neg C\}) = K^n * O(n+k)$. Since the cost is exponential in the number of constraints in a set, partitioning seems to be very effective in reducing the cost of checking for redundancy significantly for large number of constraints, that is K^n becomes $d * K^{(n/d)}$ where d is the number of partitions.

6 Checking for Contradiction

In testing redundancy, we need to see if $S \cup \{\neg C\}$ is unsatisfiable. Here, we need to test the unsatisfiability of $S \cup \{C\}$. We assume here also that the given constraint C is satisfiable but not a tautology. S is partitioned into $S_1, \cdots, S_d$ with domain sets $DS_1, \cdots, DS_d$ respectively.

As in the redundancy case, we first find the new partitioning of $S \cup \{C\}$. This is done by merging some partitions according to C=$P_1 \vee \cdots \vee P_k$. In the redundancy case, $\neg C$ is a set of k singleton clauses, and thus no partition of S was merged. Here, we have one clause C with k predicates.

Definition 5. Partitions merged by C. Let $S_1, \cdots, S_f$ be the partitions such that $DS_{S_i} \cap DS_C \neq \emptyset$ for $1 \leq i \leq f$. Then the partitions $S_1, \cdots, S_f$ are the partitions merged by C, and the rest of the partitions $S_{f+1}, \cdots, S_d$ are those that are not merged. That is, $DS_{S_i} \cap DS_C = \emptyset$ for $f+1 \leq i \leq d$. We define set $S_{1f} = S_1 \cup \cdots \cup S_f \cup \{C\}$.

Example 7. Consider the previous examples (Example 5 and 6). $DS_{S_1} = \{DOM_1, DOM_2\}$, $DS_{S_2} = \{DOM_3\}$ and DS_C=$\{DOM_2, DOM_3, DOM_4\}$. Since $DS_{S_1} \cap DS_C = \{DOM_2\}$ and $DS_{S_2} \cap DS_C = \{DOM_3\}$, S_{1f} is $(S_1 \cup S_2 \cup \{C\})$, that is, $S \cup \{C\}$.

Thus the new partitioning of $S \cup \{C\}$ is $S_{1f}, S_{f+1}, \cdots, S_d$ with pairwise disjoint domain sets $DS_{S_{1f}}$,$DS_{S_{f+1}}$,$\cdots$,DS_{S_d}. In the worst case, C merges all thc partitions, i.e. $S \cup \{C\}$=S_{1f}. It can be seen that the unsatisfiability of $S \cup \{C\}$ depends only on S_{1f} because $S_{f+1}, \cdots, S_d$ are all satisfiable. Accordingly a basic algorithm for contradiction would first find S_{1f} and then check its unsatisfiability with System R. We can find a better algorithm by observing the fact that C is the only constraint that links $S_1, \cdots, S_f$ in S_{1f}. Also notice that $(S_1 \cup \cdots \cup S_f)$ is satisfiable as it is a subset of S.

In the redundancy case, we actually checked if S implies C=$P_1 \vee \cdots \vee P_k$. We observed that S may imply a proper subclause of C, i.e. those predicates that are not in S_{rest}. Here, if S implies $\neg C$, it should imply all k singleton clauses P_1,$\cdots$,P_k as stated in the following lemma.

Lemma 6. *Let S be any set of constraints and C=$P_1 \vee \cdots \vee P_k$ be any given constraint. Then $\Box$ is derived from $S \cup \{C\}$ if and only if P_1,$\cdots$,P_k are* all *in S^*.*

We can now notice that if C has a predicate whose domain is not in domain set of any constraint in S, C is not contradictory to S.

Lemma 7. *Let S be a set of constraints partitioned into $S_1, \cdots, S_d$ with the corresponding domain sets $DS_{S_1}, \cdots, DS_{S_d}$. Let $C = P_1 \vee \cdots \vee P_k$ be a given constraint. If there is a predicate P_j in C such that $DOM_{P_j} \notin DS_{S_i}$ for all i, $1 \leq i \leq d$, then C is not contradictory to S.*

By this lemma, we should first check if C contains a predicate that belongs to a domain which is not in any domain set of partitions. If this is the case, then Lemma 7 applies. Let us assume that C does not contain such a predicate, i.e. $DS_C \subseteq DS_S$. That is, each predicate of C belongs to a domain that appears in the domain set of some partition from $S_1, \cdots, S_f$, because by the Definition 5, $DS_C \cap DS_{S_i} = \emptyset$ for $f+1 \leq i \leq d$.

Definition 8. Partitions $D_1, \cdots, D_f$ of C. Suppose S_{1f} is defined as above. Then we define D_i, $1 \leq i \leq f$ as follows:

$$D_i = \{P_j \mid DOM_{P_j} \in DS_{S_i} \text{ and } P_j \in C, S_i \subseteq S_{1f}\}$$

Then, $D_1, \cdots, D_f$ are the disjoint subclauses of C such that $DS_{D_1} \subseteq DS_{S_1}, \cdots, DS_{D_f} \subseteq DS_{S_f}$.

We said that the unsatisfiability of $S \cup \{C\}$ depends only on the unsatisfiability of S_{1f}, i.e., $S_1 \cup \cdots \cup S_f \cup \{C\}$. The following lemma shows that S_{1f} is unsatisfiable if and only if $(S_1 \cup D_1), \cdots, (S_f \cup D_f)$ are all unsatisfiable. Checking whether all of them are unsatisfiable is less costly than checking S_{1f}, similar to the arguments made in the redundancy case.

Lemma 9. *Let $S_{1f}, D_1, \cdots, D_f$ be the sets as defined above. Then S_{1f} is unsatisfiable if and only if all of the sets $(S_1 \cup D_1), \cdots, (S_f \cup D_f)$ are unsatisfiable.*

The following algorithm checks whether a constraint C is contradictory to a set S of constraints or not.

Algorithm **Contradiction.**
Input. A constraint set S partitioned into $S_1, \cdots, S_d$. A constraint $C = P_1 \vee \cdots \vee P_k$.
Output. "Yes" if $S \cup \{C\}$ is unsatisfiable, "No" otherwise.
Begin
for i=1 to k
    if $DOM_{P_i} \notin DS_S$ then return "No" /* Lemma 7 */
end;
for i=1 to d
    if $DS_C \cap DS_{S_i} \neq \emptyset$ then
        mark S_i and let D_i be the subclause of C such that $DS_{D_i} \subseteq DS_{S_i}$;
    end;
end;
for i=1 to f /* Let $S_1, \cdots, S_f$ be the *marked* partitions. */
    if $(S_i \cup D_i)$ is not found unsatisfiable (with System R) then return "No"
end; /* At this point $(S_1 \cup D_1), \cdots, (S_f \cup D_f)$ are all found unsatisfiable. */
return "Yes"
End.

In lines 1-3, the condition stated in Lemma 7 is tested. Lines 4-8 finds $(S_1, \cdots, S_f)$. The constraints in S-S_{1f} are not relevant to the unsatisfiability of $(S \cup \{C\})$. Also disjoint subclauses $D_1, \cdots, D_f$ of C are found. Then in lines 9-11, the unsatisfiability of each of the sets $(S_1 \cup D_1)$, $\cdots$, $(S_f \cup D_f)$ is tested. If all are found to be unsatisfiable, $S \cup \{C\}$ is unsatisfiable by Lemma 9.

Example 8. Consider Example 5. S_1=$\{C_1, C_2, C_3\}$, S_2=$\{C_4\}$ with DS_{S_1}=$\{DOM_1, DOM_2\}$, DS_{S_2} = $\{DOM_3\}$. The given constraint is C with DS_C=$\{DOM_2, DOM_3, DOM_4\}$. Since DOM_4 is not in DS_{S_1} or DS_{S_2}, the constraint is not contradictory to S. This is detected in lines 1-3 of the algorithm.

The Cost of the Algorithm: It is shown [14] that the cost of the algorithm is

$$O(k * |DS_S|) + d * O(k * |DS_{S_i}|) + d * K^{(n/d)} * \frac{k}{d} * O(\frac{n+d}{d}).$$

The most costly factor here is $K^{(n/d)} * k * O(\frac{n+d}{d})$. If we tested the unsatisfiability of $(S \cup \{C\})$ without partitioning , the cost would be estimated as $K^n * k * O(n+1)$.

7 Conclusion

In this paper we discussed the problem of maintaining a consistent and nonredundant set of constraints. In particular, we considered how to check whether a constraint is redundant or contradictory with respect to a constraint set. Although this is an exponential task with the number of constraints in the set, we proposed algorithms that reduce the cost significantly in most cases. The constraint set is partitioned according to the domains that attributes take values from. When a constraint is found nonredundant and noncontradictory (and also the database satisfies it), and when it is inserted into the constraint base, it may cause same other constraints to be redundant. A nonredundant subset of the constraint base is found in this case. The deletion from the constraint base does not cause problems in our method.

References

1. Aho A. V., Garey M. R., Ullman J. D., The Transitive Reduction of a Direct Graph, Siam Journal of Computing, 1:2, 1972, 31-7.
2. Bernstein P. and Blaustein B., A simplification algorithm for integrity assertions and concrete views, Proc. COMPSAC 81, 1981, pp. 90-99.
3. Böttcher S., Jarke M., Schmidt J W., Adabtive predicate managers in database systems, 12th Int. VLDB Conf., Kyoto, 1986, pp. 21-29.
4. Bry F., Manthey R., Checking consistency of database constraints: a logical basis, 12th Int. VLDB Conf., Kyoto, 1986, pp. 13-20.
5. Bry F., Decker H., and Manthey R., A Uniform Approach to Constraint Satisfaction and Constraint Satisfiability in Deductive Databases. Lecture Notes in Computer Science 303 (Proc. EDBT'88), Springer-Verlag 1988, pp. 488-505.
6. Büning H. K., Löwen U., Schmitgen S., Inconsistency of production systems, Data & Knowledge Engineering 3 (1988/89) pp. 245-260.
7. Chang C., Lee R. C., Symbolic Logic and Mechanical Theorem Proving, Academic Press, New York, 1973.
8. Elkan C., A Decision Procedure for Conjunctive Query Disjointness, ACM PODS, pp. 134-139, 1989.

9. Fagin R., Halpern J Y., and Megiddo N., A Logic for Reasoning about Probabilities, Information and Computation, 87, pp. 78-128, 1990. Springer-Verlag, 1990.
10. Gallier J H., Logic for Computer Science: Foundations of Automatic Theorem Proving, Harper & Row, Publishers, New York, 1986.
11. Hsu A. and Imielinski T., Integrity checking for multiple updates, Proc. SIGMOD Conf., 1985, pp.152-168.
12. Ishakbeyoglu N S. and Ozsoyoglu Z M., Maintenance of Semantic Integrity Constraints under Database Updates, Proc. 6th ISCIS Symposium, Turkey, 1991, pp. 125-134.
13. Ishakbeyoglu N S., Ozsoyoglu Z M., A Deduction system for implication integrity constraints, Technical Report CIS-9201, Bilkent University, 1992.
14. Ishakbeyoglu N S., Ozsoyoglu Z M., On the Maintenance of Implication Integrity constraints, Technical Report CES-92-09, Case Western Reserve University, 1992.
15. Klug A., On Conjunctive Queries Containing Inequalities, JACM 35, 1, pp. 146-160, January 1988.
16. Kung C. H., A Temporal Framework for Information Systems Specification and Verification. PhD Thesis, Univ. of Trondheim, Norway, 1984.
17. Manthey R. and Bry F., SATCHMO: a theorem prover implemented in Prolog. Proc. CADE 88 (9th Conf. on Automated Deduction), Argonne, Illinois, May 1988, also ECRC Tech. Rep. KB-21, Nov. 1987.
18. McCune W. W. and Henschen L. J., Maintaining State Constraints in Relational Databases: A Proof Theoretic Basis, Journal of the ACM, Vol. 36, No. 1, January 1989, pp. 46-68.
19. Nicolas J-M., Logic for improving integrity checking in relational data bases. Acta Informatica 18, pp.227-253, 1982
20. Ozsoyoglu Z M., Ishakbeyoglu N S., and Shenoy S T., On the Maintenance of Semantic Implication Constraints, Technical Report, Dept. of Computer Engineering and Science, Case Western Reserve University, Nov. 1991
21. Ozsoyoglu Z M., Query Optimization in Distributed Databases, PhD Thesis, Dept. of Computing Sciences, University of Alberta, Canada, 1980.
22. Rosenkrantz D J., Hunt H B., Processing Conjunctive Predicates and Queries, Proc. VLDB, 1980, pp. 64-72.
23. Sadri F. and Kowalski R., A Theorem-proving approach to database integrity, in J. Minker (ed.) Foundations of Deductive Databases and Logic Programming, Morgan Kaufmann Pub., 1988, pp. 313-362.
24. Shenoy S T., Ozsoyoglu Z M., A system for semantic query optimization, Proc. ACM SIGMOD, pp.181-195, May 1987.
25. Shenoy S T., Ozsoyoglu Z M., Design and implementation of a semantic query optimizer, IEEE Transactions on Knowledge and Data Engineering, pp. 344-361, September 1989.
26. Ullman J D., Principles of database and knowledge-base systems Vol I, Computer Science Press, 1988.
27. Ullman J D., Principles of database and knowledge-base systems Vol II, Computer Science Press, 1989.
28. Yu T C., and Ozsoyoglu Z M., On determining tree query membership of a distributed query, INFOR, Aug. 1984, pp. 261-281.
29. Yu T C., and Sun W., Automatic knowledge acquisition and maintenance for semantic query optimization, IEEE Transactions on Knowledge and Data Engineering, pp. 362-375, September 1989.

REFLEX Active Database Model: Application of Petri-Nets

Waseem Naqvi and Mohamed T. Ibrahim

Database Systems Research Laboratory
University of Greenwich, London, SE18 6PF, U.K.
{w.naqvi, m.ibrahim}@greenwich.ac.uk

Abstract. REFLEX is an active database research prototype, designed to provide a flexible and adaptive active database extension to an existing database system. This paper reviews the REFLEX model and its architecture. Some of the main contributions of the research are discussed, such as the notion of *self-activity* and of enabling investments in legacy systems to be preserved. Some current applications of petri-nets to rule management are described before the design and modelling of REFLEX using petri-nets.

1. Introduction

Active databases have generated substantive interest from the research community. In essence these systems encapsulate an enterprise's domain knowledge within the system. Generally most active prototype systems have the notions of event-condition-action (ECA) [C1]. REFLEX, is a research prototype of an active database system designed for implementation as an extension for existing organisational databases. It builds on and extends notions and concepts from other related research prototypes along a number of dimensions. The status of these extensions in the current prototype and those planned for future work are described.

The philosophy of the REFLEX architecture and design encompasses the provision of a flexible, adaptive and *active* capability to an organisation's existing database. The benefit of such an approach, in addition to the aforementioned features, is that it preserves an organisation's investment in legacy systems, resources and training.

Petri-nets [P2] have been proven as viable modelling and analysis techniques. This paper reports on the current prototype's design philosophy and features as well as the current status of modelling and analysing the REFLEX system using the Petri-net theory.

The paper is organised as follows, section 2 reviews the REFLEX model and its architecture. Section 3 briefly surveys expert and knowledge based systems. Following on, section 4 describes the application of petri-nets to the formalism of the REFLEX model. Finally section 5 concludes with future directions.

2. The REFLEX Model

An active database management system (DBMS) must be able to manage knowledge as well as other notions of its activity feature. Thus, the architecture of an active database management system, in contrast to that of a passive DBMS, must deal with *rules*. It may also support other types of knowledge representation schemes e.g. frames in order to enhance the functionality of the system as explained in later sections. Rules would then become part of the frame representation scheme. Various active monitors or daemons could then be attached to one or more of the rule's objects: events, and/or conditions and/or actions. The main types of the triggering events are given in section 2.3.

2.1. REFLEX Architecture

The main components are: the transparent interface manager, the knowledge, event and transaction/execution models. Three of these components are common to many other active prototypes. REFLEX, however, differs from other prototypes in that it provides a Transparent Interface Manager (TIM), Fig. 1, to a host DBMS. Because of this transparency, TIM contributes to the flexibility and adaptability features of REFLEX as mentioned above. Further details about TIM are explained in section 2.2.

The REFLEX knowledge model, as mentioned above, combines two schemes of knowledge representation, namely production-rules and frames [R1]. REFLEX is thus able to support the cause/effect and deep knowledge reasoning by the provision of these two types of knowledge representation .

The rule management system implements a priority mechanism. During a critical period only the highest priority rules will either be executable or can preempt other lower priority rules. The rule priority system is also used in rule conflict resolution.

Unlike POSTGRES [S1, C2], REFLEX is designed and built as an object-oriented system. It also differs from other prototypes in one important aspect. Whereas other research prototypes, such as HiPAC [C1] and POSTGRES, are tightly coupled to their underlying model, REFLEX implements a *loose coupling*. This feature is used to provide *'activity'* for many models i.e. object model, relational model and the extended relational model. A comparison of the features of a number of active database prototypes, which were not included because of space limitation, are given in [N1].

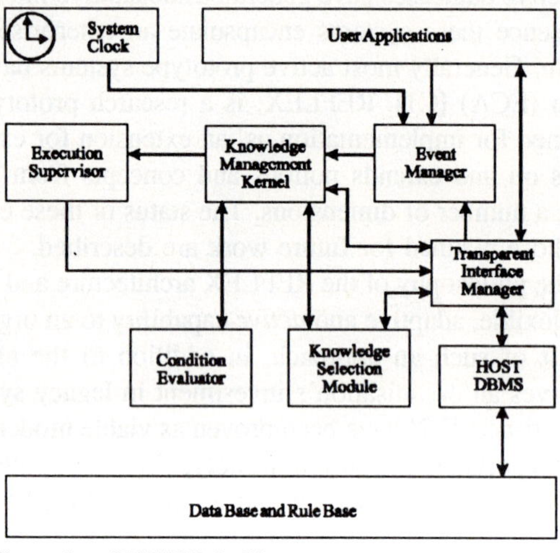

Figure 1 REFLEX Architecture

The *'active'* notion plays a dual role in our prototype. The first role, common with other prototypes, is *imparting* active capability into the application domain. The second role which, as far as we know is one contribution of this research, is that REFLEX employs a ***'self-active'*** capability to update itself. The knowledge base (KB) as well as an application database are stored within the REFLEX system. Thus the maintenance of the KB can also be subject to the notion of activity. As an example, the rule's state is monitored *actively* by the REFLEX system. Rules have three components: events, conditions and actions. The clauses for each of these components are compiled or recompiled at the point of rule creation or on rule modification. The re-compilation process being automatically triggered on a rule change. Note that the issue of knowledge base validation plays a crucial part in this case, see section 6. It will be assumed for the moment, however, that the knowledge base is consistent, valid and complete in the sense of [J4].

Since one of the main target uses of REFLEX is real-time/safety-critical systems, the REFLEX system must function in an efficient and safe manner. It must also ensure that the design of applications running under REFLEX is formally validated and verified. Petri net technology and formalism is used in the analysis of REFLEX's design and construction. A suite of tools are also being designed to support the development process.

2.2. Outline of the Model

Transparent Interface Manager (TIM). TIM allows *internal* database events to be monitored, and highlights the events to the Event Manager. Any access to the database must go through TIM. The underlying database's transaction manager has been harnessed, using *wrapper* technology, to allow the detection of transaction events and also to allow the creation of nested and sibling transactions. The transaction manager interface has special wrapper functions which trap all calls to the transaction manager, as the code wedges in symbol tables, and informs the Event Manager that a transaction based event has taken place.

Event Manager (EM). Other research prototypes, e.g. HiPAC [C1] employ the notion of primitive and composite events and both an event and '*history*' algebra in their event model. REFLEX adopts these concepts from the HiPAC model. In the following section, we describe the working of this module.

When an event is detected, the Event Manager logs it in the temporal log. Further processing steps depend on whether the event is simple or complex and will be explained in section 2.3. EM then informs the Knowledge Management Kernel that an event has occurred.

Knowledge Management Kernel (KMK). The KMK acts as the nucleus of the REFLEX architecture. KMK's major tasks are (a) as a command dispatcher to the other modules, and more importantly, (b) as a rule evaluation scheduler. REFLEX is designed to be used in many areas and particularly in the real-time application domain. Hence, it must respond very quickly to be able to influence the environment of which it is a part; e.g. in process control applications. For this reason many of the modules are designed to operate concurrently. The KMK is responsible for scheduling the cooperating modules which frequently act on the same data space. The interfaces between the KMK and the five modules are described below.

a) EM-KMK-KSM Interfaces. When the EM informs the KMK that an event occurred, KMK evaluates whether it affects any rules. The list of affected rules is passed to the Knowledge Selection Module (KSM) which returns a list of '*in-context*' rules i.e. their '*ON*'-clause are satisfied. These rules are passed to the Condition Evaluation Module, subject to the event-condition coupling mode.
b) KMK-CEM-ES Interfaces. Depending on a rule's priority level and its coupling

mode, KMK simultaneously dispatches it to the Condition Evaluation (CEM) and the KSM modules. This design strategy ensures parallelism and faster availability of the two results. If both results are true, the rule's action clause may be passed to the Execution Supervisor immediately. However, if the KSM returns an unsatisfiable rule, the CEM is preempted, and the result discarded. If the CEM returns its result first, it can be written onto the temporal log ready for use.

On return from the CEM, if the rule's condition clause has been satisfied (rule is *fireable*), it is then passed to the Execution Supervisor, subject to the condition-action coupling modes. Otherwise the rule is discarded from working memory and no further action need be taken.

Knowledge Selection Module. On being called by KMK, the KSM recalls the set of rules that the event affects. If a rule has a simple event of the kind that occurred, it is returned to the KMK with a status of *'Yes in context'*. If the rule specifies complex events, the KSM checks the temporal log for any relevant related events that occurred previously. If so, it checks if the event specification is satisfied, and informs the KMK. If a rule's event clause is part-satisfied, it is written to the *pending* log and kept for a given period of time, until its event clause is either satisfied or discharged. The log keeps a copy of the state of rule evaluation, ready for further events to be raised.

Condition Evaluation Module. The rule's condition predicate is evaluated. A condition can be in: (a) REFLEX's high level Object SQL dialect, (b) proprietary language of the host DBMS. REFLEX maps the Object SQL to the proprietary language. An application designer thus has the flexibility to write the clause in either form. The rule's condition clause is compiled, as with the other clauses, either at creation time or on modification. Examples of some rule condition clauses follow:

```
ON    update customer                        ON    update stock
IF    customer.name = 'Fred Bloggs'          IF    item.qty <= item.reorder_qty
      AND customer.credit_limit = 0          THEN  insert onorder item, reorder_qty
THEN  call Alert_No_Credit
```

Execution Supervisor. The rule's action clause is evaluated. The clause can be in one of two dialects: (i) a query in object SQL or (ii) a call to an application defined object (process module).

2.3. Event Specification

The event clause is expressed using algebra which expresses temporal relationships between events. Event histories are maintained in the temporal log to support the evaluation of complex event clauses. Our time model is based on *interval logic*, with all events having a before or after (default) granularity.

The types of events are: (i) Internal, Object events: before/after create, get, etc. Transaction events: before/after start, commit, abort (ii) Temporal events: at (specific-date/time), periodic, after (duration), sequential (iii) External events: are user-defined. Events are augmented with the concept of *validity* whereby a valid event occurs within a certain period. Example event specifications and rule syntax are:

a) $Event_1$ **AND** $Event_2$ **WITHIN MIN** 30
$Event_1$ **PRECEDES** $Event_2$ **WITHIN HOUR** 24

b) **ON** **event-algebra**
IF **either** **i) no condition** **ii) Object SQL query** **iii) proprietary language**
THEN **either** **i) call user module** **ii) Object SQL query** **iii) proprietary language**

i) event algebra clause.

update <table/class/object name>
on an update or modification of a table,class, or instance object
update <table/class/object name> AND TIME 5.00pm

ii) condition clause. The clause may be set to TRUE (i.e. no condition), or expressed in either Object SQL or the host DBMS's proprietary language.

e.g: *TRUE* i.e. no condition, just an Event-Action pair.
or *class_name.attribute* {=, <, <=, >, >=, !=} *expression*

iii) action clause. The clause may call an object module or as, with the condition clause, a more complete query may be expressed in either Object SQL or the host DBMS's proprietary language.

e.g. *call* program module (object) or *delete* object

2.4. Current Status

Phase one of the model has been implemented using AT&T C++ (v2.1) and the ONTOS object-oriented database management system. The user interface was built upon the X11R5 windowing system using a Sun Sparc Workstation running Solaris 1.1. Another implementation of the REFLEX prototype is being mirrored using the P.O.E.T. database and MS Windows on a PC platform.

3. Applications of Petri-Nets

Petri-nets and knowledge based systems have been used to help solve problems in many application areas. Applications include manufacturing, process control, planning, decision support, medical applications, etc. [L1, A1, B2, S1].

Petri-net (PN) models are abstract and formal representations of information flow [P1]. Their major use has been in the definition, design, modelling of systems that exhibit concurrent behaviour using their well known powerful modelling and analysis properties.

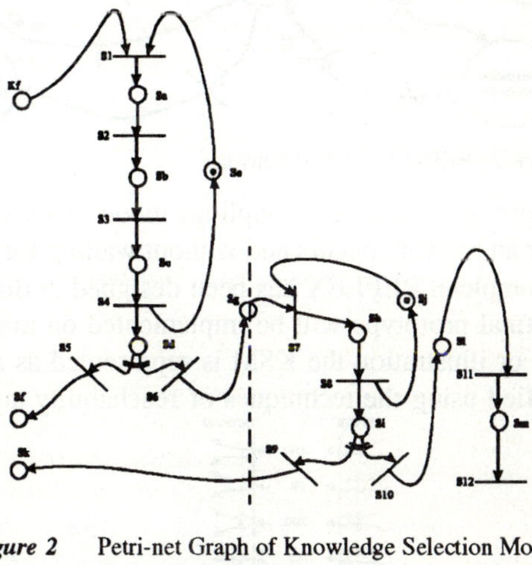

Figure 2 Petri-net Graph of Knowledge Selection Module

In their paper [B3], Bemaiza et al describe a knowledge-based Petri-net experimental tool for modelling and analysis which consists of a graphical editor to capture and edit Petri-net graphs. Their expert system is based on rules capturing the general knowledge about reachability and invariance of Petri nets. Their approach was investigated as a possible candidate for use in the analysis of REFLEX. However, whereas [B3] uses Prolog, an object oriented approach using C++ and a knowledge-based system (e.g. KAPPA) is under study.

4. Petri-nets in the REFLEX model

We share in the belief's of many others [R2, R3] that petri-nets are powerful techniques for the design and analysis of many systems. When coupled with object technology and knowledge-based systems they provide a powerful environment for many domains including active object oriented database systems. We are not aware of any research projects reported where these three technologies are being investigated and integrated in the area of active and/or object-oriented systems. Petri-nets are an instrumental technique in providing formal definitions and a sound basis for validating the design of REFLEX.

It is well known that production rules are the most widely used knowledge representation scheme. These systems, despite their many desirable features e.g. principally their simplicity, lack the power to '*model*' the behaviour of many real world systems. REFLEX aims to combine rule-based and frame-based knowledge representation schemes in order to provide cause/effect deep knowledge and reasoning mechanisms.

The notions of event-condition-action (ECA) is used in REFLEX, and other research prototypes [C1], together with the underlying architecture that includes a transaction execution model; where the coupling between groups of ECA and their execution with respect to their triggering transaction, this feature distinguishes active databases from KBs. [C1] suggest that requirements may vary with the application. Real-time applications might require an *immediate* (coupling) mode of execution to evaluate a condition as soon after an as event occurs and without waiting for the whole of the triggering transaction to complete. REFLEX has been designed in discrete units. Since it is envisioned that the final prototype will be implemented on multiprocessor hardware.

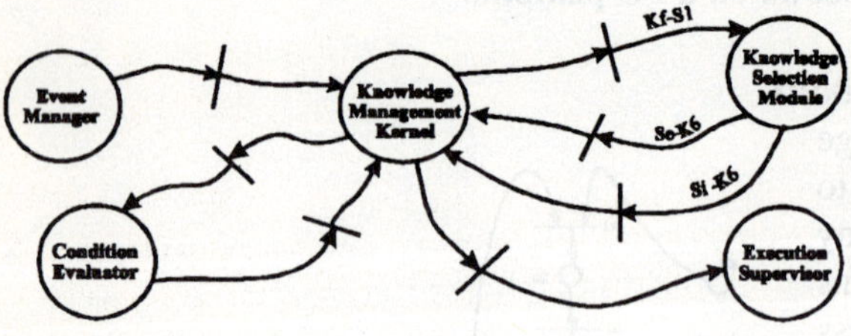

Figure 3 REFLEX Context Petri-net

For illustration the KSM is represented as a petri-net, Fig. 2. KSM was formally verified using the techniques of reachability analysis, and safeness checking.

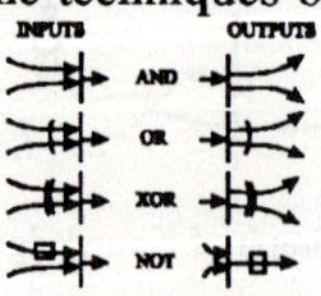

Figure 4 Petri-net Logical Notation

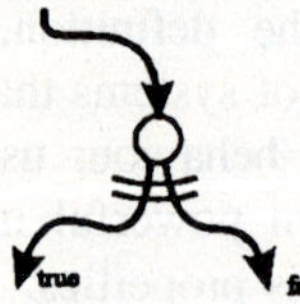

Figure 5 if-then construct

A high level context petri-net graph of the REFLEX architecture can be found in

Fig 3. For REFLEX we have adopted a similar approach to [B1] and augmented the Petri-net theory by adding the following enhancement (Fig. 4).The above can be used singularly or combined to perform additional logic. To provide an if-then or case construct, Fig. 5, is used in this paper.

A Petri-net structure, C, for the Knowledge Selection Module follows, Table 1.

From the initial markings μ = (1,0,0,0,0,1,0,0,0,0,1,0,0,0), the reachability tree is produced, see Fig 6. The reachability tree is the standard analysis technique for petri-nets, which verifies that all nodes can be reached and that infinite loops do not occur.

C = {P,T,I,O}

P = { Kf, Sa, Sb, Sc, Sd, Se, Sf, Sg, Sh, Si, Sj, Sk, Sl, Sm}

T = { S1, S2, S1, S4, S5, S6, S7, S8, S9, S10, S11, S12}

I(S1) = {Kf} O(S1) = {Sa}
I(S2) = {Sa} O(S2) = {Sb}
I(S1) = {Sb} O(S1) = {Sc}
I(S4) = {Sc} O(S4) = {Sd, Se}
I(S5) = {Sd} O(S5) = {Sf}
I(S6) = {Sd} O(S6) = {Sg}
I(S7) = {Sg} O(S7) = {Sh}
I(S8) = {Sh} O(S8) = {Si, Sj}
I(S9) = {Si} O(S9) = {Sk}
I(S10) = {Si} O(S10) = {Sl}
I(S11) = {Sl} O(S11) = {Sm}
I(S12) = {Sm}

Table 1 Petri-net Structure

The petri-net graph for structure C can be found in Fig. 2. It can be observed that the KSM can be split into two distinct modules. On the left side, the basic event-rule matching and event specification. The right side, to action and satisfy the complex event specification of the rules in context. These two modules can execute concurrently. The two modules exhibit the familiar *producer-consumer* scenario with the place Sg, Fig. 2, representing the buffer or queue between the two.

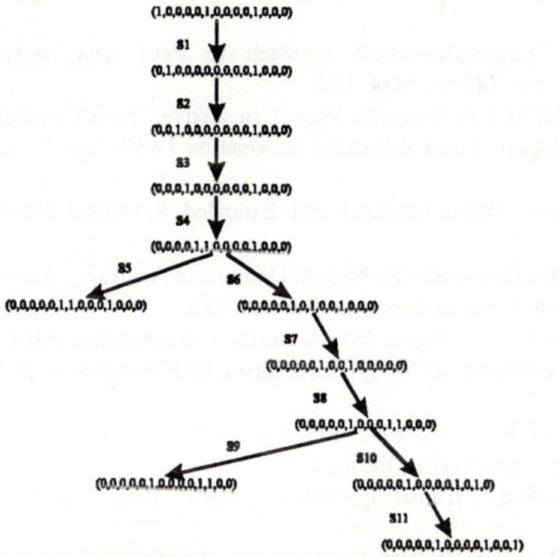

Figure 6 Reachability tree for Knowledge Selection Module

Analysis of Petri-Net Graphs

A complete analysis of petri-net graphs requires detailed study of many issues. This is especially true for a large system such as REFLEX. It must be shown that all places can be reached, that the system is safe and within specified bounds. Petri-nets offer many analysis techniques such as: safeness, boundedness, conservation, reachability and coverability [P2].

5. Conclusions and future work

This research aims to establish the feasibility of the loose-coupling approach between REFLEX and the underlying data model of a host database. This is easily achievable if REFLEX is implemented on parallel, distributed architecture. However its viability on a single-processor model, remains to be established. However, with the rapid increase in client/server popularity, it is possible for organisations to use REFLEX. As stated earlier, this will enable these organisations to preserve their investments in legacy systems and training. This is one contribution of this research in the area of active database research. Another contribution is the integration of Petri-nets, object-orientation and active database technologies.

As to future work, there are many issues still to be resolved. One important issue is the need to check that the knowledge base is valid, consistent, complete and accurately represents a problem domain.

Jafar and Bahil [J4] describe a system for interactive verification of knowledge-based systems. However, we also believe that some aspects of the validation process can be beneficially automated. Following [O1], the questions that need to be answered include: what should be validated? how is it validated? what are the procedures for validation ? how is validation integrated into development?

Version management of the knowledge base for reasoning also needs to be considered if explanation of a systems behaviour over time is to be supported.

7. References

[A1] Agarwal R. and Tanniru M., "A Petri-net based approach for verifying the integrity of production systems", International Journal of Man-Machine Studies, Vol. 36 No 3 pp 447-468, March 1992

[B1] Baer J., Bovet D. and Estrin G., "Legality and Other Properties of Graph Models of Computations", Journal of the ACM, Vol. 17, No. 3., July 1970, pp. 543-554

[B2] Brenner E., Grabner J., Moosburger M., Otschko G., Schlögl K., Seifter P., Song J., Steger Ch. and Weiss R., "Design and Implementation of a Distributed Real-Time Expert-System for Fault Diagnosis in Modular Manufacturing Systems", Microprocessing & Microprogramming, Vol. 32 No 1-5 pp 799-806, August 1991

[B3] Benmaiza, M. and Elkaraksy, M.R., "Knowledge-based approach to Petri nets analysis", Knowledge-Based Systems Vol: 4 Iss: 3, pp. 144-56, Sept. 1991

[C1] Chakravarthy S., Blaustein B., et al, "HiPAC: A Research Project in Active, Time-Constrained Database Management", Final Technical Report, Xerox Advanced Information Technology Division, July 1989

[C2] Cattell, R.G.G, "Object Data Management: Object-Oriented and Extended Relational Database Systems", Addison-Wesley, 1991.

[J1] Jensen K., "Coloured Petri Nets: A High Level Language for System Design and Analysis", Advances in Petri Nets 1990, Springer-Verlag, Lecture Notes in Computer Science, 483

[J2] Jianjun Y., Feng Z., Jiati D. and Chuaijun C., "Intelligent Manufacturing cell controller IMCC-E", Human Aspects in Computer Integrated Manufacturing Conf., Tokyo, Japan, IFIP Transaction B, Vol. B-3 pp. 745-755, 1992

[J3] Jensen, K. (Ed.), Application and Theory of Petri Nets 1992, Proceedings of the 13th international Conference, Sheffield, UK, June 1992, Springer-Verlag, Berlin 1992.

[J4] Jafar, M., Bahill, T.A, "Interactive Verification of Knowledge-Based Systems", IEEE Expert, Vol.8 No.1, Feb. 1993.

[L1] Lipp H.P., "Application of timed fuzzy Petri nets in expert systems for operative management of complerx prodyction systems", Prozessrecgensystemme '91 Conf. (Process Computer Systems '91), 1991, pp. 103-12 (in German)

[N1] Naqvi W. and Ibrahim M.T., "The REFLEX Active Database System", Database Systems Research Laboratory, University of Greenwich, Internal Report, 1992

[N2] Naqvi W. and Ibrahim M.T., "REFLEX: An Active Database Extension", BNCOD11, July, 1993

[O1] O'leary, T.J., Goul, M., Moffit, K.E., Essam Radwan, A., "Validating Expert Systems", IEEE Expert, Vol. 5 No3, June 1990.

[P1] Paterson J.L., "Petri Nets", ACM Computing Surveys, Vol. 9, No. 3, September 1977

[P2] Paterson J.L., "Petri Net Theory and the modeling of Systems", Prentice-Hall, 1981

[R1] Ringland G., "Structured Object Representation - Schemata and Frames", Approaches to Knowledge Representation, Ed. Ringland and Duce, 1987, pp 81-99

[S1] Stonebraker M. and Kemnitz G., "The POSTGRES Next-Generation Database Management System", CACM October 1991, Vol 34, No 10

Road Accident Analysis Using a Functional Database Language

J. Wu and L. Harbird

University of London Centre for Transport Studies,
University College London, Gower Street, London WC1E 6BT, UK.

Abstract. A database system for a road accident analysis application has been developed using the new functional database language PFL. This application requires extensive data validation and restructuring, and queries (and hence data retrieval patterns) tend to be of a complex and ad-hoc nature. PFL adapts functional programming to deductive databases and possesses features that are desirable for applications characterised by large volumes of both data and programs, and by complex structures of both data and queries. In this paper we describe the application domain and provide an overview of the salient features of PFL. We then discuss the development of a road accident database using PFL and comment upon the insight, this has provided in terms of both the application and the language.

Key Words: Deductive Database, Functional Programming, Information Retrieval, Governmental Information System, Engineering Application

1 Introduction

Road accident analysis is based on extensive information derived from historical records of road accidents. This application area is characterised by the fact that the data requires extensive and complicated validation; the content and organisation of the data is not suitable for all kinds of analysis so that a data restructuring involving complex inference must be undertaken; there are various kinds of analysis of road accidents and their information requirements can differ widely; and new requirements for information retrieval arise as the techniques for analysis advances. As a result queries and updates are of a complex and ad-hoc nature and thus a desirable database language should be expressive, flexible, efficient and versatile. In particular, it should support rapid prototyping and experimentation involving frequent modification of both database and programs.

The Persistent Functional Language (PFL) [1,2,3], has been used to develop a database system for this application area. PFL is a *persistent language* [4] in that all data and programs persist from one user session to the next (they are stored in a database) and do not need to be "reloaded" each time. It also allows both data and programs to be augmented *incrementally* and thus differs from conventional functional programming languages such as Miranda [5] which are not incremental. By adopting a functional formalism for both data and computation, PFL allows the combination within one uniform semantic and operational framework of the respective advantages of functional programming and relational data modelling and manipulation. In particular, in addition to conventional functions, a special class of functions called *selectors* allow the storage of *extensional relations* [2] and the representation of *intentional relations* through further functions defined over selectors

[1,3]. In this sense PFL can be considered to be a deductive database language.

Because it combines features of functional and relational programming, PFL encourages the development of clear, concise and well-structured programs whilst it accommodates large volumes of both data and programs. It enforces strong, static type checking, and supports arbitrarily complex user definable data types, the specification of defaults, automatic integrity constraint enforcement [6] as well as incremental program development. These features make PFL promising for constructing large and sophisticated database applications, and in particular for the road accident analysis application outlined above.

Little prior experience was available for the development of database applications in languages of this kind, so the main objectives of the present paper are to evaluate PFL through its application to a practical example and to identify appropriate strategies for using its features. Hence the remainder of the paper is structured as follows. In Section 2 we describe data processing requirements of road accident analysis. In Section 3 we provide a brief overview of PFL and describe the general principles of constructing a database in this language. In Section 4 we illustrate the use of PFL for road accident analysis. Finally, we present our results and give our conclusions in Section 5. We do not give a comparison of PFL with related languages here since this is discussed extensively in [1,2,3].

2 Overview of Data Processing in Road Accident Analysis

Road accident analysis involves intensive information retrieval from accident records. In Great Britain, these records are recorded as text files [7]. To provide an efficient means for the information retrieval from them, the development of a database system is essential: the volume of the data is large (eg. the total number of road accidents involving personal injury in Britain in 10 years is greater than 3,000,000 [8], and for each accident there are on average over 100 data items recorded [7]), and non-sequential access to data items is normally required. The development of this database system is complicated by several factors as described in Section 1. Among these, the most influential one is the need to restructure the data: this involves extensive and intensive searching and updating of the database and needs to be supported by sophisticated inference. We therefore give emphasis to this topic in the present paper to illustrate by example the complexity of the application.

It is not unusual for data sets to be constructed in a way which is not well suited to their intended use. The data source used by road accident analysis falls into this category. Road accident analysis for engineering purposes often requires the examination of all accidents that have occurred at a site [9,10], hence making it desirable that site identity be presented as an explicit entity in the database. However, the site entity is present only implicitly in the original data as these are sets of mutually independent accident records with no explicit connection between accidents that have occurred at the same site. A prerequisite of the analysis is therefore to derive the site entity so that those accidents which occurred at the same site can be identified readily. Our discussion of accident sites below is restricted to road junctions for simplicity.

The derivation of site entity from accident data can be conceived as a classification operation that is encountered often in database applications. Here this classification can be described as partitioning a set of accidents into subsets by matching certain accident attributes that provide locational information. These attributes include road number, grid reference and so on. A necessary and sufficient condition is therefore required to determine whether two accidents match each other: this will ensure a complete and unique partition. However, such a condition can not be established based upon the information available in the original data. Rather, only weaker conditions can be set up each of which is based upon a particular attribute. As a result, intricate inference involving the use of clustering techniques has to be adopted. This includes the following two steps which will be detailed further in Section 4 to illustrate some of the features of PFL:

1. Matching accidents according to a *disjunction principle*: the sufficient condition for a positive match between any two accidents is a logical disjunction of all sufficient conditions, each of which is based on a particular attribute.

2. Applying a *transitivity principle*: the results of matching based on the *disjunction principle* should be treated as transitive, so that if A matches B and B matches C, then A matches C as well.

Eg.1: Five accidents have occurred at a site. The values of two attributes, road_pair (two of the roads at a junction) and grid_ref (the grid reference for the location of an accident) for them are listed in Table I. Suppose the equality in either attribute is a sufficient but not a necessary condition for a match. According to the *disjunction principle*, the accident pairs that yield a positive match are {Ac2,Ac4}, {Ac2,Ac5}, {Ac4,Ac5}, {Ac6,Ac9}, {Ac4,Ac6} and these five accidents can be identified as having occurred at the same site by applying the *transitivity principle*.

Table I Values of two attributes, road_pair and grid_ref, for five accidents.

Accident	Ac2	Ac4	Ac5	Ac6	Ac9
road_pair	r_p1	r_p1	r_p1	r_p2	r_p2
grid_ref	g_r1	g_r2	g_r1	g_r2	g_r3

The complexity of the data processing is increased by factors such as insufficient precision adopted for some data items, and coding errors. These factors normally cause inconsistencies in data so can be detected and corrected in some cases. The first phase of the process is therefore a comprehensive data validation which is undertaken in three steps: (1) detecting any invalid value for data items in each accident record, (2) cross-checking between different data items in each accident record, and (3) cross-checking the site descriptive information between different accident records. The validation in the last step is particularly important because the violation of data integrity concerning the correlation of information between different accident records can often go undetected due to the non-site-oriented nature of the accident recording and reporting procedures.

3 Introduction to PFL

3.1 Overview of PFL

We now provide a brief description of PFL: more comprehensive descriptions can be found in [1,2]. PFL's type system comprises the metalevel type `Type`; the set of all types, then there are object-level types, which are either built-in or user-declared and finally the values of each object-level type. For example:

declare Acc :: Type // Acc (Accident) is an object-level type[1],
declare Ac1 :: Acc // Ac1 is a value of type Acc
declare Any :: a // and Any is a constant of every type.
The built-in types are Str, Int, Real, Bool, and Char.
declare List :: a -> Type // declares a list constructor
declare Prod2 :: a->b->Type // declares a product type
declare Tuple2 :: a->b->(Prod2 a b) // declares a 2-tuple
For syntactic clarity, n-tuples are expressed using {a,b,c} and lists using $[v_1,\ldots,v_n]$ or the ':' operator, such as 1:(2:(3:[])).

Functions are defined incrementally by the insertion and deletion of equations of the form
define <lhs>=<expression>
We can define the function if as follows :
define if True x y = x // True and False are defined as
define if False x y = y // constructors of type Bool.
Equations must be defined with unique left-hand sides and can be deleted using
delete <lhs> // specifies the syntax for deleting an equation.
delete if True x y // deletes an equation of the function if.
Functions can have local definitions introduced by the key word where, eg.
define f x y = (sqr x)+(sqr y) where sqr a = a*a
PFL provides some pre-defined functions, including arithmetic (+,-,*,/,%), relational (==,!=,<,>), and logical functions (or,and). PFL infers incrementally the type of each function, eg. the type of the above function if would be inferred as:
"if :: Bool->a->a->a".

Selectors store bulk data in PFL. They are single-argument, list-valued functions. Each selector is associated with a relation. A selector function is declared by
selector <name> :: <type>->[<type>]
where <type> is an object-level type. For example,
selector number_of_casualties :: {Acc,Int} -> [{Acc,Int}]
This selector is a relation, the first attribute of which represents an accident and the second the number of casualties incurred in the accident. Retrieval of bulk data in PFL is done by pattern matching. We describe the pattern matching in terms of the infix function ⊆, "matches", and the polymorphic "wildcard" Any. When given values p and v, the expression (p ⊆ v) yields True if p is identical to v, apart from occurrences of Any in p. Thus for example, {1,Any,3} ⊆ {1,2,3} returns True and {1,2,3} ⊆ {1,Any,3} returns False. A precise definition of ⊆ can be found in [2].

A *list abstraction* is a list-valued expression where each element is the result of evaluating an expression E that contains a number of variables that range over specified values. The values are determined by a sequence of *generator* and *filter expressions* that are evaluated in order. The general syntax of a list-abstraction is [E | E1; E2; .. ; Ek], where each Ei is either a generator or a filter expression. A filter expression is boolean-valued. A generator expression assigns to a variable the value of each element in a specified list. For each such assignment,

---

[1] The symbol '//' introduces a comment.

the filter expressions appearing to the right of the generator expression are evaluated. If any of the filter expressions evaluates to False that particular assignment is discarded. The syntax of a generator expression is:

<pattern> <- <list-valued expression>

where the pattern and the elements of the list are of the same type. Thus, given the list of integers int_list, the list abstraction,

[{x,y} | x <- int_list; y <- int_list; x > y]

defines the relationship "greater than" over the list int_list.

When a selector is declared its relation is empty. The PFL functions include (or exclude) can be used to add (or remove) tuples from a selector. In particular

include <selector> <tuple>

inserts a tuple, if it is not already there, and returns True, otherwise, it returns False, and

exclude <selector> <pattern>

deletes any <tuple> such that <pattern> ⊆ <tuple>, returning True if at least one tuple is deleted, and otherwise False. A selector's relation is queried by applying the selector to a search pattern:

selector <pattern>

The result of this is equivalent to [x | x <-relation; <pattern> ⊆ x]. When applied to an argument, a selector returns a list containing all the tuples in its relation that are matched by the argument. Consider, for example,

selector day :: {Acc,Weekday} -> [{Acc,Weekday}]

Assuming that Ac1,..,Ac4 are constructors of type Acc, Mon, Wed and Fri are constructors of type Weekday, and that the expressions include day {Ac1,Mon}, include day {Ac2,Wed}, include day {Ac3,Mon}, include day {Ac4,Fri} are the only updates to the relation Day, then (day Any), returns [{Ac1,Mon}, {Ac2,Wed}, {Ac3,Mon}, {Ac4,Fri}], and (day {Ac5,Any}) and (day {Any,Mon}), return respectively [] and [{Ac3,Mon}, {Ac1,Mon}]. If we now evaluate exclude day {Any,Mon}, we delete all the tuples whose second element is Mon and (day Any) now returns [{Ac2,Wed}, {Ac4,Fri}].

The self-consistency of a database can be ensured by specifying *integrity constraints* which have the effect of rejecting any update that would result in an inconsistency. Generally, DBMS' are rather weak on integrity. However, PFL provides a mechanism for declaratively specifying integrity constraints that are automatically enforced [6]. A *constraint selector* in PFL, which is a restricted form of a list-valued function, is used to specify an integrity constraint. A constraint selector can express any typed first-order logic formula, and can also enforce aggregate constraints. The database is assumed to be in a valid state initially and the integrity constraints ensure that any new data is consistent with that already in it.

3.2 Developing The Database

A binary relational model of the accident data is used (Fig. 1). It is characterised by binary relationships between entity types. Binary relations provide a fine level of semantic granularity making it easier for the model and the data to evolve without requiring re-organisation. However, the penalty paid is that it may be costly to compose all the information relating to a single entity. This data model is then mapped into a PFL DBMS-specific model [1,2]. Many accident record fields have enumerated types and these are represented by defining a new type whose 0-ary constructors are constants. For example,

```
declare Severity :: Type          // introduce a new type Severity
declare Fatal :: Severity         // which has three values:
declare Serious :: Severity       // Fatal, Serious and Slight.
declare Slight :: Severity
```

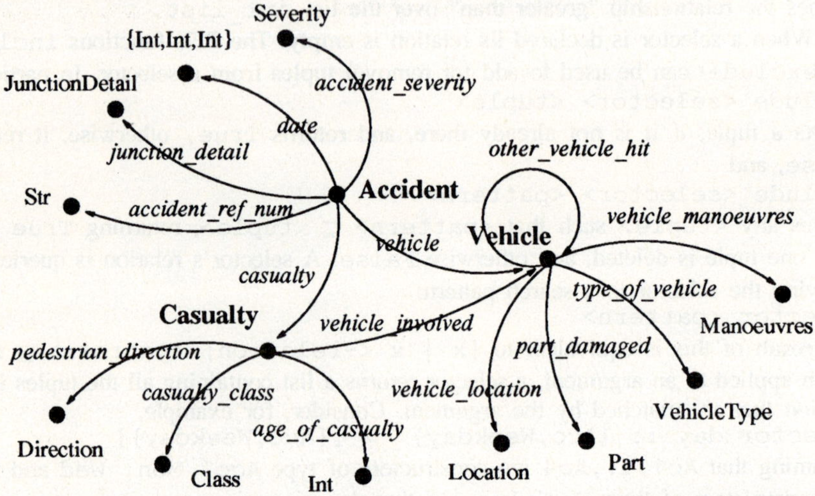

Fig. 1. Part of the binary-relational model of the accident data.

Function definitions can be made clearer by using the new constants as argument patterns and enumerated types provide a measure of security against misuse [5]. New types have therefore been defined to represent accidents, casualties and vehicles. Selectors are used to represent the relationships between data items. Most of the selectors in the database represent binary relationships but to avoid computing expensive joins some n-ary relations are also defined.

PFL allows for the representation of incomplete and default knowledge. Defaults can be defined by the use of overlapping patterns in functions. In contrast to PFL, most current DBMSs provide only rudimentary of methods for specifying default values [1]. For example, in the accident database there is a selector `junction_detail` which relates accidents to the type of junction (eg. `Roundabout`, `Sliproad`, etc) at which they occurred, if any. It is defined as,

```
junction_detail :: {Acc,Junction} -> [Acc,Junction}]
```

In fact the majority of accidents do not occur at junctions: this can be the default and therefore need not be stored explicitly. A function can be defined which given a value of type `Acc` returns the value stored in the `junction_detail` selector, if present, and returns `the default value NonJunction` otherwise.

```
define default d [] = d
define default d [x] = x
define junc_det a = default NonJunction
    [j | {a,j} <- junction_detail {a,Any}]
```

Database implementation involves loading the PFL statements to represent the accident data. A constructor is declared to represent each accident, casualty and vehicle. `Include` statements are written to store information in selectors. Here is a sample of PFL statements defined for a single accident.

```
declare Ac1 :: Acc
declare Veh1 :: Vehicle
include accident_reference_number {Ac1,"1D1129"}
include vehicle {Ac1,Veh1}
```

Views can be defined to allow data to be seen by different users in different ways, to simplify the user's perception and to provide automatic security for hidden data. A view is defined by a function that operates on selectors. PFL is computationally complete [1] and arbitrary view definitions can be specified. This contrasts with SQL [11], where a view is restricted by the capabilities of the `select` statement. For example, `view1` defines a list of tuples comprising accidents and their associated casualties and vehicles:

```
define view1 acc = [{acc, [cas | {acc,cas} <- casualty
   {acc,Any}], [veh | {acc,veh} <- vehicle {acc,Any}]}]
```

where the selector `vehicle` is defined as

```
selector vehicle :: {Acc,Vehicle} -> [{Acc,Vehicle}]
```

4 Accident Data Processing in PFL

Because it integrates database management and functional inference, PFL possesses various useful features as described in Section 1. The appropriate use of these built-in mechanisms can help to improve both the efficiency in prototyping and the performance of the database system. Some examples are discussed in detail to show how to use PFL's features to satisfy the requirements of this application. In Section 4.1 we describe how integrity constraints can be enforced in PFL. In Section 4.2 we describe how efficiency can be achieved for matching accidents using relational queries. In Section 4.3 we describe how incremental programming can be used conveniently to derive site-accident relations, and in Section 4.4 we describe the derivation of these relations using database queries and updates.

4.1 Maintaining Database Integrity Using Constraint Selectors

The types of constraints required for the accident data include range constraints, which check the value of one field within an accident record; intra-record constraints, which compare the values of several fields within a record; aggregate constraints, which operate on a collection of values from a field from a number of records; and inter-record constraints, which perform a check between records. A *constraint selector* returns a list of entities that violate it: whenever this list is empty, no constraint violation has been detected. PFL enforces each constraint by rejecting any update that would result in its violation.

An example of an aggregate constraint is to ensure that the number of vehicles involved in an accident, *n*, should be equal to the number of vehicle sub-records associated with that accident record. We store *n* in the following selector:

```
selector number_of_vehicles :: {Acc,Int} -> [{Acc,Int}]
```

Then we can define this constraint selector, called `c1`, as:

```
constraint c1 {a} = [a | {a,n}<-number_of_vehicles {a,Any};
   length (vehicle {a,Any}) != n]
```

where `length` is a function that returns the length of a list.

An example of an inter-record constraint is to ensure that accidents having the same grid reference also have the same value of junction type. We store grid reference relation (accident, easting, northing) in the selector `acc_e_n` as tuples `{Acc,Int,Int}`. Then we can define this constraint selector, called `c2`, as:

```
constraint c2 {a1,e,n} = [{a1,a2,e,n} | {a1,e,n} <- acc_e_n
   {a1,e,n}; {a2,e,n} <- acc_e_n {Any,e,n}; {a1,jd1} <-
   junction_detail {a1,Any}; {a2,jd2} <- junction_detail
   {a2,Any}; jd1 != jd2]
```

4.2 Efficient Matching of Accidents Using Relational Queries

Relational programming in PFL is facilitated by the pattern matching mechanism of selectors. By using selectors, searching bulk data can be implemented in the form of relational queries. Such implementation can be compact and efficient by virtue of the functional formalism of PFL and the underlying hashing and indexing mechanism associated with selectors, as is illustrated in the example below.

Eg.2: In order to partition a set of N accidents into subsets by the equality of M attributes according to the *disjunction principle* given in Section 2, one obvious algorithm is to match each accident against each other one in turn by testing a disjunction of M equalities each of which concerns a particular attribute, and then to derive the subsets from the results. The complexity in terms of information retrieval (eg. to retrieve the value of a single attribute for an accident) for the matching operation alone is N^2. Taking advantage of the flexibility of relational query formulation in PFL, a much more efficient algorithm can readily be implemented. Using this method, we create M partitions each of which is obtained by partitioning the set according to the equality of one of the M attributes alone. The subsets are then derived from these results (See Sections 4.3, 4.4). The PFL code for partitioning by the equality of a single attribute, in this case grid reference, is given below to illustrate this method.

// e_n_acc :: {Int,Int}->[Acc], returns all accidents associated with the given grid reference:

```
define e_n_acc {e,n} = [a | {a,e,n} <- acc_e_n {Any,e,n}]
```

// partition :: [[Acc]], returns a list of lists in each of which all accidents occurred at the same grid reference. Here, `unique` is a standard function that removes duplicates from a list:

```
define partition = [e_n_acc e_n | e_n <- (unique [{e,n} |
   {a,e,n} <- acc_e_n Any])]
```

Assume for each attribute A_j ($j = 1, 2, ..., M$), the number of possible values is K_j, then the total number of retrievals required for making the M partitions is $1 + K_1 + K_2 + ... + K_M$. In general, $K_j \ll N$ and M is a small constant, so the complexity in terms of information retrieval of this method is sublinear to N.

4.3 Modelling site-accident relations

PFL supports incremental programming so that both extensional and intentional relations can be updated without recompiling. This feature is desirable for prototyping and experimentation since both require frequent modification of the database. It also eases the storage of intermediate results in database to facilitate the use of the built-in bulk data searching mechanism as illustrated in Section 4.2. Eg.3

shows the storage of temporary relations in the database during a search.

Eg.3: The following selector is used to record the results obtained using the method described in Eg.2:

```
selector pairs1 :: {Acc,Acc} -> [{Acc,Acc}]
```

In `pairs1`, each tuple {x,y} represents two accidents x and y that match positively. The two accident identities should satisfy the inequality, `x<y`, to avoid storing the duplicate relationship `{y,x}`. In PFL, there is a system-defined ordering over all non-function types so that they can all be ordered using the "<" function. Hence we define the following function to store a list of matched accidents.

// store :: [Acc]->Int, where `sum` is a standard function that returns the sum of the given list of integers.

```
define store (h:t) = sum [1 | b<-[include pairs1 (f h x) |
   x <- t]; b==True] where
   f x y = if (y<x) {y,x} {x,y}
```

For example, the expression `store partition` records the results of function "partition" given in Eg.2. The method given in Eg.2 creates from a set of N accidents M (possibly distinct) partitions that are then recorded in turn in the selector `pairs1` using function `store`. Duplicates of any accident pair arising from the assembling of the M sets of pairs are eliminated by the insertion mechanism of selectors. For example, applying our algorithm to Eg.1 yields the results: 1) matching by the equality of road_pair: [[Ac2, Ac4, Ac5], [Ac6, Ac9]], and 2) matching by the equality of grid_ref: [[Ac2, Ac5], [Ac4, Ac6], [Ac9]]. Then we apply function `store` to Results 1) and 2) in turn, the tuples to be included are {Ac2, Ac4}, {Ac2, Ac5}, {Ac6, Ac9}, and then {Ac2, Ac5}, {Ac4, Ac6}. The tuple {Ac2, Ac5} will not be inserted the second time. Therefore the tuples being recorded are

Tuples 1: {Ac2, Ac4}, {Ac2, Ac5}, {Ac6, Ac9}, {Ac4, Ac6}.

The results recorded in this format represent implicitly a set of accidents that match each other according to the *transitivity principle*. This relation can be made explicit by converting Tuples 1 into the following format:

Tuples 2: {Ac4, Ac2}, {Ac4, Ac5}, {Ac4, Ac9}, {Ac4, Ac6}.

Where Ac4 serves as the set (or site) identity, as could any other in the set. We use another selector declared below to store this relation.

```
selector pairs2 :: {Acc,Acc} -> [{Acc,Acc}]
```

Note the condition `x<y` for any tuple `{x,y}` in `pairs2` is not required because no duplicates can be produced. Hence the following functions will resolve queries for the site-accident membership and the converse:

// site_accs :: Acc -> [Acc], site-accident membership:

```
define site_accs s = s : [a | {s,a} <- pairs2 {s,Any}]
```

// acc_site :: Acc -> Acc, accident-site membership:

```
define acc_site a = f1 a [s | {s,a} <- pairs2 {Any,a}] where
   f1 a [] = a; f1 a (h:t) = h
```

4.4 Deriving Site-Accident Relations through Database Queries and Updates

In PFL, relational programming is realised under a functional paradigm. This allows database manipulation and function transformation to be mixed naturally. As a result, complex database queries and updates can be implemented efficiently and succinctly by supporting data manipulation with functional inference, as illustrated by Eg.4.

Eg.4: The following algorithm can serve to derive selector `pairs2` from pairs1 (see Eg.3).

1) pick up arbitrarily an accident from selector pairs1.

2) find all tuples related to it from selector pairs1 using the transitivity principle.

3) remove these tuples from pairs1.

4) make a list of all accidents appearing in these tuples.

5) record the resulting list of accidents in selector pairs2.

6) repeat 1 to 5 until pairs1 is empty.

The partial implementation of the above algorithm (Steps 2 to 5) is shown below:

```
// store1site :: Acc->Int, implementing Steps 2 to 5:
define store1site a = sum [1 | b<-[include pairs2 {a,x} |
   x <- (chain a); x != a]; b==True]
```

// chain :: Acc->[Acc], implementing Steps 2 to 4. Here some built-in and standard functions of PFL are used, including append, which concatenates two lists; concat, which concatenates a list of lists; proj_1_2 and proj_2_2, which return respectively the first and the second element in a binary tuple, and error, which halts the evaluation:

```
define chain a = a:(append (f1 (pairs1 {Any,a}) proj_1_2)
   (f1 (pairs1 {a,Any}) proj_2_2 )) where
   f1 pairs take1 = f ((remove pairs)>0) error (concat
   [chain (take1 p) | p <- pairs])
// remove :: [{Acc,Acc}]->Int, implementing Step 3:
define remove xs = sum [1 | b<-[exclude pairs1 x | x<-xs];
   b==False]
```

Because the main operation involved here is searching and updating bulk data, this implementation is advantageous due to the intensive use of the built-in pattern matching and updating facilities of selectors.

5 Results and Conclusions

In this paper, we have introduced an application to road accident data analysis of PFL, a functional database language. We have described in detail some of the problems and requirements in developing this database system, and how PFL is used to provide solutions to them. The resulting database system has been tested using real data. The results of this show that the database system described in the present paper provides a useful aid for road accident analysis. As a result, the amount of routine manual work can be reduced substantially so that the analysis can be made more comprehensive. The system has achieved comparable performance to conventional languages for computation-intensive queries, and can give substantially better performance for data-intensive ones.

As a tool for developing this database system, the prototype of PFL has been found to be versatile, efficient and practical. In particular, the efficient and transparent use of secondary storage and the flexibility of query formulation have been especially useful. This example application has facilitated research into road accidents and has also served to identify useful features of PFL and appropriate ways in which to use them. These include the following:

1. In contrast to built-in types, *enumerated types* are helpful to clarify PFL codes, and, more important, they serve to enrich the collection of types in a database. This richer type set leads to better use of PFL's strong typing feature. As

a result, more data entry errors and logic errors in programs can be detected by PFL during the compilation phase thus reducing data validation and debugging overheads. Therefore enumerated types should be used preferentially.

2. PFL can model *relations* flexibly. On one hand, composite relations such as n-ary, nested and even recursive ones can be modelled directly by selectors. On the other hand, from primitive relations such as binary ones, composite ones can be derived using rules represented by functions. In general, flat relations with a small number of attributes yield better performance for selector manipulation and are preferable. However, if only a composite view is ever required for a set of data items, it is more efficient to use a single selector to represent directly this composite relation.

3. PFL supports *incremental programming* in that selectors (and other functions) can be conveniently defined or deleted. This encourages the use of temporary selectors to improve efficiency: large temporary data structures can be stored in selectors to reduce page faults, and if searching in a certain data structure is required frequently, it can be represented by a selector in order to take advantage of the built-in pattern matching mechanism of selectors to achieve both conciseness and efficiency.

4. To represent efficiently bulk data which are used temporarily, the following principles should be adopted. If only sequential access is required, it is appropriate to choose the built-in "list" type. Otherwise, a selector may be used, but in that case, frequent deletion and insertion on the same data set should be avoided (this can often be achieved by introducing an extra selector) because it may entail frequent access to secondary storage. If this is not avoidable, other data structures such as trees are preferable.

5. PFL adopts the *lazy evaluation,* so that an expression is only evaluated when its value is required. Expressions can utilize this feature to improve efficiency. For example, the components in a series of logic disjunctions can be ordered in decreasing order of their probability of yielding True.

6. PFL supports *polymorphic* and *higher order functions* which facilitate *abstraction* and *generalisation.* To take advantage of this feature, common operations involved in queries should be identified, abstracted out, and specified as general functions. A general function should be polymorphic if possible so that it can be used more widely. Based on these general functions, we can construct complex queries or different queries of the same category, thus making programs succinct, efficient and well structured.

7. A PFL expression is a tree of nested functions. The only variables are the formal parameters of functions. The communication between functions is through function values and arguments, both of which are subject to type agreement. Under such a formalism, programming is data-driven so that the types (and thus the data structures) of the value and arguments of a function must be specified before the function itself can be, and this is applied to the whole procedure of specifying hierarchically the nested functions. PFL therefore encourages the design of well-structured and efficient programs. Moreover, the absence of intermediate variables from PFL means the absence of the notion of memory address. This leads to succinctness and good structure of programs, and furthermore excludes any coding errors arising from memory addressing which often contribute a large proportion of errors in procedural language programs.

8. Defaults should be introduced where applicable in order to achieve data compaction and fast data entry.

Both PFL itself and the database system for road accident data analysis are the subject of continuing development. Major enhancements are being made to PFL to make it more efficient and versatile, for example, the introduction of *sets* [3]. For the application aspect, work is continuing to incorporate road network data into the database system to provide additional means for data validation and site entity derivation.

6 Acknowledgements

We would like to thank Carol Small, Ben Heydecker and Alexandra Poulovassilis for their useful suggestions and comments on this paper, and to thank Swarup Reddi and Fefie Dotsika for many stimulating conversations on the subject. We would also like to thank some of the above colleagues for their help on the use of PFL, and to thank Hertfordshire County Council for the use of their accident data. This work was funded by the U.K. SERC (grant No. GR/G 19596).

7 References

1. A.Poulovassilis, C.Small: A Functional Programming Approach to Deductive Databases. *Proceedings of the 17th International Conference on Very Large Databases.* Barcelona, 1991, pp. 490-500.
2. C.Small, A.Poulovassilis: An Overview of PFL. *3rd International Workshop on Database Programming Languages.* Nafplion, 1991. pp. 96-110.
3. A.Poulovassilis, C.Small: A Domain-theoretic Approach to Integrating Functional and Logic Database Languages. To appear in *Proceedings of the 19th International Conference on Very Large Databases.* Dublin, 1993.
4. M.P.Atkinson, P.Bureman: Types and Persistence in Database Programming Languages. *ACM computing Surveys.* 19(2), 105-90 (1987).
5. R.Bird, P.Wadler: *An Introduction to Functional Programming.* Prentice Hall (1988).
6. S.Reddi: Integrity Constraint Enforcement in the Functional Database Language PFL. To appear in *Proceedings of 11th British National Conference on Databases.* 1993.
7. Department of Transport of U. K.: *Instructions for the Completion of Road Accident Reports.* 1978.
8. Department of Transport of U. K.: *Transport Statistics Great Britain* (1992).
9. G.Maycock, R.D.Hall: Accidents at Four-arm Roundabouts, *TRRL Laboratory Report 1120.* Crowthorne: Transport and Road Research Laboratory (1984).
10. J.Wu, B.Heydecker: A Knowledge-Based System for Road Accident Remedial Work. To appear in *Computing Systems in Engineering.*
11. C.J.Date: *An Introduction to Database Systems.* Vol I. Addison-Wesley (1986).

DATABASE PERFORMANCE EVALUATION A METHODOLOGICAL APPROACH

N. Revell and M. W. Youssef

SCHOOL OF INFORMATICS
DEPARTMENT OF BUSINESS COMPUTING
THE CITY UNIVERSITY
LONDON

Fax: 071 477 8586
E-mail n.revell@uk.ac.city
E-mail w.youssef@uk.ac.city

Abstract. This paper presents the CITY benchmark. Its design is based on the results of several in-depth studies at several large UK organisations. These studies examined over 4800 applications, and investigated over 40,000,000 transactions accessing around 5000 tables. The work revealed a common access pattern between all the organisations, despite the different nature of these environments. The benchmark shows significant deviation from the established TPC-A script and the TPC-B script when tested in a range of environments, ranging from standalone PC to large mainframe computers and multiprocessors.

1 Introduction

The Debit/Credit (TP/1) [1] and the Transaction Processing Council (TPC) benchmarks [18, 10] have become the database market standard practice. Those benchmarks have a number of practical limitations [13]. Most of those limitations stem from the lack of background study before the benchmark design stage. The main criticism of the TPC benchmarks is that they do not provide a realistic characterisation that can be set as the target for the benchmarking process, and more than this, they do not even provide a model of the ATM systems whose performance they are supposed to simulate [15].

As benchmark results are representative of those types of transactions actually included in the benchmark set. It is impossible to generalise those results to all kinds of systems transactions. Research work has been conducted at City University to identify the main characteristics of on-line databases by examining real database performance factors. Those factors have been discussed by Ferrari [7, 8], Dongara [6], and Hawng [11]. By applying the analysis of those performance factors at several different environments, the data from that analysis can supplement the data from the live environments once the basis of this analysis has been defined to evaluate performance in a transaction processing environment.

This paper presents The CITY benchmark. The benchmark design is based on empirical studies in large database environments. The studies examined over 4800 different applications and investigated over 40,000,000 on-line transactions accessing around 5000 on-line databases. The study discovered a common pattern between the studied systems, despite the difference in activities and nature of the organisations concerned. The CITY benchmark transactions are derived from the findings from those studies.

Section 2 reviews previous benchmarks. Section 3 defines the targeted domain. Section 4 discusses the criteria of organisations selection. The findings are presented in section 5. The CITY benchmark script is presented in section 6. Conclusions are summarised in section 7. Section 8 is the paper summary.

2 Review Of Previous Work

The most frequently quoted measures of database performance in the market place have become the Debit/Credit (TPs/sec) [1] and the Wisconsin benchmark [2, 4, 5]. Eventually, the TP/1 dominated the database market and became the standard benchmark for evaluating database management systems. The benchmark modelled a banking environment and simulates random withdrawals being made against bank accounts at a large bank environment.

The Debit/Credit (TP1) benchmark later known as the TPC-A was constructed to quantify and compare the throughput and price/performance ratio of various transaction processing systems. The TPC-A benchmark measures transactions per second from the time a teller issues a request to the time a customer receives acknowledgement that the transaction has completed. It includes simulating many terminal users, their "think time" and network traffic time.

The TPC-A has become the DBMS market standard practice and almost every DBMS user runs it, in spite of being difficult to implement in its full form and includes aspects like network protocols and think-time that do not specifically relate to DBMS performance. The actual benchmark, though, is not so standard and it is clear that no two versions of TPC-A can be considered equivalent. Each user has chosen to modify parts of the benchmark without regard for the original TPC-A definition. A TPC-A transaction consists of four operations, three update operations and one insert. The benchmark has been severely criticised by several researchers from the database field [3, 12, 16, 17 and 19]. A TPC-B transaction consists of one TPC-A transaction plus one qualified retrieval.

The TPC-A and TPC-B transactions were compared to the results from several empirical studies examining typical on-line transaction behaviour at large database environments [14]. The results obtained disagreed with the TPC benchmarks scripts. It showed that TPC benchmarks scripts could be misleading if used to measure the studied environment performance. Recently, two of the largest Automatic Teller Machines (ATM) systems have been investigated [15] to identify the main characteristics of bank transactions that perform random withdrawals against bank accounts. The findings from that study also disagreed with the TPC-A benchmark script.

3 Specification Of Domain - The OLTP Environment

The domain of the studies was high-volume transaction environments. The importance of high-volume transaction environments is because of its share of the database industry. This environment is dominant in the database market and sets the rules for database standards.

High-volume transaction environments are those environments that support large number of on-line terminals that originate heavy transaction load on the running environments. The number of terminals in those environments is in thousands and the number of transactions is in thousands of transactions per hour. Those environments support large number of tables that are characterised by their large sizes. Examples of such environments include banks, airlines, government organisations, and large business organisations. Organisations that fall into the domain of high-volume transaction environments have to comply with the following criteria:

- have a large number of running applications;
- have a wide variety of those applications;

- have a large database environment;
- have a heavy transactions load;

4 Criteria For Organisation Selection

The studies examined the running systems at three of the largest UK organisations to identify the salient characteristics of actual database applications in high-volume transaction environments and to build a database benchmark that represents those environments. The research selected those organisations because they represented a good examples of high-volume transaction environments. The studied organisations were characterised by the having large number of applications; wide variety of those applications; large database environment; and heavy on-line transaction load.

4.1 The Local Authority Computer Centre

The first study took place at a large local Authority computer centre. That centre offers information technology services and software consultants to four London boroughs. Each of those has its own income sources and spending activities. This organisation was selected because of its large number of running applications, (over 300 running applications), their large database environment that comprises 150 on-line databases occupying 12.5 Gbytes and the large number of on-line terminals, (over 2500 on-line users), connected to the system.

The local authority on-line system users heavily access the systems. The on-line system utilisation could peak to reach 20,000 transactions per hour on a normal working day. On the busiest day of the period, the system load peaked to reach 23,000 transactions per hour. During the period of study, the running systems were under an average load of about 17,000 transactions per hour.

4.2 The Airlines Computer Centre

The second study took place at a large airline computer centre. The centre computing power supplied the running environment by 600 MIPS, where 286 MIPS were dedicated to on-line service. The application databases investigated comprised over 2000 hierarchical and relational databases, occupying 436 Gbytes. The running system terminal population was around 250,000 terminals, out of those, over 27000 concurrently accessed the on-line service.

On-line system load was measured over a period of fifty weeks as the average number of transactions per hour. The average number of transactions issued to the system were measured by snap shots at fifteen minutes' intervals. These snap shots were accumulated to give the average system load per hour. The average of load of the running systems at the airlines' environment was around 70,000 transactions per hour.

4.3 The Bank Computer Centre

The third study took place at a large bank computer centre. The bank computing power was divided between two production centres and a development centre. Each one of those centres produced 500 MIPS. When one of the production centres goes down, the development computer centre works as a back-up for that centre, which allows the bank to maintain 1000 MIPS of computing power to on-line service under different circumstances. The data centres serve more than 3500 branches with a terminal population of about 22,000 that supplies on-line service to over 60,000 users. The number of customers' accounts was around 17M with average accounting entries per day of around 6M accounts whereas on peak days it reaches 20M accounts per day and peak number of transactions per second that reaches 650 transactions. In addition, the system supported more than 3500 ATMs having on-line access to the system. The bank supplied its services not only to UK branches but also to several other branches all over the world, which results in 24-hour access to the computer system.

The bank branches (on-line terminals) load peak to reach 75,000 transactions per hour and the ATM transactions' load reaches a peak of 130,000 transactions per hour. The average day load of the running systems was around 90,000 transactions per hour, that system load qualified the bank environment to be selected for this research.

5 On-Line Transaction Characteristics

This paper presents the salient characteristics of a typical on-line database transaction in a high-volume transaction environment. From the authors point of view these characteristics are essential to construct a benchmark which represents that environment. These characteristics are the following:

- on-line transaction behaviour represented as number of database operations;
- JOIN operation;
- transaction complexity represented as number of nested selects;
- ratios of CPU to I/O utilisation of on-line transactions;
- number of retrieved rows per transaction;
- background workload.

5.1 On-line Transaction Behaviour Represented as Number of Database Operations

A two-way analysis of variance (ANOVA) was used to test the difference among the three organisations' patterns of behaviour. The observed value of F for the between organisations (rows) was 0.003. Clearly this value is highly insignificant indicating virtually no difference among the three organisations, (the local authority, the airlines, and the bank), transaction behaviour. The effect of these results is that overall average over the three organisations is representative for each of the organisations and this is true across the spectrum of the database operations. However, the analysis did reveal highly significant difference between the various database operations; qualified retrieval, insert, update delete, and sequential retrieval. Table 1 summarises transactions' patterns at the three organisations and Fig. 1 illustrates the calculated mean among the three organisations. A typical on-line database transaction operations tends to perform sequential retrieval and qualified retrieval more than update operations (Insert, Update and Delete).

Operation Name	Qualified Retrieval	Insert a Record	Update a Record	Delete a Record	Sequential Retrieval
The Local Authority	35%	4%	4%	1%	56%
The Airlines	39%	5%	4%	1%	51%
The Bank	50%	5%	12%	0%	33%
Average	41%	5%	7%	0%	47%

Table 1

5.2 JOIN Operation

JOIN operation was investigated by studying the number of tables accessed per on-line transaction. At both the airlines' environment and the bank environments the JOIN operation was avoided whenever possible. That was due to the negative effect of that operation on database performance. The findings from the two organisations were close enough to ignore statistical tests to check that difference. The 94% of on-line transactions accessed one database, a small percentage, 3%, accessed two databases and similar percentage accessed three databases. Table 2 and Fig. 2 present the average number of databases accessed by one transaction at the airlines and bank environments.

Number of Databases	One Database	Two Databases	Three Databases	Four Databases	Five Databases
The Airlines	93%	1%	5%	0.5%	0.5%
The Bank	94%	4%	1%	1%	0%
Average	94%	3%	3%	1%	0%

Table 2

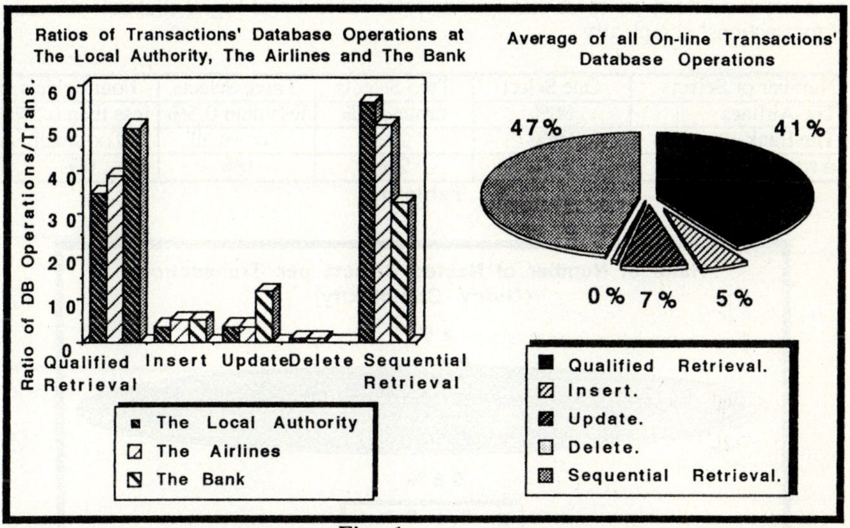

Fig. 1

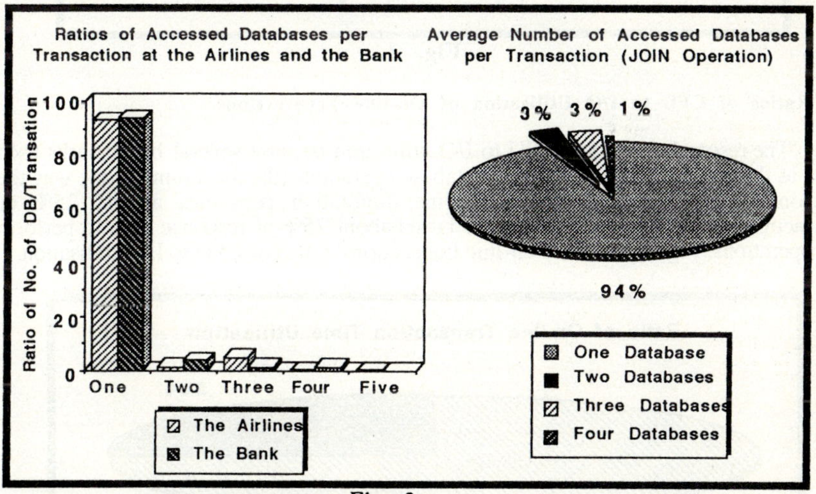

Fig. 2

5.3 Transaction Complexity Represented as Number of Nested Selects

Transaction complexity in this context is defined as the number of nested Selects in one enquiry transaction. JOIN operations might consist of one select or more than one select. The great majority of on-line transactions, around 98%, consisted of one Select and around 2% of on-line transactions consisted of two selects. Transactions that consisted of three and four selects represented a very small ratio that can be discarded. Transactions did not use more than four selects. Table 3 and Fig. 3 illustrate the ratios of transactions' complexity.

Number of Selects	One Select	Two Selects	Three Selects	Four Selects
The Airlines	98%	around 2%	less than 0.5%	less than 0.5%
The Bank	98%	2%	Too small	Too small
Average	98%	2%	0%	0%

Table 3

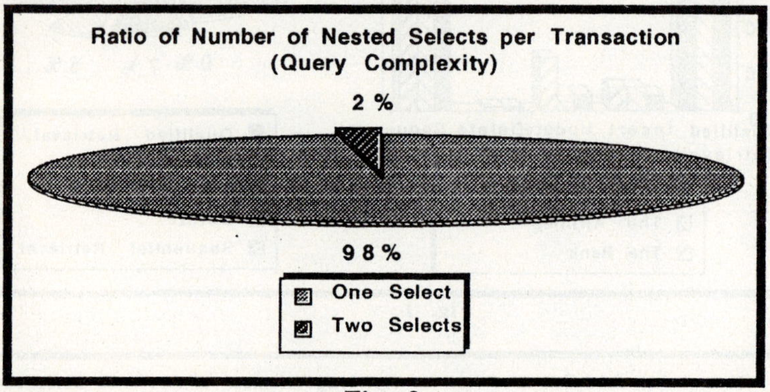

Fig. 3

5.4 Ratios of CPU to I/O Utilisation of On-line Transactions

The research examined CPU to I/O utilisation because several benchmarks used them as the main hypothesis for their database operations (the most famous one was the Wisconsin Benchmark). A typical on-line transaction consumes around 25% of transaction response time using CPU and used about 75% of response time to perform I/O operations. Fig. 4 illustrates on-line transactions' ratios of CPU to I/O utilisation.

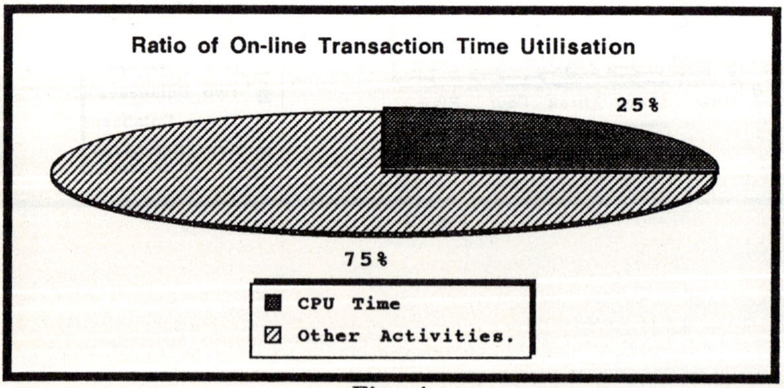

Fig. 4

5.5 Number of Retrieved Records per Transaction

An average number of retrieved rows by on-line transaction was around seven rows. The Local Authority on-line system transaction returns on average seven segments. The Airlines on-line system transaction returns on average 6.6 rows per transaction. For the Bank on-line system transaction returns on average four rows per transaction.

5.6 Background Workload

The three organisations maintained a very small background workload that is either zero or very close to zero. The local authority computer centre either separated all the off-line activities on the micro system or performed off-line jobs during night shifts when on-line service was not active. The airlines' computer centre had a processor to perform most of the off-line workload; in some rare cases the on-line processors performed part of that off-line load. The bank computer centre dedicated some processors to on-line service and dedicated some other to off-line jobs and did not perform and off-line jobs on on-line processors. As we see, the three organisations' policies were to run on-line service without background workload to enhance on-line service performance.

6 The CITY Benchmark

This section presents a summary of the CITY benchmark. The CITY benchmark is a comprehensive methodology for evaluating database management systems' performance. The CITY benchmark is a rigorous method that can test DBMS under realistic work load. The benchmark is designed to simulate on-line transactions' operations at large database environments. The benchmark design is based on the most common findings from the three studies. The benchmark design took into consideration the critiques directed towards the TPC benchmarks. Researchers such as Gray [10], and Ferrari [7], established some guidelines for evaluating systems performance, the most important one, the benchmark should be independent of the application or the architecture involved. Gray [10], recommends that a benchmark should be characterised by the following.

1. Relevant, represents the tested domain.
2. Portable, the benchmark will be easy to implement on many different systems and architectures.
3. Scalable, the benchmark should apply to small and large computer systems.
4. Simple, the benchmark should be understandable and well documented. This will allow the exact replication of the original benchmark.

Since performance implies two aspects, quantitative and qualitative. Quantitative aspects are such as speed, productivity, and capacity. Qualitative aspects are things like ease of use and the scope of functionality. The CITY benchmark measures quantitative aspects.

The City benchmark is characterised by being: representative; reproducible; system independent; simple to construct; and low in usage cost. Hence representative is defined as the accuracy of the benchmark to reflect the characteristics of real transactions at real environments, the main advantage of the CITY benchmark is being representative to high-volume transaction domain. The CITY benchmark script is a direct mapping from the on-line transaction operations as found at the discussed organisations and models a typical workload at high-volume transaction environments. The CITY benchmark is applicable to a wide range of database management systems and architecture. The benchmark results are representative of a wide variety of database management systems and database applications, and valid across different database management systems and different hardware architectures. The CITY benchmark is machine independent, database management system independent, application independent and representative to the domain of high-volume transaction environments.

6.1 The CITY Benchmark Objectives

The CITY benchmark is the first benchmark designed as a result of studying several large database systems at large database environments, regardless of the organisations nature and activities. The CITY benchmark is designed mainly for testing and comparing database systems performance in high-volume transaction environments. The CITY benchmark can serve more than one purpose and can be used to achieve several objectives, these objectives are the following.

1. To evaluate the performance of a database management system.
2. To compare different database management systems.
3. To evaluate the impact of system modifications.
4. To evaluate the effect of system parameters.

6.2 The CITY Benchmark Metrics

Generally, in benchmarks, transaction response time and transaction throughput are the most frequently used performance metrics for database systems. Transaction response time is the time elapsed between submission of a transaction to DBMS and receiving the result. Transaction throughput is the average number of transactions completed per unit of time.

The CITY benchmark metric is the system throughput. The throughput will be measured as the number of transactions performed per second under specified load. Response time, which is the reciprocal of system throughput, is used as a secondary metric. The CITY benchmark uses response time because most users are mainly interested in response time and neglecting it is neglecting important user requirement.

6.3 The CITY Benchmark Tables

The CITY benchmark database consists of five tables. The five tables divided to three enquiries tables; one table updates table and a fifth table used for record insertions. Update operations were isolated on separate table to protect enquiries tables from the effect of attributes change. The insertions table initial size is zero records when the benchmark starts. For each benchmark loop a record is inserted into the insertions table. This table should be large enough to handle all the records inserted during a complete benchmark run.

6.4 The CITY Benchmark Transaction Script

The CITY benchmark took into consideration the transaction behaviour covered by the empirical studies. The benchmark transaction script can be directly mapped to the studied systems. The CITY benchmark consist of 20 database operations distributed as follows:

- eight sequential retrievals (around 40%);
- nine qualified retrievals (around 45%);
- one insert operation (5%);
- two update operation (10%).

This previous script is fairly close to the pattern of transaction operations of the presented systems and could easily correspond with the studied system transaction behaviour.

7 Conclusion

In this paper the main characteristics of high-volume transactions at large database environments have been presented. This paper also briefly presents the CITY benchmark. The benchmark design is based on the findings from in depth studies at large database environments. The results of this work are based on a comprehensive analysis of over 4800 applications and 40,000,000 transactions. These characteristics can be summarised in the following:

1. A typical on-line transaction operations consists of 41% Qualified retrieval, Insert operation represent 5%, Update operation represents 7%, Delete operation is small enough to be zero, and Sequential search is 47%.

2. On-line transactions access at most five databases where the majority of transactions (93%) access one database, 1% of on-line transactions access two databases, 5% of on-line transactions access three databases, four databases and five databases are accessed by a very small percentage of transactions (0.5%).

3. The great majority of on-line transactions (almost 98%) consists of one Select, around 2% consists of two Selects, transactions that consists of three and four Selects represent very small ratio that can be discarded. Non of the transactions consists of more than four Selects.
4. An average number of retrieved rows by an on-line transaction is around seven rows and a typical row length is around 200 bytes.

5. All on-line systems databases are indexed.

The following sections present a comparison between a typical on-line transaction database operation as found from the studies and the benchmark scripts of the TPC-A benchmark and the TPC-B benchmarks. The comparison shows that the TPC benchmarks are biased towards some specific database operations and could be misleading when used to compare database management systems. Additionally a comparison between the CITY benchmark transaction response time and the TPC-A and the TPC-B transactions' response times are presented. The comparison demonstrated that some database management systems are significantly insensitive to the TPC benchmarks scripts even at large database sizes.

7.1 Comparison Between On-line Transactions and the TPC Scripts

The TPC-A relies on three update operations and one insert. The TPC-B benchmark is the batch transaction of the TPC-A and it has one qualified select more than the TPC-A. Table 4 presents a comparison between a typical on-line database transaction operations and transaction operations proposed by both TPC-A benchmark and the TPC-B benchmark. Both the TPC-A and the TPC-B transaction operations differ widely from the studied systems transactions which makes them not representative as a realistic performance metric for those systems.

Operation Name	Qualified Retrieval	Insert a Record	Update a Record	Delete a Record	Sequential Retrieval
The TPC-A Transaction	0%	25%	75%	0%	0%
The TPC-B Transaction	20%	20%	60%	0%	0%
On-line Transaction	41%	5%	7%	0%	47%

Table 4

The comparison shows that the TPC-A benchmark database operations are completely different from typical on-line transaction database operations. While sequential retrievals represent 88% of on-line transactions' operations at the studied environments, the TPC-A does not include records retrievals. The difference between the TPC-A database operations and typical on-line transaction database operations are large enough to ignore applying any statistical comparison between the two.

The TPC-B transaction database operations are not much different from the TPC-A transaction operations. The TPC-B transaction is a TPC-A transaction plus one qualified retrieval. A comparison between the TPC-B benchmark transaction database operations and typical on-line transaction database operations shows that the TPC-B transaction operations are still widely different from a typical on-line transaction operation. During an empirical study at the CITY university to examine the effect of different database operations one of the findings showed that qualified retrievals did not apply any realistic load on the tested system. Which makes the TPC-B transaction still too simple to test any real life environments.

To show how this might work out in practice, if there are two DBMS of which the first manages to be fast in update operations but suffer from optimisation problems when performing any other operation, and the second is equally balanced when performing all operations, TPC-A will be biased to the first one in spite of the better overall system performance of the second one. An example was given by Fox [9], DEC published Debit/Credit figures for both its own mid-range VAXs and two of IBMs competing machines, the 9377-90 and 4381-22. These figures showed that the DEC machines had three times better price/performance than the IBM systems. Accordingly, IBM countered by running its own version of TPC-A, the results they got were very different: the IBM machines processed over three times as many transactions in IBM own research centre.

7.2 Comparison Between The CITY Transaction and The TPC Scripts

The present authors conducted empirical studies to compare the behaviour of the CITY transaction script against the TPC-A and the TPC-B transactions scripts. The basic database operations of the TPC-A and the TPC-B were isolated and tested against increasing database size. The empirical studies were conducted at all levels of computer architectures from standalone PC to mainframe environments. In this paper the results from two environments are presented, the first is an IBM PC running commercial relational DBMS, and the second is a SUN SPARC Micro System running commercial relational DBMS. The tables sizes were scaled up gradually by 5000 records in the PC environment and by 10,000 records in the SUN SPARC environments. The final tables' sizes at the PC environment was smaller than that of the SUN SPARC because of disk space constraint. Record size in both environments was 200 bytes. Part of the findings are presented in Fig. 5 can be summarised in the following:

1. Despite the difference in computer architectures and test environments, the transactions took similar pattern at all environments.
2. Both the TPC-A and the TPC-B transactions transaction did not apply enough load on the tested systems even at 100,000 rows and the TPC benchmarks response time at 5000 rows is not much different than their response time at 100,000 rows.
3. There was a significant deviation between the CITY transaction response time and the TPC transactions response time specially at larger databases' sizes.

The same patterns of the CITY and TPC benchmarks behaviour were found when the test was repeated in a range of computer environments, those environments are listed below.

- Standalone PC based on 386 Intel processor running under MS/DOS operating systems and using commercial RDBMS.
- Standalone PC based on 486 processor running under MS/DOS operating systems and using commercial RDBMS.
- SUN SPARC running under UNIX operating systems and using commercial RDBMS in single user mode.
- SUN SPARC running under UNIX operating systems and using commercial RDBMS in single user mode with network connection (database management system run on a different computer to the tables).
- VAX 4000 running under VMS operating systems and using commercial RDBMS in single user mode.
- Teradata systems 3 and 4 multiprocessing computers.
- NCR 3600 (The New Teradata) multiprocessing computer running under UNIX operating systems and using commercial RDBMS in single user mode.
- IBM 3090 mainframe computer running under MVS/XA operating systems and using commercial RDBMS.

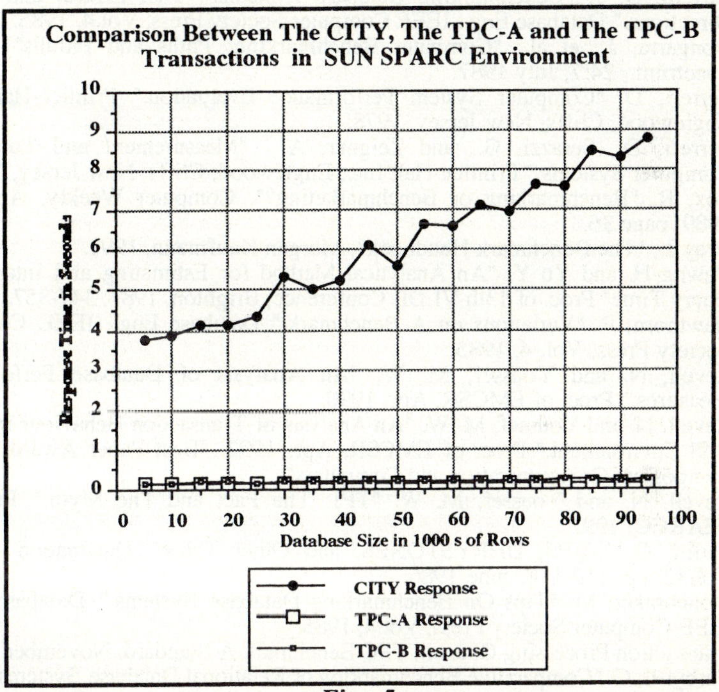

Fig. 5

8 Summary

The CITY benchmark shows significant deviation from the TPC benchmarks' scripts. The same deviation existed when the test was repeated in a range of environments from standalone PC to large mainframe computers and multiprocessors. The CITY benchmark is constructed to overcome the TPC benchmarks limitations. The benchmark is based on real on-line database transaction operations and takes into consideration all the critiques directed towards the TPC benchmarks. The benchmark design is based on in-depth studies at large database environments and simulates a typical on-line transaction operation at high-volume transactions environments (OLTP). The CITY benchmark is characterised by being relevant, portable, scalable and simple.

The CITY benchmark specification, verification process and results in comparison to other benchmarks results will be presented in future work.

9 References

1. Anon et al. "A Measure of Transaction Power." Datamation, April 1, 1985.
2. Bitton, D., DeWitt D., and Turbyfill, C., "Benchmarking Database Systems: A Systematic Approach." Proc. VLDB Conf., IEEE Press, 1983.
3. Bitton D., Hanrahan M.and Turbyfill, C., "Performance of Complex Transactions in Main Memory Database Systems" Proc. International Conf. on Third Data Engineering, Feb. 1987.
4. Haran Boral, and David J. DeWitt. "A Methodology for Database System Performance Evaluation." Proc. SIGMOD Conf., Boston, June 1984.
5. DeWitt, D. J. "Benchmarking Database Systems : Past Efforts and Future Directions." Database Eng., IEEE Computer Society Press, Vol.4, 1985.
6. Dongarra, J., et al., "Computer Benchmarking: Paths and Pitfalls" IEEE Spectrum., 24:7, July 1987.
7. Ferreri, D. "Computer System Performance Evaluation." Printice-Hall Inc., Englewood, Cliffs, New Jersey, 1978.
8. Ferreri, D., Serazzi, G., and Zeigner, A. "Measurement and Tuning of Computer Systems." Printice-Hall Inc., Englewood, Cliffs, New Jersey, 1983.
9. Fox, R. "Benchmarking or Benchmarketing?". Computer Weekly, April 20, 1989, page 36.
10. Gray J., "The Benchmark Handbook", Morgan Kaufmann, 1991.
11. Hawng H. and Yu Y. "An Analytical Method for Estimating and Interpreting Query Time" Proc. of 13th VLDB Conference, Brighton, 1987, 347-357.
12. Hawthorn, P. "Variations on A Benchmark." Database Eng., IEEE Computer Society Press, Vol. 4, 1985.
13. Revell, N. and Youssef, M. W. "An Analysis of Database Performance Measures." Proc. of EMCSR, Apr. 1990.
14. Revell, N. and Youssef, M. W. "An Analysis of Transaction Behaviour in Large IMS Environment." Proc. of EMCSR, Apr. 1992. "Best Paper Award for the Symposium Communication and Computers".
15. Revell, N. and Youssef, M. W. "TP1: The Fact and The Myth." Proc. of SEARCC, 1992.
16. Serlin, O. "MIPS, DHRYSTONES, and Other Tales." Datamation (USA), Vol.32, pp. 112-118, June 1986.
17. Stonebraker, M. "Tips On Benchmarking Database Systems." Database Eng., IEEE Computer Society Press, Vol.4, 1985.
18. Transaction Processing Council. TPC Benchmark A Standard. November 1989.
19. Turbyfill, C. "Comparative Benchmarking of Relational Database Systems" Ph.D Dissertation. Cornell University, Jan. 1988.

Design and Implementation of a DBMS Performance Assessment Tool

M.L. Kersten and F. Kwakkel
CWI, P.O. Box 4079, 1009 AB Amsterdam, The Netherlands
{mk,kwakkel}@cwi.nl

Abstract. The increasing number of advanced database management systems offered on the market requires tools to quickly assess their performance and to assure their quality. Performance measurement involves running a set of representative workloads, such as benchmarks, and quality assurance, which involves extensive testing. The SOFTWARE TESTPILOT [1] described in this paper greatly simplifies both jobs by enabling a compact specification of the workload search space, a flexible mechanism to interact with a system under study, and a fast algorithm to expose the performance bottlenecks or software instabilities.

1 Introduction

Database technology for single processor architectures has matured from file processing by a large number of individual programs to sound data models and data manipulation schemes applicable in many environments. The DBMSs are delivered as portable, single processor implementations with many techniques to obtain good performance. However, new (prototype) systems often exhibit low quality and low performance due to lack of extensive field tests in the application areas they intend to support. Inclusion of new techniques into existing architectures also hamper from unpredictable side-effects on system performance and stability. Yet, from an economic point of view it is mandatory to predict their performance and stability long before the hardware and software are installed.

The common approach to obtain performance characteristics of a DBMS is by offering it a set of carefully chosen queries and to observe its behavior. Database benchmarks such as Wisconsin[3, 2, 5] and AS3AP[8] primarily highlight the internal strengths and weakness of a system implementation. The TPC-A and TPC-B benchmarks[9] have the advantage of being based on a real application (a bank teller network), but have become divorced from the real applications requirements. They can only be used to provide a simple comparative measure of a small part of the system being tested. Current TPC work is directed towards providing benchmarks for more complex traditional application domains (e.g. Order-Entry, Decision Support) with an emphasis towards conventional systems.

The role of benchmarking to assess performance and as a means to improve software quality is limited. The known benchmarks do not directly aid users to determine the DBMS effectiveness for a particular domain. Domain-specific benchmarks are a response to this diversity of computer system use. They specify a synthetic workload

[1] The work reported here is funded by ESPRIT-III Pythagoras project (P7091)

characterizing a typical application problem domain. The OO1 [1] benchmark is a step in this direction, which addresses the perceived performance critical aspects of a Computer-Aided Design (CAD) application.

The benchmarks are complemented by test suites geared at exposure of weaknesses in the system implementation. Together they provide the basis for technical quality assessment. Extension with software quality assessment techniques, such as ISO9000, further improve the organization of software production. Finally, the alpha- and beta- test sites form the final barrier for systems to reach the market.

A major drawback of the benchmarks and test-suites, addressed in this paper, is that they represent only a few points in the workload search space. Therefore, a DBMS engineer or user with a workload characteristic slightly off those measured may face a badly performing system. Moreover, system implementors may be inclined to provide good performance on the published benchmarks. In particular, attaining good performance on the notorious complex operations may ignore the workload characteristics of the application domain. Likewise, test-suites may be biased by isolated implementation challenges, such as novel data structures or query optimization techniques, and neglect possible side-effects.

The SOFTWARE TESTPILOT described in this paper is a tool to aid the DBMS engineer and user to explore a large workload search space to find the slope, top, and knees of performance figures quickly. The approach taken is based on specifying the abstract workload search space, a small interface library with the target system, and a description of the expected behavior. Thereafter, it is up to the SOFTWARE TESTPILOT to select the actual workload parameter values and to execute the corresponding DBMS transactions, such that the performance characteristics and quality weaknesses are determined with minimal cost (=time).

The novelty of our SOFTWARE TESTPILOT is its use of a behavioral model of the target system to drive this process. The system uses the performance hypothesis and performance data gathered to identify candidate workspace parameters with high probability to (dis-) proof the hypothesis. Among the candidates it selects one of high value and low cost to reach. Moreover, the SOFTWARE TESTPILOT adjusts the behavioral model when measurements disprove the models' assumptions. Thus, the outcome of a session is both improved statistical knowledge on the performance characteristics and a (possibly) modified behavioral model of the target system.

Although testing and benchmarking [7] have received considerable attention over the last decade we are not aware of similar attempts to automate performance quality assessment at this level.

Test environments mostly focus on test-data generation, path coverage testing, or they explore the programming language properties to proof (type) assertions. The predominant pragmatic approach is to use shell scripts to capture the repetitive nature of the test runs or to rely on a small test space. The major drawback is that it often results in a brute force approach, running the script over night to obtain a few points of the performance function without adjustment or error recovery.

Performance monitors, built into the DBMS or operating system environment, are passive. They merely provide measurement data, statistical analysis, and visualization tools. Instead, the SOFTWARE TESTPILOT provides a mechanism to partially automate the interpretation of the results to prepare for and to perform the next test run.

A recent paper on I/O benchmark performance analysis [6] has some aspects in common with our approach. Like the SOFTWARE TESTPILOT , they attempt to identify the knee of a performance function as quickly as possible. However, their approach is focussed on a particular problem area. It has not been generalized into a general technique to support a larger application domain or to exploit the knowledge gained from a hypothesis.

The remainder of this paper is organized as follows. Section 2 introduces the scope of the problem, the approach taken by the SOFTWARE TESTPILOT , and the textual Test-suite Specification Language. Section 3 introduces the architecture of the SOFTWARE TESTPILOT and its core algorithms. We conclude with an outlook on future research issues.

2 A Test-suite Specification Language

In this Section we introduce the Test-suite Specification Language (TSL) for the SOFTWARE TESTPILOT . A TSL program, an object-based extension of the underlying implementation language Prolog, consists of object descriptions and their refinements. Each object type has a small number of attributes with system defined defaults.

2.1 The performance assessment problem

To obtain a better appreciation of the role of a SOFTWARE TESTPILOT in performance assessment, we use the Wisconsin Benchmark for relational DBMSs [5] as our running example. This benchmark has been designed in the early eighties to assess the performance of relational systems. It has been gradually extended to become a standard benchmark for assessing new implementation techniques [3] for relational systems.

The Wisconsin benchmark has a fixed set of 32 queries focused on single user query processing performance. One aspect being measured is the response time to access part of a table. After running many cases, two representatives were chosen. Namely, retrieval of 1% and 10% of a table with 10K tuples. Since, these numbers have become less relevant for new DBMS implementations. First, the table size has been increased to better reflect current database sizes and the hardware platform [4]. Second, selection of 1% out of a 1.000.000 tuples is probably too optimistic and the fraction may have to be scaled down as well.

This performance assessment problem can be summarized as the task to identify the shape of the performance function $Q : table\_size \times selection\_size \rightarrow response\_time$. The table size and selection size are the input variables or experimental **factors**. The selection time is the output or **response** variable. This performance function is obtained by careful selection of input parameters, setting up the environment for the experiment, and to run the experiment until a statistical stable response value has been obtained.

The SOFTWARE TESTPILOT is designed to automate a major portion of this manual task as follows. The user reformulates the task as a performance test program in terms of factor and response parameters and actions on the target system.

The action list includes descriptions to initialize the DBMS and to change its state incrementally. Given a test program, the task of the SOFTWARE TESTPILOT is then to select and execute a sequence of actions, such that the performance relationship(s) between the factors and their responses are determined with minimal cost.

The novelty of the SOFTWARE TESTPILOT is its use of an anticipated behavioral model to drive this process. That is, the user provides a **hypothesis**, i.e. a continuous function, that describes the expected performance relationship as accurately as possible. It is used by the SOFTWARE TESTPILOT to locate a point in the test space that is likely to disqualify the hypothesis given.

In general, multiple runs are required to obtain a reliable response function. If a large deviation is observed then the hypothesis is discarded by the system. Thereafter, a new hypothesis is derived from the points already measured. For example, failure to observe linear behavior may cause the SOFTWARE TESTPILOT to attempt a logarithmic distribution instead. Furthermore, a session is automatically terminated when a sufficient approximation of the hypothesis, in terms of cost and deviation, has been established.

For example, assume that the SOFTWARE TESTPILOT has already obtained responses for Q as shown in Figure 1. The straight line denotes the hypothesis for Q given by the user. To verify this hypothesis, a new point must be chosen with maximal probability to dis-qualify the claim made. A strategy is to take a point with the maximum distance from any two adjacent points already measured. In this case, the next point to be tested would be a table size of 80K (= (100+60)/2). Before this can be done 20K tuples must be inserted. Thus, the test suite program should

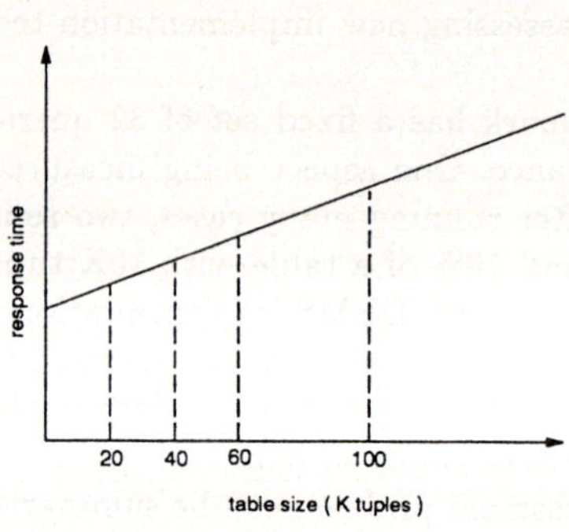

Fig. 1. Performance hypothesis and points measured

include actions to change the state of the database, i.e. to support insertion and deletion of dummy tuples. These actions are used by the SOFTWARE TESTPILOT to move the DBMS into the required state. Once the state is reached, the query can be executed to (dis) proof the hypothesis.

2.2 Factor and response definition

The basic building blocks of a test suite specification are the **factor** and **response** variables. They require a symbolic name for reference within the TSL program and a type name from the collection *(integer, symbolic, time, float, string, char, boolean)*. The type can be further constraint by specifying a sorted list of value ranges (e.g. [0..10,990..1000]) or an enumeration of categories and symbolic constants (e.g. [max,min,sum]).

The type values can also be described by a generator, i.e. a unary Prolog predicate activated upon system restart to produce a finite term list. For example, a generator can be used to produce terms for the distinct n-way joins over a relational schema.

Object refinement can be used to simplify a large test space description. A refinement is indicated by the attribute **like** bound to another variable. The attributes of the dependent variable are taken as default until they are explicitly redefined.

The mechanism to select the next value for a factor is controlled with the attribute **apply**, which is an element from the collection {**cyclic**, **random**, **optimize**}. These items can be overruled with a Prolog clause in cases where more precise control is needed on the exploration of the test space.

The partial specification shown in Figure 2 illustrates some definitions for the Wisconsin benchmark.

```
factor => [      name:           table_size,
                 type:           integer,
                 apply:          optimize,
                 range:          [ 0 .. 1000k ] ].
factor => [      name:           selection_size,
                 type:           integer,
                 range:          [ 0 .. 1000k ] ].
response => [    name:           selection_time,
                 type:           time ].
focus => [       name:           dbfocus,
                 factors:        [table_size, selection_size],
                 responses:      [selection_time:T],
                 pattern:        [table_size, selection_size, selection_time],
                 check:          (T < 1000) ].
hypothesis => [ factors:         [table_size:X, selection_size:Y],
                 responses:      [selection_time:Z],
                 guess:          Z = linear(X,Y,1)].
```

Fig. 2. Sample TSL specification

2.3 Focus definition

The test space spanned by the variables is often too large to be investigated with a single run. Therefore, the user can identify a subset as the prime **focus** of attention.

Each focus bears a name for reference within the TSL programming environment and a listing of the factor and response variables.

The variables outside the focus remain fixed at their initial value and performance relationships outside the current focus are only inspected if they involve no additional cost. The relative importance of different foci is administered by a **weight** attribute (>0), which causes the SOFTWARE TESTPILOT to balance the effort investigating the foci.

The optional attribute **check** takes a predicate to limit the space considered for experimentation. Each experiment leads to a measurement vector that can be sent to a post-processing system for further analysis. The content of the vector is described by the attribute **pattern**.

Figure 2 contains a single focus identifying interest in the (partial) performance functions over the space `table_size`× `selection_size` → `selection_time`. The constraint T<1000 indicates that the SOFTWARE TESTPILOT must avoid actions that exceed 1000 time units.[2]

2.4 Hypothesis definition

The dependency of a response variable on its factors is described with a **hypothesis** introduced by the user or deduced by the SOFTWARE TESTPILOT from earlier experiments. The current implementation only supports the former, because induction of a hypothesis from data gathered is a statistical problem initially best addressed using a (separate) statistical package.

The envisioned performance function is described by the attribute **guess**, which contains a linear, logarithmic, or exponential equation. The applicable sub-domain is described with a condition in attribute **check**. How the hypothesis can be used to select points for exploration is described in Chapter 3.2. In Figure 2 we expect `dbselect` to be linear dependent on `table_size` and `selection_size`.

2.5 Action definition

An **action** describes an experiment on the target system or a way to change the state of the target system to prepare for the next experiment. An action is characterized by its name, factor and response variable(s). Although all factors in the TSL program determine the response value, only those used as action parameters or those changed as a side-effect in an action should be explicitly mentioned.

For example, consider the action `dbselect` in Figure 3. Its body contains a call to a parameterized SQL query. This SQL command does not critically depend on the `table_size`, which is considered a constant factor taken from the focus setting.

A possible side-effect of an action is a modification of the factors to reflect the new state of the target system. These side-effects are described with the attribute `step`, which contains factors tagged with an arithmetic expression to derive the destination point in the test space. They are crucial for the SOFTWARE TESTPILOT to infer the state of the target system and, thereby, to determine the course of actions taken.

[2] An attribute can be tagged with a variable name, i.e. an identifier starting with an uppercase, to denote its value in other expressions within the same object.

The variable and focus constraints can be refined with the attribute **check** to allow for actions covering different cases. For example, the TSL program may contain two actions to insert tuples in the relation. One could generate a single tuple and another generates a batch of 100 tuples.

The **body** describes the interaction details with the target system. To support a wide range of target systems and experimentation techniques its value is a Prolog term. Interfacing the target system then depends on the foreign language facilities of the underlying Prolog implementation of the SOFTWARE TESTPILOT . A small library can be used to capture the interface requirements for a class of target systems, such as the SQL-server library currently in use.

In some cases, such as during system restart and error recovery, the SOFTWARE TESTPILOT should enquire the target system on its status. Enquiry actions are recognized by omission of **step** and **response** properties. They can be applied unconditionally at any position in the test space.

Actions come with an estimated **cost** defined by the user or inferred by the system from previous experiments. They are used to plan the course of actions.

Figure 3 illustrates the framework of several actions. The action `dbselect` represent our prime performance interest; the others are used by the SOFTWARE TESTPILOT to change the state of the DBMS. The details on how the actions interact with the SQL server are not shown.

```
action => [    name:          dbselect,
               factors:       [selection_size:S],
               responses:     [selection_time:T],
               body:          sql_select(S,T) ].
action => [    name:          dbinsert,
               factors:       [table_size:X],
               step:          [table_size:1],
               body:          sql_insert(X) ].
action => [    name:          dbdelete,
               factors:       [table_size:X],
               step:          [table_size:N],
               cost:          (N),
               body:          sql_delete( X, N )].
```

Fig. 3. Action objects

3 Design of the Software Testpilot

The SOFTWARE TESTPILOT is designed around four processes that communicate through data pools. A system overview and design rationale is given in Section 3.1. Then, the algorithm to select candidate points from the test space (Section 3.2) and the algorithm to construct a flight plan (Section 3.3) are described in greater detail. The Chapter concludes with the selection and execution of the best plan.

3.1 The Software Testpilot's Processing Cycle

The processing cycle for the SOFTWARE TESTPILOT is a repetition of flight plans during which information on the performance relationship(s) is gathered. This process stops when all interesting points have been inspected, when a fatal-error occurs, or when the user terminates further exploration of the test space.

A flight starts with selection of a target point in the test space where measurements should be taken. From the large collection of possible points the SOFTWARE TESTPILOT identifies a few candidate that provides the best information to (dis-) qualify the hypotheses applicable within the focus of interest.

Before the measurements can be taken, the SOFTWARE TESTPILOT should move the DBMS into the required state, that is, tuples must be inserted/deleted. The action(s) to reach this state is (are) inferred from the **factor** and **step** attributes of action descriptions. Often, several feasible plans exist and a choice should be made to avoid time consuming plans.

For instance, consider a TSL program to investigate tuple selection from table sizes between 0 and 100 tuples. To (dis-) qualify a linear hypothesis quickly it could investigate table sizes in the order: 0, 100, 50, 25, 75, 13, 38 etc. That is, table sizes lie far away from those already inspected. However, the corresponding flight plans are also expensive. For, after the first tuple selection 100 tuples are inserted. Then again one tuple is selected and 50 tuples are deleted to bring the database to a state of 50 tuples, etc..

A way out of this dilemma is to consider several candidate points and to apply the cheapest flight plan. For instance, if three candidate points are handled together then the execution order becomes: 0, 50, 100 .. 75, 25, 13, etc. The first batch (0,100,50) is sorted on the cost (=unit steps) to reach the point. Then the next three points are generated (25,75,13) and sorted. Now 75 is the 'cheapest' point because its distance to 100 is the minimum of the three points. The execution order becomes: 75,25,13 etc.

If we carry this idea further and allow the SOFTWARE TESTPILOT to generate all candidate points at startup then the sequence becomes: 0, 1, 2, 3 etc.. This is something we do not want either, because it provides only slow insight into the shape and validity of the performance functions. Therefore, we use a buffer of candidates and give the user a choice between an emphasis on the execution time, the 'cost' of the flight plan to reach that point, and emphasis on selecting interesting points, i.e. the 'weight' of a point (See Section 3.4).

The internal architecture of the SOFTWARE TESTPILOT uses four data pools for interprocess communication. Their roles is as follows:

- *position*, which describes the current position of the SOFTWARE TESTPILOT in the test space.
- *pointDone*, which contains the response values obtained and the setting of all TSL input variables.
- *candidate*, which contains the buffered candidate points. Each point consists of the focus input values and a **weight** of interest for this point.
- *flightPlan*, which contains a flight plan for each candidate point. A flight plan consists of the target point, a sequence of actions, and the estimated cost.

The four processes involve selection of candidate points, generation of flight plans, selection of a single flight plan, and its execution. They are described in more detail in subsequent sections.

3.2 Selection of candidate points

The first process deals with the selection of a reasonable number of candidates for inspection. Considering too many candidate makes subsequent selection of the target point expensive. Conversely, considering only a few candidates may lead to time consuming experiments, because it becomes less likely to inspect the more interesting point, as indicated in the previous section.

To solve this resource management problem, we limit the candidate pool to those with a (normalized) weight exceeding a system defined threshold. This threshold is lowered when the system runs out of good candidates. The result is a system behavior that gradually explores less-and-less interesting points up to a user interrupt or reaching a predefined termination condition. The mechanism to determine the weight is introduced by an example.

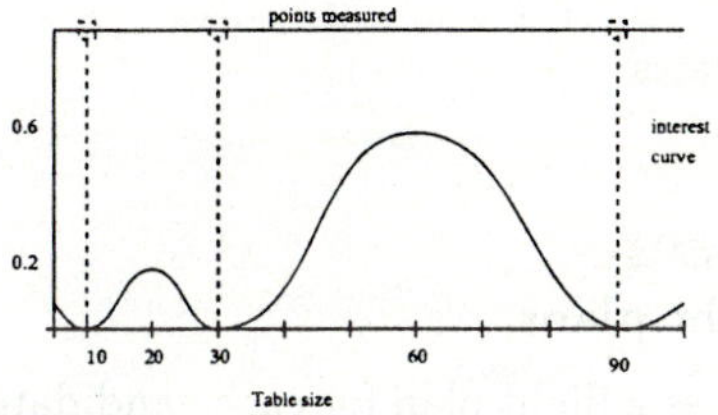

Fig. 4. The interest curve for candidate points

Assume that class *pointDone* contains the points depicted in Figure 4 on the first line. The challenge is to find a metric that identifies the interesting points. This depend on how we intend to use the SOFTWARE TESTPILOT . If we aim for identifying the shape of a performance function then the candidates close to an already measured point are of less interest, due to expected measurement errors. Conversely, if we are interested in robustness of the target system points then near the minimum and maximum of the domain are of high interest. To support a wide range of application domains, the user can specify their interest function.

In our example, we focus on identifying the shape of the continuous performance function. The interest curve for the linear hypothesis is shown in Figure 4, which favors a candidate X_i exactly in between two points X_{i-1} and X_{i+1} identified before. It is a weight proportional to the distance of its neighbors, i.e. $weight(X_i) = D * sin((X_i - X_{i-1})\pi/2D)$ with $D = X_{i+1} - X_{i-1}$. This leads to considering 20 and 60 tuples as candidates for inspection.

This idea has been generalized to deal with several hypotheses as follows. Let C denote the set of old candidates and points investigated, let H denote the set of hypothesis defined, and F the focus. Then, the algorithm in Figure 5 generates for each factor A_i in a hypothesis a candidate point between any two known points (*pointDone* and *candidate*). Factors that do not appear in a hypothesis definition do not contribute to the collection of candidates. To make the algorithm work, initial 'corners' of the test space must be stored in the candidates pool upon system initialization. The algorithm can be improved by adding points to the buffer pool after each measurement.

for each hypothesis $h : f_l \times .. \times f_r \rightarrow r_o$ **do**
    Let $c \in C$ with $c = (a_1..a_{l-1}, a_l..a_r, a_{r+1}..a_n)$
        where $a_l..a_r$ are values for the hypothesis parameters $f_l..f_r$
        and $a_1..a_{l-1}$ and $a_{r+1}..a_n$ are values for the remaining factors.
    for each $f \in \{f_l..f_r\}$ **do**
        group C by f
        def: $G_i = (a_1..a_{i-1}, a_i, a_{i+1}..a_n) \mid a_1..a_{i-1}$ and $a_{i+1}..a_n$ are constant.
        for each group $G_f[k]$ **do**
        sort $G_f[k]$ with key f
        for each subsequent pair **do**
            generate a new candidate point using the interest curve.

Fig. 5. Generation of candidates

3.3 Generation of flight plans

The second process generates a flight plan for each candidate in two phases. The first phase deals with moving the target system into the test space position identified. The second phase extends the flight plan with the actual measurement actions. At the same time the SOFTWARE TESTPILOT determines the cost and expected response time of the plan. The cost is used to order the batch of flight plans for subsequent execution. The response time is returned to an interactive user, who can use it to intervene (or have lunch). A sketch of the algorithm is shown in Figure 6.

For example, the candidate selected in the previous section requests a selection experiment of 5 tuples from a table with 90 tuples. Assume that in the current position the table size contains 60 tuples.

Then, the first phase must insert 30 tuples to reach the desired point. The eligible action is `dbinsert`, whose **factors** and **step** attributes permit table_size increments. Thus, the flight plan can be initialized with the request `dbinsert(30)`. The second phase identifies the actions whose response variable is mentioned in the focus of interest. They are added to the flight plan. In our example, we merely add the request `dbselect(90,5)`, but in general several selections are performed at once.

3.4 Selection of the best flight plan

The third process deals with selecting a flightplan for execution. This choice depends on two factors: the weight of the measuring point and the flight plan cost. The user

process makeplan()
clear flight plan FP and set cost C to zero
PHASE I:
  Let $Q(u_i..u_l)$ be current database state.
  Let $Q'(v_i..v_l)$ be the target database state.
  $S(s_i..s_l) := Q(u_i..u_l)$
  repeat
    Find an action $A = A(s_j..s_k)$ that brings S closer to Q'.
    Determine the new state S' using the **step** attribute.
    $FP := FP{+}{+}\ A(s_j..s_k)$
    $cost := cost + estimate(A(s_j..s_k))$
  until $S = Q'$
PHASE II:
  for each response r **do**
    find an action A with $A(f_c..f_e) \rightarrow r$
    substitute the relevant focus values from Q'.
    $flightplan = flightplan{+}{+}\ A(v_c..v_e)$

Fig. 6. Flight plan generation algorithm

can balance these factors using the *speed* property in the control object, which takes a value in the range 0.0 to 1.0.

A speed factor 0.0 causes the flightplan with the highest weight to be chosen; the cost to execute the flight plan is ignored. The system tries to (dis) proof the hypothesis with a minimal number of test runs. A speed of 1.0 leads to selecting the cheapest plan, but may delay insight in the precise shape of the performance function.

Actually, let F_i denote the plans under consideration then the plan taken into execution minimizes the formula, where α and β are normalized costs and weights.

$$\text{'value'} = speed * \alpha + (1 - speed) * \beta \qquad \begin{array}{l} \alpha = (cost(F_i)/maxcost) \ and \\ \beta = (weight(F_i)/maxweight). \end{array}$$

3.5 Flightplan execution

The flight plan selected above is executed on the DBMS and the results are kept for inspection by the SOFTWARE TESTPILOT . The interface between SOFTWARE TESTPILOT and target system is kept as open as possible, because it permits non DBMS tools to be considered as well, e.g. a event-queue simulation package. Moreover, we expect generic modules to defined that encapsulate interaction with a particular target system.

To aid design and debugging of a TSL program, we have included a dummy target system. This dummy uses the information within the SOFTWARE TESTPILOT to mimic the behavior of a real system. In particular, it uses the hypothesis to predict the outcome of an action with some distortion.

4 Summary

In this paper we have described a novel approach to assess the performance quality of database management systems. The technique consists of specifying a potential large test space through which the SOFTWARE TESTPILOT navigates using a behavioral model of the anticipated performance characteristics. The system automatically selects the best actions to move the DBMS into the proper experimental state by insertion/deletions. Thereafter, it performs the measurements.

The current implementation of the SOFTWARE TESTPILOT is written in SWI-Prolog [10]. It runs on Silicon Graphics workstations using the XPCE toolkit for monitoring the performance functions.

The SOFTWARE TESTPILOT is currently used for assessing the performance gains to be expected for browsing session using new query optimization techniques. This requires particular strength in the generation of symbolic data. Moreover, a prototype implementation for parallel execution of flight plans has been constructed. The SOFTWARE TESTPILOT is delivered with an SQL server module and a dummy database generator.

Acknowledgments The authors wishes to thank the members of the Database Research Group of CWI and partners in the Pythagoras project for advice on earlier versions of this systems. In particular, we thank R. Ulenbelt for his contribution on the implementation of the prototypes.

References

1. Cattell, R. "Engineering and Database Benchmark", Technical Report, Database Engineering Group, Sun Microsystem, April 90.
2. D. Bitton, D.J. DeWitt, and C. Turbyfill, *Benchmarking Database Systems: A Systematic Approach*, CS Report #526, Univ. of Wisconsin at Madison, Dec 1983.
3. D. Bitton *The Wisconsin Benchmark* in Readings on Database Systems, Editor: M. Stonebraker, Morgan-Kaufmann, 1988.
4. R.J. DeWitt, S. Ghandeharizadeh, D. Schneider, R. Jauhari, M. Muralikrishna, A. Sharma, *A Single User Evaluation of the Gamma Database Machine*, in Database Machines and Knowledge Base Machines, M. Kitsuregawa (ed.), Kluwer Academic Publ. 1988, pp. 370-386.
5. D.J. DeWitt, *The Wisconsin Benchmark*, in The Benchmark Handbook for database and transaction processing systems (by J. Gray), Morgan Kaufmann Publishers Inc., 1991.
6. P.M. Chen and D.A. Patterson, *A New Approach to I/O Benchmarks- Adaptive Evaluation, Predicted Performance* Proc. 5th Int. Conf. on Architectural Support for Programming Languages and Operating Systems (ASPLOS V).
7. Gray,J., "The Benchmark Handbook", Morgan Kaufmann Publishers Inc., 1991
8. Terbyfill C., *AS3AP - An ANSI SEQUEL Standard Scalable and Portable Benchmark for Relational Database Systems*, DB Software Corporation, 1989
9. Transaction Processing Performance Council, "TPC Benchmark, A Standard", Omeri Serlin, ITOM International Corp. Nov. 89
10. J. Wielemaker, SWI-Prolog Manual, University of Amsterdam, 1992.

Modifying Database Queries and Error Constraints[1]

Kaizheng Du and Gultekin Ozsoyoglu
Department of Computer Engineering and Science
Case Western Reserve University
Cleveland, OH 44106

ABSTRACT. In many cases, in order to satisfy constraints on a database query, the query needs to be modified. However, users' "manual" modification is an extra burden on users and, sometimes may not be correct when users lack knowledge about the database. In this paper, we discuss automated query modification techniques when modification of queries are accompanied by error constraints. We introduce an automated query modification mechanism based on superset/subset and sampling modification protocols.

1 Introduction

Query modification has long been discussed in the area of semantic query optimization, where the modified query produces the same output as the original query [Hamm 80, King 81, Chak 85]. In recent years, new research has emerged in query modification with the goal of modifying a query into another one in order to satisfy the users' expectations on the output of the query [HoOT 89, SmiL 89, Chau 90, OzDu 91, OzDG 92]. In this type of query modification, the semantics and the output of the modified query may be different from that of the original query.

Generally speaking, a database query has to be modified in order to satisfy certain constraints on the query (e.g., timing constraints, security constraints, etc.). The user specifies these constraints (also called modification constraints) to emphasize his/her expectations about the desired features of the output relation. We now give three reasons for a query to be modified:

- **Query with a Time Constraint.**

  A time-constrained query is of the form "get the information x in at most t time units". If the given query can not be finished within the given time, it needs to be modified into another query which meets the time constraint. For example, the user may need within 10 seconds the names of factory furnaces with "dangerously high" temperature readings in the last week. The database system, judging that the query cannot be evaluated in 10 seconds, may modify it into the names of "high-security furnaces with dangerously high" temperature readings in the last week.

- **Security Enforcement.**

  A given query may violate the security of the database; and needs to be modified. For instance, a query may request the average salary of

[1] This research is supported by the National Science Foundation under Grants IRI-8811057, IRI-9009897.

engineers with Ph.D. The database system may change the query to the average salary of all engineers with B.S., M.S. and Ph.D. so as to protect the salary information of a small number of engineers with Ph.D.

- **Exploratory Data Analysis.**

  Sometimes, a user may be performing exploratory data analysis, and may present an initial query with a set of constraints. The user's expectations are that if the output of the initial query does not satisfy the given constraints, the database system automatically (using pre-defined modification protocols) modifies the query such that the output of the modified query satisfies the given constraints. We give an example.

  Example 1.1. The precision of a product is determined by the precision of the machine used, and the skill level of the operator. Suppose the product with a certain precision requirement can be made by either a low-skilled operator operating a high-precision machine, or a high-skilled operator operating a low-precision machine. An exploratory data analysis query may ask at least K combinations of operators and machines such that the product precision is not less than P. Due to resource considerations, the operators are preferred to be with skill level X or low, and the machines are preferred to be with precision Y or low.

  If the number of combinations found from the operators with skill level X or low plus machines with precision Y or low is less than K, then the initial query needs to be (repeatedly) modified by relaxing the requirement either on operators' skills or machines' precision (e.g., by adding high-skilled operators and/or high-precision machines into consideration). □

In the case that the output of a user's original query does not satisfy the given constraints, the user may need to repeatedly modify his or her query until the given constraints are satisfied. The query modification work is obviously an extra burden on users. Also, users' "manual" modification may not be correct when users lack knowledge about the database. Therefore, an automated query modification mechanism may be beneficial in such environments. For instance, in example 1.1, if there are pre-defined modification protocols between the user and the database system, say, preference orders on operators and machines, then the query modification can be automatically performed by the database system.

Automated query modification (such as those in exploratory data analysis) may be beneficial in applications such as marketing analysis, decision making, industrial control, and scientific data analysis.

The purpose of this paper is to present a general automated query modification model, and a set of query modification constraints. We then discuss query enforcement issues for one specific type of query modification constraints; namely, error constraints. To simplify the problem, in this paper, we only consider relational data model and relational algebra.

2 Query Modification

2.1 Modified Queries

A modifiable database query is denoted as $\{Q(R_1, R_2, ..., R_k),\ C\}$, where $Q(R_1, R_2, ..., R_k)$ is the original (base) query (as contrasted with its modified versions), R_i is the ith relation involved in the query, C is the conjunction of a set of modification constraints on the query. $Q(R_1, R_2, ..., R_k)$ is abbreviated as Q if there is no ambiguity. For a given query $\{Q, C\}$, if Q does not satisfy C, then Q needs to be changed into a query Q_m such that Q_m satisfies C. In this paper, we assume that only the original query is to be modified, not the constraints.

From the viewpoint of query formation, modified queries are of two types, namely, the *isolog* type and the *non-isolog* type.

Definition 2.1. (Isologous queries) Two queries, $Q(R_1, R_2, ..., R_k)$ and $Q'(R'_1, R'_2, ..., R'_k)$, are said to be *isologous*, or, $Q(R_1, R_2, ..., R_k)$ is a *isolog* of $Q'(R'_1, R'_2, ..., R'_k)$, if (1) for $1 \leq i \leq k$, R_i is a superset or subset of R'_i and (2) when R'_i in Q' is replaced by R_i for all i, $1 \leq i \leq k$, we obtain Q.

Definition 2.1 implies that the parse trees $Q(R_1, R_2, ..., R_k)$ and $Q'(R'_1, R'_2, ..., R'_k)$ are identical, except at the leaves.

For example, in relational algebra, $R \cap S$ and $r \cap s$ are isologous queries if r is a subset of R and s is a superset of S. However, $R \cap S$ and R are not isologous. If we modify a query only to its isolog, then it is an *isologous query modification.* This paper discusses only isologous query modification.

2.2 Query Enlargement and Query Reduction

There are two basic strategies used in isologous query modification, namely, *query enlargement* and *query reduction.* For an arbitrary query $Q(R_1, R_2, ..., R_k)$, query enlargement means that $Q(R_1, R_2, ..., R_k)$ is transformed into its isolog $Q(R'_1, R'_2, ..., R'_k)$ such that $R_i \subseteq R'_i$ for all $1 \leq i \leq k$. Similarly, query reduction means that $Q(R_1, R_2, ..., R_k)$ is transformed into its isolog $Q(R'_1, R'_2, ..., R'_k)$ such that $R'_i \subseteq R_i$ for all $1 \leq i \leq k$. One can also use both query enlargement and reduction strategies to modify the same query, i.e., a query $Q(R_1, R_2, ..., R_k)$ is transformed into $Q(R'_1, R'_2, ..., R'_k)$ such that $R_i \subset R'_i$ for some $1 \leq i \leq k$ and $R'_j \subseteq R_j$ for $1 \leq j \leq k$, $j \neq i$. This is called *enlargement-reduction* modification.

2.3 Automated Query Modification Model

We model the automated query modification mechanism as a quadruplet (D, P, C, M), where D is a relational database instance, P is the set of query modification protocols followed by both the user and the database system during query modification, C is a set of modification constraints given by the user and satisfied by the modified queries, and M denotes modification methods such as automatic constraint enforcement strategies, query rewrite rules, etc.

A language independent query expression frame used in an automated query modification system is

Query:
{a query written in any relational database language}
Constraints:
{a set of constraints for Query to satisfy}
Protocols:
{the protocols used for modifying Query.}

with the semantics that the Query must satisfy the Constraints. Otherwise, the Query is modified into another query following the Protocols such that the modified query satisfies the Constraints.

In the following sections, we present the details of modification protocols and the modification constraints and their enforcement.

3 Modification Protocols

We give two modification protocols used for automated isologous query modification, namely, the ***superset/subset chains*** and ***samples***.

3.1 Protocol One: Superset/Subset Chain Use

A relation can be partitioned (or fragmented) into small subsets. A subset f_i, $1 \le i \le n-1$, of a relation f_n is defined using a selection formula on an attribute of f_n as

$$f_i = \{t | t \in f_n \wedge PCF(f_i)\}$$

where $PCF(f_i)$ is a Propositional Calculus Formula containing conjunctions of atoms $C_j\ \theta_j\ t.A_j\ \theta_j'\ C_j'$, $1 \le j \le k$, where A_j is an attribute of f_n and called the **fragmentation attribute**, C_j and C_j' are constants, θ_j and θ_j' are arithmetic comparison operators $=$, $<$ and $\le$[2]. A superset/subset chain involves a set of relations $f_1, f_2, ..., f_n$ such that $f_i \subset f_{i+1}$, i.e., $PCF(f_i) \wedge PCF(f_{i+1}) = PCF(f_i)$ and $PCF(f_i) \vee PCF(f_{i+1}) = PCF(f_{i+1})$. Figure 3.1.a contains the subset chain of relation Furnaces. Figure 3.1.b contains the superset chain of relation Engineer-with-PhD. Figure 3.1.c contains the subset chain Employees.

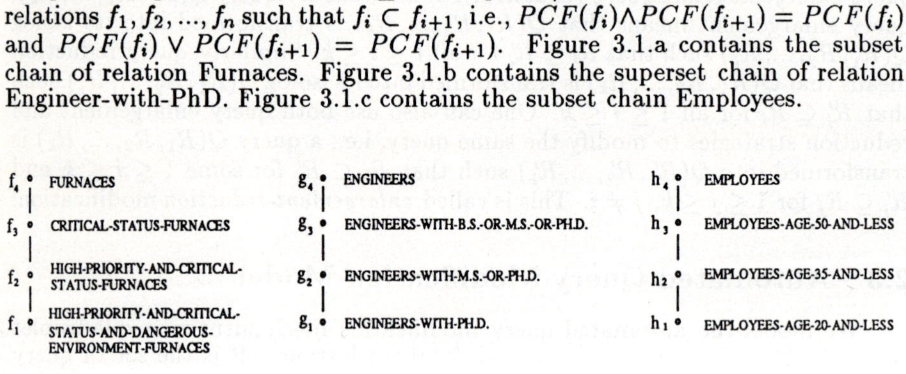

(a) Subset chain for FURNACES (b) Superset chain for ENGINEERS-WITH-PH.D. (c) Subset chain for EMPLOYEES

Figure 3.1. The Subset and Superset Chains.

Let the (finite) domain of attribute A be D_A. For a fragment f of R fragmented on A, let D_f denote the subdomain of D_A from which the tuples of fragment f get their A values. In other words, D_f is the set of A values in D_A that make formulas $PCF(f)$ true. For example, for $PCF(f)$ is $20 \le Age \le 30$, $D_f = [20, 30]$. In $PCF(f)$ and D_f, f can also be a relation, say, $PCF(R)$ and D_R. We suppose that for R fragmented on attribute A, $D_R = D_A$.

A (superset/subset) chain exists logically (conceptually) and physically. A node f_i in a logical chain is defined and located by using a selection formula

[2] **When an attribute A_j does not have a numeral domain (e.g., a character string domain), we may assume that a total ordering exists in the domain of A_j (e.g., lexicographic ordering), and treat operators $<$ and $\le$ as the "order-testing" operators.**

(PCF). However, for evaluation efficiency purposes, we maintain physical files f_i' for f_i, where $f_i' = f_i - f_{i-1}$ and $f_1' = f_1$ in the superset/subset chain. We call f_i' the **complement set** of f_i, or, the ith **physical set** in the chain. Suppose relation R is physically fragmented into n physical sets f_i', $1 \leq i \leq n$. For each f_i, $f_i = f_i' \uplus f_{i-1}$, $2 \leq i \leq n$, where $\uplus$ denotes disjoint union. Therefore, $R = f_1' \uplus f_2' \uplus \ldots \uplus f_n'$.

In this protocol, when modifying a query, we require that the new relation used for replacing the base relation must be in the superset/subset chain of the base relation. The motivation for using superset/subset chains as query modification protocols is that the superset/subset chains provide an efficient way to find a superset or a subset of a base relation in a query to be modified, making systematic and automatic query modification possible.

3.2 Protocol Two: Sampled Data Use

In some cases, a base relation may be replaced by a sample (e.g., a random sample) drawn from the base relation or its superset instead of the prefixed superset/subset chains. A typical example of using a sample to modify a query is in aggregate query estimation [HoOT 89]. In sections 6 to 10, we show other examples that use sampling protocols to enforce constraints.

4 Modification Constraints

In this section, due to space problems, we discuss only error constraints. Other constraints are discussed in [Du 93].

4.1 Error Constraints

A modified query is different from the original query in both the semantics and the output. The difference in the output is called the *modification error* (or error in short).

In terms of the expectations of the user who posed query Q, the query modification performed by the database system leads to two types of errors. First, some tuples that are in the original query Q do not appear in the output of the modified query Q_m. We call this **Deleted-Information Error**, or, **D-error** for short, and characterize it as $Q - Q_m$. Second, some tuples of the modified query Q_m are not among the tuples of the original query Q. These tuples, characterized by $Q_m - Q$, constitute **Added-Information Error**, or, **A-error** for short. We define the (relative) sizes of A- and D-errors as

$$\text{The size of A-error} = \frac{|Q_m - Q|}{|Q_m|} \quad \text{(f.4.1)}$$

$$\text{The size of D-error} = \frac{|Q - Q_m|}{|Q|} \quad \text{(f.4.2)}$$

Example 4.1. Consider the simple relational algebra query $Q = R - S$ and the modified query $Q_m = f_i - g_j$ where f_i $(1 \leq i \leq n)$ and g_j $(1 \leq j \leq m)$ are members in the superset/subset chains of R and S, respectively. For query reduction, $R = f_n$ and $S = g_m$. For query enlargement, $R = f_1$ and $S =$

g_1. Figures 4.1.a and 4.1.b illustrate the errors in query reduction and query enlargement using Venn diagrams, respectively.

Sometimes, due to various reasons (e.g., time constraint or an impatient user), an exact answer to the original query is not necessary. Instead, the user presents an error bound together with his query. Any modified query satisfying the error constraint is acceptable to the user.

For non-aggregate queries, the error constraint is specified as (A-error $\leq c_1$, D-error $\leq c_2$), where c_1 and c_2 are constants, the user can specify the desired sizes of A- and D-errors to control the error due to query modification.

A special error constraint, namely, the *safety constraint*, is useful:

Safety Constraint

In some cases, the A-error in query reduction (and the D-error in query enlargement) is unacceptable. For example, consider a time-constrained query of a hospital database asking for the names of people with blood type "O". Clearly, names of people whose blood type are not "O" are unacceptable to be included in the answer.

In the cases that the A-error in query reduction and the D-error in query enlargement are unacceptable, the user requires that the output of any modified query Q_m must be (i) a subset of the output of Q in query reduction (no A-error); and (ii) a superset of the output of Q in query enlargement (no D-error). Such a modified query is called a *safe modified query.* Such constraints are called the *safety constraints.*

A safety constraint is specified as (A-error $= 0$, D-error $\leq c_1$) for query reduction and (A-error $\leq c_2$, D-error $= 0$) for query enlargement.

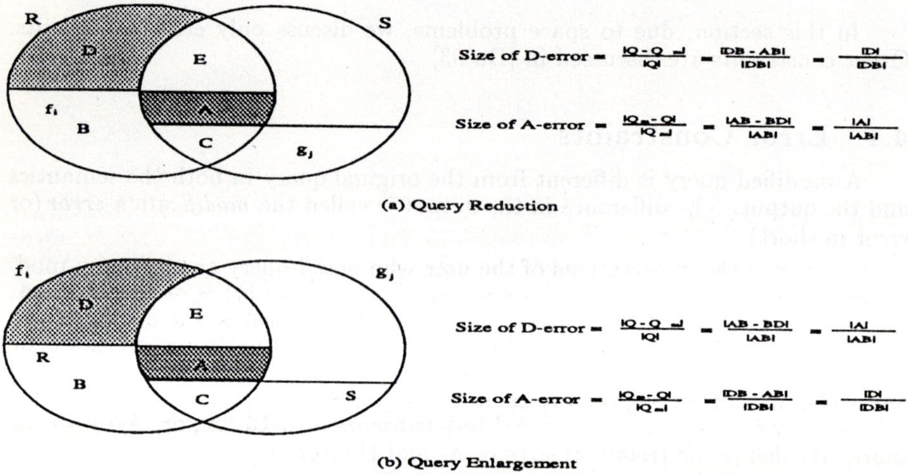

Figure 4.1. Error characterization in query reduction and enlargement of a single set difference query.

5 Enforcing Error Constraints

The error constraints are enforced by two techniques, namely, the *error removal* and the *error estimation.* Error removal eliminates the A-error in query reduction and the D-error in query enlargement. A semantic method using the

PCFs of the supersets/subsets involved in a modified query is used in error removal. When errors of certain type are chosen not to be eliminated, error estimation is used to estimate the sizes of errors. New sampling statistical techniques and estimators are designed to estimate the error in query modification.

We make two assumptions.

Assumption 5.1. For $R\theta S$, where $\theta \in \{\cup, \cap, -, \bowtie\}$, R and S are fragmented on the same attribute.

Assumption 5.2. For $R\theta S$, where $\theta \in \{\cup, \cap, -, \bowtie\}$ and R and S are fragmented on the same attribute, we have $R = f'_1 \uplus f'_2 \uplus \ldots \uplus f'_n$ and $S = g'_1 \uplus g'_2 \uplus \ldots \uplus g'_n$ with $PCF(f_i) = PCF(g_i)$, i.e., $D_{f_i} = D_{g_i}$, $1 \leq i \leq n$.

5.1 Error Removal Technique

A modified query is A_safe if it does not have any A-errors. Similarly, a modified query is D_safe if it does not have any D-errors. A- and D-errors in a modified query can be eliminated by checking the PCFs of the supersets/subsets.

A query is monotone when adding tuples to its input relations does not make it lose any of its output tuples; otherwise, it is nonmonotone. For example, RA queries with unions, intersections, projections, selection and joins are monotone [Ullman 88]. However, the inclusion of the set difference operator makes an RA query nonmonotone as shown in the lemma below.

Lemma 5.1. Consider a monotone query Q with superset/subset chains for each relation R_i in Q. For any modified query Q_m, there is no A-error in Query Reduction and there is no D-error in Query Enlargement.

Thus, we only need to perform error removal for nonmonotone queries, i.e., RA queries that contain set difference.

Let us first discuss the error removal for a simple RA query $R - S$.

Definition 5.1. (Safe Replacement Pair) Given $Q = R - S$ and $Q_m = f_i - g_j$,

(a) for query reduction, Q_m produces no A-error if $f_i - g_j \subseteq R - S$. Then, we say that $< f_i, g_j >$ is an *addition-safe pair* (denoted as a_safe pair);

(b) for query enlargement, Q_m produces no D-error if $R - S \subseteq f_i - g_j$. Then we say that $< f_i, g_j >$ is a *deletion-safe pair* (denoted as d_safe pair).

We now characterize errors of both types in terms of formulas defining superset/subset chains.

Lemma 5.2. Given $Q = R - S$, $Q_m = f_i - g_j$,

(a) there is no A-error in query reduction, i.e., $< f_i, g_j >$ is an a_safe pair, if

$$PCF(f_i) \wedge PCF(g_j) = PCF(f_i).$$

(b) there is no D-error in query enlargement, i.e., $< R, S >$ is a d_safe pair, if

$$PCF(R) \wedge PCF(S) = PCF(R) \wedge PCF(g_j).$$

Lemma 5.3. If $< f_i, g_j >$ is an a_safe pair, then for any $x \leq i$, $< f_x, g_j >$ is an a_safe pair.

Lemma 5.4. Consider $R - S$ and query enlargement. Suppose relations R and S satisfy $PCF(R) \wedge PCF(S) = PCF(R)$. For any f_i and g_j chosen from the superset chains of R and S, respectively, $f_i - g_j$ produces no D-errors.

When choosing f_i and g_j for query reduction, if zero A-error is desired then, by lemma 5.2, we should choose $PCF(f_i) \wedge PCF(g_j) = PCF(f_i)$. According to lemma 5.3, the strategy to satisfy $PCF(f_i) \wedge PCF(g_j) = PCF(f_i)$ is to assign a $\Downarrow$ operator to the minuend f_i and/or a $\Uparrow$ operator to the subtrahend g_j, and keep modifying f_i and g_j until $PCF(f_i) \wedge PCF(g_j) = PCF(f_i)$.

By using lemma 5.2.a, checking and generating an a_safe pair does not need any database access. All operations are on the given subset chains. Therefore, this approach has good time efficiency, a very important feature in real time systems.

Now we generalize error removal to the general case, i.e., for a multi-operator nonmonotone query.

For a query $Q = Q(R_1, R_2, ..., R_n)$, Q^l_m denotes a modified query of Q using fragment list $l = [f_i^{R_1}, f_j^{R_2}, ..., f_k^{R_n}]$, where $f_g^{R_i}$ is the gth fragment in the superset/subset chain of relation R_i. In modifying a multi-operator nonmonotone query, instead of finding a safe replacement pair, we find a *safe (replacement) list* for Q^l_m.

Definition 5.2. (Safe Replacement List) Given a nonmonotone query $Q(R_1, R_2, ..., R_n)$ and its modified query Q^l_m,

(a) for query reduction, l is an *addition-safe (replacement) list* (denoted as a_safe list) for Q^l_m if Q^l_m produces no A-errors;

(b) for query enlargement, l is a *deletion-safe (replacement) list* (denoted as d_safe list) for Q^l_m if Q^l_m produces no D-errors.

Let a derived fragment be an RA expression e with fragments and base relations.

Lemma 5.5. In query reduction (query enlargement) of Q, l is an a_ (d_) safe list for query Q^l_m if for any subexpression $e = e_m - e_s$ (i.e., $< e_m, e_s >$ is a subtrahend-minuend fragment pair) in Q^l_m, e_m and e_s are both A-safe (D-safe), respectively.

In order to check the safety of a fragment pair at least one of which is an RA expression e (i.e., a derived fragment), we need to derive a PCF characterizing the expression e. Similar to the query reduction safety check of a fragment pair, for $e_m - e_s$ where e_m and e_s are derived fragments, one expects that $PCF(e_m) \wedge PCF(e_s) = PCF(e_m)$ provides a sufficient condition that $< e_m, e_s >$ is an a_safe pair. Note that, using relational algebra transformation rules, we can transform a query Q into Q' such that there is no union operator in all subtrahend and minuend subexpressions in Q'. Therefore, we only need to provide PCF derivation rules for intersection, difference, join, selection and projection operations. The derivation rules are given below.

Definition 5.3 (PCF Derivation Rules). Let f and g be either base fragments (i.e., fragments of base relations) or derived fragments (of arbitrary RA expressions). The PCF derivation rules for fragments derived from intersection, difference, join, selection and projection operations are

$$PCF(f \cap g) \equiv PCF(f) \wedge PCF(g); \quad \text{(d.1)}$$
$$PCF(f \bowtie g) \equiv PCF(f) \wedge PCF(g); \quad \text{(d.2)}$$
$$PCF(f - g) \equiv PCF(f) \text{ with } PCF(f) \wedge PCF(g) \equiv PCF(f); \quad \text{(d.3)}$$
$$PCF(\sigma_C(f)) \equiv PCF(f); \quad \text{(d.4)}$$
$$PCF(\pi_X(f)) \equiv PCF(f) \text{ with } f \in X. \quad \text{(d.5)}$$

For example, consider the derived fragment $f-(g\cap h)$ where f, g and h are base fragments fragmented on the same attribute A. Suppose $PCF(f) = 20 \leq A \leq 30$, $PCF(g) = 10 \leq A \leq 40$ and $PCF(h) = 20 \leq A \leq 50$. We have $PCF(g\cap h) = 20 \leq A \leq 40$ and $PCF(f-(g\cap h)) = 20 \leq A \leq 30$.

Lemma 5.6. Let E be the original (isologous) RA expression for an arbitrary derived fragment e. $\sigma_{PCF(e)}(E) = e$.

Lemma 5.7. For $e_m - e_s$, where e_m and e_s are either base or derived fragments, $< e_m, e_s >$ is an a_safe pair if $PCF(e_m) \wedge PCF(e_s) = PCF(e_m)$.

Lemmas 5.5 and 5.7 provide an approach to perform a safety check for arbitrary nonmonotone modified queries. Based on lemmas 5.5 and 5.7, for a nonmonotone query Q, the A-error removal algorithm for a multi-operator modified query Q^l_m is now given.

Algorithm A-ERROR_REMOVAL(Q^l_m)
Input: The modified RA query Q^l_m.
Output: An A-safe modified query.
begin
  In bottom-up direction, **for** each subtree $e_m - e_s$ of the parse tree of Q^l_m **do**
    {e_m and e_s are RA expressions.}
  while $PCF(e_m) \wedge PCF(e_s) \neq PCF(e_m)$ **do**
    begin
      reduce(e_m);
      Derive $PCF(e_m)$;
    end;
  Return the resulting modified a_safe version of the query Q^l_m;
end.

Procedure reduce(e)
Input: An RA subexpression e with fragments.
Output: A modified version of e with some reduced fragments.
begin
  if e is monotone or a base relation or a fragment **then**
    assign operator $\Downarrow$ to some or all of the base relations or the fragments in e;
  else
    Traverse the parse tree of e in preorder (root-left-right) except when a set difference node $e_m - e_s$ is encountered, in which case do not traverse the subtree for e_s. During the traversal, assign operator $\Downarrow$ to some or all of the base relations and fragments that are encountered;
  Replace in e each of the fragments or relations with $\Downarrow$ operator by a subset from its subset chain;
  Return the modified e;
end.

5.2 Error Estimation Technique

In some cases, users may allow A-errors in query reduction and D-errors in query enlargement as long as the errors have a bound. In order to meet the user-specified error bounds in an error constraint, or to report the error size in a modified query, we need to design error estimation techniques.

We design estimators for D- and A-errors. Due to space considerations, we discuss the error estimation in only query reduction. Error estimation in query enlargement is quite similar.

Let us first consider the query $R-S$ and its modified version $f_i - g_j$. According to the definitions given in section 4, the sizes of D- and A-errors for $f_i - g_j$ are

$$\text{Size of D-error} = \frac{|(R-S)-(f_i-g_j)|}{|(R-S)|} = \frac{COUNT((R-S)-(f_i-g_j))}{COUNT(R-S)} \qquad \text{(f.5.2)}$$

$$\text{Size of A-error} = \frac{|(f_i-g_j)-(R-S)|}{|(f_i-g_j)|} = \frac{COUNT((f_i-g_j)-(R-S))}{COUNT(f_i-g_j)} \qquad \text{(f.5.3)}$$

where COUNT(RA-expression) gives the number of tuples in the RA-expression. We use $CO\hat{U}NT$(RA-expression) to replace COUNT(RA-expression) in f.5.2 and f.5.3, where $CO\hat{U}NT$(RA-expression) is an estimator for COUNT(RA-expression).

From the performance analysis in [OzDu 91], the accuracy of $CO\hat{U}NT$(RA-expression) is dependent not only on the sample size, but also on the sampling method used and the RA-expression structure. The variance of $CO\hat{U}NT$ for a simpler RA expression is usually smaller than that for a complicated one. Therefore, whenever it is possible, we simplify the RA-expression, i.e., make it contain as fewer operators as possible.

Stratified random sampling [Coch 77] may produce a precision gain in the estimates of characteristics of the whole population. When a population is stratified, if each stratum is homogeneous in that the measurements vary little from one unit to another, a precise estimate of any stratum mean can be obtained from a small sample in that stratum. These estimates can then be combined into a precise estimate for the whole population. Please note that the relations in our problem have already been stratified by relation fragmentation. The stratum is f_i' for unary operations and (f_i', g_i') for binary operations. According to the results from [OzDu 91], when relations are stratified (or fragmented), the stratified random sampling for COUNT outperforms significantly the other sampling plans. This is because, for union, set difference, intersection, selection and join and projection[3] operations, each stratum is more homogeneous than the whole population (higher selectivity).

Taking advantage of the relation fragmentation, we transform formulas f.5.2 and f.5.3 into the versions in which (1) the RA-expression being counted is greatly simplified; (2) the stratified random sampling can be used.

Lemma 5.8. For $Q = R - S$, $Q_m = f_i - g_j$, and query reduction

$$\text{Size of D-error} = \frac{|(R-S)-(f_i-g_j)|}{|(R-S)|} = \frac{\sum_{k=i+1}^{n} CO\hat{U}NT(f_k'-g_k')}{\sum_{k=1}^{n} CO\hat{U}NT(f_k'-g_k')} \qquad \text{(f.5.4)}$$

$$\text{Size of A-error} = \frac{|(f_i-g_j)-(R-S)|}{|(f_i-g_j)|} = \frac{\sum_{k=j+1}^{i-1} CO\hat{U}NT(f_k' \cap g_k')}{\sum_{k=1}^{j} CO\hat{U}NT(f_k'-g_k') + \sum_{k=j+1}^{i-1} |f_k'|} \qquad \text{(f.5.5)}$$

where $j < i$.

[3] The join and projection operations whose join or projection attributes include the fragmentation attribute.

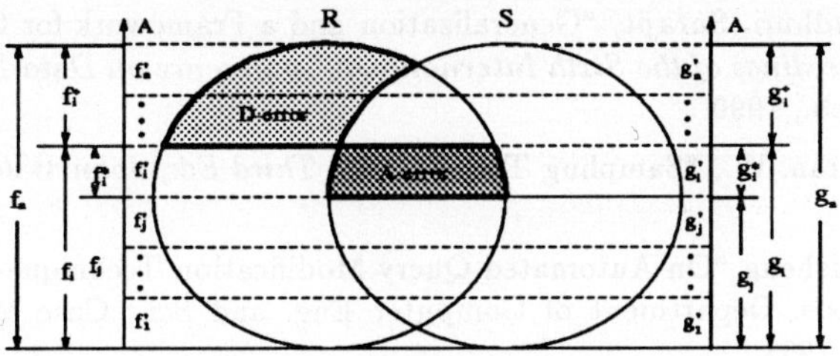

Figure 5.3. The Venn digram of $R - S$

For a given fragment list Q_m^l with an a_error bound in query reduction, suppose Q_m^l does not meet the given error bound. We design algorithm ERROR_ENFORCEMENT to make the modified query meet the given a_error constraint (bound of a_error size).

Algorithm A-ERROR_SIZE_ENFORCEMENT(Q_m^l, $\mathcal{A}$)

Input: The modified RA query Q_m^l and the a_error bound $\mathcal{A}$.
Output: A modified query satisfying the given error constraint.

begin
  if $\hat{a}(Q_m^l) > \mathcal{A}$ **then** {$a(Q_m^l)$ denotes the a_error size of Q_m^l. $\hat{a}(Q_m^l)$ denotes the estimate of $a(Q_m^l)$.}
  repeat do
    In top-down direction, **for** each subtree $e_m - e_s$ of Q_m^l **do**
    begin
      reduce(e_m);
      Estimate $\hat{a}(Q_m^l)$;
    end;
  until $\hat{a}(Q_m^l) \leq \mathcal{A}$;
  Return the resulting modified query;
end.

6 Conclusions

In this paper, we have presented an automated query modification model based on superset/subset and sampling modification protocols. Five types of query modification constraints, namely, the time constraints, the error constraints, the aggregate function constraints, the PCF constraints and the count proportionality constraints are introduced. And, for the error constraints, we have introduce its automated enforcement strategies and algorithms. The enforcement strategies for the other query modification constraints are given in [OzDG 92] and [Du 93].

References

[Chak 85] Chakravarty, U. S, "Semantic Query Optimization in Deductive Databases", *Ph.D. thesis*, University of Maryland, July, 1985.

[Chau 90] Chaudhuri, Surajit, "Generalization and a Framework for Query Modification", *Proceedings of the Sixth International Conference on Data Engineering*, Los Angeles, Feb., 1990.

[Coch 77] Cochran, W., "Sampling Techniques", *Third Ed., John Wiley & Sons, Inc.*, 1977.

[Du 93] Du, Kaizheng "On Automated Query Modification Techniques in Databases", *Ph.D. Thesis*, Department of Computer Eng. and Sci., Case Western Reserve University, 1993.

[Hamm 80] Hammer, M. Zdonik, S., "Knowledge-based query processing", *Proceedings of VLDB*, Oct., 1980.

[HoOD 91] Hou, W-C., Ozsoyoglu, G. and Dogdu, E., "Error-Constrained COUNT Query Evaluation in Relational Databases", *Proceedings of SIGMOD*, 1991.

[HoOT 88] Hou, W-C., Ozsoyoglu, G., and Taneja, B. K., "Statistical Estimators for Relational Algebra Expressions", Proc., *ACM Symposium on Principles of Database Systems*, Austin, TX, 1988.

[HoOT 89] Hou, W-C., Ozsoyoglu, G., and Taneja, B. K., "Processing Aggregate relational Queries with Hard Time Constraints", *Proceedings of ACM SIGMOD Conference*, Portland, OR, 1989.

[HouO 91] Hou, W-C., Ozsoyoglu, G., "Statistical Estimators for Aggregate Relational Algebra Queries", *ACM Transactions on Database Systems*, Dec. 1991.

[King 81] King, J., "Query Optimization by Semantic Reasoning", *Ph.D. thesis*, Stanford University, May, 1981.

[OzDG 92] Ozsoyoglu, G., Du, Kaizheng, Guruswamy, Sujatha, Hou, W-C., "Processing Real-Time, Non-Aggregate Queries with Time-Constraints in CASE-DB", *Proceedings of the Eighth IEEE International Conference on Data Engineering*, Phoenix, Arizona, February, 1992.

[OzDu 91] Ozsoyoglu, G., Du, Kaizheng, "On Estimating COUNT, SUM and AVERAGE Relational Algebra Queries", *Proceedings of the Second International Conference on Database and Expert Systems Applications*, Berlin, Germany, August 1991.

[SmiL 89] Smith, K. P. and Liu, J. W. S., "Monotonically Improving Approximate Answers to Relational Algebra Queries", *Proceedings of COMPSAC 89 Conference*, Orlando, Florida, September 1989.

[Ullman 88] Ullman, Jeffrey D., "Principles of Databse and Knowledge-Base Systems", Vol. 1, *Computer Science Press*, 1988.

[VrbL 91] Vrbsky, S. V., and Liu, J. W. S., "An Object-Oriented Query Processor That Produces Monotonically Improving Approximate Answers", *Proceedings of IEEE Data Engineering Conference*, Kobe, Japan, 1991.

Performance Evaluation System for Object Stores[1]

F. Rabitti, R. S. Sferrazza, M. G. Tori, and P. Zezula[2]

IEI-CNR,
Via S. Maria 46, 56126 Pisa, Italy

Abstract. One of the most important problems of object-oriented database management systems is efficiency. This problem becomes particularly evident with applications managing large amounts of data having complex structures and varying sizes (e.g. multimedia data). PESOS (Performance Evaluation System for Object Stores) is a software tool for estimating the cost of associative retrieval in very large and complex object stores. It enables to model various object storage organizations with respect to specific characteristics of the secondary memory hardware. It provides a simple language to specify queries on the object store structures and returns quantitative evaluations, using analytical methods, of the access performance.

1 Introduction

Object-oriented database management systems (OO-DBMS) allow their users to define the logical schema of the database that implements the application requirements. Such systems must subsequently translate the logical schema into the corresponding object storage structures. However, this process is not unique and usually several storage structure configurations can be applied. Specific implementation choices, adopted without considering important features of an application, can lead to severe performance problems. This is especially true for applications in the fields of artificial intelligence, engineering design, and multimedia. In these cases, objects can have very complex structures and extremely varying sizes.

Most of the existing OO-DBMS adopt a *fixed* strategy to build the object storage structures reflecting the logical schema specification. The only possibility to influence the physical object store design in this systems is a definition of indices and, sometimes, clustering of the physical objects. Recently, the possibility of supporting physical independence in an object database server has been investigated [1]. In this proposal, database designers are provided with mechanisms permitting to choose the most suitable physical organization for an object database in order to meet the performance requirements of particular applications.

A careful evaluation of factors relevant to the system efficiency appears to be very important during the *physical database design* phase. Such factors are also

[1] This work was funded by the ESPRIT Basic Research Action Project No. 6309, FIDE-2 (Formally Integrated Data Environment) and Progetto Finalizzato Calcolo Parallelo of C.N.R.

[2] The work was done at IEI-CNR in Pisa while on leave from the Technical University of Brno.

essential for choosing the best execution plan in the *query optimization*. In both cases, the evaluations should be performed with limited effort and in a reasonably short time.

In this paper, we propose Performance Evaluation System for Object Stores, PESOS. It allows performance evaluation of storage structures, commonly used in building object stores, without implementing the databases. Estimations are based on analytical modeling, and the models are built by simply specifying a schematic representation of the storage and index structures. PESOS aims at estimating the performance of executing queries on the specified database structures. PESOS is a typical evaluation system which allows to describe various object storage structures and indices (both value-based and navigational), specify hardware characteristics, and define *set-oriented* and *navigational* queries.

The paper is organized as follows. In Section 2, we summarize the assumptions and the techniques used in the design and implementation of PESOS. In Section 3, the architecture and functionality of PESOS are presented. Conclusions and future research plans are in Section 4.

2 Foundations

The PESOS is based on assumptions, models, and techniques concerning the data, access structures, and storage access cost estimation. In the following we summarize and reference the most important of them, directly related to our research.

2.1 Data Model

In the object store model adopted by PESOS, an *object* is considered as a sequence of *fields*. Each field contains either a value of type *simple* (*integer*, *real*, *string* or *reference*) or *complex* (*list* of simple-type values). A reference value stored in object O' identifies another object O'', and it models a reference from O' to O''. Because all objects are provided with *identity*, a reference value is constituted by a unique object identifier (*OID*), assigned by the system to each object present in the database. Objects are grouped in *collections* of objects having the same structure. Each collection is stored in a *file*; one record in the file corresponds to one object. Formally, we can write the definition as follows:

Definition 1

An Object Store, OS, is a set of collections:
$OS = \{C_1, C_2, ..., C_n\}$
Each collection, C_i, is a set of objects:
$C_i = \{O_{i,1}, O_{i,2}, ..., O_{i,card(C_i)}\}$
An object, $O_{i,j}$, has the following form:
$O_{i,j} = (OID_{i,j}, OC_{i,j}, OS_{i,j}, OV_{i,j}, OR_{i,j})$

where $OID_{i,j}$ is the j-th object of the i-th collection identifier, $OC_{i,j}$ describes the object characteristics (type of persistence, etc.), $OS_{i,j}$ is the object structure, $OV_{i,j}$ is the set of object values, and $OR_{i,j}$ is the set of identifiers of objects referenced by $O_{i,j}$. A similar approach was suggested in [8] and later also used in [1], and [9].

2.2 Associative Object Access and Navigation

Queries in an object database fall into two main categories: (1) retrieval of objects meeting particular criteria from sets (collections) and (2) retrieval by navigating along reference paths. Accordingly, we can distinguish between *set-oriented access* and *navigational access* in an object store.

A set-oriented access is typical of relational database systems. It is a process of determining and retrieving objects that satisfy a predicate or a combination of predicates based on the attribute values. Two fundamental strategies can be applied to implement access in a collection: the *sequential scan* and the *direct access*. The execution of direct access is supported by *indexing* structures (e.g. *B-tree*) or *hashing* techniques. The choice of the most suitable access method depends on several factors, such as the scanning cost, the predicate selectivity, the size of objects, and the type of query (e.g. *exact match, partial match, range query*).

A navigation process is constituted by a sequence of steps. As illustrated in Figure 1, given the set of objects, A (i.e. *starting objects*), a step of *forward navigation* determines set B (i.e. a set of objects referenced by the objects in A). Similarly, a step of *backward navigation*, starting from set A, determines set C (i.e. a set of objects referencing the objects in A).

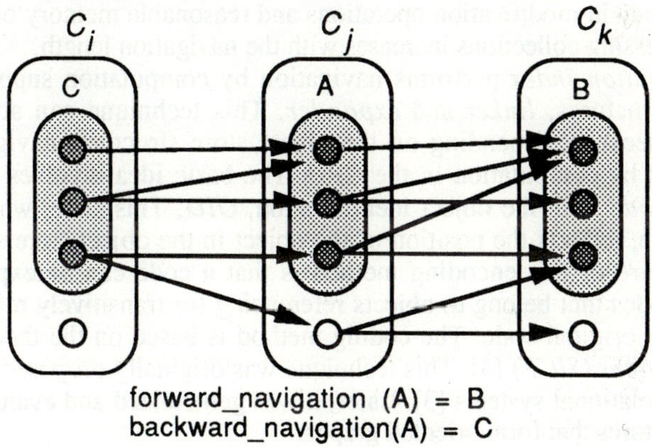

Figure 1. Navigation

Index Structures for Navigation. In object-oriented systems, navigation can be carried out in several ways. Forward navigation support is always available because values of the attributes involved (the referenced objects' identifiers) are stored in the objects themselves.

Inverse references may optionally be available. In order to avoid an excessive use of memory and a greater complexity in the system management, they are usually not stored in the objects but implemented by means of auxiliary structures (indices) based on the idea of *join index* [6]. Several specialized index structures for object stores have been proposed in the literature; they are known as *nested index, path index,* and *multi index* [2]. Another type of index, *navigation index*, was suggested in [9]. These indices are normally used for backward navigation; however, it is easy to conceive that they can also be utilized for forward navigation. As PESOS is able to model all of them, we will shortly survey the methods.

For demonstration purposes, we consider an index to be associated with a *chain* of collections, each of which (apart from the last one) references the following one through a particular object attribute. The first collection of the chain (the objects that are not referenced) is called the *top collection*, and the last collection of the chain (the objects that do not reference other objects) is referred to as the *bottom collection*. Forward navigation is performed along the *top-to-bottom* collection direction while backward navigation follows the *bottom-to-top* collection direction.

A *nested index* provides an association between objects in the bottom collection and objects in the top collection. Obviously, such an organization only provides fast access to objects in the top collection; to access objects in intermediate collections, either other indices or a forward step of navigation is needed. Memory occupancy is low, but modifications in the case of object store update are expensive.

A *path index* associates objects in the bottom collection with objects in all collections in the chain that (transitively) reference objects in the bottom collection. The main advantage is that a fast access is possible to collections at all levels; however, the modification cost is very high, and the space overhead increases.

A *multi index* is a set of indices, each of which connects objects in the collection at level *i* with objects in the collection at level *i*-1. In this case, we get the highest efficiency in modification operations and reasonable memory occupancy, but the cost of accessing collections increases with the navigation length.

A *navigation index* performs navigation by computation supported by two binary data structures, *linker* and *expander*. This technique can achieve a high performance because, depending on the object store structure, navigation can be performed just by computation in the CPU. The basic idea involves associating a fixed-length *code* with the object identification, *OID*. This code, which is unique within the store, reflects the position of the object in the object store structure. The important feature of this encoding method is that a code can be expanded into a sequence of codes that belong to objects referencing (or transitively referencing) the object with the original code. The coding method is based on the theory of *simple continued fractions* (*SICF*) [4]. This technique was originally proposed for hierarchy processing in relational systems [3]. Later, it was generalized and evaluated in [8, 9] for object structures that form oriented graphs.

2.3 Basic Performance Evaluation Support

File organization models for PESOS are obtained through a model specification of FOPES (*File Organization Performance Evaluation System*) [7]. Parameters of FOPES can describe both the implementation of files in secondary memory (with respect to the hardware) and the access mechanism that is adopted for a specific file organization. These evaluation models are used in PESOS to analyze, compare, and estimate performance-related characteristics - such as memory occupancy and query response time - for each file which is in the object store used. Performance estimations by FOPES are based on the assumptions of uniform term occurrence and query frequencies.

3 PESOS

We first present a brief, schematic summary of storage models evaluated by PESOS. Then, the use of the PESOS system will be explained in terms of both the definition of the object store models and the use of the query language. More details can be found in [5].

The definition of an object store in PESOS consists of a specification of the *collections*. A collection is a set of objects that have the same structure. The structure of an object is specified by an ordered sequence of *attributes*, each of which has a *name* (attribute identifier), a *multiplicity*, and a *type* (*integer number, real number, string of characters,* or *reference*).

Multiplicity is the average number of values which occur for a specific attribute; it can be greater than 1 if the attribute holds *lists* or *sets* of values. Moreover, for each attribute, statistical information, related to the values that are actually stored in the modelled database, is expected. Namely, the upper and the lower bound of the attribute domain set (integers and reals), the number of distinct values (i.e. the domain cardinality), and the average size of the stored values (integers, reals, and strings).

Attributes of type reference implement the link between a certain object and one or more objects of other collection; in this case, the value of the attribute, which is stored in the object, is constituted by an object identifier (*OID*). For each attribute of type reference, PESOS requires the referenced collection to be specified.

PESOS allows the specification of an *attribute index* (i.e. an *inverted file*, which can be implemented as *B-tree*, *hash* or *sequential*) for each attribute in a collection (except reference) including primary key attributes.

Structures to support navigation among objects can also be defined. Namely, *Path*, *Nested*, *Multi Index*, and *Navigation Index* are the design options. In PESOS, these indices are assumed to be used for both forward navigation and backward navigation, and their use is explicitly managed by primitives of the query language. Each of the above mentioned indices is associated with a group of collections that reference each other through their attributes.

3.1 Implementation Assumptions

As already mentioned, PESOS assumes that all the collections are stored as direct-access files, structured in records, each record equating to a physical object. The specification of the type of collection allocation can be either *contiguous*, with the records ordered by primary key, or *random*, as it is in most real cases. All objects contained in a collection are assumed to be of the same fixed length.

The data structures that implement the navigation indices are assumed to be stored as direct-access files. Their size, which is very important in determining the system's performance, is estimated as a function of the number of the objects involved in the relationship and based on a series of parameters included in the collection descriptors. These parameters serve to express (as simply and effectively as possible) the number of links that are actually stored in objects and the way how these links are distributed. In case the user does not want to specify these characteristics, PESOS attempts to perform an estimation of the parameters' values, based on certain built-in system defaults.

Hardware-related parameters (i.e. transfer time, disk latency, seek times, size of physical I/O blocks, and number of I/O buffers) are pre-defined by PESOS based on typical values, but it is possible to modify them in order to also model different machines.

3.2 The PESOS System

The basic steps that compose a PESOS session are: the definition of a *database model* (from now on, the term *database* means a database at the object-store level), the translation of the database model descriptors into an internal structure, the evaluation of the query response time, and a few other operations for the management of the *model library*. The model library is the set of all user-defined object store models; each model is stored in a file, which is accessed and used under the PESOS system's control.

The definition of a new database model is obtained by filling a template input file created by PESOS with a user-defined name. Such a template file will be referred to as *source* file, and its fundamental parts, also called *descriptors*, concern specification of the hardware characteristics, definition of the navigation indices, and description of the collections and their attributes.

Model definitions are translated into the corresponding FOPES-structured input files. Each file contains the appropriate parameters, required by FOPES to model a file organization, and the whole set of files represents the data structures for the object store model defined by the user.

3.3 Collection Descriptors

Figure 2 shows the descriptor of a collection. For each collection, a series of fields must be filled with summary information regarding the whole collection.

Number of Collections : 5

Collection N. 1.

Number of Objects	: 10000
Number of Attributes	: 5
Allocation Type	: Ord
Number of Keys	: 2
Key Attributes	: A1 A4
Key Index Type	: Bt

Ident	Type	Ref	Occ	Size	Dist	Rop	Eop	Sop	CL	Lowb	Uppb	Index
A1	Int	-	1	4	5000	-	-	-	-	10000	20000	Ht
A2	Ref	C2	10	-	4000	0.8	0.4	0.3	-	-	-	-
A3	Flt	-	1	8	8000	-	-	-	-	0.0	1.0	-
A4	Str	-	1	40	3000	-	-	-	-	-	-	Bt
A5	Str	-	2	72	100	-	-	-	-	-	-	Bt

Figure 2. Collection Descriptor

Referring to the upper part of Figure 2, collection N.1 contains 10,000 objects with five attributes. The records are ordered by a composite primary key, formed by two attributes (namely A1 and A4). An index of type B-tree supports access by the primary key.

Then, a table, containing a row for each attribute, is used to specify the characteristics of attributes. In the example shown in Figure 2, attributes "A2" and "A5" are declared as multivalued, with occurrence 10 and 2, respectively. It means that the objects are assumed to have 2 distinct strings stored in "A5", while only 40% of the objects (Eop = 0.4) are assumed to have 10 distinct references stored in "A2". 20% of the objects contain null references (Rop = 0.8) and only 30% of the referenced collection's objects are actually reached by references. The value of CL has been left unspecified, and PESOS computes a suitable value for it at compile time. Moreover, three access indices have been defined (apart from the one specified for the primary key), a hash index and two B-trees.

3.4 Reference Parameters Estimation

In object-oriented systems, the retrieval performance is greatly dependent on the cost of the navigation process, which is, in turn, influenced both by the number of steps to be performed and by the amount of links to be followed. Also, both the number and the size of the objects that are accessed during the navigation are important to determine the cost of the process. In order to make the estimation as accurate as possible, PESOS provides the possibility of specifying, related to each attribute of type reference, some "statistical" information about the database population with regard to the object references and their distribution. Such information is expressed by means of the following *Reference Parameters*:

Rop	(*Referencing Objects Percentage*),
Eop	(*Entry Objects Percentage*),
Sop	(*Shared Objects Percentage*),
Occ	(*Occurrence Number*),
CL	(*Converge of Linkage*).

Given a certain collection, *C1*, whose *N* objects globally reference (through a certain attribute) *Dist* objects belonging to another collection, *C2*, we can partition the objects in *C1* into three disjoint subsets. These three subsets contain, respectively 1) all the objects that have *Occ* references to *C2* (*entry objects*), 2) all the objects that have *one* reference to *C2*, and 3) all the objects with *null* reference. Moreover, the referenced collection, *C2*, is also partitioned into three disjoint subsets. All the objects contained in the first subset are reached by *CL* references. Those in the second subset are reached by *one* reference only, while the objects contained in the third subset are not referenced at all.

As shown in Figure 3, collection *C1*, containing *N* objects, is partitioned into three subsets: the first with *N∗Eop* entry objects, the second with *N∗* (*Rop-Eop*) single-reference objects and the third with *N∗* (1-*Rop*) non-referencing objects. *N∗Rop* is the total amount of referencing objects in *C1*. Collection *C2* contains *M* objects, among which there are *M - Dist* non-referenced objects, and *Dist* referenced objects. *Dist∗Sop* objects are shared ones, while *Dist∗* (1-*Sop*) are non-shared objects. $Dist \leq M$ must hold.

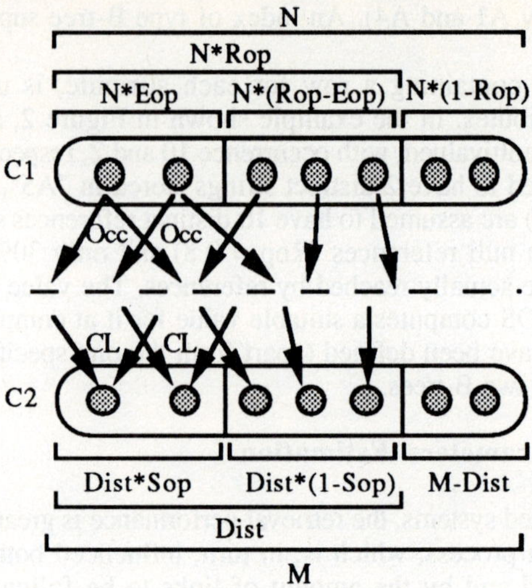

Figure 3. Reference Parameters

The parameter values must be specified according to the following constraints:

$$0.0 \leq Eop \leq Rop \leq 1.0$$
$$0.0 \leq Sop \leq 1.0$$
$$2.0 \leq Occ \leq Dist$$
$$2.0 \leq CL \leq N*Rop$$

Because all the references starting from *C1* reach *C2*, we get the following general equation, which expresses a relationship between the reference parameters and the number of objects contained in the two collections:

$$N * (Rop + Eop * (Occ - 1)) = Dist * (1 + Sop * (CL - 1)) \qquad (1)$$

It follows from the above discussion that the computation of values for the parameters (*Rop, Eop, Sop, Occ, CL*), constrained by Equation (1), may not be an easy task. As a matter of fact, each reference parameter can be left unspecified ("-"), and during the model compilation phase, the values are automatically computed by PESOS (details can be found in [5]).

3.5 Index Descriptors

In this paragraph, we describe the portion of the source file relative to the specification of the indices supporting the navigation among collections of the object store. As shown in Figure 4, this portion is composed of three tables, called *Index Descriptors*. The first and the second descriptor are related to the traditional *forward* and *backward* indices (i.e. *Nested Index*, *Multi Index*, and *Path Index*), both direct and inverse. The third descriptor is devoted to the specification of the *Navigation Indices*.

Number of Forward Indices : 3

Type	Ident	Bottom	NColl	CollectionList
M	1	C5	3	C1.A2 C2.A1 C4.A3
M	2	C5	3	C1.A2 C2.A1 C4.A3
N	1	C5	3	C1.A2 C2.A1 C4.A3

Number of Backward Indices : 2

Type	Ident	Bottom	NColl	CollectionList
M	1	C5	3	C4.A3 C2.A1 C1.A2
P	1	C5	3	C4.A3 C2.A1 C1.A2

Number of Navigation Indices : 1

Ide	NRef	ReferenceList
1	4	C1.A2:C2 C1.A1:C3 C2.A1:C4 C4.A3:C5

Figure 4. Navigation Index Descriptors

All indices have a unique identifier within the database, defined in correspondence with a group of collections connected by references. In the case of *forward* and *backward* indices, the collections are connected to form a chain, and the references are expressed by means of a sequence of collection-attribute couples (the last collection in the chain, called *Bottom Collection*, does not reference any collection). The *Navigation Indices*, instead, can be associated with collections that are connected in general graph-form. Each link is expressed through the specification of the referencing collection; the attribute of type "*Ref*", through which the reference is accomplished; and the referenced collection. Such indices can be used for both forward and backward navigation.

In general, the descriptors of type *forward* and *backward* have the following structure:

- Type - the type of index, either Nested, Multi, or Path;
- Ident - the index identifier, which, together with the index type, uniquely identifies the index (i.e. "M1", "M2", "N1", etc.);
- Bottom - the ending collection in the list, i.e. the one that is not referenced;
- NColl - the length, in number of elements, of the subsequent collection list;
- Collection List - the list of references (collections and attributes) with which the index is associated; all the elements in the list have the form "Ci.Aj", where "Ci" is the i-th collection and "Aj" is its j-th attribute; the sequence is ordered according to navigation direction (forward or backward); the bottom collection is not included in the list.

Referring to the example in Figure 4, the first row of the Backward Indices descriptor represents backward Multi-Index M1, whose bottom collection (i.e. the one from which a backward navigation starts) is C5. C5 is referenced by collection C4 through attribute A3. In turn, collection C4 is referenced by collection C2 through its attribute A1. Finally, collection C2 is referenced by collection C1 through its attribute A2.

We will now consider the descriptor for the Navigation Indices, which are used to perform navigations, both direct and inverse, by means of the *SICF* code expansion and of the two structures, *expander* and *linker* ([8], [9]). Each row in the descriptor defines one index and contains the following information:

Ide - the Navigation Index identifier (progressively increasing integer number);

NRef - the number of edges (references) that compose the graph of collections with which the index is associated;

ReferenceList - the list of references that connect the collections supported by the index; each element has the form "Ci.Aj:Ck", where "Ci" is the collection referencing "Ck" through attribute "Aj".

3.6 Query Specification

In the following, we describe how query performance evaluations can be obtained from PESOS. In fact, it is done by specifying a sequence of primitive operations representing an object store access program, i.e. the query *execution plan.*

Given a query that implies the type of navigation, different execution plans can be generated, depending on the access strategy chosen by the query-compiler's optimizer. The object store's subset that is needed to execute a certain execution plan (represented by a corresponding *access program*) is called the *access path.* An access program is composed of a sequence of steps, each consisting of exactly one *primitive operation*. Each primitive operation performs either the retrieval of a set of objects belonging to a collection, or the execution of a navigation step (either single or multiple level). In any case, the result of a primitive operation is a set of objects belonging to a collection.

PESOS provides fairly high amount of flexibility in evaluating various access strategies. The primitive operations allow specification of elementary computation steps, but they can be combined in order to model even very complex access programs. Each primitive is identified by a number that corresponds to its ordering in the input sequence. This primitive identifier is also used as the name of a variable containing the primitive's result set (together with its cardinality). In fact, each navigation primitive may refer to a previous primitive's result set by means of the previous primitive's identifier, *pi*, to determine the set of objects with which to start the navigation. The PESOS system provides the following four primitive operations to express the object store access program: FIND, MAPFW, MAPBW, and GETOBJ.

The FIND primitive selects a set of objects belonging to a specified collection based on the values of some given attributes. It has the following form:

FIND *Condition* FROM *Collection*

where *Condition* is a Boolean expression of predicates, connected in disjunctive normal form, by AND/OR operators. Each predicate has the following form:

(*Attribute_Identifier Relational_Operator Value*)

When a multivalued attribute appears in a condition, its identifier must be preceded by a *quantifier*, either "EACH" or "EXIST", which is used to decide if the predicate is satisfied by the objects that match the value in "ALL" their occurrences or in "AT LEAST" one occurrence.

The MAPFW and MAPBW primitives are used for navigation, either direct or backward, respectively. They both take the identifier of a previous primitive as an input parameter; this primitive identifier specifies a set of objects, belonging to a certain collection, that have been returned by the previous primitive. Starting with this set of objects, the MAPFW/BW primitives perform a step of forward/backward navigation, from a collection to another, along a specified chain of collections, and return a set of objects. The form of these PESOS primitives follows:

MAPFW (*Primitive_Ident* TO *Destination*) VIA *Path* [USE *Index_Ident*]
MAPBW (*Primitive_Ident* TO *Destination*) VIA *Path* [USE *Index_Ident*]

Primitive_Ident has the form *pi*, where *i* designates an issued primitive. *Destination* is a collection identifier, which indicates the collection from which the object result set of the navigation is taken (i.e. target collection). *Path* describes the forward/backward references (i.e. the sequence of collections and attributes) to be followed in order to reach the destination collection. It has the form:

$$ci_1(aj_1).ci_2(aj_2). \ldots .ci_m(aj_m)$$

where aj_k is the attribute of the i_k-th collection. The interpretation of the above expression depends on the type of primitive. In the case of a MAPFW primitive, ci_1 is the starting collection of the navigation (also specified by the primitive identifier, *pi*), and each ci_k references ci_{k+1} through aj_k, for $k = 1..m$. Collection ci_m references the destination collection through attribute aj_m. In a MAPBW primitive, ci_1 references the collection expressed by the primitive identifier (*pi*) through attribute aj_1, and each ci_k references ci_{k-1} through aj_k, for $k = 2..m$. The USE clause specifies an index to support the navigation process.

In the case of a nested index, because it only connects the top collection with the bottom collection, the path specified in the primitive must coincide with the path defined for the index (top-to-bottom or bottom-to-top navigation). The use of the path index requires the starting collection in the path to coincide with either the index top collection (forward case) or the index bottom collection (backward case); the destination collection can be any of those supported by the index. The multi index and the navigation index, for both forward and backward navigation, only require that the index path includes the primitive path .

The *GETOBJ* primitive retrieves the objects whose identifiers have been determined by means of previous operations, i.e. FIND and/or MAP primitives. The format of the GETOBJ primitive follows:

GETOBJ (*Primitive_Identifier*)

where *Primitive_Identifier* is the identifier of a previous primitive, which is associated with a set of objects belonging to a certain collection.

4 Conclusions

An analytical system for estimating performance of query execution in complex object bases has been presented. The system, called PESOS, models different implementation techniques with respect to the storage structure complexities and hardware peculiarities, such as block size, latency time, seek time, etc.

PESOS is available as a program written in C language using functions included in the C standard libraries. No graphic output routine has been used; thus, the program is easily portable with minimal modifications. In fact, both a version running on *HP Workstations*, under the UNIX operating system, and a version for IBM PC's, under MS-DOS, have been implemented.

Our future plans are to apply PESOS not only to the physical object store design and the study and evaluation of specific access methods, but also to the query optimization. In fact, some components of PESOS will be included in the query optimizer of PIOS (Physically Independent Object Server), a prototype system under development as part of the FIDE-2 project (in Esprit III Basic Research Action).

5 References

[1] N. Aloia, S. Barneva, F. Rabitti: Supporting Physical Independence in an Object Database Server. Proceedings of ECOOP-92. In: Lecture Notes in Computer Science 615. Berlin: Springer 1992, pp. 369-412.

[2] E. Bertino, W. Kim: Indexing Techniques for Queries on Nested Objects. IEEE Transactions on Knowledge and Data Engineering, Vol. 1, No. 2, June 1989, pp. 196-214.

[3] P. Ciaccia, D. Maio, P. Tiberio: A Method for Hierarchy Processing in Relational Systems. Information Systems, Vol. 14, No. 2, 1989, pp. 93-105.

[4] D. C. Olds: Continued Fractions. New Mathematical Library. New York: Random House 1963.

[5] F. Rabitti, R. S. Sferrazza, M. G. Tori, P. Zezula: PESOS: A Performance Evaluation System for Object Store Organizations. Technical Report FIDE/92/44, ESPRIT BRA Project No. 3070, FIDE (Formally Integrated Data Environment), August 1992.

[6] P. Valduriez: Join Indices. ACM Transactions on Database Systems, Vol. 12, No. 2, June 1987, pp. 218-46.

[7] P. Zezula, J. Zizka: File Organization Performance Prediction System. In: S. Ghosh, Y. Kambayashi, K. Tanaka, (eds.): Foundations of Data Organization. New York: Plenum Press 1987, pp. 399-406.

[8] P. Zezula, F. Rabitti: High Performance Object Store. Technical Report FIDE/90/4, ESPRIT BRA Project No. 3070, FIDE (Formally Integrated Data Environment), December 1990.

[9] P. Zezula, F. Rabitti: An Efficient Store for Object Basis. Twenty-fifth ACM-IEEE Hawaii International Conference on System Sciences, Kaloa, Hawaii, USA, Jan. 7-10, 1992, pp. 756-65.

An Optimization Method of Data Communication and Control for Parallel Execution of SQL Queries

A. Hameurlain, F. Morvan

Université Paul Sabatier, Lab. IRIT
118 Route de Narbonne -31062 Toulouse - France
Tél. 61 55 82 48; Fax: 61 55 62 58; E-mail: hameur@irit.fr

Abstract. *This paper describes a method for optimizing data communication and control for parallel execution of SQL queries. The optimization consists in avoiding the data communication and control which are not needed for the global parallel execution consistent with the execution plan generated by the optimizer. The basis of the method lies in the propagation of the partition attributes and of the number of processors during the relational operations parallelization phase. Performance evaluation shows the impact the propagation process has on improving response time. The main contribution of this work is the homogeneous integration in the parallelization step of the propagation process for partition attributes and number of processors in order to decrease communication volumes.*

1. Introduction and Motivation

Optimization of parallel execution in a parallel architecture now represents a critical step point in the evaluation of simple and complex SQL queries. Two types of parallel databases systems are proposed: shared nothing systems such as Teradata, Tandem NonStop SQL, Gamma, Bubba, Arbre, SDC (Super Database Computer), nCube, EDS (European Declarative System), Prisma/DB and SuperNode/ORACLE [2, 10, 5, 7, 29], and shared-memory systems such as XPRS [19, 26], DBS3 [4] and Volcano [14]. In most of these parallel database systems the programs considered are SQL or ESQL queries (ESQL: a conservative extension of SQL with deductive and object capabilities [13]), except in the Bubba system which supports the FAD language [18].

SQL relational queries are ideally suitable for parallel execution. Indeed, a SQL relational query is in general a set of relational algebra operations (selection, join,...) applied to a dataflow. Each operation uses as entry one or more relations and produces a new relation. Thus each time two operations exchange intermediate data, *pipeline parallelism* can be favoured. Indeed the execution of an operation may be started as soon as a consumed tuple is produced. This type of pipeline parallelism avoids temporary relation storage, but yields limited benefits chiefly because: (i) pipeline length is often short and (ii) some operations cannot send their first results before all the data has been processed, for example sorting or aggregation functions [12].

Another ideal approach to increase the benefits consists in distributing the operand of an operation on the nodes (node = processor, memory and disk) of the database machine and partitioning this operation over independent sub-operations (without data communication and without synchronization requirements). In this type of scheduling called *independent or partitioning parallelism*, the main problem resides in data placement.

There are two approaches for resolving the data placement problem for a set of relations in a parallel system.The first method, called *full declustering* [22], consists in distributing in a horizontal manner each relation over all the system nodes. It is used in parallel systems with relatively few processors (< 20) where compromises between communication and treatment are inexistent. Unfortunately the performance in this case are limited with complex operations such as join. Indeed each join operation is executed over all the system nodes so that it becomes impossible to exploit pipeline parallelism between the join chains and simultaneously have access to parallel disks to distribute the join operand relations. The second method, called *partial declustering*, consists in distributing each base relation over a subset of nodes. This is determined as a function of relation size [16] and eventually as a function of access frequency by applications [9]. For example for a join sequence realized by hashing, such partitioning offers best performance by allowing independent parallelism for join operand distribution and pipeline parallelism use between join operations. Such partitioning is more complex to carry out than full declustering because it requires evaluation of work loads and of changes in data distribution.

However, regardless of the data placement approach chosen, several methods exist to distribute data over a set of nodes. Generally, for the parallel systems described above, three methods of horizontal distribution are offered to the administrator:

- *Round robin*: data are distributed sequentialy to the disks with no direct means to recover them later.
- *Hash partition*: use of a random hashing function with a key related disk number.
- *Range partitioning*: use of intervals specified by the administrator by using of fragmentation predicates.

These methods present flaws which considerably impact on the load balancing. Indeed, for the hashing mechanism (Bubba, Gamma, Arbre and Teradata) the partition quality depends on proper choice of hashing function to produce a homogeneous distribution. Two critiques can be addressed to the method of administrator specified intervals: they depend on the quantitative information in the hands of the administrator and the fragmentation predicates may generate anti-parallelism by putting together tuples to be executed in parallel.

Thus, poor partition consequently unbalances load between processors. In this respect, several methods have been proposed and analysed. In [24] some aspects of data skew on parallel join methods are considered. They compare the algorithms when the join attribute are also used to distribute the relations during loading. The join algorithms are analysed in the presence of non-uniform join attribute values and bit vector filtering techniques [27]. However in their study the case where both relations to be joined have data skew was not examined. This is precisely the type of data skew which was studied and analysed in [30]. In fact, [30] present a parallel hash join algorithm based on the concept of hierarchical hashing to address the problem of data skew. The proposed algorithm adds an extra scheduling phase to the usual hash and join phases. During the scheduling phase, a heuristic optimization algorithm, using the output of the hash phase, attempts to balance the load across the multiple processors in the subsequent join phase. The algorithm identifies the hash partitions with the largest skew elements, splits them up, and assigns each one of them to an optimal number of processors [30].

However, most of this work is limited to exclusive consideration of intra-operation parallelism and only examines join operations.

In this paper, we take into account inter-operation parallelism [25, 31] which can be realized either with a pipeline execution model or with a partitioned parallelism. In addition to load balance problems due to inherently poor data distribution, we address the problem of data communication and control for parallel execution.

Let us illustrate this critical point in data communication and control with an example. Consider the parallel execution of an SQL query with the operations graph showed in figure 1. The join J and union U operations are executed respectively on 3 and 2 independent processors. The relations R1, R2 and R3 are distributed horizontally on 3, 2 and 2 disks (Figure 1).

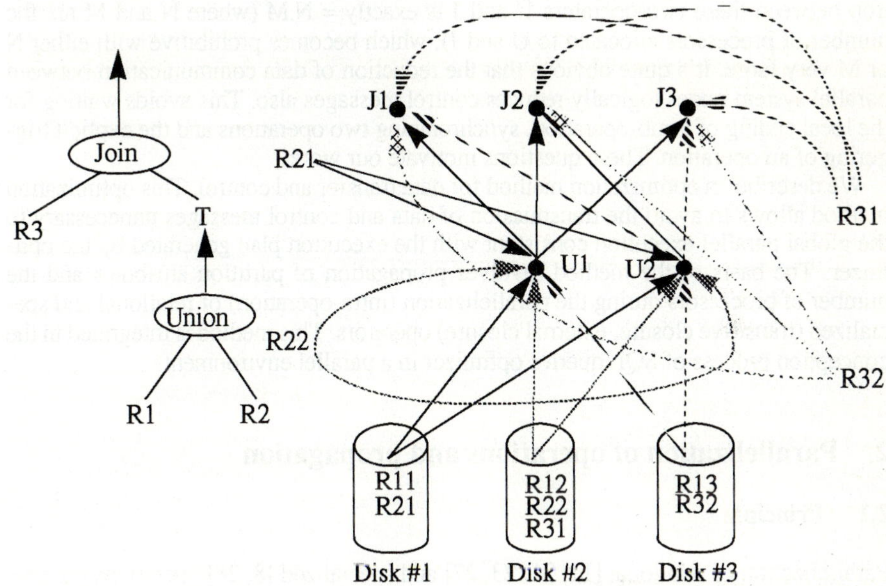

Fig. 1. A simple SQL query and associated dataflow graph

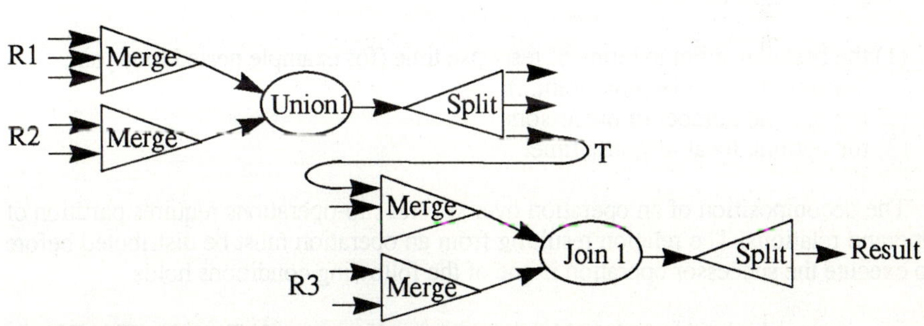

Fig. 2. Merging the inputs and partitioning the output of U1 and J1 operators

To execute these two operators U and J, we must call on the operators *Merge and Split* [12]. The Merge operator consists to combine several parallel data streams into a single sequential stream. The split operator is used to partition or replicate the stream of tuples produced by a relational operator.

Following each sub-operation of U, the system executes the Split operation. The output number of this operator is equal to the number of processors allocated to the direct successor operation J. Furthermore, before each sub-operation of J, the system executes two Merge operations in order to prepare the operands. Each Merge brings together the sub-relations from U sub-operations and from R31 and R32 sub-relations, to prepare the J sub-operation operands. As far as control messages are concerned, we must integrate local control primitives at the sub-operations level and global control primitives at the coordinator elected sub-operation.

Consequently, the execution of the sequence {U; J} requires a large number of control and data communication messages. For example, the number of data communication between these two operators U and J is exactly = N.M (where N and M are the number of processors allocated to U and J), which becomes prohibitive with either N or M very large. It's quite obvious that the reduction of data communication between parallel system nodes logically reduces control messages also. This avoids waiting for the local ending of a sub-operation, synchronizing two operations and the explicit triggering of an operation. These questions motivate our work.

We describe an optimization method for data transfer and control. This optimization method allows to avoid the transmission of data and control messages unnecessary to the global parallel execution consistent with the execution plan generated by the optimizer. The basis of the method involves propagation of partition attributes and the number of processors during the parallelization (intra-operation) of relational and specialized (transitive closure, external closure) operators. This method is integrated in the conception process of SQL queries optimizer in a parallel environment.

2. Parallelization of operations and propagation

2.1 Principle

Parallelization of relational [11, 21, 23, 27] and specialized [8, 28] operations consists in going through the query graph so that the cost evaluator [17] may determine the following for each operation:

(1) the best algorithm in terms of response time (for example nested loop join, hashing-join, sort-merge-join,...)
(2) the optimal number of processors
(3) the optimal local response time.

The decomposition of an operation over several sub-operations requires partition of operand relations. The relation resulting from an operation must be distributed before to execute the successor operation if one of the following conditions holds:

(1) a deduced relation produced by an operation (for example T= union (R1, R2)) is not consumed with the *same distribution function* by the successor operation (Join (R3, T))
(2) a deduced relation produced (for example T = union (R1, R2)) is consumed by the successor operation (join (R3, T)) with a *different distribution attribute*
(3) the *number of processors* allocated to an operation and its successor are *different*.

Such a systematic distribution generates a large number of data messages. A large number of control messages (Termination detection, synchronization,...) will be needed to control the sub-operation. All these messages must be reduced, undoubtedly as much as possible, whether they be data or control messages, in order to *improve response time* and *avoid saturating the network.*

The basic idea used to reduce communication (data and control) is to propagate the number of processors and the partition attribute for a given relation, by using *the same distribution function for all the relations*. We distinguish two type of operations, those using a join (Transitive Closure TC [20, 28], External Closure EC, Join,...) and those without a join (union, difference, selection,...). For the first type of operation C1, the only attributes on which the operand relations may be distributed are the join attributes. The join of two relations distributed over the join attribute results in a relation distributed over the join attribute (Figure 3). For the second type of operation C2, there is no constraint on the choice of a distribution attribute. The union of two relations distributed over the same attribute will result in a relation distributed the same way (Figure 4). We use these properties to propagate the number of processors for an operation and the distribution attribute of the operand relations with the same distribution function for all the relations. In figure 1, relation T produced by the union (R1, R2), will not have to be distributed to be consumed by the join (R3, T), if the following two conditions hold:

- the union (R1, R2) and the join (R3, T) have the same number of processors
- the distribution attribute of the operand relation R1, R2 corresponds to the distribution attribute of the operand relation T.

Therefore propagation helps to avoid distribution of some deduced relations. These relations remain stored on their processors or will be sent in whole to other processors.

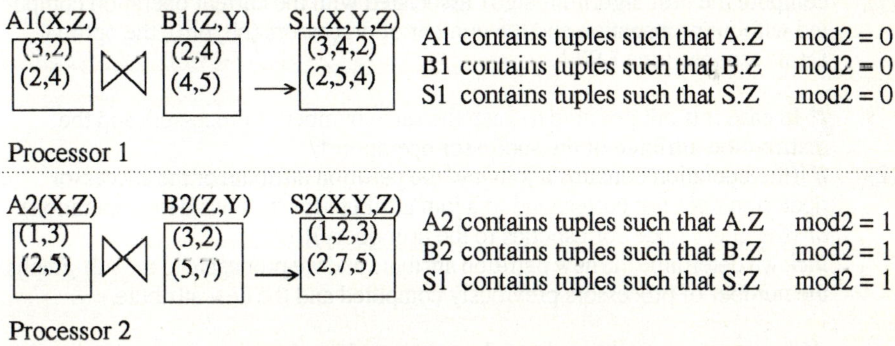

Fig. 3. Distribution of a join result relation

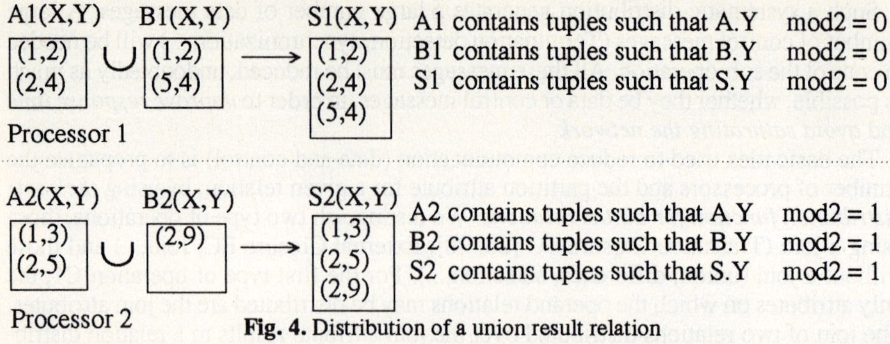

Fig. 4. Distribution of a union result relation

2.2 Algorithm selection and propagation

Our objective is to maintain as long as possible the same partition in the query graph, to avoid losing time with new distribution. To do this we propagate, as far as possible along the query graph, the distribution attribute and the number of processors.

Distribution attribute and processor number propagation depend on operation type (C1 or C2). For the first type of operation C1, the number of processors of the successor operation can be maintained, as well as the distribution attribute of its operand relation, only if the successor operation attribute corresponds to a join attribute for the considered operation. On the other hand, for the second type of operation C2, there is no constraint to conserve a distribution attribute. The propagation and algorithm selection method consists in the following steps:

(1) compute the best algorithm algo1 associated with the current operation computed without propagation and the number of processors (nb_pro), the optimal local response time LRT1.

/* In case it is not possible to keep the same number of processors and the distribution attribute of the successor operation */

(2) *if* [(the operation contains a join *and* the partition attribute of the successor operation does not correspond to a join attribute for the considered operation) *or* (the query node corresponds to the user query)]
then we determine the new partition attribute and we propagate to the sub-graphs the number of processors previously computed and the new attribute.

/* In case it is possible to keep the same number of processors and the distribution attribute of the successor operation */

(3) *else*
(a) we compute response time LRT2 and determine the algorithm algo2 as a function of the number of processors of the successor operation
(b) *if* LRT1 > LRT2 /* The propagation process is efficient */
then the current operation keeps and propagates the partition attribute and the number of processors of the successor operation to the sub-graphs.
(c) *else* we determine the new partition attribute and we propagate to the sub-graphs the number of processors computed previously and the new attribute.

3. Performance analysis and comparisons

In this section, we first describe the hypotheses which constitute the basis of the analytical model introduced by Valduriez [28]. We have extended this model in order to evaluate the number of processors [16] corresponding to an optimal parallel execution of recursive queries. Then, we evaluate the local response times, with and without propagation of the partition attribute and of the number of processors, to compute a deduced relation. We show the impact of the propagation process on response time by plotting the acceleration factor curves.

3.1 Parameters used in the analytical model

To analyse and evaluate performance obtained with the propagation method, we consider the following hypotheses:

(i) the number of tuples produced by processor is identical,
(ii) all processors have the same access method,
(iii) tuple production time is a constant,
(iv) there are no access conflicts on the network,
(v) tuple distribution time is a constant,
(vi) the buffer space is always enough for holding n tuples

The parameters used in the analytical model are:

|DT| number of tuples produced by relational operators,
di number of processors minimizing the local response time for an operation i,
t time to produce a tuple,
th time to distribute a tuple,
trf time to transfer a tuple,
msg time to send a message.

The following notations are used to compute the response times:

Tef effective time to treat an operation,
Td distribution time,
Tcom communication time from one home (= set of processors) to another home, (tuples transfer time + message communication time)
LRT local response time for an operation = Tef + Td + Tcom.

3.2. Performance analysis

The local response time LRT is the only one considered for performance analysis. It corresponds to the time elapsed from the initiation to the completion of the operation (Effective time to treat an operation + Distribution time + Communication time).

With the uniformity hypothesis (i), the processing time is: |DT| . t / di.

The communication time to send m tuples from one processor to another is given by: (m . trf) + msg.

The time to distribute $|DT|$ tuples in parallel over each processor is: $th \,.\, |DT| / di$.

In the example given in figure 1, we suppose that optimal parallel evaluation of the operator *join (R3, T)* is done on d1 processors (home 1) and that the *union (R1, R2)* is carried out on d2 processors (home 2). For $d1 \ne d2$, we assume no access conflicts occur. This hypothesis place the propagation method in the least favoured configuration.

Let us compute the local response time LRT, for example, the union operation $T = R1 \cup R2$ for $d1 > d2$ and $d1 < d2$ with and without propagation.

(a) *d1 > d2*

(1) *without propagation of d1*:

For each node of home2, the communication time is: $((|DT|/d1.d2).trf+msg).d1 = |DT|.trf/d2+d1.msg$

Therefore $LRT1 = Tef+Td+Tcom = (|DT|.t/d2)+(|DT|.th/d2)+((|DT|.trf/d2)+d1.msg)$

(2) *with propagation of d1*:

Since $d1 = d2$, the temporary relations are entirely transferred from one processor to another, hence, $Td=0$ and therefore $LRT2=Tef+Tcom=(|DT|.t/d1)+((|DT|.trf/d1)+msg)$

In addition, within the same home (same physical processors), the term $Tcom = 0$

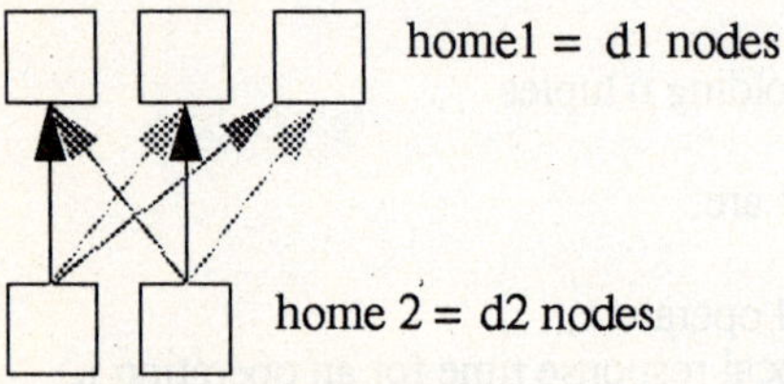

Fig. 5. case d1 > d2

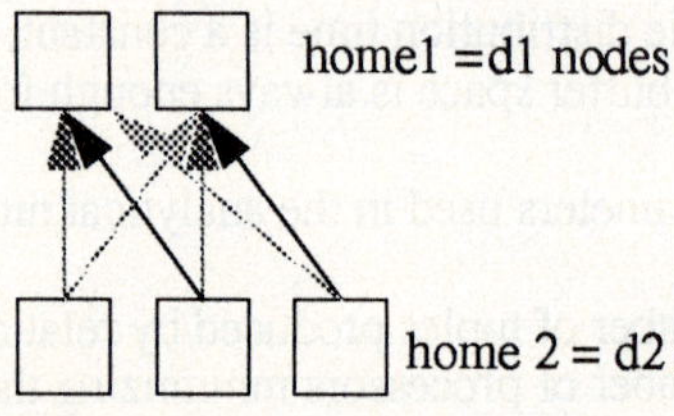

Fig. 6. case d1 < d2

(b) *d1 < d2*

(1) *without propagation of d1*:

The terms Tef and Td are the same as above. However, computation of the Tcom term is different. Indeed, if one supposes x nodes from home2 can communicate without access conflicts with x nodes of home1, then only d1 nodes from home2 can transmit in parallel at time t to the d1 nodes of home1. The first d1 nodes of home2 send in parallel to the d1 nodes of home1. Meanwhile, the remaining nodes of home2 are inactive. When the d1 nodes of home1 have completed reception, the same process is repeated with the following d1 nodes of home2 and so on. The number of iterations of this process is the closest integral value higher or equal than the number of times there are d1 nodes in home2, that is $E(d2/d1)$. Thus $Tcom = E(d2/d1).(|DT|.trf/d2+d1.msg)$

$$LRT1=Tef+Td+Tcom= (|DT|.t/d2)+(|DT|.th/d2)+E(d2/d1).((|DT|.trf/d2)+(d1.msg))$$

(2) *with propagation of d1*:

Since $d1 = d2$ the distribution time $Td = 0$.

$LRT2 = Tef + Tcom = (|DT|.t/d1)+((|DT|.trf/d1)+msg)$

In addition, within the same home, the term $Tcom = 0$.

To evaluate the contribution of the propagation algorithm, we define the acceleration factor as the ratio

$$\Omega = \frac{TRL1}{TRL2}$$

The following value are chosen to plot the graph of Ω as a function of x = d1-d2 with d2 belonging to [1, d1-1] when d1 > d2 and x = d2-d1 with d2 belonging to [d1+1, +∞[when d1 < d2.

$R = 10^6$ tuples; msg = 1 ms; trf = 5 μs; t = 0,2 ms; th = 3 μs;

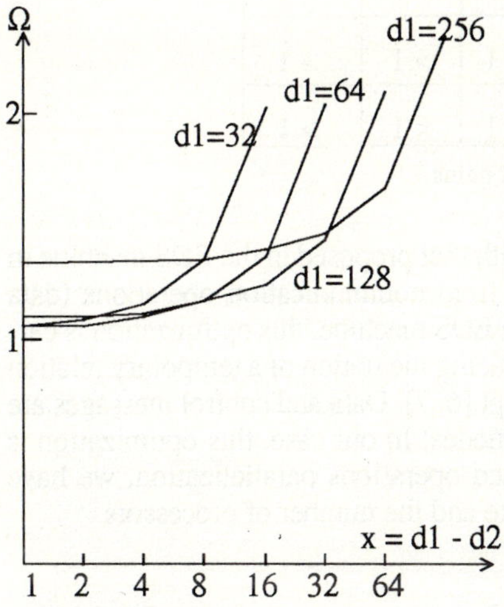

Fig. 7. Speed-up for d1 > d2

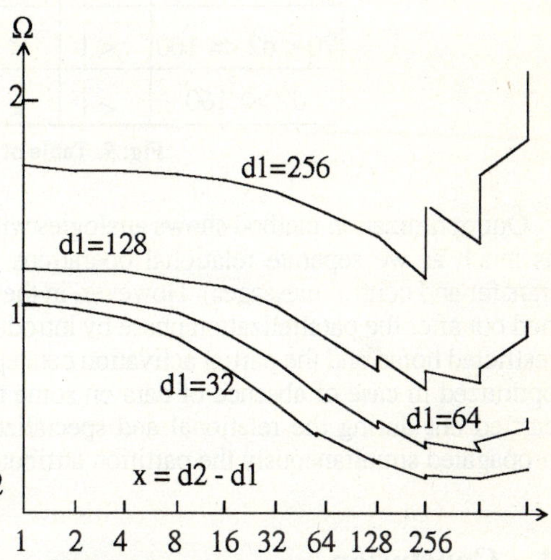

Fig. 8. Speed-up for d1 < d2

Figures7 and 8, which represent values for the acceleration factor for d1 > d2 and d1 < d2, show a propagation gain proportional to the difference between the number of processors d1 and d2. Indeed, as illustrated in figure 7, for a small difference in processors Δd = d1-d2, corresponds an acceleration of the order of 15-20% up to Δd <= 8 processors. For a larger Δd in the range 8 <Δd <= 16 the improvement is about 50-60%, and reaches 70-100% for 32 <= Δd <= 64. This is due to reduction in communication times, in effective time and of distribution time = 0 if the two homes use the same partition function, the same partition attribute and the same number of processors.

In the case where d1 < d2 (Figure 8) we distinguish 3 cases:

(a) For 1 <= Δd <= 16, the communication and distribution time saved by the propagation is greater than effective time lost because of the reduction in the number of processors.

(b) The effective time lost is more important than the time saved thanks to propagation. In such instances, propagation should not be initiated, as shown in figure 9 which illustrates the different cases where propagation is worthwhile (Ω > 1).

(c) When d1 is large enough, d1 > 200 processors, the effective time lost due to the propagation is always largely compensated by the reduction of distribution and communication times.

Figure 9 summarizes the various cases for which propagation is efficient ($\Omega > 1$). Furthermore, if we take into account termination messages in the computation of local response times, then propagation intervals increase. For example if d1 = 128, then propagation for d1 < d2 becomes efficient up to 260 processors.

d2 \ d1	32	64	128	>= 256
0 <= d2 <= 34	> 1	> 1	> 1	> 1
34 < d2 <= 70	< 1	> 1	> 1	> 1
70 < d2 <= 160	< 1	< 1	> 1	> 1
d2 >= 160	< 1	< 1	< 1	> 1

Fig. 9. Table of gains

Our optimization method shows analogies with that proposed in the EDS machine in as much as we separate relational operations from communication operations (data transfer and control messages). However, in the EDS machine, this optimization is carried out after the parallelization phase by introducing the notion of a temporary relation restricted home and the partial activation concept [6, 7]. Data and control messages are optimized in case of absence of data on some nodes. In our case, this optimization is carried out during the relational and specialized operations parallelization, we have propagated simultaneously the partition attribute and the number of processors.

4. Conclusion

In this paper we have aimed at presenting an optimization method for control and data flow which consists in avoiding the transmission of messages not needed to perform a global parallel execution consistent with the plan generated by the optimizer.

The principle of the method is based on the propagation of partition attributes and of the number of processors allocated to an operation. The advantages of this propagation lie in the considerable reduction in control and data communication, with according response time improvement and parallel system throughput increase. Furthermore, the method has been extended and generalized to take into account the fixed point operator [1,3] which allows the expression of recursive SQL queries. This implementation of a fixed point operator is based on a semi-naive method and integrates an iterative process of join, union and difference operations sequence. Such a propagation method is homogeneously integrated in the methodology of conception of SQL queries optimizer in a parallel environment.

A first version of the Parallel Inference System PARIS [15] has been conceived and implemented on a SUN stations network with ORACLE relational system. Software uses C language. The PARIS system is a shared-nothing system like Bubba and Gamma. In it's present form of PARIS system supports relational operations and the fixed point operator (transitive closure, external closure). Communication and control operations associated with Seq, End_seq, Par and End_par types of sequencing are already implanted using the communication primitives of UNIX system, in particular *sockets*.

The tools we have used are: *recvform (), sento (), socket (), bind (), gethostbyname () and gethostbyaddr ()*. The domain, type and protocol of a used socket are respectively *AF_INET, SOCK_DGRAM et UDP (User Datagram Protocol)*. We are now specifying the control operations associated with pipeline parallelism Pipe and End_pipe.

References

1. R. Agrawal, P. Denabu: Moving Selections into Linear Least Fixpoint Queries. In: IEEE Transaction Knowledge and Data Engineering. Dec. 89,Vol. 1, No. 4, pp. 424-432.
2. P. Apers, et al.: PRISMA/DB: A Parallel, Main-Memory Relational DBMS. In: IEEE, Transaction Knowledge and Data Engineering. Dec. 1992, Vol. 4, No. 6, pp. 541-554.
3. F. Bancilhon, R. Ramakrishan: An Amateur's Introduction to Recursive Query Processing Strategies. In: Proc. of ACM- SIGMOD. Washington, May 1986, pp. 16-52.
4. B. Bergsten, et al.: Prototyping DBS3: a Shared-Memory Parallel Database System. In: First intl. Conf. on Parallel Distributed Information Systems. Florida (USA), Dec. 1991, pp. 226-234
5. H. Boral et al.: Prototyping Bubba, a Highly Parallel Database System. In: IEEE Transaction Knowledge and Data Engineering. March 1990, Vol. 1, No. 1, pp. 4-24.
6. P. Borla-Salamet et al.: Compiling Control into Database Queries for Parallel Execution Management. In: First Intl. Conf. on Parallel Distributed Information Systems. Florida, Dec.91 pp. 271-279.
7. C. Chachaty et al.: A Compositional Approach for the Design of a Parallel Query Processing Language. In: 4th Int. PARLE Conf., Lecture Notes in Computer Science. Paris, June 1992, pp. 825-840.
8. J.P. Cheiney, C. DE Maindreville: A Parallel Strategy for Transitive Closure Using Double Hash-Based Clustering. In: Proc. of the 16th Intl. Conf. VLDB. Brisbane (Australia), August 1990.
9. G. Copeland et al.: Data Placement in Bubba. In: ACM SIGMOD Int. Conf. on Management of Data. Chicago (Illinois), May 1988, pp. 99-108.
10. D.J. Dewitt et al.: The Gamma Database Machine Project. In: IEEE Transaction Knowledge and Data Engineering. March 1990, Vol. 2, No. 1, pp. 44-61.
11. D.J. Dewitt et al.: An Evaluation of Non-Equijoin Algorithms. In: Proc. of the 17th VLDB Conf. Barcelona, September 1991, pp. 443-452.
12. D.J. Dewitt, J. Gray: Parallel Database Systems: The future of High Performance Database Systems. In: Communication of the ACM. June 1992, Vol. 35, No. 6, pp. 85-98.
13. G. Gardarin, P. Valduriez: ESQL2: an Extended SQL2 with F-logic semantics. In: IEEE Int. conf. On data Engineering. Phoenix (USA), Feb. 1992, pp. 320-327.
14. G. Graefe: Encapsulation of Parallelism in the Volcano Query Processing System. In: ACM-SIGMOD Int. Conf. on Management of Data. 1990.

15. A. Hameurlain, F. Morvan: Parallel Deductive Databases: Design and Implementation of a Parallel Algorithm for Computing Recursive Queries. In: SUG Ninth Annual Conf. Distributed Applications and Multiprocessor Technology. San Jose (California), December 1991, pp. 181-189.
16. A. Hameurlain et al.: An Analytical Method to Allocate Processors in High Performance Parallel Execution of Recursive Queries. In: Intl. Conf. On Database and Expert Systems Applications, DEXA92. Valencia, Sept. 1992, pp. 44-47.
17. A. Hameurlain et al.: A Cost Evaluator for Parallel Deductive Database Systems. In: Int. Conf. and Exhibition on Parallel Computing and Transputer Applications'92. Barcelona, Sept. 1992, pp. 1222-1228.
18. B. Hart, et al.: Parallelizing FAD, a Database Programming Language. In: Intl. Symp. on Databases in Parallel Distributed Systems. Austin (Texas), Dec. 1988
19. W. Hong: Exploiting Inter-Operation Parallelism in XPRS. In: ACM SIGMOD Intl. Conf. on Management of Data. USA, June 1992, pp. 19-28.
20. Y.E. Ioannidis, R. Ramakrishan: Efficient Transitive Closure Algorithm. In: Proc. of the 14th VLDB Conf.. Los Angeles (California), 1988, pp. 382-394.
21. M.S. Lakshmi, P.S. Yu: Effectiveness of Parallel Joins. In: IEEE Transaction Knowledge and Data Engineering. December 1990, Vol. 2, No. 4, pp. 410-424.
22. M. Livny et al.: Multi-Disk Management. In: ACM SIGMETRICS Conf. on Measurement and Modeling of Computer Systems. Banff (Alberta), May 1987, pp. 69-77.
23. H. Lu et al.: Optimization of Multi-Way Join Queries for Parallel Execution. In: Proc. of the 17th VLDB Conf.. Barcelona, September 1991, pp. 549-560.
24. D. Schneider and D. Dewitt: A Performance Evaluation of Four Parallel Join Algorithms in a Shared-nothing Multiprocessor Environment. In: Proc. of the 1989 ACM SIGMOD Conf.. June 1989, pp. 110-121.
25. D. Schneider and D. Dewitt: Tradeoffs in Processing Complex Join Queries via Hashing in Multiprocessor Database Machines. In: Proc. of the16th VLDB Conf. Brisbane, Australia 1990, pp. 469-480.
26 M. Stonebraker, et. al.: The Design of XPRS. In: Proceedings of the14 th VLDB Conference. 1988.
27. P. Valduriez, G. Gardarin: Join and Semi-join Algorithms for a Multiprocessor Database Machine. In: ACM TODS. March 1984, Vol. 9, No. 1, pp. 133-161.
28. P. Valduriez, S. Khoshafian: Parallel Evaluation of the Transitive Closure of a Database Relation. In: Intl. Journal of Parallel Programming. Feb. 1988, Vol. 17, No. 1, pp. 19-42.
29. D.M. Watson: Why Massively Parallel Database. In: Int. Conf. and Exhibition on Parallel Computing and Transputer Applications'92. Barcelona, September 1992, pp. 1249-1257.
30. L. Wolf, et al.: An effective algorithm for Parallelization Hash Join in the presence of Data Skew. In: 7th Int. conf. On data Engineering. Kobe (Japan), April 1991, pp. 200-209.
31. M. Ziane, et al.: Parallel Query Processing in DBS3. In: 2nd International Conf. on Parallel and Distributed Information Systems. San Diego, January 22-24, 1993.

Developing a Database System for Time-Critical Applications

Sang H. Son, David W. George, and Young-Kuk Kim

Dept. of Computer Science, University of Virginia
Charlottesville, VA 22903, USA

Abstract. Transactions in real-time database systems should be scheduled considering both data consistency and timing constraints. Since a database system must operate in the context of available operating system services, an environment for database systems development must provide facilities to support operating system functions and integrate them with database systems for experimentation. With these considerations in mind, we chose the ARTS real-time operating system kernel. In this paper we present our experience in integrating a relational database manager with a real-time operating system kernel and our attempts at providing flexible control for concurrent transaction management.

1. Introduction

Time is the key factor to be considered in real-time database systems, and the correctness of the system depends not only on the logical results but also on the time within which the results are produced. Transactions must be scheduled in such a way that they can be completed before their corresponding deadlines expire [Abb92, IEEE93, Son88]. For example, both the update and query on the tracking data for a missile must be processed within given deadlines, satisfying not only database consistency constraints but also timing constraints [Comp91].

Conventional database systems are typically not used in real-time applications due to inadequate performance and lack of predictability. These systems are designed to provide good average performance, while possibly yielding unacceptable worst-case response times [Buc89]. In addition, conventional database systems do not schedule their transactions to meet response requirements and they commonly lock data tables to assure the consistency of the database. Locks and time-driven scheduling are basically incompatible, resulting in response requirement failures when low priority transactions block higher priority transactions. New techniques are required to manage the consistency of real-time databases. These techniques should be compatible with time-driven scheduling and meet both the required temporal and data consistency constraints [Sha91, Son88, Son92, Son93].

To address the inadequacies of current database systems, the transaction scheduler needs to be able to take advantage of the semantic and timing information associated with data objects and transactions. A model for real-time transactions needs to be developed which both characterizes the distinctive features of real-time databases and

This work was supported in part by ONR, by DOE, by CIT, and by IBM Federal Systems Division contributes to the improved responsiveness of the system. The semantic information of the transactions investigated in the modeling study can be used to develop efficient transaction schedulers [Kor90, Lin90, Son90, Son93].

A database system must operate in the context of available operating system services. The correct functioning and timing behavior of database control algorithms depends on the services of the underlying operating system. As pointed out by Stonebraker, operating system services in many systems are not appropriate for support of database functions [Ston81]. In many areas, such as buffer management, recovery, and concurrency control, operating system facilities have to be duplicated by database systems because they are too slow or inappropriate. An environment for database systems development must, therefore, provide facilities to both support operating system functions and to integrate them with database systems for experimentation.

The ARTS real-time operating system kernel under development at Carnegie-Mellon University attempts to provide a "predictable, analyzable, and reliable distributed real-time computing environment." This provides an excellent foundation for a real-time database system [Tok89]. The ARTS system, which provides support for programs written in C and C++, implements different prioritized and non-prioritized scheduling algorithms and prioritized message passing as well as supporting lightweight tasks. All of these features are important when considering real-time databases.

We have investigated the issues involved in integrating a real-time database system with an operating system kernel, such as the features a database system requires from a real-time operating system kernel to provide real-time transaction support. We have used the relational database technology since it provides the most flexible means of accessing distributed data. Our research effort resulted in a new database manager for distributed real-time systems residing on top of ARTS. The result, RTDB, consists of a multi-threaded server which accepts requests from multiple clients. It provides a three-tiered approach for supported media types, offering memory-resident data options, local disk storage, and access to the UNIX file system. This support of various media types provides developers the flexibility to choose those media that best suit their needs.

ARTS provides an easily extensible real-time environment for program development. RTDB on ARTS represents a combination of desirable aspects of database technology and developmental flexibility. RTDB differs from existing database systems in a number of ways. For example, RTDB is a multi-user main-memory database while another real-time database research project, CASE-DB, was developed as a single-user, disk-based, real-time relational DBMS [Ozso90]. In this paper we present our experience in integrating a relational database manager with a real-time operating system kernel, and our attempts to provide flexible control for concurrent transaction management using a technique called *workload mediation*.

2. The ARTS Real-Time OS Kernel

Research in the area of distributed, real-time operating systems indicate that most are designed for a specific need, and as such are difficult to build, maintain, and modify; in addition, they do not afford the capability of predicting run time behavior during application design. In fact, few non-real-time operating systems provide a functionally complete set of general purpose, real-time task and time management functions, despite the fact that the user community is expressing the desire for increasingly complex applications of this type. Since the success of applications in real-time computing is primarily contingent on a system's temporal functionality, what is needed is an environment in which the system engineer can analyze and predict, during the design stage, whether the given real-time tasks having various types of system and task interactions (i.e. memory allocation/deallocation, message communications, I/O interactions, etc.) can meet their timing requirements.

In an attempt to provide such functionality, ARTS provides the process and data encapsulation that other distributed, object-oriented operating systems do, while at the same time including elements of temporal significance to the services it provides. This integration of data, thread, and concurrency control greatly facilitates real-time schedulability analysis. ARTS can support both hard and soft real-time tasks as well as periodic and sporadic ones [Tok89].

To support time-critical operations, the ARTS programming language interface allows designers to specify timing requirements and the communication structure so that they are visible at both the language and system level. This allows the system-wide ARTS environment to make scheduling decisions based on both temporal constraints and priorities of transactions. The Integrated Time-Driven Scheduler (ITDS) model of ARTS is more effective than the common priority-based preemptive scheduling of many real-time systems. Such simple schedulers become confused during heavy system loads when they are unable to decide the relative importance of tasks, and consequently cannot decide which tasks should be completed and which should be aborted. This causes unpredictability in the applications. The ITDS model, however, employs a time-varying "value function" which specifies both a task's time criticality and its' semantic importance. A hard real-time task can be characterized by a step function where the discontinuity occurs at the deadline, while soft real-time tasks are described by a continuous (linear or nonlinear) decreasing function after its deadline. In addition, ARTS' designers have separated the policy and mechanism layers, so that users can implement new scheduling policies with a minimum of effort. This decoupling allows ARTS to support scheduling policies which can be dynamically changed during run time.

The issue of priority inversion is crucial in providing semantically correct system behavior in addition to addressing temporal concerns. Priority inversion occurs when a high priority activity waits for a lower priority activity to complete. Resource sharing and communication among the executing tasks can lead to priority inversion if the operating system does not manage the available resource set properly. Significant research during the construction of ARTS was done to avoid priority inversion among concurrently executing tasks; in the processor scheduling domain, low priority servers which provide service to clients of all priorities are susceptible to inversion. For example, when a low priority request is being serviced, and a high priority task requests the same service, the high priority request waits, due to the non-preemptability of the service. Any task of higher priority than the server may preempt the server itself, however, so if a medium priority task arrives it preempts the server indefinitely, causing the high priority job to be lost in the shuffle. ARTS employs a priority inheritance mechanism to propagate information about a single computation which crosses task boundaries. That is, if a server task accepts the request of a client, the server inherits the priority of the client. Furthermore, the server should also inherit the priority of the highest priority task waiting for the service.

The notion of time encapsulation cannot be divorced from the basic structure of ARTS, in which every computational entity is represented as an object, called an *artobject*. An *artobject* is defined as either a passive or an active object. In a passive object there is no explicit declaration of a thread which accepts incoming invocation requests while an active object contains one or more threads defined by the user. In an active object, its designer is responsible for providing concurrency control among co-executing operations. When a new instance of an active object is created, its root thread will be created and run immediately. A thread can create threads within its object.

The ARTS kernel supports the notion of real-time objects and real-time threads. A real-time object is defined with a "time fence," a timer associated with the thread which ensures that the remaining slack time is larger than the worst case execution time for the operation. A real-time thread can have a value function and timing constraints related to its execution period, a worst-case execution time, a phase, and a delay value. When an operation with a time fence is invoked, the operation will be executed (or accepted) if there is enough remaining computation time against the specified worst case execution time of the operation for the caller. Otherwise, it will be aborted with a time fence error. The objective of this extension to the normal object paradigm is to prevent timing errors from crossing task or module boundaries (as often happens in traditional real-time systems which use a cyclic executive) and to bind the timing error at every object invocation.

On top of the ARTS foundation we have built a relational database manager using message passing primitives and employing the client/server paradigm. Based on the temporal urgency of the request, the server determines whether to commit the transaction or reject it.

3. The RTDB Real-Time Database Manager

RTDB is a relational database manager written in a hybrid C-based language called ARTS/C++ designed to run on ARTS. It offers not only a functionally complete set of relational operators — such as join, projection, selection, union, and set difference — but also other necessary operators such as create, insert, update, delete, rename, compress, sort, extract, import, export, and print. These operators give the user a large amount of relational power and convenience in managing the database.

We have developed two different kinds of clients for RTDB. One is an interactive command parser/request generator that makes requests to the server on behalf of the user. This client looks and behaves similarly to a single-user database manager. It is possible to run the client without knowing that any interaction between server and client is occurring. The other client is a transaction-generating "batch" client, representing a real-time process that needs to make database access requests.

The RTDB server object is the heart of the database management system. It is responsible for creating and storing the relations, receiving and acting on requests from clients, and returning desired information to the clients.

The server object defines four threads. The root thread is an aperiodic thread, which is automatically executed by ARTS upon invocation of the server. The server activates one or more worker threads. The worker threads are aperiodic and each one has a different priority which will match the priority of the messages it will service. The backup thread is a low priority periodic thread responsible for periodically backing up the relations that reside only in main memory. The lock manager thread is responsible for controlling concurrent access to the database.

The root thread of the server is responsible for binding the server's name in the ARTS name server so that the clients can find it and send requests. It is also responsible for reading the relations into its local memory, initializing the lock table and the blocked request queue, instantiating the backup thread, the lock manager thread, and the server worker threads. There is usually one worker thread created for each priority level. After completing these tasks, the root thread enters an infinite loop that accepts database requests from any client. The requests come in as packets. RTDB provides two different types of packets: *call* packets and *return* packets. The call packet, created by a client, contains all the information that the server needs to carry out the desired database access operation. Since different commands require different information, the call packet has a variant field containing different information for each command. When the server completes the processing of the request, it returns a packet to the client with the information requested. This packet is called a return packet. The return packet is created by the server and also has a variant field that carries command specific information.

The communication between the server and clients is performed by the ARTS communication primitives: Request, Accept, and Reply. The communication is synchronous; when a client issues a Request, it is blocked until the server Accepts and Replies to the message. This may cause some problems, especially in a real-time environment, for two reasons: priority inversion and data sharing.

The ARTS kernel (and thus the RTDB system) supports eight message priorities. When the root thread Accepts a message, it extracts priority information from the message packet. The root thread then enqueues the request on the message queue of the worker thread designated to service requests of that priority level. If inactive, the worker thread will be polling its queue; if active, the requests will be processed in FIFO order. Note that in this way we can easily exploit the scheduling merits of the underlying ARTS kernel without circumventing its priority-based scheduling mechanism. Since the worker thread's priority matches that of the messages it services, it will only be scheduled for the CPU in an interval where its priority is currently the highest in the system. This is a general case; for those instances where the scheduling technique is not priority based, or ARTS priority inheritance mechanism is employed, these decisions will naturally be reflected in the workers.

This technique of distributing requests among a pool of workers based on information contained in the request packet is called *workload mediation*. In our system workload mediation is realized by the server root thread which accepts the mes-

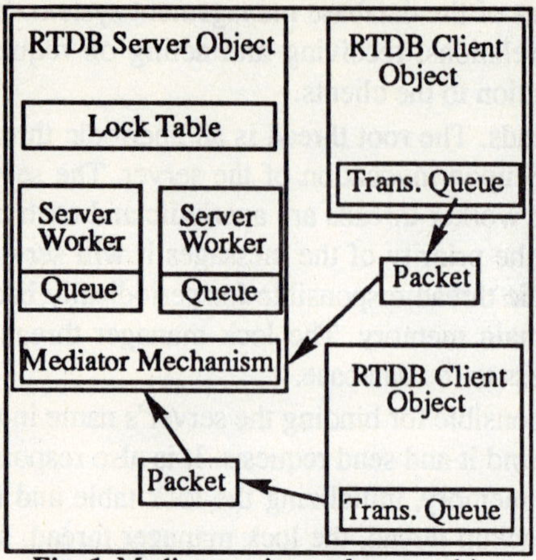

Fig. 1. Mediator as internal server object

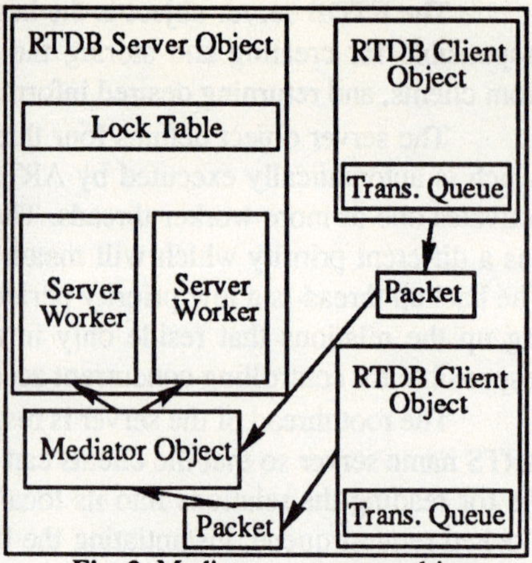

Fig. 2. Mediator as separate object

sages from the clients and puts them in the appropriate worker queue according to their priority. Figure 2 illustrates the mediator mechanism incorporated within the server object. This mechanism is unobtrusive from the view of system-wide scheduling, because it does not do any scheduling on its own. It only breaks the incoming workload up among the worker pool.

Another method of implementing this technique involves creating a dedicated object which acts as an intermediary between the RTDB client and server (Figure 3). The advantages of this implementation are enhanced abstraction for the mediation algorithms, and better modeling of the components involved. Also, algorithm implementors have a centralized repository of the routines they require and a strong definition of the communication interface they are required to maintain. However, it is our contention that the disadvantages of this scheme outweigh its merits. The primary disadvantage is a severe performance decrease due to the overhead of increased inter-object message passing. In addition, many of the data structures needed by the worker threads are also needed by the mediation algorithms.

Returning to our model, the worker thread of the RTDB server performs the client's request to access the database. It checks its request message queue, calls the appropriate database function that executes the requested operation, and replies back to the client. The worker replies to a client without completing a request when it needs to return more information than can fit in a single packet. In such a case, the worker sets a continuation flag indicating that there is more information to be sent back to the client. The client must make continuation requests to the server until it gets all the information requested. To maintain the consistency of the database, the RTDB server needs to handle conflicting requests properly. For example, a problem occurs when some request or part of a request (as in a multi-relational query) has to be blocked since it needs to lock part of relation that is already locked. RTDB handles this conflict by the use of the two phase locking protocol with priority abort. This will be covered further in section 5.

Whenever the worker becomes free, it first checks its queue of blocked requests. If there are any requests in the blocked queue that can be executed, it dequeues the request and processes it. If no request in the blocked queue is ready to be processed, the worker looks to its incoming request queue.

4. Concurrency Control

The concurrency control mechanism used in earlier versions of RTDB was a simple relation-level granularity locking scheme. RTDB is a multi-user database manager for time-critical applications and therefore the original scheme was inadequate, because it couldn't provide the high level of parallelism needed.

Experiments performed in the past showed that when the system was servicing a significant number of clients in parallel, the turnaround time for client requests would rise almost linearly with the number of clients in the system. This situation would mostly affect requests from low-priority clients, even if they were not competing with high-priority clients for the same data objects. The source of the problem was the lock granule that was used by the simple locking mechanism. By locking the entire relation it needed to access, a worker thread would lock out every other worker thread that needed to access the same relation even if the tuple sets accessed were disjoint. This was even more pronounced when there was a disproportionate number of accesses to a "hot" relation. A nearly serial execution of requests was the result exhibited by the system.

This situation was remedied by allowing the server to pick a granularity which allowed the most concurrency. The lock manager became a separate thread in the server object capable of communicating with the worker threads via message queues. The concurrency control mechanism that is employed is a version of two-phase locking (2PL) called strict 2PL. A significant disadvantage of 2PL is that it can lead to a deadlock. To avoid deadlocks the lock manager employs a high-priority abort scheme to resolve conflicts between worker threads. That scheme provides the system with a nice property: a high-priority worker never has to wait for a low-priority worker (i.e no priority inversion).

The granularity of locking for our algorithm can be modified to achieve the greatest level of performance possible. Tuple level lock granularity allows the most flexibility. By allowing worker threads to acquire a lock on a tuple basis, the number of conflicts is sharply lowered. The price to pay for this flexibility is overhead. For large relations, allocating a lock for each tuple and manipulating this lock can lead to severe performance degradation. We implemented a parameter called GRANULARITY which specifies the granularity of the 2PL locking mechanism. By varying this parameter, the server can implement anything from tuple to relation level locking. For example, if a transaction needs tuple number 123, the lock corresponding to this is $\lfloor 123/5 \rfloor$ or lock 24. The granularity a user chooses should depend upon both the type of queries done, and properties of the data being accessed. For example, if the data being accessed is distributed evenly through the relation, a lower granularity lock would be more appropriate to lessen conflicts from locking tuples not needed by the transaction. If it is known that the data the transaction is accessing is located primarily in one place or can be found in clumps throughout the database, a larger lock granularity might be appropriate. It would be easy to extend this model to support different

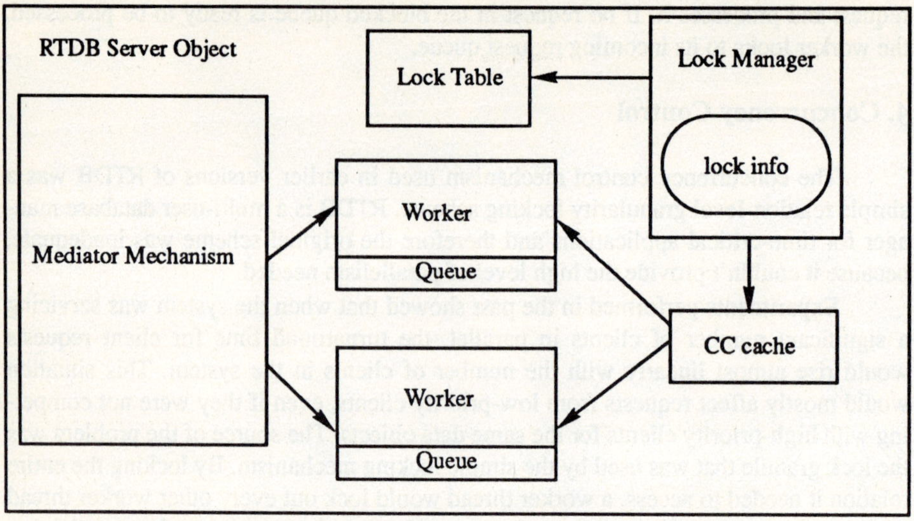

Fig 3. The Lock manager as a separate thread

lock granularity for each relation, allowing the user to fine tune the performance of the system based on a priori knowledge.

We settled on the value of five for the granularity as it provided a good compromise between lock granularity and overhead. Because of the variable granularity provided by the system, a substantial performance gain could be achieved by caching locking data. When a worker thread acquires a lock for a tuple, it is actually acquiring a lock for a block of tuples determined by the value of the granularity parameter. A worker thread asks for a lock for a tuple by executing the function call GET_LOCK. GET_LOCK maintains a local list of the locks that each worker owns. Instead of going to the lock manager for each lock request, the worker will instead check in its' local cache. If the worker has already acquired the lock corresponding to the tuple it is seeking to lock, it will proceed without sending a request to the lock manager. This saves a substantial amount of time which would otherwise been consumed in blocking and message passing.

Obviously, this requires more support from the operating system than simple relation level locking. More information needs to be kept available due to the finer lock granularity. The best way to organize and coordinate the actions to be taken to properly secure correct concurrent access to a relation was to put all the relevant data structures and operations in a separate thread in the server object (Figure 3).

The new lock manager thread still uses the lock table which is an essential part of the server. It holds important information about all the relations maintained by the server, such as the media on which the relation exists, the relation name and size, the starting address in virtual memory if it is a virtual memory relation etc. All the information concerning tuple locks and worker requests is kept inside the lock manager thread, hidden from all the other server threads.

There are two data structures that are used for communication between the lock manager and the worker thread. The first one is a priority queue where requests are

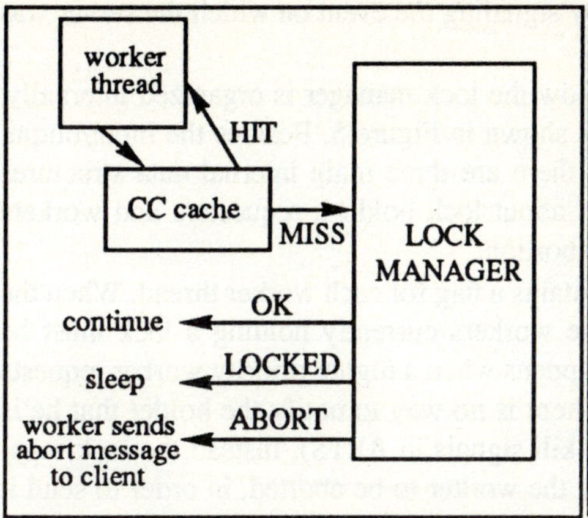

Fig. 4. Worker - Lock Manager communication

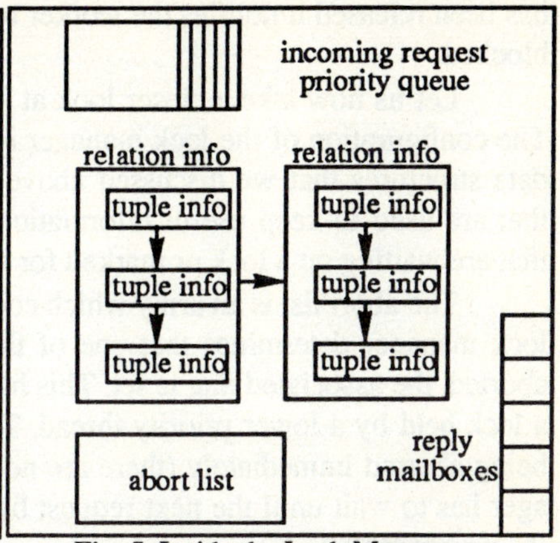

Fig. 5. Inside the Lock Manager

placed by the workers. Since the requests are ordered by priority, the lock manager always services the highest priority request at the head of the queue. Since the queue is a shared data structure, it has to be accessed in mutual exclusion by the threads that are allowed to use it. This is achieved by using special synchronization variables and primitives provided by the ARTS operating system.

The second structure used for holding the look manager's replies to the workers is an array of mailboxes, one for each worker in the server. It is not necessary to synchronize accesses to this structure, because the workers are always blocked when the lock manager accesses the mailboxes and are woken up after the lock manager has finished placing the replies in the mailboxes.

The procedure a worker follows to request a lock is described in Figure 4. The worker calls GET_LOCK to see if a lock for the required tuple has already been obtained. If a lock for the tuple has not already been allocated, the worker places a request with the appropriate information in the message queue in priority order. There are three kinds of request the worker can issue. A request for a read lock, a request for a write lock or a request to commit. If a lock has not already been granted, it blocks while waiting for a reply from the lock manager. After the lock manager has determined the reply, it places it in the mailbox associated with that worker and signals the worker. The worker either will continue, if the lock was granted, block waiting for the lock to be released or abort if there was a priority conflict.

Workers are effectively blocked while they are waiting for a reply from the lock manager or when they get a reply to block until the lock they have requested is released. An ARTS variable, called an event, is used for this blocking. A thread blocks on an event variable while waiting for an event, and will not unblock until the event corresponding to this variable is signaled. Events are used in two instances in our system. The first instance is when the request queue of the lock manager is empty. The lock manager then blocks on an event until a worker places a request and signals the lock manager, thus waking it up. The second instance is when a worker is blocked waiting for a reply from the lock manager or waiting for a lock to be released. When the lock manager has placed a reply in the appropriate mailbox or the requested lock has been released it notifies the worker by signaling the event on which the server was blocked.

Let us now take a closer look at how the lock manager is organized internally. The configuration of the lock manager is shown in Figure 5. Besides the input/output data structures that we discussed above there are three main internal data structures that are used to keep useful information about lock holders, requesters and workers that are waiting on a lock or marked for abortion.

The abort list is an array which contains a flag for each worker thread. When the lock manager determines that one of the workers currently holding a lock must be aborted, the associated flag is set. This happens when a higher priority worker requests a lock held by a lower priority thread. There is no way to notify the holder that he is being aborted immediately (there are no kill signals in ARTS). Instead the lock manager has to wait until the next request by the worker to be aborted, in order to send it the proper reply.

The tuple information structures keep information about a tuple (or group of tuples) that has been locked. This consists of the lock type, a list of workers waiting to read/write the tuple, and a list of readers or the writer with access to the tuple. The tuple information structures are statically allocated when the relation is read into memory and/or created. The first implementation of the lock manager used a linked list of these tuple information structures which was itself in a linked list. This was used for flexibility and storage efficiency. However, such an implementation resulted in seriously degraded performance. The decision was then made to go to static allocation. While static allocation results in a greater amount of wasted memory, the gain in efficiency (an order of magnitude in some cases) more than offset the slight storage inefficiency.

It is important that the modifications a worker needs to do to a relation be delayed until the worker is ready to commit, to prevent the data from being in an inconsistent state due to aborts after the state has been modified. If the modifications are written through to the stable database immediately, then a rollback mechanism would have to be invoked, in order to undo the effects of the aborted worker's actions.

In order to avoid the above situation, a local workspace is reserved for every worker, providing the basis for a *no-undo* mechanism. The local workspace is completely dynamic and grows as the worker performs modifications to the tuples. The local workspace is implemented as a linked list of structures that hold the tuples that have been modified or inserted and all the necessary information.

When the worker is ready to commit, it sends a message to the lock manager. The lock manager will respond with either an OK or an ABORT reply. In the first case, the worker will call a function that will traverse the local workspace list and write the tuples through to the stable database. In the second case, a write through is not performed and the worker sends an abort message to the client.

5. Conclusions and Future Work

A real-time database manager is one of the critical components of a real-time system. Tasks are associated with deadlines and a significant portion of the data is highly perishable, having value to the mission only if used in a timely manner. To satisfy the timing requirements, transactions must be scheduled considering both consistency and timing constraints. In addition, the system should support predictable behavior such that the possibility of missing the deadlines for critical tasks can be determined ahead of time, before the deadlines expire. Since the characteristics of a real-time database manager are distinct from conventional database managers, there are different issues to be considered. Priority-based scheduling and memory resident data are two such issues.

In this paper, we have presented an experimental database manager developed for time-constrained distributed systems. The foundation now exists for a real-time relational database manager. We have presented our experiences in implementing concurrency control algorithms appropriate for real time databases. RTDB as described in this paper with its multi-threaded server model is an appropriate research vehicle for investigating new techniques and scheduling algorithms for distributed real-time database systems.

Real time databases in general do not need all of the functionality of their non real time counterparts. For example, extensive natural join and cartesian product operations are by their very nature not very suitable to real time applications. RTDB is designed to have exceptional performance on the operations most critical to real-time database systems, namely INSERT, DELETE, UPDATE, and SELECT. Most real time database applications, such as reading and storing of sensor data, tracking and updating the location of some object etc., use only these basic commands.

We are examining the inclusion of run-time estimates for various commands within the server which will enable it to offer a choice of service to clients whose work cannot be completed in the time allotted: imprecise results or a missed deadline. Conceivably some clients might wish to simply exclude some queries which might introduce incomplete results, and terminate as quickly as possible. These execution estimates would be maintained in a table in the server and would be based on several factors such as relation file size, query type, media types involved, and current resource utilization. Properly implementing such a heuristic mechanism will require carefully controlled execution timing, and some consideration of the temporal impact of held data locks.

Future research will be in the area of concurrency control, comparing pessimistic algorithms against optimistic algorithms. The performance of these algorithms in a real system will be analyzed and compared.

References

[Abb92] Abbott, R. and H. Garcia-Molina, "Scheduling Real-Time Transactions: A Performance Evaluation, ACM Trans. on Database Systems, Sept. 1992.

[Buc89] Buchmann, A. et al., "Time-Critical Database Scheduling: A Framework for Integrating Real-Time Scheduling and Concurrency Control," Fifth Data Engineering Conference, Feb. 1989, 470-480.

[Comp91] IEEE Computer, Special Issue on Real-Time Systems, vol. 24, no. 5, May 1991.

[Grey92] Grey, J. and A. Reuter, "Transaction Processing: Concepts and Techniques," Morgan Kaufmann Publishers,1992.

[IEEE93] Tenth IEEE Workshop on Real-Time Operating Systems and Software, NewYork, New York, May 1993.

[Kor90] Korth, H., "Triggered Real-Time Databases with Consistency Constraints," 16th VLDB Conference, Brisbane, Australia, Aug. 1990.

[Lin90] Lin, Y. and S. H. Son, "Concurrency Control in Real-Time Databases by Dynamic Adjustment of Serialization Order," 11th IEEE Real-Time Systems Symposium, Orlando, Florida, Dec. 1990, to appear.

[Ozso90] Ozsoyoglu, G., et al., "CASE-DB--A Real-Time Database Management System," Tech. Rep. Case Western Reserve University, 1990.

[Sha88] Sha, L., R. Rajkumar, and J. Lehoczky, "Concurrency Control for Distributed Real-Time Databases," ACM SIGMOD Record 17, 1, Special Issue on Real-Time Database Systems, March 1988, 82-98.

[Sha91] Sha, L., R. Rajkumar, S. H. Son, and C. Chang, "A Real-Time Locking Protocol," IEEE Transactions on Computers, vol. 40, no. 7, July 1991, 793-800.

[Son88] Son, S. H., guest editor, ACM SIGMOD Record 17, 1, Special Issue on Real-Time Database Systems, March 1988.

[Son90] Son, S. H. and J. Lee, "Scheduling Real-Time Transactions in Distributed Database Systems," 7th IEEE Workshop on Real-Time Operating Systems and Software, Charlottesville, Virginia, May 1990, 39-43.

[Son92] Son, S. H., J. Lee, and Y. Lin. "Hybrid Protocols using Dynamic Adjustment of Serialization Order for Real-Time Concurrency Control," Real-Time Systems Journal, Sept. 1992, 269-276.

[Son93] Son, S. H. and S. Park. "Scheduling and Concurrency Control for Real-Time database Systems," International Symposium on Database Systems for Advanced Applications (DASFAA '93), Taejon, Korea, April 1993, 219-226.

[Ston81] Stonebraker, M., Operating System Support for Database Management, Commun. of ACM 24, 7 (July 1981), 412-418.

[Tok89] Tokuda, H. and C. Mercer, "ARTS: A Distributed Real-Time Kernel," ACM Operating System Review, 23 (3), July 1989

Object-Oriented Querying of Existing Relational Databases

Daniel A. Keim, Hans-Peter Kriegel, Andreas Miethsam

Institute for Computer Science, University of Munich
Leopoldstr. 11B, D-8000 Munich 40

Abstract: In this paper, we present algorithms which allow an object-oriented querying of existing relational databases. Our goal is to provide an improved query interface for relational systems with better query facilities than SQL. This seems to be very important since, in real world applications, relational systems are most commonly used and their dominance will remain in the near future. To overcome the drawbacks of relational systems, especially the poor query facilities of SQL, we propose a schema transformation and a query translation algorithm. The schema transformation algorithm uses additional semantic information to enhance the relational schema and transform it into a corresponding object-oriented schema. If the additional semantic information can be deducted from an underlying entity-relationship design schema, the schema transformation may be done fully automatically. To query the created object-oriented schema, we use the Structured Object Query Language (SOQL) which provides declarative query facilities on objects. SOQL queries using the created object-oriented schema are much shorter, easier to write and understand and more intuitive than corresponding SQL queries leading to an enhanced usability and an improved querying of the database. The query translation algorithm automatically translates SOQL queries into equivalent SQL queries for the original relational schema.

1 Introduction

Relational database systems are widely used in research and industry. For traditional application areas like accounting, reservation systems, etc., the relational data model seems to be adequate providing suitable modeling and performance characteristics. The main reasons for using the relational data model are: It is well known, easy to use and has a firm theoretical basis. The SQL query language, however, with its linear syntax was developed two decades ago and has not changed substantially since then. SQL has rather poor query facilities compared to the query facilities of today's object-oriented database systems. In spite of major advances in research, little has been done to improve the functionality and expressiveness of SQL. By defining the SQL2 standard [11] some of the deficiencies and inconsistencies of SQL have been removed but no major improvement of the query language has been achieved. A major problem is still the lack of an intuitive way to specify complex queries. Practical experiments with novice and experienced users show that essential and powerful concepts of SQL, such as nested queries or set operators are rarely used in a correct way [10] degrading SQL to a query language which is only useful for simple ad hoc queries. Additionally, the sometimes quite unnatural normalization of the relational data model and the missing semantic modeling capabilities make querying of relational databases even more difficult. The standardization of SQL3 [17] which shall be completed in 1996, the earliest, is aimed to improve the modelling capabilities and the query language by introducing object-oriented features. However, it is not clear how the additional features of SQL3 can be used in conjunction with existing databases.

From a practical point of view, it is very important to design query languages that allow novice and unexperienced users to query databases with little background other than some basic understanding of the schema and data. The design of graphical database interfaces is one approach to provide this kind of easy-to-use query interfaces [15]. While graphical user interfaces can greatly enhance the specification process, they can not overcome the limited capabilities of the relational model to express semantic aspects, i.e. relationships, structured entities and procedural aspects. A lot of research has been going on over the last decade to improve data models and query languages. As a result, major advances in database technology have been made, e.g. the object-oriented and extended relational database systems with their extended semantic modeling capabilities (e.g. [23], [13], [21], [16], [3]), advanced query languages (e.g. [8], [3]) and graphical user interfaces (e.g. [20], [1]). A problem, however, is the poor propagation of these systems in real world applications. Although commercial object-oriented database systems are available for some time they are rarely used in production environments. The main reason is the proliferation of relational systems. The effort and costs for migrating into a new system are very high since the application programs which have been implemented over the years and the training of users present high investments.

Our approach is a more pragmatic one and directed towards practical applications. Our starting point is the fact that, in the near future, we will be using relational systems for practical reasons; however, we need to improve the query specification process. It is possible to narrow the gap between the user's way of expressing queries and database manipulation languages like SQL without changing the system itself. Considering many examples, we found that using an object-oriented schema and query specification greatly enhances the readability and understandability of queries making it similar to the user's 'natural' view of the problem. Our idea is to automatically create an object-oriented schema from the relational one and to provide an object-oriented database query language which can be translated automatically into SQL. To query the created schema, we provide the Structured Object Query Language (SOQL), a declarative language for querying object-oriented databases. In SOQL, the user has full SQL-like access to the underlying relational database. Many object-oriented database query languages have been proposed in the literature [14], [7], [2], [22], [9], [3]. By introducing SOQL, we do not want to propose just another object-oriented query language. The main point in introducing SOQL is to define an object-oriented query language which is easy-to-use and allows to specify short and intuitively understandable queries but can be automatically translated into SQL.

At this point, we want to stress that the object-oriented schema we create is only a virtual one without having instances. The data itself completely remains in the relational system. Neither the schema transformation nor the query translation algorithm require any change to the data or the relational system. This is important since it will greatly enhance the practical applicability making our system useful for most areas where relational systems are used today.

The rest of the paper is organized as follows: Section 2 introduces the overall architecture of the system. Section 3 elaborates on the automatic transformation of relational schemas into object-oriented ones using meta information deducted from the underlying entity-relationship schema. In section 4, we introduce our Structured Object Query Language (SOQL) which provides declarative query facilities for the created object-oriented schema. In section 5, we will briefly describe the automatic query translation of SOQL into equivalent SQL queries. Section 6 summarizes our approach and points out some problems.

2 System Architecture

In this section, we want to introduce the overall architecture of our system. We designed our architecture to be used in real world environments and therefore, we had to

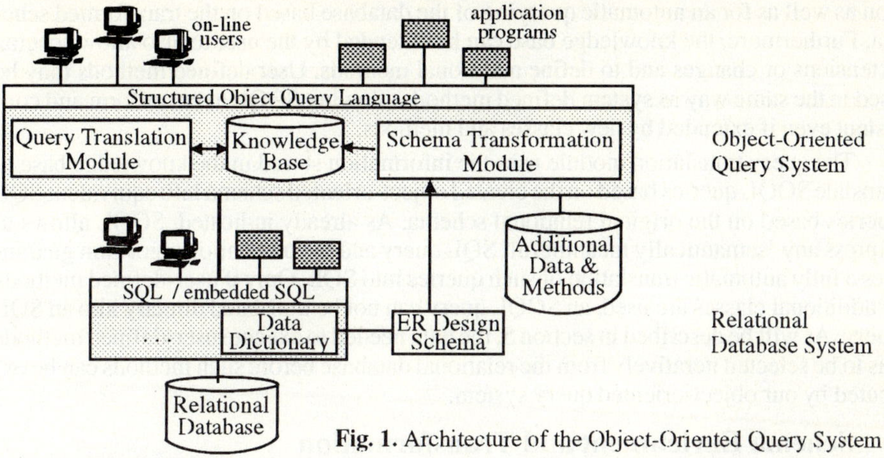

Fig. 1. Architecture of the Object-Oriented Query System

build it on top of existing relational systems like Oracle, Ingres, Sybase or others. It is important to note that, in general, such systems are used on-line with many application programs running permanently on a daily basis. In real world environments, it is important that changes of the architecture or the system do not have any impact on existing application programs because it is not feasible to rewrite them in the short- or mid-term range. Therefore, in our system we propose an additional layer which is built on top of the existing relational systems with their query language SQL (see figure 1). Our goal is to provide an advanced query interface for relational databases allowing an object-oriented querying of the database without migrating and transforming data or changing existing application programs. As shown in figure 1, in our system, pre-existing access structures remain unchanged while, at the same time, additional on-line and application program access to the database is provided by the object-oriented query system.

The main components of our system are the schema transformation module, the query translation module and the knowledge base. The schema transformation module is necessary to create an object-oriented schema from the relational schema. In general, it is not feasible to automatically create more structured and semantically richer object-oriented schemas from flat relational ones. Therefore, additional semantic information is needed, e.g. on tables implementing n-ary relationships (m:n, 1:n or 1:1), on connecting attributes implementing relationships between tables, on subtypes and so on. This additional semantic information is not modeled explicitly in the relational model but may be deducted from an underlying entity-relationship design schema. Consequently, in our schema transformation algorithm we use both, the relational schema and the entity-relationship (ER) design schema, to create the object-oriented schema. Meta information on the relational schema is usually stored in some kind of data dictionary, information about the ER schema is mostly available in the database design tool (see figure 1). Since format and access to both types of information may vary from one system to another, specific access procedures have to be implemented for the specific relational system and its design tool.

The knowledge base component is used to store all the additional semantic information deducted from the ER schema together with mapping information relating ER and relational model on one side with the object-oriented schema on the other side. The knowledge base is built during the semantic schema enrichment, the first step of the schema transformation algorithm, and provides the basis for an adequate schema transformation as well as for an automatic querying of the database based on the transformed schema. Furthermore, the knowledge base can be extended by the user to also allow schema extensions or changes and to define additional methods. User defined methods may be used in the same way as system defined methods allowing SOQL to be uniform and consistent even if extended by new classes and methods.

The query translation module uses the information stored in the knowledge base to translate SOQL queries based on the created object-oriented schema into equivalent SQL queries based on the original relational schema. As already indicated, SOQL allows to express any 'semantically meaningful' SQL query and the translation algorithm guarantees a fully automatic translation of such queries into SQL. Only if user-defined methods or additional classes are used, an SOQL query can not be translated directly into an SQL query. As will be described in section 5, the data needed to execute user-defined methods has to be selected iteratively from the relational database before such methods can be executed by our object-oriented query system.

3 Schema Enrichment and Transformation

In this section, we investigate how a relational database schema can be transformed into object-oriented class definitions. Usually a good object-oriented schema contains more semantics than a relational schema for the same application domain. If an automatic transformation process is aimed to produce adequate, well-structured object-oriented class definitions, more input than the pure relational schema is needed.

For illustrating the schema enrichment and transformation process and as a basis for the query examples in section 4, we will use the following example. Consider a relational database *FlightDB* containing information on passengers, departures, airlines, planes, planetypes and their relationships.

Passenger (pid: Integer; name: String; address: String)
Departure (did: Integer; start: Date; flight: Integer; airline-id: String; plane-id: Integer)
Pass_Dept (did: Integer; pid: Integer; booking: Date)
Airline (airline-id: String; name: String)
Plane (serial-nr: Integer; yr-built: Date; manufacturer: String; model: Integer)
Planetype (model: Integer; manufacturer: String; capacity: Integer; range: Integer)

To transform this database schema, we need additional semantic information, e.g. that *Pass_Dept* establishes an *m:n*-relationship between *Passenger* and *Departure*. Generally, we need additional semantic knowledge such as tables representing relationships (connecting tables), the type of the relationship (1:1, 1:n, n:m), attributes or groups of attributes representing foreign keys (connecting attributes), etc.

This additional semantic information is crucial for the schema transformation process to be able to replace connecting attributes and connecting tables by direct object references. Very often the domain of interest is formalized using an entity-relationship (ER) model [4]. The ER model contains the semantic information needed for our schema enrichment. If there is a formalized and standardized semantic design model together with an also standardized mapping which entity and which relationship lead to which table, a fully automatic schema enrichment is possible. If no standard ER model and no standardized mapping is available, support by the designer or administrator of the database will be necessary. In any case, part of the additional semantic information can be automatically deducted [6], [19], [18] and the user may be guided in the process of relating the ER design schema to the relational schema.

In the following, we assume that we are able to extract an ER model from the given relational schema with the following properties: Each entity E in the ER model corresponds to a table E in the relational schema, for each functional relationship R: E $\rightarrow$ F table E contains the (foreign) key of F, all other relationships R correspond to a table R connecting the respective 'entity' tables. This corresponds to the normal transformation when creating a relational schema from an ER design schema. In the following, we formally describe the transformation of the ER schema into an object-oriented schema:

1. for each entity E with attributes A_i of domain D_i, i=1,...,n and key K(E)
   $\Rightarrow$ **Class** E **with attributes** A_1:D_1; ...; A_n:D_n; **key is** (A_1, ..., A_m); **end**; is created.
2. for each functional relationship R: E $\rightarrow$ F
   $\Rightarrow$ class E is extended by a method R: $\rightarrow$ F, which applied to an object e of class E yields the corresponding object f of class F: e.R = f.
   $\Rightarrow$ class F is extended by a method R: $\rightarrow$ Set(E), which applied to an object f of class F yields the corresponding set of objects $\{e_1, ..., e_n\}$ of class E: f.R = $\{e_1, ..., e_n\}$.
3. for all other relationships R between entities E_1, ..., E_p, with possible relationship attributes A_k of domain D_k, k=1,...,q
   $\Rightarrow$ class E_i is extended by the following q+1 methods:
   - R: $\rightarrow$ Set(E_1 x $\cdots$ x E_{i-1} x E_{i+1} x $\cdots$ x E_n), which applied to an object e_i of class E_i yields the corresponding object tuples, e_i is in R-relationship with: e_i.R = $\{(\bar{e}_i)$ | R-relationship holds for $(e_1, ..., e_n)\}$, where $\bar{e}_i$ denotes the tuple $(e_1, ..., e_{i-1}, e_{i+1}, ..., e_n)$.
   - A_k: E_1 x $\cdots$ x E_{i-1} x E_{i+1} x $\cdots$ x E_n $\rightarrow$ D_k, which applied to an object e_i of class E_i and object tuple $\bar{e}_i$ as parameter yields the k-th attribute $a_k \in D_k$ of this relationship: $e_i.A_k(\bar{e}_i) = a_k$.

   Example: Let p be an object of class Passenger and d_1, ..., d_n be its departures, where p booked departure d_2 at January 1st, 1993. Then p.departures = $\{d_1, ..., d_n\}$ and, p.booking(d_2) = '01/01/93' (see also class definitions below).

Together with the creation of the object oriented schema, mapping information is stored in the knowledge base, relating classes and tables which originate at the same entity. Furthermore, each method reflecting a relationship of the ER schema is related to the corresponding connecting attributes and, if existing, connecting tables of the relational schema. We establish the mapping at class creation time by automatically linking each new class definition to its corresponding relational table. Having the mapping information, we can determine which table corresponds to which class and whether a given class attribute has to be translated to a join on the relational side. This mapping is needed for the automatic translation of queries on the object-oriented schema.

Let us now consider the schema transformation of our example database. There we have functional relationships between Plane and Planetype and between Plane and Departure and a connecting table Pass_Dept connecting Passenger and Departure, which has an attribute specifying the date of booking. The schema transformation algorithm described above will produce the class definitions given in figure 2 which represent the semantically enriched object-oriented schema.

At this point, it should be mentioned that our schema transformation may not provide a perfect object-oriented schema. There are additional possibilities e.g. identifying subtype relationships within the relational schema [18], using the aggregation paradigm of the object-oriented system more extensively[5] and so on [12]. But as it will be shown in section 4 and section 5, the schema created by our schema transformation allows to state SOQL queries which are often significantly shorter and more intuitive than corresponding SQL queries using the original tables. At this point, let us emphasize that we only generate class definitions in the object-oriented database system, whereas the instances remain in the relational database. Thus, access operations to instances of object-oriented classes have to be translated into accesses to the corresponding relational tuples which will be described in section 5.

Class** Passenger **with
***attributes** pid: Integer;*
name: String;
address: String; key is (pid);
***methods** departures: → Set (Departure);*
*booking: Departure → Date; **end;***

Class** Departure **with
***attributes** did: Integer;*
start: Date;
flight: Integer; key is (did);
***methods** airline: → Airline;*
plane: → Plane;
passengers: → Set (Passenger);
*booking: Passenger → Date; **end;***

Class** Planetype **with
***attributes** model: Integer;*
manufacturer: String;
capacity: Integer;
range: Integer; key is (model);
methods** planes: → Set (Plane); **end;

Class** Plane **with
***attributes** serial-nr: Integer;*
yr-built: Date; key is (serial-nr);
***methods** departures: → Set (Departure);*
*planetype: → Planetype; **end;***

Class** Airline **with
***attributes** airline-id: String;*
name: String; key is (airline-id);
methods** departures: → Set (Departure); **end;

Fig. 2. Object-Oriented Schema

4 Structured Object Query Language

In this section, we will give a short overview of our query language SOQL. SOQL is a declarative query language for querying the created object-oriented schema. It is similar to other declarative query languages for object-oriented database systems such as O_2SQL [3], OSQL [7] and Object SQL [9]. In addition to features available in these object-oriented database query languages, SOQL provides concepts which greatly enhance the query specification process making it more intuitive. The main point, however, in introducing SOQL is to present an object-oriented database query language which can be translated automatically into SQL (c.f. section 5).

4.1 The Query Language

As already indicated by the name, SOQL is similar to SQL. SOQL provides declarative query facilities for objects as SQL does for relations. The basic query format can be indicated by the following description

select {<range_var>{.<method>}* {.struct_expr}$^{0/1}$ }$^+$
for each {<classname>{.<method>}* <range_var>}$^+$
{ where <condition> }$^{0/1}$.

In the 'select' clause, the user has to specify the desired output of the query. According to the expression in the 'select' clause, automatically a new (temporary) object class is created. As a result of the query, all tuples fulfilling the condition are available as virtual instances of this class. The result is also available as a (nested) set and, therefore, can be directly used in subqueries. To allow an easier specification of queries with structured results, we introduce the notion of 'structured expressions'. Structured expressions extend the select-clause by providing the possibility to define the structure of the desired result which is indicated by square brackets. As we will show later in the examples, structured expressions do not only help to structure the result but may also help to avoid joins. Since structured expressions are a unique feature of SOQL, we give the exact syntax definition in the following

struct_expr ::= [{<struct_expr>}$^+$] | [{<method>}{.<method>}* {.struct_expr}$^{0/1}$] |
[<range_var>{.<method>}* {.struct_expr}$^{0/1}$]

The 'for each' clause is similar to the 'from' clause in SQL. It is necessary to define and type the class variables used in a query. The 'for each' indicates that the condition is checked for each instance of the corresponding class and in the case, an instance fulfills the condition, the desired output is created. In the 'where' clause, a condition may be specified. The condition is an expression with result type 'Boolean'. All methods, including the created access methods to attributes, may be used in the condition as long as the result of the whole expression is of type Boolean. As already mentioned, the result of a subquery may also be considered as a set. Therefore, set operations can be used to specify nested SOQL queries.

As most object-oriented systems, our system provides a set of basic object classes (*Boolean, String, Numbers, Integer, Real* and the generic classes *Set* and *List*) together with a set of basic methods. Special methods are defined for Set(Numbers) including the aggregate operations *sum, avg, min, max* (Set(Numbers) → Numbers). As already mentioned, the user may extend the system provided set of methods by additional ones. Such user-defined methods may be used in the same way as system defined methods allowing SOQL to be uniform and consistent even if it is extended by new classes and methods. In the case of user-defined methods, however, there is no automatic translation to a single SQL query based on the underlying relational database (c.f. section 5).

As indicated in the query format definition, methods are applied to class or range variables using dot-notation. For convenience, the standard infix notation is allowed for the predefined methods of the basic classes. Chains of methods may be connected in dot-notation, which allows to directly access one object class from another one without explicitly joining them. It is some kind of schema navigation in the created object-oriented schema. An advantage of the dot-notation compared to database query languages like OSQL or O_2SQL is that our queries are structured in the way the user is thinking and, therefore, they are easier to write and understand. A problem of our approach, however, is that complex methods may have many arguments which may result in queries that are hard to read. In the case of creating the object-oriented from the relational schema, most access functions do not have any argument except their class and, therefore, the problem only occurs in the rare cases of methods deducted from relationship attributes or user-defined methods.

To further illustrate the possibilities of our query language, in the following we will give some examples for SOQL queries. We will show the advantages of SOQL over SQL by comparing SOQL queries based on the created object-oriented schema with equivalent SQL queries using the original schema. For the example queries, we use the transformed example database as presented in section 3. A simple query selecting all flight numbers with a list of the corresponding passenger names for the airline "Lufthansa" on the 02/18/93 would be expressed as

Example 1: select D.flight D.passengers.name for each Departure D
where D.start = "02/18/93" and D.airline.name = "Lufthansa"

Note, that the result of the query is of the complex type Set([Integer, Set(String)]). To store the result, a temporary class with two attributes of type Integer and Set(String) is created. The nested structure of the result is a consequence of using the generalization of the dot-notation to sets. Since 'D.passengers' provides a 'Set(Passenger)' for each departure, the method 'name' is not applicable since it is only defined for objects of class 'Passenger'. The generalization of the dot-notation to sets, however, allows methods which are defined for a class O to be also used with Set(O). As a consequence, the method name in our example can also be used with 'Set(Passenger)' providing a set of passenger names for each departure. 'D.passengers.name' is equivalent to $\{x.name \mid x \in D.passengers\}$. The generalization of the dot-notation to sets will be described formally in the next subsection. In the relational system, even for the simple query example 1, four tables need to be joined in order to execute the query. An equivalent SQL query is given as the result of the query translation algorithm in section 5.

Another simple query would be to find all passengers who have at least one flight together with a passenger named "Andy Meier". In SOQL, we can write

Example 2:
```
select P for each Passenger P
where "Andy Meier" in P.departures.passengers.name
```

In this query, again we use the generalization of the dot-notation to sets. The result of P.departures. passengers.name is a set of sets of strings. The method 'in' with parameter "Andy Meier", however, requires a set of strings since it is only defined for O x Set(O) → Boolean and not for O x Set(Set(O)) → Boolean. According to the generalization of the dot-notation, we shift the method 'in' into the inner brackets until it is applicable for the first time. In the example, instead of ' "Andy Meier" in P.departures.passengers.name ', we execute { "Andy Meier" in {x.name | x ∈ d.passengers} | d ∈ P.departures} resulting in a set of booleans. Like in IRIS [7], sets of booleans in conditions are implicitly 'or'-connected providing true if at least one element is true.

While the SOQL query is still intuitive and easy to understand, corresponding SQL queries are quite difficult to read and to write. A corresponding SQL queries requires a join of at least four tables with the need to know the connecting tables and attributes

```
select distinct P.name, P.address from Passenger P, Pass_Dept PD
where P.pid = PD.pid and PD.did in
      select PD1.did from Passenger P1 Pass_Dept PD1
      where P1.pid = PD1.pid and P1.name = "Andy Meier"
```

The next query is an example of a nested query. If we want to select name and address of all passengers which have flown with all types of planes, we may use the query

Example 3:
```
select P.name P.address for each Passenger P
where P.departures.plane.planetype contains (select PT for each Planetype PT)
```

This query may be expressed in SQL as follows

```
select distinct P.name, P.address
from Passenger P
where not exists
      (select * from Planetype PT
       where not exists
             (select * from Pass_Dept PD, Departure D, Plane PL
              where P.pid = PD.pid and PD.did = D.did and
              D.plane-id = PL.serial-nr and PL.model = PT.model))
```

Another interesting query is to determine the seat utilization of all "Lufthansa" flights. The following SOQL query provides the desired result

Example 4:
```
select (D.plane.planetype.capacity - D.passengers.count) for each Departure D
where D.airline.name = "Lufthansa"
```

A corresponding SQL query is far more complicated. One possibility is

```
select D.dno, (PT.capacity - count(PD.pid))
from Departure D, Pass_Dept PD, Plane PL, Planetype PT, Airline A
where A.name = "Lufthansa" and A.aid = D.airline-id and D.did = PD.did
              and D.plane-id = PL.serial-nr and PL.model = PT.model
group by D.dno, PT.capacity
```

Note, that in the SQL query we have to select more information than actually required. We need the additional information to do the grouping which is only implicit in the SOQL query. In general, if the result for a query is a nested set with more than one nesting level, there is no one-to-one translation to an SQL query. Nested results may occur as answer for queries with structured expressions or queries where the generalization of the dot-notation is used more than once in a row.

Our last example is such an SOQL query with a nested structured expression. To select the names of all passengers who have Andy as part of their name together with all their flights as well as name and address of all co-passengers we can write in SOQL

Example 5: select P.[name, departures.[flight, date, passengers.[name, address]]]
for each Passenger P
where P.name.substring("Andy")

Since, in this case, the result has more than one nesting level, there is no possibility to express the query in SQL. As we will show in section 5, in such cases we translate the SOQL query into an SQL query which provides a superset of the data necessary to answer the query.

To summarize the advantages of SOQL over SQL: SOQL queries are much shorter, easier to write and understand and more intuitive than corresponding SQL queries. Since the created class definitions are more structured, in most cases, joins do not have to be specified explicitly and complex queries are avoided. Additionally, the results of SOQL queries can be arbitrarily structured and user-defined methods may be used like system-provided ones. In general, we believe that the created object-oriented schema together with the SOQL query language are closer to the users view of the application domain which leads to an enhanced usability and an improved querying of the database.

4.2 Semantic Issues

Before presenting the automatic query translation algorithm (c.f. section 5), in this subsection we first need to formally describe the semantics of special features of SOQL, particularly of the generalization of the dot-notation and of structured expressions.

The semantics of the 'select' clause is straightforward as long as only the system created access methods for attributes are used. For all other methods, we have to apply the method to all instances fulfilling the condition. More exactly, a query

select $a_1.op_1, ..., a_n.op_n$ for each ... with $op_i \in$ *Object-Class*(a_i) for i=1..n

results in a set of objects $(a_1.op_1, ..., a_n.op_n)$. Even in the case of having chains of methods connected in dot-notation, there is no problem as long as the methods are defined for the class to which they are applied. We found, however, that this condition is quite restrictive for practical purposes and leads to queries which are more complex than necessary. Often, it seems to be intuitive to apply methods of a class O to sets of that class (Set(O)) or even to $Set^i(O)$. Therefore, we relax the condition by generalizing the dot-notation to sets. If, for example, a method is applied to objects of class $Set^n(O)$, but is not defined within this class, we try to apply the method to each member of the outmost set. If the method is not defined for $Set^{n-1}(O)$, we try to apply the method to each member of this set and so on until the method is defined for one level. Formally the generalization of the dot-notation is defined recursively

$$m(Set^i(O)) := \{m(obj) \mid obj \in Set^{i-1}(O)\}.$$

This step is repeated as long as the method m is not applicable to $Set^i(O)$. Using this recursive definition the nesting structure of the whole expression is preserved.

The semantics of structured expressions is that all attributes on the same nesting level are related to each other if possible. As we have shown in the previous subsection, structured expressions do not only help to intuitively specify structured results, but also to avoid complicated join conditions. More formally, the semantics of a structured expression can be described as follows: Let $O.[m_1, ..., m_n]$ be a structured expression. If there is no m_i which is applicable to O and O is an object of set type, we generate the set $\{obj.[m_1, ..., m_n] \mid obj \in O\}$. This step is repeated as long as obj itself is a set and no m_i is applicable. If an m_i is applicable at the level described in the above structured expression, the final result is $\{(obj.m_1, ..., obj.m_n) \mid obj \in O\}$. According to this definition, the result type for the query in example 5 can be described as { (String, { (Integer, Date, { (String, String)}) })}. The above definition for resolving structured expressions and method applications may be used for arbitrary structured expressions.

5 Translation of SOQL Queries

This section describes the translation of SOQL queries into SQL queries and the restructuring of the result according to the complex answer type given by the SOQL select clause. It is obvious that all queries expressed in SQL over the relational schema can also be expressed by an SOQL query over the created object oriented schema, since information is added during the schema enrichment and transformation process and SOQL has more expressive power than SQL. By providing a translation *t*, we show constructively how an SOQL query Q is translated into an SQL query S = *t* (Q). The result of S may be formatted by a function *f* into the desired answer format specified by Q, where *f* basically consists of sorting and projection operations.

The main task of *t* is to resolve chains of method applications by adequate joins and subqueries on the relational side and to correctly replace the SOQL condition part by equivalent SQL constructs. In the following, we describe the translation *t* of a given SOQL-statement Q into an SQL-statement S and illustrate this process using Example 1 from section 4.1. We assume that all class variables occurring in the 'for each' clause of the query and its subqueries have pairwise distinct names; otherwise, they will be consistently renamed. New variables introduced during the transformation are denoted by V_i.

1. First, the SOQL-statement Q is transformed into a nested set expression by evaluating the chains of method applications and structured expressions as described in section 4.2. The result is an equivalent (same result) specification of the query Q, with resolved dot generalizations and resolved structured expressions.

$$\{(D.flight, D.passengers.name) \mid D \in Departure \wedge D.start = \text{“02/18/93”} \wedge D.airline.name = \text{“Lufthansa”}\} \equiv \{(D.flight, \{V_1.name \mid V_1 \in D.passengers\}) \mid D \in Departure \wedge D.start = \text{“02/18/93”} \wedge \exists V_2: V_2 = D.airline \wedge V_2.name = \text{“Lufthansa”}\}$$

2. The remaining object references are resolved in the following way: V_i *op* X.m => $V_i \in$ Type(X.m) $\wedge$ join(X, V_i), where *op* stands for '$\in$' or '=' depending on whether X.m is set or single valued. In this step, join predicates join(X, V_i) are introduced with the intended meaning: join(X, V_i) = True, if there is an object reference from the current instance of X to V_i.

$$\{(D.flight, \{V_1.name \mid V_1 \in Passenger \wedge join(D, V_1)\}) \mid \exists V_2: D \in Departure \wedge D.start = \text{“02/18/93”} \wedge V_2 \in Airline \wedge join(D, V_2) \wedge V_2.name = \text{“Lufthansa”}\}$$

3. Then, the nesting of result tuples is resolved by shifting set conditions onto the outer level and adding object identity / key information until the result tuple is flat. The structure of the result will be flattened by this transformation but can be easily reconstructed using the additional key attributes.

$$\{(D.flight, D.key, V_1.name) \mid \exists V_2: V_1 \in Passenger \wedge join(D, V_1) \wedge D \in Departure \wedge D.start = \text{“02/18/93”} \wedge V_2 \in Airline \wedge join(D, V_2) \wedge V_2.name = \text{“Lufthansa”}\}$$

4. In the next step, we transform the above tuple-calculus-like expression into an SQL statement. The attributes to be specified in the 'select' clause can be directly taken from the result part of the expression. All parts 'X $\in$ Class' of the condition are transformed into the 'from' clause. If one of these variables is existentially quantified, the 'select' clause is extended by 'X.key' for all variables occurring in the 'select' clause

and the key word 'distinct' is added to remove duplicates which are not intended. The remaining condition part has to be transformed into a permissible SQL condition. The methods on set types such as 'el in set', 'isempty(set)', 'set1 contains set2' are replaced by computing these sets in a subquery and applying the SQL constructs 'el = some (select ...)', 'exists(select ...)', 'not exists(select ... where not exists (select ...))'.

select distinct D.flight, D.key, V_1.name, V_1.key
from Departure D, Passenger V_1, Airline V_2
where join(D, V_2) and join(D, V_1) and D.start = "02/18/93" and V_2.name = "Lufthansa"

5. The join predicates join(R, S) and key expressions S.key are replaced according to the mapping information.

select distinct D.flight, D.did, V_1.name, V_1.pid
from Departure D, Passenger V_1, Airline V_2, Pass_Dept V3
where D.airline-id = V_2.airline-id and D.did = V3.did and V3.pid = V_1.pid and
D.start = "02/18/93" and V_2.name = "Lufthansa"

This is the final SQL statement to be executed on the relational database. The formatting function *f* has to sort the result by D.did and then eliminate D.did and V_1.pid.

Since SOQL has more expressive power than SQL, there are some cases where SOQL queries do not have corresponding SQL queries. Problems in the process of query translation may occur e.g. if set operations are used in conjunction with structured tuples or nested sets in the 'where' clause, if variables in the 'for each' clause range over nested sets and, as already mentioned, if user extensions (e.g. additional attributes or user-defined methods) are used in a query. In general, for such SOQL queries there is no translation to a single SQL query. Note, that the problems are only caused in cases where, in general, there is no corresponding SQL query. The details of the query translation algorithm are beyond the scope of this paper and will be presented in a future paper.

6 Summary and Conclusions

Relational database systems are widely used in research and industry. A major problem of relational systems are the poor query facilities of SQL. In this paper, we described a system which enhances the functionality and usability of existing relational databases and allows to query them like object-oriented databases. Using additional information deduced from the underlying ER schema, we automatically create a semantically enriched object-oriented schema together with the necessary mapping information relating object-oriented and relational schema. Our query language SOQL provides a uniform and convenient query interface to the database which, in addition, is easily extensible. The presented query translation algorithm is performing the automatic translation of SOQL queries into equivalent SQL queries for the original relational schema. We believe that our approach is simple, elegant and of high practical importance. We do not require any change to the relational system, the data or existing applications and therefore, systems like ours may be used in practice within a short period of time.

In our current implementation, we use the object-oriented database system O_2 as the basis for the additional layer. In O_2, we store the necessary semantic information as well as additional classes, methods and data. The created object-oriented schema is also available as O_2-schema. The implementation of the schema transformation and operation translation algorithms with complete support of user-defined methods and additional classes is currently on the way, but not yet finished. One open problem is the optimization of queries which involve user extensions to the schema or arbitrarily structured results. In such SOQL queries which have no one-to-one correspondence to an SQL query, the query optimization cannot be done on the relational side. Therefore, we have to optimize the query execution plan to reduce the amount of data which needs to be transferred between our and the relational system. Performance issues will be of high importance for such a system to be used in real world applications.

In our future work, we plan to extend the schema enrichment and query translation algorithms to cover the automatic detection and creation of subtype hierarchies or complex methods. We will further work on the optimization issue trying to provide an acceptable performance even in complicated cases. Finally, we intend to use our system as a basis for an advanced integration of relational systems into a heterogeneous multidatabase system and we plan to integrate the system itself into a network of interoperating databases.

References

[1] Agrawal R. et al.: *'OdeView: The Graphical Interface to Ode'*, Proc. ACM-SIGMOD Int. Conf. on Management of Data, Atlantic City, 1990.

[2] Alashqur A.M., Su S.Y., Lam H.: *'OQL: A Query Language for Manipulating Object-oriented Databases'*, Proc. 5th Int. Conf. on Very Large Data Bases, Amsterdam, 1989, pp. 433-442.

[3] Bancilhon F., Delobel C, Kanellakis P. (editors): *'Building an Object-Oriented Database System - The Story of O_2'*, Morgan Kaufmann, San Mateo, CA, 1992.

[4] Chen P.P.-S.: *'The Entity-Relationship Model - Toward a Unified View of Data'*, Proc. ACM Trans. on Database Systems, Vol. 1, No. 1, 1976.

[5] Castellanos M., Saltor F.: *'Semantic Enrichment of Database Schemas: An Object Oriented Approach'*, Proc. 1st Int. Workshop on Interoperability in Multidatabase Systems, Kyoto, 1991, pp. 71-78.

[6] Davis, Arora: *'Converting a Relational Database Model into an Entity-Relationship Model'*, Proc. 6th ER Conf., New York, 1987.

[7] Fishman D.H. et al: *'Overview of the Iris DBMS'*, chapter 10 in: *Object-Oriented Concepts, Databases and Applications* by Kim W. and Lochovsky F.H. (editors), ACM Press Frontier Series, Addison Wesley, Reading, MA, 1989, pp. 219-250.

[8] Haas L.M., Freytag J.C., Lohman G.M., Pirahesh H.: *'Extensible Query Processing in Starburst'*, Proc. ACM-SIGMOD Int. Conf. on Management of Data, 1989, pp. 377-388.

[9] Harris C., Duhl J.: *'Object SQL'*, chapter 11 in: *Object-Oriented Databases with Applications to CASE, Networks, and VLSI Design* by Gupta H. and Horowitz E., Prentice Hall, 1991, pp. 199-215.

[10] Hansen G.W., Hansen J.V.: *'Human Performance in Relational Algebra, Tuple Calculus and Domain Calculus'*, Int. Journal of Man-Machine Studies, Vol. 29, 1988, pp. 503-516.

[11] ISO/IEC: *'Database Language SQL'*, ISO/IEC 9075:1992 (German Standardization: DIN 66315).

[12] Kaul M., Drosten K., Neuhold E.J.: *'ViewSystem: Integrating Heterogeneous Information Bases by Object-Oriented Views'*, Proc. IEEE Int. Conf. on Data Engineering, 1990.

[13] Kim W., Ballou N., Chou H.-T., Garza J.F., Woelk D.: *'Features of the ORION Object-Oriented Database System'*, chapter 11 in: *Object-Oriented Concepts, Databases and Applications* by Kim W. and Lochovsky F.H. (editors), ACM Press Frontier Series, Addison Wesley, MA, 1989, pp. 251-282

[14] Kim W.: *'A Model of Queries for Object-Oriented Databases'*, Proc. 5th Int. Conf. on Very Large Data Bases, Amsterdam, 1989, pp. 423-432.

[15] Keim D.A., Lum V.: *'Visual Query Specification in a Multimedia Database System'*, Proc. Conf. Visualization, CS Press, Los Alamitos, CA., 1992.

[16] Lohman G.M., Lindsay B., Pirahesh H., Schiefer K.B.: *'Extensions to Starburst: Objects, Types, Functions and Rules'*, Comm. of the ACM, Vol. 34, No. 10, 1991, pp. 94-109.

[17] Melton J. (editor): *'Database Language SQL (SQL3)'*, ISO/ANSI working draft, X3H2-92-055 DBL CNB-003, July 1992.

[18] Markowitz V., Makowsky J.: *'Identifying Extended Entity-Relationship Object Structures in Relational Schemas'*, IEEE Tran. on Software Engineering, Vol. 16, No. 8, 1990.

[19] Navathe S., Awong: *'Abstracting Relational and Hierarchical Data with a Semantic Data Model'*, Proc. 6th ER Conf., New York, 1987.

[20] Rogers T.R. , Cattell R.G.G.: *' Entity-Relationship Database User Interfaces'*, in: Readings in Database Systems, ed. M. Stonebraker, 1988.

[21] Rowe L.A., Stonebraker M.R.: *'The POSTGRES Data Model'*, in: *Readings in Object-Oriented Database Systems* by Zdonik S.B. and Maier D., Morgan Kaufmann, CA., 1990, pp. 461-473.

[22] Servio Logic Development Corporation: *'Gemstone V2.0: Programming in OPAL'*, 1990.

[23] Shipman D.W.: *'The Functional Data Model and the Data Language DAPLEX'*, ACM Trans. on Database Systems, Vol. 6, 1981, pp. 140-173.

A Probabilistic Spatial Data Model *

Yoram Kornatzky   Solomon Eyal Shimony
Dept. of Mathematics and Computer Science
Ben-Gurion University of the Negev
P.O.B. 653, Beer-Sheva 84105, Israel
{yoramk,shimony}@bengus.bgu.ac.il

Abstract

Spatial information in autonomous robot tasks is uncertain due to measurement errors, the dynamic nature of the world, and an incompletely known environment. We present a probabilistic spatial data model capable of describing relevant spatial data, such as object location, shape, composition, and other parameters, in the presence of uncertainty. Uncertain spatial information is modeled through continuous probability distributions on values of attributes. The data model is designed to support our visual tracking and navigation prototype.

1 Introduction

Consider a robot operating in a real-world scenario. In order to perform anything useful, the robot must perceive the environment, plan and perform courses of action. This involves the tasks of navigation, tracking the location of objects in the environment, and other similar tasks. All these tasks require an explicit spatial model of the environment. Due to measurement errors, the uncertain dynamic nature of the world, and unknown terrain, an explicit way of dealing with uncertainty is necessary. We have developed a probabilistic spatial data model for representing such uncertain spatial information used in robot tasks. The data model describes uncertain spatial information through continuous probability distributions of spatial attributes such as object location and parameters of transformations. More generally, we allow any kind of attribute to be uncertain in which case its value is a probability distribution over the set of possible values. In most practical cases such distributions are finitely represented (e.g. by their expected value and covariance), and can be efficiently manipulated. Before describing our data model in detail, we motivate its development by presenting our application, a visual tracking and navigation prototype.

*This work is partially supported by the Paul Ivanier Center for Robotics and Production Management, Ben-Gurion University.

1.1 A Visual Tracking and Navigation Prototype

Our scenario is an office space, where most items can be approximated in a concise way with 3D models. To navigate in the environment the robot has to track the location of objects, which requires real-time efficient algorithms for calculating the pose of objects and the mapping of free-space (e.g. [5, 11]). Many existing algorithms benefit from prediction of the identity and locations of expected image features, available from models of the environment and previous images [9]. Prediction of features together with their expected quality is useful in two respects. First, it allows a-priori weighing of the quality of the features and their correlation, for use in maximum likelihood filtering schemes, such as Kalman filters (KF) or least squares (LS) approximations. Second, by predicting and looking for good features first, we can save much computation time [9]: estimating the probability of detection of a feature is useful for deciding whether trying to detect the feature is worthwhile.

An explicit 3D model of the environment that allows for limited positional and model parameter error, is used. Features are predicted, ranked according to merit, and searched for in the image locations where they are most likely to appear. Model position and parameters are then updated according to a probabilistic maximum likelihood scheme, such as Kalman filtering. The size and complexity of the world model required to describe the environment in detail motivated us to develop an object-oriented database for its representation. We intend the database to provide the basic functionality of filtering objects using size, rough location, and aggregation hierarchy information, in order to facilitate feature prediction in our robot tracking application.

1.2 The Probabilistic Data Model

Most information incorporated in the data model is known only incompletely and is subject to imprecision. Thus, values of attributes such as object location in the world, or parameters of transformations, are only estimated subject to errors. This uncertainty translates into uncertainty wrt the presence and location of features sensed by the robot's sensors. Thus, a spatial data model supporting our application has to incorporate mechanisms for representing uncertain spatial information. For example, the location attribute of an object, which is a 3D coordinate (i.e. a value in $\Re^3$), is estimated with a certain error, and hence should be represented as a probabilistic distribution over $\Re^3$. More generally, uncertain spatial information such as parameters of pose, scaling and distortion are often described as a probabilistic distribution over the values of simple attributes (e.g. real numbers), or random vectors of such attributes. Accordingly, we introduce different kinds of probability distributions as classes in our object-oriented data model, and represent uncertain spatial information using these classes. More generally, we allow any kind of attribute to be uncertain in which case its value is a probability distribution over the set of possible values.

Existence of objects in a scene is also uncertain due to imprecision of the sensing system in identifying objects from the world model in sensor images, and ascertaining the existence of particular spatial relations between objects, e.g. occlusion of image features. Such uncertain information is modeled by special *existence* attributes giving the probability of their existence. The data model is being implemented on top of the *Ode* [1] object-oriented database management system.

The rest of the paper is organized as follows: Section 2 briefly describes the object-oriented aspects of our data model. Modeling spatial information of the world model is described in section 3. The mechanisms for describing uncertainty of information within the data model are presented in section 4. Representation and manipulation of uncertain spatial information is discussed in section 5. Related work is discussed in section 6.

2 An Object-Oriented Data Model

In this section we describe the object-oriented aspects of our data model that are needed throughout the paper. These are standard and similar to the Ode [1] object-oriented data model, and we describe them briefly through examples.

The data model includes *values* and *objects*. A *value* has a *type*. This type is recursively definable from atomic types and type constructors. An object has an *identity*, a value (its state), and a behavior defined by its *methods*. It belongs to a class.

Types and Values. We assume a standard set of atomic types such as boolean, integer, and real. Complex types may be defined recursively using the *tuple* [ ], *list* $< \ >$, *array*, and *set* { } constructors. For each type, its *domain* is the set of possible values of the type. An example of a complex type is:

$$\textbf{type}\ desk\ :\ [location : 3DCoord,\ surface : Surface,\ color : Color,\ texture : Texture,\ legs : <Leg>,\ csg\_tree : CSG]$$

Classes and Objects. A class is defined by its *type* and its *methods*. An example of a class is:

class $OfficeObject$
type $[csg\_tree : CSG,\ location : 3DCoord,\ parts : set(WorldObject)]$
method $predict\_features(angle : real,\ region : ImageRegion) : \{Feature\},$
$projection(w : Window) : ImageRegion$

Each object that belongs to a class is called an instance of the class, and the set of instances of a class is called its *extent*. The extent of a class changes dynamically as new objects are being created or destroyed. When invoked in the scope of an object on a tuple of arguments, a method returns an answer and (possibly) changes the internal state of that object. For example, applying the *projection* method to a desk object wrt a window, returns an image region as a result: $region23\ :=\ desk45.projection(window1)$.

Inheritance. A class may inherit its type and methods from other classes. Such inheritance declarations generate an inheritance hierarchy over the classes. An inherited type or method can be redefined locally, as long as this redefinition respects the *subtyping* semantics. An example is:

class *WorldObject*
  type [*name* : *string*, *csg_tree* : *CSG*, *location* : *3DCoord*,
    texture : *Texture*, *parts* :< *PolyhedralObject* >]
  method *predict_features*(*angle* : *real*, *region* : *ImageRegion*) : {*Feature*}
class *desk* **inherit** *WorldObject*
  rename *parts* **as** *legs*
  type [*location* : *OfficeCoord*, *surface* : *Surface*, *color* : *Color*]

3 Spatial Aspects of the Data Model

Systems that need to perform some kind of spatial reasoning, such as our visual tracking system, require a description of the geometric properties of objects in the world model, and their predicted image features. This motivates incorporating built-in classes with associated methods for describing geometric information, such as location, size, transformations between coordinate systems, and constructive solid geometry (CSG) representations. Other classes define image features: corners, edges, and texture, and relationships between features like being collinear. The aggregation hierarchy, defining the logical composition of a complex world object from its parts, is built using the type constructors. Correspondingly, the geometric description of a complex object, such as its CSG tree, is defined as a refinement of this aggregation hierarchy. Similarly, we describe the position of parts of objects relative to their containing structure.

3.1 Geometric Models

We opt for several kinds of geometric models, which are known in the computer graphics and vision literature. These include enhanced CSG representations, extents, and generic models [2, 10]. Their representation using our powerful data model is straightforward so we omit their description here, and demonstrate them through examples. A CSG representation is constructed from primitive objects using union, intersection and similar operations, and described as a tree whose leaves are the primitive objects and whose internal nodes are the operations.

A generic model [10] is represented as a class where constraints between objects, such as the sides of the door being parallel, are implemented through methods. Computed constraints whose parameters are determined from the parameters of the objects related through the constraint, such as the angle between planes computed from their sizes, are similarly implemented through methods of the constraint class.

Example 1: A generic model of a building [10] includes a hallway that consists of two walls, where each wall contains a set of doors and a set of windows. The hallway and wall classes are:

class *Hallway* **inherit** *Building*
type [*name* : *string*, *side*1, *side*2 : *Wall*, *floor* : *plane*]
class *Wall* **inherit** *Planar_surface*
type [*location* : 3*DCoord*, *length* : *real*, *doors* : {*Door*}, *windows* : {*Window*}] □

Articulated models built from several rigid parts with constraints on their relative motion are represented using the type constructors for building a complex value, and associating appropriate transformations and constraints (that are function values) with these parts. The transformation is assumed to be of their coordinate system wrt the coordinate system of their aggregation-hierarchy parent, or any other coordinate system. Such transformation are 6-vectors, with 3 parameters for translation and 3 for rotation. Constraints exist between the transformations of the subparts, as well as their parameters. Note that there may be more that one parametrization for an object type. For example, 2D lines can be represented either by the parameters (a, b) of the line equation $y = ax + b$, or by distance from the coordinate system origin and a slope angle, etc.
Example 2: Consider a desk that has a part representing its top surface. It is represented in the data model as:

class 3*DCoord*
type [X, Y, Z : *real*]
class *Desk*
type [*position* : 3*DCoord*, *surface* : *ObjectSurface*,
legs : [*elements* :< [*leg* : *PolyhedralObject*, *position* : 3*DCoord*] >,
constraint_legs :< 3*DCoord* > → *boolean*))
class *ObjectSurface* **inherit** *PolyhedralObject*
type [*position* : 3*DCoord*]

The positions of the surface and legs of the desk are relative to that of the desk. The parameters and transformations of the legs has to be constrained: they are all at the corners of the surface, sticking out of the bottom. This constraint is implemented through the *constraint_legs* component of the legs attribute. The actual constraint function depends on the actual surface parameters of *desk*45.

To compute the absolute position of the surface we employ the method *part_abs_position* defined on the class *Desk* (where *desk*45 is a particular desk): *desk*45.*part_abs_position*(*desk*45.*surface*) □

3.2 Image Features

Images are either 2D (standard camera images) or 3D (results of stereo-pair reconstruction, depth maps from scan-line devices, etc.). Features are partitioned according to their dimensionality: 0D (points, corners), 1D (lines, curves), 2D (surfaces, textures), and 3D (volumes). Image objects are described with appropriate objects together with relationships between these objects such as being collinear, rectilinear, coplanar, etc. The image features can be computed from database objects and a projection specification. For example, for a camera focus at (X_c, Y_c, Z_c) looking along an axis oriented according to $(\theta_X, \theta_Y, \theta_Z)$ (ignoring other camera parameters, such as focal length, for simplicity, and just using a central projection), we track objects using the following class:

class *Projection*
type [*axis* : [*pitch*, *yaw*, *roll* : *angle*],
origin : [*X*, *Y*, *Z* : *distance*]]
method *transformation*(*p* : *3DCoord*) : *2DCoord*

We also allow for finding 3D objects from image features (this is an ill-posed problem in the general case). Vision systems need both kinds of manipulations.

4 Modeling Uncertain Information

Information incorporated in the data model are incompletely known and is subject to imprecision. Thus, values of attributes such as object location in the world, or parameters of transformations are only estimates. Similarly, the existence of a certain object in the scene is uncertain due to imprecision of the object recognition modules. This probabilistic knowledge is employed by the vision system to make important inferences guiding the robot in its tasks. Examining the first kind of uncertain information, that is uncertain spatial information, one can observe that it amounts to uncertainty in the values of simple attributes, or of vectors of attributes. Thus, the location attribute of some world object which is a 3D coordinate (i.e. a value in $\Re^3$), estimated with a certain error, should be represented as a probabilistic distribution over $\Re^3$. More generally, we could have any attribute of a class be uncertain, in which case its value is a probabilistic distribution over some set of values. While the focus of this paper is the probabilistic description of spatial information, we present a general approach to the semantics of probabilistic attributes below. In section 5, we deal in detail with the kind of uncertain spatial information to be incorporated in the data model.

The probabilistic distribution of the location attribute, as well as that of other information, is in principle infinite. Consequently, we need to develop finite representations of such distributions that would be used by the vision modules. Practically, such representation are implemented as classes of *probability distributions* whose instances describe instances of such distributions, e.g. a distribution of location information is represented by the expected value and covariance of the location coordinates together with methods for manipulating the distribution (by manipulating the representation). Such finite representations for several kinds of uncertain spatial information and their efficient manipulation are described in section 5.

The second kind of uncertain information is that of uncertainty in object existence and uncertainty in the composition of complex values (e.g. sets). Uncertain existence of objects is represented as an *existence* attribute giving the probability that the object exists, while uncertain composition of complex values is represented by modeling their elements as pairs whose components are the element and a *membership* attribute giving the probability that the element is indeed a component of the complex value [3].

4.1 Uncertain Attributes

Generally, an uncertain attribute A, denotes a probabilistic distribution over the instances of some type T. Such a distribution is a mapping f_A from the domain of T to $[0 \ldots 1]$, where for each $v \in domain(T)$, $f_A(v) = Pr(\ A = v\ )$. The description of this mapping depends on the type T. One should distinguish three kinds of attributes in this respect. The first one, which is the focus of this paper, are those attributes whose values are from a basic type such as the real numbers, or vectors of basic types. These attributes are the most useful for representing uncertain spatial information. However, as they range over a potentially infinite set of instances, this distribution is infinite and continuous. We would represent such a distribution by finite means such as its expected value and covariance (see Example 5.1). It turns out the useful manipulations of these attributes can be expressed by means of this finite representation as shown in section 5.

The second kind of uncertain attributes are those ranging over a user-defined class such as *Desk*. Such a class is associated with its extent, a finite set of its current instances. Consequently, uncertainty in the values of such an attribute is due to uncertainty as to which of these instances of the class is the value of the attribute. Accordingly, the probabilistic distribution assigned to such an attribute is a finite discrete distribution over the class extent. Formally, such a distribution defines an attribute A over a class C, as a mapping $f_A : extent(C) \rightarrow [0 \ldots 1]$, where for each $o \in extent(C)$, $f_A(o) = Pr(\ A = o\ )$.

Example 3: Consider the interpretation of an image in which a desk is recognized, but its identity with respect to the set of desks known to be in the office is still undetermined. The desk attribute of the interpretation is accordingly uncertain:

class *interpretation*
  type $[desk : Discrete\_Distribution\_Desk]$
class *Discrete_Distribution_Desk* **inherit** *Discrete_Distribution*
  type $[distribution : \{[d : Desk,\ probability : real]\}]$

Assuming the extent of Desk is $\{d_1, \ldots, d_n\}$, the distribution attribute has the value: $\{(d_1, p_1), \ldots, (d_n, p_n)\}$, where $p_i = Pr(\ interpretation.desk\ = d_i\ )$. □

A similar kind of distribution arises for complex-valued attributes whose composition is uncertain. In that case, as the value of a corresponding certain attribute is a complex value, the distribution is over the domain of a complex type consisting of all the complex values that can be built using the type constructor from the objects in the extents of the classes of their components.

Example 4: Consider a desk object being recognized in terms of its set of legs. The image interpretation module using an uncertain attribute giving distributions over sets of legs that it may have recognized. Thus, the legs attribute is a distribution over sets of legs: **type** *Set_Distribution* : {[*legs_set* : {*Leg*}, *probability* : *real*]}, where each tuple in the set gives the probability that a particular set of legs occurred in the image. □

4.2 Uncertainty in Object Existence and Composition

Objects are recognized in a scene with a certain degree of imprecision and consequently their existence is uncertain. We describe this situation through an *existence* attribute of such an object. Semantically, this attribute is associated with the probability that the object in which it appears exists, i.e. $Pr(\ o\ exists\ )$. For example, the *occlusion* relationship between predicted image features is often uncertain due to imprecise estimates of feature locations. Accordingly, we associate an existence attribute with the occlusion relationship objects giving the probability that one feature occludes another:

type *occlusion* : [$f1, f2$: *ImageFeature*, *existence* : *Probability*]

where *Probability* is:

class *Probability*
type [*value* : *real*]
method *threshold*(*cutoff* : *real*) : *boolean*

Composition of complex values, built using type constructors, may be uncertain, and requires associating a probability with each component, the probability that is part of the complex value. Accordingly, we assume that such complex values are built from pairs, whose first component is the element, while the second is called a *membership* attribute and contains the probability that the element is part of the complex value, e.g. {[*element* : *T*, *membership* : *Probability*]}, where for a set S and $t \in S$, $t.membership = Pr(\ t \in S\ )$.

4.3 Inheritance of Uncertain Information

Uncertain attributes and methods manipulating distributions are inherited along the inheritance hierarchy using the data model standard inheritance mechanism. Similarly, distribution classes are organized in an inheritance hierarchy which includes some basic useful discrete and continuous distributions such as the normal distribution.

5 Handling Uncertain Spatial Data

In order to handle spatial probabilistic information, we need to define the kinds of uncertain spatial data, how their probability distributions are represented, and what manipulations are performed on them. Spatial uncertainty arises from the following sources: uncertainty of position (both global and local, 2D or 3D), uncertainty of scaling or distortion parameters, and uncertainty of object (line, plane, etc.) parameters that are not positional in nature.

As objects may be parts of other objects, their position can be represented by a transformation of their coordinate system wrt the coordinate system of their aggregation-hierarchy parent. Such transformation are 6-vectors, with 3 parameters for translation and 3 for rotation (as discussed in section 3). Uncertain transformations are thus 6 dimensional random vectors. Scaling and distortion are defined wrt the shape that is the parent in the class hierarchy. As above, uncertainty in scaling and distortion is represented as a random vector. Uncertainty in parametric representations used for points, curves, and surfaces are represented by a probabilistic distribution of the parameters.

5.1 Probabilistic Representations

Having defined where distributions occur, we need to represent them. Probability distributions are either discrete or continuous. In the discrete case, they are represented by enumeration (for a small, finite set of possible values), or by specifying a known distribution type and parameters. In the continuous case, they are represented by distribution type and parameters. Distribution types are classes, of which the actual distributions are specific object instances.

Example 5: The position of a desk could be represented as a vector of random variables (X, Y, Z) that are jointly normal in distribution. It is sufficient to provide a vector of expected values $\mu = (\mu_x, \mu_y, \mu_z)$ and the covariance matrix Λ as parameters to completely specify the distribution. Accordingly, we have the $3DCoord\_normal$ class:

class $3DCoord\_normal$
type $[expected\_value : \ [\mu_x, \mu_y, \mu_z : real],$
$covariance : \ array[3,3]\ (real)]$ □

In this paper (and in the implementation), we usually stick to joint normal distributions, for the following reasons: 1) measurement errors frequently have normal distributions, 2) normal distributions are closed under linear operations, 3) the central limit theorem argues in favor of using normal distributions as approximations, and 4) much current research on manipulating spatial distributions (which we intend to use as "plug-in modules") uses normal distributions [2, 11, 7].

5.2 Data Manipulations Involving Probabilities

There are several ways in which the vision system manipulates uncertain spatial information represented in the data model. These operations on probability distributions are implemented as methods of the probability distributions' classes. These methods may be overridden in particular distribution classes. We consider the following operations: (1) Composition of distributions, (2) Expectations (immediate for normal distributions), (3) Evidential reasoning (probability updating), (4) Plausibility evaluation: finding the probability that an attribute vector is within certain extents (in special cases, one can use well known cumulative distribution functions, e.g. for normal random vectors use χ^2 distributions); and (5) Reparametrization.

We begin with a simple composition example, where everything is linear:

Example 6: Consider our desk *desk*5, at uncertain position $P = (X_P, Y_P, Z_P)$, P being a 3 dimensional random vector with joinly normal distribution (We shall ignore rotations for simplicity, for the moment). Let $\mu_P = (\mu_{X_P}, \mu_{Y_P}, \mu_{Z_P})$ be the expected values, and Λ_P be the covariance matrix of P. Let the surface of *desk*5 be uncertainly positioned relative to the desk at $Q = (X_Q, Y_Q, Z_Q)$, with Q likewise normal, with μ_Q and Λ_Q the parameters of the distribution.

We may now wish to find the absolute position R of the desk surface, in order for the robot to place something on it. The result is a composition of the above transformations, in this case a simple addition of the random vectors: $R = P+Q$. Assuming that P and Q are statistically independent (as we usually do, unless we know otherwise), R is a normal random vector, with $\mu_R = \mu_P + \mu_Q$ and $\Lambda_R = \Lambda_P + \Lambda_Q$. This is implemented using the method of the Desk class:

part_abs_position (*position* : *3Dcoord_normal*) : *3Dcoord_normal* □

In real life, not everything is linear. Rotations introduce non-linearities, as do perspective transformations. Hence, even if the transformation is exact, the distribution of a given object may become non-Gaussian. Assuming that the uncertainty is small, linearization about the expected value is possible, to get a normal approximation of the distribution for transformed object.

Example 7: An estimate of the desk's location in an image is required, in order to begin tracking it. Assume for simplicity a central projection from $(0,0,0)$ looking along the Z axis (usually the projection is more general, and the parameters may be uncertain). The transformation is:

$$(3) \qquad p(P) = (x \quad y)^T = \left(-\frac{X}{Z} \quad -\frac{Y}{Z}\right)^T$$

The location of the desk $p = (x_p, y_p)$ in the image is (almost) normal, with μ_p and Λ_p defined as follows (for small uncertainties):

$$\mu_p = \left(-\frac{\mu_{X_P}}{\mu_{Z_P}} \quad -\frac{\mu_{Y_P}}{\mu_{Z_P}}\right)^T \qquad \Lambda_p = J_{p,P}\Lambda_P J_{p,P}^T$$

Where superscript T stands for "transposed", and $J_{p,P}$ is the 2×3 Jacobian matrix of the perspective transformation $p(P)$ evaluated at μ_P. □

Updating distributions by observations is done such that the expected value of the result is the maximum likelihood estimator. Using a special case of the Kalman Filter techniques of [2, 7], this is straightforward, assuming linear transformations. We choose to represent uncertainty using normal random variables again, for the reasons stated earlier.

Example 8: Our *desk*5 has been measured to be at an uncertain location

$M = (X_M, Y_M, Z_M)$, where M is a random vector with joint normal distribution. Assume that the measurement is independent of the "measurement" P above. We would like to update the database as to the location of the desk. Call the new uncertain location P', again a normal random vector. Using the Kalman Filter equations, we have:

$$\mu_{P'} = \mu_P + K(\mu_M - \mu_P) \qquad \Lambda_{P'} = (I_3 - K)\Lambda_P$$

with I_n being an $n \times n$ identity matrix, and K being the "Kalman gain matrix", defined as $K = \Lambda_P(\Lambda_P + \Lambda_M)^{-1}$ in this special case. □

Similar methods apply to uncertain transformations, including rotations and projections. In certain non-linear cases, if the resulting uncertainty is small, it is possible to overcome the problem using iterations that converge to the correct results [7]. However, the general problem of handling large uncertainties, in the presence of non-linearities, remains open.

6 Related Work

While many spatial object-oriented data models have been suggested [12, 13, 14], they lack facilities for modeling uncertain information which is essential in our application such as uncertain location of objects. Dutta [4] have suggested a fuzzy semantics for the description of some spatial attributes and relationships in geographical information systems. For example, he suggests a fuzzy description of the notion of one object being "far away" from another. While fuzzy semantics is useful for the representation of such concepts, the representation of uncertain locations of objects is best handled by probabilistic means as one has to supply a quantitative distribution of the possible location of the object [5, 11]. Using probabilities, we can take advantage of many well understood tools, such as optimal estimators. Additionally, using probabilities makes it possible for the robot to make intelligent *decisions* in the presence of uncertainty, such as selecting one of a set of possible actions, through classical decision theoretic methods. It is unclear how that can be done with any other existing uncertainty formalism.

Previous research on the probabilistic modeling of uncertain information has concentrated on the relational model (where tuples could have probabilistic attributes), e.g. [3, 6], whose structuring capabilities are too poor for spatial database applications. Most importantly, these models incorporated only finite discrete probabilities over atomic types, e.g. integer, string, and did not consider continuous distributions of attribute values. However, these are necessary for representing uncertain spatial information.

Jagadish and O'Gorman [8] have suggested an image data model to aid in image interpretation. The description of uncertainty in object interpretation is through a confidence (probabilistic) attribute attached to each recognized object. However, they have not addressed the important problem of modeling and processing uncertain spatial information such as object pose in 3D.

References

[1] R. Agrawal and N. Gehani. ODE (object database and environment): The language and the data model. In *ACM SIGMOD Intl. Conf. on Management of Data*, pages 36–45, 1989.

[2] N. Ayache. *Artificial Vision for Mobile Robots.* MIT Press, 1991.

[3] D. Barbara, H. Garcia-Molina, and D. Porter. A probabilistic relational data model. In *Proc. of the Intl. Conf. on Extending Database Technology*, volume 416 of *Lecture Notes in Computer Science*, pages 60–74. Springer-Verlag, 1990.

[4] S. Dutta. Qualitative spatial reasoning: A semi-quantitative approach using fuzzy logic. In A. Buchmann et al., editors, *Design and Implementation of Large Spatial Databases*, volume 409 of *Lecture Notes in Computer Science*, pages 345–364. Springer-Verlag, 1989.

[5] A. Elfes. Using occupancy grids for mobile robot perception and navigation. *IEEE Computer*, pages 46–57, 1989.

[6] E. Gelenbe and G. Hebrail. A probability model of uncertainty in databases. In *Proc. IEEE Data Engineering Conf.*, 1986.

[7] Y. Hel-Or and M. Werman. Absolute orientation from uncertain point data: A unified approach. In *Proceedings of the CVPR Conference*, 1992.

[8] H. Jagadish and L. O'Gorman. An object model for image understanding. *IEEE Computer*, pages 33–41, Dec. 1989.

[9] P. Kahn, L. Kitchen, and E. M. Riseman. A fast line finder for vision-guided robot navigation. *IEEE Transaction on PAMI*, 12-11:1098–1102, November 1990.

[10] D. Kriegman, T. Binford, and T. Sumanaweera. Generic models for robot navigation. In *Proc. DARPA Image Understanding Workshop*, pages 453–460, 1988.

[11] L. Matthies, R. Szeliski, and T. Kanade. Kalman filter-based algorithms for estimating depth from image sequences. *International Journal of Computer Vision*, 3-3:209–238, 1989.

[12] J. Orenstein and F. Manola. PROBE: Spatial data modeling and query processing in an image database application. *IEEE Trans. on Software Engineering*, 14(5):611–629, May 1988.

[13] N. Roussopoulos, C. Faloustsos, and T. Sellis. An efficient pictorial database system for SQL. *IEEE Trans. on Software Engineering*, 14(5):639–650, May 1988.

[14] A. Wolf. How to fit geo-objects into databases — an extensibility approach. In *Proc. of the Intl. Conf. on Extending Database Technology*, volume 580 of *Lecture Notes in Computer Science.* Springer-Verlag, Mar. 1992.

Query Processing of Geometric Objects with Free Form Boundaries in Spatial Databases

Hans-Peter Kriegel, Stephan Heep, Andreas Fahldiek, Norbert Mysliwitz

Institute for Computer Science, University of Munich
Leopoldstr. 11B, D-8000 Munich 40

Abstract: The increasing demand for the use of database systems as an integrating factor in CAD/CAM applications has necessitated the development of database systems with appropriate modelling and retrieval capabilities. One essential problem is the treatment of geometric data which has led to the development of spatial databases. Unfortunately, most proposals only deal with simple geometric objects like multidimensional points and rectangles. On the other hand, there has been a rapid development in the field of representing geometric objects with free form curves or surfaces, initiated by engineering applications such as mechanical engineering, aviation or astronautics. Therefore, we propose a concept for the realization of spatial retrieval operations on geometric objects with free form boundaries, such as B-spline or Bézier curves, which can easily be integrated in a database management system. The key concept is the encapsulation of geometric operations in a so-called query processor. First, this enables the definition of an interface allowing the integration into the data model and the definition of the query language of a database system for complex objects. Second, the approach allows the use of an arbitrary representation of the geometric objects. After a short description of the query processor, we propose some representations for free form objects determined by B-spline or Bézier curves. The goal of efficient query processing in a database environment is achieved using a combination of decomposition techniques and spatial access methods. Finally, we present some experimental results indicating that the performance of decomposition techniques is clearly superior to traditional query processing strategies for geometric objects with free form boundaries.

1 Introduction

One essential goal in engineering applications is the storage of all product definition data in an integrated form. In mechanical engineering, a product is usually defined by a set of parts which are again described by manufacturing (CAD/CAM-) data. Thus, the description of parts and products has a complex structure and contains geometric data. For the purpose of sophisticated retrieval capabilities, a database management system for engineering applications has to offer modelling capabilities for complex structured as well as geometric data.

We will concentrate on the handling of geometric data in the way known from spatial database systems (see [Wi91]). The most relevant geometric objects in engineering applications are solids in Euclidean 3-space and surfaces in Euclidean 2-space; in both cases the objects can be considered as regular point sets. We will restrict our considerations to free form surfaces in Euclidean 2-space, free form regions for short that are described in section 2, but the concept easily can be extended to solid objects in 3-space (see [He92]).

Desirable retrieval capabilities besides standard SQL like queries are the search for similar parts (see [SK89]) and geometric queries, i.e. queries with geometric selection conditions. Geometric queries and concepts for their realization are elaborated further in section 3. The concept of a query processor is adapted to region data in section 4. The query processor is a very flexible tool increasing query performance by using different representations for regions. In section 5, we focus on possible representations for free form regions. Contrary to polygonal regions, there are no decomposition techniques known for query processing of free form regions. We propose two types of decompositions called heterogeneous and trapezoid decomposition and present some analytical results.

In section 6 results of an experimental comparison of the different representations are presented. After a comparison of the decomposition methods, we consider the construction of the different representations. Finally, we propose query processing strategies and present experimental results comparing the performance of these strategies for different representations with respect to selected types of queries, i.e. the PointQuery and the WindowQuery defined in section 3. The paper concludes with a summary of the results.

2 Definition of free form regions

As mentioned above, we will focus on surfaces in Euclidean 2-space, called regions. A region is defined by a closed, not self-intersecting curve C which may be given by a sequence of curve segments with common start and end points. According to the Jordan curve theorem, such a curve C divides the Euclidean plane into three sets: the interior, the exterior and the boundary points.

In the case of a polygonal region, the curve can be described by the vertices of the polygon. Methods for the description of smooth curves with only few information are subsumed under the notion of free form curves. Some of the most widely used methods are B-spline and Bézier curves that are defined by a sequence of control points.

We define a *free form region* as a region that is bounded by a closed, not self intersecting curve C which is described by a sequence of Bézier or B-spline curves. In this context the following properties of free form curves are essential:

- B-splines are more suitable for the interactive definition of free form curves due to the local control, i.e. the modification of a control point affects only a limited interval of the curve, and due to the simplicity of assembling patches.
- Bézier curves are better suited for computations on a readily defined curve This is due to the facts that start and end points are given explicitly and that Bézier curves pass more closely to the control points than B-splines.

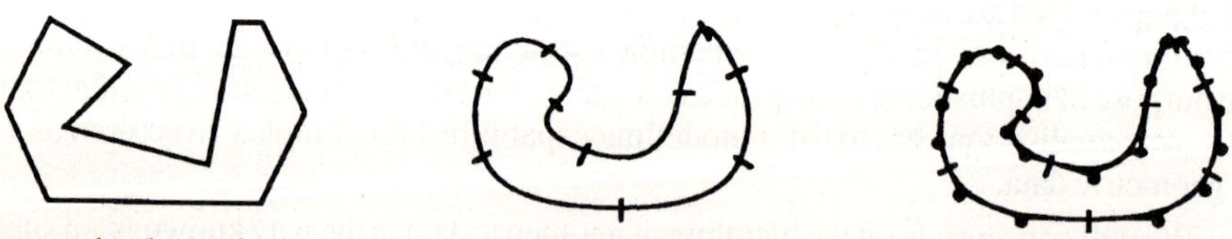

control polygon for B-spline curve — B-spline curve with segments identified — curve with Bézier control points

Fig. 1. Examples for B-spline and Bézier curves

For these reasons, we assume in the following that curves are given as B-splines and that they are stored as Bézier curves. Therefore, we focus on Bézier curves. A *Bézier curve of degree m* is defined by a sequence of m+1 points P_i (i=0(1)m):

$r(t) = \Sigma_{i=1(1)m} B_{i,m}(t) * P_i$, where $B_{i,m}(t)$ are Bernstein polynomials.

Thus the Bernstein polynomial is a weighting factor of the points varying with the value of t (over the curve). A *cubic Bézier curve* (order 4) is defined by a sequence of four points P_0, P_1, P_2 and P_3:

$$X(t) = (1-t)^3 * P_0 + 3*t*(1-t)^2 * P_1 + 3*t^2*(1-t)^2 * P_2 + 3*t^3 * P_3 .$$

For the realization of the concept proposed above, first of all we need a conversion algorithm from B-spline to Bézier curves. One solution to this problem is the so-called Oslo-algorithm (see [HL89]).

The preprocessing used for the decompositions is equal to the preprocessing of the Koparkar-Mudur-algorithm that partitions a curve in those points having a horizontal or vertical tangent (see [HL89]). In the general case, the computation of those extreme points is very costly because it involves for example the evaluation of a non-linear system of equations. Here, we only consider the computations for the simple case of cubic Bézier curves with uniform knot vectors.

A. Computation of extreme points of cubic Bézier curves

The equation of a cubic Bézier curve with a uniform knot vector is given above in vector form; if we take a look at the component functions, we see that the component functions are polynomials of degree 3. From this fact, it can be derived (see [FM92]) that a cubic Bézier curve can have at most two extreme points per axis.

B. Partitioning a cubic Bézier curve

Another problem considered here is the partitioning of a Bézier curve into two Bézier curves according to a point given by a value of t. This partitioning is an integral part of all decomposition algorithms. The basis of the algorithm is the de Casteljau algorithm to determine a point of a Bézier curve X(t) by a given value of t (see [HL89]). The border points of the de Casteljau schema are the control points of the two Bézier curves that originate from the decomposition of the Bézier curve in point X(t).

3 Known concepts from spatial databases

The demand for storing objects with geometric information (geo-objects for short) in database systems has led to the development of spatial databases. Spatial database systems are concerned with appropriate modelling and retrieval capabilities especially for sets of geo-objects which are grouped for semantic reasons (all parts of a product for example). If such a set of geo-objects is often queried with geometric selection conditions, it should be stored in a cluster (see [KH91][Wi91]). In the following we focus on the geometric information of objects ignoring other information. A set of (free form) regions embedded in the Euclidean plane is called a (two-dimensional) *scene*.

3.1 Retrieval capabilities

The abstract definition of sets of geo-objects also allows an easy definition of the required retrieval capabilities. The most relevant queries using geometric selection conditions to a given scene S of geo-objects are only summarized here (see [Wi91] or [KH91]):

PointQuery: Given a point $P \in \mathbf{R}^2$. Select all geo-objects in S containing P as interior or border point.

WindowQuery: Given a rectangle $R = ((x_1,x_2),(y_1,y_2))$ with x_1, x_2, y_1, y_2 real numbers and $x_1 \le x_2$, $y_1 \le y_2$. Select all objects in S that intersect rectangle R.

RegionQuery: Given a region R. Select all objects in S that intersect region R.

Spatial Join: Given two sets of geo-objects S_1 and S_2. Compute a new set of geo-objects containing all (regular) intersections of pairs of regions (R_1, R_2) with R_1 in S_1 and R_2 in S_2.

This set of queries for region data is easily extendable, but a full list of queries is out of the scope of this paper. Furthermore, the low level queries and operations mentioned above can be used to build complex application specific queries. For an efficient spatial join algorithm for polygonal regions we refer to [BK93a].

3.2 Methods for efficient query processing

For efficient query processing, regions should be clustered according to their spatial location using available spatial access methods (SAMs). A problem concerning region data is the lack of access methods that dirctly handle any type of region data. Because most access methods for region data are restricted to handle multidimensional rectilinear boxes (see [KS89], [Wi91]), strategies for efficient query processing of region data have to be considered more closely.

3.2.1 Approximation by minimum bounding boxes

This method is most commonly used, because it allows the direct use of spatial access methods for rectangles. A region is approximated by its minimum bounding rectilinear box (MBB for short) and this rectangle is used as spatial key in an access method for rectangles. The MBBs approximate size, location and spatial relationship of regions. This method is also applicable to free form regions. Due to the approximation, query processing is now a two step procedure visualized in figure 2:

Filter step: The rectangles which are conservatively approximating geo-objects (see [OM86]) are stored in a SAM for rectangles. A retrieval operation is represented by an appropriate query on the access method which yields a set of candidates containing all objects fulfilling the original query.

Refinement step: All candidates of the filter step are considered to determine whether they really fulfill the query condition or not.

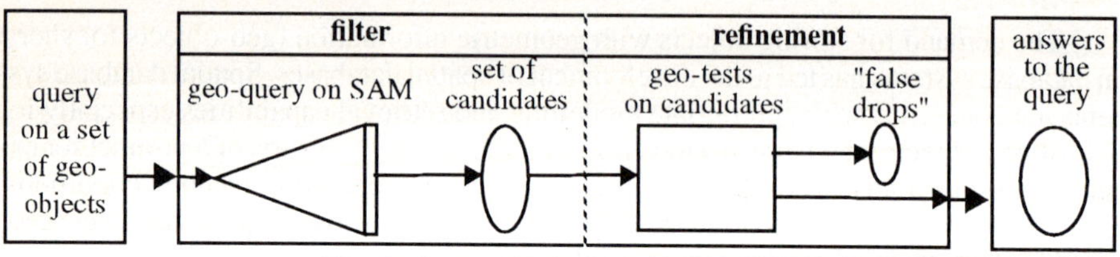

Fig. 2. Query processing using a filter

Instead of the MBB, more efficient approximations may be used if there are spatial access methods for that type of approximations. Examples of such approximations are the convex 5-corner and the rotated MBB (see [BK93b]).

3.2.2 Query processing using a z-order representation

The idea of z-order representation is to represent a region by (a set of) one-dimensional point data that can be stored as a point set in a one-dimensional index like the B^+-tree (see [OM86]). The basis is a recursive (multidimensional) spatial decomposition scheme, called quadtree, decomposing a finite part of the Euclidean plane into cells. A region is identified with the cells that intersect the region. Because the number of cells affects the approximation quality of the objects and therefore the number of candidates, a representation of one region by a set of cells is considered. In the PROBE-project (see [OM86]), the refinement step uses the original representation of the regions. A problem of the use of a redundant representation in the filter step is to eliminate the redundancy in the candidate set.

3.2.3 Query processing using a decomposition representation

The strategies considered so far all use the same refinement step; the original object is tested against the query condition. In the case of free form regions and three-dimensional objects, the amount of work in the refinement step can be enormous. The essential reason for the use of a decomposition representation as proposed in [KH91] is therefore the reduction of the processing time in the refinement step.

A *decomposition representation* as proposed in [KH91] is the combination of:
- a *decomposition technique* partitioning a region into a set of component objects of simpler shape (triangulation for example)
- a *spatial access method* to store the approximated component objects.

The filter step now yields a set of *component objects* (which are triangles in case of a triangulation) that have to be considered in the refinement step. A problem is the amount of redundancy introduced by the decomposition scheme. But a decomposition representation seems to be a good alternative especially for free form regions because the computations in the refinement step can obviously be reduced.

4 A query processor for region data

From the viewpoint of a data model of a database management system (DBMS), regions can be seen as an additional data type. It is well-known that there are some extensible database management systems which allow the integration of new data types in the form of an abstract data type. For our presentation it suffices to say that regions are integrated as abstract data types defined by an interface and an implementation.

4.1 The implementation of the query processor for region data

The interface of the new data type 'REGION' has to be comparable to other data types in the data model. In a relational DBMS the interface (used in the query language) consists of a set of predicates, functions and operations. An extensive survey for different kinds of geometric data types is given for example in [Gü89]. Some basic predicates are the test on intersection or the point-in polygon test. These predicates can be used as selection condition to define the queries on sets of geo-objects listed in section 3.1.

In contrast to a straightforward implementation of the interface of an abstract data type, we allow some degrees of freedom to achieve efficiency and data independence (see [KH91]). The concept of the query processor for regions allows us to:
- use different representations of one object in parallel
- use one or more representations to answer one query
- integrate a query optimizer for selecting an optimal strategy (query plan) to answer a given query.

The generation of the representations can be achieved by an extended version of a check-in check-out mechanism (see [Ka85][He92]). The main tasks of a query processor are the control and management of representations, the choice of a query plan for query processing, and the control of the interaction of different representations.

4.2 Types of representations and their use in a query processor

If we take a closer look at the different types of representations for sets of regions presented in section 3.2, we can identify two distinguishing features:

1.) The representation of geo-objects can be approximate or exact.
2.) The representation of geo-objects can be redundant or non-redundant.

Examples for approximate representations are the MBB- and the z-order representation of regions. While an approximate representation can only be used in an optional filter step, query processing requires at least one exact representation for the refinement.

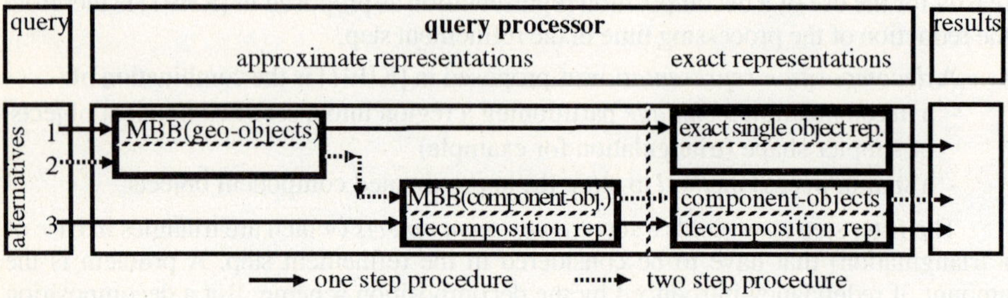

Fig. 3. Configuration of a query processor and possible query plans

Conceptually, it is possible to use more than one filter; in that case the representations used have to be ordered in a sequence of finer filters. The number of filter steps (approximate representations used) is taken to identify the procedure of query processing; the MBB-representation is called a one step procedure because it uses exactly one approximate representation.

While figure 2 visualizes the algorithmic side of query processing, figure 3 shows a query processor in a more schematic view. Figure 3 depicts a query processor using all (but one) types of representations described so far and also shows possible, alternative query plans. An open question so far is the choice of appropriate query plans, especially in the case of decomposition representations.

5 Selected representations for free form regions

In this section, the representations used in the performance comparison are described. First, we consider a non-redundant and exact representation that can be used in an MBB representation. Then we focus on representations based on decompositions.

5.1 A non-redundant and exact representation

As input for the query processor all free form regions are accepted whose boundary is given by a sequence of cubic B-spline or Bézier curves forming a closed curve (external representation). Because of algorithmic and efficiency considerations, we decided to use only cubic Bézier curves for the internal representation. Therefore, the check-in mechanism is responsible for the conversion of this description into a sequence of cubic Bézier curves applying the conversion algorithm mentioned in section 2.

For sets of geo-objects, this representation is combined with a non-redundant filter using a MBB approximation supported by a spatial access method. Thus, the most commonly used query processing strategy, here called the identity representation, is integrated into the query processor.

5.2 Decomposition-based representations

There have been many proposals for decomposition techniques for regions that were surveyed in [KS85] and [KH91] for example. While in the first survey, decomposition techniques were considered with regard to criteria used in computational geometry, the second paper analyzes decomposition techniques with respect to query processing in database systems. Most of the techniques presented there are only suitable for polygons.

Here, we present two decomposition techniques. The first is a generalization of the trapezoid method for polygonal regions (see [AA83]); the second is called heterogeneous decomposition and is derived from both, the ISOS method ([BD89]) and the heterogeneous decomposition for polygonal regions [KH91].

5.2.1 Decomposition into Trapezoid-like regions

A simple decomposition scheme for polygonal regions is the decomposition into trapezoids proposed in [AA83]. This technique was extended and tuned to be used in a query processor by [He92] and first results are presented in [KH91]. The simple decomposition method is described by the following rule (partition method H in [AA83]):

For each vertex of the polygon draw as many horizontal chords as possible.

Partition method H allows the prediction of the number of components generated in the case of polygonal regions ([AA83]): a polygon with n vertices, w holes, and h horizontal edges is decomposed into at most n+w-h-1 components.

Assuming that free form regions are given in the form of the identity representation described above (i.e. by a sequence of cubic Bézier curves), the decomposition into trapezoid-like components is given by a two step process (see [FM92] and [He92]):

1.) Determine the extreme values of the Bézier curves and decompose each curve into these points, resulting in monotonic curves.

2.) Start partition method H with the set of boundary elements derived in step 1.

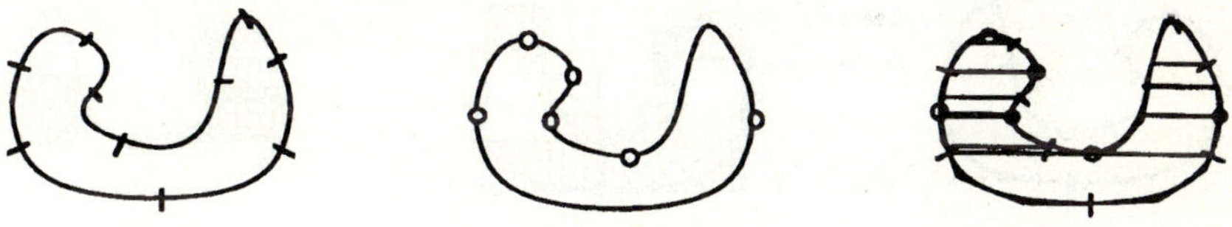

Fig. 4. Decomposition into trapezoid-like components

Because all curves are monotonic, partition method H generates *trapezoid-like regions* that are bounded by two horizontal chords and two parts of (monotonic) Bézier curves (see Figure 4 for an example). The monotonic character guarantees that the decomposition method is unique and that geometric predicates are easy to compute. For the decomposition into trapezoid-like components (T-components), we can give some analytical results:

Lemma 1: Assume, a curve is given by b B-spline curves with c control points. Then the number of T-components is bounded by 4*(c-3b).

Because the number of B-spline segments is c-3b, the conversion algorithm generates c-3b Bézier curves. Considering the maximum number of extreme values of a Bézier curve and the number of components generated by partition method H for polygonal regions, the proof is completed.

Lemma 2: The runtime of the decomposition into T-components is O(n*logn) in the worst case where n is the number of control points of the B-spline curve.

With Lemma 1 and the fact that the conversion and the decomposition of the curves can be done in constant time, the runtime of the algorithm is determined by the runtime of the application of partition method H, which is O(n*logn).

5.2.2 A heterogeneous decomposition for regions

The method is similar to the ISOS method reported in [BD89] and to the heterogeneous decomposition for polygonal regions in [KS91]. The idea is to decompose a region into two sets of components (see figure 5 for an example):

boundary components: A decomposition schema for the bounding curve is used and the components are approximated by rectangles such that the bounding curve is already contained in the rectangles.

interior components: The part of the region not covered so far is decomposed into rectangular components.

A first idea of the decomposition algorithm is given by the following three rules:

1.) Enclose all boundary elements by MBBs.
2.) In the case of pairs of overlapping MBBs, decompose the corresponding boundary elements and replace the old boundary elements by the computed components. Recompute the MBB for the new boundary elements.
3.) The difference between the original geo-object and the MBB of the boundary elements consists of one or more rectilinear regions that are decomposed.

It is obvious that the second rule has to be applied recursively. Unfortunately it is not always possible to generate a decomposition without pairs of overlapping MBBs. Solutions depend on metrical facts, so that an analytic prediction of the number of components is not possible.

Fig. 5. Example for the heterogeneous decomposition

One essential difference between the heterogeneous decomposition used for polygonal regions and the decomposition used here concerns the storage and the query processing strategy: the two sets of components (interior and exterior components) indexed by their MBB are stored in two different occurrences of the spatial access method used.

6 Experimental comparison of the representations

First, the decomposition methods are considered with respect to the number of components generated, the time used for generating the decomposition and the construction of the representation. A last criterion is based on the quality of the approximation. Finally, the query performance of the different representations is compared for the different types of queries presented in section 3.

6.1 Experimental setup

For the comparison of the different representations, we generated a set of pseudo random data. We use four sets of free form regions (scenes) varying the complexity of the regions. The complexity is measured by the number of points describing one region. We use four sets of regions that have an average number of 25, 50, 75 and 100 control points per region denoted by U25, U50, U75, and U100, respectively. The control polygons are generated in the same way as we constructed polygonal regions in [KH91].

Each scene is composed of 100 regions. The centers of the regions are distributed uniformly in the unit square given by [0..1] x [0..1]. The size of the regions was chosen such that the sum of the area of all regions is 70% of the size of the unit square. This was done to generate nearly disjoint scenes which we assumed to be realistic for CAD data.

The spatial access method used is the R*-tree which demonstrated a superior performance in the tests for polygonal regions [KS91]. The query processor was implemented in MODULA-2 and the tests were run on SUN 3/60 workstations with a local disk. Performance data were taken from the profiler available under UNIX.

6.2 Comparison of the decomposition methods

We assume that the regions are given as a sequence of Bézier curves (e.g. the internal representation). The check-in mechanism transforming the B-spline curves to cubic Bézier curves is a two step process described earlier. The parameters considered in the experimental performance comparison are:

1.) the number of components generated (C).
2.) the quality of the approximation (A).
3.) the time required for generating the decomposition in seconds (T(D)), the time for generating the representation (T) and the time required for the SAM (T(SAM)).
4.) the number of disk accesses (ACCESSES (SAM)).

The results for the different representations and for the different sets of geo-objects are summarized in table 1. The quality of the approximation is measured by an approximation index defined in the following way:

Sum up the areas of all MBBs of components generated (for the identity representation consider the MBB of the object) and divide this by the sum of the areas of all regions.

The test series reveals the following results:

1.) The heterogeneous decomposition generates twice the number of components of the trapezoid decomposition.
2.) The quality of the approximation of the decomposition methods is much better than that of the approximation of the MBB-representation.
3.) The time required for the construction of the decomposition representations is rather high. With growing complexity of the regions of a scene, this construction time increases for the heterogeneous decomposition faster than for the others.
4.) The time for and the number of disk accesses increase linearly with the number of components.

The results presented here are clearly dependent on the spatial access method used. Tests in [KS91]) have shown, that the R*-tree is relatively slow with respect to insertion, but superior for retrieval. Thus, another choice could give better results for the construction of decomposition representations. But in the opinion of the authors, query performance is more important than insertion time because the construction is considered as a check-in procedure that is performed only once. Therefore, the choice of the R*-tree with slow insertion and high query performance is justified.

Representation	Scene	C	A	T [s]	T(D)	T (SAM)	ACCESSES (SAM)
identity	U25	100	1.40	54.4	0.0	0.36	372
trapezoid		6969	1.06	3699.5	145.6	2267.29	5216
heterogeneous		13154	1.10	4513.5	713.5	1690.78	9711
identity	U50	100	1.47	84.8	0.0	0.72	381
trapezoid		15525	1.04	5835.7	426.8	2288.63	9862
heterogeneous		31254	1.08	11500.2	2508.0	3801.93	15207
identity	U75	100	1.43	108.5	0.0	0.84	360
trapezoid		22706	1.03	8537.9	708.2	3300.53	13572
heterogeneous		43478	1.05	16740.4	4129.3	5287.55	19490
identity	U100	100	1.44	135.3	0.0	1.16	414
trapezoid		31750	1.02	12484.2	1177.4	4754.35	19109
heterogeneous		62489	1.04	24269.2	7137.4	7544.58	26235

Table 1: Performance parameters of the decomposition methods

6.3 Query processing strategies

We want to take a closer look at the query processing strategies described informally by figure 2, because some algorithmic details are not contained in the figure. First, we should mention that for all required evaluations of geometric predicates, a pretest on the basis of the MBB of the geo-object or component is used.

The identity representation as well as the one step and two step procedure for the trapezoid representation are implemented in the way described earlier. For the heterogeneous representation the two types of components are stored in different occurrences of the spatial access method. This requires a strategy coordinating the use of the two filters. The implementation [FM92] uses the two filters successively.

6.4 The Point and the WindowQuery

The test for the performance of the PointQuery for the different representations is based on a point set of 100 uniformly distributed points in the unit square. For the comparison of the different query processing strategies for window queries, seven sets of rectangles with different sizes were generated. Each set contains rectangles of approximately equal size. The average size of the rectangles in the different sets is 0.01%, 0.05%, 0.1%, 0.5%, 1%, 5% and 10% of the size of the unit square, respectively. They (their centers) are distributed uniformly in the unit square. Each set consists of 100 rectangles.

Figure 6 depicts the mean value for the time required for computing of one resulting geo-object, i.e. one answer to the query, averaged over 100 window or point queries respectively. Because there are no significant differences, only the diagrams for the region files U25 and U100 are shown. The performance comparison implies:

1.) Both two step decomposition representations are superior to the identity representation in all experiments. Particularly for small query sizes, they are up to three times faster in query processing than the identity representation.

2.) The two step procedure of the trapezoid method requires the minimum time for all sizes of query windows and all types of scenes. However, the heterogeneous decomposition is not much worse than the two step trapezoid decomposition.
3.) With growing complexity of the regions in a scene, the superiority of decomposition representations over the identity representation increases.

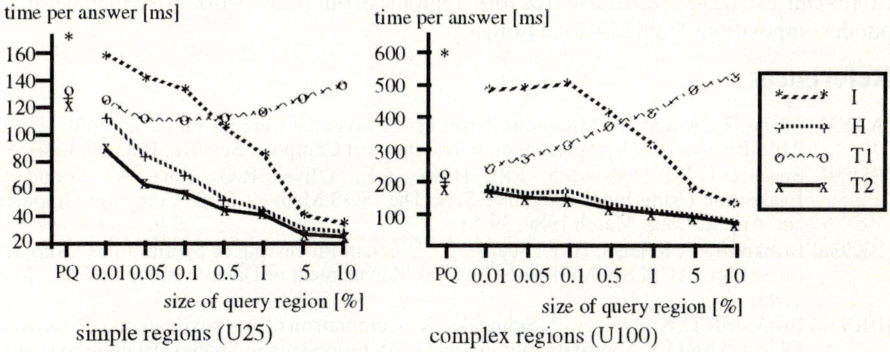

Fig. 6. Performance comparison of the Point and the WindowQuery

An interesting question arises from the fact that the time required for one answer decreases for the identity representation with growing size of the query rectangle. This decrease can be explained by some tuning features contained in the query processing strategy for the identity representation. A first test for the intersection is carried out comparing the MBB of a region with the query rectangle. In the case of large query rectangles, the MBBs are often included in the query rectangle. This suffices to decide that the region intersects the query rectangle such that no comparison with the free form region is required.

7 Conclusions

In this paper, we have proposed the concept of a query processor for the implementation of geometric queries on free form regions in a spatial database system. The query processor allows the application of different representations of regions suitable for processing a query. We survey concepts known from spatial databases and show how to use them in a query processor. We propose two decomposition methods for free form regions called heterogeneous and trapezoid decomposition. Finally, we present experimental results of different query processing strategies using different representations.

The comparison shows that the expense for a redundant representation is more than compensated by the computational savings for the geometric algorithms on free form geo-objects. This is partly due to the efficiency of the query performance of the selected spatial access method (i.e the R*-tree) which allows a fast access to locally bounded components of a scene. The results of the experiments show that the query performance of the two step procedure for the trapezoid representation is up to three times faster than the widely used identity representation (using no decomposition) and is superior to the identity representation in all experiments. For the selected scenes and queries, the two step procedure of the trapezoid decomposition is the best choice, but the query performance of the heterogeneous decomposition is only slightly worse. Another interesting fact is that the two step procedure for the decomposition into trapezoid-like regions is superior to all other techniques used. Thus, a complex query processing strategy with two coordinated filters is a good choice for the types of scenes which were investigated.

Finally, we want to mention that for the trapezoid decomposition algorithms can be derived for other geometric queries. In [He92] algorithms for the computation of Boolean operations such as the intersection of polygonal regions are presented. These algorithms can also be generalized to free form regions. In our future work, we will generalize our decompositions from 2D- to 3D-objects.

References

[AA83] Asano, T.; Asano, T.: Minimum Partition of Polygonal Regions into Trapezoids; Proc. 24th IEEE Annual Symposium on Foundations of Computer Science, 1983, 233-241.

[BD89] Beacon, G.R.; Dodsworth, J.R.; Howe, S.E.; Oliver, R.G.; Saia, A.: Boundary Evaluation Using Inner and Outer Sets: The ISOS Method; IEEE Computer Graphics and Applications, March 1989, 39-51.

[BK93a] Brinkhoff, T.; Kriegel, H.-P.; Seeger, B.: Efficient Processing of Spatial Joins Using R-trees; Proc. ACM SIGMOD Int. Conf. on Management of Data, Washington D.C., Mai 1993.

[BK93b] Brinkhoff, T.; Kriegel, H.-P.; Schneider, R.: Comparison of Approximations of Complex Objects Used for Approximation-based Query Processing in Spatial Database Systems; Proc. 9th Int. Conf. on Data Engineering, Vienna, Austria, 1993, 40-49.

[FM92] Fahldieck, A.; Mysliwitz, N.: 'Models for Processing Geometric Objects described by Free Form Surfaces in Database Systems'; Master Thesis, University of Bremen, January 1992 (in German).

[Gü89] Güting, R.H.: Gral: An Extensible Relational Database System for Geometric Applications; Proc. 15th Int. VLDB Conference, Amsterdam, 1989, 33-44.

[He92] Heep, S.: 'Queries on Geometry Data in CAD Database Systems'; Ph.D.Thesis, University of Bremen (in German).

[HL89] Hoschek, J.; Lasser, D.: 'Basics of Geometric Data Processing'; Teubner 1989 (in German).

[Ka85] Katz, R.: Information Management for Engineering Design; Springer, Berlin Heidelberg, 1985.

[KS85] Keil, J.M.; Sack, J.R.: Minimum Decompositions of Polygonal Objects; in: Toussaint, G.T. (ed.): Computational Geometry; Elsevier Science Publishers B.V. (North Holland), 1985, 197-216.

[KH91] Kriegel, H.-P.; Heep, P.; Heep, S.; Schiwietz, M.; Schneider, R.: An Access Method Based Query Processor for Spatial Database Systems; Proc. Int. Workshop on DBMS for Geographical Applications, Capri, May 16-17, 1991; in: Geoegraphic Database Management Systems, Springer, 1992, 272-292.

[KS89] Kriegel, H.P.; Schiwietz, M.; Schneider, R.; Seeger, B.: Performance Comparison of Point and Spatial Access Methods; Proc. Symposium on the Design and Implementation of Large Spatial Databases, Santa Barbara, USA, July 1989, 89-114.

[KS91] Kriegel, H.-P.; Horn, H.; Schiwietz, M.: The Performance of Object Decomposition Techniques for Spatial Query Processing; Proc. 2nd SSD´91, Zürich, August 1991; in: Günther, O.; Schek, H.-J. (eds): Advances in Spatial Databases; published as LNCS 525, Springer, 257-276.

[OM86] Orenstein, J.A.; Manola, F.A.: Spatial Data Modeling and Query Processing in PROBE; Technical Report CCA-86-05, Computer Corporation of America, Four Cambridge Center, Cambridge, MA, October 1986.

[Sa90] Samet, H.: The Design and Analysis of Spatial Data Structures; Addison-Wesley, Reading, MA, 1990.

[SK89] Schneider R., Kriegel H.P., Seeger B., Heep S.: Geometry-based Similarity Retrieval of Rotational Parts; Proc. Int. Conf. on Data and Knowledge Systems for Manufacturing and Engineering, Gaithersburg, Maryland, 1989, 150-160.

[Wi91] Widmayer, P.: Data Structures for Spatial Databases; in: Vossen, G.; Witt, K.-U. (eds.): 'Future Trends in Database Systems', Oldenbourg, 1991 (in German).

Brain Data Base (BDB) *

G. Anogianakis(1) A. Krotopoulou(2) P. Spirakis(2) D. Terpou(2) A. Tsakalidis(2)

(1) Faculty of Medicine, University of Thessaloniki, Greece
(2) Department of Computer Engineering and Informatics, University of Patras, Greece

Abstract. The Brain Data Base (BDB) is an innovative database that keeps (in a structural way) those anatomical and functional features of the human brain, suitable for applying the principles of biomagnetism in order to localize epileptic foci. It handles complex and non-uniform 3-D objects and admits efficient query evaluation through state-of the art computational geometry techniques. The proposed logical model of the BDB may serve as a framework for other specialized databases which deal with non-standard and involved topological information.

1 Introduction

This paper reports on research, currently in progress, on the design and development of a database - called *Brain Data Base (BDB)* - which intends to map the human brain. To begin with, we point out certain features that motivate our research on representing and manipulating information relative to the human brain, as an interesting data management domain.

- The use of information relative to the human brain intends to help the localization of epileptic foci. *Biomagnetism* is a modern technique which results in possible epileptic foci. Many of them, however, can be rejected by taking advantage of the existence of appropriate information relative to the human brain (a-priori information). BDB has been conceived to keep in a structural way this information, which refers to the anatomical, functional and electrical features of the brain.

- Representation and manipulation of human brain information poses a complex and difficult task, since the objects which must be handled are three dimensional with various non-uniform shapes, while - in most cases - a hierarchy exists among them. In this paper, the problem of deriving efficient data representation and access methods for these objects, is confronted.

2 Interesting Topological Entity Sets

The main task that must be considered is how to model a brain area with a certain characteristic, for example a brain area with a known anatomical name.

A reference system has been adopted (the *three dimensional proportional grid system* [1]) in order to localize the essential brain structures. With respect to this

* The experimental results that are presented in this paper have been implemented in order to derive a first prototype report, within the framework of the CEC-Program AIM, Project A2020 Magnobrain. This study conforms to the spirit of the pilot projects to be done in the U.S. Brain Mapping Initiative.

reference system, the human brain can be divided into cubes with a side of 1mm and edges parallel to the reference lines - called *basic cubes*. For every such basic cube the known and essential brain structures and features could be specified. Adopting this consideration, a brain area could be described by the set of basic cubes that it includes. This would lead to very large and non-flexible files, since the total number of the brain basic cubes is 1,5 million, approximately. Because of this and of the existence of geometric queries, which involve brain geometry, proximity and topology, the following definition of the concept of *flexible box* is necessary.

A flexible box [2] is an orthogonal parallepiped which includes a great number of basic cubes, the number of which and consequently the dimensions of the flexible box are defined according to the needs of every case. Generally, given a connected (not necessarily convex) area of the brain, the set of flexible boxes that *equivalently* represents it, is defined to be the *smallest* possible number of non-overlapped orthogonal parallepipeds (parallel to axes) of varying dimensions that covers the area. Using the concept of flexible boxes, a brain structure can now be described by the small number of flexible boxes that it includes. This is reflected in the entity set "lobe", where the brain areas described are the lobes. The entity sets "flexible-box" and "lobe" [2] may be expressed as follows:

Define entity *flexible-box* (*center-coordinates* = string, *fb-dimensions* = string)

Define entity *lobe* (*area-id* = integer, *area-name* = string, (*center-coordinates* = string, *fb-dimensions* = string)*) /* area-id indicates the code of a lobe */

Another important issue that must be considered is how to model nerve fibers. Here, we take advantage of the fact that fibers may be grouped into bundles which branch off and come in complex forms. In order to eliminate the modelling problems that branches create, we define the set of fibers that are of the same type and link the same brain areas, as *fiber bundle* . Fiber bundles are also composit objects, since they come in various non-uniform shapes, have variable width and are very long. In order to reduce the representation complexity of such composit objects, we divide them into fundamental segments, called *bundle sections*. The latter have no topological anomalies, so they do not require special design techniques. In order now to correlate topology with brain geography, that means to correlate bundle sections with the brain space they occupy, we use flexible boxes [2]. The corresponding entity set may be expressed as follows :

Define entity *bundle-section* (*bundle-id* = integer, (*center-coordinates* = string, *fb-dimensions* = string)*)

Furthermore, in order to estimate the length of a fiber bundle efficiently, we use the concept of central path [2]. The latter is consisted of successive basic cubes; each of them is the central one of a cross-section, of 1mm width, of the fiber bundle.

The way we confront fiber bundle representation is also applicable in other network applications (e.g. telephone networks and other utility-pipe based nets).

3 Adding Hierarchical Ordering to the Relational Model

Generally, there is an ordering of hierarchical type among most of the brain structures that BDB represents. This ordering can not be expressed by the use of the relational model and for this reason we use the concept of hierarchical ordering.

For the representation of the various hierarchical orderings among the relations, we use the tree structure diagram [3]. In some cases, it is important to have an ordering among children instances of a parent instance of a database tree [4]. Such an ordering is indicated by arrows from one child instance to the next one in the ordering, while each child instance has an ordinal position under its parent instance.

An ordering among the instances of certain relations improves considerably the performance. Let's focus on the ordering among the instances of the relations "lobes" and "lobe parts", which is based on the fact that the foci of epilepsy may appear with different frequency in every lobe while every lobe is divided into parts with different frequencies of epileptic foci presence. The ordering among lobes (or lobe parts in a certain lobe), is in such a way that the lobe (or the lobe part) with the greater frequency appears first in the diagram. Consequently, the search for epileptic foci will start from the most possible areas to appear.

In order, now, to ensure flexible access within the tree-structure, some special operators must be used. Such an operator [4], is called "under". The expression (c under d) is true when "c" is a child instance of "d". In this paper, three new operators are introduced. The first two of them are applied in those cases where we have an ordering among children instances of a parent instance. We define as ch(i), the ith child instance in that ordering. The definition of them is as follows:

a) The operator *after(k):*

Iff $\exists$ (i,j) $\in$ N: a=ch(i) $\wedge$ b=ch(j) $\wedge$ i=j+k (k $\in$ N) $\Rightarrow$ a *after(k)* b = TRUE

b) The operator *before(k):*

Iff $\exists$ (i,j) $\in$ N : a=ch(i) $\wedge$ b=ch(j) $\wedge$ i=j-k (k $\in$ N) $\Rightarrow$ a *before(k)* b = TRUE

Assuming that I is the set of instances of a tree-structure instance, then the operator *close(k)* is defined recursively as follows :

Iff (Q,P) $\in$ I : (a under P) $\wedge$ (b first under Q) $\wedge$ ((Q after(k) P = true) $\vee$ (P close(k) Q = true)) $\Rightarrow$ a *close(k)* b = TRUE

The OR clause ($\vee$) has to be evaluated left to right and in the basis the "after(k)" will be true first. The expression "a first under b", indicates that "a" is the first child instance which is under "b". When k=1, we call the operator *opposite*.

4 Efficient Geometric Techniques for Query Optimization

The problems needed to be solved, have a very big input size, so space - and time - efficient solutions are necessary to support the implementation of the elementary queries in BDB. Theoretical solutions included in [5,6] cover only a part of the problems which arise in the Geometry of the Brain. In most cases, customised solutions must be developed and adapted appropriately. Here, we present an example of a complex database query and we give its geometric interpretation. We consider a query in the following SQL-form:

select coordinates, flex-box-size *from* lobe *where* intersect()

The intersect() procedure finds the flexible boxes of every lobe which intersect with a given flexible box. Let I be the set of the flexible boxes that intersect the given one, say x. The answer for this query can be combined from the following subsets I_1, I_2 and I_3 of I with: I_1 = {all flexible boxes which enclose totally x}, I_2= {all flexible boxes which have at least one corner in x} and $I_3 = I - \{I_1 \cup I_2\}$.

The subset I_1 can be computed in time $O(\log^2 n \cdot \log\log n + |I_1|)$ [7]. The subset I_2 can be computed in time $O(\log^2 n + |I_2|)$ [8]. Under the aspect of the restricted universe U of the numbers used, we expect [6] that the subset I_3 can be solved in time $O(|I| + (\log \log U)^3)$.

Finally, the optimal definition of the flexible boxes of a brain area can be supported by techniques similar to the ones presented in [9].

5 Conclusion

In the course of developing an entity-relationship database scheme for efficient representation of the non-uniform 3-D brain objects, two elementary entity sets have been introduced *-flexible box, bundle section*, which are used for the construction of more complex entity sets of topological type. Also, we have used the concept of hierarchical ordering in order to represent the hierarchy among the brain structures, while three new operators are introduced in order to ensure flexible access within the produced tree-structures. In order to support efficient implementation of complex queries, efficient geometric techniques have been employed.

Finally, we mention that a classic RDBMS has been choosen, as a first approach, while we explore whether an object-oriented approach will give better results.

References

1. Talairach J., Tournoux P., "*Co-Planar stereotaxic atlas of the brain*", Georg Thieme Verlag Stuttgart, NewYork, Thieme medical publishers, 1988.
2. Anogianakis G., Krotopoulou K., Spirakis P., Terpou D., Tsakalidis A., "*The logical design of the Brain Data Base*", Technical Report MB1.2, AIM-Project, Magnobrain no A2020, September 1992.
3. Korth E., and Silberschatz A., "*Database system concepts*", McGrawhill, University of Atlas at Austin, 1986.
4. Rubenstein W. B.,"A Database Design for Musical Information", Computer Science Division, University of California, Berkley, *ACM SIGMOD* 1987.
5. Mehlhorn K. and Tsakalidis A. K., "*Chapter 6: Data Structures*", Handbook of Theoretical Computer Science, Editor J.V.Leeuwen, Elsevier Science Publishers, co-published by MIT - Press, pp. 301-341, 1990.
6. Overmars M.H. "Efficient Data Structures for Range Searching on a Grid", *Journal of Algorithms 9*, pp.254-275, 1988.
7. Bistiolas V., Sofotassios D., and Tsakalidis A., "Computing Rectangle Enclosures" Computational Geometry: Theory and Applications, 2, 1993.
8. Willard D., "New Data Structures for orthogonal range queries", *SIAM Journal on Computing*, Vol. 14, pp. 232-253, 1985.
9. Franzblau D.S. and Kleitman D. J., "An Algorithm for Constructing Regions with Rectangles, Independence and minimum generating Sets for Collections of Intervals" in Proc. 16th *ACM Symp. Theory Comput.*, pp.167-174, (1984).

Integrating Classes and Relations to Model and Query Geographical Databases[1]

Georges Gardarin

Université de Versailles and INRIA
Laboratoire MASI-CNRS
45 Avenue des Etats-Unis, 78 000 VERSAILLES, France
gardarin@masi.ibp.fr

Abstract. Geographical databases require rich data models to represent geographical entities, relationships between these entities and geometric data. Furthermore, interactive spatial query languages should allow users to pose ad hoc queries in languages close to standards with high level graphical interfaces. This paper shows that a system mixing object-oriented and relational modelling capabilities with an extended SQL to query classes and relations is appropriate for modelling geographical data and interacting between a user and a GIS. Following these lines, a system is currently being implemented on top of an object server as an outcome of the IMPRESS ESPRIT project.

1 Introduction

The appeal of object-oriented database systems for non standard applications is due to the power of the object-oriented data model to implement nested complex objects encapsulated within methods. Geographical applications are very good examples of non standard applications. They require both the management of well structured descriptive data (e.g., the description of a region) and the support of unstructured geometric data. Geographical DBMSs of the current generation (e.g., Arc Info [1]) manage two types of databases: a factual base stored in traditional relations and a geometric base of raw data stored in files. The future generation should integrate the two databases in a unique one, in order to facilitate the modelling of geographical data and queries based on attribute values or geographic location. High level non procedural query languages should be available to express such queries, for example geographical extensions of SQL.

In this paper, we analysis the requirements of geographical information systems (GIS) both on a user and technical point of views. We conclude from this analysis that a data model providing classes, relations and types organized in generalization hierarchies is appropriate for modelling geographical informations. Such a rich data model integrates the facility of object-oriented and relational systems. The ESQL2 query language [4] — which was designed for querying integrated relational and object-oriented databases — enhanced

[1] This work is sponsored by the IMPRESS ESPRIT project, N° 6355

with a geometry data type is a powerful language for querying and updating geographical data. We illustrate typical queries in ESQL2.

The idea of using extension of SQL to interact with spatial data is not new [5, 6] and is nicely surveyed in [3]. What is new is the idea of integrating in a unique model the abstract data type and class facilities of object-oriented systems and the relation concept of relational systems. This is the key idea of the new version of ESQL2, which in some sense reconciles the relational and object-oriented paradigms. It appears to give a powerful tool for modelling and manipulating geographical databases.

The paper is organized as follows. In section 2, we survey what are the functionalities required for a GIS. Section 3 is devoted to the presentation of a generic data model for geographical data which reconciles object-oriented and relational modelling capabilities. Section 4 summarizes the ESQL2 query language features and illustrate its application to geographical databases with typical queries. In conclusion, we claim that an object-oriented programming environment encapsulating ESQL2 query facilities is a good approach toward the new generation of GIS. The GEOS prototype developed in the IMPRESS ESPRIT project is implementing such an environment.

2 Geographical Information System Requirements

2.1 Overview of Functionalities

GISs manage repository of spatial objects, i.e., objects related to locations in real world space. A modern GIS should provide the following functionalities [8]:

• Data Modelling. The model should integrate geometric data types and factual data types with their relationships. It should allow the geographical database administrator to define in a simple way geometrical and non geometrical objects.

• Data Acquisition. Geographical data are available from different sources, in different formats. Data entry often requires data understanding and data fusion. The goal should be to bring together diverse sources of knowledge in a common framework.

• Preprocessing and Data Storage. The main purpose is to bring spatial objects within the database using a common representation. Data structures easy to use for retrieval and fast accelerators for query processing should be maintained.

• Manipulation and Analysis. Different types of operators should be provided to retrieve and reclassify existing information and to derive new information from the database.

• Product Generation. This function consists of displaying results of manipulation as maps, graphs and tabular information on a variety of output media.

Figure 1 summarizes the components and functions of a GIS. They are divided into functions provided by the GIS server, which manages the geographical database, and the GIS development tool, which typically supply a programming environment for developing data acquisition, preprocessing and product generation tools.

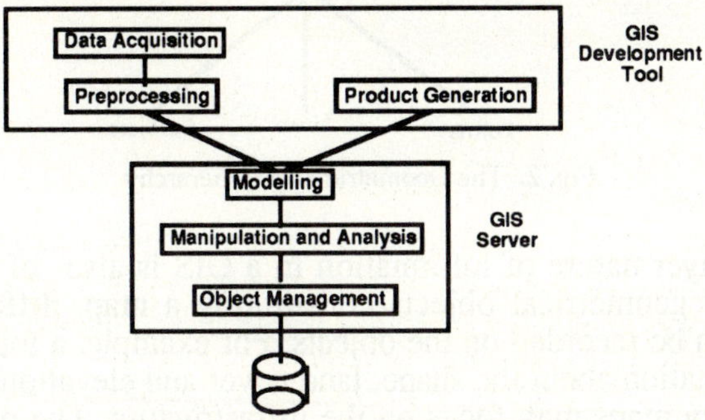

Fig. 1. Typical architecture of a GIS

2.2 Data Modelling and Storage

It is recognized that modern GISs should provide data modelling facilities to isolate classes of objects (e.g., cities, roads, counties, etc.) and relationships between these objects. Although some systems are based on the relational model, it is necessary to identify objects, to store geometric entities and to encapsulate them within specific operations.

Geographical data can be stored using a raster data structure A raster is a cellular organization of the space in which the parameter of interest (e.g., colour, type of vegetation, altitude, humidity, etc.) is given for every cell or pixel. A tessellation of the space in pixels is provided to cover the map or the image, in hexagonal, triangular or more often rectangular identical cells. Rasters are nice to store maps and retrieve local part of them without understanding the semantics of objects. They are not sufficient for modern GIS.

Vector data structures are preferable to better understand object semantics and relationships. Basic geographical entities are represented by nodes and surfaces. Relationships often correspond to edges between nodes. For example, a geographical object may be a country, a region, a river, a road, a forest, a building, etc. Such objects are represented in space, either in a two (2D), two and half (2D.5) or three (3D) dimensional space. 2D objects are projections on the ground of real objects. 2.5 D objects are 2D objects plus a maximum altitude associated to the object (e.g., by mean of level lines). 3D objects are represented with 3D points of three coordinates (X,Y,Z).

Geographical objects have a geometry that can be defined by points, lines or surfaces. Point objects can be represented as a set of isolated points. Line objects can be represented as a set of segments. Surface objects can be represented as a set of closed lines, with possible hole inside, represented as negative surfaces [2]. For being able to operate on geometric objects of different dimensions (i.e., points, lines, surfaces), it is interesting to represent them as a unique data type, called the spatial type. For example, the intersection of two spatial objects should remain a spatial object, wether it be points, lines or surfaces. Thus, we obtain a behavioural hierarchy of types as represented in Figure 2.

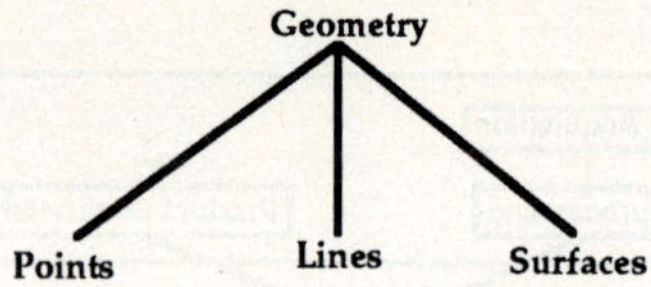

Fig. 2. The Geometric Type Hierarchy

The multi-layer nature of information in a GIS is also of great interest. Given a set of geometrical objects constituting a map, different types of information can be recorded on the objects. For example, a topographic map provides information about the shape, land cover and elevation of the terrain. Planning agency maps may focus on the infrastructure. The number of data layers to consider varies from one application to another. It might be of interest to use the modeling specialisation power of object-oriented data model to integrate various data layers.

2.3 Manipulation and Analysis

Data manipulation and analysis is one of the most important function of a GIS. A GIS should provide operators to select part of data layers and generate new data layers. The following type of operations are needed :

— Reclassification and aggregation. Reclassification is the process of grouping or splitting classes of objects in other classes (e.g., different types of forests in a unique one). Spatial aggregation requires to merge different geometric objects to generate maps at a different layer of resolution or according to different referential (e.g., a map of departments from a map of counties).

— Geometric operation. This class include intersection, union, projection of geometries as well as interpolation and rectification. It is based on the underlying geometry. Centroid determination is also useful to describe the average location of a line or a polygon.

— Topological operation. This class of operations gains from using a connexion graphs of the geometric objects. It includes connectivity and neighbourhood operations.

— Measurement. A wide variety of measurement functions is needed. Beyond lengths of lines and surfaces of polygons, several functions computing distances between objects must be provided.

– Statistical analysis. This may include mean, median and variance of attribute values in a class of objects. Histograms and frequency counts are also useful. Correlation is more sophisticated.

3 A Data Model for a GIS

To model geographical objects and their relationships, we propose to use a data model that supports the concept of type, class and relation. Types describe intentions. Complex types are used to model complex data structures handled by specific functions (e.g., geometries). Classes are extensions of identified geographical objects. Realtions are classical tables with possibly attributes of complex type. They describe logical links between classes (i.e. relationships). The data model also support generalization hierarchies of types, classes or relations. The proposed model unifies the relational, object and entity-relationship data models. It is a very rich data model, which is appropriate for specifying geographical databases.

3.1 Type and Geometric Types

We now define more precisely the concept of type. A *type* is an elementary data type (real, integer, text, etc.) or an abstract data type composed of a set of functions hiding a data structure. An abstract data type structure is specified by applying *templates* to elementary data types. The provided templates are tuple, set, bag (or multi-set), list and vector. Templates can be nested. Type structures can be hidden by functions to compose abstract data types. A type can be defined as a subtype of an existing type.

To illustrate the type construction, we now define the geometry data type. One possibility is to define every sub-type of geometry as a structural type constructed as a set of elements. Figure 3 specifies the required types to represent the spatial type hierarchy. Integrity constraints should be added, e.g., to specify that a line is a set of connected segments.

```
TYPE POINT TUPLE OF (x FLOAT,y FLOAT);
TYPE POINTS SET OF POINT;
TYPE SEGMENT TUPLE OF (ORIGIN POINT, EXTREMITY POINT)
TYPE LINES SET OF SEGMENT;
TYPE SURFACE SET OF LINES;
TYPE REGION TUPLE OF (CONTOUR SET OF SURFACE, HOLE SET OF
SURFACE);
```

Fig. 3. The Geographical Data Types

As stated above, a map is a collection of points, lines and regions. Thus, it is convenient to define a union data type including both points, lines and regions. For performance improvement when dealing with maps, it is often desirable to define the smallest containing rectangle for each geometry. This rectangle can be returned by a function without parameter as a geometry. Index structures can be based on rectangles. In summary, the GEOMETRY data type is defined in Figure 4. It provides facilities to represent any map.

```
TYPE GEOMETRY UNION OF (POINTS, LINES, REGION)
GEOMETRY function rectangle();
```

Fig. 4. The Geometry Type as a Union Type

Other functions can be added to manipulate geometries. Geographical operators are useful to handle maps. Such operators can be attached to the geometry data type. It includes:

- *Geometric functions*. Intersection, union and difference of geometries are examples of functions that return a geometry. Area, distance and length are examples that return a float.
- *Spatial predicates*. Inclusion and IsEmpty are two good examples of Boolean functions on geometries, also called predicates.
- *Spatial aggregates*. The sum of a set of geometries as a unique geometry is a good example of an aggregate.

Several other operators can be defined, which are useful to handle maps [7]. Such operators have to be included attached to the geometry class.

3.2 Database Schemas

As stated above, a class is a collection of system identified objects, while a relation is a collection of non system identified tuples. A relation implements a relationship between classes.

A database schema is a set of type, class and relation definitions. To visualize database schema, we introduce a graphical representation (which is an extension of E/R diagrams) in which types are portrayed as ovals, classes as rectangles and relations as oblongs. Single head arrows connecting classes or relations to types represent single valued attributes while double head arrows represent multi-valued attributes. Figure 5 gives an example of a geographical database using the spatial generic class GEOMETRY. It describes regions, cities, roads and forests of Europe. Three classes are created to contain the non referenced objects (Regions, Cities and Forests). Roads are represented as relations between cities. Figure 6 specifies the correspooning schema.

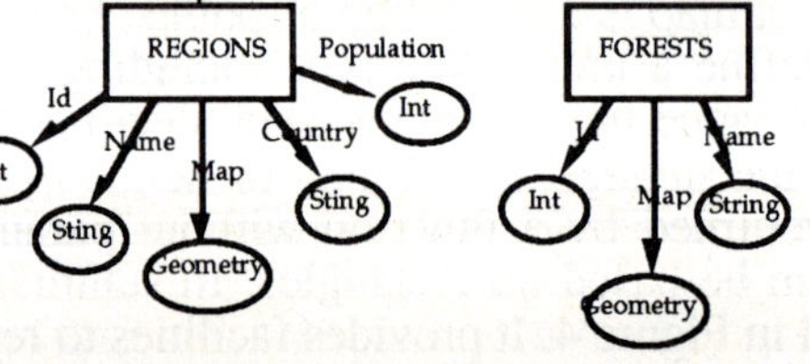

Fig. 5. Diagram of a Simple Geographical Database

CLASS REGIONS (ID CHAR(5), COUNTRY STRING, NAME STRING, POPULATION INT, MAP GEOMETRY)
CLASS CITIES (NAME STRING, POPULATION INT, REGION REGIONS, POSITION GEOMETRY)
RELATION ROADS (ID CHAR(4), NAME STRING, ORIGIN CITIES, EXTREMITY CITIES, MAP GEOMETRY)
CLASS FORESTS (ID CHAR(5), NAME STRING, MAP GEOMETRY)

Fig. 6. Definition of a Simple Geographical Database

4 A Query Language for a GIS

4.1 Querying Classes and Relations

To query classes and relations which are collections of complex tuples, we propose to use the new version of the ESQL2 query language [4]. The ESQL2 language is an upward compatible version of SQL2. The users see classes and relations and can manipulate them using an extended SQL2. Queries are of the form (+ means that several elements can be specified) :

SELECT <Value expression>+ FROM <table>+

WHERE <Qualification>

Classes and relations may be used as tables in argument of a FROM construct.When a class or relationship is referenced, the language semantics implicitly perform the union of all sub-relations or sub-classes according to the generalization hierarchies. It is also possible to manipulate data inside a complex structure using the ADT functions. Any function attached to a given type may be applied to an element of that type. SQL expressions are generalized to include the possibility of applying ADT functions at various levels. Expressions and sub-expressions must be correctly typed.

Following references from classes or relationships to classes is also possible in ESQL2 using the dot notation. Another interesting extension of SQL is the handling of recursive queries, more precisely recursive views. The UPDATE command of SQL can be used to modify complex values or objects. Complex objects are addressed through sub-queries that retrieve the object identifier in some table.

4.2 Applying ESQL2 to Geographical Databases

Typical queries on a geographical database may retrieve attribute values or maps from different kinds of selection criteria. Query qualification may involve attribute values, numerical geometric functions, geometrical geometric functions, spatial aggregation, etc. We now illustrate in ESQL2 extended with geographic operators on the Geometry data type a few typical queries on the sample geographical database.

Q1 is a classical retrieval on attribute values: it displays the map of France as the maps of the composing regions.

(Q1) Selection of maps from an alphanumeric attribute value:

```
SELECT MAP,POPULATION FROM REGIONS
WHERE COUNTRY = "FRANCE"
```

Q2 uses a geometric function with numerical results for both the selection criteria and the projection criteria.

(Q2) Selection with numerical geometric functions:

```
SELECT NAME,COUNTRY,AREA(MAP) FROM REGIONS
WHERE AREA(MAP) > 100,000 AND POPULATION < 50,000
```

Q3 uses a geometric function that returns a geometry as a join criterion. The function is the intersection denoted *. It is a typical spatial join.

(Q3) Selection with geometrical geometric functions:

SELECT NAME,COUNTRY,R1.MAP,R1.MAP*R2.MAP FROM REGIONS R1, ROADS R2
WHERE NOT EMPTY(R1.MAP * R2.MAP)

Q4 illustrates spatial aggregation: it prints a map of France without the internal frontiers between regions.

(Q4) Spatial aggregation of geometries:

SELECT COUNTRY, SUM(MAP) FROM REGIONS
GROUP BY COUNTRY

Q5 defines a geometric view in a recursive manner; + denotes the geographical union. Queries can be given against this view, such as find all paths going from Paris to Prague, etc.

(Q5) Recursive views with geometrical computation:

```
CREATE VIEW PATHS AS
    SELECT ORIGIN, EXTREMITY, MAP FROM ROADS
UNION
    SELECT R.ORIGIN, P.EXTREMITY, R.MAP + P.MAP FROM ROADS R, PATHS P
    WHERE R.EXTREMITY = P.ORIGIN
```

5 Conclusion

In this paper, we briefly analyzed the main features of a modern GIS. We showed that the integration of object-oriented and relational data models gives an appropriate tool to represent geographical data, with geometric data types, complex object instances and relationships, including multiple inheritance hierarchies. The GEOS geographical database server developed in the IMPRESS ESPRIT project supports such a model with appropriate spatial operators.

References

[1] Morehouse S., "The Architecture of ARC/INFO", Conference Auto-Carto 9, Baltimore, Maryland, April 1989.

[2] David B., "Modélisation, Représentation et Gestion d'Information Géographique", PhD Thesis, University of Paris VI, 1991.

[3] Egenhofer M., "Why not SQL !", International Journal on Geographical Information Systems, Vol. 6, N° 2, pp. 71-85, 1992.

[4] Gardarin G., "ESQL2: An Extended SQL Supporting Objects and Rules", EDS Esprit Project Report 11B.4301 Final, Paris, December 92.

[5] Güting R.H., "Gral: An Extensible Relational Database System for Geometric Applications", Proc. of 15th Very Large Database Conf., Amsterdam, 1989.

[6] Haas L.M., Cody W.F., "Exploiting Extensible DBMS in Integrated Geographical Information Systems", Lectures Notes in Computer Science N° 525, Advances in Spatial Databases, Springer Verlag, 1991.

[7] Larue T., Pastre D., Viémont Y., "Strong Integration of Spatial Domains and Operators in a RDBMS", MASI Internal Report, Paris, September 1992.

[8] Star J., Estes J., "Geographical Information Systems", Prentice Hall, Englewood, New Jersey, 1990.

Towards Cooperativeness in Geographic Databases

Andrea S. Hemerly[1,2], Antonio L. Furtado[2] and Marco A. Casanova[1]

[1] Centro Científico Rio, IBM Brasil, Av. Presidente Vargas, 824/844, 20071 Rio de Janeiro RJ - Brasil

[2] Departamento de Informática, PUC-RJ, R. Marquês de São Vicente, 225, 22453 Rio de Janeiro RJ - Brasil

Abstract. This work addresses cooperative environments for geographic databases that help users achieve their goals. The nature of geographic data, as well as the requirements for an interface to geographic databases, are first discussed. Then, the components of a rule-based cooperative environment for conventional databases are described. The core of the paper analyzes cooperativeness with respect to geographic data, separately considering query processing and the graphical display of query results.

1 Introduction

We analyze in this paper the construction of cooperative environments that help users access geographic databases. We concentrate on the novel opportunities for cooperativeness that spatial data types and their operators provide, separating the problems of query processing from those related to the graphical display of query results.

We phrase our discussion in terms of the rule-driven cooperative environment we proposed in [3]. The environment comes equipped with a set of generic rules to which the interface designer can add new application dependent rules. In either case, each rule is assigned a type that indicates when it should be invoked during the processing of a query. The central component of the environment is an algorithm that tries to apply to the query all rules that modify requests, generating a new query. Then, it executes the modified query against the database. After a successful execution, it can perform new actions as the result of the cumulative processing of the rules designed to act when queries succeed. In case of a failed execution, the algorithm tries to apply, one at a time, all rules that generate alternative queries, until one succeeds. If all alternatives fail, it also cumulatively tries rules that compensate for failures. Finally, the algorithm uses rules designed to edit query results.

Cooperative query processing in general purpose database systems is explored, for example, in [1]. But, to the best of our knowledge, there are no published papers that explore geographic data and spatial operators strictly to obtain cooperative behavior. For a fuller account of the concepts described in this paper, the reader is referred to [4].

2 Cooperative Query Formulation over Geographic Databases

The automatic correction of ill-formulated queries perhaps provides the most natural examples of cooperative query processing. But this approach can also be extended to providing alternatives or explanations to a (failed) query and to complementing a query, in the sense of retrieving more information than the user explicitly asked for. In this section we show how the cooperative approach may help in the treatment of spatial queries with ambiguous semantics, especially those formulated with the help of linguistic spatial operators whose semantics depends on context information.

All examples in this section follow a simple pattern: the semantics of an operator *op* is defined with the help of parameters whose values are fixed either in the application domain model, or in the user domain model. Moreover, the definition of *op* is expressed as a rule that reduces *op* to other known operators. This approach is naturally adequate only when the semantics of *op* is ambiguous in so far as two users may have different parameter sets and, hence, may get different answers for the same query.

Let us first consider the imprecise metric operator, *near*, considered fundamental for the definition of spatial relationships. When a user formulates a spatial query, the notion of nearness is naturally influenced by the context of the query [5]. For example, cities in a state map may appear near if they are less than one hundred kilometers apart, depending on the scale, whereas streets may appear near in a city map only if they are less than one kilometer apart. Robinson [6] pointed out that, besides depending on the context of the query, the notion of nearness may also depend on the user.

Thus, we define that P is *near* Q iff the distance from P to Q is less than *n*length_unit*, where *length_unit* is a context dependent scalar parameter, and n is a scalar parameter, that can be either unique for the application and thus defined in domain model, or specific for each class of users and therefore defined in the user models. This translational definition of *near* is easily captured by a rule to be applied before query execution.

For example, to process the query 'Retrieve all hospitals *near* school S1', the system will first apply the rule that defines *near*, which results in the final query 'Retrieve all hospitals whose distance to school S1 is less than *n*length_unit*'.

We next analyze the imprecise topological operator *between*. For simplicity, we assume in what follows that all objects involved are points. When $m > 2$, we define that the point P is *between* the points $O_1,\ldots,O_m$ iff P lies in the interior of the polygon created by connecting $O_1,\ldots,O_m$, in this order. When $m = 2$, we may give a better definition by considering that P is *between* the points O_1 and O_2 iff P lies in the ellipsis such that one of the axis is the line from O_1 to O_2 and the other axis is *n*length_unit* long. Indeed, this definition tries to capture the imprecise idea that a point between two others may not be exactly aligned with them.

We now turn to the spatial order operators *before* and *after*, whose semantics we define with the help of the concept of observation point. For example, a school may be before or after a hospital with respect to a given observation point. The system's interface may represent an observation point by a special symbol and provide specific commands to move it around the user's visual space. It may also be interesting to define multiple named points of observation in the same visual space. A possible treatment for *before* and *after* would be to reduce them to *between* as follows: P is *before* R from O iff P is *between* R and O, and P is *after* R from O iff R is *between* O and P, where O is the observation point.

3 Cooperative Presentation of Geographic Data

In this section, we focus on the cooperative presentation of geographic data. We first observe that the design of an interface for geographic databases must carefully determine a context for the presentation of the query results. To help address this question, we define the concept of a *visual space* as consisting of a *background*, which is a collection of geo-referenced geometries or pictorial data, a *length unit* and an *observation point*, The last two concepts were explained in the previous section, whereas the role of the concept of background is to help users interpret the spatial position of the geometries retrieved by queries.

We assume in what follows that the interface will exhibit the geometries of the query results superposed with those of the background. Hence, the geometries of the background must be distinguished from those explicitly requested, and the background must not be dense to avoid shifting the focus of attention from the query results. However, instead of always superposing the query results onto a background, the interface may also exhibit the query results and the background on separate windows, or present a selection menu to the user and let him decide which background he wants, if any. For example, a reasonable visual space for queries about a city might consist of just the major avenues in the city map (and not all streets) as the background, one kilometer as the length unit and a given point in the city map, as an observation point.

We assume that each geographic database includes a collection of predefined visual spaces, some of which may be specific to a given class of users. We allow visual spaces to be constructed out of virtual objects, defined over the other objects stored in the database. For example, in the above visual space, we may define the background as a (database) view over the streets of the city map, which implies that any new major avenue added to the city map will be included in the background automatically.

The interface may follow several strategies to automatically select a visual space from those predefined. For example, it may choose the visual space whose background contains all geometries of the query results, or one whose background covers the geographic area of all the geometries of the query results. If these criteria fail, the interface may try to partition the query results by geographic area before re-applying them. On the other hand, if more than one visual space meets these criteria, the interface may resort to heuristics to guide the choice, such as to select the visual space whose background has the largest scale.

The above suggestions for the automatic selection of visual spaces are sources of rules that capture cooperative behavior. For example, consider the query 'Show all schools in district D'. Assume that the database in question contains a family of visual spaces, one for each district, whose backgrounds contain the perimeter and the major avenues of the districts. The strict result of the above query naturally contains just the geometries of the schools in district D, which is not very informative. The system will then exhibit these geometries along with the visual space for district D, which is clearly suitable for the query, since its qualification indicates that all retrieved geometries belong to the geographic area of district D.

The full paper [4] also discusses the use of rules to solve presentation ambiguities and conflicts and to edit answers.

4 Conclusions and Directions for Future Research

We explored some of the new opportunities, not present in the context of conventional databases, that the spatial data types and their operators provide for cooperative query processing, including the presentation of query results. We showed, among other features, that a cooperative environment may adequately capture the semantics of spatial linguistic operators, as well as provide visual contexts for exhibiting query results.

References

1. F. Cuppens and R. Demolombe. Cooperative answering: a methodology to provide intelligent access to databases. In L. Kerschberg, editor, *2nd International Conference on Expert Database Systems*, pages 621–643. Benjamin/Cummings, 1989.
2. Max J. Egenhofer. *Spatial Query Languages*. PhD thesis, University of Maine, Orono, ME, May 1989.
3. A.S. Hemerly, M.A. Casanova, and A.L. Furtado. Cooperative behaviour through request modification. In *10th International Conference on the Entity-Relationship Approach*, pages 607–621, San Mateo, CA, USA, 1991.
4. A.S. Hemerly, A.L. Furtado and M.A. Casanova, Towards Cooperativeness in Geographic Databases. Technical Report CCR-XXX, Rio Scientific Center, IBM Brasil, Rio de Janeiro, Brasil (Jan. 1993).
5. D.M. Mark and A.U. Frank. Concepts of space and spatial language. In *9th International Symposium on Computer-Assisted Cartography*, pages 538–556, Baltimore, MD, USA, 1989.
6. V.B. Robinson, M. Blaze, and D. Thongs. Representation and acquisition of a natural language relation for spatial information retrieval. In *2nd International Symposium on Spatial Data Handling*, pages 427–487, Seattle, Washington, USA, 1986.

GeO2: Object-Oriented Contribution for a Geographical DBMS ?

Benoit DAVID, Laurent RAYNAL, Guylaine SCHORTER
IGN / COGIT & CNRS / Cassini, 2 Avenue Pasteur, BP 68
F-94160 Saint-Mandé, France
E-mail: {david,raynal,schorter}@cogit.ign.fr

Véronique MANSART
FLEXIMAGE / BDG, 43 rue de la Brèche-aux-Loups
F-75012 Paris, France
E-mail: vero@inf.enst.fr

Abstract. This paper proposes a semantic geographical data model. Localization of geographical entities is defined using an abstract data type. The geographical entities' semantic is expressed through high level concepts in an entity-relationship model extended by both inheritance and propagation mechanisms.
The system's implementation is described. It takes advantage of the object-oriented aspect of the O_2 DBMS, and in particular of the inheritance mechanism. Three different data structures allow to implement geographical entities' localization. They correspond to the topology description levels described in modern exchange formats. A principle of independence between data structures and operations is defined. This principle allows avoiding the re-questioning of the definition of a process if the data structure must be modified.
Lastly the described system has been effectively developed and is used with sets of a large volume of real data produced by the French Institut Géographique National (IGN).

1 Introduction

To date, most of the Geographical Information Systems (GIS) available on the market are built above a Relational Data Base Management System (RDBMS). The RDBMS manages the entire set of classical data types - which we call facts. At the same time, a proprietary file management system takes care of geometrical and/or topological data. A complex pointer mechanism translates links between facts and geometry. As a first consequence, this system is a single-user one since the file manager is single-user. Furthermore, there is an impedance mismatch between the two manager levels and the two query languages are not homogeneous. Arc/Info from ESRI Corp. [21] and MGE from Intergraph Corp. are such systems.

A more recent approach consists in building a GIS by extending a RDBMS. As a first step the RDBMS is extended to manage geographical objects by adding spatial data types and associated spatial functions and predicates. This architecture is more suitable for geographical data management. It eliminates previous disadvantages such as single-user, impedance mismatch and non-homogeneous query languages. System 9 from Computer Vision [9], Smallworld [4], GEO++ [25] and GeoSabrina [20] are such systems. Nevertheless, the RDBMSs are still poor regarding several aspects: concepts are simple ; the data type system is weak ; data have to be normalized in first normal form while hierarchical structures are needed ; semantic links are lost and need to be rebuilt through integrity constraints ; and the data access system is very expensive because of joins.

A third very recent approach consists in building the GIS around an Object-Oriented DBMS (OODBMS). All Object-Oriented (OO) programming benefits are available such as object identity, complex objects, property inheritance and methods. However, even if the OODBMS architecture seems to be more appropriate, it is still necessary to extend the system for managing geographical data. Specifically, geometrical data types (i.e., point, line and area) must be added to its basic structure and associated functions (union, distance, rectangle, ...), and predicates (cross, adjacency, overlapping,...) must be added to the query language.

The work presented in this paper belongs to this approach. The objective was to add the necessary functions to make a GIS using a commercially available OODBMS. We chose O_2 from O_2Technology [2] as a basis of our work. Similar works have been described in [17, 24] for example. But our work has unique aspects.

First of all, this system, we name: GeO_2, is truly operational and has been used with sets consisting of large volumes of real geographical data containing several tens of thousands of lines and several hundreds of thousands of points (40 Megabytes). Performance was therefore a main objective of our work.

On the other hand, since different data sets may be structured differently, a GIS must be capable of handling the different data structures. A GIS should not mandate its own data structure because a change of structure is never neutral, either more information is necessary, or information is lost. The described system offers different data structures and induces independence between data structures and the operations. This independence allows the operations not to be modified if data structures must. The operations need to be programmed only once, even if they must be computed with different data structures.

This paper is organized as follows. Section 2 reviews the numerous studies about the benefits of OO in geographical DBMS. Section 3 introduces our data model and section 4 describes the implementation of the data model. Section 5 concludes this paper.

2 Background

The term "object", as applied to geographical data management, has generated numerous papers these past years. Topics addressed in these papers, associated with this fashionable word, can be classified in two different categories which correspond to two approaches toward the object-oriented phenomenon.

In the first category, the OO phenomenon is considered as a technique, used for software engineering. In [19, 13, 4, 22], the benefit of OO languages for geographical DBMS software development is discussed because OO concepts have originated from programming languages. In [25] or [17, 24], one may think that OO techniques can solve all geographical data management problems. Some of the work such as described in [17] relates a set of tools to be used for application development and not ready-to-use systems. Other works, such as [24], formally define an Abstract Data Type to manage entities localisation and a map model to express operations on maps. The ADT is implemented as a class in the OODBMS and the map model is implemented using the OODBMS data model. However, in [24], the authors recognize that, due to limitations of the OODBMS, the current implementation is far from elegant.

In the second category, the OO phenomenon is considered as a model, used for semantic modelling. Some papers [12, 16, 15] highlight the various needs of geographical data management and then explain what the OO concepts can offer. But in others [14, 27, 18], authors exhibit the benefit of OO models for geographical database development. From this perspective, [14] clearly demonstrates the benefit of two mechanisms in order to specify the geographical data schema semantic. The first mechanism, *inheritance,* is widely known and therefore is not explained. The second mechanism, *propagation,* allows to determine a complex-entity property computed from the property of its components. These two mechanisms are very useful and will appear in the GeO_2 geographical data model.

3 The GeO_2 data model

The GeO_2 data model clearly separates the conceptual level from the internal level. To manage localization of geographical entities, an ADT, as in [1,7,25], named Geometry, is supplied providing independence between the two levels.

The Semantic Geographical Data Model. Regarding the semantic model, our experience with geographical information, at the IGN, showed us that the Entity-Relationship model [5] allows a correct representation of most data schemas. However, we add to the ER model the two inheritance and propagation mechanisms already cited and decribed. Any localization attribute of an entity belong to the type Geometry. So, an entity may carry several localization attributes. Such attributes may be aggregated like other attributes (originating the localization of complex objects).

The Localization Data Model. Such a model should allow processing the localization of entities. Since a predicate based model as in GEOQL [23] is not powerful enough to compose several operations, a function based model is mandatory in giving the necessary flexibility for the query resolution. In return, for the operation to be composed, every resulting value for a function must belong to the ADT. This is why the Geometry ADT is defined as a set of primitives of either point, line or polygon types [7, 20].

The Geometrical and Topological Data Model. The choice of the internal data structure is particularly important and may alter functionality and performances. Different geometrical and topological data structures have been formalized by the results of recent work on exchange format standardization, such as EDIGéO [10],

NTF, SDTS and DIGEST-VPF [26]. For example, in DIGEST-VPF, four topological levels are described : “Cartographic Spaghetti”, “Non Planar Graph”, “Planar Graph” and “Full Topology”. The need to standardize and differentiate between these different levels indicates that the levels are not compatible and that conversion of a data set from one level to a higher one cannot be performed automatically.

For this reason we have considered three levels of data structures that may match the user's needs. The simplest data structure is defined by the Spaghetti level in which the primitives are defined independently of each other. This is meant for graphical data, for which no or little analytical processing is foreseen. The Network level, which corresponds to Non Planar Graph and Planar Graph, is appropriate for networks in which the navigational aspect is essential. Lastly, the Map level, which corresponds to Full Topology, is meant for parceled data users for whom the concepts of adjacent zones and boundary sharing between parcels are rather important.

However GeO_2's critical factor consists of preserving in the structure, a hierarchy between the three levels. As a matter of fact, due to the inheritance mechanism, it is possible to use, in a transparent way, either of these structures. This leads to a unique internal model and only one implementation for each spatial operator. Furthermore, with this original technique, a user is able to update his/her data when he/she has new information about topology and he/she can also transparently integrate heterogeneous data sets into a unique GIS.

4 Implementation of GeO_2

The semantic schema given by a user has to be translated into classes in the OODBMS. Some of these classes do not depend on the semantic schema, and for the most part implement the geometrical and topological internal data structure. The other classes, however, only implement entity and relationship types as they are defined in the semantic schema.

Implementation of entity types and relationship types. Each entity or relationship type is implemented as one class in the OODBMS. Each factual attribute is implemented as an attribute of similar type. Relationships are implemented with mutual references between objects, implementing the relationship and the entity. Localization attributes are implemented by attributes referencing an object of the Geometry class .

The Geometry ADT. The Geometry ADT is implemented by a Geometry class. The data structure of the class is a set of geometrical or topological primitives. Operations on the Geometry ADT, such as intersection or union are implemented by methods of the Geometry class. New geometrical operations may be added very easily.

The geometrical or topological primitives. To represent punctual, linear, and areal data, three kinds of primitives are defined. The definition of primitives also depends on topological levels. The Spaghetti structure is limited to a persistence of object with their coordinates. The Network structure add to the Spaghetti structure the connectivity topological relationship between Node and Dart. The basis of the data structure modeling is a theory called combinatorial map theory [3, 6, 11]. Lastly, the Map structure add to the Network structure the concept of adjacency and inclusion between faces. An extension of the combinatorial map theory, called topological map, has been used. The complete schema of geometrical and topological primitives (Fig 1) is detailed in [8]

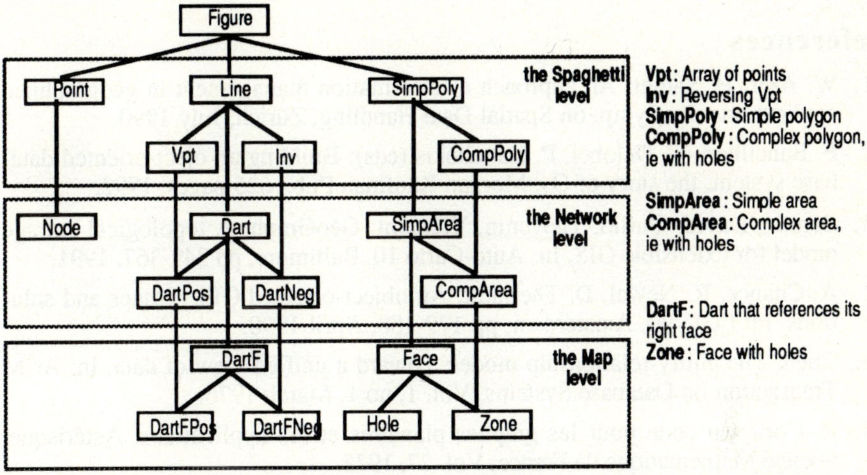

Fig. 1. Inheritance hierarchy for the geometrical and topological primitives

The aforementioned principle of independence between data structures and operations is actually achieved using inheritance provided by the OODBMS. For example, a display operator implemented on the Point, Line, and CompPoly classes will automatically work on the other primitives.

5 Conclusion

This work enabled, among other things, to assess the OO techniques for the management of geographical information and in particular the O_2 DBMS. The advantage of the OO is obvious, as shown by the extensive use of the inheritance and overriding mechanisms. Thanks to these mechanisms, the system is efficient and extensible.

The universality of the data model we have defined allows us to use the GeO_2 system for numerous studies. Work has been started to assess the coherence between geographical data input at various scales. We believe that this problem will soon become a major consideration for all users who use data at different scales and want either to assess their coherence, or to integrate data in a unique database. We consider the OO concept as a promising approach on this topic.

Lastly, we have met limitations related to the O_2 DBMS, in particular the absence of an array constructor (important to manage intermediate points in polylines and polygons) and an association constructor (which could handle inverse references between two objects).

Acknowledgements. The work stated in this paper has been partially financed by the ESPRIT BRA AMUSING n°6881. It also has been done in collaboration with the CEDRIC Department of the CNAM-PARIS. The authors wish to thank Professor Michel SCHOLL, for the discussions we had with him, and the students who worked in building and evaluating the system.

References

1. W. Aref, H. Samet: An approach to information management in geographical applications. In: Symp. on Spatial Data Handling, Zürich, July 1990.
2. F. Bancilhon, C. Delobel, P. Kanellakis (eds): Building an oject-oriented database system: the story of O_2. Morgan Kaufman Pub., 625 pages, 1992.
3. Bennis, David, Quilio, Thévenin, Viémont: GéoGraph: A topological storage model for extensible GIS. In: Auto-Carto 10, Baltimore, pp 349-367, 1991.
4. A. Chance, R. Newel, D. Theriault: An object-oriented GIS - Issues and solutions. In: EGIS'90, Amsterdam, pp 179-188, April 1990.
5. Chen: The entity-relationship model: Toward a unified view of data. In: ACM Transaction on Database Systems, Vol. 1, no 1, March 1976.
6. R. Cori: Un code pour les graphes planaires et ses applications. Astérisque, Société Mathématique de France, Vol. 27, 1975.
7. B. David: Modélisation, représentation et gestion d'information géographique: une approche en relationnel étendu. Thèse de l'université Paris 6, juillet 1991.
8. B. David, L. Raynal, G. Schorter, V. Mansart: GeO_2: Why objects in a geographical DBMS ? In: SSD'93, Singapore, 1993.
9. J W van Eck, M Uffer: A Presentation of System 9. In: Photogrammetry and Land Information Systems, Lausanne (Switzerland), pp 139-178, March 1989.
10. Norme EDIGéO AFNOR Z-13-150, 1992.
11. J Edmonds: A Combinatorial Representation for Polyhedral Surfaces. Notices of American Mathematic Society, no. 7, 1960.
12. M. Egenhofer, A. Frank: Object-oriented databases: database requirements for GIS. In: Int. Geographic Information Systems Symp, Crystal City, Nov. 1987.
13. M. Egenhofer, A. Frank: Why object-oriented software engineering techniques are necessary for GIS. In: Int. GIS Symp., Baltimore, March 1989.
14. M. Egenhofer, A. Frank: Object-oriented modelling in GIS: inheritance and propagation. In: Autocarto 9 Conference, Baltimore, pp 588-598, April 1989.
15. M. Feuchtwanger: Geographic logical database model requirements. In: Auto-Carto 9 Conference, Baltimore, pp 599-609, April 1989.
16. A. Frank: Requirements for a database management system for a GIS. In: Photogrammetric Engineering and Remote Sensing, vol. 54, no. 11, Nov. 1988.
17. M. Halstead, H. Mackenzie, P. Milne, S. Milton, J. Smith: A spatial object toolkit. In: URPIS 18, Canberra, Nov. 1990.
18. Z. Kemp: An object-oriented model for spatial data. In: Symp. on Spatial Data Handling, Zürich, vol. 2, pp 659-668, 1990.

19. D. Kjerne, K.J. Dueker: Modeling cadastral spatial relationships using an object-oriented language. In: Symp. on Spatial Data Handling, Seatle, 1986.
20. T. Larue, D. Pastre, Y. Viémont: Strong integration of spatial domains and operators in relational database systems. In: SSD'93, Singapore, 1993.
21. S. Morehouse: The Architecture of ARC/INFO. In: Auto-Carto 9 Conf., Baltimore, pp 266-277, April 1989.
22. J. A. Orenstein: An object-oriented approach to spatial data processing. In: Symp. on Spatial Data Handling, Zürich, vol. 2, pp 669-678, 1990.
23. Sacks-Davis, McDonell, Ooi: GEOQL: A query language for geographic information systems. In: Australian assoc. for science, Townsville, 1987.
24. M. Scholl, A. Voisard: Geographic applications: an experience with O_2. In: [Bancilhon 92], pp 585-618, 1992.
25. T. Vijlbrief, P. van Oosterom: The GEO++ system: an extensible GIS. In: Symp. on Spatial Data Handling, Charleston, pp 40-50, August 1992.
26. Military Standard Vector Product Format (VPF). Defense Mapping Agency, MIL-STD-600006, April 1992.
27. Worboys, Hearnshaw, Maguire: Object-oriented data modelling for spatial databases. In: Int. Journal of Geographical Information Systems, 4, 369-384, 1990.

GemCode: An Expert System Generating Mnemonic Codes for Data Elements and Data Items*

Il-Yeol Song[1], Heather M. Godsey[1], Judith Newton[2], Bruce Bargmeyer[3]

[1]College of Information Studies
Drexel University
Philadelphia, PA 19104

[2]NIST
US Department of Commerce
Gaithersburg, MD 20899

[3]EPA
PM 218
Washington, DC 20460

Abstract. Databases are a widely prevalent technology in today's industries and are not without problems. One of the major problems in managing data has been the problem of synonyms and various ways of abbreviating data elements and data items. ANSI has formed numerous committees to address such issues. In cooperation with the ANSI X3L8 Committee, we have designed and implemented GemCode, an expert system which generates mnemonic codes in an effort to standardize naming of data elements and data items. An initial prototype is presented and discussed. The GemCode has been implemented in KnowledgePro expert system shell.

Keywords. Database, Expert System, Standard, Mnemonic Code, Data Elements, Data Items.

1. Introduction

A data element is a uniquely named and defined category of data (e.g., attribute) and a data item is a particular value of a data element (i.e., a value of an attribute) [8]. As noted in [3], a lack of naming conventions and an inadequate analysis of attributes' meaning could cause tremendously redundant and inconsistent attribute names. Thus, it is strongly desirable to establish a set of rules to create consistent names that are reproducible by different people. For these reasons, a few ANSI committees have worked on the development of database naming conventions [1, 7] and developed a set of rules for the generation of mnemonic codes for data elements and data items [8].

Mnemonic codes are human readable truncated forms of original input words in English. We note that a mnemonic code is different from an abbreviation in that abbreviations do not necessarily aid the memory of a user, whereas a mnemonic will [8]. Using systematic rules for the generation of mnemonic codes will facilitate consistent and succinct, yet meaningful, names and will easily reproduce the same

* Work reported herein was supported by the National Institute of Science and Technology, US Department of Commerce, with support from the EPA, under grant number 43NANB216559 to the College of Information Studies of Drexel University.

mnemonic codes for the same input source.

For the implementation of this project, the expert system approach is considered ideal because using a rule-based expert system shell facilitates not only incremental and rapid prototyping, but also ease of maintenance of the knowledge base for further testing and expansion as well. The project was given the name of **GemCode**. GemCode has been implemented in KnowledgePro and is being successfully used in the government sector.

The paper is organized as follows: The background and need for naming conventions are discussed in sections 1.1 and 1.2. Section 2 presents initial design issues, and Section 3 discusses the implementation of the GemCode prototype system. Section 4 covers testing and evaluation, and Section 5 concludes the paper.

1.1 Background

Databases are a widely prevalent technology in today's industries and are not without problems. One of the major problems in managing data has been the problem of synonyms and various ways of abbreviating identical data elements and data items. A lack of naming procedures and an inadequate analysis of attributes' meaning could cause tremendously redundant and inconsistent attribute names. To help solve these problems, Song and Brunk developed an expert system that can keep track of names, control the use of names, and generating names based on a naming convention [4]. The ANSI X3L8 Committee has proposed the development of a system using systematic rules for the generation of mnemonic codes in a way that will facilitate consistent, succinct, and meaningful names for data elements and items and will produce the same mnemonic code given the same input [5]. After investigating what little exists in the field of mnemonics and what their own expertise had to offer, the X3L8 Committee compiled an extensive list of rules and factors considered to be relevant to generating standard mnemonic codes [8]. See section 3.3 for more on these rules.

1.2 The Need for Naming Conventions

According to Judith Newton [1, 2], the use of naming conventions for data elements provides greater efficiency when handling data, a cost savings in computer time, and enhanced cooperation and understanding among both staff and management. In promotion of this observation, ANSI X3H4 Committee proposed an Information Resource Dictionary System (IRDS) module for the verification of naming conventions used within businesses [7]. The committee's concern was that with the growth of distributed databases, "new constraints are placed on identifying redundant data and ensuring that semantic properties are preserved" [7]. Data naming standards and conventions can contribute significantly to the communication and understanding of data.

Others have observed that the problem of interoperability among databases can be solved by creating an integrated schema, or "a single description of the knowledge from the several input schemas"[6]. Yu et al. [9] propose that the semantic properties of data element names can be captured by a set of "common concepts" which aid in mapping information from one database to other, similar databases.

Given the increasing need to share data between heterogeneous and homogeneous database systems, there exists a need for a unifying manner in which to name data elements. The GemCode System proposes to fill that need by producing standard, unambiguous, easy-to-remember mnemonic codes.

2. Initial Design Issues

In this section, we discuss the conceptual design issues of the GemCode system.

2.1 Neural Net versus Expert System

Initially, the problem domain appeared to be suited to a pattern matching approach or paradigm, namely a neural network. We concluded that this approach was not feasible given time constraints and the availability of symbolic rules. Also the training set for a neural network would have been prohibitive in size given the number of possible ways of abbreviating English words and considering our resources for this project. In addition to that the training set available to us was incomplete. We have input, but not the desired output. Currently, there exists very little information with which to derive such desirable output.

The expert system approach was considered ideal because rule-based expert system shells facilitate incremental and rapid prototyping and ease of maintenance and expansion of the knowledge base [5]. The X3L8 Committee had also formulated a large set of symbolic rules which could be adapted to the knowledge base of such an expert system.

2.2 Requirements of ES Shells for GemCode

We initially identified the requirements of the expert system shell for GemCode as follows:

- Good string manipulation capability
- Good user interface (windows, fields, buttons, hypertext, mouse)
- Good control mechanism (BC/FC/parameter/weighting/rule control)
- Good external file interface (input/output/dBASE)
- Ease of maintenance of knowledge base (on/off rules, vary weighting, suspend a rule)
- Programming interface with C, Pascal, or Prolog

We surveyed a dozen commercial expert system shells, and chose KnowledgePro from Knowledge Garden, Inc. for the following main reasons:

(a) It satisfied most of the requirements listed above;
(b) The price met the suggested budget;
(c) Knowledge Garden allows us to freely distribute the developed system using KnowledgePro without any royalty.

2.3 Analysis of Rules

Since naming rules were given in [8], our project concentrated on the proper design, implementation, and test of the GemCode. In the design and implementation of GemCode expert system, we considered the following issues:

- We analyzed the given rules in two perspectives:
  - -more important (*first*) and less important (*second*) rules
  - -*easy* to implement and *hard* to implement.
- We initially focused on *first & easy* rules for the first prototyping
- We planned to implement in the order of *first & hard, second & easy, and second & hard* rules, time permitting.
- We implemented in a way that facilitated making the rules easily readable, modifiable, maintainable and testable, rather than efficient to execute.
- We also noted that:
  - a rule should be suspendible
  - weighting factors should be variable
  - the order of rules should be changeable.

3. Implementation of the GemCode

What follows is a discussion of the architecture, design details, and rules implemented by the completed GemCode prototype system.

3.1 GemCode Architecture

This section explains the conceptual structure of the GemCode system. GemCode consists of six major parts. First, program parameters are set through interaction with the user. Weighting methods, additional weighting factors, output strategies, and mnemonic code length are selected. The second part reads the file of input data into program memory and performs some minor conversions on the data. Next, the input data is compared with predefined mnemonic codes contained in an external data file. After that, the preselected weighting scheme is applied to the input data. This weighting scheme assigns a relative weight to each letter of each item. Additional weighting is assigned to the first letter of each word, the first letter of the accented syllable, the first letter of each syllable, and to infrequent consonants. After weighting is assigned, the selected output strategies are applied to the data. As referred to here, an output strategy is a procedure applied to the input data in order to reduce the number of letters until the desired mnemonic code length is achieved. After the mnemonic codes have been generated, the original input data, the resulting mnemonic codes, and the weights of the remaining letters are written to a user named output file, along with other operating facts concerning GemCode.

3.2 GemCode Weighting Scheme

The weighting scheme employed in GemCode is one labeled *Inverse Frequency Percentage* (IFP). In [8] we were provided with the relative frequencies of each letter in English text. Using these figures, an inverse value for each letter's frequency was calculated and then normalized by dividing the inverse by the sum of the inverses of all of the letters and multiplying by 100. The resulting number from this procedure is used by GemCode when assigning weights to each letter. Conceptually, the characters with the lowest IFP weights are the most frequently occurring in the English language and therefore not as valuable mnemonically, according to the rules provided in [6]. This sequence is shown below:

<u>Weighting factor scheme: Inverse Frequency Percentage (IFP) method</u>
F(Ch): frequency value of a character [6]
UnNormWF(Ch) = 1 /F(ch)
Sum_UNF = Sum of UnNormWFs from A to Z
Norm_WF(Ch) = 100 * (UnNormWF(Ch)/Sum_UNF)

Give an extra weight to the following letters:
- the first letter of a word (WF_FLW)
- the first letter of the accented syllable (WF_FLAS)
- the first letter of each syllable
- low frequency letters (WF_LFL) [6]

Three choices are provided for reducing the number of characters in a mnemonic code. These are removing the lowest weighted letter until desired mnemonic code length is achieved, compressing doublets, and removing vowels. One or more of these output strategies may be chosen by the user. However, the order of implementation of each strategy currently is not variable with relation to the others.

3.3 Rules Implemented

We have implemented the following rules from [8]:
1. Leading and trailing blanks shall be eliminated. Unnecessary embedded blanks will be deleted.
2. If the input string is equal to or less than the desired output, then the algorithm will leave that word unaltered.
7. The first letter should be retained.
8. The leading letter of a syllable has greater value for retention in a mnemonic.
9. The first character of the primary accented syllable has greater mnemonic value.
10. Low frequency consonants can be memory joggers and have greater mnemonic value.
12. Doublet compression will be incorporated.
13. Vowel deletion will be weighted.
14. Consonant deletion will be weighted.
15. The first letter of accented syllable will receive a higher weight.
16. A weighing should be assigned to specify the susceptibility of any character to deletion.
17. Characters will be deleted based weights assigned.
18. A weighing should be assigned that is inverse of the character's frequency of occurrence in the English language.

In addition to these rules, we implemented the "RmVowel" output strategy. In order to provide the users with the ability to test various possible mnemonic code generation theories, a strategy was included which removed vowels from right to left from a word. This was done in the spirit of rules 30 and 31 from [8]. Vowels at the beginning of the word and of each syllable were preserved. This strategy can be turned on or off at the input screen. See Figure 1 for the GemCode parameter setting screen.

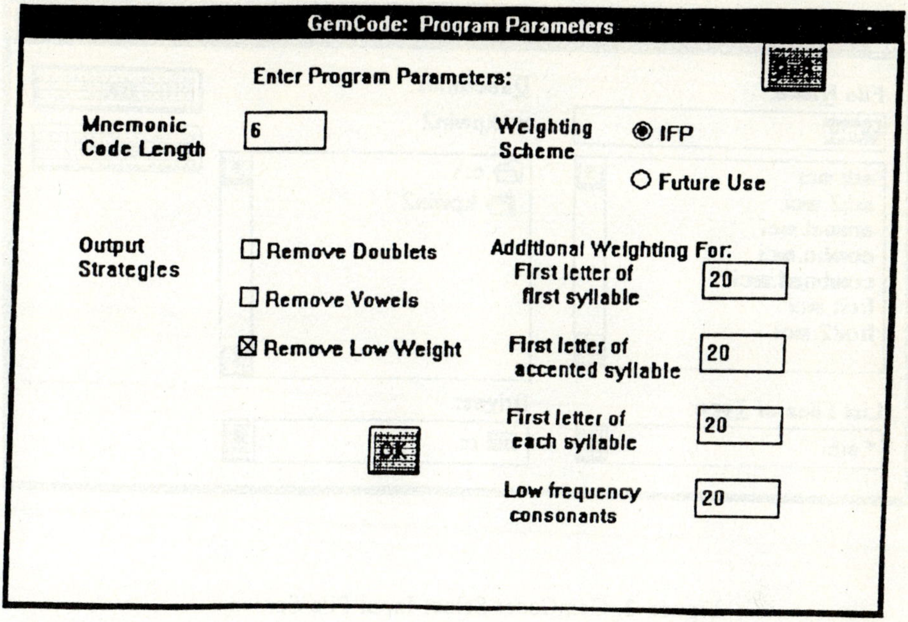

Figure 1. GemCode: Parameter Setting Screen.

4. Test and Evaluation

The following topics are discussions of test data and noted problems of the first prototype of GemCode.

4.1 Sample Data

Testing of GemCode involved the preparation of several sample input files. Input data was encoded by separating each syllable by a backslash, while an accented syllable was separated by a double backslash. This was to ease the programming by identifying each syllable and the accented syllable. Test data includes adjectives suggested to us by the ANSI X3L8 Committee, words with predefined mnemonic codes, fruit and animal names with varying length and capitalization. Using these input items, output files were prepared using a variety of different output strategies. Input files and output files can be selected from File menu of Windows. See Figure 2 for an example screen for selecting an input file and Figures 3 and 4 for the output screen generating mnemonic codes. See Appendix A for sample input word and output mnemonic codes.

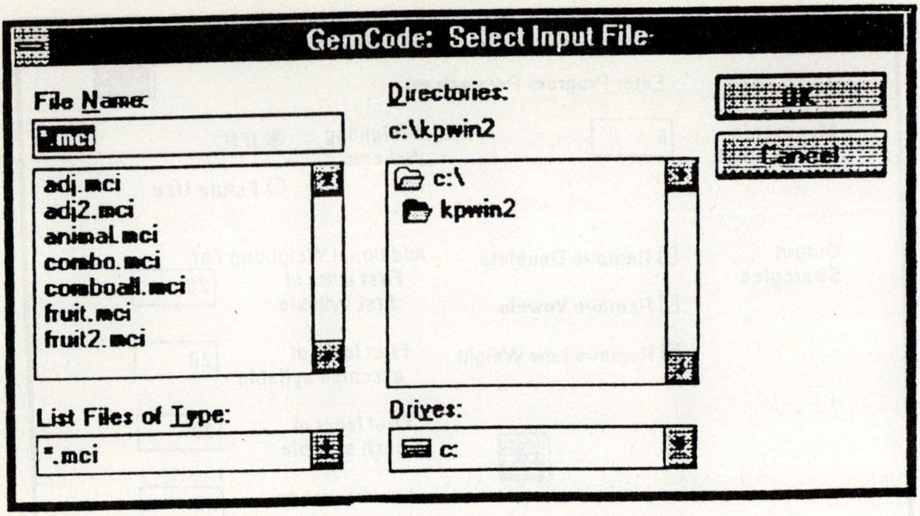

Figure 2. GemCode: Select Input File Screen.

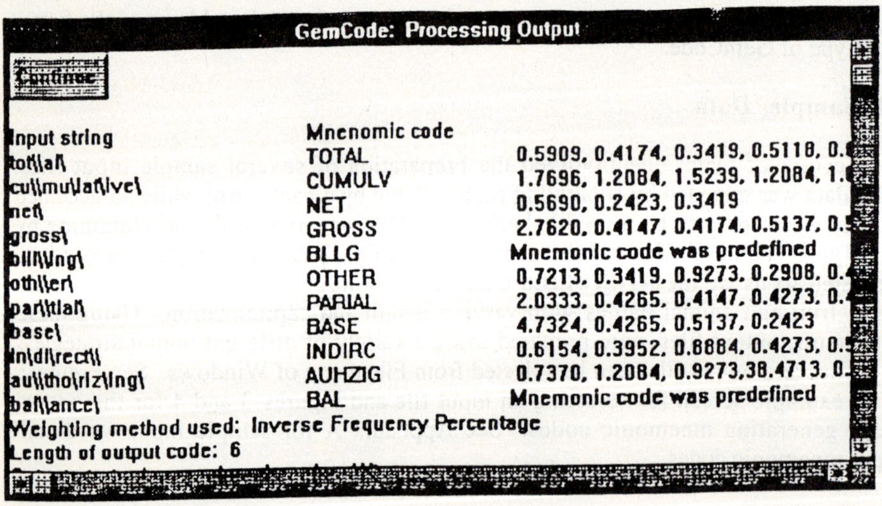

Figures 3. GemCode: Output Screen with Generated Mnemonic Codes. Part 1.

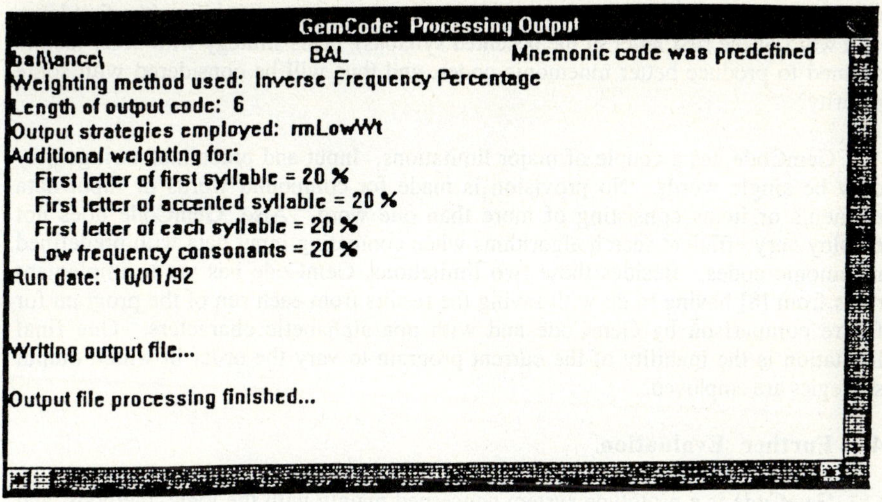

Figures 4. GemCode: Output Screen with Generated Mnemonic Codes, Part 2.

4.2 Noted Problems and Discussion

We didn't mean to test readability of the mnemonic codes generated by the GemCode, since we were given the rules and were not told to do so. We mainly focused on the correct implementation of rules provided in [8], and their user-friendly implementation. However, we would like to note several problems we feel worthy of mentioning.

(a) Removing high-frequency consonants is not always desirable. For example, STRAWBERRY was reduced to SAWBRY and PARTIAL to PARIAL. Different people might come up with different meaningful mnemonic codes for these. Certain vowels seem to be better removed than those high-frequency consonants as in this example.

(b) The current GemCode allows a user to assign various weighting factors to
- the first letter of the word
- the first letter of the accented syllable
- the first letter of each syllable

Some systematic experimental testing needs to be done to determine the optimal combination of the user input parameters to achieve good mnemonic codes.

(c) We implemented a strategy of removing vowels except certain cases (the first letter of a word or the first letter of the accented syllabus). This strategy with other factors seemed to produce better mnemonic codes, and thus will be considered with some priority.

GemCode has a couple of major limitations. Input and predefined strings may only be single words. No provision is made for compound words or input data elements or items consisting of more than one word. Also, GemCode does not employ very efficient search algorithms when comparing input data with predefined mnemonic codes. Besides these two limitations, GemCode has yet to implement rules from [8] having to do with saving the results from each run of the program for future comparison by GemCode and with non-alphabetic characters. One final limitation is the inability of the current program to vary the order in which output strategies are employed.

4.3 Further Evaluation

GemCode is a prototype system concerned mainly with the logic, methods, and knowledge used to derive mnemonic codes. Evaluation is an integral part in the process of producing an acceptable prototype. There are many different weighting schemes, output strategies, and additional weighting options employed by GemCode's knowledge base. Our goal is to come up with the best combination of factors to produce mnemonic codes with the optimum level of memory aid and usability. Evaluation will need to involve studies testing the quality of the output, enhancing the definition of good mnemonic codes, and examining domain differences in memory strategies.

5. Conclusion

GemCode is an expert system that generates mnemonic codes based on the application of 13 rules from [8]. Characters are removed from input data elements and data items based on an Inverse Frequency Percentage weighting scheme. Low weighted letters may be removed and doublets may be compressed through use of a specific output strategy. In addition, the capability to remove vowels from a word is provided by a third output strategy, "RmVowel."

Many rules have yet to be applied in this current version of GemCode. For instance, GemCode is not designed to handle input data elements and items consisting of more than one word. GemCode should provide an effective forum for discussion of mnemonic code generation and future directions of standardization efforts in the naming of data elements and items.

References

[1] J. J. Newton. *Guide on Data Entity Naming Conventions,* NBS Special Publication 500-149, October 1987.

[2] J. J. Newton. "Designing Data Entity naming Conventions," *Proc. of the Sixth Int'l Conf. on ER Approach,* S.T. March (Ed.), Nov. 9-11, 1987, New York, NY, pp. 407-417.

[3] T. Salin. "What's in a Name?," *Database Programming & Design*, Vol. 3., No. 3, March 1990, pp. 55-58.
[4] I.-Y. Song and D. Brunk. "Data Element Designer: an Expert System Front-end for Data Repositories." In *Proceedings of 29th Annual Technical Symposium of Washington D.C. Chapter of ACM on Advanced Information Interfaces: Making Data Accessible*, Gaithersburg, MD, June 1991, pp. 39-48.
[5] I.-Y. Song and H. M. Godsey. *Final report on GemCode: an Expert System Generating Mnemonic Codes for Data Elements and Data Items.* Final report to ANSI X3L8 Committee, October 1992.
[6] S. Spaccapietra and C. Parent. "Conflicts and Correspondence Assertions in Interoperable Databases." *SIGMOD Record*, 20(4):49-54, December 1991.
[7] Information Processing System Technical Report. *Information Resource Dictionary System Support for Naming Convention Verification.* American National Standard Committee X3.Information Processing System. X3/TR-11-92, 1992.
[8] X3L8 Working Paper, "A Standard for the Generation of Mnemonic Codes for Data Elements and Data Types." ANSI Working Paper on X3 Project 455-D, 1992.
[9] C. Yu, B. Jia, W. Sun and S. Dao. "Determining Relationships Among Names in Heterogeneous Databases." *SIGMOD Record*, 20(4): 79-80, December 1991.

Appendix A: Sample Input/Output Data

Input Data

```
tot\\al\
cu\\mu\lat\ive\
net\
gross\
oth\\er\
par\\tial\
base\
in\di\rect\\
au\\tho\riz\ing\
```

Output from GemCode

The three columns represent INPUT_WORD, MNEMONIC_CODE, and WEIGHTS_OF_EACH_LETTER_OF_THE_MNEMONIC_CODE, respectively.

```
tot\\al\ , TOTAL ,  0.5909, 0.4174, 0.3419, 0.5118, 0.8627
cu\\mu\lat\ive\ , CMLTIV ,  1.7696, 1.5239, 1.0352, 0.3419, 0.5128, 2.0508
net\ , NET ,  0.5690, 0.2423, 0.3419
gross\ , GROSS ,  2.7620, 0.4147, 0.4174, 0.5137, 0.5137
oth\\er\ , OTHER ,  0.7213, 0.3419, 0.9273, 0.2908, 0.4147
par\\tial\ , PARTIL ,  2.0333, 0.4265, 0.4147, 0.4103, 0.4273, 0.8627
base\ , BASE ,  4.7324, 0.4265, 0.5137, 0.2423
in\di\rect\\ , INDRCT ,  0.6154, 0.3952, 0.8884, 0.5971, 1.0241, 0.3419
au\\tho\riz\ing\ , AHRZIG ,  0.7370, 0.9273, 0.4976,38.4713, 0.5128, 1.9181
```

Weighting method used: Inverse Frequency Percentage
Length of output code: 6
Output strategies employed: rmDouble, rmVowel, rmLowWt
Additional weighting for:
First letter of first syllable =20 %
First letter of accented syllable =20 %
First letter of each syllable =20 %
Low frequency consonants =20 %
Run date: 10/04/92

Appendix B: Sample source code

The following is sample source code is one of the output strategies, "rmDouble," which reduces doublets into a single letter:

```
(*rmDouble reduces doublets to a single occurrence of the letter, as long as
max_length has not been achieved.*)
topic rmDouble(num, max).
    :rdFlag is 2.
    :temp is ?(concat (mcode, ?num)).
    :temp2 is ?temp.
    :wtTemp is ?concat(weight, ?num).
    :wtLetTemp is ?concat(weightedLetter, ?num).
    while (?rdFlag < (list_length(?temp) + 1)) and (?max < list_length(?temp2))
        then :a is element(?temp, ?rdFlag)
            and :past = ?rdFlag - 1
            and :b is element(?temp, ?past)
            and (if ?a = ?b     (*if current and past letters are the same, replace the
                                  past with a space*)
                    then temp is replace_elements (?temp, ?past, ' ')
                    and wtTemp is replace_elements (?wtTemp, ?past, ' ')
                    and wtLetTemp is replace_elements (?wtLetTemp, ?past, ' '))
            and temp2 is remove(?temp, ' ')   (*remove spaces to test length of
                                                resulting code*)
            and rdFlag = ?rdFlag + 1.
    temp is remove(?temp, ' ').          (*removes spaces introduced into code*)
    wtTemp is remove(?wtTemp, ' ').
    wtLetTemp is remove(?wtLetTemp, ' ').
    concat(mcode, ?num) is ?temp.   (*assigns temporary code back to the
                                      original mnemonic code*)
    concat(weight, ?num) is ?wtTemp.
    concat(weightedLetter, ?num) is ?wtLetTemp.
end.
```

Appendix C. Program Structure Diagram for GemCode.

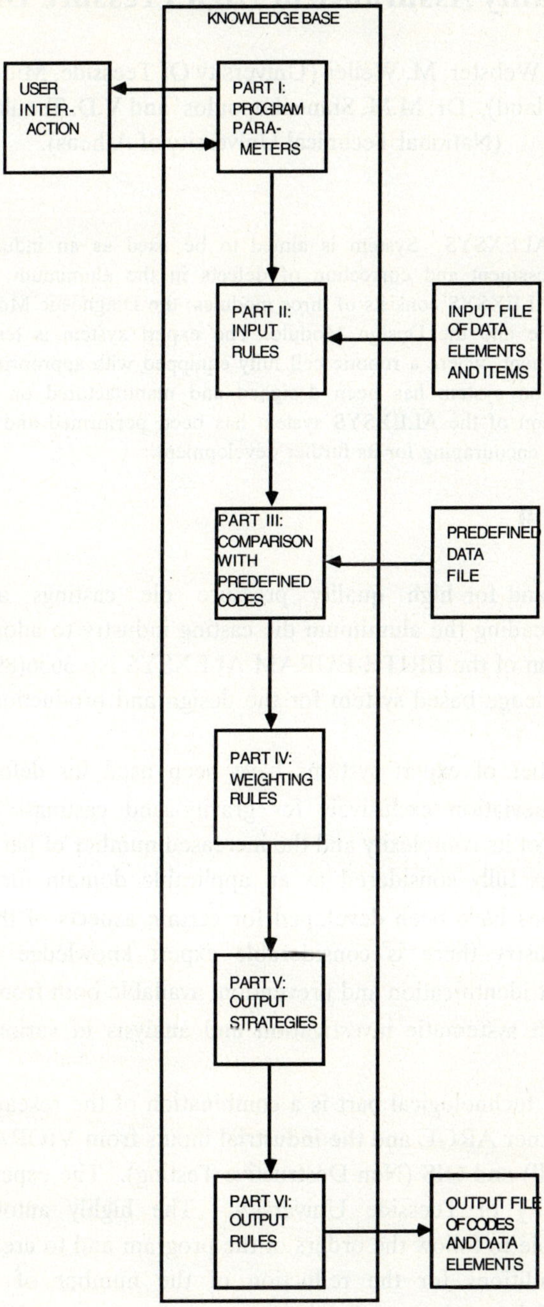

ALEXSYS - A Prototype Knowledge Based Expert System for the Quality Assurance of High Pressure Die Castings

Dr. C.A.G. Webster, M. Weller (University Of Teesside, Middlesbrough, England), Dr. M.M. Sfantsikopoulos and V.D. Tsoukalas (National Technical University of Athens).

Abstract. The ALEXSYS System is aimed to be used as an industrial tool for the identification, assessment and correction of defects in the aluminium high pressure die casting industry. ALEXSYS consists of three modules: the Diagnostic Module, the Machine Parameters Module and the Design Module. The expert system is tested within a real industrial environment, where a robotic cell fully equipped with appropriate instrumentation and data acquisition system has been designed and manufactured on this purpose. A successful validation of the ALEXSYS system has been performed and this has provided insights which are encouraging for its further development.

1. **Introduction**

Increasing demand for high quality pressure die castings and international competition is leading the aluminium die casting industry to adopt new advanced IT tools. The aim of the BRITE-EURAM ALEXSYS No 3636(89) project was to develop a knowledge based system for the design and production of high quality die castings.

A limited number of expert systems have been used for defect identification, analysis and alleviation exclusively for gravity-sand castings[1-2]. Pressure die casting because of its complexity and the increased number of parameters involved has not been as fully considered as an applicable domain for expert systems. However, systems have been developed for certain aspects of the process[3] and within the industry there is considerable expert knowledge for this process regarding defect identification and prevention, available both from the literature[4-6] and through systematic investigation and analysis in various institutes and laboratories[7].

The ALEXSYS technological part is a combination of the research results of the consortium partner ARGE and the industrial inputs from VIORAL S.A. (Robotic Die Casting Cell) and OIS (Non Destructive Testing). The expert system itself is the responsibility of Teesside University. The highly automated industrial equipment is able to follow the orders of the program and to create the necessary production conditions for the reduction of the number of defects and the improvement of the castings quality.

2. Structure of the ALEXSYS System

For the correct Expert System construction it was important to identify sub-tasks within the whole process to allow for the compartmentalisation of knowledge. It was deemed necessary to do so for several reasons. Firstly it suggests a means by which a potentially large knowledge base can be structured. Secondly with a process such as die casting which involves different people over the entire process it helps identify the various sources of expertise that it may be necessary to represent. Thirdly by performing this broad task analysis, the potential users of the system are also identified and this aids decisions regarding the user interface. After consideration of the knowledge sources, the main tasks were identified as follows:

-Diagnosis of defect.
-Corrective procedure via machine parameters.
-Die and gating design.

So the system was designed in a modular fashion according to these tasks. The system was divided into three main modules: the Diagnostic Module, the Machine Parameters Module and the Design Module.

Diagnostic Module The correct diagnosis of defects is essential for the efficient production of castings. A large number of possible defects exist and each of these has a number of possible causes. Therefore in order to reduce the search space it is worthwhile expending some effort on the initial diagnosis. The defects were divided into two main categories: surface and sub-surface (plus a third smaller category of mechanical defects). An attempt at diagnosing defects by a series of questions was made, such as; "Is it surface or internal?", "Is it a hole or a crack?", "Is it a spherical or elongated?", *etc.*

This can be somewhat tiresome for the user and more importantly the reliability of such a mode of diagnosis is questionable. There are only subtle differences between defects, and it was decided that a pictorial representation would be far more satisfactory in guiding the user through the range of defects.

The diagnostic system was constructed in a network structure with photographs of actual castings being used to illustrate different forms of each defect. The users can scan through these and select the image they deem appropriate. This is then passed back to the expert system, and the defect is named and the associated parameters listed.

Machine Parameters Module In attempting to alleviate a defect the solutions fall into two main categories, as was suggested by the breakdown of tasks mentioned above. The first is that of machine parameters that can be easily altered. These include parameters such as piston velocity, shot set point, available pressure *etc.* As such they offer the least expensive solutions as no interruption to the process is required.

The system will ask the user for pertinent information such as sleeve length, casting volume etc. and use this information to calculate optimum values to alleviate the current defect, as well as offering general advice.
The solutions were ranked according to a recommendation ratio. This was determined by obtaining a causal strength value from the expert for each Defect-Parameter pairing. This ranged from 1 (little connection) to 10 (very strong causal influence). Additionally for each parameter an "adjustability" factor was obtained which reflected the amount of time, effort and expenditure involved in altering the parameter. The recommendation ratio was then determined by dividing the causal strength by the adjustability factor.
Design Module The second aspect of alleviating defects is involved with design. There is also a sub-set of parameters that can be viewed as a middle ground between design and machine parameters, which can be termed "start-up parameters". These involve an interruption in the production process, but are not as severe as altering the die design and include parameters such as machine selection, shot sleeve length, piston diameter *etc.* They were included in the design module of the system, because it was felt the advice in this module relies to a greater extent on qualitative advice than the machine parameters module and was thus more applicable. With regards to design perhaps the most important aspect for the successful operation of a die is the positioning of the gate. Related to this is the shape of the gate and runner system and also the layout of the cooling channels. All of these will involve costly alterations and foundries are therefore reluctant to resort to such measures. The user is therefore guided to this solution after other avenues have failed. General advice is offered and optimum gating dimensions are calculated and drawn.

3. ALEXSYS: Validation and Efficiency Assessment

Improvement of the castings quality through the application of a defects diagnosis and analysis system requires the use of high performance and accuracy experimental equipment which will be able to secure the correct measurements of the machine parameter values and to react in time for the necessary corrective actions. The die casting cell, which is used for the development and validation of ALEXSYS comprises of a 280 tons locking force die casting machine, a holding furnace, an automatic lubrication system of the inner die surfaces, an automatic metal loader, a programmed oil cooling unit, a 4-axis robot extractor, a data acquisition and monitoring system for the analysis and investigation of the inter-relationships of the different die casting parameters and a process control system which is able to sense changes and make adjustments on a continuous real time basis.

The cell, in combination with the ALEXSYS system offers all the necessary functions for the correct diagnosis and alleviation of probable defects. Metal temperature, hydraulic system pressure, melt quantity, the injection velocity, die temperatures and pressures (several critical die positions), *etc.* are monitored on-line and recorded. Since all these variables interact with each other in several ways, it is difficult to detect their role individually. They must be studied simultaneously, because changes in any or all of them could affect the quality of the casting.

3.1 A Case Study

A step-by-step approach through a consultation session is demonstrated below for the case of a commercial casting. The casting was being produced with a defect on its surface at the point furthest from the gate.

The user consulted the Machine Parameters Module initially to find the least expensive and quickest solution. The pictorial gallery is selected from which the user indicates whether the defect is surface or sub-surface and the means of detection, *eg.* visual check, radiography, *etc.* After selecting one or more appropriate images the user then quits back to the Adviser system. Here the defect is diagnosed, in this case "cold flows". ALEXSYS then reasons through the rule base to find all possible related parameters, ranking them as mentioned previously. The user now selects the correction icon and chooses the parameter they wish to be given a solution for. The means of altering this parameter and thereby alleviating the defect are then inferred, the user being prompted for information when necessary.

Several parameters were suggested as possible causes, such as *gate velocity, melt temperature, 1.stage piston velocity, etc.*

It was observed that the optimal parameters to correct were the gate velocity and the 1.stage piston velocity. In order to avoid the cold flows of the previous series a new one was performed with the new parameter values corresponding to the recommendations.

The castings obtained after these alterations exhibited no, or markedly reduced cold flows. Had the defect persisted when all the solutions had been attempted then the Design Module would need to have been consulted resulting in a more expensive and fundamental alteration. So the application of ALEXSYS to this industrial sample was successful. Series of similar experiments have verified the ability of the system to diagnose the die castings' defects, to detect the reasons which cause them and to proceed to the necessary corrective actions.

The emphasis in the development of the system has now shifted towards the design of the die, with the intention of being able to offer much more specific advice regarding gating position and cooling channel layout.

References

1. H.M. Roshan, K. Sudesh: Expert System for Analysis of Casting Defects. AFS Transactions, p601-605 (1989)

2. K Sudesh, G.R. Prakash, H.M. Roshan: Knowledge Based Expert System for Analysis of Casting Defects. Proceedings of 92nd AFS Casing Congress, Paper No. 88-125, Hartford (1988)

3. S.C. Luby, J.R. Dixon, M.K. Simmons: Creating and Using a Features Data Base. Computers in Mechanical Engineering, Nov 1986

4. W.G. Walkington, R.W. Bruner: Die Casting Defects. The Society of Die Casting Engineers (1987)

5. D.L. Cocks: Assessment and Control of Die Casting Defects. Die Casting Engineer, p 26-28, January/February 1989

6. D.E. Groteke: Eliminating Hard Spots from Aluminium Die Castings. Die Casting Engineer, p 16-24, September/October 1985

7. A Mertz: Recommended Parameter Settings in Aluminium Pressure Die Casting. Arbeitsgemeinschaft Metallguss, Aalen, 1992

Viewpoints — Facilitating Expert Systems for Multiple Users

Ian Finch

Department of Computer Science, Chadwick Building, University of Liverpool, Liverpool, L69 3BX. United Kingdom

Abstract. Knowledge-based systems have not achieved the widespread usage that was originally expected from them. This is, in many cases, due to inadequate explanation facilities; particularly so in domains where the users are from a variety of backgrounds or possess different mental models of concepts.
This paper introduces the *viewpoint* as a mechanism for providing flexibility to knowledge-based systems, greatly augmenting their explanatory powers, and also providing other benefits such as increased efficiency and greater ease of maintenance.
Essentially, a viewpoint is a way of looking at a concept and a knowledge-based system with multiple viewpoints can explain a concept in a number of ways. This provides the system with a great degree of versatility, allowing it to say "let me put that another way" during an explanation.

1 Introduction

Knowledge-based systems have not achieved the widespread usage that was originally expected from them. This is, in many cases, due to inadequate explanation facilities; particularly so in domains where the users are from a variety of backgrounds or possess different mental models of concepts.

This paper introduces a new approach to explanation — the *viewpoint*. A viewpoint is a way of looking at information in a knowledge base, acting like a filter being passed over the knowledge, only allowing certain facts and concepts through. With a collection of viewpoints, the knowledge can be examined in numerous different ways. Each viewpoint highlights certain concepts and disregards others. In terms of the filter analogy, this is like examining a picture through a series of filters — the picture being seen in a different way with each filter. Some aspects of the picture may be common to a variety of filters, but other aspects will be accentuated or diminished.

The viewpoints mechanism has much merit in the construction and use of a knowledge base:

- Providing alternative explanations
- Catering to different users
- Applicability across different representations
- Applicability to existing knowledge bases
- Efficiency

- Debugging facilities for system developers
- Co-existence of multiple models
- Co-existence of multiple represenations

This paper focuses on these issues, showing how they arise from the viewpoints mechanism, how they allow a far more flexible approach to explanation, and how this is of great benefit to knowledge-based systems in engineering domains.

2 Viewpoints

Explanation can be viewed as the process of conveying understanding. The explainee must therefore be lacking some understanding and so is unable to make the connection between two concepts. The explanation system must therefore provide ways for the explainee to move from the first concept to the second. In most explanation systems, this is accomplished by supplying only one method for bridging the gap between the concepts (whether this is a rule, canned text or running a model of some sort), for example MYCIN (Shortliffe 1976) or XCON (Brownston 1985). A multi-level system (such as ABEL (Patil 1981)) can take this further, by providing an alternative explanation by adding more steps into the explanation. Whilst this approach offers an advantage over older knowledge-based systems, the multi-level explanation system can still encounter the same problem because its alternatives are not related to the characteristics or background of the user, except in a general, stereotypical way. If the user does not understand the more detailed explanation, the multi-level explanation process has reached the same block as the older knowledge-based system. It may be able to provide yet more detail but eventually it will run out of steps to elaborate, and the explanation will stall.

This can be contrasted with the approach employed by a human explainer (for example a teacher). If the explainee fails to understand some concept, the explainer often tries to approach the concept from a different perspective rather than trying to add more detail. This is an area which has been investigated in the field of *intelligent tutoring systems*, for example Goldstein's *genetic graphics* 1979 and Stevens *et al* research into different representations 1979. Wenger gives the example of two different methods of subtraction commonly used by children 1987. Figure 1 illustrates these two approaches; *regrouping* and *add and repay*.

When subtraction is performed using regrouping one is subtracted from the higher digit of the adjacent, higher order column, whereas with add and repay one is added to the lower digit of the column. A teacher thus has two approaches for explaining subtraction. If during an explanation the child fails to understand subtraction, the teacher can switch to the alternative perspective of subtraction. This is unlike the multi-level explanation system; one approach is not just a more detailed version of the other approach, it allows an alternative way of explaining the concept.

Figure 2 shows a sample rule base for electrostatic hazards, which will be used through this paper to illustrate various issues. This sample electrostatics

Borrowing by 'regrouping' ***Borrowing by 'add and repay'***

Fig. 1. Two methods of subtraction

hazards knowledge base also illustrates the idea of switching between alternative perspectives. The rules $\nu \longrightarrow \mu$ and $\lambda \longrightarrow \mu$ provide two different methods for explaining that a pipe is earthed. As with the subtraction example these two explanations are alternative approaches, rather than one being a more detailed explanation of the other. Such an approach cannot be used with existing methods, such as multi-level knowledge-based systems.

In both of these examples, the important point to note is the ability to use more than one form of explanation; more than one *viewpoint*. This allows the teacher (or knowledge-based system) to say "let me put that another way". Such an ability is very important, as expressed by researchers such as Goldstein (1979): *"the ability to explain [a] topic in more than one way is an important tutoring technique"*. This also allows the system to be used for explanation to more than one person, since each person may have a different viewpoint on the domain. Thus a physicist would view a problem in a different way to an engineer. If a human were explaining some concept and it was not being understood, they would make use of these multiple approaches to a topic, saying "let me put that another way".

This is the essential idea behind viewpoints — to allow explanation systems to use this 'let me put that another way' approach.

3 Principles of Viewpoints

Considering the example electrostatics hazards knowledge base (Fig. 2), we can see that there are four rules concerned with verifying that a pipe is earthed. One of these is a purely mechanical test ($\rho \longrightarrow \mu$), one is concerned with potential ($\nu \longrightarrow \mu$) and the remaining two are concerned with resistance ($\pi \longrightarrow \mu$ and $\lambda \longrightarrow \mu$). As with the subtraction example, different people will have been shown different ways of checking whether the pipe is earthed. A workman will be told to check the mechanical connection, an engineer may be told to check the resistance (particularly if he has had prior training with lightning, where resistances to earth are the standard way of ensuring safety) and someone from a physics background would be more comfortable being told about the potential difference between the pipe and the earth. We can thus talk about a *physicist* viewpoint or an *engineering* viewpoint. Again, these are all abstractions of the

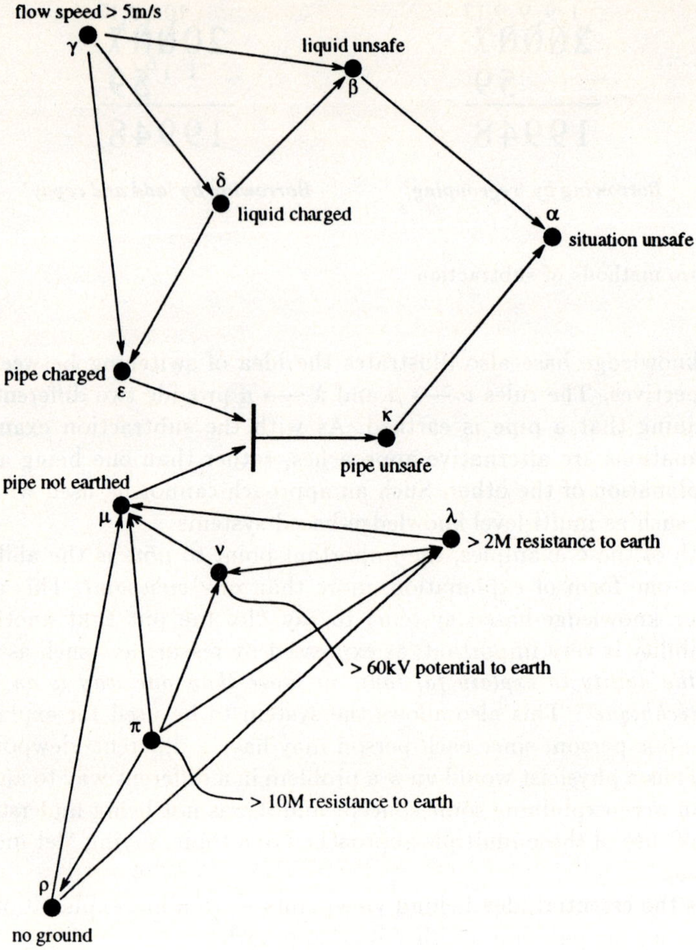

Fig. 2. A sample knowledge base

same principle, although in this case some are more straightforward and simple than others.

It must be noted that the views are not just superficially different — they are *not* just the same concept, which is merely explained with different terms, but they require all the reasoning to take place within the views too. It is not sufficient for the system to solve a problem within the physics viewpoint. If an engineer requires an explanation it may not be possible to work within the physics viewpoint and then 'look up' the corresponding engineering explanation in some sort of translation table. The system must be able to solve the problem within the engineering viewpoint so it can produce its explanation.

In simple domains, such as the subtraction problem, the viewpoints are very closely related and thus there is no real problem switching between them. With more complex domains, however, this will not always be the case. The route taken to get from the initial stage of a problem to its solution may be very different between two viewpoints and switching between viewpoints will therefore become difficult. As an example, a tank containing some liquid could be described using a charge viewpoint (how charges move in the liquid and tank) or a potential viewpoint (how lines of flux look through the liquid and the tank). Various phenomena can be explained using either viewpoint, but there is no easy way to switch between the two. Thus the expert must be able to solve a problem by considering how the charges move and how the flux lines alter. There is no way of solving the problem using the charge viewpoint and then using this solution to explain how the lines of flux are altered. So, using these ideas, we can present a definition for a 'viewpoint':

> *A viewpoint is the collection of models which comprise a person's understanding of the knowledge in a domain.*

Successful problem solving must adopt the viewpoint of the user with the bonus that explanation can also be generated within the viewpoint, providing a dialogue which the user feels comfortable with and which is thus readily comprehensible to the user. Thus we reach two important conclusions:

- To construct a knowledge-based system capable of providing appropriate explanation to a wide range of users, the system must be able to look at a problem from the viewpoints of each of the users.
  So that the system can aid different groups of people simultaneously or provide one person with more than one viewpoint, it must be able to move between viewpoints.

Figure 3 indicates some sample viewpoints for the example electrostatics rule base (from Fig. 2).

4 Implementing Viewpoints

This section will give a brief discussion of the implementation of viewpoints, both for a rule-based expert system and a deeper representation, illustrating the applicability of the viewpoints mechanism to different representations. The section will begin with an outline of the implementational requirements, leading to the application of those requirements to a rule-based system and to deeper representations.

4.1 Implementational Requirements

There are three requirements for implementing viewpoints:

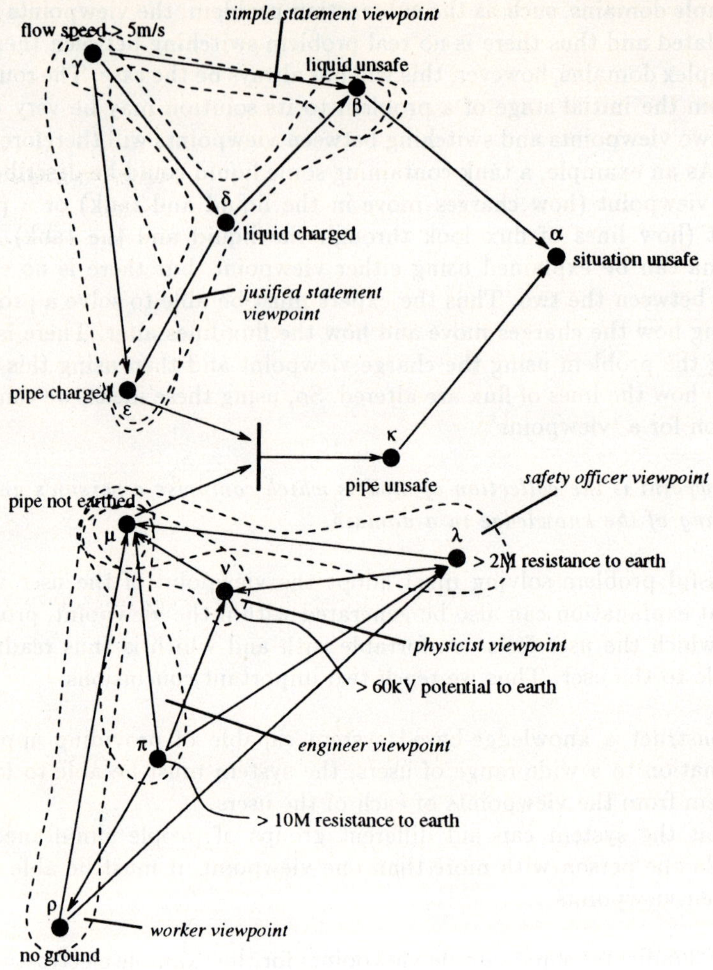

Fig. 3. A collection of viewpoints

- *A way of enabling / disabling viewpoints* — the system must be able to select certain viewpoints within which to reason and explain, so there must be a facility for enabling and disabling viewpoints.
- *A method for marking which viewpoint an entity belongs to* — for any concept to be recognised as belonging to a viewpoint, the system must mark that concept as belonging to a viewpoint (or more than one viewpoint).
- *A way of moving between viewpoints* — there are situations where one viewpoint is not capable of solving or explaining a problem. In such a case, there must be a mechanism to enable the system to move to an alternative viewpoint.

4.2 Viewpoints in a Rule-Based Approach

For a rule-based approach, there are two possibilities for the location of the viewpoints mechanism. It can be sited in the inference engine or viewpoints can be explicitly added to the rule base. Both approaches have advantages and disadvantages. For example if the viewpoints mechanism is sited in the inference engine then the knowledge engineer need not worry about how it works, but conversely has no fine control over it. Further discussion of this can be found in Finch (1992).

As a brief example, we will consider a case where the viewpoints mechanism is located in the rule base. This example will be given in PROLOG rather than an expert system shell, but the points should be clear. The rule base to be considered is that of Fig. 3, and the three requirements for implementing viewpoints (Sect. 4.1) will be discussed in turn.

Firstly, we need a way to enable and disable viewpoints. One simple way to accomplish this is to store enabled viewpoints in a list, for example:

```
viewpoints :- [simpleStatement,investigator].
```

This would imply that the *simple statement* and *investigator* viewpoints were active. To enable a viewpoint, we simply add it to this list and to disable it, we remove it from the list:

```
EnableViewpoint(X) :- append(viewpoints,X,viewpoints).
DisableViewpoint(X) :- efface(X,viewpoints,viewpoints).
```

The only other thing which is necessary is a way of telling whether a viewpoint is active. This is achieved simply by checking whether it is a member of the *viewpoints* list:

```
ViewpointEnabled(X) :- member(X,viewpoints).
```

The second requirement from Sect. 4.1 was being able to mark the viewpoint to which a rule belongs. This can be accomplished by adding a test to the condition for a rule, checking that a particular viewpoint is enabled. Thus, a rule to check whether a liquid is safe might be:

```
liquidUnsafe :- flowSpeed > 5.
```

This rule belongs to the viewpoints *simple statements*, so we can mark the rule as belonging to that viewpoint by modifying it slightly:

```
liquidUnsafe :- ViewpointEnabled(simpleStatement),
                flowSpeed > 5.
```

Note that it is also possible to mark a rule as belonging to more than one viewpoint, using a logical *or*:

```
pipeNotEarthed :- (ViewpointEnabled(safetyOfficer);
                   ViewpointEnabled(investigator)),
                  resistanceToEarth > 2.
```

The final requirement for implementing viewpoints is the ability to move between viewpoints. This is accomplished by adding an appropriate *enable viewpoint* call to the consequent of the rule (and possibly disabling other viewpoints). An investigator knows about the earthing safety margin and so can switch between the *safety officer* and *investigator* viewpoints:

```
addSafetyMargin :- ViewpointEnabled(safetyOfficer),
                   (EnableViewpoint(investigator);
                    DisableViewpoint(safetyOfficer)).

addSafetyMargin :- ViewpointEnabled(investigator),
                   (EnableViewpoint(safetyOfficer);
                    DisableViewpoint(investigator)).
```

This section has shown how the viewpoints mechanism can be implemented in a rule-based system. Notice that this approach also allows an already existing rule base to be modified so that the benefits of viewpoints are available.

4.3 Viewpoints in a Deeper Representation

Deep representations do not seek to represent the reasoning process but the knowledge underlying this process. The approaches taken may be different — for example SOPHIE (Brown *et al* 1982) views physical systems as devices whilst STEAMER (Hollan *et al* 1984) is based on physical processes — but the aims are the same. This leads to many advantages, most notably the separation of structure and function.

The separation of function and structure means that a model contains no assumption about the purpose to which it will be put. As an example, the sample knowledge base contains a rule stating that a flow speed of greater than five metres per second causes the liquid to become charged. The representation assumes that the only reason the flow speed is important is to check whether the liquid is charged. This can be contrasted with a deeper representation, where the charging process is represented as a qualitative model (although other deep representations can be used). By altering parts of the model, such as the flow speed, the liquid can become charged. However, there is no direct causal link between the flow speed and the liquid's charge; no assumption as to why flow speed is part of the model.

This separation of function and structure can be exploited by the viewpoints mechanism, by allowing different viewpoints onto the model. For example, there could be a *fault diagnosis* viewpoint for analysing why something went wrong, and a *design* viewpoint for aiding the design of a new plant (or whatever is appropriate to the domain). This would make the underlying model seem different with each selected viewpoint, reducing the complexity of the model (since it is less general).

This combats one problem frequently associated with deep representations; that they are inefficient because they must reason from first principles. The application of viewpoints to a deep representation allows the model to be made more efficient, without compromising its generality:

- The underlying model is still fully available for reasoning and explanation.
- If different viewpoints are needed, they can be added without altering the underlying model.
- The reasoning, if performed using a viewpoint, is more efficient since it need not run the full model.

Another criticism of deeper representations is that they are inefficient since reasoning from first principles is more difficult than using shallower heuristic approaches. The viewpoints mechanism provides a method for minimising this inefficiency. Two viewpoints can be provided, one for the heuristics and one for the deeper model. Not only would the system then be able to switch between the two representations, but the relationship between the two representations would also be made explicit since it is needed to make enabling and disabling of the viewpoints possible.

Deep representations generally allow a dialogue oriented approach to explanation, where questions are answered through a process of negotiation rather than a simple answer to a question. This enables the system to explain in a 'human-like' way (following the patterns discussed by researchers such as Hughes (1986) and Kidd (1985)). This ability can be greatly enhanced by the use of the viewpoints mechanism. At various times during a typical session with a human expert the focus of the explanation changes. This has been noted by researchers such as Grosz (1977) and Kidd (1985). The viewpoints mechanism can thus be used to make this co-operation between knowledge-based system and user more efficient, by attaching various models and heuristics to viewpoints and then changing viewpoints as the focus changes during the explanation process.

As a brief example, there follows an example implementation of a multi-viewpoint system using a deeper representation. The knowledge base chosen for the sample multi-viewpoint system was concerned with electrostatic hazards in the petroleum industry and used similar concepts to those in Fig. 2. An object oriented approach was taken, using the lisp-based development system *KEE* from *IntelliCorp*. The domain was divided into two classes of object; physical entities (such as liquids, pipes and containers) and concepts which acted upon those physical entities (such as Ohm's Law or pipe charging). The problem-solving was accomplished using two built-in features of *Kee*; *KeeWorlds*, which allows various states of the knowledge base to be maintained simultaneously, and an assumption-based truth maintenance system. The general approach to solving a problem was to create three worlds to test hypotheses in. The first represented the system as it was at the last known time before the incident, the second represented the system after an incident occured and the third represented a perfectly running system. A chain of worlds was then generated from the first (initial) world trying to reach the second (post-incident) world. At each stage, the newly-created world was compared with the third (perfect) world to check for inconsistencies. If an inconsistency was found, it was cited as a possible cause for the incident.

To implement viewpoints, we must once more consider the three requirements from Sect. 4.1. Firstly, we need to mark which viewpoint a concept belongs to. This was accomplished simply by creating an object for each viewpoint and then making any concept which belonged to that viewpoint a child of it. This is shown in Fig. 4.

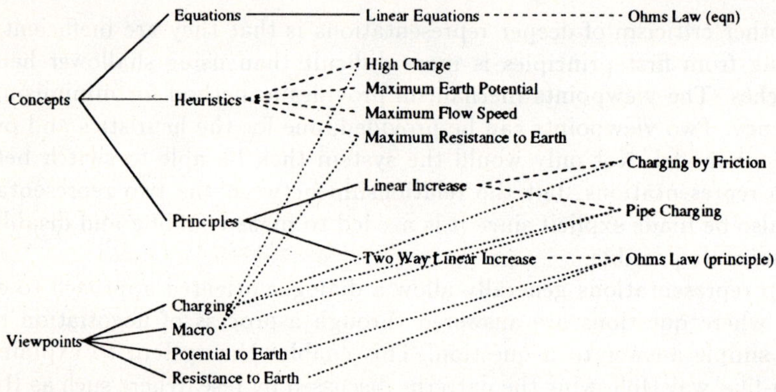

Fig. 4. Viewpoints in a deeper representation

The second requirement is to enable and disable viewpoints. This was accomplished by giving each viewpoint object an 'enabled' slot. If this was set to 'true' the viewpoint was enabled, and if it was set to 'nil' the viewpoint was disabled. Since this slot was inherited by the children of the viewpoint, each concept would also have an 'enabled' slot which could be checked before using the concept. This made enabling and disabling a viewpoint a simple matter of setting a slot value, for example to enable the *macro* viewpoint:

```
(put.value 'Macro 'enabled t)
```

The final requirement was to be able to move between viewpoints. Concepts which belong to more than one viewpoint are easily identified since they have more than one 'viewpoint' parent (for example 'Ohms Law (principle)' in Fig. 4). When a problem cannot be solved within the active viewpoint (or viewpoints), such a concept can be used as a 'pivot' to move from one viewpoint to another. This is achieved by enabling the viewpoint to move to (and possibly disabling the current viewpoint).

This example should have given an idea of how the viewpoints mechanism can be applied to deeper representations. The space available does not allow a full discussion of this example and the interested reader is directed to Finch (1992) for further details.

5 Benefits Arising from the use of Viewpoints

A list of benefits arising from the use of viewpoints was given in Sect. 1. Following on the discussion so far, this list can now be discussed in detail. This section will concentrate on the benefits relating to explanation for multiple users. The interested reader is directed to Finch (1992) for discussion of the remaining points.

5.1 Provision of Alternative Explanations

The viewpoints mechanism gives a knowledge-based system the ability to provide alternative explanations. Since the knowledge in the system is grouped into viewpoints, an explanation can be given within a viewpoint which is appropriate for the user. If that explanation is not sufficient for the user, a related viewpoint can be selected and an alternative explanation can be provided from that new viewpoint. This use of the viewpoints mechanism not only encapsulates other explanation methods (such as multi-level systems (Patil 1981), Genetic Graphs (Goldstein 1979) and Representational Viewpoints (Stevens *et al* 1979)) but offers facilities not available with other systems, such as an explanation in terms of the two viewpoints of potential and resistance.

5.2 Catering for Different Users

The viewpoints mechanism enables a knowledge-based system to provide explanations tailored to different users. In this case, each viewpoint can be tailored for a user or a group of users. Then, when the system is producing an explanation for a user, only the appropriate viewpoint is used. The example rule base illustrates this, with viewpoints such as *physicist* and *engineer*.

5.3 Co-existence of Multiple Models

It is sometimes necessary for a knowledge base to have multiple models of its knowledge. For example, more than one granularity of representation may be needed or it may simply be desireable to store the same information in different ways. The viewpoints mechanism allows such multiple models to be handled with ease. Each model belongs to a different viewpoint and the appropriate viewpoint can then be enabled for reasoning or explanation, allowing the appropriate model to be utilised.

5.4 Co-existence of Multiple Representations

The viewpoints mechanism allows the co-existence of multiple representations of knowledge. As for co-existence of multiple models, each representation belongs to a different viewpoint, and these viewpoints can be enabled or disabled to select the different representations for reasoning and explanation.

6 Conclusion

This paper has highlighted the problems which arise when knowledge-based systems have to provide explanation to people with different models of the same situation. Viewpoints provide powerful solutions to these problems, greatly enhancing the power of knowledge-based systems, providing better explanation abilities and aiding in the production and ever-growing task of maintaining knowledge bases.

References

Brownston, L., Farrel, R., Kant, E., Martin, M.: Programming Expert Systems in OPS5: An Introduction to Rule-Based Programming. Addison-Wesley (1985)

Finch, I.: Intelligent Explanation from Expert Systems. Ph.D. Thesis, University of Liverpool (1992)

Goldstein, I.P.: The Genetic Graph: A Representation for the Evolution of Procedural Knowledge. International Journal of Man–Machine Studies **11** (1979) 51–77

Grosz, B.J.: The Representation and Use of Focus in a System for Understanding Dialogues. Natural Language (1977)

Hughes, S.: Question Classification in Rule-based Systems. In M.A. Bramer, editor, *Research and Development in Expert Systems III*. Cambridge University Press (1986)

Kidd, A.L.: What do Users Ask — Some Thoughts on Diagnostic Advice. In Martin Merry, editor, *Expert Systems 85*. Cambridge University Press (1985)

Patil, R.S.: Causal Representation of Patient Illness for Electrolyte and Acid-Base. Ph.D. Thesis, M.I.T. (1981)

Stevens, A.L., Collins, A., Goldin, S.: Misconceptions in Students' Understanding. International Journal of Man–Machine Studies, **11** (1979) 145–156

Shortliffe, E.H.: Computer-Based Medical Consultations: MYCIN. Elsevier (1976)

Brown, J.S., Burton, R.R., de Kleer, J.: Pedagogical, Natural Language and Knowledge Engineering Techniques in SOPHIE I, II and III. In Sleemanm D.H., Brown, J.S., editor, *Intelligent Tutoring Systems*. Academic Press, London (1982)

Hollan, J.D., Hutchins, E.L., Weitzman, L.: STEAMER: An Interactive, Inspectable Simulation-Based Training System. A.I. Magazine **5:2** (1984) 15–27

Etienne Wenger. Artificial Intelligence and Tutoring Systems. Morgan Kaufmann (1987)

IMPROVING SHAFER-LOGAN'S ALGORITHM FOR HANDLING HIERARCHICAL EVIDENCE

J. W. Guan, D. A. Bell
Department of Information Systems
University of Ulster at Jordanstown
Newtownabbey, Co. Antrim
BT37 0QB, Northern Ireland, U.K.
E-mail: CBFM23@UK.AC.ULSTER.UJVAX

Abstract. Shafer and Logan (1987) gave an algorithm for the exact implementation of Dempster-Shafer's rule in the case of hierarchical evidence. This algorithm is computationally efficient, and it makes the approximation suggested by Gordon and Shortliffe (1985) unnecessary. However, the key steps in the Shafer-Logan algorithm (Subroutines 4 and 6) are rather complicated. In this article we improve the algorithm to make the key steps unnecessary. This makes the algorithm more attractive for embodiment in working systems.

1 INTRODUCTION

The Dempster-Shafer theory of evidence significantly generalizes Bayesian statistics as a basis for representing evidence and developing evidential reasoning systems. Unfortunately, the computation of probabilities on subsets is exponentially complex. There are special cases where better execution times are possible. For example, if we restrict our attention to a special type of subsets — singletons and their negations — we can use a linear-time computational technique developed by Barnett (1981).

However, Barnett's restriction is too strict for application to hierarchical hypothesis spaces in Artificial Intelligence, and these occur frequently in practice. So Gordon and Shortliffe (1985) suggested an approximation method to deal with the computation on subsets and their negations. However, approximation can be avoided if we use a technique introduced by Shafer and Logan (1987). This gives an exact computation for belief functions in terms of a random subset representation, and still retains the linear time character of Barnett's method.

The Shafer-Logan algorithm consists of six subroutines. The key steps in the Shafer-Logan algorithm (Subroutines 4 and 6) are rather complicated. In this article we improve the algorithm to make the key steps unnecessary. It takes 4 sections of this paper to state the Shafer-Logan algorithm in a way which permits us to explain our improvement.

Section 2 introduces Gordon-Shortliffe's concept of a hypothesis space which forms a tree hierarchy and overviews the Shafer-Logan algorithm implementing the Dempster-Shafer combination rule for hierarchical evidence. This kind of space manifests itself in many Expert Systems, especially in medical expert systems and fault diagnosis expert systems. Finally, we outline the Shafer-Logan algorithm implementing Dempster-Shafer's rule for hierarchical evidence.

Section 3 introduces the first three subroutines of the Shafer-Logan algorithm (Subroutines 1 to 3) used to combine evidence for the nodes on the top level; i.e., for the son nodes of the tree root.

Section 4 introduces the formulae used to combine evidence from a father node to its son nodes (i.e., for Subroutines 4 to 6.)

Section 5 introduces Subroutines 4 to 6 of the Shafer-Logan algorithm — used to combine evidence from a father node to its son nodes.

Now we are in a position to explain our improvement.

Section 6 proves a theorem to give a formula which allows us to eliminate the key steps (Subroutines 4 and 6) of the Shafer-Logan algorithm.

All formulae introduced in this paper are simple and easy to understand. We do not consider here their detailed derivation which involves the notion of refinement mapping (Guan & Bell 1992).

2 HIERARCHICAL EVIDENCE

This section introduces Gordon-Shortliffe's tree hierarchy and gives an overview of the Shafer-Logan algorithm implementing Dempster-Shafer's rule for hierarchical evidence.

This kind of hierarchical hypothesis space has wide application in Expert Systems, especially in diagnosis systems in medicine and in mechanical and electrical engineering.

2.1 GORDON-SHORTLIFFE'S TREE HIERARCHY

Gordon and Shortliffe introduced the concept of "tree hierarchy" as being a ubiquitous structure in application. It is characterized by set partitions.

A *tree hierarchy* on 2^{Ω} is really an upside-down tree. It is a collection

$$\mathcal{T} = \{R, ..., T, ..., S; \emptyset \subset R, ..., T, ..., S \subset \Omega\}$$

of non-empty proper subsets of Ω such that it can be represented as an inverted tree with *root* Ω on the top and the *nodes* (proper subsets)

$$R, ..., T, ..., S$$

(notice that here the root is not a node) *below*, satisfying *the tree hierarchy conditions* below.

Condition 1. *The son nodes of a node form a partition of the node.* For each node R (or root Ω) in the tree, the nodes, if any, directly below (i.e., proper subsets of) R (or Ω) $\emptyset \subset R_{s1}, R_{s2}, ..., R_{ss_R} \subset R$ (or $\emptyset \subset U, ..., V, ..., W \subset \Omega$) are called its *sons*, if they make a partition of R (or Ω); i.e., $R = \cup_{i=1,2,...,s_R} R_{si}$; $R_{si} \cap$

$R_{sj} = \emptyset$ for $i \neq j$ (or $\Omega = U \cup ... \cap V \cup ... \cup W$, where $U, ..., V, ..., W$ are mutually disjoint.) (Suppose, $s_R \geq 2$ if $s_R > 0$. Also, suppose$|\{U, ..., V, ..., W\}| \geq 2$.)

For node R, the collection of its son nodes is denoted by $\mathcal{S}_R$,

$$\mathcal{S}_R = \{R_{s1}, R_{s2}, ..., R_{ss_R}\}.$$

We also write $\mathcal{S}_\Omega = \{U, ..., V, ..., W\}$, where $U, ..., V, ..., W$ are all of the son nodes of Ω on the first level from the tree root Ω.

The collective term for all nodes below ($\subset$) node R (or root Ω) is *descendants* — its sons

$$R_{d1} = R_{s1}, R_{d2} = R_{s2}, ..., R_{ds_R} = R_{ss_R};$$

and its sons' sons, and so on ...,

$$R_{d,s_R+1} = (R_{s1})_{s1}, R_{d,s_R+2} = (R_{s1})_{s2}, ..., R_{d,s_R+s_{R,1}} = (R_{s1})_{ss_{R,1}}; ...; ..., R_{dd_R}.$$

For node R, the collection of its descendants is denoted by $\mathcal{D}_R$, $\mathcal{D}_R = \{R_{d1}, R_{d2}, ..., R_{dd_R}\}$.

Obviously, all son nodes are descendants, $\mathcal{S}_R \subseteq \mathcal{D}_R$ for each node R in the tree.

For root Ω, the collection of its descendants is denoted by $\mathcal{D}_\Omega$, and we have $\mathcal{D}_\Omega = \{R, ..., S, ..., T\} = \mathcal{T}$, the collection of all subsets in the tree hierarchy.

The nodes without any descendants are called *leaves* or *terminal* nodes.

Condition 2. *Every non-terminal node has at least two sons.* Actually, this condition is already included in condition 1 (see: $s_R \geq 2$ if $s_R > 0$, and $|\mathcal{S}_\Omega| \geq 2$).

Condition 3. *All terminal nodes are singletons in* 2^Ω.

2.2 THE SHAFER-LOGAN ALGORITHM IMPLEMENTING THE DEMPSTER-SHAFER RULE FOR HIERARCHICAL EVIDENCE

Our task is to compute $m = m_R \oplus ... \oplus m_S \oplus ... \oplus m_T$ on 2^Ω, where subsets $\emptyset \subset R, ..., S, ..., T \subset \Omega$ form a tree hierarchy on 2^Ω, and each term m_T represents a *mass function* [11] which has no focal elements other than $T, \Omega - T, \Omega$; that is, we have

$$m_T(T) = p_T, m_T(\Omega - T) = c_T, m_T(\Omega) = r_T, m_T(elsewhere) = 0;$$

where

$$p_T + c_T + r_T = 1; 0 \leq p_T, c_T, r_T \leq 1.$$

We introduce some new notation to make our presentation concise.

I. NOTATION $m_{W\downarrow}, m_{\Omega\downarrow}; p_{W\downarrow}, c_{W\downarrow}, r_{W\downarrow}$ and a_W, b_W

For every node W in the tree, denote $m_{W\downarrow} = m_{W_{d1}} \oplus m_{W_{d2}} \oplus ... \oplus m_{W_{dd_W}}$, where $W_{d1}, W_{d2}, ..., W_{dd_W}$ are all the descendants of W; i.e., all the nodes in the tree below W.

Thus, $m_{W\downarrow}$ is a function over 2^Ω (which can be evaluated at each subset $R \subseteq \Omega$ — and the value will vary between the descendants).

When W is a terminal node, $W = \{w'\}, w' \in \Omega$, we have $m_{W\downarrow} = o$, the vacuous mass function on 2^{Ω}:

$$o(\Omega) = 1, o(elsewhere) = 0.$$

We also denote the entire orthogonal sum $m_{\Omega\downarrow} = m = m_R \oplus ... \oplus m_S \oplus ... \oplus m_T$, where $R, ..., S, ..., T$ are all the nodes in the tree. It is our task to evaluate this function at each node in the tree.

Also, we have, for example,

$$bel_{W\downarrow} = bel_{W_{d1}} \oplus bel_{W_{d2}} \oplus ... \oplus bel_{W_{dd_W}}, bel_{\Omega\downarrow} = bel = bel_R \oplus ... \oplus bel_S \oplus ... \oplus bel_T,$$

the corresponding belief functions of $m_{W\downarrow}$, and $m_{\Omega\downarrow} = m$.

For every node W in the tree, denote $p_{W\downarrow} = bel_{W\downarrow}(W), c_{W\downarrow} = bel_{W\downarrow}(\Omega - W), r_{W\downarrow} = 1 - p_{W\downarrow} - c_{W\downarrow}$; and $a_W = bel(W) = bel_{\Omega\downarrow}(W), b_W = bel(\Omega - W) = bel_{\Omega\downarrow}(\Omega - W)$.

We can now re-express our task: it is to find a_W, b_W for every node W in the tree.

II. NOTATION m_{W^*} and $p_{W^*}, c_{W^*}, r_{W^*}, d_{W^*}$

For every node W in the tree, denote $m_{W^*} = m_W \oplus m_{W\downarrow}$ and

$$p_{W^*} = bel_{W^*}(W), c_{W^*} = bel_{W^*}(\Omega - W), r_{W^*} = 1 - p_{W^*} - c_{W^*}, d_{W^*} = 1 - p_{W^*}.$$

When W is a terminal node, $m_{W^*} = m_W \oplus o = m_W$; $p_{W^*} = p_W, c_{W^*} = c_W, r_{W^*} = r_W, d_{W^*} = d_W$.

Now, using the notation above, we can give an overview of the Shafer-Logan algorithm as follows. Notice that the *computation* is sometimes in the opposite direction to our *description.*

I. COMPUTATION FROM BOTTOM TO TOP (LOCAL COMPUTATION OF PARTIAL ORTHOGONAL SUM FOR ROOT OF TREE AND LEVEL 1 NODES)

The approach is to compute $a_U = bel(U), b_U = bel(\Omega - U)$ for all nodes $U \in S_\Omega$; i.e., for all nodes on the first level from the tree root Ω. We do this by a series of *reductions.* The subroutine identifiers are rather strangely ordered, for historical reasons.

Reduction 1. Local computations for the root of the tree.

(1) (Subroutine 3.) Reduce the computation of $a_U = bel(U), b_U = bel(\Omega - U)$ to the computation of $p_{U^*}, c_{U^*}, r_{U^*}, d_{U^*}$ for $U \in S_\Omega$.

When U is terminal, we know that $p_{U^*} = p_U = m_U(U), c_{U^*} = c_U = m_U(\Omega - U), r_{U^*} = r_U = m_U(\Omega) = 1 - p_U - c_U, d_{U^*} = d_U = 1 - p_U$.

(2) (Subroutine 2.) When U is not terminal, reduce the computation of $p_{U^*}, c_{U^*}, r_{U^*}, d_{U^*}$ to the computation of $p_{U\downarrow}, c_{U\downarrow}, r_{U\downarrow}$.

Reduction 2. Local computations for the first-level middle nodes.

(1) (Subroutine 1.) For non-terminal U, reduce the computation of $p_{U\downarrow}, c_{U\downarrow}, r_{U\downarrow}$ to the computation of $p_{P^*}, c_{P^*}, r_{P^*}, d_{P^*}$ for $P \in S_U$.

When P is terminal, we know that $p_{p^*} = p_P = m_P(P), c_{P^*} = c_P = m_P(\Omega - P), r_{P^*} = r_P = m_P(\Omega) = 1 - p_P - c_P, d_{P^*} = d_P = 1 - p_P$.

(2) (Subroutine 2.) When P is not terminal, reduce the computation of $p_{P^*}, c_{P^*}, r_{P^*}, d_{P^*}$ to the computation of $p_{P\downarrow}, c_{P\downarrow}, r_{P\downarrow}$.

Further reduction. Local computations for the middle nodes at other levels. We repeat this reduction, level by level, until we reach the level just above the bottom of the tree.

Final reduction. (Subroutine 1.) Local computation for the bottom.

For a father node P of terminal nodes $H, H \in \mathcal{S}_P$; $p_{P\downarrow}, c_{P\downarrow}, r_{P\downarrow}$ are reduced to $p_{H^*} = p_H, c_{H^*} = c_H, r_{H^*} = r_H, d_{H^*} = 1 - p_H$, where $H \in \mathcal{S}_P$ are all terminal, and $p_H = m_H(H), c_H = m_H(\Omega - H), c_H = m_H(\Omega)$ are already known.

II. PROPAGATION TOP TO BOTTOM (THE COMPUTATION OF THE ENTIRE ORTHOGONAL SUM)

We have now got $a_U = bel(U), b_U = bel(\Omega - U)$ for all nodes $U \in \mathcal{S}_\Omega$ on the first level from the tree root Ω. We want to compute $a_W = bel(W), b_W = bel(\Omega - W)$ for all nodes W on the other levels. We do this in a series of *rounds.*

Round 1. (Subroutines 4-6. p.293-294, Shafer, G. ; Logan, R. 1987) From $a_U = bel(U), b_U = bel(\Omega - U)$ compute $a_P = bel(P), b_P = bel(\Omega - P)$ for all nodes $P \in \mathcal{S}_U$ on the second level from the tree root Ω.

Round 2. (Subroutines 4-6.) From $a_P = bel(P), b_P = bel(\Omega - P)$ compute $a_H = bel(H), b_H = bel(\Omega - H)$ for all nodes $H \in \mathcal{S}_P$ on the third level from the tree root Ω.

Further round. We repeat this procedure round by round, level by level, until we reach the level one above the bottom of the tree.

Final round. (Subroutines 4-6.) At the bottom, the tree leaves, we compute $a_H = bel(H), b_H = bel(\Omega - H)$ for all nodes H on the bottom.

In this way we compute $a_W = bel(W), b_W = bel(\Omega - W)$ for all nodes W in the tree.

3 FORMULAE FOR THE COMPUTATION FROM BOTTOM TO TOP

In this section we present detailed formulae for use in the first part of the algorithm presented in section 2.

1. (Subroutine 3. p.293, Shafer, G. ; Logan, R. 1987) For every $V \in \mathcal{S}_\Omega$, $a_V = bel(V)$ and $b_V = bel(\Omega - V)$ are reduced to $p_{U^*}, c_{U^*}, r_{U^*}; d_{U^*} = 1 - p_{U^*}$ for $U \in \mathcal{S}_\Omega$.

(i) K is the " normalization constant " associated with the orthogonal sum. In this case it's formula is $1/K = \prod_{U \in \mathcal{S}_\Omega} d_{U^*} + \sum_{U \in \mathcal{S}_\Omega} (p_{U^*} \prod_{W \neq U, W \in \mathcal{S}_\Omega} d_{W^*}) - \prod_{W \in \mathcal{S}_\Omega} c_{W^*}$.

(ii) Belief function $bel = bel_{\Omega\downarrow}$ at V and a_V

$$a_V = bel_{\Omega\downarrow}(V) = K(p_{V^*} \prod_{W \neq V, W \in \mathcal{S}_\Omega} d_{W^*} + d_{V^*} \prod_{W \neq V, W \in \mathcal{S}_\Omega} c_{W^*} - \prod_{U \in \mathcal{S}_\Omega} c_{U^*})$$

$$(= \frac{p_{V^*}/d_{V^*} + \prod_{W \neq V, W \in \mathcal{S}_\Omega} c_{W^*}/d_{W^*} - \prod_{U \in \mathcal{S}_\Omega} c_{U^*}/d_{U^*}}{1 + \sum_{U \in \mathcal{S}_\Omega} p_{U^*}/d_{U^*} - \prod_{W \in \mathcal{S}_\Omega} c_{W^*}/d_{W^*}}$$

when $d_{U^*} \neq 0$ for all $U \in \mathcal{S}_\Omega$).

(iii) Belief function $bel = bel_{\Omega\downarrow}$ at $\Omega - V$ and b_V

$$b_V = bel_{\Omega\downarrow}(\Omega - V)$$

$$= K(\sum_{W\neq V, W\in\mathcal{S}_\Omega} (p_{W^*} \prod_{U\neq W, U\in\mathcal{S}_\Omega} d_{U^*}) + c_{V^*} \prod_{W\neq V, W\in\mathcal{S}_\Omega} d_{W^*} - \prod_{U\in\mathcal{S}_\Omega} c_{U^*})$$

$$(= \frac{\sum_{W\neq V, W\in\mathcal{S}_\Omega} p_{W^*}/d_{W^*} + c_{V^*}/d_{V^*} - \prod_{U\in\mathcal{S}_\Omega} c_{U^*}/d_{U^*}}{1 + \sum_{U\in\mathcal{S}_\Omega} p_{U^*}/d_{U^*} - \prod_{W\in\mathcal{S}_\Omega} c_{W^*}/d_{W^*}}$$

when $d_{U^*} \neq 0$ for all $U \in \mathcal{S}_\Omega$).

2. (Subroutine 2. p.293, Shafer, G. ; Logan, R. 1987) When U is not terminal, the values $p_{U^*}, c_{U^*}, r_{U^*}$ are reduced to $p_U, c_U, r_U; p_{U\downarrow}, c_{U\downarrow}, r_{U\downarrow}$. That is, we have $p_{U^*} = bel_{U^*}(U)$

$$= K(p_U p_{U\downarrow} + p_U r_{U\downarrow} + r_U p_{U\downarrow}), c_{U^*} = bel_{U^*}(\Omega - U) = K(c_U c_{U\downarrow} + c_U r_{U\downarrow} + r_U c_{U\downarrow}),$$

$$r_{U^*} = 1 - p_{U^*} - c_{U^*} = K r_U r_{U\downarrow};$$

where in this case K is

$$1/K = 1 - p_U c_{U\downarrow} - c_U p_{U\downarrow}.$$

3. (Subroutine 1. p.292, Shafer, G. ; Logan, R. 1987) When U is not terminal, values $p_{U\downarrow}, c_{U\downarrow}, r_{U\downarrow} = 1 - p_{U\downarrow} - c_{U\downarrow}$ are reduced to

$$p_{P^*}, c_{P^*}, r_{P^*}; d_{P^*} = 1 - p_{P^*}; P \in \mathcal{S}_U.$$

That is,

$$p_{U\downarrow} = bel_{U\downarrow}(U) = K(\sum_{P\in\mathcal{S}_U} p_{P^*} \prod_{R\neq P, R\in\mathcal{S}_U} d_{R^*})$$

$$(= \frac{\sum_{R\in\mathcal{S}_U} p_{R^*}/d_{R^*}}{1 + \sum_{R\in\mathcal{S}_U} p_{R^*}/d_{R^*}} \text{ when } d_{R^*} \neq 0 \text{ for all } R \in \mathcal{S}_U),$$

$$c_{U\downarrow} = bel_{U\downarrow}(\Omega - U) = K \prod_{P\in\mathcal{S}_U} c_{P^*}$$

$$(= \frac{\prod_{R\in\mathcal{S}_U} c_{R^*}/d_{R^*}}{1 + \sum_{R\in\mathcal{S}_U} p_{R^*}/d_{R^*}} \text{ when } d_{R^*} \neq 0 \text{ for all } R \in \mathcal{S}_U),$$

where K here is $1/K = \sum_{P\in\mathcal{S}_U} (p_{P^*} \prod_{R\neq P, R\in\mathcal{S}_U} d_{R^*}) + \prod_{P\in\mathcal{S}_U} d_{P^*}$.

4 FORMULAE FOR THE PROPAGATION TOP TO BOTTOM

Now we consider the formulae for the second part of the Shafer-Logan algorithm — the propagation top to bottom. This is the part of the algorithm in which our improvement appears.

From section 3 we can already compute the entire belief function at the top level nodes, $a_U = bel_{\Omega\downarrow}(U) = bel(U), b_U = bel_{\Omega\downarrow}(\Omega - U) = bel(\Omega - U)$ for $U \in \mathcal{S}_\Omega$.

So the remaining problem is how to " walk down "; propagating belief functions from each father node W to each of its son nodes P. That is, we compute $a_P = bel_{\Omega\downarrow}(P) = bel(P), b_P = bel_{\Omega\downarrow}(\Omega - P) = bel(\Omega - P)$, provided $a_W = bel(W), b_W = bel(\Omega - W)$ are known.

To solve the problem, we need some more notation and formulae. We associate the formulae with the subroutines here, and consider this a little more fully in section 5.

NOTATION

$$p_{W'} = (bel_W \oplus bel_{W'})(W), c_{W'} = (bel_W \oplus bel_{W'})(\Omega - W), r_{W'} = 1 - p_{W'} - c_{W'},$$

where $bel_{W'} = bel_{W'_1} \oplus bel_{W'_2} \oplus ... \oplus bel_{W'_{l_W}}$, and $W'_1, W'_2, ..., W'_{l_W}$ are all the nodes in the tree other than W and its descendants $W_{d1}, W_{d2}, ..., W_{dd_W}$.

Using this notation, we have the following formulae.

FORMULAE

1. First group (used in subroutine 5): $bel_{W\downarrow}(P), bel_{W\downarrow}(\Omega - P), bel_{W\downarrow}(\Omega - (W - P))$ expressed by $p_{R^*}, c_{R^*}, r_{R^*} = 1 - p_{R^*} - c_{R^*}, d_{R^*} = 1 - p_{R^*}; R \in \mathcal{S}_W$.

For $P \in \mathcal{S}_W$,

$$bel_{W\downarrow}(P) = \frac{p_{P^*} \prod_{R \neq P, R \in \mathcal{S}_W} d_{R^*}}{\sum_{R \in \mathcal{S}_W} p_{R^*} \prod_{P \neq R, P \in \mathcal{S}_W} d_{P^*} + \prod_{R \in \mathcal{S}_W} d_{R^*}}$$

$$\left(= \frac{p_{P^*}/d_{P^*}}{1 + \sum_{R \in \mathcal{S}_W} p_{R^*}/d_{R^*}} \text{ when } d_{R^*} \neq 0 \text{ for all } R \in \mathcal{S}_W\right),$$

$$bel_{W\downarrow}(\Omega - P) = \frac{c_{P^*} \prod_{R \neq P, R \in \mathcal{S}_W} d_{R^*} + \sum_{R \neq P, R \in \mathcal{S}_W} p_{R^*} \prod_{Q \neq R, Q \in \mathcal{S}_W} d_{Q^*}}{\sum_{R \in \mathcal{S}_W} p_{R^*} \prod_{P \neq R, P \in \mathcal{S}_W} d_{P^*} + \prod_{R \in \mathcal{S}_W} d_{R^*}}$$

$$\left(= 1 - \frac{(1 - c_{P^*})/d_{P^*}}{1 + \sum_{R \in \mathcal{S}_W} p_{R^*}/d_{R^*}} \text{ when } d_{R^*} \neq 0 \text{ for all } R \in \mathcal{S}_W\right),$$

$$bel_{W\downarrow}(\Omega - (W - P)) = \frac{p_{P^*} \prod_{R \neq P, R \in \mathcal{S}_W} d_{R^*} + d_{P^*} \prod_{R \neq P, R \in \mathcal{S}_W} c_{R^*}}{\sum_{R \in \mathcal{S}_W} p_{R^*} \prod_{P \neq R, P \in \mathcal{S}_W} d_{P^*} + \prod_{R \in \mathcal{S}_W} d_{R^*}}$$

$$\left(= \frac{p_{P^*}/d_{P^*} + \prod_{R \neq P, R \in \mathcal{S}_W} c_{R^*}/d_{R^*}}{1 + \sum_{R \in \mathcal{S}_W} p_{R^*}/d_{R^*}} \text{ when } d_{R^*} \neq 0 \text{ for all } R \in \mathcal{S}_W\right).$$

2. Second group (used in subroutine 4): a_W, b_W expressed by

$$p_{W\downarrow}, c_{W\downarrow}, r_{W\downarrow}; p_{W'}, c_{W'}, r_{W'}.$$

That is, $a_W = bel(W), b_W = bel(\Omega - W)$ are

$$a_W = K(p_{W\downarrow}p_{W'} + p_{W\downarrow}r_{W'} + r_{W\downarrow}p_{W'}), b_W = K(c_{W\downarrow}c_{W'} + c_{W\downarrow}r_{W'} + r_{W\downarrow}c_{W'}),$$

$$1 - a_W - b_W = Kr_{W\downarrow}r_{W'};$$

where in this case K is given by

$$1/K = 1 - p_{W\downarrow}c_{W'} - c_{W\downarrow}p_{W'}.$$

3. Third group (used in subroutine 6): a_P, b_P expressed by $p_{W'}, c_{W'}, r_{W'}$; $p_{W\downarrow}, c_{W\downarrow}$; and $bel_{W\downarrow}(P), bel_{W\downarrow}(\Omega - P), bel_{W\downarrow}(\Omega - (W - P))$.

For $P \in S_W, a_P = bel(P)$ and $b_P = bel(\Omega - P)$ are

$$a_P = K(r_{W'}bel_{W\downarrow}(P) + p_{W'}bel_{W\downarrow}(\Omega - (W - P)) - p_{W'}c_{W\downarrow}),$$

$$b_P = K(bel_{W\downarrow}(\Omega - P) - p_{W'}c_{W\downarrow} + c_{W'} - c_{W'}p_{W\downarrow} - c_{W'}bel_{W\downarrow}(\Omega - P)),$$

where again $1/K = 1 - p_{W\downarrow}c_{W'} - c_{W\downarrow}p_{W'}$ (as in 2 above).

5 THE KEY STEPS IN THE SHAFER-LOGAN ALGORITHM

We now identify the key steps in the Shafer-Logan algorithm, so that we can explain our improvement.

The main step in the algorithm is to transform the second group of formulae expressing a_W, b_W by $p_{W'}, c_{W'}, r_{W'}; p_{W\downarrow}, c_{W\downarrow}, r_{W\downarrow}$ to an expression of $p_{W'}, c_{W'}, r_{W'}$ by $a_W, b_W; p_{W\downarrow}, c_{W\downarrow}, r_{W\downarrow}$. That is the following subroutine.

(Subroutine 4. p.293, Shafer, G. ; Logan, R. 1987) Compute $p_{W'}$, $c_{W'}$, $r_{W'}$ by $a_W, b_W; p_{W\downarrow}, c_{W\downarrow}, r_{W\downarrow}$ as follows.

$$p_{W'} = \frac{\frac{1-b_W}{1-c_{W\downarrow}} - \frac{1-a_W-b_W}{1-p_{W\downarrow}-c_{W\downarrow}}}{\frac{1-a_W}{1-p_{W\downarrow}} + \frac{1-b_W}{1-c_{W\downarrow}} - \frac{1-a_W-b_W}{1-p_{W\downarrow}-c_{W\downarrow}}}, c_{W'} = \frac{\frac{1-a_W}{1-p_{W\downarrow}} - \frac{1-a_W-b_W}{1-p_{W\downarrow}-c_{W\downarrow}}}{\frac{1-a_W}{1-p_{W\downarrow}} + \frac{1-b_W}{1-c_{W\downarrow}} - \frac{1-a_W-b_W}{1-p_{W\downarrow}-c_{W\downarrow}}},$$

when $r_{W\downarrow} = 1 - p_{W\downarrow} - c_{W\downarrow} \neq 0$.

This subroutine is obtained by solving an equation of the second group of formulae.

The other two subroutines are Subroutine 5 which uses the first group of formulae, and Subroutine 6 which uses the third group of formulae.

Subroutines 4 and 6 are the key steps of the algorithm, because they are the most substantial and difficult steps required to reach son nodes P from a father node W in the evidence combination: first, Subroutine 4 gets $p_{W'}, c_{W'}$ from a_W, b_W; then, Subroutine 6 computes a_P, b_P from $p_{W'}, c_{W'}$.

6 IMPROVING THE SHAFER-LOGAN ALGORITHM

Now let us investigate the second group and the third group of formulae globally. Then we can improve the Shafer-Logan algorithm and make the key steps in the algorithm unnecessary.

THEOREM. *We can compute*

$$a_P = bel(P), b_P = bel(\Omega - P)$$

for $P \in S_W$ directly from

$$a_W, b_W; p_{W\downarrow}, c_{W\downarrow}, r_{W\downarrow}; bel_{W\downarrow}(P), bel_{W\downarrow}(\Omega - P), bel_{W\downarrow}(\Omega - (W - P)).$$

Let W be a non-terminal node in the tree, and let P be one of its son nodes. Suppose $r_{W\downarrow} = 1 - p_{W\downarrow} - c_{W\downarrow} \neq 0$. Then we can compute $a_P = bel(P), b_P = bel(\Omega - P)$ directly from

$$a_W, b_W; p_{W\downarrow}, c_{W\downarrow}, r_{W\downarrow}; bel_{W\downarrow}(P), bel_{W\downarrow}(\Omega - P), bel_{W\downarrow}(\Omega - (W - P))$$

by the following expression:

$$a_P = bel(P) = bel_{W\downarrow}(P)(1 - a_W - b_W)/r_{W\downarrow}$$
$$+\frac{(a_W - p_{W\downarrow}(1 - a_W - b_W)/r_{W\downarrow})(bel_{W\downarrow}(\Omega - (W - P)) - c_{W\downarrow})}{p_{W\downarrow} + r_{W\downarrow}},$$

$$b_P = bel(\Omega - P) = bel_{W\downarrow}(\Omega - P)(1 - a_W - b_W)/r_{W\downarrow} + b_W - c_{W\downarrow}(1 - a_W - b_W)/r_{W\downarrow}$$
$$+\frac{(a_W - p_{W\downarrow}(1 - a_W - b_W)/r_{W\downarrow})(bel_{W\downarrow}(\Omega - P) - c_{W\downarrow})}{+(p_{W\downarrow} + r_{W\downarrow})}.$$

PROOF. Consider the second and third groups of formulae given in section 4.

Summarizing these, we have the following four equations.

$$a_W = K(p_{W\downarrow}p_{W'} + p_{W\downarrow}r_{W'} + r_{W\downarrow}p_{W'}), b_W = K(c_{W\downarrow}c_{W'} + c_{W\downarrow}r_{W'} + r_{W\downarrow}c_{W'}),$$
$$1 - a_W - b_W = Kr_{W\downarrow}r_{W'};$$
$$a_P = K(r_{W'}bel_{W\downarrow}(P) + p_{W'}bel_{W\downarrow}(\Omega - (W - P)) - p_{W'}c_{W\downarrow}),$$
$$b_P = K(bel_{W\downarrow}(\Omega - P) - p_{W'}c_{W\downarrow} + c_{W'} - c_{W'}p_{W\downarrow} - c_{W'}bel_{W\downarrow}(\Omega - P)),$$

where $1/K = 1 - p_{W\downarrow}c_{W'} - c_{W\downarrow}p_{W'}$.

Now, we are given that $r_{W\downarrow} = 1 - p_{W\downarrow} - c_{W\downarrow} \neq 0$. So

$$Kr_{W'} = (1 - a_W - b_W)/r_{W\downarrow} = \frac{1 - a_W - b_W}{1 - p_{W\downarrow} - c_{W\downarrow}}.$$

This gives us four equations in four unknowns — $Kp_{W'}, Kc_{W'}, a_P, b_P$. For clarity we write $k_W = (1 - a_W - b_W)/r_{W\downarrow}$, and the four equations become

$$(p_{W\downarrow} + r_{W\downarrow})Kp_{W'} = a_W - p_{W\downarrow}k_W, (c_{W\downarrow} + r_{W\downarrow})Kc_{W'} = b_W - c_{W\downarrow}k_W,$$

$$(bel_{W\downarrow}(\Omega-(W-P))-c_{W\downarrow})Kp_{W'}-a_P=-bel_{W\downarrow}(P)k_W,$$

and

$$(bel_{W\downarrow}(\Omega-P)-c_{W\downarrow})Kp_{W'}+(1-p_{W\downarrow})Kc_{W'}-b_P=-bel_{W\downarrow}(\Omega-P)k_W.$$

Solving the equations yields:

$$a_P=bel_{W\downarrow}(P)(1-a_W-b_W)/r_{W\downarrow}$$

$$+\frac{(a_W-p_{W\downarrow}(1-a_W-b_W)/r_{W\downarrow})(bel_{W\downarrow}(\Omega-(W-P))-c_{W\downarrow})}{p_{W\downarrow}+r_{W\downarrow}},$$

$$b_P=bel_{W\downarrow}(\Omega-P)(1-a_W-b_W)/r_{W\downarrow}+b_W-c_{W\downarrow}(1-a_W-b_W)/r_{W\downarrow}$$

$$+\frac{(bel_{W\downarrow}(\Omega-P)-c_{W\downarrow})(a_W-p_{W\downarrow}(1-a_W-b_W)/r_{W\downarrow})}{+(p_{W\downarrow}+r_{W\downarrow})}. \quad \square$$

This theorem gives us an improved subroutine which enables us to compute

$$a_P=bel(P), b_P=bel(\Omega-P) \text{ for } P\in\mathcal{S}_W$$

directly from

$$a_W, b_W; p_{W\downarrow}, c_{W\downarrow}, r_{W\downarrow}; bel_{W\downarrow}(P), bel_{W\downarrow}(\Omega-P), bel_{W\downarrow}(\Omega-(W-P))$$

without using Subroutine 4 and Subroutine 6. Thus, we can improve the algorithm by making the key steps unnecessary. So Subroutines 4 to 6 are replaced by a new subroutine (following Subroutine 5) which uses the formulae in the theorem.

7 SUMMARY

A key part of the complicated Shafer-Logan algorithm consists of 3 subroutines which propagate the beliefs from the top of a tree hierarchy to the internal and leaf nodes. We have shown how to simplify the algorithm, and perhaps make it more efficient to implement, by reducing these key steps to a single step using a simple piece of algebra.

References

1. Barnett, J. A. 1981, " Computational methods for a mathematical theory of evidence ", *Proc. Seventh International Joint Conference on Artificial Intelligence (IJCAI)*, 1981, 868-875.
2. Buchanan, B. G. ; Shortliffe, E. H. eds. 1984, " Rule-based expert systems: The MYCIN experiments of the Stanford Heuristic Programming Project ", *Reading, MA: Addison-Wesley.*
3. Gordon, J. ; Shortliffe, E. H. 1985 ," A method for managing evidential reasoning in a hierarchical hypothesis space ", *Artificial Intelligence*, 26(1985) 323-357.

4. Guan, J. W. ; Xu, Y. and others, 1985, " Model expert system MES ", *Proceedings of IJCAI-85*, 397-399.
5. Guan, J. W. ; Lesser, V. R. 1987a, " The computational formulae of evidence combination scheme in a hierarchical hypothesis space ", *Proceedings of the Second International Conference on Computers and Applications*, 1987.
6. Guan, J. W. ; Lesser, V. R. 1987b, " On the evidence combination scheme in a hierarchical hypothesis space ", *Proceedings of TENCON 87*, Seoul, IEEE Region 10 Conference 1987, "Computers and Communications Technology toward 2000 ".
7. Guan, J. W ; Pavlin, J.; Lesser, V. R. 1989, " Combining Evidence in the Extended Dempster-Shafer Theory ",*Proceedings of the 2nd Irish Conference on Artificial Intelligence and Cognitive Science*, Dublin, 1989. Smeaton and McDermott (Eds.) Springer-Verlag, 1990, 163-178.
8. Guan, J. W. ; Lesser, V. R. 1989, " On probabilistic logic ", *Proceedings of the 2nd Irish Conference on Artificial Intelligence and Cognitive Science*, Dublin, 1989. Smeaton and McDermott (Eds.) Springer-Verlag, 1990, 113-131.
9. Guan, J. W. ; Bell, D. A. ; Lesser, V. R. 1990, " Evidential reasoning and rule strengths in expert systems ", *Proceedings of the 3rd Irish Conference on Artificial Intelligence and Cognitive Science*, Belfast, 1990.
10. Guan, J. W. ; Bell, D. A. ; Pavlin, J. ; Lesser, V. R. 1990, " The Dempster-Shafer theory and rule strengths in expert systems ", *IEE Colloquium on " Reasoning under Uncertainty "*, London, 1990.
11. Guan, J. W. ; Bell, D. A. 1991, " Evidence theory and its applications ", Volume 1, *Studies in Computer Science and Artificial Intelligence 7*, Elsevier, North-Holland.
12. Guan, J. W. ; Bell, D. A. 1992, " Evidence theory and its applications ", Volume 2, *Studies in Computer Science and Artificial Intelligence 8*, Elsevier, North-Holland.
13. Shafer, G. 1976, " A Mathematical Theory of Evidence ", *Princeton University Press, Princeton, New Jersey, 1976.*
14. Shafer, G. ; Logan, R. 1987, " Implementing Dempster's rule for hierarchical evidence ", *Artificial Intelligence*, 33, 1987, 271-298.
15. Shenoy, P. P. ; Shafer, G. 1986, " Propagating belief functions using local computations ", *IEEE Expert*, 1, 1986, 43-52.
16. Shortliffe, E. H. 1976, " Computer-based medical consultations: MYCIN ", *Elsevier Publishing Company*, New York.
17. Shortliffe, E. H. ; Buchanan, B. G. 1975, " A model of inexact reasoning in medicine ", *Mathematical Biosciences*, 23, 1975, 351-379.
18. Yen, J. 1986 " A reasoning model based on an extended Dempster-Shafer theory ", *Proceedings aaai-86* 125-131.
19. Yen, J. 1989, " GERTIS: A Dempster-Shafer Approach to Diagnosing Hierarchical Hypotheses ", *Communications of the ACM* 5 vol. 32, 1989, pp.573-585.

From Low-level to High-level Operations in Expert Systems

M. Popper

National Centre for Health Promotion, Bratislava, Slovakia

Abstract. The low-level universal inference operations, indifferent to knowledge substances, and higher-level task specific macro-operations for competent expert system performance are addressed. The latter ones are credited as vital and essential knowledge complements. In this respect generic reasoning templates - prescriptions related to declarative knowledge - associated in lines of reasoning are pointed out. The discussion with regard to disclosing corresponding operational patterns is followed by some illustrating examples.

1 Introduction

Both, knowledge and its efficient exploitation, are responsible for facets of competent expert system (ES) behaviour. In contrast with knowledge representation, achievements in ES operational functionality remain behind: inadequacies can be revealed when solving more complex tasks. They can be ascribed in great part to *universal knowledge processing models* providing solely *general inferential operations*. These, as well as, their control require no or very little experience with the task (domain) to which they refer. The real problem issues, the features having clear conceptual connection to the task-level manoeuvres are irrelevant to them.

We are contrasting *low-level universal* against *task-specific inferential macro-operations*, as higher-level means, sketching some aspects of their potential to approximate men's competent behaviour regarding strategy-directed problem-solving.

2 Operations generate behaviour

Operations generate (inference) processes, they are the origin for *exhibiting behaviour*, they are the *vehicle for knowledge-based and strategy-directed problem space exploration*. They should be credited as *vital and essential knowledge complements* acknowledging distinct roles of *universal and task/case devoted operations*.

Negligence of this can be illustrated on production rules. Pragmatically they are undisputed, theoretically are supported - they constitute a grammar, which can be equivalent in power to a universal Turing machine. Interpretation of the embodied knowledge is indeed based only on a small number of rather simple universal inferential operations. And yet, the process they generate is frequently not conform with demands of *efficient reasoning patterns*. Yes, their universality imposed by (and imposing) representation formalism are themselves deficient in this respect.

To surpass mechanistic knowledge interpretation the rules are usually augmented by particular *control components.* Regardless of implementation details, they compose kinds of operational *prescriptions* providing specific extra stuff affecting the inference process to comply with demands. The approach is not without potential flaws. Mainly, when *particular and casual* control components are devised instead of well conceptualized and underlain generic ones supported by reasoning strategies. Obviously, without proper *structuring and organization of universal inference operations into more complex and specific units (agents)*, neither production systems, nor other representation schemes are capable to comply with requirements.

Classes of problems and tasks, different by their nature, do not share common knowledge structures nor reasoning techniques. This suggests that corresponding *competent* ES performance, regardless of the particular knowledge substances, besides plain universal procedures, requires also invocation of various *problem or task specific - dedicated - macro-operations*.

In this respect two types of complementing *operational knowledge* components are to be discerned: the *type (1)*, corresponding to universal inference *providing general operational semantics to any declarative knowledge,* and the *type (2)*, corresponding to *various task-specific operational knowledge* in addition to the former one, to reflect the domain/task/case flavoured actions, methods, and strategies [6].

3 The macro-operations

Powerful knowledge representation schemes should be capable to accommodate knowledge modules resulting from problem decomposition so that they support recognition of their higher-level operational complements. It means disclosing *generic reasoning templates* enabling exploratory, context dependent exercise of domain and case related substance knowledge in form of specific macro-operations. They should contribute to knowledgeable performance *minimizing* the complexity of computation inherent in problem-solving by

* revealing the currently *enabled, credible, and proficient macro-operations* and inflict *situation or context dependent sequences of their invocations*,

* resolving *how, when, which, to what extent* particular instances of assertions may or should be under diverse contexts exercised,

* approaching the *same substance from various perspectives and for different needs*.

A *macro-operation*, a *prescription*, is to harmonize sequences of universal operations on and with explicit or implicit statements and propositions referring to domain subjects. As such, it *is a piece of nonuniversal operational knowledge* having the capacity to invoke other ones.

Among *descriptions* - declarative knowledge modules - and *prescriptions*, both as identifiable knowledge units, there are pairs with mutual affinity. Consequently, they in some *context or situation* (determined by currently available or missing data, their credibility and harmony, etc.) may conditionally or unconditionally, explicitly or implicitly refer to each other: *an individual description can invoke a distinctive task-specific macro-operation* and, vice versa, *such operation*, aside of its potential to invoke other related macro-operations, *can appeal a description*. Explicit articulation of such *description-prescription relations can be stated* by associated pairs of key words enabling efficient referencing.

Well designed collection of descriptions and prescriptions with potential to harmonize each other, can match strategies underlying domain-specific *competent behavioral facets*: *exploitation of task or case substances timely, properly, and topically to derive needed conclusions effectively*. It is *of advantage also regarding transparency and understandability of inference control, explanation, knowledge acquisition and representation*. In fact, it makes really visible what is otherwise dissolved at the low level formalism.

4 Lines of reasoning

In identifying existence of knowledge organizations that allow selection of highly relevant - in size limited - bodies of knowledge, one may arrive to proper conceptualization of prescriptions in context of revealed substances (descriptions). Recognising their type-type, type-subtype, case or event based dynamical precedence relations, situation specific problem solving models may show up. Being constituted by sets of propositions regarding particular situations, they are usually chained - one fuels others [2]. Consequently, the inference workings - *modelling processes for some purpose* - yield decisions resulting from procedures that order and control application of conditional statements.

Such understanding is indicating the way of step-wise assembling gradually higher-level operational constructs, actually *knowledgeable inference control reflecting well understood strategies, methods, and patterns exercised in a particular domain*.

The macro reasoning units *capturing cognitive processes in useful and meaningful ways* can be set up from *prescriptions* making up for universal operations scattered in the inference mechanism. An example is a task related situation-specific *line of reasoning*, a purposefully linked sequence of structural components, as a *goal, triggering cues, domain concepts, actions, and conclusions* [5]. Regardless of the knowledge specific to a task, such sequence is comprised from structural components, prescriptions, indeed *patterns of reasoning*. This cognizance facilitates the insight into the required knowledge, its structure, and the types of arguments underpinning actions and conclusions.

Apart of logic-based classical inferencing also the novel, less common, productive knowledge representation means, e.g. customary analytical expressions, bitmap portrayal of entity attributes and relations [4], symbolic rewriting rules, etc. demonstrate it. They associate powerful computations providing efficient macro-operations performing various processes usually needed in advanced applications.

The *patterns - specific case/event driven high-level macro-operations stated in a language of relations representing the modeled system structure and its behaviour* - in pursuing reasoning activities support decision chaining: one feeds into another and, if necessary, they retract.

It is of advantage when the patterns are generic, with instanced and/or indirectly referred variables as its parameters, and of daemon-like nature. Regarding implementation, OOP technology might prove efficient [6].

Conclusion

First let us provide some feel regarding patterns of reasoning. When a goal is given or hypothesized it may require gathering, assembling, and organizing facts in accord with network of concepts and their relations in a much more complex way comparing plain production rule interpretation. The process should support particular views respecting constraints, options, differentiation, preferences, etc. for proper process furthering. A generic pattern, say a *conceiver*, can do. When a significant portion of facts are either assembled or changed, say a *discoverer*, can be fired. Its role is to recognize whether or not a goal - a hypothesis - might be triggered under particular settings. In both cases failures in reaching the assignments invoke other supporting patterns, e.g. an *anticipator* - to recognize a partially completed task related schema in which the gaps are to be filled up, or an *proposer* - to recognize in given settings a sufficiently completed operational schema to invoke other contributing operations conditioned by present, absent, and conflicting facts. The latter one might suggest decision components e.g. for invoking a *pursuer* to refine the attained results, an *endorser* to assess their credibility, a *back-tracker* to retract the current sequence of reasoning and to shift attention in other direction, etc. An *integrator* setting up a global result based on mutual relations of partial outcomes is a significant pattern. Its profound role yields from the truth that many adequate conclusions can be developed only with a comprehensive assessing perspective covering various matters concurrently (for a motivating model see [4]).

The samples enable to perceive the discussed operational knowledge in analogy with the deep and surface level descriptive knowledge. Systems aspiring to be attentive for solving realistic problems, accommodating provisions for generic combination of a problem, representation, and inference strategies, and observant to the users' needs, are evidencing the need for *high-level* - in contrast with *universal low-level* - approach to their operational principles. It was our aim to sketch some of their contours pointing out potentially promising approaches to these affairs.

References

1. D.C. Brown, B. Chandrasekaran: Design problem solving. San Mateo: Morgan Kaufmann 1989
2. W.J. Clancey, M. Barbanson: Using the System-Model-Operator Metaphor for Knowledge Acquisition. IEEE Expert October 1991, 61-65 (1991)
3. K.C.Lun et al. (eds.): Proc. MEDINFO. Amsterdam: North-Holland 1992
4. R.A. Miller, F.E. Masarie Jr.: The Quick Medical Reference Relation Function: Description and Evaluation of a Simple, Efficient "Multiple Diagnoses" Algorithm. In [3], pp. 512-518
5. S.M. Narayan et al.: Lines and Patterns of Reasoning: New Units of Analysis for Clinical Decision Making. In [3], p. 426
6. M. Popper , M. Hauskrecht: Declarative and Operational in Knowledge Based Systems. In: K.P. Adlassnig, G. Grabner (eds.): Lecture Notes in Medical Informatics 45. Berlin: Springer 1991, pp. 299-303

Corpora as Expert Knowledge Domains: the Oxford Advanced Learner's Dictionary

Eve Wilson

Computing Laboratory, University of Kent at Canterbury
Canterbury, Kent, CT2 7NF, England

Abstract. This paper rehearses the parameters that are needed when designing an expert system for Computer Assisted Language Learning (CALL), namely:

1. expert knowledge: procedural knowledge and domain knowledge
2. student competence model
3. student's ultimate goal
4. student's current goal

It then goes on to examine the Oxford Advanced Learner's Dictionary (OALD) as an expert knowledge domain for CALL. It looks in detail at exercises that can be generated to improve:

1. clause level skills, both lexical (e.g. word usage, specialist vocabulary, and idioms) and syntactical (use of articles and verbs)
2. discourse skills.

Next, the paper contrasts briefly how the OALD as an expert knowledge domain compares with the Susanne Corpus (a collection of texts which are fully syntactically annotated) and suggests how the OALD might be improved to render the knowledge in it more accessible for the automatic generation of language exercises that are commensurate with the ability and goals of an individual student. Finally, it summarises how corpora fit into an intelligent tutoring system for CALL.

1 Introduction

If we want to incorporate in Computer Assisted Language Learning (CALL) packages an intelligent interface so that we develop an Intelligent Tutoring System (ITS), our aim must be to automate the design and implementation of the learning system. Automated systems are valuable because they afford one-to-one tutoring and facilitate thorough learning by allowing students to rehearse material until they fully understand it. However, an automated system can only be described as an intelligent system if the material in it can be tailored in a way that is uniquely appropriate to the needs of every student who uses it.

Automation would not only benefit the student: all too often, teachers who work with computer assisted learning programs have found them difficult to extend, improve or, sometimes, even to maintain: adding new exercises is too difficult and even making small changes in order or presentation demands programming skills and system knowledge that they do not have.

Intelligent tutoring activities in language learning can be roughly divided into two groups.

1. Concept understanding through instruction by an expert. Such tuition should include the explanation of linguistic principles and their illumination and clarification through example.
2. The transformation of passive information into active knowledge by practising and extending linguistic skills.

Good instruction depends upon the optimal integration of those learning techniques.

2 Parameters for Intelligent Tutoring Systems in Language Learning

The objective of most CALL packages is to teach specific skills alongside linguistic concepts in an environment where the student is motivated to learn and has unlimited opportunities to practise his skills. The study plans should accommodate individual learning differences and guide the tuition according to student need. The overall strategy should be based on four parameters: expert knowledge, student competence, student goal, and current goal.

2.1 Expert Knowledge

Many teachers still believe that the best strategy for learning is that based on what teachers believe has worked in the past for accomplishing a learning task. The expert's knowledge is used to order and structure the learning sequence and to define the knowledge domain. Traditionally in language teaching expert knowledge has been entombed in monolithic textbooks from which the student had laboriously to disinter the information required. Hypertext interfaces have revolutionised textbook use. Even if content is the same, the material is divided into logical nodes; hypertext indexes and content pages make it easier to find specific information quickly; and links make it easier to follow a trail through connected information. However, hypertext and automation stimulate us to seek more than the exhaustive explanations that introduce a topic from scratch (i.e. assuming no previous knowledge) and expound every refinement and subtlety. That such information should be available is fundamental to an educationally sound learning package. However, especially for mature students, there is also a place for brief reminders of information they have already encountered in previous sessions i.e. notes that assume previous knowledge. Only if a student finds such reminders inadequate and requests further help should the more detailed explanation be provided. In addition to reminders, a further tutorial refinement would be the pinpointing of common misconceptions and mistakes so that these can be explained as soon as students err: this is the moment when they are most receptive to instruction (A cumulative computer log of student errors could help identify most frequent mistakes).

The expert knowledge we have encountered so far might be described as *expert procedural knowledge*: i.e. it helps users to understand language and to construct their own texts. It may be the work of several authors or of one author only. The expert *domain* knowledge in language study is, in contrast, the garnered literature for that language or that dialect, i.e. the accumulated texts that are accepted by significant groups of native users of the language.

To-day, it is possible for language teachers who have *Internet* to have on-line access to substantial collections of texts from centres such as the Oxford Text Archive. Corpora such as Brown [1] give access to different textual genres which means that language courses can be constructed around texts specific to, say, science or literature. Some corpora, such as *Susanne* [6] have syntactic tagging. Yet other databases, amongst them dictionaries, are distillations of all of these sources. Much of this paper will discuss how material from one dictionary *The Oxford Advanced Learner's Dictionary of Current English* (OALD) [5] can serve as an exercise source in Intelligent Tutoring Systems to teach English as a Foreign Language.

2.2 Student Competence

Student competence is a model of the teacher's belief about what a student knows. It is based on an assessment of the student's knowledge and performance in the past, and affects both what knowledge should be offered and the form in which it should be presented. Thus, the model of student competence must incorporate student's past performance in all relevant linguistic skills so that it can be used to predict future attainment. This will be used to determine the appropriate degree of difficulty for future exercises and to define a suitable level of detail in reminders and help notes. The first task is to determine the skills which can be directly improved by computerised tuition. This was initially done in [9] and can be summarised here.

Clause Level Skills. Firstly, there are the clause level skills that enable students to understand and construct simple sentences that are morphologically and syntactically correct. Skills that are primarily morphological or lexical include:

word families and the formation of words to correspond with different parts of speech
  e.g. *reflect, reflection, reflector, reflecting*
comparison of adjectives and adverbs
  e.g. *bad, worse, worst*
irregular plurals
  e.g. *men, children, sheep, foci*
antonyms and synonyms
choosing the right verbal particle
distinguishing between pairs of words that are frequently confused
  e.g. *anticipate, expect*

Skills that are primarily syntactical include:

verbs

e.g. subject-verb agreement, tense, aspect, auxiliary and modal verbs, participles.

articles
pronouns
voice
word order
subordinate clauses

Discourse Level Skills. These are the skills needed to deal with collections of clauses. Discourse skills begin to be relevant at sentence level when we have to choose the most appropriate conjunction to join two clauses, but they come into their own at paragraph and text level. They are the skills needed to recognise the features that give coherence to a collection of clauses within a paragraph or between paragraphs within a longer text. They include such topics as:

information structure and focus
thematic structure
cohesion

Cohesion can be further broken down into:

reference
ellipsis and substitution
lexical coherence
conjunction

Some of these cannot easily be assessed automatically by computer: informatic structure and thematic structure are, perhaps, currently the most intractable. Other features that improve cohesion, word selection, choice of synonyms and collocates, use of ellipses and substitution are frequently subject to an author's stylistic preferences rather than to firm linguistic rules. Yet other cohesive techniques, e.g. cohesion through reference, are closely related to other syntactical skills. Such techniques include:

reference by pronoun
reference by demonstrative article
reference by comparison

e.g. *Jill followed a trail. On* **the** *trail* **she** *saw some bears.* **The smallest** *was black.*

The final major cohesive technique is the use of conjunctions, adverbial conjunctions and other linking frameworks. This is the discourse skill that is most easily tested by computer exercises and, for that reason, should feature prominently in the student competence model. Thus, the student model is composed of a list of skills and proficiencies in each skill. See Fig.1

Skills: Lexical	Proficiency in Skill	Skills: Syntactic	Proficiency in Skill	Skills: Discourse	Proficiency in Skill
		Verb forms	16.7		
Word families	16.7	Articles	33.3	Conjunctions	50.0
Singular/Plural	33.3	Passive	50.0	Enumeration	66.7
Comparison	50.0	Pronouns	66.7	Other frameworks	33.3
Word differentiation	66.7	Subordinate clause	83.3		
		Word Order	83.3		

Fig. 1. Student Competence Model

2.3 Student Goal

Many language learners have a goal. Learning a language may be only a subgoal of the main goal, which might be to study another discipline at a college or University where the teaching is in English. This may influence the genre of English the student wants to learn, for example technical vocabulary, how to write reports, and so on. The learner's goal may be most easily incorporated into the choice of texts around which to construct the linguistic exercises i.e. the linguistic domain might be chosen to reflect the interests of the student in Computer Science, Law, Medicine and so on. However, caution is needed: the style in many scientific and technical papers and in legal documents is regarded by many pundits as poor, if not downright bad. We must take care not to emulate by computer those English crammers who when teaching 'formal English' for tasks such as report writing persuade students to adopt a style that is verbose, impersonal, largely in passive voice, and so riddled with nominalisations it is disagreeable to read and difficult to understand.

2.4 Current Goal

Current need can best determine what should be taught next. It is the strategy for promoting learning in the current situation. It may be identified by the student through a request for help or inferred by the system from preceding events. Appropriate help should be provided and subgoals set up by way of easier or additional exercises until the student's confidence and competence have been raised sufficiently to resume the original goal.

3 An Expert Knowledge Domain: the Oxford Advanced Learner's Dictionary

In this paper, I want to concentrate on the expert domain and its use as a source of exercises to improve learner skills. Expert procedural knowledge, whether for detailed expositions, brief reminders or notes to clarify subtle usages or common misconceptions, may be culled from a plethora of standard texts that have long been available; only recently have advances in technology and the improved availability of electronic texts placed within our grasp an inexhaustible supply of exercises varying in difficulty and using specialised vocabulary. There are two main sources: corpora of texts and dictionaries. Corpora that are tagged to show the syntactic function of each word are especially useful: for an account of the use of the Susanne Corpus to construct exercises see [8]). The increased availability of packages such as the *Alvey Natural Language Tools* from the Artificial Intelligence Applications Institute, University of Edinburgh make local tagging of selected texts feasible and eventually this may be the preferred option for many language schools. Here, however, I am going to discuss the OALD as an expert domain for the English language and an on-line source for CALL exercises.

The OALD was first published in 1946. Its compiler A S Hornby taught English as a foreign language. The dictionary reflects his interests and expertise, and is deservedly popular with its target audience. (Oxford University Press claim that since 1948, of all books published in English only the Bible has sold more copies). Features that make it especially useful when designing language courses are:

1. verb patterns classify every verb according to how it can be used.
2. grammatical information is detailed and includes plurals, comparatives and superlatives.
3. idiomatic expressions and phrasal verbs are fully enumerated and well defined.
4. there are example sentences and phrases to illustrate meaning and usage.
5. words and expressions that fall into specialist English registers (e.g. accounting, aerospace, algebra etc) are labelled.

The version of the OALD available at the University of Kent is the Third Edition of 1974. In this the printers' mark-up has been replaced by tags to conform with the Standard Generalised Markup Language (SGML) [3]. While this conversion is not wholly satisfactory, it enables specific information to be easily retrieved using PAT [2], the search tool developed by Gaston Gonnet at the University of Waterloo in Canada. For example, it is possible to retrieve all occurrences of a specified verb pattern, to find all example sentences or phrases containing a given word, to search for all vocabulary that falls into a specialist register, e.g. *architecture*. Examples of searching the OALD are described in the *Electronic Handbook*, [4].

4 Exercises to Improve Lexical Skills

It is hardly surprising that the OALD should prove a particularly rich source for lexical exercises. There is not space in this paper to look at the exercises; for a more comprehensive version of the paper showing examples of exercise types and how the material for them was found, please contact the author. For a description of the interface see [7].

5 Exercises to Improve Syntactical Skills

Because the example sentences are not syntactically tagged it is not always as simple to generate syntactical exercises from the OALD as from a tagged text such as the Susanne Corpus. For a more comprehensive version of the paper showing examples of exercises and how the material for them was retrieved, please contact the author.

6 Potential of OALD as an Expert Domain

Despite technical inadequacies in the electronic version of the third edition, and difficulties in automatic selection and processing that are still to be resolved, the OALD is a very rich source of carefully constructed example sentences for students learning English as a foreign language. For lexical skills it is far better than the Susanne Corpus although for syntactical skills it is inferior because the example sentences are not syntactically tagged. Even when verb patterns give some indication of the structures likely to be found in the examples, there is no explicit link between the pattern and its instantiation. Material for testing discourse skills is scanty.

Ideally the project needs an electronic version of the OALD which:

1. has full syntactic tagging for example sentences;
2. explicitly links prototype verb patterns with instantiations;
3. dispenses with confusing contractions and abbrevations that are relevant only in a paper economy – such as example phrases rather than example sentences, and the use of $< hr >$ instead of re-printing the headword;
4. pays more attention to syntactical detail (eg. why do example sentences have no full stops? – a minor point, perhaps, but in language exercises syntactical details matter.)

Even as it stands, the electronic OALD is a resource that language teachers cannot afford to waste; with the improvements outlined above, it could become a domain for an intelligent interface that could automatically generate linguistic exercises.

However, even with these technical improvements, lexical exercises must be graded for degree of difficulty before the interface can be described as intelligent. We need to add relevance precision to the recall mechanism for the OALD, so that instead of returning a random word sample it returns a word sample appropriate to the needs and knowledge of the students. There are two ways of doing this:

1. Use a word frequency list.
2. Using word lists from texts of a genre that matches a student's goal.

7 Conclusion

The OALD cannot stand alone as a source for student exercises in every linguistic skill because it has no passages of sustained discourse. However, used in conjunction with fully syntactically tagged corpora that can be graded for readability, if offers an entirely fresh perspective on language course production (for a fuller account of the use of tagged corpora and readability coefficients in the product of graded exercises, see [8]).

The means are now available to generate on demand an infinite number of different exercises with degrees of difficulty commensurate with individual student competence levels in specific linguistic skills.

Because the computer starts with the text (i.e. the answer) and generates the exercise, the student's performance can be automatically monitored and assessed. The results can be used:

1. to provide reminders and notes of appropriate level and detail.
2. to select additional exercises to improve performance in particular skills.
3. to update the student performance model so that a study plan suitably ordered and balanced against student need can be determined and prepared in advance of the next study session.

Computer Assisted Language Learning may be the first discipline in which intelligent tutoring by computer is a reality rather than a dream of science fiction.

Bibliography

References

1. Francis, W. N., & Kucera, H., *Manual of Information to accompany a Standard Corpus of Present-Day Edited American English*, Department of Linguistics, Brown University, Providence, Rhode Island, (1989)
2. Fawcett, H., *The User's Guide to Pat*, University of Waterloo, (1988)
3. ISO, *ISO 8879 Information Processing – Text and Office Systems – Standard General Markup Language (SGML)*, ISO, Geneva, (1986)
4. Oxford University Press, *Oxford Advanced Learner's Dictionary of Current English, Third Edition, Electronic Handbook*, Oxford University Press, (1989)
5. Oxford University Press, *Oxford Advanced Learner's Dictionary of Current English*, Edited by A. S. Hornby, OUP, Oxford, (1974)
6. Sampson, G. R., *The Susanne Corpus*, University of Sussex, (1992)
7. Wilson E., et al, 'CALLGUIDE: using progammable hypertext as a shell for CALL programs', in *Computer Assisted Learning*, edited by L. Tomek, Springer Verlag, (1992)
8. Wilson, E., *An Intelligent Tutor: using the Susanne Corpus to enhance linguistic skills*, University of Kent at Canterbury, (1992), available from the University
9. Wilson, E., *The language learner and the computer: modes of interaction*, ACH/ALLC Joint International Conference, Washington, DC, (1993)

Maintenance of Knowledge Bases

Franz Lehner, Hubert F. Hofmann, Ralf Setzer, Ronald Maier

The Koblenz School of Corporate Management, Institute for Business Informatics
Burgplatz 2, D-56179 Vallendar, Germany

Abstract. To date, more and more research institutes are involved in the design, development and utilization of knowledge-based systems. Little research has, however, been published on the maintenance situation of these systems. This paper deals with the specialities of the maintenance of knowledge bases. Exemplary error sources, requests for alteration and problems are described to highlight the complex nature of this field. The activities initiated and controlled by the knowledge base maintenance management are structured. Four base and two cross-sectional activities are identified and explained in detail.

1 Introduction

Maintenance should not be regarded as being a necessary evil, and in general it is also not a sign of any defect in the product itself or in its development. Often it is the result of a changing environment (regarding tasks, technology etc.). Maintenance is an expression of the flexibility and capacity for innovation of an enterprise. The conformity of the application systems to the environment must be maintained and checked regularly if effectivity is to be guaranteed. When the environment changes, then usually the components of the application system which are affected by that change have also to be adapted to fit the new situation. Changes can also become necessary due to new or changed user requirements, errors in the software, performance problems (e.g. response-time) and for many other reasons. Errors and bad performance in particular can seriously hinder or make the use of the system impossible and so demotivate the user. Systems therefore require constant attention and further development to ensure that they do not lose their effectivity.

Conceptual modelling is to be particularly stressed as a special feature of the maintenance of knowledge-based systems. When this aspect is taken into consideration, the development of a knowledge-based system can never really be regarded as ever being completed. Ultimately, this means that the (artificial) division into phases (e.g. design phase, development-phase and operational-phase) is of little use for maintenance purposes. At present, maintenance is still generally regarded as being a part of the operational phase in the life-cycle of application systems (for both conventional application systems and knowledge-based systems). This is a simplification which does not provide a sufficient basis for a more thorough investigation of maintenance problematics. Implicit in this simplification is, for example, that the development of knowledge-based systems or components can be carried out independently from later operations and the modifications which can be expected. Recognised procedures on the designing of knowledge-based systems, e.g. KADS II (ESPRIT II Project 5248), have to some extent departed from strict phase-orientation by means of iterative development methods, prototyping-oriented procedure and the like. They do take maintenance into consideration (e.g. ensuring the possibility for expansion within the system design) but again only summarily.

The representation and storing of knowledge and knowledge-structures (Meta-Knowledge) cannot be separated from the representation formalism employed, from the programming language or from the development environment etc. Among other things, it is the fact that these links have to be taken into consideration - that they have a direct influence on maintenance activities - that makes maintenance such a difficult task. The maintenance of knowledge-based systems is, therefore, to be understood in a comprehensive sense. This will also take into account that there is a visible trend towards hybrid systems, i.e. application systems are composed more and more from components which have not only been developed with conventional technology, but also with the help of expert system technology. A further argument for the chosen perspective is the fact that in the expert system technology many elements of traditional programming are to be found and vice versa. Experience gained from the maintenance of conventional application systems can, therefore, probably in part be taken over.

There are various possibilities available for the representation of knowledge in a knowledge base. Most common is the use of rules, constraints, objects, or frames. The knowledge itself can be retained in very different forms [18]: factual knowledge, causal knowledge, conceptual structures of the object area, knowledge in the form of rules, context and explanation of rules, procedural knowledge, reasons for the applications of the rules, strategies, weighting, proofs, probabilities among others. The inference component serves the linking of knowledge elements which are managed in the knowledge base. It must, therefore, be co-ordinated with the type and special characteristics of the knowledge representation. This fact provides a further argument as to why maintenance cannot be limited to an adapting of the knowledge representation.

The integration of maintenance into the process of the development of knowledge bases is, among other things, so difficult because very often the adaptability of human specialists is not taken into account and because the effect of knowledge-based components on the work-situation is very difficult to predict [3, 9]. The users are, however, "learning systems " and subject the contents of the knowledge base to a continuously new interpretation.

2 Error Sources, Requests for Alteration and Problems

To date, a systematic structuring of important or typical error sources, requests for alteration and problems concerning knowledge bases is not yet possible. The following description is, therefore, by way of being exemplary and should give an impression of the complexity of the maintenance of a knowledge base. As a rule, it is hardly possible to obtain a general overview of potential error sources in knowledge bases; neither can these sources be precisely or completely described. This is demonstrated by the fact that testing, the most usual form for discovering errors, usually uncovers no more than 50 per cent of the errors present in a system [8]. The following descriptions, which are derived in part from experience gained from personal development projects and in part from relevant literature, can therefore only give a general overview in the form of exemplary error sources, requests for alteration and problems. Some of the points mentioned can be observed generally during the maintenance of software systems, some apply specifically to knowledge bases. In the following they are described together, because a clear division between them is for the most part neither possible nor useful.

Exemplary Error Sources:

- One typical error source is the insufficient dimensioning of variables, the origins of which are to be found in the lack of specification. For example, parts of data records which are to be worked on are loaded into matrices which were originally designed for a smaller number of data records.
- The input checking routines for user inputs are another source for error. They are essential for assuring the integrity of the knowledge base. The conducting of wrong knowledge elements can lead to wrong results in the later knowledge processing.
- Particularly during the development of expert systems, a syntax error during the input of knowledge elements (e.g. when copying facts or rules with the object of keeping the input effort low) can result in the impossibility of a later "Pattern Matching", i.e. the effective checking of syntactical conformity with the aim of constructively linking the corresponding knowledge elements. This is particularly serious when the user has no detailed knowledge concerning the contents or structure of the knowledge base and so cannot check the result or can only partially check it.
- In the development systems (e.g. Shells, Programming Environments) of expert systems there may be programming errors which can be traced back to insufficient quality standards during their development. Furthermore, errors can arise caused by incompatibilities between the development systems and the respective operational system. Unless newer, co-ordinated versions of the development environment and the operational system are available, these errors can only be avoided by changing the implementation of the software system.

Exemplary Requests for Alteration:

- A frequent request for alteration with regard to data storage is the alteration of the format in which the data is stored. An example for this is the introduction of the fifth digit in the postal codes of the Federal Republic of Germany, or the coming turn of the century which will lead to alterations in existing software systems.
- A similarly frequent request for alteration is the introduction of new objects, which are to be incorporated into an existing object category. If, for example, an object class CUSTOMER has hitherto been managed, it could become necessary due to altered requirements that this object class be split into two classes each with a different definition of a customer.
- Changes in the structure of knowledge bases which are due to changes in the environment of the software system are also a part of the maintenance process. An example for this is the combining of the contents of different data models in a common data model which is finally represented in a data base (e.g. relational, deductive, object-oriented).
- Frequent requests for alteration can be expected especially in the case of knowledge bases which are produced during the development of expert systems because of the use of an explorative construction paradigm. Maintenance also becomes more complex when in such knowledge bases not only knowledge is inserted into

existing structures, but also new structures, thereby often making a revision of the existing structure for the recording of knowledge necessary.

Exemplary Problems:

Figure 1 shows the classifying and systematizing of problems which can occur when knowledge bases are in use.

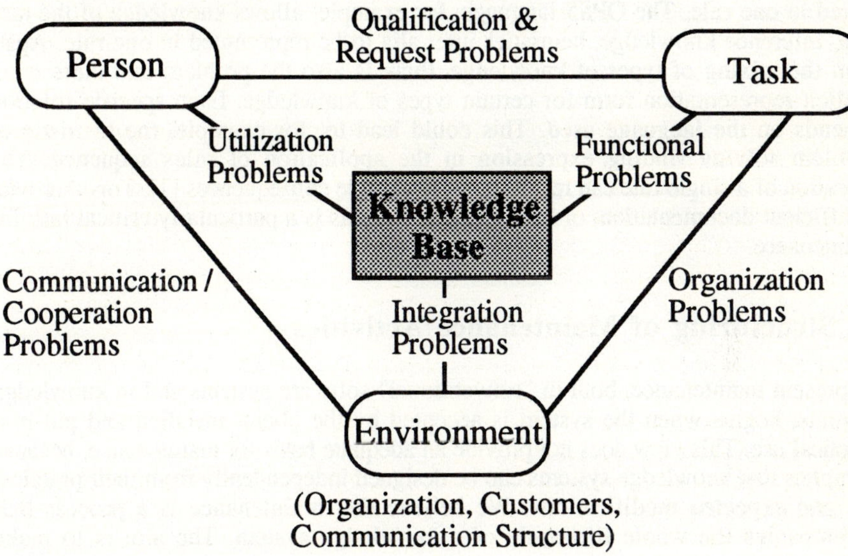

Fig. 1. Problem areas on the use of knowledge bases [3]

Some examples for the individual problem areas follow [3].

- Utilization Problems: inputs or alterations going back a long way in the dialogue, linking of consultant and handbook components, checking efficiency of the knowledge base whether it is up-to-date.
- Functional Problems: indication of threshold values, indication of provisional values, filing memoranda, modification exclusively by developer, answering of why-not questions.
- Integration Problems: linking of consultant and handbook components; indication of provisional values;
- Lack of Transparency: transparency of contents (indication of contents, modification and completeness of the contents), functional transparency (operation of system functions, applicability of system functions).

The fact that the maintenance situation concerning knowledge bases which are in practical operation is a problem which must be taken seriously is borne out by the few reports in existence on this theme. For example, four years after the XCON/R1 system which supports the configuration of DEC-computers was put into operation, four employees were still working full-time on the extension and alteration of the knowledge. The maintenance effort involved had not decreased during this period of time, in fact it had increased. However, the benefits derived from the use of the system were still valued as being higher than the costs of maintenance. SIRATAC, a support system for findings on the pest infestation of cotton plants, was replaced by a newly conceived system after several years in operation because the stored knowledge had increased to such an extent that maintenance difficulties arose [7].

Another problem area which is frequently mentioned is the documentation situation. Very often no documentation at all exists for the knowledge base. In addition, it can occur that in certain programming languages, different types of knowledge can be mixed in one rule. The OPS5 language, for example, allows knowledge of the task area, inference knowledge, heuristics inter alia to be represented in one rule. Apart from the mixing of types of knowledge, there is also the problem that there is no explicit representation form for certain types of knowledge. Each specific solution depends on the language used. This could lead to, for example, the heuristic of problem solving finding expression in the application of rules sequence. The alteration of a single rule can result in unforeseeable consequences [1]. Together with insufficient documentation, or lack of the same, this is a particularly critical task for maintenance.

3 Structuring of Maintenance Activities

At present maintenance, both in "conventional" software systems and in knowledge systems, begins when the system is accepted by the client, installed and put into practical use. This view does not provide an adequate basis for maintenance, because it implies that knowledge systems can be designed independently from their practical use and expected modifications. We believe that maintenance is a process that accompanies the whole life cycle of a knowledge system. The aim is to make maintenance and initial design as complementary as possible. If maintenance can be successfully carried out with the same methods, techniques and tools as the initial design of knowledge systems, then organisations will benefit heavily from such an approach, e.g., uniformity and standardisation, facilitation of continued education and staff training, documentation support, introduction and back-up.

We suggest the process-oriented division of work during maintenance, instead of component-oriented division of work. Component-oriented maintenance leads to division of work in the sense that different people maintain different components (e.g., knowledge base and reasoning component). Process-oriented maintenance means the division of work based on different methods for which different people are responsible. This means that the people involved in maintaining the knowledge system are assigned to working processes applying a particular method. For example, an individual or group performs enhancement or modification, verification and validation, whereas another individual or group performs quality assurance. Process-oriented maintenance helps all people involved in maintenance to understand thoroughly the knowledge system. Moreover, the responsibility for a whole work process increases the motivation of maintenance personal.

Thus, the clear, but artificial, separation of different phases in the software life cycle reveals its deficiency and is not conducive to maintenance. In the following, the maintenance which is to be initiated and controlled by the maintenance management is structured and presented in the form of activities. These activities are thought to be the most important maintenance domains, although only few empirical findings have been presented in this field until now. The following activities are differentiated (cf. fig. 2):

- modification and extension
- test and verification
- validation
- re-introduction and training

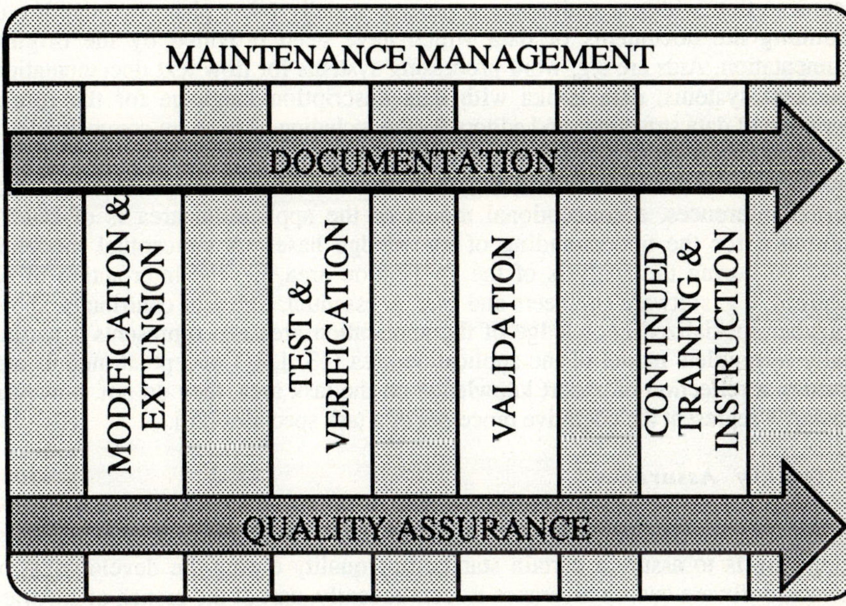

Fig. 2. Maintenance management

These maintenance activities are supplemented by two cross-sectional functions, namely documentation and quality assurance. Both are to be taken into consideration during all maintenance activities. They are not classed with maintenance management, which spans all maintenance activities, because they involve the operational performance of the individual activities and not their consideration within the management processes.

In the following, documentation and quality assurance will be described first in order to emphasize their cross-sectional character. The individual maintenance activities will then be presented.

3.1 Documentation

The documentation of the existing knowledge base is essential for a first-class, efficient maintenance performance. Ideally, this documentation will have been produced or continued parallel with the development of the knowledge base and possible previous maintenance processes. Within an actual maintenance process, the updating of documentation within the individual activity is also necessary. A subsequent documentation of alterations, i.e. a documentation after completion of the maintenance, results in an incomplete documentation or one that is not up-to-date. This can be disadvantageous to quality and efficiency. It can be expected, for example, that a test may be conducted far more accurately if, due to documentation, altered parts of the knowledge base are clearly identifiable. In addition, because of its different presentation form compared to the formal source code, the documentation accompanying the alteration can lead to an early questioning of the specification and its software implementation.

Documentation within a maintenance process usually takes place by adapting or continuing the documents or data which have been provided by the original documentation. Aids are e.g. word processing systems for flow text documentation, hyper text systems, data lexika with data description language for the formal description of data structures, and editors for the including of program commentaries.

In addition to the documentation of e.g. data structures, decision logic, interfaces and external references, a conceptional model of the application area is of crucial importance for the understanding of knowledge bases. A conceptual model is developed during the analysis of the application area, i.e. the inter-action of all concerned, e.g. software engineers and user, is essential. The user contributes above all his/her specialized knowledge of the application area and represents a partial, usually incomplete model of the application area [13, 12]. Conceptual models are, therefore, a reflection of expert knowledge on the task area, they do not, however, necessarily represent the cognitive processes of a task specialist [20].

3.2 Quality Assurance

The aim of introducing principles, methods and procedure models of software engineering is to assure a certain standard of quality during the development of software. Software quality assurance is, consequently, part of the branch of software engineering and should therefore be a planned and systematically considered part of the maintenance of software products [19].

By (software) quality, those features of a (software) product are meant which ensure that the demands made of the product are met [6]. In addition, in software production not only the features of the product itself, but also keeping to cost estimates and meeting deadlines are often seen as being part of quality. This requires a broader view of the concept of quality to include the process of software development. Quality goals are defined which are peculiar to the development process and which derive from the quality aims of the product [19].

The demand for inter-subjective testability and mechanical re-checking of software, or rather of the set quality features, led to the development of a field known as Software-Metrics or Softwaremetrie or, sometimes, Software Physics. The aim of this field is to define and apply quality standards which allow quality features to be measured objectively and, if possible, mechanically. From the vast number of quality standards for software, the following are of particular interest from the point of view of maintenance [10].

- Design-Stability Standards (e.g. PDS Yau/Collofello),
- Complexity Standards (e.g. MacCabe, Halstead, Rechenberg),

- Alteration and Extension Standards (e.g. LSP Yau/Collofello, Modifiability Metric Yau/Chang),
- Reliability Standards (Error-Prediction Standard Ottenstein, Reliability Standard, Nelson),
- Availability Standards (Error-Day, MTBF, Standard Littlewood),
- Further Standards (e.g. Portability, Modularity metrics, Standards for measuring ease-of-use, clarity of code, testability and quality of documentation).

A specialized field of research is still involved in the development of metrics for the evaluation of knowledge based components [2, 14] Two kinds of metrics are differentiated here: Task-area-oriented metrics and metrics for knowledge based components [16]. Task-area-oriented metrics measure the behaviour of knowledge based components and are analogous to the criteria applied by specialists to assess other specialists. Metrics of knowledge based components are independent of a specific software system and are concerned with the content and structure of the knowledge based components (cf. e.g. GATEWAY Project, IED Project 1751).

Experience in the field of software-metrics shows, however, that at present it is not possible to make up a complete list of quality characteristics (and thereby also quality standards), and that each organization, or rather each development environment has its own specific characteristics. This results in the fact that often only guidelines can be given for a metric. Also, it is often overlooked that the actual difficulty lies in the interpretation of the results of measuring; at present, no very well substantiated experience and results exist in this area. Nevertheless, we may now proceed on the assumption that metrics will be increasingly employed to this end. They are at present already a permanent part of object-oriented design environments, which occupy a core position in the field of knowledge based systems.

3.3 Modification and Extension

The expansion of knowledge in the application area (perfection maintenance), modification of existing functions and data (adaptive maintenance) and the elimination of detected deviations (corrective maintenance) result in a constant process of adjustment in which specialists, users and system designers together service, update and improve the knowledge bases.

These modifications and cxpansions of a knowledge base must be documented in the knowledge base itself and traceable at all times. Alterations in the user documentation, the technical documentation as well as changes in display/information material (e.g. marketing documents, training documents etc.) are also a part of the modification and expansion of the knowledge base.

According to the traditional concept of maintenance, these activities should be carried out in such a way that the design and implementation of the knowledge base is preserved as far as possible. Maintenance activities are governed usually by the level of knowledge which prevailed at the time of new development, i.e. out-dated methods are used to work on out-dated knowledge bases.

The envisaged maintenance concept has, however, a different starting point. Bcforc modification or expansion, the knowledge base is brought up to the most recent level of technology. The maintenance personnel can then proceed with the modernizcd knowledge base in the same way as with a newly-developed knowledge base, using the most up-to-date methods and aids. The modifications are specified, designed and implemented in exactly the same way as for newly-developed knowledge bases.

Ideally, not the maintenance personnel, but the user would carry out the modification with the appropriate tools after having received the system. This kind of maintenance (tuning) must, however, be taken into consideration during development [5].

3.4 Test and Verification

When modification and expansion have been carried out, then the altered knowledge bases are to be tested and verified [2, 15].

Testing is an activity for verifying the correctness of results in the software design, e.g. experimental execution for determining pre-defined characteristics. In this context it is interesting to discover that testing is a far less effective means for finding errors than is generally supposed [11]. In comparison, formal design and code inspections carried out by small groups of experienced specialists are more effective at locating errors.

Maintenance test activities differ from testing during new development primarily in that a test environment is already in existence and representative test data is available. During maintenance, however, test environment and test data have to be adapted or extended.

Verification refers to activities which can be carried out purely on the "internal" representation of a knowledge base, that is, determining the consistency, freedom from redundancy and "correctness" within the framework of the chosen representation formalism. Verification treats the knowledge base as a "white box", i.e. what matters most is to show that the internal structure of the knowledge base corresponds to its formal specification.

When new facts or rules become known, then it should be possible to correct the knowledge base with only an acceptable amount of effort involved. In order to support these activities so-called Truth-Maintenance-Systems have been developed in the field of logical knowledge representation [4]. At each extension of the knowledge base, these systems check all the contents for consistency and, if necessary, carry out corrections. The necessity for such systems arises when conclusions which have been deduced to be true and have been stored in the knowledge base later, through the addition of new knowledge, prove to be false. One speaks of monotonous logic when conclusions which have been deduced to be true and have been stored in the knowledge base can no longer prove to be false through the addition of new knowledge; at most, new, true facts can emerge. When this assumption (assumption of monotony) is not valid, then at each extension of the knowledge base all its contents must be tested for consistency and, if necessary, corrected. This procedure is called "truth maintenance" and the systems supporting it, "Truth Maintenance Systems". Without truth maintenance, non-monotonous logic leads to the intolerable situation that deduced facts and rules filed in the knowledge base can become false [17, 4].

3.5 Validation

Validation is very often confused or mixed up with verification. Verification serves to show that the knowledge base behaves in accordance with its specification and that the relevant knowledge is represented. Validation, however, is concerned with keeping the system within the application environment [14]. It is a question of whether the problems are "correctly" solved also within the context of the operational task assignment (which need not be identical with the specification). Validation treats the knowledge base as a "black box", i.e. the internal structure of the knowledge base is not taken into account during the check.

The scope of the effort which is necessary for validation within the maintenance framework is determined by the task area. Verification is a priority when a clearly defined task area is concerned which can, for example, be shown in a well-defined representation formalism; however, if the task area is first to be structured through the knowledge base, then validation activities predominate.

3.6 Re-Introduction and Training

The integration of the modified knowledge base into the operational process concentrates on the activities: re-introduction and training.

During integration, the conformity of the behaviour of the system with the required efficiency in the work situation is investigated with the use of qualitative and quantitative criteria. An important criteria for assessment is whether the re-introduction of the knowledge base brings about an improvement in the user work-situation or in that area of the business which is being supported. This improvement can be described using the criteria of quality, benefit and usability.

The quality assessment should be carried out by a group of experts who were not involved in the maintenance, or it should be undertaken by means of quantitative performance criteria and empirical tests. The benefit of the knowledge base is determined by user and management of the business area. Usability is determined, for example, by criteria such as user-acceptance, the ease with which the system answers are understood, and the adaptivity of the knowledge base.

The re-introduction of knowledge bases which have been maintained is backed-up by training activities. Due to the (technical) documentation resulting from the knowledge base analysis, the training should be less complicated than when unstructured procedures are involved. The improved quality and reliability of the knowledge base should reduce the necessity for user support.

4 Conclusions

To date, no systematic investigations of data on the maintenance situation of knowledge bases exist. This applies also to the use of methods and tools. In the relevant literature on expert systems there are to date only a few reports and suggestions concerning maintenance problems. From the few reports available, it becomes clear that the maintenance of knowledge bases represents a decisive factor for success with regard to the applicability and efficiency of the system.

In so far as insufficient documentation, or the lack of documentation, is the cause of maintenance problems concerning knowledge bases, then the situation is comparable to conventional software maintenance and requires to some extent that similar measures be taken. The remaining problems represent a combination of lack of experience and technical restrictions. An improvement of the situation is expected from new developments in the area of workable conceptional models as well as from Knowledge Dictionaries [7]. Conceptional models, which are as similar to the functioning system as possible have, among others, the following advantages with regard to maintainability: explicability, self-documentation, and comprehensibility. The contribution of Knowledge Dictionaries can be compared to the maintenance back-up of Data Dictionaries in conventional development environments [7]. Particular effort is still required in the areas of quality assurance (e.g. programming conventions, program structures) and of quality assessment (e.g. Software-Metrics for object-oriented languages).

References

1. Angele, J., Fensel, D., Studer, R.: What could the knowledge engineer learn from the software engineer? Ehrenberg, D. et al. (eds.): Wissensbasierte Systeme in der Betriebswirtschaft, Berlin 1990, pp. 285-303
2. Ayel, M., Laurent, J.-P. (eds.): Validation, Verification and Test of Knowledge-based Systems. John Wiley & Sons, Chichester/New York 1991
3. Becker, B., Herrmann, Th., Steven, E. (eds.): Zur Diskrepanz zwischen Expertensystementwicklung und -einsatz. GMD Arbeitspapier Nr. 641, GMD Bonn/St. Augustin, April 1992
4. Doyle, J.: A Truth-Maintenance System, Artificial Intelligence AI Vol 12, 3/1979, 231-272
5. Greenbaum, J., Kyng, M.: Design at work. Hillsdale, N.J.: Erlbaum, 1991
6. Heinrich, L. J., Roithmayr, F.: Wirtschaftsinformatik-Lexikon. 4th Ed., München/Wien, 1992
7. Jansen, B., Compton, P.: Data dictionary approach to the maintenance of expert systems: The Knowledge Dictionary. Knowledge-Based Systems, Vol. 2, 1/1989, pp. 14-26
8. Jones, T. C.: Verhütung und Beseitigung von Programmierfehlern. Elektrisches Nachrichtenwesen, 4/1983, pp. 295-300
9. Lamberts, K., Pfeifer, R.: Computational models of expertise. Accounting for routine and adaptivity in skilled performance. Gilhooly, K., Keane, M. (eds.): Advances in psychology of thinking, New York: Simon & Schuster, in preparation
10. Lehner, F.: Softwarewartung. München, 1991
11. Lehner, F.: Nutzung und Wartung von Software. München, 1989
12. Newell, A.: The Knowledge Level. AI-Magazine, Vol. 2, No. 2, 1981, pp. 1-20
13. Norman, D.: "Some Observations on Mental Models". In: Gentner, D. (ed.): Mental Models, Hillsdale, New Yersey, 1983, 72-113
14. O'Keefe, R. M., Balci, O., Smith, E. P.: Validating Expert System Performance. IEEE Expert, Winter 1987, pp. 81-89
15. Pfeifer, R.: Hofmann, H.F., Rademakers, R., Vinkhuyzen, E. Problemlösende Systeme: Implikationen für die Validierung. KI-Magazin 4/92, pp. 71-73.

16. Preece, A.: Towards a Methodology for Evaluating Expert Sytem. Expert Systems, Vol. 7, No. 4, pp. 215-223
17. Thuy, N. H. Ch., Schnupp, P.: Wissensverarbeitung und Expertensysteme. München/Wien 1989
18. Verein Deutscher Ingenieure (ed.): VDI-Richtlinie 5006: Bürokomunikation - Expertensysteme in betriebswirtschaftlichen Anwendungen, VDI, Düsseldorf, September 1992
19. Wallmüller, E.: Software-Qualitätssicherung in der Praxis. München, 1990
20. Winograd, T., Flores, F.: Understanding Computers and Cognition. Ablex, New York, 1986

Using Candidate Space Structure to Propose the Next Measurement in Model Based Diagnosis *

Zdeněk Zdráhal

Human Cognition Research Laboratory
The Open University, Walton Hall,
Milton Keynes. MK7 6AA.

Abstract. Model-based diagnostic algorithms consist of two steps in a loop: (1) measurement of data on the device to be diagnosed and (2) evaluation of discrepancies between the data a nd predictions provided by the model. The next measurement is selected in accordance with an entropy-base d criterion. In order to simplify its evaluation additional assumptions have been imposed. They result in easy to evaluate, but only suboptimal solutions. In the paper we show how to reduce unnecessary comput ation so that the original criterion can be calculated efficiently. Properties of diagnoses with re spect to their capacity to predict values are analysed. All diagnoses which do not predict any value for a v ariable can be represented by the set of the smallest diagnoses with this property and the rest of the diagnostic space can be organised so that it is searched efficiently. An algorithm is outlined which makes use of these results.

1 Introduction

Consistency-based diagnostic algorithms (see e.g. [1]) repeat two steps in a loop: (1) they maintain the consistency of observed data measured on the device to be diagnosed with predictions provided by its model and (2) they measure a new value for the variable which promises the best discrimination. An entropy-based criterion is usually used to propose the next measurement. In each step the variable which yields the maximum decrement of expected entropy is selected. Thus the measurement maximises in each step the expected information gain.

Proposing the next measurement is an expensive procedure since it involves a one step look ahead search of a large search space. At any state of the diagnostic process some set of candidate diagnoses is considered. The proposed measurement should reduce uncertainty within the set as much as possible. For a given variable the candidate either predicts a single value or does not predict

* This research is a part of the Vital project which is partially funded by the ESPRIT Program of the Commision of the European Communities, as project 5365. The partners in the Vital project are: Syseca Temps Reel (F), Bull Cediag (F), Onera (F), The Open University (UK), University of Nottingham (UK), Royal PTT Netherland (NL), Nokia (SF), University of Helsinki (SF), and Andersen Consulting (E).

any value. The candidates which make it possible to predict different values for the same variable have thereby produced conflict (logical inconsistency). It is the job of the diagnostic algorithm to remove the conflicts. The entropy of the candidate set depends critically on the capacity of the candidates to predict values. If the variable is selected and measured and the candidate's prediction proves to be erroneous a new conflict is found (to be subsequently eliminated by the diagnostic algorithm). In accordance with the values predicted for a variable the model can be decomposed into subsystems. The decomposition is only loosely related to the diagnostic algorithm used. This paper attempts to analyse the properties of decompositions and exploit them to better organise the evaluation of the entropy-based criterion. In particular, we will show an efficient calculation of the basic criterion given in [1].

The entropy-based criterion as described in [1] requires (1) the initial probabilities of component failure to be known and (2) independence of component failures. In order to simplify the calculation de Kleer [2] introduces additional assumptions: (3) components fail with the same probability and (4) this probability is very small. Under these assumptions the criterion is significantly simplified but the optimality is sacrificed, i. e. in some cases it is possible to find a shorter sequence of measurements if the original criterion of [1] is used instead. This especially happens if the simplifying assumptions do not hold, for example if some of the components fail with relatively higher probability. Several variations of the original entropy-based criterion are also discussed in [4].

Our approach is different. We want to achieve the efficiency by reducing the space which must be individually searched and by aggregating the rest. In section 2 we informally discuss the problem. The basic concepts and definitions are introduced in section 3. In section 4 we will formalise our intuitions and in section 5 we sketch an algorithm which exploits the properties found.

2 An Informal Analysis of the Well-known Example

Consider the familiar circuit shown in Fig. 1. Blocks M_1, M_2 and M_3 are multipliers, A_1 and A_2 are adders. Assume that no values have yet been assigned to external variables A, B, C, D, E, F and G. Therefore it does not make any sense to talk about conflicts and diagnostic reasoning. Let us analyse the possible values of variable Y. Even without knowing the values of external variables we can see that the value predicted for Y depends on 3 subsystems and their interactions. The subsystems are $S_1 = \{M_1, A_1\}$, $S_2 = \{M_2\}$ and $S_3 = \{M_3, A_2\}$. Each of them can be used to calculate a value for Y. Since there are only 3 subsystems which determine the value of Y there are only 3 possible ways of determining the value of Y. A candidate is the set of components supposed to be faulty. The candidate predicts a value for some variable if this value can be unambiguously determined in the case that the components of the candidate (and only them) are faulty. If some component of a subsystem is faulty the subsystem cannot be used to calculate the value - it is disabled. A candidate disables the subsystem if it has common components with it. Therefore the candidate predicts the value

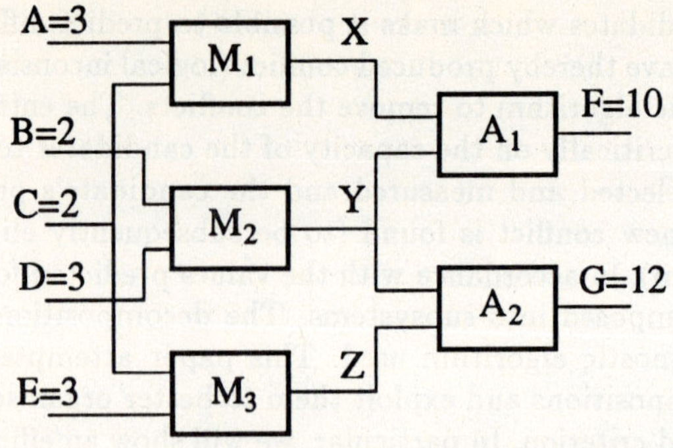

Fig. 1.: Familiar circuit

calculated by the subsystem which is not disabled. A candidate does not predict any value for a variable if it disables all subsystems which could predict a value for that variable. If n subsystems predict n different values then the diagnostic algorithm must guarantee that each candidate eliminates at least $n-1$ of them by disabling corresponding subsystems. The value calculated by the remaining subsystem is the one predicted by the candidate. For example, candidate M_1M_3 predicts for Y the value determined by subsystem S_2. If all n values are eliminated no value is predicted. Candidate $M_1M_2M_3$ disables all subsystems and thus does not predict any value for Y. For such a candidate the variable Y is "cut off" from all ways of calculating its value. Now, if two candidates predict different values for the same variable, it means that they allow two different subsystems to calculate the prediction and disable the others. The union of two candidates eliminates subsystems eliminated by each candidate. Therefore the union of candidates predicting different values cannot predict any value. This property can be used to characterise candidates which do not predict any value.

3 Preliminaries

We will need the following concepts which have been explained in detail for example in [3].

Definition 1. *[3, Definition 2.1]* A system is a triple (*Sd*, *Comps*, *Obs*), where

Sd, the system description, is a set of first-order sentences,
Obs, a set of observations, is a set of first-order sentences,
Comps, the system components, is a set of constants.

We assume that some sentences of *Sd* include $Ab(c)$ predicate, $c \in Comps$, which holds when c is abnormal. If the observations are unreliable *Obs* also include *Ab* predicates.

Definition 1 can be given a simple intuitive interpretation which explicitly distinguishes between the device and its model. *Obs* refers to the device to be diagnosed, *Sd* to its model and *Comps* indicates that components of the device are modelled by means of constants of the model.

Definition 2. *[3, Definition 2.2]* Let C_p and C_n be sets of components. We denote

$$D(C_p, C_n) = \left(\bigwedge_{c_i \in C_p} Ab(c_i) \right) \wedge \left(\bigwedge_{c_i \in C_n} \neg Ab(c_i) \right)$$

Definition 3. *[3, Definition 2.3 and 2.5]* Let $\Delta \in Comps, D(\Delta, Comps - \Delta)$ is a diagnosis for $(Sd, Comps, Obs)$, iff $Sd \cup Obs \cup D(\Delta, Comps - \Delta)$ is satisfiable. Diagnosis $D(\Delta, Comps - \Delta)$ is a ***minimal diagnosis***, if for no proper subset Δ' of Δ $D(\Delta', Comps - \Delta')$ is a diagnosis [2]. Since for a given *Comps* the diagnosis $D(\Delta, Comps - \Delta)$ and $\Delta \subset Comps$ are unambiguously bound we will also call Δ a diagnosis.

We will be interested only in systems for which the following hypothesis holds.

Minimal Diagnosis Hypothesis (MDH). *[3, Hypothesis 2.7]*
If $D(\Delta', Comps - \Delta')$ is a minimal diagnosis and if $\Delta' \subseteq \Delta \subseteq Comps$ then also $D(\Delta, Comps - \Delta)$ is a diagnosis.

The conditions under which MDH holds are discussed thoroughly in [3]. All the entropy-based methods for proposing the next measurement described in [1, 2, 4] assume that MDH holds, although they do not mention it explicitly. We will assume that the formulae of *Sd* with *Ab* predicates are implications and the *Ab* predicate is on the left-hand side. If a formula is satisfied due to the left-hand side being unsatisfied, we say that the formula is satisfied trivially.

All possible diagnoses are members of a lattice with *Comps* as a carrier and a subset-superset relation as an order. The elements of the lattice are called candidates. Diagnostic information is refined by measuring additional variables on the device, i.e. by adding new data to *Obs*. Let us assume that we can still measure variables x_i. The possible values of a variable x_i are $v_{ij}, j = 1, ..., m$.

Definition 4. *[3, p. 113]* A candidate Δ predicts a value v_{ij} for a variable x_i iff $Sd \cup Obs \cup D(\Delta, Comps - \Delta) \models (x_i = v_{ij})$. It means that Δ is eliminated if x_i is measured not to be v_{ij}. The set of all candidates which predict value v_{ij} for x_i is called *selected* and denoted as S_{ij} . A candidate Δ is ***uncommitted*** to x_i iff it does not predict any value for x_i i.e. if $\forall j (Sd \cup Obs \cup D(\Delta, Comps - \Delta) \cup (x_i = v_{ij}))$ is consistent. The set of all candidates which are uncommitted for x_i is denoted as U_i. A candidate Δ is *remaining* iff it remains after x_i has been measured to be v_{ij}. The set of all remaining candidates is denoted as R_{ij}. Obviously, $R_{ij} = S_{ij} \cup U_i$ and $S_{ij} \cap U_i = \emptyset$.

---

[2] The term ***minimal diagnosis*** refers strictly to the meaning introduced in Definition 3. The diagnosis Δ which has some property P, and no proper subset Δ' of Δ has property P, is called the ***smallest diagnosis with*** P ***(which satisfies*** P***)***.

In [1, p. 116] the following criterion is derived

$$\Delta H_e(x_i) = \sum_{k=1}^{n} p(x_i = v_{ij}) \log p(x_i = v_{ij}) + p(U_i) \log p(U_i) - \frac{np(U_i)}{m} \log \frac{p(U_i)}{m},$$

where n is the number of values predicted by x_i, m is the total number of values the variables accept, $p(x_i = v_{ij}) = p(S_{ij}) + p(U_i)/m$, $p(U_i) = \sum_{\Delta \in U_i} p(\Delta)$, $p(S_{ik}) = \sum_{\Delta \in S_{ik}} p(\Delta)$. The most promising measurement is the one which minimises the criterion over x_i.

After measuring $x_i = v_{ij}$, all $\Delta \in S_{ik}, k \neq j$ are rejected and only those of R_{ij} remain. Their posterior probabilities are updated in accordance with the Bayes formula $p(\Delta | x_i = v_{ij}) = n_{ij}\ p(\Delta)$ for $\Delta \in S_{ij}$ and $p(\Delta | x_i = v_{ij}) = n_{ij}\ p(\Delta)/m$ for $\Delta \in U_i$. The normalisation factor n_{ij} guarantees that the posterior probabilities sum to 1. Its value is

$$n_{ij} = \frac{1}{p(x_i = v_{ij})} = \frac{1}{p(S_{ij}) + p(U_i)/m}.$$

4 Predicting values for variables

Our solution is focused on the cases when the prior probabilities are known and not all of them are very small. Here the complete criterion of [1] proposes measurements which may significantly differ from those of [2] and [4]. When evaluating the criterion the expensive part is the calculation of $p(S_{ij})$ and $p(U_i)$. For large systems $|Comps|$ is a large number and so is the number of contributions to $p(S_{ij})$ and $p(U_i)$. Since we assume that not all probabilities are approximately of the same magnitude it is not easy to decide which contributions can be omitted. Our aim is to reduce the part of the candidate space which must be searched and thus arrive at the more efficient evaluation. The following theorems and lemma describe properties of the candidate space with respect to sets $p(S_{ij})$ and $p(U_i)$.

Theorem 5. *Let $\Delta_j, \Delta_k, \Delta_n \subset Comps$ be candidates. Let Δ_j predict $x_i = v_{ij}$, and Δ_n be the candidate with the following properties: $\Delta_n \supset \Delta_j$, and Δ_k exists, such that Δ_k predicts $x_i = v_{ik}, k \neq j$, and $\Delta_n \supset \Delta_k$. Then Δ_n is uncommitted to x_i, i.e. $\Delta_n \in U_i$.*

In order to prove Theorem 5 we need the following lemma.

Lemma 6. *Let $\Delta_m, \Delta_n \subset Comps$, $\Delta_n \subset \Delta_m$ and let Δ_m predict $x_i = v_{ij}$. Then also Δ_n predicts $x_i = v_{ij}$.*

Proof. $Sd_m \cup Obs \cup D(\Delta_m, Comps - \Delta_m) \models (x_i = v_{ij})$. Let us denote $Sd_m = \{f_1, ..., f_r\}$ the formulae which are not trivially satisfied for $D(\Delta_m, Comps - \Delta_m)$. Similarly we define Sd_n for $D(\Delta_n, Comps - \Delta_n)$. In accordance with the assumptions $Sd_m \cup Obs \cup \neg(x_i = v_{ij})$ is not satisfiable. From $\Delta_n \subset \Delta_m$ we get $Sd_n \supset Sd_m$, i.e. $Sd_n = Sd_m \cup \{f_{r+1}, ..., f_s\}$. Since $Sd_m \cup Obs \cup \neg(x_i = v_{ij})$ is not satisfiable neither is $Sd_m \cup Obs \cup \neg(x_i = v_{ij}) \cup \{f_{r+1}, ..., f_s\}$. Therefore Δ_n predicts $x_i = v_{ij}$. □

Proof of Theorem 5. Assume that Δ_n predicts $x_i = v_{ik}$ for some k. Then in accordance with Lemma 6 Δ_k predicts $x_i = v_{ik}$ and Δ_j predicts $x_i = v_{ik}$. This contradicts with the assumption that Δ_j predicts $x_i = v_{ij}, k \neq j$. Therefore the assumption that Δ_n predicts $x_i = v_{ik}$ does not hold, Δ_n does not predict any value for x_i, i.e. $\Delta_n \in U_i$. □

Theorem 7. *Let $\Delta_j, \Delta_k, \Delta_n \subset Comps$ be candidates. Let $\Delta_j \in S_{ij}$ and Δ_n be the candidate with the following properties: $\Delta_n \supset \Delta_j$, and Δ_k exists, such that $\Delta_k \in S_{ik}, k \neq j$ and $\Delta_n \supset \Delta_k$. Then for each Δ_l such, that $\Delta_j \subset \Delta_l \subset \Delta_n$ either $\Delta_l \in S_{ij}$ or $\Delta_l \in U_i$.*

Proof. From Lemma 6 follows that for each $\Delta_l \subset \Delta_n, l \neq j$, either Δ_l predicts $x_i = v_{ik}$ or does not predict any value. □

Theorem 8. *Let $\Delta_n \in U_i$. Then $\Delta_l \in U_i$ holds for each diagnosis $\Delta_l \supset \Delta_n$.*

Proof. The proof is trivial.

We will demonstrate some of the concepts outlined above on the familiar circuit shown in Fig. 1. The candidate lattice with prediction for Y is shown in Fig. 2. There are three possibilities: Y is predicted to be 6, Y is predicted to be 4 and Y is not predicted, i.e. the diagnoses are uncommitted. Since there is no discrepancy between prediction provided by subsystem S_2 and S_3 (both predict $Y = 6$) these subsystems merged. The uncommitted diagnoses are drawn in ovals in Fig. 2, those which predict $Y = 6$ are in normal rectangles and those, predicting $Y = 4$ are in dashed rectangles.

Theorem 5 says that if two candidates predict different values then their disjunction is uncommitted. For example, M_1M_2 predicts $Y = 6$ and A_2M_2 predicts $Y = 4$, therefore $A_2M_1M_2$ is uncommitted - see Fig. 2.

In accordance with Theorem 7 all candidates on a path from the predicting diagnosis to the uncommitted one either predict the same value or are uncommitted. For example on the path $A_1, A_1M_3, A_1A_2M_3$ all diagnoses predict $Y = 6$, on the path $A_2M_2, A_2M_2M_3$ the diagnoses predict $Y = 4$. They merge in $A_1A_2M_2M_3$ which, in accordance with Theorem 5 is uncommitted. Theorem 8 states that all diagnoses above some uncommitted diagnosis are also uncommitted. For example $A_2M_1M_2$ is uncommitted and thus $A_1A_2M_1M_2$ and $M_1M_2M_3A_1A_2$ are also uncommitted. There are smallest uncommitted diagnoses which can parsimoniously represent the whole set U_i. When climbing up the lattice we just need to identify the smallest uncommitted diagnosis to stop the search in this direction. The maximum depth of the search is limited by Theorem 5. The calculation of $p(U_i)$ is then based on the idea that as soon as all $p(S_{ik})$ are calculated, $p(U_i)$ is the complement of their sum to 1.

Unfortunately, there is no simple way of combining uncommitted sets for different variables. Since the uncommitted sets of the previous diagnostic steps are needed, after each step the set of the smallest uncommitted diagnoses is stored.

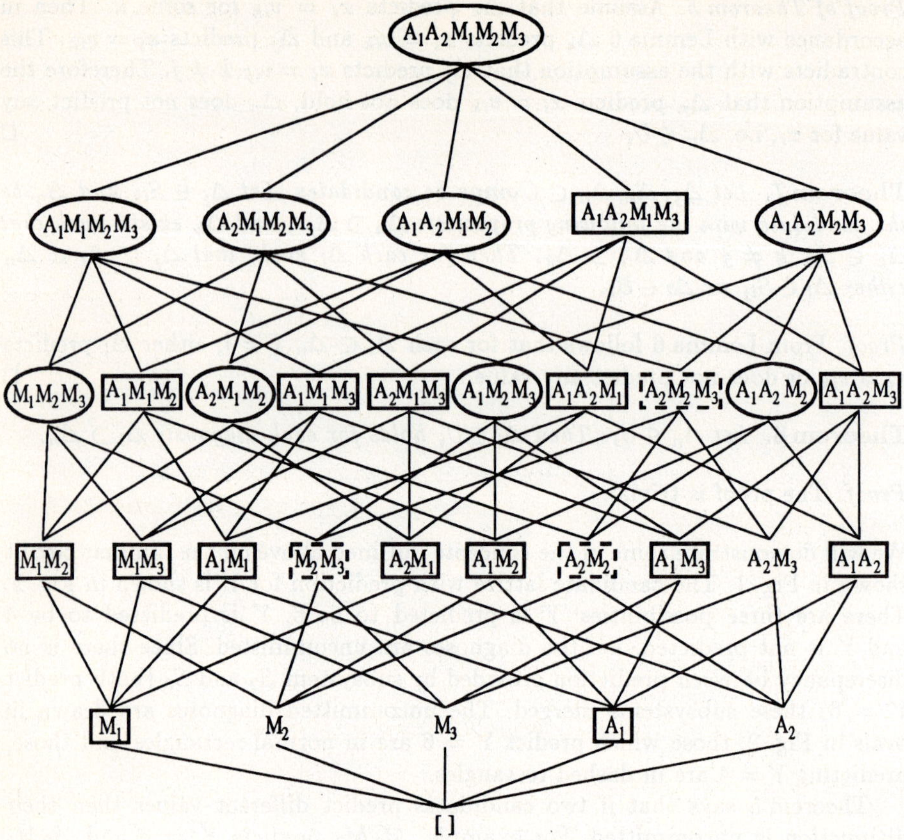

Fig. 2.: Predicting values for Y

5 An Outline of the Algorithm

If probabilities $p(S_{ik}), k = 1, ..., n$ and $p(U_i)$ are given, the evaluation of the criterion does not represent any problem. We will use the properties of diagnoses derived in the previous paragraphs to optimise the calculation of these probabilities.

Probabilities $p(S_{ik})$ are calculated as a sum of all $p(\Delta), \Delta \in S_{ik}$. Having computed all $p(S_{ik})$, $p(U_i)$ is calculated as $p(U_i) = 1 - \sum p(S_{ik})$. Since a large number of diagnoses usually belong to U_i the reduction in computation is significant. Now, the problem is how to calculate $p(S_{ik})$ efficiently. In accordance with the Bayes updating formula the current (posterior) value of $p(\Delta)$ is a product of the initial (prior) probability of Δ, the overall normalisation factor and the term $(1/m)^k$, where k expresses the number of times Δ was in previous steps a member of the uncommitted set .

The prior probabilities and m are constants throughout the diagnostic procedure. The overall normalisation factor is a product of the normalisation factors calculated in previous steps. Its value is updated in each step. However within each step the same value applies to all diagnoses. The prior probability and k are associated with each diagnosis, k being changed after each step and the prior probability remaining constant. However, if the number of diagnoses to be considered for probability calculation is sufficiently reduced, repeated calculation in each step does not represent a significant burden. In such a case previous uncommitted sets must be available for calculating k. They are represented as sets of the smallest uncommitted diagnoses (see Theorem 8). Unfortunately, these sets cannot be combined together in any simple way to produce a more parsimonious representation. The main reduction of calculations can be achieved by systematic pruning of the diagnostic space. The algorithm consists of an initialisation steps and a loop.

Let us denote:

OPEN ... the set of diagnoses which can still contribute to S_{ik}.
UNCOMMITTED ... the set of the smallest uncommitted diagnoses,
CARD ... minimal cardinality of diagnoses from OPEN,
Δ, ... a diagnosis from OPEN,
v_{ik} ... the value predicted for x_i by Δ,
EXPANDED ... the set of all expansions of Δ.

The initialisation steps:

1. Assign minimal diagnoses to OPEN.
2. Remove from OPEN all uncommitted diagnoses and assign them to UNCOMMITTED.
3. Group diagnoses in OPEN in accordance with the value they predict. Within each group order diagnoses in accordance with their cardinalities. Assign the minimal cardinality to CARD.

The loop:

Repeat until OPEN is empty:

1. Repeat for each diagnosis Δ with cardinality CARD:
   (a) Assign the expansion of Δ to EXPANDED, remove Δ from OPEN.
   (b) Remove from EXPANDED all diagnoses subsumed by any diagnosis from UNCOMMITTED (see Theorem 8).
   (c) Transfer from EXPANDED to UNCOMMITTED all diagnoses subsumed by any diagnosis with cardinality CARD from other groups, i.e. diagnoses which do not predict v_{ik}, (see Theorem 5).
   (d) For each diagnosis $\Delta' \in$ EXPANDED test whether it predicts the value predicted by Δ. If it does not, transfer Δ' to UNCOMMITTED (see Theorem 7).
   (e) For each diagnosis $\Delta' \in$ EXPANDED calculate its probability and add it to $p(S_{ik})$.
   (f) Insert each $\Delta' \in$ EXPANDED into OPEN at the position corresponding to CARD + 1.
2. Increment CARD by 1.

After the algorithm has terminated the UNCOMMITTED set contains the smallest uncommitted diagnoses and $p(S_{ik})$ have their correct values.

6 Concluding Comments

There are still several ways of optimising the algorithm sketched in the previous paragraph. The UNCOMMITTED sets produced by the previous steps are gathered for future calculation of k. After several steps the current minimal diagnosis may be subsumed by the smallest previously uncommitted diagnoses, leading to unnecessary tests. One possible improvement consists of removing these smallest uncommitted diagnoses and thus avoiding useless tests when calculating k. Much more costly is the computation which results from considering a complex description of the system while conflicts occur only in a small well-isolated subsystem and the other parts of the system do not participate. As a pathological example we can imagine the system consisting of two of the familiar circuits shown in Fig. 1 which are not interconnected in any way. Since we accept MDH, even though one of the circuits does not demonstrate any conflict, its components are considered in some diagnoses thus producing futile increase of the diagnostic space. This problem can be however solved by splitting the problem into independent parts.

We have analysed the problem of proposing the next measurement and found that the order of the candidate lattice defined by the set inclusion also describes the predictive properties of candidates and can be used to prune the space needed for calculation of entropy-based criterion. The results derived do not depend explicitly on a particular diagnostic algorithm and can be modified for other algorithms. The predictive properties of a candidate remain the same even if the candidate has already been eliminated and is not a diagnosis. Our analysis leads to the design of an algorithm which exploits the predictive properties to minimise the search needed for calculation of the entropy-based criterion. The efficient calculation of the next measurement is important for the performance of the diagnostic engine.

References

1. de Kleer J. and Williams B.C.: Diagnosing Multiple Faults, Artificial Intelligence **32** (1987), pp. 97-130
2. de Kleer J.: Using Crude Probability Estimates to Guide Diagnosis, Artificial Intelligence **45** (1990), pp. 381-391
3. de Kleer J., Mackworth A.K. and Reiter R.: Characterizing diagnoses and systems, Artificial Intelligence **56** (1992), pp. 197-222
4. Freiteag H.: A Generic Measurement Proposer, in Expert Systems in Engineering - Principles and Applications, International Workshop, Vienna, Austria, September 24- 26, 1990, Lecture Notes in AI **462**, Springer-Verlag, 1990, pp. 79-89

Decomposition of Four Component Items

John Debenham

Key Centre for Advanced Computing Sciences,
University of Technology, Sydney, PO Box 123, NSW 2007, Australia
and
CSIRO Division of Information Technology,
Locked Bag 17, North Ryde, NSW 2113, Australia

Abstract. Items are introduced as a universal formalism for describing data (ie individual things), information (ie relations) and knowledge (ie rules). A single rule for the normalisation of items is defined. The five normal forms for relational database together with the Boyce-Codd normal form provide a complete characterisation of the normalisation of 3-adic information items. New normal forms may be derived by applying our single rule of normalisation to n-adic items for n > 3.

1 Introduction

In [4] we presented a framework for modelling "data", "information" and "knowledge" using "objects". We showed that a single principle of normalisation for objects could be specified. "Objects" was defined in terms of tuples and suffered the restriction of only being able to describe a limited class of "knowledge", or "rules". Here we generalise these ideas to "items" which are capable of describing *all* rules expressible in logic, and have the important additional property of being able to represent two complex classes of constraints. We investigate the decomposition of four component items and show that this generates new rules for normalisation.

A major collaborative research project between the University of Technology, Sydney and the CSIRO Division of Information Technology has addressed the formulation of a comprehensive design methodology for knowledge-based systems. An important product of this project has been the design, construction and field testing of a Computer Assisted Knowledge Engineering tool, or CAKE tool, called "The Knowledge Analyst's Assistant" [5]. Another important result has been the demonstration of the value of the normalisation of knowledge both as a means to prevent the introduction of knowledge update anomalies and as a means of constructing knowledge bases which may be easily maintained.

2 Items

We use the terms "association", "functional association", "implicit association", "explicit association", "data", "information", "knowledge", "clause", "clause group" and "cluster" in the sense defined in [4]. We will illustrate our discussion here using Horn clause logic. Note that we are not advocating the use of logic as a practical knowledge processing language.

In [4] we introduced the notion of "objects"; those objects described data and information but only a limited range of knowledge. We now generalise the notion of "objects" to the notion of "items" which describe *all* data, information and knowledge things effectively together with two powerful classes of constraints on those things.

An *item* will be written as the named triple *A*[E,F,G]. The *item semantics* E represents the condition for labels belonging to that item. If E describes an implicit association then that item is called an *information item*, if E describes an explicit association then that item is called a *knowledge item*, and if E describes no association at all then that item is called a *data item*. If the item semantics E is trivial then the item *A* is said to be *tautological*. The item *value constraints* F is an expression that is satisfied by the labels associated with the component items. The item *set constraints* G is an expression constructed from the primitives "Card", "Uni" and "Can" that represents structural constraints on the item.

For example if *part* and *cost-price* are the names of data items then:

$$\begin{aligned}
&\textit{part/cost-price}[\ \lambda xy\bullet[\text{costs}(x\text{:part-number, } y\text{:dollar-amount})]\bullet,\\
&\quad \lambda xy\bullet[\ (1000 < x\text{:part-number} < 9999) \wedge\\
&\qquad (0 < y\text{:dollar-amount}) \wedge\\
&\qquad ((x\text{:part-number} < 1999) \rightarrow (y\text{:dollar-amount} \leq 300))\ ]\bullet,\\
&\quad (\text{Uni}(\textit{part}) \wedge \text{Can}(\textit{cost-price}, \{\textit{part}\}))_{\textit{part/cost-price}} \wedge\\
&\qquad (\text{Card} \leq 100)_{\textit{part}}\ ]
\end{aligned}$$

is an information item; the data items *part* and *cost-price* are the *components* of that information item. This information item represents the "costs" relationship between *part* and *cost-price*. It is subject to the value constraints that part numbers lie between 1000 and 9999; cost prices are non-negative dollar amounts, and if a part-number is less than 1999 then the cost will be less than or equal to $300. It is subject to the set constraints that every part-number is in this relationship, the part-number determines the cost-price and the number of different part-numbers is no greater than 100. It is important to note that items can represent data and knowledge things in the precisely same format. Thus data, information and knowledge things may be modelled using one simple formalism which includes a representation of two complex sets of constraints on those things.

In [4] we described "object composition". We have extended "object composition" to a rule for "item join" which differs in two important aspects. First, the rule now extends to a representation of all knowledge things, and second, the rule includes the composition of both the value constraints and the set constraints on those things. Given two items *A* and *B*, some of the components of *A* and *B* may be the same. Let C be the set of components where each is one of these identical pairs of components of *A* and *B*; note that C may be empty. $A \otimes_C B$ denotes the *join* of *A* and *B* on C. Using the rule of composition ⊗, knowledge items, information items and data items may be combined with one another. This item join operator is a non-trivial extension of the object composition operator described in [4]. We say that an item is *decomposable* if it can be constructed by joining two non-tautological items.

3 Normal Forms

In [4] we specified a single principle of normalisation for "objects". This principle was based on the object composition operator and extends here to a principle for "items" which is now based on the new item join operator. Principle NF: "Given a set of items discard those which are decomposable" We now explore the application of this principle to three component and to four component items.

3.1 Three component items

Suppose that item O has the three components A, B and C. There are five different ways in which the item $O = O(C, B, A)$ can be decomposed into two sub-items O_1 and O_2; these five ways are:

3NF	$O((C,B) \Leftarrow A) = O_2(C \Leftarrow B) \otimes_{\{B\}} O_1(B \Leftarrow A)$
2NF	$O(C \Leftarrow (B,A)) = O_2(C \Leftarrow B) \otimes_{\{B\}} O_1(B,A)$
BCNF	$O(B \Leftarrow (C,A)) = O_2(C \Leftarrow B) \otimes_{\{B\}} O_1(B,A)$
4NF	$O(C,B,A) = O_2(C,B) \otimes_{\{B\}} O_1(B,A)$
5NF	$O(C,B,A) = O_3(A,C) \otimes_{\{C\}} O_2(C,B) \otimes_{\{B\}} O_1(B,A)$

It should be stressed that our normal forms all apply equally well to knowledge as to data or information. Thus the classical normal forms provide a complete characterisation of the ways in which an item of three components may be decomposed.

3.2 Four component items

A four component item O can be decomposed by:

$$O(D,C,B,A) = O_2(D,C,B) \otimes_{\{B\}} O_1(B,A), \text{ and}$$
$$O(D,C,B,A) = O_2(D,C,B) \otimes_{\{B,C\}} O_1(C,B,A).$$
$$O(D,C,B,A) = O_3(A,D,C) \otimes_{\{C,D\}} O_2(D,C,B) \otimes_{\{B,C\}} O_1(C,B,A)$$
$$O(D,C,B,A) = O_4(A,D) \otimes_{\{D\}} O_3(D,C) \otimes_{\{C\}} O_2(C,B) \otimes_{\{B\}} O_1(B,A)$$

These four principles of decomposition of four component items will become rules of normalisation when the functional associations within the sub-items have been specified. Some, but not all, of the resulting rules of normalisation are not equivalent to the rules given in §3.1. Four new rules of normalisation which may be derived from each of these four principles are:

$$O((D,B) \Leftarrow (C,A)) = O_2(D \Leftarrow (C,B)) \otimes_{\{B\}} O_1(B \Leftarrow A). \quad [1]$$
$$O((D,C) \Leftarrow (B,A)) = O_2(D \Leftarrow (C,B)) \otimes_{\{B,C\}} O_1(C \Leftarrow (B,A)) \quad [2]$$
$$O(D,C,B,A) = O_3(A,D,C) \otimes_{\{C,D\}} O_2(D,C,B) \otimes_{\{B,C\}} O_1(C,B,A) \quad [3]$$
$$O(D,C,B,A) = O_4(A,D) \otimes_{\{D\}} O_3(D,C) \otimes_{\{C\}} O_2(C,B) \otimes_{\{B\}} O_1(B,A) \quad [4]$$

In rules [3] and [4] there are no functional associations present. We now illustrate these four normal forms with an example.

These four rules can be applied to the normalisation of data, information and knowledge. For example, we apply normal form [1] to knowledge; consider the following rule [a]:

part/sale-price(x, y) ← part/cost-price(x, z), part/part-type(x, v),
part-type/mark-up-factor(v, w), $y = (z \times w)$ [a]

Buried within this rule is the sub-rule that "the mark-up factor for a part is the mark-up factor associated with that part's type". This sub-rule could be represented as:

part/mark-up-factor(x, y) ← part/part-type(x, z),
part-type/mark-up-factor(z, y) [b]

Now it should be clear that rule [b] is buried within rule [a], and that rule [a] should thus be re-expressed as:

part/sale-price(x, y) ← part/cost-price(x, z),
part/mark-up-factor(x, w), $y = (z \times w)$ [c]

References

1. Date, C.J., "An Introduction to Database Systems" (4th edition) Addison-Wesley, 1986.
2. Debenham, J.K., "Knowledge Systems Design", Prentice Hall, 1989.
3. Debenham, J.K., "Knowledge Systems: A Synthesis of Database Systems and Expert Systems Technologies", in proceedings International Conference on Database and Expert Systems Applications, Vienna, 1990, pp 315-321.
4. Debenham, J.K.(1992), "Modelling Knowledge Systems", in proceedings International Conference on Database and Expert Systems Applications, Valencia, 1992.
5. Debenham, J.K. and Lindley, C., "The Knowledge Analyst's Assistant: A Tool for Knowledge Systems Design", in proceedings of the 4th Australian Joint Conference on Artificial Intelligence, Perth, 21-23 November 1990, pp 343-354.
6. Gray, P.M.D., "Expert Systems and Object-Oriented Databases: Evolving a New Software Architecture", in "Research and Development in Expert Systems V", Cambridge University Press, 1989, pp 284-295.
7. Ito, H., "Interface for Integrating a Knowledge-Based System and Database Management System Using Frame-Based Knowledge Representation", in proceedings Expert Systems World Congress, J. Liebowitz (Ed), Pergamon Press 1991.
8. Kowalski, R.A., "Logic Programming in Artificial Intelligence", in proceedings International Joint Conference on Artificial Intelligence, Sydney, August 1991.
9. Walker, A., Kowalski, R., Lenat, D., Soloway, E. and Stonebraker, M., "Knowledge Management", in (L. Kerschberg, Ed.), "Proceedings from the Second International Conference on Expert Database Systems", Benjamin Cummings, 1989.

Intelligent Inference For Debugging Concurrent Systems

Mike Brayshaw[1]

Human Cognition Research Laboratory
The Open University
Milton Keynes, England, MK7 6AA.
Tel: [+44] (0)908 65 5015
FAX: [+44] (0)908 65 3169
email: m.c.brayshaw@open.ac.uk

Abstract: This paper gives an overview of a program visualisation system which allows users to build up agents to perform detection and inference about the symptomatic behaviours of their concurrent programs. The system allows users to graphically describe program behaviours and then to use these descriptions within a inference engine. Temporal relations are introduced between agents in order to allow the system to deal with concurrent behaviours. Finally we show how these can be combined with standard knowledge engineering techniques to debug programs, and how explanations can be graphically presented.

1 Introduction

The work reported in this paper is part of a system called MRE [2, 3, 4, 5, 6]. It represents a continuing evolution of program visualisation systems for logic programming (e.g. see [7, 9, 11]). In each of these systems a program is run and a trace history generated (non-termination being specially catered for). This trace history can then be reviewed by animation, manipulated according to grain-size of information, or customised. This representational environment allows both novice and experts access to a wide body of information, arranged around the concept of a visual execution model. Such a system for Prolog is now available commercially, freely for Macintoshes™ [16], and is used for teaching on our undergraduate and post-graduate courses. The work reported here has now moved on to consider parallel logic programming. We shall give a brief overview of the current state of this work, before moving on to focus on the use we have made of inference within the current debugger. In this paper we will introduce the following:

• visually programmed search *agents* that allow large information areas to be searched, either upon request or via continual monitoring.

• *agents* can be augmented by a simple temporal logic in order to allow users to reason about time in relation to the occurrence of symptomatic clusters of behaviours.

• such an architecture can then be incorporated into a conventional rule-based system to produce knowledge bases capable of debugging a concurrent system.

• such inference can be built into a large Program Visualisation System permitting users graphical explanation of the outcome of this diagnostic process.

---

[1]This work was supported by a MRC/SERC/ESRC UK Joint Research Council Grant #89/CS31, which is gratefully acknowledged.

The paper will develop each of these points in turn. First let's start with a brief description of the kernel system, as this forms the basis upon which we shall build in the rest of the paper.

2. Program Visualisation in MRE

MRE is an attempt to find new and improved ways to understand and debug software by simultaneously looking for new representational media (sound and graphics) to describe software execution and (correspondingly) new and more flexible information accessing and manipulation techniques. It is currently implemented for a commit choice parallel logic language, PARLOG [13]. Of interest from the point of view of visualisation are problems presented by showing the effects of AND- and OR-parallel search, dynamic events like process deadlock and suspension, inter-process communication and mutual dependencies, together with clause selection and unification, data-flow, and commitment to various solution routes. Special events, like the race at various choice points between competing alternatives to satisfy critical preconditions, need to be shown, and their dynamics captured. As a result a series of visual representational techniques have been used, of which an overview is shown below. A full account of the PARLOG visualisation is in [4]

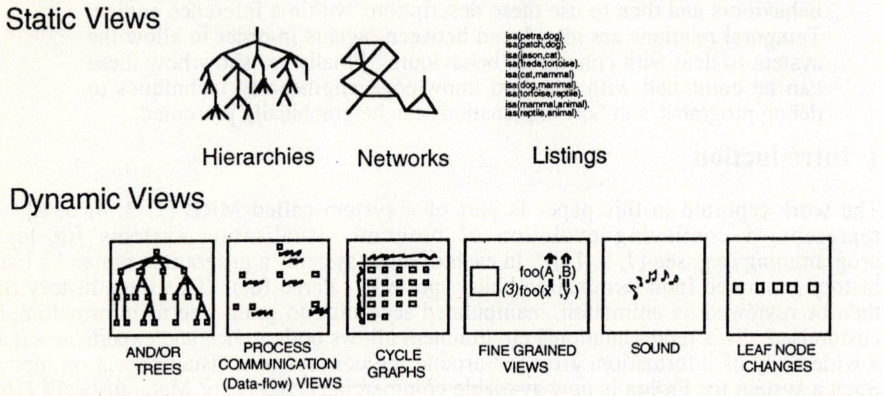

If you look at the diagram above, you will note that we distinguish between static and dynamic program visualisations. Static visualisations are source code or data structure browsers designed to let the user develop better models of their code. The dynamic models aim to give views of the code in action. All the dynamic views are closely tied together by an overall execution model. They can also be animated in order to capture the history of the execution. Great efforts have been made to emphasise that each dynamic view is just a perspective on the same execution model and virtual machine. The aim is thus to provide representational flexibility whilst at the same time avoiding multiple models of the virtual machine or multiple perspectives whose interrelationship is not readily apparent. The dynamic views aim to show (from left to right) parallel search (including process interdependency), process communication, repetitive dynamics, clause selection and unification, and latest changes (conceptually, a continually updated stop press column). Additionally the tracer can be augmented by an audio soundtrack, with every event in the trace having an associated sound.

Upon this graphical kernel we will now start to add some more complex information accessing and retrieval functionality. In the next section we will start this by looking at how we can index and pinpoint particular behaviours of our program.

3. Agent Based Information Location

We here use agents in the manner suggested e.g. by Kay [14], i.e. something that shares the user's goals and to which the user can delegate part of their task. One reason they are important is that as data repositories, be they knowledge bases or databases, get even larger, it will become increasingly harder to find information, or in the more extreme scenario, know where to start looking. For this reason agents offer a great opportunity to search and order banks of information at the behest of the user. The agents in this scenario are divided into two different sorts. The first is a feature detection system that can look out for things on behalf of the user. The second is a much more sophisticated kind of agency which can perform inference using a standard inference engine. Novelly, this inference can be about the behaviour of a concurrent system.

MRE's agency menu is shown below. Simple information search and retrieval agents are shown on the left. More complex inference based ones on the right. We shall now go on to describe each type in turn.

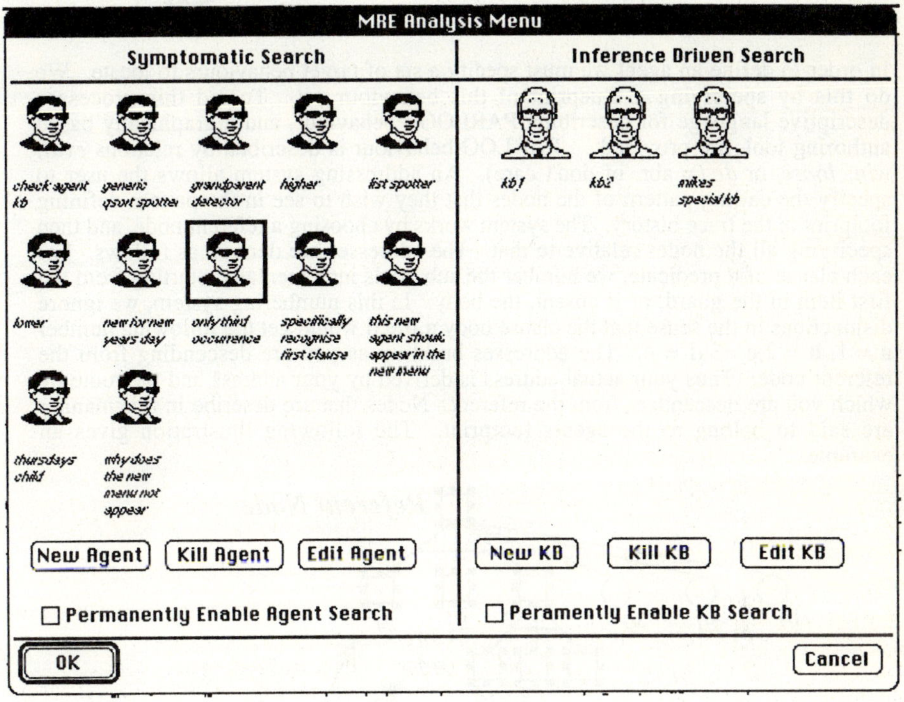

4.1 Symptom Search Agents

Symptom search is a method of rapidly finding areas of interest. Influenced by Eisenstadt's [8] suspicious symptom detectors, here they allow us to automate the process of detecting particular behaviours on the part of the program. Note that the patterns that we are talking about may be a very complex series of events over a large execution history. The system thus goes beyond the functionality of a simple feature detection system: complex patterns, implicit within a much large visual story may be readily found. Users may set up agents to continually monitor for states either that they anticipate or have seen before. Patterns can either by coded by hand, or visually as described below.

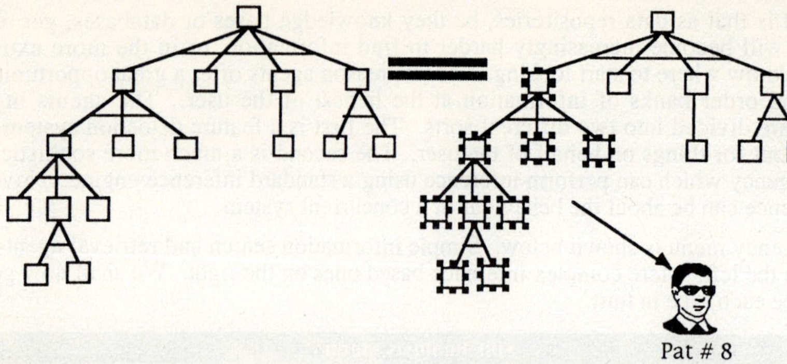

In order to define an agent we must specify a set of target behaviours to locate. We do this by specifying a blueprint of this behaviour set. To aid this process a descriptive language for describing PARLOG's behaviour, and a graphically based authoring tool, are provided. PARLOG behaviour is described by relations *eval, win, loose,* or *dc* (= abr. of don't care). An addressing system allows the user to specify the calling pattern of the nodes that they wish to see in the pattern defining footprint in the trace history. The system works by choosing a referent node, and then specifying all the nodes relative to that. The addresses are derived as follows. For each clause of a predicate, we number the sub-goals incrementally, starting from the first item in the guard, or if absent, the body. In this numbering system, we ignore disjunctions in the sense that the clause body **a,b;c,d** would get the following number **a** = 1, **b** = 2,**c** =3,**d** = 4. The addresses build up as you are descending from the referent node. Thus your actual address is derived by your address and the route by which you are descendant from the referent. Nodes that are describe in this manner are said to belong to the agents footprint. The following illustration gives an example.

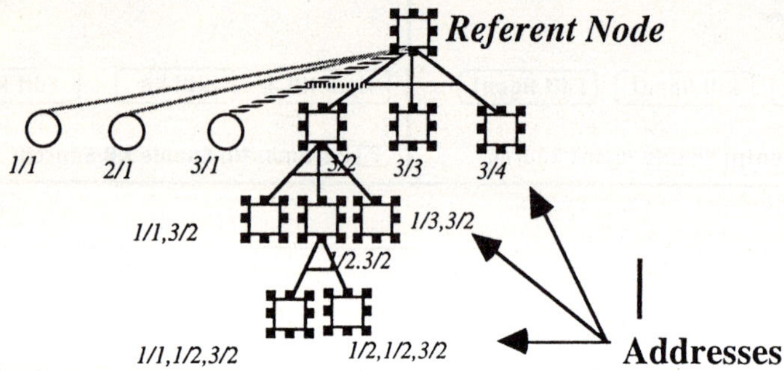

We can define a pattern for an agent to look out for us by using an existing trace. In the above diagram, we can see on the left the trace of some hypothetical program. Suppose this contained some particularly noteworthy behaviour. What we can do is to record the behaviour of interest (the highlighted nodes in the tree on the right) and place this pattern into the head of a new agent. This new agent will then become available on the *MRE Analysis Menu* that we saw previously. If we select that menu, and that agent, we then have a way of rapidly (re-)locating this set of eventualities should they ever reoccur.

In certain sets of circumstances the particular behaviour we wish to describe may not yet have been observed. This might be the case when we are dealing with a possible machine state which we anticipate and to which we want to be alerted, but cannot guarantee will occur. To cater for this users can define agents by hand or indeed refine existing agents defined graphically, if they so wish to. This is because all agents are written out to a file using the following syntax.

```
agent(<Name String>,
<list-of-name-in-special-print-format>,
<referent>,
<footprint>)
```

The first two arguments contain the name of the agent. Normally automatically generated, the first contains the name as a string, the second in an internal print format. The various patterns located in the referent and footprint following the pattern and referencing scheme that we discussed above. Multiple definitions of agents with the same name allow users to specify alternative solutions to the agents search. To take an example, suppose that we were interested in a quick sort spotting agent, which in our particular program wants to see the third invocation of **qsort** when called with the list **[2,1,3]**. Our definition would be as follows.

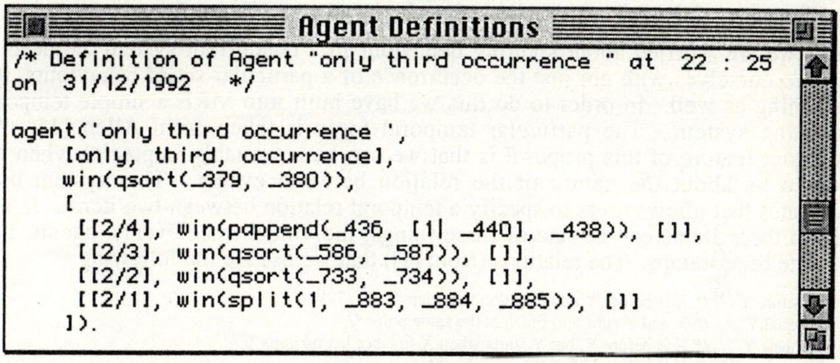

If we were to select this agent from the menu, then we would get the following:

The system starts from the top and finds each instance of the described pattern, prompting the user whether to find the next instance of the pattern or quit. This allows the user to search their code for particular symptomatically-defined patterns of activity, and not just the usual single line of information.

4.3 Inference Driven Search

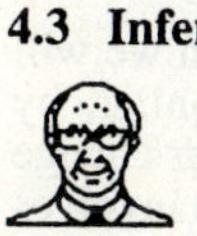

Inference Driven Search can be thought of as an extension of symptomatic driven search. The agents that we saw in the earlier section can here be combined with inference rules in order to infer or deduce a particular conclusion from the state of their program. Once inferred, this conclusion can then be passed on to users. Thus by using such a system users can compile into the machine intelligent inference that otherwise they might have to do, and set up special agents to continually check if these inferences can be made about a program's execution. This could be used both for debugging or setting up warning devices within the development environment.

The idea here is not necessarily to write large knowledge bases about a program. Instead the idea is that you can have easily conditioned handles on the execution history looking for eventualities of various degrees of complexity. The user is thus able to compile into the interface high level information about the programs desired performance and design specifications, and automate this knowledge for their own later benefit. Heuristic information may be treated likewise, so that the user can also get intelligent inferences support for supplying additional hunches. More specifically, the use of a series of different rules lets us do additional (conditional) checks, make intermediary hypotheses, or consider more than one manner of manifestation of the behaviour you wish to find.

Since we are worried about spotting behaviour in a concurrent system we need to concern ourselves with not just the occurrence of a particular set of behaviours, but the timing as well. In order to do this we have built into MRE a simple temporal reasoning system. The particular temporal logic is taken from Allen [1]. An important feature of this proposal is that we can be reasonably imprecise when we need to be about the nature of the relation between events. This system uses predicates that allows users to specify a temporal relation between two items. In our system these items can be one of three things, individual trace events, agents, and absolute time stamps. The relations (from [1]) that we use are the following

```
X before Y    /* X is before Y and they don't overlap */
X equal Y     /* X and Y start and finish at the same point */
X meets Y     /* X is before Y, but Y starts when X finishes i.e. no gaps */
X overlaps Y  /* X is before Y, but they overlap */
X during Y    /* the event X happens within the span of event Y */
```

additionally we include the following

```
X at Y /* event X happens at time Y */
X near Y      /* Y happens in a user defined interval from the outset or ending of Y */
X after Y     /* X occurs after Y */
```

In the trace history we know when the time events occur (this is how we can produce the execution animation). When the system is given either a particular behaviour, be it in the form of an event e.g.. **win(quicksort([2,1,3],[1,2,3]))** or a more macro behaviour described such as an agent, the system transforms this information into these internal time stamps. User need not use them themselves. They can program the system merely by specifying information relationally. However the **at** relation allows users to retrieve the actual internal time stamp for a particular event. Actual time stamps of this form can then be used explicitly with the other temporal relations, if users so choose.

Now that we can recognise temporal relation between events in a program, we now have to concern ourselves with how to perform inference. MRE contains within it and embedded version of MIKE [10, 11]. MIKE (Micro Interpreter for Knowledge Engineering) includes forward and backward chaining rules with user-definable conflict resolution strategies, and a frame representation language with inheritance and 'demons' (code triggered by frame access or change), plus user-settable inheritance strategies, a RETE-based rule compiler, probabilistic reasoning and resolution strategies, hypothetical worlds, and a truth maintenance system (TMS).

In this paper we are just going to use the MIKE rule interpreter. In addition we will also need to extending MIKE KR to include agent and temporal reasoning, by allowing rules to contain the temporal logic syntax we saw above. A further change is optionally available to the user effecting MIKE's inferencing regime. This involves how choices of action are made. One of our specific requirements for AI agents is that they can, if you wish, perform inference according to some individual criteria, as befits their character. This can be modelled in terms of attractor states that influence the agents trajectory through a state space (e.g. after Kiss, [15]). We shall use a similar concept here to allow us to define agents with individual axiological concerns. At any point of a state-space traversal there may be a choice of which operator (rule) to employ. MIKE uses standard conflict resolution techniques (after Forgy, [12]) to make a choice about what to do next. Additionally here however we can allow agents to customise the choice using criteria based on more specific semantic considerations (as relating to the particular agency under consideration). Thus users can specify particular rules or patterns that they think are particularly attractive and give them a numerical ranking. Items that can be ranked either per rule, or per component parts of a rule. The ranking should reflect the correspondence of that particular item to the achieving of some particular attractor state deemed good for that agent e.g. consider the following two patterns that we might observe as elements in a rule.

```
conclusion(_) rank 10
hypothesis(_) rank 2
```

This says that rules that contain statements about conclusions will be ranked highly, although to a lesser degree we will also favour rules that allow hypothesis formation (when placed in a position to choose between a set of rules containing these features). Notice that these ranking will produce an agent that favours rapidly focusing on a conclusion. If we were to reverse them, we could instead create an agency, containing the same rulebase as before, which instead favours exploring the space of possible hypotheses before narrowing on to a conclusion. We can thus alter the behaviour of our agents by altering the way they choose their actions. If this is done systematically we can thus alter the character of an agent. For example, causing one to be cautious (e.g. about reaching a conclusion in the above scenario), another eager, depending upon the character rôle we have ascribed for them.

Now that we have looked at the various components in the system, we can now turn our focus onto how they can be used. Lets illustrate this by considering a simple example. The purpose of this example is to show how we can combine agents and other knowledge engineering techniques to produce simple diagnostic inference. Suppose we wish to monitor the print demon in some hypothetical concurrent operating system. Conceptually we could model it as follows:

```
/* simple hypothetical rulebase diagnoses synchronisation problem in printer spool queue
agent1 detects the issuing of a print command
agent2 detects when we spool the document concerned
agent3 detects when we attempt to print spooled documents
clock tick 45 allows us to look at some specific series of events */
rule rule3 forward
    if after(45,agent1) & /* does pattern-1 occur after some clock tick 45 */
        before(agent1,agent2) /* and pattern-1 before pattern-2 */
    then add printer_spool(ok). /* make fwd chaining memory assertion */
rule rule4 forward
    if after(45,agent1) & /* does pattern-1 occur after some clock tick 45 */
        before(agent2,agent1) /* WHOOPS pattern-2 before pattern-1 */
    then add printer_spool(error_in_synchronisation ).
rule rule6 forward
    if near(agent2,agent3)
    then add printing_demon(ok).
rule rule7 forward
    if not(near(agent2,agent3)) then add printing_demon(slow).
rule rule8 forward
    if agent2 /* check that agent2 occurs by just calling it */
        & not agent3 /* agent3 is a no show */
    then add printing_demon(not_happening).
rule rule30 forward
    if printer_spool(ok) &
        printing_demon(not_happening)
```

then annonce('Highlight Printer Demon Bugs',['There seems to be a problem with you printer demon. The command is being detected and the file is being spooled in the correct way. However, this is not being detected by the printer demon, which fails to find the file and print it']).

Suppose in some scenario we reached the conclusion described by **rule30**. The conclusion we reached can be graphically described back in terms of the program trace, and related to the actual nodes involved. We can use an agent, in this example '**Highlight Printer Demon Bugs**' to locate the part of the trace to highlight (this being the describing agents referent and footprint), and also specify a specific message to display at that time. The specification is shown on the Right-Hand-Side of **rule30** and the consequences in terms of the trace demonstrated in the following snapshot:

Currently, experiments have been limited to simple reasoning regimes (i.e. rule chaining), but there is no technical reason why you could not attempt to use TMS inferencing, for example. An area for future work is to see if you can adapt such inferencing techniques to software trouble-shooting in the current domain and demonstrate how this would work.

5. Conclusions

This paper has presented a series of techniques aimed at producing intelligent and co-operative interactions between the user and a large program trace history. This history can be thought analogous to a large database contained information about the program's behaviour and temporal synchronisation. As information systems get larger and the user population expands we think it imperative that we worry not just about representing information, but how to make it more accessible to the user. Although the focus here has been on debugging a concurrent system, the types of information access and managing facilities develop here are of potential interest to other information rich environments. Here we have demonstrated ways of adding inference techniques, both built in and user supplied, that allow the user to delegate intelligent diagnosis to the machine. The overall aim of this work is thus to attempt to find (a) better ways of talking about and represent information, (b) to explore new and more adaptable interactive techniques, and (c) provide for intelligent behaviour within the interface, for the benefit of information systems of the future.

6. References

1. Allen, J.F. An Interval-Based Representation of Temporal Knowledge, in *Proceedings of the Seventh International Joint Conference on Artificial Intelligence (IJCAI'81)*, pp. 221-226, Vancouver, B.C. Canada, 1981.
2. Brayshaw, M. An Architecture for Visualising the Execution of Parallel Logic Programming. *Proceedings of the Twelfth International Joint Conference on Artificial Intelligence (IJCAI-91).* Los Angeles: Morgan Kaufmann, 1991.
3. Brayshaw, M. Program Visualisation and Knowledge Negotiation, R. Moyse and M.T. Elsom-Cook (Eds.) *Knowledge Negotiation*, Academic Press:London, 1991.
4. Brayshaw, M. Visual Models of PARLOG Execution. Submitted for Publication, Submitted for Publication, Available as, *Technical Report 64*, Human Cognition Research Laboratory, The Open University, Milton Keynes, England.

5. Brayshaw, M. MRE: An Information Management Framework for Monitoring Program Execution, To appear in proceedings British Human-Computer Interface Conference, 1993.

6. Brayshaw, M. Seeing Parallel Logic Programs in Action , in prepn.

7. Brayshaw, M. and Eisenstadt, M. A Practical Graphical Prolog Tracer. *International Journal of Man-Machine Studies.,* **55**, pp. 597-631, 199.

8. Eisenstadt, M., Retrospective Zooming: a knowledge based tracing and debugging methodology for logic programming. *Proceedings of the Ninth International Conference on Artificial Intelligence (IJCAI-85).* Los Angeles: Morgan Kaufmann, 1985.

9. Eisenstadt, M. and Brayshaw, M. The Transparent Prolog Machine (TPM),*Technical Report 21*, Human Cognition Research Laboratory, The Open University, Milton Keynes, England.

10. Eisenstadt, M. and Brayshaw, M. Build your own Knowledge Engineering Toolkit *BYTE: The Small Systems Journal)*, McGraw-Hill, Hightstown NJ, Part 1 : October 1990, Part 2 : November 1990a & b.

11. Eisenstadt, M., and Brayshaw, M. The Transparent Prolog Machine (TPM): an execution model and graphical debugger for logic programming. *Journal of Logic Programming*, *5*(4),pp. 277-342, 1988.

12. Forgy, C. L. A Fast Algorithm for the Many Pattern/Many Object Pattern Matching Problem. *Artificial Intelligence*, 19:17-37, 1982.

13. Gregory, S. *Parallel Logic Programming in PARLOG: The language and its implementation.* Wokingham, UK: Addison-Wesley, 1987.

14. Key, A, User Interface: A Personnel View, In B. Laurel and S.J. Mountford (Eds.) Thc Art of Human-Computer Interface Design, page 191-208, Addison-Wesley, 1990

15. Kiss, G.R. Autonomous Agents, AI, and Chaos Theory. In J-A Meyer and S. Wilson, *From Animals to Animats*, Cambridge, Massachusetts:MIT Press, 1991.

16. TPM for Macintosh, Public Domain Software, c/o Human Cognition Research Laboratory, The Open University, Milton Keynes, England, 1991.

Sharing Temporal Knowledge by Multiple Agents

V.Botti, F. Barber, A. Crespo, D. Gallardo, I. Ripoll,
E.Onaindía, L. Hernández

Dpto. de Sistemas Informáticos y Computación.
Universidad Politécnica de Valencia
E-46022 Valencia Spain

Abstract: The multi-agent system paradigm emerges as an interesting approach in the Knowledge-Based System (KBS) field, when distributed problem-solving techniques are required for solving problems that can be represented as a collection of groups of cooperating intelligent individuals. This paper presents a framework for agent communication based on the blackboard paradigm, and it provides its multiple access and coherence management protocols.

1 Introduction

The Multi-agent system paradigm [5] emerges as an interesting approach in the Knowledge-Based System (KBS) field, when distributed problem-solving techniques are required for solving problems. A key concept in the multi-agent paradigm is the interaction between agents, which cannot only be considered by single message exchange. Usually, communication occurs through sophisticated protocols for informing, requesting or convincing [4]. On the other hand, temporal representation and reasoning arise in areas where time plays a crucial role, such as process control and monitoring, fault detection, diagnosis etc., in order to obtain conclusions about the problem.

In this paper, a Temporal Blackboard (TBB) framework for a multi-agent world, including concurrence control protocol, is described. The TBB provides a framework for sharing coherent information between agents. The TBB is structured for organizing communications at various levels of abstraction, and an agent communicates with another one by writing on the blackboard. These agents are activated when given patterns of information are present on the blackboard. The TBB is a component in a real time expert system shell under development in the framework of the REAKT Esprit project Nº 5146 [6].

2 System Architecture

The system is built around a Temporal Blackboard for a Real-Time Knowledge Based Architecture[2], named **Knowledge Data Manager** (KDM). The architecture of this temporal blackboard provides storage and management of application objects used by a set of *knowledge sources* (KS) running concurrently (Figure 1). The main components in the architecture are:

• **ICM**: The Intelligent Communication Manager is a task that provides the interface with external processes for sending and receiving external data.

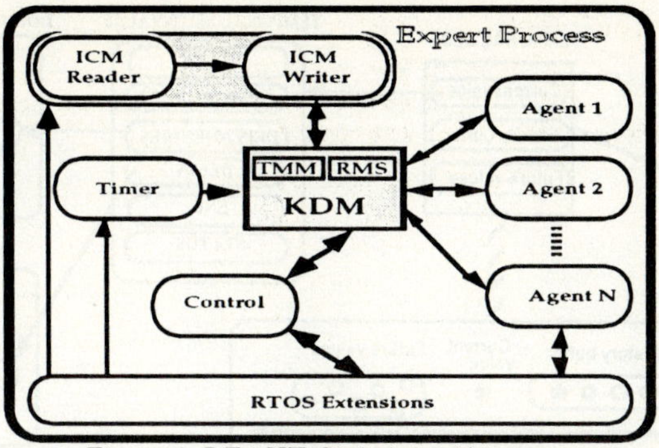

Figure 1. REAKT Global Architecture.

• **KDM**: The KDM implements a Blackboard (shared memory) for temporal data. Temporal constraints are managed by means of a *Time Map Manager* (TMM) module and a *Reason Maintenance System* (RMS) module is in charge of maintaining the logical coherence of temporal data [1].

• **Agents** are the executable components in the system from Knowledge Sources (KS). A KS in the REAKT architecture can be procedural or rule-based. Each KS instance is structured as an independent task called *agent*.

• **Control:** this module receives significant events in the system and, in consequence, creates and schedules *intentions* (like Knowledge Source instances, or cooperating agents) for solving a situation.

• **Real-Time Operating System (RTOS) Extensions:** this module provides system calls to create, communicate and synchronize internal processes.

• **Timer:** It provides timing signals and message manipulation to execute actions at determined instants with respect to a real time clock.

3 Blackboard Structure

The KDM data structure [2] is an **object-oriented** approach (Figure 2). Each object in the blackboard has a set of static and temporal slots. The structure of a temporal slot is formed by three sets of pointers [past, current, future] to **Temporal-value** structures. Each temporal value is defined by means of a *value* and its *begin* and *end* points. These time points (*tmnodes*) are defined as the time points between where the value was, is, or will be taken. Each *tmnode* represents a time point and it has a set of temporal constraints with other ones, which are represented in a temporal graph (*Time Map*). Furthermore, each temporal value records its logical dependencies from other temporal values by means of *rms-nodes,* which are represented in a dependency graph. these dependencies denote that the belief of a temporal value depends on the belief of other temporal values [1,3].

The *Blackboard Interface* [1,3] provides a set of functions that can be used by a user language to express actions, such as class definition, object instances , and temporal updates and queries.

a) *query functions*: left-hand side rule predicates in rule-based agents

• *when (object slot value begin end)*: This predicate is satisfied for those temporal values (current or predicted) which, belonging to the temporal slot, match the value.

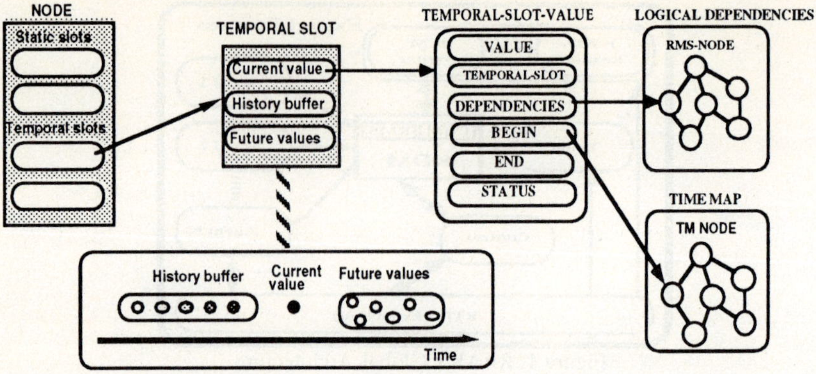

Figure 2 .- KDM Internal Data Structure

• *past_value (object slot value begin end)*: This predicate is satisfied when a current value in the defined slot is outdated and is moved from current to past.
• *temporal_test (any temporal expression):* Time-test function is used for asking about temporal relations between temporal values.

b) *update functions:* called from right-hand side of rules in rule-based agents
• *predict_value (object slot value begin end dependencies)*: Adds a predicted (future) value to a temporal slot.
• *put_value (object slot value begin end dependencies):* This function sets a value to a slot.

4 Multiple Access and Coherence Management

The multiple access and coherence management requiriments in REAKT are very similar to the concurrence control in databases [7]. The KDM has to serve queries (transactions) from agents to read or write data, which have timing and consistency constraints that must be accomplished.

The execution of each transaction is based on the Two-Phase Locking protocol [7] with three different phases: the *read,* the *wait* and the *write phases.* During the *read phase,* a transaction can read from the database and write to its own local memory (prewrite). Before the transaction can perform a reading, it must obtain the *read-lock* on the data object it is interested in. To perform a write (prewrite) operation in its local memory, the transaction also has to obtain the *write-lock* on the data object. The read and prewrite operations can be done at any moment during the read phase.

After the transaction is completed, previous to writing the results in the database,it has to wait in the wait phase. When its turn has been granted, the process shifts to the write phase and downloads all the prewrite objects into the database. The protocol with priorities is based on the principle that higher priority transactions should be completed before lower ones. If two transactions conflict, the higher priority transaction should precede the lower priority transaction. Several possible conflicts can be found [2]: several write operations, a read operation before a write operation of a higher priority agent, a write operation before a read operation of a higher priority agent, etc. Other cases in the serialization are not considered due to the scheduling policy and the assumption about non input/output blocking of agents.

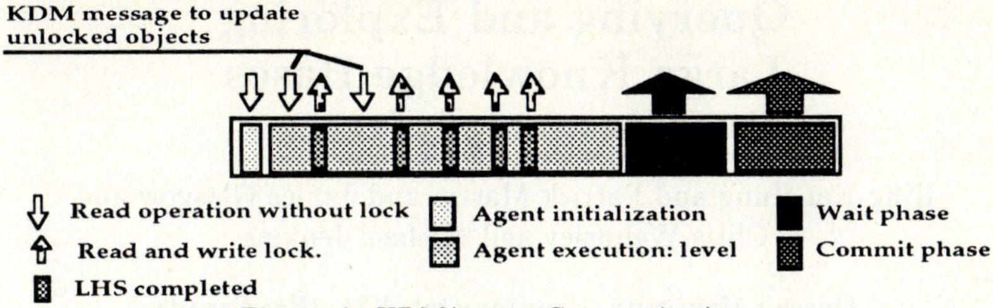

Figure 3. KDM/Agent Communication.

At the initialization, each agent receives the values of all the slots it is interested in. As soon as a slot value is updated into the KDM and no read lock has been requested by the agent, it is sent to all agents in the same condition. When a LHS of a rule is satisfied, slot values in the LHS are read-locked while slots in the RHS are write-locked. At the end of the commit phase, all locks are released.

CONCLUSIONS

In this paper, a temporal blackboard for a multi-agent world has been presented. Temporal information is associated to the temporal attributes of stored objects using a model based on time points. A proposal for multiple access and coherence management has been described. The following issues can be considered in the protocols: the lowest granularity level is at the slot level, and concurrence control and coherence are managed. The method proposed is appropriate for working with agents as the timing constraints of agents are met as much as possible, and the protocol allows working with agents when no computation time or resources are known in advance.

References

1. F. Barber, V. Botti, A. Crespo, D. Gallardo,E.Onaindía. "A temporal Blackboard structure for Process Control". *3th IFAC/IFIP Symposium on Artificial Intelligence in Real Time Control.* Delft. 1992.
2. V. Botti, F. Barber, A. Crespo, D. Gallardo, I. Ripoll, E.Onaindía, L. Hernández. 'A Temporal Blackboard Model for Multi-Agent Environments'. Internal Report DSIC-II/13/1993. Universidad Politécnica de Valencia.
3. A. Crespo, F. Barber, V. Botti, D. Gallardo,E.Onaindía. "Temporal Reasoning in Process Control". Engineering Applications of Artificial Intelligence, Pergamon PressLtd., 1993.
4. Demazeua Y., Müller J.P. "Decentralized Artificial Intelligence", in Decentralized A.I. North-Holland. 1990. pp 3-13.
5. Georgeff M.P., Lansky A.L., editors, "Reasoning about actions and plans". Morgan and Kaufman Pub. 1987.
6. Thomson, Syseca, Crin, GMV, UPV, Marconi, Etnoteam. "*REAKT: Environment and Methodology for Real-time Knowledge Based Systems..* ESPRIT II 4651. 1990-93
7. A.van Tilborg, G. Koob. 'Foundations of Real-Time Computing: Scheduling and Resource Management'. Concurrency Control in Real-Time Database Systems. Kluwer Academic Publ.1991.

Querying and Exploring Large Knowledge Bases

Hing-Kai Hung and Patrick Martin and Janice Glasgow and Chris Walmsley and Michael Jenkins

Queen's University, Kingston Ont. K7L 3N6, Canada

Abstract. This paper presents three aspects of information retrieval from large knowledge bases: the abstraction mechanisms, the modes, and the interface model. To reduce retrieval complexity, we investigate the view and viewpoint abstraction mechanisms. We consider and discuss querying and exploring as two major modes of knowledge base retrieval.

1 Introduction

We are designing and implementing a large knowledge base of protein structures. The knowledge base consists of individuals and concepts. Individuals are protein molecules, fragments, and other objects of interest. A concept groups the individuals with common structures and properties into a collection. The members are called instances. Both individuals and concepts are represented by the frame data structure which consists of a collection of slots like database attributes. Inheritance is used to provide sharing of information.

Abstraction mechanisms are needed for retrieving meaningful portions of a large knowledge base. One well-known problem is that the retrieval of the building components of a large structure leads to explosion of information. This paper presents a way of handling the problem by views and viewpoints.

Views define a subset of instances from a source concept. The slots of the instances are chosen from the slots of the source concept. The syntax of views is as follows.

(**view** *view-name* (?*x* **in** *source-concept*) (**select** *slot-name**) (**where** *query*))

Sample View

(**view** `non_sheet_structure` (?*x* **in** `structure`)
 (**select** `weight` `angle_phi` `pH_val` `part`)
 (**where** (**and** (**not** (?*x* **in** `sheet`)) (< (`angle_phi` **of** ?*x*) 30))))

The sample view `non_sheet_structure` contains a sub-collection of the instances of `structure` that satisfy the query. Only the selected slots: `weight`, `angle_phi`, `pH_val` and `part` are visible in the instances. Inside the queries, views can be used in the same way as concepts.

Viewpoints define a heterogeneous collection of concepts and instances that are related in the knowledge base according to a certain perspective. Viewpoints cannot be used inside sub-expressions of the queries. The syntax of viewpoints is as follows.

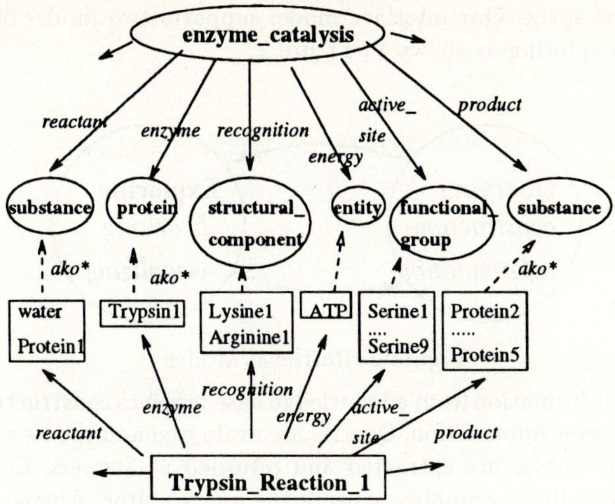

Figure 1. As_A_Kind_Of Viewpoint

(viewpoint (*viewpoint-name variable∗*) *query*)
Sample Viewpoint
(viewpoint (`as_a_kind_of` ?*x* ?*c*1 ?*r* ?*v* ?*c*2)
(and ((codomain of ?*r* of ?*c*1) is ?*c*2) ((?*r* of ?*x*) is ?*v*) (?*v* in ?*c*2))
Sample Query
(`as_a_kind_of Trypsin_Reaction_1 enzyme_catalysis` ?*r* ?*v* ?*c*)

The `as_a_kind_of` viewpoint [1] provides a means for finding an approximate membership relation between individuals and concepts. In Figure 1, rectangles are used to stand for values, ellipses for concepts, and arrows for slots. The individual `Trypsin_Reaction_1` is not an instance of the concept `enzyme_catalysis` according to the particular domain organization under discussion. It is because `enzyme_catalysis` has more slots than `Trypsin_Reaction_1`. However, they have some slots in common. Figure 1 shows how `Trypsin_Reaction_1` can be related approximately to `enzyme_catalysis`. The common slots of them are found, and the relationship between the individual's slot values and the concept slot codomain is given by the transitive closure of the *ako* links. The non-common slots are ignored.

2 Interface Model

Traditionally, database queries have to be well specified in order to access relevant information. However, many users find it difficult to express their task-related problems with the system's formal languages. Furthermore, when the information space is large, the users may easily become disoriented. To narrow the gap between users and knowledge bases, an articulation interface is necessary to facilitate the interactions. In this interface, queries can be reformulated incrementally based on the critiques of their answers. At appropriate points of querying, users can switch to another mode and use a browser to explore the information space. Our interface model supports two modes of interaction: querying and exploring as shown in Figure 2.

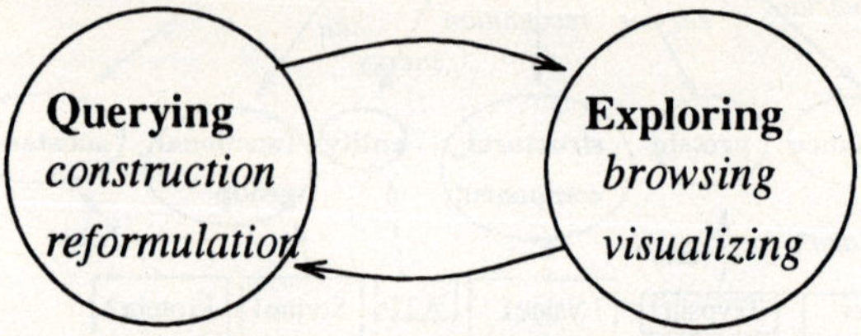

Figure 2. Retrieval Modes

Retrieving information from a knowledge base involves construction of queries to describe relevant information. Queries are evaluated and the items that match and satisfy the queries are extracted and returned as answers. Queries can be formulated textually or graphically using the query editor. Answers can be displayed graphically in the browser window. Users can judge the relevance of the answers and reformulate the queries in the editor window. This can be continued until the user is satisfied with the answers. When the answer is large, views and viewpoints are used to help refining the queries.

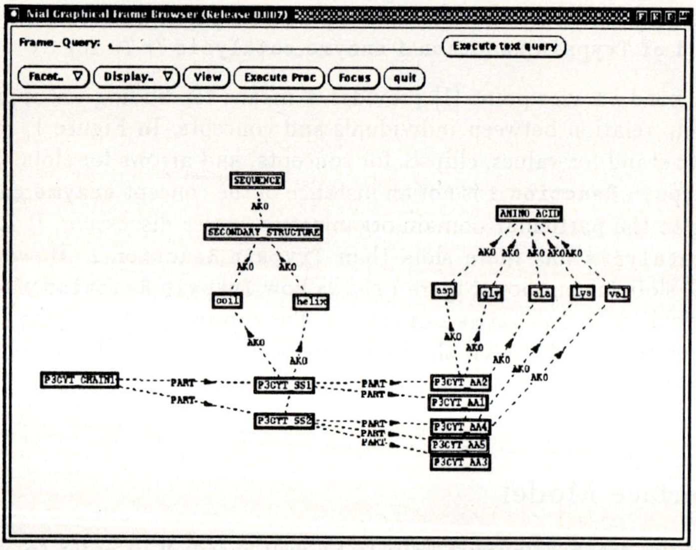

Figure 3. Sample Answer Using Views and Viewpoints

A sample graphical answer to the query (`component_v P3CYT_CHAIN1` ?*p* ?*c*) which uses both viewpoints and views is shown in the browser window in Figure 3. The definition of the viewpoint `component_v` is given as follows.

(viewpoint (`component_v` ?*x* ?*p* ?*c*)
  (and ((`part of` ?*x*) **is** ?*p*) (?*p* **in** `only_coil_helix`) (?*p* **in** ?*c*))

The **part** slot denotes the whole-part relation between individuals. It is declared as transitive. The query processor retrieves recursively all subparts $?p$ of the object $?x$. It also retrieves concept names $?c$ of which the component $?p$ is an instance. The explosion of the components will fill up the display window easily. To focus on a smaller subset of the instances, we use the view `only_coil_helix` to avoid all instances of `SECONDARY_STRUCTURE` except `coil` and `helix`. To highlight the concept hierarchy and the part hierarchy, concepts of the same level are put on the same row and individual components of the same level are put on the same column.

The display in the answer window serves as a starting point of exploring. Exploring can be done in two ways.

1. **Frame Browser:** Browsers view the knowledge base as a graph or a network where nodes represent individuals or concepts and arcs represent relationships. Users can explore the knowledge base by following the arcs to access connected nodes. Techniques and designs for supporting efficient browsers are discussed in detail in [3].
2. **3-D Object Viewer:** Methods can be attached to the slots to provide a task level layer of abstraction for goal-oriented users. This implies that once a frame is located, the user can access its associated displaying methods. This ability adds power to our exploring paradigm. By sending messages to a protein structure being browsed, we can visualize its three-dimensional structure graphically on screen.

3 Conclusion

We have prototypes of the query editor, the query processor, the frame browser and the 3-D object viewer. They are written in the Nested Interactive Array Language (Nial) [2]. With the support of view and viewpoint abstraction mechanisms, our interface model is considered more powerful than the traditional query-by-reformulation models [4]. Furthermore, we include the ability to switch between querying and exploring modes, the ability to depict queries and answers with graphical representation, and the ability to edit textually and graphically.

Acknowledgment This work is supported by the IRIS Federal Network Centre of Excellence of Canada. We thank Jack Bikker for the discussions on protein biochemistry.

References

1. Acker, L.E.: Access Methods for Large, Multifunctional Knowledge Bases. Ph.D. Thesis, Department of Computer Sciences, University of Texas at Austin (1992).
2. Jenkins, M.A.: Nial Language Manual. Nial Systems Ltd. Kingston Ontario (1984)
3. Martin, P.T., Hung, H.K., Walmsley, C.: Supporting Browsing of Large Knowledge Bases. Proceedings of the 3rd International Conference on Database and Expert Systems Applications 92 (1992) 402–408
4. Patel-Schneider, P.F., Brachman, R.J., Levesque, H.J.: ARGON: Knowledge Representation meets Information Retrieval. Proceedings AAAI'84 (1984) 280–286

Managing Text Objectively

Stuart Watt

Human Cognition Research Laboratory
The Open University, Walton Hall,
Milton Keynes. MK7 6AA.

Abstract. Complex development environments which use languages of diverse styles and purposes have special problems efficiently managing their data. Generally there are two alternatives; first, marking the text with extra codes, and second, using a tool capable of structuring the data, such as an object management system. For many purposes, something between the two is appropriate, in which plain text files can be read and used as if stored in an object management system. This paper describes a technique which can be used to implement this kind of data management substrate, and how it can be used to help in the construction of one such complex environment, the VITAL workbench.

1 Introduction

Data structuring is a critical aspect of complex computer systems. Unfortunately, the tools which have evolved to manage these complex structures tend to hide the contents of the data at the expense of the structure. On the whole, data management tools have always been less accessible than, say, file systems, so inevitably people have resorted to using simple text files with well defined structures; this allows programs to manipulate the contents according to the structure, but at all times people remain in control, because they can see exactly what the files contain.

The same problems arise when developing systems which operate on complex plain text formats, like programming languages. Again, there is a complex structure in the syntax of the programming language which is easily apparent to the user of the text, even though the support tools which are used (syntax-directed editors, for instance) are very different.

The VITAL project is developing just such a workbench [9], and although the programming languages are for the development of knowledge-based rather than conventional software systems the principles are the same. The project is defining a methodology for the development of knowledge-based systems as a series of phases, each of which is supported by a set of specially designed languages. For conceptual modelling, for instance, there are informal and formal languages which the development team can use to describe the conceptual models. There are similar special purpose languages to support the other phases involving, among others, specification, design, and implementation.

Apart from providing these languages, the workbench must help people to move a project between the phases, so it is organised as a set of assistants, each of which has built-in knowledge about how the languages belonging in one phase can be transformed (as far as possible automatically) into those required in the next phase. A key feature of these assistants, therefore, is their ability to recognise, manipulate, and generate information in different languages.

In order to build this kind of workbench it is clear that a substrate capable of manipulating many different languages is appropriate, and the rest of this paper shows how this substrate can be designed and used to help in the development of these assistants.

2 The Structure of Text

Two broad strategies have been followed in the path towards the management of more structured data. The first is that of augmenting basic text with additional data about its structure; this is the approach followed largely by the Standard Generalized Markup Language (SGML) standardisation route [6]. This involves marking the text with additional tags indicating the types of the different parts of the text. To some extent this can be done automatically, in that SGML can be partially configured to the syntax of the text by means of a 'document type definition' file, or DTD, which uses the syntax to tag the file directly.

The second strategy is to put the structure in data storage capabilities; this is the strand which has evolved from traditional database management systems and is today represented by object management systems (or OMSes). OMSes are usually not so finely grained as marked text, but usually provide additional facilities like as network file access and advanced searching systems.

Neither solution is ideal. Marking the text with additional tags is difficult, as it really needs support from an underlying editor so that the users aren't required to be aware of the added codes. This requires editor technology which is advanced and still not widely available (many editors use this strategy internally, but only recognise their own tag formats.) Object management systems also have their drawbacks, notably that they are following in the footsteps of their database management system ancestors, and so aren't as openly visible as plain text would be. An approach is needed that has the advantages of both, so that plain text can be used as if with tagging and that the files which are used can appear to have all the complex structure that could be provided by an object management system.

There is one further advantage to using plain text as a canonical form, the clean and consistent structure makes sharing the data much easier. Because there are so few operations needed to operate on the plain text (one, to be precise, the *replace-selection* operator used in modern text editors) it is possible to use non-locking techniques for sharing the data, such as the dOPT algorithm [4].

3 The Advantages of Being Syntax

For a file to have structure, it must have syntax. This syntax may be very simple or very complex, it may be context-free or context-sensitive, but the syntax must be there. When this syntax is implemented in a parsing program, a file can be decomposed into segments and syntactic categories assigned to these segments; the syntax gives the file structure. The problem is to bind the structure inherent in the syntax into a form explicit enough to be useful in manipulating files.

People naturally use the syntax of a file as a way of referring to elements within it. If the file is natural language text, these references will be of the form "the *n*th word of the *m*th sentence of the *p*th paragraph". If the file is C source code, references will be more direct, usually by name "the procedure *foo*" or "the structure *bar*". References to elements in text by properties found through their syntactic categories is not only possible, it is how people work. What we need is some way of turning this informal strategy into an approach that can be used by programs.

As the examples show, there are broadly two strategies that can be used in references: reference by name (or some set of properties) or reference by index, although neither kind by itself is sufficient for all applications. However, in both examples syntactic categories (such as `word` and `procedure`) are used in combination with parameters to provide a unique reference to a particular segment of text. Further, the type of the segment of text is clearly implicit in the reference, the referenced object in the first case is a `word` and in the second case a `procedure`. Finally, as the first example shows, references to objects can be nested; there is a clear path to an object through its enclosing objects (although this path may not be unique.)

In order to implement this a parsing system is needed that can scan text and build references of these two kinds by setting up property values and element sequences in some external indices into the text file. These must then be capable of being composed into compound references.

4 Implementing the Text Object Manager

In order to map text into a structured system it first needs to be parsed, so a traditional parser can be used. A parser-generator should be used so that the grammar can be written as data rather than hard-coded into the parser. As with most parsers, a lexical grammar is usually a help in tokenising the text so that the parser has an easier time. Tagging the text is then simply a matter of assigning properties in the grammar, so that the syntactic categories are marked with the right tags. Parsing the text is then a two-stage process; in the first stage the text is tokenised and in the second properties in the grammar are used to mark up the text with appropriate tags.

This approach differs from SGML in that it is not intrusive, the tags never need to exist implanted in the text. The key difference is that an entirely different set of structures is generated. Instead of marked-up text, the process of parsing generates a set of *namers*.

A namer is a reference to an object in text; usually implemented as a first-order object in the host programming language or environment. The namer keeps the mapping between tags in the syntax and segments in the text file, so that changing some property of a namer can change the corresponding text. A typical namer would be printed like this in Common Lisp.

```
#N"FileSystem:pavlov:monkey.file;success.frame"
```

This describes an object of class **frame** with name **success**, defined in the file **/monkey**, in a file system on host **pavlov**. The fields defined are, in order *tool*, *host*, *path*, *name*, *type*, and *version*. The *host* and the *version* fields are optional. (The **#N** is the Lisp notation for a namer.)

The *tool* provides a general interpretation to be placed on the rest of the namer. If it is **FileSystem**, as in the example above, the interpretation is that of a file system starting at the root directory. Other tools can be added, for instance referring to a database or object management system. The space of namers allows heterogeneous references to objects which are stored in many different forms. **FileSystem** is the one common tool which is guaranteed to be defined, and is the gateway to the access of text files.

The *host* field is available to let distributed systems specify which host is to be used, **pavlov** in the example above. By default, the current host is used.

More important are the *path*, *name*, and *type* fields which form the bulk of a reference to a particular object. The *name* and *type* fields, together with the optional *version*, form a tuple referring to a unique object within that indicated by the *path*. In the example above, the namer references an object named **success** of type **frame**. The version is optional, and defaults to the newest version available. Versions are defined so that a version management facility can be added for object management systems even though plain text files can't really support multiple versions. Instead of using a name, an index can be supplied to be combined with the type, so that references of the form "the *n*th **rule**" are possible.

The *path* consists of a set of *name*, *type* and *version* tuples which trace a path of nested objects from the root provided by the *tool*; in **FileSystem** the root directory. The objects in a **FileSystem** are files or directories; once a file has been referenced the contents of the file are made available by switching to types defined by grammar systems according to the syntax of the file. As with a file system, wildcards can be used in namers, and then these namers may not provide a unique reference, but they can be searched and used to provide lists of more accurate namers which can be used as unique references.

Consider a simple example—that of an OPS5 rule base [5]. Files containing OPS5 code mostly contain only two kinds of definition, **literalize** forms (which are a bit like frames or structures) and rules. A complete syntax for OPS5 can be written, following that of Forgy, and the grammar augmented to indicate that top-level forms beginning with **literalize** are mapped to the type **frame**, and forms beginning with **p** are mapped to the type **rule**. The same grammar will also mark the category corresponding to the name parameter to the **name** property.

5 Using the Text Object Manager

Like the pathname system in Common Lisp [8], there are a number of functions defined which can be used to access and manipulate namers and the objects that they refer to.

The most important function is that which allows properties of a namer to be queried and changed if appropriate. For instance, if the name of a rule is to be changed, it could be done using the following code:

```
(setf (get-property
       #N"FileSystem:pavlov:monkey.file;congratulations.rule"
       'name)
      "well-done")
```

The effect of this is to change the value of the **name** property for the rule **congratulations** to be **well-done**. This will implicitly change the section of the original text bound to the name property for this rule.

All namers are structured like this; they have a set of properties and a sequence of elements. Properties have values, and are accessed by name. Elements also have values, but are accessed by index. Elements are used rather like directories. The following query, for instance, will return a sequence of the elements in the file **/monkey**. Each of the returned elements will be a namer with the name and version component **monkey.file** in its path field. One of these will be the namer shown above referring to the (newly renamed) rule **well-done**.

```
(get-elements #N"FileSystem:pavlov:monkey.file")
```

Since **FileSystem** namers start at the file system root the directory structure will be followed. Directories and files can be specified just as in a hierarchical file system. Up to this point, namers provide a superset of pathnames capable of referencing files. This ends the space of references possible with filenames, but the capabilities of namers are only just beginning. Namers extend the same kind of path, allowing it to explore the contents of a file rather than just the directory structure of a file system. Definitions and language text defined inside files become accessible through the use of namers.

Finally, as with pathnames, namers do need not refer to objects that exist. Namers can be constructed component by component to refer to objects which don't yet exist, and then these objects can be created by the namer functions. As would be expected, this uses the grammar to complete the textual representation from the supplied properties, and from then on the namer refers to an existing object which can be manipulated just like any other.

6 Interfaces to Text Objects

Namers provide an abstract interface to text files, allowing them to be presented as structured systems of nested objects. This kind of abstract interface is exactly what is required for the development of visual interfaces to many languages. By looking inside text files to see their constituent parts it is possible to present these parts using graphical displays, where the namers are used to indirect between the information that is presented on the screen and the information that is available in the underlying representation.

The VITAL workbench contains a generic editor, called Dale, which works in exactly this way. Dale contains information in buffers rather than files (buffers are a convenient representation of a file in memory) but the approach is just the same. The text is split into namers in the parsing process and the name/type combination is used to choose an appropriate graphical representation. Usually the graphical representation is either icon- or graph-based, and the type of the namer is used to choose an appropriate icon or node or link style which is then used as the presentation in a window. A user, by manipulating the presentation, makes changes to the namer, and so, indirectly, modifies the underlying object. In Dale, for instance, just changing the name (in Macintosh Finder style, by typing a new name and pressing ENTER) will change the textual representation to contain the new name.

Using text as a canonical representation has one further advantage for the VITAL workbench. As already noted, non-locking algorithms can be used for data sharing because text is simple to manipulate. Groupware can be added to the editors presenting these languages graphically by simply sharing the textual representation and so implicitly sharing the objects [10].

Finally, there is one other enhancement that can be made to traditional editing techniques; in the use of advanced typography in the presentation of text [1]. As the syntax tags the text according to its syntactic category a further mapping from syntactic category to typographic style is possible. For instance, names used in defining OPS5 rules could always be presented in 12-point Times Bold, with the rest of the rule source text in 12-point Monaco. As the syntactic categories are kept generic, like `rule` and `name`, the typographic information can provide both an immediate graphical cue as to the type of that segment of the text and a common link between equivalent syntactic forms. The same techniques that are required to provide the structuring needed to recognise segments of text can be used to make the text itself easier to use. The distinction between text and graphics is blurred by the common structure used to help in the presentation of both.

Since the primary reasons for the development of this approach are the restrictions imposed both by the harshness of plain text and the inaccessibility of typical object management systems it is gratifying that the intermediate solution does indeed seem to provide for good interfaces both on textual and object-based views of the same data.

7 Applying the Text Object Manager

So far, the strategy has been described with respect to a single example, that of OPS5. While this is fairly representative, much of the power of this approach is in that it can work with different languages in an abstract form. For instance, the types `frame` and `rule` used in OPS5 can be related to equivalent types in other languages, for instance the rule language ERI in the KEATS environment [3]. The abstract types `frame` and `rule` are common, although the textual representations of the two classes of object will vary depending on the syntax of the underlying text.

A simple example of how this works would be in converting a file from OPS5 syntax to ERI syntax. The first stage is to get a list of all the objects in an OPS5 file, and then a new set of namers can be created for each of these objects in an ERI file. All that remains is to copy all the properties and contained objects of corresponding namers from the OPS5 referencing namer to the ERI referencing namer. All properties that are common will be used to generate ERI text, and any that aren't will be ignored. Using namers creates an abstract space of object representations in many different kinds of text when the objects that are being represented are largely equivalent.

In development environments like the VITAL workbench, though, the transformations are more likely to be between phases in the development cycle than between roughly equivalent forms such as OPS5 and ERI. A more typical example would be the automatic transformation of a detailed design into a set of template rules which could then be filled out with implementation details. Here again the strategy of copying properties from one set of namers to another is viable; the difference is that the objects and their properties will *not* be equivalent, and so a significant amount of program transformation is needed. Even so, with the direct access that namers provide to the detailed structure of the underlying text, this kind of transformation is significantly easier to develop.

8 Conclusions

The problem which this paper sets out to address is how to manage complex structured text files *as if* they were implemented in some object management system. The approach outlined allows segments in the file to be presented to a program as objects through references called namers which can be used to manipulate the underlying object, rather like a filename is a reference to a file.

The advantages of this approach are that plain text files can be used directly, and so people can always resort to their favourite text editor if things go wrong. Text is generally easier to recognise and manipulate with today's tools, so using text rather than advanced object management systems is generally a very safe option.

The disadvantages are largely ones of performance; parsing text to split it into chunks is computationally expensive. There are two approaches to easing these problems; first, incremental parsing can be used so that only the sections of the text which have changed need to be parsed. Algorithms for this exist [2] but are really only appropriate within an environment which is aware of which sections of the text have changed, and this requires special text editors.

The second approach is to throw more processing power at the problem, and to carefully optimise the procedures used.

If the performance problems can be overcome, as it appears they can be, this approach to the management of data has significant benefits; it is safe, it is powerful, and it is the data can be shared between many users. It is this combination of features that makes it an ideal approach for the development of a complex system like the VITAL workbench.

Acknowledgements

This research was part-funded by the Commission of the European Communities ESPRIT-II Project 5365 - VITAL.

References

1. Baecker, R. M., and Marcus, A.: Human factors and typography for more readable programs. ACM Press. (1988)
2. Degano, P., Mannuci, S., and Mojana, B.: Efficient incremental LR parsing for syntax-directed editors. ACM Transactions on Programming Languages and Systems, 10(3), (1988) 345–373.
3. Eisenstadt, M., Domingue, J. B., Rajan, T., and Motta, E.: Visual knowledge engineering IEEE Transactions on Software Engineering. 16(10) (1990)
4. Ellis, C. A., and Gibbs, S. J.: Concurrency control in groupware systems. In the proceedings of the ACM SIGMOD '89 Conference on the Management of Data, Seattle, Washington. (1989)
5. Forgy, C. L.: OPS5 users manual. Technical Report CMU-CS-81-135. Department of Computer Science, Carnegie-Mellon University. (1981)
6. Goldfarb, C. F.: The SGML handbook. Oxford University Press. (1990)
7. Motta, E., O'Hara, K., and Shadbolt, N.: Grounding GDMs: A structured case study. Knowledge Acquisition (to appear).
8. Steele, G. L., Jr: Common Lisp: the language. Digital Press. (1990)
9. Watt, S. N. K., Motta, E., and Domingue, J. B.: Architecture of the VITAL workbench. HCRL Technical Report V92. (1993)
10. Watt, S. N. K.: Role conflict in groupware. In the proceedings of the first International Conference on Intelligent and Cooperative Information Systems.

Legal Expert System KONTERM - Automatic Representation of Document Structure and Contents

Erich SCHWEIGHOFER, Werner WINIWARTER

Institute of Public International Law and International Relations,
Institute of Applied Computer Science and Information Systems
University of Vienna, Austria

Abstract. Our legal expert system KONTERM contains a selective thesaurus and a knowledge base for the automatic representation of the structure and the contents of the document. The thesaurus takes into account the necessary degree of formalism of legal language and therefore overcomes the *untidiness* of natural language and represents automatically the expert knowledge of a lawyer about legal terminology. The required selectivity of the individual descriptors is achieved by distinguishing between precise legal terms and words with fuzzy meanings as well as by detecting *hidden* word senses. This thesaurus, together with the expert rules for structuring the document, provides the user with an analytical document representation. In addition to that, hypertext links will be supplemented in order to offer the lawyer a convenient tool for efficient information retrieval.

1 Introduction

Overcoming the so-called information crisis of law is the main aim of database and expert system applications in the field of law. The explosion of relevant legal materials was realized in the late sixties and has led to the problem that lawyers cannot cope with the vast amount of relevant information sources by using the traditional information techniques.[1] The avalanche of legal norms and judicial decisions is so extensive that the practise of law can be based only on fragmentary information.

The information crisis was the stimulus for the creation of legal information systems. Many of these databases with conventional information retrieval logic are now available but the utilization is quite disappointing. In our view the main reason lies in the fact that these information systems are only large electronic text collections, whereas lawyers who have to face strict time-limits are mainly interested in well structured analytical commentaries. They provide not only the document collection but the analysis of the material itself (documentation of the legal rules as well as relevant clarification by means of judicial decisions or literature).

Lawyers are very often not aware that the information system is unable to understand the legal vocabulary[2] with its particular terms and specific connotations which they take for granted in the process of working with legal databases. This deficiency of the information system can be solved only by the use of very sophisticated retrieval strategies.

Conceptual information retrieval systems represent an interesting approach, but are restricted to small databases so far.[3] Our method is based on statistical analysis techniques and hence applicable also on huge legal information systems.

2 Idea

KONTERM is a prototype of an intelligent IR-system which is designed to overcome the problems stated above. The main hypothesis of our approach is the assumption that a combination of a legal thesaurus with selective descriptors, special search techniques, and conventional information retrieval can provide automatically the necessary structure of legal information.[4] The documents are described by use of the knowledge base of KONTERM. The resulting representation is used not only for a short and accurate overview of the document but also for search possibilities equivalent to those supplied by a commentary.

Nobody will really read the commentary from beginning to end. The user has a specific legal problem and will search by means of the register or the citations. KONTERM provides these features. The register is replaced by the thesaurus and the document descriptions, whereas the citation and searching for very specific terms can be solved by simple boolean information retrieval.

The descriptors of our intellectually created thesaurus have been checked with regard to their selectivity. We also wanted to capture all distinct dimensions of meanings for a specific descriptor especially those *hidden* word senses which are not noticed in the process of intellectual indexing. KONTERM automatically produces descriptions for all different uses of the thesaurus entries to clarify the specific connotations. Only precise descriptor clusters have been incorporated in our final thesaurus.

The special structure of legal documents can be used for further document analysis. The presence of certain words and phrases within a special context will be interpreted according to context-based rules contained in the knowledge base.

3 Method

The analytical document representation contains the title data, the structural analysis, and a summary of the contents which is generated by use of the selective thesaurus and the knowledge base. The document is segmented into chapters (articles) to which the context-sensitive rules are applied in order to retrieve the position of special structural elements that indicate document parts of particular interest for the user. In the same way the thesaurus entries that are present in the document are attached to the concerned text segments.

The thesaurus of KONTERM has been produced intellectually and is composed of selective descriptors (also capturing compound descriptors and synonyms) whereby all distinct word senses are taken into consideration by creating descriptor clusters for the various specific connotations. In a further step of analysis, clusters with fuzzy meanings are eliminated to achieve the required precision.

The similarity between two occurrences of the same descriptor which is the basis for the process of clustering is computed as a function of the number of properties that they have in common. As properties of a descriptor occurrence we defined the presence or absence of the index terms included in the database with regard to the surrounding context (i.e. 50 words before and after the concerned descriptor). Thus, according to the vector space model of information retrieval, we represented each descriptor occurrence by means of a vector whereof the components represent the properties in that they take the value *1* if the term in question is present in the context and a weight of *0* otherwise (referred to as binary indexing).

Thus one of our basic assumptions was that the meaning of a specific descriptor use is determined by the context in which it is situated. Likewise the contexts of the cluster elements form the basis for the creation of cluster descriptions which consist of the 5 most frequent terms occurring in these text segments and are used for clarifying the word senses of the different descriptor clusters.

4 Implementation

The ideas and methods that were developed in the preceding chapters were implemented under consideration of the principles of modular programming and stepwise refinement. Our final process model consists of five steps of analysis (see fig. 1):

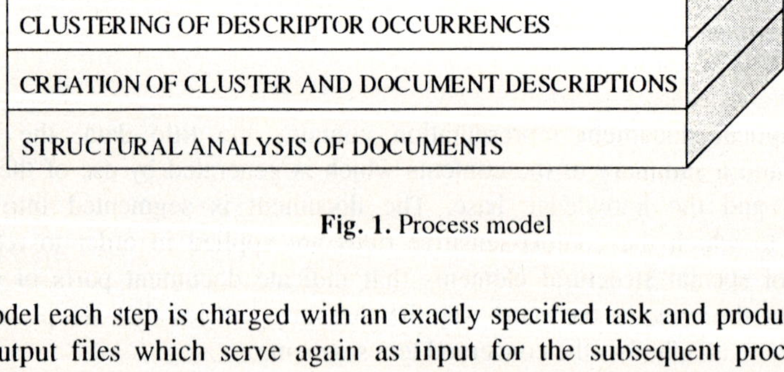

Fig. 1. Process model

In this model each step is charged with an exactly specified task and produces well-defined output files which serve again as input for the subsequent process. The relations and dependencies between the individual data files that exist in our model are shown in fig. 2. With only one exception (dotted arrow) all transformations take place by completely automatic processing. So our model guarantees the observance of the principle of modular programming by supplying precisely determined interfaces between the various steps of analysis. Explanations of the functionality of the five main modules as well as the definitions for all the distinct data files are provided in the following sections.

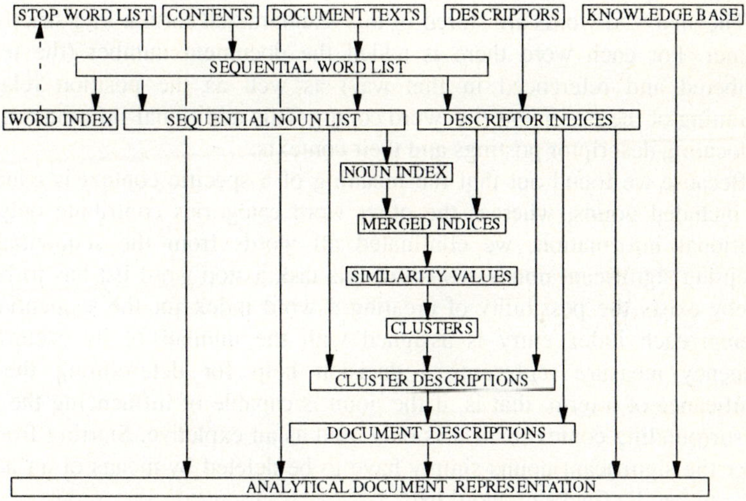

Fig. 2. Relationships between data files

4.1 Creation of Sequential Lists

The initial step of our prototype system is the transformation of the original document texts (stored as files in ASCII-format) into a sequential word list whereby, with regard to full flexibility, no naming conventions were introduced, but instead of that a contents file with references to the individual text files was employed.

In order to separate the single words in the document texts, i.e. to find the boundaries between words, the simplifying heuristic was used that words only consist of alphabetic characters, that is all non-alphabetic characters were regarded as separating elements. Especially for the application on legal documents this approximation produced very reasonable results. The only remarkable discrepancy was the separation of the components of compound words. However, it turned out to be of no significant influence to the quality of the final output.

To get rid of all the abbreviations that do not contribute to the meaning of context, we set a lower bound of at least two characters so that all abbreviations consisting of only one character (or several characters separated by dots) were not taken into consideration.

In addition to these selection criteria we transformed the German special characters (ä, ö, ü, ß) into their international transcriptions (ae, oe, ue, ss) because both styles of writing appeared in the evaluated document set. Furthermore this standardization was very helpful for the development of our comparison module in order to get hold of all inflexions with vowel-gradation. For the same reason (the simplification of word comparisons) we finally converted all characters into their uppercase representation.

The analyzed words are stored in this standardized format in a strictly sequential manner. For each word there is added the document number (the text files are numbered and referenced in this way) as well as the position relative to the beginning of the document (i.e. word count). This additional information is essential for locating descriptor postings and their contexts.

Because we found out that the meaning of a specific context is concentrated in the included nouns, whereas the other word categories contribute only peripheral additional information, we eliminated all words from the sequential word list excepting significant nouns. To fulfill this task a stop word list has to be produced. Hereby exists the possibility of creating a word index for the sequential word list, whereat each index entry is assigned with the number of its occurrences. This frequency measure represents a decision help for determining the degree of significance of a term, that is, if the noun is capable of influencing the meaning of the surrounding context or if it is only used as an expletive. Starting from this word index the significant nouns simply have to be deleted by means of an arbitrary text editor to get the final stop word list.

With the initial sequential word list and the stop word list as input the former is now reduced to the sequential noun list by eliminating all insignificant terms. If there is already a stop word list available (as the result of any prior analysis) then one first has to delete those stop words, before he can continue with the above described procedure on the basis of the resulting intermediate word list.

4.2 Generation of Indices

The sequential noun list is condensed to a noun index where each term is supplemented with a list of all postings for that entry. The information which characterizes a specific posting is the document number and the position in the document. Instead of using a simple string matching algorithm to check the equality of two words from the sequential noun list we created a comparison module that deals with the following two important phenomena:

Spelling Errors. As result of our pretests we found out that legal texts are already free from spelling errors to a high degree. In the remaining erroneous words the insertion of one wrong character represented the error type which occurred most frequently. So we accepted two words as equal if they contained only one divergent additional character (with the exception of the sensitive first letter). This heuristic also takes the vowel-gradation (e.g. a to ä respectively ae) into account.

Suffixes and Inflexions. The treatment of all different word shapes is of great importance, especially for an inflective language like German. So we added a collection of all valid German inflexions and suffixes which is applied in the comparative analysis of the words in question.

As a result of our extensive test cycles we achieved a very high precision, so that nearly all of the above mentioned cases were noticed, and not a single incorrect unification took place. In comparison with other approaches dealing, for example, with thresholds for absolute or relative measures of diversity, our method turned out to be significantly superior.

The descriptors used for the representation of the document contents are provided by means of a descriptor file. Each descriptor is hereby searched in the sequential word list (by use of our comparison module) resulting in a numbered list of postings which yields a set of descriptor indices. The user is not restricted to single word descriptors but can also apply compound descriptors and synonyms. The former are entered in the description file in a natural way, in that the individual parts are separated by blanks while the latter are marked by use of equal signs between the various synonyms. The feature of the search for synonyms can hereby also be employed for the detection of irregular declensions not captured by the comparison module.

Finally, for each descriptor the noun index and the concerned descriptor index are merged. All the noun postings are compared with the different descriptor postings for checking if the noun in question is situated in the context (surrounding text range of ⊥ 50 words) of the considered descriptor. The result of this step of analysis is merged indices for all descriptors that assign to each noun a list of all descriptor postings of which it influences the meaning, that is the noun is part of the context of that descriptor occurrence (see fig. 3).

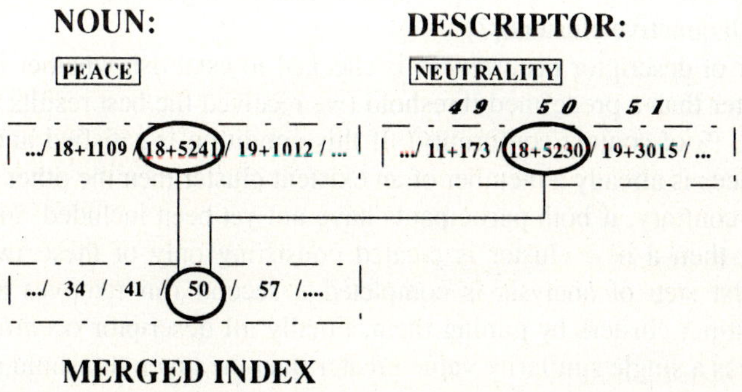

Fig. 3. Example for building a merged index

4.3 Clustering of Descriptor Occurrences

In conformity with the vector space model of information retrieval[5] for every descriptor occurrence *i* a vector D_i is calculated. This vector is assumed to represent the specific meaning whereby the components (referred to as properties) are determined by the presence or absence of the individual nouns in its context (*t* signifies the number of nouns contained in the merged index for the considered descriptor):

$$D_i = (TERM_{i1}, TERM_{i2}, TERM_{i3}, \ldots, TERM_{it})$$

$TERM_{ik}$ takes the value *1* if the noun occurs in the context and *0* otherwise, a simple weighting method referred to as binary indexing.[6] With the help of these vectors the similarity between two descriptor occurrences is now calculated as function of the number of congruous properties (i.e. vector components). As a result of pretests we found that of all the numerous similarity measures proposed in literature[5] the symmetric coefficient of *Dice* is most suitable for our purposes:

$$SIM(D_i, D_j) = \frac{2\sum_{k=1}^{t}\left(TERM_{ik} \cdot TERM_{jk}\right)}{\sum_{k=1}^{t} TERM_{ik} + \sum_{k=1}^{t} TERM_{jk}}$$

The value range for the coefficient of Dice is the interval *[0,1]*. The coefficient value reproduces exactly the percentage of nouns which the two contexts have in common. To capture distinct dimensions of word senses of one descriptor we collected them according to the calculated similarity values. This grouping procedure was done by the help of a simple quick cluster algorithm that created non-hierarchical disjunctive clusters.[7]

Each pair of descriptor occurrences is checked to establish whether its similarity value is greater than a predefined threshold (we received the best results with a value of 0.2, i.e. 20 % of context conformity). If this condition is satisfied and one of the two occurrences is already a member of an existent cluster then the other is appended to it. On the contrary, if both participants have not yet been included in the process of clustering then a new cluster is created consisting only of these two elements. After this first step of analysis is completed a second run removes all duplicate entries in distinct clusters by joining them. Finally all descriptor occurrences which did not possess a single similarity value greater than the given threshold are added as single element clusters.

Although this approach does not use sophisticated statistical methods, we obtained very reasonable clusters which were superior even to more complicated algorithms, as our comparative pretests showed.

4.4 Creation of Cluster and Document Descriptions

To get a meaningful representation of the different dimensions of meaning for a specific descriptor, we supplemented each cluster with a list of those five nouns which occurred most frequently in the concerned contexts.

For the retrieval of those five terms we extracted the associated contexts of the postings for each cluster element. Out of all the contexts for one cluster a noun index (each entry assigned with the number of occurrences) was produced which yielded the basis for obtaining the five most frequent terms as cluster description.

In the next step the descriptor clusters were used for a representative description of the contents of the individual documents. In order to arrange the descriptor clusters which are included in a specific document according to their relevance, several ranking algorithms were tested.[8] The most reasonable results were achieved by the use of the inverse document frequency as weighting factor.

The basic idea of this approach is the assumption that the relevance of a term is proportional to the number of occurrences of the term k in the document i ($FREQ_{ik}$) and indirectly proportional to the number of documents which contain the term k ($DOCFREQ_k$). Thus the applied weighting function has the following appearance (n signifies the number of documents):[5]

$$WEIGHT_{ik} = FREQ_{ik} \cdot \left[\log_2(n) - \log_2(DOCFREQ_k) + 1 \right]$$

The final result of this step of analysis was a list of the most relevant descriptor clusters for each document (we found a number of 20 to be sufficient) whereby the individual clusters were completed by the actual cluster descriptions. So we obtained by means of a fully automatic indexation process an accurate and clear summary of the contents of a document.

4.5 Structural Analysis of Documents

The processing of the documents was extended one degree further by producing a complete analysis of the document structure. The condensed representation created consists of five main sections which are explained in full detail in the following.

Extraction of Title Data. In order to obtain the basic information contained in the initial segment of a document, the first 50 words are used for the beginning part of the structural description.

Segmentation of the Document. The document is searched through for the appearance of chapter headings; i.e. the string *ARTICLE*, a corresponding numbering, and optional additional heading text. According to the retrieved positions, the document is separated into several segments.

A special case hereby presents the treatment of preambles. As the presence of a preamble is facultative and the positioning in the text is not so clearly emphasized as chapter headings, we applied the following procedure: After the first chapter heading is detected (i.e. the end of the initial part of the document is reached) a context-sensitive rule (see below) is applied to search for the existence of a preamble. If this search is successful the initial part is divided into a preamble and the remaining initial part, as well as including information about the presence of a preamble in the structural representation.

Special Structural Elements. Some parts of the documents are of particular interest to the user. These text segments are identified by means of special structural elements out of which we selected the three most important cases for our prototype: *entry into force*, *ratification*, and *signature*.

To differentiate between the specific use of these terms as structural elements and other word meanings, the search is supplemented by context-sensitive rules which are stored in a knowledge base. These rules are applied to the retrieved surrounding contexts (±50 words) of the structural elements to test for the presence of other significant terms which support the hypothesis that the concerned term is really a valid indicator.

The knowledge base consists of rule files in which the context-sensitive rules can easily be entered as boolean expressions by means of a simple text editor. The inference machine parses the rule file and captures the following features:

- combination of several operands by the boolean operators *AND* and *OR*
- changing the precedence of the operators by use of parenthesis
- unlimited right-hand truncation of the operands symbolized by an asterisk

So an example of a very simple context-sensitive rule for provisions on *ratification* could look like this: *ARTICLE AND (APPROV* OR ACCEPT*)*

For each structural element a corresponding message is reported in the document representation, whether it occurs in the document or not. In the former case the heading information of all document segments in which it is present is supplied as additional information.

Formal Descriptors. Formal descriptors fulfill an additional indicating function for structural analysis in that they characterize the scope of certain document segments. Examples of applied formal descriptors are: *application, interpretation, consultation, dispute, reservation etc.* Those formal descriptors that are present in the document text are appended to the structural document information.

Material Descriptors. The document description obtained in the previous step of analysis forms the basis for the output of the material descriptors. According to the results of relevance ranking they are displayed supported by their cluster description and the corresponding heading information. Although we limited our content summary to the processing of material descriptors, the flexibility of our knowledge base incorporates the possibility to extend the representation by applying context-sensitive rules analogous to those we used for structural analysis.

5 Evaluation

The database *Austrian Treaties 1988 - 1992* consists of 77 complete documents of Austrian public international law. A representative list of 89 test descriptors has been created intellectually whereby both compound descriptors and synonyms were included. Descriptor clusters with fuzzy meanings have been eliminated intellectually.

As a result of the application of our prototype system KONTERM quite reasonable document representations were generated. The following figure shows in full detail the analytical representation of a sample document, namely the *European Data Protection Convention* (for reasons of convenience the example has been translated into English).

Extraction of Title Data

The National Council (Nationalrat) has decided:

1. The sanctioning of the following Treaty with interpretative declarations and notifications is approved.

2. This Treaty shall be implemented by the issue of laws according to art. 50 para. 2 B-VG (Austrian Federal Constitution).

(Translation)

CONVENTION

FOR THE PROTECTION OF INDIVIDUALS WITH REGARD TO AUTOMATIC PROCESSING OF PERSONAL DATA

PREAMBLE

Document structure

Preamble exists.

Provisions concerning the entry into force:

Article 21: Amendments
Article 22: Entry into force
Article 23: Accession by non-member States
Article 24: Territorial clause
Article 27: Notifications

Provisions concerning accession:

Article 23: Accession by non-member States
Article 27: Notifications

Provisions concerning denunciation:

Article 26: Denunciation

Provisions concerning reservations:

Article 25: Reservations
Article 27: Notifications

Content analysis

Information

Article 2: Definitions
Article 3: Scope
Article 27: Notifications
Cluster description: Contracting parties, accident, measures, co-operation, implementation

Security

Article 9: Exceptions and restrictions
Article 15: Safeguards concerning assistance rendered by designated authorities
Article 16: Refusal of requests for assistance
Cluster description: Rights, Security Council, international peace, protection, measure

Good faith

Article 5: Quality of data
Cluster description: Treaties, principles, rights, contracting party, approval

Measures

Article 4: Duties of the parties
Article 13: Co-operation between parties
Cluster description: Rights, contracting parties, governments, Security Council, meeting

Public policy (ordre public)

Article 16: Refusal of requests for assistance
Cluster description: Rights, security, interest, reasons, protection

Scientific research

Article 9: Exceptions and restrictions
Cluster description: Antarctic, contracting parties, co-operation, purpose, moon

Freedom

Article 9: Exceptions and restrictions
Cluster description: Right, convention, protection, human rights, committee

Fig. 4. Sample document representation

6 Conclusion

Our research prototype KONTERM consists of two main components: the selective thesaurus and the knowledge base. The former distinguishes all distinct connotations of a specific descriptor whereas the latter provides context-sensitive rules which determine the document structure. Therefore, the produced analytical representations of the contents as well as the structure of the documents turned out to be of comparable quality to traditional content summaries.

Of particular interest with respect to user-friendliness is the addition of hypertext links[9] which provide relations between a reference in the condensed analytical document representation and the corresponding position in full text. Other useful links could be established between thesaurus entries and concerned document positions. These extensions are subject to ongoing research.

The results that we achieved in our extensive testing cycles were quite motivating. KONTERM satisfied to a high degree our initial expectations that it could be an important assistance in overcoming the problem of capturing the formalism of legal language, and thus an efficient representation tool for well structured expert knowledge about legal terminology.

Acknowledgements

Our work is funded by the Jubiläumsfonds of the Oesterreichische Nationalbank - research project no. 4225: *Expert System for Public International Law.*

References

1. S. Simitis: Informationskrise des Rechts und Datenverarbeitung. Karlsruhe: Müller 1970
2. H. Hatz: Rechtssprache und juristischer Begriff. Stuttgart: Kohlhammer 1963
3. J.P. Dick: Representation of Legal Text for Conceptual Retrieval. In: Proc. Int. Conf. on AI & Law. Baltimore: ACM Press 1991, pp. 244-253
4. L. Reisinger: Rechtsinformatik. Berlin: de Gruyter 1977
5. G. Salton, M.J. McGill. Introduction to Modern Information Retrieval. New York: McGraw-Hill 1983
6. H.R. Turtle, W.B. Croft: A Comparison of Text Retrieval Models. Comp. Journal 35, 279-290 (1992)
7. J. Panyr: Vektorraum-Modell und Clusteranalyse in Information-Retrieval-Systemen. Nachr. Dok. 38, 13-20 (1987)
8. G. Salton, C. Buckley. Term-Weighting Approaches in Automatic Text Retrieval. Information Processing & Management 24, 513-523 (1988)
9. M. Agosti, P.G. Marchetti: User Navigation in the IRS Conceptual Structure through a Semantic Association Function. Comp. Journal 35, 194-199 (1992)

Matrim, an expert system on marital law

José Félix Muñoz, Fernando Galindo

Seminario de Informática y Derecho
University of Zaragoza, 50009, ZARAGOZA, SPAIN.
e mail: cfa@cc.unizar.es

Abstract. MATRIM is a computerized system which helps lawyers to adopt a strategy when about to press a judicial or extrajudicial resolution on concrete divorce cases, in view of Spanish legislation. The system offers judicial documentation which is capable of justifying different types of claims, in the light of the characteristics of the specific case, which are established in the dialogue which takes place between the lawyer who uses the system and the programme, the legal texts and the jurisprudence which govern the cases and the interests of the lawyer's client who is seeking advice. The lawyer can decide, in the light of all these points, whether or not to place a claim and, if he decides to proceed, what form it should take. Once the option has been taken, the programme offers the corresponding writ and the relevant documents to justify the claim.

1 Introduction

The MATRIM system is a tool for the retrieval of judicial texts, which guides the user through a dialogue in which the characteristics of the case are defined and which provides the documents which prove to be applicable. The first implementation, performed in VPEXPERT, applies only to legal texts (Code of civil law and Bill 30/1981 of July 7th). At present it is being imported into to KEE (Knowledge Engineering Environment), which will allow it, similarly to other systems which have been developed by members of our group [1], to accede to the jurisprudence of the content of the database of the company Colex Data.

On presentation of the application, our intention is to go into greater depth on two points. The first of these is the study of the isomorphism between the norm and the rules [2]. This isomorphism is at first reflected in the similarity between the legal text and the list of rules [3]. However, in our opinion, the concept can be broadened to include greater levels of development. This entails making use of the systematizations of Law performed by jurists and in particular by the science known as Dogmatics when it comes to designing the expert systems in the judicial sphere [4]. Civil Law is particularly suited to this line of work.

The second aspect to be considered is related to the need to define the different types of users as well as their activities before setting out an expert system for judicial matters [5]. The principle of isomorphism can also be applied to the activities and the study of the suitability of designing the systems in such a way that they simulate the "modus operandi" of the different subjects of judicial activity.

2 Working of the programme and activity of the jurist

The claim is the document which initiates the trial and in it the question to be dealt with is decisively defined. In order that the Judge be informed as to this question, the facts are recounted and the legal grounds which are considered applicable are brought forward. Normally the first of these grounds refers to the competence of the Judge to deal with the case. This order has not been respected in the MATRIM system, which analyses in the first place the merits or otherwise of the divorce and/or separation. This means of proceding is more similar to that of a "consultation" and to the way of reasoning of lawyers. Both the competence of the Judge and the procedure are examples of "formal" aspects, that is, those which regulate the manner in which a claim should be materialized. The separation between "formal" and "material" (or background) aspects should be taken into consideration when the groups of rules are being created, with a view to separating the two types of knowledge since, for example, very different developments in time can take place.

MATRIM is divided into two modules, the first of which tackles the basic question (merits or otherwise of the divorce and/or separation) and examines whether the related questions (children or spouse under age or incapacitated) concurr with the case and, as a result, together with the pertinent documents, provides a set of items which are included in the initial menu of the second module, in which the user decides which of these items he wishes to discuss in greater depth.

The aim is to create systems which do not follow a single dialogue, keeping track at all times of those topics which can be associated with the topic in hand and which can be incorporated into the field of knowledge of the system, in order to offer subsequently the possibility to the user of acceding to the corresponding knowledge base. The problem of how to inform the already existing modules of the possible broadening of the field of knowledge is posed. A first solution would be to group the items into classes and associate these classes, rather than specific items, with the rules. This classification is transparent for the user since the menu does not reflect it but simply presents the related items. Both the definition of classes and that of items are tasks which should be commended preferably to the jurists.

3 Implementation

Among Law professionals, within the continental sphere, it is normal to refer to the judicial figures by mentioning the article in which they are defined. On certain occasions, this reference constitutes the only name which is given to the figure, for example, the action of Article 41 of the Mortgage Bill. By using this technique in the implementation, the code becomes more legible for the jurists but, above all, a clear definition of the judicial concepts associated with each variable is achieved. The appearance of a MATRIM rule is as follows:

```
RULE CC_81_1_01
    IF          Agreement_81_1 = yes AND
                Duration_Marriage <> less_than_1_year
    THEN        Cause_Sep_81 = CC_81_1
                Options = Agreement
                Procedure = L_30_81_DA_6
                Options = Procedure;
```

The title of the rule indicates that it is the first of those which contain the knowledge of the first paragraph of Article 81 of the Code of civil law in which it is stated that if both spouses are in agreement and if more than a year has passed since the celebration of the marriage, it is fitting to decree the separation. Article number CC_81_1 is associated with two other identifiers. The first refers to the agreement mentioned in the Article, the contents of which are determined directly by the Law and should, therefore, be clearly differentiated from any other case of agreement which might be incorporated into the system. The identifying segment, constituted simply by the reference to the article, is associated to its content. The identifiers of this type indicate, when they are accumulated on the variables which are designed to gather the conclusions, that the norm referred to is applicable to the case, as occurs in the example, with Cause_Sep_81 and Procedure.

The variables of the Options type also act as piles onto which the associated topics are stored throughout the dialogue. The system will subsequently offer the possibility of going into greater depth on these topics, as has already been described in the previous section. As can be observed, the Procedure indicator receives the value of the norm which contains that which is applicable to the case (L_30_81_DA_6), and on the other hand the same Procedure identifier is loaded on Options. The second module, on recovery of the identifiers loaded on Options also has access to the values associated with each of them and will be able, therefore, to propose to the user as items of the menu, on the one hand the general aspects of the procedure on recovery of the Procedure value and on the other the precise procedure which the first module would have chosen (a value which is associated with the Procedure identifier).

On mentioning the concepts in this way, the incorporation of new groups of rules is facilitated in such a way that they can be communicated with those already in existence, by means of a common and precise language. Generally in the Code of civil law, when a figure is identified in an article, the specific aspects of its working are developed in the following articles in such a way as to facilitate both the definition of the concepts and, by means of the titles of the rules, the localization of those which are associated with the definition of a specific concept. The numerous "remissions" which pertain to the legal texts which are autodocumented in a certain way are also clarified, since, once the rule is observed we know both the remitting and the remitted article. Other concepts which have to do only with de facto details (Duration_Marriage) or which apply to all of the Law and which do not enter into collision with others of similar denomination (Public_Writ, Minor) can be mentioned directly without giving rise to ambiguities.

This method facilitates the structurization of the system in which the rules in groups are implemented in "dictionary" form. The mission of each of the groups is that of assigning a final value to specific variables. The progressive development of the systems is also facilitated, so for example, one of the MATRIM questions alludes to the Public_Writ Concept which is not defined in the application and it is left to the judgment of the use to decide whether or not a document belongs to this category. On creating a group of rules associated with this concept, one of two paths can be chosen: either to introduce the variable on the premise of the rule, in which case the module would enter into action each time the system alludes to a public writ or, more advisable in this case, it would be sufficient to load the item Public_Writ onto Options, so that the user could dispute the term if he has any doubts about it. This form of structuring the dialogue is flexible and allows a logical course to be followed without obliging the user to answer groups of questions whose answers could be obvious to him and therefore lacking in interest.

4 Isomorphism, dogmatics and civil law

The mechanics adopted in the implementation of MATRIM show the virtualities offered by taking as a reference in the structuring of the stored judicial documentation in a database, the substantive traditional judicial categories and not only, as has been the case up to the present in commercialized databases, formal details such as the date of the promulgation of the norms, or their category: legal, administrative or jurisprudence or the meaning of the words contained in the document. These are the only categories or abstractions which govern the storage or classification of information in current judicial databases and, therefore the access to the information contained therein. In MATRIM the content of the judicial texts is attended to, which can be an important fact for jurists who have graduated recently. This is possible because use is made of the systematics of Codification, expressed in the form of specific institutions: divorce in Spain in this case, which are firmly rooted in the professional habits of present-day jurists. This is of great importance for Law in general, it must be born in mind that the foundations of civil codification lie in the structure of civil Law, regulated from Roman Law and converted in the usual practice of judicial life from Medieval times up to the present.

The judicial peculiarity of MATRIM resides, however, in that in it, the limititations pertaining to the exclusively normative visions of the Law which are merely passive or static or exclusively theoretical are attended to. As has been indicated, MATRIM does not focus attention only on a formal vision of the Law. Its starting point is constituted preferably by concrete activities or habits of the jurists or by their way of operating in practice, the freedom of which does not narrow but, on the contrary, broadens. Ultimately, it is thought that the civil judicial clauses are general principles rather than norms. It must be born in mind that the user's opting for one or other of the proposals of the programme depends only and exclusively on the constellation of interests, values and norms which, according to the judgment of the lawyer who uses the system are pertinent in order to solve a specific case. From a judicial point of view, this involves MATRIM's being consistent with an argumentative/communicative theory/explanation [6, 7] of the judicial practice and the experience acquired by means of its use and adapted to the SIREDOJ background will facilitate the projection of the experiences gained in this way into the construction of a judicial information system of storage and retrieval of judicial documents which have a common end .

5 Conclusions

The structuring of the information necessary to devise an expert system such as MATRIM which is designed to aid judicial decision and which in reality advises the jurist, throws the importance of initiating the construction of an architecture of judicial databases into relief, which might attend to the traditional judicial categories as long as these can be translated with little judicial effort into classes or items or, which amounts to the same thing, into programmes capable of documenting judicial responses to different real situations, conversations or dialogues [8].

References

1. D. Bercovich: Documentacion tecnica de SIREDOJ, Zaragoza, Seminario de Informatica y Derecho, 1992.
2. T. Bench-Capon, F. Coenen, P.E.S. Dunne: Integrating Legal Support Systems Through Document Models, Expert Systems with Applications, vol. 4, 1992, pp. 355-362.
3. T. Bench-Capon, F. Coenen: Isomorphism and legal knowledege based systems, Artificial Inteligence and Law, vol. 1, nº 1, 1992, pp. 65-88.
4. F. Galindo, P. Lasala, M. Vazquez, J.F. Muñoz: Construcción de un sistema de resolución documentada de casos en materia contractual. Primeros Pasos", Zaragoza, Seminario de Informatica y Derecho, Documento 1/1993.
5. F. Galindo: La distribución de fondos públicos para la promoción de empleo, Zaragoza, Seminario de Informatica y Derecho, Documento 3/1992.
6. R. Alexy: Begriff und Geltung des Rechts, München: Albert, 1992, p. 201.
7. K. D. Ashley: Case-Based Reasoning and its Implications for Legal Expert Systems, Artificial Intelligence and Law, vol. 1, 1992, pp. 148-161
8. J. Bing: Conceptual text retrieval, Complex 9/88, Institutt for Rettsinformatikk, Oslo, 1988.

Contradiction and Confirmation

Daniel Poulin[1],Pierre St-Vincent[2] and Paul Bratley[2]

[1] Centre de recherche en droit public

[2]Département d'informatique et de r.o.

Université de Montréal, C.P. 6128, Succursale A
MONTRÉAL (Québec), Canada H3C 3J7

Abstract. In most expert systems, efforts are made to keep the rules in the knowledge base free from contradictions., because a logical system that generates even a single contradiction may collapse. We argue that not only can contradictions be tolerated, but in fact they are useful. An excellent test of an argument is to compare it with the best argument for the opposing view. Accordingly, we propose a multilevel architecture, where the object level may include contradictory rules, and the metalevels resolve these conflicts. Once such an architecture exists, there are advantages to allowing contradictions in wider contexts. In a legal context we may want to examine both sides of an argument. In administrative applications, we may need systems that 'look over a clerk's shoulder' to check that he is following one of several plausible, but not necessarily compatible, approaches. We are currently implementing these ideas.

1 Introduction

In most existing designs for expert systems, contradictions are avoided like the plague. The reasons for this are not far to seek. On the one hand, it may be feared that a system supposed to offer advice will only confuse the user if its recommendations are not clear and unambiguous. On the other, contradictions cause classical logic to collapse: once a contradiction has been derived from a theory (a set of axioms), then any formula whatsoever can also be derived, and there is no longer any meaningful distinction between theorems and non-theorems. Since expert systems typically employ some variant of classical logic as their inference mechanism, they are subject to the same limitation: if the knowledge base contains rules that lead directly or indirectly to a contradiction, then the system can justify giving any answer whatsoever.

The influence of this attitude can be traced in other areas of artificial intelligence, too. Such names as truth-maintenance systems, or belief-revision systems, strongly suggest that there exists an single, incontrovertibly true state of the world, and that it is the job of the system to find this true state and to ignore any competing interpretations of reality. Even modal systems using a "possible worlds" semantics do not admit direct contradiction: while they may concede that, for some proposition P, possibly P is true and possibly P is false, they do not allow both P and *not*-P to be asserted in the same world.

In this paper we argue that not merely is it unnecessary to avoid contradictions, but that including them in the rule-base of an expert system can be positively advantageous. In section 2 we outline our reasons for believing this, and in section 3 we outline how a system including contradictions might be implemented. Once such an architecture is in place, we can see further advantages to be gained; sections 4 and 5 describe some of these, and section 6 sums up.

2 Contradictions and Confirmation

In many aspects of everyday life, when time and cost do not preclude it, the best way to take a complex decision is to take advice from several sources and to compare the different arguments that are offered. One 'expert' may have a better reputation or a more competent air than another. Among the defensible conclusions that may be reached, some may rely on rules more universally accepted, or more commonly applied, than others. It is therefore essential to judge the force of the different arguments, and perhaps to order them accordingly.

Suppose you are about to buy a new car, but that you don't want anything too expensive. Being a cautious sort of soul, you consult two friends that you consider to be experts in the area. The first gives you a rule that can be summarized as

if a car costs more than 40,000$, *then* it is too expensive,

while the second proposes the rule

if a car has a high resale value, *then* it is not too expensive.

In your opinion, your friends are both reliable judges, so you incorporate both these rules into your decision procedure. What should you do when, after a visit to your local Mercedes dealer, you realize that both the rules apply in this case?

What you clearly should *not* do is to argue that since the rules furnished by your experts lead to a contradiction, you are entitled to conclude anything you want (as you could if you relied on classical logic), so you might as well go out and buy that 1935 Hispano-Suiza you have always longed for. Contradictions in classical logic lead the system to collapse, but in everyday life this is not the case. We all manage to live with contradictory beliefs and conflicting tastes without this leading to a breakdown of reason.

It is more sensible temporarily to ignore one of the contradictory rules, and see where that leads you, and then to ignore the other, and follow that argument to its logical conclusion. If you are lucky you may find that in both cases the system suggests the same conclusion: the question of expense may not be the decisive factor in your choice, so that preferring one rule or the other is irrelevant. If on the other hand choosing one rule leads to one conclusion, while choosing the other leads to a different answer, you will be obliged to opt for one conclusion or the other. However this may be easier than choosing between the two original rules.

There are several reasons for this. For example, if you are faced with two coherent, complete arguments leading to different conclusions, it may be that either choice is good, and that a distinction must be made on the basis of relatively minor criteria that you had not thought worthwhile to include in your system. If this is the case, then you can accord whatever weight you now choose to these minor criteria, confident that whichever decision you take can be justified. On the other hand it may be that when you look at the details of the two conflicting arguments, you see that one of them, although derived in accordance with the rules in your system, seems shakier than the other: perhaps at some stage a rule is applied in an inappropriate context, or perhaps some arbitrary cut-off point seems to carry too much weight.

In such a situation the presence of contradictory rules in the system has actually led you to make a better decision. Instead of relying blindly on the rules in the knowledge base, you have in effect used the system to obtain the best argument in favour of one conclusion, and then to obtain the best argument in favour of a different conclusion, before looking at both these arguments in detail and making an overall judgement of their value. Our contention is that contradiction, used in this way, is not a fault in a system, but rather a positive quality to be exploited.

We believe that producing contradictory or conflicting arguments is a better way of allowing the user to make intelligent decisions than attempting to attach certainty measures, probabilities, or some other form of weight to rules in the knowledge base. It is notorious that system designers have great difficulty in assigning such weights in such a way that they are useful and uncontroversial. It is equally clear that even an experienced user can make little of a recommendation along the lines "You should buy a Toyota with certainty 0.73." To be told, "You should probably buy a Toyota, but on the other hand you might just prefer a Mercedes. Here are the arguments in favour of each of those choices," conveys much more information.

In short, we believe that an expert system that, except in clearcut cases, provides only one conclusion or only one point of view is not as useful as one that routinely sets out alternative conclusions, or that gives the best arguments both in favour of and against some proposed course of action. The problem now, of course, is how to implement such a system.

3 Implementation

To implement an expert system capable of handling such considerations, we propose using a multilevel architecture, where basic knowledge is supplied at the object level, and the inference mechanism is controlled at one or more metalevels. This kind of architecture is called 'subtask-management' in [van Harmelen 89].

At the lower, or object level, basic knowledge supplied in the customary way by one or more experts in the appropriate area is expressed using rules. The rule base can be structured in any suitable way; for instance, maintenance may be easier if all the rules supplied by one particular expert are kept together, or alternatively it may be more convenient to group rules concerning the same topics. In areas such as the law, where texts have authority simply by virtue of their existence, isomorphic methods can be used to formalize knowledge [Sergot 86; Bench-Capon 87, 92].

Where we differ from the usual approach, however, is that we take into account the possibility that different experts may have different opinions, so we make no attempt to enforce consistency among the rules. Thus for any particular topic, there may be several corresponding rules in the knowledge base. These object level rules are augmented with attributes representing their relationships and allowing the metalevel to manipulate them. For each rule, these attributes include four lists of identifiers: of directly contradictory rules, of opposed rules, of supporting rules, and of alternate rules. These lists can be constructed during compilation of the knowledge base. Other attributes may be added in the future.

At the object level, the system works in the usual way. Inferences can be made either by forward or backward chaining, depending whether the call from the metalevel is trying to deduce all the consequences of a given situation, or to establish some particular conclusion. Above the object level, we propose using one or more metalevels to take account of inferential, procedural, and general knowledge.

3.1 Procedural

Giving good advice to a user requires more than the ability to produce one or more acceptable arguments. An expert system must also include representations of procedural and methodological knowledge related to particular situations. For instance, a human expert knows that he must first determine whether the current situation falls into some particular class, whether some unusual exception must be considered in this case, and so on. Knowledge of this type, intimately related to the skills of the human expert, reduces the search space, and helps organise the dialogue with the user. However it cannot conveniently be incorporated within the object level rules. The structure of the object level rules can only provide local guidance as to how these rules should be used.

Several advantages arise when procedural knowledge is separated from the representation of the rules. Aiello [Aiello 88, pp. 246-247] notes that if the way the rule base is to be applied is encoded implicitly at the object level, then this single use is the only one possible. It is preferable to maintain the generality of the rule base. However 'general' rules cannot easily be used in practice unless the system incorporates procedural knowledge. A rule base free from control information is easier, too, to modify than one where other considerations, such as control of the inference mechanism, complicate the rules. Moreover the separation of procedural knowledge brings other benefits. For instance, the object level rules can be verified and tuned more easily if the user does not have to consider 'control.' Also, differing procedural rules, operating on the same object rules, can be used to implement different tasks.

3.2 Inferential

Much as for procedural knowledge, we propose to use metaknowledge to represent the different strategies of argument that can be based on the rules depending on the point of view of the user. In a knowledge base purged of conflicting rules, such 'points of view' would be unthinkable, and whatever line of argument the user wished to adopt, the result would be the same. In the system we propose, the presence of alternative rules allows different inferences starting from the same facts. It is at the metalevel that this flexibility is invoked, giving more or less weight to the various principles involved. Although two parties to a dispute may found their arguments on essentially the same rules, with only a limited number of differences of emphasis, there is frequently a considerable difference in the conclusions they reach. Even if one party is convinced he is right, he may still be interested to know what arguments can be advanced against his position, to prepare answers in advance. The rules of inference at the metalevel must implement a similar strategy for using the object level knowledge.

For an expert, the ambiguity inherent in many rules poses no serious problem. An expert system must also be capable of giving a plain answer based on the most straightforward reading of the situation. Even with a knowledge base incorporating contradictory rules, such plain answers must be possible. Thus the system must know which rules represent on the face of things the most evident items of expertise, so as to give the 'straightforward' answer when required. Using the attributes mentioned earlier, the system will favour the initial use of rules that are not contradicted. It may also accumulate different lines of reasoning supporting one particular conclusion, whether final or intermediate. When no single, obvious answer can be found, it must also be able to build alternative chains of reasoning, sorted according to their persuasive strength.

Finally, it must be able to produce an argument supporting a predetermined point of view. In this context, the metarules guide hypothetical arguments. At each choice point, where it is possible to derive contradictory conclusions and where backtracking will most often occur, they should choose the direction that best promises to achieve the required goal. They will also be used to produce the best possible argument against a given conclusion, for it is often insufficient to know that an argument can be constructed showing that X is A; it is also necessary to ensure that no better, contradictory arguments showing that X is not A are available.

Alternatively, if such arguments *do* exist, then the user had better be aware of them. To achieve this, the system must identify points in an argument where a different course might have been taken, and indicate the consequences of following the alternative path. The metalevel will use the attribute of the object level rules that contains the identifiers of contradictory rules. With such a mechanism, the system can produce alternative inferences leading to different conclusions.

In this connection there is an interesting analogy between the logician's 'closed world assumption' [Reiter 78] and what lawyers call 'the burden of proof'. In many current systems, it is assumed that an individual mentioned in the knowledge base does not have some particular property (is *not* a student, say, to use one familiar example), unless the contrary is explicitly stated or is derivable by the rules. In many situations one side has the burden of proof: in the criminal courts, for example, one is *not* guilty unless this can be explicitly proved. As a less dramatic example, an investment adviser selling mutual funds must show why it is actually better to move out of the investments the client already has. In other contexts the burden of proof may shift: when buying a car, you probably don't need to consider pickup trucks unless there is a good argument to the contrary; once you have heard that argument, if you detest pickups, you may search for a good argument to take you back to your original position; and so on. Thus the inferential metarules in our system must be able to use the closed world assumption on different sides of an argument at different stages.

Throughout this discussion we have assumed that the system will be capable of explaining and justifying the inferences it has made in any particular case. Indeed the whole approach to confirming an argument by contradicting it requires a change in emphasis from *what* the system recommends to *how* it arrives at its conclusions. Conventional expert systems, of course, do explain their reasoning, partly for the very reasons we have set out: certainty factors and such-like devices are better than nothing for evaluating an argument, but an explanation is preferable. We believe that an explanation of the arguments both for and against a given position is better still.

3.3 General

Our proposal provides additional benefits when an attempt is made to model inherently imprecise domains such as the law, economics, financial planning, and so on. Some of the models developed in these domains can be integrated as metalevel knowledge. In legal reasoning, this metalevel knowledge may prove useful to structure valid legal arguments.

A system such as the one we propose would have little chance of success were everyday reasoning as complicated and subtle as proving complicated theorems in mathematics. However it is increasingly accepted that while everyday arguments are, generally speaking, quite broadly based, with a wide choice of rules that can be applied, they are on the other hand not usually deep, and conclusions are reached after the application of a relatively small number of rules. When buying a car, you are more likely to consider several arguments, each quite short, than to construct an elaborate logical edifice depending on a long chain of reasoning. Thus for many purposes it is feasible to use inference mechanisms that might prove impossible to apply in a field characterized by longer chains of reasoning. We believe that, besides legal reasoning, there are many other areas where the chains of reasoning are wide and short: sociology, economics, and the political sciences are examples.

4 Contradiction and Legal Expert Systems

Our team in the Faculty of Law at the University of Montréal is engaged, among other things, in the design of expert systems to give advice to lawyers, clients, and officials in such areas as unemployment insurance, consumer rights, and so on. Legal reasoning, not merely the law itself, has been an object of study for centuries, and there are few fields where the participants are so acutely concerned not merely with the conclusions of their arguments, but with the methods of argument involved. An expert system which, when presented with a set of facts, replied simply, "Your client is right: go to court," or "Your client is wrong: take no action," without being able to explain how the conclusion was reached, would be even less acceptable in the legal domain than elsewhere.

Furthermore lawyers are famous—notorious even—for their ability to take both (or several) sides of an argument. An advocate's job is to defend his clients' interests. To this end he requires advice not on how to attain some abstract notion of justice, but how, within the limits set by professional ethics, to defend one particular point of view. If he is wise, he also takes advice about how his opponent is likely to defend a contradictory position, so as to be ready to refute this counterargument. Thus a useful legal expert system must be able to find and explain arguments both for and against any given position: in other words, it must be able to reason in a context where contradictions are the rule rather than the exception. Indeed, Ashley [Ashley 90] used case-based reasoning to argue with legal precedents. This work was extended to a combination of case-based and rule-based reasoning in CABARET [Rissland 91]. The problem they tackled was to decide upon the meaning of 'open-textures', which are hard to define concepts.

It is almost universally accepted by jurists that not all the law applicable in a particular area is found in the source texts. Lawyers use not merely the text of the law, but also rules of interpretation: general principles concerning what is and is not legal, common-sense concepts, and so on. Depending on the rules of interpretation, different, and often contradictory, meanings may be ascribed to the same legal text. In some cases all, or almost all, these principles may indicate that some particular interpretation is to be preferred; but there are also situations where different principles lead to different results [Côté 90].

In a legal expert system, situations of the first type, where one interpretation seems indisputably preferable, are relatively easy to handle. Situations of the second type, where contradictions arise, create difficulties. Many lawyers believe these conflicts can be solved using metarules of interpretation [Wróblewski 83; MacCormick 91].

An adequate legal expert system must be able to handle arguments based on differing, possibly contradictory, interpretations both of the law and of the facts in any particular case. If different arguments lead to different conclusions, then the system must be able to discover at least the most plausible reasoning that could be employed by each side. It must therefore neither eliminate contradictions from its knowledge base, nor collapse into incoherence when a contradiction is encountered.

This point is underlined in [Bench-Capon 88], where an example is given of two conflicting formalizations of the British Nationality Act. For Bench-Capon and Sergot, as for us, "the requirement for conflicting rules, which argue both for and against a conclusion, is essential" [*op. cit.*, page 53]. However, beyond noting that "the implementation problems that arise from this are severe", they give no hint how this is to be achieved.

We propose using the metareasoning architecture described in section 3 to implement a legal reasoning system that can handle the adversarial dimension of legal reasoning and the contradictory interpretations. This last topic has recently become a subject of interest. The use of meta-knowledge has been proposed to resolve rule conflicts in legal expert systems. Hamfelt [Hamfelt 89; 92] uses metareasoning, but does so to derive more specific rules of law from general ones, this process being controlled by the judgment of the user. It remains to be seen if suitable general rules can be produced. Breuker and den Haan [Breuker 91], Mariani and her team [Guidotti 92] and Yoshino and Kakuta [Yoshino 92] implement priority criteria between legal norms using metareasoning.

5 Advise or Consent?

An expert system that can function in the presence of contradictory rules offers still more possibilities. We envisage, for example, using such a system not to give advice, but rather to give a stamp of approval to a series of decisions, as Bench-Capon suggests [Bench-Capon 87].

Imagine a civil servant working in a government office, filling out a form or taking details for a client's file. The kind of task we have in mind is not totally routine, but may require that the clerk take decisions about how to classify the case, what actions to set in train, and so on. It is normal for a computer system to check the plausibility of raw data entered in a particular field of a form. What we propose now, however, is that the system should use the rules in its knowledge base to "look over the clerk's shoulder" and verify that the decisions made are coherent and sensible.

For the level of task we envisage, there may be no simple right or wrong answer to every question that comes up, so the user cannot be constrained to follow a single, undeviating line. At some point a choice may have to be made that leads to divergent, and maybe indeed conflicting, courses of action. Within limits, the system cannot simply decide that the user is wrong, and constrain him or her to act correctly: some decisions may be too subtle for the machine. However it is not unreasonable to expect the system to verify that the decisions made in the course of entering the data, and the conclusion finally reached by the clerk, correspond to an argument that could be made using at least one interpretation of the facts.

To do this, it is once again necessary that the knowledge base of the system hold conflicting or contradictory rules. As before, these can be held in the object level of the knowledge base, while the metarules for verifying consistency of the argument reside in the metalevels. The metarules can be made very tight when the user is to be allowed little discretion in the procedures to be followed, while more tolerant metarules can be used as looser checks on the activities of experienced or more professional users. Bourcier [Bourcier 92, p. 44] has suggested the use in the legal context of a hierarchy of 'lawyer's assistants' with differing levels of skill and responsibility. The architecture we propose is a step towards achieving this.

If such an architecture is to be used to implement an approval system, then it should respond in 'real-time' to the actions of the clerk. A batch system, working on idle time, would be unsatisfactory. These time considerations could force us to consider using a 'bounded rationality' scheme [Russell 91], where the quality of the solution is limited by the available computing time. It should also be able to accept 'special cases' if the user so wishes, and refer them to the appropriate authority. Finally, in case of refusal, it must justify its decision so the user can identify his mistake.

6 Conclusion

We have proposed an architecture for expert systems that allows contradictory rules to be kept in the knowledge base, using metarules to ensure that any arguments produced are nevertheless coherent. We believe that producing arguments both for and against any given recommendation is a better way of estimating the strength of a case than simply stating one side of the question.

A prototype to test our ideas is currently being implemented at the Université de Montréal. This preliminary version uses an object level and a single metalevel, which is used to implement the different types of metaknowledge. The prototype is written in Prolog, which, while not ideal, is sufficient to allow experiment. For later versions, after we have gained some experience, we believe it will be worthwhile to implement a special language for the metalevel, and possibly to increase the expressiveness of the object level. Sources of inspiration for a specialized language abound: LLD (the Language for Legal Discourse) for the object level [McCarty 89], and the ideas of Bowen [Bowen 85] and Qu-Prolog [Cheng 91] for the meta-level, to cite only a few.

Although much remains to be done, results so far suggest that there is no serious difficulty in principle in implementing what we now call 'a contradiction management system.'

Acknowledgements

The work described here is supported by grants from the Social Sciences and Humanities Research Council of Canada, and from Quebec's *Fonds FCAR*.

References

[Aiello 88] Aiello, L., Levi, G., "The uses of metaknowledge in AI systems", in *Meta-level architectures and reflection*, eds P. Maes, D. Nardi, North-Holland, 1988

[Bench-Capon 87] Bench-Capon, T.J.M., Robinson, G.O., Routen, T.W., Sergot, M.J., "Logic Programming for Large Scale Applications in Law: A Formalization of Supplementary Benefits Legislation", in *Proceedings of the First International Conference on Artificial Intelligence and Law*; Northeastern University, Boston, ACM Press, 1987

[Bench-Capon 88] Bench-Capon, T.J.M, Sergot, M., "Toward a Rule-Based Representation of Open Texture in Law", in *Computer Power and Legal Language*, ed. C. Walter, Quorum Books, New York, 1988

[Bench-Capon 92] Bench-Capon, T. J.M., Coenen, F., "Isomorphism and Legal Knowledge Based Systems", *Artificial Intelligence and Law* ,1 (1), 1992

[Bourcier 92] Bourcier, D.,"De la règle de droit à la base de règles. Comment modéliser la décision juridique?", *Actes du Séminaire Sciences du texte juridique*, Far Hills, Québec, 1992, to appear in : *Sciences du texte juridique*, Yvon Blais, Cowansville, 1993

[Bowen 85] Bowen, K.A., "Meta-level Programming and Knowledge Representation", *New Generation Computing*, 3, 1985

[Breuker 91] Breuker, J., den Haan, N., "Separating world and regulation knowledge: where is the logic ?", in *Proceedings of the Third International Conference on Artificial Intelligence and Law*, St. Catherine's College, Oxford, ACM Press, 1991

[Cheng 91] Cheng, A.S.K., Robinson, P.J., Staples, J., "Higher Level Meta Programming in Qu-Prolog 3.0", in *Proceedings of the 8th International Conference on Logic Programming*, ed. K. Furukawa, MIT Press, 1991

[Côté 90] Côté, P-A, *Interprétation des lois*, 2ième édition, Yvon Blais, Cowansville, 1990.

[Guidotti 92] Guidotti, P., Mariani, P., Sardu, G., Tiscornia, D., "Meta-level Reasoning - The Design of a System to Handle Legal Knowledge Bases", in *Settimo Convegno Sulla Programmazione Logica*, GULP 92, Tremezzo, 1992

[Hamfelt 90] Hamfelt, A., *Building Modular Legal Knowledge Systems. The Multilevel Structure of Legal Knowledge and its Representation*, The Swedish Institute of Law and Informatics Research, IRI-Rapport 1990:2, 1990.

[Hamfelt 92] Hamfelt, A., "Metalogic Representation of Multilayered Knowledge", PhD Thesis, Uppsala Theses in Computer Science 15, Uppsala University, 1992

[Lenat 83] Lenat, D. *et al.*, "Reasoning about Reasoning", in *Building Expert Systems*, eds F. Hayes-Roth, D. A. Waterman, D. B. Lenat, Addison-Wesley, 1983

[MacCormick 91] MacCormick, D.N., Summers, R.S. *Interpreting Statutes: A Comparative Study*, Dartmouth Publishing, Aldershot, 1991

[McCarty 89] McCarthy, L.T., "A Language for Legal Discourse: 1 - Basic Features", in *Proceedings of the Second International Conference on AI and Law*, UBC, Vancouver, ACM Press, 1989

[Reiter 78] Reiter, R., "On Closed World Data Bases", in *Readings in Artificial Intelligence*, eds B.L. Webber, N.J. Nilsson, Morgan Kaufmann, 1981

[Routen 91] Routen, T.W., Bench-Capon, T.J.M., "Hierarchical Formalizations", *International Journal of Man-Machine Studies*, 35, 1991

[Russell 91] Russell, S., Wefald, E., "Principles of metareasoning", *Artificial Intelligence*, 49, 1991

[Sergot 86] Sergot, M.J., Fariba, S., Kowalski, R.A., Kriwaczek, F., Hammond, P., Cory, H.T.. "The British Nationality Act as a Logic Program". *Communications of ACM*, 29(5), 1986

[van Harmelen 89] van Harmelen, F., "A Classification of Meta-level Architectures", in *Meta-Programming in Logic Programming*, eds H. Abramson, M.H. Rogers, MIT Press, 1989

[Wróblewski 83] Wróblewski, J. "Paradigms of Justifying Legal Decisions", in *Theory of Legal Science, Proceedings of the Conference on Legal Theory and Philosophy of Science*, Lund, Sweden, December 1983

[Yoshino 92] Yoshino, H., Kakuta, T., "The Knowledge Representation of Legal Expert System LES-3.3 with Legal Meta-inference", in *Proceedings of the 6th International Symposium on Legal Knowledge and Legal Reasoning Systems*, Tokyo, October 1992

Meta-reasoning in Law: a computational Model

Daniela Tiscornia
Istituto per la Documentazione Giuridica
del Consiglio Nazionale delle Ricerche
Via Panciatichi 56/16
50121 Florence- ITALY
e-mail DANIELA@VM.IDG.FI.CNR.IT

Abstract
The legal decision- making process can be reproduced by a model in which the deductive structure that justifies the decision is integrated with other formal aspects of legal reasoning , able to represent the concept of applicability, that is strictly related to the dynamic evolution of the normative systems; it may creates anomalous situations, as incompatibility (normative conflicts) or legislative gaps (lacunas). The solution of such a phenomena requires meta-level criteria to be formalised and correctly handled.

1 Introduction

The objective of this article is to analyse the legal decision- making process for the purpose of obtaining a model in which the deductive structure that justifies the decision is integrated with other formal aspects of legal reasoning ; and to specify, through such an analysis, the contents of the concept of applicability.
The concept of applicability is strictly related to the dynamic evolution of the normative systems: the introduction of new norms in a system of complex logical/normative relations creates anomalous situations, that lawyers must analyse and solve in the phase of identifying the norm (or norms) to be applied: in particular situations of incompatibility (normative conflicts) or legislative gaps (lacunas). The tools offered to the lawyer for solving these phenomena are defined by the same legal order through *metanorms* or, in other words, norms that have other norms as their object. These provide the legal sources on wich to base the analysis of the two processes here analized: *conflict solving* process and reasoning by *analogy*[1]. On the level of formal representation, they have some similar, and other complementary aspects; on the cognitive level they may be placed in the category of *plausible* reasoning, to which both experts in Cognitive Science and experts in Artificial Intelligence have given great attention, because it constitutes a large part of common reasoning.

2 Definition of normative conflicts

In civil (*statutory*) law normative systems, the new norms that are added to the system provide for a defined space-time area of applicability. When, in relation

---

[1]For reason of space, I will examine here only the conflicts-solving problem; the analysis of the analogical reasoning is in [Tiscornia 1993].

to a case, two norms may be applicable as alternatives we talk about *normative conflict*; logically we define two norms as inconsistent when both the facts of the cases of these may be met by the case at the hand, and the consequences of these are inconsistent. Along with the *logical* concept of *inconsistency*, we will broaden the definition of inconsistency to include cases of *legal inconsistency* (for example, a contract cannot be both void and voidable at the same time) and *pragmatic inconsistency* (for example, where the norms provide for two contradictory kinds of behaviour: to sleep or to stay awake).

The criteria for conflict solving are classified by legal authority as follows:

- the hierarchical criterion: *lex superioris legi inferiori derogat*;
- the chronological criterion: *lex posterioris legi anteriori derogat*;
- the speciality criterion: *lex specialis legi generali derogat*;

to which the criteria that regulate spatial conflicts, more precisely defined conflicts between legal orders, object of international law, are to be added.

The interrelationships between the criteria are not completely defined but are integrated by two supplementary principles:

- the prior general law does not abrogate previous special norms :*lex generalis posterior legis speciali non derogat;*
- unless the new legislation aims at regulating *ex novo* the subject matter by eliminating all the pre-existing norms (absolute norms).

3 Formal structures for conflicts-solving: non-monotonic logic

The normalisation of a part of a normative system into a logic model is usually defined as an operation of translating normative, interpreted, sentences in logic formulas that constitute the axioms of the theory; from which, by applying the inference rules of that logic, infer theorems (in legal terms: to verify that a given decision is the legal consequence that follows deductively from the norms chosen as premises). If, therefore, we can think of a logic model of a normative subsystem as a theory of classical logic, the properties of completeness and consistency required by the theory contrast with a legal reality of inconsistency (conflicts between norms) and non completeness (gaps). Inconsistency of the normative system, in particular, can be overcome: either by *selecting a subset* that is consistent with it (normative system in force obtained by applying hermeneutic or meta criteria for conflict solving); or by accepting the notion of *defeasible* logical consequence. that derogates the monotonicity of classical logic[2]. One of the typical cases of non-monotonic reasoning is that in which there are *exceptions* to general knowledge; a valid piece of information (either a belief

[2] In traditional logic the formulas that are the logical consequences of a set of premises do not change by augumenting the set of premises. This means that the addition of new knowledge (for example, a new norm or the ascertaining of new facts) cannot invalidate the formulas that have logically been inferred from the original premises

or rule), generally and in normal conditions, it is understood as being able to be asserted (or inferred) in the absence of information about the existence of exceptional conditions and, consequently, it is *defeated* from the time the abnormal event comes into being or is recognised.
In the law, an exception is made by the legislator when he believes it to be advisable to limit the range of the general norm when there are more specific fact situations. Consequently, the general norm is applicable in the absence of information about the applicability of the exception.
Before analysing some of the approaches to dealing with exceptions, we should distinguish between *weak* and *hard* exception[3]: that is, between exceptional circumstances that, where they occur, produce the effect of blocking the application of the general norm (weak exception), so that *nothing* can be inferred in relation to the situation in course, and exceptions (hard exceptions) that produce the verification of the *complementary effect*, to that provided for by the general norm . The corresponding legal distinction between (weak) *exceptions to norms* and (hard) *exceptions to the effects* can be found in [Sartor 90].
In many cases, the above mentioned distinction depends on the interpretation (in a weak or hard sense) of expressions such as "provided that...","except...", etc. For example, art. 1626 Civil Code: *The lease terminates for the interdiction, incapacity or insolvency of the tenant, unless suitable guarantees are given to the landlord for the exact performance of the duties of the tenant.*
A hard interpretation of the expression "unless"` in our example would attribute the meaning of a hard exception to the sentence introduced by it (in other words, in the case where suitable guarantees are presented, the contract is not terminated); while a weak interpretation would be limited to blocking the application of art. 1626 when guarantees are given.

2.1 Classification of the approaches to non-monotonic reasoning

Various criteria have been used for classifying the approaches to non-monotonic reasoning: the traditional distinctions between syntactical and semantic approaches and that (almost coinciding) between credulous and sceptical approaches. Another distinction based on properties most relevant for the law refers to the nature of the initial assumptions: a) the pre- condition is the consistency of the premises and the objective is to extend the derivable consequences (theorems): b) the starting point is the inconsistency of the premises and the scope is to identify which theorems can be inferred from a consistent subset of them. In any case both approaches have to consider cases in which multiple consequences (mutually conflicting) can be inferred by default, or more than one consistent subset can be constructed; according to the methods of selection used in these situations, a transversal criterion distinguishes :

[3]The distinction is to be found in [Brewka 1991].

approaches based on *exception clauses, and* approaches where a wider *criterion of priority* between formulas is fixed.

The extension of inference

We shall cite two of the approaches based on the principle of extension of inferences, *default logic* and *logic programming*. Both, it seems to us, permit the relations between general rule and exception to be dealt with, but not the introduction of more general criteria of priority.

At the basis of default logic(DL) (Reiter 80), there is the assumption that it is possible (and necessary) to draw inferences by using available knowledge, always that the new inferred knowledge be consistent with the known facts, in other words, that there is no information contrary to the inferred conclusions. In order to explain this idea, a new *rule of inference* is used. Given a default theory *T* made up of a set of defaults *D*[4] and the set of facts *W* (closed formulas of first order logic), an *extension* is constituted from all the formulas obtained by applying the defaults that can be added to W maintaining consistency. In general a theory of default permits more than one extension: it derives from them a concept of *strong validity* (a formula is in all the extensions) and *weak validity* (a formula is in at least one extension).

To express the exceptions (hard exceptions), *seminormal defaults* are required: for example, art. 1626 can be translated:

$$\frac{\text{non\_\_complying(tenant)}: \neg\, \text{gives\_guarantees(tenant)} \wedge \text{terminates(contract)}}{\text{terminates(contract)}}$$

In fact, it means blocking a general default when the conditions of exception are proved, but also of being able to use the general default when we know nothing about the conditions of exception. The *seminormal defaults* have problems at the level of the proof theory, due to the fact that they do not have semimonotonicity; another disadvantage is that, if a more specific default (a new exception) is added, the general default must be rewritten as all the exceptional facts must be explained in the justification.

Logic programming has proved to be a particularly suitable structure for analysing non-monotonic reasoning, firstly for the implementation in Prolog of the form of non-monotonic negation (*negation as failure*: NAF): proposals for handling of some of these aspects in the context of logic programming can be found in [Kowalski 1989][5] where the possibility of dealing as constraints clauses

---

[4]The formulas are not considered to be universally quantified but, rather, are considered the set of all possible instances of the variables; it means that asserting the negation of an instance does not imply the falsity of the formula.

[5] [Kowalski 1989], pp. 11-15.

with a negative conclusion is demonstrated and, therefore, the possibility to eliminate them through transformation; and in [Kowalski-Sadri 1990][6], where the exceptions are explained by using clauses with the consequent classically negated[7]. It is shown how, by assuming the *priority* of the clauses with negative head over clauses with positive head, it is possible, through transformation, to obtain an equivalent logic program, for example:

terminates(contract) :- non_complying(tenant).

¬terminates(contract) :- gives_guarantees(tenant).

and then:

terminates(contract):-non_complying(tenant), not (¬ terminates).

and finally: terminates(contract):-non_complying(tenant), not (gives_guarantees(tenant)).

Theory Construction

The alternative approach considers the situation of inconsistency that is generated, not by the incompleteness of the knowledge as by "too much" knowledge (and, it is said, the normative conflict may be seen as a situation in which two norms or set of norms are applicable to the same case).

In order to do this it is necessary to change the concept of inference, by substituting it with that of *provability*: instead of extending the derivable theorems, it means reducing the number of the derivable formulas, that is, only those that can be proved. A formula can be proved if it is possible to build a consistent argument based on the most *reliable* hypotheses[8]. In contrast with Default Logic that introduces a new rule of inference, Poole's approach[9] stays within the sphere of classical first order logic, but by dividing the formulas into *facts* (true) and *default*: the defaults are possible hypotheses in theory construction (maximal consistent subsets): a *scenario* is a consistent set of formulas obtained by adding all the facts that can be inferred form defaults and maintaining consistency. A formula is *explainable* if there is a scenario that implies it (it should be noted that all the logical consequences that can be derived from a *scenario* corresponds to an *Extension* in *DL* and that Poole's defaults correspond to Reiter's without prerequisites). In order to express the exceptions, *constraints* are introduced that block the application of a default when there is new information. In practice, they function as seminormal defaults of DL., where every default becomes an hypothesis (or assumption) and every

---

6 [Kowalski Sadri 1990], pp. 598-613.

7 The introduction of classical negation is based on [Gelfond, Lifschitz 1990] who suggest a appropriate adaption of the semantics of stable models; in [Kowalski Sadri 1990] it is shown how it is possible to extent the *answer-set semantics* of Gelfond and Lifschitz to dealing with exceptions (*e-answer-set*).

8 The approach is based on the views of [Rescher 1964].

9 [Poole 1988], pp. 27-47.

condition found in the justification is considered *abducible*. The technique of *naming* is also used for retaining atomic formulas, e.g.:

D (art.1626): non_complying(tenant) >terminates(contract).

Constraints: ¬(gives_guarantees(tenant) ∨ terminates(contract)).

(or, interpreting art. 1626 as a weak exception:)

Constraints: gives_guarantees(tenant)> ¬ *D(art.1626).*

Multiple extensions

The problem of multiple extensions (or scenarios), as we have seen, is solved by introducing an (internal) criterion of speciality or, as in the approaches that will be analysed here defining an (external) criterion of priority through which to order the formulas of the theories.

Brewka's approach[10] is a generalisation of Poole's defaults; in fact, compared with Poole, we go from two levels(refutable and inconsistent default; true and consistent facts) to a partition of the knowledge within a theory on more than one level, where every level contains first order formulas at different levels of reliability (from the bottom to the top). A *preferred subtheory* is a maximum consistent subset obtained by adding all the formulas that can possibly be added retaining consistency to lower level formulas:

- a formula is *strong provable* if can be inferred from all the maximum subsets;
- is *weak provable* if can be inferred from a subset .

In this way, a criterion of priority can be expressed on the basis of the reliability of the knowledge, by putting the more specific formulas on a lower (more reliable) level, and by assuming that the facts have a higher priority. This, therefore, allows the speciality relation between formulas to be expressed, and exceptions in the strict sense to be dealt with, placing the formula that contains the exception on a higher level of priority than the general norm. It should be noted that the approach based on preferred subtheories, in contrast with DL, allows exceptions to exceptions to be dealt with, because the knowledge that is inconsistent with new beliefs is not eliminated but only put on a lower level of plausibility, which allows it to be restored where the new knowledge is, in turn, eliminated.

In [Eshghi,Kowalski 1989][11], the construction of theories in the paradigm of logic programming is approached in an abductive context, where the choice between the different *abductive hypotheses* (seen as defaults) is guided by special constraints. The possibility of mapping general logic programs in an abductive structure, enables the relationship general rule/ exception to be transformed in the hypotheses formulation: the general rule is in force until the facts provided

---

10 [Brewka 1989].

11 [Kowalski Eshghi 1989],pp. 234 ff. It shows how the abduction can be seen as the generalization of *negation by failure*, which allows a semantics for the NAF to be formulated.

for in the exception are not shown to be true, therefore, the abductive hypotheses remain valid until the constraints are satisfied.

2.2 Theory revision

Another approach to normative conflicts could be within the scope of *theory revision.* Having been developed within the field of epistemic logic[12], theory revision deals with problems caused by the addition of new knowledge to a set of presumably consistent beliefs.

One of the better known approaches[13] presumes that a set of consistent epistemic states (the *set of beliefs*, or *theory*), is logically equivalent to a set of deductively closed logical formulas; the changes produced in the belief set by the elimination of knowledge, the addition of new knowledge, or by the introduction of knowledge inconsistent with the old one, must preserve the consistency of the theory. The criteria on which the revision is based are those of *rationality* (retaining consistency) and *economicity* (the changes and the elimination of beliefs are minimal)[14]. It means, therefore, eliminating a small number of beliefs and, on the basis of an ordering criterion, the beliefs that have less epistemic relevance*(entrenchment)*.

The two approaches, that based on non-monotonic and that on theory revision, have many points in common on a logical and methodological level[15], but they start off, as we have already mentioned, from a different theoretical approach. From a legal perspective, if we are considering, the problem of selecting the normative system that is applicable to a case, a perspective common to both the work of the judge and the lawyer, the most natural reference seems to be that of the derivation of plausible conclusions, through the selection of premises that are consistent within a theory (the set of all the norms) ;the objective is not to re-establish consistency but to obtain a logically valid (and, therefore, logically grounded) justification for the decision.

Theory revision approaches the phenomenon of legislative drafting: a definition of the legal system as a set of all statutory norms, plus all norms that can be inferred from these, seems close with a model made up of logically closed theories. Furthermore, the *normative system in force* is the system of norms that have validly been enacted and from which all the norms explicitly or implicitly abrogated have been removed. It becomes obvious how a requisite of this system is consistency, and how a structure becomes necessary, that enables consistency

---

12 But the ideas underlying it originate in the legal field: [Alchourron 1981].

13 Known as AGM from the names of the authors: [Alchourron, Gardenfors, Makinson 1985].

14 . A different approach, based on the concept of justification (every belief is valid in as far as there is another valid belief that justifies it) is developed in TMS (*Truth Maintenance Systems*) , see [Doyle 1979].

15 For a comparison between the two aspects, see [Brewka 1989, pp. 217 ff.; Brewka 1991 pp. 77 ff]; [Gardenfors Makinson 1989]; [Sartor 1991].

to be restored after the addition of new sentences.

3 Dealing with conflicts as a process of metareasoning

As the analysis has pointed out, the exploitation of priority criteria of the premises (or the inferences) constitutes one of the most crucial tasks; in the proposal above mentioned just *one* ordering criterion is taken into consideration, whether it is that of speciality or the general criterion of priority(whatsoever it is the meaning) . In law, instead, as we have said, the criteria of choice between norms in conflict are more than one, and in relations such that they can, in turn, be in conflict. It means, therefore, defining a structure that manages and controls the relations between the criteria, solves any conflicts between them and, therefore, applies the selected criterion to solving the normative conflict. It is evident that this requires making a distinction between *object knowledge* and *metaknowledge*, and a further definition of *metaevaluation rules* that manage both kinds of knowledge.

The logic programming paradigm is considered a capable representation formalism of the legal domain; it seems also a suitable framework for handling the multilevel features of legal knowledge. The use of metaprogramming techniques for introducing extensions in general logic programs has considerable advantages, both formal and computational [Kowalski 1990]. In [Nute 1988] we have a concrete application of these considerations, through the definition of a logic (meta)program that reproduces non-monotonic reasoning. In [Guidotti, Mariani, Sardu, Tiscornia 1992] a similar approach is described, applied to normative conflicts.

4 Conclusion

As we have mentioned, by considering working on a "logical model" of a system of norms, the treatment of incompatibility between norms, like the process by analogy, can incertain way be brought down to a verification of consistency and completeness of a theory. Proposals for solving in metatheoretical terms some of the problems linked to the processing of plausible reasoning seem acceptable , on the legal level, with regard to the natural nature and fidelity of the representation: from the analysis, it is evident that the concept of *applicability*, also like that of *speciality* or *priority*, *similarity*, *defeasability* are metaconcepts, and , as a consequence, require representation through metaknowledge. One of the particular features is the coparticipation, in such a structure, of metaknowledge on the processes and metaknowledge on the contents, which requires deeper investigation about the nature and the relations existing between them.

References

[Alchourron,.Gardenfors, Makinson 1985]: Carlos E. Alchourron, Peter Gardenfors, David Makinson, *On the Logic of Theory Change: Partial Meet Functions for Contraction and Revision,* Journal of Symbolic Logic, 50, 1985.

[Alchourron 1981] : Carlos E. Alchourron, *Ordinamento normativo e abrogazione*, in Preproceedings of the First International Conference on Logica, Informatica, Diritto, Florence, 1981, pp.3 - 57.

[Brewka 1989]: Gerhard Brewka, *Preferred subtheories: an extended logical framework for default reasoning*, Proc. IJCAI 1989, pp. 1043 -8.)

[Brewka 1991]: Gerhard Brewka, *Nonmonotonic Reasoning: Logical Foundation of Commonsense*, Cambridge University Press, Cambridge,1991.

[Doyle 1979]: Jon Doyle, *A Truth Maintenance System*, Artificial Intelligence ,12, 1979..

[Gardenfors 1988] : Peter Gardenfors, *Knowledege in Flux*, MIT Press, Cambridge, MA, 1988.

[Gardenfors, Makinson 1988]: Peter Gardenfors, David Makinson: *Revision of Knowledge Systems Using Epistemic Entrechment*, in Proceedings of the Second Conference on Theoretical Aspects of Reasoning about Knowledge, Morgan Kaufmann , Los altos, 1988.

[Gelfond, Lifschitz 1988] M. Gelfond, V. Lifschitz, *The Stable Model Semantic for Logic Programming*, in Proc. AAAI 1987, pp. 207 - 211.

[Gelfond, Lifschitz 1990): M. Gelfond, V. Lifschitz, *Logic Programs with Classical Negation*, in. Proc. 7th Int. Conf. on Logic Programming , 1990, pp. 579- 597.

[Guidotti, Mariani, Sardu, Tiscornia 1992]: Paolo Guidotti, Paola Mariani, Giuseppe Sardu, Daniela Tiscornia, *Metalevel Reasoning. The design of a System to Handle Legal Knowledge Bases*, in Proceedings of the 7th Italian Conference on Logic Programming(GULP 92, Citta Studi Editore, Milano, 1992.

[Kowalski 1989]: Robert A. Kowalski, *The treatment of negation in logic programs for representing legislation*, Proceedings of the Second International Conference on Artificial Intelligence and Law , ACM, 1989, pp. 11-15.

[Eshgi Kowalski 1989]: K Eshgi, Robert A.Kowalski, , *Abduction compared with negation by failure*, Proceedings of the 6th Int. Conf. of Logic Programming. , 1989, pp. 234 ff.

[Kowalski Sadri 1990], Robert Kowalski, Fariba Sadri, *Logic Programming with exceptions*, in Proceedings of the Seventh International Conference on Logic Programming, MIT press, 1990, pp598-613.

[Nute 1985] : Donald Nute, *A nonmonotonic Logic based on Conditional Logic*, ACMC Research Report n. 01-007, University of Georgia, 1985.

[Poole 1988] :Poole D.L., *A logical Framework foe Default Reasoning*, Artficial Intelligence, 36:1(!988), pp. 27 - 47)

[Reiter 1980]:R.Reiter: *A Logic for Default Reasoning*, Artificial Intelligence, 13, 1980, pp. 81 - 132)

[Rescher 1964] Rescher Nicholas: *Hipothetical Reasoning* , North-Holland Amsterdam, 1964.

[Sartor1991] : Giovanni Sartor , *The Structure of Norm Conditions and Nonmonotonic Reasoning in Law*, in Proc. of the 3th. Int, Conf. on Artificial Intelligence and Law, ACM Press, 19991, pp. 155 - 164.

[Tiscornia 1993]: Daniela Tiscornia, *Un modello computabile del concetto di applicabilità normativa*, in Informatica e Diritto,Firenze, 1993,forthcoming.

The Application of Kripke-Type Structures to Regional Development Programs

Matthias Baaz[1], Fernando Galindo[2],
Gerald Quirchmayr[3], Manuel Vázqez[2]

[1] Institute of Algebra and Discrete Mathematics, TU Wien
Wiedner Hauptstr. 8-10, A-1040 Wien

[2] Seminario de Informática y Derecho, University of Zaragoza
E-50009 Zaragoza

[3] FAW, University of Linz
Altenbergerstr. 69, A-4040 Linz

Keywords: Modal logic, Kripke-type frames, legal expert systems.

Abstract. Legal and administraitve decision making are characterized by conflicting laws, statutes and internal regulations making the process extremely difficult to formalize. Defining strategies for modelling priorities and their allocation is of major importance in such an environment. Modal logic and multiple-valued logic are therefore used in our approach to design a priority-oriented model.

1. Introduction

Research concerning priority-oriented models of legal and administrative decision making have for a long time been only theoretical. With the example of formalising strategies used by INEM (the Spanish national institute for employment) and the EEC for allocating subsidies we show one possible way for putting formal logic-based models to work in legal environments. To be able to represent contradictions naturally occurring between the interests of different applicants and different institutions granting subsidies, we use Kripke-type frames based on the concept of possible worlds.

2. Decision Making at INEM

Given the present situation in Spain, the major goal of INEM is to fight unemployment by supporting regional development in the form of grants. The allocation for these grants has to based on the most promising strategy in order to successfully reduce unemployment and strengthen the local industry. The strategies can in an advanced form be based on philosophical principles of decision making, in our example a utilitarian and an impartial one. It is assumed that INEM follows the utilitarian and the EEC the impartial philosophy (for detailed description of the philosophies cf. [Galindo 1992]). It is obvious that the model can easily be extended by other philosophies.

From a utilitarian point of view an application should be classified according to the following ranking of criteria:

a) number of new permanent positions created (1)
b) number of contracts issued to unemployed people (2)
c) number of people employed (3)
d) number of apprenticeships and educational contracts (4)
e) type of positions created (5)

Following an impartial philosophy, the decision making strategy has to follow a different ranking of criteria:

a) number of apprenticeships and educational contracts (4)
b) number of new permanent positions created (1)
c) number of people employed (3)
d) number of contracts issued to unemployed people (2)
e) type of positions created (5)

3. Decisions as Morphism Chains of Possible-World Structures

Basically, there are many ways of representing decisions, but it is reasonable to keep the chosen structures as simple as possible. As only the most general structures do guarantee a focus on the essential, they alone can prevent redundant overhead. That mainly is why possible-world semantics introduced by Kripke (cf. [Kripke 1963], [Kripke 1965] and [Chellas 1980]) are chosen for modelling conflicts between internally consistent parties. As not the parties themselves, but their relationships are of major interest, modal operators acting on these relationships are the basic components which a solution can be developed from. A decision process (the dynamic aspect of a decision) is therefore represented by the simplest transformation on relationhips, namely cancelling connections between worlds. As other representations lead to incorporating redundancy, this approach is chosen in order to be able to cope with high volumes of data in an abstract manner.

4. A Formal Model of Regional Development Programs

The construction consists of a static part used for describing and a dynamic part used for deciding situations of allocation of grants:

a) the static part:

- the situation of allocation of subsidies is represented by a Kripke-type frame;
- the representatives consist of totally ordered non-empty sets of worlds, where a representative stands for all grants given by an institution or all companies a person is handling the application for;
- the truth values determining the priorities are elements of $\mathbf{C}_1 \times \ldots \times \mathbf{C}_r \times \{0,1\}$, where $\mathbf{C}_1, \ldots, \mathbf{C}_r$ are the components of an application; $\mathbf{C}_1, \ldots, \mathbf{C}_r$ are totally ordered non-empty sets representing the criteria according to which an application is evaluated;
- we represent the application of a local corporation to an institution α as follows:

  a) a true statement $APP_{c,\alpha}$ valued at c by the actual situation of the company (i. e. the value $\langle \mathbf{c}_1, \ldots, \mathbf{c}_r, 1\rangle$ is assigned to $APP_{c,\alpha}$, $c \in \alpha$, $\mathbf{c}_i \in \mathbf{C}_i$, $i = 1, \ldots, r$);

  b) all elements of α are connected to c by arrows;

  c) a false statement $APP_{c',\alpha}$ for all $c' \neq c$, $c' \in \alpha$, valued at $\mathbf{c}$ by the actual situation of the local corporation (i. e. the value $\langle \mathbf{c}_1, \ldots, \mathbf{c}_r, 0\rangle$ is assigned to $APP_{c',\alpha}$, $\mathbf{c}_i \in \mathbf{C}_i$, $i = 1, \ldots, r$); the underlying assumption is that one grant can be given to only one corporation;
- $\Box APP_{c,\alpha}$ is true for some elements (is false for all elements) of the institution α if α does (not) grant a subsidy for the representative β, $c \in \beta$.

b) the dynamic part:

- for finite situations derivations are defined by cancelling

  a) applications which have already been successful (= have already received a grant)

  b) applications with the weakest arguments; the weakest argument is determined by the lexicographic order of the ring of $\langle \mathbf{c}_1, \ldots, \mathbf{c}_r, 1\rangle$ which follows the total ordering of the criteria $\mathbf{C}_1, \ldots, \mathbf{C}_r$ representing the philosophy on which the decision making process is based.

  The result has the following properties:

  a) $\Box APP_{c,\alpha}$ or $\neg\Box APP_{c,\alpha}$ is true at every $c \in \alpha$;

  b) if $\Box APP_{c,\alpha}$ is true at $c \in \alpha$, then it is not true at any $c' \neq c \in \alpha$, which means that the institution grants the subsidy to a corporation c iff $\Box APP_{c,\alpha}$ is true at c.

  The derivations produce a normal form which uniquely determines all decisions of granting subsidies.

Enlarged sets of truth values are useful for the representation of priorities without influencing the set of logically valid propositions determined in this context by an adequate two-valued modal logic (cf. [Baaz/Quirchmayr 1987] and [Baaz/Quirchmayr 1988] for a related approach modelling contradictory situations in legal procedures).

5. Notations and Definitions

For reasons of simplicity only propositional logic is considered. The *truth values* **V** are elements of $\mathbf{C}_1 \times \ldots \times \mathbf{C}_r \times \{0,1\}$. $\mathbf{C}_1, \ldots, \mathbf{C}_r$ are totally ordered non-empty sets.

$\langle \mathbf{c}_1, \ldots, \mathbf{c}_r, 1 \rangle$ are designated to be true. (As a consequence of this definition the properties of usual classical modal propositional logics will be saved, cf. [Rescher 1969]). Generalisations to other systems of multiple-valued (first order) logic are obvious.

Let **L** be a propositional language with variables **Var** and operations $\neg, \wedge, \vee, \Box$. A *presituation* is a frame $F = \langle \mathrm{D}, \mathrm{PHIL}, \mathrm{R}, \mathrm{v} \rangle$, where

$\mathrm{D} = \{\alpha_1, \alpha_2, \ldots\} \neq \{\}$; α_i are disjoint non-empty totally ordered sets of worlds (the representatives); $U = \bigcup \alpha_i$ denotes the *universe*;

$\mathrm{PHIL} : \mathrm{D} \to \mathbb{P}(\{\mathbf{C}_1, \ldots, \mathbf{C}_r\} \times \{\mathbf{C}_1, \ldots, \mathbf{C}_r\})$ has the property that $\mathrm{PHIL}(\alpha)$ is a total order of $\mathbf{C}_1, \ldots, \mathbf{C}_r$. $\mathrm{PHIL}(\alpha)$ therefore induces a lexicographic order $<_1$ on $\mathbf{C}_1 \times \ldots \times \mathbf{C}_r \times \{1\}$ that can be extended to **V** by

$u <_{\mathrm{PHIL}(\alpha)} w \quad \Leftrightarrow$
$u <_1 w$ and u and w are designed to be true, or
u is not designed to be true and w is designed to be true, or
$w <_1 u$ and u and w are not designed to be true;

$\mathrm{R} \subseteq U \times U$;

$\mathrm{SIT} : U \to \mathbf{C}_1 \times \ldots \times \mathbf{C}_r$ is used to describe the *situation* of the corporation;

$\mathrm{v} : U \times \mathbf{L} \to \mathbf{V}$ is inductively defined by
$\mathrm{v}_c(A) \in \{\mathrm{SIT}(c)\} \times \{0,1\}$ for all $A \in \mathbf{Var}$,
$\mathrm{v}_c(\neg A) = \langle \mathbf{c}_1, \ldots, \mathbf{c}_r, 1-e \rangle$ for $\mathrm{v}_c(A) = \langle \mathbf{c}_1, \ldots, \mathbf{c}_r, e \rangle$,
$\mathrm{v}_c(A \wedge B) = \min <_{\mathrm{PHIL}(\alpha)} \{\mathrm{v}_c(A), \mathrm{v}_c(B)\}$ for $c \in \alpha$,
$\mathrm{v}_c(A \vee B) = \max <_{\mathrm{PHIL}(\alpha)} \{\mathrm{v}_c(A), \mathrm{v}_c(B)\}$ for $c \in \alpha$,
$\mathrm{v}_c(\Box A) = \min <_{\mathrm{PHIL}(\alpha)} \{\mathrm{v}_d(A) \mid \langle c, d \rangle \in \mathrm{R}\}$ for $c \in \alpha$, the only condition where different philosophies lead to different results;

A *situation of allocation of subsidies* is a presituation extended by an injective function $\mathrm{APP} : U \times \mathrm{D} \to \mathbf{Var}$ such that $\mathrm{v}_c(\mathrm{APP}_{c,\alpha})$ is designed to be true and $\mathrm{v}_c(\mathrm{APP}_{d,\alpha})$ is designed to be false for all $d \neq c$.

6. The Formal Evaluation of a Given Situation

In the previous chapter we have defined the formal basis necessary to develop a procedure for achieving a unique decision in a situation where different corporations are applying for different grants given by different institutions.

Relation-based stability: $\langle d,c\rangle \in R$ excludes $\langle d,c'\rangle \in R$ for $c \neq c'$, $\langle d,c\rangle \in R$ excludes $\langle d',c\rangle \in R$ for $d \neq d'$, $d,d' \in \alpha$. $F' = \langle D, PHIL, R', v', APP\rangle$ is a *relation-based derivation* of $F = \langle D, PHIL, R, v, APP\rangle$ iff $\langle d,c\rangle \in R$ and $\langle d',c\rangle \in R$ for different $d,d' \in \alpha$, $\langle d,c'\rangle \notin R$ for all $c' \neq c$ and $R' = R - \{\langle d,c\rangle\}$ or otherwise $\langle d,c\rangle \in R$; d is maximal in $\{e \mid e \in \alpha, \langle e,k\rangle \in R, \langle e,k'\rangle \in R$ for some $k \neq k'\}$; $SIT(c) * \langle l\rangle = \min_{<_{PHIL(\alpha)}} \{SIT(e) * l \mid \langle d,e\rangle \in R\}$ and $R' = R - \{\langle d,c\rangle\}$.

Valuation-based stability: at least one of $\Box A$ and $\Box\neg A$ is true at every element of U and if $\Box APP_{c,\alpha}$ is true at $d \in \alpha$ then $\Box APP_{c,\alpha}$ is not true for all $d' \in \alpha$, $d' \neq d$. $F' = \langle D, PHIL, R', v', APP\rangle$ is a *valuation-based derivation* of $F = \langle D, PHIL, R, v, APP\rangle$ iff $\Box APP_{c,\alpha}$ is true for $d' \in \alpha$, $\langle d,c\rangle \in R$, $d \in \alpha$, $d \neq d'$ and $R' = R - \{\langle d,c\rangle\}$ or otherwise $\langle d,c\rangle \in R$, $d \in \alpha$; $\Box A$ and $\Box\neg A$ are not true for some A at d where d is maximal in α with this property; $SIT(c) * \langle 1\rangle = \min_{<_{PHIL(\alpha)}} \{SIT(e) * \langle 1\rangle \mid \langle d,e\rangle \in R\}$ and $R' = R - \{\langle d,c\rangle\}$.

A situation is *coherent* iff $\langle d,c\rangle \in R$ for some $d \in \alpha$ implies $\langle d,c\rangle \in R$ for all $d \in \alpha$. A situation is *acyclic* iff there is no sequence $\langle d_1,d_2\rangle \in R, \ldots$ $\ldots, \langle d_{k-1},d_k\rangle \in R$ for d_1, d_k in the same α. The *application criteria are distinct* iff $SIT(c) = SIT(d)$ implies $c = d$.

Theorem. *Assume that the situation of allocation of subsidies F is finite, coherent, acyclic and that the application conditions are distinct; all relation- and valuation-based derivation chains are finite and terminate with a relation- and valuation-based stable normal form F^*.*

Proof (Sketch). Reductions obviously terminate because of the finiteness of F and all resulting frames have relation- and valuation-based stability. If different derivation steps are possible at a certain stage, these derivation steps possess the diamond property (i. e. there are derivation chains to a common frame F°).

Corollary. *In F^* all grants are uniquely allocated if the number of applicants is greater than or equal to the number of grants (formally: an institution α allocates a subsidy to a corporation c if $\Box APP_{c,\alpha}$ is true in F^* at some $d \in \alpha$).*

7. Example: The Application to Regional Development Programs

In our example we have three corporations A, B and C which apply for grants of two institutions, INEM and EEC. The 5 criteria described in Chapter 2 are denoted by the sets $\mathbf{C}_i = \{\mathbf{a}_i, \mathbf{b}_i, \mathbf{c}_i\}$, where $\mathbf{a}_i$ ($\mathbf{b}_i, \mathbf{c}_i$) do express the actual position of A (B, C) relative to the corresponding criterion $\mathbf{C}_i$. ($SIT(A) = \langle \mathbf{a}_1, \ldots, \mathbf{a}_5\rangle$, $SIT(B) = \langle \mathbf{b}_1, \ldots, \mathbf{b}_5\rangle$, $SIT(C) = \langle \mathbf{c}_1, \ldots, \mathbf{c}_5\rangle$). Criteria $\mathbf{C}_1, \mathbf{C}_2, \mathbf{C}_3$ are ordered by $\mathbf{c}_i < \mathbf{b}_i < \mathbf{a}_i$, criteria $\mathbf{C}_4, \mathbf{C}_5$ are ordered by $\mathbf{b}_i < \mathbf{a}_i < \mathbf{c}_i$. All corporations are applying to both institutions; INEM has two grants to allocate, the EEC has one subsidy to give to one of the applicants. (INEM = $\{g_1, g_2\}$, say $g_1 < g_2$, EEC = $\{g_3\}$. For the INEM decision makers we assume a utilitarian philosophy, for the EEC we assume an impartial one (PHIL(INEM) = $\mathbf{C}_5 < \mathbf{C}_4 < \mathbf{C}_3 < \mathbf{C}_2 < \mathbf{C}_1$, PHIL(EEC) = $\mathbf{C}_5 < \mathbf{C}_2 < \mathbf{C}_3 < \mathbf{C}_1 < \mathbf{C}_4$). Our formal model takes the following form:

$$F = \langle\{\text{INEM}, \text{EEC}, A^\circ, B^\circ, C^\circ\}, \text{PHIL}, R, v, \text{APP}\rangle,\ A^\circ = \{A\},\ B^\circ = \{B\},\ C^\circ = \{C\}.$$

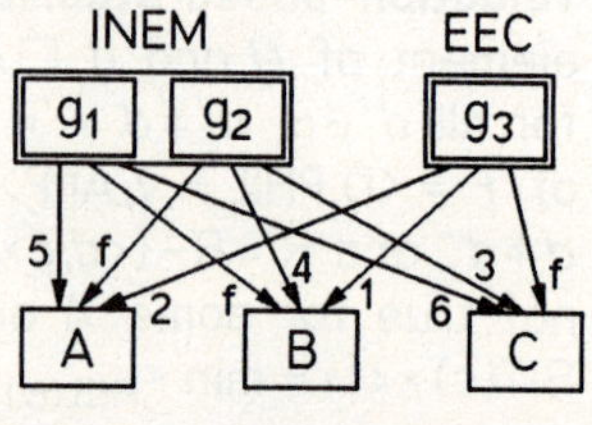

R is given by the arrows, APP is defined in the obvious way. F is obviously coherent, acyclic and the application criteria are distinct. The numbers associated to the arrows represent their cancellation in a possible derivation chain. The arrows to which "f" is associated are present in the stable normal form. Consequently $\Box \text{APP}_{A,\text{INEM}}$ is true at g_2, $\Box \text{APP}_{B,\text{INEM}}$ is true at g_1, $\Box \text{APP}_{C,\text{EEC}}$ is true at g_3. Therefore INEM grants a subsidy to A and B and not to C ($\Box\neg \text{APP}_{C,\text{INEM}}$ is true at g_1 and g_2) and the EEC grants a subsidy only to C ($\Box\neg \text{APP}_{A,\text{EEC}}$ and $\Box\neg \text{APP}_{B,\text{EEC}}$ are true at g_3).

8. Conclusion

Currently an implementation is undertaken in Double Helix, a database system which allows to graphically model rules and queries. The first prototype is tested at the University of Zaragoza in cooperation with INEM and will be used for simulating the consequences of applying different philosophies as described in Chapter 2.

References

[Baaz/Quirchmayr 1987] M. Baaz and G. Quirchmayr: *The application of multiple valued logic in supporting legal decision making.* In: Proc. of the 17th Int. Symp. on Multiple-Valued Logic, pp. 234-248, IEEE Washington 1987.

[Baaz/Quirchmayr 1988] M. Baaz and G. Quirchmayr: *Models of juridical decisions based on the concepts of possible worlds.* In: Proc. of the 8th Int. Workshop on Expert Systems and their Applications, pp. 165-174, EC2, Nanterre 1988.

[Chellas 1980] B. F. Chellas: *Modal Logic.* Cambridge 1980.

[Galindo 1992] F. Galindo: *La distributión de fondos públicos para la promocion del empleo. Principios básicos.* Zaragoza, Seminario de Informática y Derecho, Documento 3/1992.

[Kripke 1963] S. A. Kripke: *Semantical analysis of modal logic I. Normal modal propositional calculi.* In: Zeitschrift für mathematische Logik und Grundlagen der Mathematik, vol. 9/1963, pp. 67-69.

[Kripke 1965] S. A. Kripke: *Semantical analysis of modal logic II. Non-normal modal propositional calculi.* In: J. W. Addison, L. Henkin and A. Tarski (eds.): The Theory of Models, Amsterdam 1965.

[Rescher 1969] N. Rescher: *Many-Valued Logic.* New York 1969.

Data Management Tools for Genomic Applications: A Progress Report *

Victor M. Markowitz and I-Min A. Chen

Information and Computing Sciences Division
Lawrence Berkeley Laboratory, Berkeley, CA 94720

Abstract

We report in this paper on the development of data management tools that allow scientists to construct and manipulate genomic databases in terms of application-specific objects and protocols. We are developing tools for specifying genomic database structures, as well as for entering, changing, maintaining, browsing and querying data in genomic databases. These tools are based on the Object-Protocol Model (OPM) developed by us and target commercial relational database management systems which are widely used in molecular biology laboratories. OPM allows scientists to interact with genomic databases in terms of their own frame of reference, namely genomic objects and protocols. Databases developed using the data management tools are easier to use, manage, and adapt.

1 Introduction

The information controlling the development of biological organisms is encoded in their *genome* in the form of polymeric molecules known as DNA. DNA information is encoded as a sequence of *nucleotides*. Regions of the DNA called *genes* specify the information for protein molecules. In higher organisms (yeast, plants, animals, humans) the DNA is organized into several linear *chromosomes*.

Several projects are attempting to determine the complete DNA sequence of various organisms. These projects require databases for managing DNA data and related information. Typically, the structure of a genomic database can be modeled in terms of *objects* characterized by (having) *attributes* that take values from a *domain* (set of values); objects that share common attributes can be organized (*classified*) into homogeneous sets of objects. For example, consider the *contig maps* used in determining the complete DNA sequence of various

---

*Issued as Technical Report LBL-33706. This work is supported by the Office of Health and Environmental Research Program of the Office of Energy Research, U.S. Department of Energy under Contract DE-AC03-76SF00098.

organisms, and consisting of ordered *DNA fragments*[1]. Contig maps can be modeled as objects that have attributes such as **`contig_id`**, **`owner`** (representing owners of contig maps), and (**`fragment, position`**) (representing component fragments and their positions in contig maps); similarly, fragments can be modeled as objects that have attributes such as **`fragment_id`** and **`owner`**.

Genomic databases also contain data on *protocols* representing experimental laboratory procedures. Given an input, a protocol instance (i.e., an elementary experiment) results in an output. Protocols often involve a series of subprotocol steps. The recursive specification of protocols in terms of component subprotocols is called *protocol expansion*. Protocol expansion reveals the composition of component subprotocols and/or alternative ways of performing the protocol. For example, consider a *construct* protocol for constructing contig maps of ordered DNA fragments: such a protocol is applied on DNA fragments (input) and result in contig maps (output). Protocol *construct* can be expanded into two alternative protocols, *overlap* and *constraint*, both followed by protocol *assemble*: protocol *overlap* compares two DNA fragments using a computer program, protocol *constraint* compares manually two DNA fragments according to certain constraints, and protocol *assemble* assembles DNA fragments into a contig map according to information in the connection tables regarding possible connecting positions of two DNA fragments.

Most genomic databases developed in the past few years use commercial relational database management systems (DBMSs). Relational DBMSs do not provide constructs for representing directly genomic-specific objects and protocols. These objects and protocols are usually represented in relational databases by several disconnected tuples scattered among multiple tables, logically tied together by primary key-foreign key references. Such representations are not only hard to comprehend, but also entail the development of large procedures for assembling data on application-specific objects from (i.e., by joining) several relations. Furthermore, because of the complexity of the relational representations for objects and protocols, the development, maintenance, and modification of such databases are tedious, error-prone, and time-consuming processes.

Data models such as the *Extended Entity-Relationship Model* (EERM) [10] and the *Semantic Data Model* (SDM) [4] provide constructs for modeling objects, sets of objects, and object associations, and therefore are better suited than relational DBMSs for specifying the structure of genomic databases. For example, in EERM atomic objects called entities are classified into *entity-sets*, and are qualified by *attributes* that take values from value-sets. Associations of entities are modeled as *relationships* classified in *relationship-sets*. EERM has a *generalization* mechanism that allows viewing similar (*specialization*) entity-sets as a single *generic* entity-set.

We have explored using EERM for describing genomic databases [9], and found that it is too restricted for specifying accurately their object structure. Such restrictions can be overcome by using *auxiliary* entity-sets and relationship-

[1] Since existing technology permits sequencing only fragments of a few hundred nucleotides, chromosomal DNA is cut into smaller fragments, the fragments are propagated as clones, and then assembled into contig maps.

sets. For example, contig maps, fragments and their owners can be represented by three EERM entity-sets called CONTIG_MAP, FRAGMENT, and PERSON, respectively. However, representing that contig maps and fragments can be owned by persons requires an auxiliary entity-set generalizing CONTIG_MAP and FRAGMENT, OWNED_OBJECT, together with an auxiliary relationship-set, OWNED_BY, associating OWNED_OBJECT with PERSON. Auxiliary constructs do not represent application-specific objects and therefore unnecessarily increase the complexity and obscure the semantics of databases.

The need to employ a diversity of continuously evolving mapping and sequencing strategies require facilities for efficiently constructing genomic databases that are easy to use and change. In order to attain the desired level of flexibility and adaptability, we decided to develop data management tools that allow scientists to rapidly construct and manipulate genomic databases in terms of genomic objects and protocols. The underlying data model for these tools is provided by the Object-Protocol Model (OPM) developed by us.

OPM has similarities with other object data models (cf. [5]), especially with SDM [4]. Similar to SDM, in OPM objects are classified into object classes and are qualified by attributes that take values from value classes. Unlike SDM, however, in OPM attributes can be *composite*, that is, consisting of multiple component simple attributes, and can be associated not only with single value classes, but also with *unions* of value classes. These constructs allow avoiding the creation of object classes that do not have an application-specific counterpart. Furthermore, unlike other data models (e.g., such as those reviewed in [5] or [6]), OPM provides a *protocol class* construct for modeling laboratory experiments. A protocol class in OPM can be associated with regular attributes as well as *input* and *output* attributes used for specifying input-output protocol connections. OPM also supports a *protocol expansion* mechanism for specifying a protocol class in terms of component subprotocol classes.

The data management tools we develop will benefit several molecular biology laboratories and genome centers. In particular, our project supports directly the large-scale sequencing project at University of Washington, Seattle, for characterizing up to six million bases of the human and mouse T-cell receptor loci and the development of the Integrated Genomic Database at the German Cancer Research Center, at Heildelberg.

The rest of the paper is organized as follows. Our approach to developing data management tools is described in section 2. The status of our work is reviewed in section 3. Section 4 briefly discusses future plans.

2 Approach

The data management tools are based on a data model developed by us, the *Object-Protocol Model* (OPM). OPM is briefly reviewed below. A complete description of OPM is provided in [1].

2.1 The Object-Protocol Model

OPM allows describing database structures in terms of *objects* characterized by *attributes* taking values from *value classes*, and classified into *object classes*. For example, the contig maps mentioned in the previous section can be represented in OPM by object class **CONTIG_MAP** having attributes **contig_id**, **owner**, and (**fragment**, **position**). Similarly, fragments can be represented by object class **FRAGMENT** having attributes **fragment_id**, **sequence**, **length**, and **owner**; and owners can be represented by object class **PERSON** having attributes **person_id**, **name** and **owns** (see figure 1).

Object classes can have subclass-superclass relationships. For example, one can specify a class **SCIENTIST** as a subclass of **PERSON**.

Attributes in OPM can be:

1. *atomic*, such as attribute **contig_id** of object class **CONTIG_MAP**, or *composite*, that is, consisting of aggregations of atomic attributes, such as attribute (**fragment**, **position**) of **CONTIG_MAP**;
2. *single-valued*, such as attribute **person_id** of object class **PERSON**, or *multi-valued*, such as attribute **owns** of **PERSON**;
3. *local*, such as attribute **sequence** of object class **FRAGMENT**, or *referential*, that is, representing references to other objects, such as attribute **owner** of **FRAGMENT**, representing references to **PERSON**;
4. associated with a *single* domain, such as attribute **name** of object class **PERSON**, or with a *union* of different domains, such as **owns** of **PERSON** whose domain is the union of object classes **CONTIG_MAP** and **FRAGMENT**;
5. *derived*, that is, attributes that have values derived from the values of other attributes using a derivation expression, such as attribute composition, arithmetic expressions, aggregate functions, or attribute inversion; for example, attribute **owner** of **CONTIG_MAP** in figure 1 is specified as the inverse of attribute **owns** of **PERSON** (i.e., the value of **owner** for a given contig map m is the person whose **owns** value contains m).

In addition to objects, OPM supports modeling laboratory *protocols*. Protocols are classified in protocol classes and can be qualified by both regular and special, input and output, attributes. For example, protocols *construct*, *overlap*, *constraint*, and *assemble* mentioned in the previous section can be described in OPM by the protocol classes shown in figure 2, where their inputs and outputs are modeled by the object classes shown in figure 1. Thus, the experiments for constructing contig maps of ordered DNA fragments can be represented by the instances of protocol class **CONSTRUCT** having an output attribute **contig_map** representing the result of construct protocols applied on fragments, where fragments are represented by input attribute **fragments**.

OPM has a protocol expansion mechanism for the recursive specification of protocols in terms of *alternative* protocols, *sequences* of protocols, and *optional* protocols; "*or*", ",", and "[ ]" are used to denote alternative, sequences

```
OBJECT CLASS FRAGMENT
   DESCRIPTION: DNA fragment
   ID: fragment_id
   ATTRIBUTE fragment_id: INTEGER                 not null     single-valued
   ATTRIBUTE sequence: VARCHAR(750)                            single-valued
   ATTRIBUTE length: INTEGER                                   single-valued
   ATTRIBUTE owner: PERSON                                     single-valued
             DERIVATION: inverse of PERSON.owns
OBJECT CLASS CONNECTION_TABLE
   DESCRIPTION: connection table
   ID: table_id
   ATTRIBUTE table_id: INTEGER                    not null     single-valued
   ATTRIBUTE left_entry: FRAGMENT
   ATTRIBUTE right_entry: FRAGMENT
   ATTRIBUTE distance: INTEGER
OBJECT CLASS CONTIG_MAP
   DESCRIPTION: contig map
   ID: contig_id
   ATTRIBUTE contig_id: INTEGER                   not null     single-valued
   ATTRIBUTE (fragment, position): (FRAGMENT, INTEGER) multi-valued
   ATTRIBUTE owner: PERSON                                     single-valued
             DERIVATION: inverse of PERSON.owns
OBJECT CLASS PERSON
   DESCRIPTION: person
   ID: person_id
   ATTRIBUTE person_id: INTEGER                   not null     single-valued
   ATTRIBUTE name: CHAR(80)
   ATTRIBUTE owns: CONTIG_MAP or FRAGMENT                      multi-valued
```

Figure 1: Object Classes Representing the Input and Output for Protocols

of, and optional protocols, respectively, and parentheses are used for specifying complex protocol compositions. For example, consider protocol classes **CONSTRUCT**, **OVERLAP**, **CONSTRAINT**, and **ASSEMBLE** shown in figure 2. The expansion of **CONSTRUCT** in terms of **OVERLAP**, **CONSTRAINT**, and **ASSEMBLE** is expressed as follows (see figure 2): **EXPANSION**: (**OVERLAP** or **CONSTRAINT**), **ASSEMBLE**.

Input and *output* attributes associated with protocols represent the input and output of protocols, respectively, and can be used to express the inheritance of input or output attributes by component subprotocols from their generic protocols and the input–output connection of directly related protocols. Input–output attribute inheritance is expressed using *'input is-a ...'* statements (e.g., see attribute **fragments** of **OVERLAP** in figure 2) and *'output is-a ...'* statements (e.g., see attribute **contig_map** of **ASSEMBLE** in figure 2) in the specification of the input and output attributes associated with subprotocols. If a protocol is followed directly by another protocol, then the input of the latter may include some or all of the output of the former. Such input–output

```
PROTOCOL CLASS CONSTRUCT
   DESCRIPTION: construct a contig map
   ID: construct_id
   EXPANSION: (OVERLAP or CONSTRAINT), ASSEMBLE
   ATTRIBUTE construct_id: INTEGER      not null   single-valued
   ATTRIBUTE fragments: FRAGMENT        not null   multi-valued    input
   ATTRIBUTE contig_map: CONTIG_MAP     not null   single-valued   output
PROTOCOL CLASS OVERLAP
   DESCRIPTION: compare fragments using computer programs
   ID: overlap_id
   ATTRIBUTE overlap_id: INTEGER          not null   single-valued
   ATTRIBUTE fragments: FRAGMENT          not null   multi-valued
                                 input isa CONSTRUCT.fragments
   ATTRIBUTE connect_table: CONNECTION_TABLE   not null              output
   ATTRIBUTE (program_name, program_version): (CHAR(40), CHAR(6))
PROTOCOL CLASS CONSTRAINT
   DESCRIPTION: manually compare fragments using constraints
   ID: constraint_id
   ATTRIBUTE constraint_id: INTEGER       not null   single-valued
   ATTRIBUTE fragments: FRAGMENT          not null   multi-valued
                                 input isa CONSTRUCT.fragments
   ATTRIBUTE connect_table: CONNECTION_TABLE    not null   output
   ATTRIBUTE constraint_type: CHAR(80)          single-valued
PROTOCOL CLASS ASSEMBLE
   DESCRIPTION: assemble contigs
   ID: assemble_id
   ATTRIBUTE assemble_id: INTEGER         not null   single-valued
   ATTRIBUTE connect_table: CONNECTION_TABLE  not null
                                 input from OVERLAP via connect_table
                                         or CONSTRAINT via connect_table
   ATTRIBUTE contig_map: CONTIG_MAP       not null   single-valued
                                 output isa CONSTRUCT.contig_map
```

Figure 2: Protocol Classes Representing Protocol Construct and its Components

attribute connections are expressed using '*input from ... via ...*' statements (e.g., see attribute `connect_table` of `ASSEMBLE` in figure 2) in the specification of input attributes associated with protocols taking their input from other protocols.

2.2 Data Management Tool Development

Developing data management tools based on OPM and targeting relational DBMSs, involves mapping OPM constructs and data manipulation operations (retrievals and updates) into relational DBMS constructs and SQL queries. This mapping is very complex because of the discrepancy between the OPM and relational DBMS constructs, but can be simplified by introducing an intermediate EERM level that allows decomposing the OPM to relational DBMS mapping into simpler mappings between OPM and EERM, and between EERM and relational DBMS, respectively. The OPM to EERM mapping is easier to develop than the direct OPM to relational DBMS mapping because EERM schemas and queries are specified in terms of objects and object associations, and therefore are inherently more concise and simpler to specify than relational DBMS schemas and queries. Furthermore, EERM schemas and queries are independent of a specific DBMS, and therefore can be used across different DBMS platforms. The EERM version we use is the EERM described in [10], extended with two constructs (unary relationship-sets and a new form of directly associating entity-sets) described in [2].

We have developed a mapping of OPM schemas that generates EERM schemas together with queries for constructing OPM objects and protocols from entities and relationships. These queries are expressed in the *Concise Object Query Language* (COQL) [11], and involve associating a (primary) entity-set with attributes of other (auxiliary) entity-sets and relationship-sets, where the primary entity-set is associated with the auxiliary entity-sets and relationship-sets either directly or via other entity-sets and relationship-sets. Thus, a primary entity-set, its local and inherited attributes as well as the attributes of auxiliary entity-sets and relationship-sets can be specified in COQL using an OUTPUT statement, while the association of a primary entity-set with auxiliary entity-sets and relationship-sets can be expressed using CONNECTIONS statements. COQL also allows setting conditions on entity-sets and relationship-sets. Suppose that the contig maps and their owners mentioned above are represented by entity-sets `CONTIG_MAP` (with attribute `contig_id`) and `PERSON`, connected by relationship-set `OWNED_BY`. Then the following COQL query expresses the association of contig maps with their owners:

```
OUTPUT        CONTIG_MAP: contig_id, PERSON;
CONNECTIONS   CONTIG_MAP OWNED_BY PERSON;    END
```

In the COQL query above, `PERSON` is an auxiliary entity-set whose attributes are associated with `CONTIG_MAP` via relationship-set `OWNED_BY`.

Regarding the mapping of EERM schemas and queries into relational DBMS schemas and queries, we have developed tools that can automatically carry out the EERM to relational DBMS schema and query mapping. The EERM schema to relational schema mapping is presented in [10] and has been implemented as part of an EERM schema translation tool called SDT [8]. SDT automatically translates EER schemas into schema definitions for several relational DBMSs: Sybase, Ingres, Informix, and Oracle. The DBMS database definitions generated by SDT include procedures (e.g., triggers in Sybase) necessary for maintaining referential integrity and value constraints. The information about schemas and their mapping is subsequently stored in a *metadatabase*.

The COQL to SQL mapping is described in [11], and has been implemented as part of a COQL translation tool. Based on the metadatabase generated by SDT, the COQL translator maps a COQL query into one or several queries in the SQL dialect of the underlying relational DBMS. The COQL translator has been implemented for Sybase and will be implemented for other relational DBMSs as well.

3 Development Status

In this section we briefly review the status of the OPM data management tools.

3.1 The OPM Schema Editor

We have developed a graphical schema editor for interactively specifying, displaying, modifying, merging, and browsing OPM schemas.

The OPM schema editor allows specifying incrementally complex object and protocol structures by providing facilities for defining new schemas, modifying existing schemas, and merging schemas. A schema can be browsed using an Object Classes Listbox that lists in the main window the object classes of the schema (see figure 3). This listbox can be switched into a Protocol Classes Listbox or a Controlled Value Classes Listbox for browsing protocol classes and controlled value classes, respectively.

For an object class selected in the Object Classes Listbox, its connections to other classes (via attributes), and its superclasses and subclasses are displayed in the drawing area of the main window. This graphical display can be also used for browsing a schema by recursively expanding value classes associated with displayed attributes.

An object class can be defined or modified by double clicking on the name of an object class in the listbox or in the drawing area, or by selecting the `OPM Object Class` option of the `Define` menu item in the main window. The Object Class Definition window shown in figure 3 illustrates the definition of object class `CONTIG_MAP`. The `Define Attribute` option in this window allows defining or modifying attributes of the current class.

The Composite Attribute Definition and Component Attribute Definition windows shown in figure 3 illustrate the definition of a composite attribute, namely attribute `(fragment, position)` of `CONTIG_MAP`. The Attribute Inverse Definition window shown in the same figure allows specifying object cross referencing by defining attributes as inverses of other attributes.

Protocol classes can be browsed, defined or modified in a similar way. For a protocol class selected in the Protocol Classes Listbox, its connections to other classes via attributes, as well as the graphical representation (in a DFD like notation) of its expansion (if any) are displayed in the main window drawing area. A protocol object class can be defined or modified by double clicking on the name of a protocol class in the listbox or in the drawing area, or by selecting the `OPM Protocol Class` option of the `Define` menu item in the main window. Figure 4 illustrates the definition of a protocol class (`CONSTRUCT`) and its subprotocols. The Input/Output Attribute Definition window allows specifying the input and output attributes of protocols. Protocol expansion can be defined or modified using the Protocol Expansion window. The Input From Definition window allows specifying '*input from ... via*' connections. For example, in figure 4) attribute `connect_table` of protocol class `ASSEMBLE` is specified as: from `OVERLAP` via `connect_table` or from `CONSTRAINT` via `connect_table`

A schema can be saved in a text file by selecting `Generate OPM` option of the

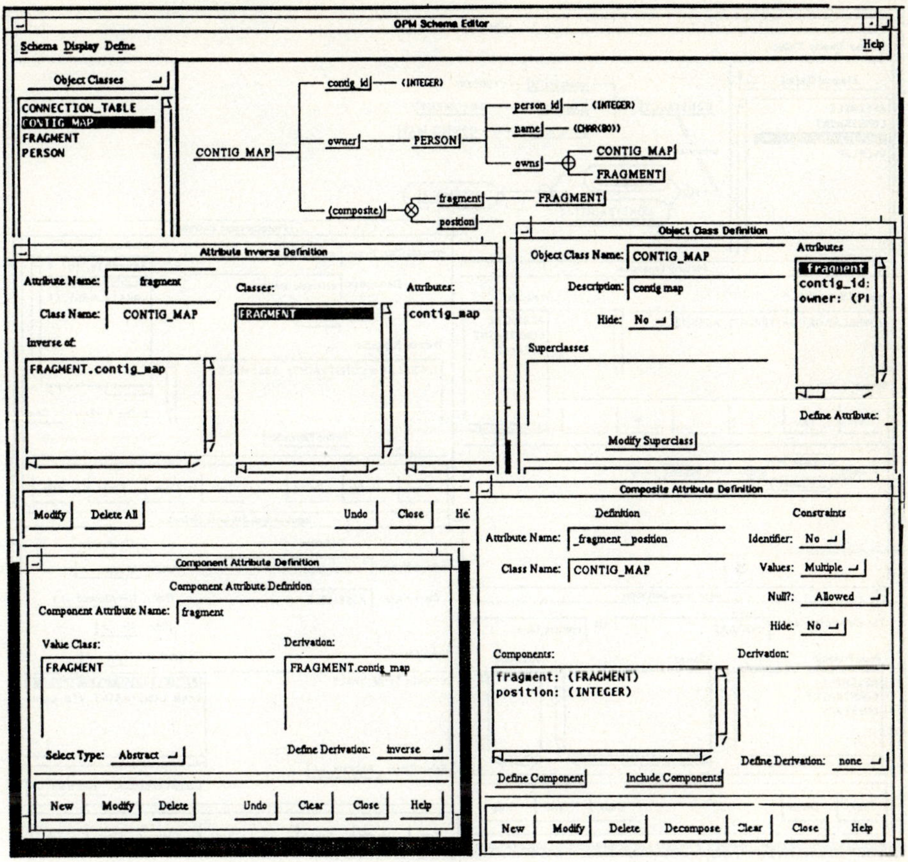

Figure 3: Specifying Object Classes using the OPM Schema Editor

Schema menu item in the main window. This file contains the schema definition in the OPM data definition language, and can be passed to the OPM schema translator described below, for generating the corresponding EER schema and COQL queries.

The OPM schema editor has been implemented on Sun SPARCstations using C++ and the X11 Motif graphical user interface toolkit and is described in [3].

3.2 The OPM Schema Translator

Since scientists in most molecular biology laboratories use commercial relational DBMSs (mainly Sybase), the tools we develop target relational DBMSs. Consequently, these tools involve mapping OPM schemas into relational schema definitions and SQL queries that express basic manipulations (retrievals and updates) of OPM objects and protocols.

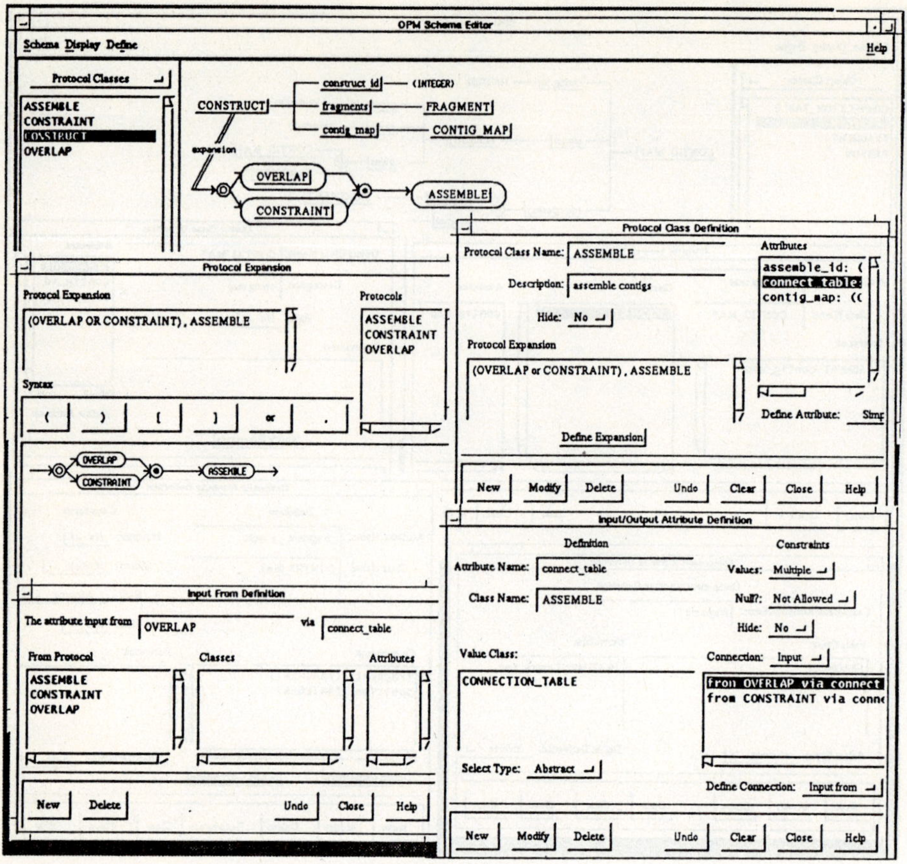

Figure 4: Specifying Protocol Classes using the OPM Schema Editor

As already mentioned above, our approach to mapping OPM schemas into relational definitions and queries is to use an intermediate EERM level, so that OPM schemas are mapped first into EERM schemas and queries, and then EERM schemas and queries are mapped into relational database schema definitions and queries. This approach allows reducing the development of a complex OPM to relational DBMS mapping to a simpler OPM to EERM mapping, while taking advantage of the existing EERM to relational DBMS translation tools [8, 11] for generating relational database definitions and queries from EERM schemas and queries.

The complete specification of the OPM schema mapping procedure and examples can be found in [2]. Informally, mapping OPM into EERM consists of mapping every OPM object or protocol class into an entity-set, and of incrementally constructing COQL queries associated with these entity-sets, that express the construction (retrieval) of OPM objects and protocols from EERM entities and relationships. Depending on their type (primitive, abstract, simple, composite, etc.), non-derived attributes of object or protocol classes are mapped into EERM attributes, direct entity-set associations, or relationship-sets. Derived attributes are not mapped into EERM schema components (with the exception of some inverse attributes) and entail only modifying COQL queries. For each (object or protocol) class, the mapping generates a COQL query for retrieving the instances in this class, including the values for all their non-derived, derived, and inherited attributes. The mapping also generates a *metadatabase* that contains information on the correspondence between the components of the OPM schema and the components of the generated EER schema and COQL queries. The OPM browsing and query tools we plan to develop will be based on this metadatabase.

The OPM schema translator has been developed on Sun SPARCstations in C++ using Lex++ and Yacc++.

4 Summary and Future Plans

We have briefly discussed the development of data management tools that allow specifying genomic database structures. These tools are based on the Object-Protocol Model (OPM) developed by us and target commercial relational database management systems. These tools have been applied to the development of a genomic database supporting the sequencing project at University of Washington, Seattle.

We are currently developing OPM data entry and browsing tools. These tools will provide facilities for: (i) inserting, deleting, and updating objects and protocols; (ii) selecting and displaying objects and protocols that satisfy certain conditions; (iii) browsing through selected sets of objects and protocols; (iv) recursively displaying, for a given object or protocol, related objects or protocols.

We also plan to develop a more complex OPM query language and a query tool based on this language. This tool will allow querying genomic databases in terms of objects and protocols, and will consist of two main components: (i) an OPM-based graphical interface will allow users to browse through OPM schema specifications and incrementally specify queries in terms of object and protocols; and (ii) a translator will map OPM queries into COQL queries, and subsequently into SQL queries.

The data management tools we develop are currently targeting the Sybase DBMS, mainly because Sybase is widely used in molecular biology laboratories and centers worldwide. We recognize that relational databases are cumbersome for implementing genomic databases. Since object-oriented DBMSs are more amenable to represent complex protocols and DNA sequences and provide mechanisms for incorporating application-specific (e.g., sequence alignment) operators, we plan to use such DBMSs for genomic databases. We will experiment with one of the C++ based object-oriented DBMSs, such as Object Store, and will extend our tools in order to ensure an easy transfer of genomic databases to these DBMSs.

Acknowledgements. The OPM schema editor was implemented by Ofer Ben-Shachar, Francis Pang, and Carol Jean Smith. SDT was implemented by Weiping Fang and Jun Wang. The COQL translator has been implemented by Ernest Szeto. We greatly appreciate their excellent work.

References

[1] Chen, I.A., and Markowitz, V.M., The Object-Protocol Model, Lawrence Berkeley Laboratory Technical Report LBL-32738, 1993.

[2] Chen, I.A., and Markowitz, V.M., Mapping Object-Protocol Schemas into Extended Entity-Relationship Schemas and Queries, Lawrence Berkeley Laboratory Technical Report LBL-33048, 1993.

[3] Chen, I.A., Markowitz, V.M., Ben-Shachar, O., and Pang, F., OPM Schema Editor 1.1: A Graphical Editor for Object-Protocol Schemas, Lawrence Berkeley Laboratory Technical Report LBL-33410, 1993.

[4] Hammer, M., and McLeod, D., Database Description with SDM: A Semantic Database Model, *ACM Transactions on Database Systems*, **6**, 3, (1981), pp. 351-386.

[5] Hull, R., and King, R., Semantic Database Modeling: Survey, Applications, and Research Issues, *Computing Surveys* **19**, 3 (1987), pp. 201-260.

[6] Ioannidis, Y.E., and Livny, M., MOOSE: Modeling Objects in a Simulation Environment, *Information Processing 89*, G.X. Ritter (ed), Elsevier Science Publishers B.V., 1989, pp. 821-826.

[8] Markowitz, V.M., Fang, W., and Wang, J., SDT 6.0. A Schema Definition and Translation Tool for Extended Entity-Relationship Schemas, Lawrence Berkeley Laboratory technical Report LBL-27843, 1993.

[9] Markowitz, V.M., Lewis, S., McCarthy, J., Olken, F., and Zorn, M., Data Management for Genomic Mapping Applications: A Case Study, *Proc. of the 6th International Conference on Scientific and Statistical Database Management*, 1992, pp. 45-57.

[10] Markowitz, V.M., and Shoshani, A., Representing Extended Entity-Relationship Structures in Relational Databases: A Modular Approach, *ACM Transactions on Database Systems*, **17**, 3, (1992), pp. 423-464.

[11] Markowitz, V.M., and Shoshani, A., Object Queries over Relational Databases: Language, Implementation, and Applications, *Proc. of the 9th International Conference on Data Engineering*, 1993, pp. 71-80.

Resolution of Constraint Inconsistency with the Aim to Provide Support in Anaesthesia

Ernest Rotterdam,* Sieger van Denneheuvel,†
Pim Hennis‡ and Peter van Emde Boas§

Keywords: Constraint Satisfaction, Expert Systems Architecture, Medical Information Systems.

Abstract

We have investigated the possibilities to use constraints to provide decision support in Anaesthesia. It became apparent that concepts are required to deal with inconsistency due to three causes: differences between defaults and specific information, imprecision in measurements or knowledge, and incompatibility of different preferences. Differences between defaults and specific knowledge can be resolved by attaching priorities to constraints. Imprecision in measurements or in knowledge can be resolved by using intervals instead of point values. For resolution of inconsistency due to incompatibility of preferences, next to priorities and intervals, relaxation is required. Thus, the constraint satisfaction system must support three concepts for inconsistency resolution: priorities, intervals and relaxation.

For constraint-satisfaction a number of methods has been developped: local propagation, relaxation, constraint propagation, backtracking, and symbolic rewriting. For each of these methods we investigated which of the concepts required for inconsistency resolution they can support. Furthermore it was investigated how different constraint satisfaction methods can be combined such that two or all three of the forementioned concepts can be supported.

1 Motivation for using constraints

After defining constraint problems, their application to provide decision support to anaesthetists is discussed. A constraint satisfaction problem can be denoted as a tuple $\langle C, K, W \rangle$. C is a set of constraints. K is a set of *known* variables, i.e., variables whose values are known. W is a set of *wanted* variables, i.e., variables whose values are requested. The task of a constraint satisfaction system is to infer the values of the wanted variables from the values of the known variables with the constraints. Simple examples of constraint problems are:

*University of Groningen, dept. of Medical Information Science, PO Box 30.001, 9700 RB Groningen
†Syllogic, PO Box 26, 3990 DA Houten
‡University Hospital Groningen, dept. of Anaesthesiology, PO Box 30.001, 9700 RB Groningen
§University of Amsterdam, dept. of Information Science, Plantage Muidergracht 24, 1018 TV Amsterdam

$C = \{a = b + c\}$ $K = \{a, c\}$ $W = \{b\}$
$C = \{a = b \wedge c\}$ $K = \{a, c\}$ $W = \{b\}$

In the first constraint problem, the involved variables are reals, in the second they are booleans. Next to K and W, two derived sets of variables U and I are distinguished. U is the set of *unknown* variables: $U = var(A) - K$. I is the set of *intermediate* variables: $I = U - W = var(A) - K - W$. The function $var(A)$ denotes the variables appearing in constraint set A.

This paper focuses on equational constraints. This class of constraints is important to us since we want to base decision support mainly on data obtained from measurement equipment in the operating theatre. These data can be obtained without asking attention from the anaesthetist such that he can concentrate on the patient. Most data generated by measurement equipment are numerical. It is general practice in decision support to map numerical data to a limited number of symbolic values. However, equational constraints, connecting measured variables with 'deep variables' permit to extract more information from the available numerical data. Examples of equations between physiological variables are:

$CO = HR \times SV$	*CO*	: Cardiac Output
$PArtM - CVP = CO \times SVR$	*CVP*	: Central Venous Pressure
	HR	: Heart Rate
	PArtM	: Mean Arterial Pressure
	SV	: Stroke Volume
	SVR	: Systemic Vascular Resistance

CO, *CVP*, *HR* and *PArtM* are measureable. *SV* and *SVR* are un-measureable. A simple physiological equation model is given in [4].

Below, for four support functions, it is outlined how it can be based on a physiological model consisting of equations.

Inferring values of 'deep' variables.
Deep variables are variables whose values are interesting to the anaesthetist, but which can not be measured. Equations connecting deep variables with measureable variables permit computation of the values of deep variables.

Artifact detection. When enough variables can be measured, equations connecting them can be used to check their consistency. When a set of measurements is inconsistent, part of the measurements must be artifactual, i.e., not reflecting the real value of the measured variable.

Simulation. In simulation, values of variables at future moments are computed with equations connecting past and present values with future values. Simulation can be used to assess the effect of an action intended by the Anaesthetist. When the action is administration of a drug, the effect is usually related to the dose administered.

Dose computation. In dose computation, the dose of a drug to be administered to obtain a particular effect within a certain period is computed. This function can be provided with the same equations as used for simulation of the effect of a particular dose of the drug; the equations are used in the opposite direction.

The constraint problems corresponding to the different support functions mainly differ in their sets of known and wanted variables. Since, whenever possible, the same model equations are used to provide the different support functions, the support functions will be consistent. E.g., the dose computed to obtain a particular effect is consistent with the effect forecasted for that dose. Furthermore, the constraint approach modular: the model can be changed by adding or deleting equations.

2 Resolving inconsistencies from different sources

There are four causes that can make a constraint problem, constituted to provide one of the desired decision support functions, inconsistent: artifacts, differences between defaults and specific information, imprecision, and incompatibility of aspired goals. Below, it is shown how inconsistencies due to the latter three causes can be resolved with priorities, intervals and relaxation. For imprecision, it is also demonstrated how this cause of imprecision can be distinguished from artefacts. This is important, since artifact detection is one of the decision support functions that we want to provide.

Difference between defaults and specific information can be resolved with priorities. A form of inconsistency is that a difference may exist between defaults and specific information. Suppose that a model contains a default value for a variable. When, in a particular operating theatre, equipment is present to measure the variable, the specific information from this equipment should be used. Another example is that it may be assumed by default that a variable will keep its actual value in the future. However, when a drug has been administered which is known to influence the value of the variable, knowledge about the action of the drug rather than the default assumption must be used to forecast the future value of the variable.

Inconsistency due to differences between defaults and specific information can be resolved with priorities [2]. A higher priority is given to the constraints and to inputs representing specific information than to the constraints representing defaults. As a consequence, defaults are only used to determine the value of a variable when insufficient specific information is available to determine the value of the variable.

Imprecision in measurements or knowledge can be resolved with intervals. Each measurement method has some error. Therefore, a measured value need not be entirely consistent with the other values measured simultaneously or earlier according to the equations of the model. Inconsistency stemming from imprecision can be resolved by using intervals instead of point values. When a value is measured for a variable, an interval around the value is associated with the variable. The more precise the measurement method, the smaller the interval. With intervals, imprecision can be distinguished from artifacts. When not only the point values but also the interval values associated with variables are inconsistent according to the physiological model, one or more of the measured values must be artifactual. A simple example is when there are two methods to measure the same variable, e.g., the heart rate can be deduced from the ECG (Electro CardioGram) and from the pletysmogram. When the intervals, implied by measurements with two different methods, are consistent, which in this case means that they overlap, the value of the variable must be in the intersection of the two intervals. When the intervals do not overlap, one or both of the measured values must be artifactual. In general, inconsistency due to measurement imprecision may present when the value of a particular variable can be deduced from different subsets of the available measurements. When no measurement information is available at all about a variable, an interval value deduced for it must still overlap with its physiological range.

Knowledge as well as measurements may be imprecise. For example, the effect of a drug can not be forecasted exactly from its dose. It can be forecasted in which interval the value of a variable will reside after administration of a particular dose of the drug.

Incompatibility of aspired effects can be resolved with a combination of priorities, intervals, and relaxation. The third cause of inconsistency to be considered is incompatibility of preferences. This kind of inconsistency presents in constraint problems constituted for drug dose computation. The dose is computed with the dose–effect relation for the drug from the effect(s) that an Anaesthetist wants to bring about. When more than one effect is aspired, no dose may exist that can bring about the desired effects simultaneously.

Incompatibility of aspired effects can be resolved with priorities, intervals, relaxation or a combination of these concepts. Priorities can be used when the aspired effects can be ordered according to their importance. Using intervals prevents incompatibilities: when intervals rather than point values are used to express the desired effects, it is less likely that the different aspired effects are incompatible. Relaxation can be used to find a compromise between incompatible desired effects of equal priority.

3 Constraint satisfaction methods

As outlined above, the task of a constraint satisfaction system is to infer values for wanted variables from the values of known variables with constraints. A large number of methods have been developed to perform this task: local propagation, relaxation, constraint propagation, backtracking, and symbolic rewriting. For choosing between these methods, the following points are important.

Variable domain properties. The following dichotomies concerning the domains of variables involved in constraint problems are relevant:

- discrete – continuous
- finite – infinite
- symbolic – numerical.

As outlined above, we are mainly interested in numerical physiological variables. The domains of these variables are also continuous and infinite. Therefore, bactracking, which relies on finity of value domains is unsuitable for our puposes [13], [10].

Efficiency. Apart from how fast a solution is found for a particular constraint problem, it is also important whether a constraint problem can be compiled with the satisfaction method. Compilation of a constraint problem means that one or more procedures are derived to compute values for the wanted variables from values of the known variables. This is possible when the satisfaction method is not influenced by the actual values of known variables. Evaluation of the derived procedures with values for the known variables permits direct computation of the values of the wanted variables. Compilation is possible with local propagation and symbolic rewriting but not with constraint propagation and error minimization.

Solution of circular constraint problems. Local propagation can not solve some circular constraint problems [8].

Resolution of inconsistencies. Above it was demonstrated that three concepts for resolution of inconsistency are required to provide constraint-based decision support in Anaesthesia: priorities, intervals and relaxation.

Borning and coworkers have developped versions of local propagation and error minimization supporting priorities [2]. Error minimization also supports relaxation for continuous numerical variables. Constraint propagation supports intervals. Below it is demonstrated that symbolic rewriting can also support priorities and intervals.

Systems for constraint satisfaction usually combine different constraint satisfaction methods to benefit from the good qualities of each. In the next sections, it is investigated how different methods for constraint satisfaction can be combined and which concepts for inconsistency resolution can be supported by different methods or combinations of methods.

We have tested only part of the (combinations of) methods with an implementation. The constraint satisfaction system of Thinglab [1] [2], which combines local propagation and error minimization, has been reimplemented in Smalltalk, which is also the implementation language of the original version of Thinglab. Constraint propagation for intervals has been implemented in C++. Combination of symbolic rewriting with error minimization and the version of symbolic rewriting supporting intervals have not been implemented.

4 Local propagation + error minimization

Thinglab [1] [2] solves constraint problems with a combination of local propagation and error minimization. When possible, local propagation is used, because it is efficient. Error minimization is used to solve parts of the constraint problem that can not be solved with local propagation due to either cyclicity or inconsistency. In Thinglab both local propagation and error minimization have been adapted to support priorities [2] [6].

The principle of local propagation is that a constraint is used for propagation, i.e., to compute the value of one of its variables, when all its other variables are known [8]. The variable whose value is computed is added to the set of known variables such that additional constraints may become useable for propagation. Local propagation can be used to compile a constraint problem, since for the question whether a constraint can be used for propagation it only matters whether a variable is known, not what its value is. As mentioned before, some cyclic constraint problems can not be solved by local propagation [8].

In error minimization, the error of a constraint set is minimized by iteratively choosing a variable and adapting its value [8]. The error of a constraint is a measure of the degree to which a constraint is not satisfied. Error minimization can solve any cyclic constraint problem. When a constraint problem is inconsistent, its error can not be reduced to 0; minimization of the error in that case means that a compromise is found between the inconsistent constraints. A drawback of error minimization is that it can not be used to compile constraint problems, since the choice of the value in a particular iteration depends on the actual values of other variables. Another drawback of error minimization is that the total error which is a function of all variables may reach a local minimum rather than its absolute minimum.

5 Symbolic rewriting + error minimization

An advantage of symbolic rewriting over local propagation is that it can solve circular constraint problems provided that sufficient mathematical knowledge is available to rewrite the mathematical relations involved. This motivated us to investigate whether symbolic rewriting can replace the local propagation part of Thinglab. First CS, the symbolic rewriter of RL/1 is described. Then it is shown how CS can be extended to HCS; the H stands for hierarchy, which signifies that priorities are supported. Furthermore, it is outlined how CS and HCS can be combined with error minimization.

5.1 RL/1's symbolic rewriter

A symbolic rewriter uses substitution to express wanted variables in terms of known variables. The symbolic rewriter discussed below has been implemented as part of RL/1. RL/1 is a prototype of the language RL. In this language, it must be possible to define relations in three ways: (1) with tables, like in relational databases, (2) with Horn clauses, like in logic programming languages, and (3) with algebraic constraints, like partly implemented in spreadsheets. Next to equations, algebraic constraints also comprize inequalities (*term1* [> | < | >= | <=] *term2*). The first ideas for RL date back to 1985 [11], [12]. In 1991, the prototype RL/1 became available [5].

A high level description of CS, the symbolic rewriter used in RL/1, is given in figure 1. A more detailed description of CS is given in [5]. This reference also describes how algebraic constraints are satisfied in combination with tabular constraints and Horn clauses.

CS has three inputs, A, K and W, and two outputs, Φ and B. A, a constraint set, K, a set of known variables, and W, a set of wanted variables, constitute the constraint problem to be solved. Φ is a solution set and B a condition set. For each of the wanted variables $x \in W$, Φ contains an element $x = t$, where t is an expression containing only known variables. Thus, Φ is a compiled form of the constraint problem. The conditions in B also apply only to known variables; they can be used to test whether a particular set of input values is consistent according to the constraints in A. Inconsistent input values must not be used to evaluate the solutions in Φ.

In the CS description, the following notation for substitution is used. The function $\Psi(C)$ performs substitution in constraints. Ψ is a solution set $\{x_1 = t_1, x_2 = t_2, \cdots\}$,

```
CS(A, K, W, Φ, B)
Input: A, set of algebraic constraints
       K, known variable set, W, wanted variable set
Output: Φ, solution set, B, condition set
begin
    Φ = ∅; B = ∅; C = A
    for a ∈ C do
        if ISOLATE(a, var(A) − K, x, t) then
            C = C − {a}
            if x ∈ W then Φ = Φ ∪ {x = t}
            Φ = {x = t}((Φ))
            C = {x = t}(C)
        else
            C = C − {a}
            B = B ∪ {a}
        endif
    endfor
end
```

Figure 1: CS: The RL/1 Constraint Solver

and C a constraint set. In the constraints of C, each occurrence of one of the head variables x_i of Ψ is replaced by the corresponding tail t_i. For example $\{a = p + q, b = r + s\}(\{a + x = b + y\}) = \{p + q + x = r + s + y\}$. The function $\Psi((\Upsilon))$ performs substitution in solutions. Both Ψ and Υ are solution sets. In the tails of Υ, each occurrence of one of the head variables x_i of Ψ is replaced by the corresponding tail t_i. For example, $\{a = b + c\}((\{x = a + c\})) = \{x = b + 2c\}$.

The procedure ISOLATE(a, U, x, t), used in CS, has two inputs, a, a constraint, and U, a set of unknown variables, and two outputs, $x \in U$, and t, a term, such that $a \equiv x = t$. If ISOLATE(a, U, x, t) succeeds, a is removed from the remaining set of constraints C, t is substituted for x in the tails of the solutions in Φ and in the constraints in C. If x is an element of W, $x = t$ is added to Φ. If ISOLATE(a, U, x, t) does not succeed, constraint a applies to known variables only. Thus it is a condition that must be satisfied between the known variables and is therefore moved from C to B. To implement ISOLATE mathematical knowledge is required. The quantity of knowledge required increases with the complexity of the constraints to be solved; for example, constraints containing logarithms with complex arguments are hard to deal with.

5.2 Extension of symbolic rewriting for priorities

HCS is a version of the symbolic rewriter CS that takes the priorities of constraints into account (see figure 2). Like CS, HCS has three inputs A, K and W and two outputs Φ and B. A is a constraint hierarchy, that is a set $\{A_0, ..., A_n\}$, where each A_i is a set of constraints of priority i. Priority number 0 represents the highest priority and n the lowest [2]. K is a knownness hierarchy $\{K_0, \cdots, K_n\}$, set K_i contains inputs of priority i. W a set of wanted variables. Φ is a solution hierarchy $\{\Phi_0, \cdots, \Phi_n\}$ and B a condition hierarcy $\{B_0, \cdots, B_n\}$. When a set of values for the variables in $K_0 \cup \cdots \cup K_i$, satisfies the constraints in $B_0 \cup \cdots \cup B_i$, the solutions in Φ_i can be used to compute values for wanted variables.

HCS(A, K, W, Φ, B)
Input: A, hierarchy of algebraic constraints $\{A_0, \cdots, A_n\}$,
    K, a knownness hierarchy $\{K_0, \cdots, K_n\}$, W, wanted variable set
Output: Φ, solution hierarchy $\{\Phi_0, \cdots, \Phi_n\}$, B, condition hierarchy $\{B_0, \cdots, B_n\}$
begin
    $C = A; \Upsilon = \emptyset$
    for $i = 0$ **to** n **do**
        $B_i = \emptyset$
        for $a \in C_i$ **do**
            if ISOLATE($a, var(C_i) - K_0 - \cdots - K_i, x, t$) **then**
                $C_i = C_i - \{a\}$
                if $x \in W$ **then** $\Upsilon = \Upsilon \cup \{x = t\}$
                $\Upsilon = \{x = t\}((\Upsilon))$
                for $j = i$ **to** n **do** $C_j = \{x = t\}(C_j)$
            else
                $C_i = C_i - \{a\}$
                $B_i = B_i \cup \{a\}$
            endif
        endfor
        $\Phi_i = \{x = t \mid x = t \in \Upsilon \wedge var(t) \subset K_0 \cup \cdots \cup K_i\}$
        $\Upsilon = \Upsilon - \Phi_i$
    endfor
end

Figure 2: HCS: Hierarchical version of CS

Both the constraints that HCS uses for constructing Φ and the inputs used in the solutions of Φ are of the highest possible priority. First only the constraints in A_0 —with the highest priority— are used in the rewriting process; those in $A_1, \cdots, A_n$ are added successively. In parallel, first only the variables in K_0 are considered known and those in $K_1, \cdots, K_n$ are added successively. The solutions under construction are stored in Υ. After processing constraint set A_i, the solutions in Υ of which all variables in the tail belong those considered known ($K_0 \cup \cdots \cup K_i$) are moved to Φ_i. Conditions found during processing of A_i, are stored in B_i. Thus the solutions in Φ_i are based on the constraints in $A_0 \cup \cdots \cup A_i$, use $K_0 \cup \cdots \cup K_i$ as knowns and these knowns must satisfy the conditions in $B_0 \cup \cdots \cup B_i$.

5.3 Combination with hierarchical error minimization

Symbolic rewriting can be combined with error minimization to relax inconsistent parts of a constraint problem. Relaxation is applied to the condition set derived by CS or the condition hierarchy derived by HCS. For hierarchical relaxation the same procedure is used as in Thinglab. The compromise values found for the known variables in this relaxation, are substituted in the solutions of Φ to compute values for the wanted variables. Combination of relaxation with symbolic rewriting is more fully described in [7].

6 Constraint propagation

Constraint propagation is a constraint satisfaction method which can support the interval concept for inconsistency resolution. In constraint propagation a domain is associated with each variable. The domain of a variable is iteratively deminished by deleting values that are inconsistent with a constraint applying to the variable given the domains of other variables to which the constraint applies [9] [10]. If the domains of all variables are finite, constraint propagation may find a unique value for each variable. Here we consider the case that the domains are intervals and the relations are equations.

For this type of constraint problems an expression evaluation function *eval* accepting and returning intervals as well as point values is required. Examples of how such an expression evaluator should operate are:
$eval([-1,2]+[3,4]) = [2,6]$,
$eval([-1,2]\times[3,4]) = [-4,8]$,
$eval([1,2]/[-3,4])$
$= eval([1,2]/[-3,0)) \cup eval([1,2]/(0,4]) = (-\infty,-\frac{1}{3}] \cup [\frac{1}{4},\infty)$ and
$eval([-1,1]^2) = [0,1]$.

Initially, with each variable an input interval is associated, which can be derived without knowledge of the equations that must be satisfied among the variables. For physiological variables, the input interval is determined by the physiological range of the variable, measurements available for the variable and the precision of these measurements.

The evaluator is used to compute the interval for a variable x which is compatible with a constraint c applying to x and the intervals associated with the other variables to which c applies: $var(c)-\{x\}$. With an isolation procedure as used in CS, a term t is sought such that $c \equiv x = t$. Evaluation of t after substitution of the intervals associated with its variables, yields an interval for x which is consistent with c and the intervals associated with the variables in $var(c)-\{x\} = var(t)$. This interval is intersected with the current interval of x to obtain a new interval for x. Constraint propagation finishes when, in a complete pass over all variables, for none of them the associated interval has been reduced.

Constraint propagation with intervals as domains has two drawbacks: Firstly, it may loop infinitively [3]. Secondly, because it is inferred for each equation in isolation whether the intervals associated with its variables are consistent, the intervals derived for variables may not be as tight as implied by the equations when considered simultaneously [7].

7 Extension of symbolic rewriting for intervals

Symbolic rewriting can support resolution of inconsistencies with intervals. Condition set B derived by CS, which is meant to test consistency of point values, is used as a starting point for computing a consistent set of intervals for known variables. These consistent intervals are then substituted in the solutions found by CS or HCS.

To get an idea of how intervals for known variables can be made consistent with a condition set consider the condition $x = y$. The intervals x_{I_0} and y_{I_0} are the input intervals for x and y. This means that the true values of x and y are confined to x_{I_0} and y_{I_0} respectively. The intervals x_I and y_I can be made consistent with the input intervals and with the constraint $x = y$ by setting both to $x_{I_0} \cap y_{I_0}$.

In more general cases there is a set of known variables K, and a set of conditions, B, that must be satisfied among them. For each of the known variables, an input interval is given. To make intervals consistent in such situations, procedure UNWIND is used. UNWIND(x, B, t) has two inputs, x and B, and one output t. Input x is one of the known variables. Output t is an expression to compute the interval for x implied by the input intervals for other knowns and the conditions in B.

```
UNWIND(x, B, t)
Input: x, variable, B, constraint set.
Output: t, expression to compute the interval of x
        from the input intervals associated with variables
        in var(B) − {x}
begin
    CS(B, var(B) − {x}, {x}, {x = t}, D)
    for y ∈ var(D) do
        UNWIND(y, D, t')
        t = {y = y ∩ t'}(t)
    endfor
end
```

Figure 3: UNWIND: Procedure for unwinding the mutual dependencies between variables

UNWIND(x, B, t) calls CS with B as constraint set and x as wanted variable. CS returns one solution, expressing x in terms of other variables in $var(B)$ and a set of conditions D that must be satisfied among the variables involved in t. When D is not empty, UNWIND must be called recursively for each of the variables $y \in var(D)$. The recursive call UNWIND(y, D, t') returns an expression t' for computing the interval implied for y by the intervals associated with the variables in $var(D) - \{y\}$, the other variables involved in D. The recursion ends, since the number of variables in $var(D)$

is smaller than in $var(B)$, such that a level of recursion must exist where D is empty. In t, y is substituted by $y \cap t'$, such that both the interval associated with y and the intervals associated with the other variables in D are taken into account in computation of the interval implied for x.

UNWIND is called for each of the knowns and for each of them the implied interval expression found by UNWIND is intersected with its own input interval to obtain an expression for an interval that is consistent with all input intervals and with the conditions. These expressions are then substitued in the solutions found by CS for wanted variables. This method for propagation of intervals through a network of constraints does not have the disadvantages mentioned for constraint propagation; space limitations prohibit further elaboration of this statement.

To support priorities next to intervals, UNWIND must be applied to the condition hierarchy derived by HCS. In the solutions of Φ_i, interval expressions must be substituted derived by application of UNWIND for variables in $K_0 \cup \cdots \cup K_i$ and conditions in $B_0 \cup \cdots \cup B_i$.

8 Conclusion

In this paper, it has been shown that three concepts for inconsistency resolution are required for providing constraint-based decision support in Anaesthesia: priorities, relaxation and intervals. The method or combination of methods used for constraint satisfaction must support these concepts for inconsistency resolution. For a number of combinations of constraint satisfaction methods it has been investigated which of the concepts for inconsistency resolution they can support. Thinglab, which combines local propagation and error minimization to solve constraint problems, supports priorities and relaxes inconsistencies. It has been demonstrated that the local propagation part of Thinglab can be replaced with symbolic rewriting. This has the advantage that error minimization, an imprecise and inefficient method for constraint satisfaction, will only be used for relaxation of incompatible constraints, and not to satisfy cyclic constraint problems.

Constraint propagation is a constraint satisfaction method supporting intervals. However, it has two drawbacks: infinite loops may occur and, because each constraint is considered separately, the intervals associated with variables are not confined as much as implied by the set of constraints as a whole. It has been demonstrated that symbolic rewriting can be extended to support intervals and then does not have the disadvantages of constraint propagation.

Next to the advantages of symbolic rewriting over local propagation and constraint propagation, it also has disadvantages: it is less efficient and harder to implement. In choosing a (combination of) constraint satisfaction methods, the importance of the advantages and disadvantages of a method for the application at hand must be assessed. In our opinion, decision support in Anaesthesia is a domain where the balance for symbolic rewriting is positive.

References

[1] Alan Borning. *Thinglab: A Constraint-Based Simulation Laboratory*. PhD thesis, Computer Science Department, Stanford University, 1979.

[2] Alan Borning, Robert Duisberg, Bjorn Freeman-Benson, Axel Kramer, and Michael Woolf. Constraint hierarchies. In Norman Meyrowitz, editor, *Proc. OOPSLA-87*, pages 48–60, New York: NY, 1987. ACM Press.

[3] Ernest Davis. Constraint propagation with interval labels. *Artificial Intelligence*, 32:281–331, 1987.

[4] S. van Denneheuvel, K.L. Kwast, P. van Emde Boas, F. de Geus, and E. Rotterdam. Symbolic computation in RL/1. In *Proc. DEXA-91*, pages 559–564, Berlin, 1991. Springer Verlag.

[5] Sieger van Denneheuvel. *Constraint Solving on Database Systems; Design and Implementation of the Rule Language RL/1*. PhD thesis, University of Amsterdam, department of Mathematics and Information Science, October 1991.

[6] Bjorn N. Freeman-Benson, John Maloney, and Alan Borning. An incremental constraint solver. *Communications of the ACM*, 33(1):54–63, January 1990.

[7] A. Fred de Geus and Ernest P. Rotterdam. *Decision Support in Anaesthesia*. PhD thesis, State University of Groningen, Faculty of Medicine, The Netherlands, December 1992.

[8] Wm. Leler. *Constraint Programming Languages; Their Specification and Generation*. Addison Wesley, 1988.

[9] A.K. Mackworth. Consistency in networks of relations. *Artificial Intelligence*, 8(1):99–118, 1977.

[10] A.K. Mackworth. Constraint satisfaction. In Stuart C. Shapiro, editor, *Encyclopedia of AI*, pages 205–211. John Wiley & Sons, 1987.

[11] Peter van Emde Boas. RL, a language for enhanced rule based database processing, working document. RJ 4869 (51299), IBM Research Laboratory, San Jose: CA 95193, 1985.

[12] Peter van Emde Boas. A semantical model for integration and modularization of rules. In *Proc. MFCS 12 Bratislava*, pages 78–92, Berlin, August 1986. Springer Verlag.

[13] Pascal Van Hentenryck. *Constraint Satisfaction in Logic Programming*. MIT Press, Cambridge: MA, 1989.

An Object-Oriented Implementation for a Semantic System (CANDID)

TOURE Famory, SCHNEIDER Michel

Laboratoire d'Informatique
Université Blaise Pascal Clermont-Ferrand II
Complexe Scientifique des Cézeaux
63177 Aubière CEDEX, FRANCE

Abstract:
CANDID is the name of a project that has for goal the definition and the implementation of a graphical interface for database manipulation. It is based on a conceptual semantic model. This paper deals with the implementation which is achieved through an object oriented kernel. This kernel is based on a uniform model with one kind of objects and one kind of control structures. To facilitate the development, the kernel is enriched by a multiwindowing graphical toolbox and an extended set of algebraic operators.

Keywords: graphical query language, semantic model, graphical interface, object-oriented database, persistence.

1. INTRODUCTION

This paper deals with the implementation of the graphical query language CANDID [9] which is based on a semantic data model. We have chosen to install CANDID as the upper layer of a specific kernel. It appears that this kernel must be object-oriented since most of the object-oriented approach matches most the semantic data model concepts (inheritance, composite objects, etc...). There are several ways to built such a system. A first solution consists of extending a relational database system like in IRIS [4]. Another solution consists of adding persistence to an existing programming language like in GEMSTONE [6] and PS-ALGOL. We have chosen to use a uniform system with one kind of object (all is object, even classes) and one kind of control structure (messages). This approach can be developed in many programming languages like PASCAL, C, LISP, ADA, C++. Its major originality is to include both static and dynamic inheritance for variables. We have implemented this kernel on an APOLLO network of stations. Persistence is treated in a transparent way with a client-server model. We have also installed a complete multiwindowing system on the kernel. Manipulation of databases is achieved through an extended set of algebraic operators.

The paper is organized as follows. First, we recall the semantic data model on which CANDID is based. Then, we present the object-oriented model of the kernel and its implementation. We provide also some details on the implementation of the graphical toolbox and the extended complex object algebra. Finally, we illustrate the use of the kernel for the implementation of the CANDID graphical interface.

2. THE SEMANTIC DATA MODEL

In this chapter we shall present shortly the semantic data model on which CANDID is built. More details on these different parts are given in [9].

The semantic model on which CANDID is built, resembles GSM as defined in [5]. The principal differences concern the use of constructors and binary relationships exclusively. It can also be compared to the semantic data models presented in [7] or [8]. The graphical representation of a schema uses a certain number of symbols that are illustrated in figure 1.

The Mediatic Object Type (MOT) is essentially used to describe other objects. It is attached to one and only one AOT or COT and has several properties (name, predefined type, frames). Its type is predefined and it can be shown or heard by the user (string, integer, real, picture, sound, etc...).

The Abstract Object Type (AOT) corresponds to something abstract or concrete from the real world that we wish to modelize. It is described by attributes.

An attribute is a relationship used to describe an aspect of an object by a semantic link with another object. It is a directed binary relationship between two types. The reverse attribute always exists.

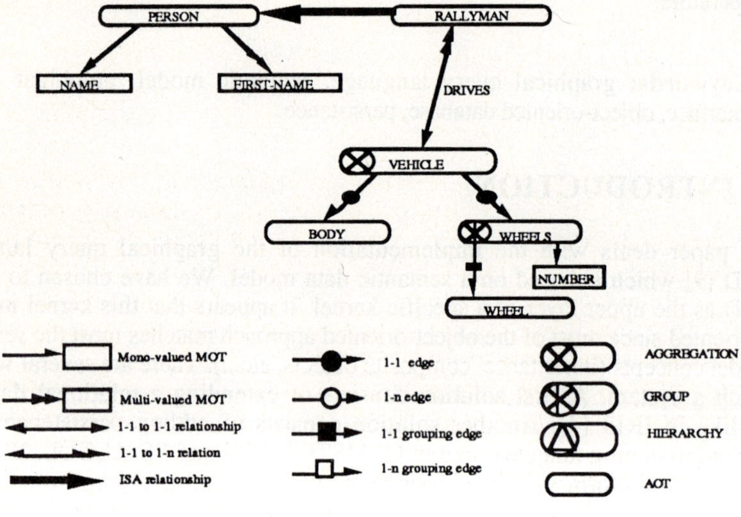

Fig. 1. CANDID symbols through a sample database

A Constructed Object Type (COT) is characterized by a construction relationship on other types (abstract or constructed) of the schema. There are three kinds of constructors: aggregation, grouping and hierarchization.

Aggregation: This constructor always requires at least two subjacent types. A same type can be used several times. The edges of the relationship are named to remove any ambiguity. The edges look like attributes, but are strictly monovalued from the aggregation to the target and can be multivalued in the reverse direction. Some systems allow a value propagation between the constructor and its subjacent types.

However, this propagation is not systematic. We prefer to define a derived MOT to compute the desired value whenever it is necessary.
Grouping: This is a relationship with one argument that defines a finite set of same type instances. Instances of a group are classes, and group attributes can be considered as class-attributes for the new instances of the grouping. Thus a group can be considered as a metaclass, where all the subclasses will have the subjacent type of the group in their supertype list. The default subjacent type is the OBJECT type.
Hierarchization: Hierarchization makes it possible to build trees based on a cyclic attribute. Simultaneously, it solves the linear recursive queries problem.

Defined between two types, sub and super, an ISA relationship indicates that any instance of sub is also an instance of super. SUB is called a subtype of SUPER and SUPER is the supertype of SUB. We give specific semantics for this relationship. First, a subtype inherits all the attributes of the supertype. Second, inheritance is transitive. Third, two types can have a common subtype without having a seeable common ancestor, because we consider that the root of the inheritance tree is the OBJECT class. Fourth, inheritance can be either dynamic or static.

Similar constraints to the ones presented in [3] can be defined. For this purpose we define a derived subtype using union, intersect or minus operations and we specify that this subtype must always be empty.

3. THE OBJECT-ORIENTED MODEL

3.1. General principles

The object-oriented model on which CANDID is built is similar to the SMALLTALK and OBJVLISP [2] models. However, it is a strongly, dynamically typed model that allows multiple inheritance and also dynamic inheritance for both variables and methods. The integers, reals and other standard types are managed in a different way from the other objects for reasons of speed and memory occupation. They can however receive messages just like any other object.

Some of the system's characteristics are as follows:
Persistence: Data are saved between two working sessions.
Complex objects: A complex object is made of several other objects related by relationships.
Object identity: an object is identified independently of its value and of its physical address.
Types and classes: Types in our model are considered as abstract classes that cannot be instantiated. They are, for example, predefined types like integers, reals, strings and so on. Classes are those that are issued from class languages and which support instantiation, inheritance, ... A new object can be attached to its class or otherwise.
Multiple inheritance: The inheritance is the same as the ISA inheritance in semantic data models. A class inherits of all the properties of another class (called its superclass) with respect to the encapsulation principle. Muliple inheritance raises the problem of property search, since a property can be defined in several superclasses. We use a particular search method to obtain a quasi-total order between the different superclasses.
Hiding, overloading and dynamic binding: Hiding is the manner by which a property can be redefined in a subclass. The property search method will see the subclass

property before the superclass property. The superclass property is hidden. Overloading consists of giving the same name to different functions with different parameters. It especially concerns operators. Dynamic binding is almost a consequence of the previous principles. It looks for the method to execute at runtime according to the receiver and the parameter types.

Uniformity: Our system is built by auto-booting. The CLASS and VARIABLE classes are defined by themselves. Except predefined types like integers, reals, booleans, ..., all the objects of the model are instances of a class that is itself the instance of a class. To avoid an infinite regression, the CLASS class is itself instance.

Query facilities: An easy learning graphical query language is available and an SQL like textual query language is in preparation.

3.2. The inheritance graph

The inheritance graph root is the OBJECT class as shown in figure 2.

The OBJECT class has the GET and SET methods to modify or to read the value of an object attribute. This choice calls into question the principle of encapsulation so dear to object-oriented languages. However, we wish to point out that many object-oriented languages propose encapsulation, but only very few of them really make it an obligation. In the domain of databases for example, we must be able to treat queries like:

```
UPDATE emp
    SET job='Manager', sal=sal+100, depno=20
    WHERE empno=7934.
```

It seams obvious that for such a query, we will have to break the encapsulation principle.

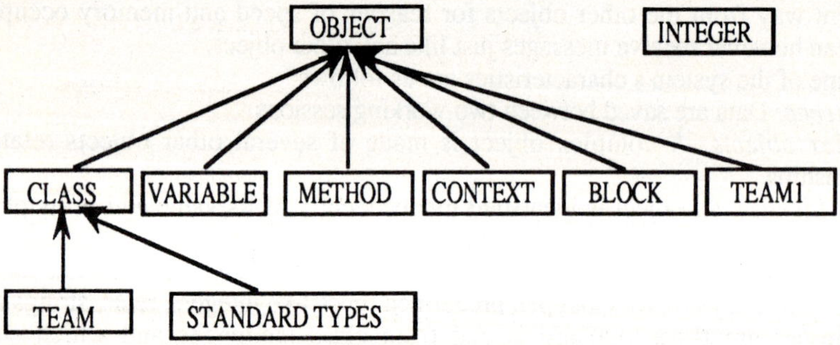

Fig. 2. The inheritance graph

3.3. The instantiation graph

The root of this hierarchy is the CLASS class as shown in figure 3. It possesses the NEW method that makes it possible to create a new instance.

The OBJECT, VARIABLE, METHOD, CONTEXT, BLOCK and TEAM classes are instances of the CLASS class. The TEAM class, which is a group, is considered as a metaclass. The TEAM1 and TEAM2 classes will have TEAM class instance variables as class instances.

The CLASS class is its own instance. Such a hierarchy allows us to define metaclasses, and so to create classes during execution time.

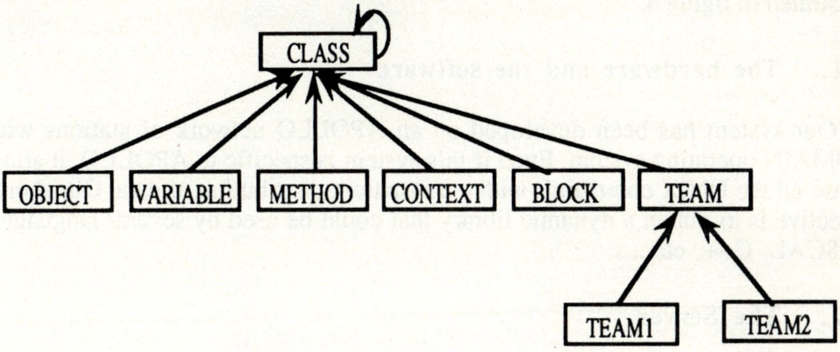

Fig. 3. The instantiation graph

Each object has a KIND-OF field which is statically inherited from the OBJECT class. This field is managed by the system so that at any moment the object owner can be known.

An object is made of a header which contains information managed by the system and static inherited variables, dynamic inherited links, and instance variables.

3.4. The primitive classes

We just have six primitive classes to describe our model.

The OBJECT class is an abstract class that is especially used to maintain the coherence of the model. All the classes statically inherit from this class. It possesses a field that contains the class identifier of the instances.

The CLASS class is its own instance. It is described with its instance variables. This class possesses the NEW method to create new instances.

The VARIABLE class makes it possible to describe an attribute. Variables are used in class descriptions as in the description of method parameters or local variables. It is also used for its own description, that is another example of the system auto-booting. GET and SET methods can be used to personalize field access as in frame languages.

The BLOCK class resembles a lambda function in LISP. It can be manipulated completely to be passed as a parameter or to be executed simultaneously with another block and so to obtain intra object parallelism. The instructions are stored in a PCODE form. The BLOCK class has the DO method to execute a block.

The METHOD class is only used to name a BLOCK. A method is not only identified by its name. Because of overloading, the parameter types also, must be taken into account. No methods are associated to this class. It only reacts to messages by executing its list of instructions.

The CONTEXT class is used to execute a method. It corresponds to stack contexts in classical languages.

4. THE IMPLEMENTATION OF THE KERNEL

In this chapter, we will describe the implementation of the object-oriented kernel achieved on an APOLLO network of stations. The architecture of the system is illustrated in figure 4.

4.1. The hardware and the software

Our system has been developed on an APOLLO network of stations with the DOMAIN operating system. Even if this system is specific to APOLLO, it allows us to use all the UNIX commands with a transparent distribution of data. Our short term objective is to obtain a dynamic library that could be used by several languages like PASCAL, C++, etc... .

4.2. The Server

The server is the lower level of the persistent memory. Its role is to read, write and add objects on the disk and to transfer them to the different clients. We have deliberately chosen an object-server for different reasons. First, it is easier to develop. Second, an object size can exceed the size of a page. Third, the object locking granularity is finest. The server doesn't have to know the structure of the objects.

4.3. The client/server communication

The client to server communications are done by mailboxes. Mailboxes are reliable interprocess communication mechanisms. Our communication model is the well known client-server model that we use to make remote procedure calls.

4.4. The memory manager

We can distinguish several kinds of objects storing areas. Our system actually provides four kinds of areas, but it is easy to add some others. The first area and the most elementary one is the stack that is used to store execution contexts including the parameters and the receiver of a method. The stack is of course managed with a LIFO strategy.

The second area is the temporary objects heap. The third area is a transit zone for virtual objects that can be transferred on the disk. The fourth and more complicated area is used for the persistent objects. A garbage collector is available for the three last areas. This is of course not necessary for the stack. The garbage collection is very easy to manage by means of internal identifiers. The memory management primitives are: getmem, freemem and maxmem.

4.5. The object manager

The object management concerns the object modification, creation, access, suppression, locking and unlocking functionalities. All these functions are available for any kind of object, even if they have no effect (suppression of an object has no effect for the objects of the stack since they are unstacked). The translation from an internal identifier to a memory address is achieved by means of a table. This table is a direct access table for the stack and memory objects, and a hashing table for virtual and persistent objects.

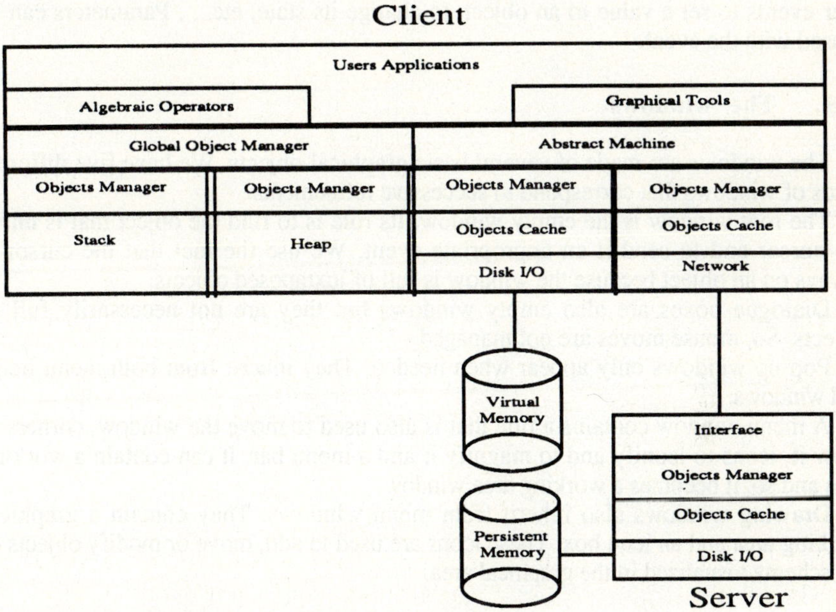

Fig. 4. The general architecture of the system

4.6. The abstract machine

The CANDID abstract machine allows us to execute a method or a block. The methods and block body is made of our PCODE instructions. This solution avoids an external compilation and execution of the code and so, allows us to dynamically execute queries. The PCODE is made up of very few instructions essentially to send messages. The code can be generated from a graphical query language, or a textual query language (SQL like), or a textual programming language. We have actually developed two of them: the graphical query language and the textual programming language.

4.7. The graphical objects

Graphical objects are made of basic objects that shall be gathered in windows. These basic objects are : the box, the disc, the icon, the mono or multi-line editor, the vertical and horizontal scrolling box. Each of theses objects can be considered as an actor that reacts to the external events by means of a special procedure called "WNDPROC". It resembles in this many other windowing systems like WINDOWS or XWINDOW. An object can receive the following events: WM_PAINT, WM_MOUSE, WM_KEYBOARD, WM_SET_FOCUS, WM_KILL_FOCUS, WM_DELETE. The WM_PAINT event indicates that the object must be redrawn. The WM_MOUSE and WM_KEYBOARD events signals a mouse or keyboard event (mouse move, key stroke, etc...). The WM_SET_FOCUS and WM_KILL_FOCUS events gives control to an object or takes the control from an object. We can also add user events to set a value to an object, to change its state, etc... . Parameters can be passed with the event.

4.8. The windows

The windows are made of several basic graphical objects. We have five different kinds of windows that correspond to successive refinements.

The root window is the empty window. Its role is to find the object that is under the cursor and to send it an appropriate event. We use the fact that the cursor is always on an object because the window is full of juxtaposed objects.

Dialogue boxes are also empty windows but they are not necessarily full of objects. So, mouse moves are not managed.

Pop-up windows only appear when needed. They inherit from both menu items and windows.

A menu window contains a title that is also used to move the window, corners to grow it, icons to iconify and to magnify it and a menu bar. It can contain a working area and so, it becomes a working area window.

Drawing windows also inherit from menu windows. They contain a graphical working area and an icon box. These icons are used to add, move or modify objects of the schema visualized in the graphical area.

5. THE IMPLEMENTATION OF THE INTERFACE

5.1. The CANDID interface

CANDID is the first drawing interface we have developed using this kernel. The CANDID interface is made of five different windows. The first one, called Schema Window, allows us to design a conceptual schema of the database. It is a drawing window. The second one, called BROWSER, is used to instantiate the database and to introduce instances. Several instances can be presented together in an ARRAY format. Another window makes it possible to present each instance separately. The third window, called Query Window (see figure 7) is used to perform subqueries corresponding to an algebra operation. The fourth window, called the Recapitulative Window, contains the skeleton of the query. Complex queries are decomposed into smaller subqueries through successive steps. The Recapitulative Window contains, in a summarised form, the final query of the user. The last window, called the Result Window, is used for displaying the results in a bucket format.

All these windows, except the Result Window and the BROWSER, have the same graphical aspect. They all seems like drawing windows, even if they are not all.

5.2. The CANDID algebra

The CANDID algebra is the direct support for the implementation of the graphical language. It includes the operations defined in [1] for complex objects and takes also into account the algebra proposed in [10]. Recursive queries, nest, unnest and grouping operations are available. We have voluntarily chosen a non-minimal algebra to offer the greatest ease of use. It is important to note that, for our algebra, results of operations are based on derived subtypes. The space saved by using it is therefore very significative, comparing with other algebras where results are based on tuples. We now list the different operators.

Selection: It defines a new subtype of the selected type and allows the user to eliminate non-desired values according to a selection predicate.

E=select[Pr](E_1).

Cartesian product: It defines an aggregation of two types or more. The result is made of as many subtypes as types taking place in the cartesian product.

E=Product[N_1, ..., N_n](E_1, ..., E_n)

Join: It is just a cartesian product followed by a selection.

E=Join[Pr, N_1, ..., N_n](E_1, ..., E_n).

Projection: It has the same effect as the relational operation. The result has no redundant values.

E=Project[X_1, ..., X_n](E_1).

Extension: It adds a derived attribute to a class that is computed each time its value is read.

E=Extension(E_1, $attr_1$=$Formula_1$, ..., $attr_n$=$Formula_n$).

Union: It makes it possible to gather in a same type, two or more supertypes having a common supertype. The union will be composed of instances of the common supertype that are related to one of the subtypes.

E=Union[Sp](E_1, ..., E_n).

Minus: It returns all the instances of a supertype that are related to the first subtype but not to the others.

E=Minus[Sp](E_1, ..., E_n).

Intersect: It gives all the instances of a supertype that are related to all the subtypes.

E=Intersect[Sp](E_1, ..., E_n).

Nest: It structures an originally flat class.

E=Nest[id=N, N_1, ..., N_n](E_1).

Group of parts: This is the same operation as the "set of parts" operation, except that it returns classes.

E=Group-of-parts(E_1).

Grouping: This operation groups instances of same values.

E=Group[id=N, N_1, ..., N_n](E_1).

Set of parts: It constitutes all the possible combinations we can obtain with the instances of a type. This operation is very expensive and has only been introduced to prove that our algebra is able to take into account recursive queries.

E=Set-of-part(E_1).

Hierarchization: It is obtained from a cyclic attribute and constitutes a more convenient way to solve recursive queries.

E=Hierarchization[attr, father=N_1, son=N_2](E_1).

Collapse: This operation transforms a class into a list that contains all the instances of the class.

E=Collapse(E1)

Unnest: It flattens an originally structured class.

E=Unnest[id=N, N_1, ..., N_n](E_1).

Ungrouping: This corresponds to the unnest operation applied to groups.

E=Ungroup[id=N, N_1, ..., N_n](E_1).

Remark: Null values are treated as exceptions.

5.3. The schema creation

CANDID offers, through the Schema Window, the facilities to design and test the conceptual schema of an application quickly. The user has at its disposal all the tools defined in the upper sections and can assemble them as he wishes, as if he were using an object-oriented drawing software (MACDRAW for example). Once placed, an object can be moved, enlarged, erased, modified, etc... . The working area in which the schema is designed can be larger than the window (see figure 5). From this window, it is also possible to enter instances with the BROWSER and to formulate a query.

The first time it is used, the BROWSER generates a database corresponding to the schema. The user can then enter, add, modify, delete or insert instances. The entering of an instance is done field by field. For fields that do not correspond to a predefined type (ISA relationships and attributes), the user can move among the database by selecting the arrow that represents the indirection.

We envisage to improve the schema readability by using an automatic drawing method like those described in [12].

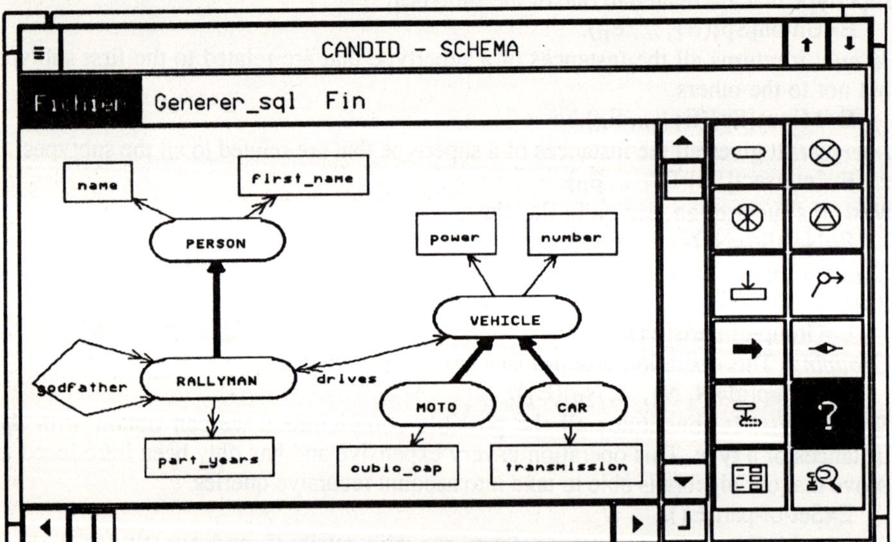

Fig. 5. The CANDID schema editor

5.4. The Recapitulative Window

The query graph display is done automatically as shown in figure 6. Our essential criteria for this drawing is the minimization of the number of crossings between the edges in the graph. The algorithm we used is inspired from [11]. This algorithm is composed of two heuristics, the first one to minimize the number of crossings and the second one to place nodes in an acceptable manner.

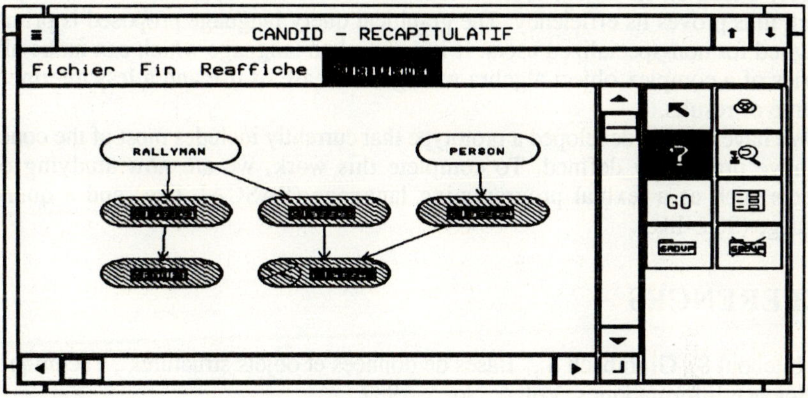

Fig. 6. The Recapitulative Window

This method does not guarantee a minimum for the total number of intersections, but it has the great advantage of providing a good solution quickly. However, depending on the initial configuration, this procedure does not give the best solution for simple cases. So, we have decided to associate to it an exhaustive search for the best solution when the maximum number of nodes at each level is less than 7. A simulated annealing method is used in other cases.

An example of a query graph is shown in figure 7.

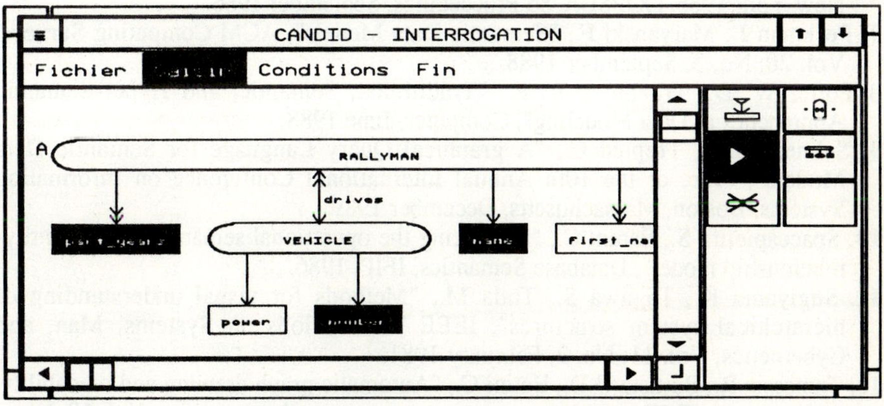

Fig. 7. The Query Window

6. CONCLUSION

The CANDID system is a fully, uniform object-oriented system. It is able to deal with many problems related to the database domain. Its particularities, such as persistence, associations and metaclasses offer the developers capabilities that are available in only very few languages.

The other great particularity of CANDID is its multiwindow graphical interface entirely based on its object system. It is in fact the first application of the system, which thus proves its efficiency. The graphical query language proposed is primarily designed for non-specialized users. It is a complete language which can make all the queries of a complex object algebra with greater ease of use and a less intermediate volume of results.

We have already developed a prototype that currently includes most of the concepts we have previously defined. To complete this work, we are now studying other aspects such as a textual programming language (PASCAL-like) and a querying language (SQL-like).

REFERENCES

1. Abiteboul S., Grumbach S., "Bases de données et objets structurés", Technique et Science Informatiques, Vol. 6, No. 5, 1987.

2. Cointe P., "Metaclasses are first class: the ObjVlisp Model", in Proceedings of the 2nd OOPSLA, Orlando, Florida, 1987.

3. Davist J. P., Bonnell R.D., "Modeling semantics with concept abstraction in the EARL data model", Proc. of the Entity-Relationship Approach, November 1989.

4. Fishman D.H. and al, "Iris: An object-oriented database management system", in Readings in Object-Oriented Database Systems, Morgan Kaufman Publishers, 1990.

5. Hull R., King R., "Semantic database modeling : survey, applications, and research issues", ACM Computing Surveys, Vol. 19, No. 3, September 1987.

6. Maier D. and al., "Developpement of an object-oriented DBMS", ACM/SIGPLAN New-York 1986, OOPSLA '86 Proceedings, September 1986.

7. Peckman J., Maryanski F., "Semantic Data Models", ACM Computing Surveys, Vol. 20, No. 3, September 1988.

8. Potter W. D., Trueblood R. P., "Traditional, Semantic, and Hyper-Semantic Approaches to Data Modeling", Computer, June 1988.

9. Schneider M., Trepied C., "A graphical Query Language for Semantic Data Models", Proc. of the 10th Annual International Conference on Information Systems, Boston, Massachusetts, December 1989.

10. Spaccapiettra S., Parent C., "Enhancing the operational semantics of the entity-relationship model", Database Semantics, IFIP, 1986.

11. Sugiyama K., Tagawa S., Toda M., "Methods for visual understanding of hierarchical system structures", IEEE Transactions on Systems, Man, and Cybernetics, Vol. 11, No. 2, February 1981.

12. Tamassia R., Battista G.D., Batini C., "Automatic graph drawing and readability of diagrams", IEEE transactions on systems, man, and cybernetics, Vol. 18, No. 1, January/February 1988.

Distributed Schema Management in a Cooperation Network of Autonomous Agents

Hamideh Afsarmanesh *, Frank Tuijnman, Michiel Wiedijk, L.O. Hertzberger

Computer Systems Department, University of Amsterdam,
email: hamideh@fwi.uva.nl, frankt@fwi.uva.nl, wiedijk@fwi.uva.nl, bob@fwi.uva.nl

Abstract. For data-intensive, computation-intensive, collaborative engineering application environments such as computer-integrated manufacturing, a natural architecture is a network of loosely-coupled, autonomous, and heterogeneous agents, where each agent runs on a single workstation. Each agent is autonomous in its decision to keep a part of its information private and to share another part of its information with some other agents. Loose and tight interdependencies among agents' information can be defined through the integration and interrelation of agents' schemas. Complex derivation/integration of agents' schemas and their referential integrities can be supported by a schema management mechanism. This facility, that we claim to be essential for cooperating teams in industrial automation applications, is the novel feature presented in this paper. The integrated schema created locally at each agent is a coherent view on the local and the global information accessible by this agent. Hence, the physical and logical distribution of information through the network is entirely hidden from the end user of the network and absent from their queries. The schema management mechanism supports the definition of complex derived types and derived mappings, remote referencing among information stored in various agents, and their referential integrities. The schema management mechanism described here is developed as a part of PEER. PEER is designed and prototypically implemented as part of the Archon abstract machine, which provides an environment for the integration of heterogeneous cooperating expert systems [2].

keywords: object-oriented databases, federated databases, cooperation network, distributed schema management

1 Introduction

In a wide variety of recent application environments (e.g. CAD, CAM and CIM), management of information requires support for exchange and sharing of data and knowledge in a network of inter-related, loosely-coupled, heterogeneous, and autonomous *agents*. Agents have their own independent resources and capabilities, and a team of agents have to accomplish certain tasks. An agent may be completely automated, such as an

---

* On leave from California State University.

[2] The work described here has been partially supported by the ESPRIT II project P2256 (ARCHON) whose partners are: Atlas Elektronik GMBH, JRC Ispra, Framentec-Cognitech SA, Labein, IRIDIA, Iberdrola SA, EA Technology Ltd, Amber SA, Tech. Univ. of Athens, Univ. of Amsterdam, CERN, Queen Mary and Westfield College and Univ. of Porto.

expert system for the control of a plant, but will typically include a human user who is the actual locus of semi-autonomous decision making. In CIM applications, a designer together with a set of design tools, such as drawing programs, viewing tools and stress analysis programs, is modeled as a single agent, that interacts with other agents involved in the same activity (design) or different activities, such as production engineering, production planning, machine control, market analysis, or manufacturing. The typical situation in CIM is that each agent has its own workstation, and many agents store and process a huge amount of data locally. The computing environment to support teams of cooperating agents has to be an open, interactive, distributed environment.

So far, the distributed object-oriented database systems developed (such as in [11]), do not fully support the requirements imposed by a cooperative engineering environment. The cooperation architecture suggested there is a 'restricted' federated database system, in the sense that it supports a relatively tight integration of homogeneous distributed database systems. A single global schema is introduced to support the entire network of database systems. The global shared database is accessible by all users and receives input from all users on the information they are willing to share.

PEER [5] is a federated, object-oriented database management system designed and implemented primarily to support the industrial automation application environments. The design of PEER is influenced by [10], where a federated database system is described as a loose federation of autonomous, heterogeneous distributed database systems without a global schema. The approach suggested by the research described in [6], is related to our approach since it emphasizes the importance of site autonomy, and the problems associated with a single global schema for the network, however it is designed specifically for the relational database systems. The methodologies for distributed database integration presented in [8, 12, 13, 1, 9] can also be mentioned, however the schema integration and the schema derivation primitives of PEER are more elaborate than the 'view definition' and 'view update' described in these publications and only more restricted if an efficient implementation of some features were not feasible in PEER; some of these cases will be later described in the paper.

The significance of this paper lies primarily in defining a schema derivation and integration mechanism for a federated database architecture to support the specification of interdependencies among activities in industrial automation applications. The schema management mechanism is based on an object-oriented data model and language. Complex definition of derived types and derived mappings are supported by a set of derivation/integration primitives. Remote referencing among agents can be established and their referential integrities are supported through the extension of local schemas. The subject of complex object-representation, -identification, and -boundary, and a linearization mechanism developed for complex object transformation into messages is described in [15]. The subject of agents' negotiation on access rights to sharable information and action levels in case of data updates as well as propagation of these rights to support their referential integrities are described in [14]. Detailed description of the distributed query evaluation; namely, conversion algorithms for derived types and derived mappings, kernel-storage of the converted information, query decomposition, and query rewriting are presented in [5]. Other topics, outside the scope of the paper are the data update problems regarding the shared schemas, optimization of distributed query processing and distributed concurrency control that are subjects of forthcoming papers.

A prototype implementation of the PEER federated system has been developed in the C language that runs on a network of SUN-4 workstations. This implementation of PEER is a part of the ESPRIT-Archon project, which develops a system to integrate cooperating expert systems [16]. This prototype is being tested at the control rooms of power distribution networks in two different industries in Spain and England.

The remainder of this paper is organized as follows. First we give an overview of the PEER architecture in Section 2, and its data model and query language in Section 3. An outline of the schema management mechanism is presented in Section 4. In section 5, we discuss the problems that must be resolved by the schema integration mechanism. A set of primitives are defined and exemplified in Section 6 that specify an integrated schema as a collection of derived types and derived mappings. The rationale for definition of these primitives is to support the most practical problems that can be implemented efficiently. Section 6 also describes extending the local schema to support and represent references to remote objects in other agents.

2 The PEER Architecture

PEER [5] defines an information access/sharing mechanism that uses as the base a *global data model*, the object-oriented 3DIS model [3], to represent the information of each agent, and a *global language*, the object-oriented 3DIS/ISL language [4, 7], defined on top of the data model to support agents' interactions. By using the global model, agents' heterogeneous schemas are made homogeneous. However, the homogeneity of schema representation does not address the semantic interrelationships (loose or tight integration) that may exist among the data and knowledge of different agents. These interrelationships are established systematically and incrementally through a set of derivation/integration operations defined for distributed schema management of PEER. Clearly, the query language and its capabilities play a major role in the specification of schema integration among the PEERs. The architecture of the PEER system is shown in Figure 1.

Every PEER is represented by several schemas; one local schema, a number of import and export schemas and one integrated schema. The PEER network has a community dictionary. Its function is to provide up-to-date information on agents. It contains the network addresses of its active agents and their current state. For every agent, it also stores its export schemas, and the access rights and schema modification action levels that the agent supports. The dictionary is also used as the general store for other static information that concerns the entire community such as objects' name-tables. The community dictionary is represented as a separate agent, however, agents can keep local copies of parts of its information.

2.1 Object Identifying and Object Naming

Every object in the PEER network has a globally unique object-identifier (object-id), generated by the agent where it is created. The object-id encodes the 'agent' (PEER-id) and the 'type' (type-id) of the object in the local schema.

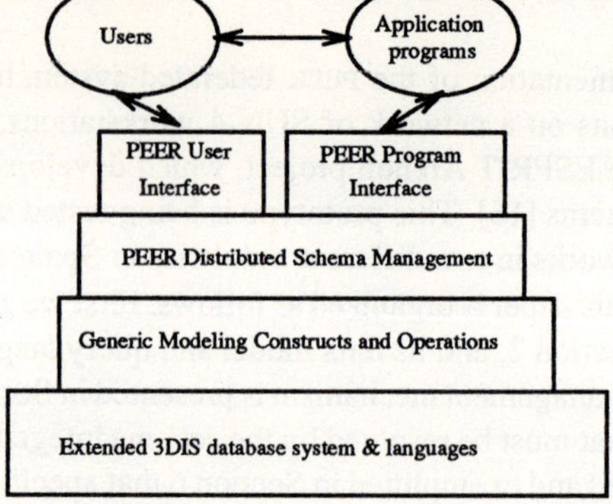

Fig. 1. Architecture of an individual PEER site.

Additional unique identifiers (object-names) can be defined for objects. Object-names are unique within a certain scope. Scopes can be defined for different purposes. A scope may represent a certain schema or a type in the schema, for example to cover all instances of a derived type in the integrated schema. On the other hand, scopes can be defined to support an interest area of: one 'user' (the agent), a project with a 'team' of cooperating users (several agents), or the entire cooperation 'network'. Names known within each scope are stored in one 'name-table', which associates an object-name with an object-id. Every name-table has a network-wide unique name. Name tables that are used by several agents are stored in the community dictionary. Agents can consult the remote name-table (in the community dictionary) whenever a query is evaluated.

3 Data Model and Query/Update Language

The 3DIS [2, 3] is an object-oriented binary-based data model. It supports the fundamental abstractions of instantiation, generalization, and aggregation. Any identifiable piece of information is uniformly represented as objects and different kinds of objects are distinguished by the set of structural and non-structural (data) relationships defined on them. The 3DIS supports multiple inheritance; the schema forms a Directed Acyclic Graph (DAG). The 3DIS data model is extended to support the representation of concepts and entities of the industrial engineering applications and to support the kernel structure of the distributed architecture of PEER.

The 3DIS/ISL information retrieval/manipulation language [4, 7], supports the local access and modification of agents' information, and is used by PEER to support the remote access and sharing of information among agents. The 'retrieval' of information is simply formulated as an ordered triple with: domain-object, mapping-object, and range-object, being its three elements, and in a typical query one or more of these elements is replaced by a '?'.

The 3DIS/ISL language has been extended primarily to facilitate both the specification of the derived/integrated schemas and the rewriting of queries for distributed query evaluation. Two specific extensions that are of particular relevance here are (1) the possibility to use path expressions (mappings separated by dots) as mappings in a query to denote indirect relationships between objects; for example 'retrieve (? , parts-used.designer.name , "Smith")', and (2) the possibility to specify the schema context against which a particular query must be evaluated, either by appending the schema name as the fourth argument in the query itself, or by appending the sign '@' followed by the schema name to each type name and map name that appears in a query. This second extension, together with the rule of uniqueness of names (for types and mappings) in any 3DIS schema, provides a 'globally unique naming system' for all the type names and mapping names of all schemas in a PEER.

4 Distributed Schema Management

The 'local' schema is the private schema defined on the physical data in an agent. Derived from the local schema are 'export' schemas that each define a particular view on some local objects. Export schemas restructure and represent several related concepts in one schema. For every export schema, the exporter agent manages the information on agents who can access it, by keeping their agent-id, their access rights on the exported information, and the agreed schema modification conditions to notify the agents who use this export schema of its changes. To obtain access to data in another agent's export schema, an agent has to input it as 'import' schema.

Originally, an agent's 'integrated' schema is derived from its local schema and various import schemas. In later stages of integration, instead of the local schema, the previous integrated schema will be used as base. At the level of the integrated schema, the physical distribution of information becomes hidden, and the contributing agents are no longer directly visible to the end user. Different PEERs can establish different correspondences between their own schema and other agents' schemas, and thus there is no single global schema for the network.

A query is always evaluated within the context of a single schema specified within the query itself. Queries that originate within an agent (local queries) can in principle be evaluated against any of the schemas in the agent. But, the default schema to process a local query is the agent's integrated schema. Queries that come from another agent (remote queries) are always first evaluated against the appropriate export schema and then (after rewriting) evaluated against the agent's local schema. Notice that actual real transfer of data occurs only when the importer agent tries to access the instances of the imported type, the same way as accessing the instances of the types local to the agent. Therefore, the information is not stored redundantly in the network.

5 Defining an Integrated Schema

In creating a new integrated schema obviously, designers' preference is always to keep the structure defined locally in its own integrated schema as the base and incrementally integrate a part of other import schemas to it. In this section, for simplicity, we only consider the integration problem of two schemas (i.e. the integrated and an import schemas). We discuss the complexities of this process through some examples and for each example describe an integration solution. Later, in Section 6 we define schema derivation/integration primitives that formulate these solutions and more complex kinds of schema integration examples. Please notice that in every case, there are several ways that the integration can be established however, the final decision on how to integrate two schemas is made by the database designer.

Three cases of integration are distinguished:

case 1 Integrating 'semantically unrelated' information systems; for example, a system containing information about old catalogs and another about modern aircraft. In this case, each "object" will only be represented in one of the two systems, and the objects are totally unrelated.

An integrated schema is obtained by simply placing the top level types of both schemas under a new *root* (the highest node in the 3DIS-kernel hierarchy [3]). Logically the two systems remain completely separated, but the outcome of integration is that the physical distribution becomes transparent to the user.

case 2 Integrating 'semantically related but, with disjoint context and schema' information systems. These are the information systems where an "object" will only be represented in one of the two systems, but the objects that are represented in one system can be related to those represented in another system. For example, a system containing information about catalogs on modern aircraft, and a different system containing information about modern aircraft. Catalogs are only represented in the first system, aircrafts only in the second, but one may wish to represent that certain catalogs are on certain aircrafts.

An integrated schema is again obtained by placing the top level types of both schemas under a new root. However, in this case mappings to remote schema must be introduced to relate the types from one system to the other (remote references). As a result, objects defined in one system will become related to objects in the other system. Remote reference 'access rights' must be negotiated between the two databases to support the referential integrities.

case 3 Integrating 'semantically related, with common context but distinct schema' information systems. These are the information systems where an object can be represented in both systems. For example, two systems containing information about modern aircraft with partially overlapping information.

This is the most complicated form of schema integration of the two systems. Some of the problems that arise in this case are exemplified below. In the solution presented for each integration example, inside the parenthesis we add the names of the *derivation primitives* (described in Section 6) that can be used to formulate these derivations.

- Semantically equivalent entities with similar or distinct names. For instance, when the two types 'PRODUCT' and 'COMPONENT' with mappings 'capacity' and 'has-capacity' are respectively defined in the integrated and an import schema. A new type PRODUCT must be defined in the integrated schema containing all instances of the other two types (*type union*). A new mapping must be defined representing both of the other two mappings (*map union*). There may be some differences in the set of characteristics that describe each object in the two systems, for instance, integrated schema may represent the 'estimated-cost' as a mapping of type PRODUCT while imported schema may not represent it at all. Of course in this case, the mapping estimated-cost will be defined on PRODUCT.

- Different classification principles on semantically related entities. The type structures in the two systems may imply a different classification strategy for objects. For example, the integrated schema may have the two types 'UNDER-DEVELOP' and 'COMPLETE' as subtypes of 'PRODUCT', where 'COMPLETE' has a mapping 'price-paid' that represents the price of products bought from other suppliers. Now, the import schema may have the two subtypes 'IN-HOUSE' and 'PROCURED' for its type 'PRODUCT'. An integration that captures all the semantics represented in these two schemas defines a type PRODUCT with two subtypes INHOUSE and PROCURED, where the INHOUSE type has the two subtypes UNDERDEVELOP and COMPLETE. The type PROCURED contains all instances of 'PROCURED' from import schema and all instances of 'COMPLETE' from integrated schema except for those instances where the 'price-paid' is "0" (*type restrict*). Similarly, the type COMPLETE contains all instances of 'COMPLETE' from integrated schema except for those where 'price-paid' is not "0" (*type restrict*).
- Different definition principles on semantically equivalent entities. Even though the description of the information represented in both systems is the same, the two systems may have different notions of the objects. For example, an import schema may represent the catalog-entry of a product as a separate object; thus 'PRODUCT' has a mapping 'catalog-entry' relating it to type 'CATALOG-ENTRY' with three mappings of 'year', 'section', and 'page' defined on it. While the integrated schema has the mappings 'catalog-year', 'catalog-section', and 'catalog-page' defined for type 'PRODUCT', without grouping those attributes together in a single object. A new type PRODUCT must be defined with the catalog-year, catalog-section, and catalog-page mappings defined on it, where catalog-year represents both the 'catalog-year' of the original integrated schema and the 'year' of the 'catalog-entry' (*threaded map*) of the 'PRODUCT' from the imported schema.

In all of the above cases, duplicate names of semantically unrelated derived types and derived maps must be renamed (*type rename* and *map rename*) for uniqueness in the integrated schema. Semantically related types and maps with duplicate names must be handled case by case as shown above.

The schema integration/derivation primitives of PEER (described in Section 6) are designed to deal with these and other integration complications. An integrated type is constructed from other types by the union, restrict, and subtract primitives. Map integration is accomplished by specifying a map as either a union of other maps, or as a threaded map, or some combination of these two primitives. This derivation process supports deriving a type while hiding some of its member objects, but it prohibits the creation of objects that do not have *physical existence* in the network. For instance, it is not possible to aggregate arbitrary maps to form new types as it is described in [1] to create 'imaginary' objects. This restriction is put on the current design of PEER partially due to the semantic problems associated with creating arbitrary objects, and partially due to the implementation inefficiencies. The naming conflict problem among schemas are simply resolved by the naming strategy of PEER described in Section 3.

6 Schema Integration/Derivation Primitives

The following schema derivation/integration primitives define the relationships between the types and maps in the derived (or integrated) schema[3] and the types in the base schemas (called the base types). For example, to derive the agent's integrated schema for the first time, the base schemas are the local schema and the import schemas. Now first, the integrated types must be defined from their base types to appropriately classify all objects in the integrated schema; this is specified by type derivation expressions. The next step is to use map derivation expressions to define mappings (derived mappings) for each derived type, using the base mappings originally defined on the base types.

6.1 Type Derivation

A derived type is defined by a type derivation expression as follows:

derived-type-definition := *derived-type-name* = <*T-expr*>
T-list := <*T-expr*> | <*T-expr*> , <*T-list*>
T-expr := *type-name@schema-name* | **union** (<*T-expr*> , <*T-list*>) |
subtract (<*T-expr*> , <*T-expr*>) | **restrict** (<*T-expr*> , *restriction*)

Below, the semantics of the type derivation primitives are provided, where every 'T_i' stands for a "type-name@schema-name", 'I(T_i)' represents the set of all members of type T_i, 'a' represents a member object, and the 'restriction(a)=TRUE' denotes a 3DIS/ISL query that checks if 'a' satisfies the restriction. In this query, the restriction will be transformed into a regular 3DIS/ISL 'condition' defined on members of type T_i, [4] contains the definition and examples of these conditions. In the examples that follow 'LOC' is the local schema and 'IMPn' is the import schema 'n'.

1. Type Rename
   T = T_1
   interprets as: a $\in$ I(T) $\Leftrightarrow$ a $\in$ I(T_1),
   where T is the derived type and T_1 is a type in a base schema S_1.
   example: PRODUCT = COMPONENT@IMP3
2. Type Union
   T = **union** (T_1, ..., T_n)
   interprets as: a $\in$ I(T) $\Leftrightarrow$ a $\in$ I(T_j),
   where 1 <= j <= n, T is the derived type and T_j is a type in a base schema S_j.
   example: UNFINISHED-PROD = union (UNDER-DEVELOP@IMP3,
   UNFINISHED-PROD@LOC)
3. Type Subtract
   T = **subtract** (T_1, T_2)
   interprets as: a $\in$ I(T) $\Leftrightarrow$ a $\in$ I(T_1) $\wedge$ a $\notin$ I(T_2),
   where T is the derived type and T_1 and T_2 are types from base schemas S_1 and S_2.
   example: GS-PRODUCT = subtract (COMPONENT@IMP3,
   PROCURED-COMPONENT@IMP3)

   Due to the support of multiple inheritance in 3DIS, T_2 does not have to be a subtype of T_1 in to apply the subtract primitive to them.

[3] referred to as either derived types and integrated types in the remaining of this section.

4. Type Restrict

   T = restrict (T1, restriction)

   interprets as: $a \in I(T) \Leftrightarrow a \in I(T1) \wedge$ restriction(a)=TRUE,

   where T is the derived type and T_1 is a type in a base schema S_1.

   example: MAJOR-PRODUCT = restrict (PRODUCT@IMP2, [estimated-cost > 3000])

Following is a BNF-like description of restrictions, where '=E' denotes an 'element of' and '!E' denotes 'not an element of'.

restriction := [<predicate>]
predicate := <simple-predicate> | <complex-predicate>
simple-predicate := <mapping-object> <RE> <range-object> |
<mapping-object> <SE> <set-of-range-objects>
complex-predicate := NOT (<predicate>) | (<predicate>) AND (<predicate>) |
(<predicate>) OR (<predicate>)
RE := = | <> | > | >= | < | <=
SE := =E | !E

6.2 Map Derivation

A derived mapping is defined by a map derivation expression as follows:

derived-map-definition := *derived-map-name* = *<m-expr>*
m-list := *<m-expr>* | *<m-expr>* , *<m-list>*
m-expr := *map-name@schema-name* | { *<m-list>* } | *<m-expr>* . *<m-expr>*

Semantics of the primitives defined for map integration are provided below, where the union primitive is represented by '{ , }', the treading primitive is represented by '.', every 'm_i' in the following definitions stands for a "mapping-name@schema-name" and 'a.m' stands for the range-object (value) related to object 'a' by mapping 'm'.

1. Map Rename

   m = m_1

   interprets as: a.m = b $\Leftrightarrow a.m_1 =$ b,

   where m is a mapping of type T in the derived schema and m_1 is a mapping of type T_1 in a base schema S_1, and where T and T_1 are not disjoint.

   example: designer-name = designer@IMP1

2. Map Union

   m = { $m_1,\ldots,m_n$ }

   interprets as: a.m = b $\Leftrightarrow a.m_i =$ b,

   where m is a mapping of type T in the derived schema, 1 <= i <= n and m_i is a mapping of type T_i in schema S_i, and where for all i, 1 <= i <= n, T and T_i are not disjoint.

   example: capacity = { capacity@LOC, has-size@IMP1 }

3. Map Threading

   m = $m_1.m_2. \ldots .m_n$

   interprets as: a.m = k $\Leftrightarrow a.m_1 = b \wedge b.m_2 = c \wedge \ldots \wedge j.m_n =$ k,

   where m is a mapping of type T in the derived schema, and m_i is a mapping of type T_i in a base schema S_i, and where T and T_1 may not be disjoint.

   example: subpart-producer = parts-used@IMP1 . manufacturer@IMP1

```
define-schema LOC used-schema —
type FINISHED_PRODUCT
    price: INTEGER
    catalog_no: INTEGER
    parts_used: FINISHED_PRODUCT
end-schema LOC
----------------------------------------------------------------
define-schema IMP1 same-as-export-schema EXP3 from-agent A4
type PRODUCT
    product_no: INTEGER
    OEM_subparts: PRODUCT
    locally_manufactured_subparts: PRODUCT
    value_estimate: VALUE
    model: STRING
type UNDER_DEVELOPMENT_PRODUCT subtype-of PRODUCT
    designer: STRING
    release_date: STRING
type VALUE
    market_price: INTEGER
    date: STRING
end-schema IMP1
----------------------------------------------------------------
derive-schema INT from-schema LOC, IMP1
type FINISHED_PRODUCT
    price: INTEGER
    catalog_no: INTEGER
    parts_used: FINISHED_PRODUCT
    model_description: STRING
- - - - - - - - - - - - - - - - - - - - - - - - -
derivation-specification
FINISHED_PRODUCT =
    union(FINISHED_PRODUCT@LOC,
        subtract(PRODUCT@IMP1,
                UNDER_DEVELOPMENT_PRODUCT@IMP1))
price = {price@LOC, value_estimate@IMP1.market_price@IMP1}
catalog_no = { catalog_no@LOC, product_no@IMP1 }
parts_used = { parts_used@LOC, OEM_subparts@IMP1,
             locally_manufactured_subparts@IMP1 }
model_description: model@IMP1
end-schema INT
----------------------------------------------------------------
```

Fig. 2. Example of schema integration

```
define-schema LOC used-schema IMP8
type CATALOG
    ...
    has-entry: APPLIANCE-PROD
extended-local-type APPLIANCE-PROD
- - - - - - - - - - - - - - - -
derivation-specification
APPLIANCE-PROD = PRODUCT@IMP8
end-schema LOC
----------------------------------------------------------------
define-schema IMP8 same-as-export-schema EXP4
                                    from-agent A2
type PRODUCT
    p-number: STRING
    description: PRODUCT-DSCRPT
    type PRODUCT-DSCRPT
    color: STRING
    size: INTEGER
    model: STRING
end-schema IMP8
----------------------------------------------------------------
derive-schema INT from-schema LOC, IMP8
type CATALOG
    ...
    has-entry: ITEM
type ITEM
    item-no: STRING
    item-model: STRING
- - - - - - - - - - - - - - - -
derivation-specification
CATALOG = CATALOG@LOC
...
has-entry = has-entry@LOC
ITEM = PRODUCT@IMP8
item-no = p-number@IMP8
item-model =
has-entry@LOC.description@IMP8.model@IMP8
end-schema INT
----------------------------------------------------------------
```

Fig. 3. Example of extended local types

A derived/integrated schema must preserve the properties that are common to all 3DIS database schemas. These properties include: (1) two types in one schema are either disjoint (have no common instances) or have a common subtype, (2) all instances of a subtype are also instances of all its supertypes, and (3) the two objects related by a mapping m, are instances of the domain type and the range type of that mapping respectively. The designer of derived schemas must consider these properties, however, PEER system also automatically checks if the inter-schema and intra-schema properties are maintained [5].

Figure 2 is an example to demonstrate the schema integration language and the specification of different schemas for one agent. In this example, we refer to the local-schema as LOC; the integrated-schema as INT; the import-schemas are represented by IMP concatenated with a number, e.g. IMP1 and IMP6; and the export-schemas are similarly named, for example EXP2 and EXP4. Different *schema definition environments* specify the defined and derived schemas.

6.3 Extending the Local Schema

There is an important case of schema integration between two agents that requires extending the local schema by a special kind of derived type called 'extended-local type'. Extended local types are defined to establish remote references among specific objects of this agent and some other agents. Essentially, the local schema defines only the type structures that describe locally stored objects. We make an exception to this: when instances of a local type are related by a mapping m_1 to some remote objects in another PEER, the range type of m_1 (an imported type at this agent) has to be defined in its local schema as an extended local type. Mappings cannot be defined on extended local types, so that their instances are locally represented only by their object-identifiers.

An example is the case where agent A_1 has the information on CATALOG and agent A_2 has the information on PRODUCT. An export schema of A_2 (EXP4) contains the type PRODUCT and the agent A_1 imports it into its IMP8 schema. Now in A_1 as shown in Figure 3, in order to establish the relationship between the catalog and their entry-items, we must add a new mapping 'has-entry' on the type CATALOG in its local schema. The range type for this mapping will be defined as an extended local type APPLIANCE-PROD, derived from the PRODUCT type in IMP8. An extended local type is defined in the local schema through specifying its derivation expression. Now, the (remote) object-ids of objects of type APPLIANCE-PROD related to CATALOG, are (physically) stored in A_1. In the INT schema of A_1, the derivation specification of the 'item-model' mapping for the type ITEM (renamed type for PRODUCT@IMP8) uses the 'has-entry' mapping at LOC to establish the remote reference to the actual 'model' description of ITEM.

7 Conclusion

This paper presents a distributed schema management mechanism to support the requirements set by the cooperating teams of autonomous agents in an industrial engineering application. Interdependencies among agents are defined through the integration and interrelation of agents' schemas. A federated architecture is presented to provide mechanisms for complex information sharing and information interrelationships, while supporting agent's autonomy. Agents can import the information shared by other agents in order to respond to local and remote queries. Since each agent defines its own 'integrated' schema, several views on the entire application can easily coexist, and there is no need for a single schema to be agreed upon and administered centrally. The schema management mechanism described here supports various kinds of tight and loose coupling among agents, and the complex derivation/integration of agents' schemas and their referential integrities. The schema management mechanism described here is developed as a part of PEER [16]. PEER is designed and prototypically implemented as part of the Archon abstract machine, which provides an environment for the integration of heterogeneous cooperating expert systems.

Acknowledgments

The authors wish to thank Martin Bergman and Peter Trenning for their work on the implementation of PEER, and their contributions to its design. Additionally the authors thank the partners of the Archon project for many fruitful discussions.

References

1. S. Abiteboul and A. Bonner. Objects and Views. In *Proceedings ACM SIGMOD91*, pages 238–247, May 1991.
2. H. Afsarmanesh, D. Knapp, D. McLeod, and A. Parker. An Extensible Object-Oriented Approach to Databases for VLSI/CAD. In *Proceedings 11th International Conference on Very Large Data Bases*, pages 13–24, 1985. reprinted in "Readings in Object-Oriented Database Systems" (S. Zdonik and D. Maier, editors), Morgan Kaufmann Publishers, 1990.
3. H. Afsarmanesh and D. McLeod. The 3DIS: An Extensible Object-Oriented Information Management Environment. *ACM Transaction on Information Systems*, 7:339–377, October 1989.
4. H. Afsarmanesh, F. Tuijnman, P. Trenning, and G. Wiedijk. The 3DIS/ISL User Manual. Technical Report CS-92-08, Dept. of Computer Systems, University of Amsterdam, June 1992.
5. H. Afsarmanesh, F. Tuijnman, and G. Wiedijk. PEER: A Distributed Object Management System for Industrial Automation. Technical Report CS-93-05, Dept. of Computer Systems, University of Amsterdam, March 1993.
6. R. Alonse, D. Barbará, and S. Cohn. Data Sharing in a Large Heterogeneous Environment. In *Proceedings Seventh Int. Conf. on Data Engineering*, pages 305–313. IEEE, April 91.
7. M. Bergman. Design Document for the NetISAM Implementation of the 3DIS Database System and Language. Technical Report Archon/UvA/TN12/7-92, Dept. of Computer Systems, University of Amsterdam, July 1992.
8. R. Elmasri, J. Larson, and S.B Navathe. Integration algorithms for federated databases and logical database design. Technical report, Honeywell Corparate Research Center, 1987. submitted for publication.
9. S. Heiler and S. Zdonik. Object Views: Extending the Vision. In *Proceedings Sixth Int. Conf. on Data Engineering*, pages 86–93. IEEE, February 1990.
10. D. Heimbigner and D. McLeod. A Federated Architecture for Information Management. *ACM Transaction on Information Systems*, 3(3):253–278, July 1985.
11. W. Kim, N. Ballou, J.F. Garza, and D. Woelk. A Distributed Object-Oriented Database System Supporting Shared and Private Databases. *ACM Transaction on Information Systems*, 9(1):31–51, January 1991.
12. W. Litwin. From database systems to multidatabase systems: Why and how. In *Proc. The 6th British National Conference on Databases*, pages 161–188, July 1988.
13. A. Motro and P. Buneman. Constructing Superviews. In *Proceedings of ACM SIGMOD International Conference on the Management of Data*, April 1981.
14. F. Tuijnman and H. Afsarmanesh. Distributed Objects in a Federation of Autonomous Cooperating Agents. In *Int. Conf. on Intelligent and Cooperative Information Systems*. IEEE/AAAI, May 1993.
15. F. Tuijnman and H. Afsarmanesh. Sharing Complex Objects in a Distributed PEER Environment. In *13th Int. Conf. on Distributed Computing Systems*. IEEE, May 1993.
16. T. Wittig, editor. *ARCHON: An Architecture for Multi-agent Systems*. Ellis Horwood, 1992.

A Distributed AI System for Job Shop Control

Werner Dilger, Stephan Kassel

European Business School, Schloss Reichartshausen
D-6227 Oestrich-Winkel, Germany

Abstract. Self Organizing Production Processes (SOPP) are an alternative to the job shop control, i.e. they follow the time- and capacity management of PPS systems. The basic idea with the SOPPs is to regard the units involved in the production process as autonomously acting agents that compete with each other for orders that are to be processed. The objectve of each unit is to maximize the added value by minimizing processing time, down times, stores etc. The communication between the single units, required for the organization of the production process, is managed by a blackboard like agent, called the broker. In order to fit to this principle of process organization, a production process must be based on flexible manufacturing cells having partly identical functions thus creating a parallel manufacturing environment.

1 Introduction

Multi–agent systems have been suggested for the solution of complex problems. Using several agents instead of a single system can improve the problem solving abilities by increasing the efficiency of the problem solving process and by making complex problems tractable. Flexible manufacturing systems (FMS) allow for manufacturing of relatively small lot sizes and for rapidly reorganizing the lines of production according to the demands of the customers. They are based on the cooperation of flexible manufacturing cells and automated guided vehicles. The cells and the vehicles have their own control programs coordinating their activities with the overall process control. Thus they are to some degree autonomous, but not very far.

Usually control structures of FMSs follow the lines of a global plan, which requires time consuming replanning in case of disturbances. The concept of *Self Organizing Production Processes* (SOPP) for FMS control is aimed to avoid this drawback. The basic idea of SOPP is to regard the units involved in the FMS as a community of autonomously acting agents that organize themselves to reach the objectives of the production plan. The agents behave like separate business units, each of them trying to increase its own profit. SOPP has two main advantages over conventional process control. Firstly, no global process plan and centralized control is needed, and secondly, events such as disturbances or changes of plant configuration have no influence on the progress of the process as long as there are some entities available for each function that is needed in the process, thus no replanning is required.

In the next section the broker concept is introduced which is central for the SOPP approach. Section 3 presents models of the two main types of agents that are needed. The effect of the profit–oriented mode of operation of the single agents (SOPP) is described in section 4. The implementation of SOPP is sketched in section 5. Finally in section 6 we compare our approach with others.

2 The broker concept

In the world of markets, a broker acts as a mediator between several participants in the market process. He manages the exchange of goods, money, real estates, or informations. In SOPP, the broker has to handle the exchange of informations between the agents, which is exclusively done via the broker, i.e. it is centralized. This restricts the ways of possible communication. Therefore the agents need not know each other, they just have to know the broker, like in the market process. This has the advantage that the set of available agents need not be fixed. This corresponds to the fact that in an FMS the number of available production units changes very often due to breakdowns that may occur for different reasons.

The broker also serves as a blackboard. As such, he exhibits at any time the actual status of the manufacturing process. As a special agent, he has also some important additional tasks like announcing jobs to the production agents, accepting their bids, evaluating the bids, an selecting the agent with the best bid. He can also manipulate the priorities of the jobs to make them more attractive for the production agents.

3 Modeling the agent types

The class of SOPP agents can be divided into the subclasses of *production agents* and *mediating agents*. The class of production agents can be divided into the subclasses of manufacturing and transport agents, which may have a number of instances. The class of *mediating agents* consists of the subclasses of *planning agents* and *brokers* with just one instance each. The hierarchy of agents is illustrated in figure 1.

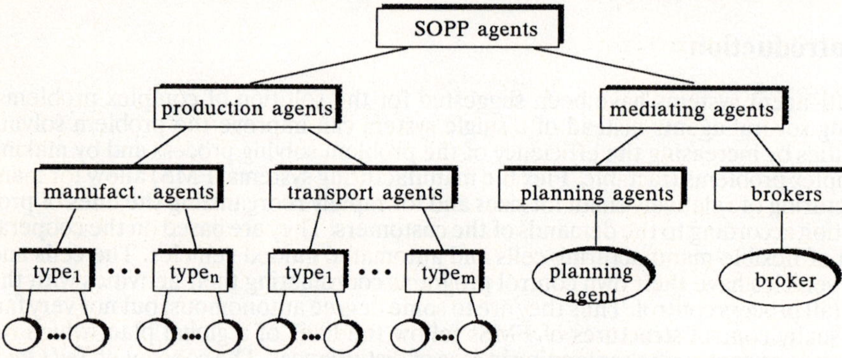

Figure 1: The hierarchy of SOPP agents.

The flow of information between the agents is illustrated by figure 2. The broker is the center of information exchange and the planning agent serves as the link between the production planning system and the community of agents via the broker. In the following subsections the main types of agents are described in more detail.

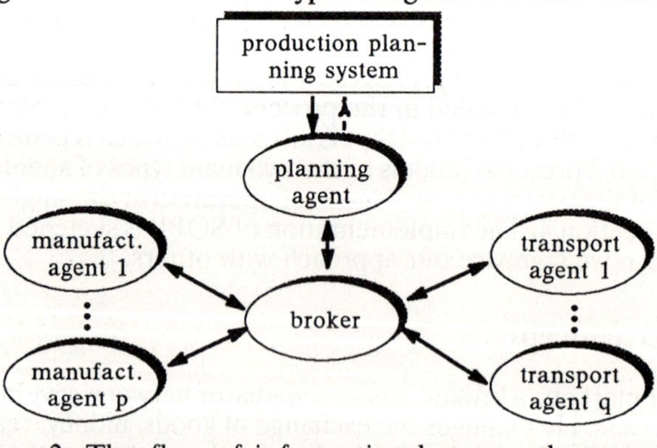

Figure 2: The flow of information between the agents.

3.1 The Broker

The broker concept was described in section 2. The structure of the broker agent is shown in figure 3. The broker agent has to handle the work-orders from the planning agent, processing bids from the manufacturing agents, transportation bids from the transport agents, he has to show the actual process state, and he has to handle all the messages that he receives from and sends to the other agents. The broker's central role in the progress of a SOPP process is described in section 4.

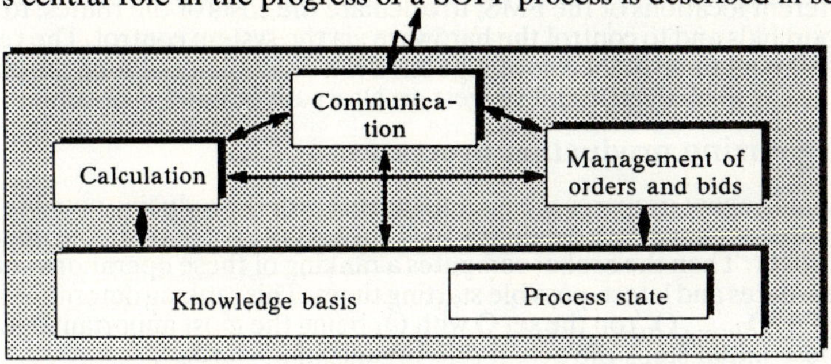

Figure 3: The structure of the broker agent.

3.2 The Production Agents

The structure and behavior is basically the same for all manufacturing agents, therefore it is described once for the whole class of those agents and we speak of *the* manufacturing agent, correspondingly for the transport agents. The structure of both types of agents is roughly the same, it is shown in figure 4.

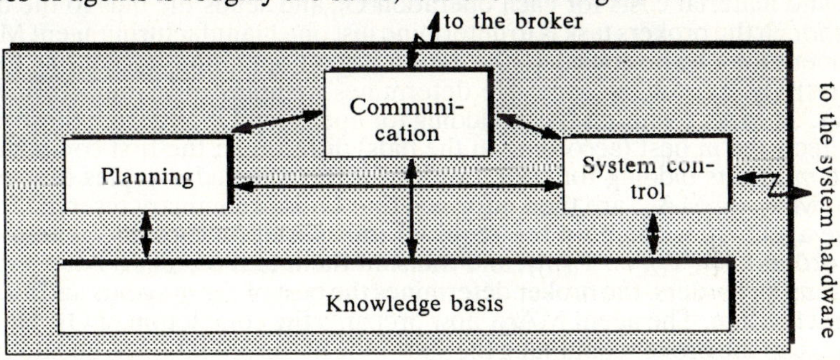

Figure 4: The structure of the production agents.

The manufacturing agent. The communication component manages the communication with the broker. It receives announcements of tasks that can be processed by the agent and transfers them to the planning component. The planning component has to calculate costs and to determine an optimal schedule for the machines. The best result is transferred to the broker agent via the communication component. When the manufacturing agent is informed that a task has been reserved for him, the planning component has to create the transport orders for needed tools, materials, and parts. A due-date is assigned to each of them, that is used by the transport agents to decide if the order is acceptable to them. The system control is the link between the planning facilities and the hardware of the manufacturing cell. It receives the information about the actual states of all parts of the manufacturing cell by appropriate sensors and controls the activities of these parts. In particular it is responsible for the correct handling of materials from and to the transport agents, for quality control, and for the dialogue with the human operator.

The transport agent. The task of the transport agent is to carry goods between different locations. For this purpose he must know the environment in which he moves and he must be able to react to disturbances that may occur. In addition, he has to communicate with the broker, to receive transport orders and to calculate bids for these orders, i.e. to calculate costs of routes, and to return them to the broker. The system control handles the communication between the hardware of the transport agent and the planning component The planning component has to plan routes between different locations of the FMS, to calculate the costs of the routes, to generate transport bids and to control the hardware via the system control. The required knowledge is contained in the knowledge base. If a disturbance occurs, the planning component has to analyze it and suggest an alternative route, if possible.

4 Self organizing production processes

The planning agent prepares the manufacturing orders producing possible operation sequences assigned with deadlines and transfers the set of treatable operations **O** to the broker. Then the broker computes a ranking of these operations considering the due–dates and latest–possible starting times. This ranking determines a total ordering $(O_1, O_2, \dots, O_p)$ on the set **O** with O_1 being the most important operation.

After these initial steps the actual self–organization starts:

The manufacturing agents which soon will be ready to work on some new operations, send messages to the broker containing their communication address, their abilities, and the earliest time when they can start to work on a new operation. For each manufacturing agent M_k the broker determines a subset $\{O_{k1}, O_{k2}, \dots, O_{kl}\} \subseteq \mathbf{O}$ of operations that fit to the abilities of the manufacturing agent and are considered as the most urgent ones. He transmits this subset to the manufacturing agent. If the transmitted subset was not empty, the manufacturing calculates the expected time and material costs for each operation O_{ij} and sends the bids to the broker.

Although the brokers task is to determine just one manufacturing agent MA_{O1} for the operation O_1, he considers the *n* most urgent operations (according to certain criteria) $O_1, \dots, O_n$ at once. He determines *n*–tuples of manufacturing agents $(MA_{j1}, \dots, MA_{jn})$, where MA_{ji} is bidding for operation O_i, and from those *n*–tuples he selects the *m* best (according to the bids) differing in the first component.

The *m* agents bidding for operation O_1 in the selected *n*–tuples of agents, say $MA_1, MA_2, \dots, MA_m$, are then informed that O_1 is preliminary reserved for them. These agents now compute the required transportation capacity, generate transport orders $\{T_{i1}, T_{i2}, \dots, T_{ik(i)}\}$, and transmit them to the broker. After evaluating the transport orders, the broker determines the best of the *m* agents and awards the contract to him. The agent MA_{O1} now prepares the completion of O_1. He sends a message to the broker containing the start time of the operation to update the global database of the PPS system. With this update, the planning agent can determine new operations with their earliest possible starting times and transmit these new operations to the broker starting a new round of the game.

The transport orders are handled in a similar way. Each transport agent which soon will be ready for a transport job, sends a message to the broker containing the possible goods he can carry, his id, and the possible start time for doing a job. The broker then computes a subset $\{T_{i1}, T_{i2}, \dots, T_{in(i)}\}$ for each transport agent TA_i with appropriate transport orders for the agent. This subset is transmitted to TA_i.

The transport agent computes the time he needs to handle each job T_{ik}. Then he transfers his bids for the most preferable jobs to do. He can handle at most one job for each manufacturing agent, because normally the transport orders for one manufacturing agent have to be done at the same time. However, a transport agent can deliver bids for several manufacturing agents with the same reserved operation, because only one of the *m* agents will be awarded with the contract and the other bids are rejected. If in this first turn there are transport orders without bids from any transport agent, these orders will be announced again with a higher priority.

The broker again waits for a period to give each interested agent a chance to send his bids for the due transport jobs. After that he determines the best bids for each outstanding transport order. When all transport orders assigned to the same manufacturing operation, say O_1, are bidded for, the broker determines the best of the *m* bids of the manufacturing agents that got a preliminary reservation for this operation, say MA_{O1}. He awards the contract for operation O_1 to MA_{O1} and the contracts for the required transport jobs to the corresponding transport agents. The transport agents respond sending messages about their starting and completion time to the broker for updating the global database of the PPS system.

5 Implementation

The SOPP system has been implemented on a Siemens WS–30 Workstation with the UNIX operating system. The graphics window system was X11, Release 3, with the Motif Window Manager. The implementation language was C++. We decided to use C++, because this language is object-oriented and uses features of C. The use of C simplified the programming of the communication routines for all agents. For the handling of multiple processes we used the inherent facilities of UNIX to achieve a quasi-parallelism of the agents.

Each agent is implemented as a separate process. The processes are conducted by the operating system. To achieve a simulation environment, we built a master process. It starts all agents, simulates a clock and allows to bring disturbances to the system. The production agents simulate their own behavior in the manufacturing process by an appropriate delay. This delay is managed by the progress of the simulated clock of the master. The human user of the system can give new work-orders to the system, create or abolish production agents, which corresponds to a change in the manufacturing environment, and control the progress of simulated time, which allows him to fasten up or slow down the simulation speed of the system.

6 Comparison with other approaches

SOPP is basically a "Decentralized AI" approach [2], [3], [4]. According to this approach, the existence of a community of autonomous agents is assumed. Each of the agents exists and acts independently of the other agents and has its own intentions. The same holds for the SOPP agents. A means for the communication between autonomous agents is the contract net [6]. In the contract net, an agent can take on the roles of a manager and a contractor. As a manager he has to divide a given task into subtasks and to announce them to potential contractors that feel able to solve any subtasks. Then he must select the best of the potential contractors according to their bids. A contractor can either solve the subtask or can himself take on the role of a manager and divide the subtask into sub–subtasks etc. A prototypical system for the control of manufacturing on the basis of the contract net was developped by Parunak [5]. The contract net has two major drawbacks: a lot of communication is needed to solve a non–trivial task and the agents must know each other, at least in part. By means of the broker concept, both disadvantages are avoided in SOPP.

Sycara et al. developped a prototypical control system where the agents communicate to limited extent [7]. They partly know their environment and take it into regard in their decisions. The communication is mainly needed for the solution of conflicts and the access to shared resources. Resources are passive units but the access to them is controlled by special supervisor agents. In contrast to this approach, resources are modeled in SOPP as autonomous agents. They must have the intention to satisfy the lines of the production plan with respect to the priorities of access as good as possible.

SOPP as a production management model has some similarities with the Kanban principle (cf. [1]) and with load–oriented production control (LOPC) [8]. According to Kanban, a production process is initiated by the retrieval of finished goods from the stock. The retrieval starts a chain of production requests in order to replace the kind and quantity of the retrieved final product. Kanban processes are to a high degree self organized, like SOPP processes. However, Kanban fits best to processes with clearly defined seqences of operations, as in belt production. On the other hand, LOPC is a centralized process control. It controls the queues at the manufacturing cells and depending on the lengths of the queues it decides when the next operation is handed over to a cell. Thus LOPC is well suited for FMSs. However as a centralized control system, it can not sufficiently exploit the modularity of FMSs.

7 Conclusion

We have described a system of autonomous agents that are able to control a manufacturing process in a highly flexible way. The control is achieved just by the fact that each agent follows his own intentions. Therefore a manufacturing process controlled in this way can be regarded as self organizing. We have described the structure of each agent type and have indicated their functioning and the progress of the SOPP process. We plan to develop the SOPP model further by providing the agents with intention modules, limited facilities for direct communication with other agents and learning capability to acquire some knowledge about their environment.

Acknowledgements. We want to thank Alexander Cappius, Hans-Peter Güllich, Cristopher Herzfeld, Ralf Peters, Burkhard Schüttler, and Frank Ziech who have made substantial contributions to this work.

References

1. J. Browne, J. Harhen, J. Shivnan: Production management systems, a CIM perspective. Addison–Wesley Publ., Wokingham 1988.
2. C. Castelfranchi: Social power, a point missed in multi-agent, DAI, and HCI. In: Y. Demazeau, J.-P. Müller (eds.): Decentralized A.I. Proceedings of the First European Workshop on Modelling Autonomous Agents in a Multi-Agent World. Cambridge, England, Aug. 1989; Elsevier Science Publ. B.V., Amsterdam, 1990, 49 - 62.
3. Y. Demazeau, J.-P. Müller: Decentralized Artificial Intelligence. In: Y. Demazeau, J.-P. Müller (eds.): Decentralized A.I. Proceedings of the First European Workshop on Modelling Autonomous Agents in a Multi-Agent World. Cambridge, England, Aug. 1989; Elsevier Science Publ. B.V., Amsterdam, 1990, 3 - 13.
4. J.-R. Galliers: The positive role of conflict in cooperative multi-agents systems. In: Y. Demazeau, J.-P. Müller (eds.): Decentralized A.I. Proceedings of the First European Workshop on Modelling Autonomous Agents in a Multi-Agent World. Cambridge, England, Aug. 1989; Elsevier Science Publ., Amsterdam, 1990, 33 - 46.
5. H.V.D. Parunak: Manufacturing experience with the contract net. In: M.N. Huhns (ed.): Distributed Artificial Intelligence. Pitman Publ., London 1987, 285 - 310.
6. R.G. Smith: The contract net protocol: High level communication and control in a distributed problem solver. In: A.H. Bond, L. Gasser (eds.): Readings in Distributed Artificial Intelligence. Morgan Kaufmann Publ., San Mateo 1988, 357 - 366.
7. K.P. Sycara, S.F. Roth, N. Sadeh, M.S. Fox: Resource allocation in distributed factory scheduling. In: IEEE Expert, Febr. 1991, 29 - 40.
8. H.-P. Wiendahl: Belastungsorientierte Fertigungssteuerung. Grundlagen, Verfahrensaufbau, Realisierung. Hanser-Verlag, München 1987.

Expert System for Production Planning of Perishable Goods

Andrzej Gospodarowicz, Ewa Kania, Stanisław Krawczyk, Mieczysław Rymarczyk
University of Economics, Wrocław, Poland

A Min Tjoa
University of Vienna, Institute of Statistics and Computer Science

Abstract. This paper presents a computer system of production planning for perishable goods industry (e.g. meat products). The demand for the products of such industries exhibits short-term seasonalities, usually of one-week length. Therefore, short-term forecasting is very important to provide the planning department in an enterprise with up-to-date information about the expected demand. The expert procedures for the evaluating of forecasts and of customers are applied.

1 General System Assumptions

The basic goal of a production enterprise in free economy is to provide the market with products that will be purchased by customers. Any decision to start production relies therefore on the conviction that a product will be sold for sure. A producer can be sure about it if customers put their orders in advance. In the case of mass production (like meat products and other consumption goods) such orders are only a part of the actual demand for it. The rest is determined by anonymous buyers who take their individual decisions about a purchase while products are on market.

The proper production planning significantly depends on the exact determining of that additional demand. Therefore, we are going to take the demand forecasts from the past data as a basis to determine the expected demand. We shall also assume that the production of a given day can be stored in order to satisfy the next day(s) demand provided the storage requirements for meat products are fulfilled. Thus, the value of expected demand determined as the sum of orders and forecasts should first be compared with the state of storehouse and if stock-list is not satisfying, a new production should replace stock in short supply. On the other hand, even if demand is not uniformly distributed we are still able to accordingly plan production in advance so that it does not much vary from day to day.

The computer system of production planning under study contains three equivalent modules: forecasting the demand, maintaining and supporting the orders, and operating the storehouse. All data processed in those modules are used in the main module of production planning. All four modules have access to the common database which is supported by the separate module.

2 Description of the Forecasting Module

2.1 General Assumptions

We assume that the forecasts of demand for meat products with short storage periods will be determined basically for a 6-day horizon or for a 3-week horizon (or shorter). Past data about sales and/or orders from customers are stored as time series for each product in a file with specified structure.

In the classic approach to forecasting with time series $Y_1,...,Y_n$ we specify a procedure of determining a forecast $\hat{Y}_{n+p}$, $p \geq 1$, whereas the value $\hat{Y}_{n+p}$ is of *the same type* as every element of the time series. Such approach will be called here *a direct forecasting* comprising usually the following steps:

1) Time series input
2) Time series analysis
3) Forecasting method selection
4) Determining a forecast $\hat{Y}_{n+p}$

Working with standard statistical packages, a user activates solely numerical procedures of time series analysis and of forecasting method selection, and it is user who is responsible for any premises and conclusions resulting from his choice. The experience with forecasting shows clearly that we can formulate unambiguous inference rules of expert-system type, for time series analysis. For selection of a forecasting method we can give some selection rules using the conclusions drawn from autocorrelation analysis and from the information about the length of time series. The useful information can be obtained from the forecasting simulation taking time series generated from the original time series $Y_1,...,Y_n$.

The forecasting simulations with true data taken from enterprises indicate that direct forecasting in many cases yield forecasts distorted by large errors, thus questioning the usefulness of forecasting. Usually, a judgment follows that in such cases forecasting is not possible at all. Such conclusion may be justified, but only as far as forecasting of the value $\hat{Y}_{n+p}$ is concerned. Forecasting may become much more practicable if we abandon a paradigm of strict compatibility between time series data and a result of forecasting. In cases when direct forecasting does not produce an adequate estimate of demand, we should try to build a new time series, say $W_1,...,W_m$, from the original one, and build a forecast $\hat{W}_{m+r}$ which may be used indirectly to determine $\hat{Y}_{n+p}$. Such a procedure will be called here *an indirect forecasting*. The issue how to build a time series $W_1,...,W_m$, is decided upon in a due analysis of the process under study.

In the case of food products with limited storage periods, we have two important characteristics used in indirect forecasting procedures:

1) A standard week consists of six days of production followed by a holiday.
2) A surplus of production may be deposited in a storehouse.

The first instance means that weekly data should display cycles. The second one suggests that production planning may also account the cumulative demand over several days. Thus, we have developed a procedure for indirect forecasting which is based on a cumulative time series of sales data from Monday to a given day of the week. This procedure is applied when the original time series analysis indicates that the direct forecasting cannot ensure correct results. Usually, it is the case of white-noise type series.

2.2 Procedures of the Module

We assume that time series $Y_1,...,Y_n$ is known.

A. Time series analysis

For a given time series the usual coefficients of autocorrelation r_k, $k=1,...,K$, $K=n/3$, with time lag k, are calculated. The analysis of r_k employs the following inference rules:

R1 : If $r_1 \geq 0.6$
and $r_1 > r_2 > ... > r_K$
then trend

R2 : If $r_1 \geq 0.6$
and $r_1 > r_2 > ... > r_m$
and $m < p$
and $r_p > r_{p+1} > ... > r_K$
then trend

R3 : If $m_1 = \text{bending\_point}()$
and $m_1 < -0.4$
and $m_2 = \text{bending\_point}()$
and $m_2 > 0.4$
and $m_3 = \text{bending\_point}()$
and $m_3 < -0.4$
then seasonality

The function bending_point() returns the number of the autocorrelation coefficient r_v for which we have:

either $r_{v-1} < r_v$ and $r_v > r_{v+1}$
or $r_{v-1} > r_v$ and $r_v < r_{v+1}$

Then $m_3 - m_1$ determines the period of seasonality.

R4 : If $|r_i| < 0.3$ for i=1,..,K,
then white_noise

R5 : If trend
then procedure trend()

R6 : If seasonality
then procedure seasonality()

R7 : If white_noise
then procedure white_noise()

B. Procedure trend()

The simulations of diverse cases have shown that the trend test should not refer to the entire time series but to subseries detected by the bending points as returned from function bending_point(). The argument of that function should be therefore the time series after smoothing. We employ the following moving averages:

M3 : $M3_t = (Y_{t-1} + Y_t + Y_{t+1})/3$
M33 : $M33_t = (M3_{t-1} + M3_t + M3_{t+1})/3$
M333 : $M333_t = (M33_{t-1} + M33_t + M33_{t+1})/3$
M5 : $M5_t = (Y_{t-2} + Y_{t-1} + Y_t + Y_{t+1} + Y_{t+2})/5$
MH : $MH_t = -0.073Y_{t-2} + 0.294Y_{t-1} + 0.558Y_t + 0.294Y_{t+1} - 0.073Y_{t+2}$

After smoothing, we determine the bending points for the smoothed time series GM_t. Let m_k be the last bending point. The procedure trend() is applied now to the time series $Y_{m_k}, \ldots, Y_n$. We used least squares method to determine the linear trend, Brown's exponential smoothing of second order, and recursive equations to determine the quadratic trend.

C. Procedure seasonality()

It follows from our assumptions about time series under study that they exhibit seasonality induced by the weekly pattern of production. This fact simplifies the calculation of seasonality coefficients. Our simulations show, however, that one should calculate them with the smoothed series of $M33_t$ or $M333_t$ type. The procedure comprises the following steps:

1) Time series smoothing with moving averages
2) Calculating the seasonality coefficients
3) Adjusting for seasonalities
4) Adjusted time series analysis
5) Forecasting with adjusted time series
6) Modifying the forecast with seasonality coefficients

D. Procedure white_noise()

When we find out that the original time series does not justify any trend or cycles and that the autocorrelation coefficients are near zero, it means that a forecast in such cases may be distorted by large error and as such, it must be carefully verified and modified. As direct forecasting is not possible, our system automatically switches to indirect forecasting. One of the numerical procedures invoked from the white_noise procedure is the technique of forecasting with cumulative weekly sums of past sales data.

Let m denote the number of a week for which sales data are available. We build the following cumulative sums:

$$S[m*6+1] = Y_{m*6+1}$$
$$S[m*6+k] = Y_{m*6+k} + S[m*6+k-1], \text{ for } k=2,\ldots,6.$$

Then we calculate the indices showing the fraction of the k-th day sum in the total weekly sum:

$$s[m*6+k] = S[m*6+k] \,/\, S[m*6+6], \quad k=1,\ldots, 6$$

In full procedure these coefficients are smoothed.

Let j denote the number of a day in next week, j=1,..,5 and $Y_{(m+1)*6+j}$ be the sales in j-th day. Using S[(m+1)*6+j] and s[m*6+k], k=j+1,...,6, we determine a forecast of the weekly cumulative sum:

$$\hat{S}[(m+1)*6+6] = S[(m+1)*6+j] \,/\, s[m*6+j],$$

and from it we obtain the forecasts of cumulative sums:

$$\hat{S}[(m+1)*6+k] = \hat{S}[(m+1)*6+6] * s[m*6+k], \text{ for } k=j+1,..,6.$$

The foreacast Y will be found by subtracting the respective cumulative sums:

$$\hat{Y}_{(m+1)*6+k} = \hat{S}[(m+1)*6+k] - \hat{S}[(m+1)*6+k-1] \quad \text{for } k > 1.$$

The cumulative sum $\hat{S}[(m+2)*6+6]$ necessary to determine the first forecast $\hat{S}[(m+2)*6+1]$ when the quantity $Y_{(m+2)*6+1}$ is yet not known, should be predicted in a separate run in a (m+1)-th week.

The above procedure proved very reliable and promising in view of simulations conducted so far.

2.3 Analysis of Forecasts in Special Situations

A usual situation has it that both days: t_z for which we calculate a forecast, and $t_z - t_p$ when the respective production must start, are normal workdays. Obviously, this condition must be checked in advance. In the case when either of two: t_z or $t_z - t_p$ is not a workday, we deal with a special situation which must be considered separately.

We assume that on day t_0 we check all the days $t_0 + t_p + 1, \ldots, t_0 + t_p + t_s$, for which forecasts are calculated, and respective days of production start $t_0 + 1, \ldots, t_0 + t_s$, whether there are any holidays among them.

We distinguish the following special situations:

S1 :	t_z is not a workday	and	$t_z - t_p$	is not a workday
S2 :	t_z is not a workday	and	$t_z - t_p$	is a workday
S3 :	t_z is a workday	and	$t_z - t_p$	is not a workday

In both situations S1 and S2 we must not start production on day $t_z - t_p$ because otherwise it would have been stored at least till day $t_z + 1$. For that day, however, we start production on day $t_z - t_p + 1$. We do not wish to double production and so we apply the rule that the demand calculated is to be replaced by zero.

Let B_{t_z} denote the predicted value of demand for day t_z. The rule follows:

R8 : If $t_0 + t_p + 1 \le t_z \le t_0 + t_p + t_s$ and (S1 or S2) then $B_{t_z} = 0$

In situation S3 the procedure is ambiguous. Now, the day of production start is not a workday whereas the demand is not equal zero. In order to satisfy the expected demand, it is necessary to start production earlier and then to store it. Such case must be recognized in good time, and the day $t_0 + 1$ must be a workday. In addition, the earlier start of production will result in increasing its quantity on days before $t_z - t_p$, which in turn might violate the production capacity restrictions.

The following rules are therefore to be applied:

R9 : If $t_0 + t_p + 2 < t_z \le t_0 + t_p + t_s$
and S3 and $t_s > 2$
then $B_{t_z - 2} = B_{t_z - 2} + 0.3 B_{t_z}$ and $B_{t_z - 1} = B_{t_z - 1} + 0.7 B_{t_z}$

R10 : If $t_0 + t_p + 2 < t_z \le t_0 + t_p + t_s$
and S3 and $t_s = 2$
then $B_{t_z - 1} = B_{t_z - 1} + 0.8 B_{t_z}$

3 Description of the Production Planning Module

The main functions of this module are:
- determining the draft plan based on forecasts and available production capacities,
- determining the expected quantities of production in order to classify the existing orders,
- modifying the draft plan when the orders exceed production capacities.

On day t_0 we use information about demand and orders on days $t_0 + t_p + 1, \ldots, t_0 + t_p + t_s$. Of course, production periods t_{p_1}, t_{p_2} for two products P_1 and P_2 and storage periods t_{s_1}, t_{s_2} are usually different. We only redirect the data for product P_1 from day $t_0 + t_{p_1} + t_{s_1} + 1$and for product P_2 from day $t_0 + t_{p_2} + t_{s_2} + 1$to the information valid on day t_0.

We apply the following notation:

B_k - predicted demand on day $t_0 + t_p + k$, $k=1,..,t_s$
$\tilde{B}_k$ - modified forecast of demand on that day
SZ_k - sum of orders requested for day $t_0 + t_p + k$
$Z_k[\ ]$ - order for day $t_0 + t_p + k$
$Z_k[i]$ - i-th order for day $t_0 + t_p + k$
R_k - raw material supply for day $t_0 + k$
S - matrix of input quantities
$S{*}B_k$ - raw materials required for production B_k

The start situation is following: $SZ_{t_1} = 0, \ldots, SZ_{t_s} = 0$. Given the predicted values of demand $B_1, \ldots, B_{t_s}$, we determine the required quantities of raw materials, $S * B_1, S * B_2, \ldots, S * B_{t_s}$. We assume that at least R_1 and R_2 are accurate and reliable data. Data $R_3, \ldots, R_{t_s}$can be underestimated.

R1 : If $S * B_1 \le R_1$
and $S * B_2 \le R_2$
:
and $S * B_{t_s} \le R_{t_s}$
then draft plan of production $B_1, B_2, \ldots, B_{t_s}$

This rule says that given the adequate supply of raw materials, the draft plan of production simply agrees with demand forecasts. The draft plan may be modified when orders exceed the forecasts.

R2 : If $S * B_1 > R_1$
then $B_1 = \tilde{B}_1$

In order to modify the forecast (determine the value of $\tilde{B}_k$) we solve the optimization problem:

$$c^T x \rightarrow \min$$
$$S * (B_k - x) \leq R_k$$
$$0 \leq x \leq B_k$$

Let x_k^0 be the solution to this problem. Then we have:

$$B_k = B_k - x_k^0$$

The coefficients of the function $c^T x$ may be e.g. the prices of products.

R3 : If $S * B_1 \leq R_1$
and $S * B_2 > R_2$
then $B_2 = \tilde{B}_2$

where $\tilde{B}_2$ is calculated as $\tilde{B}_k$ above.

Following the procedure of determining the draft plan we know the expected quantities of production which can be used as guidelines for the approval of orders.

Let us now assume that the following orders are known:

$Z_1[1], .., Z_1[k_1 - 1]$ for day $t_0 + t_p + 1$

$$SZ_1 = \sum_{i=1}^{k_1-1} Z_1[i] \leq B_1$$

$Z_2[1], .., Z_2[k_2 - 1]$ for day $t_0 + t_p + 2$

$$SZ_2 = \sum_{i=1}^{k_2-1} Z_2[i] \leq B_2$$

....

A. Procedure Order $Z_1[k_1]$

R4 : If $SZ_1 + Z_1[k_1] \leq B_1$
then $SZ_1 = SZ_1 + Z_1[k_1]$
and $Z_1[k_1]$ approved

R5 : If $SZ_1 + Z_1[k_1] > B_1$
and $S * (SZ_1 + Z_1[k_1]) \leq R_1$
then $SZ_1 = SZ_1 + Z_1[k_1]$
and $B_1 = SZ_1$ and $Z_1[k_1]$ approved

R6 : If $SZ_1 + Z_1[k_1] > B_1$
and $S * (SZ_1 + Z_1[k_1]) > R_1$
then $Z_1[k_1] = Z_1[k_1] - x_1^0$
and $SZ_1 = SZ_1 + Z_1[k_1]$ and $B_1 = SZ_1$
and $Z_1[k_1]$ approved

where x_1^0 is calculated with procedure $\tilde{B}_k$.

B. Procedure Order Z_2 [k_2]

R7 : If $SZ_2 + Z_2[k_2] \leq B_2$
then $SZ_2 = SZ_2 + Z_2[k_2]$
and $Z_2[k_2]$ approved

R8 : If $SZ_2 + Z_2[k_2] > B_2$
and $S * (SZ_2 + Z_2[k_2]) \leq R_2$
then $SZ_2 = SZ_2 + Z_2[k_2]$
and $B_2 = SZ_2$ and $Z_2[k_2]$ approved

This rule considers the case when the order Z_2 [k_2] may be approved, despite the exceeded forecast, because the raw materials are in adequate supply.

Next, we deal with the case when a part of the order Z_2 [k_2] is fulfilled on day t_0 +2, and another part on day t_0 +1.

Let us denote:

PZ[ ] - approved part of the order Z[ ], and

NZ[ ] - disapproved part of the order Z[ ]

R9 : If $SZ_2 < B_2$ and $S * (SZ_2 + Z_2[k_2]) > R_2$
then $PZ_2[k_2]$ is approved
and $SZ_2 = SZ_2 + PZ_2[k_2]$
and $NZ_2[k_2] = Z_2[k_2] - PZ_2[k_2]$
and $B_2 = SZ_2$

In this case we treat a disapproved part NZ as an additional order for day t_0 +1 and we check if it is possible to fulfill it earlier.

C. Procedure PZ[k]

The start situation is described as:

$$S * SZ < R$$
and
$$S * (SZ + DZ) > R$$

We solve the problem:

$$c^T x \rightarrow \min$$

subject to:

$$S * (SZ + DZ - x) \leq R$$
$$x \leq DZ \quad x \geq 0$$

and from the optimal solution x^0 we obtain:

$$PZ = DZ - x^0$$

R10 : If $S * (SZ_1 + NZ_2[k_2]) \leq R_1$
then $SZ_1 = SZ_1 + NZ_2[k_2]$
and $Z_1[k_1 + 1] = NZ_2[k_2]$
and $NZ_2[k_2]$ approved
and $B_1 = SZ_1$

R11 : If $S * (SZ_1 + NZ_2 [k_2]) > R_1$
then $PNZ_2 [k_2]$ approved
and $SZ_1 = SZ_1 + PNZ_2 [k_2]$
and $Z_1 [k_1 +1] = PNZ_2 [k_2]$
and $NZ_2 [k_2] - PNZ_2 [k_2]$ disapproved
and $B_1 = SZ_1$

The quantity $PNZ_2 [k_2]$ is determined by the procedure PZ[k] where $DZ=NZ_2 [k_2]$ is assumed. We do not suppose it is worth trying to generalize the above procedures for horizons longer than 2 days because of small informativeness of data $R_3, ..., R_{t_s}$ and also because the forecasts $B_3, ..., B_{t_s}$ are repeatedly modified as new data arrive.

4 Some Features of the Expert Procedure in the Orders Maintenance Module

In this module customers' orders are registered, approved and/or cancelled. The expert procedure is applied in order to answer the question: "What priority should be assigned to a customer whose order is to be approved?" The possible answers are: special, normal, basic, conditional.

We consider the following characteristics of customers:

1) category of customer
2) rank of order
3) way of payment
4) degree of credibility
5) frequency of orders
6) value of order

Each characteristics can be described by appropriate facts. For example, frequency of orders can be represented by means of the following facts: every day, almost every day, constant-cyclical, often-irregular, sporadic, no orders so far. Value of order can be described as: low, average, high, very high.

The facts about characteristics such as: *category of customer, way of payment, degree of credibility, frequency of orders* and *value of order* are determined from database, whereas the facts connected with characteristics *rank of order* are determined by rules which consider such characteristics as *category of customer, frequency of orders* and *value of order.* There are several hundred rules of determining the priority of customer in our system.

5 Concluding Remarks

The system under consideration does not include the entire activity of an enterprise. Its cardinal goal is to supply an aggregate production plan. The production plan is only formally separated as the ultimate goal of the system. In practice, other goals achieved simultaneously are not less important, like registering and supporting the orders, operating the storehouse of finished goods and acquiring the information about transactions performed. In some of the system's modules, computational procedures play the essential role, especially in the FORECASTS module and the PRODUCTION PLANNING module which we tried mainly to present in this paper. In other modules, data processing is more important, such as creating data sets, updating them or appending new items of information.

References

1. A Min Tjoa, R.R. Wagner, K. Macho, L. Winkelbauer: Lernen aus Beispielen. In: Künstliche Intelligenz und Expertensysteme, S. Savory (ed.), München-Wien: R.Oldenbourg Verlag 1985, pp.201-210.

2. A. Gospodarowicz, E. Kania, S. Krawczyk, M. Rymarczyk: Ein Expertensystem für die Fertigungsplanung im Betrieb. In: Nichtlineare Modelle in der Ökonometrie, Wydawnictwo AE Wrocław 1991, pp.71-79.

An Expert System as a Manager in the Application of Production Planning and Control Software in CIM Environments

N.D. Mekras, A.G. Malama, G.P. Parnassas, I.P. Tatsiopoulos

National Technical University of Athens,
Dept. of Mechanical Engineering, Sector of Industrial Management & O.R.,
28is Octovriou 42, 10682 Athens, Greece

Abstract. This paper presents the way that expert system technology has been used for the development of a consulting tool in the National Technical University of Athens, aiming to support those who want to apply Production Planning and Control (PPC) software in their manufacturing firm. In the knowledge base that has been created, both a production systems taxonomy and a generic software package with specific modules and functions are presented. The inferences are based on rules, that express the need for the existence of certain software, when a set of production systems characteristics is found in the production system that is under consideration. The results that are given by the expert system include the whole architecture of PPC software package that is applicable in a certain manufacturing setting.

1 Introduction

The different types of production systems and the lack of standardization on both the production systems and the PPC software, makes the problem more difficult considering the fact that new managerial principles and methods are applied in the industrial environments. Managers and consulting experts, have difficulty in taking the right decision for the appropriate software that should be applied in a specific industry.

A few efforts for the evaluation of PPC software and design of computerized production systems have been reported that have their origin in different science fields using different approaches. An example of the industrial engineering approach is the system BAPSY of the TH Aachen [10], [22], which uses multicriteria and value analysis methods to compare different PPC software packages. Another tool that has been developed under the Esprit project 5424, is the software package FTM [20], that helps the user to determine his functional requirements for PPC software and compare them with functions of existing PPC software packages.

Two other efforts for the design and optimization of the behavior of computerized PPC systems, based on Artificial Intelligence concepts, are the Eloranta [7] and GRAI methodologies [2], [3], which have been developed in the

University of Helsinki and Bordeaux respectively. For the implementation of the above methods [10], the researchers are using AI tools [1], [5], that help them to organize, classify and process knowledge by which the representation and improvement of PPC systems is achieved.

In this paper, a method, based on expert system techniques [12], [15], that can be used for the selection of PPC software is presented. By this method, expert knowledge concerning production systems and PPC software is gathered and classified. Also, logical rules are used to relate characteristics of the production systems with the functions of PPC software. For the realization of the method an expert system has been constructed that gives as inference results the needed PPC software functions and the structure of the whole software package that these functions belong to. Explanation procedures have been embodied in the expert system that show the way the results have been obtained.

Semantic networks and rules are the basic knowledge representation structures [9], [18], used for the creation of the expert system's knowledge base. The programming language that has been used for the construction of the whole expert system, is the Prolog language [14], [25], due to its capabilities for the creation and processing of the knowledge representation structures we mentioned before [13], [16].

Section 2 of this paper contains a description of both the production systems taxonomy and the PPC software, including the way that they have been represented in the knowledge base.

Section 3 presents the basic steps of the inferencing process and the possibilities that the user has, for describing and classifying his production system in the production systems taxonomy knowledge base. Also examples of inferencing results are given for certain types of manufacturing settings.

2 Knowledge base

The knowledge base consists of two semantic networks which contain descriptions of several production systems and the representation of a generic PPC software package. Entities of the two semantic networks are linked with rules that express relations that exist between the production systems taxonomy and the software functions. These rules are necessary for the inferencing process because they drive the expert system to the conclusions concerning the appropriate software for a certain manufacturing setting.

2.1 Production systems taxonomy

For the creation of the production systems taxonomy a set of 9 classes of attributes has been used [19], [23]. These attributes express the functional characteristics of the production systems and are used to represent their structure in the knowledge base, including forms of product structure, types of shop layout, complexity of production processes etc. The 9 classes of the production attributes are :

01 Product standardisation
- 01.1 Non-catalogued customized products
- 01.2 Catalogued products with non-standard, customized options
- 01.3 Catalogued products with standard options
- 01.4 Standard products

02 Product structure
- 02.1 Single component products
- 02.2 One-level bill of materials
- 02.3 Multi-level bill of materials
- 02.4 Scrap recycling
- 02.5 Yield variability

03 Form of independent demand (products)
- 03.1 Production of individual order
- 03.2 Production of blanket order
- 03.3 Non-seasonal production to stock
- 03.4 Seasonal production to stock
- 03.5 Assembly to order

04 Form of depend demand (components, raw materials)
- 04.1 Dependent on the customer order
- 04.2 Mixed mainly dependent on the customer order
- 04.3 Mixed mainly independent of the customer order
- 04.4 Independent of the customer order

05 Form of Purchasing
- 05.1 Insignificant buy
- 05.2 Mixed
- 05.3 Mainly buy

06 Process form (time dimension)
- 06.1 One-off production with transfer
- 06.2 One-off production without transfer
- 06.3 Small Batch Production
- 06.4 Serial intermittent batch production
- 06.5 Machine-paced line flow
- 06.6 Worker-paced line flow
- 06.7 Lot Production (raw material dependent)
- 06.8 Lot Production (products dependent)
- 06.9 Batch flow process
- 06.10 Continuous flow
- 06.11 Production with by-products and co-products

07 Shop-layout (space dimension)
- 07.1 Construction shop
- 07.2 Functional organization (job-shop)
- 07.3 Functional layout with sequenced operations
- 07.4 Cellular layout
- 07.5 Flexible manufacturing system
- 07.6 Product line layout

08 Process complexity
- 08.1 One operation per component
- 08.2 A few operations per component
- 08.3 Many operations per component
- 08.4 Sequential routing
- 08.5 Networked form of routing

09 Warehouse structure
- 09.1 Single warehouse
- 09.2 Multiple warehouses geographically adjacent
- 09.3 Multiple warehouses geographically distant
- 09.4 Receiving warehouse geographically distant
- 09.5 Assembly components from multiple warehouses
- 09.6 Quality status tracking important

In the knowledge base exist descriptions of :

a. Production systems found in sectors and subsectors of the Greek Industry, which are classified according to the Greek National Statistical Service (e.g. food industry, plastics industry, metal industry, etc).

b. The four basic types of production systems *(Repetitive, Discrete, Process & Project)* with specializations and subcategories for each one [17].

c. Production systems found in specific Greek industries.

The above form the production systems taxonomy which is described and classified in one of the two semantic networks of the knowledge base. In the next figure, some examples are given that show the structure of the taxonomy.

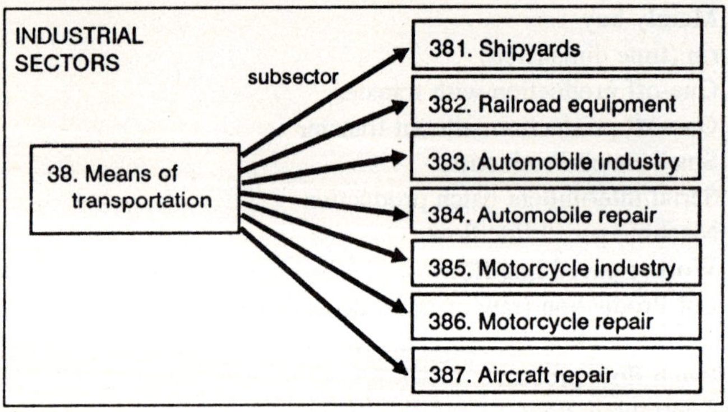

Figure 1

Examples of functional characteristics found in subsector *"383.Automobile Industry"*.

1) 01.3 Catalogued products with standard options
2) 02.3 Multi-level bill of materials
3) 03.5 Assembly to order
4) 04.1 Demand of components and raw materials, dependent on the customer order

5) 05.3 Mainly purchasing of components
6) 06.6 Worker-paced line flow
7) 06.8 Lot production (products dependent)
8) 07.6 Product line layout
9) 08.2 A few operations per component

Examples of the *"Repetitive"* production system subcategories are the following :

1. With product line layout
2. In cellular layout
3. Based on customer orders
4. For non-seasonal production to stock
5. With assembly of semifinished parts based on customer orders
6. Of multi-level bill of material products
7. Of standard products
8. With mainly purchasing of finished parts for assembly
9. With in-house-production of finished parts

For each of the above subcategories or combinations of them, a set of functional characteristics is defined, that gives the structure of the production system that the user wants to describe.

The knowledge representation structures, that we used for the creation of the whole production systems knowledge base give the following possibilities :

1. Hierarchical classification of industrial sectors and subsectors.
2. Introduction and study of a production system indepentently from the sector or subsector it belongs.
3. Hierarchical classification of subcategories of the four basic types of production systems.
4. Inheritance of attributes found in a higher classified level production system.
5. Description of production systems found in specific industries.
6. Study of systems that are not included in the knowledge base, with the help of extra questions asked by the expert system.
7. Linking of the production systems taxonomy with PPC software functions in an easy and comprehensive manner through logical rules.

2.2 Production Planning and Control software

For the representation of the PPC software in the knowledge base, an ideal generic PPC software package has been considered for three main reasons :

a. It is quite common, that the proposed information system embodied in the production management generic software package, may be fundamentally different from existing patterns in the factory (in its content, form, complexity, etc.), so that anchoring on an existing information system or existing observations of information needs, will not yield a complete and correct set of "ideal" requirements.

b. In practice, there is not usually enough time at this stage to proceed to a detailed analysis of the company's current information processing and organisational procedures.
c. A database of existing commercial packages would not be practical to maintain, given the continuous release of updated versions and new products in this field.

This ideal and generic software package is analyzed in modules, submodules and functions. The above analysis is based on both managerial principles of the MRPII design philosophy and software functions found in existing commercial PPC software packages [8], [21], [24].

The main modules of this package are :

Production Data Management (PDM)
Forecasting of Demand
Order Processing
Master Production Scheduling (MPS)
Capacity Requirements Planning (CRP)
Materials Requirements Planning (MRP)
Shop Floor Control (SFC)
Inventory Control
Purchasing

For the creation of the generic software package knowledge base, a second semantic network has been used on which the structure of its module has been represented. In figure 2, in the next page the structure of the *Shop Floor Control (SFC)* [4] module is presented.

Examples of software functions of two SFC submodules are listed below.

Submodule : *Order_Release*
Software functions

1) *Selection_of_alternative_routings*
2) *Rescheduling_and_release_part_of_the_order*
3) *Release_of_bill_of_materials*
4) *Release_of_construction_drawings*
5) *Release_of_workers_instructions*
6) *Release_of_movement_and_transportation_instructions*

Submodule : *Job_assignment_in_work_centers*
Software functions

1) *Creation_of_job_lists*
2) *Determination_of_job_priorities*
3) *Listing_of_critical_jobs (time dimension)*
4) *Assignment_of_jobs_to_machines*
5) *Assignment_of_workers_to_machines*
6) *Balancing_of_capacity_load_in_the_work_center*

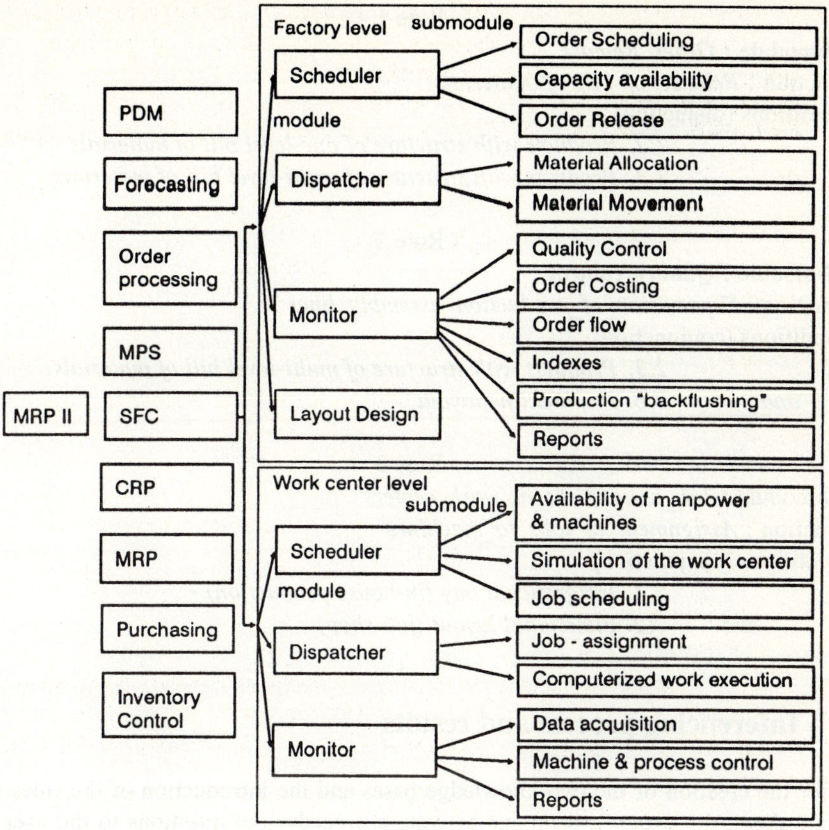

Figure 2. Structure of the *Shop Floor Control* module.

2.3 Rules for linking PPC software with Production systems

The third part of the knowledge base consists of a set of logical rules that link the functions of the PPC software with the production systems attributes. These rules express the need for the existence of certain functions when a set of attributes is present in a production system.

The conditions of the rules are joined with *"conjunction (and)"* or *"disjunction (or)"* logical relationships, giving by this way the possibility to create any kind of condition combinations of all the classes of the production systems functional characteristics. Only for the Shop Floor Control (SFC) module (Fig. 2), a total of 435 rules has been defined, that are necessary for all of its software functions.

In the next page, examples of rules are given that have as results functions of the SFC module.

Rule 1

Submodule : *Order_Release*
Function : *Release_of_bill_of_materials*
Conditions (disjuction)
1) *2.2. Products with structure of one-level bill of materials*
2) or *2.3. Products with structure of multi-level bill of materials*

Rule 2

Submodule : *Quality_control*
Function : *Supervision_of_production_assembly_lines*
Conditions (conjunction)
1) *2.3. Products with structure of multi-level bill of materials*
2) and *7.6. Product line layout*

Rule 3

Submodule : *Job_assignment_in_work_centers*
Function : *Assignment_of_jobs_to_machines*
Conditions (conjunction)
1) *5.1. Insignificant buy (in-house-production)*
2) and *7.2. Functional layout (job-shop)*

3 Inferencing process and results

After the creation of the two knowledge bases and the introduction of the rules that relate them, the expert system can activate a procedure of questions to the user for the determination and description of his production system. The answers coming from the user, are based on both the existing knowledge of the production systems taxonomy and on extra queries concerning functional characteristics not included in the already classified production systems. By this way any exceptions and special characteristics of production systems are considered, before the inference procedures are activated.

A set of starting menus and questions helps the user to give a first description of his production system. The menus and questions that follow, depend on the answers given previously. For example, if the user defines his production system as of type *"Repetitive"*, then the questions that follow, concern its subcategories and its special characteristics (e.g. Repetitive production based on customer orders).

The rules that exist in the knowledge base, are used by the inference engine and drive the expert system to those software functions that are appropriate for each manufacturing setting. For each selected function, the explanation mechanism shows how it was selected and the rules that were responsible for this selection. The explanation process is necessary to make clear the usefulness of each selected software function.

The results that can be obtained concern sectors and subsectors of the Greek industry, types of production systems and their specilizations, or structures of production settings found in specific industries. By this way, results for the appropriate software of any structure of manufacturing system, can be given by the expert system. The results include the whole architecture of the modules and submodules that contain the selected functions. By this way modules and submodules that contain not needed software are excluded from the proposed solutions.

Examples of results, for the *discrete type production system, with functional organized layout for small batch production that is based on customer orders* are the following :

Submodule : Order_scheduling
Software functions
1) Forward_scheduling_of_production_orders
2) Backward_scheduling_of_production_orders
3) Creation_of_order_priorities_based_on_due_dates
4) Simulation_of_production_orders_before_release

Submodule : Capacity_availability
Software functions
1) Simulation_of_mater._usage_for_several_prod._quantities
2) Check_of_tools_availability
3) Check_of_work_centers_availability
4) Simulation_of_work_centers

Submodule : Order_release
Software functions
1) Selection_of_alternative_routings
2) Orders_split
3) Rescheduling_and_release_part_of_the_order
4) Release_of_construction_drawings
5) Release_of_workers_instructions
6) Release_of_movement_and_transportation_instructions

Submodule : Material_allocation
Software functions
1) Lot_allocation_of_materials_per_job
2) Reallocation_of_materials_between_orders

Submodule : Material_movement
Software functions
1) Forward_scheduling_of_material_movement
2) Backward_scheduling_of_material_movement
3) Hierarchy_of_priorities_for_material_movement
4) Reports_for_received_materials_in_work_position

Submodule : Quality_control
Software functions
1) Scheduling_and_release_of_quality_control_work_orders
2) Reporting_of_scrap_quantities
3) Reason_codes_for_scrap_creation

Submodule : Order_costing
Software functions
1) Machine_costing
2) Costing_of_materials
3) Costing_of_direct_labor
4) Costing_of_indirect_labor
5) Calculation_of_total_indirect_cost
6) Work_center_groupings_for_accounting

Submodule : Indexes_of_factory_level_monitor
Software functions
1) Indexing_of_machine_utilization
2) Indexing_of_machine_efficiency
3) Indexing_of_workers_utilization
4) Indexing_of_workers_efficiency
5) Indexing_of_scrap_percentage
6) Work_center_performance_reporting
7) Comparison_indexes_between_scheduled_and_real_prod.

Submodule : Job_assignment_in_work_centers
Software functions
1) Creation_of_job_lists
2) Determination_of_job_priorities
3) Listing_of_critical_jobs (time dimension)
4) Assignment_of_jobs_to_machines
5) Assignment_of_workers_to_machines
6) Balancing_of_capacity_load_in_the_work_center

Submodule : Data_acquisition
Software functions
1) Job_interruptions
2) Working_machine_hours
3) Set_up_machine_hours
4) Production_quantities
5) Unused_quantities_of_materials
6) Scrap_quantities
7) Work_repetition

Submodule : Machine & process control
Software functions
1) Control_of_machine_working_conditions
(Temperatures, pressures, on-off state, etc.)

4 Conclusions

The method and the expert system developed, can be valuable to those who plan to buy/develop and implement PPC software package in a manufacturing firm. Such evaluation and selection decisions are far too complex to be faced either by quantitative multi-criteria methods or by simple guessing. AI technology techniques have been applied for the creation and processing of a knowledge base, needed for the systemization of the software selection process. The whole knowledge can be updated when new managerial principles must be included, new software functions are considered or new rules must be added.

The results of the method can be used as a guide for consulting experts, production managers and PPC software developers, helping them to determine the apropriate software for a certain type of manufacturing setting. Through the explanation mechanism, the relation of each software function with the structure of the production systems is given, helping to determine the way it can be used in the production process.

The developed expert system is expected to be also a significant educational tool, for those who want to apply new managerial principles and new production planning methods in several production environments.

References

[1] Akif, J.C., and Doumeingts, G., 'Computer Aided GRAI Method' in Advances in Production Management Systems, Eloranta E. (Ed), Elsevier/North-holland, IFIP, Amsterdam, Netherlands, 1991.

[2] Akif, J.C., 'Consistency analysis of Production Management system (P.M.S.) based on GRAI Modelling' in Computer Applications in Production and Engineering : Integration Aspects, Doumeingts G., Browne J. and Tomljanovich M. (Editors), Elsevier/North-holland, IFIP, Amsterdam, Netherlands, 1991.

[3] Berard, C. and Nguyen, P., 'A specification system for analysis and design methods of production systems' in Computer Applications in Production and Engineering : Integration Aspects, Doumeingts G., Browne J. and Tomljanovich M. (Editors), Elsevier/North-holland, IFIP, Amsterdam, Netherlands, 1991.

[4] Browne, J., Shop Floor Control - An Architectural View, CIMRU, U.C.G., Ireland, 1990.

[5] Doumeingts, G. et al, 'Knowledge-based System for the Design of Production Management Systems', in: J. Browne (Ed), Knowledge Based production Management Systems, Elsevier (North-Holland), IFIP, 1989.

[6] Doumeingts, G., Roboam, M., Wagner, J.L. and Darricau, D., 'Knowledge based system for the design of production management systems' in Knowledge Based Production Management Systems, Browne. J. (Editor), Elsevier/North-holland, IFIP, Amsterdam, Netherlands, 1989.

[7] Eloranta, E. et al, 'Model-based reasoning in manufacturing systems design' in Browne, J (ed), Knowledge Based Production Management Systems, Elsevier/North-Holland, Amsterdam, Netherlands, 1989.

[8] Foerster, H., Hoff, H. and Missen, E., Marktspiegel PPS-Systems auf- dem Pruefstand, Verlag, Koeln, Germany, 1986.

[9] Frost, R.A., Introduction to Knowledge Base Systems, William Collins & Sons, London, UK, 1986.

[10] Hackstein, R., and Virnich, M., 'Selecting standard systems of production and inventory control (PIC) with the aid of utility value analysis (BAPSY model)' in Information Technology for Organisational Systems, H.J. Bullinger et al (ed), Elsevier/North-Holland, Brussels, 1991.

[11] Huber, A. and Bluenz, D., 'Using GRAI to specify Expert Systems for the Control and the Supervision of Flexible Flow Lines' in Knowledge Based Production Management Systems, Browne. J. (Editor), Elsevier/North-Holland, IFIP, Amsterdam, Netherlands, 1989.

[12] Keller, R., Expert System Technology, Prentice-Hall, Englewood Cliffs, NJ, USA, 1987.

[13] Levesque, H.J., 'Knowledge Representation and Reasoning' in Artificial Intelligence and Databases, Mylopoulos, J. and Brodie, M. (Editors), Morgan Kaufmann Publishers, Inc., San Mateo, California, 1989.

[14] Malpas, J., Prolog: A relational language and its applications, Prentice-Hall, Englewood Cliffs, NJ, USA, 1987

[15] Meyer, W., Expert systems in Factory Management - Knowledge based CIM, Ellis Horwood Ltd., Chichester, West Sussex, England, 1990.

[16] Rowe, C.N., Artificial Intelligence through Prolog, Prentice-Hall International Inc., Enlewood Cliffs, New Jersey, USA, 1988.

[17] Schmitt, T.G., Klastorin, T. and Shtub, A., Production classification system: concepts, models and strategies, Int.J.Prod.Res., 1985.

[18] Schneider, H.J., and Karagiannis, D., 'Intelligent Knowledge Bases of CAD Environments : The Hybrid System KANON', NATO ASI Series, Vol. F49, pp 161-196, Springer-Verlag, Berlin, 1988.

[19] Schomburg, E., Entwicklung eines Betriebstypologischen Instrumentariums zur Systematischen Ermittlung der Anforderungen an EDV - Gestuetzte Productionsplanungs - und - Steuerungssysteme im Maschinenbau, Dissertation, TH Aachen, Germany, 1980.

[20] Shemwell, A., Shepherd, N., and Wood, A., 'Consultancy tools - Affordable CIME solutions for SMEs (FTM)', Kewill Group Consultancy Services, ESPRIT II project 5424.

[21] Sepehri, M., 'Newest manufacturing software packages offer modules which meet specialized needs', Ind. Eng. Vol 28, pp 32-43, 1985.

[22] Speith,G. and Brief, U., BAPSY - ein Instrumentarium zur Beurteilung und Auswahl von Produktionsplanung - und steuerungs - Systemen, FIR mitteilungen , TH Aachen, Nr. 43 (Juni), 1982.

[23] Tatsiopoulos, I.P., 'Requirements analysis of production management software systems' in Computer Integrated Manufacturing Systems, Vol 3, pp 207-215, Betterworth-Heineman Ltd, 1990.

[24] Tatsiopoulos, I.P. and Pappas I.A., 'Design of fault-tolerant production management systems for small and medium sized firms' in Eloranta, E (ed), Advances in production management systems, Elsevier/North-Holland, Amsterdam, Netherlands, 1990.

[25] Weiskamp, K. and Hengl, T., Artificial Intelligence Programming with Turbo Prolog, John Wiley & Sons, New York, USA, 1988.

Composition and Dependency Relationships in Production Information System Design

C. Djeraba **, A. Ait Hssain *, B. Descotes-Genon *

** Laboratoire de Genie Informatique-IRIMAG,
B.P. 53X, 38401, Grenoble Cedex, France. e-mail : djeraba@imag.fr

* Laboratoire d'Automatique- ENSIEG,
BP 46, 38402 St Martin d'Hères, France. e-mail ait@lag.grenet.fr

Abstract Flexible Manufacturing System provides many alternative machines and conveying paths to manufacture a given part. Thus control of such complex systems must be bent, via an effective Production Information System (PIS), to a powerful Decision Making System (DMS) which has to compute the best alternatives in real-time. This paper presents such a Production Information System (PIS) for Flexible Manufacturing Systems. First it is briefly shown how the PIS incorporates models of both data sources (the FMS) and information requirements of planning, scheduling and control functions. Then structure and semantics modelling of information are emphasized using concepts of the knowledge-based system SHOOD. Utility of the system semantic relationships among objects, especially those of composition and dependency, is stressed.

1 Introduction

This paper deals with a global architecture and integrative modeling of Production Information System (PIS). The proposed PIS comprises: - a Petri-net-based control model to manage the interactions among all the various sub-systems (decision making agents, data/knowledge entities, FMS resources) modelled with objects, - an object-oriented description of, on one hand, both structure and semantic relationships of data and knowledge compounding the PIS core, and on the other hand, the elements of DMS. For this purpose some concepts of the knowledge-based system SHOOD, especially the semantic relationships, are employed. The composition and the dependency relationships are particularly useful here. It is our belief that, on one hand, this system control is a key issue to simplify complexity and, on the other one, semantic relationships permit expression of generic triggers and hence efficient consistency control among information objects. Indeed, the SHOOD concepts applied here for data/knowledge structuring have already been used to CAD/CAM systems design [10, 11]; and Petri net has been employed to describe an interaction scenario among MRP (Manufacturing Requirement Planning), CAM and CAD packages [4].

2 System Architecture and Global Modelling Methodology

Petri nets are powerful tools for modelling, simulation, validation and control of discrete event systems [2]. An Interpretation of Colored Petri Net (ICPN) have been used for control and monitoring of FMS [1]. Indeed it is concise (coloration) and acts on the

FMS resources (external operations) taking into account FMS actual state (marking, events, status variables). These elementary data are processed by the PIS so as to supply appropriate information to the decision makers.

The ICPN-based control consists of : - Initializing the ICPN modelling the system (marking, values for status variables). - Updating the ICPN taking into account the real-time process status (event occurrences, updated values of the variables).
When updating the ICPN, there may be a conflict among transitions to be fired with respect to tokens/colors [1]. This is a decision making problem which moreover must be solved in real-time by DMS. The alternatives are the transitions and the criteria are defined in the used selecting procedure.

In addition to time constraints and complexity, the DMS must cope with random disturbances (unscheduled orders, resource failures). Hence it should be decomposed to a set of decision making objects (men and/or software) cooperating according to a model. Hierarchical DMS (Fig. 1) is a solution to these requirements [5, 2].
In general, a decision maker [12] may be modelled by an object. Among its attributes are the decision criteria, parameters for expression of the alternatives and a strategy (method) to select the best alternatives (s) with respect to those criteria.

As a result, ICPN has been chosen to specify a coordination strategy among objects corresponding to DMS levels [1]. The strategy is more general and more efficient than classical top-down planning and scheduling. It includes, in particular, a feedback from the shop floor. The same ICPN will be used to implement the strategy and then guarantee a coherence with the ICPN based control and monitoring.

The PIS of FMS generally involves the following elements, listed with some properties related to production processes: - Machines (including conveyors) with MTTF (Mean Time To Failure), MTBF (Mean Time Between Failure), set-up time, ... - Tools with total time of use, ... - Operators with names, skills, ... - Products/parts with their manufacturing routings, ... - Production orders with concerned set of products/parts, quantities, delays, ... The main relationships among these elements are in the following (Fig. 1): Products are manufactured according to consumer orders. A product is a set of parts assembled according to a routing which is a sequence of manufacturing operations. A part is also manufactured according to a routing. An operation needs some tools and it is performed on a machine or workstation. This requires some worker skills. Machines compose workcells, etc.

The PIS core is a database which should be specified in such a way that it may apply to most FMSs. This requires appropriate models to describe both structure and semantic relationships among the entities. The object paradigm is enough rich and thus could provide such facilities. In addition, two important relationships, namely composition and dependency, are particularly useful for PIS design. The former is a link between a pair of objects (a set of objects related by the composition relationship is collectively called a composite object).

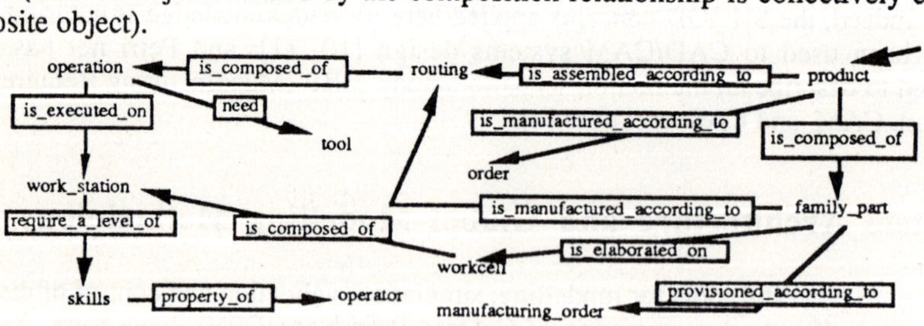

Fig. 1. PIS elements

The latter presents SHOOD, a Knowledge-Based System [10, 11, 12] which supports an Object oriented Data Model extended with the composition and dependency relationships. It eliminates the shortcomings while retaining the advantages of the existing systems which seem more limited models [8]. For all these reasons, we shall use SHOOD concepts to specify the PIS core.
Section 3 presents briefly these concepts and section 4 shows their application for PIS.

3 SHOOD Concepts

SHOOD is based on three principles [11, 12]: 1) every thing is an object, every object is an instance of another object, and any information concerning an object is stored in its attributes. The use of principles mentioned previously for the design of shood has given rise to a powerful, reflexive and meta-circular model.

A class has a number of attributes. The value of an attribute is itself an object which belongs to a class. A class may be a primitive class without any attributes (e.g integer, character), or may have any number of attributes (the attributes of the class "workcell" include the "name" and the "space-localization"). An attribute is itself a class which has class variables (descriptors) [10]. These descriptors define the class where the attributes take their values, their restrictions and the different ways to be computed (constraints and inferences). The instance variables of an attribute define the local properties for an attribute instance.

We say that an object "object1" has a reference to another object "object2", if object2 is a value of an attribute of object1. The instance that acquires values will be called a receptor (e.g object1) and the instances from which values are acquired will be called transmitters (object2).

For example, the class "workcell" has a reference to the domain "factory" through the attribute "space_localization". The "workcell1" (instance of the class "workcell") has a reference to "factory1" (instance of the class "factory") through an instance of the attribute class "space_localisation". We can also say that the space localization of "workcell1" is "factory1" or "factory1" is the value of the attribute "space_localization" of the"workcell1" instance. Here, "workcell1" is a receptor and "factory1" is a transmitter.

4 SHOOD Concepts in the PIS

4.1 Relationship and Graph of Composition

In the production information system design domain, an important type of semantic relations is the relation between the parts of things and the whole entities which they comprise. While knowledge of parts and whole entities can be expressed in many specialized ways [5], we will focus on the relation expressed by the terms "component-of" or "part-of", as in "The X is component of the Y", "X is a component of Y" and similar expressions, such as "Operations are component of routing ", "A work_station is a component of a workcell", "Family of parts is a component of product", etc. We will refer to relationships that can be expressed with the term "component-of" in the above frames as "composition relationship".

From a logical point of view, composition relationships are usually understood to express strict partial ordering relations [5]. These logical properties of composition relationships make them particularly important to our understanding of the composition relationship structure. Strict partial ordering relations are transitive, irreflexive, and antisymetrical, that is, if CR is the relation expressed by "is a component of", then, - if x CR y, and y CR z, then x CR z (transitivity); - x CR x (irreflectiveness); and - y CR x (antisymetry).

4.2 Dependency Relationship

PIS core specification requires a facility for defining and manipulating dependency relationships which describe semantics superimposed on relations between objects [4, 5]. The basic constructs of the dependency collection are shared dependency (S), exclusive dependency (X), and existential dependency (E) which impact upon in creation, search, deletion, changing , and duplication operations. For example, the existence of a production depends on the existence of water. If water ceases to exist, the production is stopped. The link between production and water is an existential dependency relationship. The dependency relationships can be superimposed on the attribute when it is created.

a. Shared dependency relationship: An essential concept in modeling the dependency between objects is that of a shared dependency. A shared dependency relationship between an object (receptor) and another object (transmitter) means that the transmitter is referenced by the receptor and possibly other receptors. We say that the transmitter is a value of a receptor attribute and probably other receptor attributes. Let us consider this example. Suppose that a skill is linked to operators (Fig. 1). A skill may share operator with other skills. "operator1" is shared by "skill1" and "skill2". From the user's point of view, these skills ("skill1" and "skill2") are related to the same operator ("operator1"). Therefore, the deletion of "operator1" of "skill1" must not implicate the deletion of the same operator ("operator1") related to "skill2".

b. Exclusive Dependency Relationship: We also need a notion of exclusive dependency relationship between an object (receptor) and another object (transmitter). This is closely related to the idea which means that the transmitter is referenced by only one receptor. It allows a receptor to be the single owner of a transmitter. The transmitter is a value of only one receptor attribute and therefore can not be a value of another attribute merged with exclusive or shared dependency relationships. Let us consider the example of a workstation. We require that a set of skills may be used by only one workstation. A workstation may be used for only one operation. The set of skills {"skill1", "skill2", "skill2", etc} is required by "workstation1", it can not be required by "workstation2".

c. Existential Dependency Relationship: It is sometimes desirable to free the user applications from having to search for and delete all objects which depend existentially on a deleted object. This feature impedes the reuse of objects in an PIS design. The semantics of an existential dependency is refined on the basis of wether the existence of a receptor depends on the existence of a transmitter (existential_t_r) or the existence of a transmitter depends on the existence of a receptor (existential_r_t).

When the existence of a transmitter object depends on the existence of a receptor object, we talk about existential dependency relationship from the receptor object to the transmitter object *(existential_r_t)*. Therefore, if the receptor is deleted, the transmitter object is also deleted. The deletion of the receptor involves the deletion of the transmitter only if all other shared dependencies to the transmitter have been removed. For example, the destruction of a consumer order implicates the destruction of its compounding products. The receptor is the order and the transmitter is the component object product. This component is destroyed only if all other shared dependencies to this component have been removed.

Existential dependency relationship from a transmitter object to a receptor object *(existential_t_r)* means that the existence of a receptor object depends on the existence of a transmitter object. If the transmitter is deleted, the receptor object is also deleted. The deletion of a transmitter causes the deletion of a receptor only if all other shared dependencies to the receptor have been removed. Let us consider the example where the components of a product include parts. The destruction of the part involves the destruction of the product. The receptor is the composite object "product" and the transmitter is the component object "part". The product is destroyed only if all other shared dependencies to the product have been removed.

d. Generic and Specific Dependency: Generic dependency relationship consists of common dependencies for all instances of an attribute class. All instances undergo the dependencies of the attribute class. We call it generic dependency or strong dependency, in a sense that the semantic dependency on the attribute class can not be overridden on the instances.

In some complex PIS designs, it is not interesting to have a generic dependency. Not all instances will have the same dependency. We call it specific or weak dependency, in a sense that, a dependency of an attribute class can be overridden in the instances. A specific dependency is declared with default dependency. For examples, a workstation require a set of skills through a level of skill. Generally, the dependency relationship between the object "workstation" and the objects "skills" means that a skill is reserved exclusively to a workstation. the skill is connected to the workstation with the exclusive dependency relationship. This dependency relationship is generally true, but there is some situations where it is not overridden. For financial considerations, it is possible that a skill will be shared between several work-stations. For example, the skill (skill1) is generally reserved to only one work-station (workstation1). However, there is specific situation where the skill (skill1) is shared by two work-stations "workstation1" and "workstation2".

4.4 Changes to Dependency Relationship

Frequently, the user has to change the dependency relationship from source dependency to target dependency. For example, a workcell in the production management (FMS) concerns several work-stations which correspond respectively to different components of the workcell. The component "work-station" is reserved exclusively to the composite "workcell". Consequently, the component "work-station" is connected to the composite "workcell" with an exclusive dependency relationship. Because they found it expensive, the managers decide to share "work-station" to other "workcell". The managers change the dependency relationship from exclusive dependency to shared-dependency. Now, the component "work-station" can be shared by two composites (workcell1 and workcell2).

Globally, the changes may be of two types : state-independent and state-dependent changes. Roughly, a state-independent change is a change which removes a constraint from a dependency relationship, while a state-dependent change adds a constraint to a dependency relationship. A state-dependent change requires verification of the exclusivity involved in the change. The notion of state-dependent and state-independent are introduced by [8], but they are limited to generic dependency relationships. In SHOOD system, they are extended to specific dependency relationships.

5. Conclusion

A Production Information System (PIS) for FMS has been presented. It is a part of a global object-oriented architecture incorporating Petri-net-based models for both data sources and information destinations. Design of the PIS core (a database) employes concepts of the knowledge-based system SHOOD especially the original semantics of dependency and composition relationships. As a result, complexity is reduced and integration is facilitated. Indeed, first, this systemic approach specifies the interactions involving the PIS and thus requests are known in advance; then the behavior of the dependency relationships, occurring in operations such as creation, deletion, dependency change, and duplication, reduces the number of stored objects. The functionalities of composition and dependency relationships are implemented and used in two other laboratories. Ongoing works aim at performance evaluation (using ICPN) and complete implementation of the architecture.

References

1. Ait Hssain A. and B. Descotes-Genon, Production Monitoring Integration in Planning and Control of FMS, IFAC-INCOM'92, Toronto (Canada).
2. David R., Modelling of Dynamic Systems by Petri Nets, ECC'91, Grenoble (France).
3. Djeraba, C., Composition and Dependancy Relationships. Intern. Conf. of Artificial Intelligence in Engineering, Jun 93, Toulouse (France).
4. Harhalakis G., H. Hillion, K.Y. Moy, Development of a Factory Level CIM Model, J. of Manufacturing Systems, Vol. 9, no 2, 1990.
5. Harhalakis G., R. Nagi and J.M. Proth, Hierarchical Modelling Approch for Production Planning, IFAC-INCOM'92, Toronto (Canada).
6. Hsu, C. and L. Rattner, Information Modelling for Computerized Manufacturing, IEEE Transactions on Syst., Man and Cyb., Vol. 20, No. 4.
7. JEAN P., Manipulation d'objets composites dans les bases de connaissances. Rapport de DEA INPG 1989.
8. KIM W., BERTINO E., GARZA J. F., Composite objetcs revisited . SIGMOD 1989 Proceedings Volume 2.
9. Nagi G., Design and Operation of Hierarchical Production Manufacturing Systems, Ph.D Thesis Report, Univ. of Maryland.
10. Nguyen G.T, Rieu D., Representing Design object . Proc 1th Int. Conf Arificial Intelligence in Design, Edinburgh (UK), 1991.
11. NGUYEN G.T, RIEU D., Multiple object representations. Proc 20th ACM Computer Science Corporation. Kansas City (USA) March 1992.
12. Rieu D., T Nguyen G.,Culet A.,Escamilla J. and Djeraba C., Représentations Multiples d'objets évolutifs, RFIA, 1991.

Vehicle Transactions

Makoto Takizawa†, Satoshi Hamada†, and S. Misbah Deen ‡

† Dept. of Computers and Systems Engineering, Tokyo Denki University
Ishizaka, Hatoyama, Saitama 350-03, Japan
e-mail {taki, hama}@takilab.k.dendai.ac.jp

‡ Dept. of Computer Science, Univ. of Keele
Keele, Staffs ST5 5BG, England
e-mail misbah@cs.kl.ac.uk

Abstract. A vehicle space where vehicles move around is structured in a *space* tree whose nodes are space objects. Higher-level objects denote broader area than lower level ones. Each vehicle first decides a *broad* path which includes higher-level objects, and the path is made more detailed as the vehicle is approaching to the destination. Vehicles are modeled as transactions which hold objects. There are kinds of vehicles, on three points, *removable*, *stoppable*, and *retreatable*. In this paper, we discuss three schemes, i.e. *close*, *semi-open*, and *open* ones for locking and releasing objects with respect to types of vehicles.

1 Introduction

A *vehicle system* is composed of *vehicles* which move around in a *vehicle space*. [1] discusses a *broad path decision* where each vehicle v first decides the *broad* path to the destination, and then the path is more detailed as v is approaching to the destination. The space is structured in a tree whose nodes are objects. Children of an object o are *component* ones of o.

Each vehicle v moves on objects by locking them. A movement of v is modeled as a transaction which holds objects. There are types of vehicles. For example, airplanes cannot stop, and automobile cars in motorways cannot back. The vehicles which cannot back do not need to hold the objects which the vehicles have passed already. In this paper, we discuss three schemes, *open*, *semi-open*, and *close* ones for locking and releasing objects with respect to types of vehicles.

In section 2, we present a system model. In section 3, we present three synchronization methods i.e. *open*, *semi-open*, and *close* ones.

2 System Model

2.1 Vehicle space tree

A space is structured in a tree named a *space tree* whose nodes are space objects. For each objects o, let $level(o)$ be a number of nodes in a path from o to the root. o_1 is *higher* than o_2 ($o_1 \succ o_2$) iff $level(o_1) < level(o_2)$. Higher objects denote *broader* paths than the lower objects. Each object o has a set of ports. Each pair of ports is a *primitive* path of o, written as $\langle o \rangle$. A vehicle v can move from a port to a port of o, written as $\langle o \rangle$. A *path* is a sequence of primitive paths, i.e. $\langle \langle o_1 \rangle, \ldots, \langle o_n \rangle \rangle$where every $\langle o_i \rangle$ and $\langle o_{i+1} \rangle$ are directly connected. Figure 1 shows an example of the space tree. o is composed of a, b, ..., g. d is further composed of d_1, d_2, ..., d_4. p_1 and p_2 are ports of o. The double lines between objects indicate links.

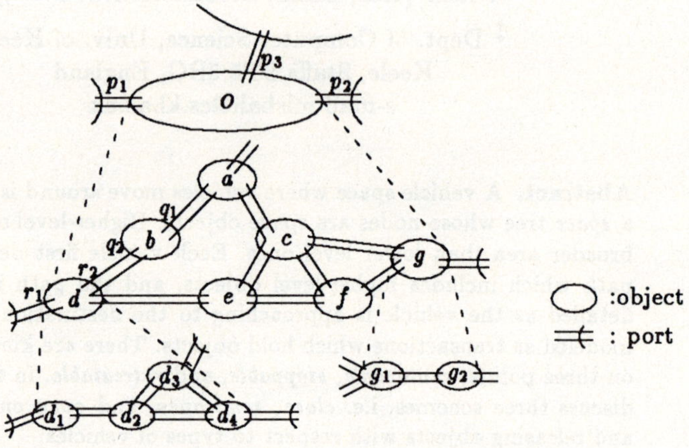

Fig. 1. Space object

2.2 Types of vehicles

There are types of vehicles, i.e. *removable*, *stoppable*, and *retreatable* ones. Some vehicles cannot be removed from the vehicle space, e.g. automobile. The other point is concerned with whether vehicles can stop or not. For example, airplanes cannot stop. For each *unstoppable* vehicle v, farther objects which v would take have to be obtained. On the other hand, objects farther from a stoppable v need not be obtained by v because v can wait on some objects. The last point is concerned with whether or not v can back along the path which v has passed. As soon as an *unretreatable* v passes an object o, v can release o since v never backs. On the other hand, if v is retreatable, v can hold o.

3 Synchronization

We model the movement of each vehicle v as a transaction which locks objects.

3.1 Locking scheme

For each primitive path $\langle o \rangle$ of an object o, the *capacity* of $\langle o \rangle$, $cap(\langle o \rangle)$ represents how many vehicles $\langle o \rangle$ can admit at the same time. $hold(\langle o \rangle)$ denotes a number of vehicles in $\langle o \rangle$ ($hold(\langle o \rangle) \leq cap(\langle o \rangle)$). In order to make sure that v can pass o, v locks o before arriving at o. If $cap(\langle o \rangle) - hold(\langle o \rangle) \geq 0$, o can accept the lock request of v. Suppose that v in o_1 would like to pass through $\langle o \rangle$. First, v

sends the lock request to o. Here, suppose that v makes a success in locking $\langle o \rangle$. If v locks o which is farther from v, another vehicle v_2 may not hold o even if v_2 is nearer to o than v. Furthermore, even if v holds o, v may not arrive at o due to some accident. Hence, v sends o a lock with a level $olevel(o_1, o)$. $olevel(o_1, o)$ represents the lock level on $\langle o \rangle$. In order for v to pass $\langle o \rangle$ nearer to v, v has to hold o more strongly with bigger *olevel*. $olevel(o_1, o)$ depends on the distance of o from o_1. $olevel(o_1, o)$ is computed as presented in [1].

(1) If $cap(\langle o \rangle) - olevel(o_1, o) \geq 0$, o accepts the lock request from v. If locked, $cap(\langle o \rangle) = cap(\langle o \rangle) - olevel(o_1, o)$.
(2) If $cap(\langle o \rangle) - olevel(o_1, o) < 0$, o rejects the lock request from v. □

As v is approaching to o, the lock level for o is increased according to the definition of *olevel*. It is a *lock augmentation* on $\langle o \rangle$.

3.2 Releasing schemes

The movement of v is modeled as a transaction which locks objects. v locks o before arriving at o and releases o after leaving o. If v is a *strict* two-phase locked (*2PL*) [2] one, v does not release objects until v arrives at the destination. The *2PL* decreases the space utilization. On the other hand, if v releases objects which v has passed through, the objects can be used by another vehicles.

After locking $\langle o \rangle$, v requires o to decide a detailed path $\langle \langle o_1 \rangle, \ldots, \langle o_n \rangle \rangle$where o_i is a component of o. v is a sequence of subtransactions $v_1, \ldots, v_n$, where each v_j is concerned with movement on $\langle o_j \rangle$[Fig. 2]. Thus, v is *nested*. When v passes through o, v commits. There are three ways to release objects when v commits.

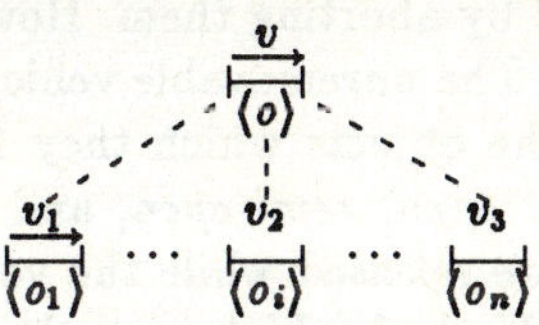

Fig. 2. Vehicle transaction

1. If v is a root of the vehicle and v arrives at the destination, all the locks held by v are released. Otherwise, no objects are released.
2. $\langle o_1 \rangle, \ldots, \langle o_n \rangle$ held by the $v_1 \rightarrow v_n$ are released.
3. $\langle o \rangle$ is released. □

The first is a *close* scheme, i.e. strict *2PL*. The second is a *semi-open* one. It is noted that $\langle o \rangle$ is not released although $\langle o_1 \rangle, \ldots, \langle o_n \rangle$ are released. The third is an *open* scheme, where all the objects obtained by v are released. It depends on the type of v which scheme is adopted[Table 1]. Suppose that v is *unretreatable*. As soon as v passes objects, v can release them. Hence, unretreatable vehicles can adopt the open scheme. On the other hand, a retreatable v may back to some object which v has passed. If the objects which v has passed are released by the open scheme, v cannot back. Therefore, v can adopt the semi-open or close scheme.

If o cannot accept v, v waits on o until v can hold, or gives up to hold o and tries to find another way. As stated before, only stoppable vehicles can take the *wait* action. The unstoppable vehicles like airplanes cannot take the wait action and have to go ahead without stopping. The second is a *re-planning* action. If o is farther from the current object, v may move on the path. If o is nearer to v v tries to find another path to escape o.

Table 1. Releasing schemes and vehicle types

Releasing schemes	Concurrency degree	Treatable	Vehicle types	
			Treatable	Nontreatable
close	×	○	○	×
semi-open	△	△	○	×
open	○	×	×	○

○ : good. △ : marginal. × : not good.

4 Concluding Remarks

In this paper, each vehicle movement is modeled as a transaction which holds objects in the space tree. The vehicles are classified with respect to three points, *removable*, *stoppable*, and *retreatable*. In the conventional database systems, transactions can be removed by aborting them. However, vehicles like automobile cars cannot be removed. The unremovable vehicles have to move to another objects in order to release the objects which they hold. We have shown three synchronization schemes, i.e. *open*, *semi-open*, and *close* ones. In the open or semi-open one, the objects are released while the vehicles are moving. We have discussed what scheme each kind of vehicle can adopt.

References

1. Deen, S. M., Hamada, S., and Takizawa, M., "Broad Path Decision in Vehicle System," *Proc. of the 3rd International Conf. on Database and Expert Systems Applications (DEXA'92)*, 1992, pp.8-13.
2. Eswaren, K. P., Gray, J., Lorie, R. A., and Traiger, I. L., "The Notion of Consistency and Predicate Locks in Database Systems," *CACM*, Vol.19, No.11, 1976, pp.624-637.
3. Moss, J. E., "Nested Transactions: An Approach to Reliable Distributed Computing," *The MIT Press Series in Information Systems*, 1985.
4. Takizawa, M. and Deen, S. M., "Lock Mode Based Resolution of Uncompensatable Deadlock," *Proc. of the Far-east Workshop on Future Database Systems*, 1992, pp.168-175.

An Approach to Image Retrieval for Image Databases

T. Gevers and A.W.M. Smeulders

Faculty of Mathematics & Computer Science, University of Amsterdam
Kruislaan 403, 1098 SJ Amsterdam, The Netherlands
e-mail: gevers@fwi.uva.nl

Abstract. In this paper, a method is discussed to store and retrieve images efficiently from an image database on the basis of the data structure called E() representation. The E() representation is a spatial knowledge representation preserving the spatial information between objects embedded in symbolic images as an iconic index for the purpose of efficient image retrieval.
The image retrieval method is invariant under, at least, the affine transformation (i.e. translation, rotation and scale) and is able to deal with substantial object occlusion. A metric is defined to express similarity between symbolic images.
Initial experiments carried out for two applications show that the image retrieval method is very efficient and robust to similarity retrieval in image databases. Together with the inherent high parallelism, it makes the method a promising image retrieval method.

keywords: image database, image indexing, similarity retrieval, spatial relations, E() representation, metric, spatial query language.

1 Introduction

Research in the design of image database systems has increased significantly in the last decade [3], [12], [21]. Much attention has been paid to the problems of how to store images and to retrieve them efficiently from an image database. Many data structures have been proposed at the level of pixels, such as pixel-based [7], R-trees [13], quadtrees [20] together with their spatial processing operations. Most of the image database systems combines these spatial processing capabilities with DBMS capabilities for the purpose of storage and retrieval of complex data (e.g. range queries). Other image database systems are still based on the paradigm to store a key-word description of the image content, created by some user on input, in a relational DBMS in addition to a pointer to the raw image data. Image retrieval is then based on the relational DBMS capabilities. However, another approach is required if we consider the wish to retrieve images on the basis of objects and their spatial relations. To that end, an object-oriented data structure is required to represent images preserving information about objects and their spatial relations in a robust way to enable efficient image indexing and retrieval [4],[5],[19].

In this paper, a method is presented to retrieve images based on the E() indexing scheme. The E() representation preserves the spatial information between objects, embedded in images, as an index. The image retrieval method is invariant under, at least, the affine transformation (i.e. translation, rotation and scale) and is able to deal with substantial object occlusion. A query specification method is discussed to enable the formulation of a query in terms of objects and their spatial relations. Because the query as well as every image in the image database are represented by an E() representation, image retrieval is reduced to E() representation matching. A metric is given to express similarity between two E() representations. For the purpose of image retrieval, the metric can be used to compare a picture query with each E() representation of every image in database and order the images by their proximity to the query. Images with a low metric are considered the same or similar to the query.

This paper is organized as follows.
Section 2 will start with the E() representation scheme for image indexing. In Section 3, a comparison scheme is discussed to retrieve images on the basis of directional relations between object pairs. Section 4 will present another comparison scheme for the purpose of image retrieval based on the sequence in which objects are situated around each other. A spatial query specification method is discussed in Section 5. In Section 6, applications and experiments are presented to illustrate the nature of the method and how the method can be applied to real-world problems. Finally, a summary will be given.

2 Image Indexing: the E() Representation

Retrieval of images is one of the most important issues of image database design. In this paper, we approach this problem on the basis of the observation that images can be discriminated by the presence of objects and their spatial relations. Therefore, a query should be defined in terms of objects and their spatial relations. A typical query is for example "retrieve all images with a car left to a house". Image retrieval is then the process to compute to what extent the images in the database, described by objects and their spatial relations, correspond to the query. To realize the image retrieval process, a data structure is needed to represent the images. The data structure must capture the information about the objects as well as the spatial information in images in a robust way to enable efficient image indexing and retrieval. To that end, a representation scheme is discussed in this section.

The architecture of the image database system consists of a physical image store and a logical database. A symbolic description is obtained for every raw digital image in the physical image store by applying image processing and pattern recognition techniques or by manually tracing outlines of objects. The symbolic description of an image includes the identity of objects and their position in image space. In this paper we make no distinction between low-level objects such as corners, points of inflection and t-junctions [18] or high-level objects such as a rectangular box, a chair, a table etc. We assume that objects have already been recognized automatically or interactively and unique symbolic labels have been assigned to them, yielding a symbolic picture.

More precisely, a symbolic picture f is defined as a mapping $M\text{x}N \rightarrow S$, where $M = (1, 2, ..., m)$ and $N = (1, 2, ..., n)$. S is the power set of V, where V is a set of symbols called the vocabulary. Each symbol represents an object.

A data structure is required to efficiently store symbolic pictures for the purpose of flexible image indexing and retrieval. The data structure should be able to preserve the spatial relations between objects in an elegant and flexible manner. Various different spatial relations have been proposed in literature [1], [15]. The most typical spatial relations are topological relations, describing (partly) overlapping objects, adjacency relations, describing to what extent objects are touching each other, and directional relations such as north, east, south and west. In this paper, we concentrate on directional relations.

From now on, we consider point objects which give an unambiguous account of directional relations. For objects larger then points, we consider their centroids as indicators.

An intuitive understanding of how a symbolic picture f of point objects is represented, is given in the following example.

Consider the symbolic picture shown in fig. 1. The coordinate system plane may be quantized at different resolutions, making the directional relations between objects as precise or fuzzy as apt for the domain at hand. If simple directional relations north-east, south-east, south-west and north-west are considered, it is sufficient to quantized the

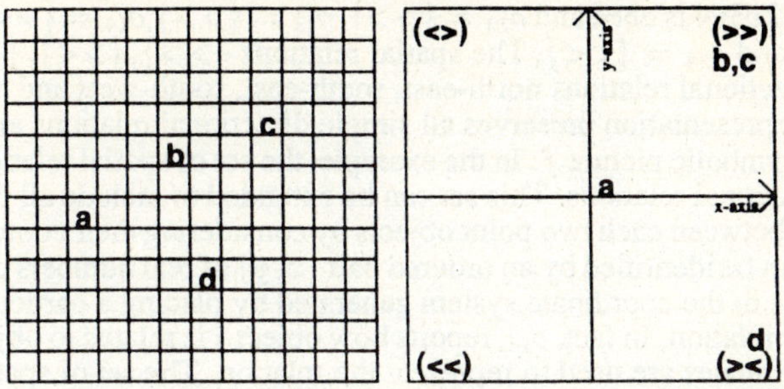

Fig. 1. a: symbolic picture b: object a placed at the origin of a rectangular coordinate system

coordinate space in four quadrants. First, we place object a at the origin of a rectangular coordinate system where the direction of the x-axis and y-axis corresponds to that of the symbolic picture, as shown in fig. 1.b. All other objects are lying in one of the four quadrants. Let's record in which of the four quadrants each of the objects is lying. Object b will be recorded as lying east of object a along the x-axis and north along the y-axis. The two dimensional directional relation north-east is recorded for object b with respect to object a and will be represented as the string $a :>> b$. Further, object c is also north-east with respect to a, yielding the following string $a :>> b >> c$. Finally, we obtain the string $a :>> b >> c >< d$, where the substring $a :$ denotes that the following substring records how the other objects b, c and d are positioned with respect to a. Similarly, this process is repeated for the other objects as being placed at the origin of the coordinate system, yielding the strings $b :<< a >> c >< d$, $c :<< a << b << d$ and $d :<> a <> b >> c$. The entire set of strings, denoted by $E(a, b, c, d)$, is

$$E(a,b,c,d) = \begin{array}{l} \{\ (a :>> b >> c >< d) \\ \ \ \ (b :<< a >> c >< d) \\ \ \ \ (c :<< a << b << d) \\ \ \ \ (d :<> a <> b >> c)\ \} \end{array} \tag{2.1}$$

This coding scheme is inefficient, because the spatial information between any object pair is recorded twice (e.g. north-east(x, y) implies south-west(y, x)). Therefore, the following set of strings is necessary and sufficient to represent the symbolic picture f:

$$E(a,b,c,d) = \begin{array}{l} \{\ (a :>> b >> c >< d) \\ \ \ \ (b :>> c >< d) \\ \ \ \ (c :<< d)\ \} \end{array} \tag{2.2}$$

A more formal definition of $E()$ is as follows. Let V be a set of symbols. Each symbol represents an object. Let O be a set of spatial operators which specify spatial relations among objects, then

$$E(v_1, v_2, ..., v_n) = \begin{array}{l} \{\ (v_1 : o_{12} v_2 o_{13} v_3 ... o_{1n} v_n) \\ \ \ \ (v_2 : o_{23} v_3 o_{24} v_4 ... o_{2n} v_n) \\ \ \ \ \vdots \\ \ \ \ (v_{(n-1)} : o_{(n-1)n} v_n)\} \end{array} \tag{2.3}$$

where $v_1, v_2, ... v_n$ are symbols in V and $o_{ij} \in O$ for $i < j \leq n$. For the example above, the vocabulary is $V = \{a, b, c, d\}$ and $O = \{>>, ><, <>, <<\}$ is the set of simple directional relations:

$$E(v_1, v_2, ..., v_4) = \begin{array}{l} \{\ (v_1 : o_{12} v_2 o_{13} v_3 o_{14} v_4) \\ \ \ \ (v_2 : o_{23} v_3 o_{24} v_4) \\ \ \ \ (v_3 : o_{34} v_4)\ \} \end{array} \tag{2.4}$$

where $v1v2v3v4$ is *abcd* and $o_{12} = \{>>\}, o_{13} = \{>>\}, o_{14} = \{><\}, o_{23} = \{>>\}$, $o_{24} = \{<>\}$ and $o_{34} = \{<<\}$. The spatial relations $\{>>\}, \{><\}, \{<>\}$ and $\{<<\}$ denote the directional relations north-east, south-east, south-west and north-west.

The $E()$ representation preserves all simple directional relations among objects induced by the symbolic picture f. In the example, the set of spatial relations, O, is the set of simple directional relations. This set can be extended to include all possible geometrical relations between each two point objects by considering their coordinates (i.e. each point object can be identified by an ordered pair (x, y) of real numbers corresponding to the coordinates in the coordinate system generated by placing a particular object at the origin) as their relation. In fact, o_{ij}, reports how object j is related to object i. For spatial relations, coordinates are used to represent the relation. The set of spatial relations, O, can also be extended to include the sets of topological and adjacency relations as well.

To perform image retrieval, each symbolic image for every image in the image database is translated to an $E()$ representation as well as the query. The query can be specified by drawing an iconic picture on the screen. The iconic picture consists of icons representing objects and their spatial relationships, similar to a symbolic picture, see Section 5. After the user has specified the query graphically, the query is converted into an $E()$ representation. The problem of image retrieval then becomes the matching of two $E()$'s.

3 Image Retrieval by E() Matching

A metric between two $E()$'s is necessary to express to what extent two images, represented by E_1 and E_2 respectively, are similar. If two object embeddings with different sets of objects have to be compared, only those objects which are common to both are considered to contribute to the metric. The advantage to take objects which are common to both embeddings to compute the metric, is that the method is able to deal with substantial occlusion of objects. This is desirable for general image retrieval.

Let two $E()$ representations $E_1(v_1, v_2, ..., v_n)$ and $E_2(v_1, v_2, ..., v_n)$ contain the same set of n distinct objects $V = \{v_1, v_2, ..., v_n\}, v_i \neq v_j, \forall i \neq j \leq n$. Further, let O_1 and O_2 denote the sets of spatial operators of respectively E_1 and E_2. Then the distance is defined as follows:

$$d(E_1, E_2) = \sum_{i=1}^{i=n} \sum_{j=i}^{i=n} w_{ij} f(o_{ij}, p_{ij}), o_{ij} \in O_1, p_{ij} \in O_2 \tag{3.1}$$

where, w_{ij} is a weight factor.

If we use a 2D relation table to store each $E()$ representation, the elements on and below the diagonal of the matrix are zero. The matrix is triangular with total number of elements is $\sum_{i=1}^{i=n}(i-1)$ for n objects. In each entry $E_{ij}, i < j \leq n$ of E(), the coordinate is recorded of object j in the coordinate system generated by placing object i at the origin. The coordinate system is a rectangular coordinate system, usually the Euclidean L_2. In the 2-D case, the coordinate vector $\mathbf{x} = (x, y) \in R^2$ is stored in each entry expressing the directional relation between object pairs.

Thus, mathematically, we can model the distance between two directional relations as a function $f \in R^2$ of a two dimensional spatial vector $\mathbf{x} = (x_2 - x_1, y_2 - y_1) = (\Delta x, \Delta y) \in R^2$, where $\mathbf{x}_1 = (x_1, y_1)$ is the coordinate vector recorded at entry (i, j) for E_1 and $\mathbf{x}_2 = (x_2, y_2)$ is the vector recorded at the corresponding entry for E_2. For each vector $\mathbf{x}$, the value $f(\mathbf{x})$ equals the distance between two directional relations. When $f(\mathbf{x})$ has been chosen to express the minimum number of directional relations violated to transform relation $\mathbf{x}_1$ into $\mathbf{x}_2$, the function f corresponds to the magnitude distance function:

$$f(\mathbf{x}) = |x| + |y| \tag{3.2}$$

or the Euclidean distance function:

$$g(\mathbf{x}) = \sqrt{x^2 + y^2} \tag{3.3}$$

Let E_1 and E_2 be the symbolic representations of two object embeddings of the same distinct objects. Let $d(E_1, E_2)$ denote the total minimum number of directional relation violations required to transform E_1 into E_2, then $d(E_1, E_2)$ is a metric and implies that for every E_i other $E_1, E_2, ..., E_n$ not equal to E_i can be ordered in their proximity to E_i. For the purpose of image retrieval, E_i can be seen as the representation of a query and $E_1, E_2, ..., E_n$ the representations of the images in the image database. In this way, images are shown on the screen to the user in accordance to their metric value, where images having a low metric are considered the same or similar to the query.

3.1 Invariance under the Affine Transformation

Till now, the method is invariant under translation. For general image retrieval, the method should be invariant, at least, under the affine transformation such that object embeddings can be recognized even if they are transformed (rotated, translated, scaled and sheared).

We first extend the method to be invariant under rotation. An rotation transformation is uniquely defined by the transformation of two non-collinear objects [17]. Therefore, each combination of two non-collinear objects can be chosen to represent all other objects. Specifically, let p_0 and p_1 be two non-collinear objects extracted from a symbolic picture, then any other object from the same symbolic picture can be represented in the 2D space spanned by the basis (p_0, p_1). The origin is chosen to be the middle of p_0 and p_1, see fig. 2.

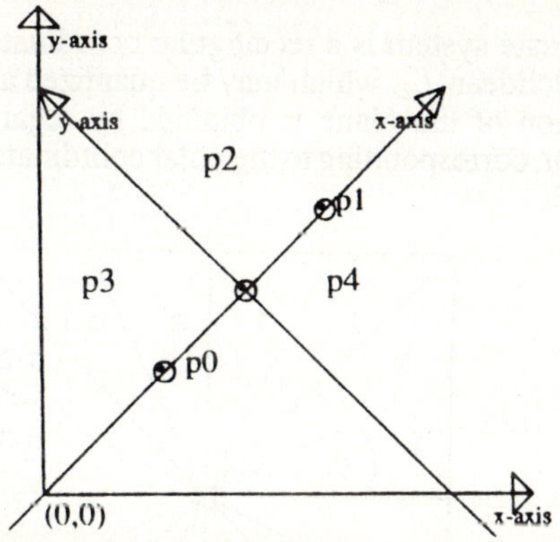

Fig. 2. Basis for transformation.

Let n be the number of objects. The coordinates are computed for all other $n-2$ objects in the new coordinate frame defined by the basis objects. In this way, the coordinates of all $n-2$ objects undergo a rotational transformation equal to the system and therefore the coordinates remain the same with respect to the basis (p_0, p_1). To compare two object embeddings of two images for the purpose of image retrieval, two non-collinear objects common to both object embeddings are chosen and the coordinates of all other objects are calculated with respect to the basis, yielding two $E()$ representations which can be matched. Due to object occlusion or noise, one or more objects may not be present or may be translated in the images to be compared. Hence, not only one basis pair should be taken, but each ordered non-collinear pair of objects must be taken to be the basis of a new coordinate frame. When n is the number of distinct objects, then there exists a maximum of n^2 different basis pairs, yielding n^2

$E()$ representations. Because the time complexity to match two E()'s is $O(n^2)$, the time complexity of the method to be translation and rotation invariant is $O(n^4)$, because n^2 $E()$ representations must be matched, each with complexity $O(n^2)$ in order to compute the best translation- rotation invariant match.

To allow the method to be invariant under the affine transformation (translation, rotation, scale and sheare), a three object basis is required. Let p_0, p_1 and p_2 be three non-collinear objects in 2D extracted from a symbolic picture, and $(p_1 - p_0, p_2 - p_0)$ is the basis with p_0 as the origin spanning the 2D space. The maximum number of basis triplets is n^3 to represent the other $n-3$ objects. For each ordered non-collinear triplet an $E()$ representation is generated. Hence, the number of $E()$'s for an arbitrary image with n objects is n^3 and the time complexity to match two images, both having n identical distinct objects and required to be invariant under the affine transformation, is $O(n^5)$. The great advantage of this approach is that it suitable not only for the affine 2-D case, but also to other useful transformations in 2-D and 3-D, as required by the application, by simply changing the number of basis objects. For example, 4 basis objects is needed for a projective transformation [8]. Because only the number of objects to be taken as a basis for a new coordinate frame differ, it is important to know to what extent the time complexity is affected by the number of basis objects.

More specifically, let k be the number of basis objects needed for the desired transformation. All other $n-k$ objects have transformation invariant coordinates with respect to the k-tuple basis. Then the time complexity of the method is $O(n^2)$, $k=1$, and $O(n^{k+2})$, $k>1$.

4 Circular Coordinate System

Till so far, the coordinate system is a rectangular coordinate system (i.e. the Cartesian plane), usually the Euclidean L_2, which may be quantized at different resolutions.

Another tessellation of the plane is obtained by regarding the space around the origin as being circular, corresponding to the polar coordinate system without magnitude information, see fig. 3.

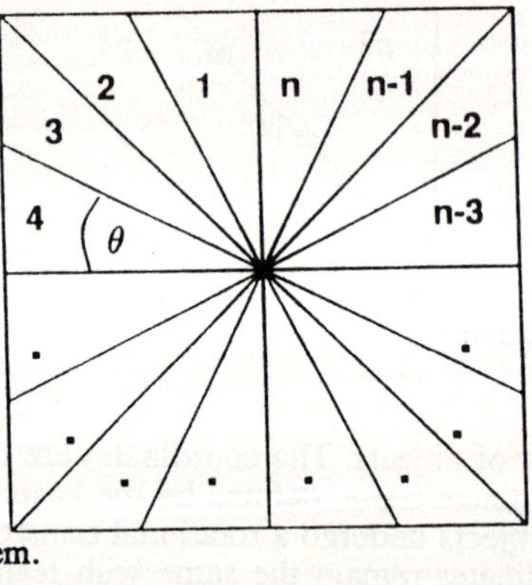

Fig. 3. Circular coordinate system.

The bins are equally sized and for $\theta = \frac{2\pi}{2^n}, n = 2$, the simple directional relations are represented. As opposed to the rectangular system, each location consists of only one coordinate. For $n > 2$, the resolution of the coordinate system increases. For large n, relations are more precisely described.

The $E()$ representation is generated by placing each object at the center of the circular coordinate system and all object coordinates are recorded and stored as an entry. Let

$\mathbf{x}_1 = (x_1) \in N^+$ be the one-dimensional vector of entry E_{ij} of $E_1()$ describing in which bin object j lands with respect to object i placed at the origin of the circular coordinate system. $\mathbf{x}_2 = (x_2) \in N^+$ is the one-dimensional vector of entry E_{ij} of $E_2()$. Then $\mathbf{x} = (x_2 - x_1)$ and $f(\mathbf{x}) \in N^+$ is defined as:

$$h(\mathbf{x}) = |x| \quad (4.1)$$

and the distance $d(E_1, E_2)$ is defined as:

$$d(E_1, E_2) = \sum_{i=1}^{i=n} \sum_{j=i}^{i=n} w_{ij} h(o_{ij}, p_{ij}), o_{ij} \in O_1, p_{ij} \in O_2 \quad (4.2)$$

where O_1 and O_2 denote the sets of spatial operators of respectively E_1 and E_2.

The method is already translation and scale (i.e. the magnitude of the polar coordinate system is discarded) invariant. To allow the matching of two $E()$'s to be also rotation transformation invariant, two non-collinear objects are taken as a basis. All other objects are represented by the new coordinate frame defined by the basis.

4.1 Matching E()'s on the Basis of Object Sequence Information

In this section, we discuss another comparison scheme, based on the circular coordinate system, to match E() representations. The paradigm of the comparison scheme is that the gestalt of an image is described by the sequence in which objects occur around each object. This information is preserved in the $E()$ representation generated from a circular coordinate system, see fig. 4.

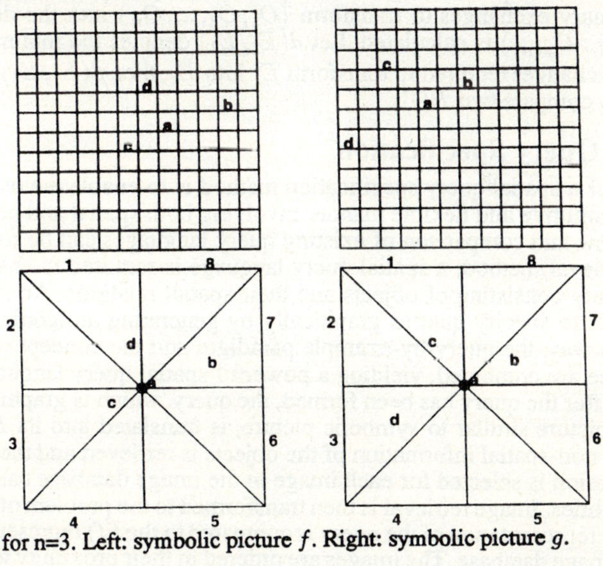

Fig. 4. Example for n=3. Left: symbolic picture f. Right: symbolic picture g.

For example, the sequence of all objects around a for the symbolic picture f, see fig. 4, is denoted by the string $a : d_1 c_3 b_7$. Because the relative ordering of the objects in the sequence is important, we consider the relative string $a : d_1 c_2 b_3$, where $a :$ denotes that the following substring describes the relative ordered sequence of objects in which they occur by scanning the space around a in a counterclockwise manner. In a similar way, the set of strings for b, c and d are obtained for f and g:

$$f = \begin{Bmatrix} (a : d_1c_2b_3) \\ (b : d_1a_2c_2) \\ (c : a_1b_1d_2) \\ (d : c_1a_2b_3) \end{Bmatrix} \quad g= \begin{Bmatrix} (a : c_1d_2b_3) \\ (b : c_1a_2d_2) \\ (c : d_1a_2b_3) \\ (d : a_1b_1c_2) \end{Bmatrix} \tag{4.3}$$

The sequence in which objects occur with respect to an object is easily derived from an E() representation, because the one-dimensional coordinates of objects coming from the same row, is a natural number corresponding to a bin. Hence, the entries E_{ij} for row i containing the lowest coordinate value, is the first object j detected if the space around object i is scanned in a counterclockwise manner.

For the purpose of image retrieval, two $E()$'s are declared to be the same, if each object in both $E()$'s has the same set of objects situated in the same sequence around it. In order to compute the distance between two $E()$'s, the indexes of the objects of $E_g()$ have to be changed to correspond to the indexes of the objects in $E_f()$.

The distance between two $E()$'s is defined as the minimum of total number of binary exchanges to transform each string of $E_g()$ into an ordered sequence. A binary exchange is defined as the exchange of the position of two objects in the sequence of objects. Notice that circular shifts are not counted.

More formally, consider the string of objects $(O_1, O_2, ..., O_n)$. Each object, O_i, has key value K_i. The key values correspond to natural numbers corresponding to the bins (i.e. coordinates). Therefore, it is obvious that for any two key values K_i and K_j either $K_i = K_j$, $K_i < K_j$ or $K_i > K_j$ (i.e. there exist a transitive ordering relation on the key values). The problem is then to find a permutation, σ, such that $K_{\sigma(i)} \leq K_{\sigma(i+1)}$, $1 \leq i \leq (n-1)$, to obtain the ordering $(O_{\sigma(1)}, O_{\sigma(2)}, ..., O_{\sigma(n)})$. Notice that key values may be identical (i.e. two objects are lying in the same bin), and therefore the above defined, σ, is not unique. During the computation of permutation, σ, the minimum number of binary exchanges to transform $(O_1, O_2, ..., O_n)$ into the desired ordering $(O_{\sigma(1)}, O_{\sigma(2)}, ...O_{\sigma(n)})$ is calculated. Let $d(E_1, E_2)$ denotes the minimum number of total binary exchanges required to transform E_1 into E_2, then $d(E_1, E_2)$ is a metric and can be used to compare two $E()$'s.

5 Spatial Query Specification

The purpose of a spatial query specification method is to enable the user to formulate queries in an intuitive and flexible manner involving both spatial and non-spatial predicates. A review and comparison of existing query languages can be found in [9]. For the image retrieval method, a spatial query language is required to enable the formulation of a query consisting of objects and their spatial relations. An intuitive way to achieve this, is to specify queries graphically by generating an iconic picture on the screen. In this way, the query-by-example paradigm and the concept of icon-oriented visual interface are combined, yielding a powerful spatial query language suitable for the method. After the query has been formed, the query, which is graphically described by an iconic picture similar to symbolic picture, is translated into its $E()$ representation. Then the non-spatial information of the objects is retrieved and the corresponding $E()$ representation is selected for each image in the image database based on standard DBMS capabilities. Image retrieval is then transformed to the problem of $E()$ matching, where the $E()$ representation of the query is compared to the E() representation of every image in the image database. The images are ordered in their proximity to the query and presented to the user. The following techniques can be used to formulate a query.

5.1 Query by Example Image

This technique is based on the query-by-example-image paradigm, which means that images are retrieved on the basis of an example image. The example image is selected by the user at run time and corresponds to an image in the image database. The selected image is represented by its symbolic picture. The user is allowed to specify the following image retrieval parameters:

- 1. The coordinate system (i.e. rectangular or circular).
- 2. Resolution of the coordinate system.
- 3. The distance function between the objects.
- 4. Comparison schema.
- 5. Viewing transformation (i.e. translation, rotation, scale and so on).

Then the $E()$ representation is generated by deducing the spatial relations between the objects, induced by the symbolic picture of the query and the retrieval parameter settings. Because every image in the image database is properly described by its $E()$ representation, image retrieval is reduced to $E()$ matching. The metric is used to order the images with respect to the example image.

5.2 Query by Iconic Picture

A large set of icons is available to the user. Each icon represents an object. To each icon a set of attributes is assigned. The user can select an icon and set the desired attribute values. For example, the user can select an icon representing a city with the attribute "*population*" attached to it. Once the desired icons (i.e. objects) are selected and their attributes are properly set, the user is allowed to move the icons around and place them properly on the screen with respect to their spatial relations. In this way, the non-spatial predicates are specified by the selection of icons and their attributes and the spatial predicates are expressed by the locations of the icons on the screen with respect to each other. The user is allowed to specify the image retrieval parameters. The $E()$ representation of the iconic picture query is generated by deducing the spatial relations induced by the iconic picture query and the image retrieval parameter settings. Then the non-spatial information of the objects is retrieved for each image and their corresponding $E()$ representation is matched against the query. The images are ordered in accordance to their metric and shown on the screen.

5.3 Query by Iconic Example

The difference between this mode and the query-by-iconic-picture mode is that it does not matter how the icons are located with respect to each other on the screen, because the user has to specify the spatial relations between the icons explicitly. After the desired icons have been selected and their attributes are properly set, the user may specify zero or more relations, in addition to a distance function for directional relations, between each two objects. To allow the specification of distance functions between each two icons, queries can be constructed having partial embeddings which may be precisely defined and other partial embeddings more fuzzy. After the retrieval parameters have been set for each two icons in the query, the E() representation is generated and matched with those of the images in the image database.

6 Applications & Experiments

The image indexing and retrieval method has been implemented and integrated as a part of a larger prototype information system [10]. The purpose of the information system is that it is used as a research vehicle to investigate important issues with regard to image database design. The information system has been implemented in C in combination with the X widget set, on a SUN-SPARC workstation with UNIX as operating system. The ScilImage package, [16], provides the image processing functionality.

In this section, applications are discussed to illustrate the nature of the method and its importance in real-world situations. We discusses both image database and computer vision problems, that need a means of comparing images, represented by their object embeddings, to their benefit.

6.1 Object Indexing and Retrieval

The method can be used for model-based recognition of rigid and deformable 2-D and 3-D objects under different viewing transformations in cluttered scenes and is able to deal with substantial occlusion.

Object recognition is an important problem for image databases as well as for computer vision. The model-based approach to object recognition, in which a predefined model of an object is matched with an input image, has been proved very useful[2],[6]. In the sequel, we consider flat object recognition which is the case when the object is orthogonally projected on the retina (i.e. viewing plane). In this way, 2-D objects can be recognized from 2-D data. Although the 2-D data might be obtained by different sensors, we assume that the 2-D data is the output of a camera (i.e. images).

The starting point for object recognition, is the way an object can be described. We assume that the object to be recognized can be represented by local geometrical features. Those features may be domain independent, such as corners, high curvature points, T-junctions and so on or domain dependent[10]. Domain dependent features are features from which the object is composed. All of these local geometrical features can be automatically extracted from each image in the image database. The type of features to be extracted from every image depends on the object to be recognized. In general, the features should be specific for the particular object to be recognized and the more different types features are used the more effective the method will be. Because the object is also represented by the chosen features, the problem of object recognition is then to find a match between the image features and the object features. For general object recognition, the match should be invariant under, at least, the affine transformation.

Taking this approach as starting point, the method can be used as follows. First, after extracting the appropriate features from every image in the image database, an E() representation is generated for each image preserving the identity of the features and their geometrical relations as an index. Then, the object modeling step consists of formulating the geometrical model, consisting of features and their spatial relations, as a query to the image database. For example, the user may select an icon representing a local feature such as a corner with the attribute "*angle*" attached to it. After the user has selected the icon and the attributes are properly set, spatial relations may be specified with other icons (i.e. query-by-iconic-example). To allow the specification of distance functions between each two icons, a geometrical object model can be obtained consisting of subsets of features which are defined as precise as necessary enabling the recognition of partly or completed rigid or deformable objects. After the user has specified the retrieval parameters (i.e. coordinate system, resolution, comparison schema and the required viewing transformation), the E() representation of the object model is obtained. Then the method is used to discover a match, consistent with the transformation, of the subset of object features and each compatible subset of the features in every image in the database indexed by their E() representation. The metric information is used to order the candidate objects found in the images. The candidate object with the lowest metric are expected to be the same or similar to the model object.

Tentative experiments have been carried out to test the usefulness and performance of the system. A picture query have been specified to retrieve images containing different electronic components. The query consisted of domain dependent features and their directional relations. The goal was to recognize the different electronic components in a small image database of 20 images of electronic schemes. The system found all images in descending order of quality of resemblance containing the components and relationships as specified by the search request. It took approximately 0.2 seconds per image on a standard SUN-SPARC station to retrieve the non-spatial information of the objects, executing the matching method and ordering the images in descending order of resemblance.

6.2 Similarity Retrieval for Medical Images

The second application discussed in this paper, to present an example of how the method can be applied to real-world problems, is similarity retrieval in medical image databases. The problem at hand is to retrieve images from a medical image database, containing MR images of the heart, that have the same tomographic sections. Retrieval of images with similar tomographic sections is a very common problem in cardiac image databases [14]. Is is known that the embeddings of chambers and blood vessels are important indicators to determine the tomographic section of a cardiac image. It is desirable for the radiologist to compare an example image at hand with images taken from the same tomographic section in order to establish a more reliable diagnosis. Therefore, the radiologist should be able to retrieve images from a medical image database with the same tomographic section in an intuitive and flexible way for comparison. In the context of the method, the user is able to formulate the desired tomographic section by means of the geometrical model, consisting of most informative objects (i.e. called parts in medical terms) and of course their spatial relations. The choice of parts that have to be present in the tomographic section model is made by the user. For example, the most relevant parts of a tomographic section of a MR image of the heart are: left ventricle, right ventricle, left atrium, right atrium, ascending aorta and the pulmonary artery. At run time, the user selects the icons representing these parts and sets the appropriate attributes. After the user has selected the parts, represented by icons and their attributes, he or she is allowed to place the parts properly with respect to each other determining the spatial relation between them. The retrieval parameters are entered and the E() representation of the tomographic section model is constructed. The E() representation is then matched with those of the images in the image database and ordered in accordance to their metric.

Experiments have been carried out on an image database of more than 200 MRI images taken from the chest containing a variety of planar cross-sections through a large variety of patients. The images have been recorded at the Yale University Medical School facilities. A search request was made which consisted of four icons, representing the parts left ventricle, right ventricle, left atrium and right atrium, and their directional relations. With this search request, it was the aim to find in the database those images which contained the same tomographic section. The result was that 7 out of the first 7 highest ranked images rightfully contained the desired plane.

7 Summary

In this paper, a method is discussed to retrieve images efficiently based on the data structure called E() representation. The method is invariant under, at least, the affine transformation and is able to deal with substantial object occlusion. The E() representation preserves the information about objects and their spatial relations as an index. Because the query as well as every image in the image database can be described by an E() representation, image retrieval is reduced to E() representation matching. E() matching is the process that computes to what extent two E() are similar. To that end, two comparison schemes are discussed. First we consider the paradigm that the overall configuration of objects in an image can be described by the combination of spatial relations between each object pair. The second comparison scheme is based on the information expressed by the sequence in which objects are situated around each other. For both comparison schemes a metric is given. For the purpose of image retrieval, the metric can be used to compare a picture query with each E() representation of every image in database and order the images by their proximity to the query. Images with a low metric are considered the same or similar to the query. A query language is discussed to enable the formulation of a query in terms of objects and their spatial relations. Two applications are discussed, that need a means of comparing images, to illustrate the nature of the image retrieval method in real-world situations. Experiments carried out for the two applications show that the method is very robust and efficient and together with the inherent high parallelism it makes the method a promising one.

Acknowledgements

The research project is supported by NIH: NLM-Ep(1 R01LM05007-01A1)

References

1. Ballard D. H. and Brown C. M., **Computer Vision**, Prentice-Hall, 1982.
2. Besl, P. J. and Jain, R. C., **Three-Dimensional Object Recognition** , ACM Computing Surveys, 17(1), 1985, pp. 75-154.
3. Chang, S. K., **Principles of Pictorial Information Systems Design**, Prentice-Hall, Englewood Cliffs, NJ.
4. Chang, S. K., Shi, Q. Y. and Yan, C. W., **Iconic Indexing by 2-D Strings**, IEEE Trans. Pattern Anal. Machine Intell., vol. 9, no. 3, 1987, pp. 413-428.
5. Chang, S. K. and Jungert, E., **A Spatial Knowledge Structure for Image Information Systems using Symbolic Projections**, Proc. Fall Joint Comp. Conf., Dallas, TX, 1986, pp. 79-86.
6. Chin, R. T. and Dyer, C. R., **Model-Based Recognition in Robot Vision** , ACM Computing Surveys, 18(1), 1986, pp. 67-108.
7. Chock, M., Cardenas, A., F. and Klinger, A., **Database Structure and Manipulation Capabilities of the Picture Database Management System (PICDMS)** , IEEE Trans. Pattern Anal. Machine Intell., vol. 6, no. 4, 1984, pp. 484-492.
8. Delone, B. N. and Raikov, D. A., **Analytic Geometry** , Vol. 2, Moscow, 1949.
9. Egenhofer, M., **Spatial Query Languages** , PhD Thesis, University of Maine, Orono, 1989.
10. Gevers, T. and Smeulders A. W. M., **Enigma: An Image Retrieval System** , International Conference on Pattern Recognition, The Hague, The Netherlands, vol. II, 1992, pp. 697-700.
11. Grimson, W.E.L, **Object Recognition by Computer**, Cambridge, MA: MIT Press, 1990.
12. Guenther, O. and Buchmann A., **Research Issues in Spatial Databases** , SIGMOD RECORD, vol 19, no. 4, 1990, pp. 61-68.
13. Guttman, A., **R-trees: a Dynamic Index Structure for Spatial Searching** , Proc. ACM-SIGMOD Int. Conf. Management of Data, June 18-21, 1984, pp. 47-57.
14. Hemant, D. T., Jaffe, C. C. and Duncan, J. S., **Arrangements: A Spatial Relation Comparing Part Embeddings** , International Conference on Pattern Recognition, The Hague, The Netherlands, vol. I, 1992, pp. 91-94.
15. Hildreth, E. C. and Ullman, S., **The Computational Study of Vision in Foundations of Cognitive Science**, M.I.T. Press, 1989.
16. Kate ten, T., Balen van, R., Smeulders, A.W.M., Groen, F.C.A., Boer den, G., **SCILAIM: a Multi-level Interactive Image Processing Environment**, Pattern Recognition Letters 11, 1990, pp. 429-441.
17. Klein, F., **Elementary Mathematics from an Advanced Standpoint; Geometry**, Macmillan, NY, 1925.
18. Lamdan, Y, Schwartz. J. T. and Wolfson, H. J., **On Recognition of 3-D Objects from 2-D Images**, Proc. of IEEE Int. Conf. on Robotics and Automation, Philadelphia, Pa., 1988, pp. 1407-1413.
19. Lee, S. Y. and Hsu, F. J., **Picture Algebra for Spatial Reasoning of Iconic Images represented in 2D C-string**, Pattern Recognition Letters, 12, 1991, pp. 425-435.
20. Samet, H., **The Quadtree and Related Data Structures**, ACM Computer Surveys, vol. 16. no. 2, 1984, pp. 187-260.
21. Tamura, H. and Yokota, N., **Image Database Systems: A Survey**, Pattern Recognition, Vol. 17, no. 1, 1984, pp 29-43.

FACILITATORY PROCESS FOR CONTRAST DETECTION

Candela S., García C., Muñoz J., and Alayon F.

Department of Informatica y Sistemas
Campus Universitario de Tafira.
University of Las Palmas de Gran Canaria
Las Palmas, Canary Islands, E-35017 Spain.

Abstract. We present in this work an image process technique that we call facilitatory effect. This technique is a multiplicative mechanism which improves the response of a previous process. It is based on a statistical process computing averages and variances This technique is an invariant process to noise and to illumination changes. It is also concluded that this technique is a type of generalized high pass filter since image areas with high grey variations are contrasted. We present results of this technique for a practical case of defects detection in leather.

1. Introduction.

This paper belongs to the field of Artificial Vision , and more specifically to the field of Computer Aided Vision Systems (C.A.V.) [1] for defects detection in materials in an industrial environment. In this context, it is frequently necessary to preprocess the input images before executing the defect detection process. This transformation is necessary because the input have undesirable characteristics, such as noise and not uniform illumination. Preprocessing is also necessary when the defects to be detected have a poor visual intensity.

In general, the problem of defect detection in materials, using both the techniques of a CAST system [2] and the artificial vision tools, consists of the detection of small changes in textures. Even, this fine changes are apparent with a poor visual intensity; making it necessary to develop methods such as the technique presented here.

2. Facilitatory process.

From the point of view of system computational theory [3], image processing can be modeled as a system formed by a input space, an output space, and a relationship structure between them. In our case the input space is formed by a matrix (y,x) where the row dimension, y, varies between [1..N], and the column dimension, x, varies between [1..M]. Each point of the matrix address a variable, I(x,y), which stores a grey level; with a range between 0 to 255.

A facilitatory process is defined as a process that aids a facilitatory action for

the other process output. This facilitatory action consists of modifying the output of a previous process for producing an optimum response.
In our case, it is needed to emphasize certain areas of the input image, especially areas where fine texture changes are produced; a facilitatory process, which is a multiplicative mechanism between two local processes, is proposed. The first process computes for each local area, the offset between the grey level of the center point and the average in the periphery. The second process computes the variance of each local area. The value, F(u,v), is obtained as an output space; this value is the product of the output of the two processes [3].

Details of the used technique are as follows. The method is a transformation on images. First it is necessary to establish the local area, W(y,x). Assuming that it is rectangular and that (y,x) are the coordinates of the central point, we need to define the horizontal dimension, dx, and the vertical dimension, dy. Then, for each local area, W(y,x), defined in the original image, the average and the variance of W(x,y) are computed, by means of the expressions [4,5]: the average of W(y,x) is $X_w(y,x)=1/Np^* \sum \sum I(p,q)$, and the variance of W(y,x) is $V_w^2(y,x)= 1/Np^* \sum \sum (X_w - I(p,q))^2$. Np is the number of pixels of the local area, W(y,x), and I(p,q) represents the grey level of each pixel of the area.

When the values of $X_w(y,x)$ and $V^2{}_w(y,x)$ are computed, a value $F(y,x) = | I(y,x) - Xw | * V_w^2$, is assigned to each point (y,x) of the resulting image. I(y,x) is the grey level of the central point of the local area, W(y,x), in the original image. The following aspects are to be emphasized. First, the transformation is defined on pixels, (y,x), in the original image, which is carried out under the following restriction: $dy/2 \leq y \leq N-dy/2$ and $dx/2 \leq x \leq M-dx/2$ (N is the vertical dimension and M is the horizontal dimension of the original image). And second, the transformation produces a result image that has the following dimensions: the vertical dimension is N - dy + 1, and the horizontal dimension: M - dx + 1.

3. Method implementation.

The main aspects of the computational implementation of the method follows [6]. Peculiarities are: the method has a fast algorithm and the method can be implemented by a parallel neuronal net. To show this, the variance is expressed as a function of the average. This new expression of the variance is:

$$V^2 = 1/Np^* \sum \sum I^2(p,q) - X^2_w$$

fast algorithm. The method can be implemented through an algorithm that is a "fast algorithm" . The structure of the algorithm is based on the fact that the parameters of the local area can be and are computed in terms of the parameters of the nearest peripherical areas in the 180° and 90° directions. With this algorithmic structure, it is achieved that the number of operations to be computed in the local area (which has peripherical areas in the previous directions) is independent of the area dimension of the area, and therefore, independent also of the number of pixels of the local area .

Parallel granular net. For a dimension of 8, it is showed in the following figure.

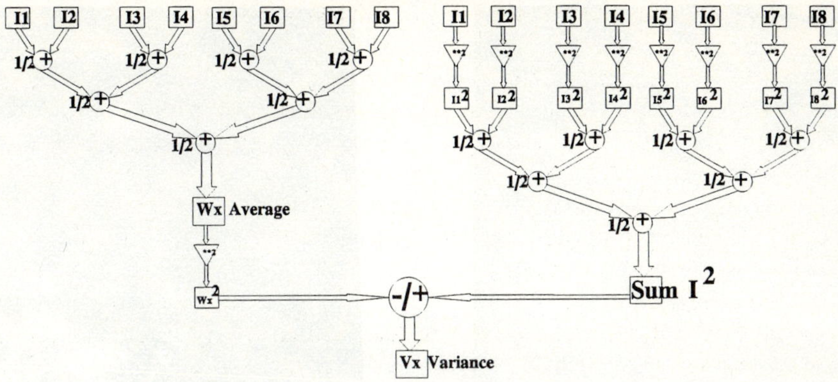

Fig. 1. Parallel granular net

4. Results of the processing.

As mentioned above, the technique is used in a prototype for defect detection in leather. To illustrate the behaviour of the method, two examples with images of leather are presented. In these examples, it can be seen that defects located by using the described process can be achieved relatively easily. Original images (figures 2 and 4) and the associated result images (figures 3 and 5) are showed.

Fig. 2. Original image

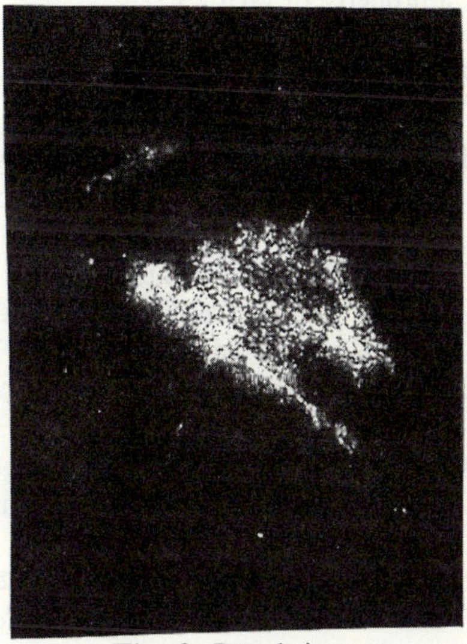

Fig. 3. Result image

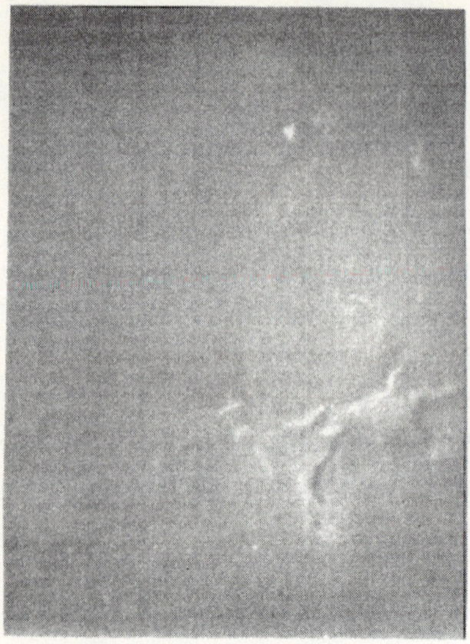

Fig. 4. Original image

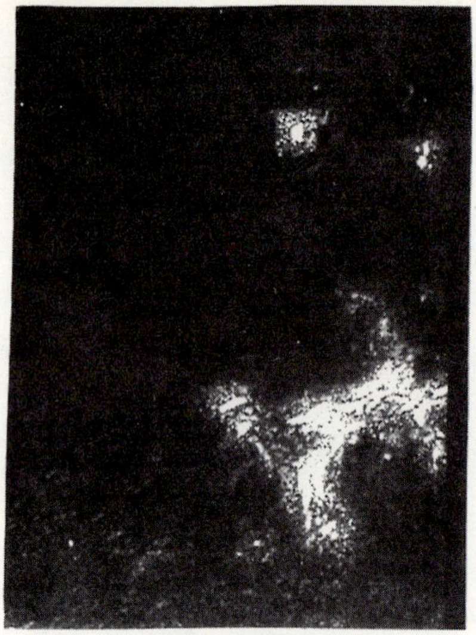

Fig. 5. Result image

Acknowledgement. The authors wish to acknowledge the guidance of Prof. Roberto Moreno-Díaz during the preparation of this work. This work presented in this paper has been partially supported by the project Brite 2195. The leather catalog used is a property of GUCCI.

References

[1] Candela, S., Muñoz, J., Alayon, F., Garcia C. "Un Sistema de Visión para la detección de defectos". Actas de Panel´92 p. 240-247. Las Palmas de G. Canaria.1992. Universidad de Las Palmas de Gran Canaria

[2] Pichler, F."Compuetr Aided System Theory: A Framework for Interactive Method Banks. Cybernetics and Systems 88 (ed. R. Trappl) KluwerAcademic Publishers Dordrecht, The Netherlands, 1988 pp 731-736.

[3] Moreno-Diaz, R. "Natural and Artificial Neural Nets". AIWAN, opening lecture. Granada Sept. 1991.

[4] Rao, K., Ahmed, N. Orthogonal Transforms for Digital Signal Processing. IEEE International Conference on Acustics, Speech and Signal Processing P 136-40, 1976.

[5] Haralick, R. Statistical and Structural Approaches to Texture. Proccedings of the IEEE, vol 67, no 5, May 1979.

[6] Candela, S. Transformaciones de Campo Receptivo Variable en Proceso de Imagenes y Visión Artificial. Tesis Doctoral. Nov 1987.

Object-oriented Database Management Systems for Construction of CASE Environments*

Wolfgang Emmerich, Petr Kroha and Wilhelm Schäfer

University of Dortmund, Dept. of Computer Science
D-44221 Dortmund, Germany
{emmerich|kroha|wilhelm}@ls10.informatik.uni-dortmund.de

Abstract. We argue that a fully object-oriented database management system is a very suitable basis of every modern CASE environment. We describe how the features provided by an OODBMS are exploited to build a CASE tool or environment. We discuss especially problems concerning inter-document consistency constraints and multi-user support. We finally sketch the features which are still missing in OODBMSs.

1 Introduction

The enormous increase in the size of software and the reliability required from modern software intensive systems has focussed attention on languages and corresponding tools which do not only support programming but also specification, design, and documentation of software. In fact, specification or design documents have become equally important as the final code in order to check and verify correctness, completeness and reliability of a delivered software product. In addition, the industrial-scale production of software today requires teams of developers who should be supported by tools which organise access to a large amount of shared and frequently changing information. This information consists of the above mentioned documents for the various phases of the software production process. Examples for such documents are data-flow diagrams, state-transition diagrams, petri-nets, entity-relationship diagrams, and modular design descriptions.

Tools supporting the construction of documents usually work in a syntax-directed mode, which is the adequate support for those mostly graphical languages. In more detail, the user selects a graphical element from a panel, places it on a drawing board and can possibly annotate it with textual explanations. This mode especially enables the tool to check the correct syntactic construction during editing.

Even for textual input, syntax-directed manipulation is useful, because it avoids a lot of typing errors (templates for the concrete syntax of a language are generated automatically) and, more than that, static semantic consistency

* This work has been partly funded by the CEC under contract No. 6115 (ESPRIT-III project GOODSTEP)

can immediately be checked, e.g. the use of a variable is checked against its declaration and the user is immediately informed about errors.

In general, syntax-directed tools support the syntactically and static semantically correct construction of documents which is often denoted as *intra-document consistency*.

An integrated software development or CASE-environment is a collection of tools supporting various phases of the production process. It has two main additional features compared to tools supporting the construction of single documents in a single language.

The first feature is the possibility to handle *inter-document consistency*, e.g. a name of a function or a parameter should be the same in the requirements specification, in the interface definition of a module, in the design document and in the implementation. Even more, changing the name in one document can result in a propagation of this change into the other documents concerned. If an environment maintains such inter-document dependencies, it is able to support an incremental intertwined development and maintenance of the documents. As a further illustration for the advantage of an incremental production process assume that a programmer may have detected an error in the code which is due to a wrong requirements specification of a particular function. If then the specification is changed, the environment could inform the user about all other places in all other documents which are affected by this change. In contrast, doing such a small incremental change in a phase-oriented environment is rather tedious, because such an environment is usually based on a complete transformation of all documents concerned from one phase into the next one. For more details we refer to [8].

The second main feature of an environment is *multi-user support* which means document change in general and in particular the above sketched change propagation must be subject to concurrency control and access rights defined for a team of developers, e.g. an automatic immediate update of one document as a consequence of a change in another document can not be performed in any case.

The two features of an environment, i.e. maintaining inter-document dependencies and even inter-document consistency and providing multi-user support demand complex-structured, persistent data and thus the use of a sophisticated database management system as a key architectural component of a CASE-environment. In commercial CASE-environment development this demand is often not (yet) taken very seriously, i.e. a lot of existing tools or environments are still based on rather rudimentary extensions of file systems. This is, to our view, due to the lack of appropriate database management systems for CASE (cf. Section 5 and and [7]).

This paper argues that fully object-oriented database management systems (OODBMSs) like O_2 or GEMSTONE are the most appropriate ones and it will illustrate how an integrated CASE environment is built on top of such a database system, i.e. it will explain the construction of the database scheme, and the exploitation of other database features like transaction management, and the performance capabilities offered by OODBMs. Thus, the next section will sketch the concept of an integrated CASE environment, whereas section 3 describes the scheme construction in terms of a class hierarchy of an object-oriented data definition and manipulation language. Section 4 explains how OODBMs have to be extended in order to fully meet the requirements of CASE environments. Section 5 sketches related work. Section 6 reports about the implementations we used for evaluating the results described in this paper.

2 The Concept of Integration in a CASE-Environment

Syntax-directed document manipulation and maintenance of inter-document consistency is based conceptually on a graph-like representation scheme of a document. The graph (usually called abstract syntax graph) describes the syntactic structure of each document [8, 1]). Additional edges describe inter-document dependencies. Operations which are performed by the user of a CASE-environment, are conceptually graph operations. They have to be defined in a way that they respect static semantics and inter-document consistency. Note, that consistency is given by the definition of those operations. For example, an operation which changes the name of a function in a design document could be defined in such a way that it performs the corresponding name change in all other documents concerned by traversing the graph along the edges connecting various occurrences of a function name in different documents.

As an example for a graph scheme (without considering the definition of the operations) see Fig. 1. It sketches the dependencies within and between three documents which are technical documentation, modular design and implementation of the module bodies. The solid arrows represent the syntactic structure of each document, i.e. the so-called abstract syntax tree. This tree is usually turned into a graph by indicating inter- and intra-document dependencies also by (dashed) edges. Finally, node attributes describe values like e.g. names of identifiers, modules etc.

More generally speaking, a project-wide ASG is a directed attributed graph which conceptually consists of a subgraph for each document. Each document subgraph in turn is spanned by a tree which is determined by the grammar of the language, the document is written in. Subtrees of this spanning-tree that are units for manipulation at the user-interface are called *increments*. An example of an increment of the design document depicted above is the procedure `InitWindowManager` with its identifier and parameter list. Edges of this spanning-tree are called *syntactic edges*. All other edges which consequently describe inter- and intra-document dependencies between nodes are called *non-syntactic edges*.

For the scope of this paper the given informal explanation of ASGs should do. A few languages have been developed (e.g. PROGRESS developed in the IPSEN project [8]) which allow to formally specify such rather complex graph schemes and especially the consistency preserving operations on those schemes.

The whole concept of integration is becoming more complicated if different users work on different documents at the same time. Then the execution of a particular operation on the graph by a particular user is subject to an access right which was granted to this user and allows the execution of the operation.

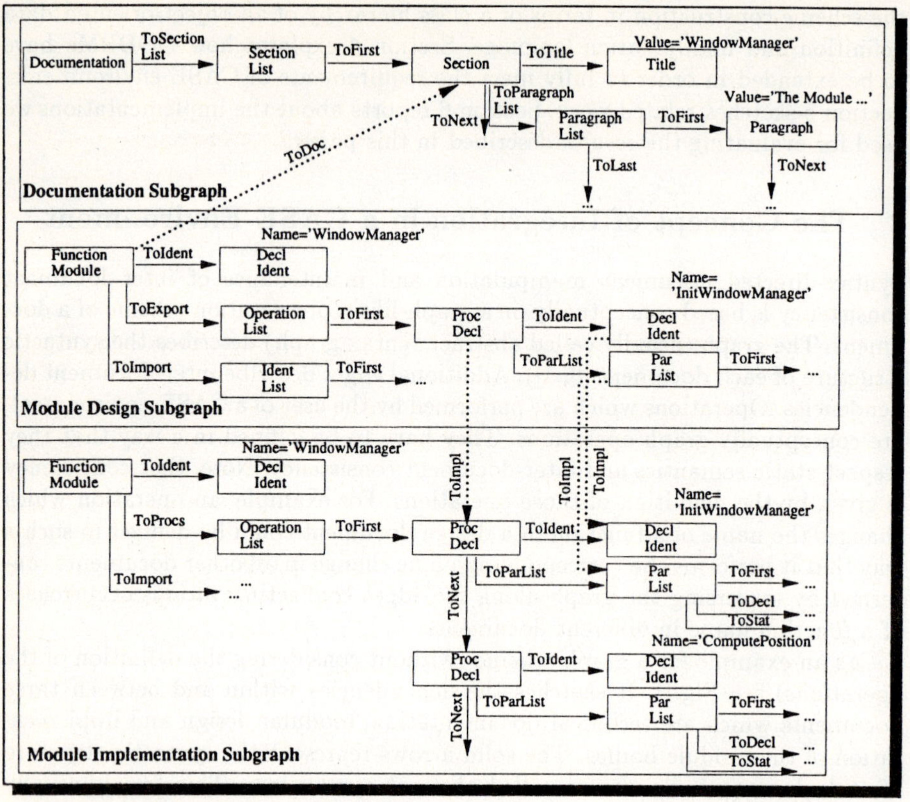

Fig. 1. Intra- and inter-document consistency

In addition, automatic change propagation across document boundaries have to be treated differently depending on the particular document, the owner of the document, and the state of the document. For example, if one user works on some specification and another one started already to develop a corresponding implementation, then change propagation should only happen after both have finished a major piece of their work and explicitly require the environment to renew document consistency (maybe only partly automatically). Thus the environment just has to keep track of inconsistencies for some time and it may only display warnings to users about possible inconsistent states.

In more sophisticated environments which however only exist as research prototypes so far, the concurrent manipulation of (integrated) documents is supported by versioning, i.e. users may change different versions of the same document concurrently. Then strategies for handling merging versions have to be defined as well. In addition, versioning is, of course, already a useful concept even in the single user case.

Finally, document representation and integration schemes as described undergo changes even during the construction of documents according to the defined scheme. For example, a user may add new document dependencies which have not been anticipated or the syntax definition of a language could change.

3 OODBMSs in a Multi-User CASE Environment

3.1 Scheme Definition and Generation

The objects stored in a database of a CASE environment represent user's documents, and, as we have argued, they have to be stored persistently in a structured way according to their syntax.
Consequently, a database scheme for a CASE environment firstly defines all possible syntactical constructions as classes according to the language definitions. The scheme defines additional classes for representing objects describing static semantics, e.g. a symbol table. Further a scheme defines syntactic and non-syntactic relationships among classes.

The overall integrity constraint of a database which all tools must obey is that document subgraphs must represent syntactically correct documents in which static semantics and inter-document consistency constraints are only violated in a controlled way. To enforce this constraint, we implement the constraints within the database scheme and exploit the fact that each tool (as a database application) can only perform those modifications that are in-line with the scheme defined.

We now present how we define the structure of abstract syntax graphs using an object-oriented scheme definition language. The common properties of nodes are defined within *classes* of the database scheme. Nodes are *complex objects* whose instance variables represent edges. Navigation along these edges is done by dereferencing instance variables. In case the number of edges that may start at a node is not known in advance, object constructors such as lists or sets are used. For navigation purposes a *query language* is used then.

The type-compatibility in the scheme should be checked at compile-time in order to achieve safety and better performance. The set of target nodes of a particular edge should therefore be restricted to those types of nodes which are allowed according to syntax and static semantics of the language. Therefore, we exploit the *type-system* provided by typed OODBMSs (such as O_2) to define the types of instance variables.

For further scheme simplification, *inheritance* is used to define common properties of nodes such as outgoing syntactic or non-syntactic edges or attributes in a superclass only once. In addition, edges connect not always nodes of the same type. In case of alternative productions in grammars such as `A::=B|C`, we have edges that may connect different types of nodes. We must therefore allow that all edges which point to nodes of type A can also point to nodes of type B or C. In the example, we declare the classes which represent node types B and C to inherit from the class derived from A. Exploiting *polymorphism*, we can then assign instance variables of class A also values of class B and C.

Integrity constraints are enforced by *encapsulation*, i.e. applications are not allowed to modify instance variables directly, but must use the methods defined.

For example, terminal increment classes have a **scan** method which guarantees that values assigned to lexem attributes obey the lexical syntax. In case of the non-syntactic edge, we can declare a method with which a declaring identifier can be changed. That method may additionally perform a propagation of the change along all non-syntactic edges to all objects that represent the identifiers' usage. In the multi-user case, this method can additionally test whether the identifiers are contained in documents which the user is allowed to modify or not. Depending on that decision the method performs a change propagation or marks the identifier as inconsistent. Hence, we define multi-user support statically already in the scheme.

The computations necessary for performing these methods, however, require *computational completeness* of the scheme definition language.

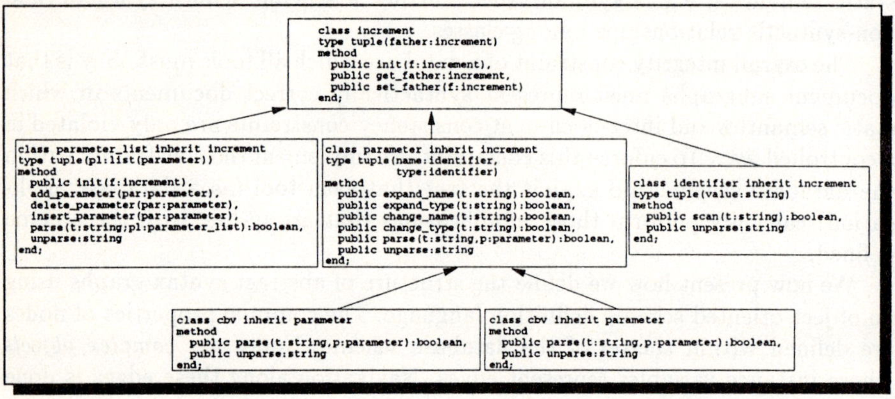

Fig. 2. Example of a Scheme Definition

A major advantage of scheme construction for CASE environments is that normalised grammars [8] of the languages can be used for deriving the scheme partly automatically. Each terminal and non-terminal symbol of the grammar is translated into a class. An instance variable of type string (for textual languages) used to store the value of lexems is attached to each terminal class. Instance variables for storing syntactic edges are attached to each non-terminal class according to the production on which the respective non-terminal appears on the left-hand side. The types of these instance variables are defined as the classes derived from the symbols on the productions' right-hand side. Classes which represent optional increments are declared to inherit from a predefined class representing the properties of optional increments. Symbols that appear on the right-hand side of an alternative production are transformed into subclasses of the class representing the symbol on the left-hand side. Productions like {A} are transformed into a class with an instance variable that is a list constructed from the class derived from the repeated symbol.

Methods for scanning lexems are generated from regular expressions and are

provided by each terminal class. Methods for parsing and construction of the spanning-tree which represents an increment are generated for each non-terminal class using parser-generation techniques. Methods for unparsing (i.e. to compute the external representation of data structures) are attached to all classes. Also, methods for expanding and collapsing increments which are frequently used in template-based editors can be attached to each non-terminal class.
The algorithm sketched is the basis of our scheme generator. So far, the definition of static semantics, inter-document consistencies and multi-user support has to be added manually by defining the respective methods.

Fig. 2 depicts an O_2 schema for parameter lists in PASCAL. Instance variables and method heads are depicted within solid boxes. Arrows denote inheritance.

3.2 Transaction Management

When users start a CASE tool, they start a session (as part of a long-durating transaction), that lasts until they quit the tool. Such a session can not be performed within one conventional database transaction (with ACID properties) for three reasons: Firstly, other users would not be able to use intermediate results produced within the session. Secondly, concurrency control conflicts would cause that other users would not be able to access those parts of their documents which have incoming or outgoing non-syntactic edges to the documents edited in the session. Finally, there is a likely chance to loose significant human effort in case of hard- or software failures.

Instead, we split a session into a number of short conventional transactions with ACID properties each of which executes the computations caused by a short user interaction. For example, changing a name of a type would be such an interaction which modifies the lexem attribute and all attributes of objects that represent identifiers that use the type. This strategy achieves that firstly, other users immediately see the effect of an interaction after transaction commit. Secondly, concurrency control conflicts become fairly rare, because they occur only if two sessions access the same nodes within two concurrent short transactions. Finally, there is no danger of loosing significant effort.

To implement the requirement of distributed access of users to documents, we can not execute tools on the machine on which the projects' database is stored. We would overload the server, since tools opposed to standard applications perform significant computation in order to create textual or graphical representations of the ASG, to compute context-sensitive menus and to display them on the screen. Instead we can exploit the client/server architecture offered by most OODBMSs in order to achieve process distribution.

3.3 Performance Capabilities

OODBMSs can only be used, if they achieve reasonable performance. To investigate this, we defined a software engineering application specific benchmark in order to evaluate the performance of OODBMSs. The Opus-Benchmark [6] accesses and modifies an ASG composed of several hundred document subgraphs with a high number of non-syntactic edges in between them. The benchmark simulates template based editing operations such as insertion, modification and deletion of increments as well as analysis operations which require massive traversals through the graph. The application of this benchmark to a few systems in particular an archetypical OODBMS like GemStone justifies the statement that those systems perform reasonably well with respect to software engineering applications. The description of the GemStone implementation as well as a detailed discussion of the results is out of the scope of this paper. Instead we only sketch the main results and refer to [5] for a detailed discussion.

With respect to space, storing ASGs in GemStone for instance is excellent. It required only about 2.5 times the space than storing a textual representation in a file system.

With respect to time, the response-time of tools increases with the number of transactions executed per time unit. In single-user case (i.e. no concurrent transactions at all) we observed that template-based editing operations perform in less than 100 milliseconds[2]. Unparsing medium-sized documents (up to 500 nodes) takes less than 500 milliseconds. Committing an optimistic transaction requires about 500 milliseconds. If incremental unparsing is chosen (i.e. only those parts of the textual document representations are redisplayed which have changed), interactions can be executed in about half a second and users are not going to recognise them as delays.
In multi-user case, we observed that response times become unacceptably worse, if more than four users work intensively (i.e. without significant thinking periods between successive interactions) on the same project-wide ASG.

4 Necessary Extensions of object-oriented DBMSs

4.1 Transaction Management

A major reason for the bad performance in multi-user mode is that the database spends unnecessary effort on achieving isolation of transactions. This is illustrated now.

One major paradigm in software engineering is information hiding. This means that users designing and implementing a large software system divide it into small modules with well defined small interfaces. As an example consider class definitions in C++ shown to other users while method implementations are hidden. Conceptually, those parts that represent hidden documents or fragments thereof do not have any non-syntactic edges to nodes of other documents. Usually, only one user modifies a document at a time. Therefore concurrency control conflicts can only be caused by transactions which access nodes along such non-syntactic edges (in order to check or preserve inter-document consistency).

[2] The times have been captured on a Sun SparcStation II with a medium-sized local SCSI disk.

Hence, in many transactions, there is no need for the DBMS to perform concurrency control. Tools can tell the DBMS at transaction start whether or not concurrency control is required. Note, that it is inappropriate to define this on session level, as both transactions with and without concurrency control may have to be executed.

Less time is needed if concurrency control is abandoned, because locking of objects or maintenance of conflict sets with conflict detection at commit-time need not be done. Note, that other transaction properties such as atomicity and durability must still be supported.

4.2 Version Management

Versioning of documents implies versioning of the corresponding subgraphs. As a prerequisite to have the database management system maintaining versions and revisions of subgraphs, the scheme definition language must offer means to define the notion of subgraphs. This can either be done at scheme generation time or at run-time. In the first case composite instance variables which lead to component objects are distinguished from non-composite instance variables which refer to objects [11]. We would then declare each instance variable which implements a syntactic edge as composite instance variable while non-syntactic edges are implemented as non-composite instance variables. In the second case, objects are added to a container that implements the composite object. Note, that in both cases the requirement that in a composite object, a dependent object is a component of only one composite object holds, because syntactic edges define a spanning-tree in the subgraph. We have then managed to implement document representing subgraphs as composite objects. The first solution sketched must be supported by the scheme definition language (as in the ORION system) whereas the second solution can be added as a general class for composite objects without modifying the OODBMS.

The operations which must be provided for versioning composite objects [12] must offer transparent versioning (i.e. to establish a current version), derivation of new versions, merging of alternate versions or retrieval of a particular version.

4.3 Scheme Evolution

In order to achieve changes of the syntax of documents, their static semantics and changes of inter-document consistency constraints during an ongoing software production process, the database must be able to perform incremental scheme updates. As an example consider the definition of a new reviewing strategy for module interfaces, which requires that documents are now annotated by the reviewers' name and have an additional relationship to a new document type "review report".

Implementing changes of documents' structure, requires to add, rename or delete classes, to change the inheritance relation between classes, to add instance variables, to change their names and types, and to delete instance variables, and finally to create, change and delete methods. To cope with the above mentioned example, we have to add new classes which define the structure of the review report and to add new instance variables for storing reviewers names and the relationship to the review report to the class which represents module interfaces.

In order to preserve the integrity of existing documents the objects of the database must migrate to the new scheme. In the above example, module interface definitions must neither be deleted, nor manually be transformed to the new scheme.

The scheme evolution facilities available in current databases, however, do not fully cover those requirements. In GemStone for instance, objects are not affected by a scheme update, i.e. an object can only be accessed with the scheme that was established when the object was created. In O_2, objects must be manually transformed to conform to the new scheme.

5 Related Work

A major piece of work in CASE tool construction during the last ten years focussed on tool generators (e.g. [15, 1] which are similar to compiler-compilers in compiler construction. Those approaches do not consider to use a database system at all. All information produced during a working session with such a tool is just dumped into a file after the end of a session. Those approaches provide no multi-user support. In addition, inter-document consistency is also a problem, because the generators only work for a particular language and corresponding single documents and not for the definition and manipulation of document dependencies, i.e. project-wide abstract syntax graphs.

A few research projects in environment construction have built their own dedicated database systems like GRAS [13]. Those approaches, however, focus on an adequate persistent graph representation of the abstract syntax graphs. Thus, they enable a quick manipulation of arbitrary large graphs by smart caching techniques. They do not adequately support multi-user access. As a first step towards more sophisticated support, GRAS has been recently extended to deal with version management.

Some of the available commercial CASE tools or environments respectively use relational databases. They end up with the well-known performance problem of relational technology when being used for storing highly complex objects as abstract syntax graphs [14].

More recent research work has focussed on building dedicated software engineering database systems like PCTE/OMS [9] or DAMOKLES [4]. Unfortunately, these systems are only strong in efficiently supporting coarse-grained dependencies between documents. They do not adequately support the efficient manipulation of such fine-grained information.

In general, none of the mentioned systems offers a fully object-oriented data definition and manipulation language and thus lack the adequate modelling power for describing these complex structured software engineering data.

6 Implemented Systems and Further Work

We started using object-oriented DBMSs in an experimental evaluation of their performance. In [3] we describe a simple OMS benchmark we implemented on top of several structurally object-oriented databases (such as PCTE/OMS, Damokles, GRAS and Cadlab/OMS) as well as on GemStone and VBASE. It turned out that GemStone performed very well with small grained objects. Based on the results of that benchmark, we implemented the Opus benchmark [6] for those systems that performed well with fine-grained objects. According to the results we obtained, we selected GemStone for our further developments. We then ported the commercially available OPUS environment which supports design and implementation phase from GRAS to GemStone [10]. Thus, we were able to change OPUS from a single-user system to a multi-user system which is called Groupie. Using this environment, we also experienced the limits concerning transaction throughput mentioned in section 3.3. Furthermore, we implemented a generator which automatically derives a set of C++ classes that define the common properties of increments from a grammar written in a normalised BNF [2]. The C++ classes are generated in the way sketched in Section 3.1. These classes are then registered by GemStone's C++ Interface to become a part of the scheme definition.

We have just started implementing a generator which takes conceptual specifications of the syntax, static semantics, inter-document consistency and multi-user support and generates a database scheme. This work is a part of our activity in the ESPRIT-III project GOODSTEP (General Object-Oriented Database for SofTware Engineering Processes). In this project, O_2 will be enhanced in a way that it overcomes the deficiencies identified in section 4.

Acknowledgements

We are grateful to all members of the GoodStep consortium for intensive discussion about OODBMSs in CASE environments. In particular, we appreciated the discussions with Prof. C. Ghezzi and Prof. A. Fugetta about basic transaction mechanisms required from an OODBMS. Initial ideas regarding versioning evolved during discussions with Dr. J. Madec, Prof. J. Welsh and Prof. C. Delobel. Dr. S. Even, Ms. S. Sachweh, Prof. R. Zicari and Dr. R. de By provided us with deep insights in the topics of scheme updates and type safety.

We enjoyed working with a number of students working on this subject. F. Buddrus did a great job when implementing the first scheme generator. When implementing Groupie, M. Kampmann showed what is feasible and discovered the limits in the use of current OODBMSs.

References

1. P. Borras, D. Clément, T. Despeyroux, J. Incerpi, G. Kahn, B. Lang, and V. Pascual. CENTAUR: the system. *ACM SIGSOFT Software Engineering Notes*, 13(5):14–24, 1988. Proc. of the ACM SIGSOFT/SIGPLAN Software Engineering Symposium on Practical Software Development Environments, Boston, Mass.

2. F. Buddrus. Generierung von syntaxgesteuerten Werkzeugen auf der Basis eines objektorientierten Datenbanksystems. Master's thesis, University of Dortmund, Dept. of Computer Science, June 1992.
3. S. Dewal, W. Emmerich, and K. Lichtinghagen. A Decision Support Method for the Selection of OMSs. In *Proc. of the 2nd Int. Conf. on Systems Integration, Morristown, N.J.*, pages 32–40. IEEE Computer Society Press, 1992.
4. K. R. Dittrich, W. Gotthard, and P. C. Lockemann. Damokles – a database system for software engineering environments. In R. Conradi, T. M. Didriksen, and D. H. Wanvik, editors, *Proc. of an Int. Workshop on Advanced Programming Environments*, volume 244 of *Lecture Notes in Computer Science*, pages 353–371. Springer, 1986.
5. W. Emmerich and M. Kampmann. The Merlin OMS Benchmark - Definition, Implementations and Results. Technical Report 65, University of Dortmund, Dept. of Computer Science, Chair for Software Technology, 1992.
6. W. Emmerich and W. Schäfer. Dedicated Object Management Benchmarks for Software Engineering Applications. In R. Welland, editor, *Proc. of the Software Engineering Environments '93, Reading, UK*, 1993. To appear.
7. W. Emmerich, W. Schäfer, and J. Welsh. Databases for Software Engineering Environments — The Goal has not yet been attained. In I. Sommerville, editor, *Proc. of the 4th European Software Engineering Conference, Garmisch-Partenkirchen, Germany*, Lecture Notes in Computer Science. Springer, 1993. To appear.
8. G. Engels, C. Lewerentz, M. Nagl, W. Schäfer, and A. Schürr. Building Integrated Software Development Environments — Part 1: Tool Specification. *ACM Transactions on Software Engineering and Methodology*, 1(2):135–167, 1992.
9. F. Gallo, R. Minot, and I. Thomas. The object management system of PCTE as a software engineering database management system. *ACM SIGPLAN NOTICES*, 22(1):12–15, 1987.
10. M. Kampmann. Werkzeuge zur Unterstützung gruppenorientierter Arbeit beim Softwareentwurf. Master's thesis, University of Dortmund, Dept. of Computer Science, January 1993.
11. W. Kim, N. Ballou, H.-T. Chou, J. F. Garza, and D. Woelk. Features of the ORION Object-Oriented Database. In W. Kim and F. H. Lochovsky, editors, *Object-Oriented Concepts, Databases and Applications*, pages 251–282. Addison-Wesley, 1989.
12. P. Kroha. *Objects and Databases.* McGraw-Hill, 1993. To appear.
13. C. Lewerentz and A. Schürr. GRAS, a management system for graph-like documents. In *Proc. of the 3rd Int. Conf. on Data and Knowledge Bases.* Morgan Kaufmann, 1988.
14. M. A. Linton. Implementing Relational Views of Programs. *ACM SIGSOFT Software Engineering Notes*, 9(3):132–140, 1984. Proc. of the ACM SIGSOFT/SIGPLAN Software Engineering Symposium on Practical Software Development Environments, Pittsburgh, Penn.
15. T. W. Reps and T. Teitelbaum. *The Synthesizer Generator – a system for constructing language based editors.* Springer, 1988.

Summary Data Representations in Application Developments

Ten-lee Hwang

Andersen Consulting
Taipei, Taiwan, R.O.C.

Abstract. We included summary entities in ER models and proposed an analysis framework for summary data. Instead of examining the representations from the viewpoint of relational algebra or SQL queries, we took user requirements, identified during early phases of application developments, as constraints in modeling summary data. We used statistics requirement matrices to group identified statistics in summary entities. The concepts of data groups, aggregation operators, and underlined directed aggregation graphs, were developed accordingly. We showed how to model data and processes in the framework, and, as a real example in application developments, we described how we applied the framework as a guideline in developing an aggregation system for OAS Telecom Australia.

1 Introduction

Summary data is a summary of source data. For example, the yearly rainfall in a nation is a summary of the monthly rainfall by regions. Due to the aggregated nature, summary data are important in statistical databases owned by governments and commercial corporations, for operational control and strategic planning. There have been several works with regards to summary data. Johnson [5] extended the entity-relational model (ER model), proposed a query language to retrieve summary data, and argued for summary entities in the ER model. As he pointed out, with extra storage for summary data, we would achieve lower response time (direct retrieval from summary data) and higher security (keeping source data private). As an example of summary data, in a commercial corporation, we may record sales of each product type and for each sales person. As shown in Figure 1, entity *sales group* is a summary entity of the underlined entity *sales person*. In this case, *product type* and *sex* are called category attributes; while *total sale* and *avg sale* are called statistics attributes. For illustration, we will use the example throughout the paper. Other researchers [8, 4, 10] represented summary data in either tabular or graphical forms. However, the category attributes in their representations have to be orthogonal.

We will follow Johnson's proposal and use ER models to represent summary data. Using ER models, we will naturally lift the common assumption that category attributes are orthogonal. Instead of being motivated by simplifying lengthy queries and developing query languages, we will use information requirements acquired during system analysis, as constraints in data modeling. This approach will enable our results directly applicable as a guideline in application developments involving complicated data aggregation.

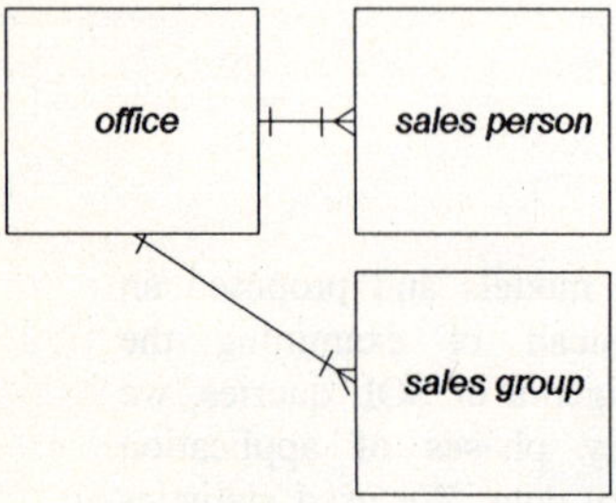

office

office name

sales person

sales name	*product type*	*sex*	*sales*

sales group

office name	*product type*	*sex*	*total sales*	*num of sales persons*	*avg sales*

Figure 1. Johnson's extended ER model

We will assume that the original source data are available after aggregation. They are stored as part of the active databases, recoverable from archived backup, or calculable from some aggregated data. For the case that source data are *not* available after aggregation, please refer to works by Sato [9] and Malvestuto [7]. Also, we will assume that commercial RDBMS's can handle extensive computational and storage requirements in data aggregation. The rationale is that database and hardware vendors will strive to provide faster and better products, as they have been doing successfully [3]. Application developers could then concentrate on re-engineering business functions and meeting the associated information requirements. For alternative data structures and different system architectures, please refer to works by Chen and MaNamee [2] and Baru [1].

The remainder of the paper is organized as follows. In section 2, we propose *statistics requirement matrices* to record identified statistics in summary entities and introduce the concept of data groups to group statistics. We define aggregation operators to aggregate statistics from one data group to another and propose directed graphs, *underlined aggregation graphs*, to graphically show how data groups related to each other. In section 3, we describe how summary data are represented in ER models. In section 4, we show how aggregation processes for summary data can be derived from the underlined aggregation graphs for all summary entities. Finally, as a real example from our practice, we show how we successfully implemented an aggregation system for Operator Assistance Service (OAS), Telecom Australia.

2 Information Requirements

Information requirements of an application generally cover both data and processes. Following our example in the introduction, to build an application monitoring the sales operations, we have to specify at least what source data, such as individual sales for each product type by each sales person, feed into the system; what summary data, such as total sales for each product type, interest managers using the system, and how summary data are obtained from the source data, a simple summation in this case. The first two are part of critical business data and the third, the aggregation processes, are from the business rules of the corporation.

Summary data tend to be layered. For example, in Figure 1, *total sales* could be for (1) each office, each product type, and each sex; (2) each office and each product type; (3) each office; and (4) the whole corporation. We do not list all possible layers. For instance, *total sales* can be for the whole corporation and each product type. *Total sales* for (4) can be aggregated from those for (3), which can be aggregated from those for (2), and so on. We define *total sales* for (1) are at the lowest layer because they are for the most detailed and complete list of category attributes. The aggregation from (1) to (2) is on the category attribute *sex* and we say that *sex* of *total sales* for (2) is empty. As far as the aggregation from (3) to (4), it is on the category attribute *office name* and we say that *office name* of *total sales* for (3) becomes more parental. These kinds of category attributes are hierarchical. They may describe a discrete organizational structure, as in this example, or as in the case that machines are made of parts. In other cases, they are different artificial units along a continuous dimension, such as seconds, minutes, and hours in time.

In general, let summary data have category attributes $\mathbf{k_1}, \mathbf{k_2}, .., \mathbf{k_m}$ and statistics attributes $\mathbf{s_1}, \mathbf{s_2}, ..., \mathbf{s_b}, \mathbf{s_{b+1}}, ..., \mathbf{s_n}$. $\mathbf{s_1}, \mathbf{s_2}, ..., \mathbf{s_b}$ are called basic statistics in the sense that each instance s_i, i = 1, 2, ...,b, depends on associated category attributes $k_1, k_2, .., k_m$ only. $\mathbf{s_{b+1}}, \mathbf{s_{b+2}}, ..., \mathbf{s_n}$ are called derived statistics in the sense that each instance s_i, i = b+1, b+2, ..., n, depends on some of the corresponding basic statistics $s_1, s_2, ..., s_b$ and possibly associated category attributes $k_1, k_2, .., k_m$. Category attributes are not necessarily orthogonal. Take Figure 1 as an example, for summary data in summary entity *sales group*, $\mathbf{k_1}$ = *office name*, $\mathbf{k_2}$ = *product type*, and $\mathbf{k_3}$ = *sex* (m = 3); $\mathbf{s_1}$ = *total sales* and $\mathbf{s_2}$ = *num of sales persons*; and $\mathbf{s_3}$ = *avg sales* (n = 3). Average sales can be calculated from total sales divided by number of sales persons, so b = 2. During system analysis, analysts will identify required summary data and statistics from the application requirements. Some of them are identified in order to reduce on-line retrieval or batch aggregation operations. Some of them are defined for faster statistical analysis time, or utilizing additive properties under statistical operations [4].

D	$\mathbf{k_1}$	$\mathbf{k_1^p}$	...	$\mathbf{k_2}$	...	$\mathbf{k_m}$	...	$\mathbf{s_1}$	...	$\mathbf{s_b}$	$\mathbf{s_{b+1}}$	...	$\mathbf{s_n}$
D_1	x			x		x		x			x		x
D_2		x		x		x		x			x		
			...		...	...			...			...	

Figure 2. A statistics requirement matrix

We propose to group required summary data by a matrix, the *statistics requirement matrix*, for each summary entity. As shown in Figure 2, we list category attributes and statistics attributes at the row heading, including parental attributes, such as $\mathbf{k_1}^{\mathbf{p}}$, the parental attribute of $\mathbf{k_1}$. The column heading **D** is to group summary data in groups, $D_1, D_2, ..., D_i, ...$ We use **x** to denote non-empty category attributes and required statistics. Each group of summary data share the same set of category attributes. For instance, the data group D_1 contains summary data with category attributes $\mathbf{k_1}, \mathbf{k_2},.., \mathbf{k_m}$ non-empty. In D_1, statistics attributes $\mathbf{s_1}, \mathbf{s_2}, ..., \mathbf{s_{b-1}}, \mathbf{s_{b+1}}, ...,$ and $\mathbf{s_n}$ are identified as required. The data group D_2 contains summary data with category attributes $\mathbf{k_1}^{\mathbf{p}}, \mathbf{k_2},.., \mathbf{k_m}$ non-empty. In D_2, only statistics attributes $\mathbf{s_1}, \mathbf{s_2}$, and $\mathbf{s_{b+1}}$ are identified as required. During identifying user requirements, the matrix is useful to summarize what statistics are needed, and what category attributes these statistics are associated with. Following our example, we may identify that *total sales* for (1), (2), (3), and (4); *num of sales persons* for (2), (3), and (4); and *avg sales* for (3) and (4), are required, then the statistics requirement matrix in Figure 3 can be created for the summary entity *sales group*.

D	k_1	k_1^p	k_2	k_3	s_1	s_2	s_3
D_1	x		x	x	x		
D_2	x		x		x	x	
D_3	x				x	x	x
D_4		x			x	x	x

Figure 3. A statistics requirement matrix for sales group in our example

Let us describe the dependencies between category attributes and statistical attributes by the following notations:

$\mathbf{s_i} = \mathbf{s_i}\ (\mathbf{k_1}, \mathbf{k_2},.., \mathbf{k_m})$ $\quad i = 1, 2, ..., b$ $\quad$ Equation (1)
$\mathbf{s_i} = g_i\ (\mathbf{k_1}, \mathbf{k_2},.., \mathbf{k_m}, \mathbf{s_1}, \mathbf{s_2}, ..., \mathbf{s_b})$ $\quad i = b+1, b+2, ..., n$ $\quad$ Equation (2)

For summary data at the lowest level, we assume that the basic statistics $\mathbf{s_1}, \mathbf{s_2}, ..., \mathbf{s_b}$ are simply aggregated from source data, collected from other systems (applications), or entered by clerks. Derived statistics $\mathbf{s_{b+1}}, \mathbf{s_{b+2}}, ..., \mathbf{s_n}$ are then calculated by (n-b) functions g_i. For summary data aggregated to higher layers, some of their category attributes become empty or more parental. Without loss of generality, if the aggregation is on $\mathbf{k_1}$ and $\mathbf{k_1}$ becomes empty, then the aggregation of basic statistics can be represented by $\mathbf{s_i}\ (, \mathbf{k_2},.., \mathbf{k_m}) = A_{(1)}\ \mathbf{s_i}\ (k_1, \mathbf{k_2},.., \mathbf{k_m})$. If $\mathbf{k_1}$ becomes more parental, then, $\mathbf{s_i}\ (\mathbf{k_1}^{\mathbf{p}}, \mathbf{k_2},.., \mathbf{k_m}) = A_{(1p)}\ \mathbf{s_i}\ (k_1, \mathbf{k_2},.., \mathbf{k_m})$, where $A_{()}$ is the aggregation operator aggregating basic statistics to higher levels. The subscript *(1)* means that the aggregation is on the first category attribute $\mathbf{k_1}$ and the letter *p* means that the aggregation is toward parental.

This notation can be naturally generalized for aggregations on multiple attributes. In our example, $\mathbf{s_1}$ for D_4 can be aggregated from $\mathbf{s_1}$ for D_2 by $\mathbf{s_1}(\mathbf{k_1}^{\mathbf{p}},,) = A_{(1p, 2)}\ \mathbf{s_1}\ (k_1, k_2,)$. Let us assume that each product type is sold by all offices, then $\mathbf{k_1}$

and $\mathbf{k_2}$ are orthogonal, and $\mathbf{s_1}(\mathbf{k_1}^{\mathbf{p}}, ,) = A_{(1p)}\, A_{(2)}\ \mathbf{s_1}\ (k_1, k_2,)$. Because the aggregation for $A_{(1p)}$ and $A_{(2)}$ is a simple sum and addition operators are commutative, $\mathbf{s_1}\ (\mathbf{k_1}^{\mathbf{p}}, ,) = A_{(1p)}\, A_{(2)}\ \mathbf{s_1}\ (k_1, k_2,) = A_{(2)}\, A_{(1p)}\ \mathbf{s_1}\ (k_1, k_2,)$. The aggregation for $\mathbf{s_2}$ is the same with that for $\mathbf{s_1}$. Once $\mathbf{s_1}$ and $\mathbf{s_2}$ for D_4 are available, $\mathbf{s_3}$ can be calculated by a simple division ($\mathbf{s_3}\ (\mathbf{k_1}^{\mathbf{p}}, ,) = g_3\ (\mathbf{k_1}^{\mathbf{p}}, , , \mathbf{s_1}, \mathbf{s_2}) = \mathbf{s_1}\ (\mathbf{k_1}^{\mathbf{p}}, ,) / \mathbf{s_2}\ (\mathbf{k_1}^{\mathbf{p}}, ,)$).

Inductively, if some of category attributes become empty or more parental, we first aggregate basic statistics and then calculate derived statistics in the same data group D_i by functions g_i. Basic properties of the aggregation operations, such as orthogonality and commutativity, can be derived, depending on functional relationships between category attributes and statistics attributes. Data groups D_i naturally bind basic and derived statistics together. Hence, we may represent aggregations as follows:

$$D_j = A\ D_i \qquad \text{Equation (3)}$$

This means that required statistics in data group D_j can be aggregated from required statistics in data group D_i. Required statistics and their relationships are described in Figure 2 and g_i are not expressed explicitly again. In Figure 3, $D_3 = A\ D_2$, $D_4 = A\ D_2$, and $D_4 = A\ D_3$. Because basic statistics $\mathbf{s_2}$ in D_2 cannot be aggregated from statistics in D_1, we cannot write $D_2 = A\ D_1$.

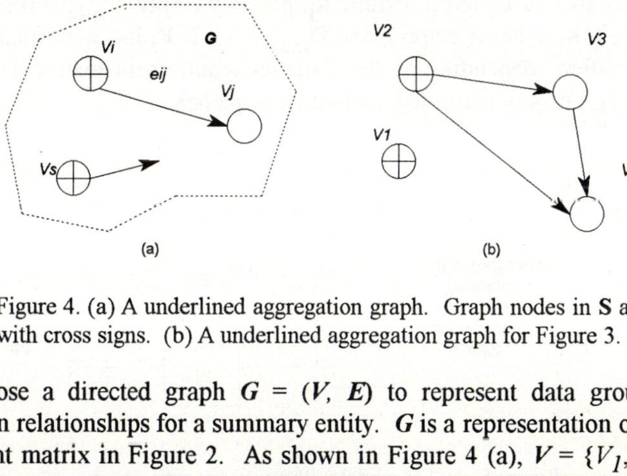

Figure 4. (a) A underlined aggregation graph. Graph nodes in **S** are nodes with cross signs. (b) A underlined aggregation graph for Figure 3.

We propose a directed graph $\boldsymbol{G} = (\boldsymbol{V}, \boldsymbol{E})$ to represent data groups and their aggregation relationships for a summary entity. $\boldsymbol{G}$ is a representation of the statistics requirement matrix in Figure 2. As shown in Figure 4 (a), $\boldsymbol{V} = \{V_1, V_2, , V_i, \ldots\}$, where V_i corresponds to a data group D_i; and $\boldsymbol{E} = \{ e_{ij} \mid e_{ij}$ is a directed edge from V_i to V_j, if and only if $D_j = A\ D_i$ }. Let $\boldsymbol{S}$ be the set, $\{ V_s \mid V_s$ has no directed edge pointing to it}. Graph nodes in $\boldsymbol{S}$ correspond to the data groups at the lowest level, and those not accumulable from them. The graph $\boldsymbol{G}$ is called the *underlined aggregation graph* because it shows all possible aggregation paths from one data group to another. Our example in Figure 3 can be represented by the underlined aggregation graph in Figure 4 (b), where $\boldsymbol{S} = \{ V_1, V_2\}$.

3 Data Modeling of Summary Entities

We will examine entity-relational models for summary data and show the relationships between statistics requirement matrices in Figure 2 and the ER models.

Following Johnson's proposal to include summary entities in ER models [5], we use $\mathbf{E_s}$ for summary data, as shown in Figure 5. The summary entity $\mathbf{E_s}$ contains category attributes $\mathbf{k_1}$, $\mathbf{k_2}$,.., and $\mathbf{k_m}$; and statistics attributes $\mathbf{s_1}$, $\mathbf{s_2}$, ..., $\mathbf{s_b}$, $\mathbf{s_{b+1}}$, ..., and $\mathbf{s_n}$, defined in the statistics requirement matrix in Figure 2. There may be more than one summary entity in an ER model, but we only show one of them in Figure 5. All other entities are partitioned into two parts, entities with some $\mathbf{k_i}$'s as unique identifiers (defined as *category entities*, such as $\mathbf{E_i}$ and $\mathbf{E_j}$), and other entities. Category entities are created to best group category attributes (Helman has shown that grouping attributes into entities for some cost function is NP complete [6]) and to further describe them. Other entities may include entities for source data, and even other summary entities.

As shown in Figure 5, each category entity, such as $\mathbf{E_i}$, has a relationship $\mathbf{R_{is}}$ with the summary entity $\mathbf{E_s}$. Each relationship $\mathbf{R_{is}}$ has a cardinality sequence ($\mathbf{f^i_{min}}$, $\mathbf{f^i_{max}}$, $\mathbf{f^s_{min}}$, $\mathbf{f^s_{max}}$), where $\mathbf{f^i_{min}}$ ($\mathbf{f^s_{min}}$) and $\mathbf{f^i_{max}}$ ($\mathbf{f^s_{max}}$) are the minimum and the maximum cardinalities from $\mathbf{E_i}$'s ($\mathbf{E_s}$'s) side. Because each instance of $\mathbf{E_i}$, with unique identifiers of some $\mathbf{k_i}$'s, must correspond to at least one instance of summary data in $\mathbf{E_s}$ (otherwise $\mathbf{k_i}$'s would not be included as category attributes), $\mathbf{f^i_{min}} = 1$ and $\mathbf{f^i_{max}} = N$. On the other hand, if $\mathbf{E_i}$ has a single $\mathbf{k_i}$ as the unique identifier, because each instance of $\mathbf{E_s}$ has a definite $\mathbf{k_i}$, possibly empty, $\mathbf{f^s_{min}} = 0$ (if $\mathbf{k_i}$ could be empty) or 1 (if $\mathbf{k_i}$ is never empty), and $\mathbf{f^s_{max}} = 1$. If $\mathbf{E_i}$ has more than one $\mathbf{k_i}$ as the unique identifiers, depending on the statistics requirement matrix, $\mathbf{f^s_{min}} = 0$, 1 and $\mathbf{f^s_{max}} = 1$, N, i.e., any permitted cardinality sequence.

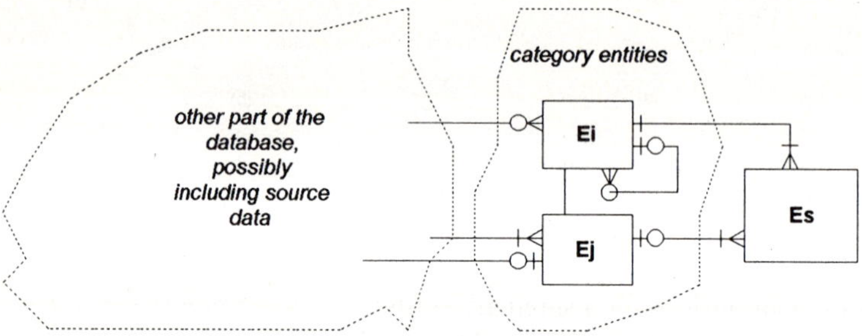

Figure 5. An ER model with summary entities

Similarly, category entities may have relationships with each other. In the case that all category attributes $\mathbf{k_i}$'s are orthogonal, we will have at most $\mathbf{m}$ category entities, each containing corresponding $\mathbf{k_i}$ as its unique identifier. Because of orthogonality, these entities will be isolated, meaning there are no relationships between them. Some of the category attributes, such as *sex* (including male and female) and *time* (including seconds, minutes, etc.), are well-defined and do not need category entities to further describe them. We call these manifest category attributes *self-evident*. In general, there may be a relationship between two category entities $\mathbf{E_i}$ and $\mathbf{E_j}$. It can have any permitted cardinality sequence, so its cardinalities are not shown in Figure 5. A category attribute $\mathbf{k_i}$ may contain parental attributes, such as $\mathbf{k_i^p}$, so the corresponding category entity may have a relationship with itself, as $\mathbf{E_i}$ in Figure 5, and $(\mathbf{f^i}_{\mathbf{min}}, \mathbf{f^i}_{\mathbf{max}}, \mathbf{f^i}_{\mathbf{min}}, \mathbf{f^i}_{\mathbf{max}}) = (0, 1, 0, N)$. Because category entities may be used by other entities (other than $\mathbf{E_s}$) for different reasons, their relationships with other entities can have any permitted cardinality sequences.

Category entities and their relationships are identified usually at the same time when the statistics requirement matrices for the summary data are being constructed. In our example, category attributes of the summary entity *sales group*, i.e., *office name*, and *product type*, can be unique identifiers of the category entities, *office* ($\mathbf{E_i}$), and *product type* ($\mathbf{E_j}$), as shown in Figure 6. We assume that category attributes *office name* and *product type* are orthogonal, so there is no relationship between $\mathbf{E_i}$ and $\mathbf{E_j}$. If the relationship between category attributes *office name* and *product type* becomes more complex, we may either add a relationship between $\mathbf{E_i}$ and $\mathbf{E_j}$, or use a single category entity to hold these two attributes together.

Let us discuss the case that there is more than one summary entity in the ER model, e.g., $\mathbf{E_s}$ and $\mathbf{E_s}'$, and each has its associated statistics requirement matrices, e.g., $\mathbf{M_s}$ and $\mathbf{M_s}'$. As shown in Figure 7, let $\mathbf{E_i}$ and $\mathbf{E_i}'$ be the category entities of $\mathbf{E_s}$ and $\mathbf{E_s}'$, connected by thin and thick lines respectively. The relationships between $\mathbf{E_s}$ and $\mathbf{E_s}'$, can be summarized as the follows (corresponding to Figure 7):

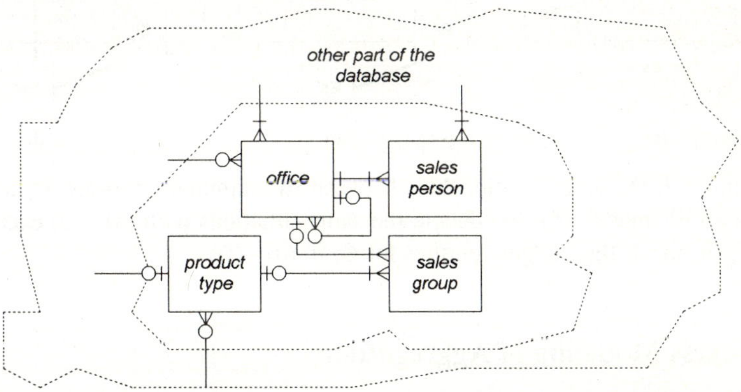

Figure 6. Another (extended) view of the ER model in Figure 1.

In (a), $\mathbf{E_s}$ and $\mathbf{E_s}'$ are two independent summary entities. All category entities for $\mathbf{E_s}'$ are not for $\mathbf{E_s}$. They often do not share any category attributes in $\mathbf{M_s}$ and $\mathbf{M_s}'$. Even if they do, the shared category attributes are self-evident, such as *time*. In (b), $\mathbf{E_s}$ and $\mathbf{E_s}'$ share some, but not all, category attributes, as defined in $\mathbf{M_s}$ and $\mathbf{M_s}'$. Some of the shared category attributes are not self-evident, and they are unique identifiers of some category entities, such as $\mathbf{E_i}'$. $\mathbf{E_i}$ contains non-shared, and not self-evident, category attributes as unique identifiers. Except for self-evident ones, category attributes in $\mathbf{M_s}'$ intersect with those in $\mathbf{M_s}$ (As a special case, category attributes in $\mathbf{M_s}'$ may form a subset of those in $\mathbf{M_s}$). In (d) and (e), except for self-evident category attributes, the set of category attributes in $\mathbf{M_s}'$ is a subset of those in $\mathbf{M_s}$ (the former, as a whole, is either empty or non-empty in the latter). (c) and (f) are like (b), but the same set of category entities are shared by both $\mathbf{E_s}$ and $\mathbf{E_s}'$. Except for self-evident ones, category attributes in $\mathbf{M_s}'$ are the same as those in $\mathbf{M_s}$.

$\mathbf{E_s}$ and $\mathbf{E_s}'$ can be combined as one summary entity, and their statistics requirement matrices can be combined too. They are separated as different summary entities, because they describe functionally separate statistics, or because statistics requirements (data groups) are such that entity separation makes functional senses or definitely leads to performance improvement, etc.

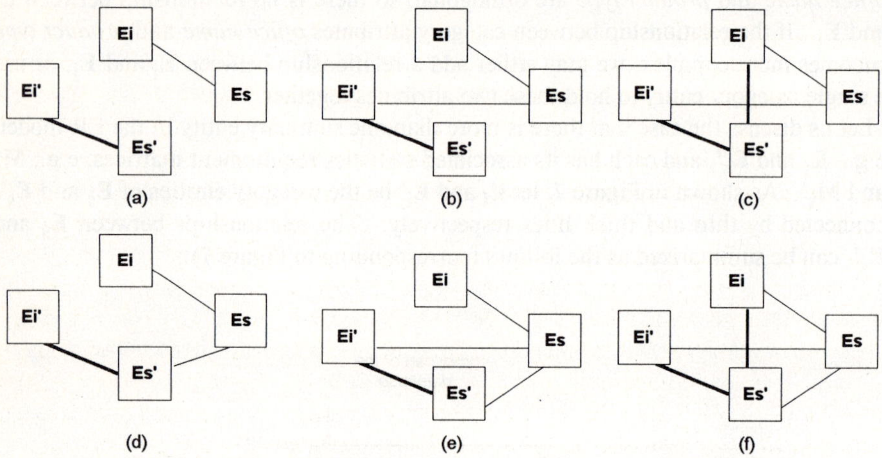

Figure 7. Different relationships between two summary entities, $\mathbf{E_s}$ and $\mathbf{E_s}'$, in an ER model. (d) - (f) denote the same situations with (a) - (c) except that $\mathbf{E_s}'$ is one of the category entities for $\mathbf{E_s}$ in (d) - (f).

4 Process Modeling of Aggregations

For each summary entity **Es** in an ER model, a underlined aggregation graph G as Figure 4 (a) can be created from Equation (3), derived from the associated statistics requirement matrix. For a system as a whole, a *combined underlined aggregation graph* may be created for all summary entities in the ER model. It is a union of the underlined aggregation graphs for all summary entities.

Let $\mathbf{Es}^1$, $\mathbf{Es}^2$, ..., $\mathbf{Es}^j$,... be summary entities of an ER model; $\mathbf{Ms}^1$, $\mathbf{Ms}^2$, ..., $\mathbf{Ms}^j$,... the corresponding statistics requirement matrices; and G^1, G^2, ..., G^j,... the corresponding underlined aggregation graphs. Let us represent each G^j as (V^j, E^j). As in section 2, $V^j = \{V_i^j \mid V_i^j$ corresponds to a data group D_i^j in $\mathbf{Ms}^j\}$; and $E^j = \{$

$e_{ij}^{j} \mid e_{ij}^{j}$ is a directed edge from V_i^j to V_j^j, if and only if $D_j^j = A\ D_i^j$ }. For a combined underlined aggregation graph $\boldsymbol{G} = (\boldsymbol{V}, \boldsymbol{E})$, $\boldsymbol{V} = (\mathrm{U_j}\ \boldsymbol{V}^{\mathbf{j}}) - \boldsymbol{V}_{\mathbf{c}}$ and $\boldsymbol{E} = (\mathrm{U_j}\ \boldsymbol{E}^{\mathbf{j}}) + \boldsymbol{E}_{\mathbf{c}}$, where **U** is a set union operator over its operands; - a set difference operator; and + a set union operator. $\boldsymbol{V}_{\mathbf{c}}$ is the set of graph nodes to be merged, so they are removed from the union of $\boldsymbol{V}^{\mathbf{j}}$'s. $\boldsymbol{E}_{\mathbf{c}}$ is the set of extra directed edges to be added.

We will show how two underlined aggregation graphs can be combined. As discussed in section 3, two different summary entities, $\mathbf{Es^j}$ and $\mathbf{Es^k}$, with statistics requirement matrices $\mathbf{Ms^j}$ and $\mathbf{Ms^k}$, have relationships as in Figure 7 (a) - (f):

(a) Any of category attributes in data groups D_j^j in $\mathbf{Ms^j}$, except the self-evident ones, is not the same with any category attribute in any data group D_i^k in $\mathbf{Ms^k}$, so data groups, hence corresponding graph nodes in $\boldsymbol{V}^{\mathbf{j}}$ and $\boldsymbol{V}^{\mathbf{k}}$, cannot be merged, and statistics in D_i^k cannot be aggregated from statistics in D_j^j. Combining the underlined aggregation graphs of these two summary entities will not add elements to $\boldsymbol{V}_{\mathbf{c}}$ and $\boldsymbol{E}_{\mathbf{c}}$.

(b-f) Category attributes, as a whole, in some data group D_j^j in $\mathbf{Ms^j}$ may be the same as the category attributes in a data group D_i^k in $\mathbf{Ms^k}$. There are a few possibilities in creating combined underlined aggregation graphs. First, we may ignore these relationships and create the combined underlined aggregation graph by simple unions as (a), i.e., no elements are added to $\boldsymbol{V}_{\mathbf{c}}$ and $\boldsymbol{E}_{\mathbf{c}}$. Second, we may keep graph nodes in $\boldsymbol{V}^{\mathbf{j}}$ and $\boldsymbol{V}^{\mathbf{k}}$ intact, and pursue the statistical relationships between data groups in $\mathbf{Ms^j}$ and $\mathbf{Ms^k}$. If statistics in some data group in $\mathbf{Ms^j}$ are accumulable from statistics in a data group in $\mathbf{Ms^k}$, we may add extra elements to $\boldsymbol{E}_{\mathbf{c}}$ but $\boldsymbol{V}_{\mathbf{c}}$ is still empty. Third, we may combine $\mathbf{Ms^j}$ and $\mathbf{Ms^k}$ in an attempt to merge some of their data groups, including D_j^j and D_i^k. We could draw a new underlined aggregation graph for the combined statistics requirement matrix. However, we may combine their underlined aggregation graphs as follows. The corresponding nodes for D_j^j and D_i^k, V_j^j and V_i^k, could be perceived as one in the combined underlined aggregation graph, so one of them, say V_j^j, is an element of $\boldsymbol{V}_{\mathbf{c}}$. Because the statistics in both D_j^j and D_i^k will be concatenated for the merged node, some of existing edges into the merged node, say e_{ij}^{j}, denoting aggregation from D_i^j to D_j^j, may be removed. The reason is that required statistics in both D_j^j and D_i^k may not be accumulable from required statistics in D_i^j alone. On the other hand, all existing edges out of the merged node, say e_{ij}^{k}, denoting aggregation from D_i^k to D_j^k, will be preserved. The reason is that required statistics in D_j^k could be aggregated from required statistics in D_i^k alone, not to say from required statistics in both D_j^j and D_i^k. This suggests a heuristic that nodes in $\boldsymbol{S}^{\mathbf{j}}$ and $\boldsymbol{S}^{\mathbf{k}}$, or nodes closer to those in $\boldsymbol{S}^{\mathbf{j}}$ and $\boldsymbol{S}^{\mathbf{k}}$, should be first considered as candidates for node merging.

While creating the combined underlined aggregation graph, we should inspect the business data and functions to decide if some of graph nodes can be merged, and if directed edges can be added. This is actually performed at the same time when we decide if summary entities in the ER model should be combined or separated. Functional relationships between statistics, such as Equation (1) and (2), should be considered. It may not be important to find out all aggregation processes, namely all directed edges in the combined underlined aggregation graph, but it is critical to produce all required statistics efficiently. We will assume that there exists at least one traversal path from a node in **S** to any node in **G**. This assumption is reasonable because there must be a way to generate required statistics from source data, otherwise they could not be required. To generate the required statistics in each data group, we have to identify a set of aggregation processes during process modeling. In addition to the processes for statistics in **S**, union of **S**^{j}'s for all **G**^{j}'s, other aggregation processes correspond to a set of the traversal paths connecting all nodes in **G**, starting from nodes in **S** (the number of these processes is equal to the number of nodes in **G**, but not in **S**). For instance, in Figure 4 (b), in addition to the processes for statistics in **S**, nodes V_1 and V_2, we need two aggregation processes, corresponding to either edges e_{23} and e_{34}, or edges e_{23} and e_{24}, to generate statistics in data groups for nodes V_3 and V_4. If we associate each directed edge in **G** a positive cost, identifying these aggregation processes is equivalent to finding a set of traversal paths in **G** under some constraints, e.g., the sum of costs over traversed edges is minimized. It can be performed while creating the combined underlined aggregation graph and modifying summary entities in the ER model.

During system design, after database tables are generated from the ER model, each aggregation process from a data group, say D_i, to another, say D_j, either within the same summary entity or across different summary entities, can be easily implemented by SQL queries involving summary tables [4, 5] and calculations for derived statistics. For SQL queries, in most cases, simple SELECT statements with standard aggregation operators such as SUM and COUNT (for basic statistics in D_j), GROUP BY clauses (for category attributes in D_j), and WHERE clauses (for category attributes in D_i), on summary tables are sufficient. If category entities for the summary entities have complicated relationships, join operations between summary tables and the category tables (generated from the associated category entities) may be needed, especially when a category attribute is aggregated toward parental. Because each aggregation process is fairly regular this way, the system as a whole can be easily designed, coded, tested, and maintained.

5 Exemplar Engagement

We were engaged in 1992 to build a management information system (MIS) for Operator Assisted Services (OAS), Telecom Australia. OAS provides services including Directory Assistance, National and International Call Connect, etc. The MIS system, a client-server application across a wide area network, is to provide managers at national, regional, area and even local levels, source and aggregated operational statistics, so that OAS can improve its services. Each night, the MIS extracts four kinds of feeder files from switches across Australia. The feeder files contain operational statistics at local and switch levels, such as number of calls answered, number of calls refused, mean service time, number of positions staffed, number of calls per position staffed, etc. After extracting the feeder files, the MIS will aggregate these statistics to higher organization levels, by service, and by different periods of time, such as months and years. MIS users across Australia can then enquire and extract these statistics through the system.

During system analysis, we identified statistics requirements in OAS and summarized information requirements in forms like Figure 2, Equations (1) and (2). It turned out that there are two summary entities, one for machine related operational statistics ($\mathbf{E_s}$), such as number of calls answered, and the other for human related productivity statistics ($\mathbf{E_s}$'), such as number of positions staffed. In the statistics requirement matrix for $\mathbf{E_s}$, $\mathbf{M_s}$, there are five category attributes, namely *organization unit*, *service type*, *switch name*, *switch queue type*, and *time*. The attribute *organization unit* has three parental attributes according to OAS's organizational structure. The attribute *time* (days) has two parental attributes, months and years. There are 15 basic statistics and 5 derived statistics in $\mathbf{M_s}$. In the statistics requirement matrix for $\mathbf{E_s}$', $\mathbf{M_s}$', there are three category attributes, i.e., *organization unit*, *service type*, and *time*. The category attributes *organization unit* and *time* have parental attributes, as in $\mathbf{M_s}$. There are 7 basic statistics and 5 derived statistics in $\mathbf{M_s}$'. The associated mathematical relationships for statistics in $\mathbf{M_s}$ and $\mathbf{M_s}$' are described by additions, subtractions, multiplications, and divisions.

There are four category entities for summary entities $\mathbf{E_s}$ and $\mathbf{E_s}$', namely, *service type*, *organization unit*, *switch name*, and *switch queue type*. Except for the attribute *time* (self-evident), other four category attributes are not orthogonal and have complicated relationships, particularly between *organization unit*, *service type*, and, *switch queue type*. Summary entities $\mathbf{E_s}$ and $\mathbf{E_s}$' share category entities as in Figure 7 (b) and except for *time*, category attributes in $\mathbf{M_s}$' form a subset of those in $\mathbf{M_s}$.

There are totally 35 data groups in $\mathbf{M_s}$ and $\mathbf{M_s}$', so there are 35 nodes in the combined underlined aggregation graph. We did not draw all of the edges in the graph. Instead, we chose about the same amount of edges directly from $\mathbf{M_s}$ and $\mathbf{M_s}$' to generate the needed data groups. Information requirements in $\mathbf{M_s}$ and $\mathbf{M_s}$' and relationships between category entities *organization unit*, *service type*, *switch name*, and, *switch queue type*, are such that three types of aggregation processes, aggregation by *organization unit*, aggregation by *service type*, and aggregation by *time*, are sufficient. Because of the relationships between category entities and statistics, some aggregation processes are complex.

Oracle database tables are created following the summary entities and category entities in the ER model. There are about 1.5 million and 0.1 million rows in tables from $\mathbf{E_s}$ and $\mathbf{E_s}$' respectively. Although the aggregation processes are in batch, choices of the table indexes, created according to the access patterns of the aggregation processes, turned out critical to have the aggregation finished within the allowed time window. In addition to separate modules for error handling and date handling, we designed aggregation modules around data groups. They are modular and structured that 12 aggregation modules are sufficient. The aggregation programs are about 8,000 lines, written in Oracle's SQL-embedded C, running in Ultrix Unix.

With statistics requirement matrices and data groups, people not coding the aggregation programs were able to understand the aggregation requirements quickly and to perform system tests of aggregation programs efficiently. During stress testing with real data, we were able to quickly identify the aggregation bottleneck (from a particular data group to another), and to change the associated SQL queries.

With the framework, when there were enhancements, we were able to update our analysis (design) documents and to modify the programs productively.

6 Conclusion

We summarized different representations of summary data in literature, including Johnson's proposal to include summary entities in ER models. Instead of examining the representations from the veiwpoint of relational algebra or SQL queries, we started from user requirements. We proposed statistics requirement matrices to arrange identified statistics in data groups and represented aggregation processes by underlined aggregation graphs. We described summary entities in ER models and derived aggregation processes from the underlined aggregation graphs. Finally, we described how we implemented an aggregation system for OAS Telecom Australia, as an example applying this framework. This systematic treatment on summary data can be used as a guideline in system analysis of an aggregation system and will facilitate its design and installation.

References

1. C. Baru, S. Su: Performance Evaluation of the Statistical Aggregation by Categorization in the SM3 System: Proc. of ACM SIGMOD, 1984, pp. 77-89
2. M. Chen, L. McNamee: A Data Model and Access Method for Summary Data Management: Proc. International Data Engineering, 1989, pp. 242-249
3. D. Dewitt, J. Gray: Parallel Database Systems, the Future of High Performance Database Systems: Communications ACM, vol. 35, no. 6, June 1992
4. S. Ghosh: Statistical Relational Tables for Statistical Database Management: IEEE Transactions on Software Engineering, No. 12, Dec. 1986, pp. 1106-1116
5. R. Johnson: Modelling Summary Data: Proc. of ACM SIGMOD, 1981, pp. 93-97
6. P. Helman: A Family of NP-Complete Data Aggregation Problems: Acta Informatica 26, 1989, pp. 485-499
7. F. Malvestuto, M. Moscarini: Aggregate Evaluability in Statistical Databases: Proc. of VLDB Conference, 1989, pp. 279-286
8. G. Ozsoyoglu, Z. Ozsoyoglu, F. Mata: Language and a Physical Organization Technique for Summary Tables: Proc. of ACM SIGMOD, 1985, pp. 3-16
9. H. Sato: Handling Summary Information in a Database:Derivability: Proc. of ACM SIGMOD, 1981, pp. 98-107
10. A. Shoshani: Statistical Databases: Characteristics, Problems, and Some Solutions: Proc. of VLDB, 1982, pp. 208-222

REUSABLE PROCESS CHUNKS*

Colette Rolland
Université de Paris Sorbonne
17, rue de la Sorbonne
75231 Paris Cedex 5
France

Naveen Prakash
Delhi Institute of Technology
Kashmere Gate, Old IG Block
110006 Delhi
India

Abstract. Reusability of project components, either at the code level or at the conceptual specification level, is considered a fundamental aspect in application development. More recently it as been argued that project histories can support reuse of design decisions. We propose a solution based on so-called process chunks which are generic process frames to resolve the issue stated by a generic requirements engineering (RE) situation. Chunks are classified into micro-chunks and macro-chunks. The latter support the decision making process whereas the former help in implementing the decision. The RE activity based on these chunks consists of (1) recognising a situation as belonging to the class of situations treated by a chunk and (2) the instanciation of the process frame. The benefit expected from this approach is threefold : (1) to speed up the requirements engineering process; (2) to improve the quality of the conceptual specifications; and (3) to offer an extensible way for capturing generic RE process knowledge.

1 Introduction

Reuse of project components is being put forward as a promising approach in the application development process [Biggerstaff1987], [ACM1990], [Gibbes1990] . In fact it facilitates both effective development of good quality applications by exploiting existing validated components, and easy re-development of applications by promoting a modular approach. It is commonly agreed that reuse does not only concern code, but any development artifact. Thus, requirements specifications, design decisions, logical specifications are also candidates for reuse. A more recent claim is that the development process itself is candidate for reuse (and not only the artifacts which result of the process). A common characteristic of recent proposals is the representation of the development history as a set of decisions which transform the state of artifacts [Jarke1988], [Jarke1992], [Potts1989], [Balasubramanian1992] and the argumentation for reusing design decision in subsequent projects.

In this paper we address the problem of reusing generic pieces of the Requirements Engineering Process which are called Process Chunks. Requirements Engineering is this early part of the system development which involves investigating the problems and requirements of the users community and developing the conceptual specification of the future system, the so-called conceptual schema. The Requirements Engineering process is the route to reach the conceptual schema. It has the purpose of abstracting and conceptualizing relevant parts of the application domain. This is guided by requirements [Dubois1987].

---

* This work has been partially supported by the ESPRIT project NATURE

A process chunck is a piece of generic knowledge reusable for requirements engineering issues of the same kind. It is in the form <situation, decision, argument, action> and associates to a common situation in requirements engineering, the decisions the requirements engineer can take in that situation, the arguments to choose among the possible decisions and the action which is a schema transformation that is triggered by the engineer choice. A process chunk is a knowledge store which is structured according to a process model. The process model underlying process chunks is presented in section 2. In section 3, the notion of process chunck is defined and examplified. The RE-by-reuse methodology is sketched in section 4. Our concluding remarks are given in section 5.

2 The process model

According to Dowson [Dowson1987] existing process models can be classified into three categories:

-*Activity-oriented models* [Royce 1970], [Boehm 1988], [Henderson-Sellers & Edwards 1990] come from an analogy with problem solving, i.e. finding and executing a plan of actions leading to the solution. They are sequential in nature and provide a frame for manual management of projects developed in a linear fashion. Such a linear view of the design process is inadequate for methodologies which support backtracking, reuse of previous designs and have to support parallel engineering activities.

-*The product-oriented process models* [Finkelstein & al. 1990], [Peugeot and Franckson 1991]. represent the development process through the evolution of the product. They promote a view of development processes which is still centred around the notion of development activity but emphasises the linkage between the development activities and their output, the product.

-A more recent class of process models follows a *decision-oriented paradigm*. The successive transformations of the product are looked upon as consequences of decisions. The process model of the DAIDA project [Jarke & al. 1990; Rose & al. 1991] and of [Potts 1989] fall into this category. Such models are semantically more powerful than the previous ones because they explain not only how the process proceeds but also why transformations happen. They provide a more complete knowledge about the process which is particularly useful for reuse of developed products, or of design decisions, and for backtracking purposes when a modification in requirements has to be considered either during the design process itself or during the maintenance of the information system

Considering the highly non-deterministic nature of the Requirements Engineering process we do believe that only the last of these approaches appears to be partially appropriate. It is probably difficult to impossible to write down a realistic state-transition diagram that adequately describes what has to happen or actually happens in requirements engineering. But relying on the pure artifact history is also insufficient. Even the decision-based approaches offer only limited hints about when and how to decide on what.

Analysts react *contextually* according to the domain knowledge they acquire and react by analogy with previous situations they have been involved in. In order to take into account the very nature of the RE we have chosen to emphazise the contextual aspect of decisions. Our process modeling approach strongly couples the context of a decision to the decision itself, otherwise we loose information about the decision. This approach aims at capturing not only activities performed during the RE process but also why these activities are performed (the decisions) and when (the decision contexts).

The central aspect of our process way of modeling is therefore that it makes the notion of *situation* (in which to decide) explicit and relates it to the broader question of context handling. Figure 1 gives an overview of the process model, introducing its key concepts and their relationships (with a binary E/R based notation).This approach is an extension of the one presented in [Grosz&Rolland1990] and implemented in the ALECSI prototype [Rolland&Cauvet1991].

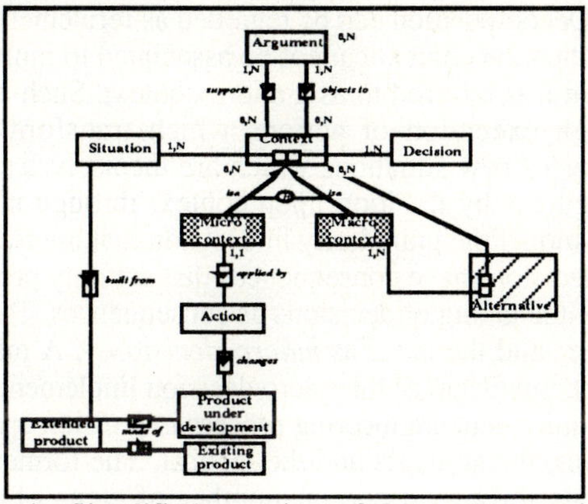

Fig.1 : Simplified overview of the process model

The four basic concepts are the ones of situation, decision, action and argument :
- *situation* to explain the decision context,
- *decision* to guide the RE process,
- *action* to perform the product transformations,
- *argument* to support decision-making.

A *situation* is most often a part of the product under development it makes sense to take a decision on. It represents the context of a decision. It can be a statement about the application domain or a requirement. It can also refer to part of existing products resulting from previous developments or a piece of generic domain knowledge. Accordingly, in figure1, the situation *is built on* either the *product under development* or *existing products.* A complete product model is presented in [Schmitt1993].
A *decision* reflects a choice that a requirement engineer makes at a given point in time of the RE process. A decision can be looked upon as the intention of product transformations. It explicitly represents the resolution of an issue.

An *action* performs a transformation on the product. It is a materialisation of the decision. Performing it changes the product and may generate new situations which, in turn, are subjects of new decisions.
Arguments are statements which support or object to decisions within a given context.

The model emphasises the dimension of decisions and introduces the notion of context as a main concept of process modelling .A *contex;*t is a couple <situation,decision> which amplifies the decision semantics by refining the "when" part of the decision.
Furthermore, the process model has to handle different levels of granularity of contexts, i.e. granularity of situations, as well as of decisions. This leads to the specialisation of the context into *macro* and *micro* ones. The former corresponds to a situation which requires to explore alternatives in decision making for its treatment. This is represented in Figure 1 by the loop upon context through macro context and alternative. This introduces the decomposition of a macro context into its more elementary context. Decomposition can be regarded as refinement in decision making. On the other hand, when the context cannot be associated to multiple ways of solving the issue it raises then it is referred to as a micro context. Such a context implements one decision through execution of actions which transform the product under development. This raises new situations which are themselves subjects of decisions. This is shown in Figure 1 by the loop upon context through micro context, action, and situation. In this model the granularity in decision making relates to consequences of decisions. Some decisions have consequences that are only product transformations whereas others imply the taking of decisions as consequences. The former are referred to as *micro decisions* and the latter as *macro decisions* ; A macro decision can be qualified as a strategic one whereas the micro decision implements a tactic.
Consequently, the requirement engineering process is decision oriented and recognises two kinds of decisions, the strategic and the tactical. The former needs to be refined into tactical decisions through a certain number of steps of decision making. A tactical decision can be immediately implemented through a set of actions.

3 The notion of process chunk

A process chunk captures generic process knowledge. It is context-targeted and intends to provide help to the requirements engineer for reacting to the RE situations he is faced to, through decision making and associated actions. A process chunk is concerned with one generic context composed of one generic situation that might occur in the RE process and an associated generic decision. According to the classification of contexts introduced earlier, chunks will be classified into macro and micro chunks.

The macro chunk corresponds to a situation which requires the exploration of alternatives in decision making. Each alternative is an approach or a strategy for the resolution of the issue being faced by the engineer in the current situation. The chunk supports the requirement engineer in the exploration of these strategies and in the selection of the most appropriate one. By definition, a macro chunk offers a choice among a set of strategies all of which achieve the same purpose. In this sense, one can look upon the macro chunk as being goal oriented.

A micro chunk refers to a situation for which the strategy to be followed has been decided. It supports the implementation of the tactic associated with the strategy through the ordering of actions to be performed on the product under development.

3.1 The Macro Chunk

The structure of the macro chunk is given in Figure 2. As can be seen the main notion underlying a macro chunk is that of macro context. Basically, the macro chunk provides support to decompose the initial macro context into other contexts. This is done through deliberation on the produced contexts by arguing in favour of or against them. Thus the key concepts underlying the macro chunk are the ones of context, alternative, and argument.

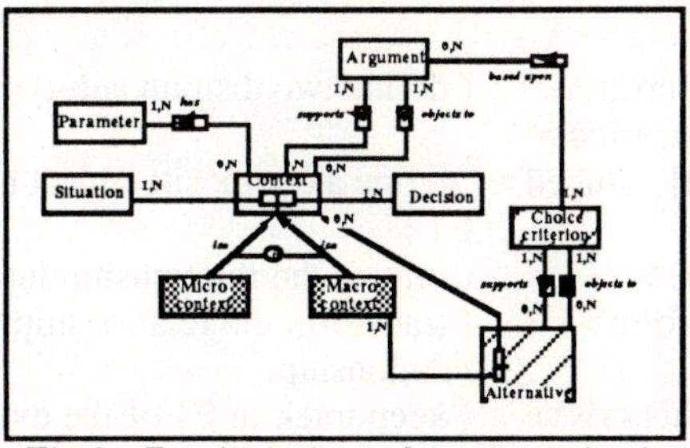

Fig 2 : Detailed view of a macro chunk

A macro chunk is associated to a macro context that shall be referred to as the mother context. This is composed of a generic pair, <situation, decision> and associated parameters. As an example, consider the mother context, MC, shown in Figure 3 consisting of

- the generic situation defined by the binary relationship between two entity-types,
- the generic decision, 'structure', and
- the parameters which characterise the relationship using cardinalities. Cardinalities are of three types, totality, valuation, and permanency. The first two of these are the usual ER ones and take on values as follows

totality : *partial* (p) or *total* (t), {0 or 1 respectively of the ER minimum cardinality }

valuation :*simple* (s) or *multiple* (m) {1 or N respectively of the ER maximum cardinality } The third one is specific and takes on the following values

permanency :*variable* (v) or *permanent* (p)

The relationship between E1 and E2 is said to be *permanent* if an instance of E2 which is associated with an instance of E1 remains permanently linked to it during the full life cycle of E1. The relationship is said to be *variable* when an instance of E1 is related to different instances of E2 during its life cycle.

As shown in Figure 3, there are two triplets of cardinalities which characterise respectively the relationship from E1 to E2 and the one from E2 to E1.

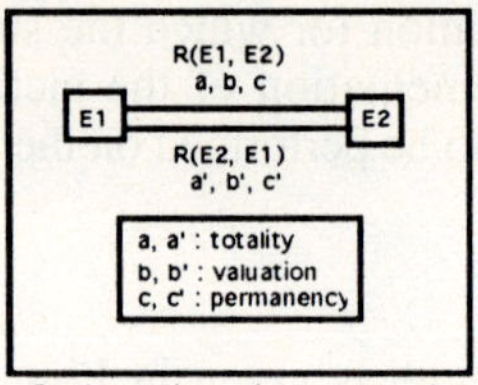

Fig 3: Example of situation in a mother macro-context,

The macro chunk aims at refining the decision of the mother context by considering various alternatives all of which are relevant to the resolution of this decision. This is modelled in terms of the decomposition of the mother context into other contexts. For instance a partial list of contexts resulting from the decomposition of MC is as follows:

- < {E1, R(E1,E2)}, 'partition'> (define two disjoint sub-types)
- < {E2,R(E2,E1)}, 'partition'>
- < {E1, E2, R(E1,E2)}, 'embed'> (define a composite object by embedding E2 into E1)
- < {R(E1,E2)}, 'retype'> (mutate the relationship into an entity type)
- < {R(E1,E2)}, 'transform'> (transform the relationship into an ISA relationship)
- < { E1, R(E1,E2)}, historise> (keep track in E1 of the evolution of its reltionship with E2)
- < { E2, R(E2,E1)}, historise> (keep track in E2 of the evolution of its relationship with E1)

In order to help in the selection of the appropriate alternative, the chunk provides criteria for choosing among these (hatched box in Figure 2). A choice criterion combines arguments which support/object to the decision within a context. Taken together, the choice criterion and arguments make explicit the deliberation behind the decision making process. Along the lines of the IBIS model [Conklin&Begeman1992] the chunk helps the requirement engineer in acting according to the rationale of decisions. In the example considered above, the arguments will be based on values of cardinalities. For example the cardinalities triplet

< p, -, - > where '-' could take on any of the allowed value

associated with the relationship R(E1,E2) in the forward direction supports the partition of E1. Similarly, when associated with the relationship in the backward direction, this triplet supports the partition of E2.

It is possible to base the arguments associated with 'embed' in a similar manner. The two cardinality sextuplets

< < t,m,p> <t,s,p > > and < <t,m,v> <t,s,p,> >

associated with the relationship between E1 and E2 support the embedding of E2 into E1. Due to the valuation, m, there shall be multiple instances of E2 embedded in one instance of E1. Similarly, the two cardinality sextuplets

< < t,s,p> <t,s,p > > and < <t,s,v> <t,s,p,> >

associated with the relationship between E1 and E2 support the embedding of E2 into E1. Due to the valuation, s, there shall be one instance of E2 embedded in one instance of E1.

The choice criterion is built up using arguments. For instance, a criterion could be formulated as follows
< if the argument supporting specialisation of an entity type holds then this decision has a higher priority over any other decision supported by another argument >. One can therefore notice that a choice criterion has to be formulated when several arguments hold at the same time. The choice criterion gives, in fact, a priority to one of the arguments.

3.2 The Micro Chunk

A micro chunk is associated with a micro context, i.e., to a pair <situation, decision> which implies only one way of solving the issue it raises. One can say that the micro chunk is only concerned with the manner in which the decision shall be implemented and not with exploring alternatives. The implementation of the decision of the micro context will be performed by actions that transform the product under development. There are two major differences between the macro chunk and the micro chunk : the first one lies in the absence of any alternatives in the latter and the second one is that a macro chunk has no direct consequence on the product under development.

The structure of a micro-chunck is shown in Figure 4. As can be seen the main concept underlying the micro-chunk is that of micro-context. The micro-chunk provides the procedure to perform the transformations of the product under development resulting of the decision stated by the initial micro-context. This is merely achieved through the execution of actions but may require the decomposition of micro-contexts into more atomic micro-contexts. Thus the key notions of a micro-chunck are those of micro-context and action.
A micro-chunk is associated to a micro-context that will be referred to as the mother-context. Each of the contexts resulting of the decomposition of the macro-context < {E1, R(E1,E2), E2}, 'structure' > introduced in the previous paragraph are examples of such micro-contexts. A context consists of a decision and the situation subject to this decision. For instance the context < {E1,R(E1,E2)}, 'Partition' > is based upon a situation composed of an Entity-type E1 and the decision to partition E1.
If the consequence of the decision stated in the micro-context consists of a unique action, it is referred to as an *atomic context*. An *atomic context* triggers only one action which can be in turn (cross-hatched boxes in figure 4) *compound* (composed of several actions) or *atomic* (changing only one product element). In this case, the decision is directly implemented. Even though a commitment to implementing the decision has been made, it is possible that the implementation is complex requiring transformations of several elements of the product under development. In this case the context is said a *compound context*. A compound context is itself a pair <

situation, decision> that has to be further decomposed into more atomic contexts. This decomposition proceeds till atomic contexts are reached, which, by definition, are immediatly implementable. This is modelled through the decomposition of contexts ("composed of" relationship in figure 4).

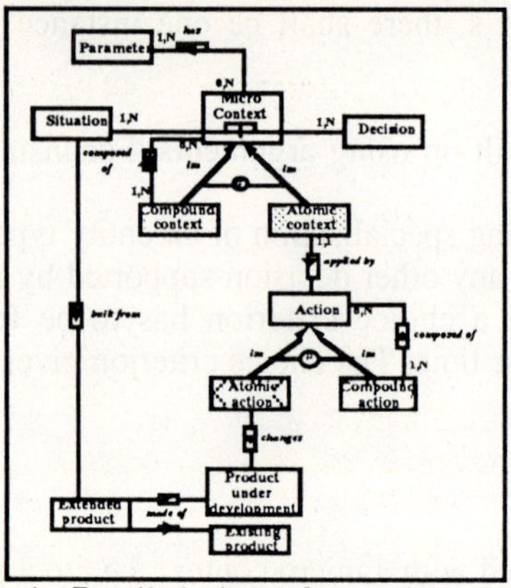

Fig 4 : Detailed view of the micro chunk

For instance, the decomposition of the compound context < {E1, R(E1,E2)} ,'partition' > is as follows :

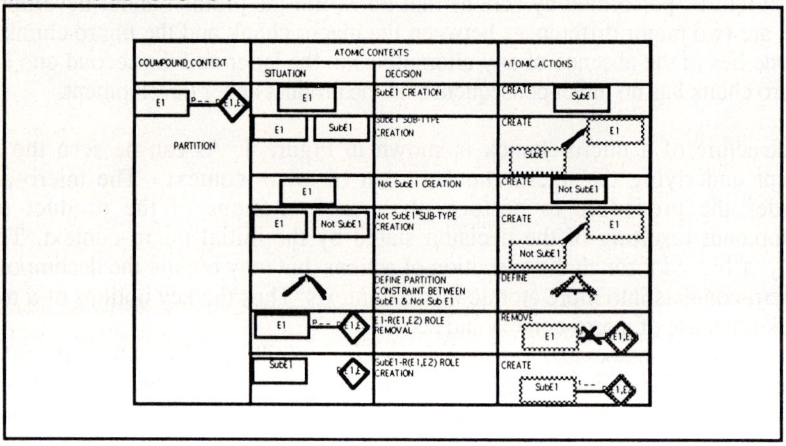

The mother micro-context <E1, R(E1,E2), 'partition'> is further decomposed into seven atomic contexts including each, a sub-micro situation of the initial one and the corresponding micro-decision. Each micro decision is implemented through the execution of one action which creates or removes elements of the product under development. For instance the first atomi-type E1 and the micro-decision 'SubE1 Creation' which results in the creation of a sub-type of the Entity-type E1 . The fith atomic context associates to the two sub-typing links introduced to the Entity-type E1, the decision of defining a partition constraint which is immediatly implemented by the correspondig action.

5 Reusing process chunks

In this section we address the problem of reusing process chunks. Reusability can be considered from two different perspectives. According to a *design-by-reuse* perspective an application can be obtained by tailoring existing components extracted from an available repository. According to a *design-for-reuse* perspective, a repository must be populated with reusable components, properly defined to be exploitable for developing new applications not from scratch. We sketch in this section a RE-by-reuse approach in which the Requirements Engineering process is guided by the reuse of process chunks. Process knowledge is captured into a Process Knowledge Base wich consists of a collection of process chunks.

From an operational point of view, the Chunk definition is aimed at providing guidance for method engineers It helps these engineers in defining the way-of-working of the specific methodology they have to develop. The way-of-working of a given methodology will be obtained by instanciating macro and micro chunks as defined in the previous section The result of such an instanciation consists of a collection of chunks such as the macro chunk <{ E1, R(E1,E2), E2}, 'structure'> and the micro-chunk <{ E1, R(E1,E2) }, 'partition' > previously .discussed They will be stored in the Process Knowledge Base.

Once fully defined, the Process Knowledge Base can be used to *guide* the Requirements Engineering. Guidance will be provided by the Process Assistant by performing pattern matching. Indeed, the chunks of the process knowledge base can be matched against the current state of the product under development and help the developer in considering relevant situations and in taking the right decisions. Selection of a macro-chunk will help the requirements engineer in developing a top-down decision making.process This will allow him to select the rigth strategy to solve the issue he is faced to during the RE process When the initial macro-context has been further decomposed into micro-contexts, the corresponding micro-chunks will support the engineer in the tactical implementation of the chosen decisions.

Some experiments of this approach have been made through the development of the design expert system ALECSI [Cauvet&Rolland1991], [Rolland&Proix 1992] We examplified it with part of an Object-Oriented schema construction.
Let assume that the data schema under development is currently composed of the relationship R(Client, Product) as stated in Figure 5.1. The cardinality triplet is < *p*, *m* ,*v* > in the forward direction : a client may not have associated product(p), may have ordered several products (m) and is not always associated with the same products (v). The cardinality triplet in the backward direction is < *p*, *m*, *v* >: a product is not necessarily associated with a client (p), it may be linked to a number of clients (m) which vary in time (v).

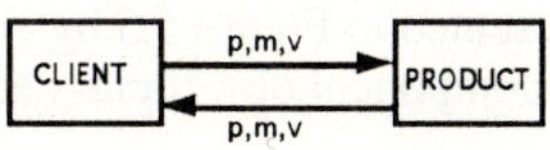

Fig.5.1 Example of situation

The macro-chunk MC1 : < {E1, R(E1,E2), E2}, 'structure' > presented in section III holds in this case .The situation considered in Figure 5.1 belongs to the class of situations of the mother context of MC1. According to the parameter values of the context *<p,m,v>* *<p,m,v>*, the macro-chunk suggests two possible kinds of decisions : either to partition the Entity-type Client as well as the Entity-type Product, or to refine the schema by retyping the Relationship-type into an Entity-type. Let assume that the decision chosen by the engineer is to refine the schema by retyping the relationship into the Entity-type Order. This corresponds to the decomposition of the mother context into the micro-context < {R(Client, Product)}, 'mutate' > which is instance of the micro-chunk <{R(E1,E2)}, 'retype' >providing the procedure to implement the 'retype' decision. This leads to the transformation of the schema as simply graphically showned in Figure 5.2 Some of the cardinalities are automatically infered, some have to be introduced by the engineer.

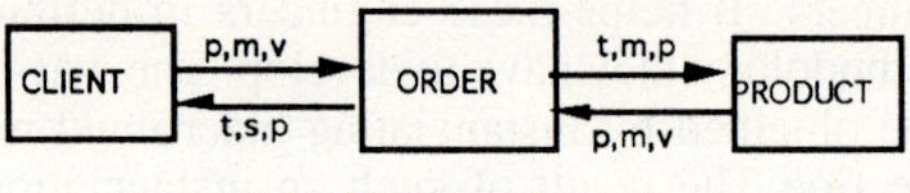

Fig. 5.2 Mutation of the relationship

Again the two relationships R(Client, Order) and R(Order, Product).match the situation of the macro-chunk MC1 and can be structured accordingly the advices provided by the chunk. Due to the sextuplet of cardinalities of the former relationship, the macro-chunk suggests three alternatives : partitioning Entity-types, historising the relationship-type and transforming it into a reference link between two object classes. Let suppose that the engineer chooses the last one. Figure 5.3 shows the resulting schema.

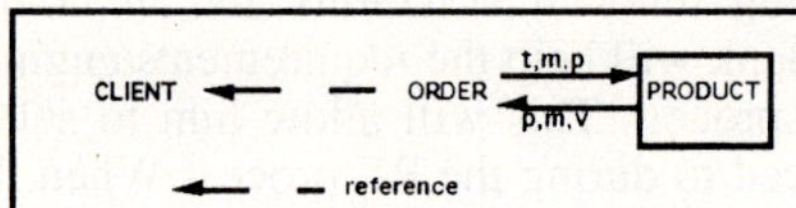

Fig. 5.3 Creation of object classes and a referencing link

According to the cardinalities of the relationship R(Order,Product), the possible decisions are : 'historise', 'referencing' and 'retype'. Figure 5.4 shows that the requirements engineer has found relevant to retype the relationship-type into the Entity-type Order-Line.

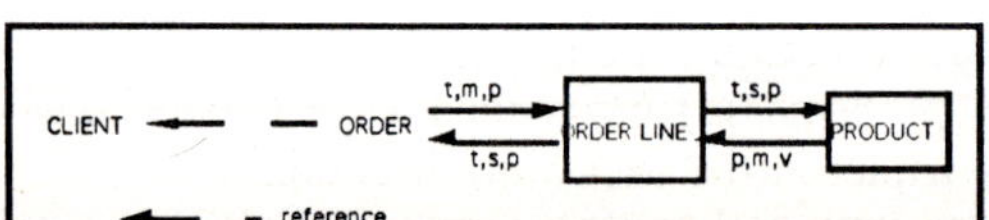

Fig. 5.4 Introduction of the Entity-Type Order-Line

The relationship R(Order, Order-Line) matches the situation of the macro-chunk MC1 and is transformed as presented in Figure 5.5 by embedding the order-lines into orders. Order-line becomes a component object class embendded into the composite object class Order.

Finally according to the cardinalities of the relationship R(Order-line, Product) the macro-chunk MC1 suggests the following decisions : 'historise', 'retype', 'partition' Product or objectify Product with 'referencing' Product from Order-line. The latter is chosen and the resulting schema is presented in Figure 5.5.

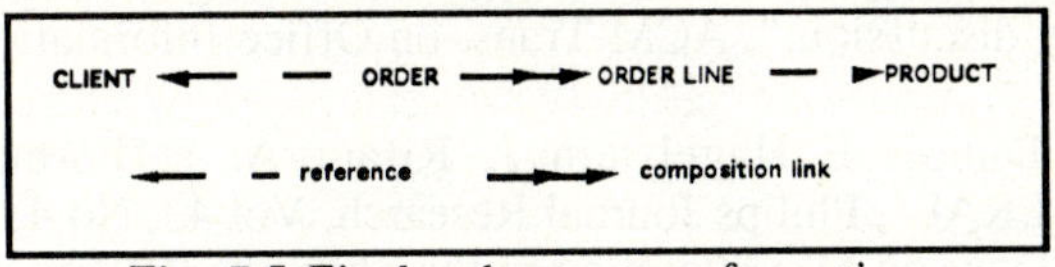

Fig. 7.5 Final schema transformation

As illustrated in this example, macro-chunks guide the RE process by matching situations which appear in the product under development with generic situations of mother contexts. The RE-by-reuse approach consists then, of suggesting possible decisions to the RE engineer and performing the consequences of the selected decision following the procedure stored in the corresponding micro-chunk.

5 Conclusion

In this paper, we presented an innovative and operational approach to build conceptual specifications. It is based on the reuse of RE process chunks. A chunk is a parametrized frame representing the possible ways to solve the issue raised in a common situation of requirements engineering. A chunk is expressed in a way which facilitates its reuse in subsequent projects.

The use of chunks changes the requirements engineering process. Building conceptual specifications is no longer a tedious composition of elementary concepts (e.g entity, event, operation, etc.), but rather the recognition of a particular situation as belonging to a chunk context and the instanciation of the process frame corresponding to the chunk.

In this paper we presented chunks in an informal way; However, it is clear that they can be expressed in different formalisms. As a matter of fact , we expressed chunks using the TELOS language and we are currently implementing the Process Assistant using the Knowledge Base System "Concept Base" [Jarke&al1992]

Our work goes on the same line as the ones defined for instance by Fugini [Fugini&al1991] in the Ithaca project or Pietro-Diaz [Pietro-Diaz1991] for domain analysis. With chunks, we are definitely "*identifying and structuring information for reusability*" . However, with chunks we are focusing on reuse of process patterns and not on reuse of domain knowledge or conceptual specifications.

We are currently working on the extension of the existing library to fully support the NATURE [Jarke&al1992] way-of working. We are also studying how process chunks could be discovered in a semi-automatic way using a learning by example tool.

6 References

[ACM1990] : ACM Issue on Object-Oriented Design, 1990

[Balasubramaniam1992] : Balasubramaniam. R., Vasant. Dhar " Supporting Systems Development by Capturing Deliberations During Requirements Engineering", IEEE Transactions of Software Engineering, Vol 18, No 6, 1992.

[[Biggerstaff1987] : Biggerstaff.T et al, " Information Management Challenges in the Software Design Process", IEEE Database Engineering, Vol 10, 1987.

[Boehm1988] : Boehm B.W. : "A Spiral Model of Software Development and Enhancement"; IEEE Computer 21.,1988.

[[Conklin&Begeman1992] : Conklin. J., Begeman. M. " gIBIS : a hypertext tool for exploratory policy discussion ", ACM Trans. on Office Information System, Vol 6, 1988.

[Dubois1989] : Dubois E.,Hagelstein J, Rifaut A. : "Formal Requirements Engineering with ERAE", Philips Journal Research, Vol 43, No 4, 1989.

[Dowson1987] : Dowson M. : "Iteration in the Software Process. Proc 9th Int Conf on Software Engineering", Monterey, CA,1988.

[Finkelstein et al. 1990] : Finkelstein A., Kramer J., Goedicke M.; "ViewPoint Oriented Software Development"; Proc. Conf "Le Génie Logiciel et ses Applications", Toulouse, p 337-351, 1990.

[[Gibbes1990] : Gibbes S, Tsichritsis.I, Casais.E, Nierstrazs. O, Pintado.X : "Class Management for Software Communities", Com. ACM, Vol 33, No 9, 1990.

[Grosz&Rolland1990] : Grosz G., Rolland C. : " Using Artificial Intelligence Techniques to Formalize the Information System Design Process"; Proc Int Conf on Databases and Expert Systems Applications, 1990.

[Henderson-Sellers and Edwards 1990] : Henderson-Sellers B., Edwards J.M.; "The Object-oriented Systems Life-Cycle"; Comm. ACM, 09, 1990.

[Jarke1988] : Jarke. M., Rose. T.," Managing Knowledge about Information System Evolution", Proc. ACM SIGMOD, 1988.

[Jarke et al1992] : Jarke M., Bubenko J, Rolland C., Sutcliffe A., Vassiliou Y.; "NATURE Initial Integration Report", NATURE.D-I, 1992.

[Jarke et al.1992] : Jarke M., Mylopoulos J., Schmidt J.W., Vassiliou Y.; "DAIDA : An environment for evolving information systems", ACM Transactions on Information Systems, Vol. 10, No. 1, 1992.

[Peugeot and Franckson 1991] : Peugeot C., Franckson M.; "Specification of the Object and Process Modelling Language", ESF Report n° D122-OPML-1.0, 1991.

[Potts 1989] : Potts C.; "A Generic Model for Representing Design Methods"; Proc. 11th International Conference on Software Engineering, 1989.

[Rolland&Cauvet1991] : Rolland C., Cauvet C. : "ALECSI : An Expert System for Requirements Engineering", in "Advanced Information Systems Engineering", R.Andersen, J.A.Bubenko, A.Solvberg (Eds), Springer Verlag, 1991.

[Rolland&Proix1992] : Rolland C, Proix C. : "A Natural Language Approach for Requirements Engineering", in "Advanced Information Systems Engineering", P. Loucopoulos, K; Jeffery, J.A Bubenko, A.Solvberg (Eds), Springer Verlag, 1992.

[Rose et al1991] : Rose T., Jarke M., Gocek M., Maltzahn C., Nissen H. : " A Decision-Based Configuration Process Environment", Software Engineering Journal, 6, 5.

[Royce1970] : Royce W.W.; "Managing the development of large Software Systems"; Proc. IEEE WESCON 08/1970.

[Schmitt1993] : Schmitt J.R., " Product Modelling for Requirement Engineering Process Modelling", IFIP Int. Conf. on " Information System Development Process", Rolland C., Prakash N., Pernici B. (eds), North Holland (pub), 1993.

From Analysis to Design in a Deductive and Object-Oriented Environment

Oscar Pastor López, Isidro Ramos, José H. Canós
Departament de Sistemes Informatics i Computació
Universitat Politecnica de Valencia. e-mail: {plo, iramos, joseh}@dsic.upv.es

Abstract. In this paper we present an Object-Oriented (OO) methodology for software production, and we focus on the analysis to design transition. OO-METHOD provides software tools covering the classical development phases of analysis, design and implementation, all this within a graphical, user-friendly working environment. Starting from a graphical system specification as the product of the OO analysis step, we produce the corresponding system specification in OASIS (a formal and OO specification language used as design tool). Finally, depending on the chosen working environment (logic or OO), we can obtain a final software product automatically by using the corresponding translator.

1 Introduction

To solve the *Crisis of Software*, we aim to change the methodological perspective by developping a Software Production Environment that focus on:

1. Life cycle modification via the introduction of rapid prototyping and automated programming [1].
2. The use of formal specification languages, in a deductive approach [2].
3. The use of an OO model.
4. The development of advanced graphical working environments.

In this paper we present an OO Methodology for Software Production (OO-METHOD), and we focus on the analysis to design transition. This OO system view is maintained throughout all the phases of the software life cycle provided by OO-METHOD.

The idea of blending the Object-Oriented and the Logic Programming paradigms within an automated programming life cycle and a deductive approach is within the basis of our proposal.

Section 2 on this paper constitutes its core, and introduces the main features of OO-METHOD, focusing on the transition from the analysis to the design, and stating how to obtain the resulting OO specification in OASIS. The basic concepts of the underlying OO model that we use can be found in [9,7].

2 The methodology

OO-METHOD generates two OO graphic specifications: one dealing with structural system aspects and the other dealing with the behavioural counterpart. In

[7,8] the analysis phase in OO-METHOD is presented in depth. The products resulting from the OOA step must be translated into an OASIS specification. OASIS [6] is a formal and OO Specification Language, used by OO-METHOD as its OO-design tool (see 2.2). Within a logic programming environment, and with an OASIS specification being equivalent to a formal dynamic logic theory [9,5,8,13], the animation of the logic program that represents this theory constitutes the system implementation. This logic program is obtained directly from the OASIS specification by means of a translator. In fact, we automatically produce the final implementation from the graphical specifications built in the analysis phase.

An interesting extension is accomplished when the chosen implementation tool is an OO Programming Language (OOPL). The final goal is to provide an OO-CASE tool covering the development phases of analysis, design and implementation with a high level of automation, and within an OO and deductive framework.

In the remainder of this work , we use the following example. Let's consider a (simple) hospital consisting of doctors, patients and individual rooms. When a patient goes into hospital, (s)he occupies an available room. During his/her stay, one or more doctors look after him/her. Doctors provide services, labelled with a date and a price. When patients leave the hospital, an invoice is made up of their associated set of services.

2.1 OO Analysis

OO-METHOD proposal. Object-Oriented Analysis (OOA) emphasizes the building of real-world models, using an object-oriented view of the world. We define OOA from a twofold view: first as a *classification* process for identifying which classes compose our System Domain and which relationships exist between them. Second, as a process of identifying which are the *available states* for the detected classes, and how *changes of state* can be produced (i.e. which *events* will be relevant for a given class). Fulfilling an OOA has three main advantages over the classical structured analysis methods ([3,11]).

1. We have the same model dealing with both the structural, static system aspects (data) and the behavioural, dynamic ones (processes).
2. We are using a model closer to the working of human cognition, consisting basically in capturing our understanding of the problem domain by means of a classification process.
3. Within an OO framework, the boundaries between analysis and design are somewhat fuzzy, dealing in both cases with classes, objects and their relationships and reducing the gap from analysis to design. Design is just a step along the way in the incremental, iterative development of a System that OO approaches provide.

The results of our OO-METHOD analysis process [7] will be the generation of two kind of graphics:

1. a *Class Configuration Diagram* (CCD). It is an extended semantic model showing the static system structure but also including the relevant events for every class.
2. for each class in a CCD, a *Classchart* (CCh) that represents its available states and the events that will cause the transition from one state to another.

This section is closed by presenting the CCD corresponding to our example and the CCh corresponding to the room class (figure 1). In (a), the system component classes are represented graphically (`doctor`,`patient`,`room`) with their shared events (`give-service`, `leave-room` and `occupy`) and a many-to-many aggregation relationship between doctors and patients labelled `services`.

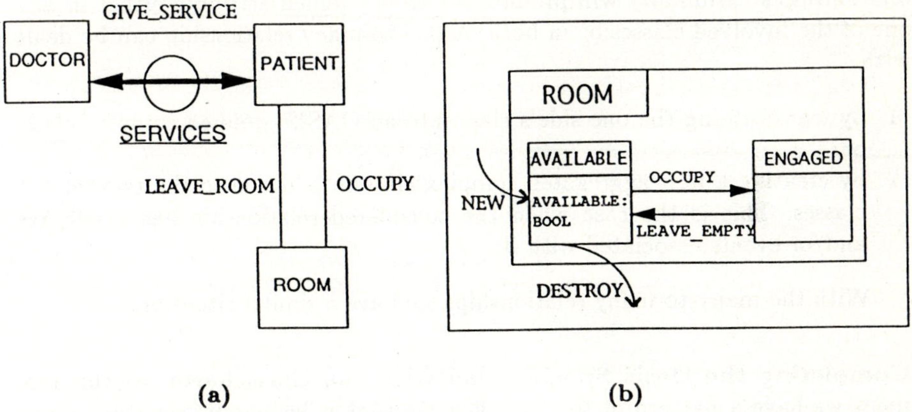

Fig. 1. Class Configuration Diagram (CCD) and Classchart (CCh) corresponding to the `room` class of the Hospital example

In (b), two potential states are considered for the `room` class (to be `available` or `engaged`), representing the events that can change any room object state (`occupy` , `leave-empty`).

2.2 From Analysis to Design : OO Design

OASIS is an OO specification language [6,10] that provides a set of syntactic constructs to declare the classes that constitute the system domain viewed as a society of interacting objects. Briefly, OASIS has three main constructs:

- *domains* (primitive classes), used as object surrogates and attribute classes.
- *elementary classes*, and
- *complex classes*, those defined using the set of *class operators* provided by OASIS: aggregation, inheritance, association and parallel composition.

Every class has a set of *attributes* (state variables), *events* (private or shared class messages sent by agents), *preconditions* (admissibility laws associated to events) and *triggering relationships* (actors implementation).

Next, we map the graphical diagrams coming from the previous OOA phase into OASIS constructs, showing how we can obtain the corresponding OASIS specification in an automated way.

Starting from the Class Configuration Diagram. Every elementary class is transformed into an OASIS elementary class. Inheritance relationships introduce specialization, declared in OASIS by means of `using` statements. The situation with the aggregation relationships is richer: depending on the cardinality associated to the aggregation we have different design time choices. A one-to-one relationship's cardinality will produce an object-valued attribute either in any one of the involved classes or in both. A one-to-many relationship can be dealt with

1. by transforming the one side's class into an OASIS grouped complex class, or
2. by creating a new aggregated complex class in addition to the two related classes. This is the case when the considered relationship has attributes and/or events associated with it.

With the many-to-many relationships we have a similar situation.

Completing the Oasis Specification with the Classcharts. At this moment we have a pattern of the Specification that is lacking information about the System behaviour in terms of variable attribute definition, preconditions associated with class events and triggering relationships. We get this information from the CCh associated to every class.

Variable attribute definition. In OO-METHOD, there are four categories of attributes depending on how their relevant events modify them.

1. *Boolean-valued* attributes checking if the object is in a given state, reached by an `event1` occurrence and left by another `event2` occurrence. For an attribute `a` :

```
        attribute(a,t)=b if (event1(a,t) and b=true) or
    (event2(a,t) and b=false) or
    (t1=t-1 and attribute(a,t1)=b)
```

   An example is the `available` attribute of the `room` class.

2. *Push-Pop* attributes, that have an `event1` *incrementing* their value and an `event2` *decrementing* it. We would have:

```
        attribute(a,t)=n if (t1=t-1 and attribute(a,t1)=n1) and
    (event1(a,n',t) and n=n1+n') or
    (event2(a,n',t) and n=n1-n'))
```

The Doctors' attribute `number-of-services` is an example of this kind. It has an incremental event (`give-service`) and no decremental event.

3. *State-valued attributes*: those attributes whose value is given by the event that has brought the object to the given state:

```
attribute(a,t)=v if (event1(a,v',t) and v=v') or
(t1=t-1 and attribute(a,t1)=v)
```

   For example, if an event occupy of a Patient class leads a patient instance to the *in-hospital* state, a state-valued attribute would be the associated room number, an integer parameter of the occupy event.

4. Mixed attributes, defined in terms of the previous types.

Preconditions. The CCh associated to every class includes information about state transitions caused by the occurrence of events. This representation states a first component for the precondition associated to the event: the affected object must be in the source state of the event transition state. Additional components appear in the transition's label after the *if'* symbol, stating other conditions that must hold for having a correct event occurrence.

Triggering relationships. Associated with any event label, every CCh includes information about which other events may be triggered as a consequence of the state transition. This will produce the following OASIS sentence:

```
object::trigger-event if event1
```

where `object` is the addressee, `trigger-event` is its triggered event and `event1` is the actual event causing the change of the object's state. To close this section the specification in OASIS for the `doctor` class of our simple Hospital example is given:

```
domains: string,int,bool,time
elementary class doctor
   attributes
    constant
code:integer key
name:string
start-date:time
speciality:string
    variables
number-of-services(doctor,time):int
   formulas:t,t1:time;d:doctor;
    p:patient;s:string;i:int;
number-of-services(d,t)=i:-
t1=t-1,number-of-services(d,t1)=n1,
(give-service(p,d,s,t),n=n1+1 or n=n1)
```

```
   events
    private
contract(d,t) new
dismiss(d,t) destroy
    shared
give-service(p,d,s,t)
   preconditions
contract(d,t):-not exists(d,t)
dismiss(d,t):-exists(d,t)
give-service(p,d,s,t):-
    exists(p,t),exists(d,t),
    speciality(d,t)=s
end class doctor
```

3 Conclusions

OO-METHOD provides a software production environment with the following relevant aspects:

- It starts from an OO system view that develops basic Information System concepts, according to the most recent Information Systems concepts.
- A graphical notation to represent the analysis products is given. This notation includes static and dynamic graphical models that constitute a clear specification of the system to be designed.
- Within the OO approach used by OO-METHOD, the transition from analysis to design can be done in an automated way. The chosen OO specification language is OASIS, and the specification in OASIS corresponding to the Analysis products is directly obtained.
- As a specification in OASIS is equivalent to a dynamic logic theory (clausal or equational), the logic program equivalent to the specification constitutes an executable system prototype obtained directly from the specification.
- If our working environment is based on the use of OO Programming Languages, an advanced pattern of the final software product can be obtained in an automated way.

At the moment, an OO-METHOD implementation is being tested in several large software projects to check its real capacity as a software production methodology.

References

1. R. Balzer et al.:*Software Technology in the 1990s: Using a New Paradigm.* IEEE Computer Science Press,Nov.1983.
2. J. A. Bubenko, A.Oliv é: *Dynamic or Temporal Modelling? an illustrative comparison.* SYSLAB Working Paper 117,Nov.1986.
3. C.Gane,T.Sarson: *Structured System Analysis.* Englewood Cliffs,NJ:Prentice Hall,1979
4. O.Pastor,I.Ramos,J,Canós: *Object Oriented and Relational Specification of Information Systems.* Second International Workshop on the Deductive Approach to Information Systems and Databases. Aiguablava,Sept.1991.
5. O.Pastor,F.Hayes,S.Bear: *OASIS: An Object-Oriented Specification Language.* In the Proceedings of the CAiSE-92, Manchester,UK.
6. O.Pastor,A.Gonz ález: *OO-METHOD: An OO Methodology for S oftware Production.* Proceedings of DEXA-92, Valencia
7. O.Pastor. *Diseno y Desarrollo de un Entorno de Producción Autom ática de Software basado en el Modelo OO.* PhD Thesis, U.P.V., Valencia 1992.
8. I.Ramos: *Logics and OO-Data Bases: a declarative approach.* Proceedings of DEXA-90, Springer-Verlag,1990 pag. 348-363.
9. I.Ramos,O.Pastor: *OO and Active Formal Information System Specification.* Proceedings of DEXA-91, Berlin (1991)
10. E.Yourdon: *Modern Structured Analysis.*Englewood Cliffs,NJ:Prentice Hall,1989
11. R.J. Wieringa, *A formalization of objects using equational dynamic logic*, Proc. of the 2nd DOOD Conference, Springer-Verlag, 1991.

A Case Study for an Open CASE System: The TROLL *light* Development Environment

Nikolaos Vlachantonis*

Technische Universität Braunschweig,
Informatik, Abt. Datenbanken
Postfach 3329, W–3300 Braunschweig, Germany
e–mail: vlachant@idb.cs.tu-bs.de

Abstract. In this paper[2], the TROLL *light* development environment is described as a special computer aided software engineering (CASE) system. In particular, it serves the formal development of information systems on the basis of the object-oriented specification language TROLL *light* [CGH92] which in turn allows to describe the Universe of Discourse (UoD) as a community of concurrently existing and communicating objects. TROLL *light* which is a dialect of the language TROLL [JSHS91] is especially suited for the specification of information systems but is not restricted to this application field. Within the compound project KorSo [Bro92] our team is concerned with the research on techniques and methods for the development of reliable information systems on the basis of formal specifications [VHG+93].

1 Introduction

The development of large software systems is a very expensive process. Different methods and techniques were developed to minimize time and costs of development. Because software development is a stepwise process comprising different methods and techniques, certain methodologies (sets of interrelated methods) resulted from that. Stand-alone software tools support the application of the different methods and techniques. While their number and complexity increases, the software developer is affected by the task of managing and coordinating the different tools in the right way. Therefore, different CASE systems have been developed which support methods and techniques belonging to a selected methodology.

One problem that arises with CASE systems is that there is a low acceptance on the users' side because the supported methodologies are very often not adequate enough and the handling of the system and its methods is unsuitable, restricting and difficult from the ergonomic point of view [WH90]. To overcome these problems new approaches have been developed towards open and adaptable CASE systems. The so-called CASE-Shell [VHW91, PG92] systems offer the user the possibility to adapt existing tools to his or her requirements and to add new tools in order to extend or to improve the methodology of the system [SLTM92].

* Work reported here is supported by the German Ministry for Research and Technology (BMFT) under Grant No. 01 IS 203 D (KorSo = Korrekte Software)

[2] This paper is an extended abstract of the original submission, which can be accessed via ftp (ftp.ips.cs.tu-bs.de:/ips/papers/korso/DEXA93-CaseStudy.ps.Z)

However, the problem of adapting existing tools or adding new ones is not a trivial one. One of the main problems concerns the aspect of tool integration [SN92]. Different tools are interacting with each other on the one hand by a given communication protocol and on the other hand by exchanging the documents that represent the results of the different development steps. Making changes to the CASE system requires profound knowledge of the current methods, techniques and their relationships from the semantic point of view. With regard to technical aspects knowledge is needed about interfaces and structures of documents.

In the following section the methodology of the TROLL *light* development environment is described and in Section 3 a conceptual overview of the system will be given.

2 Methodology of the TROLL *light* development environment

A certain model of the software development process is the methodological basis of a CASE system. A given model is described by means of a selection of stages and methods for developing software. CASE systems are designed to appropriate support the selected stages and methods.

The TROLL *light* development environment supports the creation of TROLL *light* specifications especially with respect to correctness. Starting with a first TROLL *light* specification the following development steps may be performed.

1. **Validation/Animation:** This step consists of prototyping a TROLL *light* specification in a certain environment called animator. An animator provides object windows which enable the user to observe attributes, to open new object windows by following sub-object relationships or object-valued attributes, to initiate state transitions by clicking at events, to formulate queries, etc. This should help the developer to compare the informal view of the real-world fragment that is to be modeled with the current specification.
2. **Verification:** This means to check the TROLL *light* specification with regard to inconsistencies, deficiencies and assertions given from outside of the specification.
3. **Modification:** The current specification may be modified after the verification or validation phase.
4. **Transformation:** At last the specification may be transformed, possibly in several steps, towards executable code.

The above steps can be performed in a cycle until the desired level of correctness and completeness is reached by the specification.

3 Concepts of the TROLL *light* development environment

The TROLL *light* development environment is an open CASE system (see Fig. 1) which allows the user to integrate new tools and to adapt existing ones to new requirements. Here, the notion "to integrate" means that there exist certain requirements concerning technical and conceptual aspects. Conceptual requirements concern the logical integration or adaptation of tools, i.e., new or adapted

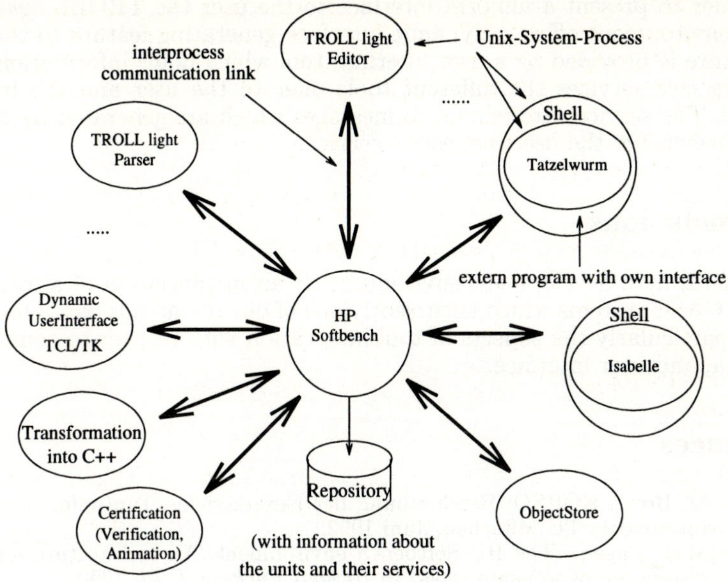

Fig. 1. Architecture of the TROLL *light* development environment

tools should be able to work with documents (specifications, source code, etc.) created by other tools. This is a very important requirement because documents have certain structures and certain semantics to the CASE system. Moreover, they may be stored in a structured way in a repository (this is also a technical aspect).

For preserving the openness of the environment tools have to be as independent as possible of the environment. The tasks they support must be clearly outlined. Therefore, the TROLL *light* development environment supports a loose coupling of tools. This is achieved on the one hand by a process of interchanging messages (HP Softbench [Cag90]) and on the other hand by an object-oriented documents repository (ObjectStore [LLOW91]) which is accessible by each tool and which has clear and open interfaces to the different documents.

Messages are not a means for interchanging data but more a means for interchanging integrity preserving information. A tool which performs changes to a document, for instance, has to generate a message for informing other tools about the change. The process of interchanging messages is managed by a server by broadcasting the messages to all tools which are interested in them. A tool does not know which other tools are interested in its messages. New tools could be integrated in the TROLL *light* development environment without changing existing ones. Only the message broadcasting information of the message server has to be extended by new message definitions.

The concept of broadcasting messages to other tools in the case of incidents frees the user of working in a fixed way with the TROLL *light* development environment. The tools are able to preserve the integrity of the different documents and the correctness of their interrelations. This aspect is particularly important for a multi-user version of the TROLL *light* development environment. At the time being, it is not planned to include this feature in the environment because of time and capacity constraints.

In order to present a uniform interface to the user the TROLL *light* development environment offers a dynamic interface generating feature to the tools. This feature is provided by a user interface tool which holds information about the interactive services the different tools offer to the user and the interface structure. The services are related to messages which are generated by the user interface whenever the user requests a service.

4 Conclusions

The TROLL *light* development environment is an instantiation of a framework for open CASE systems which is currently one of our research topics. Our efforts concern particularly the aspects of tool integration with respect to communication, data, and user interface.

References

[Bro92] M. Broy. KORSO: Beschreibung der Gesamtziele. Tum-info, Institut für Informatik, TU München, Juni 1992.

[Cag90] M.R. Cagan. The HP Softbench environment: An architecture for a new generation of software tools. *in Hewlett Packard J. 41*, 1990.

[CGH92] S. Conrad, M. Gogolla, and R. Herzig. TROLL light: A Core Language for Specifying Objects. Informatik-Bericht 92–02, Technische Universität Braunschweig, 1992.

[JSHS91] R. Jungclaus, G. Saake, T. Hartmann, and C. Sernadas. Object-Oriented Specification of Information Systems: The TROLL Language. Informatik-Bericht 91–04, Technische Universität Braunschweig, 1991.

[LLOW91] C. Lamb, G. Landis, J. Orenstein, and D. Weinreib. The ObjectStore Database System. *Communications of the ACM*, 34(10):50–63, 1991.

[PG92] S. Papahristos and W.A. Gray. Federated Case Environments. In R. Anderson, J. A. Bubenko jr., and A. Sølvberk, editors, *Advanced Information Systems Engineering*, Springer LNCS series, Vol. 498, pages 461–478, May 1992.

[SLTM92] K. Smolander, K. Lyytinen, V.-P. Tahvanainen, and P. Marttiin. MetaEdit - A Flexible Graphical Environment for Methodology Modelling. In R. Anderson, J. A. Bubenko jr., and A. Sølvberk, editors, *Advanced Information Systems Engineering*, Springer LNCS series, Vol. 498, pages 168–193, May 1992.

[SN92] K.J. Sullivan and D. Notkin. Reconciling Environment Integration and Software Evolution. *ACM TOSEM*, 1(3):229–268, July 1992.

[VHG+93] N. Vlachantonis, R. Herzig, M. Gogolla, G. Denker, S. Conrad, and H.-D. Ehrich. Towards Reliable Information Systems: The KORSO Approach. In C. Rolland, editor, *Proc. 5th Int. Conf. Advanced Information Systems Engineering*. Springer, LNCS Series, 1993. *To appear.*

[VHW91] T. F. Verhoef, A.H.T. ter Hofstede, and G. M. Wijers. Structuring modelling knowledge for CASE shells. In R. Anderson, J. A. Bubenko jr., and A. Sølvberk, editors, *Advanced Information Systems Engineering*, Springer LNCS series, Vol. 498, pages 502–524, May 1991.

[WH90] G.M. Wijers and H. Heijes. Automated Support of the Modelling Process: A View Based on Experiments with Expert Information Engineers. In B. Steinholtz, A. Sølvberk, and L. Bergman, editors, *Advanced Information Systems Engineering*, Springer LNCS series, Vol. 436, pages 88–108, 1990.

Meta Data Model for Database Design

Tatjana Welzer and Johann Eder

Tehniska fakulteta
Univerza v Mariboru
Smetanova 17
SLO-62000 Maribor
Slovenija

Institut für Informatik
Universität Klagenfurt
Universitätsstr. 65
A-9020 Klagenfurt
Austria

Abstract. Software re-use has become a major issue in software engineering research to overcome the so called application backlog in software production. In this paper we introduce a meta data model as a tool to apply re-use concepts also to database design. The main idea is to provide a structured repository of data models such that a database designer can use models or submodels of previous projects in his actual design and thus accelerating the design process. In this meta data model objects are thus organized according to their similarity. In particular, the structure supports the search for similar objects.

1 Introduction

Database design is a process of analyzing the information-needs of the members of an organization, designing external and conceptual models in some semantic data model, mapping them to database schemas, and developing internal schemas for them.

In principle each of the models is used only once, i.e. within a single project, although a model or parts of a model derived for one project could be used in future projects. While re-use is a well established field in software engineering to increase quality and productivity of software development, comparatively little work has been reported on re-use in the area of database design.

For applying re-use concepts to database design we have to take care of the following:

1. Design databases in a way that the resulting models are reusable.
2. Developing a repository of models, so that the designer is assisted in his search for relevant models of previous projects.
3. Integrate re-use in the design process.

In this paper we will focus on the second item. For designing reusable components it is necessary to abstract from the actual project to be able to reason about commonalities between different models and different projects. Domain analysis seems to be a good candidate for this task [Eder 92].

The main objective of our paper is to introduce an object oriented meta data model. Integrating the results of previously developed concepts (i.e. meta data model [Eder92], changeable part of conceptual database model [Welz91]) in an object oriented structure. Both concepts focus on the problem to provide a framework to classify and to compare objects of an application domain (enterprise) based on their similarity as well as to use them for database design and software development. In this paper we briefly sketch the MetaBase concept, for details we refer to [Welz92].

2 Previous Research

In the knowledge based design model [Welz91] a (relational) database is discussed as a joining of three parts: the unchangeable part, the changeable part and the non-alignment part. In the first one the same attributes for the resembling databases (databases for resembling enterprises - domains) are considered. A basic aim of this part is to enable a direct transfer of the same attributes from the existing conceptual model into new (similar) one. The second one, the changeable part addresses similar attributes which are usually different with respect to the names and domains but according to common sense they describe similar objects. In the non-alignment part a remainder of attributes is stored representing attributes which are unique for each application.

This concept has some commonalities with the concept of a meta data model based on similarity [Eder92]. It was constructed in order to reason about similarities between different models. The central building block of the meta data model is the conceptual model, which consists of entities and relationships between them. Both entities and relationships are discussed as semantic objects.

However, each semantic object is characterized by several properties which can be found in the description of different semantic objects. Similarity - as a semantic property - depends on the point of view and the purpose for which similarities are expressed. For this reason we define a generalization hierarchy for semantic objects. We consider two objects to be similar if they have a common ancestor in the generalization hierarchy. By defining a generalization hierarchy for semantic objects we are able to determine similarities of both objects and models. However, it can be found that all specializations of a certain semantic object may contain properties which are different with respect to their names and domains but have similar semantics. Therefore, we introduce the concept of generic properties and a generalization hierarchy of properties.

3 MetaBase

The structure of the MetaBase (Fig. 1) consists of three levels, object level, enterprise level, and function level. The central enterprise level contains the conceptual models, the external models as well as information about the enterprises. The application domain links function and enterprise level. External models represent the view of application systems and user groups on the database. Like conceptual models they consist of a set of related objects. An external model is a submodel of one or more conceptual models. Conceptual models as well as external models are connected with a respective application domain.

In the function level each application domain is characterized by a classification in two dimensions: the business domain (e.g. banking, tourism, airline) and the functional domain (e.g. accounting, order processing, etc.), both organized in a generalization hierarchy, the functional domain, furthermore, in an aggregation (part-of) hierarchy.

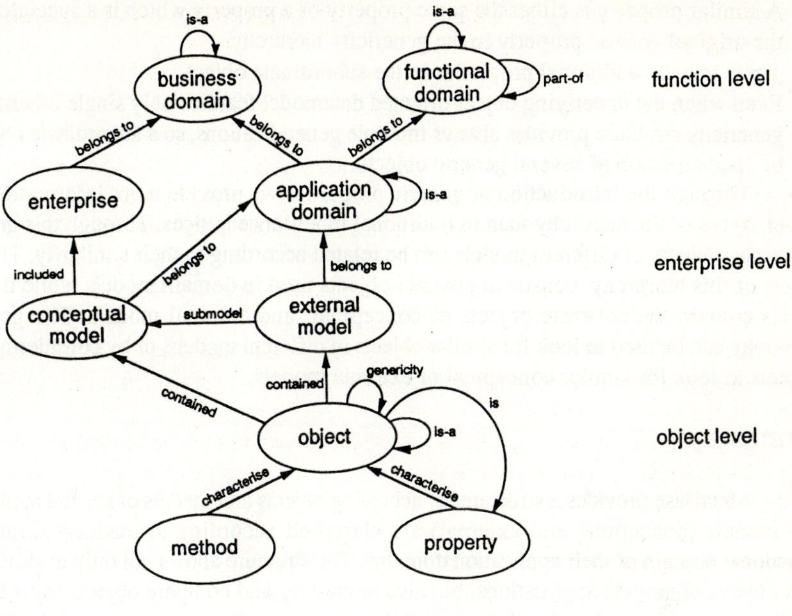

Fig. 1. Structure of the MetaBase

To give an example for functional level, we presume a tourism domain to have different kinds of sub-business domains like accommodation and transport. Each of these subdomains has again subdomains (subsubdomains) in the sense of is-a hierarchy (accommodation -> hotel, motel, youthostel). Similar functional domains like book-keeping by single and double entry book-keeping are presented as specializations of book-keeping in the is-a hierarchy, while the functional domains credit, debit, and transfer are subordinate domains of book-keeping in the part-of hierarchy.

The rationale of this structure which is a conclusion of the usefulness of domain analysis for discussing similarities is to assist the search for reusable models. Based on the observation that the possibility of reusing models is greater within the same application domain or very similar application domains [Free83], a designer can start searching for reusable models by first identifying the application domain in terms of business and functional domains.

The object level reflects the associations usually found in object oriented data models, i.e. generalization and aggregation. The is-a relationship between objects represents the generalization (inheritance) lattice of an object oriented data model. The aggregation hierarchy is modeled through the properties relationship, i.e. the components of a composite object are its properties. In our structure an object is characterized by several properties. Some of the properties are values, but some of them are objects themselves.

Our object level structure is able to represent the objects and their associations of a single model. In order to relate the objects of different models we introduce another relationship, the genericity hierarchy.

A subordinate object in this hierarchy is a specialization of the superordinate object according to the following rules:

- For each property of the superordinate object there is a similar property in the subordinate object.

- A similar property is either the same property or a property which is a specialization of the original generic property in the genericity hierarchy.
- There may be additional properties in the subordinate object.
- Even when the underlying object-oriented datamodel features only single inheritance the genericity structure provides always multiple generalizations, so a subordinate object may be specialization of several generic objects.

Through the introduction of generic properties we provide more information in the upper layers of the hierarchy than in traditional inheritance lattices. Through this genericity hierarchy objects of different models can be related according to their similarity. The upper levels of this hierarchy consist of abstract objects used in domain models while the lower levels contain the concrete objects of conceptual and external models. The genericity hierarchy can be used to look for similar objects in different models, or by considering sets of objects to look for similar conceptual or external models.

Summary

MetaBase provides a structure for achieving objects and models of several applications. All models (conceptual and external) are classified according to business domain and functional domain of their application domains. The structure allows not only to store models and objects of several applications, but also to classify and compare objects from different applications and models through the genericity hierarchy. The main purpose of the MetaBase is to facilitate the application of re-use concepts to the area of database design. Powerful search strategies aid the designer to efficiently use the MetaBase for retrieving models and objects which may be used directly or adapted in a new design. Furthermore, the MetaBase is considered as a basis for design tools and data-dictionaries.

Acknowledgement. It is gratefully acknowledged that the work on the present paper of Tatjana Welzer was supported by an Alpe-Adria grant provided by the federal state Carinthia (Austria).

References

[Eder90] J. Eder, W. Rossak: An Archive of Semantic Data Models as Basis for Software Re-use, In Proc. 8th International Symposium on Applied Informatics, Innsbruck, Austria, pp. 284-287, February 1990.

[Eder92] J. Eder, W. Rossak: Using a Data-Oriented Approach to Decide on Similarity of Objects During Domain Analysis, Appear in Proc. 11th European Meeting on Cybernetics and System Research, 1992.

[Free83] P. Freeman: Reusable Software Engineering Concepts and Research Directions, Proc. Workshop on Reusability in Programming, Newport RI, Sept., pp. 1-15, 1983.

[Welz91] T. Welzer, B. Stiglic, J. Gyorkos, I. Rozman: Knowledge Based Model of Relational Database Design, Mathematical and Intelligent Models in System Simulation, IMACS, pp. 227-231, 1991.

[Welz92] T. Welzer, J. Eder: MetaBase for Schema-Re-Use. Technical Report, Universität Klagenfurt, Institut für Informatik, 1992.

Extending PCTE with Object-oriented Capabilities*

Xuequn Wu and Jan Neuhaus

Fraunhofer Gesellschaft, Institute for Software Engineering and Systems Engineering
c/o University of Dortmund, Software Technology, D-44221 Dortmund

Abstract. In this paper we briefly describe our work accomplished for the Eureka ECMA PCTE project. Our task was to define an object-oriented extension to the well-known and internationally standardized Portable Common Tool Environment (PCTE) [3]. The PCTE types are extended to be associated with methods. High-level types are introduced and their mappings to the PCTE data model are discussed.

1 Introduction

Recently performed research has identified many requirements pertaining to object management systems (OMS), which are only partially met by PCTE, and which could be fulfilled by a fully object-oriented OMS [2, 6, 7, 4]. Because of its important position in the OMSs area, and in order to overcome weaknesses in its current form, we present an object-oriented extension to PCTE. This extension will allow the current PCTE to migrate smoothly towards a fully object-oriented OOPCTE. To follow this text some basic knowledge of PCTE is needed.

2 Object-oriented Extension of PCTE

Our work extends the PCTE type definition mechanisms to enable the definition of methods to be attached to types. Method inheritance is allowed, which supports overloading, overriding, and late binding. Access and manipulation of objects and communication between objects can be done by invoking methods. Moreover, high-level types are provided, which emerge from object-oriented modelling and which are required to support aggregations for fine grained data.

2.1 Introducing Behavior to PCTE

Defining Methods To fit the PCTE concepts, methods are introduced as method types. Method types can be imported like any other types. This decision enables our method concept to inherit the view mechanisms of PCTE.

According to the PCTE view concept, we define a method type always in the context of a Schema Definition Set (SDS). A method type is associated to an object type and has a name and a signature that specifies the parameter types and the optional result

* This research work is partially funded by the Eureka ECMA PCTE project (EU 710).

types of the method. The SDS must include all types in SDS, which are needed as parameter types or result types. Method types differ from other types in that their names are significant. So these names can not be modified in an SDS and thus are stored with the method type. Each method type is connected to an object type, not to an object type in SDS. The method type has links to the types of the parameters and a link to a file that contains the source code of the method. An indexed link models the relations to the files containing the object code suitable for each workstation type. So a method is associated with both the source code and the executable code which implements the method. The methods are implemented within a process using the information in the current working schema (WS). The implementation of a method can use all previously defined types in this WS.

Method Invocation Concerning the PCTE View Concept The method concept does not conform well with the PCTE view concept. So we have to adapt the method concept to PCTE. If a message is sent, the corresponding method is searched. The method to be executed is determined based on both the message name and the type of the object to which it is applied. The message handler starts the method search in the type hierarchy at the node that is the type of the target object. If a match is found, it is the method corresponding to the message. Otherwise, the search is continued by the parent types along the inheritance hierarchy. If the search reaches the root type and the corresponding method is not found, then the search fails and an error occurs.

Because the methods must be able to call methods and use attributes which are not found in the current WS, we deduce that method search and execution must be performed in a special environment which reduces much of the restrictions that a normal PCTE process has. To support such an environment all methods are searched and executed by a message handler. So the access rights of the executing process are unmodified, but the method execution is able to bypass the restrictions enforced by the WS concept. A good way to allow a method to access all needed types, methods, and attributes is to store the WS of the creating process along with the method type. The message handler is then able to install this schema during method execution and it guarantees that a method is always executed with the correct WS.

This does not imply that a process can bypass or violate security restrictions by abusing the method concept. A process can only define a new method if the method body accesses only types and methods which are in the WS of the process. So it is impossible to create and execute a method that has more rights than the defining process. A method type must be imported according to the normal PCTE conventions. So security risks can be avoided in the normal PCTE manner.

2.2 High-Level Types in OOPCTE

The PCTE OMS provides good means for modelling coarse grained data such as documents and interconnections between them. Thus we find a rather small type system. If fine grained modelling is done, however, there will be a much larger type system and it will be too complicated for the existing type mechanisms to define hundreds of types, which may be needed for data structures used by a syntax directed editor. Requirement analyses for SDEs have shown that three basic type constructors are needed to fulfill most data modelling needs: sets, lists, and aggregations. The PCTE data model distinguishes clearly between large unstructured data (BLOBs) and basic types, which can only be used as attributes. Object-oriented data models do not make this distinction. We propose a high-level type system including: sets, lists, and aggregations, on top of PCTE.

A New Concept for Links There is a huge number of possible different link types by PCTE. Some of these concepts for link definition are only rarely used. We have decided to allow only a reduced number of link types. The two categories, composition and reference, are sufficient for the modelling of most data structures. An implicit reverse link is always assumed. This reduces the complexity of data type definition, enabling the construction of much larger type systems with less efforts.

Providing Conventional Attributes Object-oriented database systems or relational database systems handle attributes always in a local context. The PCTE data model defines attribute types which can be included into SDSs and attached to many different object or link types. These two concepts do not fit well together, although both have their own merits.

We provide a coexistence of both concepts. The new high-level types provide attributes which have the semantics known from other database systems, while the PCTE attribute types are still usable. The PCTE concepts require that each type used in an SDS must be included in that SDS explicitly. We define the new high-level types together with their attributes as units. So there is no implicit inclusion on the conceptual level. However, as these high-level types are implemented with PCTE mechanisms, there is implicit inclusion on the implementation level. The high-level types themselves are treated as any other object type.

In our extension, the attributes of a high-level type are specified with a name, a reference specification, and a type. The reference specification identifies the link category. The type can be a basic type, a BLOB, an object type or a high-level type.

Mapping the New High Level Types to PCTE Our new types have to be mapped to the existing PCTE concepts for various reasons. First, we want to provide a basis for coexistence, so that applications which do not use the extension can share data with OOPCTE based applications. Second, we want to define our extension using terms that are already known to the PCTE community. Third, it enables a fast partial implementation of OOPCTE for feasibility studies.

An aggregation is described through a list of names, reference specifications, and types. We have two different reference specifications, namely `PART` and `REFERENCE`. They are abbreviated to $\mathcal{P}$ and $\mathcal{R}$ respectively. The types can be divided into three categories. In the first one we find the so called complex types. This category includes all PCTE object types and all high-level types and is denoted as $\mathcal{C}$. The second category includes all basic types ($\mathcal{B}$) with the exclusion of BLOBs. These BLOBs ($\mathcal{L}$) must be handled separately, so they are considered as a special case. The following table gives the mappings for aggregations. For lists and sets a similar approach is used.

Table 1. Mapping for Aggregation

Ref.	Type	Mapping
$\mathcal{P}$	$\mathcal{B}$	An attribute of that base type is created
$\mathcal{P}$	$\mathcal{C}$	A composition link to such a type is created
$\mathcal{P}$	$\mathcal{L}$	A composition link to an object of a special longfield type is created
$\mathcal{R}$	$\mathcal{B}$	This is not possible and will result in an error message at definition time
$\mathcal{R}$	$\mathcal{C}$	A reference link to such a type is created
$\mathcal{R}$	$\mathcal{L}$	A reference link to an object of type longfield is created

3 Related Work, Conclusions and Acknowledgements

There is little research which provides object-oriented extension to PCTE, e.g. OOTIS [5] and ATIS [1]. In contrast to our work, none of these approaches has investigated extensions to the PCTE data model.

We have shown that the data model of PCTE can be extended with object-oriented capabilities to fulfill the needs of future SDEs. Solutions have been given to adapt the method concept to the existing concepts of PCTE. This enables the coexistence of applications based on our new approach and conventional applications. We have also investigated the solutions to the problems that result from the special characteristics of PCTE.

Many ideas addressed in this short paper arose during intensive discussions with our colleagues in the Eureka ECMA PCTE project. We are particularly indebted to our colleagues Holger Schween and Gabriele Wehrsdorfer in Berlin and Bernhard Holtkamp in Dortmund.

References

1. A. Argento, C. Bonferini, F. Dematté, and S. Manca. ECMA PCTE, CORBA and ATIS 'the easy way to O-O ECMA PCTE services'. *PCTE Newsletter*, (10):20–27, June 1992.
2. P. A. Bernstein. Database system support for software engineering. In *Proc. of the 9th Int. Conf. on Software Engineering*, pages 166–178, Monterey, CA, 1987.
3. Portable common tool environment – abstract specification. ECMA Standard 149, European Computer Manufacturers Association, Rue du Rhône, CH-1204 Genf, 1990.
4. W. Emmerich, W. Schäfer, and J. Welsh. Suitable databases for process-centered environments do not yet exist. In J. C. Derniame, editor, *Proc. of the 2nd European Workshop on Software Process Technology*, LNCS 635, Trondheim, Norway, Sept. 1992. Springer Verlag.
5. W. Harrison, M. Kavianpour, and H. Ossher. Integrating coarse-grained and fine-grained tool integration. In *CASE'92*, June 1992.
6. L.-C. Liu and E. Horowitz. Object database support for a software management environment. In *Proc. of the 3rd ACM Symposium on Practical Software Development Environments*, volume 13 of *ACM SIGSOFT Software Engineering Notes*, pages 85–96, Nov. 1988.
7. X. Wu, G. Wehrsdorfer, H. Schween, and J. Neuhaus. Towards OOPCTE. ISST Bericht 7, FhG, Institut für Software- und Systemtechnik, Dortmund, Germany, Mar. 1993.

A New Hypermedia Data Model

H. Maurer*, N. Scherbakov, P. Srinivasan

Institute for Information Processing and Computer Supported New Media,
Graz University of Technology, Schieszstattgasse 4a,
A-8010 Austria.
Tel.: 43/316/83-25-52/ext.12 Fax:43/316/82-43-94

Abstract. The general-purpose data models in use today are well-suited to the management of structured data. However, most of the current data models are often inadequate to handle effective processing of rather complex forms of information. Very often such data models do not provide efficient and suitable data structure types for complex hypermedia objects such as documents containing textual, pictorial, sound and other multimedia components.
In this paper we describe a new hypermedia data model for such ill-structured data. The model is based on the notion of abstract data objects called structured collections (S-collections) and combines browsing-based data manipulation facilities with information retrieval techniques.

1 Introduction

In the vague world of hypermedia systems (vague, since such systems are used by different groups for an amazingly variety of different tasks) it is this notion that "a hypermedia system consists of nodes and links, the links allowing to navigate through the universe of nodes" that seems to be embraced by most hypermedia experts.

We assume the reader to be familiar with the basic notion of a hypermedia system and refer for details not discussed here to [3, 9, 10, 20] for survey papers, to [2, 14, 7, 16] for books on hypermedia systems, and to [11] for an extensive hypermedia bibliography.

The most serious problems encountered in today's hypermedia systems could be enlisted as:

(i) The network of links is responsible for the well-known "getting lost in hyper space" phenomenon;

(ii) The editing of links (when inserting new nodes) is tedious [9, 18], to say the least; Deleting nodes can cause serious consistency problems with links pointing to and emanating from that node [9, 18, 19];

(iii) When combining a set of nodes with other existing nodes the semantics of the links attached to the various nodes is not visible to the users [4, 8, 9, 10, 20].

---

*- The support of the Austrian Federal Ministry of Science and Research for the work behind this paper is gratefully acknowledged. Part of this paper was written while the first author was on leave at the University of Auckland, New Zealand.

We believe that the basic hypermedia paradigm (i.e. "node-link" model) makes hypermedia systems feel more confusing than they have to be; the notion of a link as something physically existing is potentially limiting our view to a very low, implementation oriented level much like thinking of addresses, pointers or branches has driven many programmers in earlier days too close to implementational details until higher levels of abstraction have made programming easier and more productive.

We feel that the situation may be similar with respect to hypermedia systems: that the notion of a "physical" link is bogging us down, that a higher level of abstraction where links play no or a much smaller role is necessary to obtain better usable hypermedia systems [5, 19].

The rest of this paper is structured as follows: in the next Section 2 we present a brief description of the HM-data model (a fuller version is contained in a technical report [13]) and give examples as basis of concrete discussions; in Section 3 we give some further examples and show how problems (i) - (iii) mentioned above can be reduced in hypermedia systems based on our approach; in section 4 we briefly discuss the combination of browsing and retrieval techniques available within the HM-data model. The paper ends with a short conclusion and references.

2 The HM-Data Model

In accordance with the HM-data model, a hypermedia database is a number of complex data objects called structured collections (abbreviated as S-collections). Note that the links cannot be defined on the level of database (see fig.1).

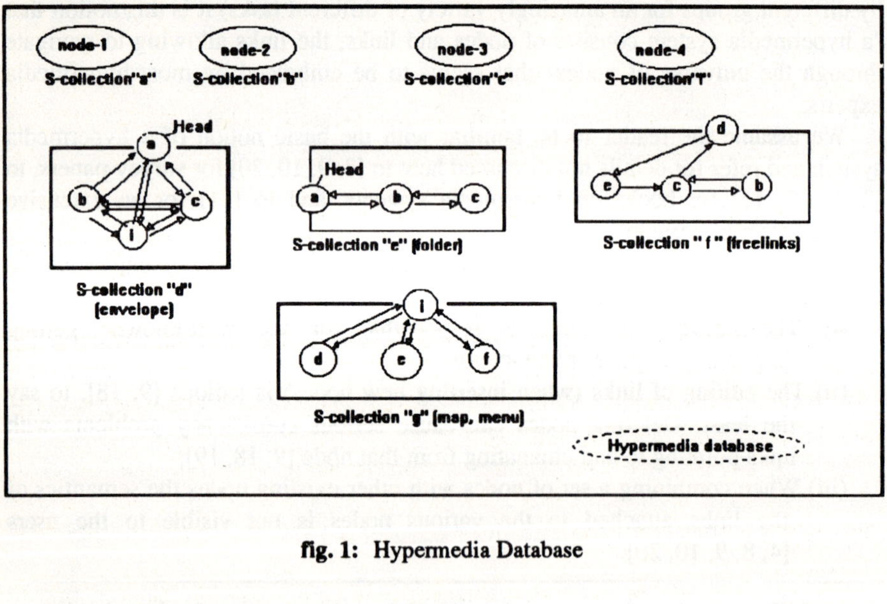

fig. 1: Hypermedia Database

Each S-collection has a unique identifier (i.e. a name) and a so-called *head*. The head can be a primitive node or another S-collection. A primitive node consists of a *name* and a *data unit*. Both terms are not formally defined any further: this is the task of specific implementations or more detailed papers such as [13]. The main part of a primitive node is its data unit. Accessing a primitive node implies executing its data unit: this will ordinarily cause some information to be presented (text, pictures, audio, video-clips) but can also result in a more complicated interactive dialogue with the user. In fact, any kind of action may happen because of the execution of a data unit. It is, however, atomic in the sense that no navigation is supported by the hypermedia system within such a data unit.

The head of S-collection is visualized when the S-collection is accessed. If the head in its turn is a complex S-collection (i.e. not a primitive node), then the above procedure of visualization is applied recursively.

An S-collection encapsulates a particular navigable structure. The navigable structure is a set of other S-collections related by a number of computer-navigable links (see fig.1). Note that we connect S-collections but not primitive nodes.

Links are encapsulated within a particular S-collection. Thus, links may be defined only between members of a certain S-collection; and in this sense, they belong to the S-collection, but not to a hypermedia database or to members that are related by means of links. An S-collection devoid of an internal structure is called a primitive S-collection.

At any particular moment in time the user can navigate only through a concrete S-collection which is called *user view*, by means of links defined within this particular S-collection. The navigation consists of a certain number of steps. A concrete S-collection is the current one for each particular navigation step. More precisely, on each navigation step the user can access a certain S-collection within the user view. To "access" means to visualise a certain S-collection. The S-collection most recently accessed (visualized within the user view) is called *current S-collection*.

For instance, consider the navigation through the previously defined S-collection "d" (see fig. 1). In this case, the user can access the S-collections "a", "b", "c" and "i" by means of links available within the user view (i.e. within the S-collection "d").

More precisely, if the S-collection "a" is a current S-collection, then it is visualized (in this particular case, node-1 is displayed by means of some internal procedure of visualization), and the user has the links to the members "b", "c" and "i" available (i.e. accessible on the next step of navigation).

Since links are encapsulated within an S-collection, they become available for navigation only if the S-collection has been "entered". Thus, during navigation the current S-collection can be "zoomed" or "entered" in order to navigate by means of links defined within this "zoomed" S-collection.

In other words, if the current S-collection is a complex S-collection (i.e. most recently accessed member of user view is a complex S-collection) then the user can apply the operation "zoom in" in order to make this member new user view (see fig. 2).

That is, a head automatically becomes the current S-collection if the S-collection including this head becomes user view by means of the "zoom in" operation.

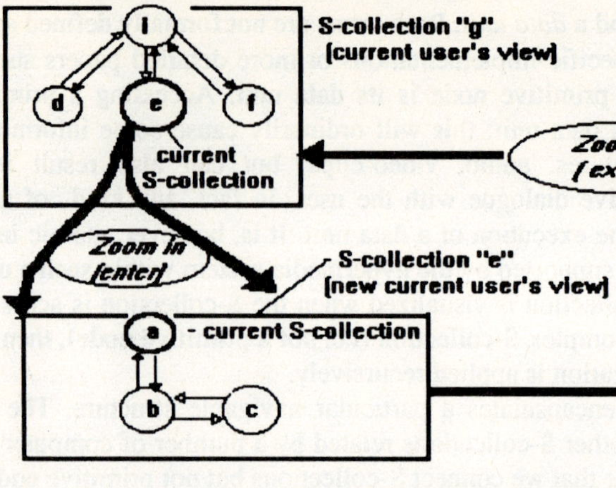

fig. 2: "ZOOM IN" and "ZOOM OUT" Operations.

The operation "zoom out" is complementary to the last "zoom in" action. More precisely, the operation "zoom out" restores user view and current S-collection to a state which they had just before the last "zoom in" operation.

Let us summarize the notion of S-collections.

An S-collection is the main "building block" (i.e. an abstract data object) within the HM-data model.

From one point of view, an S-collection can be seen as a "primitive" node. The S-collections can be linked by computer navigable links without taking into consideration their internal structures. Note that a link emanates from an S-collection and is directed to another S-collection.

On the other hand the S-collection is a sophisticated navigable structure. An S-collection encapsulates a set of other S-collections and links. Note that links can be defined only between members of the S-collection and, in this sense, the S-collection is a particular context for such encapsulated links. When S-collection is accessed in some way, it is visualised as a whole, but its internal structure is hidden from the user.

Links are encapsulated within a particular S-collection. Hence, the links do not belong to the whole hypermedia database as such (i.e. they are not global) but belong to a certain S-collection. Such an encapsulation of links within an S-collection offers a gross simplification to the otherwise tedious and complicated process of link maintenance within a hypermedia database. The hypermedia database is no more a huge network (or a web) of nodes but a number of S-collections (see fig. 1).

Surprisingly, despite the absence of such "global" links we will see that the recursive structure inherent to S-collection is sufficiently powerful to express all that is usually done using "wild cross-reference" links, in a more orderly and more user-friendly fashion.

The HM-data model supports a finite number of so-called types of S-collection, where each type defines a set of properties common to all S-collections belonging to this type.

For the purpose of this paper it suffices to explain the situation using five types of special S-collections: *envelope, folder, menu, map and freelinks*. Note that the types may be combined.

Type of S-collections can be seen as the definition of a particular regular structure of links encapsulated within each S-collections of this type (see fig. 1).

Thus, all members of an *envelope* are fully related (i.e. each member of an "Envelope" includes links directed to all other members).

An S-collection of the type "folder" is a sorted (sequential) set of members (i.e. each member includes the links directed to the "next" and "prior" members of the same S-collection).

An S-collection of the types "menu" or "map" is a simple hierarchical structure (i.e. head of such S-collection includes links to all other members and each member is provided with link directed to the head). In the case of "map", the user has to define fixed sensitive areas on the screen as "names" of links. When the head is a current S-collection, a particular link can be activated by means of "clicking on" such a sensitive area. The obvious example of such an S-collection is a map (i.e. a digitized image of the map within the head data unit) where the user can select regions in order to obtain detailed information.

New S-collections are created as instances of these types; the user assigns a name, type and head. Once the S-collection has been created, new members can be inserted or existing members can be removed. Note that all links within S-collections belonging to previously mentioned types, are maintained automatically in accordance with the selected regular structure.

Of course, the previously defined types of S-collections do not restrict us from using of S-collections having arbitrarily connected members. Thus, the S-collection type *freelinks* requires manual editing of links and does not impose any restriction to the internal structure of links.

Observe, in passing, that hypermedia systems are sometimes just considered to be systems containing "a set of arbitrarily linked nodes". By defining all such nodes as belonging to a single S-collection of type *freelinks* our HM-data model provides exactly this kind of functionality.

All primitive S-collections (or primitive nodes) belong to the type "void".

When a certain S-collection (say, "g" from the fig. 2) is entered (it becomes the user view), type determines how the user will be able to work with the structure at issue.

Observe that S-collections may be nested arbitrarily. This not only permits constructs such as folder of envelopes or folder of maps or maps of menus (and if the intuitive meaning of above is not clear at this point we will explain above by means of examples, shortly), but it also permits an S-collection to be part of a number of other S-collections, and even recursive memberships are possible and very meaningful as we will see in section 3.

Before continuing with a more detailed discussion let us now look at a few concrete examples.

Suppose we have a number of digitized pictures (each with just a short description of what it is) of various sights in cities in European countries. To be specific, let us assume we have as countries at least e.g., Austria, Germany, and France. For each country we have a number of cities represented. In Austria, say, the capitals of the provinces; in Germany quite a few and their location on a map of Germany is known, and in France a long list of cities but no map of France.

A typical hypermedia database according to the HM data model might contain all the pictures at issue as primitive S-collections. The pictures in a particular city will be organised in an S-collection, typically in a collection of type *envelope*, *folder*, *menu*, *map* or *freelinks*.

If these pictures are organised as an S-collection of type folder with name "Pictures of Vienna", then the head of the collection should typically include the symbol of Vienna and textual description of the contents of the S-collection as a whole such as "This collection consists of pictures of Vienna. To look through them one-by-one click now on *enter*".

Suppose that the S-collection "pictures of Vienna" is a member of the S-collection "pictures of Austria". In this case, when "Pictures of Vienna" is accessed, some information (as defined in the data unit of the head) is displayed (i.e. the above mentioned symbol of Vienna and the text "This collection consists of pictures of Vienna. To look through them one-by-one click now on *enter*"). If the user clicks on *enter*, all pictures can be now looked at by choosing next or previous, or by choosing *exit*, in which case the user is back in the S-collection "Pictures of Austria". However, observe that the S-collection "Pictures of Austria" containing "Pictures of Vienna" also contains pictures of other cities in the form of S-collections and has a certain navigational strategy associated with it. Rather than clicking on *enter*, the user may also choose another city according to this strategy, or can even choose *exit* to leave the S-collection "Pictures of Austria".

Note that types can be combined in many ways. If "Pictures of Vienna" is e.g. organised as S-collection of types {*folder*, *menu*}, then the menu allows to enter the folder at an arbitrary point but the additional options *next* and *previous* for traversing the folder would also be available.

To finish our example, the nine collections representing the capital cities of the nine provinces of Austria may well be combined in an S-collection "Pictures of Austria" of type *menu*, the many cities of Germany into an S-collection "Pictures of Germany" of type *map*, and the many cities of France into an S-collection "Pictures of France" of type *folder* (assuming that this is for some reason more convenient than using the type map). All countries of Europe might be organised in an S-collection "Pictures of Europe" of type {*map*, *folder*}, the type *folder* allowing to go from a particular country to the alphabetically next or previous one (sorted by name of country), or to use the name of desired country as a keyword.

3 More Details and Examples

The collection of pictures described in the example of section 2 is structured completely hierarchically: each picture belongs to exactly one city and each city is located in the one specific country. Such a specific hierarchical view is fine in some instances, but in real life the situation is often more complicated.

Suppose the S-collection "St. Stephen's Cathedral" belongs to the S-collection "Pictures of Vienna". If it is desirable to also include it into other collections like "Large European Cathedrals" or "Gothic Art" this is (conceptually) done so; and it is done so without considering whatever links are emanating from it: new links are added automatically (see above), and additional ones manually, if so desired.

There are three important issues to understand:

(1) The fact that, conceptually, an S-collection $\mathcal{X}$ can be member of $n \geq 1$ other S-collections $\mathcal{Y}_1, \mathcal{Y}_2, \ldots, \mathcal{Y}_n$ does not mean that $\mathcal{X}$ has to be physically stored n times; whether this is the case or whether some clever pointer-mechanism or whatever is used instead is part of the implementation and of no concern to the user. In this important sense the HM-data model offers a higher level of abstraction than models involving arbitrary links much in analogy to programming languages where e.g. abstract data types offer a higher level of abstraction than data-structures based on explicit pointers.

(2) Not only primitive nodes but also structures - i.e. arbitrary S-collections - can be members of more than one S-collection. And this is indeed how bigger "chunks" of information (including links or particular navigational strategies encapsulated in such "chunks") can be used in various parts of a hypermedia system. Thus, the S-collection "Pictures of Austria" could be member of the collection "Pictures of Europe" but also member of the S-collection "Information on Austria". Moreover the S-collection "Information on Austria" may well be included into the S-collection "Pictures of Austria" (note, the recursive membership). To understand this basic property of the HM-data model let us simulate the steps of a typical user session when entering the S-collection "Pictures of Europe" (see fig. 3). The head of the S-collection is responsible for displaying a map of Europe. A user clicking on Austria (i.e. activating link to the S-collection "Pictures of Austria" within the S-collection "Pictures of Europe") will obtain detailed map of Austria, list of 9 cities of Austria or whatever as it was defined within the head of S-collection "Pictures of Austria". Note that the navigational paradigm associated with the S-collection "Pictures of Europe" is still active. The user has the possibility to access another country by clicking at it. After selecting a particular country (say, Austria), the user can "enter" this S-collection. Once "entered", the user obtains links encapsulated within the S-collection "Pictures of Austria" (i.e. a menu indicating the choice of 9 cities of Austria and of the S-collection "Information on Austria").

Each choice from the menu (note in passing that the S-collection "Pictures of Austria" is the user view and belongs to the type menu) results in the presentation of information defined by the head of the corresponding S-collection. If the user has selected and entered the S-collection "Information on Austria", a number of members including the S-collection "Pictures of Austria" becomes available. This situation is typical for hypermedia systems where a particular information can be seen in different contexts [15, 20]. Also consider the possibility to insert the S-collection "Information on Austria" into other S-collections (say, "Information on Europe", "Encyclopedia", "Tourist attractions" etc.).

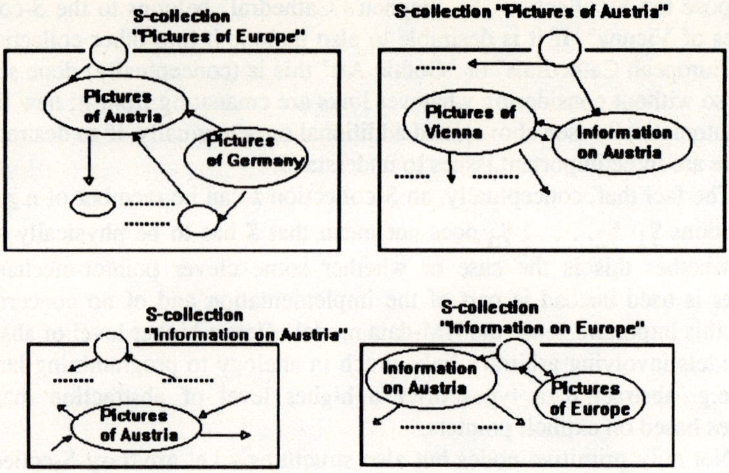

fig. 3: A sample hypermedia database

(3) S-collections need not be "stratified". An S-collection may well consist of some primitive S-collections and some other complex S-collections. As an example, a S-collection "Pictures of Vienna" of type folder may well contain a number of primitive S-collections (individual pictures) and two complex S-collections, also of type folder, "St. Stephen's Cathedral" and "Castle Schoenbrunn", each consisting of a sequence of pictures of the object at issue.

An S-collection may be further developed or modified at any time, whether it is a member of other S-collection or not. For instance, new members which are either primitive or complex S-collections can be inserted into the S-collection "St. Stephen's Cathedral" in order to detail existing information. At any moment, primitive S-collections can be rearranged into complex ones by means of assigning a particular type (say, "envelope", "folder", etc. instead of the type "void"). Note that this process does not affect participation of S-collections being under development within other S-collections because links are encapsulated into such S-collections.

4. Queries in the HM-data Model

The mechanisms of the HM-data model described sofar do not suffice to cover all important situations encountered in hypermedia systems. After all, one of the important features of ordinary hypermedia systems is that one can click at highlighted words or buttons to obtain additional information on the area specified. And in usual hypermedia systems this is done by having a reference to the appropriated part of the hypermedia database or by means of a stand-alone Information Retrieval (IR) mechanism. By "stand-alone" we mean that information retrieval is normally seen as an alternative to "browsing" of a hypermedia network [1, 6]. In terms of basic hypermedia paradigm, the information retrieval can be seen as a selection of a particular subset of nodes from the current hypermedia database. Information retrieval within a hypermedia system is described in the form of so-called *queries* that represent short-term interest of particular users. Note that in conventional hypermedia systems, queries can be applied at any point in time as an alternative to a link-based browsing. In the HM-data model a powerful query mechanism is fully incorporated into the navigational paradigm. Queries are integrated into the general structure of a hypermedia database through the concept of so-called *dynamic* S-collections: according to the HM-data model the definition of a particular query is a parameter of such a dynamic S-collection. The result of the query is a "dynamic" S-collection where members are those S-collections satisfying the query at issue. Such a dynamic S-collection includes a head defining a visible description of the particular query and belongs to a certain type (*envelope, folder*, . . .), but it has no "static" structure (i.e. has no predefined members inside).

A dynamic S-collection may be a member of other S-collection in the normal way. Thus, the user can access such a dynamic S-collection by means of links defined within other S-collections, in this case, head is visualized (i.e. description of a corresponding query becomes visible). The query description can be seen, normally, as a number of highlighted words of text, as a demand to type in a combination of words, etc. A dynamic S-collection can be "entered" (or "zoomed in"), this actions is regarded as a request to carry out the corresponding query.

When the user initiates a query (i.e. "enters" a dynamic S-collection); all S-collections in which a "hit" is obtained are "inserted" into the dynamic S-collection. Now the user may "browse" the dynamic S-collection as usual, i.e. in accordance with the navigational strategy defined by the type.

The user selects one of the S-collections (which of course can be a complex or dynamic one) within the dynamic S-collection and obtains some information relevant to the search at issue by means of the normal browsing procedure. Note that using this query mechanism the set of S-collections the user has navigated through is completely replaced by another set of S-collections, i.e. a "jump" from one part of the hypermedia database to another is carried out. In this case, the dynamic S-collection can be seen as a "bridge" between different parts of a hypermedia database. Thus, the conventional "exit dynamic S-collection" option leads back to the previous "environment" and supports normal navigational process even when queries of arbitrary complexity are used.

There exist another important aspect of the HM-data model which should be mentioned here. Thus, a hypermedia database can be supplemented with an additional meta-information which is called a semantic dictionary. Categories used in a particular hypermedia database, should be defined in the semantic dictionary. When an S-collection is created, it can be assigned to a certain category (or a number of categories). In other words an S-collection is created as an instance of particular category.

For instance, in the previously discussed example the following categories exist: *continent, country, city, building, picture, topic*. Obviously, when the S-collection "Pictures of Vienna" is created, it should be assigned to the category *city*. In analogy, the S-collection "Pictures of Austria" belongs to the category *country*; the S-collection "St.Stephen's Cathedral" belongs to the category *building* and so on.

Of course, there can exist S-collections which belong to two or more different categories. For instance, if the categories *cathedral* and *church* have been defined in the semantic dictionary, the S-collection "St. Stephen's Cathedral" would belong to all three categories: *building*, *cathedral* and *church*.

Generally, the semantic dictionary can be seen as a semantic network which defines categories and semantic relationships between them. There can exist semantic relationships of different types. Typical types of semantic relationships are: "is a" and "is a part of".

The semantic relationship "is a" defines participation of a particular S-collection within different categories. For instance, there can be defined the following semantic relationships: "*cathedral* is a *building*", "*church* is a *building*" and "*cathedral* is a *church*". In this case, if a particular S-collection is created as an instance of the category "cathedral", the S-collection is automatically considered to be also instance of the categories "church" and "building".

Another important type of semantic relationship is the so-called "is a part of" relationship. When an S-collection participates within another S-collection as a member, such a membership can be seen as an instance of this particular semantic relationship. This semantic relationship in not to be confused with the link that can be installed independently. For instance, the semantic relationships "is a part of" between previously discussed categories can be seen as follows: "*city* is a part of *country*", "*building* is a part of *city*"; "*picture* is a part of *building*" or "*picture* is a part of *city*" etc.

Thus, the participation of the S-collection "Pictures of Vienna" within the S-collection "Pictures of Austria" can be seen as an instance of the semantic relationship "*city* is a part of *country*".

Of course, the semantic dictionary should not be regarded as a predefined metastructure of whole hypermedia database as in the case of conventional database schema. Thus, S-collections which do not belong to previously defined categories or facts of membership which do not belong to predefined semantic relationships, may well exist within a hypermedia database. In analogy, a list of categories or semantic relationships can be extended at any point in time. The semantic dictionary is used for so-called intelligent navigation, semantic filtering and structured querying in the HM-data model.

A structured query is incorporated into a head of dynamic S-collection and includes: type of the query; parameters of the query; scope of the query; resultant categories.

Type of a query defines a particular kind of comparison (i.e. exact match, prefix match, phonetic match etc.) and subject of comparison that can be names of S-collections, stated keywords or full textual part of a head. Parameters of a query can be seen as a predefined set of words (i.e. the words are highlighted within a text and the user can click on one or more on them) or as an input window where desired combination of words can be typed in.

Scope of a query is defined in terms of the semantic dictionary. More precisely, a number of categories and a number of semantic relationship between them can be stated as such a scope.

If a number of categories has been selected as a scope, all S-collections belonging to the selected categories are scanned. Only information which has been directly pinned to a particular S-collection (i.e. name, keywords, and text within a head), is used for the comparison. Note that the members of such S-collections do not take part in the process of comparison. Members of the S-collections can be included into the comparison by explicitly pointing to corresponding semantic links within definition of the scope.

For instance, if scope of the query "find all objects having the word *St.Stephen* within textual part" is defined as the category *city*, the hit is obtained for S-collections belonging to category *city* and having the stated word directly within the head. But if the scope of the query was defined as the category *city* including the semantic relationship "*building* is a part of *city*", then all members are also searched, and the hit for a particular city is considered to be obtained when the word has been found within a head or an arbitrary member.

Finally, definition of a query includes a number of resultant categories. The resultant categories define S-collections that are actually selected and inserted into the dynamic S-collection. Thus, for the previously discussed example the category *city* could be stated as a resultant one. In this case, the dynamic S-collection includes such S-collections of the category *city* where the word "St.Stephen" has been found either within a head or members (i.e. S-collections of the category *building*).

Both the categories *building* and *city* may be pointed out as resultant ones. In this case, separate buildings where hit has been obtained (i.e. S-collections of the category *building* without taking into account their participation in other S-collections of the category *city*) are also included into the dynamic S-collection. Thus, the user can either navigate through cities and access desired buildings, or directly access the buildings having the stated keyword within a textual description.

In analogy, the scope can be defined as the category *cathedral*; but another category related to this one by a particular semantic relationship (say, the category *city*), can be used as a resultant one. In this case, only limited number of S-collections belonging to the category *cathedral* will be scanned and only S-collections belonging to the category *city* where the desired *cathedrals* (result of the query) participate as members, are inserted into the dynamic S-collection. We believe that this mechanism provides the users with possibility to conserve the coherence of the hypermedia information in the context of information retrieval [15, 20].

Summary

In this paper we contend that the multitude of links available in ordinary hypermedia systems [7, 16] are often more confusing than helpful for users of such systems. When analyzing links available, it turns out that some can (and should) be replaced by introducing structure rather than links; others (often called "dynamic links") can be replaced by query mechanisms; remaining links become simpler and do not lead to the "lost in hyper-space" problem.

We discuss our approach for the reduction of links called HM-data model in this paper in general terms and explain how the model can be used to obtain powerful yet easy to use hypermedia systems.

References

1. Belkin, N. J., Croft, W. B.: Information filtering and Information Retrieval: two sides of the same coin? C. ACM 35, 12 (1992), 29-38.
2. Berk, E., Devlin, J. (Eds.): Hypertext/Hypermedia Handbook; McGraw Hill Software Engineering Series, New York (1991).
3. Conklin, E.J.: Hypertext: An Introduction and Survey; IEEE Computer 20 (1987), 17-41.
4. Conklin, J., Begeman, M.: gIBIS -- A Hypertext Tool for Exploratory Policy Discussion; Proc. CSCW (1988), 140-152.
5. De Young, L.: Links considered harmful; Proc. ECHT, Versailles 1990, Cambridge University Press (1990), 238-249.
6. Foltz, P.W., Dumais, S.T.: Personalized Information Delivery: An analysis of Information Filtering Methods. C. ACM 35, 12 (1992), 51-60.
7. Goodman, D.: The complete Hypercard Handbook. Bantam books, New York (1987).
8. Halasz, F., Moran, T., Trigg, R.: NoteCards in a Nutshell. Proc. ACM Conf. Human Factors in Computer Science (1987), 45-42.
9. Halasz, F.: Reflection on Notecards: seven issues for the next generation of hypermedia systems; C. ACM. 31, 7 (1988), 836-852.
10. Kappe, F.: Aspects of a Modern Multi-Media Information System; IIG Report 308, Graz (1991).
11. Maurer, H., Tomek, I.: Hypermedia Bibliography, J.MCA 14, 2 (1991), 161-216.
12. Maurer, H.: Why Hypermedia Systems are Important; Proc. ICCAL'92, Wolfville, Canada, LNCS 602, Springer Pub. (1992), 1-15.
13. Maurer, H., Scherbakov, N.: The HM-Data Model; IIG Report, Graz (1992).
14. Nielsen, J.: Hypertext and Hypermedia; Academic Press (1990).
15. Stotts, P.D., Furuta, R. : Adding browsing semantics to the hypertext model. Proc. ACM Document Processing Systems Conf., Santa Fe, NM (1988), 43-50.
16. Using Toolbook, Version 1.0, Asymetrix Corporation, Bellevue, WA (1989).
17. Tomek, I., Khan, S., Muldner, T. Nassar, Novak, G., Proszynski, P.: Hypermedia - introduction and survey; J.MCA 14, 2 (1991), 63-103.
18. Tomek, I., Kappe, F., Maurer, H.: Links in Hypermedia Systems; Proc. of the 7th Joint Conference of the Austrian Computer Society (OCG) and NJSZT (1992), 197.
19. Van Damm, A.: Hypertext'87 Keynote Address, C.ACM 31, 7 (1988), 887-895.
20. Yankelovich, N., Haan, B., Meyrowitz, N., Drucker, S.: Intermedia: The concept and the construction of a seamless information environment, IEEE Computer, 21, 1 (1988), 81-96.

Linearisation Schemata for Hypertext

T.J.M. Bench-Capon P.E.S. Dunne G. Staniford*

Department of Computer Science
University of Liverpool
Liverpool L69 3BX
Great Britain

Abstract: Hypertext systems typically contain massive volumes of textual information. This information is structured as a labelled directed graph, so that progression from one item of text to another is via labelled edges in the hypertext network. A user, faced with this quantity of material, must cull the information required by carefully navigating through the nodes of the network. Even experienced hypertext users can become disorientated when navigating a complex network structure. A formal aid to hypertext navigation (with particular reference to the problem of linearisation) was presented in [1]. The mechanism described, however, has the drawback that the linkage structure on which it is built must be already present in the hypertext. In this paper we describe a formal extension to the earlier work which provides greater navigational flexibility through a higher level approach to user profile specifications.

1. Introduction

The last decade has seen considerable expansion in the range of hypertext systems produced. There are now several large hypertext systems available, e.g. Writing Environment [9] and gIBIS [3], as well as a number of commercial systems for creating hypertext e.g. Apple's HyperCard system has been supplied with the Macintosh microcomputer since 1987 and the third party Guide system produced by OWL and introduced in 1985. Some hypertext systems (e.g. hypercard) have their information presentation paradigm based squarely around the concept of a card or window of fixed size while others allow a more flexible approach to the amount of text and or graphics that can be accommodated and presented from one node.

So called linear text can be presented both in traditional paper and electronic form. It is well established that educated readers have highly developed skills for information retrieval with traditional texts, skills that have been developed from childhood onwards. Studies have been carried out, for one example see [6] which compared information retrieval tasks on the same information presented on paper, as linear electronic texts and on two different designs of hypertext. The tasks were designed so that a range of retrieval strategies would be employed by the experimental subjects. The results indicate that paper and linear electronic texts scored almost the same on each count, being significantly better than both hypertexts for accuracy and on average all four mediums were similar on speed of working; hypertext was found to be better when a specific piece of information was being

* This research was supported by SERC research grant No. 90309983

searched for. These results seem to fairly typical of such experiments and show that at present there is no overall best method for presenting and retrieving information from textual matter. We contend that there is now, and will be for the foreseeable future, an excellent case for presenting text selectively retrieved from a hypertext in a linear form either electronically on screen or as a traditional paper document.

In this paper we are primarily concerned with larger hypertext systems where we would typically expect the hypertext to contain the equivalent of a large number of different linear documents embedded within a rich mix of material, much of which would not be required, nor suitable, for output as a coherent exposition in relation to a given need.

The linearisation problem in hypertext can be described at the user level as the problem of producing a sensible linear rendering, as an orthodox textual document, of some desired portion of the information stored within the hypertext. Formally it may be viewed as extracting a linear path from a directed graph structure. Producing such linearisations and the more general problem of hypertext navigation, presents considerable problems even to experienced users of hypertext systems. The navigation of paper documents, by readers, has been studied by a number of workers; the work of [4] on a model of discourse comprehension is worthy of note. Through experience, in this model, readers acquire schemata ('superstructures' based upon the formation of a macropropositional hierarchy) that allow readers to predict the likely grouping and positional protocols inherent within and between the constituent structures of the document. It is generally agreed that this sort of ability, developed over centuries and a property of the cultural inheritance of the reader, does not carry over when a person is faced with the relatively new medium of hypertext. See, e.g. [2], [7] and [8] on the difficulties faced by users in navigating a highly intricate and convoluted virtual space. With the complex systems, that are nowadays becoming commonplace, the information required in textual form by different groups of users may vary considerably depending on the backgrounds they possess. For example, an information assistant may wish to browse through a list of titles, keywords and abstracts, while the person making the query will need to linearise complete sections of documents or even complete documents. Faced with such a multiplicity and variety of user needs linearisation mechanisms must have some profile of user requirements supplied to them allied to a mechanism for satisfying those requirements, or face being found unusable by the majority of clients.

[1] introduced a formal concept of such a profiling mechanism. In this approach the linearisation system works from a specification of the target linear structure and extracts material from the hypertext graph in a manner that is forced to be consistent with the supplied specification. Thus differing user needs can be accommodated by designing appropriate specification templates and the difficulties of linearisation are shifted from the computational task of guiding the hypertext traversal to the human task of constructing an appropriate specification for each user class. Experimental investigations of this specification mechanism, however, reveal some disadvantages when

certain types of linear ordering are required. In particular, since the description of the target structures constrains these to utilise only the linkage structure that is explicitly present, it is possible that textual orderings that are *implicitly* present in the hypertext cannot be recovered since there is no explicit path which traverses the relevant nodes in the desired order. A further drawback is that the mechanism operates on the lowest level of node and edge label content, and thus if a selective traversal based on a hierarchical structuring of the hypertext nodes is desired, then this, although possible, is not straightforwardly catered for.

In order to surmount these difficulties, we extend the formalism presented in [1] by incorporating it as the lowest level of a richer specification structure. We demonstrate that this extended specification language offers three significant advantages over the purely graph based system on which it is built: implicit orderings can be represented and recovered, hierarchical structures within a hypertext can be imposed, and specifications can be written in a more transparent manner. The remainder of this paper is organised as follows. Section 2 introduces some formal definitions used subsequently, briefly reviews the specification mechanism (target graph specifications) referred to earlier, and presents examples of linearisation requirements that it cannot easily deal with. In Section 3, we describe the elements of a specification language, expressions in which are called *linearisation schemata*, that employs target graph specifications as a foundational formalism. Examples of linearisation schemata in practice are then given and discussed followed by a brief discussion of the approach taken to the practical testing of the ideas (which will form the subject of a forthcoming paper). Finally, conclusions are given in Section 4.

2. Target Graph Descriptions and Hypertext Linearisation

Throughout we use the following formal definitions of hypertext, from [1]

Definition 2.1: A *hypertext*, H, over the character set (or *alphabet*) Σ is defined by a quintuple:

$$H \equiv (V; E; \lambda_V; \lambda_E; \chi)$$

where $V = \{1, 2, \ldots, n\}$ is a finite set of graph nodes; $E \subseteq V \times V$ is a finite set of graph edges; $\lambda_V : V \rightarrow \Sigma^*$ is a *node-labelling* function; $\lambda_E : E \rightarrow \Sigma^*$ is an *edge-labelling* function; and $\chi : V \rightarrow \Sigma^*$ is the mapping describing the textual content stored at each node.

For a mapping λ_R from some set R onto Σ^*, we define the set $Names(\lambda_R)$ by

$$Names(\lambda_R) =_{def} \{\alpha : \exists\, x \in R \text{ such that } \lambda_R(x) = \alpha\}$$

Hence, $Names(\lambda_V)$ is the set of node labels used and $Names(\lambda_E)$ the set of edge labels used. We assume throughout that there is a null (empty) label in both sets. •

From the definition it is apparent that a hypertext is a labelled, directed graph that may contain cycles or may be structured as a hierarchy. Each edge and node has associated with it a label constructed from the alphabet Σ. Σ may be specified at one of a number of levels, eg. $\{0,1\}$, the ASCII character set, or the 16 bit multicode, etc., allowing a hypertext to be created that contains documents in almost any machine readable representation or human language. The sets $Names(\lambda_V)$ and $Names(\lambda_E)$ in the general definition have no restrictions placed upon them. In practice they may be distinct or, more commonly, $Names(\lambda_E) \subseteq Names(\lambda_V)$ so that the edge labels have meaningful form and be used to provide navigational information.

Definition 2.2: An *extended regular expression* over an alphabet of terminal symbols, Σ and *connection set*, Λ, is any expression built in accordance with the following:

1. $\forall\, \sigma \in \Sigma$: σ is an extended regular expression.
2. If S and T are extended regular expressions, then so are:
   - 2.1. $S \oplus T$ (*alternative*)
   - 2.2. $S \rightarrow T$ (*connection*)
   - 2.3. $S \overset{\lambda}{\rightarrow} T$, $\forall\, \lambda \in \Lambda$ (*labelled connection*)
   - 2.4. (S) (*bracketing*)
   - 2.5. S^* (*repetition*)
3. All that are extended regular expressions arise by reason of (1) and (2) alone.

We denote by $ERE(\Sigma, \Lambda)$ the set of all extended regular expressions with alphabet Σ and connection set Λ. •

The extended regular expressions that may be produced using this definition can be mapped onto labelled tree structures; this affords a relatively low level pattern matching facility for sub-graphs of a hypertext. This enables Definition 2.3 to be used in a mapping from $ERE(\Sigma, \Lambda)$ onto suitable sub-graphs of $H \equiv (V; E; \lambda_V; \lambda_E; \chi)$.

Definition 2.3: A *target graph specification* is an extended regular expression with alphabet $Names(\lambda_V)$ and connection set $Names(\lambda_E)$, i.e. an element of $ERE(Names(\lambda_V); Names(\lambda_E))$. •

The approach used in [1] can be described as follows: extended regular expressions may be used to define a (family of) directed *acyclic* graphs; there is then a correspondence between paths from source to sink nodes in these directed graphs and the strings in the set generated by the corresponding extended regular expression. By viewing a hypertext linearisation as a constrained total ordering of a subset of hypertext nodes and by regarding an extended regular expression as a specification, a linearisation is defined as conforming to a specification if the sequence of node and edge labels used within it give rise to a string within the defined extended regular set of strings.

Experimental studies involving this formalism, however, reveal some weaknesses that would arise in practical situations. These may be summarised as follows.

- Specific orderings of hypertext nodes can only be produced if the linkage structure of the network connects them. Thus linear orderings that are implicit in the network linkage cannot be specified.
- Hypertext systems may be constructed as a hierarchy of node classes. Target graph specifications operate only on the lowest node level and thus cannot combine sub-levels of different hierarchies together easily.

As an example of these difficulties, consider the possible hyperisation of a bibliography in Figure 1 below.

One may wish to produce either a list of the titles on which a specific writer is co-author or of all the information associated with a particular title. Clearly this information is present in the network of Figure 1, but since there are no explicit *Title→Title* or *Author→Author* links neither of these can be realised by a target graph specification. Thus, even in a small example such as the one below, there are difficulties when using only the linkage structures present.

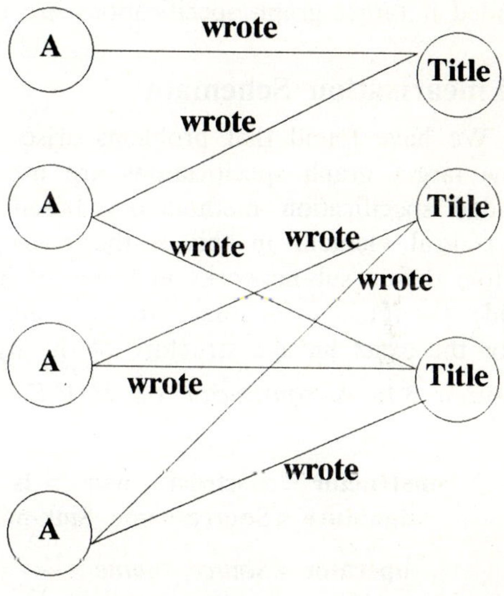

Figure 1. Implicit Information

In the same way the information in the bibliography might be represented hierarchically within a hypertext, e.g Figure 2

Again it is not possible to cater for certain natural linear orderings of the hypertext, since the hierarchical representation is not expanded by the regular expression formalism.

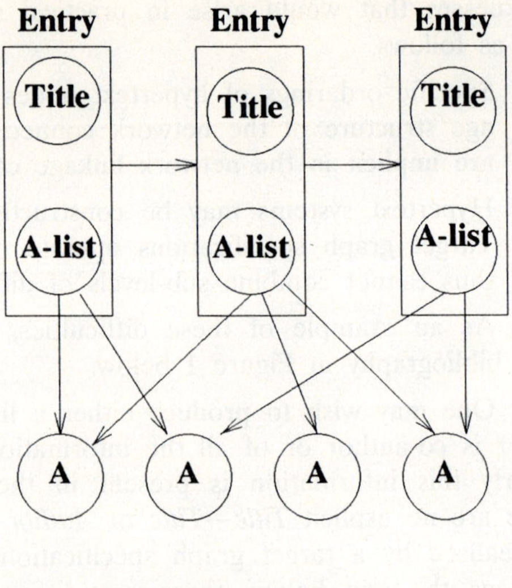

Figure 2. Hierarchical Bibliography

The two problems illustrated above mean that in order to extract particular orderings the hypertext representation itself would have to be amended if target graph specifications are to be used.

3. Linearisation Schemata

We have found that problems arise in constructing some linearisations if raw target graph specifications are used. In this section we describe an extended specification methodology based on extended regular expressions. The central element in this is the concept of *constructor definitions*. Constructors define sub-networks in terms of hypertext node and edge labels but provide the facility for these to be combined in a manner that need not mirror the exact linkage structure of the hypertext.

Definition 3.1: A *constructor* on $H(V,E,\lambda_V,\lambda_E,\chi)$ is a specification of the form:

constructor <constructor-name> **is**
signature <Source-name, Sink-name> **by** {<edge-label>}
operator $<Source-name>^{*} \overset{\lambda}{\rightarrow} <Sink-name>$ |
operator $<Source-name> \overset{\lambda}{\rightarrow} <Sink-name>^{*}$
end

where $Source-name$ and $Sink-name$ are elements of $Names(\lambda_V)$ or previously defined constructor-names; $edge-label$ is an member of $Names(\lambda_E)$.

A *linearisation schema* for H is a sequence of constructors

$$C = < C_1, \ldots, C_m >$$

together with an expression

$$\Lambda \in ERE\,(\,C \bigcup names\,(\,\lambda_V\,)\,;names(\,\lambda_E\,)\,)$$ •

Constructor definitions, when executed, return a set of directed acyclic graphs 'implicitly consistent' with the structure of the hypertext being linearised. The above definition gives a syntactic form for schemata. The semantic interpretation is as follows. The signature of a constructor, *C*, specifies the node labels and edge labels that may occur in the sub-network being defined. The operator acts as follows if the operator definition is of the form

$$<Source-name>^{*} \xrightarrow{\lambda} <Sink-name>$$

Case 1: Both source and sink names are element of $Names(\lambda_V)$. In this case the resulting directed acyclic graph templates are formed by identifying all occurrences of nodes labelled with *sink – name*. For each such occurrence, *v*, all nodes labelled *source – name* that have a directed link labelled λ into *v* are formed into a linear chain with the last node in this chain being directed into *v* by a link labelled λ.

Case 2: At least one of the source and sink names is a constructor name. In this case the directed graph is formed by expanding the relevant constructor definition, as above, and chaining the resulting graphs into a linear order.

The mapping from constructors to graphs in the alternative operator definition is performed in a similar manner.

For some examples we return to the fragment of a hypertext shown in Figure 1. Using this fragment we can define two schemata corresponding to publication lists.

constructor publication **is**
  signature A, Title **by** wrote
  operator $(A)^{*} \xrightarrow{wrote} Title$
end

constructor bibliography **is**
  signature publication **by null**
  operator $(publication)^{*}$
end

schema bibliography

Example 1: Linearisation of bibliography by ordering titles

constructor authors-work **is**
  signature A, Title **by** wrote
  operator $A \overset{wrote}{\rightarrow} (Title)^*$
end

constructor bibliography **is**
  signature authors-work **by null**
  operator $(authors\_work)^*$
end

schema bibliography

Example 2: Linearisation of bibliography by ordering authors

In the case shown in Figure 1, the first schema (Example 1) would identify 3 instances of the constructor **publication**: two with two co-authors and one with three co-authors; expanding the constructor definition for **publication** would yield the linearisation of Figure 1, shown in Figure 3 below:

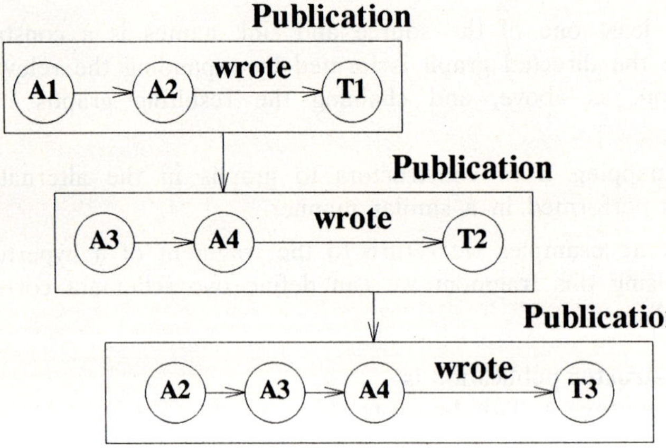

Figure 3: Action of – **constructor** publication.

One the other hand, the second schema (Example 2) would identify 4 instances of the constructor **authors-work** and expanding the constructor definition for these would yield the linearisation of Figure 1, shown in Figure 4 below:

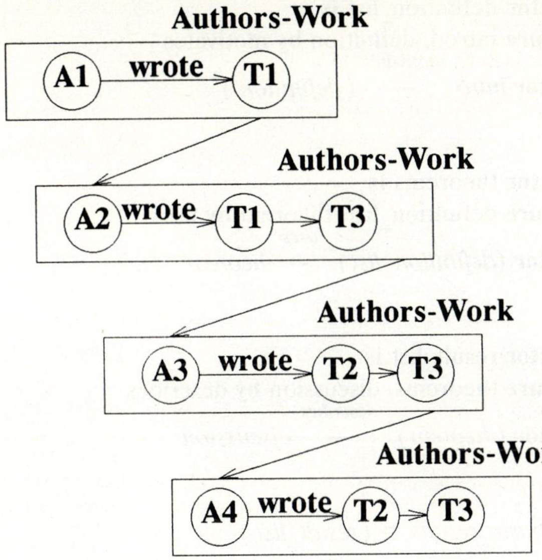

Figure 4: Action of – **constructor** authors_work.

The examples above show that linearisation schemata offer the possibility of specifying text orderings that cannot be recovered directly from the hypertext structure. As a more complex example such schemata also allow for hierarchies to be represented by defining new constructors in terms of previously defined ones. Thus for a mathematical paper we may wish to group together introductory motivation, definitions, theorems and discussion material without including detailed proofs. A schema such as the following would provide an appropriate linearisation in this case.

constructor definition_list **is**
  signature introd, definition **by** motivates
  operator *intro* $\xrightarrow{\textit{motivates}}$ $(\textit{definition})^*$
end

constructor theorems **is**
  signature definition_list, theorem **by** uses
  operator $(\textit{definition\_list})^*$ $\xrightarrow{\textit{uses}}$ *theorem*
end

constructor result_list **is**
  signature theorems, discussion **by** describes
  operator $(\textit{theorem})^*$ $\xrightarrow{\textit{describes}}$ *discussion*
end

schema *basic_results* $\equiv$ $(\textit{result\_list})^*$

Example 3: Hierarchically Organised Specification of Mathematical Paper

The experimental implementations of these formalisms are based upon the idea of *non-deterministic finite pushdown automatons.* Briefly, a *finite pushdown automaton* can be, and is in the form of an *augmented transition network* (ATN) used as a parsing mechanism for sentences and represents a grammar as a graph or network. ATN's allow both recursion and backtracking and it is possible to show formally that a given ATN is equivalent to some particular grammar. An *extended regular grammar* that defines how the extended regular expressions may be combined together to form *extended regular sets* has been developed for this purpose. When used in the parsing of sentences an ATN consumes words off the input string as an arc in the network is traversed and augments a syntactic parse tree to include the new word and its grammatical attributes. In this application the ATN generates a linearisation of the hypertext by consuming edge and node labels and augmenting a linear graph with the textual content of the nodes in accordance with the constructor definition and the lower level extended regular expressions.

A non-deterministic finite pushdown automaton allows for the parallel generation of alternative paths through the hypertext by forking off copies of itself to handle each alternative; as in all practical implementations of parallelism heuristic control is necessary to manage resource allocation during this process. This enables the production of a finite set of linearisations that satisfy the specification supplied to reflect the user's needs.

4. Conclusions

The problems that users face while navigating hyperdocument spaces to extract information are unlikely to be solved within the short term, nor are they likely to admit of a single solution. The empirical work that has been carried out so far in the field is of limited extent, with most researchers and designers failing to concern themselves with the mental representations that users would need to possess in order to be able to build up a cognitive map of the information space. The difficulties faced by designers—caused by the lack of an authoritative cognitive model that would provide a description of the user for the designer—have not as yet been much recognised in the literature. The users difficulties, on the other hand, are beginning to be recognised and studied empirically. The formation of such a cognitive model is a difficult, open question for cognitive scientists and psychologists to grapple with.

In this paper we have proposed a practical route to one possible solution to the problems, based upon ideas that have been current in other spheres for some time. The notion of a profile is often used and the mechanism described here using extended regular sets as the lower level pattern matching input for higher level specifications in the form of linearisation schemata should provide a useful means of building up user profiles. These profiles allow particular users to have the information output they desire specified in a manner that is suited to the needs of the task that forms their current objective in trawling a complex information space. The specification schemata are at once understandable to to us as humans and capable of being mapped onto the complex graph of the hyperdocument space by the use of automata.

The design of suitable automata has been briefly indicated and the detailed theoretical correctness proof of the design and the practical implementation and testing will be the subject of future work. The authors have been developing a large hyperdocument, for use with a document management system ([5]), using prolog databases for flexibility. The practical testing of the efficacy of different types of user profile and the classifying of the tasks that may be assisted by the use of the profiles will, we believe, be a useful direction for future work to follow.

Another very interesting line of enquiry which could be built upon the work presented here, and which may have considerable general application, is the extraction of implicit information from within a graphical information space. We have demonstrated that linearising schemata acting as a metalevel specification over extended regular expressions can be used to extract useful implicit information from some commonly occurring structures found within documents.

Finally, we contend that the work presented here provides a useful basis upon which to build part of the hyperdocument management tools that must surely be provided for users as hypertexts increase in size and complexity in the coming years.

5. References

1. T.J.M. Bench-Capon, P.E.S. Dunne, G. Staniford: Linearising Hypertext through Target Graph Specifications, Proc. Dexa92, Valencia, Springer-Verlag 1992, pp173–178
2. J. Conklin J: Hypertext – An Introduction and Survey, Computer, September 1987, 17–41.
3. J. Conklin, M.L. Begeman: **gIBIS**: A Hypertext Tool for Exploratory Policy Discussion, ACM Transactions on Office Information Systems, 6(4), 303-331. (1988)
4. T.A. van Dijk, W. Kintsch, W: Strategies of Discourse Comprehension, Academic Press, New York, (1983)
5. P.E. Dunne, G. Staniford: CASS — a Cooperative Authorship Support System, Proc. Sixièmes Journeés internationales des Sciences Informatiques: Les Systèmes d'Information de l'ideé à la concrétisation, Tunis, (May 1992) , 129-140
6. C. McKnight, A. Dillon, J. Richardson: A comparison of linear and hypertext formats in information retrieval, in R. McAleese & C. Green (eds), Hypertext: State of the Art, Oxford, Intellect, 1990.
7. A. Simpson: Navigation in Hypertext: design issues, Paper presented at International Online 89 Conference, London, December 1989.
8. A. Simpson, C. McKnight: Navigation in Hypertext: Structural cues and mental maps, in R. McAleese & C. Green (eds), Hypertext: State of the Art, Oxford, Intellect, 1990.
9. J.B. Smith, S.F. Weiss, G.J. Ferguson: A hypertext writing environment and its cognitive basis, Proceedings of Hypertext '87, University of North Carolina, Chapel Hill, (1987), 195-214.

HyperPATH/O2: Integrating Hypermedia Systems with Object-Oriented Database Systems*

B. Amann[1], V. Christophides[2] and M. Scholl[2]

[1] INRIA F-78153 Le Chesnay Cedex France
[2] Cedric/CNAM 292 rue St Martin 75141 Paris Cedex 03 France

Abstract. We describe an integration of the hypermedia system HyperPATH with the object-oriented DBMS (OODBMS) O_2. Providing persistence to a hypertext system was the first motivation of this work. More generally, we were interested in a better understanding of the connection of hypertext systems with OODBMS. One of our goals was to define an abstract interface between HyperPATH and a variety of OODBMS's. The solution adopted shows that opening HyperPATH to different OODBMS's is not possible without major rewriting of existing C++ code.

Keywords: hypertext, hypermedia, object oriented database, system integration, persistence, C++ code reusability

1 Introduction

This paper describes an integration of the hypermedia system HyperPATH (formerly called MultiCard) [12] with the object-oriented database management system (OODBMS) O_2 [7]. Providing persistence to a hypertext system was the first motivation of this work. More generally, we were interested in 1) gaining a better understanding of the connection of hypertext systems with object-oriented database systems and 2) providing hypertext systems with typed nodes and links [11] in order to introduce new query facilities [2]. The latter issue will not be addressed in this paper. Instead we shall concentrate on providing persistence to HyperPATH by connecting it to the OODBMS O_2. One challenge was to verify whether an integration between a significant piece of code written in C++ (HyperPATH) and the OODBMS O_2 could be implemented quickly and easily. In particular, it should not require major rewriting. Another issue was to check whether there exists a general solution which is independent of the OODBMS used for the integration. In parallel with our work, an integration of HyperPATH with the OODBMS ONTOS has been done by Bull [1].

According to the HAM model [4], hypertext systems can be divided into three distinct layers : a) a *storage layer* providing persistence to the hypermedia

* Work partially supported by the French *Programme de Recherche Coordonnée BD3*.
V. Christophides and M. Scholl are also affiliated with INRIA.
Email: <Bernd.Amann|Vassilis.Christophides|Michel.Scholl>@inria.fr

objects, such as nodes, links and anchors b) a *management layer* (Hypertext Abstract Machine) providing system functionalities, such as the creation, update, deletion and display of the hypermedia objects and c) a *presentation layer* providing a high-level interface for human-machine interaction. In a further step, the DEXTER model [10] proposes the separation of the hypertext structure (storage layer) from the node contents (within-component layer). In this approach, since the range of possible document types is large (text, image, sound, etc.) and hard to be modeled in a generic way, the within-component layer is not part of the hypertext model *per se*. This architecture as well as the growing demands on the storage layer to provide concurrency control, transaction management, object versions, distribution or even efficient query language facilities [9], leads to two main research directions.

The first investigates the integration of existing hypertext systems with current database systems (relational or object-oriented). Examples of such persistent hypertext systems are described in [8, 14, 5]. The second research direction attempts to create an open hypermedia database platform for a variety of connections with existing hypertext systems. Examples of such platforms can be found in [6, 13]. Recent evolution in this direction allows new objects and operations to be added at run-time [16]. The integration of HyperPATH with O_2 pertains to the first direction. To our knowledge this is the first attempt to provide a hypermedia system with a persistence module built on top of a commercial OODBMS. Current hypertext systems are generally closed systems that cannot be easily integrated with other programs and data. On the other hand, it is evident that the extensibility of hypertext systems is crucial for interoperability reasons, in particular for the exchange of hyperdocuments stored in various systems and applications. For example, with our integration of HyperPATH with O_2 we have the possibility to visualize the structure of a hypertext by using the O_2Graph application tool. In this direction we have also investigated the definition of a minimal interface between the management layer and the storage layer in order to implement the latter by a variety of OODBMS's.

O_2 is an object-oriented DBMS developed and distributed by O_2Technology. It combines the traditional advantages of DBMS's (persistence, secondary storage management, concurrency, recovery and ad hoc query facility) with those of object-oriented programming (encapsulation, extensibility, computational completeness, etc.). HyperPATH is a set of hypermedia software tools that allows the development of interactive hypermedia applications. It has been developed at Bull as a part of the Esprit project Multiworks. In HyperPATH, a *hypertext* (hypermedia application or hyperdocument) is a graph with nodes containing multimedia documents, hereafter referred as *documents*. Following the DEXTER model, documents are strictly separated from the hypertext structure.

Prior to our integration, the persistence of the HyperPATH hypermedia objects was provided by an *ad hoc* distributed system, called *mwdbms* (Multiworks Data Base Management System). The developers' objective was not to implement a complete database system but an open and flexible module that allows hypertexts to be stored and retrieved on different hosts. In order, then, to extend HyperPATH with full database functionalities (query facilities, security, recovery, etc.) as well as for a better understanding of the relationship between hypermedia systems and object-oriented database systems, we use the O_2 DBMS for implementing the persistence of HyperPATH objects.

Section 2 presents the architecture and the hypertext model of HyperPATH as well as its initial persistence mechanism. The C++ interface of O_2 which is used to connect both systems is described in Section 3. In Section 4 we present different levels of integration among which one was chosen for the integration of HyperPATH and O_2. Section 5 points out the main issues of an "open" integration of HyperPATH with OODBMS's while Section 6 describes the solution that was finally adopted.

2 HyperPATH

2.1 The HyperPATH Architecture

A general overview of the architecture of HyperPATH [12] is given in Figure 1. A hypermedia application can be constructed by using the following modules:

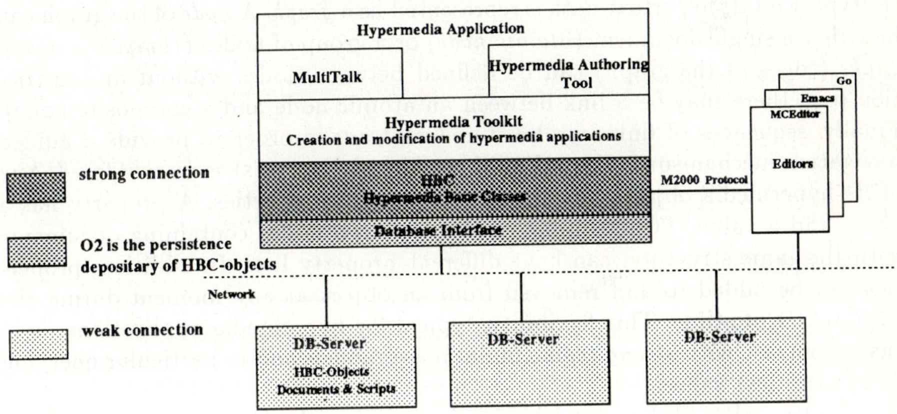

Fig. 1. HyperPATH Architecture

1. The *Hypermedia Authoring Tool* is a **Motif**[3] application built on top of the *Hypermedia Toolkit* (see below) and allows a) authors to create and modify hypertexts by using specific editors, and b) readers to browse through existing hypertexts. Different documents are separately prepared with specific editors and then linked together interactively.
2. With the programming language *MultiTalk* it is possible to write simple programs, called *scripts*. These are attached to objects like nodes and anchors, and are triggered by events such as a display of a node or an anchor selection.

[3] **Motif** is a registered trademark of the Open Software Foundation, Inc.

3. The *Hypermedia Toolkit* is a library of C functions for the creation and manipulation of persistent distributed hypermedia objects (such as nodes, anchors and links).
4. The *M2000 Protocol* and the *Compliant Editors* allow a user to edit the information contents of a node. Each node is associated with a specific editor (for example MCEditor, GO, Emacs, etc.) that is not included in HyperPATH but is "extended" in such a way as to communicate with HyperPATH via the predefined communication protocol *M2000*. It is then possible to create HyperPATH applications with any kind of node contents (text, image, audio, graphics, etc.) whose editor is compatible with the *M2000 protocol*.

The *Hypermedia Basic Classes (HBC)* module, written in C++, manages all objects representing the structure of a hypertext. Their persistence is provided by *mwdbms* running on several servers (DB-Server) which are connected by a network. An application represents a client that communicates with mwdbms using remote procedure calls (RPC).

2.2 The Data Model of HyperPATH

In HyperPATH, hypertext data is represented as a *graph*. A *node* of the graph can be either a single document (*atomic node*) or a group of nodes (*composite node*). *Links* (edges of the graph) can be defined between nodes without any restriction (e.g. there may be a link between an atomic node and a composite node). Finally, sequences of links can be stored as *trails* in order to provide a guided navigation mechanism to HyperPATH readers. A hypertext is *weakly typed*. Any of its hypermedia objects has an arbitrary list of properties. A property has a name and a value. Two "similar" nodes, e.g. two nodes containing documents with the same structure, can have different property lists. In addition, properties can be added to and removed from an object at any moment during the hypertext's life-time. This flexibility, typical for hypermedia applications, is in sharp contrast with *strong typing* in database models and in particular querying by (properties) values.

The HyperPATH data model is implemented in the C++ programming language. Objects are defined through composition and inheritance mechanisms resulting in the schema shown in Figure 2 : dashed lines represent inheritance relationships (e.g. the class `Link` is a subclass of `HyperObject`) and solid arcs represent composition. The labels of these arcs are the attribute names. Multi-valued attributes are distinguished from single-valued attributes by an additional <> symbol. For example, the arc from `Anchor` to `Node` labeled with *node* denotes that each anchor has an attribute with name *node* and whose value is the `Node` object containing the anchor. On the other hand, each node has an attribute *anchors* with the list of its anchors (class `Anchor`).

All classes are subclasses of the class `HyperObject`. The user semantics of each object, i.e. its list of properties, is represented by the attribute *propertylist* which is inherited from `HyperObject`. HyperPATH hypertexts are objects of the class `Hypergraph`. Atomic nodes (class `Node`) and composite nodes, hereafter

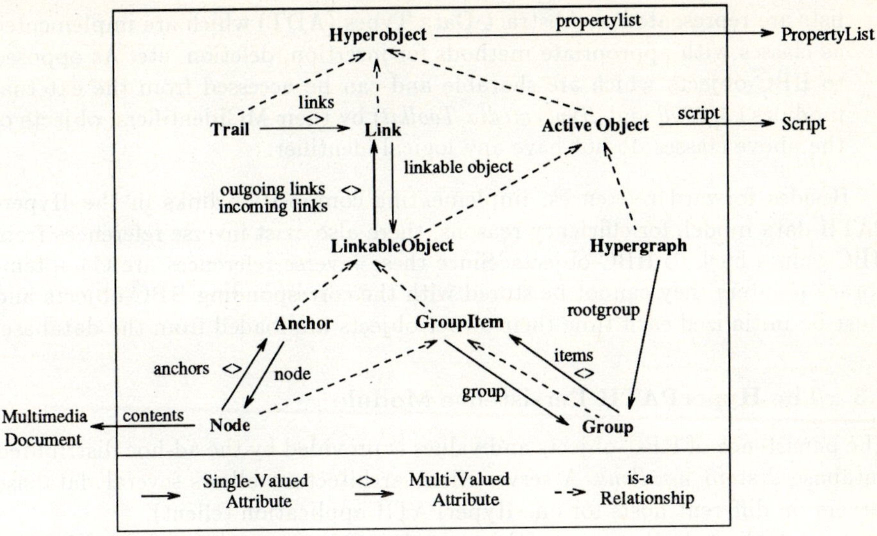

Fig. 2. Hypermedia Basic Classes (HBC)

called groups (class `Group`), form the instances of the class `GroupItem`[4]. The components of a group (nodes and groups) are stored in the *items* attribute. HyperPATH links (class `Link`) can be defined between groups, nodes and anchors (common superclass `LinkableObject`) without any restriction. A HyperPATH trail (class `Trail`) is then a list of links followed during user navigation in the hypertext. Objects of the class `ActiveObject` can receive events triggering the execution of an attached *script* (attribute *script*). Finally, the contents of a HyperPATH atomic node is not an object of the class hierarchy but is stored, for example as a UNIX file, by the corresponding compliant editor of the node.

The HyperPATH data model contains not only objects from the Hypermedia Basic Classes (HBC) hierarchy but also values such as scripts and property lists. From now on, we will distinguish between *HBC-objects* and *classes* and *HBC-values* and *types*. Both have to be rendered persistent. More precisely,

a) HBC-objects are created and managed by the persistence module (*internal interface*) and have a "global" identifier, called the *MCIdentifier* of the object. The MCIdentifier is also used by the *Compliant Editors* and the *Hypermedia Toolkit* (*external interface*) and it is composed of a) the *host* name, b) a hypertext identifier, called the *stack*, and c) an identifier for the object inside the hypertext, called the *local identifier* of the object.
b) HBC-values represent non sharable and non encapsulated attribute *values* of HBC-objects. However, they are also implemented as C++ objects (e.g. class `Script` and `PropertyList`). Since C++ does not provide bulk data types,

[4] Atomic nodes can be compared with files and groups with directories containing files and other directories.

lists are represented as Abstract Data Types (ADT) which are implemented as classes with appropriate methods for insertion, deletion, etc. As opposed to HBC-objects which are sharable and can be accessed from the external modules (*M2000* and *Hypermedia Toolkit*) by their MCIdentifiers, objects of the above classes do not have any logical identifier.

Besides forward references, implementing composition links in the HyperPATH data model, for efficiency reasons, there also exist inverse references from HBC-values back to HBC-objects. Since these inverse references are C++ temporary pointers they cannot be stored with the corresponding HBC-objects and must be initialized each time their owner objects are loaded from the database.

2.3 The HyperPATH Persistence Module

The persistence of HBC-objects and values is provided by the ad-hoc distributed database system *mwdbms*. A server-client architecture allows several database servers on different hosts for one HyperPATH application (client).

In each client, a *dbmsserver* (object of class `DbmsServer`) guarantees the persistence of all HBC-objects of one hypertext. It communicates with mwdbms by remote procedure calls (RPC). An *object manager* (object of class `ObjManager`) renders distribution of objects transparent to the above layers by handling a list of dbmsservers.

Each time the object manager needs an HBC-object with MCIdentifier *mcoid*, it sends a request to the dbmsserver. The latter initializes a new object with the database value obtained from mwdbms unless there is already an object with the same identifier *mcoid* in the *dictionary* of loaded objects. Each object has a reference to its dbmsserver. This allows faster access to an HBC-object of the same hypertext (e.g. a link accessing its source node) by calling directly the related dbmsserver, i.e. without passing by the object manager.

A hypertext can be saved only in its entirety. Each HBC-object receives from the dbmsserver the message to save itself. An object is saved only when its state has been modified. Saving a node also includes saving its contents. Obviously, an HBC-object is saved with its HBC-values.

3 C++ Interface of O_2

O_2 provides a C++ programming interface [15] which allows an O_2 database to be linked with an external application written in C or C++. By this, writing and reading to and from the database are transparent to the programmer. The *import* command takes an existing C++ declaration file as an input and generates its image schema in O_2. The *export* command renders O_2 objects visible to external applications. In general, each C++ class is extended by two methods *read* and *write*, which allow an object to be read/written from/to the O_2 database. Additionally, for each C++ class K a twin C++ class (*persistent pointer class*) o2_K is created and whenever an application wishes to access a persistent object, it might use the persistent pointer instead of the C++ temporary pointer.

C++ member functions (methods) are not imported. In contrast to O_2C methods, they are neither changed nor stored in the O_2 database. Nevertheless, it is possible to call O_2C methods from a C++ method. A named object (O_2 persistence root) is automatically available to the external C++ application when its class is exported. In the imported classes, temporary pointer declarations are automatically replaced by persistent pointer declarations. Non-imported classes are not modified. For example, if we define the `class A {B *b;}`, `class B {C *c;}` and `class C {A *a;}`, the importation of class `A` and `B` implies the following changes in the upgraded class definitions and methods : the attribute `B *b` in class `A` is replaced by the O_2 persistent pointer `o2_B b`. On the other hand the attributes `C *c` in class `B` and `A *a` in the non-imported class `C` remain unchanged. The methods of both imported and non imported classes are not modified. For an exhaustive description of O_2 persistent pointers structure and management see [3].

4 HyperPATH/O_2 : Three Levels of Integration

One of our requirements was to make as few changes as possible in the HBC module and definitely no changes in the *Hypermedia Toolkit*. Additionally, the node's contents (documents) are not stored in the O_2 database since in HyperPATH the persistence of the documents is under the responsibility of the compliant editors. We have examined the following solutions for the integration of HyperPATH with O_2 (see Figure 2):

1. **Weak connection** : O_2 only replaces some DB-Server and communicates with a HyperPATH client via remote procedure calls (RPC).
2. **O_2 is the persistence depositary of the HBC-objects** : We modify the C++ schema of the HBC-classes as little as possible, i.e. only the methods concerning the persistence module.
3. **Strong connection** : The HBC schema and thus the hypertext management itself is implemented in O_2. Note that most of the hypermedia functionalities of HyperPATH are implemented outside HBC (*M2000 protocol*, *Hypermedia Toolkit*).

The simplest solution for storing the HBC-objects is the substitution of mwdbms by an "O_2 database server" that simulates the interface of mwdbms (weak connection). The disadvantages of this solution become clear when we look at the steps necessary for storing an HBC-object. The database interface a) copies the C++ structure into a C structure and b) sends it by a remote procedure call (RPC) to the database server that c) receives the RPC, d) copies the C structure into a C++ structure and e) stores the structure in the O_2 database. Such a mechanism results in an extremely low performance (at least two data transformations each time) and low reliability (the transaction mechanism of O_2 is not used).

The second solution suggests that an O_2 database is the persistence depositary of the HBC-objects. The main idea is to build a persistent module that uses

O_2 in a transparent way to the rest of the HyperPATH architecture. This solution requires a redefinition of the front-end (database interface), i.e. the classes and the methods implementing the persistence of the HBC-objects.

The third solution (strong connection) makes possible to avoid the traditional type mismatch between programming languages and database systems. However it was not chosen in a first step since it requires a major rewriting of the existing code and because it is in contradiction with the objective of opening HyperPATH to various OODBMS's.

Finally, the second solution was adopted because of the encountered problems which will be described in detail in the following section. In the sequel we shall see that even in this case, the integration was not trivial and led us to three possible implementations of the HBC module.

5 "Open Integrations"

We first planned to provide persistence to the HBC hierarchy with different DBMS's (O_2 and ONTOS [1]). This heterogeneity should have been transparent to the above HyperPATH layers. The idea was to define for each DBMS and HBC-class a *persistent subclass*. For example, to the HBC class `Node` we add two subclasses `NodeO2` and `NodeONTOS`, which allow a node to be stored either in an O_2 or an ONTOS database. Then, after the importation of the existing HBC-class hierarchy into O_2, a HBC-class schema with multiple inheritance, as shown in Figure 3, is created.

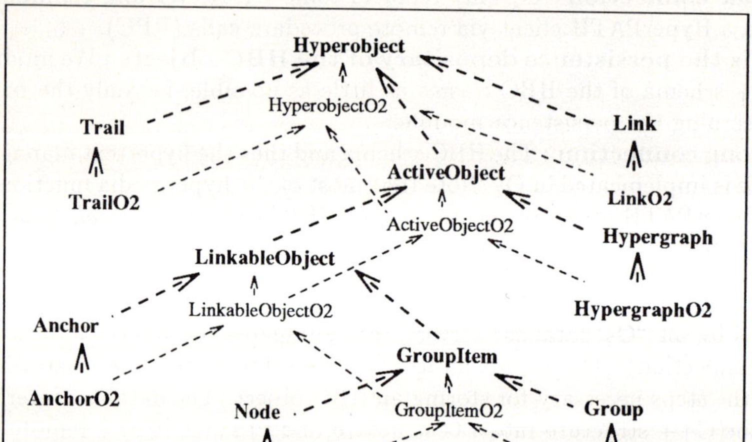

Fig. 3. HBC-Class Schema with Multiple and Simple Inheritance

Even if the use of multiple inheritance increases the complexity of the resulting C++ schema, it leads to a very natural solution for coupling HyperPATH with a variety of OODBMS's. It simply requires the definition of a minimal abstract interface between the HBC classes and their persistent subclasses whose implementation depends on the OODBMS used. But existing C++ restrictions for explicit casting rendered the implementation of this solution practically impossible. For a better understanding of the C++ inheritance mechanism and the difficulties encountered with this solution see [3].

In order to avoid the difficulties with multiple inheritance and keep the persistent module extensible to other OODBMS's we have investigated a schema based on simple inheritance where all HBC attributes that have to be stored are redefined in persistent subclasses. Looking at the resulting class hierarchy (bold classes and inheritance arcs in Figure 3) we can see that, at the O_2 level, we do not have any inheritance hierarchy and we create only 6 persistent subclasses for each of the HBC-classes that can be instantiated (**`Link`**, **`Hypergraph`**, **`Anchor`**, **`Node`**, `Group` and `Trail`). Likewise, HBC-values become persistent by adding the subclasses `ScriptO2`, and `PropertyListO2`.

The resulting C++ structure of each persistent subclass contains pairs of HBC-values with the same semantics : one attribute is defined at the database level (i.e. is an O_2 object) and one is inherited from the corresponding superclasses in the C++ schema (i.e. is a C++ temporary pointer). In order then to ensure consistency between non persistent and persistent HBC-values we are obliged to impose supplementary constraints during the object's creation and management. This solution turned out to be impractical because of the mismatch in object construction and management between C++ and O_2 [3].

In conclusion, the two possible solutions for providing HyperPATH with the possibility of using a variety of OODBMS's were abandoned. The following section describes the final solution that was chosen for the integration. It has the advantage that no rewriting of the *Hypermedia Toolkit* is necessary but it loses the generality of the "persistent subclass" solutions. The solution is specific to O_2 and does not represent an abstract interface to different DBMS's.

6 An O_2 Tailored Integration

6.1 The Hypermedia Basic Classes Schema

This solution consists in using the result of the importation of the whole HBC hierarchy as such. This implies that all HBC-classes become persistent via the O_2 persistent pointers. The C++ schema finally constructed is the same as the initial one given in Figure 2. After importation, the HBC-classes include the necessary methods for implementing the minimal interface with the rest of the HyperPATH modules as well as the methods for the persistence functionalities (`create`, `load`, `save` and `delete`). Thus the database interface and the persistence module still remain independent from the other HyperPATH modules.

6.2 Mapping of Object Identifiers

The mapping between object identifiers (MCIdentifiers) used in a hypermedia application and object identifiers of the database is another important issue. Since HBC-objects are accessed through their MCIdentifiers, one solution for a uniform integration of the two systems was the substitution of the MCIdentifier by the *OID* provided by O_2. In that way, we could "directly" access the HBC-objects in the O_2 database. This solution was rejected for two reasons :

1. The MCIdentifier is not only used by the HBC module but also to a large extent by the external interface. Thus, the uniform usage of the O_2 *OID* implies important modifications of HyperPATH modules that were not intended to be modified (e.g. *Hypermedia Toolkit* and *M2000 protocol*).
2. With a replacement of the MCIdentifiers with O_2 *OID*'s, we are faced with the same problem when attempting to read other hypertexts stored in different OODBMS (managing different *OID*'s).

Therefore, at least for reasons of openness, to each OODBMS system $\mathcal{S}$ associated with HyperPATH corresponds a table (dictionary) mapping MCIdentifiers to *OID*'s of system $\mathcal{S}$. When an object needs to be accessed, either there is an entry in the dictionary, or it has to be loaded from the database. Since each object has an attribute whose value is the MCIdentifier, loading is performed by querying the objects on their MCIdentifier attribute.

6.3 The Persistence Module

We have seen in Section 2.3 that the persistence of the HBC-objects in a hypertext is guaranteed by an object of the class `DbmsServer`, i.e. the dbmsserver loads and saves the HBC-objects. One way to represent this functionality in O_2 is to render the dbmsserver persistent and extend it such that it contains all HBC-objects of the corresponding hypertext. Since it is not possible to create an O_2 name for each new dbmsserver (C++ interface restriction), we define a named variable which contains a list of dbmsservers. In this way and because of the O_2 persistence transitivity, all HBC-objects become persistent together with their dbmsserver.

Now, all hypertexts can be accessed by the object manager through the persistent list of dbmsservers. Note that for HBC-values that are always attached to some HBC-object, access is provided implicitly by O_2. Each time we load a persistent HBC-object, its corresponding persistent HBC-values are loaded automatically by the C++ interface of O_2. Since we have replaced all temporary C++ pointers by persistent pointers, inverse references also become persistent and do not need to be reinitialized each time the dbmsserver loads an object from the database.

7 Conclusion and Future Work

One objective of the integration HyperPATH/O_2 was to deeply understand both products, in order to supply HyperPATH with query facilities. The integration has turned out to last much longer than expected and is not satisfactory as far as the performance is concerned. The major issues encountered during this experiment are related to the difficulties in reusing C++ code. Since HyperPATH uses C++ both as an object-oriented programming language and as an extension of C, we first encountered difficulties related to incompatibilities between object-oriented and imperative programming. In particular the coexistence of strong typing as implied by object-oriented models and explicit casting of C++ objects led to unexpected dead ends. We think that one major drawback of C++ is the lack of consistency in the type system conversion.

In addition, the mapping between two object identifiers (one for HyperPATH objects and one for O_2 objects) results in performance discrepancy. There is also some mismatch in object construction and management between C++ and O_2[3]. Thus, guidelines to let HyperPATH support both C/C++ and C++/OODBMS interfaces are quite ambitious and currently not easily implementable. This is why we advocate for a higher level interface between hypertexts and OODBMS's. For a more powerful integration between HyperPATH and O_2 (strong connection, see Section 4), the HBC layer of HyperPATH should be written in O_2C. Currently, the document's content is not stored in the O_2 database.For that, we plan to add a compliant editor able to communicate both with O_2 and HyperPATH. This experiment will also be useful for our next goal of providing HyperPATH with query capabilities [2].

In conclusion, constructing a HyperPATH persistence module extensible to a variety of commercial OODBMS's turned out to be a difficult task. Nevertheless, we believe that it was a necessary step towards the specification of common hypertext storage requirements for current database technology.

Acknowledgments

We are grateful to O_2Technology, Bull and Euroclid France for their support during this integration. Thanks also go to D. Plateau, A. Rizk, L. Sauter and A.M. Vercoustre for helpful discussions and to M. Ahedo and P. Dagand from Bull for fruitful exchanges on HyperPATH and their integration of HyperPATH with ONTOS.

References

1. M. Ahedo, P. Dagand, and L. Sauter. private communication, 1992.
2. B. Amann and M. Scholl. GRAM: A Graph Model and Query Language. In *Proc. of the ACM Conference on Hypertext (ECHT'92)*, pages 201–211, Milano, Italy, December 1992.
3. B. Amann, V.Christophides, and M. Scholl. HyperPATH/O2: Integrating Hypermedia Systems with Object-Oriented Database Systems (extended version). Technical Report 93-07, CEDRIC CNAM, Paris, France, April 1993.
4. B. Campbell and J. M. Goodman. HAM: A General Purpose Hypertext Abstract Machine. *Communications of the ACM*, 31(7):856–861, July 1988.

5. J. C. Chen, T. W. Ekberg, and C. Thompson. Querying an Object-Oriented Hypermedia System. In R. Mc. Aleese and C. Catherine, editors, *Hypertext: State of the Art*, pages 231–238. Billing & Songs, 1990.
6. N. Delisle and M. Schwartz. Neptune: A Hypertext System for CAD Applications. In *Proc. of the ACM Conf. on the Management of Data (SIGMOD'86)*, pages 132–143, Washington, D.C., May 1986.
7. O. Deux et. al. The Story of O_2. *IEEE Transactions on Knowledge and Data Engineering*, 2(1), March 1989.
8. L. Gallagher, R. Furuta, and P. D. Stotts. Increasing the Power of Hypertext Search with Relational Queries. *Hypermedia*, 2(1):1–14, 1990.
9. F. G. Halasz. Reflections on Notecards: Seven Issues for the Next Generation of Hypermedia Systems. *Communications of the ACM*, 31(7):836–852, July 1988.
10. F. G. Halasz and M. Schwartz. The Dexter Hypertext Reference Model. In *Proc. of the NIST Hypertext Standardization Workshop*, pages 95–133, Gaithersburg, National Institute of Standards and Technology, January 1990.
11. J. Nanard and M. Nanard. Using Structured Types to Incorporate Knowledge in Hypertext. In *Proc. of the ACM Conference on Hypertext (HYPERTEXT'91)*, pages 329–343, December 1991.
12. A. Rizk and L. Sauter. Multicard: An Open Hypermedia System. In *Proc. of the ACM Conference on Hypertext (ECHT'92)*, pages 4–10, December 1992.
13. H. A. Schütt and N. A. Streitz. *Hyperbase*: A Hypermedia Engine Based on a Relational Database Management System. In *Proc. of the European Conference on Hypertext (ECHT'90)*, pages 95–108, Versailles, France, November 1990.
14. K. E. Smith and S. B. Zdonik. Intermedia : A Case Study of the Differences between Relational and Object-Oriented Database Sytems. In *Proc. of the Conf. on Object-Oriented Programming (OOPLSA'87)*, pages 452–465, October 1987.
15. O_2 Technology. *The O_2 User's Manual, version 3.4*, June 1992.
16. U. K. Wiil and J. J. Leggett. *Hyperform*: Using Extensibility to Develop Dynamic, Open and Distributed Hypertext Systems. In *Proc. of the ACM Conference on Hypertext (ECHT'92)*, pages 251–261, Milano, Italy, December 1992.

Integrating Knowledge-based Hypertext and Database for Task-oriented Access to Documents

Jocelyne Nanard, Marc Nanard, Anne-Marie Massotte, Alain Djemaa, Alain Joubert, Henri Betaille, Jacques Chauché

LIRMM, UM CNRS/Université Montpellier II,
161 Rue Ada, 34392 Montpellier, FRANCE

Abstract. Dealing with huge technical document bases is a very hot topic for high-technology industry. We focus on a *full integration* of database, knowledge-based system and hypertext techniques to provide task-oriented-access to documents. An external semantic-driven structure is mapped onto documents owing to knowledge-based hypertext techniques. A database is used to keep the elements describing this structure and to help access documents. The overall structure organization is specified by a task model. A hypertext-like interface to the document base is used to navigate within the task-organized information space. Links dynamically result from complex computed relationships handled by the knowledge representation system between concepts and from the concepts anchorage into the text. A medium scale prototype for a real document base about nuclear engineering has been developed. The paper describes the principle of integrating the three techniques and discusses the implementation.

1 Introduction

Dealing with huge technical document bases is a very hot topic for high-technology industries such as space, nuclear engineering, electronics and so on. Tools that facilitate accessing, linking and sharing documents would greatly enhance engineers abilities to design and manufacture better products faster [7].

Databases are well suited to handling huge amounts of strongly structured information. Nevertheless, they are not so efficient at managing weakly structured information such as texts, pictures, videos, or sounds: rich but complex semantic structures which implicitly exist within documents are rarely represented in the database. Furthermore writing textual queries is not quite natural for a user. Thus, a lot of interface styles and techniques have tried to improve efficiency of the man-machine dialog. They often rely on an intelligent pre-processing of queries. Natural (or supposedly) user interactions, based on semi-natural or visual language, are turned into database queries. Such approaches are not truly integrated: they only take advantage of the pipe-lining of independent but complementary tools.

In this paper, we focus on another kind of approach which relies on a *full integration* of three techniques: databases, knowledge-based systems and hypertexts. The resulting unified tool provides a task-oriented access to technical documents. The underlying idea is to map an external semantic-driven structure onto documents owing to knowledge-based hypertext techniques [10]. A database is used to keep the elements describing this structure and to help access documents: it manages the anchoring between parts of texts and the associated concepts used in the knowledge representation system. A hypertext like interface to the document base is used to navigate within a task-organized information space. The overall organization of the structure is specified by the task model. For the user, such a system behaves like a hypertext: the user browses from one piece of information to another. But links are not static: they dynamically result both from complex relationships handled by the knowledge representation system between concepts and from the anchorage of concepts into the text. These relationships are specified as generic path expressions.

In order to prove the feasibility of the approach, we have developed a medium scale prototype for a real document base concerning nuclear engineering[1]. An abstract model of the approach is described in [11]. Two implementations sharing a similar structure have been developed, one relying on the knowledge-based hypertext engine MacWeb [10], the other one relying on Sybase. We have compared their behavior.

2 Task-oriented Access to Documents

2.1 Information Is Changing and Distributed in Several Documents

Engineering activities involve dealing with large and intertwined sets of structured documents. Industrial effectiveness and security directly depend on the delay to access a pertinent and usable piece of information according to a given situation.

Let us consider the official rule book that an engineer has to follow during design time. The slow but gradual evolution of the rules leads experts to frequently append application notes, as well as notes on new specifications or notes on exceptions that the designer should take care of.

Consequently information one needs is rarely described in a single document, but is distributed in a wide set of notes. Sometimes one note explicitly refers to a previous one, but semantic relationships between documents are rarely explicit within the documents themselves. Thus many tasks require expertise which is not due to their real complexity but to the lack of centralized up-to-date information.

The aim of the work is to take advantage of a task model to dynamically build *views* of the information available in the document base and to mask the evolution and the distribution of information in the initial document set for the user.

2.2 What Techniques Are Available to Help Access Documents?

Databases. Document management which relies directly on databases has two major drawbacks: they do not take advantage of document internal semantics and the interfaces are either too rigid or boring. Databases have been used for a long while to manage technical documents, and even to integrate documentation handling within design activity as it is done in Software Engineering Environments. The schema of such databases mainly relies only on the document *logical structure* [13, 3] which is specified by the SGML DTD of the documents [15]. However rich semantic structures between parts of texts are rarely elicited in document descriptions. Thus, document databases organized according to document structure do not take advantage of internal semantics to help access document content.

Ad hoc interfaces developed for specific applications such as CASE are efficient but lack generality and flexibility. Besides, writing general purpose queries is not exactly simple for a user. Graphical approaches such as those provided by Graphtalk [6] are useful for improving the man-machine dialog but only replace a textual formalism by a

---

[1] This work has been supported by Framentec (France)

visual one [14]. Even though these are more attractive, they are nearly as difficult to use as textual ones to correctly express complex queries. They do not really match the user's feeling and do not offer a task-driven interface to database.

Information Retrieval. Information retrieval is a classical method to find pertinent information in a document base. Techniques often rely on signature, which is a statistical characterization of a document profile. They uses probabilistic approaches to select the answer elements. Whereas they are now well tuned, their statistical foundations make them better suited to characterize large documents matching some query rather than to determine which part of a document contains the answer to the user's current problem. A lot of advanced work has been done in information retrieval [18], in order to take into account information embedded in hypertext structures. Attempts have also been done to take advantage of flexible hypertext interfaces to build graphical structure-oriented queries [5], based on the hypertext structure of documents, but they still lack powerful knowledge representation and reasoning means.

Text Understanding. Text understanding approaches, such as those based on Sowa graphs [2] seem promising for natural language based interfaces for the long term. They are currently more used to intelligently answer questions about toy texts rather than to help intelligent access to a wide documents base. Accordingly either the user has to express his queries in a very artificial "natural" language or the system fails to understand the real meaning of really free sentences.

Hypertext. Hypertext approaches rely on the notion of link between information. They provide a very efficient interaction metaphor known as navigation. First generation hypertext systems offer only hard-wired links. Second generation systems such as Aquanet [8] and MacWeb rely on a knowledge representation approach to describe relationships between information. Since this aspect is the main concern of the paper, it is no longer detailed here.

None of these approaches is by itself adequate and sufficient to provide the user with a task driven view of his document base. We propose to combine them into an integrated tool. The next section describes the aim of this tool.

2.3 What Kind of Task-oriented Access is Proposed?

Man is still the most important part of every industrial system. Increasing his efficiency implies the design of "user-centered systems" [12] *i.e.* systems that should rely on a task model. When a user is searching for information, he is less concerned with raw information than with data organized according to "his task current context". Thus, both querying and answering should be *adapted* to the task context. Among the many possibilities that provide a user with a task driven environment, we have studied the use of virtual documents that are organized as a hypertext to structure the user's information space according to an explicit task model.

Notion of Virtual Documents. Any user who has struggled with a document base may have hoped to find "the document part" specific to his current task context. Producing on the fly specific documents from existing knowledge is still a complex problem; it relies on techniques which are tuned on toy examples. Accordingly, we use a *simplified* solution to produce virtual documents. It consists in organizing *selected* *parts of existing documents*, collected as answers to a set of queries parameterized by a knowledge representation system into a specified document structure.

Generic Document Specification Based on a Task Model. The rules responsible for the document structure and the queries, which deliver its content, are *generic specifications for virtual documents.* Such specifications are kept in the task model: they characterize what kind of information is needed in a given task-context regardless to the distribution of information in the actual documents. Building such virtual documents involves a database accessing primary document parts and knowledge management to decide the document structure and contents.

Hypertext Interface Style. In order to reduce the burden on the user, it is preferable that accessing virtual documents is as simple as if the documents existed in the document base. The user has not to write queries but only to navigate, like with a hypertext, in an information space in which some documents are real and others virtual and in which links represent semantic relationships between informations. The user selects parts of a document as his new interest focus. According to the generic task model, the system proposes a list of documents connected to the selected focus, each of them concerning a specific task aspect. The user selects the new virtual document to be generated according to the information base. Then he goes on browsing, on his own.

The next section describes the technique used to build up the information space. It presents an overview of the system and describes its model.

3 An Approach Based on Macroscopic Semantics

The proposed approach relies on the "generalist metaphor" introduced in [11]. As opposed to an *expert*, a *generalist* has a wide but shallow view of a domain. He has in mind only limited but general knowledge *connected* to factual knowledge. This lets him know where he can find, *when needed*, some additional specific *information*.

Since the knowledge conveyed by the document base is too complex to be handled efficiently by an expert system, a generalist approach has been chosen: it takes advantage of general knowledge of the domain, (which is far easier to acquire and handle) and of factual knowledge about document contents which help select the relevant parts of documents with respect to a given task. It is then up to the user to deal with the provided information. The system does not intend to behave as an expert by reasoning on knowledge conveyed by documents but it will make a reasoning *about documents* to help the user find pertinent information.

3.1 The Approach Overview

In this section we present an overview of the functional model of the system. We show how integrating each technique (database, knowledge-based system and hypertext) contributes to modelling macroscopic semantics on a document base and thereby to providing task-oriented access to documents. As shown in fig. 1, a virtual hypertext organization is mapped onto the document base, but, unlike most hypertext systems, links between parts of documents are not hard-wired: they result from computed relationships that take advantage of general domain knowledge and of factual knowledge about documents. The model of the system relies on a three level organization:

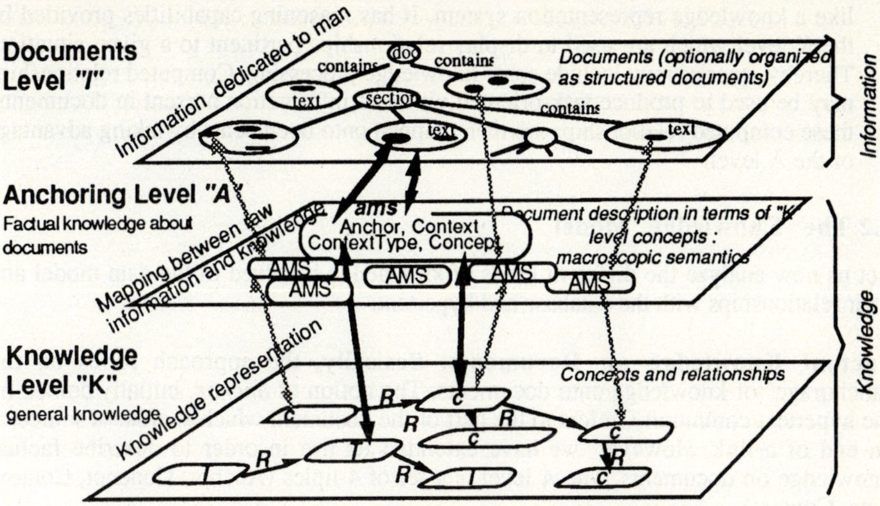

Fig. 1: Macroscopic knowledge about documents.

- The Information Level (noted *I*) contains documents which are considered as raw information mainly dedicated to man. Only man gives it sense: the picture of an engine in a document may be interpreted by man but is raw information for the system which is not concerned with image recognition. The *I* Level is accessed by a screen-oriented document server which provides anchor handling facilities.
- The Knowledge Level (noted *K*) helps reasoning. It contains general knowledge about the domain and about the tasks concerning the documents: the useful concepts and their relationships, as well as the task model. It is implemented as a knowledge representation system and uses an object-oriented formalism.
- The Anchorage Level (noted *A*) represents the macroscopic semantic of documents. It defines a mapping between *I* and concepts of *K*. It describes the anchorage of concepts within documents. For instance, it states that a given part of a picture is a 'sprinkler', or that a given paragraph specifies an 'exception' to a 'security rule'. This mapping is used as factual knowledge *about* documents but it does not aim at expressing the "knowledge embedded *in* "documents. The *A* level is implemented as a database.

The system behavior results from the *integration* of the three levels. Their activities are strongly intertwined. The system integrated architecture differs basically from those based on the pipelining of an autonomous intelligent preprocessing and a database. The different levels do not act individually, but they cooperate to help the user access pertinent information. Thus, the system functionalities cumulate the advantages inherent to its three levels. It may be used simultaneously:

- like a hypertext. The user starts from the *I* level and gets its answer in the *I* level. Semantic relationships between documents, elaborated by the cooperation of the *A* and *K* levels, provide dynamic hypertext links allowing the user to select an anchor in a document and browse through other documents.
- like a data base. Explicit queries sent to the A level are used to select parts from documents which directly match given properties.

- like a knowledge representation system. It has reasoning capabilities provided by the *K* level which are used to display relationships pertinent to a given situation. Thereby, queries may include some knowledge processing. Computed relationships may be used to produce task-oriented views of information present in documents: these computed relationships are then mapped onto documents by taking advantage of the A level.

3.2 The Knowledge Model

Let us now analyze the different kinds of knowledge involved in the data model and their relationships with the database and hypertext.

Factual Knowledge on Documents. Basically, the approach relies on the "anchorage" of knowledge onto documents. The notion of *anchor*, initially coined by the hypertext community, refers to the part of the document which is either a source or an end of a link. However, we have extended its use in order to describe factual knowledge on documents. The *A* level is a set of 4-uples (Anchor, Concept, Context type, Context):

- a *Concept* is an abstraction denoted by words, word groups or even sentences in texts. It corresponds to a meaningful concept for the domain or for the considered task. Concepts are represented as classes at the K level. The valid concepts list is initially provided by the documentation experts and incrementally updated and controlled as and when new concepts appear in new texts.
- an *Anchor* is a small part of a text which denotes a valid concept. Any part of a sentence which represents a given concept is its anchor in the text. Parts of text which do not denote valid concepts are insignificant for the system but convey information for the user. Anchors are used as triggers for browsing.
- a *Context* is the smallest part of a document, surrounding an anchor, which has an autonomous full meaning. Informally, a context is the minimal information which must be given to the user when its anchor is the target of the dialog. For instance, on a carburetor picture, a small part of the drawing is the anchor associated to the concept "idle mixture screw", its context is the part of the drawing that helps the reader identify its location on a real carburetor. Contexts, as well as concepts and anchors are not necessarily textual even though our system currently operates on textual anchors.
- a *Context Type* is an equivalence class defined on contexts, regardless of their associated concepts. It characterizes the average meta-speech present in the context. For instance, the notions of "definition", "exception" "proof",... are Context Types. Context types constitute the most original notion in this approach: they strongly enhance the semantics conveyed by instances of concepts. For instance, knowing that a given context in a document concerns an "exception to" a "security rule" is a rich piece of factual knowledge about the document.

Each of these 4-uples used to represent factual knowledge about documents (*A* level) is called an *anchor macroscopic semantic* abbreviated as AMS. AMS is far more detailed than a simple indexing by weighted key-words, as often used in information retrieval systems, but is far less detailed than a conceptual-graph based description needed for text understanding. For this reason we speak of *macroscopic semantics*.

For instance, let us consider the sentence: "*The valve Z48 should never be closed before the agent has previously checked... The previous rule may be overridden in case of emergency : if the fire alarm rings this valve has to be closed unconditionally.*"

This sentence is described as:

anchor	concept	context type	context
valve Z48	VZ48	general rule	*The...checked...*
this valve	VZ48	exception	*The valve...unconditionally*
fire alarm	FireAlarm	considerations	*The valve ...unconditionally*

Sets of AMSs precisely characterize the content of documents, but are not planned to elicit the text meaning. The original documents are not modified. We have used a relational database to implement AMSs which are queried when traversing hypertext links (e.g. : select "the contexts which have this type and concern the concept of this anchor"). The database contributes to the global system mechanisms but is neither its center nor one of its layers, it is just one of the integrated components. Description of AMSs results from a knowledge acquisition process based on a semi-automatic linguistic analysis of texts, run under the control of the documentation expert [11].

General Knowledge. Factual knowledge is connected to general knowledge on the domain, on the task and on documents and is used to improve the querying of the base. Complex queries takes advantage of general knowledge to represent generic hypertext links and constitute the basis for generic document specifications.

An Object-Oriented Knowledge Representation Model: An object-oriented model is used to represent the general knowledge and the task environment model. Each domain concept or task concept (e.g.: "hydraulic valve", "hand operated Valve", "security", ...) and each type of context (e.g.: "location", "operating rule"...) is described as a class. They are the *primary objects* of the K level. Inheritance between classes describes specialization between concepts (e.g: "an hydraulic valve" is a "Valve").

Direct relationships between concepts are described as Class attributes. For instance, the concept "Security" has an attribute <is concerned by> which is a set of concepts which contains the concepts "fire event" and "Chemical leak event"....

The task model currently involves the task of reading the documents. It relies on the notion of focus which characterizes the concepts that the user is currently concerned with. The kind of information accessible from a given focus depends upon the class organization of the concepts. Methods are used to specify what kind of virtual documents the reader can access from an instance of the concept. Methods are implemented as scripts which contain path expressions. The simplest methods are simple database queries, the most complex ones are generic document specifications. The reader expresses his focus by selecting an anchored text and traversing one of its links to a concept. The inherited methods become available in a menu. For instance, any concept for which a context "definition" is present in the document base, has a method named "give me examples about this".

Semantic Path Expressions: A *Semantic path expression* is a generic specification of semantic relationships between anchors and contexts. Path expressions specify generic hypertext links and have similarities to Hyperwalk [1]. The result of the evaluation of a semantic path expression on a given anchor, is the set of contexts which match the described relationship, i.e. the end of the actual path. As shown on fig. 2, an actual path is the concatenation of three elementary paths:

- a path from the source anchor to the concepts, according to context types. This first elementary path is specified by a parameterized database query.
- a path from concepts to other concepts. This elementary path is specified as a logical relationship between concepts that relies upon the K level description.
- paths from the destination concept to its associated context, according to the desired context types. These last elementary paths are also specified by a parameterized database query.

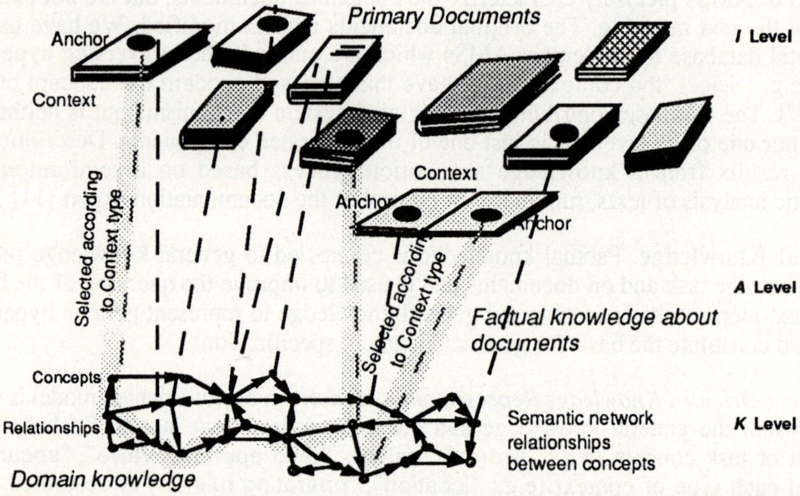

Fig. 2: Documents, anchorage, facts, knowledge, and paths. The light gray lines represent an actual path from a given anchor in a document to contexts in other documents, going through domain knowledge.

Let us consider the path expression named "give me examples of this", which is attached as a method to some concepts in the task model description. When the user selects a focus as anchor in a document, the associated concept class is considered and its methods become accessible to the user as part of his subtask environment. When the user triggers the method, the actual path is evaluated. It starts from the concept associated to the selected anchor and then as specified in the generic path, it reaches any of the concept specializations, and then returns to the document level through the context type "example". The answer is a set of parts from documents that contain examples of the given concept.

According to the hypertext metaphor, the answered information seems to be a document connected to the initial anchor by a link named "give me examples of this". Indeed only a generic specification of this link class is kept at the K level as a part of the task environment model. The same single script can be used on any given anchor.

Scripts may contain several path expressions which are organized into a document structure in order to produce more complex answers. They are then considered as generic document specifications leading to virtual documents which are evaluated only when they are accessed. Thus, they are always up to date and reflect the most recent information contained in documents introduced to the base. They are *views* of the information present in the base.

Generic Document Specifications. Generic document specifications are given in method scripts associated to concepts. They are used to synthesize virtual structured documents. This feature is the most powerful function of the system. The script language is WebTalk [9, 10]. Scripts specify both the logical structure [13] of the document (which is expressed by the SGML like part of the script), and the semantic structure (expressed by semantic path expressions).

Unlike a DTD, a WebTalk script provides a *constructive* description of the document. It specifies in an algorithmic manner the semantic conditions which cause a node to be present, omitted or repeated by taking advantage of path expressions. Furthermore, the content of a terminal node is specified as a mix of constant text and semantic path expressions results. Semantic path expressions may include variables.

The results of a script interpretation are in the form of a tree-structured document. The generation of the actual structure is controlled by the evaluation of the results of queries. The document content is typically built from *contexts* selected as semantic path expressions values. Thus, in a document produced by the evaluation of a script, information (i.e. "Contexts" which have been selected in the document base as matching some properties) is organized into a specific document structure. Scripts specify *task-oriented views* of the document base. Note that the term "Views" may be seen as a generalization of the database view notion : it has the same purpose but does not rely on the same technique.

4 The System Architecture

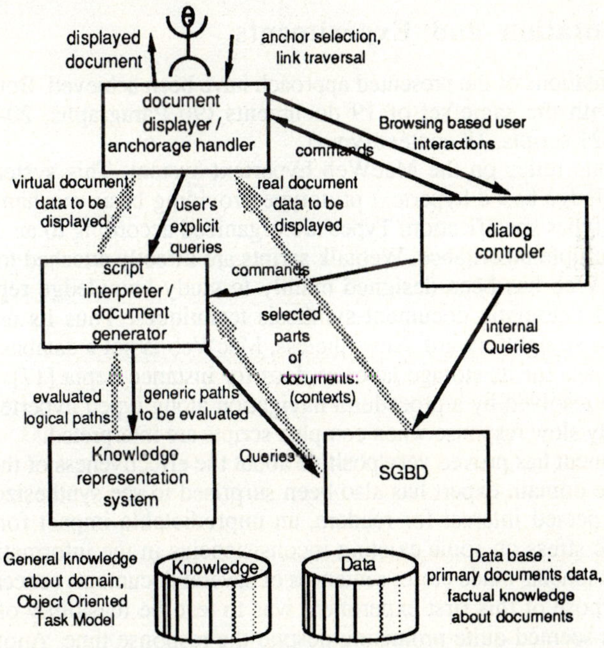

Fig. 3: The system architecture.

The global architecture of the system has important similarities with the Dexter model [4]. It contains five main components (fig. 3):

- the *dialog-controller* manages the coordination between the four other modules. It is usually called the "RunTimeLayer" in the Dexter model.
- the *script interpreter* produces structured documents by concatenating constant data specified in the scripts and variable values obtained as answers to queries specified in scripts. The script language looks like a SGML markup in which the document text is replaced by queries which specify the intended semantics. Structures like alternative and iteration help express complex document semantic structures. Scripts are parameterized by variables which are set by the dialog-controller.
- a *screen-oriented interactive document displayer*, with the organization and functionalities being very similar to those specified for the "Within Component Layer" of the Dexter model, including the anchoring mechanisms.
- a *database* which stores the description of anchorage, the documents and the elementary relationships between primary objects.
- a *knowledge representation system* which computes semantic relationships between the *primary objects* of the K level.

The database and the knowledge representation system both act as a Dexter "Storage Layer". The dialog controller is responsible for the global intelligent behavior of the system. Its primary function is to convert user interactions with documents into semantic path expressions. Another important function is to send scripts to the interpreter to prepare specific documents.

5 Implementation and Experiments

Two implementations of the presented approach have been achieved. Both of them have been tested with the same set of 19 documents (90 Paragraphs, 204 concepts, 20 relationships, 21 scripts, 18 context types).

The first one relies on the MacWeb hypertext system. This system is a general purpose knowledge based hypertext prototype providing basic mechanisms to handle link and node types specification. Types are organized according to an object-oriented model with multiple inheritance. Webtalk scripts are directly attached to node types as methods. MacWeb has been designed mainly to study knowledge representation in hypertexts and automatic document synthesis techniques. Thus its use for such an application was straightforward. Nevertheless, MacWeb is not a database and does not rely on a database for its storage layer as does for instance Sepia [17]. Thus, most of the queries are resolved by a procedural navigation along typed hypertext links which causes a slightly slow response when complex scripts are interpreted.

The experiment has proved very positive about the effectiveness of the approach for readers and the domain expert has also been surprised to see synthesized documents: beyond the expected interest for readers, an unpredictable impact for authors is to directly put the stress on some existing inconsistencies in the information base since synthesized documents made closer sentences of several documents concerning the same point! The purpose of this first experiment was to test the feasibility of the approach and the results seemed quite promising despite the response time. Another important point concerns the semi automatic elicitation of AMS from the initial document base. Improving this point is currently under way.

In order to progress towards a real use of this approach, a second implementation has been tested on a Next computer. It relies on Sybase. Since the stress was on the test of the response time, little effort has been done at the K level which has been, for the first time, simulated in Sybase at the price of an obvious lack of efficiency for that level. Scripts directly include SQL queries. The results of this experiment stressed the need to optimize the script language in order to minimize the number of queries sent to the base. The response time is quite correct when the user navigates with a simple browsing relying on only a few queries for each interaction. But it is not as good as expected when a script needs many queries to build a complex path needed by a document. The experiment has shown that the response time is far more determined by the number of queries sent to the database server than by the size of the base or by the complexity of the queries. For complex scripts the response time for both systems is surprisingly similar (i.e. about 20 seconds to generate a 5 page specific document). As a result of this experiment, it seems necessary to use both a database to handle the AMS, which are very numerous when working on large document sets, and a knowledge representation system which operates faster on the concept sets whose size remains small and is not proportional to the document base.

6 Discussion

This approach is naturally very different from an intelligent query preprocessor. It relies on a deep integration and cooperation between the different tools which boost their own efficiency. The whole approach is task-oriented. It aims at providing the user with a simple means to access the needed information according to a given situation. Such information is pre-classified into generic specifications of documents according to a model of the task environment. The most probable or frequent queries are abstracted as path expressions and kept in the system as scripts attached to concept classes.

The whole system behaves like a hypertext. The knowledge described in the K level makes it possible to provide its generic description in terms of an object-oriented task environment model. Generic specifications of documents and generic path expressions are the projection of the nodes and the links of this virtual hypertext on the task environment model. They express the kind of information that a user may access in a given context. Thus, this hypertext is not a simple set of hard wired links on the initial document base. It is a task-oriented organization mapped onto the information which was initially present in the documents. The user triggers the synthesis of a virtual document by selecting a focus and a script in a previous one and navigates in an information space. Since documents are virtual, they are always up to date and reflect any elicited information present in the existing documents as and when new documents are introduced in the base.

Nevertheless, these predefined path expressions are not the only way to navigate. When needed, the user can write his own queries to explicitly pilot the underlying mechanisms, like in a classical database, but this is not the real aim of the system. Preparing scripts, as well as eliciting domain knowledge is a task which has to be conducted with the help of a domain expert. Nevertheless, the chosen object-oriented structure makes it possible to enhance the task environment model incrementally by adding new methods as and when the user highligths missing helpful scripts.

This experiment has shown that complex techniques such as databases, hypertext and knowledge representation systems are complementary and can be usefully mixed to build task oriented environments. It also clearly indicates that the fundamental basis of the second generation hypertext approach is the mapping of a strong structure onto an initially weakly structured set of information.

The basis of the approach is now well mastered but a lot of improvements have to be made to turn the prototype into an actual full scale system. Both the response time of document synthesis and elicitation of the knowledge about the primary documents are still to be tuned up.

7 References

1. Amann B., Scholl M. "Gram: A graph data model and query language", Proc. ECHT'92, 4th ACM Conf. on Hypertext, D. Lucarella, J. Nanard, M. Nanard, P. Paolini (edts), ACM Press, Milano, Dec. 1992.
2. Bérard-Dugourd A. et al., "Natural language analysis using conceptual graphs", Proc. Int. Computer Science Conference'88, Hong Kong, 1988.
3. Glushko R.J., Proc. 2nd ACM Conf. on Hypertext HTX'89, ACM Press, Baltimore, p. 51-60, 1989.
4. Halasz F., Schwartz M., "The Dexter hypertext reference model", Workshop on hypertext standardization, 1990, pp. 95-133.
5. Hoffman M., Achmezko S., "Graphical Structure-Oriented Search in a Hypertext System", Proc. 3rd Int. Conf. DEXA'92, Springer-Verlag, Valencia, 1992.
6. Khlat M., Jeulin P., *Graphtalk Reference Manual*, Rank Xerox, 1987.
7. Malcolm K.C. et al., "Industrial strength Hypermedia: Requirements for a large engineering enterprise", Proc. of the 3rd ACM Conf. HTX'91, ACM Press, San Antonio (Tx), p.13-24, 1991.
8. Marshall 91 et al. "Aquanet, a hypertext tool to hold your knowledge in place", Proc. of the 3rd ACM Conf. HTX'91, ACM Press, San Antonio (Tx), 1991.
9. Nanard M., Nanard J., "MacWeb, a tool for building documents", Proceedings of WOODMAN'89 (Workshop on Object-Oriented Document Manipulation), Rennes (France), Mai 1989, in BIGRE n° 63-64, Mai 1989, ISSN 0221-5225.
10. Nanard J., Nanard M., "Using types to incorporate knowledge in Hypertext", Proc. of the 3rd ACM Conf. HTX'91, ACM Press, San Antonio (Tx), 1991.
11. Nanard M., Nanard J., Massotte A.M., Chauché J., Djemaa A., Joubert A., Betaille H., "The generalist metaphor : Macroscopique Knowledge Acquisition and Use on a Technical Document Base", JAVA'93, St Raphaël (France), 1993.
12. Donald A. Norman, S. Draper edts, *User Centered Systems Design*, Lawrence Erlbaum Associates, Publishers, 1986.
13. Quint V., Vatton I., "Combining Hypertext and Structured Documents in Grif", Proc. 4th ACM Conf. on Hypertext ECHT'92, D. Lucarella et al. (edts), ACM Press, Milano, Dec. 1992.
14. Ramos H.B., "Design and implementation of a graphical SQL with generic capabilities", Proc. 1st Int. Work. on Interfaces for Database Systems, Springer-Verlag, R.E. Cooper (ed.), Glasgow, 1992.
15. Information Processing - Text and Office systems - Standard Generalized Markup Language (SGML), ISO 8879, 1986.
16. Silberschatz A., Stonebraker M., Ullman J., "Database Systems: achievements and opportunities", CACM Vol. 34, n°10, Oct. 1991.
17. Streitz N. et al., "Sepia: a collaborative hypertext writing system", Proc. 4th ACM Conf. on Hypertext ECHT'92, D. Lucarella et al (edts), ACM Press, Milano, Dec. 1992.
18. Thompson R.H., Croft W.B., "Support for browsing in an intelligent text retrieval system", Int. J. Man Machine Studies, 30, 1989, p. 639-668.

Reengineering of User Interfaces for the Migration of Database Applications

Dimitris Karagiannis, Eckhard Ortwein, University of Vienna
Jochen Gag, Ploenzke Systeme GmbH, Wiesbaden

University of Vienna, Dept. of Knowledge Engineering,
Bruennerstr. 72, A-1210 Vienna
e-mail: dk@ifs.univie.ac.at

Abstract. Reengineering of user interfaces (RUI) integrates useful, old technologies and modern concepts of UI design. In particular, RUI can be applied for the migration of business relevant database applications on host systems. Their life-cycle can be extended by distributing presentation and dialogue functionality to an intelligent front-end. Operationally, direct benefits can be realised by increasing the user's productivity. Strategically, RUI can trigger the stepwise migration of old software systems. RUI-strategies minimise migrational risk and can be flexibly applied where user acceptance is minimal or the economical benefits are maximal. However, the realisation of a successful RUI-project requires complex knowledge in a broad range of subjects. This knowledge has to be covered by a generic process model. Our goal is to present an integral approach that involves an extensive preliminary analysis, a reverse engineering process and a forward engineering process. This concept - currently developed with Ploenzke, Inc. - can be generically applied for dialogue solutions differing in complexity.

1. Introduction

The demand for integrated and open applications based on distributed hardware- and software-architectures is the consequence of the revolution in IC technologies. The replacement of monolithic host systems by client server systems should be a mere question of time.

1.1. Generational change

However, the generational change from transaction-controlled host systems to event-driven workstation applications is a slow process. The replacement of an old system by a newly developed application is a high-risk procedure since most of the analytical knowledge about the old system's functionality is implicitly embedded in the details of its implementation. Furthermore, why should old systems be entirely redeveloped, if the new systems just fulfil the same functionality. This is particularly true for the useful database systems in administrational work environments. A stepwise migration seems to be the appropriate approach for complex systems in order to meet the challenges of the IC-revolution.

Innovation and migration. Innovation is the "narrow path between stagnation and revolution" which simultaneously has to control the stepwise introduction of new technologies and the support of the existing [1]. Migration examines in which ways new technologies can be feasibly and economically integrated in the existing hardware, software and network infrastructure of an organisation. Thus, migration concepts are not only important for the applying side but also for the developing one. In organisations, concepts of migration are applied in different situations and at different levels of abstraction [2]:

- Hardware downsizing, e.g. from Unisys-Host to AS/400 and PC-LANs,
- Migration from a hierarchical DB to a relational one, e.g. from IMS to DB-2,
- Language Transformation, e.g. from COBOL 74 to COBOL 85 and
- Outsourcing of personnel activities, e.g. Third Party Maintenance.

This paper focuses on UI migration from terminal interfaces of transaction controlled database systems to dialogue interfaces of modern workstation applications [3].

Requirements for migration. The essential basis and the most important requirement for a successful migration project of any kind is the broad knowledge of the existing information processing environment. In order to provide this knowledge, methods, concepts and tools of *reengineering* - in particular *reverse engineering* - have to be applied for program understanding, redevelopment, restructuring or recycling and reuse of software components.

The significant processes of change in software development have to be covered by methods of "forward" engineering. These involve a new orientation in application development, the evolution of efficient network architectures and the use of improved process models. The methods, particularly, have to encompass new and high requirements for the UI design that are incorporated by usability engineering. The diversity of integrated systems aimed at can only be achieved if the use of systems is easy to handle, quick to learn and standardised.

UI migration. The upgrading and qualified enhancement of the UI of an existing system is induced by different motivations and objectives, e.g.

- complicated interaction mechanisms are to be easied,
- functional enhancement of existing systems requires intelligent workstations,
- migration from batch processing to interactive systems requires a new UI,
- distribution of task control between user, UI and functional core is inefficient.

In order to achieve user friendly mechanisms in human-computer interaction (HCI), terminals have to be replaced by intelligent workstations. The ultimate goal is the system-wide standardisation of HCI. This unfolds a new dimension in the use of workplace technologies, e.g. by the use of standard software. The transmissions between host and workstation will be reduced to pure application data and the number of host-terminal-transactions will decrease. In this way, network resources will be set free and networking cost reduced.

1.2. Generic methods

It has become clear that the migration of existing systems is a complex task which involves a broad range of activities. The generic methods described below represent the state-of-the-art in RUI and have partly influenced our own work. Each method, however, covers just partially the requirements drawn above.

REDO: Process model for reengineering. The REDO method (Reengineering, Validation and Documentation of Systems) was developed within the ESPRIT project and describes the generic activities to analyse existing applications through reengineering techniques. A system of integrated (or at least integratable) methods and tools eases software maintenance and, thereby, improves its efficiency [4]. On the data level a repository assures the consistency of the data for all methods and tool and fulfils more functionality than a simple data dictionary. The reverse engineering concepts, developed in REDO, can generally be applied for the analysis of existing software-systems. This is specifically true for UI migration.

ANDES: Analysis and redesign of user interfaces. The ANDES method (UI Analysis and Redesign) was developed within REDO to support the analysis and redesign of user interfaces, primarily of technical applications like systems in production, design or simulation [5]. It was intended to make concepts of software ergonomics transparent and applicable for software engineers. A paper based tool-set (checklists) and a tool for the analysis process were developed. ANDES differentiates the three phases *analysis*, *redesign* and *implementation*. It focuses on the analysis and redesign phase and does not discuss implementation details (since the implementation is extremely dependent on the UI tools used).

FOCUS: Knowledge-based Front Ending. FOCUS (Front Ends to Open and Closed User Systems) is another ESPRIT project and introduces a generic, in this sense platform independent, software architecture for the front ending of mainly scientific and technical host systems [6]. A front end has to combine some host systems or back ends in one UI and to integrate enhanced functionality and co-operative, knowledge-based assistance. These front ends are referred to as knowledge-based front ends (KBFE). The software architecture has been modeled to meet the criteria distribution, modularity and portability. The central component is the Communication Module acting as an associated communication protocol. FOCUS assumes that the host system is a black box, i.e. reverse engineering activities are restrained to the analysis of input and output. Thus, the HCI mechanisms and the full potential of UI migration are hard to explore.

CRIM: Reverse Engineering and reengineering of user interfaces. The CRIM (Centre de Recherche Informatique de Montréal) pursues the development of an open tool for the reverse engineering of source code and RUI from a very technical point of view [7]. It is assumed that reverse engineering is not yet completely automatable. An interactive processing approach was chosen to support the developer in understanding the program. It differentiates four levels of abstractions for the representation of source code and combines methods for structural representations on

the implementation and structural level and methods for behavioural representation on the functional and the domain level.
In comparison to ANDES and FOCUS, this approach does not centre on the qualitative description of a process model. The major goal is the automatic transformation of the UI from the source code into a designated UI specification language which can then be used as input for the design of the new UI.

2. Reengineering of User Interfaces

2.1. Definition

We define *RUI* for existing software systems as a migration process which comprises

- the integration of the UI of one or more host systems in a modern application architecture, particularly by distributing their dialogue functionality,
- the replacement of terminals by workstations and
- the possible distribution of the system's functionality to several platforms by restructuring, modification or enhancement.

The term *front ending* is more comprehensive. It comprises the notion of a new development. *Terminal emulation*, in contrast, cannot be described as RUI since two different UIs with divers functionality coexist.

Business relevance. We examine transaction-controlled database applications with alphanumeric interfaces as target systems for RUI. The goal is the realisation of an event-driven system with a direct manipulative UI [8]. The number of workstations can be variably set up, even a stepwise migration process is possible. The coexistence of workstations and terminals is guaranteed. Terminals can be operated where they are still functional and economical. The initial resistance of older users and the demand of the new user generation can be met at the same time. The know-how of development and maintenance personnel can be diversified and suited to the new requirements.

Organisational change. The introduction of modern UIs is not only justified by the job enrichment originating from user-friendly systems. It also has to meet the strategic challenges to develop IC-systems like DSS and MIS. Since management tasks regularly do not follow a scheme, a UI based on an intuitive interaction model is the critical factor of success for strategic systems.

2.2. Design options

The idea of co-operative and distributed systems is based on the concept to exploit the benefit of the single components and avoid their setbacks. The benefits of a workstation as a front end to a host system result in an increased *user acceptance*, the *distribution* and *integration* of applications and strategic and operative payoffs. These benefits can be accomplished in many cases of organisational change by RUI. They can be defined as design options for different dialogue solutions. These options have to be determined in an organisation-wide *dialogue concept* for software ergonomics, integration and distribution.

Software ergonomics. Many systems provide a remarkable amount of "hidden" know-how and user benefits because the usability of the system is too complicated. RUI can recover user acceptance by the integration of a new, ergonomically designed UI. The more workstations with GUIs are installed, the harder it is to preserve the acceptance for the terminal interfaces. An organisation-specific ergonomic concept has to determine general methods for the integration of usability engineering mechanisms within the development routines of the organisation. Direct manipulation has become a de-facto standard for HCI. The several metaphors are mainly realised by GUIs. The ergonomic characteristics that can be accomplished just by the use of these windowing systems are:

- UI design supporting a particular look & feel (e.g. standards like CUA),
- "simultaneous" run of different applications in multiple windows,
- context-sensitive on-line systems for help and error handling,
- manual data exchange between applications by cut-copy-paste techniques,
- undo-redo mechanisms to avoid errors and support exploitative learning,
- syntactic and semantic macro support to combine commands and make individual customising possible,
- static and dynamic default values to simplify HCI and reduce error inputs.

Integration. The integration of applications is implicitly possible by manual data exchange which is realised by the underlying window systems. Additional mechanisms which have to be explicitly implemented represent a higher level integration concept:

- automatic data exchange, e.g. DDE and OLE in Windows 3.x,
- the integration of host systems with standard software functionality,
- the integration of system-wide communication services like e-mail, fax, auto-dialling systems and teleconferencing,
- data integration among host systems by the new UI.

In this sense, RUI can play a major role to substantiate office communication systems that have to achieve a functional integration or symbiosis with standard applications. This often implies a solution that adds an office communication system to the existing environment.

Distribution. By distributing the UI to a workstation, RUI can produce directly measurable benefits. Local processing offers a much better response performance than host processing. Host resources are set free and can be used for mass data storage and processing. On a conceptual level, integration and distribution are two views on the same problem. Integration combines functions and data of different network knots. By distribution, autonomous but logically coherent systems are designed and destined on different network knots [9]. For RUI, three different concepts are the focal points for a generic distribution concept:

- semantic and syntactic evaluation of the integrity of input data,
- assistance functionality by providing local static data that can be periodically updated (uploaded or downloaded), e.g. for symbolic representation of data, additional information or on-line retrieval systems (CD-ROM etc.),

- completion of functionality by the development of autonomous add-on-systems, e.g. hypertext systems as front ends to relational databases, forecast and statistical systems or knowledge-based configuration systems.

2.3. Dialogue solution

In adjustment to the concepts of ergonomics, integration and distribution, we present a three-step, business-relevant concept for RUI. In general, the described design options can be accomplished by the three dialogue solutions non-integrating, application-integrating and server-based [10] (fig. 1).

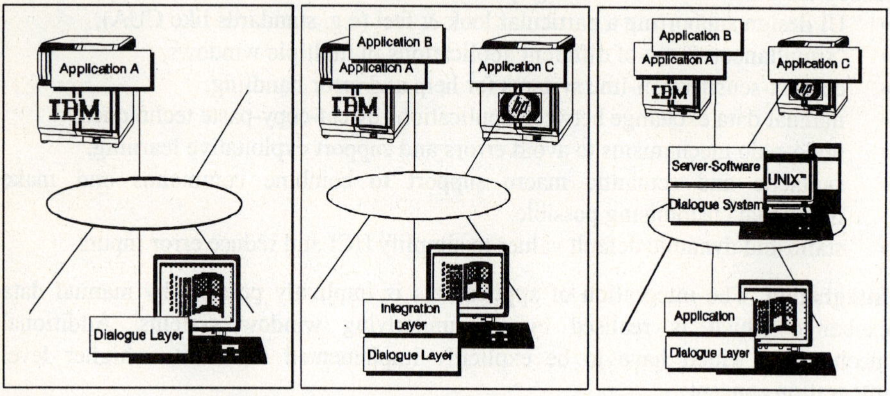

Figure 1 (a) (b) (c): Diverse Dialogue solutions

We point out that the non-integrating dialogue solution is the basis for the application integrating solution. A server-based solution already goes beyond a reengineering variant, but can be build upon an application-integrating solution.

Non-integrating solution. A non-integrating dialogue solution represents besides terminal emulation the easiest way to blend a conventional host systems by a GUI (see fig. 1a). The host application does neither have to be modified nor integrated with other applications. Technically, we distinguish two possibilities to develop a non-integrating solution. A *presentation-oriented* solution captures the screen data stream (e.g. the virtual terminal protocol IBM-3270). Map objects interpret the behaviour of the host application by passing data to the UI and transforming the user input in host system commands. This solution is barely bound to any premises. The use of mainframe resources can be reduced by 5-35%. A *dialogue-oriented* solution uses the fact that many transaction controlled systems comprise a transaction processing part and a dialogue part (often the TP-monitor). By replacing the dialogue software on the workstation, the communication processes can be modified (e.g. using LU 6.2 under APPC reduces use of mainframe resources by 60-80%). A dialogue oriented solution, however, may be constrained by the structure of the host systems and the necessity that the system still has to run on host terminals.

Application-integrating solution. On the basis of a non-integrating solution several host systems can be logically integrated as one front end in the UI. In addition to the dialogue software, an integrating mini-application is realised (see fig. 1b). All integrational design options discussed above can be realised. In contrast to the expensive and technically pretentious development of co-operative systems on the host side, co-operative processing of several host applications through data integration on the workstation side is relatively easy to accomplish. This solution, however, bears the drawback that redundant and superfluous data is transferred and the performance may be influenced.

Server-based solution. A very elegant dialogue solution promising higher performance for the development of complex systems like DSS is represented by the server-based solution (see fig. 1c). A server takes the role as a flexible data platform. The front end controls the data access of the server on the host. The server can access the data in all ways described above or by additional methods like embedded SQL-statements and complete or selective file transfer. For the front end the data access has to be transparent. The difficult updating and locking mechanisms also have to be implemented on the server. A server-based solution yields an entirely new system structure. The front end is no longer host-controlled. The server programs are small and simple and the whole system can be comfortably modularised.

3. Management process model for RUI

A software engineering (SE) concept - which integrates proved conventional concepts of SE and innovative, knowledge-based approaches in reverse and forward engineering - is the foundation for a RUI management process model. Likewise, the different dialogue solutions which are build up on each other but vary heavily in complexity call for a generic and modular process model that can be applied for all RUI processes.

3.1. Conceptional SE base

A conceptual SE base involves primarily methods of information engineering, reverse engineering and usability engineering in order to ensure software quality in terms of classical features like robustness and fault tolerance and new features, in particular usability, integration and distribution. These methods have to mutually correspond and embed innovative concepts described below.

Information engineering. Information engineering supports the organisation wide design of data and function models by use of repositories. In this case, the design of meta knowledge is extraordinarily important. A RUI meta model - using a RUI repository - has to fulfil the standard requirements of data dictionaries and CASE-repositories and, additionally, integrate the reverse life cycle by using CARE tools (Computer Aided Reverse Engineering). Suited CARE tools have to invert knowledge which is embedded in the implementation of the host system and transfer it into the repository. This data can be modified and used as input for another CASE cycle. The information management model of our RUI approach involves *four levels* *of abstraction* for the reverse engineering of the host system which are matched by *four equivalent development phases* for the forward engineering of new applications (see fig. 2). Knowledge and reasoning techniques are related to every level. The overall idea is the integration of CASE, CARE, hypertext and knowledge-based technologies. The basis for an efficient development process is the transformation of the source code of the host system into an intermediary, context-free language and its storage in a repository [11]. This means that every tool involved in the development process has to place its data at the disposal of the other tools.

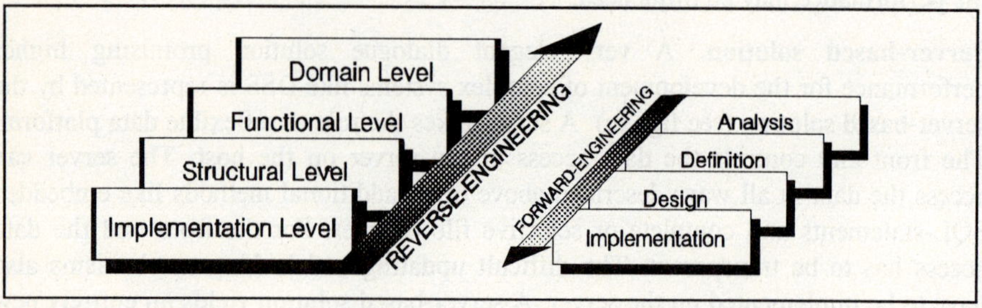

Figure 2: Levels of abstraction and phases of development

Reverse engineering. The idea of reverse engineering originated to solve the maintenance problem, e.g. to reduce the cost of program understanding of undocumented systems. We claim, however, that reverse engineering is a necessary complement for the entire system life cycle. The concepts of reverse engineering and reengineering for RUI aim at the integration of the old system into a new architecture. Most systems have been developed following a process model, e.g. the waterfall model. Therefore, it seems necessary to invert this process to recover the specification of the system. It is not absolutely clear if reverse engineering will be completely automatable in a reasonably efficient way, but - as shown at the CRIM- a systematic, machine-assisted methodology can be developed. Formal methods help to realize migrational tasks at the source code level. They can be used to restructure (e.g. to eliminate unconditioned branches) and remodularize the system, to separate I/O or DB interfaces calls (e.g. to make a system portable) and to recover reusable components. Related work in design recovery recreates design abstractions from a combination of code, existing documentation, human expertise and general knowledge about problem and application domains [12].

Usability engineering. The UI design can amount to an essential share of cost (50-70%) in software development. A standardised approach and the use of tools for design and implementation of UIs are therefore obligatory. Usability engineering is an enhanced SE concept covering these requirements and taking an expanded life cycle into consideration (e.g. analysis of predecessor systems and analysis after operation) [13]. Although usability engineering just complements the conventional SE techniques, it must be accompanied by organisational changes in software development since user centred design techniques and user participation are employed [14]. Specifically, UI prototyping becomes an inherent element of the development process. Concerning knowledge-based approaches, we are focusing on the rule-based generation of the UI from the specification of the old interface and the data model of the new system. This generation must follow ergonomic guidelines.

3.2. Generic model

Having set up the conceptual SE framework, we can present our generic RUI model. The model clearly goes beyond the approaches described above, but certainly has not reached the necessary depth yet [15]. It represents the substructure of a detailed process model and can be used as starting point for a pilot project in RUI. It has to be detailed and refined in several iterations. Besides, an integral, business-relevant perspective is created by including a preliminary analysis which can be incorporated in the business strategies of the organisation.

Management process. The generic model encompasses three main processes:

- the *preliminary analysis* to identify potential target systems for RUI,
- the four-step *reverse process* to analysis the targeted systems on the different levels of abstractions (see fig. 2), and
- the four-step *forward process* to develop the new dialogue application following the guidelines of usability engineering.

As a result of the preliminary analysis, the most suited dialogue solution is assigned to any chosen target system. Depending on this choice, the reverse process is just partly executed. For all dialogue solutions the first two reverse steps on the implementation and the structural level are mandatory. For the non-integrating solution, the transfer to the forward process can then be made. For an integrating application, more valuable knowledge can be acquired by passing to the functional level. On the fourth abstraction level, knowledge has to be obtained for a server-based solution. The first phase of the forward process (the analysis) can be started at the same time when the reverse process is entered. But the forward process can only proceed to the design phase after the reverse process has been completed. Since the model gives the impression of a linear sequence, it has to be stated that evaluation is a central activity of each activity in the model. Neither is reverse engineering a clear bottom-up and automatable process, nor is forward engineering a strict top-down process. Interactive analysis and iterative development are key issues to be modelled. Task analysis and task modelling are central and integrated processes which overlap the reverse and the forward process.

Preliminary analysis. The preliminary analysis is a complex process that combines the following main activities:

- classification of workplace types to identify the *business-relevant* target systems,
- portfolio analysis to identify the *technically relevant* target systems, and
- assignment of the targeted systems to the appropriate dialogue solution, their combination to integral packages and a cost-benefit analysis for the packages.

A pilot project serves to specify the organisational changes in application development and to form the organisation wide concepts for applying the design options described above.

Reverse processing. The reverse process contributes to program understanding, i.e. the analysis of the host system, by answering the questions what, why, how and where in the system things do happen. These questions are asked on the four levels of abstractions to which methods, knowledge and reasoning can be related. The answers raise enough meta and reference knowledge for a profound understanding of the system. The activities on the first two levels of abstraction - mandatory for all dialogue solutions - represent knowledge in structural form and are data-driven. The activities on the third and fourth level represent knowledge in behavioural form and are model-driven.

On the implementation level, the *transformation* of the source code produces a technical and syntactical understanding which, ideally, is recorded in the repository. Views on this level are generated by compiler technology, syntactical manipulation and semantic knowledge of the programming language. All views on the following levels are derived from the transformational results. Optionally, the system may be technically redocumented and formal methods may be applied for restructuring.

On the structural level, the *structure analysis* explicitly identifies dependencies among program components and represents its knowledge in different views, in particular data and function models. A first but superficial semantic understanding is created. The structural analysis is the central concept of the understanding process and involves three many activities:

- a logical reverse analysis to gain detailed insight into the system by applying reverse engineering techniques (to derive the data and the function model),
- a communication analysis to examine the physical system components (OS, DB, TP monitor etc.) and to locate function specific bottlenecks, and
- a task analysis of the system's UI to investigate the HCI components (user, presentation, dialogue).

The task analysis of the HCI is the starting point to design RUI-specific automatable processing mechanisms. By capturing the screens of the host system and modeling the dependencies among the screens, the UI of the host system can be stored in the repository (based on a suited scheme). This *user interface model* which must be linked to the data model is the basis for an automated, particularly rule-based, generation of the new UI.

The *functional analysis* - on the third abstraction level - describes the functionality and logic of the system much more detailed which is important for the integration of systems. Each view on this level is the abstract representation of functional equivalents but different implementations. The task analysis is continued by examining the dialogue control, especially the transaction mechanisms, and the functional quality of the system. The UI model is expanded by these results. The transaction model can semantically be classified on a higher level than the function model. Overall, techniques of program slicing and pattern matching have to be applied and are future interests to cover on this level [16.].

The *domain analysis* serves to link implementation details and functionality to domain-specific concepts, i.e. to recover the requirement specification of the system. If a system is to be changed, the task analysis is continued by examining the access rules for the system (user, user groups etc.) and the user acceptance for the different system's functionalities. Techniques applied on this level go beyond reverse engineering methods and embody knowledge-based design-recovery issues [12].

Forward processing. The forward process comprises four standard development phases that incorporate the results of the reverse process and usability engineering techniques for the RUI. The major phase of this process is the definition phase in which the results of the reverse process and the requirement analysis of the new system are matched against each other. A dialogue model and a storyboard are developed to specify the requirements that can be realised on processes which already exist. These results and the use of refining prototyping techniques in the following phases can be effectively used to push user testing. It has to be mentioned that only an integral, user-participative development of the UI - focusing on the user *and* the software - can succeed. The process has to look ahead to the implementation to recognise technical problems in an early phase (in particular regarding the performance). This also implies the significance of the overall evaluation [17.]

In the *requirement analysis*, the "ideal" requirements for the new system are described as explicitly as possible. Corresponding goals for the usability and utility of the system are defined, and the ideal task model based on a thorough user model is specified. Although this phase is lined up with a usual, user-centred requirement analysis, the progress of the reverse process and the design options which are achievable by the targeted dialogue solution have to be taken into account. Storyboarding considerably improves the comprehensiveness of the analysis.

The definition phase *adaptive requirement specification* - as described above - joins the "optimum" requirements of the requirement analysis and the results of the reverse process and leads to a practicable dialogue model and an adjusted storyboard. The dialogue model is the final step of the task analysis and task modelling process and determines which requirements are fulfilled by the old system, which can be fulfilled by a modification of the old system, which have to be re-implemented and which cannot be realised. Based on the UI model and the data model of the host system, dialogue views can be defined. This approach extends methods of rule-based generation of UIs from data models[18, 19].

The design phase or *redesign* heavily depends on the chosen architecture since the software objects representing the specified dialogue task model have to be designed. The major layers of an interactive system, i.e. the functional, the dialogue and the presentation layer, seem to form an appropriate basic architecture [17]. It is worth integrating adaptive components that enable e.g. the use of high-level knowledge-based front ends and user models. By specifying dialogue views, a prototype can be developed.

The prototype can be used as input for the *implementation* phase. It can be refined in an iterative process using object-oriented technology for the UI design. Coding depends on the tools applied. Besides coding, testing and evaluation are equally relevant activities. Furthermore, a training concept has to emphasize the changes that have been made towards the old system. A maintenance concept has to establish change mechanisms that determine how changes to the system effect the UI part and the host part.

4. Evaluation

This approach for RUI has to be evaluated from two perspectives: a business and a technical one, i.e. two questions have to be answered:

- Does RUI represent a business-relevant approach towards a new development?
- Is RUI feasible? In other words, is the process of RUI sufficiently automatable by use of the techniques represented in this paper ?

4.1. Business Perspective

From an operative point of view, RUI is a promising approach to realise direct benefits - in particular higher productivity and user acceptance. From a strategic point of view, RUI unbars the risk-minimising way of a stepwise migration of old, but valuable database systems. A detailed cost/benefit analysis has to incorporate both views. In order to calculate the operative value of RUI, the simplified handling of the system, the increased efficiency of business processes and the reduction of capacity of central computing resources have to be taken into account. For the strategic value, the system's significance within the organisation's strategic business plans, its future life-cycle and the maximal life-span of the system environment have to be examined.

The decision for RUI can only be validated by taking alternatives into account, i.e. the extremes - keeping the actual status (*endurance mode*) and going to redevelop (*new development mode*). Related criteria are the cost, the system's value, the risk of the decision and the system's life span [2]. In comparison to redevelopment, RUI enables a stepwise migration from terminals to workstations. Hardware investments can, therefore, be optimised regarding the necessary workplace technologies. After distributing the dialogue part of an application, further distribution of the system may be considered and planned. On the other hand, a new development does not only cause higher cost, but also potentially higher benefits (at least conceptually).

4.2. Technical Perspective

Each technique, method and concept described has a proved technical validity for itself. The key factor in RUI projects, however, is the management process model that links the different concepts. Our model describes the activities involved still in qualitative terms. The next step is the design of a formalised and generic meta model based on the four levels of abstraction and the four development phases. It defines the interfaces between the different activities and can be applied for all dialogue solutions described above.

We think that the concept based on a meta model proves feasible if it is possible to support the process by efficient tools. This is particularly true for the reverse process. It still has to be verified that there are tools which can sufficiently support the reverse process by including the methods and knowledge-based techniques described. In contrast, there are already handy tools available for the forward process, in particular for the UI design. The transition between the CARE and the CASE life cycle rests to be modeled.

References

1. R. Thurner: Beherrschung des Technologie-Wechsels mit Reengineering, in: R. Thurner (ed.): Reengineering, AIT, Hallbergmoos, 1990, pp.11-20
2. H. Sneed: Economics of Software-Re-engineering, Communications of the ACM, Vol.3, pp.163-182, 1991
3. J. Grudin: The computer reaches out, CHI'90 Proceedings, 1990, pp.339-384
4. H. Zuylen (ed.): The REDO Handbook - A Compendium of Reverse Engineering for Software Maintenance, Esprit Project 2487, Aug. 1991
5. E. Smit: ANDES - Method for user interface ANalysis and reDESign, Report 2487-TN-WL-1071, Esprit project 2487: REDO, Feb. 1992
6. S. Hague, I. Reid: FOCUS - Esprit II Project: P2620 - Third Annual Report Summary of Progress, Esprit Project 2487, Jan. 1992
7. R. Mori et alii: Programm Understanding through Structural and Behavioral Recognition and User Interaction, Proceedings CASE 1992, p.21992
8. Ploenzke Systeme GmbH: Expertise - Dialog-Reengineering, Wiesbaden, 1992
9. S. Eicker et alii: Einbindung von Software-Altlasten durch integrations-orientiertes Reengineering, WI, No.2, Vol.34, pp.137-145, Apr. 1992
10. R. Marty: Reengineering des Benutzerinterface, in: R. Thurner (ed.): Reengineering - Ein integrales Wartungskonzept, pp.115-123
11. L. Richter: Wiederbenutzbarkeit und Restrukturierung oder Reuse, Reengineering und Reverse Engineering, WI, No.2, Vol.34, pp.127-136, 1992
12. T. Biggerstaff: Design Recovery for Maintanance and Reuse, IEEE Computer, No.7, Vol.22, pp.36-49, July 1989
13. J. Nielsen: The Usability Engineering Life Cycle, IEEE Computer, No.3, Vol.25, pp.12-24, March 1992
14. B. Curtis, B. Hefley: Defining a Place for User Interface Engineering, IEEE Software, No.2, Vol.9, pp.84-86, 1992
15. E. Ortwein: Reengineering von Benutzerschnittstellen in existierenden Software-Systemen, Diplomarbeit, Institut für Angewandte Informatik, Universität Karlsruhe, Feb. 1993
16. W. Hausler, R. Linger, M. Pleszkoch: Using Function Abstraction to Understand Programm Behavior, IEEE Software, No.1, Vol.7, pp.55-63, 1990
17. L. Bass, J. Coutaz: Developing Software for the User Interface, Addison-Wesley, Reading, Massachusetts, 1991
18. J. Foley et alii: UIDE - An Intelligent User Interface Design Environment, in: J. Sullivan, S. Tyler (eds.): Intelligent User Interfaces, ACM, 1990, pp.339-384
19. A. Weisbecker: Regelbasierte Generierung softwareergonomischer Benutzer-schnittstellen, GI Ergonomie & Informatik, No.16, pp.19-28, Juli 1992

User Interface of Knowledge Based-DSS Development Environment, Some Further Developments

Michel R. Klein
HEC School of Management
78350 Jouy en Josas, France

Roland Traunmüller
Johannes Kepler University
Universität Linz , Austria

Abstract : Knowledge Based Decision Support Systems (KB-DSS) have achieved maturity in theory and practice. In a KB-DSS development environment the separation of modelling and interface specification should be done in the right way. We wish to provide a tool which will allow present spread sheet users and KB-DSS professional designers to implement easily more advanced application of the KB-DSS type which are impossible to implement with standard DSS or spread sheet technology. We also wish to provide professional designers with a tool to improve their productivity when they are required to develop the application because users often wish to delegate this task. We are interested here to support the task of KB-DSS design by a development environment which is integrated. It is the same system which support the interface design and the modeling. Interface design and modeling being two subtasks of KB-DSS design.

1.The KB-DSS Framework

1.1. The KB-DSS Conceptual Framework

The conceptual framework of knowledge based decision support systems (KB-DSS) comprises several functional parts which together build an architecture as described in Klein, Methlie, [1] Principal functional parts are the following ones :

- Data bases store information on entities, attributes and their relationships.
- Knowledge bases store information on rules, metarules and heuristics.
- Inference engine provides inference and ensures verification and consistency of the knowledge.
- Report generators deliver elaborate business reports customized to particular demands for content and outlay.
- Special subsystems provide such functions as e.g. statistics, forecasts, optimization, editors and debuggers.
- Computer-Human-Interfaces (CHI) combine all these parts into an overall system presented to the user. Thereby an intertace should be created for accessing easily all these functions so that the system can be used without problems and applied efficiently.

1.2. KB-DSS Development Environments and User Interface

As an example of KB-DSS Development Environments OPTRANS-EXPERT from SIG [10] provides the basis for producing systems according to the architecture given above . Our experience has been that the user interface characteristics is second only in importance to the real capacity of the KB-DSS to help in decision support . This experience is based on our observation of improvement in system acceptability following user-interface improvement in systems such as Finsim [9] or Siad Mairie [15].

2.Expectations of the User Concerning the Interface

2.1. User Interface Requirements

The expectations of the users concerning the interface have substantially changed in recent years. Users will no longer show any willingness to adapt to the system. Rather they demand that it is the system that has to adapt. For a person in charge of a particular task it is of great importance that the decision problem can be solved in a way that meets the work procedures he is accustomed to. In the literature many requirements guiding the interface design are given (cf. J.P. Meinadier, [2], Coutaz [3], [4]. Qualities that should be mentioned have been recalled in Klein, Traunmüller [16]. In particular we share the opinion of Jones [17] according to which graphical interfaces are now a necessity for DSS and KB-DSS.

Three points of particular interest should be emphasized for DSS and KB-DSS :

- For KB-DSS it is very important that a diversity of interface types can be user defined. So the form of a menu is appropriate for the selection of objects or options while for modeling a language for defining relations between variables equation suits best.
- When working with decision models the user needs a system which will enable him to work on a text which is only made of the relations between variables of the model and is not mixed with instructions the role of which is to define the application interface or overall logic.
- The weak point of most DSS development environment is that they do not provide a way to define sophisticated reports mixing different kinds of objects by direct action as with spread sheets. However even advanced spread sheets such as Excel 4 do not provide a way to define reports mixing text intertwined with variable values coming from the decision models , the data base , tables and diagnosis from the expert.

2.2. New Basic Technologies for Computer Human Interfaces

Fulfillment of these user needs requires major efforts. It only became possible through new concepts emerging and new products coming onto the market. Competitive advantage can be achieved through graphical user interface (GUI) that comprises the following features : capacity to mix several interface types, icons representing objects, direct manipulation of these objects, window management system, menus pulling down or popping up on demand, congruence of representation (WYSIWYG), use of methaphor (e.g. desktop) when working on concrete objects.
All these things have been used in now available commercial products. Leading computer companies and software firms have introduced powerfull products to the market such as the MacIntosh user interface, Windows, OS2 Presentation Manager, Next Interface Builder...
We would like to stress here that KB-DSS application development is a rather abstract task, as a consequence the use of metaphors is not as useful as in office automation applications. Also we share the opinion of Holsapple [14] according to which a DSS interface must be able to mix command driven, menu driven, form oriented, question/answer, and direct manipulation interface .
It must be stressed that a GUI is not an advantage in itself. So it does not suffice to have for example Windows as a basic system on top of which the decision support system is implemented. A spread sheet such as Excel even used under Windows does not give much assistance to the user to define simply the interface of his application apart from the constitution of unreadable "programs" using macros and the "dialog Editor" which very few users will be able to use. In particular the overall logic of the application is impossible to define and make clear in such environments. Much more important is that the KB-DSS development environment integrates a User Interface Development System (UIDS) that is as simple as possible to use. So it is the user or the Kb-DSS designer who will be able to specify and generate automaticaly from the specifications the desired interface for his application. In fact such a UIDS was already available in a KB-DSS development

environment such as Optrans Expert. However the UIDS of Optrans (version 2) had two drawbacks : it was not graphical and it was integrated in the modeling language. The consequence of the last point was that it was not easy to have a clear separation between the text (instructions) of the models and the text defining the application interface. It was in fact possible to simulate this separation by writing the model equations in submodels but it was not very convenient.

3.Importance for Separation of Modeling and Interface

3.1. Ease of Modeling by Users

In building a KB-DSS the presentation of data and results to the user and the structure of the dialogue are the most time consuming task. It has been our experience that up to 80 percent of the development time may go into the building of the computer-human dialogue. So for the user (who is primarily interested in the model and not in the interface structure) it means a heavy burden with much involvement in creating displays, reports formats and dialogues.

3.2. Model-Interface-Independence

As a consequence it is necessary that the modeling part and the interface part are as independent as possible. In fact the goal is that the interface definition constitutes a new resource in the application and so is created, deleted, and modified like other resources such as data bases, knowledge bases and models. In this way independence is achieved.

With model-interface-independence several important gains are achieved :

- Major alterations of the model can be made with no or only minor influence on the interface. Changes in the model can be due to a refining of the model.
- Often alterations are enforced from outside for administrative and legal reasons. Such enforced changes may be highly critical in time and volume.
- Providing new interfaces to existing models is also an interesting aspect. Reasons for such a change may range from mere cosmetic updates to transfer to other computers or adaptation to new environments (e.g. a company policy might be to choose OS2 as new operating system).
- Re-use (as a whole or in parts) of the interface for analogous problems can be envisaged. When under time pressure the re-use capacity could be of some considerable advantage.

3.3. Requirements of the Development Environment

The development of the application will usually imply the following resources: data bases, models, reports, graphics, knowledge bases, user-interface.
The typical designer of the application is a specialist in a domain (financial manager assistant, controler, marketing analyst, financial analyst...) as well as a professional KB-DSS designer.The designer may wish to design his application starting by any of the resources ,i.e. he may be willing to start by modeling the data (the data base), the relations between variables, the interface, the knowledge, the reports etc.. However to the contrary of the spread sheet which forces the user to start with the reports; a good environment should help the user to start by designing the user interface adding the models, data bases, reports, knowledge bases progressively and as a function of the caracteristics of the application itself. The development environment should comprise a nucleus to which can be added at will the other ressources: DBMS, KBMS, etc... The environment is seen as one unique system to the designer and users.

4. Example From Financial Planning

For the discussion an example from financial planning is described in what follows. The model will be used to describe the relations between the variables of the income statements,

balance sheets and fund flows of a company. We shall just here give a simplified example of income statement relations. The readers interested to have the relations defining the balance sheets variables and funds flow used in the full example are refered to Klein [16]. The main assumptions are described in the following income statement relations :
sales t= sales t-1 * (1+g)
margin t = sales t * perc.margin t
salary.expenses. t = R1 * sales t
profit.bf.deprec.t= margin t - salary expenses t
cum.deprec. t = cum.deprec. t + deprec.funct. (invest, type, duration)
interests. t = long.term.Debt t * mean.rate.int.
profit.bf.tax. t = margin t - salary.expenses. t - deprec. t - interests. t
income.tax. t = if benefit.bf.tax. t > 0 benefit.bf.tax. t / 2 else 0
profit.after.tax. t = profit.bf.tax t / 2 if profit.bf.tax. >= 0
loss t = - profit.bf.tax. if profit.bf.tax. < 0

5. Application Interface Design

5.1. Role of the User in the Model-Interface Interaction

The design of the interface is derived from the analysis of the model-interface interaction. Thus the user will wish to :

- Provide the historical values of variables of the model,
- Present the historical variable values in different ways (tables, graphs),
- Provide forecasted values of some environmental model variables,
- Solve the model to obtain the values of criteria and other system variables .
- Provide the values of decision variables to simulate financial policies,
- Present the historical and forecasted values to detect trends,
- Obtain a financial diagnosis of the company (by financial diagnosis we mean here the result of some logical reasoning based on criteria provided by an expert module).

5.2. Interface Design Corresponding to the Above Interactions

The application interface will be made of several parts :

- A hierarchical sequence of menus and,
- Reports mixing different objects (tables, graphics, text with variables values computed by the models or the data bases) .
- conclusion or explanations of the expert subsystem.
- Interaction with the development environment through multiple windows when working within the modeling , expert or data base subsystems.

5.3. Design of the Menus

The main menu (fig. 1) presents the user with the basic options which can support the tasks during the process of financial analysis : entering historical values for the variables of the model (DATA INPUT), display of reports (REPORT), display of various graphics (GRAPHICS), moving to the forecast and simulation analysis (SIMULATE), leaving the application (QUIT).The option is selected using the cursor or mouse. The report menu shows the possibility of selecting the display for the Income statement (INCOME), Balance sheet (BALANCE), Fund flow statement (FUNDS FLOW).The simulation (fig 2) menu shows the possibilities to select : The entering of hypotheses (HYPOTHESES),the display of reports (REPORTS),the display of graphics (GRAPHICS), the entering of financing decisions (FINANCING), the return, to the main menu (QUIT).
The pull down menu corresponding with the HYPOTHESES keyword shows the selection possibilities of the elementary variables for which estimated values have to be given.

5.4. Design of the Screen Displays

With respect to the display of the variable values two situations may be met : display during

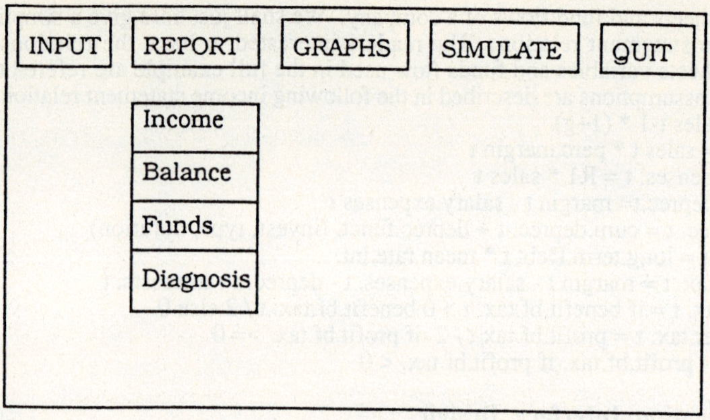

Fig.1 Historical analysis & report menu

the input phase and display during the output phase. The display needed after solving the model (output phase) is the trivial, well known case. The user wishes to display a report or a graphic of the numerical value of one or several variables . The display during the *input phase* is needed when the designer wants (and he really should do this) to present to the user estimates of variables. So the system has to be designed to provide estimates of the

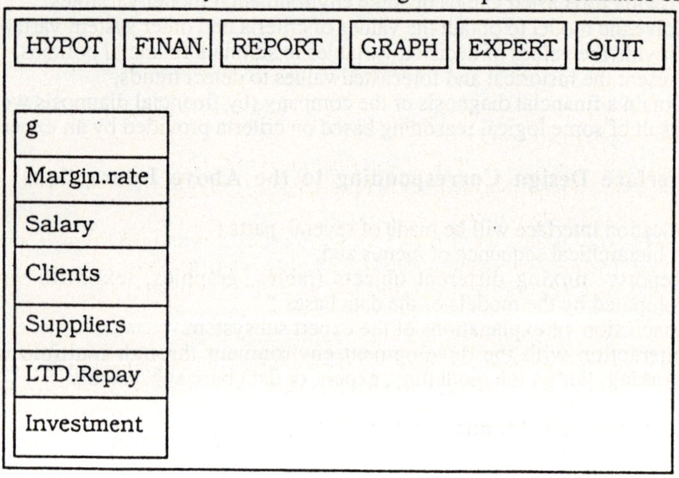

Fig.2 Forecast analysis & hypothesis menu

value of a variable over a given horizon and then let the user free to make his own choice by keeping the estimate or entering a different value.

5.5. Interwining the activities

An interface that allows interwining activities in the input phase brings two advantages :

- The supply of good estimates can involve much knowledge (modelling knowledge such as pertinent explanarory variables etc.) and is usually considered as an important progress in the ability of the system to provide support in the input phase. The use of the expert module of the development environment can be here of great help.
- On the other hand the user remains free to accept or modify the estimate. So - according to his judgement or other reasons as for instance external information - the user can have his own choice for the variable value considered.An example for such intertwining is given in figure 3. The screen is divided in four windows :

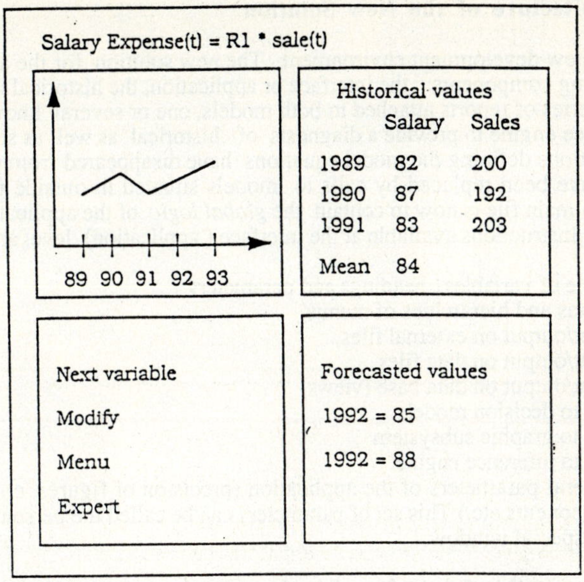

Fig. 3 Screen presentation for entering forecast hypothesis

- Window 1 : displays of the graphics of the historical value of the variable in question (e.g. salary expense),
- Window 2 : displays of the numerical historical value of the variable salary expense as well as the explanatory variable of salary expense (sales) with some statistics such as mean, standard deviation etc.,
- Window 3 : displays of the proposed forecasted value of the variable (the user can accept the forecast or change it according to his judgement),
- Window 4 : displays of the text of comments on the variable for which an input is expected.

After the user has accepted or changed the estimate the system will display the modified graphics up to the forecasted horizon in window 1 and the numerical value in window 3. In window 4 the new options will be displayed : move to the next variable, re-enter the values, activate help from the expert, return to the preceeding menu.

6. Application Solution Using a Second Generation KB-DSS

An implementation of the above simplified application defined with a first generation KB-DSS (version 2 of OPTRANS Expert) is described in Klein, Traunmüller[16] as well as some of the first results concerning the structure and implementation using the new second generation development environment. The architecture of the second generation development environment is described in more details in Klein [6].We shall present here some recent results concerning the second generation user interface and functionalities of such systems using the same simplified example.

6.1. Architecture of the New Solution

Using the new development environment The new solution for the application is made of the following components: the interface or application, the historical model, the simulation model, a series of reports attached to both models, one or several knowledge bases used by the inference engine to provide a diagnosis of historical as well as simulation results. All the instructions defining the model equations have disappeared from the application main file and have been replaced by calls to models situated in outside files. The role of the application main file is now to contain the *global logic* of the application and the *interface definition*.. Instructions available at the interface (application) level are there to let the user define :

- Name of variables , headings and parameters
- Menus and hierarchies of menus,
- Input/output on external files,
- Input/output on data files,
- Input/output on data base (views)
- Call to decision models
- Call to graphic subsystem
- Call to inference engine
- General parameters of the application (precision of figures, colour of the windows components etc.) This set of parameters can be called the personalisation and appears in a special window.

7.2. New graphical interface for the development environment

The environment appears to the user as presented in the top menu of figure 4 . Five key words designate the resources which can be used in an application : Application (overall logic & UIMS), Data File (Données), Data Base(Base) , Report Generator (Rapport) , Expert (or KBMS), Personalisation (Terminal). The option Application of the menu gives the user the possibility to open , run , close or edit the application.
The options can also be selected using the mouse. Fig 4 shows a "command window " which is available for the user to type his commands. An "output window " is open on the

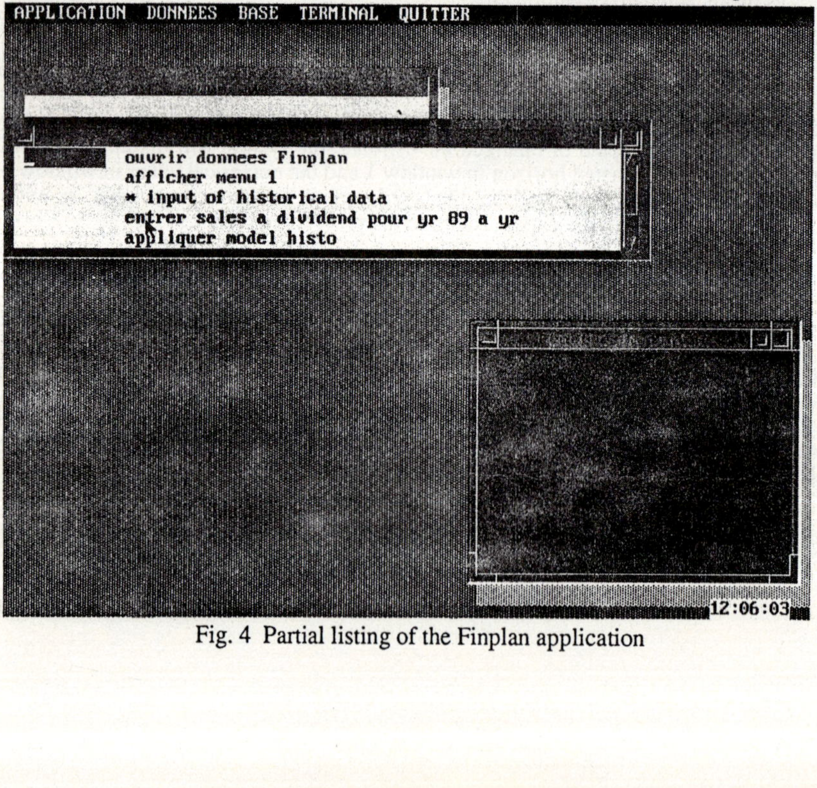

Fig. 4 Partial listing of the Finplan application

right hand side to present the resources of the application with which the user is interacting: decision models, reports , data files, data bases, knowledge bases, etc...Fig. 4 also shows the beginning of the text of the application (interface). As can be seen the text does not contain anymore instructions defining the model .Fig 5 shows the beginning of the text of the forecast model. This screen is obtained by clicking on the solve (appliquer) instruction of the interface .

7.3. Comments on the interface

. Menu definition at the application level

One of the strategy to define an application is to start by defining the user interface of the application through a hierarchy of menus. One of the goal of the system is to achieve a good balance between instructions to define the application's hierarchy of menus and direct action on the objects created by these instructions or readily available in the system.

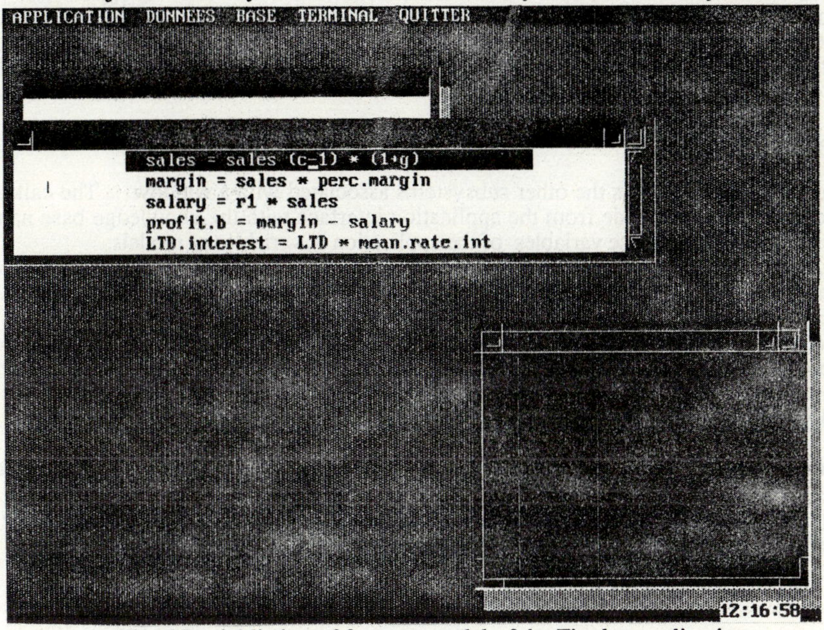

Fig. 5 Partial listing of forecast model of the Finplan application

For example three instructions only can be used to define a hierarchy of menus that the user can position on the screen using the mouse while he is defining its application interface. These instructions are:
CREATE MENU < menu n° N>
MENU < menu n°> "Text" : GO TO <label>
MENU <menu n°> "TexT": EXECUTE <label>
MENU <menu n°> "Text": MENU < menu n°>

To define the key words and hierarchies of menus. The display of menus is performed by the DISPLAY instruction : DISPLAY MENU < menu n°>

When this application is executed the hierarchy of menus will be displayed on the screen and the user will be able to finish positioning the menus and submenus on the screen using the mouse. As a consequence the user is completely free to position the menus on the screen by direct action.

Report generator.

One of the difficult problems which remained to be solved was how to provide an easy way for the user to define sophisticated reports associated with the application since in many cases the reports the users wish to define are fairly complex . In the preceding version of the system it was possible to define sophisticated reports using a report definition language [10] . However the reports where mainly rectangular in format and could not mix at will tables of figures, text and images. Such a mixture could be done as a "composite" screen to display a table in a window, a graph in an second window, an image in a third etc... but could not be catalogued as a single object .In the new report generator the basic concept is that of the white page which constitutes a background on which can be placed several types of objets : tables, text, graphics and images.The tables are defined in an interactive way by selecting, using the cursor, the variable names and heading names of the application which each appear in a separated window. The variables and headings can be selected one by one or by blocks. The selected variables and heading appear in another window . When the OK button is used the table is automatically placed on the blank page where the user can move it where he wishes using the mouse.Text can be typed on the page as background. This text can contain parameters which take the value of certain variables of the application.

. Expert module.

The expert module is as the other subsystems associated with a window . The call of the inference engine is made from the application interface with the knowledge base name as parameter. Rules can use variables of the application & variables of models.

. Data base module.

The multidimensional data base module is associated with a window like the other subsystems. The definition of the views of the data base is now entirely menu driven.

7.4. Implementation

The implementation of the system was done in C preparing the ground for a version in C++. The reader interested by the design strategy of the new version and the new implementation is refered to Klein [6]. The system is running under MS-DOS . Given the graphical library used It should be available under OS/2 by simple recompiling .

8. Experience and Future Research Directions

At the time of writing this paper a first version of the system is near completion. The implementation of the graphical interface of the development environment is finished. The separation between the modeling subsystem and the interface definition is done. The syntax of the development environment for defining the application interface is implemented. The system is still at an early stage of testing and important applications such as FINSIM [9] running under previous versions of Optrans have not yet been transferred . Measurement of performance has not been possible yet. The present research directions are consistent with the research agenda proposed in Klein [8]. There is presently one kind of solver for the decision model . A better separation between the decision models definition and the model solver is another goal of the research. In the future we wish to be able to use a library of model solvers.

9. Conclusions

The system we have briefly presented shows that it is possible to implement in a fully integrated KB-DSS development environment a clear separation between the user-interface definition and overall logic of the application and the rest of the application resources: decision models, data files, data bases, knowledge bases, report,...

We believe that the proposed structure should have important consequences by improving : the application capacity to evolve,the ease of implementation of an equation reasoning subsystem embedded in the modeling language, the ease of implementation of a rational decision theory support function. We provide with the new graphical interface for the KB-DSS development environment and resulting applications :
- windows and associated functions for each resources (application, decision models, report, data bases, knowledge bases...)
- greater ease to specify the user interface of the application in terms of hierarchy of menus and screen partitioning using multiple windows.
We believe that with this new structure we have provided the user and professional developpers more freedom to decide on the best design strategy for a specific application since they can at will , by stepwise refinement , define in an iterative way :
- the interface and overall logic of the application.
- the decision models.
- the presentation of data and results in reports mixing : tables , text , graphics and images.
- the data structures of the data bases.
- the rules of the knowledge bases.

10. Acknowledgements

We would like to thank Cyrille Danes , Henry Guibert and Yvon Garandeau for programming . Victor Hargreaves for some pertinent remarks on stylistics. The company Decision Research for financing this research.

10. References

[1] KLein M., Methlie L., Expert Systems : A Decision Support Approach, Addison Wesley 1990
[2] Meinadier, l'Interface Utilisateur, Dunod 1991
[3] Coutaz J. A paradigm for user interface architecture, Carnegy Mellon University, 1984
[4] Coutaz J. Interface Homme Ordinateur, Conception et Realisation, Dunod 1990.
[5] Howard R.A. The Foundation of Decision Analysis, IEEE, SSCA, 3, 1968
[6] Klein Michel, Danes Cyrile, Design of a Second Generation Knowledge Based Decision Support System, Communication at the 2nd ISDSS Conference, Exploring the Next Generation of Decision Support, FAW, University of Ulm 22-25 June 1992.
[7] Excel 4, User Manual Microsoft (ed) 1992
[8] Klein Michel, Research Issues for Second Generation Knowledge Based DSS, Proceedings NATO Advanced Summer Institute on DSS , Lucca Italy, June 1991.
[9] Klein Michel, FINSIM Expert : A Knowledge Based DSS for Financial Analysis and Planing in Proceedings Eurinfo 88, North Holland 1988.
[10] Optrans Expert version 2 , User Manual , SIG (ed), 4 bis rue de la Libération , 78350 Jouy en Josas ,France.1988
[11] Pfaff G.E. (ed) User Interface Management Systems, in proceedings EurographicsSeminars, Springer Verlag, 1985
[12] Webster B.F. The NeXT Book, Addison Wesley 1989.
[13] Window 3.1 , Programmer's Manual, Microsoft (ed)
[14] Hosapple G.W., Park S.,Whinston A.B., Framework for DSS Interface Development Recent Developments in Decision Support Systems. (C..W. Holsapple, A.B. Whinston ed) Springer Verlag 1993.
[15] KLein Michel, Decision Support for Financial Management in Local Government, in Decision Support in Public Administration (P. Bots, H. Sol, R. Traunmüller editors) Proceedings IFIP Transactions n° 26, North Holland 1993 .
[16] Klein Michel, Traunmüller Rolland , Architecture and User Interface of Knowledge Based -DSS Development Environment in Proceedings of the 26 th Annual Hawai International Conference on System Science, IEEE Computer Society Press 1993.
[17] Jones Christopher, User Interface Development Environment and Decision Support Systems in Recent Developments in Decision Support Systems, (C. Holsapple, A.B. Whinston ed.) Springer Verlag 1993.

A Highly-Customisable Schema Meta-Visualisation System for Object-Oriented (O-O) Database Schemas - Overview

M A Qutaishat* W A Gray N J Fiddian
Department of Computing Mathematics, University of Wales College of Cardiff, U.K.
* Department of Computer Science, University of Jordan, Amman, Jordan

Abstract. Many researchers have addressed the problem of reverse-engineering a relational database schema to produce an Entity Relationship graphical representation of its structure. This paper describes the development of a schema meta-visualisation system for O-O database schemas, which processes a textual schema to generate a relevant graphical representation (view) of the schema. This system is designed to be highly customisable as it employs a common internal intermediate schema representation, generalised object meta-knowledge and flexible meta-translation techniques in the production of the graphical views. Thus it can produce a wide range of types of visualisation (graphical view) from the structural components and semantic contents of a wide range of types of textual O-O database schema.

1 Introduction

Conceptual visualisation of schemas using graphical notation and diagrams has proved to be an important step during the initial stages of database design [4], during schema evolution and modification, and in heterogeneous database integration [10,11,7,3]. The desire of database users to see a visual picture of their database structure instead of textual descriptions of the defining schema led to the production of graphical representations of the schema information by means of reverse-engineering. In all these situations, graphical data models constitute an ideal vehicle for conceptualising and modelling schemas by employing a set of data modelling concepts and a language-independent graphical notation (e.g. the Entity Relationship (E-R) model [2], Enhanced Entity Relationship (EER) model [4] or the Object Modelling Technique (OMT) [9]). Given the large number of conceptual elements that comprise a typical database schema, manual production of such graphical representations by users is difficult and tedious. The potential usefulness of tools that automate this task is therefore readily apparent.

In this paper we will be concentrating on a powerful and flexible tool which is designed to help in the reverse-engineering of database schemas, i.e. the transformation of the textual representation of a schema into a corresponding graphical form. This tool is specifically designed for a heterogeneous database environment. In such an environment there are two situations which are facilitated by graphical presentations of schema information: the integration of multiple schemas from a set of pre-existing heterogeneous databases; and the visualisation of individual schemas that exist only in textual form, which the database users are able to assimilate more easily in graphical form (particularly when the schemas concerned are non-local ones).

2 Scope and Objective

The advanced nature of O-O data modelling approaches has stimulated the need for rich and higher level concepts, tools and techniques to be used in the process of designing and developing O-O databases. Graphical data models (GDMs) represent an ideal vehicle in this respect. Consequently, a growing number of O-O graphical data models have appeared recently for supporting the conceptual design and development of O-O databases. The Object Modelling Technique (OMT) and the Enhanced Entity Relationship (EER) model are two of these. Due to limitations of space we concentrate our discussion on OMT, as a representative example, while referring to other models if necessary. OMT uses three models spanning the development life cycle; here we are mainly concerned with the object model, which consists of a set of object data modelling concepts and a language-independent graphical notation. This notation combines O-O concepts (i.e. classes and inheritance) with information modelling concepts (i.e. entities and associations).

In recent work at Cardiff, a meta-programmed translation technology was developed using Prolog to address and solve some of the problems associated with integrating heterogeneous sets of databases. Application of this technology to the generation of language inter-translators in the database systems context has proved in practice to be very efficient and productive [5,8]. Encouraged by this success, we decided to use the same general approach to tackle the schema visualisation problem in a heterogeneous environment. We concluded from our previous experience that it should be possible to develop a generalised schema meta-visualisation system (SMVS) for the construction of graphical views of textual O-O schemas. This system would be based on the application of the meta-translation technique with a common internal intermediate representation of schemas as a frame based structure which represents the object meta-knowledge contained in a schema, and it would use Prolog as the system implementation language.

3 SMVS Development

A highly customisable system is one that can be applied to diverse domains in its area of application with minimal changes being required to the system. Our approach to minimising the domain dependency of SMVS can be explained in terms of the following two (simplified) figures, which represent possible scenarios in a heterogeneous (O-O) database environment.

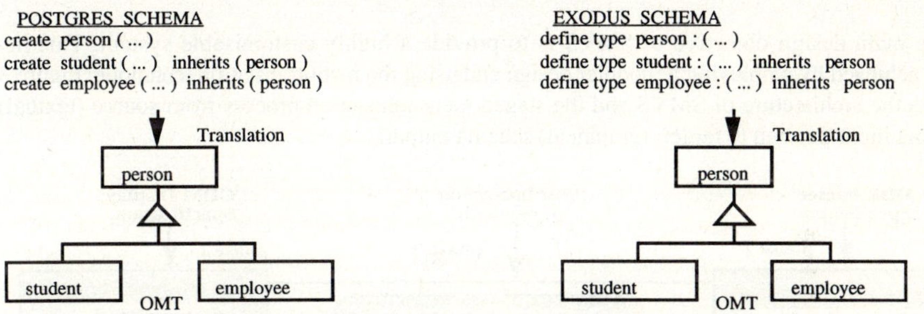

Fig. 1. Texts and OMT visualisations of equivalent POSTGRES [12] and EXODUS [1] schemas

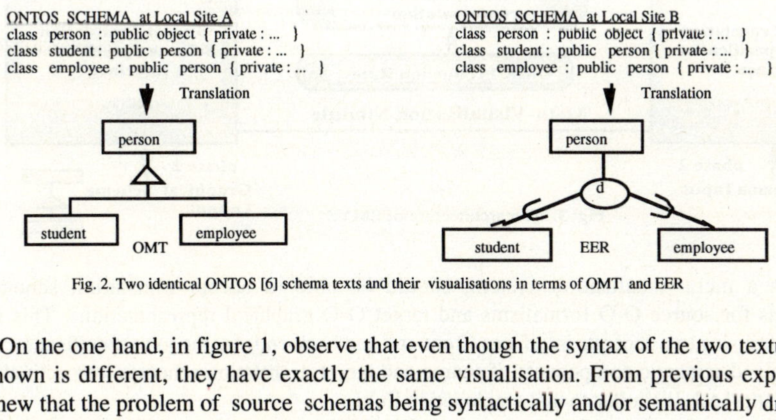

Fig. 2. Two identical ONTOS [6] schema texts and their visualisations in terms of OMT and EER

On the one hand, in figure 1, observe that even though the syntax of the two textual schemas shown is different, they have exactly the same visualisation. From previous experience, we knew that the problem of source schemas being syntactically and/or semantically diverse could be solved by utilising a generalised front-end interface that can accept a wide range of types of schema syntax and semantics and transform them into a common internal representation. We have developed such a front-end interface by identifying a schema syntactic/semantic meta-model for the O-O paradigm. This was done by analysing many implemented variants of that paradigm and abstracting their concepts into a composite set of variant-independent schema information concepts which we refer to as object meta-knowledge (OMK). In the context of SMVS we needed an intermediate modelling scheme that was capable of accommodating the rich semantic information content of an O-O schema in a way that is independent of any specific O-O data model implementation, and that was also suitable for manipulating this content throughout the visualisation process. Having identified OMK, we could then express its concepts in terms of a suitable formalism and design a corresponding schema translation meta-language for use in translating source schemas into OMK form.

On the other hand, in figure 2, observe that even though the syntax and semantics of the two textual schemas shown are exactly the same, different users at two distinct sites of a heterogeneous database environment may wish to visualise these schemas in different graphical data model terms. In this example, one user chooses OMT and the other EER; such diversity may derive from their local site standard practice, their training or personal preference. Again from previous experience, we knew that the problem of target schema graphical representation diversity could be solved by utilising a generalised back-end interface that can transform a common internal representation to produce a wide range of types of visualisation. We have developed such a back-end interface by means of a template-driven internal representation traverser, which processes the OMK internal form and, by acting upon the relevant templates, produces a corresponding target visualisation as desired.

3.1 SMVS Architecture and Operation

The main design objective of SMVS is to provide a highly customisable system. This has been achieved by employing a modular design and using the meta-translation technique. Figure 3 shows the architecture of SMVS and the staged meta-translation process from source (textual) schema input through to target (graphical) schema output.

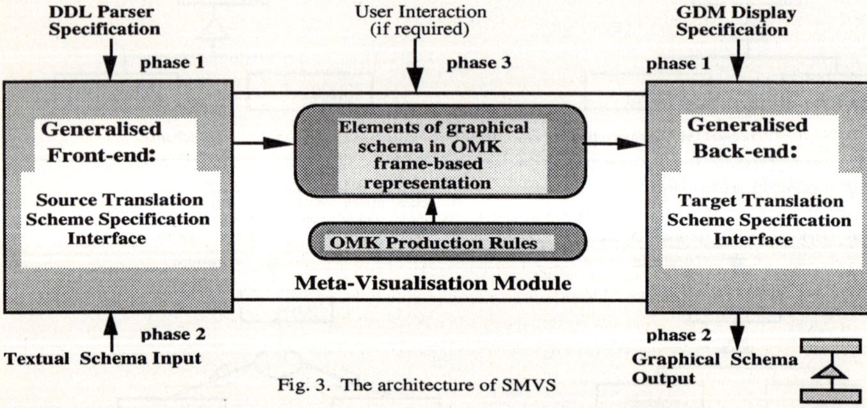

Fig. 3. The architecture of SMVS

SMVS, as a meta-visualisation system, should be able to accept translation scheme specifications for source O-O formalisms and target O-O graphical representations. This is achieved by utilising two separate interfaces (front-end and back-end) for the joint specification of the syntactic and semantic components of source and target translation schemes, respectively. The general approach is similar to that employed in [5,8].

The set of schema information concepts used within SMVS is known as object metaknowledge (OMK), i.e. knowledge about objects. This is of two types: facts and rules. Facts are represented in a frame structured language (as Prolog facts) and rules in a production rule-based system (as Prolog rules). Together, these provide a suitable organisational form for the knowledge concerned.

In operation, the system has three distinct phases, cf. figure 3. In the first, translation specification phase, a source and target translation scheme specification pair is linked into the meta-visualisation system. In the second, visualisation application phase, an O-O schema in the specified source formalism is entered, then it is translated into the specified target representation, from which the required visualisation can be displayed. The third phase, invoked in parallel with the second if necessary, is an interaction with the database designer which can be used to supply additional information specifying semantic relationships that cannot be resolved automatically. The schema visualisation application process (phase 2) begins with the parsing stage, which accepts the source schema and decomposes it into its basic elements (e.g. classes, properties and associations). These elements and their relationships are represented in the OMK common internal intermediate form. This internal representation is then traversed by the display stage to produce the desired visualisation.

In an overall operational setting, SMVS has access to a number of translation schemes from various types of O-O DDL formalism to OMK and from OMK to various types of graphical data model (GDM). However, in mapping use it is linked to only one source O-O formalism and one target graphical data model translation scheme at a time.

4 Current Project Status and Initial Results

A prototype implementation of SMVS has been successfully tested for a variety of schemas ranging from simple to complex examples, where the latter include richer concepts such as different types of association multiplicity; multiple inheritance; fixed, variable, recursive and transitive aggregation; alerters and triggers. We have used the ONTOS, EXODUS and POSTGRES DBMSs as source domains and the OMT and EER graphical data models as target domains. This system has proved to be relatively domain independent and therefore highly customisable (i.e. minimal changes are required to support any new DBMS or graphical data model from within the O-O paradigm).

References

1. M. Carey, D. DeWitt: An Overview of the EXODUS Project. *in* [13]
2. P. Chen:The Entity-Relationship Model: Towards a Unified View of Data. ACM TODS 1(1), 1976
3. B. David, G. Jane: Distributed Database Systems. Addison-Wesley, 1992
4. R. Elmasri, S. Navathe: Fundamentals of Database Systems. Benjamin Cummings, 1989
5. D.I. Howells, N.J. Fiddian, W.A. Gray: A Source-to-Source Meta-Translation System for Relational Query Languages. Proceedings of 13th VLDB Conference, 1987
6. ONTOS Reference Manual. Ontologic Inc., Massachusetts, 1989
7. M. Ozsu, P. Valduriez: Principles of Distributed Database Systems. Prentice-Hall, 1991
8. A. Ramfos, N.J. Fiddian, W.A. Gray: A Meta-Translation System for Object-Oriented to Relational Schema Translation. Proceedings of 9th British National Conference On Databases, 1991
9. J. Rumbaugh, *et al*: Object-Oriented Modelling and Design. Prentice-Hall, 1991
10. A. Sheth, J. Larson, A. Cornelio, S. Navathe: A Tool for Integrating Conceptual Schemas and User Views. Proceedings of 4th International Conference on Data Engineering, 1988
11. P. Sheth, J. Larson: Federated Database Systems for Managing Distributed, Heterogeneous, and Autonomous Databases. ACM Computing Surveys 22(3), 1990
12. M. Stonebraker, *et al*: The Implementation of POSTGRES. IEEE Transactions on Knowledge and Data Engineering, March 1990
13. S. Zdonik, D. Mair: Readings in Object-Oriented Database Systems. Morgan Kaufmann, 1990

Walkthrough using Animation Database System MOVE

Susumu Kuroki, Katsuhiko Kikkawa, Kunihiko Kaneko,
and Akifumi Makinouchi

Dept. of Computer Science and Comm. Eng., Kyushu University
Hakozaki, Higashi, Fukuoka 812, Japan
kuroki@csce.kyushu-u.ac.jp

Abstract. This paper discusses walkthrough as an advanced application of the object-oriented animation database system MOVE, which is developed so as to make producing computer animation easier. Since MOVE offers computer animation facilities as well as data management facilities in encapsulated form, users can use them without knowing the details. We introduce a graphics model in MOVE. Using this, we produced a walkthrough animation in our university and evaluated the system.

1 Introduction

Virtual reality is one of the most challenging research areas in computer science. Walkthrough is an application of virtual reality technologies and is often used for architectural simulations. The walkthrough is a computer animation to visualize what a person sees walking around in a virtual space.

However, producing an animation requires special techniques and knowledge of computer graphics, computer animation, and computer programming. And they are restricted to professional animators, artist, and computer scientists. To make producing a computer animation easier, we began to study an animation database system MOVE [1, 2]. We designed and are implementing MOVE based on an object-oriented database management system (OODBMS) ONTOS [3], because OODBMSs are said to be good tools for handling so-called multimedia data such as images, graphics, sounds, and alphanumeric data in a natural and efficient manner.

Various computer animation systems, languages, and toolkits are proposed. And some of them are based on object-oriented concepts [4, 5, 6, 7]. However, they often lack database facilities. Since MOVE is based on ONTOS, animation data are stored in the database and can be used repeatedly. Such reusability of the data guaranteed by the DBMS makes MOVE suitable for cooperative work, too.

From the database point of view, a frame of a computer animation can be considered as visualization of the result of a spatial query to a spatial database, because the only visible objects are retrieved from the spatial database and visualized. In this aspect, spatial database techniques are important for MOVE.

This paper is organized as follows. Section 2 introduces our graphics model implemented in MOVE. Section 3 describes walkthrough implemented on MOVE. Implementation issues and some evaluation results are given in Section 4. Section 5 concludes the present study and states further research topics.

2 Graphics Model of MOVE

In computer animation, spatial entities may be constructed using geometric modeling techniques. Spatial entities are lightened by light sources and viewed through a camera. In order to represent animation entities such as spatial entities, light sources, and the camera, MOVE provides a graphics model. Attribute values of the animation entities such as location, orientation, size, shape are stored in MOVE.

As MOVE is an object-oriented animation database system implemented in C++, the model is also implemented as classes in C++. There are twelve fundamental classes in MOVE to define animation entities. Technical details, see [1, 2].

2.1 Graphics Model

Using the graphics model, animation entities are represented. They are defined by their attribute values. In order to define animation entities, MOVE provides eight classes Vector, Color, Polygon, Surface, Solid, SolidDB, Camera, and LightSource as in ASAS [4]. ASAS is based on the actor theory and also an extended Lisp. Our model is similar to that of ASAS, but class SolidDB in our system is implemented as type Group in ASAS. An instance of class SolidDB is a concatenation of instances of the class Solid and expressed as a complex object in MOVE. On the other hand, instances of class Solid are primitive objects. They are polyhedra, spheres, cylinders and so on.

Once the geometrical structure of a spatial entity is specified, its location is to be

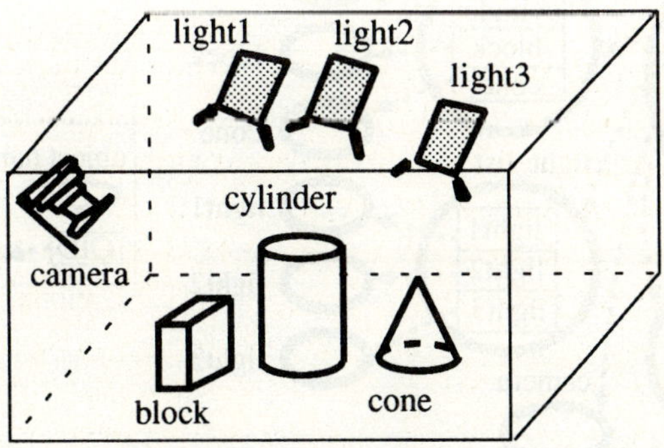

Fig.1. Model of three dimensional space

given. Three dimensional spatial entities such as buildings, telephone booths, gates, and trees should be located according to a global coordinate system as well as two dimensional spatial entities such as roads and parks.

To describe which entities are contained in a scene, how they are illuminated, and how they are visualized, a scene object is used. The scene object contains every information about spatial objects to be displayed in the scene (see Fig. 1. and Fig. 2.). To visualize a scene, a user has only to give values to attributes of a camera and light sources. Once the attributes of the camera and the light sources are given, the spatial objects which are to be displayed are automatically selected and registered to the scene object.

Knowledge and techniques of computer graphics are distributively represented. They are implemented as methods in each entities. For example, algorithms to solve hidden line and surface elimination problem and visibility problem are implemented as methods of camera objects.

2.2 Graphics Data Access

As MOVE manages all the entities as database objects, they may be frequently accessed and modified. As they are manipulated implicitly through ONTOS, they can be used from every application on ONTOS. Frames of an animation are stored as image objects. Since a frame is generated from the corresponding scene object, the frame has as much information as the scene object. Due to the relationship between the frame and the scene object, image search problem could be transformed into a search problem in the scene objects.

3 Walkthrough

Walkthrough is a computer animation and shows the scenes which a person in a

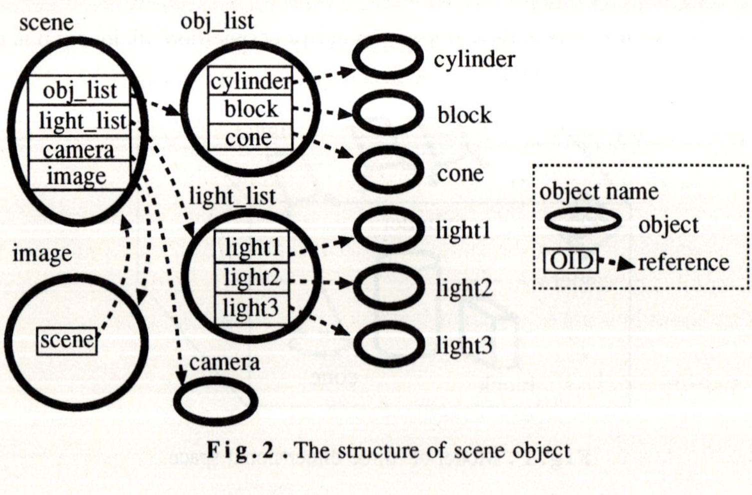

Fig. 2. The structure of scene object

virtual space sees. When walkthrough is projected, an illusion of walking along the street and watching buildings occurs to spectators. As a consequence, they can understand visually the situation as if they were in the virtual space. For example, he can understand what colors of a walls of a building is, how tall it is.

3.1 Walkthrough

Walkthrough is realized by the following three activities:

- Determination of movement of a camera and light sources
- Selection of the spatial entities which are visible from the camera
- Visualization of the selected spatial entities

First, a user has to specify positions and orientations of the camera and light sources at each time in order to determine their movement. For example, the user has to specify a location of the sun as well as a camera. Second, the visible spatial objects are retrieved using spatial selection. The selection is formulated as a spatial query to a spatial database. Finally, scenes are visualized according to the scene objects. This process is performed automatically, too. To help spectators of walkthrough, camera view and top view can be displayed at the same time to show where the camera is and which direction the camera is going to.

3.2 Visibility Problem

Solving visibility problem is the main activity of walkthrough. To solve this efficiently, many algorithms are proposed [8]. The problem is formulated as follows: From a spatial database, select the spatial objects which are visible from an observer in a known position.

When the position of the camera is determined, its visible space is also determined. Suppose the screen of the camera is a circle, the visible space is a cone. Let us call the cone a view cone. Then the solution of the problem involves a set of all the spatial objects that intersect the view cone. Let us call the set potentially visible set. From the potentially visible set, hidden surfaces must be eliminated to visualize a scene. Consequently, solving visibility problem consists of the following two procedures; determination of the potentially visible set and elimination of the hidden surfaces from potentially visible set.

From the spatial database point of view, the above procedures are formulated as a complex spatial queries to the spatial database. For efficient processing of such queries, many algorithm are proposed [9, 10]. In MOVE, these spatial query processing algorithms are implemented as methods of camera objects.

3.3 Multiple Views

To understand a scene correctly, we provide two kinds of views; camera view and top view. The camera view shows local information and the top view shows global information. The camera view shows the spatial relationships between the spatial entities around the camera. On the other hand, the top view shows overall area of walkthrough. It also shows the absolute location of the camera in a global coordinate system. The combination of the camera view and the top view makes an environment around the camera easier to be understood.

4 Implementation and Evaluation

To implement a walkthrough in our university, principal buildings, gates, telephone booths, trees, and walls are modeled and stored in the spatial database as well as roads, lawn and baseball ground. In order to represent 135 buildings, 2236 polygons are used. In average, a building consists of 24.6 polygons and a telephone booth is represented by 74 polygons, etc. (see Table 1). This means that buildings and trees are roughly modeled, while gates and telephone booths are precisely modeled, since telephone booths and the gates are few and remarkable.

Frames of walkthrough are displayed at real-time rate. However, it is impossible for MOVE to display them directly to the screen of a CRT terminal. Instead, the animation is produced frame by frame and then recorded in the database as a sequence of image objects. MOVE automatically produces frames using the mechanism of scene objects, that helps users to produce animation easily. We have developed the walkthrough "The road to multimedia lab.". Its venue is Kyushu University which we are working for. The animation consists of 200 frames and animates the scenes which a person sees walking from the gate of our university to our laboratory. In average, it takes about 347 seconds to produce one frame, which consists of 800*800 pixels. All the frames of the animation was produced frame by frame on the workstation SUN Sparcstation 2 without using special hardware.

Walkthrough is produced by the C++ program in only 320 lines, while MOVE is implemented in about 12000 lines.

5 Conclusion and Future Work

We discussed walkthrough using MOVE and showed that it could make it easier to

Table 1 . Modeled spatial entities

	buildings	tel. booths	gates	trees
# of registered entities	135	4	4	266
# of registered polygons	3326	296	128	1064
# of polygons per entity	24.6	74	32	4

implement a computer animation. As animation entities are stored in MOVE and managed by ONTOS, they can be used by other applications. As MOVE provides various kinds of computer graphics facilities as encapsulated objects, users have only to know interfaces of the objects. Due to this feature, users can make abstract description in application programs.

As for future work, we are planning to add the following facilities to MOVE;

1. More precise model of the animation entities such as trees, clouds, and so on .
2. Advanced user interface and environment for defining spatial objects.

More precise models will make walkthrough more realistic. And the advanced user interface helps the user to define spatial entities more easily.

Acknowledgements

We would particularly like to thank Yusuke Kondo and Shirou Takayama, who helped us produce the animation. This research was partially supported by the Japanese Ministry of Education, Science and Culture under Grant-in-Aid for Scientific Research (B) (Grant-No. 03858007).

References

[1] K. Kaneko, S. Kuroki, and A. Makinouchi: Design of 3D CG Data Model of "MOVE" Animation Database System, *Proc. 2nd Far-East Workshop on Future Database Systems*, pp. 364-372, 1992.

[2] K. Kaneko, S. Kuroki, and A. Makinouchi: Towards Dynamics Animation on Object-Oriented Animation Database System "MOVE", *Proc. 3rd Int. Symp. on Database Systems for Advanced Applications*, pp.3-10, 1993.

[3] ONTOS Inc.: ONTOS DB 2.2 Reference Manual, ONTOS, Inc., 1992.

[4] Reynolds CW: Computer Animation with Scripts and Actors, *Proc. SIGGRAPH'82*, pp.289-296, 1982.

[5] N. Thalmann and D. Thalmann: CINEMIRA: a 3D computer animation language based on actor and camera data types, Technical Report, University of Montreal, 1984.

[6] N. Thalmann, D. Thalmann, and M. Fortin: MIRANIM: An Extensible Director-Oriented System for the Animation of Realistic Images, *IEEE Computer Graphics and Applications*, Vol.5, No.3, pp.61-73, 1985.

[7] P. Strauss and R. Carey: An Object-Oriented 3D Graphics Toolkit, *Proc. SIGGRAPH'92*, pp.341-349, 1992.

[8] S. Teller and C. H. Sequin: Visibility Preprocessing For Interactive Walkthroughs, *Proc. SIGGRAPH'91*, pp.61-69, 1991.

[9] D. Rotem: Spatial Join Indices, *Proc. Data Engineering'91*, pp.500-509, 1991.

[10] O. Guenther, H. Noltemeier: Spatial Database Indices for Large Extended Objects, *Proc. Data Engineering'91*, pp.520-526, 1991.

Author Index

Springer-Verlag and the Environment

Lecture Notes in Computer Science

Recent Volumes on Databases and Information Systems

Vol. 701: P. Atzeni (Ed.)
LOGIDATA+: Deductive Databases with Complex Objects
1993. ISBN 3-540-56974-X

Vol. 696: M. Worboys, A.F. Grundy (Eds.)
Advances in Databases (BNCOD 11)
1993. ISBN 3-540-56921-9

Vol. 692: D. Abel, B.C. Ooi (Eds.)
Advances in Spatial Databases (SSD '93)
1993. ISBN 3-540-56869-7

Vol. 685: C. Rolland, F. Bodart, C. Cauvet (Eds.)
Advanced Information Systems Engineering (CAiSE '93)
1993. ISBN 3-540-56777-1

Vol. 646: J. Biskup, R. Hull (Eds.)
Database Theory – ICDT '92
1992. ISBN 3-540-56039-4

Vol. 645: G. Pernul, A M. Tjoa (Eds.)
Entity-Relationship Approach – ER '92
1992. ISBN 3-540-56023-8

Vol. 639: A.U. Frank, I. Campari, U. Formentini (Eds.)
Theories and Methods of Spatio-Temporal Reasoning ... (GIS)
1992. ISBN 3-540-55966-3

Vol. 611 (LNAI Subseries): M.P. Papazoglou, J. Zeleznikow (Eds.)
The Next Generation of Information Systems: From Data to Knowledge
1992. ISBN 3-540-55616-8

Vol. 595: Mark Levene
The Nested Universal Relational Database Model
1992. ISBN 3-540-55493-9

Vol. 580: A. Pirotte, C. Delobel, G. Gottlob (Eds.)
Advances in Database Technology – EDBT '92
1992. ISBN 3-540-55270-7

Vol. 566: C. Delobel, M. Kifer, Y. Masunaga (Eds.)
Deductive and Object-Oriented Databases (DOOD '91)
1991. ISBN 3-540-55015-1

Springer-Verlag Berlin Heidelberg New York London Paris Tokyo Hong Kong Barcelona Budapest

Lecture Notes in Computer Science

For information about Vols. 1–645
please contact your bookseller or Springer-Verlag

Vol. 646: J. Biskup, R. Hull (Eds.), Database Theory – ICDT '92. Proceedings, 1992. IX, 449 pages. 1992.

Vol. 647: A. Segall, S. Zaks (Eds.), Distributed Algorithms. X, 380 pages. 1992.

Vol. 648: Y. Deswarte, G. Eizenberg, J.-J. Quisquater (Eds.), Computer Security – ESORICS 92. Proceedings. XI, 451 pages. 1992.

Vol. 649: A. Pettorossi (Ed.), Meta-Programming in Logic. Proceedings, 1992. XII, 535 pages. 1992.

Vol. 650: T. Ibaraki, Y. Inagaki, K. Iwama, T. Nishizeki, M. Yamashita (Eds.), Algorithms and Computation. Proceedings, 1992. XI, 510 pages. 1992.

Vol. 651: R. Koymans, Specifying Message Passing and Time-Critical Systems with Temporal Logic. IX, 164 pages. 1992.

Vol. 652: R. Shyamasundar (Ed.), Foundations of Software Technology and Theoretical Computer Science. Proceedings, 1992. XIII, 405 pages. 1992.

Vol. 653: A. Bensoussan, J.-P. Verjus (Eds.), Future Tendencies in Computer Science, Control and Applied Mathematics. Proceedings, 1992. XV, 371 pages. 1992.

Vol. 654: A. Nakamura, M. Nivat, A. Saoudi, P. S. P. Wang, K. Inoue (Eds.), Parallel Image Analysis. Proceedings, 1992. VIII, 312 pages. 1992.

Vol. 655: M. Bidoit, C. Choppy (Eds.), Recent Trends in Data Type Specification. X, 344 pages. 1993.

Vol. 656: M. Rusinowitch, J. L. Rémy (Eds.), Conditional Term Rewriting Systems. Proceedings, 1992. XI, 501 pages. 1993.

Vol. 657: E. W. Mayr (Ed.), Graph-Theoretic Concepts in Computer Science. Proceedings, 1992. VIII, 350 pages. 1993.

Vol. 658: R. A. Rueppel (Ed.), Advances in Cryptology – EUROCRYPT '92. Proceedings, 1992. X, 493 pages. 1993.

Vol. 659: G. Brewka, K. P. Jantke, P. H. Schmitt (Eds.), Nonmonotonic and Inductive Logic. Proceedings, 1991. VIII, 332 pages. 1993. (Subseries LNAI).

Vol. 660: E. Lamma, P. Mello (Eds.), Extensions of Logic Programming. Proceedings, 1992. VIII, 417 pages. 1993. (Subseries LNAI).

Vol. 661: S. J. Hanson, W. Remmele, R. L. Rivest (Eds.), Machine Learning: From Theory to Applications. VIII, 271 pages. 1993.

Vol. 662: M. Nitzberg, D. Mumford, T. Shiota, Filtering, Segmentation and Depth. VIII, 143 pages. 1993.

Vol. 663: G. v. Bochmann, D. K. Probst (Eds.), Computer Aided Verification. Proceedings, 1992. IX, 422 pages. 1993.

Vol. 664: M. Bezem, J. F. Groote (Eds.), Typed Lambda Calculi and Applications. Proceedings, 1993. VIII, 433 pages. 1993.

Vol. 665: P. Enjalbert, A. Finkel, K. W. Wagner (Eds.), STACS 93. Proceedings, 1993. XIV, 724 pages. 1993.

Vol. 666: J. W. de Bakker, W.-P. de Roever, G. Rozenberg (Eds.), Semantics: Foundations and Applications. Proceedings, 1992. VIII, 659 pages. 1993.

Vol. 667: P. B. Brazdil (Ed.), Machine Learning: ECML – 93. Proceedings, 1993. XII, 471 pages. 1993. (Subseries LNAI).

Vol. 668: M.-C. Gaudel, J.-P. Jouannaud (Eds.), TAPSOFT '93: Theory and Practice of Software Development. Proceedings, 1993. XII, 762 pages. 1993.

Vol. 669: R. S. Bird, C. C. Morgan, J. C. P. Woodcock (Eds.), Mathematics of Program Construction. Proceedings, 1992. VIII, 378 pages. 1993.

Vol. 670: J. C. P. Woodcock, P. G. Larsen (Eds.), FME '93: Industrial-Strength Formal Methods. Proceedings, 1993. XI, 689 pages. 1993.

Vol. 671: H. J. Ohlbach (Ed.), GWAI-92: Advances in Artificial Intelligence. Proceedings, 1992. XI, 397 pages. 1993. (Subseries LNAI).

Vol. 672: A. Barak, S. Guday, R. G. Wheeler, The MOSIX Distributed Operating System. X, 221 pages. 1993.

Vol. 673: G. Cohen, T. Mora, O. Moreno (Eds.), Applied Algebra, Algebraic Algorithms and Error-Correcting Codes. Proceedings, 1993. X, 355 pages 1993.

Vol. 674: G. Rozenberg (Ed.), Advances in Petri Nets 1993. VII, 457 pages. 1993.

Vol. 675: A. Mulkers, Live Data Structures in Logic Programs. VIII, 220 pages. 1993.

Vol. 676: Th. H. Reiss, Recognizing Planar Objects Using Invariant Image Features. X, 180 pages. 1993.

Vol. 677: H. Abdulrab, J.-P. Pécuchet (Eds.), Word Equations and Related Topics. Proceedings, 1991. VII, 214 pages. 1993.

Vol. 678: F. Meyer auf der Heide, B. Monien, A. L. Rosenberg (Eds.), Parallel Architectures and Their Efficient Use. Proceedings, 1992. XII, 227 pages. 1993.

Vol. 679: C. Fermüller, A. Leitsch, T. Tammet, N. Zamov, Resolution Methods for the Decision Problem. VIII, 205 pages. 1993. (Subseries LNAI).

Vol. 680: B. Hoffmann, B. Krieg-Brückner (Eds.), Program Development by Specification and Transformation. XV, 623 pages. 1993.

Vol. 681: H. Wansing, The Logic of Information Structures. IX, 163 pages. 1993. (Subseries LNAI).

Vol. 682: B. Bouchon-Meunier, L. Valverde, R. R. Yager (Eds.), IPMU '92 – Advanced Methods in Artificial Intelligence. Proceedings, 1992. IX, 367 pages. 1993.

Vol. 683: G.J. Milne, L. Pierre (Eds.), Correct Hardware Design and Verification Methods. Proceedings, 1993. VIII, 270 Pages. 1993.

Vol. 684: A. Apostolico, M. Crochemore, Z. Galil, U. Manber (Eds.), Combinatorial Pattern Matching. Proceedings, 1993. VIII, 265 pages. 1993.

Vol. 685: C. Rolland, F. Bodart, C. Cauvet (Eds.), Advanced Information Systems Engineering. Proceedings, 1993. XI, 650 pages. 1993.

Vol. 686: J. Mira, J. Cabestany, A. Prieto (Eds.), New Trends in Neural Computation. Proceedings, 1993. XVII, 746 pages. 1993.

Vol. 687: H. H. Barrett, A. F. Gmitro (Eds.), Information Processing in Medical Imaging. Proceedings, 1993. XVI, 567 pages. 1993.

Vol. 688: M. Gauthier (Ed.), Ada-Europe '93. Proceedings, 1993. VIII, 353 pages. 1993.

Vol. 689: J. Komorowski, Z. W. Ras (Eds.), Methodologies for Intelligent Systems. Proceedings, 1993. XI, 653 pages. 1993. (Subseries LNAI).

Vol. 690: C. Kirchner (Ed.), Rewriting Techniques and Applications. Proceedings, 1993. XI, 488 pages. 1993.

Vol. 691: M. Ajmone Marsan (Ed.), Application and Theory of Petri Nets 1993. Proceedings, 1993. IX, 591 pages. 1993.

Vol. 692: D. Abel, B.C. Ooi (Eds.), Advances in Spatial Databases. Proceedings, 1993. XIII, 529 pages. 1993.

Vol. 693: P. E. Lauer (Ed.), Functional Programming, Concurrency, Simulation and Automated Reasoning. Proceedings, 1991/1992. XI, 398 pages. 1993.

Vol. 694: A. Bode, M. Reeve, G. Wolf (Eds.), PARLE '93. Parallel Architectures and Languages Europe. Proceedings, 1993. XVII, 770 pages. 1993.

Vol. 695: E. P. Klement, W. Slany (Eds.), Fuzzy Logic in Artificial Intelligence. Proceedings, 1993. VIII, 192 pages. 1993. (Subseries LNAI).

Vol. 696: M. Worboys, A. F. Grundy (Eds.), Advances in Databases. Proceedings, 1993. X, 276 pages. 1993.

Vol. 697: C. Courcoubetis (Ed.), Computer Aided Verification. Proceedings, 1993. IX, 504 pages. 1993.

Vol. 698: A. Voronkov (Ed.), Logic Programming and Automated Reasoning. Proceedings, 1993. XIII, 386 pages. 1993. (Subseries LNAI).

Vol. 699: G. W. Mineau, B. Moulin, J. F. Sowa (Eds.), Conceptual Graphs for Knowledge Representation. Proceedings, 1993. IX, 451 pages. 1993. (Subseries LNAI).

Vol. 700: A. Lingas, R. Karlsson, S. Carlsson (Eds.), Automata, Languages and Programming. Proceedings, 1993. XII, 697 pages. 1993.

Vol. 701: P. Atzeni (Ed.), LOGIDATA+: Deductive Databases with Complex Objects. VIII, 273 pages. 1993.

Vol. 702: E. Börger, G. Jäger, H. Kleine Büning, S. Martini, M. M. Richter (Eds.), Computer Science Logic. Proceedings, 1992. VIII, 439 pages. 1993.

Vol. 703: M. de Berg, Ray Shooting, Depth Orders and Hidden Surface Removal. X, 201 pages. 1993.

Vol. 704: F. N. Paulisch, The Design of an Extendible Graph Editor. XV, 184 pages. 1993.

Vol. 705: H. Grünbacher, R. W. Hartenstein (Eds.), Field-Programmable Gate Arrays. Proceedings, 1992. VIII, 218 pages. 1993.

Vol. 706: H. D. Rombach, V. R. Basili, R. W. Selby (Eds.), Experimental Software Engineering Issues. Proceedings, 1992. XVIII, 261 pages. 1993.

Vol. 707: O. M. Nierstrasz (Ed.), ECOOP '93 – Object-Oriented Programming. Proceedings, 1993. XI, 531 pages. 1993.

Vol. 708: C. Laugier (Ed.), Geometric Reasoning for Perception and Action. Proceedings, 1991. VIII, 281 pages. 1993.

Vol. 709: F. Dehne, J.-R. Sack, N. Santoro, S. Whitesides (Eds.), Algorithms and Data Structures. Proceedings, 1993. XII, 634 pages. 1993.

Vol. 710: Z. Ésik (Ed.), Fundamentals of Computation Theory. Proceedings, 1993. IX, 471 pages. 1993.

Vol. 711: A. M. Borzyszkowski, S. Sokołowski (Eds.), Mathematical Foundations of Computer Science 1993. Proceedings, 1993. XIII, 782 pages. 1993.

Vol. 712: P. V. Rangan (Ed.), Network and Operating System Support for Digital Audio and Video. Proceedings, 1992. X, 416 pages. 1993.

Vol. 713: G. Gottlob, A. Leitsch, D. Mundici (Eds.), Computational Logic and Proof Theory. Proceedings, 1993. XI, 348 pages. 1993.

Vol. 714: M. Bruynooghe, J. Penjam (Eds.), Programming Language Implementation and Logic Programming. Proceedings, 1993. XI, 421 pages. 1993.

Vol. 715: E. Best (Ed.), CONCUR'93. Proceedings, 1993. IX, 541 pages. 1993.

Vol. 716: A. U. Frank, I. Campari (Eds.), Spatial Information Theory. Proceedings, 1993. XI, 478 pages. 1993.

Vol. 717: I. Sommerville, M. Paul (Eds.), Software Engineering – ESEC '93. Proceedings, 1993. XII, 516 pages. 1993.

Vol. 718: J. Seberry, Y. Zheng (Eds.), Advances in Cryptology – AUSCRYPT '92. Proceedings, 1992. XIII, 543 pages. 1993.

Vol. 719: D. Chetverikov, W.G. Kropatsch (Eds.), Computer Analysis of Images and Patterns. Proceedings, 1993. XVI, 857 pages. 1993.

Vol. 720: V. Mařík, J. Lažanský, R.R. Wagner (Eds.), Database and Expert Systems Applications. Proceedings, 1993. XV, 768 pages. 1993.